SPORTS IN SOCIETY

SPORTS IN SOCIETY

Issues and Controversies

THIRTEENTH EDITION

Jay Coakley, Ph.D.
University of Colorado
Colorado Springs

SPORTS IN SOCIETY: ISSUES AND CONTROVERSIES, THIRTEENTH EDITION

Published by McGraw Hill LLC, 1325 Avenue of the Americas, New York, NY 10121.

This book is printed on acid-free paper.

1 2 3 4 5 6 7 8 9 LCR 24 23 22 21 20

ISBN 978-1-260-24066-5 (bound edition)
MHID 1-260-24066-5 (bound edition)
ISBN 978-1-260-83455-0 (loose-leaf edition)
MHID 1-260-83455-7 (loose-leaf edition)

Portfolio Manager: *Francesca King*
Marketing Manager: *Meredith Leo Digiano*
Content Project Managers: *Danielle Clement, Lisa Bruflodt*
Buyer: *Laura Fuller*
Designer: *Egzon Shaqiri*
Content Licensing Specialists: *Jacob Sullivan*
Cover Image: *"HIGH ASPIRATIONS" Copyright © 1972 Ernie Barnes Family Trust*
Compositor: *MPS Limited*

All credits appearing on page are considered to be an extension of the copyright page.

Library of Congress Cataloging-in-Publication Data

Cataloging-in-Publication Data has been requested from the Library of Congress.

mheducation.com/highered

To Nancy Coakley who has supported me and this project since 1975 and provided substantial assistance and critique for each of the thirteen editions. As a life partner and co-parent, she has always been irreplaceable.

ABOUT THE AUTHOR

Jay Coakley

Jay Coakley is a Professor Emeritus of Sociology at the University of Colorado in Colorado Springs. He received a Ph.D. in sociology at the University of Notre Dame and has since taught and done research on play, games, and sports, among other topics in sociology. Dr. Coakley has received many teaching, service, and professional awards, and is an internationally respected scholar, author, and journal editor. In 2007 the Institute for International Sport selected him as one of the 100 Most Influential Sports Educators, and the University of Chichester in West Sussex, England awarded him an Honorary Fellowship in recognition of his outstanding leadership in the sociology of sport; in 2009, the National Association for Sport and Physical Education inducted Coakley into its Hall of Fame; and in 2015 he was named an Honorary Member of the International Sociology of Sport Association.

Coakley continues to use concepts, research, and theories in sociology to critically examine social phenomena and promote changes that make social worlds more democratic and humane. He currently lives in Fort Collins, Colorado with his wife, Nancy.

ABOUT THE COVER ARTIST

Artist Ernie Barnes was born July 15, 1938, in Durham, North Carolina during the height of the Jim Crow Era. He lived in a section of the city called "The Bottom" with his parents and younger brother, James. His father, Ernest Barnes, Sr. was a shipping clerk for Liggett & Myers tobacco company. His mother, Fannie Geer, supervised the household for a prominent attorney who shared his extensive art book collection with the young Barnes so by elementary school, Barnes was already familiar with the Master painters.

Bullied as a child for his shyness and sensitivity, Barnes found solace in drawing. In his freshman year, a weightlifting coach put Barnes on a fitness program. By his senior year at Hillside High School, Barnes was captain of the football team and state champion in the shot put.

Barnes earned a full athletic scholarship to North Carolina College (now North Carolina Central University) and majored in art, where his art instructor, sculptor Ed Wilson, encouraged Barnes to create images from his own life experiences.

Barnes only attended segregated schools. In 1960, he was one of 30 African-Americans drafted into the National Football League–one of nine players selected that year from a Historically Black College and University. For five seasons, Barnes was an offensive lineman for the New York Titans, San Diego Chargers and Denver Broncos. In 1965 New York Jets owner Sonny Werblin paid Barnes a season's salary "to paint" and sponsored the first Ernie Barnes art exhibition in a prestigious New York City gallery. After the success of the show, at age 28, Barnes settled in Los Angeles, California.

Barnes is the first American professional athlete to become a noted painter. From his sports experience and the study of anatomy, Barnes' unique style of elongation captures the movement, energy, and grace of his subjects. This earned him numerous appointments, including "Sports Artist of the 1984 Olympic Games" in Los Angeles and "America's Best Painter of Sports" by the American Sport Art Museum & Archives. He was commissioned to paint artwork for the National Basketball Association, Los Angeles Lakers, Carolina Panthers, New Orleans Saints, Oakland Raiders, educational institutions, corporations, musicians, celebrities and professional athletes. Barnes' beloved painting, "The Bench," that he created before his rookie season, was presented to the Pro Football Hall of Fame in 2014.

In pop culture, the art of Ernie Barnes appears in television, movies and music album covers, including his famous dance hall scene, "The Sugar Shack." His pride of North Carolina also is evident in his images of pool halls, barbershops, porch ladies, church, street singers, sandlot games and other memories of growing up in the South.

Barnes died on April 27, 2009. He is survived by his wife Bernie and his five children, Deidre, Michael, Sean, Erin, and Paige.

This is the eighth consecutive cover of *Sports in Society* that presents the art of Ernie Barnes. He spoke to students regularly, bringing his work to show that art, sport, and academic learning could come together in their lives.

For more information, please visit his official website: www.ErnieBarnes.com. My thanks go to Ernie's longtime personal assistant, Luz Rodriguez, and his family for sharing *High Aspirations* for this edition of *Sports in Society*.

CONTENTS

PREFACE

PURPOSE OF THIS TEXT

The thirteenth edition of *Sports in Society: Issues and Controversies* provides a detailed introduction to the sociology of sport. It uses sociological concepts, theories, and research to raise critical questions about sports and explore the dynamic relationship between sports, culture, and society. The chapters are organized around controversial and curiosity-arousing issues that have been systematically studied in sociology and related fields. Research on these issues is summarized and cited so that readers can critically examine them.

Chapter content is guided by sociological research and theory and based on the assumption that a full understanding of sports must take into account the social and cultural contexts in which sports are created, played, given meaning, and integrated into people's lives. At a time when we too often think that an online search provides everything we need to know, I intend this text as a thoughtful scholarly work that integrates research on sports as social phenomena, makes sense of the expanding body of work in the sociology of sport, and inspires critical thinking.

FOR WHOM IS IT WRITTEN?

Sports in Society is written for everyone taking a first critical look at the relationships between sports, culture, and society. Readers don't need a background in sociology to understand and benefit from discussions in each chapter; nor do they need detailed knowledge of sports jargon and statistics. My goal is to help readers identify and explore issues related to sports in their personal experiences, families, schools, communities, and societies.

The emphasis on issues and controversies makes each chapter useful for people concerned with sport-related policies and programs. I've always tried to use knowledge to make sports more democratic, accessible, inclusive, and humane, and I hope to provide readers with the information and desire to do the same.

WRITING THIS REVISION

Media coverage and general awareness of social issues and controversies in sports have increased dramatically over the past decade. There has been a similar increase in research on sports as social phenomena as scholars now ask a wide array of questions and study aspects of sports that were overlooked or avoided in the past. Tracking and reading this material has become a full-time job for me. Trying to include in this book all the issues I think are important has become impossible. When I add something, I must delete something. Making those choices is difficult. I try to anticipate the issues and controversies that will have important social implications and present them in ways that will spark the interest of students reading the book.

As in past editions, I break up text with photos, cartoons, 19 *Reflect on Sport* boxes, and 42 figures and tables related to chapter content.

In this edition, I've added materials related to global issues and controversies. Sports have become more interconnected worldwide, and information about sports around the world is more accessible to us than ever before. I hope that discussions and analyses of sport-related phenomena outside the United States helps readers understand that the ways of doing and thinking about sports vary from culture to culture.

CHANGES TO THIS EDITION

This edition builds on and updates the twelfth edition. New chapter-opening quotes, photos, and examples maintain the timeliness of content.

New research and theoretical developments are integrated into each chapter. There are over 1600 references, nearly 900 of which are new to this edition. A significant change is that references are now listed at the end of each chapter to assist those writing papers and doing research. Most new references identify materials published after 2016.

The sociology of sport has expanded so much in recent years that *Sports in Society* is now an introduction to the field more than a comprehensive overview.

The editors at McGraw-Hill collect data from self-tests taken by students to identify sections in the book that are difficult for students to fully understand. Those data are passed on to me and I pay special attention to revising and clarifying those sections. This is very helpful to me and should benefit all readers of the book.

Revision Themes and New Materials

This edition updates all time sensitive materials and continues to provide readers with provocative chapter opening quotes, a brief Chapter Outline, and Learning Objectives. At the end of each chapter are lists of Supplemental Readings that are accessible through the Instructor Resources section in Connect, along with selected sport management discussion issues related to the chapter content. Finally, five chapters–socialization, youth sports, sports and the media, and school sports–have been largely or entirely rewritten and most others contain significant new materials. Chapters 1 and 2 are the only ones with minimal changes.

Chapter 1 contains only minor revisions as it lays out the general framework for the book. Likewise, Chapter 2 remains much the same with revisions made to clarify issues related to sociological theory and research methods.

Chapter 3 has been shortened and made more concise. The focus continues to be on socialization through the life course with a special emphasis on childhood through early adulthood. There is new material on the role of physical literacy as a factor that influences choices about sport participation. The section on Changing or Ending Sport Participation has been rewritten with a greater emphasis on factors that influence participation through adulthood.

Chapter 4, has been completely rewritten to highlight three models around which youth sports are currently organized. These are the *Skills and Excellence* model, the *Physical Literacy and Lifelong Participation* model, and the *Personal Growth and Development* model. This was done to show that youth sports are not all the same and to identify important efforts to make youth sports more child-centered.

Chapter 5 continues to focus on deviance on and off the field among athletes and those connected with governing bodies. With the increasing legalization of gambling in the United States there is new material on match-fixing and prop-fixing. Institutional corruption in sports receives additional attention as well. The sections on the use of performance-enhancing substances have been made more concise with new information on the use of technology and enhancement.

Chapter 6, on violence in sports, has been revised to focus more on the consequences of violent actions during events. There is a new section on the ways that some coaches incorporate violence in their relationships with players and a major addition that covers the sexual abuse and assaults that have occurred in USA Gymnastics and the Michigan State athletic department.

Chapter 7, on gender and sports, is organized to highlight changes in gender ideology in connection with the "me too" movement worldwide. There is new material on girls and women claiming space in sports and updates on intersex and transgender issues in sports. The discussion of gender and access to power in sports has also been updated to account for positive changes as well as new forms of resistance.

Chapter 8, on race and ethnicity, received minor revisions with a continuing emphasis on race and ethnic relations at all levels of organized sports. This chapter has remained timely with the current global expressions of racist attitudes and actions and with the continuing inclusion of people of color into elite level mainstream sports.

Chapter 9, on social class, also remains timely. It is organized around the idea that meritocracy is not all it's cracked up to be. Applying this idea to sports is difficult because people believe that it offers everyone a level playing field. However, this is not the case for athletes, spectators, coaches, or those who control sports as owners, managers, and executives in governing bodies. The dynamics of social class are built into the very structures in which we live our lives, and this is highlighted in the chapter.

Chapter 10, written with Elizabeth Pike, my colleague from the University of Chichester in England, continues to focus on issues and controversies related to age and ability in sports. The framework of this chapter is built on research showing how social definitions of age and ability impact the provision of sports participation opportunities and the decisions made by people to become and stay involved in sports. The sections on masters events, the Paralympics, the Special Olympics, and related forms of sport provision illustrate the complexity of sports when they are viewed in a general social and cultural context in which age and ability influence how people are perceived and how they include physical activities in their lives.

Chapter 11 deals with the commercialization of sports. It explains how the great sport myth is used to appropriate public money to build sport venues and subsidize sport teams. Labor relations, collective bargaining agreements, lockouts, and the role of players' associations are discussed along with new topics including the responses to commercialization in sports by athletes and fans and the impact of legal gambling on the business of sports.

Chapter 12, on sports and the media, continues to focus on the changing media landscape and how it is related to sports. There are new sections on how fantasy sports, sports video games, and esports are changing the ways that we watch and experience sports and how sports are covered by the media. Additional new sections cover the difficulties of including the play element of sports into media coverage and the pressures placed on sports journalists to "stick to sports" and stay away from social issues in their coverage.

Chapter 13, on politics, government, and global processes, contains new sections on the use of sports in nation-building processes and on athletes as political activists. The movement that was given new life by NFL player Colin Kaepernick is discussed in depth with an eye to how it may influence the connections between sports and society. This edition retains an emphasis on the ways that globalization impacts the composition of sports teams, the allegiance of spectators, and the tensions around the perceived sanctity of national boundaries. Research is presented to show that these realities are linked with corporate expansion, the global flow of capital, the business strategy of global media companies, and processes of *glocalization* through which global sports are integrated into people's everyday lives on a local level.

Chapter 14, on high school and college sports, has been fully revised. There are new sections on the challenges faced by young people who must manage dual academic and athletic careers now that training in elite sports has become more demanding. Managing dual careers in the context of the NCAA and Division I sports and how this can be done successfully is discussed and the diversity of college athlete experiences is highlighted. Additional new topics include esports in US high schools and colleges and how esports teams may impact student culture as well as popular definitions of *sports*. There are also major new sections on head injuries in schools sports, scandals and rule violations in NCAA universities, and issues related to player rights and compensation. Government intervention in the form of laws focused on the rights and freedoms of college athletes is also discussed. Finally, there is a new section on challenges faced by black women participating in college sports in the US and the strategies being developed to meet those challenges.

Chapter 15, on religion and sports, presents information on world religions and how they influence conceptions of the body, evaluations of physical movement, and sports participation. The chapter has been carefully edited with revisions in sections where clarifications are warranted.

Chapter 16 continues to focus on the process of making change in sports rather than describing what the future of sports might be. This is because there is a need for us to acknowledge the power of corporations in shaping sports to fit their interests and to develop strategies for creating sport forms that directly serve the needs of individuals and communities.

Supplemental Readings and New Website Resources

Each chapter is followed by a list of Supplemental Readings that provide useful information about topics in the chapters. The Supplemental Readings for each chapter can be accessed through the Instructor Resources within Connect.

New Visual Materials

There are 120 photos, including 52 new ones, 20 figures, and 20 cartoons in this edition. These images are combined with updated tables to illustrate important substantive points, visually enhance the text, and make reading more interesting.

Mc Graw Hill connect®

The thirteenth edition of *Sports in Society,* is now available online with Connect, McGraw-Hill Education's integrated assignment and assessment platform. Connect also offers SmartBook® 2.0 for the new edition, which is the first adaptive reading experience proven to improve grades and help students study more effectively. All of the title's website and ancillary content is also available through Connect, including:

- A full Test Bank of multiple choice questions that test students on central concepts and ideas in each chapter
- An Instructor's Manual for each chapter with full chapter outlines, sample test questions, and discussion topics
- Supplemental Readings that add depth and background to current chapter topics
- Group projects
- Previous chapters on coaches, competition, history (from the tenth edition), and social theories (from the ninth edition)
- True/false self-tests for each chapter
- A cumulative 350-page bibliography that lists all references from this and the last seven editions of *Sports in Society*
- A complete glossary of key terms integrated into the index

ACKNOWLEDGMENTS

This book draws on ideas from many sources. Thanks go to students, colleagues, and friends who have provided constructive criticisms over the years. Students regularly open my eyes to new ways of viewing and analyzing sports as social phenomena.

Special thanks go to friends and colleagues who influence my thinking, provide valuable source materials, and willingly discuss ideas and information with me. Elizabeth Pike, Chris Hallinan, and Cora Burnett influenced my thinking as I worked with them on versions of *Sports in Society* for the United Kingdom, Australia/New Zealand, and Southern Africa, respectively. Peter Donnelly, co-author of past Canadian versions, has provided special support for many years and influenced my thinking about many important issues. Thanks also go to photographers and colleagues, Lara Killick, Barbara Schausteck de Almeida (Brazil), Elizabeth Pike (UK), Michael Boyd (Northern Ireland), Basia Borzecka (Mexico), Alaei Forough (Iran), Claudio Echeverria (Chile), Paul W. Harvey IV and the University of Oregon, Coaches Across Continents, The Aspen Institute and Project Play, the Challenged Athletes Foundation, and my daughter, Danielle Hicks, for permission to use their photos. Thanks also to artist Fred Eyer, whose cartoons have been used in this and previous editions.

Thanks also to Sandeep Rawat, Francesca King, and Katie Roman for their willingness to work with me on revision issues and schedules, and the entire McGraw-Hill team for their help during the course of this revision.

Finally, thanks go to Nancy Coakley, who has lived through all thirteen editions of *Sports in Society* and assisted with each one in more ways than I can list here. She keeps me in touch with popular culture sources related to sports, and tells me when my ideas should be revised or kept to myself–a frequent occurrence. This edition is dedicated to her.

My appreciation also goes to the following reviewers, whose suggestions were helpful in planning and writing this edition:

Stephen Bronzan, University of California, Davis
Kay Daigle, Southeastern Oklahoma State University
Susan Dargan, Providence College
Fitni Destani, Keene State College
Kristi M. Fondren, Marshall University
Donna Grove, York College of Pennsylvania
Phil Lewis, University at Albany
Anne Marx, Loras College
Dominic Morais, Trinity University
Anthony Rosselli, Texas A&M University-Commerce

Finally, thanks to the students and colleagues worldwide who have e-mailed comments about previous editions and ideas for future editions. I take them seriously and appreciate their thoughtfulness–keep the responses coming.

Jay Coakley
Fort Collins, CO

FOR INSTRUCTORS

You're in the driver's seat.

Want to build your own course? No problem. Prefer to use our turnkey, prebuilt course? Easy. Want to make changes throughout the semester? Sure. And you'll save time with Connect's auto-grading too.

65%
Less Time Grading

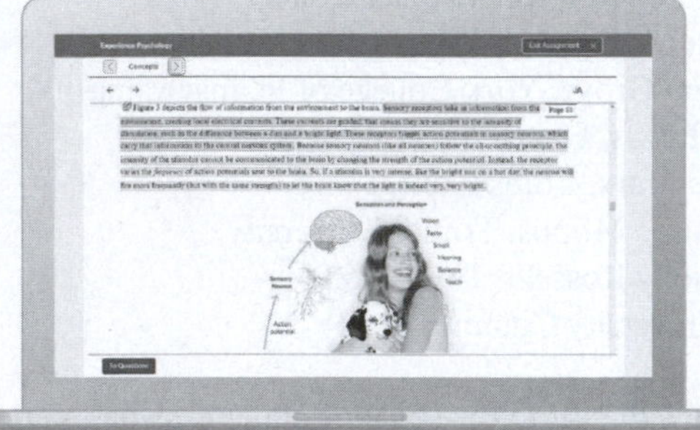

Laptop: McGraw-Hill; Woman/dog: George Doyle/Getty Images

They'll thank you for it.

Adaptive study resources like SmartBook® 2.0 help your students be better prepared in less time. You can transform your class time from dull definitions to dynamic debates. Find out more about the powerful personalized learning experience available in SmartBook 2.0 at **www.mheducation.com/highered/connect/smartbook**

Make it simple, make it affordable.

Connect makes it easy with seamless integration using any of the major Learning Management Systems—Blackboard®, Canvas, and D2L, among others—to let you organize your course in one convenient location. Give your students access to digital materials at a discount with our inclusive access program. Ask your McGraw-Hill representative for more information.

Padlock: Jobalou/Getty Images

Solutions for your challenges.

A product isn't a solution. Real solutions are affordable, reliable, and come with training and ongoing support when you need it and how you want it. Our Customer Experience Group can also help you troubleshoot tech problems—although Connect's 99% uptime means you might not need to call them. See for yourself at **status.mheducation.com**

Checkmark: Jobalou/Getty Images

FOR STUDENTS

Effective, efficient studying.

Connect helps you be more productive with your study time and get better grades using tools like SmartBook 2.0, which highlights key concepts and creates a personalized study plan. Connect sets you up for success, so you walk into class with confidence and walk out with better grades.

Study anytime, anywhere.

Download the free ReadAnywhere app and access your online eBook or SmartBook 2.0 assignments when it's convenient, even if you're offline. And since the app automatically syncs with your eBook and SmartBook 2.0 assignments in Connect, all of your work is available every time you open it. Find out more at **www.mheducation.com/readanywhere**

"I really liked this app—it made it easy to study when you don't have your text-book in front of you."

–Jordan Cunningham,
Eastern Washington University

Calendar: owattaphotos/Getty Images

No surprises.

The Connect Calendar and Reports tools keep you on track with the work you need to get done and your assignment scores. Life gets busy; Connect tools help you keep learning through it all.

Learning for everyone.

McGraw-Hill works directly with Accessibility Services Departments and faculty to meet the learning needs of all students. Please contact your Accessibility Services office and ask them to email accessibility@mheducation.com, or visit **www.mheducation.com/about/accessibility** for more information.

Top: Jenner Images/Getty Images, Left: Hero Images/Getty Images, Right: Hero Images/Getty Images

chapter

1

(*Source:* Lara Killick)

THE SOCIOLOGY OF SPORTS

What Is It and Why Study It?

Our sports belong to us. They came up from the people. They were invented for reasons having nothing to do with money or ego. Our sports weren't created by wealthy sports and entertainment barons like the ones running sports today.

–Ken Reed, Sport Policy Director, League of Fans (2011)

Why should we play sport? Why not just have everyone exercise? [. . . Because sport] takes you to the edge of a cliff, and it's at that edge of the cliff where you understand your creative soul.

–Brian Hainline, chief medical officer, NCAA (in Wolverton, 2014)

The National Federation of State High School Associations (NFHS) and the NFHS Network have entered into a partnership with PlayVS to begin the rollout of esports competition in high schools throughout the nation.

–NFHS (2019)

Sports is almost like a religion beat. People are really, really passionate about it, and they really, really care. That can be a blessing or curse.

–Mary Pilon, sports journalist (in Guinee, 2019)

Chapter Outline

Learning Objectives

- Explain what sociologists study about sports and why sociology of sport knowledge is different from information in sports media and everyday conversations.
- Understand issues related to defining sports and why a sociological definition differs from official definitions used by high schools, universities, and other organizations.
- Explain what it means to say that sports are social constructions and contested activities.
- Understand the definition of the great sport myth, how it impacts sports in society, and how it influences the sociology of sports.
- Explain why research and knowledge in the sociology of sport may be controversial among people associated with sports.
- Understand the meaning of "ideology" and how ideologies related to gender, race, social class, and ability are connected with sports.

ABOUT THIS BOOK

If you're reading this book, you have an interest in sports or know people who play or watch them. Unlike most books about sports, this one is written to take you beyond scores, statistics, and sports personalities. The goal is to focus on the "deeper game" associated with sports, the game through which sports become part of the social and cultural worlds in which we live.

Fortunately, we can draw on our experiences as we consider this deeper game. Take high school sports in the United States as an example. When students play on a high school basketball team, we know that it can affect their status in the school and the treatment they receive from teachers and peers. We know it has potential implications for their prestige in the community, self-images and self-esteem, physical health, future relationships, opportunities in education and the job market, and their overall feelings about life.

Building on this knowledge enables us to move further into the deeper game associated with high school sports. For example, why do so many Americans place such importance on sports and accord such high status to elite athletes? Are there connections between high school sports and widespread beliefs about masculinity and femininity, achievement and competition, pleasure and pain, winning and fair play, and other important aspects of US culture?

Underlying these questions is the assumption that sports are more than games, meets, and matches. They're important aspects of social life that have meanings going far beyond scores and performance statistics. Sports are integral parts of the social and cultural contexts in which we live, and they provide stories and images that many of us use to evaluate our experiences and the world around us.

Those of us who study sports in society are concerned with these deeper meanings and stories associated with sports. We do research to increase our understanding of (1) the cultures and societies in which sports exist; (2) the social worlds created around sports; (3) the experiences of individuals and groups associated with sports; and (4) the social aspects of sports and physical culture.

ABOUT THIS CHAPTER

This chapter is organized to answer four questions:

1. What is sociology, and how is it used to study sports in society?
2. What are sports, and how can we identify them in ways that increase our understanding of their place and value in society?
3. What is the sociology of sport?
4. Who studies sports in society, and for what purposes?

The answers to these questions will be our guides for understanding the material in the rest of the book.

USING SOCIOLOGY TO STUDY SPORTS

Sociology provides useful tools for investigating sports as social phenomena. This is because **sociology** *is the study of the social worlds that people create, maintain, and change through their relationships with each other.*[1] The concept of **social worlds** refers to *identifiable spheres of everyday actions and relationships* (Unruh, 1980). Social worlds are created by people, but they involve much more than individuals doing their own things for their own reasons. Our actions, relationships, and collective activities form patterns that could not be predicted only with information about each of us as individuals. These patterns constitute identifiable ways of life and social arrangements that are maintained or changed over time as people interact with one other.

---

[1]Important concepts used in each chapter are identified in **boldface.** Unless they are accompanied by a footnote that contains a definition, the definition will be given in the text itself. This puts the definition in context rather than separating it in a glossary. Definitions are also provided in the Subject Glindex.

Social worlds can be as large and impersonal as an entire nation, such as Saudi Arabia or Brazil, or as personal and intimate as your own family. But regardless of size, they encompass all aspects of social life: (a) the values and beliefs that we use to make sense of our lives; (b) our everyday actions and relationships; and (c) the groups, organizations, communities, and societies that we form as we make choices, develop relationships, and participate in social life.

Sociologists often refer to **society,** *which is a relatively self-sufficient collection of people who maintain a way of life in a particular territory.* In most cases, a society and a nation are one and the same, such as Brazil and Brazilian society. But there are cases where a society is not a nation, such as Amish Mennonite society as it exists in Ohio, Pennsylvania, and other parts of the United States.

The goal of sociology is to describe and explain social worlds, including societies–how they are created, re-created, and changed; how they are organized; and how they influence our lives and our relationships with each other. In the process of doing sociology we learn to see our lives and the lives of others "in context"–that is, in the social worlds in which we live. This enables us to identify the social conditions that set limits or create possibilities in our lives and the lives of others. On a personal level, knowing about these influential conditions also helps us anticipate and sometimes work around the constraints we face at the same time that we look for and take advantage of the possibilities. Ideally, it helps us gain more control over our lives as well as an understanding of other people and the conditions that influence their lives.

Key Sociology Concepts

Sociologists use the concepts of culture, social interaction, and social structure to help them understand sports as social activities.

Culture consists of *the shared ways of life and shared understandings that people develop as they live together.* Once a culture exists, it influences relationships and social interaction.

Social interaction consists of *people taking each other into account and, in the process, influencing each other's feelings, thoughts, and actions.* Through interaction, we learn to anticipate the thoughts and actions of others and predict how others may respond to what we think and do.

Social structure consists of *the established patterns of relationships and social arrangements that take shape as people live, work, and play with each other.* This is the basis for order and organization in all social worlds.

These three concepts–culture, social interaction, and social structure–represent the central interconnected aspects of all social worlds. For example, a high school soccer team is a social world formed by players, coaches, team parents, and regular supporters. Over time every team creates and maintains a particular *culture* or a way of life consisting of values, beliefs, norms, and everyday social routines. Everyone involved with the team engages in *social interaction* as they take each other into account during their everyday activities on and off the playing field. Additionally, the recurring actions, relationships, and social arrangements that emerge as these people interact with each other make up the *social structure* of the team. This combination of culture, social interaction, and social structure comprises the team as a social world, and it is connected with the larger social worlds in which it exists.

Peer groups, cliques, and athletic teams are social worlds in which participants are known to one another. Communities, societies, concert crowds, and online chat rooms are social worlds in which participants may not be well known to each other. This means that the boundaries of social worlds may be clear, fuzzy, or overlapping, but we generally know when we enter or leave a social world because each has identifying features related to culture, social interaction, and social structure.

We move back and forth between familiar social worlds like a sport management class, a club team practice, and a gender-mixed dorm without thinking. We make nearly automatic shifts in how we talk and act as we accommodate changing cultural, interactional, and structural features in each social world.

However, when we enter or participate in a new or unfamiliar social world, such as a concert venue, we usually pay special attention to what is happening. We watch what people are doing, how they interact with each other, and we develop a sense of the recurring patterns that exist in their actions and relationships. If you've done this, then you're ready to use sociology to study sports in society.

Sociological Knowledge Is Based on Research and Theory

My goal in writing this book is to accurately represent research in the sociology of sport and discuss issues of interest to students. At a time when online searches provide us with infinite and sometimes questionable facts, figures, and opinions about sports, I am primarily interested in the knowledge produced through systematic research. I use newspaper articles and other media as sources for examples or to raise issues, but I depend on research results when making substantive points and drawing conclusions. This means that my statements about sports and sport experiences are based, as much as possible, on studies that use surveys, questionnaires, interviews, observations, content analyses, and other accepted methods of research in sociology (see Chapter 2).

In the space of a few decades, the world has come to take sport more seriously than ever before. —Simon Kuper, journalist, *The Financial Times* (2012)

The material in this book is different than material in blogs, talk radio, television news shows, game and event commentaries, and most of our everyday conversations about sports. It is organized to help you critically examine sports as they exist in people's lives. I use research findings to describe and explain as accurately as possible the important connections between sports, society, and culture. I try to be fair when using research to make sense of the social aspects of sports and sport experiences. This is why nearly 1700 sources are cited as references for the information and analysis in this book.

Of course, I want to hold your attention as you read, but I don't exaggerate, purposely withhold, or present information out of context to impress you and boost my "ratings." In the process, I hope you will extend your critical thinking abilities so you can assess what people believe and say about sports in society. This will enable you to make informed decisions about sports in your life and the social worlds in which you live.

DEFINING SPORTS

Most of us know enough about the meaning of sports to talk about them with others. However, when we study sports, it helps to precisely define our topic. For example, is it a sport when young people choose teams and play a baseball game in the street or when thirty people of various ages spend an afternoon learning and performing tricks at a skateboard park? These activities are sociologically different from what occurs at major league baseball games and X Games skateboard competitions. These differences become significant when parents ask if playing sports builds the character of their children, when community leaders ask if they should use tax money to fund sports, and when school principals ask if sports are valid educational activities.

When I say that I study sports, people ask if that includes jogging, double-dutch, weight lifting, hunting, scuba diving, darts, auto racing, chess, poker, ultimate fighting, paintball, piano competitions, ballroom dancing, skateboarding, Quidditch, and esports. To respond is not easy, because there is no single definition that precisely identifies sports in all cultures at all times (Lagaert & Roose, 2016).

According to definitions used widely in North America and much of Europe, **sports** *are physical activities that involve challenges or competitive contests.* They are usually played according to rules and organized so that participants can assess their performances and compare them to the performances of others or to their own performances from one situation to another. However, the organization, meaning, and purpose of sports often vary from one cultural context to another.

(*Source:* Jay Coakley)

Is "Competitive Cheer" and sideline cheerleading a sport? The answer to this question is important because it impacts the budgets, participation rates, and gender equity decisions in US high school and college sport programs. Sociologists study why certain activities are considered to be sports, who has the power to make such decisions, and how those decisions affect people's lives (Lamb & Priyadharshini, 2015).

Some sports are organized to emphasize free-flowing, playful action and exist primarily for the pleasure of the participants. Examples include 5K fun runs, spontaneous games of Ultimate in open areas, and skateboarding in the streets or local skate parks. In contrast, other sports are organized to include scheduled and regulated action with participants displaying their skills for the pleasure of spectators. These include professional and other elite sports that people follow through media and pay to see in person. NFL games, matches in professional soccer leagues, and major golf tournaments are examples.

Most sports, however, are organized in ways that fall somewhere between these two extremes. They are formally organized and, even though people may watch them, they exist mostly for participants, who enjoy them, value the skills needed to play them, and receive external rewards, such as peer or family approval, social status, or formal awards for playing them. Softball leagues, scheduled volleyball tournaments, and most organized youth sports are examples.

Scholars who study sports as social phenomena generally use a flexible and inclusive definition of sport. Although past research in the sociology of sport has focused mainly on what you and I would describe as "organized sports," current research often focuses on **physical culture,** *which includes all forms of movement and physical activities that people in particular social worlds create, sustain, and regularly include in their collective lives.* This could be tai chi done in a Beijing park, capoeira in a Sao Paulo plaza, parkour in a Paris neighborhood, or breakdancing in New York City's Central Park.

Of course, organized sports are a central and often dominant component of physical culture in many societies today, but it has not always been this way and there continue to be societies in which traditional folk games, locally organized contests, and expressive forms of movement are more important than formally organized, competitive sports. Research on physical culture is important because it helps us understand how people think and feel about their bodies and how they define movement and integrate it into their lives. Additionally, it provides a foundation for critically examining the deeper game associated with sports in society.

Official Definitions of Sports

Defining *sports* in official terms and choosing specific activities that qualify as sports is an important process in organizations, communities, and societies. Being classified as an official sport gives special status to an activity and is likely to increase participation, funding, community support, and general visibility. For example, in Switzerland and the Scandinavian countries, walking, bicycling, and certain forms of general exercise are considered to be "sports." Therefore, those who participate regularly in these activities often see themselves as "sportspersons" and are treated that way by their peers. Additionally, public policies are likely to provide common spaces for these activities and financial support for events that include them.

The official definitions of sport used by organizations and officials in the United States are more exclusive in that they give priority to formally organized, competitive activities. Therefore, even though walking is encouraged for general health purposes, most people in the United States would not consider walking a sport, nor would they ever describe walkers as sportspersons. This is important because it also may mean that walking trails and walking events will receive much less financial and political support than stadiums and arenas in which elite and professional sports are played and watched—because these are seen as the "real" or official sports. This, in turn, may be related to obesity rates and general health in a society.

According to most people in wealthy, postindustrial societies, sports involve rules, competition, scoring, winners and losers, schedules and seasons, records, coaches, referees, and governing bodies that set rules and sponsor championships. In the United States, for example, organizations such as local park and recreation departments, state high school athletic federations, the National Collegiate Athletic Association (NCAA), and the United States Olympic and Paralympic Committee use their own criteria for defining *sport* and selecting activities for official recognition as sports for purposes of funding and support.

Official definitions of sports have important implications. When a definition emphasizes rules, competition, and high performance, many people will be excluded from participation, and decide that they are not fit to play, or avoid other physical activities that are defined as "second class." For example, when a twelve-year-old is cut from an exclusive club soccer team, she may not want to play in the local league sponsored by the park and recreation department because she sees it as "recreational activity" rather than a real sport. This can create a situation in which most people are physically inactive at the same time that a small number of people perform at relatively high levels in front of spectators—a situation that negatively impacts health and increases health-care costs in a society or community. When sport is defined to include a wide range of physical activities that are played for pleasure and integrated into local expressions of social life, physical activity rates will be high and overall health benefits are likely.

Sports Are Social Constructions

Understanding the sociology of sport is easier if you think of sports as **social constructions**—that is, as *parts of the social world that are created by people as they interact with one another under particular social, political, and economic conditions*. This means that the kinds of sports that exist and gain popularity often tell us much about the values and orientations of those who play, watch, or sponsor them. They also tell us about who has power in a social world.

Just as defining and identifying *official* sports is part of a political process, with outcomes that benefit some people more than others, so is the process of creating and sustaining sports in a social world.

This becomes apparent when we examine the struggles that often occur over whose ideas will be used when making decisions about the following sport-related issues:

1. What is the meaning and primary purpose of sports, and how should sports be organized to fit that meaning and purpose?
2. Who will play sports with whom, and under what conditions will they play?
3. What agencies or organizations will sponsor and control sports?

Heated debates occur when people have different answers to these questions. History shows that some of these debates have caused conflicts and led to lawsuits, government intervention, and the passage of laws. For example, people often disagree about the meaning, purpose, and organization of cheerleading in US high schools. School officials have traditionally said that cheerleading is not a sport because its primary purpose is to support high school teams. But as competitive cheer teams have been organized to train and compete against other teams at least 34 state high school activities associations now define "cheer" as an official sport. This is important because the stakes are high: being designated an official sport brings funding and other support that changes its status and meaning in schools, communities, and society. For example, as I write this, high school officials in many school districts are planning to sponsor and fund esports teams in high schools across the United States, and organizers of the 2024 Olympic Games in Paris are hoping to include breakdancing (i.e., "bboying" and "bgirling") as a new sport.

Disagreements and struggles over the purpose, meaning, and organization of sports occur most often when they involve the funding priorities of government agencies. For example, if the primary purpose of sport is to improve health and fitness for everyone, then funding should go primarily to sports with widespread participation resulting in net positive effects on physical well-being. But if people see sports as "wars without weapons" with the purpose being to push the limits of human ability, then funding should go to sports organized to produce high-performance athletes who can achieve competitive victories. This issue is regularly contested at the national and local levels of government, in universities and public school districts, and even in families, as people decide how to use resources to support physical activities and sports.

These examples show that sports are **contested activities**–that is, *activities for which there are no timeless and universal agreements about what they mean, why they exist, or how they should be organized.* This is also illustrated by historical disagreements over who is allowed to play sports and the conditions under which certain people can play. Cases involving extended struggles are listed in the box, "Who Plays and Who Doesn't" (p. 10).

The third issue that makes sports contested activities focuses on who should control them and provide the resources needed to play them. When people see sports contributing to the common good, it is likely that sport facilities and programs will be supported by government agencies and tax money. When people see sports as primarily contributing to individual development, it is likely that sport facilities and programs will be supported by individuals, families, and private-corporate sponsors. However, in both cases there will be struggles over funding levels, the extent to which sponsors control sports, and the extent to which sports are organized to be consistent with community values.

Struggles over these three issues show that using a single definition of sports may lead us to overlook important factors in a particular social world, such as who has the power and resources to shape the meanings given to particular activities at different times in a community or society. Being aware of these factors enables us to *put sports into context* and understand them in the terms used by those who create, play, and support them. It also helps us see that the definition of sports in any social world usually represents the ideas and interests of some people more than others. In the sociology of sport, this leads to questions and research focusing on whose ideas and interests count the most when it comes to determining (1) the meaning, purpose, and organization of sports; (2) who plays under what conditions; and (3) how sports will

Who Plays and Who Doesn't
Contesting a Place in Sports

Being cut from a youth sport team is a disappointing personal experience. But being in a category of people that is wholly excluded from all or some sports is more than disappointing–it is unfair and occasionally illegal. Most cases of categorical exclusion are related to gender and sexuality, skin color and ethnicity, ability and disability, age and weight, nationality and citizenship, and other "eligibility" criteria. Struggles about inclusion occur in connection with questions such as these:

- Will females be allowed to play sports and, if they are, will they play the same sports at the same time and on the same teams that males play, and will the rewards for achievement be the same for females and males?
- Will sports be open to people regardless of social class and wealth? Will wealthy and poor people play and watch sports together or separately?
- Will people from different racial and ethnic backgrounds play together or in segregated settings? Will the meanings given to skin color or ethnicity influence participation patterns or opportunities to play sports?
- Will age influence eligibility to play sports, and should sports be age integrated or segregated? Will people of different ages have the same access to participation opportunities?
- Will able-bodied people and people with a disability have the same opportunities to play sports, and will they play together or separately? What meanings will be given to the accomplishments of athletes with a disability compared to the accomplishments of athletes defined as able-bodied?
- Will lesbians, gay men, bisexuals, and transsexuals play alongside heterosexuals and, if they do, will they be treated fairly? What if they do not fit clearly into popular definitions of sex and gender?
- Will athletes control the conditions under which they play sports and will they have the power to change those conditions to meet their needs and interests?
- Will athletes be rewarded for playing, what form will the rewards take, and how will they be allocated?

Federal and local laws may mandate particular answers to these questions. However, traditions, local customs, and personal beliefs often support various forms of exclusion. The resulting struggles for more inclusion illustrate that sports can be hotly contested activities.

Think about sports in your school, community, and society: how have these inclusion questions been answered?

be sponsored and controlled. Material in each of the following chapters summarizes the findings of this research.

WHAT IS THE SOCIOLOGY OF SPORT?

The **sociology of sport** *is primarily a subdiscipline of sociology and physical education that studies sports as social phenomena.* Most research and writing in the field focuses on "organized, competitive sports," although people increasingly study other forms of physical activities that are health and fitness oriented, informally organized, or done just for the fun or challenge of it. These can include recreational, extreme, adventure, and virtual sports as well as the new phenomenon of esports.

Research in the sociology of sport generally seeks to answer the following "top ten" questions:

1. Why are some activities, and not others, selected and designated as sports in particular groups and societies?
2. Why are sports created and organized in different ways at different times and in different places?
3. How do people include sports and sport participation in their lives, and does participation affect individual development and social relationships?

4. How do sports and sport participation affect our ideas about bodies, human movement work, fun, social class, masculinity and femininity, race and ethnicity, ability and disability, achievement and competition, pleasure and pain, deviance and conformity, and aggression and violence?
5. How do various sports compare with other forms of movement in producing positive health and fitness outcomes?
6. How do sports contribute to overall community and societal development, and why do so many people assume that they do?
7. How is the meaning, purpose, and organization of sports related to the culture, social structure, and resources of a society?
8. How are sports related to important spheres of social life such as family, education, politics, the economy, media, and religion?
9. How do people use their sport experiences and knowledge about sports as they interact with others and explain what occurs in their lives and the world around them?
10. How can people use sociological knowledge about sports to understand and participate more actively and effectively in society, especially as agents of progressive change?

For those doing research to answer these and related questions, sports provide observation sites for studying the societies and cultures in which they exist. This means that the sociology of sport tells us about more than sports in society; in reality, it tells us about the organization and dynamics of relationships in society, and about how people see themselves and others in relation to the world around them.

The *Great Sport Myth* and Resistance to the Sociology of Sport

As organized sports have spread around the world, so has the myth that sport is essentially pure and good, and that its purity and goodness is automatically transferred to all who participate in it (Coakley, 2015). This myth supports related beliefs that sport builds character, and that anyone who plays sport will be a better person for doing so. The great sport myth and its implications are outlined in Figure 1.1.

FIGURE 1.1 The great sport myth.

Evidence that will be presented in the following chapters clearly shows that the essential purity and goodness of sport is a myth and that merely participating in or consuming sports does not guarantee any particular outcomes related to character development or increased purity and goodness. In fact, we hear every day about cases and situations that contradict the great sport myth. But that doesn't seem to weaken its uncritical acceptance by many people. In fact, when the actions of athletes, coaches, spectators, and others associated with sports are inconsistent with the perceived inherent purity and goodness of sport, those who accept the myth dismiss them as exceptions—as the actions of people so morally flawed that they resist the lessons that are inherent in sports.

The great sport myth implies that there is no need to study sports or seek ways to make them better. The sociology of sport is unnecessary, say the myth-believers, because sports are inherently positive. The source of problems, they say, is the morally flawed individuals who must be purged from sports so that goodness and purity will prevail. Sports, according to myth believers, are already as they should be—a source of inspiration and pure excitement that is not available in any other activity or sphere of life.

Throughout this book, we will see how the great sport myth influences many important decisions—from creating and funding organized sport programs for "at-risk" youth to making multibillion-dollar bids to host the Olympic Games, the FIFA World Cup (for men), and other sport mega-events with public money. The myth supports a strong belief in the power of sports to bring purity and goodness to individuals in the form of positive character traits and to cities and nations in the form of revitalized civic spirit and desired development.

Using the Sociology of Sport

Knowledge produced by research in the sociology of sport can be useful to athletes, coaches, parents, and people in sport management, recreation, physical education, public health, and community planning and development. For example, it can inform parents and coaches about the conditions under which youth sport participation is most likely to produce positive developmental effects among children and teenagers (NASPE, 2013). It explains why some sports have higher rates of violence than others and how to effectively control violence in sports and among spectators (Young, 2019).

Like knowledge produced in other fields, knowledge in the sociology of sport can be used for negative and selfish purposes unless it is combined with concerns for fairness and social justice. For example, it can inform football coaches that they can effectively control young men in US culture by threatening their masculinity and making them dependent on the coaching staff for approval of their worth as men. And it also shows that this strategy can be used to increase the willingness of young men to sacrifice their bodies "for the good of the team"–an orientation that some coaches favor and promote.

This example shows that the sociology of sport, like other scientific disciplines, can be used for many purposes. Like others who produce and distribute knowledge, those of us who study sports in society must consider why we ask certain research questions and how our research findings might affect people's lives. We can't escape the fact that social life is complex and characterized by inequalities, power differences, and conflicts of interests between different categories of people. Therefore, using knowledge in the sociology of sport is not a simple process that automatically brings about equal and positive benefits for everyone. In fact, it must also involve critical thinking about the potential consequences of what we know about sports in society. Hopefully, after reading this book you will be prepared to do the following:

1. Think critically about sports so you can identify and understand the issues and controversies associated with them.
2. Look beyond performance statistics and win–loss records to see sports as social activities that can have both positive and negative effects on people's lives.
3. Learn things about sports that enable you to make informed choices about your sport participation and the place of sports in your family, community, and society.
4. See sports as social constructions and strive to change them when they systematically and unfairly disadvantage some categories of people at the same time that they privilege others.

Controversies Created by the Sociology of Sport

Research in the sociology of sport can be controversial when it provides evidence that changes are needed in the ways that sports and social worlds are organized. Such evidence threatens some people, especially those who control sports organizations, benefit from the current organization of sports, or think that the current organization of sports is "right and natural."

People in positions of power know that social and cultural changes can jeopardize their control over others and the privileges that come with it. Therefore, they prefer approaches to sports that blame problems on the weaknesses and failures of individuals. When individuals are identified as the problem, solutions emphasize the need to control individuals more effectively and teach them how to adjust to social worlds as currently organized.

The potential for controversy created by a sociological analysis of sports is illustrated by reviewing research findings on sport participation among women around the world. Research shows that women, especially women in poor and working-class households, have lower rates of sport participation than do other categories of people (Ahmad, 2015; Cailliau, 2013; Elling and Janssens, 2009; UNESCO, 2017; Van Tuyckom et al., 2010). Research also shows that there are many reasons for this, including the following (Taniguchi and Shupe, 2012):

1. Women are less likely than men to have the time, freedom, money, and "cultural permission" needed to play sports regularly.
2. Women have little or no control of the facilities where sports are played or the programs in those facilities.
3. Women have less access to transportation and less overall freedom to move around at will and without fear.
4. Women often are expected to take full-time responsibility for the social and emotional needs of family members–a job that seldom allows them time to play sports.
5. Most sports programs around the world are organized by men and around the values, interests, and experiences of men.

These reasons all contribute to the fact that many women worldwide don't see sports as appropriate activities for them to take seriously.

It is easy to see the potential for controversy associated with these findings. They suggest that opportunities and resources to play sports should be increased for women, that women and men should share control of sports, and that new sports organized around the values, interests, and resources of women should be developed. They also suggest that there should be changes in ideas about masculinity and femininity, gender relations, family structures, the allocation of child-care responsibilities, the organization of work, and the distribution of resources in society–and that's quite a disruptive list of changes!

People who benefit from sports and social life as they are currently organized are likely to oppose and reject the need for these changes. They might even argue that the sociology of sport is too critical and idealistic and that the "natural" order would be turned upside down if sociological knowledge were used to organize social worlds. However, good research always inspires critical approaches to the social conditions that affect our lives. This is why studying sports with a critical eye usually occurs when researchers have informed visions of what sports and society could and should be in the future. Without these visions, often born of idealism, what would motivate and guide us as we participate in our communities, societies, and world? People who make a difference and change the world for the better have always been idealistic and unafraid of promoting structural changes in societies.

Despite controversies, research and popular interest in the sociology of sport has increased significantly in recent years. This growth will continue as long as scholars in the field do research and produce knowledge that people find useful as they try to understand social life and participate effectively as citizens in their communities and societies (Boykoff, 2018; Burawoy, 2005, 2014; Cooky, 2017; Donnelly et al., 2011).

WHY STUDY SPORTS IN SOCIETY?

We study sports because they are socially significant activities for many people, they reinforce important ideas and beliefs in many societies, and they've been integrated into major spheres of social life such as the family, religion, education, the economy, politics, and the media.

Sports Are Socially Significant Activities

As we look around us, we see that the Olympic Games, soccer's World Cups, American football's Super Bowl, Rugby World Cups, the Tour de France, the tennis championships at Wimbledon, and other sport mega-events attract global attention and media coverage. The biggest of these events are watched by billions of people in over two hundred countries. The media coverage of sports provides

Families and family schedules often are shaped by sport involvement, sometimes interfering with family relationships (left) and sometimes creating enjoyable time together (right).

vivid images and stories that entertain, inspire, and provide for people the words and ideas they often use to make sense of their experiences and the world around them. Even people with little or no interest in sports cannot ignore them when family and friends insist on taking them to games, watching sports at home, and talking about sports.

People worldwide talk about sports at work, at home, in bars, on campuses, at dinner tables, in school, with friends, and even with strangers at bus stops, airports, and other public places. Relationships often revolve around sports (see cartoons above). People identify with teams and athletes so closely that the outcomes of games influence their moods, identities, and sense of well-being. In a general sense, sports create opportunities for conversations that enable people to form and nurture relationships and even enhance their personal status as they describe and critique athletes, games, teams, coaching decisions, and media commentaries. When people use sports this way, they often broaden their social networks related to work, politics, education, and other spheres of their lives. This increases their **social capital,** that is, *the social resources that link them to social worlds* in positive ways (Harvey et al., 2007).

When people play sports, their experiences are often remembered as special and important in their lives. The emotional intensity, group camaraderie, and sense of accomplishment that often occur in sports make sport participation more memorable than many other activities.

For all these reasons, sports are logical topics for the attention of sociologists and others concerned with social life today.

Sports Reaffirm Important Ideas and Beliefs

We also study sports because they often are organized to reaffirm ideas and beliefs that influence how people see and evaluate the world around them. In fact, a key research topic in the sociology of sports is the relationship between sports and cultural ideologies.

We are not born with ideologies. We learn them as we interact with others and accept ideas and beliefs that are generally taken for granted in our culture. An **ideology** *is a shared interpretive framework that people use to make sense of and evaluate themselves, others, and events in their social worlds.* We learn ideologies as people around us consistently give meaning to and make sense of social phenomena in certain ways. Even if we don't agree with a particular ideology it represents the principles, perspectives, and viewpoints that are widely shared in our culture.

Most ideologies serve the interests of particular categories of people and are presented as accurate and truthful representations of the world as it is or as influential people think it should be. In this way, ideologies serve a social function in that they can be used to justify certain decisions and actions.

When we study sports in society, it is important to know about four ideologies that influence how sports are organized and who controls and participates in them. These ideologies are organized around ideas and beliefs about gender, race, social class, and ability. Each of these ideologies is explained in terms of how it is related to sports in our lives.

(*Source:* Paul W. Harvey IV)

Women in sports such as rugby, weightlifting, shot put, discus, pentathlon, roller derby, and other sports that require bursts of power have destroyed the myth of female frailty. As gender benders, these women have inspired females world wide to redefine their bodies and what they can do.

Gender Ideology

Gender ideology consists of *interrelated ideas and beliefs that are widely used to define masculinity and femininity, identify people as male or female, evaluate forms of sexual expression, and determine the appropriate roles of males and females in society.* The dominant or most widely shared gender ideology used in many societies is organized around three central ideas and beliefs:

1. Human beings are either female or male.
2. Heterosexuality is nature's foundation for human reproduction; other expressions of sexual feelings, thoughts, and actions are abnormal, deviant, or immoral.
3. Men are physically stronger and more rational than women; therefore, they are more naturally suited to possess power and assume leadership positions in the public spheres of society.

Debates about the truth of these ideas and beliefs have become common worldwide and they are part of (a) larger struggles over what it means to be a man or a woman; (b) what is defined as normal, natural, moral, legal, and socially acceptable when it comes to expressing gender and sexuality; and (c) who should have power in the major spheres of life such as the economy, politics, law, religion, family, education, health care, and sports. Today, many people have come to realize that dominant gender ideology privileges heterosexual males, gives them access to positions of power, and disadvantages women and those not perceived and classified as heterosexual.

Fortunately, ideologies can be changed. But those whose interests are directly served by a dominant ideology usually possess the power and resources to resist changes and demonize those advocating alternative ideas and beliefs. For example, the girls and women who first challenged gender ideology by entering the male world of sports were generally defined as abnormal, immoral, and unnatural (see Chapter 7). The demonization of these "gender benders" was especially strong in the case of women who played sports involving power and strength and women who did not conform to norms of heterosexual femininity. Men with power and resources banned females from certain sports, refused to fund their participation, excluded them from sport facilities, labeled female athletes as deviant, and promoted ideas and beliefs that supported their discrimination against females (Allison, 2018; Lewis, Roberts, & Andrews, 2018; Mansfield et al., 2017; Schultz, 2014).

The struggles around gender ideology also influence the lives of men—most directly, those who don't conform to prevailing ideas and beliefs about heterosexual masculinity (Anderson, Magrath, & Bullingham, 2016). In this sense certain sports, such as American football, ice hockey, boxing, and mixed martial arts, are organized, played, and described in ways that reaffirm an ideology that privileges certain boys and men over others. But as women and gender nonconforming men increasingly demonstrate their physical skills, they raise questions about and discredit dominant gender ideology (Aiba, 2017; Knijnik, 2015; Liu, Baghurst, & Bradley, 2018; Roberts, Anderson, & Magrath, 2017). This means that sports are *sites,* or *social places,* where ideas and beliefs about gender are reaffirmed at the same time that oppositional ideas and beliefs are expressed. In this way, sports are important in sites for ideological struggles related to the meanings and implications of gender in society and our everyday lives.

Racial Ideology

Racial ideology consists of *interrelated ideas and beliefs that are widely used to classify human beings into categories assumed to be biological and related to attributes such as intelligence, temperament, and physical abilities.* These ideas and beliefs vary greatly from culture to culture, due to historical factors, but racial ideologies are usually divisive forces that privilege particular categories of people and disadvantage others.

Racial ideology in the United States has been and continues to be unique. Its roots date back to the seventeenth century, but it was not fully developed until slavery came to an end and white people faced a new reality in which former slaves could claim citizenship and the rights that came with it. Fear, guilt, ignorance, rumors, stereotypes, and a desire to retain power and control over blacks led whites to develop a complex set of ideas and beliefs promoting white superiority and black inferiority as "facts of nature." The resulting ideology was organized around these three major ideas and beliefs:

1. Human beings can be classified into races on the basis of biologically inherited or genetically based characteristics.
2. Intellectual and physiological characteristics vary by race, with white people being intellectually and morally superior to black people and all people of color.
3. People classified as white have only white ancestors, and anyone with one or more black ancestors is classified as a black person.

The ideology based on these ideas and beliefs was used to justify segregation and discrimination based on skin color and deny that black people were real "Americans" in the full legal sense of the term.

The connections between racial ideology and sports are complex and they vary from one society to the next (see Chapter 8). Through much of the twentieth century whites in the United States used racial ideology to exclude African Americans and other dark-skinned people from many sports, especially those occurring in gender-mixed social settings, such as golf, tennis, and swimming.

For many years whites also believed that blacks had physical weaknesses that prevented them from excelling in certain sports. But, when blacks demonstrated physical skills that rivaled or surpassed those of whites, dominant racial ideology was revised to describe blacks as less evolved than whites and, therefore, more dependent on their innate physicality for survival. At the same time, whites saw themselves at a more advanced stage of evolution and dependent primarily on their innate intellectual abilities for survival–abilities they believed were not possessed to the same degree by blacks.

This racial ideology has been challenged and factually discredited during struggles over civil rights. But its roots are so deep in US culture that it continues to influence patterns of sport participation, beliefs about skin color and abilities, and the ways that people view sports and integrate them into their lives.

Social Class Ideology

Social class ideology consists of *interrelated ideas and beliefs that are widely shared and used by people to evaluate their material status; explain why economic success, failure, and inequalities exist; and* *what should be done about economic inequalities in a group or society.* The dominant class ideology in the United States is organized around three major ideas and beliefs:

1. All people have opportunities to achieve economic success.
2. The United States is a **meritocracy** *where deserving people become successful and where failure is the result of inability, poor choices, or a lack of motivation.*
3. Income and wealth inequality is normal and inevitable because some people work hard, develop their abilities, and make smart choices and others do not.

Although some people question the truth of these ideas and beliefs, the class ideology that they support is heavily promoted and remains in existence because it serves the interests of people with power and wealth.

Competitive sports in the United States have been organized and described to inspire stories and slogans that reaffirm this ideology and help sustain its popularity (see Chapter 9). Coaches, media commentators, and sport fans consistently proclaim that people can achieve anything through hard work and discipline, and that failure is the result of laziness and poor choices.

This way of thinking leads to the conclusion that wealth and power are earned by hardworking people of good character and that poverty befalls those who are careless, unwilling to work, or have weak character. As a result, there is little sympathy for the poor at the same time that winning athletes and coaches–and wealthy people generally–are widely seen as models of smart choice-making and strong character. To the extent that people accept this class ideology, socioeconomic inequality is justified and the wealth and privilege of economic elites is protected. Therefore, economic elites and the corporations they control are major sponsors of high profile, competitive sports that are organized and presented in ways that inspire widespread acceptance of this class ideology.

Ableist Ideology

Ableist ideology consists of *interrelated ideas and beliefs that are widely used to identify people as physically or intellectually disabled, to justify treating them as inferior, and to organize social worlds and physical spaces without taking them into account.* In many cultures today this ideology is organized around two major ideas and beliefs:

1. All people can be classified as either enabled *or* disabled.
2. People with a disability are inferior to and more needy than enabled people.

Underlying these ideas and beliefs is the general perspective of **ableism,** that is, *attitudes, actions, and policies based on the belief that people perceived as lacking certain abilities are inferior and, therefore, incapable of full participation in mainstream activities.* When people use ableist ideology, they tend to patronize, pathologize, or pity those whose abilities don't "measure up" to their standards of normality. This ideology leads to forms of social organization in which people are sorted into the categories of *enabled* and *disabled.*

Ableist ideology denies that there is natural variation in the physical and intellectual abilities of human beings, that abilities are situation- and task-specific, and that the abilities of all human beings change over time. As noted in *Reflect on Sport* (pp. 18–19), sports influence the meanings that are given to bodies in connection with their appearance and abilities.

Everyday experience shows us that there are many different abilities used for many different purposes, and each of us is more or less able, depending on the situation or task. Additionally, people often forget that being *enabled* is not a permanent condition, because abilities change due to accidents, disease, and the normal process of aging. This means that we cannot neatly categorize everyone as either enabled or disabled. We can rank people from low to high on a particular ability in a particular situation or when doing a specific task, but it is impossible to have one ability-based ranking system across

The Body Is More than Physical
Sports Influence Meanings Given to the Body

Until recently, most people viewed the body as a fixed fact of nature; it was biological only. But many scholars and scientists now recognize that a full understanding of the body requires that we also view it in social and cultural terms (Adelman & Ruggi, 2016; Andreasson & Johansson, 2019; van Amsterdam, Claringbould, & Knoppers, 2017; Wellard, 2016). The meanings given to the body and body parts in any culture are the foundation for people's ideas and beliefs about sex, gender, sexuality, beauty, self-image, body image, fashion, hygiene, health, nutrition, eating, fitness, ability and disability, age and aging, racial classification systems, disease, drugs and drug testing, violence and power, and other factors that affect our lives.

Cultural definitions of the body influence deep personal feelings such as pleasure, pain, sexual desires, and other sensations that we use to assess personal well-being, relationships, and quality of life. For example, people in Europe and North America during the nineteenth century identified insensitivity to physical pain as a sign that a person had serious character defects, and they saw a muscular body as an indicator of a criminal disposition, immorality, and lower-class status (Hoberman, 1992).

Cultural definitions of the body have changed so that today we see a person's ability to ignore pain, especially in sports, as an indicator of strong moral character, and we see a muscular body as proof of self-control and discipline rather than immorality and criminal tendencies. But in either case, our identities and experiences are inherently embodied, and our bodies are identified in connection with social and cultural definitions of age, sex, sexuality, race, ethnicity, and ability, among other factors.

Definitions of the body are strongly related to sports in many societies. For example, our conception of the "ideal body," especially the ideal male body, is strongly influenced by the athletic body (van Amsterdam et al., 2012). In fact, the bodies of athletes are often used as models of health and fitness, strength and power, control and discipline, and overall ability.

In today's competitive sports, the body is measured, monitored, classified, conditioned, trained, regulated, and assessed in terms of its performance under various

(*Source:* Quality Sport Images/Contributor/Getty Images)

The ideal male body? Christiano Ronaldo, a professional soccer player ("footballer"), is captain of the Portuguese national team and currently under contract with the Italian football club, Juventus. Reportedly, his 322 million followers on social media make him the most popular athlete in the world. His frequent shirtless presentations of self have had a worldwide impact on ideas about the male body and its representation of power and strength. However, ideas about the body change over time *and* are shaped by many social and cultural factors.

conditions. Instead of being experienced as a source of pleasure and joy, the body is more often viewed as an object used to achieve important goals. As an object, it must be developed, maintained, monitored, and repaired. Additionally, when the athletic body fails due to injuries, impairments, and age, it is reclassified in ways that alter a person's identity, relationships, and status.

Socially constructing the body in this way emphasizes control and rationality. It leads people to accept forms of body regulation such as weigh-ins, measuring body-fat percentage, testing for aerobic and anaerobic capacity, observing physiological responses to stressors, doing blood analysis, dieting, using drugs and other substances, drug testing, and self-monitoring with measuring devices attached to the body. For example, the members of some elite teams must now wear heart monitors and GPS devices in specially designed shirts or sport bras during practices so coaches and trainers can determine how hard they work, their fitness level, and their on-field strategy awareness (Gilmore, 2016; Millington, 2017). Similar technologies are even being used by some parents–for example, devices that count steps and calories expended–to "discipline" the bodies of their children so they can achieve performance goals and shape their bodies to meet parents' expectations (Tidén, Redelius, & Lundvall, 2017).

Cultural conceptions of the *body as a machine-like object* and *sport as performance* make it likely that athletes will use brain manipulations, hormonal regulation, body-part replacements, and genetic engineering as methods of disciplining, controlling, and managing their bodies. Measurable performance outcomes then become more important than subjective experiences of physical pleasure and joy. As a result, the ability to endure pain and stay in the game becomes an indicator of the "disciplined body;" and bodies that are starved to reduce body fat to unhealthy levels are viewed as "fit" and "in shape" (Brown, 2017).

When we realize that human life is embodied and that bodies are socially constructed in the context of culture, we ask the following critical questions in our sociology of sport research:

1. What are the origins of prevailing ideas about natural, ideal, and deviant bodies in sports and in society?
2. What are the moral and social implications of the ways that the body is protected, probed, monitored, tested, trained, disciplined, evaluated, manipulated, and rehabilitated in sports?
3. How are bodies in sports marked and categorized by gender, skin color, ethnicity, (dis)ability, and age, and what are the social implications of such body marking and categorization?
4. How are athletic bodies represented in the media and popular culture, and how do those representations influence identities, relationships, and forms of social organization in society?
5. Who owns the body of an athlete, including the athletes' tattoos, and under what conditions can bodies or tattoos be used to promote products, services, beliefs, or ideas?
6. If moving the body were seen primarily as a source of pleasure rather than tool for achievement, would more people engage in physical activity?

These questions challenge taken-for-granted ideas about nature, beauty, health, and competitive sports. Ask yourself: *how have my ideas about bodies, including my own, been influenced by sports and the culture in which I live?*

all situations and tasks encountered in everyday life, or even in sports.

Variations across all physical and intellectual abilities are a normal part of human life. But ableist ideology and ableism obscure this fact and prevent us from realistically dealing with ability differences in society.

In summary, ideologies are important parts of culture. People are usually unaware of them because they are simply taken for granted in their lives. As ideologies are widely shared and used as a basis for establishing, organizing, and evaluating social relationships and all forms of social organization, they are woven over time into the fabric of culture and the organization of society. This makes them different from the ideas and beliefs of individuals or those shared only with family members and friends.

Sociology has always attempted to defatalize and denaturalize the present, demonstrating that the world could be otherwise. –Editor, *Global Dialogue* (2011)

Ideologies also resist change. They are defended by those who use them to make sense of the world and those whose privilege depends on them. Sometimes they are connected with religious beliefs and given intrinsic moral value, which fosters intense resistance to change. Although we rarely acknowledge our ideologies, we frequently recognize the ideologies of people whose assumptions and perspectives are different than ours. When this occurs we often criticize their ideologies while we leave our own unexamined. However, in this book we will take a critical look at dominant gender, racial, class, and ableist ideologies and their implications for sports in Chapters 7-10.

Sports Are Integrated into Major Spheres of Social Life

Sociology is also used to study sports because sports are clearly connected to major spheres of social life. This will become increasingly clear in the following chapters. For example, Chapters 3 and 4 deal with family relationships and how they influence sport participation and how sports influence family life today. Issues involving the economy are covered in most chapters, and Chapter 11 is dedicated to examining the commercialization of sports and the changes that come with it. The media are closely connected with contemporary sports, and new social media are now changing the ways in which fans engage athletes and consume sports. This is explained in Chapter 12.

Government and politics are no strangers to sports, although their influence has changed as sports have become increasingly global and less dependent on nation-states. This is the topic of Chapter 13. The connections between interscholastic sports, the lives of students, the academic mission of schools, and the organization of high schools and colleges is the focus of Chapter 14. Finally, Chapter 15 deals with the complex relationships between major world religions and sports. Overall, sports are not only visible and important activities in themselves, but they are linked to major spheres of life in today's societies.

summary

WHY STUDY THE SOCIOLOGY OF SPORT?

This book is based on the premise that sports are socially significant activities worthy of critical investigation. To do so I use the concepts and theories of sociology to identify the patterns and processes that are the stuff of our lived experiences.

Sociology is the study of *the social worlds that people create, organize, maintain, and change through their relationships with each other.* Sociologists use concepts, research, and theories to describe and explain social worlds. In the process, they enable us to put the lives of individuals and groups into context. This makes us aware of the circumstances that set limits and create possibilities in people's lives. For most sociologists, the ultimate goal is to create and distribute knowledge that enables people to understand, control, and improve the conditions of their lives and the social worlds in which they live.

Sociologists use the concepts of culture, social interaction, and social structure as they investigate social worlds. Sociological knowledge about sports and other social worlds is based on data systematically collected in research. This makes it different from statements about sports based only on personal experiences and feelings.

Defining sports presents a challenge. If we use a single definition that emphasizes organization and competition, it can lead us to ignore people who have neither the resources nor the desire to develop formally organized and competitive physical activities. For this reason, many of us in the sociology of sport prefer an alternative definitional approach based on the assumption that sports are social constructions and that conceptions of sports vary over time and from one social world to another. Therefore, we try to explain why certain activities, and not others, are identified as sports in a particular group or society, why some sports are more strongly supported and funded than others, and how various categories of people are affected by commonly used definitions of sports and related funding priorities.

This alternative approach to defining sports also emphasizes that they are contested activities, because people can disagree about their meaning, purpose, and organization. Furthermore, people often have different ideas about who should play sports and the conditions under which participation should occur. Debates over who plays and who is excluded can create heated exchanges and bitter feelings, because they are tied to notions of fairness and the allocation of resources in social worlds. Finally, people can also disagree over which sports will be sponsored, who will sponsor them, and how much control sponsors should have over sports.

Asking critical questions is the starting point for doing the sociology of sport. When I say that we use a critical approach to think about sports in society, I mean that we move away from the question, "Is this good or bad?" and instead ask, the following: (a) "Is it working or not working? (b) For whom is it working or not working? (c) Whom does it harm or disadvantage? (d) What is the value of sport as it is organized, and could value be increased if it were changed?"

The sociology of sport often struggles for acceptance in societies where many people accept the *great sport myth*–that is, the beliefs that sports are pure and good and that all who play or consume them will share in this purity and goodness. These beliefs lead to the conclusion that it is not necessary to study and critically evaluate sport because it is essentially good as it is.

When sociologists study sports in society, they often discover problems related to the structure and organization of sports or the social worlds in which sports exist. Additionally, our research-based recommendations may threaten those who benefit by maintaining the status quo in sports. This leads some people to see the sociology of sports as controversial, but we continue to do research and produce knowledge that can be used to promote fairness and social justice.

People study sports in society because sports are socially significant activities for many people. They provide excitement, memorable experiences, and opportunities to initiate and extend social relationships. Sports also reaffirm and sometimes challenge important ideas and beliefs, especially those related to gender, race and ethnicity, social class, and ability.

Finally, sports are studied sociologically because they are closely tied to major spheres of social life such as family, economy, media, politics, education, and religion.

Overall, sports are such an integral part of everyday life that they cannot be ignored by anyone concerned with the organization and dynamics of social life today.

SUPPLEMENTAL READINGS:

Reading 1. Why should I take sociology of sport as a college course?

Reading 2. The sociology and psychology of sport: what's the difference?

Reading 3. Play, games, and sports: They're all related to each other

Reading 4. Professional associations in the sociology of sport

Reading 5. Where to find sociology of sport research

Reading 6. Basketball: An idea becomes a sport

Reading 7. People's sports versus Prolympic sports: What are the differences?

SPORT MANAGEMENT ISSUES

- You work for a sport management consulting firm. A client wants to invent a new sport that will attract participants as well as eventual media coverage, and asks you to submit a proposal covering what must occur and how long it might take. Describe the points you will present in your "create a sport" proposal.
- You have a teaching assistantship as you enter a graduate program in sport management. Your advisor says that you must teach a sociology of sport course to the first-year undergraduate sport management students. Describe what you will say on the first day of class to convince your students that it is important for them to take the course seriously.
- One of the major challenges faced in sport management is to deal with the influence of the great sport myth in contemporary cultures. Explain why this myth should be questioned by giving three examples of how sports have not automatically produced positive consequences for individuals and/or schools and communities.
- You are an advisor to a state high school activities association in the United States. The National Federation of High School Activity Association has just announced that they have partnered with PlayVS, Inc. to establish esport leagues and state championships nationwide. The head of the state association asks for your advice on forming or not forming an esport league and sponsoring a state championship as they do with basketball, volleyball, and other sports. She believes that esports are not sports and should not be treated as such. Do you agree or disagree with her, and how do you explain your decision?

references

Adelman, Miriam, and Lennita Ruggi. 2016. The sociology of the body. *Current Sociology* 64(6): 907–930.

Ahmad, Rather Hilal. 2015. Women sports in India: Constraints, challenges, complications, and its remedies. *International Journal of Applied Research* 1(13): 656–659.

Aiba, Keiko. 2017. *Transformed bodies and gender: Experiences of women pro wrestlers in Japan*. Osaka: Union Press of Japan.

Allison, Rachel. 2018. *Kicking center.* New Brunswisk, NJ: Rutgers University Press.

Anderson, Eric, Rory Magrath, and Rachael Bullingham. 2016. *Out in sport: The experiences of openly gay and lesbian athletes*. London: Routledge.

Andreasson, Jesper, and Thomas Johansson. 2019. Triathlon bodies in motion reconceptualizing feelings of pain, nausea and disgust in the Ironman Triathlon. *Body & Society* 25(2): 119–145.

Boykoff, Jules. 2018. Riding the lines: Academia, public intellectual work, and scholar-activism. *Sociology of Sport Journal* 35(2): 81–88.

Brown, Seth. 2017. 'Tidy, toned and fit': Locating healthism within elite athlete programmes. *Sport, Education and Society* 22(7): 785–798.

Burawoy, Michael. 2005. For public sociology. *American Sociological Review* 70(1): 4–28.

Burawoy, Michael. 2014. Introduction: Sociology as a combat sport. *Current Sociology* 62(2): 140–155.

Cailliau, Valentine. 2013. Worldwide barriers to women's participation in physical activity. *sportanddev.org* (January 30): https://www.sportanddev.org/en/article/news/worldwide-barriers-womens-participation-physical-activity

Coakley, Jay. 2015. Assessing the sociology of sport: On cultural sensibilities and the great sport myth. *International Review for the Sociology of Sport* 50(1): 402–406.

Cooky, Cheryl. 2017. "We cannot stand idly by": A necessary call for a public sociology of sport. *Sociology of Sport Journal* 34(1): 1–11.

Donnelly, Peter, Michael Atkinson, Sarah Boyle, and Courtney Szto. 2011. Sport for development and peace: A public sociology perspective. *Third World Quarterly* 32(3): 589–601.

Elling, Agnes, and Jan Janssens. 2009. Sexuality as a structural principle in sport participation negotiating sports spaces. *International Review for the Sociology of Sport* 44(1): 71-86.

Gilmore, James N. 2016. Everywear: The quantified self and wearable fitness technologies. *New Media & Society* 18(11): 2524-2539.

Guinee, Sarah. 2019. Dark side of sports journalism as fans harass female reporters online. *CPJ.org* (February 28): https://cpj.org/blog/2019/02/sports-fans-harass-female-journalist-online.php

Harvey, Jean, Maurice Levesque, and Peter Donnelly. 2007. Sport volunteerism and social capital. *Sociology of Sport Journal* 24(2): 206-223.

Hoberman, John M. 1992. *Mortal engines: The science of performance and the dehumanization of sport*. New York: Free Press.

Knijnik, Jorge. 2015. Femininities and masculinities in Brazilian women's football: Resistance and compliance. *Journal of International Women's Studies* 16(3): 54-70: http://vc.bridgew.edu/jiws/vol16/iss3/5

Lagaert, Susan & Henk Roose. 2016. Exploring the adequacy and validity of 'sport': Reflections on a contested and open concept. *International Review for the Sociology of Sport* 51(4): 485-498.

Lamb, Penny & Esther Priyadharshini. 2015. The conundrum of C/cheerleading. *Sport, Education and Society* 20(7): 889-907.

Lewis, Colin J., Simon J. Roberts, and Hazel Andrews. 2018. 'Why am I putting myself through this?' Women football coaches' experiences of the Football Association's coach education process. *Sport, Education and Society* 23(1): 28-39.

Liu, Hung-Ling, Timothy Baghurst, and Michael Bradley. 2018. Female roller derby athletes' athletic identity and systematic pursuit of leisure. *Journal of Amateur Sport* 4(1): 108-128.

Mansfield, Louise, Belinda Wheaton, Jayne Caudwell, and Rebecca Watson. 2017. Sportswomen still face sexism, but feminism can help achieve a level playing field. The *Conversation* (July 28): https://theconversation.com/sportswomen-still-face-sexism-but-feminism-can-help-achieve-a-level-playing-field-76748

Millington, Brad. 2017. *Fitness, technology and society: Amusing ourselves to life*. London: Routledge.

NASPE. 2013. *Maximizing the benefits of youth sport (Position Statement)*. Reston, VA: National Association for Sport and Physical Education.

NFHS. 2019. Esports in high school. National Federation of State High School Associations: http://www.nfhs.org/sports-resource-content/esports/

Reed, Ken. 2011. *A sports manifesto: Citizenship through sports activism.* Washington DC: League of Fans.

Roberts, Steven, Eric Anderson, and Rory Magrath. 2017. Continuity, change and complexity in the performance of masculinity among elite young footballers in England. *British Journal of Sociology* 68(2): 336-357.

Rogers, Nick. 2019. Holding court: The social regulation of masculinity in university pickup basketball. *Journal of Contemporary Ethnography* 48(6): 731-749.

Schultz, Jaime. 2014. *Qualifying times: Points of change in US women's sport*. Champaign, IL: University of Illinois Press.

Spaaij, Ramón, Jonathan Magee, and Ruth Jeanes. 2014. *Sport and social exclusion in global society.* London: Routledge.

Taniguchi, Hiromi & Frances L Shupe. 2014. Gender and family status differences in leisure-time sports/fitness participation. *International Review for the Sociology of Sport* 49(1): 65-84.

Tidén, Anna; Karin Redelius & Suzanne Lundvall. 2017. The social construction of ability in movement assessment tools. *Sport, Education and Society* 22(6): 697-709.

UNESCO. 2017. *Worldwide barriers to women's participation in physical activity*. Paris: United Nations Educational, Scientific and Cultural Organization: http://www.unesco.org/new/en/social-and-human-sciences/themes/physical-education-and-sport/women-and-sport/

Unruh, David R. 1980. The nature of social worlds. *Pacific Sociological Review* 23(3): 271–296.

van Amsterdam, Noortje, Annelies Knoppers, Inge Claringbould, and Marian Jongmans. 2012. A picture is worth a thousand words: Constructing (non-)athletic bodies. *Journal of Youth Studies* 15(3): 293–309.

Van Tuyckom, Charlotte, Jeroen Scheerder, and Piet Bracke. 2010. Gender and age inequalities in regular sports participation: A cross-national study of 25 European countries. *Journal of Sports Sciences* 28(10): 1077–1084.

Washington, Jesse. 2019. Born out of competition, breaking is a natural for the Olympics. (February 27): https://theundefeated.com/features/born-out-of-competition-breakdancing-is-a-natural-for-the-paris-olympics/

Wellard, Ian, ed. 2016. *Researching embodied sport: Exploring movement cultures*. London: Routledge.

Wolverton, Brad. 2014. At meeting of Knight Commission, old ideas are new again. *The Chronicle of Higher Education* (September 9): http://chronicle.com/article/At-Meeting-of-Knight/148709/

Yang, Nicole. 2019. Adam Silver says NBA is a melancholy place. *Boston Globe* (March 2): https://www.bostonglobe.com/sports/celtics/2019/03/01/adam-silver-says-nba-melancholy-place/lHMiD4fH6mD2FoxAJhAQDN/story.html

Young, Kevin. 2019. *Sport, violence and society* (2nd edition). London: Routledge.

chapter

2

(*Source:* John Flournoy/McGraw-Hill Education)

PRODUCING KNOWLEDGE ABOUT SPORTS IN SOCIETY

How Is Knowledge Produced in the Sociology of Sport?

It is foolish to be convinced without evidence, but it is equally foolish to refuse to be convinced by real evidence.

—Upton Sinclair, journalist and author, 1930 (p. 138)

[K]nowing what scientists think is ultimately no substitute for actually believing it. . . . [People] just aren't willing to endorse [scientific] consensus when it contradicts their political or religious views. . . . With science as with politics, identity often trumps the facts.

—Brendan Nyhan, political scientist, University of Michigan (2014)

In science, when human behavior enters the equation, things go nonlinear. That's why Physics is easy and Sociology is hard.

—Neil deGrasse Tyson, astrophysicist (2016)

We all work with concepts. . . . We have no choice. . . . Without concepts, you don't know where to look, what to look for, or how to recognize what you were looking for when you find it.

—Howard Becker, sociologist (1998)

Chapter Outline

Producing Knowledge in the Sociology of Sport

Doing Research and Using Theory in the Sociology of Sport: A Case Study

The Impact of Sociology of Sport Knowledge

Using a Critical Approach to Produce Knowledge

Summary: How Is Knowledge Produced in the Sociology of Sport?

Learning Objectives

- Understand how and why our personal theories about social life differ from theories used in the sociology of sport.
- Identify the five steps involved in the production of knowledge.
- Explain the differences between cultural, interactionist, and structural theories.
- Understand what it means to say that gender exists as meaning, performance, and organization.
- Know the differences between a quantitative approach and qualitative approach and when it would be best to use one over the other when doing social research.
- Identify and describe the three major research methods used in the sociology of sport.
- Describe what it means to say that sports are more than reflections of society.
- Know the key features of a critical approach to producing knowledge in the sociology of sport.

The sociology of sport focuses on the deeper game associated with sports in society. We learn about that deeper game by using research and theories to understand the following:

1. The social and cultural contexts in which sports exist.
2. The connections between those contexts and sports.
3. The social worlds that people create as they participate in sports.
4. The experiences of individuals and groups associated with those social worlds.
5. The organization of sports and how people are influenced by sports

Our research is motivated by combinations of curiosity, interest in sports, and a desire to know more about social worlds. Most of us also want to use what we know about sports in society to promote social justice, expose and challenge the exploitive use of power, and empower people who lack the resource to effectively participate in political processes and improve the quality of their lives.

As we study sports, we use research and theories to produce knowledge. **Social research** consists of *investigations in which we seek answers to questions about social worlds by systematically gathering and analyzing data.* Research is the primary tool that we use to expand what we know and to develop and refine theories about sports in society.

Social theories are *logically interrelated explanations of the actions and relationships of human beings and the organization and dynamics of social worlds.* Theories provide frameworks for asking research questions, interpreting information, and applying the knowledge we produce about sports.

Research and theories go hand in hand because we use research to create and test the validity of theories, and we use theories to help us ask good research questions and make sense of the data we collect in our studies.

The goal of sociology is to describe and explain social worlds logically and in ways that are consistent with systematically collected and analyzed evidence. This makes knowledge in the sociology of sport a more valid and reliable source of information than what we read or hear in the media and online, where much of the content is based on a desire to entertain and attract a large audience.

In practical terms, knowledge produced in the sociology of sport helps us understand more fully the actions of individuals, the dynamics of social relationships, and the organization of social worlds. This, in turn, enables us to be more informed citizens as we participate in our schools, communities, and society.

The goal of this chapter is to answer these questions:

1. How is knowledge produced in the sociology of sport?
2. What are the primary research methods used by scholars who study sports in society?
3. Why do scholars often use a critical approach when doing research and developing theories in the sociology of sport?

PRODUCING KNOWLEDGE IN THE SOCIOLOGY OF SPORT

All of us manage our lives and navigate social worlds by using personal, practical knowledge. We acquire this knowledge by keeping our eyes and ears open and developing explanations of everyday experiences and events. For example, consider how you manage your life at home, school, work, and with friends. What strategies do you use to understand what occurs around you, and how do you make decisions about what to do in connection with the people and events in your life?

We learn to navigate social worlds and manage our lives by observing how others act and what occurs in various situations. Then we use this information to develop experience-based explanations or "personal theories" about our own actions, the actions of others, and the social worlds we encounter. These **personal theories** *are summaries of our ideas about and explanations of social life and the contexts in which it occurs.* We use them as guides when we make decisions and interact with others throughout the day.

Think about your family life as an example. You collect information and develop explanations to make sense of your family and your involvement in it. You may even consider how your family is related to the larger community and society in which you live. In the process, you develop "educated hunches" for why your family is more or less loving, strict, organized, wealthy, poor, or supportive than other families. The goal of your personal, experience-based data collection and theorizing is to make sense and gain control of your life and the social worlds in which you live.

Personal theories are forms of practical knowledge that we use to anticipate events, the actions of others, and the consequences of our own actions in various situations. Without them, we would be passive responders in our social worlds—victims of culture and society. But with theories, we become potentially active agents with the ability to participate intentionally and strategically in social worlds, reproducing or changing them as we take action alone and with others.

When Pierre Bourdieu, a famous French sociologist, discussed the practical knowledge that people develop through their personal experiences, he referred to it as "cultural capital" (Bourdieu, 1986). He explained that each of us can acquire and accumulate cultural capital as we expand our social and cultural experiences and make sense of them in ways that increase our understanding of ourselves, our relationships, and the dynamics of social worlds. Although each of us has different opportunities and experiences, we can convert our personal theories into cultural capital. Like money, cultural capital has value as we use it to navigate, manage, and control our lives; unlike money, cultural capital can be used over and over again without running up our bills.

As you consider these points, you may wonder how your personal observations and theories about sports and sport experiences compare with research and theories in the sociology of sport. Personal research focuses on our immediate social worlds. We gather and analyze information, but we don't use carefully developed methods and follow systematic and rigorous guidelines as we do so. Similarly, we develop personal theories for our own use. We don't systematically test them, compare them with related theories, and make them public so that others can examine them and determine their overall validity in different social worlds.

Research in the sociology of sport, unlike personal research, is designed to answer questions that go beyond the experiences and the social situations encountered by one person. In sociological research, we collect data from people or in situations that are chosen because they can provide information to answer particular questions. We then analyze the data by using methods that have been developed and refined by other sociologists. If the analysis leads to clear conclusions, we try to connect them with the conclusions and theories of other sociologists in the hope of expanding knowledge about the dynamics and organization of social life. Finally, we are expected to publish our studies so that others can critically examine them to see if they have flaws that would invalidate our findings.

People in the sociology of sport may study particular topics because they have a personal interest in them, but the process of doing research involves using methods that minimize the influence of our personal values and experiences on the findings and conclusions. Basic research methods used in sociology of sports research are described later in the chapter (pp. 32–44), but first we will examine a case study that illustrates how social research is done and how theory is used in the process of producing knowledge in the sociology of sport.

DOING RESEARCH AND USING THEORY IN THE SOCIOLOGY OF SPORT: A CASE STUDY

Micheal Messner is a well-known and respected sociologist at the University of Southern California. One of his books, *Taking the Field: Women, Men, and Sports* (2002), was named best book of 2002 by his colleagues in the sociology of sport. In the first chapter of Messner's book, he described a situation

(*Source:* Jay Coakley)

The social worlds created around sports are so complex that it helps to have systematic research methods and logical theories to study and understand them. When I attend youth sports events I use knowledge produced by Micheal Messner and others in the sociology of sport to help me make sense of what occurs there.

that, in part, inspired him to do in-depth sociological research on the connections between sports and gender in the United States. The situation occurred as he accompanied his son to the opening ceremony of a youth soccer season. Here is what he observed:

> The Sea Monsters is a team of four- and five-year old boys. Later this day, they will play their first ever soccer game. . . . Like other teams, they were assigned team colors–in this case, green and blue–and asked to choose their team name at their first team meeting. . . . A grandmother of one of the boys created the spiffy team banner, which was awarded a prize this morning. While they wait for the ceremony to begin, the boys inspect and then proudly pose for pictures in front of their new award-winning team banner. The parents stand a few feet away, some taking pictures, some just watching. . . .
>
> Queued up one group away from the Sea Monsters is a team of four- and five-year-old girls in green and white uniforms. . . . They have chosen the name Barbie Girls and they too have a new team banner. But the girls are pretty much ignoring their banner, for they have created another, more powerful symbol around which to rally. In fact, they are the only team among the 156 marching today with a team float–a red Radio Flyer wagon base, on which sits a Sony boom box playing music, and a three-foot-plus tall Barbie doll on a rotating pedestal. Barbie is dressed in the team colors; indeed, she sports a custom-made green and white cheerleader-style outfit, with the Barbie Girls' names written on the skirt. Her normally all-blond hair has been streaked with Barbie Girl green and features a green bow with polka dots. Several of the girls on the team have supplemented their uniforms with green bows in their hair as well.
>
> The volume on the boom box nudges up, and four or five girls begin to sing a Barbie song. Barbie is now slowly rotating on her pedestal, and as the girls sing more gleefully and more loudly, some of them begin to hold hands and walk around the float, in synch with Barbie's rotation. Other same-aged girls from other teams are drawn to the celebration and, eventually, perhaps a dozen girls are singing the Barbie song. . . .

While the Sea Monsters mill around their banner, some of them begin to notice and then begin to watch and listen when the Barbie Girls rally around their float. At first, the boys are watching as individuals, seemingly unaware of each other's shared interest. . . . I notice slight smiles on a couple of their faces, as though they are drawn to the Barbie Girls' celebratory fun. Then, with side glances, some of the boys begin to notice each other's attention on the Barbie Girls. Their faces begin to show signs of distaste. One of them yells out, "NO BARBIE!" Suddenly, they all begin to move, jumping up and down, nudging, and bumping one another, and join in a group chant; "NO BARBIE! NO BARBIE! NO BARBIE!" They now appear to be every bit as gleeful as the girls as they laugh, yell, and chant against the Barbie Girls.

The parents watch the whole scene with rapt attention. . . . "They are SO different!" exclaims one smiling mother approvingly. A male coach offers a more in-depth analysis: "When I was in college," he says, "I took these classes from professors who showed us research that showed that boys and girls are the same. I believed it, until I had my own kids and saw how different they are." "Yeah," another dad responds. "Just look at them! They are so different!"

The girls meanwhile, show no evidence that they hear, see, or are even aware of the presence of the boys, who are . . . loudly proclaiming their opposition to the Barbie Girls' songs and totem. The girls continue to sing, dance, laugh, and rally around the Barbie for few more minutes, before they are called to reassemble in their groups for the beginning of the parade.

After the parade, the teams reassemble on the infield of the track, but now in a less organized manner. The Sea Monsters once again find themselves in the general vicinity of the Barbie Girls and take up the "NO BARBIE!" chant. Perhaps put out by the lack of response to their chant, they begin to dash, in twos and threes, invading the girls' space and yelling menacingly. With this, the Barbie Girls have little choice but to recognize the presence of the boys; some look puzzled and shrink back, some engage the boys and chase them off. The chasing seems only to incite more excitement among the boys. Finally, parents intervene and defuse the situation, leading their children off to their cars, homes, and eventually to their soccer games (from Messner, 2002, pp. 3-6).

As Messner observed these things, it caused him to think critically about youth sports. As a father, he was concerned about how his son would make sense of these experiences as a five-year-old boy in twenty-first-century America. He even thought about how to help his son define them in ways that would impact his development positively. But as a sociologist, Messner's thoughts went beyond his immediate experiences and his role as a father. He wondered why parents at the soccer ceremony accepted the idea that boys and girls are naturally different, even though many of the boys were initially interested in the playful actions of the girls and their use of the Barbie icon. Taking this thought a step further, he wondered if people who use "nature" to explain the actions of their children tend to overlook similarities between boys and girls and feel no need to discuss strategies to help their children understand that boys don't "naturally" try to intimidate girls.

Even though the boys' "playful actions" did not physically hurt anyone, Messner wondered if certain sports are organized to reaffirm ideas about masculinity and femininity so that they make it seem normal for boys and men to express aggression and intimidate others. This also made him think about the decision of the American Youth Soccer Organization (AYSO) officials to segregate soccer teams by sex, thereby eliminating opportunities for boys and girls to play together and discover that they often share interests and other characteristics. Without such opportunities, are boys and girls more likely to grow up thinking that males and females are naturally "opposites," even though they share many attributes? And if this is so, what implications does it have for how we identify ourselves, form relationships, and organize our social worlds? As Messner asked these critical questions about sports and gender, he decided to do a study to expand sociological knowledge about this topic.

At this point, Messner was at the beginning of a five-step process for producing knowledge in the sociology of sport. These steps are listed in Figure 2.1, and we can use them as a guide as we discuss this case study.

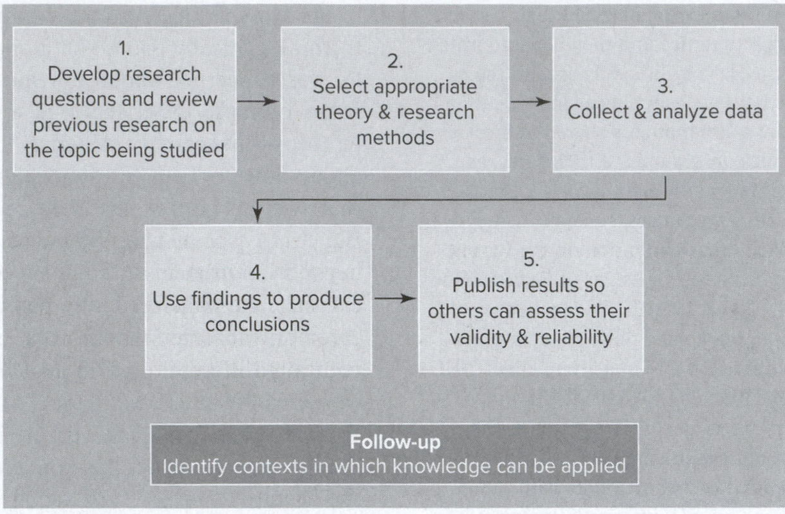

FIGURE 2.1 Producing knowledge in the sociology of sport.

Step 1: Develop Research Questions

Producing knowledge always begins with observations of the world followed by questions about what is and is not observed. In this case, Messner observed a particular event and combined what he witnessed with his previous observations and knowledge of sports.

As he thought more deeply about his observations, he asked a series of critical questions about culture, social interaction, and social structure–the three concepts around which much sociological knowledge is organized. In connection with culture, he asked these questions:

- What gender-related words, meanings, and symbols do American children learn to use as they identify themselves and others?
- How do children learn and use cultural ideas and beliefs to separate human beings into two sex categories that they see as "opposites," even though males and females share many social, psychological, and physiological attributes and are not biological "opposites"?

In connection with social interaction, he asked:

- How do children perform gender in their everyday lives, and how do they learn to successfully present themselves to others as boys or girls?
- What happens in their relationships when they don't perform gender as others expect them to?

In connection with social structure, he asked:

- How is gender a part of the overall organization of the AYSO (American Youth Soccer Organization) and other sport programs?
- How does the organization of sports at all levels create constraints and possibilities that influence the lives of boys and men in different ways than they influence the lives of girls and women?

To see if other researchers had already answered these questions or developed theories to guide his study, Messner reviewed many of the 326 sources he listed as references in his book. This "review of the literature," as it is called by researchers, indicated that there was a need to know more about the relationship between sports and how people learn and incorporate ideas about gender into their identities, relationships, and the organization of social worlds.

Step 2: Select Appropriate Theory and Research Methods

This is a crucial step in the knowledge production process. When you have selected a theory, or a combination of theories, you then have a guide for thinking about your research questions and connecting them to what is already known about the organization and dynamics of social worlds. Additionally, there are different research methods that can be used to collect and analyze the information that will help you answer your research questions.

Selecting Theories As he designed his research project, Messner knew that human beings, social relationships, and social worlds are complex and must be viewed from different angles and vantage points to describe and explain them accurately. Therefore, he used a combination of cultural, interactionist, and structural theories as guides for conceptualizing his project. Each of these theories focuses on different aspects of social life. Table 2.1 summarizes the central features of these theories, showing that each one explains different aspects of social worlds, has a different focus of

Table 2.1 Central features of major types of theories used in the sociology of sport

Type of Theory	Help to Explain	Major Focus of Analysis	Major Concepts Used	Examples of Research*
Cultural Theories	Processes through which people create, maintain, and change values, norms, ideas, and beliefs as they play and watch sports	The ways people define and make sense of their bodies, experiences, and relationships as sport participants and consumers	Values, norms, ideas, beliefs, ideology, symbols, and narratives associated with sports	– imagery and narratives used in the media coverage of men's and women's sports – impact of racial ideology on the sport participation choices of individuals
Interactionist Theories	Social interaction and relationships in the social worlds created in connection with sports	Social development; the relationships through which people give meaning to sport experiences and integrate them into their lives	Interaction, socialization, role models, significant others, self-concept, identity, labeling, deviance, and stereotyping	– process of normalizing pain and injury when playing sports – process of developing and maintaining athletic identities
Structural Theories	The social organization and patterns of relationships that influence opportunities, decisions, and actions in sports	Impact of social organization on access to power, authority, status, resources, and economic opportunities in sports and society	Status, roles, groups, authority, power relations, social control, social inequality, social institutions, organizations, and societies	– gender equity in school sport programs – who benefits when public money builds stadiums for pro sport teams

*Source: See Messner (2002) Chapters 2, 3, and 4 for examples of these and other studies. Chapter 4, "Center of Attention: The Gender of Sports Media," summarizes studies guided by cultural theories. Chapter 2, "Playing Center: The Triad of Violence in Men's Sports," summarizes studies guided by interactionist theories. Chapter 3, "Center of the Diamond: The Institutional Core of Sport," summarizes studies guided by structural theories.

analysis, uses different concepts, and addresses different issues.

Messner used **cultural theories** because they *explain what we know about the ways that people think and express their values, ideas, and beliefs as they live together and create social worlds.* Research based on cultural theories focuses on the processes through which people create, maintain, and change ideas and beliefs about their lives and the social worlds in which they live.

Cultural theories emphasize that people create symbols and give meaning to aspects of their worlds that are important to them; in turn, those symbols and meanings influence their feelings, thoughts, and actions.

Cultural theories utilize concepts such as values, norms, ideas, beliefs, ideology, symbols, and language because they are the tools and reference points that people use to make sense of and give meaning to themselves, their experiences, and the world around them. In most cases, people who use cultural theories assume that culture is messy–its boundaries are fuzzy and difficult to identify, it contains inconsistencies and contradictions, and it is dynamic, meaning that culture is always changing as people develop new ideas, beliefs, values, and norms.

Cultural theories alerted Messner to the importance of symbols, such as the names, colors, uniforms, banners, songs, and chants that were used to represent teams in the AYSO. Further, they directed his attention to specific **narratives,** which are *the explanations that people use–or the stories they tell–to explain and make sense of their choices and actions.* Therefore, Messner focused on the ways that ideas and beliefs about masculinity and femininity were included in the narratives used in the context of youth sports.

Messner also used **interactionist theories** because they *explain what we know about the origins, dynamics, and consequences of social interaction among people in particular social worlds.* These theories focus on processes of social learning and development. They deal with how social relationships are the contexts in which people come to know and give meaning to themselves, others, and the things and events in their lives.

Interactionist theories use concepts such as social interaction, socialization, role models, significant others, self-concept, identity, labeling, deviance, and stereotyping to study social development during childhood, adolescence, and adulthood. This alerted Messner to the ways that youth sports are **sites,** that is, *identifiable social places or contexts,* where people learn what it means to be male or female, how to perform masculinity or femininity as they interact with others, and the ways that ideas and beliefs about gender are integrated into the organization of social worlds.

Finally, Messner used **structural theories** because they *explain what we know about different forms of social organization and how they influence actions and relationships.* These theories focus on how relationships are organized and influence people's access to power, authority, material resources, economic opportunities, and other resources.

Structural theories help us identify and understand the social impact of recurring social relationships and patterns of social organization that exist in different spheres of everyday life, such as the family, religion, education, the economy, politics, and the media. They emphasize concepts such as status, roles, authority, power, social class, and social inequality to explain that the constraints and opportunities that exist in social worlds affect people differently, depending on their social positions and relationships with others. These structural theories alerted Messner to the ways that sport organizations are "gendered" in terms of the jobs done by women and men, and who has authority and power on AYSO teams and in the AYSO administration.

Like many researchers in the sociology of sport, Messner's research was also shaped by feminist theory which is explained on pp. 35–36)

Selecting Research Methods After selecting the theories he would use to guide his research, Messner selected a combination of research methods for collecting and analyzing data. Depending on the topic studied, most researchers use either quantitative or qualitative methods, but Messner was asking such a variety of questions that he decided to use both.

Feminist Research and Theory
From Margins to Mainstream in the Sociology of Sport

Prior to the 1970s, science was much like sport–it was a man's world, created by and for men and based on their interests and experiences. Men dominated all fields of study and produced knowledge based on their questions, observations, analyses, and theorizing about the world. This did not make science wrong, but it certainly made it incomplete, and occasionally it was so biased that it misrepresented physical and social realities.

When women entered science and pointed this out, many male scholars became defensive and used their power to question the ability of female scientists and the quality of their work. This led to conflicts between men and women in most scientific disciplines, from biology to sociology. These conflicts are less common today because many male scientists now realize that female scholars using a feminist approach raised valid points and did research that made important contributions to their fields. In fact, many male scholars today use feminist theories to inform their own work. In the sociology of sport, feminist theories have become mainstream with few questions about their legitimacy or usefulness when trying to understand sports in society.

During the 1970s and 1980s, feminist research and theory in sociology focused on making apparent the patriarchal organization of nearly all societies and explaining how the values, experiences, and interests of men, especially men with power, had shaped social relationships and social life generally. They showed that the privileges accorded to men were directly linked to systemic disadvantages experienced by women. In other words, relationships and society were organized around particular meanings given to gender.

There are several different forms of feminist theory (Thorpe, Toffoletti & Bruce, 2017), but most scholars in the sociology of sport favor critical feminist theory because it focuses on issues of ideology, power, and the need to ask critical questions about the meaning, purpose, and organization of sports in society.

In the sociology of sport, critical feminist theory explains that sports are gendered activities–their meaning, purpose, and organization tend to celebrate a form of masculinity in which aggression, violence, physical domination, and conquest are highly valued. It also explains how and why the bodies, abilities, orientations, and relationships of girls and women are systematically devalued in sports. Finally, it explains why gender equity and the transformation of the culture and structure of sports are in the best interests of both females and males.

Like all theories, critical feminist theory is revised as its weaknesses and oversights are identified. For example, today it focuses more directly on understanding gender in terms of how it is connected with other categories of experience, including age, sexuality, race and ethnicity, social class, ability, religion, and nationality–in order to gain a full understanding of its importance in everyday life. Additionally, critical feminist theory is no longer just about women because scholars also study masculinity and how it is constructed, reaffirmed, and challenged (Anderson, 2008a, 2008b, 2011a, 2011b; Martin, 2012; Messner, 2011; Thorpe, 2009a). Much of the focus is now on social justice, and how gender has influenced the organization of society and culture in ways that perpetuate and legitimize gender inequalities. For this reason, critical feminist research now looks at how gender intersects with other socially significant factors–including social, class, race and ethnicity, and sex identification– to influence people's lives (Nash, 2019).

Younger scholars today often use critical feminist theory, but they are less likely than their older peers to describe themselves as feminists. They accept feminist principles, but want to move beyond the weaknesses and oversights of past feminist approaches that often focused too much on the lives of upper-middle-class, enabled, white, heterosexual women and were not as inclusive as they should have been. They know that the meaning and real-life implications of gender vary in the lives of people who face different social circumstances depending on their access to resources, jobs, medical care, and community support. Therefore, feminism may be less visible today than in the 1980s and 1990s because so many people now take it for granted, but feminism and critical feminist theory remain as viable as ever.

Continued

reflect on SPORTS Feminist Research and Theory (*continued*)

We have not yet entered what some describe as a postfeminist world. Gender and gender relations remain contentious issues in many spheres, and they continue to be central concerns for those of us who study sports in society. Since the beginning of this century feminist theories have been increasingly integrated into sociology and the sociology of sport and combined with other theories to the point that feminism is no longer considered a separate project seeking legitimacy and challenging the way social research is done. In this sense, the emerging legacy of feminism influences our lives and makes us aware of the problems associated with systematically excluding particular categories of people as we try to understand sports in society.

Finally, from a practical standpoint, as people in organizations, communities, and societies seek to revive physical activity and sport participation in everyday life, the concepts and research inspired by critical feminist theory are invaluable tools. Without awareness of the challenges faced when seeking inclusion and participation, people who manage or work in sport programs often find that they serve a select few and reproduce existing patterns of inactivity. Young people hoping to work in sport programs are much more likely to find jobs if participation rates increase in all demographic sectors. *How might knowledge created through critical feminist theory and research help bring about increased participation in sports?*

Quantitative methods *involve collecting information (data) about people and social worlds, converting the information into numbers, and analyzing the numbers by using statistical procedures and tests.* Data may be collected by using a written questionnaire administered to a randomly selected sample of people that represents a larger population, or by quantifying particular facts in a sample or series of official records, reports, documents, or media content. The facts or data are usually presented in graphs and tables to represent statistical profiles and the quantifiable aspects of people, relationships, events, and social worlds (Aubel and Lefevre, 2013; Borgers et al., 2013).

Quantitative methods are used when social realities can be explained and understood by creating an overall view—a "big statistical picture"—of a population, media content, event, or social world. For example, they would be used to study general patterns and relationships, such as the differences between the family incomes of children who participate in youth sports and those who do not, or the patterns of keywords used in newspaper articles about youth sports.

Qualitative methods *involve collecting information about specific people, media content, events, or social worlds; identifying patterns and unique features; and analyzing information by using interpretive procedures and tests.* Data are usually collected by doing in-depth interviews with a carefully selected sample of respondents, by observing particular events and social worlds, or by collecting a sample of documents or media content for analysis. These data are analyzed to provide detailed descriptions of what people say and do, and what occurs in social events and social worlds.

Qualitative methods are used when researchers want to discover the meanings and ideologies that underlie what people say and do, or when they want to understand the precise details of what occurs in specific kinds of relationships, groups, and social worlds. For example, qualitative methods might be used to discover and understand why young people drop out of sports, the meanings people give to their sport experiences, or athletes' decisions to play when injured.

When sociologists study sports in society, they generally use surveys and interviews, observations, and text analysis to collect data (see Figure 2.2). Examples

SURVEYS	OBSERVATIONS	TEXT ANALYSIS
• **Written questionnaries** that participants complete by checking response options or providing brief written responses	• **Nonparticipant observation** — the researcher is an outside observer who documents what is seen and heard	• **Scan** text, audio, or video content to identify keywords, themes, and patterns
• **Interviews** in which participants are asked questions that are answered by phone, online, or face-to-face	• **Participant observation** — the researcher is a full participant in a social world and documents what is seen and heard	• **Deconstruct*** texts to identify the logic, values, ideological assumptions, and contradictions that are built into them

* Text deconstruction is a special method of analyzing documents, literary materials, webpages, ads, billboards, graffiti, paintings, photographs, and all forms of media content. It uses defined strategies to uncover the logic, values, and assumptions underlying the narratives and/or images that constitute *the text*. This method also identifies the ideology that informs the text and the contradictions that are contained in it.

FIGURE 2.2 Data collection methods for studying sports in society.

of these methods and how they are used in actual research are provided in the following sections.

SURVEYS AND INTERVIEWS: ASKING PEOPLE QUESTIONS

Social scientists often collect data by using surveys, which involve asking people questions through written questionnaires or person-to-person interviews. Questions must be clearly worded so that all respondents understand them in the same way, and formulated so they do not influence or bias the answers given by study participants.

Each of us has responded to survey questionnaires in which we are asked about our attitudes, opinions, preferences, backgrounds, or current circumstances. Additionally, we're usually asked to provide demographic data such as our age, gender, education, occupation, income, race and ethnicity, and place of residence. The goal of many surveys is to construct statistical profiles of the characteristics, attitudes, beliefs, and actions of respondents who represent or statistically match a larger collection of people. Researchers then compare and analyze those profiles to describe and even predict the patterns of how people will think and act in particular situations.

Survey questionnaires are also used to identify recurring patterns and relationships in social life and to see if they support or contradict predictions based on a particular theory. As more people have computers and smart phones, questionnaires are more often being sent and replied to online.

In Messner's research project, he used data collected in a national survey of 800 boys and 400 girls, ten- to seventeen-years-old, equally distributed across four ethnic backgrounds: White, African American, Latinx, and Asian. The data were collected through written questionnaires, and they indicated that boys were five times more likely than girls to regularly watch sports on television. Thirty percent of boys across the four ethnic groups watched sports every day, whereas only 6 percent of girls did so.

When it isn't practical to use written questionnaires, or when the goal is to do an in-depth investigation of people's feelings, thoughts, and actions, data may be collected through interviews. In-depth interviews are used instead of written questionnaires when researchers seek open-ended information about the details and underlying meanings of what people say and do. Conducting in-depth interviews is a time-consuming method of collecting data. Usually, they are done with people who have been chosen because of their experiences, positions in an organization or community, or vantage point for viewing one or more social worlds. Interviewers attempt to develop trust and rapport to maximize the truthfulness of responses. Interview questions are presented in a clear, understandable manner, and the interviewer listens carefully to what *is* and *is not* said. Usually interviews are recorded for later transcription and analysis, but in the case of interviews done in the field, notes may be taken by hand.

Messner used data from in-depth interviews that he conducted with thirty men who were former elite athletes (Messner, 1992). He learned that these men began playing sports with already-gendered identities, that is, with certain ideas about how to be a man in US culture. As their athletic careers progressed, the men had experiences and formed attitudes consistent with dominant ideas about manhood. They believed that gender was grounded in nature and biological destiny, and this belief influenced the ways they performed masculinity in public, defined and interacted with women, and evaluated their position and relative privilege in the overall organization of social worlds.

In summary, when data are collected by using questionnaires or interviews, researchers seek knowledge about general patterns and relationships in social worlds or knowledge about the details of everyday experiences and the meanings that people give to them.

OBSERVATIONS: SEEING AND HEARING WHAT PEOPLE DO AND SAY Researchers in the sociology of sport often collect data by observing people in everyday life situations. They do this as (1) "nonparticipants" or outside observers, who are detached from the people and situations being studied, or as (2) "participant observers" who are or become personally involved in the social worlds being studied. For example, Matt Atencio and three of his colleagues at California State University, East Bay spent three and a half years as outside observers studying the changing skateboarding scene in the San Francisco Bay area. They collected data through intense observations at skateparks and in-depth interviews with young skaters, their parents, and skatepark leaders and city staff members to understand the social significance of a popular urban youth sport (Atencio et al., 2018).

Collecting data through observational methods is time intensive. Relationships must be established so there is trust and rapport developed with the people being studied. Actions, relationships, and social patterns and dynamics must be studied over time and from different vantage points so the data accurately depict the people and social worlds being studied. The goal of some sociologists who do observational research is to extend or challenge our knowledge of familiar groups and social worlds or introduce us to marginalized groups and unique social worlds about which we have little or no knowledge (Anderson, Magrath & Bullingham, 2016; Anderson & Travers, 2018; Atencio et al., 2018; Capous-Desyllas & Johnson-Rhodes, 2017; Sparkes, Brighton & Inckle, 2018; van Amsterdam, Knoppers & Jongmans, 2015; Willing et al., 2018).

Observational methods generally involve **fieldwork,** that is, *"on-site" data collection.* An **ethnography** *is fieldwork that involves both observations and interviews;* in fact, ethnography literally means writing about people and how they live with each other (Adler and Adler, 2003; Hammersley, 2007). Ethnographies may take years to complete. They provide detailed descriptions and analyses of particular people and social worlds, such as sport teams, organizations, and communities.

Ethnographies are limited because they focus on particular social worlds, and it is difficult to know if the knowledge they produce can be used to understand other social worlds. However, they provide detailed information about the organization and dynamics of the social worlds studied. This enables us to understand how actions and relationships create, sustain, and change those worlds; how they become unique; and how the meanings created in them influence the decisions and actions of the people who inhabit them.

TEXT ANALYSIS: STUDYING DOCUMENTS AND MEDIA Research in the sociology of sport often involves some form of text analysis in which data are collected from sources in which there are narratives and images that represent ideas, people, objects, and events associated with sports. **Narratives** are *the stories that people tell about themselves and their social worlds.* They are an integral part of conversations, social interaction, and the media. They represent factual or fictional realities and they're often combined with **images**–that is, *visual representations of ideas, people, and things.*

These narratives and images are pervasive in connection with sports in society today. For example, Messner and his colleagues analyzed the content of network sports news from 1989 through 2009 (Table 2.2), and they also analyzed at regular intervals during 2009 the content of ESPN's one-hour evening *Sports Center* program and sports coverage by two network stations (Table 2.3). The data indicated that stories about men's sports dominated television coverage between 1989 and 2009, despite dramatic increases in women's sport participation during that period. For example, during ESPN's prime time *Sports Center* program, only 1.3 percent of total airtime was given to women's sports (Cooky et al., 2013). Messner and his colleagues concluded that this type of mainstream television news coverage perpetuates the notion that elite sports is a masculine activity in US culture.

Table 2.2 Gender focus of network sports news stories, 1989–2009 (in percentages)

Stories	1989	1993	1999	2009
About men	92.0	93.8	88.2	96.3
About women	5.0	5.1	8.7	1.6
Neutral/About both	3.0	1.1	3.1	2.1

Source: Cooky, Messner, and Hextrum, 2013.

Table 2.3 Percentage of 2009 sports coverage, by sex, on ESPN *Sports Center* and KCBS and KNBC (Southern California)

	ESPN	KCBS and KNBC
Men's Sports	96.4	95.9
Women's Sports	2.7	3.2
Both/Neutral	1.0	1.0

Source: Cooky, Messner, and Hextrum, 2013.

Messner and his colleagues also did a more in-depth analysis in which they *deconstructed* narratives and images to identify the logic, values, assumptions, and underlying ideologies used by those who produce media content about sports (Messner et al., 2000). This method of analyzing data enabled them to identify a master narrative that media people used to describe masculinity. This narrative emphasized the following: sports are a man's world, sports are wars and athletes are warriors, boys will be boys, boys are basically violent, aggressive guys win and nice guys lose, women are sexy props, men sacrifice their bodies for their teams, and the measure of a man is his "guts." Messner and his colleagues concluded that these assumptions formed a "Televised Sports Manhood Formula" that was consistently presented in sports programming.

These quantitative and qualitative methods of investigating the content of documents and media help us understand the complex connections between sports and other spheres of our lives. Scanning, analyzing, and deconstructing narratives and images associated with sports enables researchers to identify widely accepted ideas and beliefs about competition, authority structures, teamwork, dedication, achievement, and success.

Step 3: Collect and Analyze Data

Using cultural theories as a guide, Messner also collected information on the team names that players and coaches selected for the 156 AYSO teams that season. Names, along with colors, uniforms, banners, and songs or chants, are symbols that people often use to represent sport teams in US culture. **Symbols** are important to sociologists because they *are concrete representations of the values, beliefs, and moral principles around which people organize their ways of life.*

When Messner analyzed the 156 team names, he found that 15 percent of the girls' teams and 1 percent of the boys' teams chose sweet, cutesy names such as the Pink Flamingos, Blue Butterflies, Sunflowers, and Barbie Girls. "Neutral" or paradoxical names such as Team Flubber, Galaxy, Blue and Green Lizards, and Blue Ice were selected by 32 percent of the girls' teams and 13 percent of the boys' teams; and power names such as Shooting Stars, Raptor Attack, Sea Monsters, Sharks, and Killer Whales were selected by 52 percent of the girls' teams and 82 percent of the boys' teams.

Overall, boys were much more likely to avoid cutesy and "neutral" names in favor of power names. This is consistent with past research showing that people represent themselves and their groups with symbols and names that reaffirm their favored identity. In this case, the boys and girls selected names that fit their gendered sense of who they were and how they wished to be perceived in the social world of AYSO youth soccer.

When Messner used interactionist theory as a guide, he observed the actions of people at AYSO events to see how they performed gender as they interacted with others. His observations of the children indicated that their performances clarified *and* blurred traditional gender distinctions. But the most noticeable gender performances occurred when the boys vocally objected to the girls' celebration of their Barbie icon and attempted to physically disrupt the girls' celebration. At the same time, the girls were surprised by the boys' actions and either withdrew due to fear or stood their ground to challenge the boys. The parents reaffirmed the normalcy of these performances by attributing them to natural differences between boys and girls; they did not consider that the children's actions could be due to cultural norms, the interactional dynamics of the opening AYSO ceremony, or the overall social organization of the soccer league and most sports in the United States.

Using structural theory as a guide, Messner also collected data on the adult divisions of labor and who held power positions in the AYSO and on each of the 156 teams. He found that the commissioner and assistant commissioners were men, as were twenty-one of thirty board members. Over 80 percent of the head and assistant coaches were men, whereas 86 percent of the team managers, or "team moms," as most people referred to them, were women. The coaches had formal authority at the league and team levels, and the "team moms" performed support roles that were labor and behind the scenes.

Even when the soccer experiences of women surpassed those of men, they were less likely to volunteer as coaches. Men volunteered because they believed it was appropriate for them to play such a role, whereas the women felt less so–and men didn't see themselves as "team dads" doing what team moms did.

As Messner collected and analyzed data on the organization of the AYSO, he also found that patterns of authority were *informally* gendered by the adults, whereas gender was *formally* and officially used to segregate boys and girls into separate leagues. According to AYSO leaders, the teams at all age levels were segregated by sex "to promote team unity." For the leaders, this made gender "appear to disappear" in the organization and in the decision-making processes of the leagues. By using sex to segregate the leagues and teams, gender was minimized in the day-to-day consciousness of coaches, officials, parents, players, and administrators, even though it was the primary organizing principle for the entire AYSO and the experiences of nearly 2000 young people.

Messner pointed out that this type of social structure creates highly gendered experiences while they give everyone the impression that gender is irrelevant. For example, as the children played on sex-segregated teams, they had no opportunities to observe similarities in the skills, personalities, interests, and emotions of boys and girls or to be teammates and friends with differently gendered peers. Coaches treated boys as they felt boys should be treated and girls as they felt girls should be treated without realizing that ideas and beliefs about gender influenced the entire social context in which they coached. Gender was minimized in their awareness at the same time that it organized and structured the experiences of everyone associated with the AYSO.

(*Source:* Jay Coakley)

What does it mean when five-year-old girls choose Barbie as a representation of their team? Barbie represents traditional feminine values and ideals in US culture, but the girls in Messner's study connected Barbie to their sport participation. Is this a sign that traditional feminine values are changing, that the girls are creating a new form of femininity, or that the girls value traditional femininity more than playing sports? The sociologists most likely to ask these questions are guided primarily by cultural and feminist theories.

Collecting and analyzing data about the AYSO was a very small part of Messner's overall research project. He had already done many studies of sports and gender in different contexts, and he and his colleagues had studied gender in media coverage of sports, commentaries during sport events, ads during sport events and in sport publications, and patterns of corporate sponsorships for sports. In other words, his systematic collection and analysis of data went far beyond the opening ceremony, the Sea Monsters and Barbie Girls, and the AYSO.

Step 4: Use Findings to Produce Conclusions

Messner's analysis of all the data he collected enabled him to present detailed explanations of the connections between gender and sports in the United States. He used cultural, interactionist, and structural theories to make sense of these connections and make knowledge statements about gender in social worlds. Messner's overall conclusion was that **gender** is much more than a social category or trait that identifies a person; instead, it *consists of interrelated meanings, performances, and organization that become important aspects of social worlds.*

Figure 2.3 depicts Messner's description of gender as a multidimensional concept. *Gender as meaning* refers to the fact that in a particular culture people often learn to identify certain colors, names, and objects as "masculine" or "feminine." Gestures, actions, and elements of physical appearance may also be identified in this way. These socially agreed-upon cultural meanings are part of a larger cultural process of constructing the gender categories that people use to identify themselves and make sense of what occurs in their relationships and experiences. For example, males in the United States don't select pink as a team color because they have learned that it is associated with femininity. The five-year-old boys observed by Messner had already learned *gender as meaning* to the extent that they did not name themselves the "Barbie Boys" or "Pink Monsters." This example may seem trivial, but *gender as meaning* influences people's choices and interpretations of the world around them. Significant here is the fact that sports serve as an important site at which this meaning is learned, reaffirmed, and sometimes even challenged and changed.

Gender as performance (Figure 2.3) refers to the fact that people "do" gender as they interact with others. In the process they reproduce existing meanings and organization, or they offer alternatives. The five-year-olds observed by Messner had clearly learned to perform gender in certain ways and evaluate each other in terms of what it meant for them to "act like a boy" or "act like a girl" in their

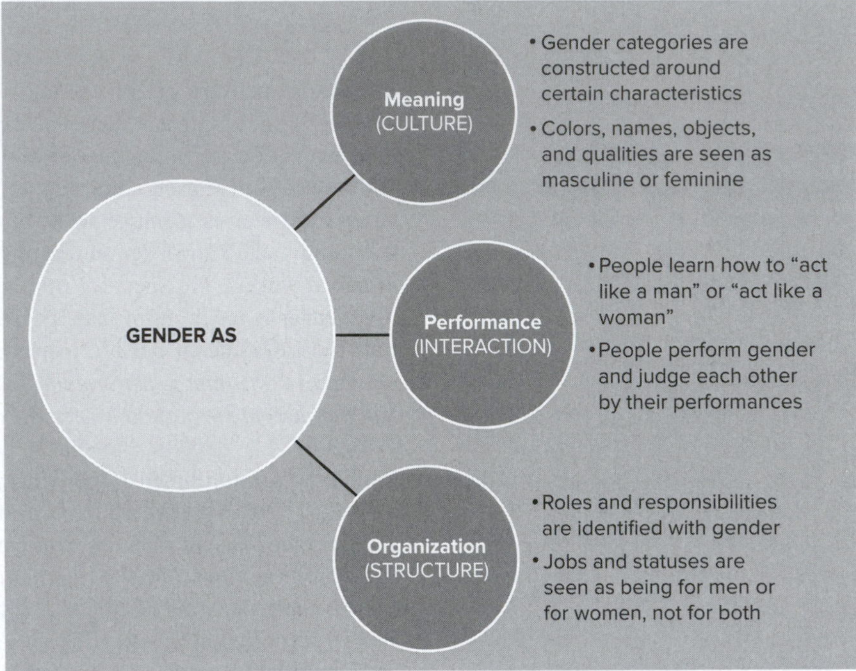

FIGURE 2.3 Gender as meaning, performance, and organization in social worlds.

social worlds. In this sense, *gender is performance.* For example, a coach might use feminine references to boys on his team when they don't perform well. Similarly, a player on a girls' team who spits regularly on the field may be told by her coach to "act like a lady"–meaning that she is not performing gender as expected in US culture.

Gender as organization (Figure 2.3) refers to the ways that positions, roles, and responsibilities are structured around gender. For example, in most sports the coaches are more likely to be men than women, because it is widely believed that masculinity is more compatible with the demands of coaching than femininity is. This is why men coach nearly all men's teams and most women's teams, whereas women coach a minority of women's teams and almost no men's teams.

The pattern of men in positions of control and women in support positions was clear in the AYSO, where the commissioner and assistant commissioners were men, as were twenty-one of the thirty members of the board of directors, and 85 percent of the 156 head coaches. In this sense, organization is clearly gendered.

Part of Messner's contribution to what we know about gender and sport is showing us how gender constitutes a combination of meaning, performance, and organization in social worlds, especially those constructed around sports. This is important because it explains why it is so difficult to "ungender" sport. As long as we uncritically accept current meanings, performances, and organization, sport will remain gendered in ways that preclude equal treatment for men and women. However, once we see gender in critically-informed terms, it's possible to develop strategies to create equity.

Step 5: Publish Results

After completing his project, Messner wrote research papers that explained what he had done and what he had discovered about gender and sports in the United States. At least three of these papers were written as articles and submitted for possible publication in academic journals, and a long manuscript was written as a possible book and submitted to the University of Minnesota Press. The journal and book editors each asked scholars who were experts on the topic of gender and sports to critically review Messner's manuscripts and recommend whether they should be published. These reviewers assessed the overall quality and accuracy of Messner's work: Did he ask good questions, collect useful data from appropriate sources, analyze the data with care and accuracy, come to logical conclusions based on the data, and make thoughtful knowledge statements about sport and gender?

After receiving favorable reviews calling only for minor revisions, each of Messner's manuscripts was accepted for publication. Even though Messner was an established scholar and had tenure at the University of Southern California, he, like most researchers, was expected to publish his work so that his contributions to sociology knowledge could be verified by a community of scholars who study gender, sports, and related topics. This is because knowledge production in science is never a one-person job; it always depends on the critical review of a community of scholars. Messner understood this and published his research so that others could evaluate it. Although his manuscripts were published, most manuscripts submitted for publication are rejected because reviewers find them lacking in quality or not contributing to knowledge production in a particular field.

Messner's claim that gender was more than a social category and should be viewed as a combination of meaning, performance, and organization was an important addition to sociological knowledge, and very useful for people who study gender. In his own research, Messner used this knowledge to theorize about sports as sites where ideas and beliefs about gender are created, maintained, and sometimes challenged and changed.

This knowledge is important because many people describe sports simply as a reflection of society–sites where aspects of culture and society are revealed to those who take a close look. But Messner's research findings challenged this view and provided evidence that sports are more than reflections of society; in fact, they are sites where ideas and beliefs about gender and other important aspects of our lives are created, reproduced, and changed. Therefore, sports constitute a significant social world to study, and the people associated with sports are most accurately viewed as agents actively involved in shaping social worlds rather than passive subjects determined by culture and society.

(*Source:* Jay Coakley)

It is widely believed that sports have a positive impact on people and society–that "a ball can change the world." Is this true? In the following chapters we will use published research in the sociology of sport to help us answer this question.

Messner's research made an important contribution to knowledge and is frequently used by others as they develop ideas and do their own research on gender, sports, childhood, and related topics.

THE IMPACT OF SOCIOLOGY OF SPORT KNOWLEDGE

After reading about *how* to do research in the sociology of sport, it is reasonable to ask *why* we do this research–in other words, for what purpose do we produce knowledge about sports in society?

Those of us who do research on the social aspects of sports hope that the knowledge we produce does not just sit on the pages of journals and books. When considering the application of this knowledge, it is important to be aware of the following:

1. Social science research does not produce "ultimate truth" in the form of knowledge that eliminates all doubt and uncertainty in everyday life.
2. Research, theories, and knowledge in the sociology of sport will never lead to the creation of a single strategy to prevent social problems and forever guarantee fairness and justice in sports and sport organizations.
3. Knowledge about social worlds is never complete, and using knowledge to solve current problems does not mean that the solutions will be free of challenges and problems.

This does not mean that social research and theories should be ignored in our personal decisions about sports or in planning, making, and funding policies and programs related to sports, but it reminds us of our limitations as social scientists.

With that said, sociology of sport knowledge can help us detect oversights as well as bias and validity problems in our personal theories and enable us to make more fully informed choices about sports in our lives. For example, the research of Micheal Messner and others (see Chapters 3 and 4) is clearly useful when we select sport programs for our children, become coaches in schools or youth programs, create policies to increase healthy sport participation in our communities, develop sport programs for employees at our workplaces, or vote on ballot issues regarding the use of public money to build local recreational centers or new stadiums for men's professional teams. Overall, knowledge produced in the sociology of sport enables us to view sports from multiple perspectives that go beyond our personal experiences and vantage points in social worlds.

It is difficult to know whether and how sociology of sport knowledge is used. Although many of us work with sport programs and serve as sources of information for people who make decisions about the provision and organization of sports, we don't control how that knowledge is used in all circumstances. We may produce science-based knowledge, but we seldom have official power in sport organizations, so we generally depend on others to apply sociology of sport knowledge in real-world situations.

There is resistance to the application of research-based knowledge when it raises questions about the status quo. Such knowledge–usually produced by researchers who ask critical questions–is often seen as threatening or even subversive by those who benefit from the current organization of sports. This is why it is important for access to knowledge to be widespread so that decisions about putting knowledge to use can be part of a democratic political process rather than part of a strategy to enhance the control exercised by powerful people. In this sense, research and knowledge production are a starting point rather than an end point for many of us in the sociology of sport. We want to see knowledge used for the common good and to make sports more humane, democratic, and inclusive.

What inspired Micheal Messner to do his research were his initial observations of the youth soccer program in which his son wanted to participate. These observations led to questions about what his son might learn as he played soccer, why the leagues and teams were sex-segregated, why parents and coaches supported this segregation, how gender was performed by the children and adults, how gender was integrated into the organization of the leagues and teams, and how gender is related to more general forms of social organization in society.

Messner knew that widely held ideas and beliefs about femininity, masculinity, and male-female relationships created constraints for males and females and supported a system of social organization that often privileged men and disadvantaged women, especially in terms of their access to positions of power in most spheres of social life, including sports. Therefore, he was inclined to use a critical approach as he designed his research project. He wanted to understand and explain why the meanings that people give to sports, the actions of females and males in sports, and the organization of sports are gendered and how this might affect other parts of society. Using a critical approach, Messner's goal was to produce knowledge that could be used to find solutions to social problems, identify and eliminate injustices, and shrink the "the gap between what is and what could be" in social worlds (Burawoy, 2004). Therefore, he wanted that knowledge to empower people as they participate in a process of creating sustainable, just, and equitable ways of life.

USING A CRITICAL APPROACH TO PRODUCE KNOWLEDGE

When using a critical approach to study sports in society, our research is guided by one or more of the following questions:

- What values, ideas, and beliefs are promoted through sports, and who is advantaged or disadvantaged by them?
- What are the meanings currently given to sports and sport participation, and who is advantaged or disadvantaged by those meanings?
- How are sports organized, and who is advantaged or disadvantaged by existing forms of organization in sports?
- Who has power in sports, to what ends do they use their power, and how are various categories of people affected by power relations associated with sports?
- Who accepts and who resists the organization of mainstream sports, and what happens to those who resist?
- What strategies effectively foster progressive changes in sports and the social worlds around them?

These questions show that a critical approach is organized around an awareness that people are positioned differently in social worlds, and they are affected differently by the meaning, purpose, and organization of mainstream sports. In other words, everyone does not benefit from sports in the same ways, and some people may be disadvantaged by how they are organized and played in a particular social world. For example, an emphasis on high-performance or elite sports in a society may exclude or discourage participation among many people who could benefit from sports organized for recreational purposes.

Additionally, a critical approach heightens one's awareness that knowledge about social worlds can be applied in many ways. For example, Messner understood that knowledge about the relationship between masculinity and the cultures that exist in certain sports could be used to transform those cultures, thereby reducing male-on-male violence and the serious injuries that boys and men often learn to accept as a normal part of the game. Therefore he organized the last chapter of his book to answer the question: "Just do *what?*" The chapter presents thirty pages of recommendations for critically informed actions to make sports more humane, equitable, and democratic.

Referring to the Nike marketing slogan *"Just do it!,"* Messner emphasizes that without critically assessing what "it" is, we reproduce sports as they are rather than actively changing and developing them to be fair and equitable as they provide people with excitement, physical challenges, and joy. For example, he called for more activities that give boys and young men opportunities to make healthy, respectful connections with others (2002, p. 166). Similarly, he urged that we must reorganize certain sports so that boys and men do not have their "need

(*Source:* Michael Boyd, Irish Football Association)

A critical approach to knowledge production in Northern Ireland focuses on the role of sport in eliminating sectarian (Protestant versus Catholic), racial, and interpersonal violence. Administrators in the Irish Football Association have consulted with scholars in the sociology of sport to develop strategies to make soccer more inclusive, just, and supportive of the well-being of athletes and spectators.

for closeness, intimacy, and respect thwarted [and] converted into a narrow form of group-oriented bonding based on competitive one-upmanship, self-destructive behaviors, silent conformity to group norms, and sexually aggressive denigration of others" (2002, p. 166).

Along with Messner and many of my colleagues in the sociology of sport, I also use a critical approach to guide my thinking and research on sports in society. Our sense is that if we only did research that reflected and reaffirmed sports as they are, there would be no point to our professional existence. Unless our work is based on a critical approach, raises questions about sport, and causes people to think about the place of sports in our lives, we contribute nothing of value to the world around us. This is why you will notice that the following chapters often focus on issues and controversies that deal with fairness, access to sport participation, and equity. Underlying these critical discussions is my desire to make available to more people the excitement, physical challenges, and joy that can be part of sport participation.

summary

HOW IS KNOWLEDGE PRODUCED IN THE SOCIOLOGY OF SPORT?

Sociology of sport knowledge is produced through research and theories. Research provides data and systematic analyses to answer questions and validate or revise existing theories about sports in society. Theories provide logical explanations of people's actions and relationships and the organization and dynamics of social worlds. Additionally, theories guide research and the interpretation of research findings. This makes knowledge in the sociology of sport more valid and reliable than most of what we read, see, or hear in the media and discuss in our everyday conversations about sports.

Personal experience is a useful starting point for understanding the role of research and theory in knowledge production. This is because each of us gathers information about the people and things around us and uses it to develop experience-based explanations or "personal theories" about people, relationships, events, and social worlds.

We use personal theories to anticipate events, the actions of others, and the consequences of our actions in various situations. But these theories are limited because they focus on our individual circumstances and immediate social worlds. On the other hand, research and theories in the sociology of sport take us beyond the limitations of our own experiences and worlds.

Social research follows systematic and rigorous guidelines for collecting and analyzing data, and social theories are systematically tested, compared with related theories, and presented for others to examine. The goal of social research and theory in the sociology of sport is to develop logical and verifiable explanations of the social worlds created in association with sports and the actions and relationships of people in those social worlds.

The case study of Michael Messner's research illustrates that scholars in the sociology of sport use systematic and carefully planned methods as they study and develop explanations of sports. The five-stage process of producing knowledge consists of (1) developing research questions; (2) selecting appropriate theory and research methods; (3) collecting and analyzing data; (4) using research findings to produce conclusions; and (5) publishing results so that others may assess their validity and reliability.

Three types of theories guide most sociology of sport research. *Cultural theories* help us study and understand the meanings that people give to sports, sport experiences, and relationships formed in and through sports. *Interactionist theories* help us study and understand the origins, dynamics, and consequences of social relationships connected with sports. And *structural theories* help us study and understand how various forms of social organization influence actions and relationships in sports and the social worlds associated with sports in society.

Depending on the research topic and the goals of the project, researchers use either a quantitative or a qualitative approach when collecting and analyzing data, or a combination of the two. Data in sociology of sport studies are usually collected through surveys, interviews, observations, or text analysis.

Many people in the sociology of sport use a critical approach as they do research and develop theory. This means that they are committed to producing knowledge that can be used to promote fairness and equity in sports and society, expose and challenge exploitation, and empower those who are disadvantaged by the current organization of sports in society. Overall, critical scholars are dedicated to the idea that sociological knowledge should be used to create and sustain social worlds in which basic human needs can be satisfied fairly and equitably.

Research and theories in the sociology of sport help us understand that sports are more than mere reflections of society. Instead, sports are sites where meanings, relationships, and forms of social organization are created, maintained, and changed. Learning about the knowledge production process in the sociology of sport is part of the process of thinking critically about the issues and controversies discussed in the following chapters. When we use research and theories critically, we become aware of the deeper game associated with sports in society and this makes us more informed participants in our families, schools, communities, and societies. How we use this knowledge depends on how we are engaged as citizens of our schools, communities, and society.

SUPPLEMENTAL READINGS:

Reading 1. Sociologists use more than one theoretical approach
Reading 2. Sports are more than a reflection of society
Reading 3. The meaning of pain: Interactionist theory as a research guide
Reading 4. Specific theories used in the sociology of sport
Reading 5. Feminist theories in the sociology of sport
Reading 6. Sociology of sport research today is based on a critical approach
Reading 7. A European approach: Figurational theory

SPORT MANAGEMENT ISSUES

- You are hired to study why athletes are willing to play while they are in pain or injured. Explain which theory (cultural, interactionist, and structural) you would use to guide your research. What research questions would you ask, what would be the focus of your analysis, and what concepts would you use in your study?
- You are hired to study the pros and cons of intercollegiate sports on your campus. Today you report on the steps in your research project. Identify the steps and briefly explain each as you will do them.
- As a sport management consultant you are hired by the Women's Center at a major university to study gender and sports on their campus. You use some of Messner's work as a model for your project. Explain the data collection methods you will use.
- Research using a critical approach may produce findings that challenge individuals in sport management positions. Identify examples of possible research findings that might be rejected or ignored by executives for a professional sport team.

references

Adler, Patricia A. and Peter Adler. 2003. The promise and pitfalls of going into the field. *Contexts* 2(2): 41–47.

Anderson, Eric. 2008a. "Being masculine is not about who you sleep with . . .": Heterosexual athletes contesting masculinity and the one-time rule of homosexuality. *Sex Roles* 58: 104–115.

Anderson, Eric. 2008b. "I used to think women were weak": Orthodox masculinity, gender segregation, and sport. *Sociological Forum* 23: 257–280.

Anderson, Eric. 2011a. Inclusive masculinities of university soccer players in the American Midwest. *Gender and Education* 23(6): 729–744.

Anderson, Eric. 2011b. Masculinities and sexualities in sports and physical cultures: Three decades of evolving research. *Journal of Homosexuality* 58(5): 565–578.

Anderson, Eric, Rory Magrath, and Rachael Bullingham. 2016. *Out in Sport: The experiences of openly gay and lesbian athletes in competitive sport*. London: Routledge.

Anderson, Eric and Ann Travers, eds. 2018. *Transgender athletes in competitive sport.* London/New York: Routledge.

Atencio, Matthew, Becky Beal, E. Missy Wright, and ZáNean McClain. 2018. *Moving borders: Skateboarding and the changing landscape of urban youth sports*. Fayetteville, AK: The University of Arkansas Press.

Aubel, Olivier and Brice Lefèvre. 2015. The comparability of quantitative surveys on sport participation in France (1967–2010). *International Review for the Sociology of Sport* 50(6): 722–739.

Becker, Howard. 1998. *Tricks of the trade: How to think about your research while you're doing it.* Chicago: University of Chicago Press.

Borgers, Julie, Erik Thibaut, Hanne Vandermeerschen, Bart Vanreusel, Steven Vos, and Jeroen Scheerder. 2015. Sports participation styles revisited: A time-trend study in Belgium from the 1970s to the 2000s. *International Review for the Sociology of Sport* 50(1): 45–63.

Bourdieu, Pierre. 1986b. The forms of capital. In J. G. Richards, ed. *Handbook of theory and research for the sociology of education* (pp. 242–258). New York: Greenwood Press.

Burawoy, Michael. 2004. Public sociologies: Contradictions, dilemmas and possibilities. *Social Forces* 82(4): 1603–1618.

Capous-Desyllas, Moshoula and Marina Johnson-Rhodes. 2018. Collecting visual voices: Understanding identity, community, and the meaning of participation within gay rodeos. *Sexualities* 21(3): 446–475.

Cooky, Cheryl, Ranissa Dycus and Shari L. Dworkin. 2013a. "What makes a woman a woman?" Versus "Our first lady of sport": A comparative analysis of the United States and the South African media coverage of Caster Semenya. *Journal of Sport and Social Issues* 37(1): 31–56.

Cooky, Cheryl, Michael A. Messner and Robin H. Hextrum. 2013b. Women play sport, but not on TV: A longitudinal study of televised news media. *Communication & Sport* 1(3): 203–230.

deGrasse Tyson, Neil. 2016 (on Facebook & Twitter); https://twitter.com/neiltyson/status/695759776752496640

Hammersley, Martyn. 2007. Ethnography. In George Ritzer, ed., *Encyclopedia of sociology* (pp. 1479–1483). London/New York: Blackwell.

Martín, Montserrat. 2012. The (im)possible sexual difference: Representations from a rugby union setting. *International Review for the Sociology of Sport* 47(2): 183–199.

Messner, Michael A. 1992. *Power at play*. Boston: Beacon Press.

Messner, Michael A. 2002. *Taking the field: Women, men, and sports*. Minneapolis, MN: University of Minnesota Press.

Messner, Michael A. 2011. Gender ideologies, youth sports, and the production of soft essentialism. *Sociology of Sport Journal* 28(2): 151–170.

Messner, Michael A., Michele Dunbar and Darnell Hunt. 2000. The televised sports manhood formula. *Journal of Sport and Social Issues* 24(4): 380–394.

Nash, Jennifer C. 2019. *Black feminism reimagined: After intersectionality*. Durham NC: Duke University Press.

Nyhan, Brendan. 2014. When beliefs and facts collide. *New York Times* (July 5): https://www.nytimes.com/2014/07/06/upshot/when-beliefs-and-facts-collide.html

Sinclair, Upton. 1930. *Mental radio.* Monrovia, CA: Published by the Author.

Sparkes, Andrew C., James Brighton, and Kay Inckle. 2018. Imperfect perfection and wheelchair bodybuilding: Challenging ableism or reproducing normalcy? *Sociology* 52(6): 1307–1323.

Thorpe, Holly. 2009. Bourdieu, feminism and female physical culture: Gender reflexivity and the habitus-field complex. *Sociology of Sport Journal* 26(4), 491–516.

Thorpe, Holly, Kim Toffoletti, and Toni Bruce. 2017. Sportswomen and social media: Bringing third-wave feminism, postfeminism, and neoliberal feminism into conversation. *Journal of Sport and Social Issues* 41(5): 359–383.

van Amsterdam, Noortje, Annelies Knoppers, and Marian Jongmans. 2015. 'It's actually very normal that I'm different'. How physically disabled youth discursively construct and position their body/self. *Sport, Education and Society* 20(2): 152–170.

Willing, Indigo, Andy Bennett, Mikko Piispa, and Ben Green. 2018. Skateboarding and the 'tired generation': Ageing in youth cultures and lifestyle sports. *Sociology* 53(3): 503–518.

chapter

3

(*Source:* Jay Coakley)

SPORTS AND SOCIALIZATION

Who Plays and What Happens to Them?

If you're around [an NBA] team in this day and age, there are always headphones on. "[The players] are isolated, and they have their heads down. . . . I think it's a generational issue.

–Adam Silver, NBA Commissioner (in Yang, 2019)

Esports is about more than just playing games–it can be used to help students grow their STEM interests and develop valuable life skills; . . . it's about time we foster this pastime in an educational setting.

–Delane Parnell, CEO and founder of PlayVS (NFHS, 2019)

. . . so many kids don't even know what they could be good at because they're only playing one sport since they were eight years old. So, I look back and I'm grateful that I had the opportunity to play those other sports.

–Jennie Finch, Gold medalist softball pitcher (Jacobson, 2010)

If I have a shot at the championship and there's two races to go and my head is hurting and I just came through a wreck . . . I'm not going to say anything.

–Jeff Gordon, NASCAR driver (Moore, 2012)

Chapter Outline

What Is Socialization?

Becoming and Staying Involved in Sports

Changing or Ending Sport Participation

Participation in Sports: What Happens?

Socialization as a Community and Cultural Process

Summary: Who Plays and What Happens To Them?

Learning Objectives

- Describe what occurs during the socialization process and explain why it is important to study socialization as an interactive learning process.
- Identify key factors involved in the process of becoming and staying involved in sports.
- Describe key factors involved in the process of changing or ending sport participation and explain when the retirement process is most likely to be difficult for a former athlete.
- Understand why sport participation does not have the same socialization effects for everyone who plays sports.
- Differentiate pleasure and participation sports from power and performance sports and explain why it is important to know these differences when discussing socialization in sports.
- Identify the conditions under which sport participation is most likely or least likely to have positive socialization effects on those who play sports.
- Explain why sport participation does not automatically lead to physical fitness and well-being and why it may not reduce obesity rates in a society.
- Explain what sociologists mean when they say that socialization is a community and cultural process.

When and why do people play sports?

When and why do they stop playing them?

What happens to them when they play sports?

How do sports influence ideas and beliefs in communities and societies?

When researchers in the sociology of sport try to answer these questions we focus on the process of social learning and development that sociologists call socialization.

For more than half a century, researchers in the sociology of sport have focused their attention on four topics that are central to discussions of sports and socialization:

1. The process of becoming involved and staying involved in sports.
2. The process of transitioning out of active sport participation.
3. The consequences of being involved in sports.
4. Socialization as a community and cultural process.

This chapter is organized around these topics. As you read, you'll see that we've learned much, but our understanding of the learning and development processes associated with sports remains incomplete. Some of what we've learned is so complex that our discussions will carry over to subsequent chapters.

WHAT IS SOCIALIZATION?

Socialization *is a process of learning and social development that occurs as we interact with one another and become familiar with the various social worlds in which we live.* It is through this process that we form ideas about who we are and what is important in our lives.

We are *not* simply passive learners in this learning and development process. We actively participate in our own socialization as we form relationships and are influenced by others at the same time that we influence them. We actively interpret what we see and hear, and we accept, resist, and revise messages that we receive from others about who we are and how we are connected with social worlds. Therefore, socialization is not simply a one-way process of being molded and shaped by our social environment. Instead, it is an interactive process through which we make decisions about our relationships, our interpretation of information that comes to us through interaction, and what we will say and do. It is through these decisions that we become who we are and influence other people and the social worlds in which we participate.

Each of us experiences socialization as we learn about social worlds and use our knowledge to construct our own lives. In this sense, socialization, social development, and identity formation are part of an interconnected process. We make choices in this process, but our choices are influenced by the options available to us, the resources we have to assess them, and the context in which we act on them (Van de Walle, 2011).

For example, some people might have opportunities to play many different sports and choose the one in which they have the best chances of succeeding, whereas others might have opportunities to play only one sport. Additionally, some people might have excellent coaching, good support from others, and good mentors in their chosen sports, whereas others might play in a context where there is no one to be their coach or mentor. Therefore, some of us are in better positions than others when it comes to using socialization experiences to our advantage and extending our knowledge, experience, and developmental opportunities.

This explanation of *socialization* is based on a *social interaction model* that is organized around a combination of cultural, interactionist, and structural theories. It leads researchers to assume that human beings learn values and norms and develop as individuals as they interact with others and participate in social worlds. For example, as children interact with their parents, other family members, teachers, and peers, they learn norms about safety and risk-taking and they learn to give meaning to the pain that comes with the bumps, bruises, and cuts that are a part of childhood. However, if they play organized sports, their interaction with

"I know this is starting early, but I can't let him get too far behind the other kids if he's going to succeed in life."

Research guided by structural theories focuses on who influences the sport participation patterns of children. Fathers and other family members are usually identified as *significant others* who influence when, how, and where children play sports.

coaches and teammates may lead them to define pain as a normal part of playing sports and to see sports injuries as symbols of their commitment to a team and their identity as an athlete. In this way sense, socialization can be is a powerful and influential process.

Much of the research on sports and socialization provides detailed descriptions of sport experiences as they occur in people's lives and then analyzes the processes through which people make decisions about sport participation and give meaning to their sport experiences. Ultimately, the goal of research is to connect those decisions and meanings with the cultural and structural contexts in which sports and sport participation exist. This approach captures the complexity of the processes through which people become and stay involved in sports, change or end sport participation, and incorporate sports into their lives. The rest of this chapter focuses on what we know about sports and socialization today.

BECOMING AND STAYING INVOLVED IN SPORTS

Who plays sports consistently over time, who plays and drops out, and who never plays? This three-part question is important today, as many societies deal with health problems that are partly related to a lack of regular physical exercise (Nike, Inc. 2012; Guthold et al., 2018; Piggin and Bairner, 2016; Project Play, 2018).

Research on socialization has found that sport participation is related to three sets of factors: (1) a person's abilities, physical and psychological characteristics, and resources; (2) the influence of significant others, including parents, siblings, teachers, peers, and role models; and (3) the availability of opportunities to play sports that are personally satisfying. It also indicates that participation is connected to multiple processes that make up people's lives, and it occurs as people interact with others and make decisions based on opportunities and the meanings they give to sports in their lives. These decisions and meanings shift with age and with changes in social conditions and relationships.

These factors are highlighted in the following sections.

Physical Literacy as a Pathway in Sports

The process of becoming involved in sports has changed dramatically in recent years. Children today are less likely than peers in previous generations to have the freedom or encouragement to engage in unsupervised physical play and games outside and away from the home. In response, many children now turn to attractive and engaging forms of new media and other relatively sedentary activities to occupy their time. This restricts the frequency and range of their physical activities and opportunities to become ***physically literate,*** that is, *to have the ability, confidence, and desire to be physically active for life* (Farrey & Isard, 2016).[1]

With a decline in child-controlled physically active play and games, organized sports have emerged to become the primary context for introducing children to the benefits and enjoyment of physical activities. This shift is also a reflection of decisions to reduce or eliminate physical education programs in many schools. Parents now see organized youth sports as the primary sites for their children to be physically active, learn physical skills, maintain good health, and have fun to the point that they will value physical activities and sports through their lives.

Evidence from developed nations suggests that this strategy has failed to keep children physically active enough to meet minimum standards of health, and this failure is higher in the United States than in other wealthy societies (Guthold et al., 2018; O'Donnell, 2018; Farrey & Solomon, 2018). This has led professionals in public health, physical education, and sports across a number of countries to hypothesize that the majority of young people are physically illiterate and that the most effective way to put them on a pathway into physical activities and youth sports is to increase their physical literacy (Dudley et al., 2017; Farrey & Isard, 2016; Malina, 2012; Roetert et al., 2017a; 2017b). Their reasoning is that unless people, especially children, know how to run, balance, hop, jump, skip, crawl, roll, throw, catch, kick, dodge, glide on ice and snow, fall, swim, and develop eye-hand, eye-foot, and general body coordination, they won't be inclined to play sports or engage in any physical activities that require basic movement skills. Without them, children won't feel confident running forward, backward, sideways, falling without fear, and doing many of the other physical things that would make it easier to try various sports and experience enough success to continue their participation. Similarly, without knowing how to throw, catch, kick, and dodge flying objects a child would not have the physical literacy needed to try and experience enjoyment in multiple sports.

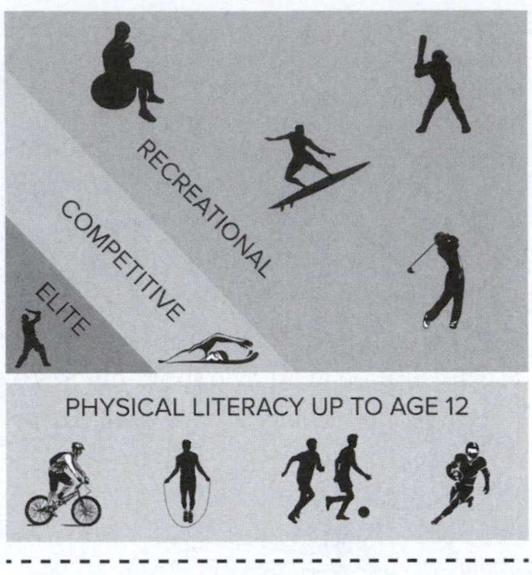

(*Source:* Project Play (2015, p. 8))

FIGURE 3.1 Physical literacy: The foundation for lifelong sport participation.

With many children not being active enough to maintain good health, it makes sense to create new programs and revise physical education and youth sports so that teaching physical literacy is a high priority. Furthermore, maintaining physical literacy over the life course makes it easier for adults to begin or resume forms of sport participation that have multiple benefits. This approach is illustrated in Figure 3.1 which shows that when physical literacy is the primary focus in youth sports for children up to 12 years old, it serves as the foundation for participating and enjoying elite, competitive, and recreational sports throughout their lives.

Research suggests that physical literacy is associated with becoming and staying involved in sports (Belanger et al., 2018; Malina, 2012; Spengler & Cohen, 2015). But more research is needed to identify the most engaging ways to develop and maintain physical literacy for different populations of people across the lifespan. In the meantime, nationwide

[1]This is a basic definition of physical literacy. For more complete definitions that are now being tested, used in research, and applied in programs, see International Physical Literacy Association (2016), Longmuir et al. (2018), Trembley et al. (2018); Whitehead (2010, 2013).

organizations, such as the national governing bodies for Olympic sports in a number of countries, including the United States, Canada, and the United Kingdom are revising their sport development programs for children so that physical literacy and lifelong participation across multiple sports are emphasized. Of course, many organized sport programs for children and young people will continue to emphasize intensity, competitive success, selective tryouts, and year-round specialization in a single sport, but it is unlikely that this approach will increase rates of participation in sports and physical activities. It hasn't worked so far, and some youth sports focus on performing such specialized physical skills that they undermine the level of physical literacy among young athletes. This, in turn, has a negative impact on participation through the life course (Belanger et al., 2018; Dudley et al., 2017; Whitehead, 2010).

The concept of physical literacy is not new (Corbin, 2016; Whitehead, 2001). However, there is growing support for the idea that developing and maintaining physical literacy is key to increasing sport participation in societies where sedentary lifestyles create health problems and limit the range of activities that bring enjoyment into people's lives.

Family Culture and the Sport Participation of Children

Sociologist Sharon Wheeler studies sport education and development in England. In one of her research projects she conducted semi-structured interviews with elementary school children for whom playing sports was important for them and their parents. She found that the parents in each family defined sport participation as important for young people and willingly dedicated considerable family time, money, and energy to support their children as they played sports. Transporting them to practices and games and attending games were

(*Source:* Jay Coakley)

When physical activities and sports participation are incorporated into everyday family life, children are more likely to remain physically active through their lives. The four children in this family are learning that running is an enjoyable activity for men and women, young and old. The positive memories from "fun runs" such as this are factors that encourage these children to be active in the future.

part of the family routine and overall lifestyle. Most of the parents did not coach or critique their children nor did they provide anything other than verbal encouragement (Wheeler, 2012, 2014).

Unlike some parents in the United States, these parents were not obsessed with pushing their children to excel so they might obtain athletic scholarships to college. These UK families also had the resources to sustain a lifestyle that included sport participation. This lifestyle was linked with a culture created and sustained by a network of families with similar beliefs, resources, and lifestyles. This culture served as a context in which playing sports was seamlessly integrated into the lives of the children. Sports for these children were simply a taken-for-granted part of family life.

Of course, families with fewer resources for pay-to-play sport programs would have different lifestyles in which such a culture would be more difficult to create and sustain. This would also be the case for single-parent families and families in which sports were given a low priority for the expenditure of resources.

Wheeler notes that it is important to study families as the immediate contexts in which sport participation is initiated and nurtured. This is especially the case as publicly funded sport programs are eliminated and selectively replaced by private fee-based programs that require parental support and family resources for transportation, uniforms, equipment, and paid coaches.

Wheeler's findings are consistent with other research in which family culture has been found to provide a context in which children see sport involvement as a normal part of their everyday lives and continue playing sports as they become adolescents and young adults (Hayoz et al, 2019; Pot et al., 2016; Stuij, 2015). Her findings also suggest that short-term interventions designed to increase sport participation among young people outside of this culture are likely to fail if they ignore the extent to which families now serve as the contexts in which participation decisions are made and supported. For example, young people cannot develop or sustain a commitment to sport participation if their families lack the resources to pay for their opportunities to sample different sports and select one or more programs that suit their interests. Additionally, if they don't become involved during childhood or early adolescence, they are less like to feel comfortable playing sports later in their lives.

Wheeler's research shows us that the process of becoming and staying involved in sports is closely tied to family dynamics and decisions, and these are influenced by structural and cultural factors.

Structural factors include socio-economic status and the availability of sport facilities, equipment, financial support, coaching, and competition opportunities (Wheeler and Green, 2014). Cultural factors include the importance given to particular sports and to the ways that one's age, gender, race, ethnicity, sexuality, and ability influence the meaning of being an athlete. For example, data from a national sample of young people in the United States indicates that African American youth are more likely than their white, Latino, and Asian counterparts to receive encouragement for sport participation through all their relationships, including family, teachers, coaches, peers, and friends (Shakib and Veliz, 2013). This is partly because many people have been socialized to uncritically assume that there is a connection between sport and race and that African Americans are either better at or more interested in sports than others, and that sports provide them with mobility opportunities that are less accessible in their lives.

Making Choices to Participate During Adolescence

During one of the times when I worked in England, my colleague Anita White and I did a study on why most young people did not participate in a highly publicized, state-sponsored sport program. We used in-depth interviews to explore how British adolescents in a working-class area east of London made decisions about what they did in their free time (Coakley and White, 1999).

Data from our interviews indicated that the young people took a combination of factors into account as they made decisions about sport participation. These factors included the following:

1. Their ideas about the connection between sport participation and their own growth and development.
2. Their desires to develop and display competence so they could gain recognition and respect from others.
3. Family and peer support for participation
4. Their access to the resources needed for participation (time, transportation, equipment, and money).
5. Their memories of past experiences with physical activities and sports.
6. The social and cultural significance of sports in their social worlds.

Overall, the young people decided to play sports when it helped them extend control over their lives, achieve development and career goals, and present themselves to others as competent. We also found that young women who often had bad experiences when playing sports in physical education classes were less likely than young men to imagine that they could accomplish those things by playing sports. Therefore, they took sports less seriously and chose to participate less often than young men did.

The young people in our study made their decisions by determining if sport participation would add something positive to their lives. They didn't passively respond to the world around them, so their decisions and sport participation patterns shifted over time, depending on access to opportunities, available resources, and changes in their identities. Therefore, socialization into sports was a *continuous, interactive process* grounded in the social and cultural contexts in which they lived.

Our study also found that people make decisions to participate in sports for different reasons at different points in their lives. This is consistent with theories stating that personal growth depends on accomplishing developmental tasks associated with various stages of childhood, adolescence, young adulthood, and adulthood. Therefore, the issues considered by seven-year-olds as they make decisions about sport participation differ from the issues considered by 14-year-olds, 40-year-olds, and 60-year-olds. Furthermore, when seven-year-olds make decisions about sport participation today, they do so in different social and cultural contexts than the contexts in which 7-year-olds lived in 2000 or will live in 2050.

After analyzing our interview data, it was clear that sport participation decisions among these young people were tied to their perceptions of the cultural importance of sports and the links between playing sports, gaining social acceptance, and achieving personal goals. Therefore, when we study why people become and stay involved in sports, we take into account their perceptions of how sport participation is related to their own growth and development, how sports are integrated into their social worlds, and the extent to which participation is viewed in their culture.

I was reminded of these points when I read that some parents in Ethiopia, a patriarchal society, now accept competitive running as a way for their daughters to achieve financial success. This change has allowed girls to take up running as a strategy to stay in school, avoid an arranged marriage (as a young teen), and seek a life that consists of more than doing laundry, preparing food, and obeying a husband who is likely to define her as a form of property. Running, for girls lucky enough to be identified as talented, opens up developmental opportunities, gives them more control over their lives, and enables them to claim their bodies as their own. This is why thirteen-year-old Ethiopian girls are more likely to define competitive distance running as a desirable activity than thirteen-year-old girls living in air-conditioned homes in Beverly Hills, California. The context and consequences of their choices are much different.

Identity Formation and Being Accepted as an Athlete

Two decades ago, sociologists Peter Donnelly and Kevin Young (1999) combined data from two qualitative studies in which they did in-depth interviews.

Donnelly interviewed expert rock climbers, and Young interviewed elite rugby players. As continuing or former participants in those sports, their goal was to learn about the process through which people become accepted members of specific sport cultures.

Their analysis of the data led them to conclude that becoming and staying involved in a particular sport occurs in connection with the process of forming and maintaining an athlete identity through interaction with established participants in that sport. This, in turn, occurs through four phases of continuing socialization:

1. Acquiring knowledge about the sport.
2. Interacting with athletes in the sport.
3. Learning how participation occurs and what athletes expect from each other in the sport.
4. Becoming recognized and fully accepted as an athlete in the sport culture.

This finding indicates that becoming an athlete in a particular sport depends on learning to "talk the talk and walk the walk" so that one is identified and accepted as an athlete *by other athletes.* This process of identification and acceptance is continuous; it doesn't happen once and for all time. When athletes can no longer talk the talk and walk the walk, interaction with other athletes declines, and support for their identity fades. Membership in a sport culture is always temporary; it depends on what you do today and are expected to do tomorrow, not what you did in the past.

To understand Donnelly and Young's findings, observe skateboarders, in-line skaters, snowboarders, football or basketball players, race car drivers, or members of any sport culture. Each culture has a unique vocabulary, unique ways of thinking about and doing their sports, and special understandings of what athletes expect from each other. New participants in a sport are tested and "pushed" by the "veterans" before being accepted as true skaters, riders, boarders, football players, ballers, or Formula 1 drivers. Vocabularies may change over time, but the process of being accepted as an athlete exists in most sport cultures that participants take seriously.

The work of Donnelly and Young helps us understand that becoming and staying involved in a sport depends on establishing social connections, being accepted in a sport culture, and receiving social support for the formation and maintenance of an athlete identity. This finding also helps explain why males outnumber females in alternative sport cultures. Many boys and men have defined riding on a board, whether it is down a mountain, a wave, or a rail as an activity that conveys a form of masculinity. In the process, they created cultures in which it is difficult for females to be accepted as authentic "board athletes." Acceptance of females in these sports has increased in recent years, but it has occurred primarily because girls and women have demonstrated that they can do the sports as boys and men do them. In other words, becoming and staying involved in sports is a complex, interactive socialization and identity formation and maintenance process.

In summary, the research described in the previous four sections indicates that people don't make decisions about sport participation once and for all time; they make them day after day as they consider how participation is related to their lives and their level of physical literacy. These decisions are made in particular social and cultural contexts and they are influenced by access to resources and the meanings attached to gender, class, skin color, ethnicity, age, and physical abilities.

CHANGING OR ENDING SPORT PARTICIPATION

Those of us who play or have played sports know that changing or ending our participation in a sport are common occurrences. We are cut from teams, lose interest and drop out, suffer injuries and face physical challenges that force us to stop playing, and we make choices based on changes and time conflicts in our lives. However, some of us stay involved in some form of sport as long as we can, and others–most of us–stop and restart sport participation multiple times during our lives.

(*Source:* Jay Coakley)

Although people may drop out of sports at one point in the life course, they may return at a later point. This team of women, all over seventy years old, is playing an exhibition game against a group of younger women. The team is raising funds to travel to the national finals in the Senior Games. Most of these older women had not played competitive basketball for thirty to fifty years. This process of reinvolvement in sports is discussed in Chapter 10, Age and Ability in Sports.

Research helps us understand these changes and transitions. Studies done in the sociology of sport and related fields have identified factors that enable people at all levels of competition to change or transition out of active sport participation more smoothly and with less disruption to their lives. This research is also useful for professional athletes anticipating the end of their competitive careers; by their friends and family members, by social workers, psychologists, and others who provide guidance during these transitions; and by sports organizations as they assist athletes facing the end of careers.

The next four sections summarize studies that explain when and why people change or end sport participation. The studies I've chosen focus on (1) normal life changes that impact sport participation, (2) burnout and the factors that cause it, (3) stopping and restarting participation, and (4) factors influencing the quality of transitions out of competitive sport careers.

Getting on with Life and Getting out of Sports

"*Why do so many young adults stop practicing sport?*" This was the question asked by three researchers as they studied the impact of regular life events on decisions made by young people between the ages of 18 and 35 in The Netherlands (van Houten, Kraaykamp & Breedveld, 2017). Previous studies had generally ignored changes in sport participation patterns after childhood and adolescence. But these researchers knew that these decisions were related to important health outcomes and the types of services and opportunities provided by governments, non-profit organizations, and private businesses.

The study used complex quantitative methods to collect and analyze data from a national sample of the Dutch population. Their focus was very specific: how do four major life events–*beginning to work, living independently, cohabiting or getting married,* and *becoming a first-time parent*–impact participation in sports and membership in local sport clubs that are a key provider of sport participation opportunities in the Netherlands and nearly all of Europe? What they found was that there were 2,854 times that people in their sample stopped playing a sport and 1,447 times that people dropped their membership in a sport club.

Their statistical analysis showed that the risk of ending sport participation and dropping a sport club membership overlapped. However, young adults were more likely to stop playing sports than leaving a sport club where they had friends and be around the sports they had enjoyed. The data also indicated that each of the four life events they studied did influence decisions to stop playing sports and that this influence impacted women more than men, suggesting that women continue to be more involved than men in doing domestic tasks and caregiving.

The general conclusion of the study was that the sport participation patterns of young adults change with "shifting needs, resources and restrictions" (p. 871). But the researchers also noted that just as life events reduce sport participation at certain points in the life course, they can also provide opportunities to initiate or resume sport participation at other points. In other words, when people at any age stop playing a sport due to changing life circumstances, they may not stop forever, and they often maintain connections associated with their previous participation, a factor that may facilitate future participation. Additionally, decisions to stop sport participation are not always the result of negative experiences, poor or abusive coaching, injuries, or declining abilities. Related research that is discussed in Chapter 10, *Age and Ability,* indicates that people often turn to different and less intense sports as they become older and revise their interests and priorities (Gayman et al., 2017; O'Connor, 2018; Ronkainen, Ryba & Selänne, 2015; Ronkainen & Ryba, 2018; Willing et al., 2018).

For the researchers in The Netherlands their findings indicated that there is a need for policy-makers, program developers, and sport providers to be responsive to the changing needs, resources, and the everyday life circumstances of young adult sport participants so they can offer "less time-consuming and more flexible forms of sports" to include couples participating together, and provide on-site childcare and programs linked with workplaces where physical activity is emphasized for employees. This makes sense in any society where youth sport programs are seen as a gateway to lifelong sport participation; such a gateway is irrelevant unless opportunities for adult sport participation are provided in ways that accommodate changing life circumstances through adulthood.

Love it or Leave it: Burnout Among Adolescent and Young Adult Athletes

As youth and junior level sports have become more intense, competitive, and selective, burnout has become a common problem. During the 2000s this was the case among select 16- to 18-year-old inter-county Gaelic football players in Northern Ireland. It attracted the attention of Lynette Hughes, herself a former top footballer, as she was selecting a topic for her Ph.D. dissertation at the University of Ulster. She requested and received funds from the Gaelic Games Association to collect data from 524 elite level football players in the 16- to 24-year old competition categories, and from a sample of coaches, team administrators, and others familiar with this level of Gaelic football. Her goal was to identify the reasons for unexpectedly high burnout rates among top players in the younger age categories (Hughes and Hassan, 2017).

Hughes knew that the causes of burnout in sports were (1) exhaustion due to intense training and competition, (2) a devaluing of sport participation and performance, and (3) a sense that achieving performance goals and improving performance was not possible. Overall, burnout was explained by using a "vocabulary of stress." Her interviews with a sample of players indicated that this was the case: stress *was* related to burnout. But as she probed further in the interviews, she discovered that these stress-related conditions were rooted in the social organization of Gaelic football itself. Statements from the players indicated that they lacked control over any of their sport participation. Furthermore, the demands of their sport allowed them no opportunities to be anything other than a football player at a time in their lives when developing autonomy and multiple identities was important. The players lacked power in their sport and this created the stress typically associated with burnout.

When Hughes gave her report to the GAA and the men who controlled Gaelic football, she noted that the high rate of burnout among players was explained more accurately through a "vocabulary of empowerment" than a "vocabulary of stress." However, this is not a message that people who control athletes and sport organizations want to hear. Reducing the power of coaches, managers, and administrators so athletes can more effectively control their lives requires major changes in the organization of most elite sports. Therefore, burnout is primarily seen as an athlete problem rather than an organizational problem. This, in turn, perpetuates conditions that increase overuse injuries: with no control over their training and competition, there is no time for physical and emotional recovery–unless the athletes drop out of a sport in which they have willingly participated. In the meantime, burnout is treated with stress management strategies that do not change the underlying organizational and development barriers that set the stage for burnout.

Stopping and Starting: Sporadic Participation Until Going Out for Good

A common pattern of sport participation involves playing sports during childhood, stopping during early-to-mid-teen years, and playing sports on and off at various recreational levels during much of adulthood. In some cases, people move into adulthood with an identity in which *being an athlete* is central to who they are. However, most adults, even young adults have multidimensional identities in which being an athlete is not a significant part of their everyday lives. They may see themselves as being athletic without tying their sport participation to an identity as "an athlete." Generally, they participate in one or more sports for an enjoyable physical experience, staying healthy, meeting people, and maintaining friendships. To achieve these outcomes, they tend to choose sports in which goals and challenges can be adjusted and controlled as their physical skills and life circumstances change, and they may regularly switch participation from one sport to another as seasons change. But over time, they also stop, restart, and change sports as their lives change.

There is little research on patterns of sporadic or seasonal sport participation among 25–50-year-olds, partly because it isn't associated with any serious personal or social problems. There are occasional injuries that require medical attention or recovery time away from sport participation, but most people see these as temporary interruptions in their lives. Even though sporadic sport participation during adulthood doesn't cause transition trauma, it is worth knowing who engages in various patterns of participation, how those patterns are related to youth sports experiences, how they influence friendships and family relationships, and if they are associated with other factors such as community involvement, buying season tickets to sports events, coaching in youth sports, and general health and well-being.

There have been a handful of studies focused on older "skaters" (skateboarding), some of whom retain a strong self-identity with skateboard culture as young and middle-aged adults (O'Connor,

2018; Snow, 1999; Willing and Shearer, 2016; Willing et al., 2018). Paul O'Connor, a sociologist from Australia used online video chats to interview 23 skaters from 6 countries to identify patterns of participation. The skaters were between 36 and 55-years-old, all but one was white, and all but two were male. They had varying participation histories with seven having continuous involvement in skateboarding since childhood or early adolescence, 13 had resumed skating after breaks of 5–20 years, and 3 began skating after their mid-30s. Combining his interview data with ethnographic observation, and discourse analysis of skateboard media, O'Connor found that skateboarding was an important element in the biographies and identities of most middle-aged skaters and that long-term experiences in skateboarding were seen by other skaters as an indicator of their authenticity in skateboard culture. In turn, the older skaters used their skating experience as a resource in managing their status in the culture.

Building on the work of O'Connor and others, a team of scholars at the Griffith University Centre for Social and Cultural Research in Australia studied older–mostly middle-aged–male skaters represented in *The Tired Video* and its two sequels, each focusing primarily on older skaters (Willing et al., 2018; Tired Skateboards, 2014, 2015a, 2015b). Their analysis found that aging in skateboarding was as much a cultural phenomenon as a biological one. The men continued to skate even though they were not experts. They tried to maintain their skills, despite falls and injuries, and they sustained their skater identity by dressing and talking like skaters. Their identity was linked with opportunities for creativity and self-expression as they skated. Rather than competing, they passed on their knowledge and learned from younger skaters in settings characterized by a playful spirit. To manage and reaffirm their skater identity, they used four strategies:

1. *Modification* in the form of controlling their clothing and presentation of self to accommodate their changing bodies, and regulating the difficulty of their tricks to match declines in their agility.
2. *Dedication* as they displayed persistence and enthusiasm during their repeated attempts to perform tricks successfully.
3. *Humor* in their presentations of humility and self-deprecation as they attempted difficult tricks that challenged their abilities.
4. *Homage* in the way they acknowledged classic tricks, the reputations of top skaters, and knowledge of skating events and stories enshrined in the history of skateboard culture.

The successful use of these strategies indicated that skateboard culture was fluid and open to identity claims and lifestyles that included age-related changes. Physical skill was not the only criterion for cultural membership. As Lance Mountain, a 51-year-old original Bones Brigade team rider and professional skater explained: *"Skateboarding doesn't make you a skateboarder. Not being able to stop skateboarding makes you a skateboarder"* (https://cuttingthestone.wordpress.com/2013/02/27/lance-mountain-quote/ see also, Peralta, 2012).

An important point about skateboarding is that it is a *lifestyle sport* (Wheaton, 2013). This means that it is enjoyed for its own sake with an emphasis on individual skill development, creativity, playfulness, self-expression, peer support, and cooperative learning; and it does not involve formal competition or power dynamics based on a hierarchical structure of authority (Wheaton, Roy & Olive, 2017).[2] Other examples include a long list of challenging individual sports, such as surfing, skiing, parkour, mountain biking, trail running, snowboarding, rafting, kayaking, windsurfing, snowboarding, mountain and rock climbing–all of which can be enjoyed at various ages and with different levels of ability (Falcous, 2017).

Research done in Finland suggests that people who participate in lifestyle sports, even at high skill levels, have markedly different attitudes and values than athletes in traditional competitive sports (Salasuo et al., 2016). Participants in lifestyle sports

[2]Later in this chapter, there is a discussion of *pleasure and participation sports,* a sport form that is similar to lifestyle sports in certain respects.

don't see themselves as athletes or as elite performers, even when participation is important in their lives. Additionally, participation is self-regulated so it can continue even as skills decline; and ending or retiring from participation is usually part of a gradual process based on personal decisions made over time. This connects the transition out of the sport with other life changes so that it does not cause identity trauma.

Game Over: Being Forced Out, Injured Out, and Voluntarily Ending Sport Careers

Careers in high performance and professional sports always end. Many of them end involuntarily and sooner than expected, whereas others end voluntarily for various reasons. But in most cases, there is a transition period during which retiring athletes must adjust to life without training and competition, without coaches and others supervising their lives, and without the recognition and status that they may have enjoyed during their careers.

An impressive number of studies have focused on these transitions with the goal of identifying factors that cause problems or make them successful. The findings reported in these studies are sometimes contradictory, but there are general patterns reported across multiple studies.

The transition out of high school sports has not been studied, although there is anecdotal evidence that some people have self-concepts that are partly dependent on memories of high school "glory days". But there are informative studies of college, elite amateur, and professional athletes and how they handle the transition out of their competitive sport careers. A review of these studies found that

(*Source:* Lara Killick)

Many factors influence decisions to drop out of sports or shift participation from one sport to another. Although identity changes, access to resources, and life course issues are involved, injuries often force people to make changes. In all these cases, as our circumstances change, so do our ideas about ourselves and about sports and sport participation.

there are six major factors that influence the quality of the transition experience (Fuller, 2014):

1. *The centrality and importance of athletic identity.* An athlete identity that dominates a person's overall self-concept is associated with difficulties in the transition process. After years of being identified and strongly self-identifying as an athlete, it is necessary to renegotiate the self by establishing new relationships and developing identities outside of sport. This may be challenging for young people whose lives as athletes separated them from peers other than teammates and from developmental experiences unavailable in sports. The goal is to move beyond one's former athlete identity or use it as a tool when first establishing new relationships and identities.

   Although all transitioning athletes experience this identity challenge, female athletes generally deal with it more effectively and quickly than male athletes do (Smith & Hardin, 2018; Tinley, 2015). For example, female athletes may depend less on their athlete identities than their male peers, and they know that there are few opportunities at the professional level. This encourages them to cultivate relationships and identities outside of their sports. Young men, on the other hand, are more likely to assume that there will opportunities to continue their sport careers, so they spend less time developing relationships and identities unrelated to sports.
2. *Anticipating and preparing for the transition.* Compared with athletes who don't anticipate and prepare for transitioning out of sport, those who do anticipate and prepare face far fewer problems that disrupt their lives and undermine their sense of purpose. Athletes who have focused exclusively on sports may lack the motivation, knowledge, and resources to do this. However, if coaches and administrators working for teams and sport organizations were really concerned about the well-being of the athletes they supervise or employ, they would provide them with guidance and resources for dealing constructively with the transition process. Of course, this is especially imperative for athletic departments in colleges and universities because they are part of higher *education*.
3. *Exploring opportunities and possibilities for future growth and development.* This process of exploration is crucial for making a positive transition out of sport careers. Those who ignore it often end up feeling lost at a time in their lives when important choices are made. The likelihood and effectiveness of this exploration process depend partly on the athlete's relationships with age peers who are actively considering non-sport career possibilities and opportunities. The demands of training and competition often preclude experiences that make them aware of what is realistically possible for them in the future.
4. *Being satisfied with athletic performance.* Regrets about sport performance during a sport career may decrease the quality of transition experiences. Dissatisfaction related to unmet goals can reduce a person's motivation to get on with life after a sport career. The likelihood and intensity of this dissatisfaction are related to the importance of a person's athlete identity. When being an athlete is the most important thing in a person's life, failing to achieve goals or having negative feelings about their performance during their careers can decrease confidence and self-esteem in ways that make the transition process more difficult. This is especially the case when athletes feel like they've let other people down with their performance.
5. *Creating strategies for maintaining desired connections with teammates.* The transition process is more likely to go smoothly if the retiring athlete creates plans for maintaining relationships with teammates who are friends. This helps to overcome the loss of camaraderie that they often experienced when they are no longer a member of a team. When the loss of these connections is upsetting, it helps to have strong social and emotional support from friends and family outside of sport. The emotional intensity and feelings of togetherness that exist on some sport teams are relatively unique, and a successful transition

involves being able to put them in perspective and effectively establish and maintain relationships that do not depend on sports.

6. *Having social and emotional support systems.* Any challenging transition is made easier when a person has an established network through which they receive social and emotional support. The effectiveness of these networks and support systems depends on a retiring athlete's willingness to share personal feelings to be vulnerable in the process. The most effective support systems are based on a combination of trust and reciprocity, so if an athlete has difficulty sharing emotions and giving and receiving support in relationships outside of sports, transitions are more difficult.

The transition challenges experienced by college athletes ending their intercollegiate careers are generally less severe than the challenges faced by professional athletes who have longer careers during which they (and their families) have depended on sport-related income for their livelihoods. This was documented by Scott Tinley as he interviewed forty-six people–"29 athletes (18 men, 11 females) from 16 professional sports, 9 sport administrator/managers, and 8 sport media journalists" over an 18-month period (Tinley, 2015, p. 270). Tinley undertook this project that also involved fieldwork, ethnography, and media analyses, to make sense of his life as he experienced continuing problems in his own transition out of a 25-year career as one of the top triathletes in the world. He had won the Ironman and other major championships multiple times and supported himself and his family with what he earned. As he struggled to figure out who he was outside of constantly training and competing, he entered a Ph.D. program and did his research to learn from the transition experiences of his peers in other sports. His previous connections with them enabled him to extend interviews and do follow-ups over many hours and days.

His findings reaffirmed and went beyond the six factors identified by Fuller (2014, see above). For example, he found that money alone did not ease the retirement transition. Like other resources, money had to be used strategically to develop new skills and initiate activities with meaning that transcended the former athlete identity and opened opportunities for growth. Being able to drive an Escalade or Mercedes did not improve the retirement transition. Good health also improved transitions. Being forced to end careers due to an injury or an accumulation of injuries often created emotional trauma that undermined efforts to do what is needed to experience successful transitions (Turner, 2018). Consistent social support was also a positive factor; it did not eliminate trauma, but it helped to deal successfully with it.

A few people of color encountered difficulties caused by prejudice and discrimination, but this was more the exception than the rule among the athletes interviewed by Tinley. On the basis of his data, he concluded that the access barriers faced by people of color when they entered professional sports were greater than the barriers they faced when transitioning out of sports careers. Important for a few of the retiring athletes was an opportunity to create a reflexive autobiography in which they reviewed their careers and clarified issues and experiences that had been inaccurately or incompletely covered in the media. Being able to tell their stories verbally or in print was a healing experience that served as an "identity bridge" linking who they were as an athlete with emerging new identities in retirement. Also related to identity issues was that most retiring athletes interviewed by Tinley decided to wait 2–5 years before interacting with athletes still playing. This gave them time to make an "identity break" from being an athlete before reconnecting with active athletes and simply reminiscing about their playing days. Making this identity break was a major challenge for most of the retiring athletes. For example, a former NFL player had this to say about it: "Without football, without my ability to express myself through football I am nobody. I will disappear. Football has been my life and I have so little else" (Tinley, 2015, p. 133). Moving past this self-appraisal is not easy, and it takes more time than most former athletes anticipate.

Finally, interaction with fans seldom improved the quality of retirement transitions because fans treated the former athletes as commodities rather than human beings facing issues having little or nothing to do with sports. However, former athletes who had critically examined commercial sports and their role in it were more likely to interact with fans without experiencing trauma. They knew what to expect and they felt relief in being away from a sport in which they were evaluated primarily as a piece of property (Jones & Denison, 2017). This helped them come to terms with retirement and find meaning in their post-retirement lives.

Future retirement transitions from high performance sports may be more difficult than they have been in the past because athletes now must devote much more time and energy to training and competition. No longer are there "off seasons" during which they can expand their experiences, relationships, identities, and knowledge about life after sport. Self-concept and identity are grounded in sports first and foremost. This means that they are likely to face retirement transitions with few resources. Unless teams and sports organizations take responsibility for providing meaningful transition assistance involving more than a few lectures from retirement experts, the quality of future transitions will decline and post-retirement problems will increase (Tennant, 2014).

In summary, research shows that ending or changing sport participation often involves the same interactive and decision-making processes that occur as a person becomes and stays involved in sports. Changes in participation are often the result of decisions associated with other life events, social relationships, and cultural expectations related to development. This means that theories explaining why people play sports and change their participation over time must take into account identity issues and developmental processes that are part of the social and cultural contexts in which people make decisions about sports in their lives (van Houten et al., 2015).

Furthermore, theories must take into account the personal, social, and material resources that former athletes possess as they make transitions to other relationships, activities, and careers. When problems occur during this transition, they are associated with an unwillingness to transition into identities unrelated to sports and a lack of the personal and social resources needed to successfully negotiate the transition challenges they face (Tinley, 2015).

Research suggests that changes and retirement transitions are less likely to involve problems if sport participation has *expanded* a person's identities, experiences, relationships, and resources outside of sports. Difficulties are most likely when athletes have never had the desire or the chance to live outside the culture of elite sports and learn to successfully navigate their way in nonsport social worlds.

PARTICIPATION IN SPORTS: WHAT HAPPENS?

Beliefs about the consequences of sport participation vary from culture to culture, but many people accept what was described in Chapter 1 (p. 11) as the *great sport myth.* In other words, they believe that playing sports leads to a long list of positive outcomes with little chance that there will be any negative outcomes. This belief creates encouragement for children to play sports, and generates support for funding sport programs in schools, building stadiums, promoting teams and leagues, and sponsoring international events such as the Olympic and Paralympic Games, world cups, and national championships. In the following sections, we will critically examine this belief and come to a realistic understanding of the influence that sport participation has in people's lives.

Do Sports Build Character?

For the past 70 years, researchers have tried to prove that "sport builds character," find the conditions under which certain personal attributes are likely to be developed, or refute the notion that there is a connection between sport and character development. Their studies have often compared the traits, attitudes, and behaviors of those who play organized sports with those who don't. However, these one time snapshot comparisons have produced inconsistent and confusing findings. This is because researchers have generally used inconsistent definitions of *character* based on two faulty assumptions (McCormack and Chalip, 1988). First, they've wrongly assumed that *all* athletes have the same or similar experiences in *all* sports. Second, they've wrongly assumed that organized sports provide unique experiences that are not available in other activities. These assumptions have caused researchers to overlook the following important things when they study sports and socialization:

1. *Sport experiences are diverse*. Because sport programs and teams are organized in vastly different ways, we cannot make generalizations about the consequences of sport participation. This point is explained further in Reflect on Sports, pp. 68–70.
2. *Selection processes exist in sports.* People who choose or are selected to play sports often have personal characteristics that differ from those who do not choose to play or are not selected by coaches. Therefore, sport participation may not *build* character as much as sports are organized to *select* people who already possess traits valued by coaches and compatible with highly organized, competitive, physical activities.
3. *The meanings given to sport experiences vary from person to person.* Even when people play in the same program and on the same team there are important variations in what they learn as they participate and how they apply it to their lives.
4. *People change*. The meanings given to sport experiences may change over time as people develop new values and understandings of themselves and the world.
5. *Relationships and context matter*. The meaning and importance of sport experiences in a person's life are influenced by other people and the contexts in which participation occurs.
6. *Sport experiences are not unique*. The learning that occurs in sports can also occur in other activities. Therefore, it is possible for people who do not play sports to have developmental experiences similar to those of athletes.

Due to these six oversights, studies that compare "athletes" with "nonathletes" have produced inconsistent and misleading research results about the impact of sport participation in people's lives. After evaluating these studies, I've concluded that sport participation is most likely to have positive socialization consequences when it provides athletes with the following:

- Opportunities to explore and develop identities apart from sports.
- Knowledge-building experiences that go beyond the locker room and playing field.
- New relationships, especially with people who can be mentors and advocates outside of sports.
- Training that shows how lessons learned in sports can be applied to situations unrelated to sports (that is, skills transfer lessons).
- Opportunities to develop and display competence in nonsport activities.

In other words, positive developmental outcomes *do not* occur automatically when people participate in sports.

My review of research also suggests that when sport participation is organized so it *constricts* opportunities, experiences, relationships, and developing competence in non-sport activities and situations it will have negative consequences for a person's overall development. Therefore, we cannot make a general statement that sport participation leads to specific positive or negative outcomes. Sport experiences are diverse, and they are given meaning and incorporated into people's lives in various ways, depending on the social and cultural contexts in which people live.

This conclusion does *not* mean that sports and sport participation are irrelevant in people's lives.

Power and Performance *versus* Pleasure and Participation

Different Sports, Different Experiences, Different Impact and Learning

Sport experiences are diverse. It's a mistake to assume that all sports are organized around the same goals and orientations, played in the same spirit, or given meaning in the same way. For example, there are highly organized competitive sports, informal sports, adventure sports, recreational sports, lifestyle sports, extreme sports, alternative sports, cooperative sports, indigenous sports, contact sports, artistic sports, team sports, individual sports, and so on. However, at this point in history, the most dominant sport form in wealthy postindustrial nations is organized around a **power and performance model.**

Power and performance sports are highly organized and competitive; they emphasize the following factors:

- Using strength, speed, and power to push human limits and achieve competitive success
- Proving excellence through competitive success and attributing success to dedication, hard work, and sacrifice
- Being willing to risk physical well-being and play with pain
- Exclusive processes through which participants are cut from teams if they do not meet elite performance standards
- A chain of command in which owners and administrators control coaches, and coaches control athletes
- Competing against opponents and defining them as enemies to be conquered

These points exaggerate the characteristics of power and performance sports to show that they provide experiences that are very different from experiences in other sport forms. Although, many people use the power and performance model as a standard for defining "real" sports, it is not the only model around which sports are organized. For example, people worldwide also participate in other forms of sport.

The sport forms most unlike power and performance sports today are organized around a **pleasure and participation model,** and they emphasize the following factors:

- Active participation that revolves around connections between people, integration of mind and body, and harmony with the environment
- A spirit of personal expression, enjoyment, growth, good health, and mutual concern among participants

(*Source:* Jan Kruger/Getty Images)

Power and performance sports involve the use of strength, speed, and power to dominate opponents in the quest for competitive victories.

(*Source:* Jay Coakley)

Pleasure and participation sports emphasize connections between people and personal expression through participation. This is often seen at skateboard parks where participants support and encourage each other.

- Personal empowerment created by gaining knowledge about and pleasure from the body
- Inclusive processes through which participation is encouraged by accommodating ability differences
- Democratic decision-making structures in which relationships are characterized by cooperation and sharing power
- An emphasis on seeing competitors as partners in creating and meeting physical challenges

Again, these points exaggerate the characteristics of pleasure and participation sports, but they show that experiences in these sports are very different from experiences in power and participation sports.

These two sport forms represent only two of the many ways that sports might be organized, played, and defined. There are sports that contain elements of both forms and reflect diverse ideas about what is important in physical activities. However, power and performance sports remain dominant today because they receive the most attention, support, and sponsorship. When people play or watch these sports, their socialization experiences are different from their socialization experiences in pleasure and participation sports.

WHY ARE POWER AND PERFORMANCE SPORTS SO DOMINANT TODAY?

Power and performance sports are dominant today because, they foster the interests of people and organizations with the resources to sponsor and stage large sport events. History shows that wealthy and influential people in societies around the world have used different strategies to maintain their privileged positions. Some have used coercive strategies such as employing the police and military to maintain control over resources and people, but most have used cultural or "soft" strategies that foster the belief that they deserve their wealth and power and that society benefits from their resources.

In countries where wealth and power have been controlled by a monarchy, the privileged position of the royal family is based on the belief that it is their birthright to rule over others. Therefore, kings and queens maintain their privileged positions as long as their "subjects" believe that birthrights represent legitimate claims to wealth and power. This is why the church and state have usually been closely aligned in societies with monarchies–kings and queens use the clergy to promote the belief that their position was bestowed on them by a divine, supernatural source, such as a god.

In democratic countries, most people use *merit,* or "personal achievement," as a standard when judging whether the possession of wealth and power is legitimate. Therefore, it is only when most people believe that wealth and power are rightfully earned that those who possess them are seen in a positive way. When a democracy is characterized by widespread inequality, people with wealth and power promote the idea that they have earned their privileged positions through hard work and intelligence and that society as a whole benefits from their control and influence. In recent history, this idea has been promoted by emphasizing that *competition* is a natural part of social life and the only fair basis for determining who gets what in society. When there is widespread acceptance of this idea, people generally idealize and defer to wealthy and powerful people and believe that they deserve what they have.

Power and performance sports are widely promoted and sponsored by people with wealth and power because these sports are based on an ideology that celebrates competitive winners and defines competition as the only fair and natural way to distribute rewards. This ideology also explains and justifies economic inequalities as part of the natural order of things. The executives of major corporations realize this and collectively allocate billions of dollars annually to sponsor power and performance sports worldwide. They personally believe that rewards should go to winners, that winners deserve wealth and power, and that the ranking of people on the basis of wealth and power is fair and natural. By sponsoring power and performance sports and making them a major source of enjoyment and excitement in people's lives, they promote these beliefs at the same time that they profit from selling the vehicles, fast food, soft drinks, and beer advertised during sports events.

Continued

reflect on SPORTS Power and Performance *versus* Pleasure and Participation (*continued*)

The sport forms that challenge this ideology may be popular among some people, but they don't receive many sponsorship dollars from wealthy and powerful people. For example, alternative sports such as skateboarding and disk sport (Frisbee) were often banned and associated with deviance until they were organized around a power and performance model. Free-flowing, expressive alternative sports that don't produce winners and losers receive little attention from powerful sponsors. But when ESPN used a power and performance model to restructure these sports in the X Games, corporate sponsors came forward to support them. Today, many of these sports have lost their alternative character. Celebrity athletes now hawk corporate products and lifestyles of consumption. At the same time, participation comes to be tied with brands and the quest for the latest piece of equipment, clothing, or energy drink endorsed by the athletes. The masses watch and idolize the select few at the top. This raises questions about who benefits from the ways sports are currently organized and supported worldwide.

Are there ways to preserve and promote pleasure and participation sports under these circumstances? Is this important to do in today's societies? From a policy and management perspective these are important questions to answer. *What do you think?*

We know that sport participation often involves memorable experiences that impact people's lives. However, we cannot separate those affects from the meanings that people give to sports and how they integrate them into their lives. Therefore, if we want to know what happens in sports, we must study sport experiences in the contexts in which they occur. This type of research provides insights into the complex connections between sports and socialization and helps us understand the conditions under which positive or negative outcomes occur among those who play sports (Holt, 2016; Overman, 2019).

When discussing what happens during sport participation it is important to recognize that the conditions of participation have changed dramatically in recent years. At all age levels, the time, energy, and emotional commitments required for being selected and retained in sport programs have increased significantly compared to expectations for athletes in previous generations (Burlot, Richard & Joncheray, 2018). Athletes today, compared with athletes from even a few years ago, spend more time practicing, competing, weight/strength/speed training, treating injuries, "rehabbing," studying game and performances strategies and films of themselves and opponents, and meeting with performance psychologists and nutrition experts. Additionally, the stakes associated with their performances have increased; they are more tightly supervised and controlled by coaches, parents, and team support personnel; and they experience more pressure in sports. These changes have altered the sport experience for so many athletes that we need new data on how they define their experiences and integrate them into their lives as well as how their participation influences non-sport activities and relationships that in the past helped athletes keep their sport participation in perspective.

These changes have implications for those of us doing research in the sociology of sport. The findings reported in previous studies are less relevant for understanding the impact of sport participation on athletes today. New studies are needed to see if these changes have shifted the impact of participation in a positive or negative direction.

Sport Participation and Health

The relationship between sports, exercise, and health has been widely studied (Malm et al., 2019). When sociologist Ivan Waddington (2000a, 2000b, 2007) reviewed research on this topic, he concluded that the healthiest of all physical activities were rhythmic, noncompetitive exercises in which individuals control and regulate their own body movements. The research also indicated that health benefits decline when there is a shift from self-controlled exercise to competitive sports. This is because the injury rates in competitive sports are high enough to increase health costs above what is considered "average" in most populations. This cost-benefit ratio becomes even less favorable when there is a shift from noncontact to contact sports and from recreational sports to elite sports in which participants train intensely for more than 15 hours per week, play while injured, and perceive their bodies as tools for achieving competitive success.

These points were outlined in a report by the Physical Activity Guidelines Advisory Committee (2008) for the US Department of Health and Human Services. The expert on the committee concluded that "competitive athletes who participate and train at high levels (e.g., elite, professional sports, National Teams, Olympic athletes) in sports requiring high joint impact (e.g., football, track and field, soccer) for many years have higher rates of incident knee or hip OA [osteoarthritis] than do non-athletes" (p. G5–20). These athletes also incur abnormally high rates of joint injuries that result in eventual surgeries, including tendon and ligament repairs and shoulder, knee, and hip replacements, over the life course.

The connection between sport and health is being viewed more critically now that mainstream media have published numerous stories about concussions, brain trauma, sudden cardiac arrest, heat stroke, overuse injuries, ACL injuries, and other injuries sustained regularly by athletes (Turner, 2018). For example, during a typical mid-season week in the NFL, nearly 25 percent of the 2000 players on team rosters are too injured to play, and some of them are already out for the season. Cumulative injuries have longterm consequences as one-third of retired NFL players are diagnosed as disabled at some level. Injury rates in Division I college football are so high today that coaches insist they cannot reduce team size or the allowable number of scholarships because they need many replacement players during a normal season.

Dr. Edward Wojtys, director of sport medicine at the University of Michigan, notes that ACL injuries are so frequent among athletes that they are becoming a public health problem in the United States (Longman, 2011). Athletes tear or rupture ligaments in over 250,000 knees each year and sustain between two and four million concussions. Knee surgeries and rehabilitation are major healthcare costs in the US health care system. Overuse injuries among child athletes are increasingly common and it costs nearly $2 billion to treat them. Additionally, about 5000 former NFL players and their families sued the NFL in 2013 for withholding information about the consequences of head trauma and other injuries that are causing them chronic problems and leading to massive health care costs. College athletes have filed over 100 lawsuits against the NCAA for similar reasons. Football, hockey, lacrosse, and other sports now publicize new efforts to make participation safer for athletes. Research on these issues is discussed in Chapter 6, but at this point people must clarify what they mean when they say that "sports improve health."

When adults no longer have regular access to physical and health education experts, they sometimes assume that they can participate in sports without a sufficient level of physical literacy, without conditioning to strengthen and keep muscles flexible, and without setting reasonable limits on exertion levels when they begin new forms of participation. Although informed participation is almost always good for a person's overall health, uninformed participation often creates health problems.

In practical terms, if you lack health insurance, it is best to stay fit by doing aerobics, walking, swimming, and jumping rope; and if you play football, rugby, hockey, or other competitive contact sports, you should have good health insurance because your medical bills are likely to be higher than average. If you play sports in which you sustain concussions, receive repetitive hits to the head, or collide violently with other players, you may also want to have long-term-care insurance in case you develop chronic traumatic encephalopathy (CTE) and are not able to function on your own in later life. Even if you play golf, softball, soccer, and other sports that require sudden and forceful twisting motions or sprinting from a dead stop, injuries may require medical care.

The Sport-Obesity Connection

Obesity is a highly publicized health problem today in a growing number of countries. Nearly every discussion of this issue ends with the conclusion that eating right and exercising regularly is the best way to avoid unhealthy weight gain. Some people think that as sports become increasingly popular in a society, obesity rates will decline. However, data in the United States indicate that obesity rates among young people and adults have more than doubled between 1985 and 2012–a period when participation in organized competitive sports increased. This means that the popularity of sports in a society does not automatically inspire people to exercise or change their eating habits in ways that reduce obesity.

Like the connection between sports and health, the connection between sports and obesity rates is complex. Some competitive sports such as wrestling and gymnastics emphasize extreme forms of weight control; others emphasize weight gain for some or all participants. Many football players at the high school, college, and professional levels are encouraged to "bulk up" to the point that they would be classified as overweight according to the body mass index (BMI). Although BMI is not always a good measure for assessing the relationship between weight and health, there is good reason to believe that playing football does not routinely promote healthy weight control.

Expectations in US football today often encourage excessive eating, taking untested nutritional supplements, or using drugs to gain muscle and size. A consequence of these expectations is illustrated in Table 3.1. Unlike in 1920–1985, when no more than eight NFL players weighed over 300 pounds, in 2010 there were 394 players over 300 pounds, and they claim to have gained weight by overeating. This takes a toll on overall health (Belson, 2019; Churchill et al., 2018; Gabler, 2018).

Similar patterns of weight gain exist in college and high school football, which together have by far the most participants of all school-sponsored sports.

For example, a health survey of 3,500 former NFL players showed that for every 10 pounds the players gained during their high school to college years or during their college to professional years, there was a 14 percent greater risk of heart disease

Table 3.1 Number of 300-pound players in the NFL, 1970–2012

Year	Number of Players
1970	1
1980	3
1990	94
2000	301
2010	394
2012	361
2016	354
2018	357*

Source: Associated Press, 2010; Manfred, 2014.

* The number of players over 300 pounds stabilized when speed has became more central in offensive and defensive game plans.

(*Source:* Jay Coakley)

The physical movement that occurs during participation in recreational sports has a positive impact on health and well-being. However, participation in elite sports, especially those involving heavy contact and intense training more than 20 hours per week often have negative consequences for health.

than was the case among players who experienced only minor weight changes during the same periods; rates for other later-life health problems were also higher among players who bulked up (Churchill et al., 2018).

Of course, US football is unique, but like other sports, it exists in a social world where expectations focus on competitive success rather than healthy actions and overall fitness. If playing sports is to have a positive impact on the long-term physical well-being, regardless of age, it should be accompanied by information about nutrition and health combined with effective encouragement to use this information in connection with sport participation. As it is now, participation in certain power and performance sports sometimes involves weight control strategies that create both acute and chronic health problems for athletes.

SOCIALIZATION AS A COMMUNITY AND CULTURAL PROCESS

Socialization research has focused mostly on what occurs in the lives of individuals within specific social worlds. However, researchers now use a combination of cultural theories and text analysis to study *socialization as a community and cultural process.* These studies go beyond investigating the experiences and characteristics of athletes and what happens in sports. Instead, they focus on sports as sites at which people collectively create and learn "stories" that they use to give meaning to and make sense of realities in the world around them. These stories are sociologically relevant because many people use them as vehicles for presenting ideas and beliefs about everything from morality and work to capitalism and lifestyles of consumption. Researchers in the sociology of sport conduct studies to identify these stories, explain how they fit into the culture, and show how people use them as a guide for what they think and do.

Researchers using cultural theories are primarily concerned with whose stories about sports become dominant in a culture and whose stories are ignored. The dominant or most widely told stories are important because they are based on ideological assumptions of what is natural, normal, and legitimate in social worlds; therefore, they promote ideas and beliefs that often privilege some people more than others. For example, sports stories often revolve around heroic figures—warriors who are big, strong, aggressive, record-setting competitors. As researchers have examined the logic, values, and ideological assumptions on which these stories are based, they've found that many of them celebrate ideas and beliefs that serve the interests of capitalist expansion and traditional notions of masculinity based on the ability to dominate others through the use of physical strength, power, and speed (Burstyn, 1999).

This type of research is difficult to do because it requires a deep knowledge of history and the conditions under which sports and sport stories are integrated into people's lives. But it is important in the knowledge-building process because it deals with the ways that sports influence culture, society, and the lives of people even when they don't participate in or care about sports.

Sports as an Ideology Delivery Tool

Critical research on socialization as a community and cultural process is partly inspired by the ideas of the Italian political theorist Antonio Gramsci. When the fascist government in Italy imprisoned Gramsci for speaking out against their oppressive policies, he used his time in prison (1928–1935) to think about why people in Italy and elsewhere had not revolted against the exploitive forms of capitalism as they existed in Western societies during the early twentieth century. Gramsci concluded that revolutions had not occurred because people accepted ideas and beliefs promoted by their political leaders and supported their leaders' actions even when those actions exploited and oppressed them (Gramsci, 1971, 1988).

After carefully studying historical evidence from countries around the world, Gramsci explained that fascist and autocratic leaders often maintained power by convincing the people that they governed of three things: (1) that life was as good as it could be under present conditions; (2) that all positive things that people experienced were due to the benevolence and power of current leaders; and (3) that changing leaders would threaten everything that people valued.

Although Gramsci never talked about sports, he used historical data to conclude that fascist and autocratic leaders could effectively maintain power by providing people with exciting and pleasurable experiences that perpetuated ideas and beliefs supportive of the status quo. Using this strategy enabled these leaders to retain their power without controlling people through intimidation and brute force. In other words, people would not want to do anything that might eliminate a primary source of their positive experiences in their lives.

Gramsci's analysis explains why large corporations spend billions of dollars every year to sponsor power and performance sports and present their commercial messages through national and global media coverage. For example, Coca-Cola and McDonald's each spent about $2.6 billion sponsoring the International Olympic Committee (IOC) and presenting advertising messages during the Olympic Games from 2000 through 2018. These expenditures were made to promote sales, but more important, they used the Olympics as a site for delivering cultural messages that encouraged people to see these global corporations as benevolent providers of exciting entertainment. If these messages were successful, people would be less likely to criticize the corporations or support legislation that would curb their power and influence.

The corporate executives who made the decision to sponsor the Olympics wanted people who attended or watched the events to agree that competition was the only fair way to allocate rewards in society. The executives and their advisors realized that this belief supported the free market ideology that was the foundation of their personal status and wealth as well as the long-term success of Coca-Cola and McDonald's. For them, the Olympic Games reaffirmed an ideology that supported the global expansion of corporate capitalism.

The people who run Coca-Cola and McDonalds want to sell Coke and fast food, but they don't spend billions of sport sponsorship dollars only to boost sales figures. More important to them is effectively promoting lifestyles organized around consumption and the use of corporate brands and logos as status and identity symbols. They also use sponsorships to convince people that corporations provide them with positive experiences, and support the athletes, teams, and sports that they follow. Management at Coke and McDonald's want people to connect their soft drinks and fast food with strong athletes, healthy physical activities, and the positive spirit of the Olympic Movement. Additionally, they want influential people around the world to promote physical activity as a strategy for eliminating obesity and weight-related diseases, and to ignore the need to reduce consumption of soft drinks overloaded with sugar and fast food overloaded with fat and calories. To the extent that people make these connections, the power of global corporations is perpetuated. This is why the marketing departments of major corporations often use power and performance sports as sites to promote their interests.

Sports as a Tool for Maintaining Power and Control

TV viewers of the Super Bowl and the FIFA World Cups may not realize it, but the biggest stakes associated with those events have nothing to do with the score and everything to do with how viewers integrate into their lives the cultural messages that are embedded in the narratives and images presented in media coverage of the events.

Many sociologists refer to this process in which one group strategically persuades one or more other groups to accept their power and view of the world as establishing hegemony (heh-ǧem-ō-nee). In political science and sociology, **hegemony** is a *process of maintaining leadership and control by gaining consent and approval from those who are being led or controlled.* For example, American hegemony in the world exists only if people worldwide accept US power and influence as legitimate. Hegemony is never permanent, but it can be maintained as long as most people feel that there is no compelling reason to challenge the power of those who are in control.

Similarly, corporate hegemony is maintained as long as most people accept a view of the world that discourages them from objecting to corporate policies, profits, and executive pay packages. Like Gramsci, corporate executives know that preserving corporate power depends on establishing "ideological outposts" in people's heads. Sports, because they are exciting forms of entertainment for so many people, are important sites for creating these mental outposts. Once they are established, the outposts serve as relay terminals for delivering corporate messages directly into everyday consciousness and conversations. To highlight Gramsci's conclusion about hegemony, it can be said that "it is difficult to fight an enemy that has outposts in your head."[3] As long as this is true, those who possess power in the world will endorse, sponsor, and directly fund high-profile power and performance sports.

[3]This phrase was popularized by Sally Kempton, a feminist and spiritual teacher.

(*Source:* Jay Coakley)

When corporations invest money to have their names, logos, and products associated with sports, they are looking for more than sales. In the long run, their executives hope that people will believe that their enjoyment of sports depends on corporations. This will make people more likely to support and less likely to interfere with corporate interests.

In summary, the significance of sports in the socialization processes that occur at the community and cultural level can be understood only in connection with local history, ideologies, and power relations. In other words, the influence of sports on people's lives cannot be captured in a single statement about building character, bringing people together, creating responsible citizens, promoting conformity, or fostering warfare. The connection between sports and socialization is complex and can be explained only by studying sports in the contexts in which people give them meaning and make them a part of their lives.

summary

WHO PLAYS AND WHAT HAPPENS TO THEM?

Socialization is a complex, interactive process through which people learn about themselves and the social worlds in which they participate. This process occurs in connection with sports and other activities in people's lives. Research indicates that playing sports is a social experience as well as a physical one.

Becoming involved and staying involved in sports occur in connection with general socialization processes in people's lives. Decisions to play sports are influenced by the availability of opportunities, the existence of social support, processes of identity formation and affirmation, and the cultural context in which decisions are made.

Research also indicates that people do not make decisions about sport participation once and for all time. They make them day after day, as they set and revise priorities throughout their lives. Research on sport-related decisions indicates that significant others influence those decisions and that reasons for staying in sports change over time as people's lives change. Therefore, to understand sport participation patterns it is important to study the changing contexts in which these decisions are made.

Changing or ending active sport participation also occurs in connection with general socialization processes. These processes are interactive and influenced by personal, social, and cultural factors. Changes in sport participation are usually tied to a combination of identity, developmental, and life course issues. Ending sport participation involves a transition process, during which a person disengages from sport, redefines personal identity, reconnects with friends and family members, and uses available resources to become involved in other activities and careers. Just as people are not socialized into sports, they are not simply socialized out of sports. Research shows that changing or ending a career as a competitive athlete occurs over time and is often tied to events and life course issues apart from sports. These connections are best studied by using research methods that enable us to identify and analyze long-term transition processes.

Socialization that occurs as people participate in sports has been widely studied, especially by people wanting to know if and how sports build character and promote positive development. Much of this research has produced inconsistent findings because it has been based on oversimplified ideas about sports, sport experiences, and socialization.

Reviews of this research indicate that the most informative studies of sports and socialization take into account variations in the ways that sports are organized, played, and integrated into people's lives. This is important because different sports involve different experiences that influence socialization outcomes. For example, the experience and meaning of involvement in power and performance sports is different from involvement in pleasure and participation sports. The continued visibility and popularity of power and performance sports are related to issues of wealth and power in society because they promote an ideology that supports the interests of powerful people and corporations.

Most scholars who study sports in society now see sports as sites for socialization experiences, rather than the causes of specific socialization outcomes. This distinction recognizes that powerful and memorable experiences can occur in connection with sports, but the impact of those experiences depends on the relationships through which they are given meaning and the social and cultural factors that influence how those meanings are integrated into people's lives. Therefore, the most useful research in the sociology of sport focuses on the importance of social relationships and the contexts in which sport experiences occur.

SUPPLEMENTAL READINGS

Reading 1. Socialization and sports: A brief overview
Reading 2. Making decisions about sport participation during adolescence
Reading 3. Burnout among adolescent athletes: A sociological approach
Reading 4. Sport and character development among adolescents
Reading 5. Why do people believe that "sport builds character"?
Reading 6. Using Mead's theory of the self to organize youth sport programs

SPORT MANAGEMENT ISSUES

- You work in the parks and recreation department of a city with a high rate of obesity among people of all ages. Your job is to create programs that will increase physical activity rates across the general population. Using research as support, outline your plan and specify how it will interface with sport programs in the city.
- You are the athletic director of a new private school with a student body of fewer than 600 students. The parents and teachers want to discuss with you whether the new sports program will emphasize power and performance sports or pleasure and participation sports. You plan to identify the pros and cons of each alternative from the perspective of the students' overall educational experience. Create a handout that does that.

- You work as a sport management intern in the athletic department of a major university in the United States. The athletic director has asked you to prepare a "white paper" on the need for a program that will assist athletes in their retirement out of intercollegiate sports. List and explain the major points that you will cover in the paper.
- You are now working for an NFL team, and you want to thoughtfully consider the ideological impact of the team on its fans and the surrounding community. Identify at least three of the ideological messages that are highlighted in the media coverage of the NFL and discuss who is most likely to be advantaged or disadvantaged by each of them.

references

Associated Press. 2012. 2010. Number of 300-pound NFL lineman still ballooning. ESPN.com (August 6): http://www.espn.com/espn/wire/_/section/nfl/id/5443459

Belanger, Kevin et al. 2018. The relationship between physical literacy scores and adherence to Canadian physical activity and sedentary behaviour guidelines. *BMC Public Health* 18(Supplement 2): https://doi.org/10.1186/s12889-018-5897-4

Belson, Ken. 2019. The N.F.L.'s obesity scourge. *New York Times* (January 17): https://www.nytimes.com/2019/01/17/sports/football/the-nfls-obesity-scourge.html

Burlot, Fabrice; Rémi Richard & Helene Joncheray. 2018. The life of high-level athletes: The challenge of high performance against the time constraint. *International Review for the Sociology of Sport* 53(2): 234–249.

Burstyn, Varda. 1999. *The rites of men: Manhood, politics, and the culture of sport*. Toronto, ON: University of Toronto Press.

Churchill, Timothy W. et al. 2018. Weight gain and health affliction among former National Football League players. *The American Journal of Medicine* 131(12): 1491–1498.

Coakley, Jay & Anita White. 1999. Making decisions: How young people become involved and stay involved in sports. In Jay Coakley and Peter Donnelly, eds., *Inside Sports* (pp. 77–85). London: Routledge.

Corbin Chuck B. 2016. Implications of physical literacy for research and practice: A commentary. *Research Quarterly for Exercise and Sport* 87(1):14–27.

Donnelly, Peter, and Kevin Young. 1999. Rock climbers and rugby players: Identity construction and confirmation. In Jay Coakley and Peter Donnelly, eds., *Inside Sports* (pp. 67–76). London: Routledge.

Dudley, Dean, John Cairney, Nalda Wainwright, Dean Kriellaars & Drew Mitchell. 2017. Critical considerations for physical literacy policy in public health, recreation, sport, and education agencies. *Quest* 69(4): 436–52.

Falcous, Mark. 2017. Why we ride: Road cyclists, meaning, and lifestyles. *Journal of Sport and Social Issues* 41(3): 239–255.

Farrey, Tom & Jon Solomon, 2018. *State of Play 2018: Trends and development*. Washington DC: The Aspen Institute, Sports & Society program and Project Play; online, https://assets.aspeninstitute.org/content/uploads/2018/10/StateofPlay2018_v4WEB_2-FINAL.pdf

Farrey, Tom & Risa Isard. 2016. *Physical literacy in the United States*. Washington DC: Aspen Institute Sports & Society Program.

Fuller, Rhema D. 2014. Transition Experiences out of Intercollegiate Athletics: A Meta-Synthesis. *The Qualitative Report, 19*(46), 1–15. Online, https://nsuworks.nova.edu/tqr/vol19/iss46/1

Gabler, Nathanael. 2018. A weighty issue: NFL linemen must contend with post-football pounds. *GlobalSportMatters.com* (August 7): https://globalsportmatters.com/health/2018/08/07/nfl-linemen-contend-post-football-pounds/

Gayman, Amy M.; Jessica Fraser-Thomas, Rylee A. Dionigi, Sean Horton & Joseph Baker. 2017. Is sport good for older adults? A systematic review of psychosocial outcomes of older adults' sport participation. *International Review of Sport and Exercise Psychology* 10(1): 164–185.

Gramsci, Antonio. 1971. *Selections from the prison notebook* (Q. Hoare and G. N. Smith, Trans). New York: International Publishers (Original work published in 1947).

Gramsci, Antonio. 1988. *Selected writings: 1918-1935* (D. Forgacs, ed.). New York: Shocken.

Guthold, Regina, Gretchen A Stevens, Leanne M Riley & Fiona C Bull. 2018. Worldwide trends in insufficient physical activity from 2001 to 2016: a pooled analysis of 358 population-based surveys with 1·9 million participants. *Lancet Global Health*, published online, https://www.thelancet.com/pdfs/journals/langlo/PIIS2214-109X(18)30357-7.pdf

Hayoz, Christelle, Claudia Klostermann, Jürg Schmid, Torsten Schlesinger & Siegfried Nagel. 2019. Intergenerational transfer of a sports-related lifestyle within the family. *International Review for the Sociology of Sport* 54(2) 182–198.

Holt, Nickolas L., ed. 2016. *Positive youth development through sport* (2_{nd} edition). New York: Routledge.

Hughes, Lynette & David Hassan. 2017. Wearing their chains willingly: Athlete burnout and the case of adolescent Gaelic footballers in Ireland. *International Review for the Sociology of Sport* 52(7): 839–857.

International Physical Literacy Association 2016. https://www.physical-literacy.org.uk/

Jacobson, David. 2010. Insights from softball star Jennie Finch on playing multiple sports. *Positive Coaching Alliance Connector* (August 17): 1.

Jones, Luke & Jim Denison. 2017. Challenge and relief: A Foucauldian disciplinary analysis of retirement from professional association football in the United Kingdom. *International Review for the Sociology of Sport* 52(8): 924–939.

Longman, Jeré. 2012b. For Lolo Jones, everything is image. *New York Times* (August 4): http://www.nytimes.com/2012/08/05/sports/olympics/olympian-lolo-jones-draws-attention-to-beauty-not-achievement.html

Longmuir, Patricia E. Katie E. Gunnell, Joel D. Barnes, Kevin Belanger, Geneviève Leduc, Sarah J. Woodruff & Mark S. Tremblay. 2018. Canadian assessment of physical literacy second edition: A streamlined assessment of the capacity for physical activity among children 8 to 12 years of age. *BMC Public Health* 18(Supplement 2): 1047. Online, https://bmcpublichealth.biomedcentral.com/track/pdf/10.1186/s12889-018-5902-y

Malina, Robert. 2012. Movement proficiency in childhood: Implications for physical activity and youth sport. *Kinesiologia Slovenica* 18(3):19–34.

Malm, Christer, Johan Jakobsson & Andreas Isaksson. 2019. Physical Activity and Sports–Real Health Benefits: A Review with Insight into the Public Health of Sweden. Sports 7(5): 127; doi: HYPERLINK "https://dx.doi.org/10.3390%2Fsports7050127"10.3390/sports7050127

Manfred, Tony. 2014. One GIF that shows how NFL players are exploding in size. *Business Insider.com* (July 29): https://www.businessinsider.com/nfl-player-size-over-time-2014-7

McCormack, Jane B. & Laurence Chalip. 1988. Sport as socialization: A critique of methodological premises. *The Social Science Journal* 25, 1: 83–92.

Moore, David Leon. 2012. Head games. *USA Today* (October 12): 1–2C.

NFHS. 2019. Esports in high school. No date: https://www.nfhs.org/sports-resource-content/esports/

O'Connor, Paul. 2018. Beyond the youth culture: Understanding middle-aged skateboarder through temporal capital. *International Review for the Sociology of Sport* 53(8): 924–943.

O'Donnell, Jayne. 2018. Federal government announces new physical fitness guidelines; fewer than one in three Americans meet standards. *USA Today* (November 12): https://www.usatoday.com/story/news/health/2018/11/12/physical-fitness-aerobic-activity-sports-social-media-health-human-services-department/1943318002/

Overman, Steven J. 2019. *Sports crazy: How sports are sabotaging American schools*. Jackson MS: University Press of Mississippi.

Peralta Stacy. 2012. *The Bones Brigade*. USA: Non Fiction Unlimited Productions.

Physical Activity Guidelines Advisory Committee. 2008. *Physical activity guidelines advisory committee report*. Washington, DC: US Department of Health and Human Services. Online: health.gov/paguidelines/report/pdf /committeereport.pdf

Roetert, E Paul, Dean Kriellaars, Todd S. Ellenbecker & Cheryl Richardson. 2017. Preparing students for a physically iterate life. *Journal of Physical Education, Recreation and Dance* 88(1): 57-62.

Roetert, E Paul, Todd S Ellenbecker & Dean Kriellaars. 2017. Physical literacy: Why should we embrace this construct? *British Journal of Sports Medicine* 52(20): http://dx.doi .org/10.1136/bjsports-2017-098465

Ronkainen, Noora & Tatiana V. Ryba. 2018. The role of setting in the field: The positioning of older bodies in the field of elite women's gymnastics. *Sociology* 52(4): 727-743.

Ronkainen, Noora J. & Tatiana V. Ryba. 2017. Is hockey just a game? Contesting meanings of the ice hockey life projects through a career-threatening injury. *Journal of Sports Sciences* 35(10): 923-928.

Säfvenbom, Reidar, Belinda Wheaton & Jennifer P. Agans. 2018. 'How can you enjoy sports if you are under control by others?' Self-organized lifestyle sports and youth development. *Sport in Society* 21(12): 1990-2009.

Salasuo, Mikko, Mikko Piispa & Helena Huhta. 2016. *Exceptional Life Courses: Elite Athletes and Successful Artists in 2000s Finland*. Finnish Youth Research Society/Finnish Youth Research Network, publications 177, internet publications 97. Helsinki: Finnish Youth Research Society.

Smith, Allison B. & Robin Hardin. 2018. Female student-athletes' transition out of collegiate competition. *Journal of Amateur Sport* 4(3): 61-86.

Snow, D. 1999. Skateboarders, streets and style. In: White R (ed.) *Australian Youth Subcultures: On the Margins and in the Mainstream*. Hobart: Australian Clearinghouse for Youth Studies, 16-25.

Spengler, John Otto & Jacob Cohen. 2015. *Physical literacy: A global environmental scan*. Washington, DC: Aspen Institute Sports & Society Program, June 2015.

Stuij, Mirjam. 2015. Habitus and social class: A case study on socialisation into sports and exercise. *Sport, Education and Society* 20(6): 780-798.

Tennant, Kelli. 2014. *The transition: Every athlete's guide to life after sports*. Scotts Valley CA: CreateSpace Independent Publishing Platform

Tinley, Scott. 2015. *Racing the sunset How athletes survive, thrive, or fail in life after sport.* New York: Skyhorse Publishing.

Tired Skateboards. 2014. *The Tired Video. Thrasher Magazine* (December 25): YouTube Channel, online, https://www.youtube.com /watch?v=5BRZoqUTD5M

Tired Skateboards. 2015. *The Tired Video Two. Thrasher Magazine* (June 19): YouTube Channel, online, https://www.youtube.com /watch?v=QwhS17INkEY

Tired Skateboards. 2015b. *The Tired Video 3. Thrasher Magazine* (December 24): YouTube Channel, online, https://www.youtube.com /watch?v=SXk4VWjXvtw

Tremblay, Mark S., Christa Costas-Bradstreet, Joel D. Barnes, Brett Bartlett, Diana Dampier, Chantal Lalonde, Reg Leidl, Patricia Longmuir, Melanie McKee, Rhonda Patton, Richard Way & Jennifer Yessis. 2018. Canada's physical literacy consensus statement: Process and outcome. *BMC Public* Health 18 (Supplement 2): 1034, online at https://doi.org/10.1186/s12889-018 -5903-x (retrieved 3-21-19)

Turner, Robert W. 2018. *Not for long: The life and career of the NFL athlete*. New York/London: Oxford University Press

Van de Walle, Guy. 2011. 'Becoming familiar with a world': A relational view of socialization.

International Review of Sociology 21(2): 315–333.

van Houten, Jasper MA; Gerbert Kraaykamp & Koen Breedveld. 2017. When do young adults stop practising a sport? An event history analysis on the impact of four major life events. *International Review for the Sociology of Sport* 52(7): 858–874.

Waddington, Ivan. 2000a. Sport and health: A sociological perspective. In Jay Coakley and Eric Dunning, eds. *Handbook of sports studies* (pp. 408–421). London: Sage Publications.

Waddington, Ivan. 2000b. *Sport, Health and Drugs : A Critical Sociological Perspective*. London: Routledge.

Waddington, Ivan. 2007. Health and sport. In George Ritzer, ed., *Encyclopedia of sociology* (pp. 2091–2095). London: Blackwell.

Weinberg, Ben, ed.. 2013. Physical literacy. *Journal of the International Council of Sport Science and Physical Education* (ICSSPE) Bulletin 65 (October): Special issue.

Wheaton, Belinda. 2013. *The cultural politics of lifestyle sports*. London: Routledge.

Wheaton, Belinda, Georgina Roy & Rebecca Olive. 2017. Exploring critical alternatives for youth development through lifestyle sport: Surfing and community development in Aotearoa/New Zealand. *Sustainability* 9, 2298; online, https://core.ac.uk/download/pdf/154363749.pdf

Whitehead, Margaret. 2001. The concept of physical literacy. *European Journal of Physical Education* 6(2), 127–138.

Whitehead Margaret, ed. 2010. *Physical literacy: Throughout the lifecourse*. New York/London: Routledge.

Whitehead, Margaret. 2013. The history and development of physical literacy. *ICSSPE Bulletin* 65(October): 22–28.

Willing, Indigo & Scott Shearer. 2016. Skateboarding activism: Exploring diverse voices and community support. In Lombard KJ (ed.) *Skateboarding: Subcultures, sites and shifts*. New York/London: Routledge (pp. 44–58).

Willing, Indigo, Andy Bennett, Mikko Piispa & Ben Green. 2018. Skateboarding and the 'tired generation': Ageing in youth cultures and lifestyle sports. *Sociology* May 24, 2018 | OnlineFirst

chapter

4

(*Source:* Jay Coakley)

ORGANIZED YOUTH SPORTS

Whose Interests Do They Serve?

Coaches can often be more helpful to a young player's development by organizing less, saying less, and allowing the players to do more. . . . Be comfortable organizing a session that looks like pick-up soccer.

—US Soccer (2010, p. 4)

The perception is you train early and only do a single sport and do as much as you can until you're better than everyone else. I think it's pretty clear from the injury and performance-data side that that's a terrible developmental model.

—Neeru Jayanthi, Medical Director, Primary Care Sports Medicine, Loyola University Health System (in Reddy, 2014).

Among richer families, youth sports participation is actually rising. Among the poorest households, it's trending down. . . . This isn't a story about American childhood; it's about American inequality. . . . Youth sports has become a pay-to-play machine.

—Derek Thompson, Economics writer, *The Atlantic* (2018)

[Today's youth sports] emphasize performance over participation well before kids' bodies, minds, and interests mature. And we tend to value the child who can help win games or whose families can afford the rising fees. The risks for that child are overuse injuries, concussion, and burnout.

—Project Play Report (2015, p. 7; http://youthreport.projectplay.us/the-problem)

Chapter Outline

Learning Objectives

- Explain how social changes related to family and childhood have influenced the growth of organized youth sports in the United States since 1950.
- Identify the goals around which each of the three models of youth sports are organized.
- Explain how the skills and excellence model of youth sports has come to be popular in the United States, and identify problems associated with this model.
- Explain why some people prefer the physical literacy and lifelong participation model over the skills and excellence model.
- Distinguish the major differences between the Long-term Athletic Development Model, the American Development Model, and the model proposed by Project Play.
- Explain why the approach used by Coaches Across Continents has become a model for other "sport for development" youth sport programs in regions where children are in crisis.

Participation in organized youth sports is seen worldwide as an important activity in the lives of children. However, there is growing disagreement about the goals of youth sports and how they should be organized. Media today are full of articles, blogs, videos, editorials, and studies that criticize the actions of parents and coaches and call for changes in the organization of teams and programs. These criticisms vary from one country to the next, depending on who controls youth sports and the goals around which they organize programs.

After reviewing research and observing youth sports in a number of countries it appears to me that there are three primary models for organizing youth sports today, depending on the goals that program organizers want to achieve. One is a *Skills & Excellence* model organized around achievement at progressively higher levels of competition. It is endorsed by people who see youth sports as a form of training that enables children to enter a developmental pipeline in which they learn the skills they need to move successfully from one level of competition to the next. For a sizable minority of young people, along with their parents and coaches, the ultimate goal of participation is to become high-performance athletes who earn rewards or gain access to valued opportunities based on their skills in a sport.

The second model is organized around the goal of producing *Physical Literacy & Lifelong Participation* in sports and physical activities that improve health and wellness in the population of a country. It is endorsed by people who think that youth sports should provide children with opportunities to play so they develop Physical literacy, that is, the ability, confidence, and desire to stay active throughout their lives. In a growing number of countries, including the United States, this model has gained popularity because programs organized around the Skills and Excellence model have failed to create sufficient levels of physical literacy and failed to produce high performance athletes that are successful in national and international competitions.

The third model is organized around the goal of producing *Personal Growth & Development* among children living in poor urban and rural areas where there is a lack of sport participation opportunities. It is endorsed by social reformers and community developers who use sports to intervene in the lives of young people and provide them with guidance, role models and mentors. Sports for these reformers are developmental tools that can inspire positive changes in the lives of young people and the communities where they live. Programs that fit this model are usually funded by governments agencies; non-governmental organizations (NGOs), including influential sports organizations; faith-based and university groups; and crisis intervention teams that help children cope with the effects of war, natural disasters, ethnic cleansing, and extreme poverty.

In this chapter, we don't assume that all youth sports programs fit neatly into only one of these three models. Some programs include elements from more than one model because they have multiple goals that reflect the values of a sponsoring organization, such as the YMCA, a religious organization, or an organization serving young people with special needs. But the three models described in this chapter represent the primary goal-oriented approaches around which many youth sports programs are organized worldwide.

The goal of this chapter is to provide a critical overview of youth sports today–why they are organized as they are, how they impact the lives of young people, and whether they are worth the all the time, effort, and funding that people and organizations put into them. To do this we will focus on two general topics:

1. The historical and social contexts in which youth sports were created and have become so popular over the past half-century.
2. Descriptions and critical analyses of the three models around which most youth sports programs are organized.

As we discuss youth sports, keep in mind your experiences and the experiences of your friends and family members. Do they fit into one or more of the three models, and were they worth the time, effort, and financial resources that went into them?

THE ORIGINS OF ORGANIZED YOUTH SPORTS

During the latter half of the nineteenth century, people in Europe and North America began to realize that child development was influenced by the social environment. This created a movement to organize children's social worlds with the goal of building their character and turning them into hardworking, productive, and patriotic adults in rapidly expanding capitalist economies (Chudacoff, 2007).

It wasn't long before organized sports for young boys were organized and sponsored by schools, communities, and church groups. The organizers hoped that sports, especially team sports, would teach boys from working-class families to obey rules and work together productively. They also hoped that sports would toughen middle- and upper-class boys and turn them into competitive men, despite the "feminized" values they learned from their stay-at-home mothers. At the same time, girls were provided activities that taught them to be good wives, mothers, and homemakers. The prevailing belief was that girls should learn domestic skills rather than sport skills when they went to schools and playgrounds.

There were some exceptions to this general pattern, and after World War II, the men who organized youth sports youth sports assumed that sport participation would build the character of boys and young men without being too concerned about how teams and programs were organized. To most of them, sports were sports and their job was to give boys opportunities to share in the purity and goodness that shaped all sport experiences. They believed the great sport myth and this led them to ignore critical questions about how to organize youth sports to achieve what they wanted to achieve.

The Postwar Baby Boom and the Growth of Organized Youth Sports

The baby-boom generation was born between 1946 and 1964. Young married couples during these years were optimistic about the future and eager to become parents. As the first wave of baby boomers moved through childhood during the 1950s and 1960s, organized youth sports grew dramatically in the countries of Western Europe and North America. Programs were sponsored by public and private organizations. Parents also entered the scene, believing that organized competitive sports would build the character of their sons. Fathers became coaches, managers, and league administrators. Mothers did laundry and became chauffeurs and short-order cooks so their sons were ready for practices and games.

Most programs were for boys eight to fourteen-years-old, and they were organized with the belief that playing sports would prepare them to be upstanding citizens and economically successful men. Until the 1970s, girls were largely ignored by these organizers. They sat in the bleachers during their brothers' games and, in the United States, they were encouraged to become cheerleaders. Then came the women's movement, the fitness movement, and government legislation prohibiting sex discrimination in education, including school-sponsored sports. These changes stimulated the growth of sport programs for girls beginning in the mid-1970s. By the 1990s most countries had organized youth sports for girls and most of them resembled the programs provided for boys.

Participation in organized youth sports between 1950 and the 1980s became a valued part of growing up in most wealthy nations. Parents and communities used their resources to sponsor, organize, and administer a variety of youth sports. However, some parents began to question the benefits of programs in which winning was more important than overall child development; other parents sought out win-oriented programs, hoping their children would become winners. A few parents encourage their children to engage in unstructured, noncompetitive physical activities–an alternative that a few young people preferred over adult-controlled, organized sports.

Recent Social Changes and the Continued Growth of Organized Youth Sports

Beginning in the 1980s an increasing amount of children's after-school time and physical activity occurred in adult-controlled organized programs. This growth was partly related to changing ideas about family life and childhood. These changes were influenced by ***neoliberalism***—an ideology emphasizing free markets and economic deregulation, privatization and the reduction of government power, the pursuit of self-interest, and competition to boost efficiency and stimulate progress.

As a shared interpretive framework, neoliberalism influenced how people made sense of and evaluated themselves, others, and events in their social worlds. It had an impact on economic and political policies, individual orientations, and personal and family decisions. Individualism and material success became more important for many people. Publicly funded programs and services, including city-funded youth sports, were cut back or eliminated and selectively replaced by private programs supported by use-fees and dues-paying members, and non-profit programs supported by grants, foundations, and charitable donations. Overall, this neoliberal cultural turn led to or intensified six social changes that impacted youth sports.

First, the number of families with both parents working outside the home increased dramatically. This created a demand for organized and adult supervised after-school and summer programs. Organized sports grew because many parents believed they offered their children opportunities to have fun, learn adult values, become physically fit, and acquire positive status among their peers.

Second, there was a change in what it meant to be a "good parent." Good parents were those who could control and account for the whereabouts

(*Source:* Jay Coakley)

To meet cultural expectations for the "good parent," mothers and fathers are often attracted to youth sport programs that use symbols of progressive achievement and skill development. Karate, with achievement levels signified by belt colors, is appealing to some because the visible and quantifiable achievements of their children can be used as proof of their parental moral worth.

and actions of their children 24/7—an expectation that led many parents to seek organized, adult-supervised programs in which their children were monitored and controlled. Organized sports were also favored by parents because they provided predictable schedules, adult leadership, and measurable indicators of a child's accomplishments. When children succeeded, parents could claim that they met important cultural expectations. In fact, many mothers and fathers felt that their moral worth as parents was associated with the visible achievements of their children—a factor that further intensified parental commitment to youth sports.

Third, many people believed that informal, child-controlled activities inevitably led to trouble—much like what occurred in the novel, *Lord of the Flies.* As young people were increasingly seen as threats to social order, organized sports came to be seen as ideal activities to keep them occupied, out of trouble, and under control.

Fourth, many parents, responding to fear-producing news stories about murders and child abductions saw the world outside the home as increasingly dangerous for their children. They regarded organized sports as safe alternatives even if they had. high injury rates and uncertified coaches. Due to perceived dangers lurking outside the home, parents felt compelled to use organized youth sports to protect their children.

Fifth, the visibility of high-performance and professional sports increased awareness of organized competitive sports as a valued part of culture. As children watched sports on television, listened to parents and friends talk about sports, and heard about the wealth and fame of popular athletes, they came to see organized youth sports, especially those modeled after professional sports, as attractive activities. When children said they wanted to be gymnasts or basketball players, parents were expected to nurture these dreams by seeking the best-organized programs in those sports. In this sense, organized youth sports grew in popularity partly because children saw them as enjoyable and culturally valued activities that would enhance their status among peers and adults.

Sixth, the culture of childhood play faded and nearly disappeared in most segments of post-industrial society, especially in the United States. Children were less encouraged and had fewer opportunities to engage in spontaneous play—activities that involved creativity, expressiveness, joy, and "ownership" possessed by the participants themselves (Gray, 2013). Children were put into structured, achievement-oriented activities earlier and earlier in their lives (Hyman, 2012). These activities, including organized sports for preschoolers, were controlled by adults and provided few opportunities for children to play, which often was seen as a "waste of time." Instead, the focus was on improvement and measurable development that would pay off for a child in the future. Parents sought developmental activities that they thought would improve their children's academic and future occupational success.

Together, these six social changes boosted the popularity of organized youth sports in recent decades. Knowing about them helps to explain why parents invest so many family resources into the organized sport participation of their children. The amount of money that parents spend on participation fees, equipment, travel, personal coaches, high-performance training sessions, and other items defined as necessary in many programs has skyrocketed in recent years (Barone, 2017; Bogage, 2018; Cohen, 2019; Gregory, 2017; Keshner, 2019; Project Play, 2018; Shell, 2017; Thompson, 2018). Parents justify their expenditures as investments into the development of their children, and parents who can't afford to do so are viewed as failing to meet expectations for good parenting. This pressure has led some parents to take second jobs and borrow money to nurture the sport dreams of a child and pay for expensive training, travel, and equipment (Fatsis & Levin, 2018; FlipGive, 2019; Hyman, 2012; Thompson, 2018; Weir, 2006).

In this way, organized sports for children have become linked to political issues and debates about family values and the comparative moral worth of parents in lower-income households—parents who cannot afford to nurture the sport dreams of their children and therefore fail to meet current expectations for being "a good parent."

THREE MODELS OF ORGANIZED YOUTH SPORT PROGRAMS

Youth sports come in many forms, but we can begin to understand them as social phenomena if we view them in terms of the primary goals around which they are organized. This approach is not perfect, because programs worldwide have diverse goals depending on the characteristics of participants, the priorities of sponsors, and the cultures in which they exist. However, my observations combined with a review of research on youth sports have led me to identify three main goals that influence the organization and culture of most youth sport programs today.

First, there are programs that focus primarily on developing physical skills so that young people can achieve excellence in a particular sport. *Second*, there are programs that emphasize physical literacy so that young people would develop the ability, confidence, and desire to engage in healthy physical activities through their lives. *Third*, there are programs that emphasize growth and development so that young people will make responsible life choices and become productive members of their communities.

I refer to these three goal-based organizational frameworks as *models* even though there are variations in each of them. The following sections discuss issues and controversies associated with youth sport programs that generally fit into one of these three models.

Skills and Excellence Model

Organized youth sports today often focus on developing sport-specific skills and excellence to a much greater extent than programs did in the past. Young people are expected to make greater commitments of their time, energy, and intellectual focus to "their sport" than ever before. The stakes associated with participation are higher, feelings of pressure are greater, injury rates and corrective surgeries have increased, parents' involvement and stress levels are higher, coaches are more serious about training and winning, and the cost of participation has skyrocketed.

These programs emphasize the ***performance ethic,*** *a perspective in which the experiences of young people are evaluated in terms of the progress made in developing on-the-field skills in a specific sport, moving up to higher levels of competition, and building a record of competitive success*. To some degree, this approach to youth sports is a global phenomenon with important variations by country and cultural region. However, in this section, I focus mostly on the United States because it provides a clear and extreme example of youth sports that emphasize this approach to youth sports.

The use of a *Skills and Excellence model* of youth sports has increased over the past four decades as publicly funded local programs have faced budget shortages and were forced to cut back on their provision and management of programs. This reduction went hand-in-hand with the increasingly popular neoliberal belief that big government was bad and that public programs are not needed if individuals and families were more responsible and accountable for their own actions (Coakley, 2011a). The impact of this belief has been especially significant in the United States because it was combined with an anti-tax movement that reduced the revenues that local governments used to provide social services and manage recreational programming, including low- or no-cost youth sports for young people. This meant that parents felt compelled to find sport participation opportunities for their children in programs that charged dues and other fees—a situation that gives rise to a professionalized form of youth sports.

The Emergence of the Skills and Excellence Model As the shift toward a neoliberal political approach occurred during the 1980s and 90s, park and recreation departments were reduced to being brokers of public spaces, including sports fields and other publicly owned sports venues. Instead of providing and managing youth sports, they issued permits to private programs organized mostly by relatively wealthy parents and youth sports entrepreneurs eager to establish careers for themselves by creating youth sport programs that generated enough revenue for them to make a living.

Selling privatized, pay-to-play youth sport programs to parents who could afford them was not difficult because parents wanted their children to reap all the benefits they believed were offered by sports. This began a major shift in how parents thought about youth sports: when they paid for the programs, they evaluated them more closely and wanted the most for their money. In response, the programs used a marketing approach emphasizing that *their* method of producing skilled athletes would create the excellence that parents expected when they paid their dues and other training fees. This quickly led to the formation of exclusive club teams that were promoted by program managers and coaches as pipelines leading to success at higher levels of competition through childhood, adolescence, and beyond.

Some of these programs paid to use public facilities, and others, especially in high-income areas, built their own. At the same time, for-profit commercial programs entered the scene with fancy facilities and relatively high-cost programs in gymnastics, tennis, soccer, and other sports that could be played indoors year-round. As this business approach grew across multiple sports, the programs became a career track, mostly for young men with a desire to work in sports. These men were mostly well-intentioned and committed to enabling young people to excel in the sport they had grown to love. However, they also had to create a rationale to establish year-round programs because they needed to support themselves and their families for the entire year.

(*Source:* THOMAS COEX/AFP/Getty Images)

As publicly funded youth sports were slashed or eliminated, high-cost nonprofit and private commercial clubs became popular. Membership fees were too costly for most families, and some children were put off by the heavy emphasis on the performance ethic in these programs. This is especially true in gymnastics where costs and demands for excellence are extreme.

This meant that dues-paying parents had to be sold on the idea that year-round specialization in one sport was good for their children. In response, program managers and coaches emphasized competitive success and assured parents that longer seasons, more demanding practices and competition schedules, mandatory summer and holiday camps, and extensive travel to play top teams and enter tournaments was *the* way for their children to achieve excellence. The inference in this sales approach was that early specialization in a sport would pay-off by leading to success in high school sports, admission into college, reception of athletic scholarships, and possibly a chance to play at a professional level.

This sales approach by organizers and coaches was so successful that a national survey in 2019 found that 80 percent of US parents with children in competitive activities–mostly youth sports–thought their children would eventually earn money in their activity (Schulz, 2019). The more money that parents spent on their child's participation, the more they believed that it would lead to a future financial payoff. As a result, about two-thirds of the parents felt stressed out by expenses for their children's participation; over half said they spent more money than they could afford, and half of those parents said they had no regrets because they were investing in their children's future. A more selective survey of relatively wealthy investors who had children playing competitive youth sports, reported that 40 percent of these parents felt that their child had a good chance of receiving a college athletic scholarship and about one-third thought that their child would make the US Olympic team or become a professional athlete (TD Ameritrade, 2016). In reality, only 2 percent of the older investors reported that a child actually made an Olympic team or reached some level of professional status in their sports, and less than 25 percent reported that a child received a college athletic scholarship–and this was in families that could afford high-priced participation and training opportunities for their children.

Despite the dismal reality about future payoffs, these privatized programs grew rapidly and changed the culture of youth sports in the United States in a single generation. They also altered the daily schedules of families that had to plan around the timing of practices, games, camps, and tournaments. The desire to improve the performance of their children also led many parents to seek out private coaches and specialized training facilities with fees of $100 per hour or more. Unsurprisingly, child athletes, who looked to pro athletes as models, expected their parents to buy the clothes and equipment that would make them look like the athletes they dreamed of becoming (Strashin, 2017). These changes boosted new businesses that sold sports swag in a US youth sports industry that was valued at over $17 billion annually in 2018 (Gregory, 2017; Thompson, 2018). At the same time, youth sports in Canada had become an $8.7 billion business–a much higher per capita cost due to expenses for ice time needed to play hockey, one of their national sports (Curtiss & Eustis, 2018).

These changes and the cultural shift toward neoliberalism had a dramatic impact on youth sport parents. They now lived in a culture where they were expected to know the whereabouts and activities of their children 24/7, year-round–an expectation that no parents had ever faced in human history. They knew that their social reputations and moral worth as parents depended on them becoming sports chauffeurs, altering work lives and meal times so they could attend practices and games, and dedicating weekends and vacation times to training camps and tournaments in addition to an increasing number of practices and games. This put pressure on parents who, in turn, expected more from the sports programs and from their own child-athletes. As a result, some of them, mostly fathers, became demanding and occasionally obnoxious in their sports parenting and spectating.

The Changing Landscape of Youth Sports The growing promotion and acceptance of the skills and excellence model were associated with other social and cultural changes as well (Coakley, 2019). The patterns and priorities in children's play shifted so that free play and informal child-controlled games faded and nearly disappeared in most neighborhoods. Parents began to feel that if they parented correctly, their children would not need a village to raise them. Responsibility for child care and development shifted from the community to the family, and most US parents came to believe that this was culturally appropriate. This neoliberal shift put great pressure on parents and often created tension in parent-child relationships as parents felt compelled to micro-manage their children's lives. For example, in the case of youth sports, mothers and fathers felt obliged to be sideline coaches, agents, advocates, and advisors for their children because it was their moral responsibility to do so (Strandbu et al., 2019; Holst & Stuhlsatz, 2017).

At the same time, coaches focused more and more on competitive success in sport-specialized, year-round programs. They knew that if children in their programs had better winning records than children in other programs, their revenue would increase as parents dug deeper in their pockets to pay higher dues and additional fees to train with the best. Managers and coaches increased the visibility and reputations of their programs by entering teams in regional, state, and national tournaments. Over time, this led a number of cities and towns to sponsor multi-day tournaments to attract customers for local businesses. Some even built multiplex sports venues to bring in as many teams as possible to all the impressively-named championships they could organize.

This description does not fit all youth sport programs, but during this time in the United States, there were no regulations to guide program

(*Source:* Jay Coakley)

Coaches who constantly shout directions during games can be described as "joysticking" their players, and some parents do the same as they watch games. As pawns in this joysticking process, children will not feel comfortable engaging in personally expressive actions. This makes it nearly impossible for them to emotionally identify with and claim ownership of a sport. Instead, many of them learn to view organized sports as an adult thing that they'll eventually outgrow–much like braces on their teeth (Farrey, 2008).

organizers and coaches and no means of official oversight to check on what they were doing with children. Government officials influenced by neoliberal ideas did not favor regulating the programs, and parents generally accepted the myth that sports are essentially pure and good activities needing no oversight to evaluate programs, coach behaviors, or the practices of trainers and sport medical staff.

Although certain neoliberal ideas were accepted by people in other wealthy nations, most were more cautious than Americans when applying them to youth sports. Many of them thought that youth sports should be publicly funded, evidence-based, and regulated by national sports ministries and government agencies concerned with child welfare. When this occurred, youth sports were organized to reflect research-based guidelines that gave priority to the needs of children. Unlike the United States, priorities were not given the revenue needs of program managers and coaches, parental desires to affirm their moral worth as parents by creating child prodigies, and the profit targets of businesses selling uniforms, hats, equipment, backpacks, warmup suits, and team flags, tents, shirts, and car bumper stickers in team colors.

The most dramatic changes associated with unregulated, pay-to-play youth sports in the United States was that it reduced participation by children from families that lived paycheck to paycheck—about 78 percent of American families (CareerBuilder, 2017). Unsurprisingly, a 2019 national survey found that 80 percent of US parents with children in organized youth sports made major financial trade-offs to offset the costs of youth sports, and doing so became a major stress point for 87 percent of all families (Verduzco, 2017; FlipGive, 2016). The study reported that parents even worked extra shifts, took second jobs, reduced spending for groceries, and sold family possessions to nurture and support their children's sports dreams. Overall, the study indicated that most parents were "burning it at both ends" (Verduzco, 2017).

The pay-to-play approach that is built into the skills and excellence model in the United States and more than a few other countries reproduces the patterns of income and wealth inequality in the society as a whole (Vandermeerschen et al., 2016). For example, between 2008 and 2018 the participation of children in families with an annual income of $100,000 or more steadily increased, whereas it decreased among children in families with average and lower annual incomes (Bogage, 2017, 2018; Shell, 2017). Additionally, pay-to-play programs deepen racial and ethnic segregation and exclusion. Even when programs are formed in lower-income neighborhoods, it is often difficult to recruit the teams to make the league sustainable, and a lack of affordable transportation generally rules out travel to distant locations to play other teams.

The children who participate in skills and excellence programs quickly realize they are part of an "up or out" system (Bogage, 2018). If they are selected for a competitive club travel team at 9-years-old, they may not be selected the following year. Those who do not move up are cut out of the program. Children who fail to make the cut often drop out of organized youth sports altogether because they consider the recreational programs to be second class. As a result, most publicly funded recreational sports for children and teens have disappeared. In effect, wealthier American parents have taken "their children, their resources, and their own time away from the local level" to the point that neighborhood, recreational leagues are not able to exist (Thompson in Fatsis & Levin, 2018; Thompson, 2018). This has reduced sport participation opportunities for young people in poor and lower-income families and given young people in wealthy families an advantage when competing for college athletic scholarships. This situation caused Hope Solo, former goalkeeper on the US national soccer team, to point out that the cost of youth soccer excludes young people in lower-income ethnic minority communities so that soccer "has become a rich, white kid sport"–an outcome that hurts the "state of the game" (in Gleeson, 2018). A similar pattern of exclusion exists in most privatized youth sport programs (Solomon & Farrey, 2018a).

After over 30 years of promoting and expanding youth sports organized around a privatized and commercially driven skills and excellence model in the United States, participation has declined slightly in recent years. Overtraining, burnout, and injury rates have increased. There is no formal coordination between youth sports and other programs that provide recreation, physical education, and elite sports training. Additionally, the time that children spend in sedentary activities has increased, fewer young people meet the recommended guidelines for daily physical activity, and childhood obesity rates are higher in the US than other wealthy, post-industrial societies. The young people who participate in competitive youth sports now say that they experience anxiety, and research shows that their enjoyment decreases as parents spend more money on their participation (King & Rothlisberger, 2014). Additionally, many programs face a growing shortage of referees as coaches and parents have become more vocal and critical of their calls. Referees are frequently demeaned and even threatened with bodily harm to the point that resignations have increased and fewer people are willing to submit themselves to crude and foul-mouthed critiques from the sidelines (Adelson, 2019; Eilerson, 2017; Froh, 2018).

The United States as an Exceptional Case Most countries have been slower than the US to accept neoliberal ideas and turn youth sports into big business. Even when they established youth sport programs that stressed skills and excellence, those who managed and coached were expected to follow guidelines issued by a central sports ministry or another government agency. For example, some of the 194 national governments that signed the 1989 UN Convention on the Rights of the Child used it as a guide. This global document declared that governments would "protect and enhance the basic rights of children through their policies, programs, and services,"

(*Source:* Jay Coakley)

As the stakes associated with youth sports increase, decisions made by referees are questioned more regularly and strongly by parents and coaches. As referees face this and occasional threats from players, coaches, and spectators, they are quitting in record numbers. This has left many youth sport programs with serious referee and umpire shortages.

and that the "right to play is fundamental in the lives of children" worldwide. Although this commitment was voluntary and has no formal enforcement provision, it was meant to remind people that children had rights, that youth sports should be child-centered, and that adults must listen to the voices of young people as they organize and manage programs (Eliasson, 2017). Only two countries in the world refused to sign the Convention on the Rights of the Child: Somalia and the United States.

The Norwegian government preceded the United Nations when it created in 1987 a Children's Rights in Sport document that outlined a framework that remains the foundation for their national sports system (Farrey, 2019; Thompson, 2018). This statement on the rights of children required youth sport programs to provide age-appropriate opportunities for all children to be physically active in safe environments where the formation of peer friendships is nurtured by adults. Federal funding depended on meeting these requirements. Having been successful with this approach, Norway's population ranks high for overall health, and 93 percent of Norwegian children participate in sports (Farrey, 2019). Additionally, Norway set a record in 2018 for the most medals ever won by a nation in a winter Olympic Games (39), despite having a population (5.3 million) smaller than the state of Colorado (5.7 million in 2018).

Although Norway is unique, other nations have also developed guidelines for youth sports. One of these is to mandate education for all coaches working with young people. Some youth sports organizations in the United States have initiated coaching education programs, but most of them are superficial and focus primarily on how to administer CPR and how to organize practices and teach tactics and techniques. This approach limits the financial liability for leagues and helps coaches feel more prepared, but it contains little or no information about child development, physical literacy and how to assess and teach it, age-appropriate expectations, explanations of emotional and physical abuse, or what to do when they witness possible abuse by others. Overall, the majority of youth sport coaches in the United States have no coaching education and use their own sports experiences as their guide (Bogage, 2017, 2018; Hall, 2019; Solomon and Farrey, 2018). This means that most practices are highly structured with little time for free play, informal games, and other activities that increase creativity, personal expression, and a child's sense of ownership of the sports they play (Epstein, 2019). In many cases, coaches spend so much time giving verbal instructions and critiques that a one-hour practice involves less than 20-min of the physical activity that children should have on a daily basis.

The outcome of this approach is that the experiences of children in youth sports vary greatly from one team and program to the next. There is no cohesion, continuity, or general principles serving as a framework for the provision of positive experiences or overall child development. Of course, many children do manage to have positive experiences, but there is little to ensure that this occurs. The lack of oversight, transparency, and accountability in the programs means that coaches can do things for years that undermine positive development among young participants without receiving constructive feedback or losing their positions when they abuse children. In most cases, a winning record is taken as proof of a coach's ability to work with children–an evaluation approach that would be unacceptable in childcare or elementary education.

This lack of oversight can be dangerous in highly competitive club sports and in elite training programs sponsored by national governing bodies (NGBs) like gymnastics, swimming, and taekwondo (Pinheiro et al., 2014). In most cases, these athletes travel with coaches to competitive events or live at training facilities without their parents. As a result, they are regularly left alone with coaches, trainers, and team doctors. Under these conditions, children whose success and identities depend on coaches and staff members become vulnerable to exploitation and abuse. Although we don't know how often this occurs, recent reports indicate that it is much too common.

Beginning in the early to mid-1990s a steady stream of abuse reports was submitted to USA Gymnastics, but they were filed away by federation

The Silver Lining: *Increased Interest and Participation in Alternative Sports*

As youth sports became increasingly structured and controlled by adults, some young people sought alternatives allowing them to engage more freely in physical activities on their own terms (Johnson, 2019). Because organized sports programs are the most visible and widely accepted contexts for youth sport participation, these unstructured, participant-controlled activities are referred to as *alternative sports*—alternatives, that is, to organized sports.

Alternative sports encompass a wide array of physical activities, and they have been referred to with many terms, including, action, adventure, extreme, whiz, new, postmodern, and lifestyle sports, among other terms. These terms are being sorted out and clarified as research is done. They refer to slightly different activities, but they tend to share certain characteristics (see Gilchrist & Wheaton, 2016, 2017). For example, they are not controlled by adults, they lack formal rules and authority structures, and they are generally democratic in that participants negotiate the norms that coordinate their activities. Participation is voluntary and does not occur on a fixed schedule. In most cases, they combine physical activity with relaxing and interacting with friends. A research team from Norway, New Zealand, and the United States describe them as "self-generated, self-organized, self-structured and collaborative" (Säfvenbom et al., 2018, p. 2002).

The popularity of alternative sports is based in part on young people rejecting the highly structured character of adult-controlled, organized sports. For example, when legendary skateboarder Tony Hawk was asked why he chose to skateboard rather than play mainstream youth sports, he said, "I liked having my own pace and my own rules . . . and making up my own challenges" (in Finger, 2004, p. 84). Similarly, when Sonja Catalano, the president of the California Amateur Skateboard League, was asked why young people choose alternative sports, she explained, "It's a lifestyle, a culture. It's art. It's music. I'm a firm believer in mind and body. If you keep both busy, then you have a happy kid" (in Steinhardt, 2012). More to the point, a young down-hill biker said, "How can you enjoy sports if you are under control by others?" (in Säfvenbom et al., 2018, p. 1999).

(*Source:* Jay Coakley)

Many young people seek alternatives to adult-controlled youth sports. Skateboarding, BMX biking, and snowboarding are among a growing assortment of popular alternative sports that young people use to creatively express themselves as they learn skills on their own terms. The experience of creating your own sports agenda is very different from the experience of playing organized youth sports under the supervision of parents, coaches, referees, and league administrators.

Alternative sports involve self-selected challenges without keeping score. Failures are accepted as a necessary part of learning moves and tricks. Participants track their own progress in skill development and define success in their own terms without depending on adults for recognition and approval. The age-integrated aspect of many alternative sports creates opportunities for learning that don't exist in age-segregated organized youth sports.

Because alternative sports are self-controlled by young people, and often involve the appropriation of spaces not created or reserved for them, they were initially perceived as disorderly, disruptive, and deviant. But this perception has changed as the activities have become more familiar and more often take place in designated spaces, such as

Continued

reflect on SPORTS — The Silver Lining: (*continued*)

skate and BMX parks, disk golf courses, snowboard terrain at ski areas, and climbing gyms. The downside of these changes is that alternative sports have also become more commercialized and, in some cases, prohibitively expensive for many young people.

Most participants in alternative sports claim that they are inclusive, but they tend to be male-dominated. Females are welcomed and supported if they conform to the informal norms created by males. Changing those norms is difficult, but it can be done with support from informal leaders, and those who manage the spaces in which the sports occur (Atencio et al., 2018). Similar challenges are faced when a sport is dominated by a particular racial or ethnic population due to its history and place of origin. New participants from different racial or ethnic backgrounds may be defined as outsiders unless there are intentionally created norms and processes that prevent this from occurring.

Finally, media coverage has increasingly shaped the dynamics and cultures of certain alternative sports. ESPN's X-Games coupled with the inclusion of some alternative sports in the Olympic Games have added institutionalized elements such as scoring, formal training with coaches, sponsorships, scheduled events, prize money, and high profile awards. All of these elements make these sports less alternative and more organized around a skills and excellence model. This raises a question about the future of alternative sports. Will they remain alternatives to adult-controlled youth sports, or will they become part of them? *What do you think?*

officials with little or no investigation. It wasn't until 2016 that sports journalists at the *Indianapolis Star* discovered this long-term coverup and by 2018 found women willing to come forward and describe the abuses they had endured over many years (Evans et al., 2018; Orbey, 2019; Snider, 2018). This resonated with hundreds of other current and former gymnasts who came forward with their stories of sexual abuse by the team doctor, Larry Nassar, and additional stories of physical, emotional, and sexual abuse by dozens of coaches (North, 2019). These and hundreds of similar cases of abuse in USA Swimming and over a dozen other NGBs served as a wakeup call and signaled the need for effective oversight. However, as I write this in 2020, national guidelines for youth sports have not been created, formal systems of oversight have not been put into place, and comprehensive coaching education is not mandatory in most organized youth sports.

Overall, programs in the United States remain unregulated, exclusive, fragmented, and inconsistent. Most are organized around the ideas of the men who manage them. Many parents continue to seek and pay dearly for the best programs they can find for their children and expect returns on their investments. Young people who participate in youth sports often struggle to distinguish encouragement from pressure as they interact with parents and coaches. Many of them enjoy their experiences, make friends with teammates, appreciate the attention they receive, and benefit from the status they gain if they are successful. But too many others experience more anxiety than enjoyment, drop out, and don't see sport participation as a desirable lifelong activity. Interestingly, and to the benefit of commercial sports, they usually remain fans of high-performance athletes and teams and spend little time thinking critically about reforming youth sports for their children.

Physical Literacy and Lifelong Participation Model

As the visibility and popularity of youth sport programs based on the skills and excellence model increased, so did the criticism of them. Child development experts asked critical questions about the programs and their impact on young people. Disillusioned parents and coaches, along with educators, psychologists, sociologists, public health officials, pediatricians, and other experts called for reforms to make the programs child-centered and age-appropriate.

The urgency of these calls for reform increased as research indicated that children in post-industrial, wealthy societies were becoming more sedentary, overweight, and obese to the point that health problems related to poor physical fitness were reaching crisis levels among young people in certain demographic categories. Among these societies, the United States was the worst example, mostly because of economic inequalities that influenced diet and nutrition in addition to participation opportunities in physical activities and organized sports. Ironically, at the same time that children were becoming less physically active, more time, energy, and resources were invested in youth sports by those who could afford them. But people with power and influence were slow to recognize that health issues among children might be related to youth sports that had become costly, exclusive, and focused on adult priorities rather than the needs of children.

The critics that were the first to initiate reforms were those who noticed that youth sports focused on producing skills and excellence were not producing the high-performance athletes expected by NGBs and other organizations that depended on the competitive success of elite athletes. Young people with athletic potential were being selected out, burned out, and injured out, or they were dropping out due to intense training and competition schedules over which they had no control. As scholars did research and worked with coaches looking for explanations, there was a growing awareness that the adult-centered skills and excellence model did not provide a positive starting point for the achievement of excellence or nurturing lifelong participation in sports and physical activities.

Play, Physical Literacy, and Informal Games, as Starting Points Health and Excellence One of the first issues considered by reformers was that youth sports had eliminated free play, overlooked the need to develop physical literacy, and ignored the informal games that provided children with pleasure, friendship, and a sense of control as they engaged in physical activities. Over the past century, research consistently identified the importance of play and child-controlled games in the process of human development. In summarizing the current relevance of this research, psychologist Peter Gray explained the role of play in the social and emotional development of children in this way:

> *Playing with other children, away from adults, is how children learn to make their own decisions, control their emotions and impulses, see from others' perspectives, negotiate differences with others, and make friends. In short, play is how children learn to take control of their lives* (Gray, 2013, p. 157).

Gray and others noted that free play, despite how it looks to outside observers, has a structure based on rules that exist in each player's mind. When children engage in physical play, they see patterns and purpose in their own actions that parents and coaches see as chaotic and pointless movement. But parents and coaches don't realize that play occurs because of self-created rules that are based on "mental concepts that often require conscious effort to keep in mind and follow" (Gray, 2013, p. 146). During extended play, and in play from one situation to the next, these rules are created again and again to fit the circumstances and enable the players to express themselves and experience pleasure, excitement, self-satisfaction, and other positive emotions as they engage in physical activities (Brown & Patte, 2013; Henricks, 2015). When adults don't understand this, they organize youth sports that meet *their* interests rather than the interests and needs of children. In turn, this undermines the process through which young people claim ownership of their sport participation and define physical activity as an important part of their lives.

Informal games are an action-centered form of play that occurs when children agree to the rules they will follow as they play together. Coming to this agreement is a process packed full of learning experiences related to creativity, social interaction, negotiation, compromise, cooperation, conflict

(*Source:* Rachel Spielberg)

Information about concussions and injury rates in certain youth sports has led some parents to be less supportive of high-intensity youth sports for children. Will this lead them to demand programs that give priority to physical literacy and long-term health and fitness over winning records and age-group championships?

resolution, and the importance of following agreed-upon rules (Bowers & Green, 2013; Bowers et al., 2014; Gray, 2013). Most important, children learn that cooperation is the foundation for the existence of competitive games and sports. Unless everyone agrees to the rules and follows them, the game doesn't begin or it ends quickly and deprives the players of exciting and pleasurable experiences.

When children are put into organized sports before they learn how to cooperate through informal, player-controlled games, they don't understand why rules exist or why they should follow them during games. Without this understanding, there is little internal or self-enforcement of the rules, and youth sports come to depend on external rule enforcement by referees and umpires. But neither the rules nor rule enforcement by referees makes much sense to children who have not experienced the process of creating, modifying, and enforcing rules as they played informal games.

Without this learning, the foundation for fair play and sportspersonship is missing in organized youth sport programs.

Informal or pickup games also depend on physical literacy. The greater the physical literacy among players, the more options they have when creating games that are exciting and action-filled (Berlanger et al., 2018; Roetert et al., 2017). Previous generations of children developed physical literacy as they played in settings where they felt free to be spontaneous, self-expressive, and calculating risk-takers. But this sense of freedom and self-controlled risk-taking declined as parents were expected to be totally responsible for the whereabouts and actions of their children 24/7. Consistent with neoliberal attitudes, allowing children, especially those perceived as vulnerable, to engage in free play and informal games away from home and without adult supervision was defined by many people as negligent and irresponsible parenting. To meet this expectation and claim moral worth as parents, mothers and fathers felt compelled to put their young children in organized sports before they were physically literate enough to feel capable and had enough control over their bodies to enjoy their experiences (Hopple, 2018). As a result, many children became less eager to try other sports or see physical activity as pleasurable. If they did remain in organized sports, nearly 70 percent of them dropped out during early adolescence.

New Models of Youth Sports Strategies for reforming youth sports were initially formulated during the early-1990s. Inspired by previous studies showing that the process of talent development begins with childhood exploration, play, self-expression, and experiences across multiple activities (Bloom, 1985; Epstein, 2019), Istvan Balyi, a sport scientist at the National Coaching Institute in British Columbia (Canada), created a four-stage model for training athletes. He described it as a *Long-Term Athlete Development* (LTAD) model and identified the four stages as (1) FUNdamentals, (2) Training to Train, (3) Training to Compete, and (4) Training to Win. The model called for age-appropriate activities and emphasized play, the acquisition of physical literacy, and basic experiences in different sports from early childhood through age 12. Structure and competition were de-emphasized during the first two stages. Organized training and competition did not occur until early adolescence, and specialization in a chosen sport began only during mid- to late-adolescence.

This model was interesting to researchers but people in sports organizations, and especially in youth sports, refused to use it as a guide (Holt et al., 2018). However, this changed in Canada after their national team failed to meet expectations at the 2004 Olympic Games. Balyi and other sport scientists came together in 2005 to revise LTAD and create a 7-stage model that outlined the talent development process in more detail (Balyi, Way & Higgs, 2013; Ford et al., 2011). This model is presented in Table 4.1. The timing was right, and more coaches in Canada were willing to try LTAD in their programs. As word about the model spread, Balyi introduced it to coaches and sports officials in England, Ireland, Australia, New Zealand, and other countries over the next few years.

Variations of the LTAD model became and remain popular worldwide, but they have been used almost exclusively to develop elite athletes rather than nurturing lifelong participation in sports and physical activities–a job that coaches and sports officials continue to think belongs in recreation, not sports. Additionally, priority in LTAD was given to physiological development rather than factors related to overall health and well-being. Inserting LTAD into sports cultures that were highly structured and performance-oriented meant that it produced only minor changes in organized youth sports and did little to improve general health and wellness for young people or adults. The potential was there but the goal of nurturing lifelong participation in physical activities was not a priority in sports organizations where coaches focused on producing high-performance athletes and competitive success (O'Sullivan, 2018).

Sports organizations in the United States were slow to consider LTAD and resisted embracing it. However, the men who controlled USA Hockey

Table 4.1 Seven-stage *Long-Term Athlete Development* (LTAD) Model

Stage	Age in Years	Description
1. Active Start	0–6	Combine fun with learning the *ABCs* of movement – Agility, Balance, Coordination, and Speed in an unstructured but supervised setting.
2. FUNdamental	girls 6–8 boys 6–9	Focus on fun, self-expression, improving fundamental movement skills, and learning to use them in different sports.
3. Learn to Train	girls 8–11 boys 9–12	Add structure and focus on physical coordination and converting fundamental movement skills into sport skills.
4. Train to Train	girls 11–15 boys 12–16	Training becomes more formalized and is combined with learning strategies to maintain health and fitness for life.
5. Train to Compete	girls 15–21 boys 16–23	Focus on achieving excellence in a specific sport, use competitions for self-evaluation, develop cognitive and emotions strategies to deal with competition.
6. Train to Win	girls 18+ boys 19+	A choice is made to train as a serious athlete and work with coaches, trainers, therapists, and physicians to achieve success.
7. Active for Life	Any age	This stage mostly overlaps with Stage 4 or 5 as the adolescent participates in multiple recreational and competitive physical activities and sports.

(USAH) were impressed with the 7-stage model and decided to use it in an effort to save youth hockey programs that were rapidly losing participants across the country. They modified LTAD and in 2009 and presented it to the hockey community in the United States as ADM–the *American Development Model*. Although youth hockey coaches nationwide actively resisted using the new model, the men at USAH headquartered in Colorado Springs worked tirelessly with a team of open-minded hockey coaches to change the culture of youth hockey. It took nearly 10 years to see significant changes, but as they were implemented, participation among young people increased, parents saw that their children having fun and learning to love hockey, and the quality of elite hockey players increased (USA Hockey, 2019).

Under the ADM motto, *Play, Love, Excel,* youth hockey programs embraced an age-appropriate approach and emphasized free play and informal games for children through age 12. One of their most significant changes was to show coaches how to convert a regulation ice rick surface into three smaller surfaces going across the width of the rink (https://www.admkids.com/page/show/915460-practice-plans). Low-profile barriers separated the three surfaces with different play activities for skaters on each one. As physical literacy increased, the players were introduced to pickup-like games with small goals and no goalies. With three surfaces across the rink, team members enjoyed more time on the ice, more touches on the puck and shots on goal, and less time standing around, doing drills, and traveling to distant locations for games and tournaments. When coaches and parents saw that these changes increased fun, improved skating skills, boosted the passion for playing hockey, and provided more ice time per skater for the same rental fee, they were impressed.

These and other changes, including a new policy that encouraged children to sample multiple sports in addition to hockey and a policy that banned participation in competitive tournaments turned things around for USAH. It took a decade of hard work to defuse resistance and implement changes. Most important for USAH, the decline in youth participation was halted and participation among children 8 and under increased by 33 percent between 2009 and 2019. Participation and retention rates during those years also increased in all age categories and reached record numbers in 2019. Plus, the talent pool and the skills of top players began to increase.

After the success experienced by USAH, people in other NGBs in the United States began to take notice. With support from the USOC and its coaching programs, some NGBs are adapting ADM to their sports. This was an important step forward, but these changes did not increase participation opportunities among children in lower-income families because the programs remained costly. Nor did they transform the culture of youth hockey so that lifelong participation in recreational hockey was as important as playing college and professional hockey in the minds of coaches and parents. Creating transformative changes required an even larger long-term effort.

Project Play: Reimagining Youth Sports When only a handful of Americans were aware of LTAD and ADM, Tom Farrey, an award-winning investigative journalist at ESPN, was studying how youth sports were organized in countries with successful sport systems. He found that countries with the best elite athletes also had youth sports based on versions of LTAD, especially for children under 13-years-old. His 2008 book, *Game on: The all-American race to make champions of our children*, discussed the details of these programs and showed how they were different from programs in the United States. After a few years of speaking and writing about his vision for transforming youth sports in the US, he joined with The Aspen Institute in 2012 to organize Sports and Society as a new topic for study and innovation. Farrey spent over three years learning and listening to experts nationwide and working with an advisory board to develop Project Play, which he described as a social movement to reimagine youth sports in the United States.

The Project Play report, *Sport for all, play for life: A playbook to get every kid in the game* was published in 2015. It, like LTAD and ADM, was based on the dual notion that (a) play and physical literacy were prerequisites for the successful recruitment and retention of young people in youth sports, and (b) lifelong participation in sports and physical activities was crucial for improving the health and well-being in the US. Project Play went beyond LTAD and ADM in that it gave voice to young people and directly addressed the need to provide participation opportunities to all children, regardless of ability and the zip code where they lived. Most important, *Project Play gave explicit priority to the goal of lifelong participation over the goal of producing elite athletes.* Improving health and fitness was the underlying primary goal that attracted the financial support from the foundations and corporate funders that supported public health goals in the US.

The Project Play strategy for changing the culture of youth sports and linking them to lifelong

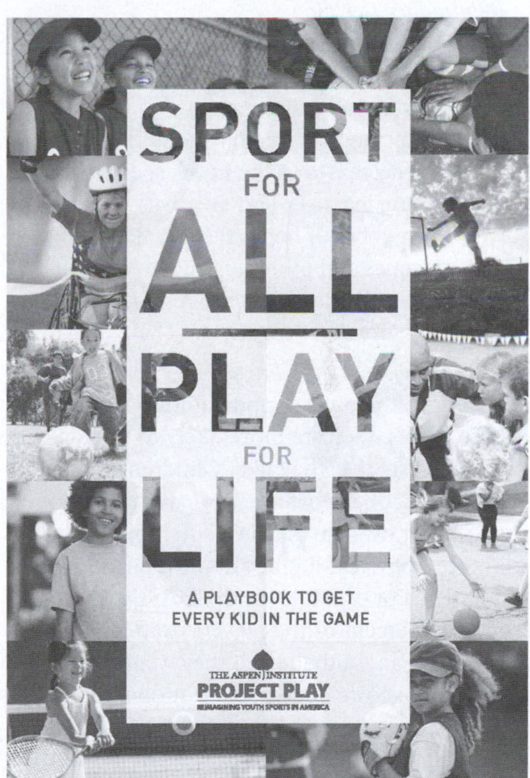

(*Source:* Aspen Institute)

This is the cover of the 46-page report that outlined the reform strategy of Project Play. It is available online at https://assets.aspeninstitute.org/content/uploads/2015/01/Aspen-Institute-Project-Play-Report.pdf involvement in physical activities is organized around a "playbook" consisting of the following eight guidelines:

1. *Ask kids what they want*
   This guideline refers to three things: (a) consulting research that has investigated children's priorities in youth sports; (b) talk with children and ask them what they like best and least about their experiences during a youth sport season, game, and practice; and (c) watch children play informal games and identify their priorities by analyzing how they create and play their games (Coakley, 1983; Hopple, 2018; Visek et al., 2015).
2. *Reintroduce free play*
   Children will play if they feel free, unjudged, and connected with playmates. Free play gives them opportunities to be spontaneous and self-expressive as they move. Research shows that children's creativity decreases as the hours spent in organized sports increase; and creativity increases with the number of hours they spend playing pickup games and other unstructured, child-controlled activities (Barreiro & Howard, 2017; Bowers & Green, 2013; Bowers et al., 2014).
3. *Encourage sport sampling*
   When children have opportunities to play multiple sports, they are more likely to find one or more sports that they like. Children who play more than one sport are *less likely* to burnout and suffer overuse injuries, and more likely to improve physical literacy and overall athletic abilities. For example, in the 2019 NFL Draft over 90 percent of the players drafted did not specialize in football until they went to college. Research shows that specialization seldom leads to long term success in a sport (DiFiori et al., 2017; Epstein, 2019; Jayanthi & Brenner. 2017).
4. *Revitalize in-town leagues*
   Reviving and expanding low-cost community leagues and neighborhood teams provides widespread access to youth sports, especially in areas where parents have non-negotiable work hours and lack easy access to personal transportation. Making it safe to walk and bike to practice and games is important for these programs to thrive. Inclusion is not just a buzz word; it is an ongoing process of fostering access for all (Project Play, 2014).
5. *Think small*
   Abandon the notion that "God created the official dimensions of sports surfaces" and make youth sports so they are "player size." The best soccer players in the world grew up playing on small surfaces where they learned ball control skills and to pass and shoot with pinpoint accuracy. Why have one game on a full-size surface for less than full-size players when you can have 2–4 small sided games on the same surface with modified boundaries and equipment? Creating neighborhood spaces for small-sided games and physical activities increases participation, physical literacy, and more equal access (Kessel, 2019; see also the video, https://www.usahockey.com/news_article/show/354670-video-from-child-s-view-adults-find-full-ice-no-fun).
6. *Design for development*
   Nearly all children are drawn into *age-appropriate* activities that involve action, personal involvement in the action, controlled challenges, and time with friends (Coakley, 1983). Creating playful activities that build physical literacy is crucial for children under 12 (Epstein, 2019), and physical literacy is ultimately a foundation for becoming an athlete and being active for life (Farrey & Isard, 2015; Meadors, 2012).
7. *Train all coaches*
   Coaches are the most important adults in youth sport programs. Like teachers, they must have a basic background in child development and know how to work with children in activities adapted for the children's ages and abilities. Recruiting women as coaches is key to building and maintaining successful programs. Properly trained coaches have much better participant retention rates than do untrained coaches (Langan et al., 2013; Sullivan et al., 2012).

8. *Emphasize prevention*
   All coaches must know CPR, basic first aid, general safety and injury prevention strategies, age-appropriate physical conditioning activities, and concussion management protocols. Pushing children to the edge of exhaustion increases injuries, and ignoring them when they describe pain is to miss valuable teachable moments that help young people understand their bodies and the difference between pain and injury (Malina, 2009; Jayanthi & Brenner, 2017).

When LTAD and ADM were created, they were taken directly to the people who worked in elite sports development. But Farrey used a different approach with Project Play. Guided by collective impact theory (Pierce, 2019), he emphasized the goal of building healthy communities–a goal that everyone would support. Once the Project Play report was published and received national publicity, he and his staff identified major stakeholders that would benefit from youth sports organized to produce physical literacy and lifelong participation. Table 4.2 lists the eight stakeholders he identified and the benefit each would experience if Project Play's *Sport for all/Play for Life* approach was embraced and implemented in their communities.

Farrey and his staff worked strategically to recruit key people in each stakeholder category. In the process, hundreds of organizations across the eight stakeholder categories made commitments to reform youth sport programs by using the 8 guidelines in the report. Others gave impressive donations to support *Project Play 2020* (https://www.aspenprojectplay.org/project-play-2020), a long-term plan in which research is done to identify communities where there was a severe shortage of youth sport participation opportunities. Data were collected in selected communities to identify specific needs, resources, and other baseline information related to four "Key Play Indicators" (KPIs) for children 12 and younger. These indicators were the metrics to be used in annual evaluations of the impact of a customized Project Play program over multiple years. They consist of the following:

- Sport participation rates among young people.
- The number of youth sports coaches trained in basic competencies.
- The average number of different team sports played by young people.
- The number of young people engaged in no physical activity.

The first set of targeted communities are in relatively poor urban and rural areas where there is a high proportion of children in low-income families (e.g., see https://communityfoundationsa.org/project-play/ and http://projectplaysemi.org/). During the community selection process, Project Play identifies local partners/stakeholders that will support and provide funding to make changes in youth

Table 4.2 Stakeholders and benefits identified in Project Play

Stakeholder	Benefit
Community Recreation Groups	*Participation creates sustainability*
National Sport Organizations	*Kids are your future*
Policymakers & Civic Leaders	*Thriving communities and engaged citizens*
Education	*Active kids do better in school*
Parents	*Active kids do better in school and at home*
Public Health	*Sport and physical activity are preventive medicine*
Business & Industry	*It's always good business to invest in kids*
Tech & Media	*Youth sports is ripe for disruption; so be disruptive*

Sitting Children Down
Smartphones, Laptops, and Video Games

In societies where young people have easy access to smartphones, laptops, and video games, inducing them to play organized sports is a challenge. When parents tell them to stay close to home, young people have few opportunities to meet with friends to organize informal games. After school, most young people see their tech devices as tools that put them in virtual touch with friends and connect them with an infinite stream of entertaining media content.

Young people are attracted to their devices and video games for many reasons. The people who design apps and games do extensive research and testing to discover how young people use their phones and other devices, what they find entertaining, what holds their attention, what brings them back to apps and games day after day, and what leads them to integrate their use of apps and games into their relationships with peers. Developing and marketing these products is expensive and time-consuming; therefore, convincing young people to use or buy them is serious business.

Assuming that an app or video game will be a hit with young people because the designers and financial investors like it will not lead to success! But this is the approach used by most of the men who organize youth sport programs today. They don't stop to think that sports created generations ago may not be attractive to young people who live in a social and cultural context that is completely different from the context in which their great grandparents or even their parents lived. Just because a specific sport has become a traditional activity in a cultural region does not mean that every new generation will accept it with as much enthusiasm as previous generations did.

This point did not escape the people who developed Project Play. In fact, the first three guidelines in the Project Play playbook are: (1) asking young people about their likes and dislikes in physical activities and organized sports, (2) giving them opportunities to play on their own terms, and (3) encouraging them to try multiple sports—even new and alternative sports. If these guidelines were taken seriously and if we followed the example of video game designers there would be a large body of research to help us understand how young people create and play physical games, what they find entertaining, what holds their attention, what brings them back to physical activities and sports day after day, and what leads them to integrate those activities and sports into their relationships with peers (Mulcahy, 2019).

Unfortunately, only a handful of studies begin to touch on these issues. Additionally, doing studies that obtain valid and reliable data from young people is a challenge today. They have heard the same sport-related narratives so many times from parents and sports commentators that they tend to repeat what they've heard without thinking deeply about their experiences or preferences. However, obtaining permission to study children in situations where they are not watched by parents or teachers is difficult if not impossible in some communities and countries. Creating methodologies and research designs that give young people opportunities to be spontaneous and self-expressive as they create physical activities and games on their own terms is another challenge; and if you collect data while watching children play during school recess or in a park, you may be perceived as a pervert instead of a youth sports reformer.

Game designers pay money to young people who respond to surveys, participate in focus groups, and test their products. Parents can watch through a one-way viewing window so their children cannot see them, and parents are assured that game content will not hurt their children. But adults assume that young people will choose to play organized sports without doing research to learn what they like and dislike about their experiences during practices and games, and what will lead them to be active through their lives. Research on the experiences of children who eventually reach elite status in sports, music, and science suggests that the skills and excellence approach that emphasizes early specialization and structured training is largely ineffective and counterproductive. *What do you think?*

sports; in fact, local "buy-in" was seen as a crucial factor in the community selection process.

Communities in relatively wealthy areas were not selected during this stage of implementation. Project Play staff realized that reforms were often needed in those areas, but they also knew that the children there had multiple choices for playing sports and that parents collectively possessed the resources needed to make changes if they wanted to do so. It was also clear that parents and coaches in relatively wealthy areas had strong vested interests in programs emphasizing skills and excellence; in fact, they were the ones who had created those programs thinking that they would benefit their children. This meant that many of them would resist changes that might interfere with the investment payoffs they expected for their children who played on elite club teams.

At this point, Project Play remains an ambitious social experiment with the goal of increasing physical activity rates in a country of 325 million people. This is a long-term undertaking, but it is off to an encouraging start. It is difficult to predict how successful it may be, but there are influential individuals and organizations that support the goal of making make sport participation accessible and attractive to young people regardless of their ability or where they live. In the meantime, people living in relatively wealthy areas will not see Project Play guidelines implemented unless parents and youth sports entrepreneurs decide to do so.

Growth and Development Model

Sport for development is a buzz phrase that has morphed into a global social movement in the 21st century (Darnell, 2012; Darnell et al., 2018; Hartmann & Kwauk, 2011). This movement has led to the creation of thousands of programs that use sport to intervene in the lives of children and adolescents perceived to be in need (IHRB, 2018). For the most part, these young people are coping with poverty and personal trauma, war and dislocation, and a range of medical, psychological, and social problems. The missions of these programs vary, depending on their location, who they serve, and the priorities of organizations that sponsor and fund them. But all of them emphasize various forms of growth and development.

Youth Sports Interventions in Wealthy Countries
When people and organizations go into low-income areas in wealthy countries and create youth sport programs, the programs often take the form of interventions in the lives of children living there. They may involve one-day or short-term experiences in selected sports, or longer-term programs, such as 3-on-3 basketball leagues or track and field clubs. Most of these programs provide safe, adult-supervised opportunities to play sports after school, on weekends, and during school breaks. Consistent with neoliberal values, the programs are based on the assumption that participation in organized sports contributes to *personal* growth and development and provides coaches and staff members opportunities to mentor young people and teach them how to make responsible choices and avoid situations that could get them into trouble.

These programs may also be designed to give young people access to resources and opportunities that don't exist where they live. However, some of them are organized around a deficit-reduction approach in which it is assumed that the personal characteristics and behaviors of young people must be improved so that they can eventually escape their immediate environments and become productive citizens in the same social and economic system that limited their lives in the first place (Hartmann, 2003, 2012; Batlle et al., 2018; Coalter, 2013a; Coakley, 2002; Darnell, 2012; Sukarieh & Tannock, 2011; Whitley et al., 2019).

Except in rare cases, these programs do not focus on advocating social justice, building strong community institutions, increasing economic resources in the community, or politicizing and empowering young people to be effective change agents in their communities. Instead, they focus on increasing self-esteem and confidence among young people so they can pull themselves up by their athletic shoelaces and escape the conditions that led others to label them as "at-risk" and decide that an organized sports program is what they need to change the reality of their lives.

Youth Sports for Development and Peace The growth and development model is also used by organizations and governments that deliver youth sport programs to regions of the world where people are desperately poor, escaping war or ethnic cleansing, or living in communities devastated by natural disasters. These programs grew rapidly through this century as media coverage alerted people in the Northern hemisphere to the plight of children–mostly in the Southern hemisphere–facing trauma, abuse, starvation, and the absence of opportunities to play. Additionally, the United Nations, the International Olympic Committee, and FIFA (the global governing body for soccer) published declarations and sponsored conferences emphasizing that "the power of sport" can be used to support the rights of children, including their right to play sports, along with a range of global goals related to development and peace (Blom et al., 2015; Sanders, 2016; Sanders and Coakley, 2020).

The idea that sports can be used as a tool to change the world is based on the great sport myth (see Chapter 1, p. 11) and the neoliberal belief that individuals and their families are responsible for shaping their own lives. Without critically examining either of these factors, hundreds of universities along with faith-based, charitable, and sports organizations created thousands of "sport for development and peace" programs worldwide (IHRB, 2018; Jessop et al., 2019). Nearly everyone associated with these programs thought that sports could heal people suffering from trauma, bring people together and reinvigorate communities, eliminate intergroup hostilities and gang violence, provide respite from the tedium of everyday life, and give children and young people supervised opportunities to play sports, develop useful skills, and eventually contribute to community development.

Although sports can be useful tools when working with young people and their communities, there is a need to critically examine when and how they are associated with positive changes for individuals and communities.

(*Source:* Jay Coakley)

Belief in the power of sport is widely accepted without question. This has led governments, corporations, and non-governmental organizations (NGOs) to spend billions of dollars in the hope that sports would eliminate certain global problems and contribute to the development of young people worldwide.

Critical Assessment of the Growth and Development Model Youth sports organized to produce growth and development generally focus on (a) building the knowledge needed to make good choices, (b) reforming habits put young people "at-risk," and (c) creating physical and social skills that are useful in achieving personal success. The programs that focus on building knowledge assume that sport participation has a *fertilizer effect* on young people—that is, if it is tilled into their lives, it will increase self-confidence, create personal responsibility, and lead to constructive choice-making. The programs that focus on reforming the habits of at-risk youth assume that sport participation produces a *car wash effect*–that is, it washes away negative attitudes and deviant tendencies so that young people stay out of trouble and become accountable for their choices and actions. The programs that focus on physical and social skills assume that sport participation has a *guardian angel effect*–that is, it provides adult role models and mentors that put young people on a path to education, personal achievement, and occupational success.

Another assumption underlying many of these youth sport programs is that the combined influence of the fertilizer, car-wash, and guardian angel effects will create personal growth and development among the young people who will eventually contribute to their communities. This contribution usually refers to increased social integration and economic expansion rather than increased social justice, community activism, and structural changes that promote the common good of local populations (Coakley, 2011b).

There are notable exceptions to this description of sport for development and peace programs. But the commitment to neoliberal ideas about individualism and personal responsibility runs deep in the United States and countries where there are many organizations that fund and provide the staff and volunteers who work in "sport for development and peace" programs (Peachey et al., 2018; Sanders & Coakley, 2020). These programs often use a "we know best," top-down, outside in, deficit-reduction approach in which outsiders from relatively wealthy countries bring their sports, equipment, staff and "volun-tourists" to create sports programs for young people in resource-deprived regions around the world. Local government officials usually approve these programs because they temporarily care for vulnerable young people in their communities (Rosenberg, 2018). But these programs are seldom guided by a theory of change or a theory-based methodology for integrating youth sport programs into a larger process of social change that involves local people taking control of their lives. As a result, sport for development and peace programs often have a more lasting impact of the program staff and volunteers than on the children who participate in them; additionally, most communities lack the resources to sustain youth sport programs over time (Coalter 2013a, 2013b).

The purpose of this critical assessment is to point out that bringing a youth sport program into a region does not automatically lead to positive outcomes. In a worst-case scenario, it represents a form of neo-colonialism that increases the dependency of people in poor regions of the world on the goodwill of people in wealthy nations (Darnell & Hayhurst, 2011). It is clear that playing sports can bring joy into the lives of young people living with scarcity, but it takes much more than sports to empower young people to join with others to create the changes desperately needed in their communities (Lindsey, 2017; Meir & Fletcher, 2019; Spaaij & Jones, 2013; Spaaij et al., 2016).

Coaches Across Continents: Sport for Social Impact

One of the few organizations with an explicit theory of change and a methodology for facilitating change is *Coaches Across Continents* (CAC). It's guiding theory is that meaningful and sustainable change occurs through a bottom-up, inside-out, community-building process (https://coachesacrosscontinents.org/wp-content/uploads/2016/11/CAC-Theory-of-Change.pdf). This process is driven by local people who learn to critically assess their own cultural practices and social policies as they "identify, address, and solve problems specific to their communities (Gates & Suskiewicz, 2017; https://coachesacrosscontinents.org/curriculum/). Through a 3-year "organizational development and sport for social impact education" program, people in selected communities become self-directed experiential learners with the ability to identify, analyze, and deal with local issues in ways that positively impact their collective future.

CAC was formed in 2008 by Nick Gates, a former junior national soccer player in the United Kingdom who also played at and graduated from Harvard University in 1991. After working in international service organizations, he assembled a team of coaches who were experts in organizational development, cultural dynamics, and social change to develop a curriculum in which sports and games were used to create social awareness, knowledge about public health, conflict resolution and social inclusion strategies, female empowerment and gender equity, and general life skills. These coaches then served as mentors and facilitators in programs designed to empower local people as agents of change.

CAC uses a unique version of the growth and development model (Cho, 2017). Instead of focusing exclusively on changing individuals, it emphasizes a continuous and sustainable process of social impact controlled by local people. This allows them to avoid an approach to "development" that has been shaped to fit the neoliberal idea that change involves growth in economic productivity rather than empowering a local population to control their own future (Fuller & Zapata, 2019; Jessop et al., 2019; Sanders and Coakley, 2020). This is why CAC emphasizes a bottom-up, insider-initiated transformation at the community level. For example, when working in regions where women have few rights, CAC uses games and sports that are strategically organized to empower girls and women; and at the same time, they use variations of games and sports that enable boys and men to understand how current social and cultural practices oppress girls and women in ways that disadvantage everyone in the community. When the boys and men understand this and realize that gender relations must change, the girls and women who *feel* empowered have real opportunities to *be* empowered.

(*Source:* Coaches Across Continents)

When using sports and games to create a critical awareness of community issues, Coaches Across Continents often works with age-integrated groups of young people. This puts older participants in positions of responsibility as they help younger participants understand the issues that need to be addressed.

Whenever there are significant changes in the organization of social relationships, there will always be internal pushback. This is why CAC has developed a 3-year social impact program in which many variations of games and sports are used to stimulate critical awareness and identify all the ways that their current social and cultural practices interfere with the achievement of their collective goals. Over time this builds community capacity for collectively identifying, making, and taking collective ownership of change. Additionally, when people experience this process first hand, they also acquire the skills to effectively address unanticipated outcomes that negatively impact some community members.

When working with children, CAC has for the past 10 years (2009-2019) developed a strategy named *Purposeful Play*. It was created while its staff and leaders worked for nearly three decades with 16 million children in 60 countries (Suskiewicz, 2019). Purposeful Play is a theory-based self-directed learning methodology that establishes educational environments in which children have control over the games and sports that they play with each other, and are responsible for dealing with challenges, resolving conflicts, and sustaining group participation in he action. With the help of staff facilitators, playing fields are transformed into outdoor classrooms where young people learn to develop critical thinking skills as they play. The evaluation research commissioned by CAC has documented that Purposeful Play is effective because it is fun and engaging for both children and facilitators as it develops lifelong learners with the capacity to be involved citizens and community leaders (Suskiewicz, 2019).

In 2019 CAC launched *Purposeful Play: Creating Education Outside the Classroom,* an organizational accreditation program for leaders working in sport for development organizations around the world. The program consists of an applied curriculum through which the leaders learn to effectively use

(*Source:* Coaches Across Continents)

When a youth sport for development program is created in a community, it is important connect first with community leaders so the program can be linked to a larger social impact process in the community as a whole. This is an important part of the Purposeful Play approach used by Coaches Across Continents.

CAC theory and methodologies as social impact tools in their own work. The success of the Purposeful Play education program over the past decade has established CAC as the Global Leader in Education Outside the Classroom, and it has earned them 26 major awards, including the 2018 Beyond Sport Global Impact of the Year Award. The next goal is to create a global network of organizations that share information about their experiences in adapting and implementing social impact programs in diverse situations. Ideally, this process of sharing information will provide the data needed to effectively use and refine the CAC theory of change and its methodologies in programs that define growth and development in terms of social impact.

Maximizing Social Impact in the Sport for Development and Peace Sector Coaches Across Continents is not the only organization working effectively in the sport for development and peace sector. There are others, and this number will grow with CAC's accreditation program. But many organizations still use an approach in which people from wealthy post-industrial societies bring their versions of youth sports into regions where they do not have detailed knowledge of the culture, people, and communities. They generally measure their success in terms of the number of participants they attract, the teams they create, the coaches they train, and the sports fields they build. Staff, volunteers, and participants have fun, but the programs are usually short-term and are not designed to have a lasting social impact on the communities in which the young people live.

The sport for development and peace sector has a short history. Most of the organizations in this sector are created by well-meaning people who believe in the power of sport and assume that sports will automatically contribute to the growth and development of young people living in challenging conditions. But participation in organized youth sports does not change those conditions unless there is a plan to strategically connect youth sports with a larger project of social impact. When done without critical reflection and planning, SFD programs can mislead young people by encouraging them to have uninformed and unrealistic expectations about becoming professional athletes. They can also mislead people in a community by introducing a form of sport that is incompatible with their culture and unsustainable with their resources. For example, investing local resources into training high-performance athletes and having young people–mostly young men–invest all their time and energy into seeking a career that will take them away from their communities with no guarantees of success is not a strategy that will have a positive social impact (Abbot, 2018).

summary

ARE ORGANIZED PROGRAMS WORTH THE EFFORT?

Although physical activities exist in all cultures, organized youth sports are a luxury. They require resources and discretionary time among children and adults. They exist only when children are not required to work fulltime and when adults believe that experiences during childhood influence growth and development. Youth sports have a unique history in every society where they exist, but they characteristically emphasize experiences and values that are central to the dominant culture.

The emergence of organized youth sports in North America and Europe was nurtured by new ideas about children, childhood, and character development at the beginning of the twentieth century. These programs began to grow rapidly after World War II as parents during the 1950s saw participation in organized sports as an important developmental activity for their children. Changes in the family, acceptance of neoliberal ideology, parental fears that their children would cause trouble or face danger outside the home, the decline of childhood play, and the growing visibility of high-performance and professional sports increased the popularity of organized, adult-controlled youth sports.

Youth sports worldwide today are organized around three models that emphasize skills and excellence, physical literacy and lifelong participation, or growth and development. In wealthy post-industrial societies, and especially the United States, youth sports have been organized primarily around a skills and excellence model. As local, public programs lost funding due to the acceptance of neoliberal ideas and policies, they were replaced by privatized programs that depended on revenue coming from dues-paying families. For economic reasons these programs encouraged early specialization in a specific sport and high-intensity training and competition schedules organized around the performance ethic–an approach embraced by parents hoping that it would benefit their children.

As youth sports became more costly and professionalized fewer families could afford them. Children in wealthy families had multiple choices for participation, whereas children in working-class and poor families had few or no opportunities. As programs became more competitive and were seen as gateways to future success, more pressure was felt by participants, parents, and coaches. Parents saw dues and other expenses as investments in their child's future and coaches used the success of their athletes to recruit more dues-paying families to their programs.

These changes in the US occurred without oversight, transparency, or accountability. Whereas official agencies in other countries provided and enforced guidelines for working with children in youth sports, the United States had none. As a result, children overtrained, injury rates increased, passion for playing their sport declined, expectations for achieving excellence were seldom met, and program participants became vulnerable to exploitation and abuse.

In response to highly structured, adult controlled programs, some young people turned to alternative sports that they could play on their own terms. Critics of the skills and excellence model identified its weaknesses and sought a more effective approach to youth sports. Using research on play, physical literacy, childhood development, and the achievement of excellence as a guide they created a model organized to emphasize play, physical literacy, and lifelong participation in physical activities.

The first version of this model was Long-term Athletic Development. LTAD was based on the idea that talent development was most likely if children between 6 and 12-years old were involved in physical activities that were fun, self-expressive, and designed to improve movement skills through increasingly structured and diverse sports. Coaches and sports organizations rejected this approach, but after the model was expanded to clarify more details in a 7-stage development process, it came to be widely accepted in organizations that developed and trained high-performance athletes.

LTAD was generally ignored in the United States until USAH adapted it to fit its development program. It was named the American Development Model, or ADM. Like LTAD, it emphasized play, movement skills, and informal games. Other NGBs and youth sport programs developed an interest in ADM after USAH showed that it increased participation and retention in their programs. However, both LTAD and ADM were used in programs that prioritized elite athlete development rather than lifelong participation in physical activities, and neither approach reduced program dues enough to make participation accessible to all young people.

In 2015, The Aspen Institute introduced Project Play, a plan to inspire a social movement to reimagine youth sports. It also used a model organized around play and physical literacy but it emphasized other factors that made youth sports more accessible to all children regardless of ability and family income and focused lifelong participation and public health than producing elite athletes. Project Play strategy is based on collective impact theory and involves engaging stakeholders in multiple sectors to support public health and evidence-based sport participation opportunities for all children. Project Play is currently creating youth sport programs in communities and regions where participation opportunities are scarce and local leaders are willing to support programs designed to give young people the abilities, confidence, and desire to stay physically active through life.

Changing the culture and organization of youth sports in the United States is a wildly ambitious goal, but the people and organizations supporting Project Play are committed to achieving it. In the process, they will have to make youth sports as attractive to young people as social media and video games–a challenge that will be met only if sport programs are contexts in which they can connect with friends and continuously experience exciting challenges that they are prepared to meet.

Growth and development is the third set of goals around which youth sports are organized. Most recently, these goals have been emphasized in programs designed as interventions into the lives of young people. In wealthy countries, these programs exist primarily in lower-income urban and rural areas where young people are perceived to be in need of support. In other parts of the world, usually in the southern hemisphere, where children face poverty and crises created by war, ethnic violence, or natural disasters these programs are funded by governments and non-government organizations (NGOs) in the Northern Hemisphere as aid that helps vulnerable children.

As interventions, youth sports emphasizing growth and development often reflect a desire by people with resources to help disadvantaged children develop habits and make choices that will make their lives better. This deficit-reduction approach usually focuses on changing children rather than the contexts in which they live. It is commonly used by organizations in the rapidly growing sector of "sport for development and peace" that is based on the belief that the power of sport can be used to improve the lives of children.

Among the organizations in this sector, Coaches Across Continents is one that has (re)defined development in terms of social impact rather than personal growth. Its programs focus on building community capacity for change by using sports and games in a bottom-up, inside-out, community-building process driven by local people empowered to transform the social and cultural organization of their communities.

Youth sports worldwide appear to be at a possible transition point involving a shift in goals. In wealthy countries, there is a move to replace adult-centered, revenue-driven programs organized around a skills and excellence model with accessible child-centered programs that emphasize physical literacy and lifelong participation in physical activities. Globally, there are efforts to use an approach to growth and development that prioritizes social impact over changing individuals. These shifts will not come easily. Theories of change and methodologies supported by research are essential in this process.

Overall, organized sports for children *are* worth the effort–*if* adults put the needs and interests of children ahead of the organizational needs of sport programs and their own needs to gain status through their association with successful and highly skilled child athletes.

SUPPLEMENTAL READINGS

Reading 1. Youth sports: What we know
Reading 2. Youth advocacy guidelines: Do we need them in sports?
Reading 3. George H. Mead's theory on the development of the self: Implications for organized youth sport programs
Reading 4. A self-assessment tool for youth sport parents
Reading 5. Guidelines for participation in youth sport programs: Specialization versus multiple-sport participation (a 2010 position statement by NASPE–the National Association of Sport and Physical Education)
Reading 6. The "logic" of sport specialization: Using children for adult purposes
Reading 7. Citizenship through Sports Alliance: Youth sports report cards
Reading 8. Project play: Re-creating youth sports in the United States

SPORT MANAGEMENT ISSUES

- You work in the sport and recreation division of a city government. As it faces a budget crisis, you are asked to present arguments for and against privatizing all the city's youth sport programs. List the major points you would include in your presentation.
- You work in the main office of a youth soccer organization that has programs in five US states. The actions of players' parents have become increasingly troublesome and extreme in those programs. Coaches want you to tell them why parents are so obnoxious today and what can be done to minimize their troublesome actions. Outline the points you will include in your explanation and recommendations.
- As the director of programs in a park and recreation department, you have an opportunity to hire two people. They will work with you to reform the youth sport programs in the city. Write the job description for these two positions and identify the skills you are seeking in applicants.
- Project Play has hired you to identify the top five reasons why young people play video games and to use those reasons as a basis for modifying or expanding the 8 strategy guidelines in the Project Play report. List what you think those five reasons might be and explain how they can be used to support or add to the 8 strategies.
- You have just graduated from college with a degree in sport management. You have an opportunity to take a "gap year" before entering a graduate degree program in the same field. You have an opportunity to do a one-year internship working in a youth sports program that is part of a project being done by Coaches Across Continents in Johannesburg, South Africa. As you study the theory of change and methodology used by CAC, list the factors that you like or dislike about the CAC approach to sport for development.
- You are part of a consulting team hired to create youth sport programs in lower-income areas of a major city in your country. Identify the three models (as described in the chapter) you will consider as a framework for your programs, explain the goals of the programs, choose the model you will use, and explain why you chose it.
- You are interviewing for a job in the youth sport development program at USA Volleyball. During the interview, you are asked how you would design a volleyball program for 6-10-year-olds. Explain why you would include certain elements in the program.

references

Abbot, Sebastian. 2018. *The away game: The epic search for soccer's next superstars.* New York/London: W.W. Norton & Company, Inc.

Adelson, Eric. 2019. The hidden officiating crisis: How the NFL's problems trickle down to youth sports. *Sports Illustrated* (March 29): https://www.si.com/nfl/2019/03/29/football-officiating-crisis-video-replay-impact-youth-sports-florida

Atencio, Matthew, Becky Beal, E. Missy Wright & ZáNean McClain. 2018. *Moving Borders: Skateboarding and the changing landscape of urban youth sports.* Fayetteville AK: The University of Arkansas Press.

Atencio, Matthew, Becky Beal, E. Missy Wright & ZáNean McClain. 2018. *Moving Borders: Skateboarding and the changing landscape of urban youth sports.* Fayetteville AK: The University of Arkansas Press.

Balyi, Istvan, Richard Way, and Colin Higgs. 2013. *Long-term athlete development.* Champaign IL: Human Kinetics.

Barone, Emily. 2017. The astronomical cost of kids' sports. *TIME* (August 24): http://time.com/4913284/kids-sports-cost/

Barreiro, Joshua A., and Rick Howard. 2017. Incorporating unstructured free play into organized sports. *Strength and Conditioning Journal* 39(2): 11–19.

Belanger, Kevin, Joel D. Barnes, Patricia E. Longmuir, Kristal D. Anderson, Brenda Bruner, Jennifer L. Copeland, Melanie J. Gregg, Nathan Hall, Angela M. Kolen, Kirstin N. Lane, Barbi Law, Dany J. MacDonald, Luc J. Martin, Travis J. Saunders, Dwayne Sheehan, Michelle Stone, Sarah J. Woodruff, and Mark S. Tremblay. 2018. The relationship between physical literacy scores and adherence to Canadian physical activity and sedentary behaviour guidelines. *BMC Public Health* 18(2): https://bmcpublichealth.biomedcentral.com/articles/10.1186/s12889-018-5897-4

Blom, Lindsey C., Lawrence Judge, Meredith A. Whitley, Lawrence Gerstein, Ashleigh Huffman, and Sarah Hillyer. 2015. Sport for Development and Peace: Experiences Conducting US and International Programs, *Journal of Sport Psychology in Action*, 6(1): 1–16.

Bloom, Benjamin S. 1985. *Developing talent in young people.* New York: Ballantine Books.

Bogage, Jacob. 2017. Youth sports study: Declining participation, rising costs and unqualified coaches. *Washington Post* (September 6): https://www.washingtonpost.com/news/recruiting-insider/wp/2017/09/06/youth-sports-study-declining-participation-rising-costs-and-unqualified-coaches/

Bogage, Jacob. 2018. Youth sports still struggling with dropping participation, high costs and bad coaches, study finds. *Washington Post* (October 16): https://www.washingtonpost.com/sports/2018/10/16/youth-sports-still-struggling-with-dropping-participation-high-costs-bad-coaches-study-finds/

Bowers, M.T., and B.C. Green. 2013. Reconstructing the community-based youth sport experience: How children derive meaning from unstructured and organized settings. *Journal of Sport Management* 27(6): 422–438.

Bowers, M.T., B.C. Green, F. Hemme, and L. L Chalip. 2014. Assessing the relationship between youth sport participation settings and creativity in adulthood. *Creativity Research Journal* 26(3): 314–327.

Brown, Fraser and Michael Patte. 2013. *Rethinking children's play*. London/New York: Bloomsbury Academic.

CareerBuilder. 2017. Living paycheck to paycheck is a way of life for majority of US workers. *PRNewswire*; Online: http://press.careerbuilder.com/2017-08-24-Living-Paycheck-to-Paycheck-is-a-Way-of-Life-for-Majority-of-U-S-Workers-According-to-New-CareerBuilder-Survey

Chudacoff, Howard. 2007. *Children at play: An American history.* New York: New York University Press.

Cho, JK. 2017. Second-time global citizen. *Coaches Across Continents* (November 30): https://coachesacrosscontinents.org/the-ultimate-challenge-of-the-perpetual-social-impact-machine/

Coakley, Jay. 1983. Play, games and sports: Developmental implications for young people. In Janet C. Harris, and Roberta J. Park, eds., *Play, games and sports in cultural contexts* (pp. 431–450). Champaign, IL: Human Kinetics.

Coakley, Jay. 2002. Using sports to control deviance and violence among youths: Let's be critical and cautious. In Margaret Gatz, Michael A. Messner, and Sandra J. Ball-Rokeach, eds., *Paradoxes of Youth and Sport* (pp. 13–30). Albany, NY: State University of New York Press.

Coakley, Jay. 2011. Ideology doesn't just happen: Sports and neoliberalism. *Revista de ALESDE* 1(1): 67–84.

Coakley, Jay. 2011b. Youth sports: What counts as "positive development?" *Journal of Sport and Social Issues* 35(3): 306–324.

Coakley, Jay. 2019. Sports and the development of youth: Canada and the United States. In Joseph Maguire, Mark Falcous and Katie Liston eds. *The business and culture of sports: Society, politics, economy, environment, vol. 3: Community* (pp. 257–269). Boston MA: Cengage Learning.

Coalter, Fred. 2013a. 'There is loads of relationships here': Developing a programme theory for sport-for-change programmes. *International Review for the Sociology of Sport* 48(5): 594–612.

Coalter, Fred. 2013b. *Sport for development: What game are we playing?* London: Routledge.

Cohen, Kelly. 2019. Kids aren't playing enough sports. The culprit? Cost. *ESPN.com* (August 11): https://www.espn.com/espn/story/_/id/27356477/kids-playing-enough-sports-culprit-cost

Curtiss, Ellen T., and Susan Eustis. 2018. Youth team, league, and tournament sports: Market shares, strategies, and forecasts, worldwide, 2018 to 2024. *WinterGreen Research* (September): http://wintergreenresearch.com/youth-sports

Darnell, Simon C. 2012. *Sport for development and peace: A critical sociology*. New York: Bloomsbury Academic.

Darnell, Simon, and Lyndsay Hayhurst. 2011. Sport for decolonization: Exploring a new praxis of sport for development. *Progress in Development Studies* 11(3): 183–196.

Darnell, Simon C., Megan Chawansky, David Marchesseault, Matthew Holmes, and Lyndsay Hayhurst. 2018. The state of play: Critical sociological insights into recent 'Sport for Development and Peace' research. *International Review for the Sociology of Sport* 53(2): 133–151.

DiFiori, John P., Joel S. Brenner, Dawn Comstock, Jean Côté, Arne Güllich, Brian Hainline, and Robert Malina. 2017. Debunking early single sport specialisation and reshaping the youth sport experience: An NBA perspective. *British Journal of Sports Medicine* 51(3): 142–143.

Eilerson, Nick. 2017. Verbal abuse from parents, coaches is causing a referee shortage in youth sports. *Washington Post* (June 16): https://www.washingtonpost.com/sports/highschools/verbal-abuse-from-parents-coaches-is-causing-a-referee-shortage-in-youth-and-high-school-sports/2017/06/16/cf02a016-499a-11e7-a186-60c031eab644_story.html

Eliasson, Inger. 2017. The gap between formalised children's rights and children's real lives in sport. *International Review for the Sociology of Sport* 52(4): 470–496.

Epstein, David. 2019. *Range: Why generalists triumph in a specialized world*. New York NY: Riverhead Books.

Evans, Tim, Joe Guillen, Gina Kaufman, Marisa Kwiatkowski, Matt Mencarini, and Mark Alesia. 2018. Larry Nassar: The making of a monster who abused gymnasts for decades. *USA Today Network* (March 9): https://www.usatoday.com/story/news/nation-now/2018/03/08/larry-nassar-sexually-abused-gymnasts-usa-gymnastics-michigan-state-university/406044002/

Farrey, Tom. 2019. Does Norway have the answer to excess in youth sports? *New York Times* (April 28): https://www.nytimes.com/2019/04/28/sports/norway-youth-sports-model.html

Farrey, Tom, and Risa Isard. 2015. *Physical literacy in the United States: A model, strategic plan, and call to action.* Washington DC: Aspen Institute Sports & Society Program.

Fatsis, Stefan and Josh Levin. 2018. How rich parents spending big on their kids' sports teams hurts lower-income families. *Slate.com* (November 23): https://slate.com/culture/2018/11/youth-sports-income-inequality-child-investment.html

Finger, Dave. 2004. Before they were next. *ESPN The Magazine* 7.12 (June 7): 83–86.

FlipGive. 2016. The rising cost of youth sports: Is your child being priced out? *FlipGive.com* (June 21): https://www.flipgive.com/stories/the-rising-cost-of-youth-sports-is-your-child-being-priced-out

FlipGive. 2019. FlipGive & Scotiabank report on the real cost of hockey. *FlipGive.com* (October 1): https://www.flipgive.com/stories/flipgive-scotiabank-report-on-the-real-cost-of-hockey

Ford, Paul, Mark De Ste Croix, Rhodri Lloyd, Rob Meyers, Marjan Moosavi, Jon Oliver, Kevin Till and Craig Williams. 2011. The Long-Term Athlete Development model: Physiological evidence and application. *Journal of Sports Sciences* 29(4): 389–402.

Froh, Tim. 2018. 'My under-10 matches are the worst': no end in sight to youth referee abuse.

The Guardian (April 16): https://www.theguardian.com/sport/2018/apr/16/my-under-10-matches-are-the-worst-no-end-in-sight-to-youth-referee-abuse

Fuller, Sarah and Juliana Zapata. 2019. Getting the 'development' right in sport for development. (April 6): https://blogs.unicef.org/evidence-for-action/getting-development-right-sport-development/

Gates, Judith and Brian Suskiewicz. 2017. Soccer changes lives: From learned helplessness to self-directed learners. *Soccer & Society* 18(2/3): 418–430.

Gilchrist, Paul and Belinda Wheaton. 2016. *Lifestyle and adventure sport among youth* In Ken Green & Andy Smith, eds. *Routledge handbook of youth sport* (pp. 186–200). London/New York: Routledge; Online: http://eprints.brighton.ac.uk/15968/1/GILCHRIST%20%26%20WHEATON%20FINAL%20RHYS.pdf

Gilchrist, Paul, and Belinda Wheaton. 2017. The social benefits of informal and lifestyle sports: A research agenda. *International Journal of Sport Policy and Politics* 9(1): 1–10.

Gleeson, Scott. 2018. Hope Solo says youth soccer in the US has become a 'rich, white kid sport.' *USA Today* (June 28): https://www.usatoday.com/story/sports/soccer/2018/06/28/hope-solo-youth-soccer-united-states-cost/741378002/

Gray, Peter. 2013. *Free to learn.* New York NY: Basic Books.

Gregory, Sean. 2017. How kids' sports became a $15 billion industry. *TIME* (August 24): http://time.com/4913687/how-kids-sports-became-15-billion-industry/

Hall, Brandon. 2019. A shocking number of youth sports coaches are unqualified for the gig. *Stack.com* (April 10): https://www.stack.com/a/a-shocking-number-of-youth-sports-coaches-are-unqualified-for-the-gig

Hartmann, Douglas. 2003. Theorizing sport as social intervention: A view from the grassroots. *Quest* 55(2): 118–140.

Hartmann, Douglas. 2012. Beyond the sporting boundary: The racial significance of sport through midnight basketball. *Ethnic and Racial Studies* 35(6): 1007–1022.

Hartmann Douglas and Christina Kwauk. 2011. Sport and development: An overview, critique, and reconstruction. *Journal of Sport & Social Issues* 35(3): 284–305.

Henricks, Thomas S. 2015. *Play and the human condition*. Champaign IL: University of Illinois Press.

Holst, Marissa E. and Greta L. Stuhlsatz, 2017. Parenting and motocross: The whoops and downs. *Journal of Amateur Sport* 3(3): 45–63.

Holt, Nicholas L., Kurtis Pankow, Martin Camiré, Jean Côté, Jessica Fraser-Thomas, Dany J. MacDonald, Leisha Strachan, and Katherine A. Tamminen. 2018. Factors associated with using research evidence in national sport organisations. *Journal of Sports Sciences* 36(10): 1111–1117.

Hopple, Christine J. 2018. Top 10 reasons why children find physical activity to be unfun. *Strategies: A Journal for Physical and Sport Educators* 31(3): 40–47.

Hyman, Mark. 2012. Why kids under 14 should not play tackle football. *Time* (November 6): http://ideas.time.com/2012/11/06/why-kids-under-14-shouldnot- play-tackle-football/

IHRB (with Guido Battaglia). 2018. Rights through sport: Mapping "Sport For Development and Peace." Institute for Human Rights and Business (April): Online: https://www.ihrb.org/focus-areas/megasporting-events/report-mapping-sport-for-development-and-peace

Jayanthi, Neeru and Joel Brenner. 2017. Caring for the young athlete: past, present and future. *British Journal of Sports Medicine* 51(3): 141.

Jessop, Nadia, Cirenia Chavez, Juliana Zapata, and Sarah Fuller. 2019. *Getting into the game: Understanding the evidence for child-focused sport for development. Report summary.* Florence, Italy: UNICEF Office of Research. Online: https://www.unicef-irc.org/getting-into-the-game

Johnson, Courtney. 2019. Athletic options for kids who have no interest in traditional team sports. *Washington Post* (April 19):

Keshner, Andrew. 2019. 90 percent of towns qualifying for the Little League World Series reveal an uncomfortable truth about organized sport. *MarketWatch.com* (August 26): https://www.marketwatch.com/story/most-us-towns-qualifying-for-the-little-league-world-series-have-one-concerning-thing-in-common-2019-08-15

Kessel, John. 2019. Teach novice players the love of volleyball. *USA Volleyball* (May 8): https://www.teamusa.org/USA-Volleyball/Features/2019/May/08/Kessel-Teach-Novices

King, Michael, and Kevin Rothlisberger. 2014. Family financial investment in organized youth sport. Research On Capitol Hill. *Research on the Hill (Salt Lake City).* Paper 17; Online: http://digitalcommons.usu.edu/poth_slc/17

Langan, Edel, Catherine Blake, and Chris Lonsdale. 2013. Systematic review of the effectiveness of interpersonal coach education interventions on athlete outcomes. *Psychology of Sport and Exercise* 14(1): 37–49.

Lindsey, Iain. 2017. Governance in sport-for-development: Problems and possibilities of (not) learning from international development. *International Review for the Sociology of Sport* 52(7): 801–818.

Malina, Robert M. 2009. Organized youth sports – background, trends, benefits and risks. In Manuel J. Coelho e Silva, António J. Figueiredo, Marije T. Elferink-Gemser, and Robert M. Malina, eds. *Youth Sports: participation, trainability and* readiness. Coimbra, Portugal: Coimbra University Press; Online, https://digitalis-dsp.uc.pt/bitstream/10316.2/32076/1/1-CHAPTER%201.pdf

Meadors, Larry. 2012. Practical application for long-term athletic development. *National Strength and Conditioning Association,* Online, https://www.nsca.com/education/articles/practical-application-for-long-term-athletic-development/

Meir, David, and Thomas Fletcher. 2019. The transformative potential of using participatory community sport initiatives to promote social cohesion in divided community contexts. *International Review for the sociology of Sport* 54(2): 218–238.

Mulcahy, Glen. 2019. Why do kids play video games? *Paradigmsports.ca* (March 21): https://www.paradigmsports.ca/why-do-kids-play-video-games/

North, Anna, 2019. Beyond Larry Nassar: hundreds of athletes are fighting USA Gymnastics in court over abuse. *Vox.com* (April 29): https://www.vox.com/2019/4/30/18287522/larry-nassar-usa-gymnastics-bankruptcy-usag-assault

Orbey, Eren. 2019. The victims of Larry Nassar who dared to come forward first. *The New Yorker* (May 25): https://www.newyorker.com/culture/culture-desk/the-victims-of-larry-nassar-who-dared-to-come-forward-first

O'Sullivan, John. 2018. In Youth Sports, there is no LTAD without STAE. *ChangingTheGameProject.com* (April 28): http://changingthegameproject.com/youth-sports-no-ltad-without-stae/

Peachey, Jon Welty, Allison Musser, Na Ri Shin, and Adam Cohen. 2018. Interrogating the motivations of sport for development and peace practitioners. *International Review for the Sociology of Sport* 53(7): 767–787.

Pierce, Alan. 2019. 3 reasons why the collective impact model is the future of social change. *SOPACT.com* (April 16): https://www.sopact.com/perspectives/collective-impact-evaluation

Pinheiro, Maria Claudia; Nuno Pimenta, Rui Resende & Dominic Malcolm. 2014. Gymnastics and child abuse: an analysis of former international Portuguese female artistic gymnasts. *Sport, Education and Society* 19(4): 435–450.

Project Play. 2014. *Designing for universal access: How to reach all kids? Project Play Roundtable Summary.* Washington DC: The Aspen Institute. Online, https://www.aspeninstitute.org/publications/designing-universal-access-how-reach-all-kids/

Project Play. 2015. *Sport for all. Play for life*. The Aspen Institute, Sports and Society section; Online: https://assets.aspeninstitute.org/content/uploads/2015/01/Aspen-Institute-Project-Play-Report.pdf

Project Play. 2018. *State of play 2018: Trends and development*. The Aspen Institute, Sports & Society section; Online: https://assets.aspeninstitute.org/content/uploads/2018/10/StateofPlay2018_v4WEB_2-FINAL.pdf

Reddy, Sumathi. 2014. Guidelines for young athletes to reduce injuries. *WSJ Wall Street Journal* (November 24): http://www.wsj.com/articles/guidelines-for-young-athletes-to-reduce-injuries-1416869652

Roetert, E. Paul, Todd S. Ellenbecker, and Dean Kriellaars. 2017. Physical literacy: Why should we embrace this construct? *British Journal of Sports Medicine* 52(20): http://dx.doi.org/10.1136/bjsports-2017-098465

Rosenberg, Tina. 2018. The business of voluntourism: Do western do-gooders actually do harm? *The Guardian* (September 13): https://www.theguardian.com/news/2018/sep/13/the-business-of-voluntourism-do-western-do-gooders-actually-do-harm

Säfvenbom, Reidar, Belinda Wheaton, and Jennifer P. Agans. 2018. 'How can you enjoy sports if you are under control by others?' Self-organized lifestyle sports and youth development. *Sport in Society*, 21(12): 1990–2009.

Sanders, Ben. 2016. An own goal in sport for development: Time to change the playing field. *Journal of Sport Development* 4(6): Online: http://repository.uwc.ac.za/bitstream/handle/10566/2166/Sanders_own%20goal_2016.pdf

Sanders, Ben, and Jay Coakley. 2020. Levelling the playing field: Investing in grassroots sports as the best bet for sustainable development. In Joseph Maguire, Katie Liston and Mark Falcous, eds., *The Palgrave handbook of globalization and sport*. London: Palgrave.

Schulz, Matt. 2019. 8 In 10 parents think kids' extracurricular activities may one day lead to income. *CompareCards.com* (April 24): https://www.comparecards.com/blog/8-in-10-parents-think-kids-extracurricular-activities-may-lead-to-income/

Shell, Adam. 2017. Why families stretch their budgets for high-priced youth sports. *USA Today* (September 5): https://www.usatoday.com/story/money/2017/09/05/why-families-stretch-their-budgets-high-priced-youth-sports/571945001/

Snider, Mike. 2018. Investigation by 'Indianapolis Star' hailed as proof of local journalism's impact. *USA Today* (January 25): https://www.usatoday.com/story/money/media/2018/01/25/investigation-indianapolis-star-hailed-proof-local-journalisms-impact/1066040001/

Solomon, Jon, and Tom Farrey. 2018a. *10 Charts that show progress, challenges to fix youth sports.* The Aspen Institute. https://www.aspeninstitute.org/blog-posts/10-charts-that-show-progress-challenges-to-fix-youth-sports/

Spaaij, Ramón, Sarah Oxford, and Ruth Jeanes. 2016. Transforming communities through sport? Critical pedagogy and sport for development. *Sport, Education and Society* 21(4): 570–587.

Spaaij, Ramón and Ruth Jones. 2013. Education for social change? A Freirean critique of sport for development and peace. *Physical Education and Sport Pedagogy* 18(4), 442–457.

Steinhardt, Ken. 2012. Skating league returns to Huntington Beach. *Orange County Register* https://www.ocregister.com/2012/06/03/skating-league-returns-to-huntington-beach/

Strandbu, Åse, Kari Stefansen, Ingrid Smette, and Morten Renslo Sandvik. 2019. Young people's experiences of parental involvement in youth sport. *Sport, Education and Society* 24(1): 66–77.

Strashin, Jamie. 2017. Pricey 'swag' is driving kids' sports costs up. *CBC Sports* (March 9): http://www.cbc.ca/sports/kids-sports-swag-costs-1.4017409

Sullivan, Philip, Kyle J. Paquette, Nicholas L. Holt, and Gordon A. Bloom. 2012. The relation of coaching context and coach education to coaching efficacy and perceived leadership behaviors in youth sport. *The Sport Psychologist* 26(1): 122–134.

Sukarieh, Mayssoun & Stuart Tannock. 2011. The positivity imperative: a critical look at the 'new' youth development movement. *Journal of Youth Studies* 14(6): 675–691.

Suskiewicz, Brian. 2019. CAC's Purposeful Play creates education outside the classroom. *coachesacrosscontinents.org* (February 15): https://www.sportanddev.org/en/article/news/cacs-purposeful-play-creates-education-outside-classroom

TD Ameritrade. 2016. *Parent perspectives on the cost of competitive youth sports*. TD Ameritrad Investor Survey (July): Online, https://s1.q4cdn.com/959385532/files/doc_downloads/research/Sports-Parents-Survey-Report_2016.pdf

Thompson, Derek. 2018. American meritocracy is killing youth sports. *The Atlantic* https://www.theatlantic.com/ideas/archive/2018/11/income-inequality-explains-decline-youth-sports/574975/

USA Hockey. 2019. 10 years ago today: USA Hockey approves American Development Model. *USA Hockey.com* (January 18): https://www.usahockey.com/news_article/show/986127

US Soccer. 2010. Best practices for coaching soccer in the United States: Player development guidelines. *USSoccer.com* Online: https://www.ussoccer.com/stories/2014/03/17/11/45/us-soccer-and-ea-sports-launch-updated-free-online-soccer-resource

Vandermeerschen, Hanne, Steven Vos, and Jeroen Scheerder. 2016. Towards level playing fields? A time trend analysis of young people's participation in club-organised sports. *International Review for the Sociology of Sport* 51(4): 468–484.

Visek, Amanda J., Sara M. Achrati, Heather M. Mannix and Karen McDonnell. 2015. The fun integration theory: Toward sustaining children and adolescents sport participation. *Journal of Physical Activity and Health* 12(3): 424–433.

Weir, Tom. 2006. Rookie always in a hurry. *USA Today* (June 30): C1–2.

Whitley, Meredith A. (with William Massey, Martin Camiré, Lindsey Blom, Megan Chawansky, Shawn Forde, and Simon Darnell). 2019. *Sport for Development: The Road to Evidence: A Systematic Review & Comparative Analysis*. Laureus Sport for Good and the Commonwealth Secretariat.

chapter

5

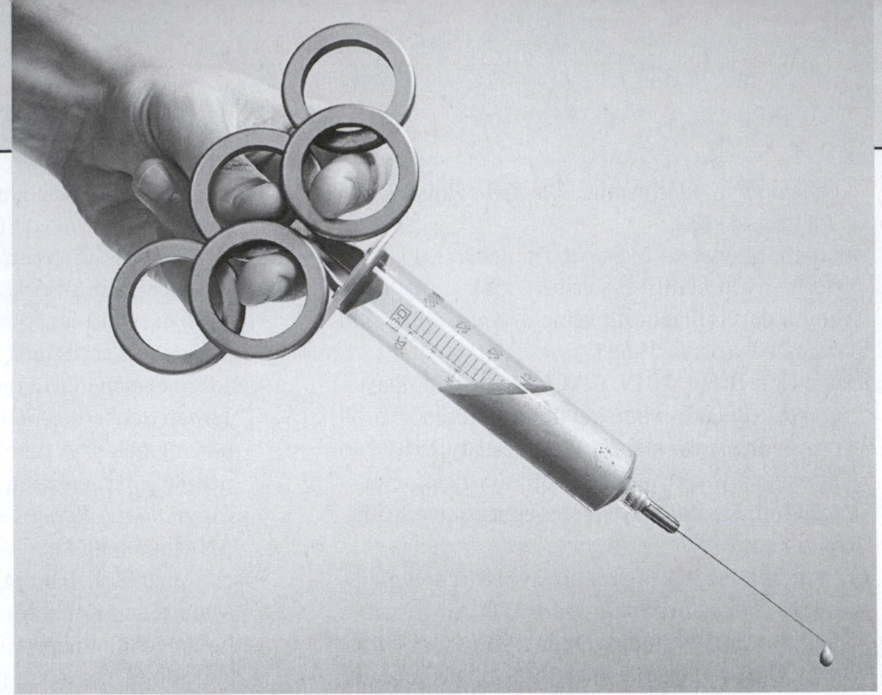

(*Source:* C.J. Burton/Corbis/Getty Images)

DEVIANCE IN SPORTS

Is It Out of Control?

We were definitely paying players . . . Everyone was paying players. . . . They are the only people in college basketball who can't get paid.

–Christian Dawkins, defendant in college basketball scandal (in Powell, 2019)

These individuals and organizations [connected with FIFA] engaged in bribery to decide who would televise games, where the games would be held, and who would run the organization overseeing organized soccer worldwide.

–US Attorney General Loretta E. Lynch (in Clifford and Apuzzo, 2015)

History is clear: As long as there have been sports, people have bet on them–and tried to fix them.

–Scott Eden, ESPN (2019)

The Olympic Training Center [in Colorado Springs] was the Wild West. It was really bad . . . You train six to eight hours a day . . . You had a two hour workout on Saturday morning. Saturday nights and Sundays was drinking and mischief and hooking up.

–Anna Kim, USA Taekwondo (in Fuchs, 2018)

Chapter Outline

Defining and Studying Deviance in Sports
Challenges Faced When Studying Deviance in Sports
Research on Deviance in Sports
Performance-Enhancing Substances: A Case Study of Deviant Overconformity
Summary: Is Deviance in Sports Out of Control?

Learning Objectives

- Define deviance and identify challenges faced when studying deviance in sports.
- Explain the absolutist and constructionist approaches to deviance in sports.
- Define the sport ethic, and identify the norms of the sport ethic.
- Distinguish between deviant overconformity and deviant underconformity.
- Identify the athletes most likely to overconform to the norms of the sport ethic.
- Understand the research findings on the major forms of deviance in sports and identify examples that do not involve athletes.
- Explain why performance-enhancing substance use is so prevalent among athletes today.
- Outline the phases in a professional sport career and indicate when performance-enhancing substances become important in that career.
- Understand why the current system of drug testing in sports will not eliminate the use of performance-enhancing substances.
- Outline and evaluate new strategies to control doping in sports.

Media stories about drug use, on-the-field rule violations, and off-the-field criminal actions are so common today that deviance is seen by many as out of control in sports. For those who accept the great sport myth these stories create a dilemma: Either they must admit that their belief in the purity and goodness of sports is wrong or they must conclude that sports are being undermined by money, greed, undisciplined athletes, and corrupt management.

Few people are willing to abandon the great sport myth, so they express outrage at offending individuals and insist that they be banned from sports to preserve their essential purity and goodness. In the face of this outrage and the extent to which it is expressed in mainstream media, it is difficult to have a research-based sociological discussion of deviance in sports. But that is the purpose of this chapter.

Our discussion will focus on four questions as we deal with the issue of deviance:

1. What challenges do we face when studying deviance in sports?
2. What is deviance, and how does sociological knowledge about it help us understand sports as a social phenomenon?
3. Are rates of deviance in sports out of control?
4. Why has the use of performance-enhancing substances become such a persistent problem in many sports?

DEFINING AND STUDYING DEVIANCE IN SPORTS

When a softball player punches an umpire after a disputed call, it's a deviant act because it violates a norm. Similarly, when a college football coach hires prostitutes for high school recruits or when an Olympic judge alters scores to ensure a victory for a particular figure skater, we know that deviance has occurred. In each case, norms have been violated.

A **norm** is *a shared expectation that people use to identify what is acceptable and unacceptable in a social world.* Norms exist in all social worlds and serve as the standards that people use to identify deviance. **Deviance** *occurs when a person's ideas, traits, or actions are perceived by others to fall outside the normal range of acceptance in a society.*

Studying deviance is often tricky because norms take different forms, vary in importance, change over time, and differ from one social world to another. **Formal norms** *are official expectations that take the form of written rules or laws,* whereas **informal norms** are *customs or unwritten, shared understandings of how a person is expected to think, appear, and act in a social world.*

When basketball players foul an opponent or shove a referee in anger over a foul call, they violate formal norms that are written in the official rule book. These norms are enforced by "officials" given the authority to sanction or punish violators. When two college basketball players don't face the US flag during the national anthem or don't participate in a pregame team ritual, they violate unwritten, informal norms. In response, fans may deride players who don't conform to flag-related customs, and teammates may refuse to talk with players that don't meet their expectations for togetherness. This means that there are two forms of deviance. **Formal deviance** involves a *violation of an official rule or law, and is punished by official sanctions administered by people in positions of authority.* **Informal deviance,** on the other hand, involves a *violation of an unwritten custom or shared understanding, and is punished by informal sanctions administered by observers or peers.*

These definitions of norms and deviance appear to be straightforward, but there are different ways to interpret norms and identify deviance when studying sports in society.

CHALLENGES FACED WHEN STUDYING DEVIANCE IN SPORTS

Studying deviance in sports presents challenges for four reasons. First, *the types and causes of deviance in sports are so diverse that no single theory can explain them all* (Atkinson and Young, 2008). For example, think of the types of deviance that occur just among male college athletes: failing to show up for a scheduled practice, violating rules or committing fouls on the playing field during a match or game, taking performance-enhancing substances, hazing rookie team members by demeaning them and forcing them to do illegal things, binge drinking, fighting in bars, harassing women, engaging in group sex, sexual assault, turning in coursework prepared by others, betting on college sports, using painkillers to stay on the field, destroying hotel property during a road trip, taking money from boosters, and going home over a holiday to meet an agent who gives money to their parents.

This list includes only a sample of cases reported for athletes at one level of competition over the past decade. The list would be more diverse if we included all athletes and if we listed examples of deviance by coaches, administrators, team owners, and spectators. Therefore, it is important to study deviance in the context in which it occurs and not expect that a single theory will explain all cases.

Second, *actions accepted in sports may be defined as deviant in other spheres of society, and actions accepted in society may be defined as deviant in sports.* Athletes are allowed and even encouraged to do things outlawed or defined as criminal in other settings. Some things that athletes do in contact sports would be classified as felony assault on the streets. Ice hockey players would be arrested for actions defined as normal during their games. Racecar drivers would be ticketed for speeding and careless driving. Speed sking and motocross racing would be defined as criminally negligent in everyday life. Even when serious injuries or deaths occur in sports, criminal charges are seldom filed, and civil lawsuits asking for financial compensation are rare and generally unsuccessful when they go to court (Atkinson and Young, 2008; Young 2019).

Coaches treat players in ways that would be defined as deviant if teachers treated students or employers treated employees similarly. Team owners in North American professional sports don't abide by antitrust laws that apply to other business owners. Fans act in ways that would quickly alienate friends and family members in other settings or lead people to define them as out of control.

On the other hand, if athletes take the same drugs or nutritional supplements used by millions of normal citizens, they may be banned from their sports and defined as deviant, even by the people using the same products to enhance performance in their non-sport jobs. Athletes who miss practices or games due to sickness or injury often are defined as deviant by coaches and teammates, even though taking "sick days" is accepted as normal in everyday life. College athletes with scholarships violate formal NCAA rules if they hold jobs during the school year, and coaches may punish players who fail to attend class, whereas other students work and cut classes without violating formal rules. Youth league players may be benched for a game if they miss practice to attend a family picnic, despite the value given to the family outside sports. The fact that norms are applied and enforced differently in sports makes it difficult to use studies of deviance in other contexts to understand what occurs in sports.

Third, *deviance in sports often involves overconformity to norms, rather than rejecting or not conforming to them.* Athletes often go overboard in their dedication to sport and their willingness to do whatever it takes to perform at a level that allows them to stay on the field, do what they love to do, and gain acceptance from teammates and coaches. Their attitudes and actions in these cases are *supranormal* in that they overconform to norms widely accepted in society as a whole. Instead of setting limits on what they are willing do as athletes, they evaluate themselves and their peers in terms of their unqualified willingness to go over-the-top and exceed normative limits, even if they jeopardize health and well-being in the process.

This "over-the-top deviance" is often dangerous, but athletes learn to accept it as part of the game they love to play and as the basis for being accepted into the culture of high-performance sports. When this normative overconformity takes the form of extreme dedication, commitment, and self-sacrifice, it brings praise rather than punishment from coaches and fans. It's even used to reaffirm cultural values related

(*Source:* Jeff Chiu/AP Photo)

Understanding deviance in sports is a challenge because athletes often do things that are not accepted in other settings. Many actions of mixed martial arts fighters, boxers, football and hockey players, racecar drivers, and wrestlers would be criminal acts off the field.

to hard work, competition, achievement, and manliness. In the process, people overlook its negative consequences for health, relationships with family and friends, and overall well-being.

This practice of overconformity among athletes makes it difficult to understand certain cases of deviance because they contradict the assumption that deviance always involves *subnormal* or *underconforming* attitudes and actions based on a rejection of norms. However, *supranormal* attitudes and actions also are *abnormal* and deviant (Heckert and Heckert, 2002, 2007; West, 2003). When people don't distinguish between these different forms of deviance, they often define athletes as role models, even though much of what they do is dangerous to health and well-being and beyond the limits of acceptance in other spheres of life.

Fourth, *training and performance in sports are based on such new forms of science and technology that people have not yet developed norms to guide and evaluate much of what occurs today in sports.* Science and medicine once used only to treat people who were sick are now used regularly in sports. The everyday challenge of training and competition in sports often pushes bodies to such extremes that continued participation and the achievement of performance goals requires the use of new medical treatments and technologies.

Using nutritional supplements is now a standard practice in nearly all sports. As one high school athlete explained, supplements "are as much a fixture in sports participation as mouth guards and athletic tape" (Mooney, 2003, p. 18). Ingesting substances thought to enhance performance is a taken-for-granted part of being an athlete today–a strategy for living up to the time-honored motto of the Olympics: Citius, Altius, Fortius, which is Latin for "Faster, Higher, Stronger."

A survey of the ads for performance-enhancing substances online (see www.t-nation.com) or in any *Flex, Muscle and Fitness, Planet Muscle,* or *Iron Man* magazine leads to the conclusion that strength and high performance are just a swallow or syringe away. Online promotions push protein drinks, amino acids, testosterone boosters, human growth hormone boosters, insulin growth factor, vitamins, energy drinks, and hundreds of other supplements that supposedly will help athletes get the most from their workouts, recover more quickly from injuries, and build a body that can adjust to overtraining and become stronger in the process.

Using the Internet to obtain various substances has occurred since the early 1990s, and this makes it difficult to determine just what actions are deviant and what actions are accepted parts of athletic training; in fact, "normal training" is now an oxymoron because high-performance training involves exceeding boundaries accepted as normal in society as a whole.

Two Approaches to Studying Deviance

When norms are viewed as representing absolute, unchanging "truths" about right and wrong and good and evil, deviance is identified differently than when norms are viewed as social constructions that people create as they interact with each other and organize their social worlds to meet individual and collective needs.

The unchanging, right or wrong perspective, or **absolutist approach** to deviance *assumes that social norms are based on essential principles that constitute an unchanging foundation for identifying good and evil and distinguishing right from wrong.* According to this approach, all norms represent *ideals,* and whenever an idea, trait, or action departs from an ideal, it is deviant; the greater the departure from the ideal, the more serious the deviance. This approach is illustrated in Figure 5.1, where the broad vertical line signifies a particular ideal, and the horizontal hash line represents increasing deviations from the ideal. The most extreme deviations from the ideal are often described as evil or perverse ideas, traits, or actions. For example, if obedience to the coach is a team norm, any form of disobedience is deviant. The greater and more frequent the disobedience, the more serious the deviance; chronic or consistent deviance would eventually be seen by absolutists, including most coaches, as evil or a sign of perverted character.

The absolutist approach has not contributed to a sociological understanding of deviance in sports, but it is often used by fans, media people, and the general public as they discuss rule violations and crimes by athletes and coaches.

It's important for us to understand this approach because it helps us explain how people respond to deviance and why there are so many disagreements when people discuss deviance in sports. For example, if you and I use an absolutist approach but hold

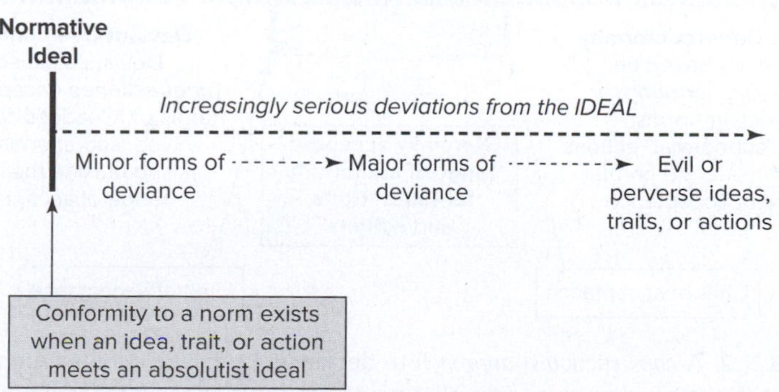

FIGURE 5.1 An *absolutist approach* to deviance: Using ideals as a basis for identifying deviant ideas, traits, and actions.

different ideals, it becomes difficult for us to jointly study deviance. Let's say that my ideal is fair play, and your ideal is achieving excellence as demonstrated through winning. According to my ideal, all violations of game rules would be deviant, whereas you would say that a player was deviant if your team lost because she refused to commit a strategic foul (a "good" or "smart" foul) in the closing minutes of a game. If we don't share the same ideals, we identify *deviance* differently.

Another problem with an absolutist approach is that it leads many people to see deviance as caused by the character weaknesses of individuals. Therefore they think that controlling deviance always requires more rules, better rule enforcement, and increasingly severe penalties for deviations from the ideal. However, this approach ignores that people with strong moral character have engaged in civil disobedience, violated unjust laws, and challenged unfair and biased norms to produce important changes and innovations in all social worlds, from classrooms to entire societies. It also overlooks that a rigid system of rules and rule enforcement creates fear and guilt to a point that people avoid being spontaneous, self-expressive, and creative.

Despite these problems with an absolutist approach, many people use it when they discuss deviance in sports. For example, when the actions of athletes don't match people's ideals, they define the athletes as deviant. They argue that the only way to control deviance is to "get tough" and eliminate the "bad apples" that lack moral character. In the process, they don't ask critical questions about justice, about the ways that laws and rules are created and who creates them for what reasons.

Most sociologists reject an absolutist approach and use a constructionist approach to define and understand deviance. A **constructionist approach** states that **deviance** occurs when *ideas, traits, or actions fall outside the boundaries that people create and use to decide what is acceptable and unacceptable in a social world.* This approach is based on a combination of cultural, interactionist, and structural theories in sociology, and it emphasizes the following six points:

1. **People create norms and laws**. This occurs as they interact with each other and use their values to determine a range of acceptable ideas, traits, and actions. This point is illustrated in Figure 5.2, where the vertical hash marks crossing the horizontal line represent the boundaries that separate what is accepted from what is considered deviant. Note that the gray range of acceptance in the middle of the figure is broad enough so that everyone is not forced to think, look, and

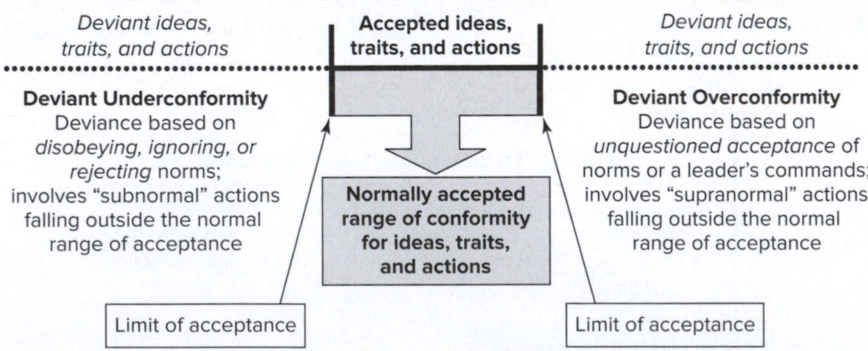

FIGURE 5.2 A *constructionist approach* to deviance: Deviance occurs when ideas, traits, or actions are determined to fall outside the limit of acceptance on either side of the range of conformity. Therefore, deviance can involve *underconformity* or *overconformity* to a norm or law

act exactly alike to avoid deviance. Of course, the range of acceptance may be very narrow in authoritarian social worlds such as high security prisons, military combat training, and systems of slavery where no deviations are tolerated.

2. **Norms and laws can be changed**. This occurs when people agree to temporarily or permanently shift the boundaries (the dark vertical lines in Figure 5.1) that define the range of acceptance. Deviance is socially constructed as people negotiate the boundaries of their acceptance. The ideas, traits, and actions that fall outside the range of acceptance are defined as deviant. However, boundary negotiation occurs continuously, and the vertical lines that represent normative boundaries move one way or the other over time as norms change.
3. **The establishment of normative boundaries is influenced by who has power**. People with power and authority generally have the most influence in determining, changing, and enforcing norms and laws. In democracies these people can be challenged without violating norms, whereas challenging these people in a dictatorship or autocracy would be defined as deviance because there is no tolerance of dissent.
4. **There are two kinds of deviance: underconformity and overconformity**. Both involve ideas, traits, or actions that fall outside the normal range of acceptance in a social world.
5. **Deviant underconformity** *occurs when ideas, traits, and actions indicate a rejection of norms or ignorance about their existence*, such as bar fighting, sexual assault, or referring to a person with an intellectual disability as "stupid." do not measure up to expectations based on norms or laws. A coach yelling nasty obscenities in the face of a referee and pushing the ref into the scorer's table are examples of deviant underconformity. **Anarchy** is *the condition that exists when there is widespread deviant underconformity to the point of general lawlessness in a social world.*
6. **Deviant overconformity** *occurs when ideas, traits, and actions* go beyond expectations in ways that are defined by most people as unacceptable. For example, when an athlete obeys *without question* a coach's command to continue running in the heat until he collapses from heat exhaustion and faces possible death is an example of deviant overconformity (Hruby, 2018). **Fascism** *is the condition that exists when there is widespread deviant overconformity based on unlimited obedience to norms or to the commands of an autocratic leader.*

A constructionist approach is useful when studying deviance in sports because athletes are just as likely to go overboard in their conformity to expectations as they are to reject expectations when they participate in their sports, even though deviant overconformity is often dangerous or harmful to themselves or others.

Deviant Overconformity in Sports

Research shows that deviant overconformity is a significant problem in sports. When sociologists Ewald and Jiobu (1985) studied men who were seriously involved in bodybuilding or competitive distance running, they found that some of the men engaged in unquestioned overconformity to norms related to training and competition. The men trained so intensely and so often that their family relationships, job performance, and/or physical health deteriorated, yet they never questioned their actions or the norms of their sport cultures.

This study was published over 35 years ago, but athletes today are just as likely, if not more likely, to ignore normative limits and do anything it takes to train and participate in sports. Former NFL player Matt Millen explained it this way:

> You have to be selfish, getting ready for a game that only a handful of people understand. It's tough on the people around you. . . . It's the most unspoken but powerful part of the game, that deep-seated desire to be better at all costs, even if it means alienating your family or friends. [Athletes] will do anything to [stay in the game], even if it means sacrificing their own physical or mental well being (in Freeman, 1998, p. 1).

More recently, a former member of the USA Gymnastics team, explained her training with these words:

> . . . we are taught to soldier on through intense training sessions, . . . though injury and fatigue, through pain . . . Pain was a fact of life for me . . . but so was silence (Williams, 2018).

Research has identified many forms of deviant overconformity, including self-injurious overtraining, extreme weight-control strategies, taking untested or dangerous performance-enhancing substances, and playing while injured (Coker-Cranney et al., 2018; Platts & Smith, 2016). When studying deviance in sports, it's important to distinguish between actions based on indifference to or rejecting norms and actions based on a blind, uncritical acceptance of norms to a point that most people define as unacceptable. Such a distinction is identified only by examining the organization and dynamics of sport cultures and the meanings that athletes give to their sport participation (Aubel et al., 2019). For example, in the culture of high-performance sports, athletes are expected to live by a code that stresses dedication, sacrifice, and a willingness to put their bodies on the line for the sake of their sport and their teammates. Conforming to this code is seen as a mark of a true athlete (Bloodworth, McNamee & Tan, 2017). However, when athletes do not set limits on how far they will go with their conformity, they are likely to engage in deviance, and this is especially likely in contemporary power and performance sports.

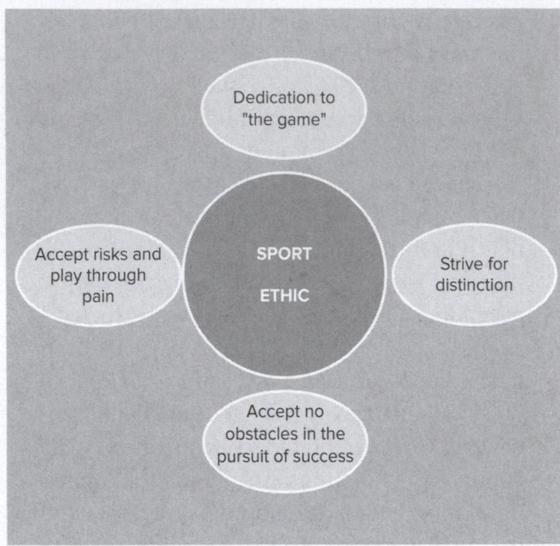

FIGURE 5.3 The four primary norms of the sport ethic.

The Sport Ethic and Deviance in Sports

An **ethic** is *an interrelated set of norms that a collection of people use to guide and evaluate ideas, traits, and actions in a social world.* Elite athletes and coaches use a **sport ethic** to guide and evaluate attitudes and actions in the social world of power and performance sports. This ethic is formed around four general norms (see Figure 5.3):

1. *Athletes are dedicated to "the game" above all other things.* This norm stresses that athletes are expected to love "the game" and prove it by giving it top priority in their lives, making sacrifices to stay in their sport, and facing the demands of training and competition without backing down. Pre-game pep talks and locker-room slogans proclaim the importance of this norm. It was explained in these terms by NFL player Brandon Stokley, who said, "I just love it. I can't see myself giving up football because I think I might have something (bad) happen to me or my brain. . . . I am going to live in the here and now and have fun at what I am doing" (Brennan, 2012).
2. *Athletes strive for distinction.* The Olympic motto *Citius, Altius, Fortius* (faster, higher, stronger) captures the meaning of this norm. Athletes are expected to relentlessly strive for improvement by pushing limits and doing what it takes to maximize their potential. This norm is highlighted by Justin Wadsworth, a top US Nordic skier in the 30-kilometer race, who pushed his body so hard during the 2002 Olympics in Salt Lake City that he suffered internal bleeding. From his hospital bed he said, "It's pretty special to push yourself that hard," and his coaches and fellow athletes agreed with him (Berger, 2002).

3. *Athletes accept risks and play through pain.* According to this norm, athletes are expected to endure pressure, pain, and fear without quitting. When athletes talk about this, they simply say that "this is part of the game." In the process of saying this, athletes develop a narrative that normalizes pain and injuries as an unavoidable part of what they do and who they are. This is clearly illustrated in the comments of X Games athletes who endure pain and injury as they push limits. Levi LaValee, a medal-winning snowmobile athlete, said, "I've been injured so many times . . . [but] every time I'm injured, I can't wait for the moment until I can get back on the sled [and] drive again" (George, 2013).

   For many elite athletes, the endurance of pain comes to be seen as an indicator of inner strength and commitment; eventually, many athletes view pain as positive–as a sign that they are alive and doing what they were meant to do. Coaches in most high-performance sports seek athletes who feel this way and then use them as examples of what they expect from everyone on the team.
4. *Athletes accept no obstacles in the pursuit of success in sports.* This norm stresses "the dream" and the obligation to pursue it at all costs. Athletes don't accept obstacles, they work to overcome them. Dreams, they say, are achievable only if you work hard and never quit. Champion boxer Lucia Rijker (who starred in the film *Million Dollar Baby*) stated this norm succinctly as she trained for a bout: "I use obstacles as wood on a fire" (Blades, 2005, p. 96).

Most people in society, me included, accept these four norms. They are not unique to sports. I taught them to my children when I told them they should be dedicated to their goals, work hard to achieve them, suck it up when things get difficult, and persevere when obstacles are in the way. But I also taught them to set limits and avoid deviant overconformity: *that is*, be dedicated but not obsessive, work hard but know when to stop, suck it up but don't sacrifice your health, pursue your dreams but be realistic in the process. In other words, *be sensible, don't engage in deviant overconformity*.

The danger of overconformity was explained by Alberto Salazar, a former marathoner and coach for Mary Decker Slaney, a legendary middle-distance runner during the 1970s and 1980s. After multiple injuries and nineteen sport-related surgeries, Slaney attempted a comeback while she lived in constant pain; she trained excessively, hoping to make the US Olympic team. Salazar understood Slaney's deviant overconformity to the norms of the sport ethic, but he also recognized its dangers with this comment:

> The greatest athletes want it so much, they run themselves to death. You've got to have an obsession, but if unchecked, it's destructive. That's what it is with [Slaney]. She'll kill herself unless you pull the reins back (Longman, 1996, p. B11).

The importance of Salazar's insight, from 25 years ago, has been vividly supported by current research on concussions and brain injuries in sports a topic that is discussed in Chapter 6, *Violence in Sports*. When athletes overconform to the norms of the sport ethic by enduring repeated head trauma, they risk permanent brain damage, chronic memory loss, and early-onset dementia that can affect them long before old age. This is in addition to the arthritis and joint injuries that result from intense daily training that pushes their bodies beyond normal limits. This suggests that deviant overconformity is more dangerous than deviant underconformity and is a central problem in sports today. Without critically assessing the culture of high-performance sport, this form of deviance will remain common.

Of course, deviant underconformity also is a problem in sports, but when athletes underconform, they are punished immediately. As a result, underconformers are usually pushed out of high-performance sport cultures, whereas overconformers are praised. Additionally, media stories glorify overconforming athletes as role models–as warriors who play with broken bones and torn ligaments, endure surgery after surgery, and willingly submit to injections of painkilling drugs to stay in games. Spectators express awe when they hear these stories, even though they realize that athletes have surpassed the normative limits that they use to define what is deviant. But people seldom object to deviant overconformity in sports because it is entertaining to watch and it reaffirms the importance of the sport and values such as dedication, hard work, and achievement. However, they condemn deviant underconformity because it threatens the sport and their values. Therefore, most athletes avoid asking critical questions and setting limits on their conformity to the norms of the sport ethic, even though it creates problems, causes pain, disrupts family life, jeopardizes health and safety, and may even shorten their life expectancy. This illustrates how powerful the sport ethic can be when athletes internalize it and use their own overconformity as a basis for evaluating themselves and sustaining their identity among peers.

Who is Most Likely to Overconform to the Norms of the Sport Ethic?

Overconforming to the norms of the sport ethic is a significant form of deviance in high-performance sports, but not all athletes overconform. Those most likely to overconform are athletes who have a strong need for approval and respect from other athletes and their coaches. This need is most characteristic among the following athletes:

Being an athlete, you're always like—what can I do more? What can I do better? —Aly Raisman, gymnast, Team USA (in Kimes, 2018)

1. Those with low global self-esteem and a strong need to be recognized and accepted as athletes by their peers in sport.
2. Those who perceive achievement in sports as the surest way to be defined as successful and gain the respect of others.
3. Those who link their identity as an athlete to their masculinity so that being an athlete and being a man are merged into a single identity.
4. Those who play on teams in which coaches and teammates make overconformity an important feature of acceptance as a team member.

These four hypotheses have not been tested. However, there are coaches who create a team environment in which athletes are kept in a perpetual state of adolescence by withholding acceptance. For some athletes, this creates identity insecurity and makes them dependent on the coach for approval as an athlete and team member. Challenging the masculinity of male athletes is also used as a strategy to encourage overconformity as athletes seek identity reaffirmation as a man. When this becomes a part of team culture, overconformity to the norms of the sport ethic will be common among team members. But research is needed on this topic.

Deviant Overconformity and Group Dynamics

Being an athlete is a social experience as well as a physical one. At elite levels of competition, athletes form special bonds with each other, due in part to their collective overconformity to the norms of the sport ethic. When team members collectively dedicate themselves to a goal and willingly make sacrifices and endure pain in the face of significant challenges, they create a social world in which overconformity is "normalized," even as it is defined as deviant in society as a whole (Smith, 2017). As they push the envelope together, the bonds between athletes become extraordinarily powerful. Their overconformity sets them apart culturally and physically from the rest of the community, and this leads them to assume that people outside of their sport cannot understand who they are and why they do what they do.

Athletes may appreciate fan approval, but they don't look to fans for reaffirmation of their identity as athletes because they know that fans don't really understand what it takes to perform at the level that they perform. Only other athletes understand this, and this makes everyone else peripheral to an athlete's life in sports, even spouses and family members.

The separation between athletes and the rest of the community makes the group dynamics associated with participation in high-performance sports very powerful. Other selective and exclusive groups, usually groups of men, experience similar dynamics. Examples are found in the military, especially among Special Forces units. Former soldiers sometimes talk about these dynamics and the powerful social bonds formed while they faced danger and death with their "teams." These bonds and the desire to remain connected with the select men that share these unique and intense experiences can be so strong that group members support increasingly extreme behaviors among themselves.

As high-performance athletes strive to maintain their identities and membership in their elite in-group, they often develop the sense that they are unique and extraordinary people. They often hear this day after day from coaches to fans and people on the street. They read it in newspapers and social media, and they see it on TV and the Internet. And when this sense of being unique and extraordinary becomes extreme, as it often does among high-profile athletes, it can take the form of **hubris**–that is, *pride-driven arrogance and an inflated sense of self-importance that leads one to feel separate from and superior to others.*

The dynamics leading to hubris among athletes are clear. First, they bond together in ways that encourage and normalize deviant overconformity. Second, collective overconformity creates a sense of specialness that separates athletes from the rest of the community at the same time that it inspires awe and admiration from fans. Third, the unique experiences associated with team membership leads athletes to feel a sense of entitlement. Fourth, athletes see people outside their sport culture as incapable of understanding them and their lives, and therefore undeserving of their concern or, in some cases, their respect.

The hubris that emerges on some sport teams can create serious problems, because it leads athletes to support each other in a general belief that community norms don't apply to them (Tracy & Barry, 2017). But this possibility has not been studied, so we don't know if there may be a relationship between the dynamics of collective overconformity to the norms of the sport ethic and high rates of deviant underconformity off the playing field.

Controlling Deviant Overconformity

Deviant overconformity presents special social control problems in sports. Coaches, managers, owners, and sponsors–people who create and enforce rules–often benefit when athletes overconform to the norms of the sport ethic. In their eyes, athletes who willingly put their bodies on the line for the team are a blessing, not a curse. In the eyes of the athletes, overconformity is proof of their dedication and commitment; and in the eyes of fans and media people it is seen as exciting, a way to win games, and a wonderful boost to media ratings. Therefore, deviant overconformity usually goes unpunished, even though it often consists of dangerous actions that everyone sees as falling outside normative boundaries. For example, few directors of national sports federations, such as the United States Olympic and Paralympic Committee, will tell national team coaches that their athletes are too dedicated to their sports, too focused on achieving distinction, too willing to play in pain, or too concerned with overcoming obstacles to win medals for the United States.

Complicating matters further is that *neither money nor the desire to win is the primary reason that athletes push themselves beyond the normative limits.* Instead, it is their desire to play their sport in a way that sustains the athlete identity around which their entire lives–their relationships, experiences, and everyday decisions and routines–have been organized. J.J. Watt (2016), a noted NFL player expressed this desire when he said this:

> Football has been everything to me since I was 10 years old. . . . the money, the fame, the awards, the people talking about me on TV, none of that matters. None of those things have any effect on why I love this game and why I give everything I have to it.

Legendary Ironman, Scott Tinley, uses slightly different words to explain his motivation in a sport that pushed him beyond his limits on a daily basis for over 20 years:

> . . . as the winningest triathlete in the world in 1985, I was earning less than a moderate living . . . It wasn't the material compensation I coveted, but the respect commensurate with the amount of pain I suffered each and every day in training. . . . [The] motives required to accept high levels of pain . . . were firmly steeped in issues of identity . . . It was a kind of external branding of my skills as an endurance athlete and I had somehow internalized that identity with the support of the signifying and surrounding culture Tinley, 2019, pp. 64–65).

Of course, winning, money, and fame are important to athletes, but they are secondary to reaffirming the identity that has been at the core of their existence ever since they focused on becoming an elite athlete. Every time people repeat the rhetoric about "winning at all costs" and "money" as explanations for everything that athletes do, they obscure two important things: (1) the deeper meaning and personal issues linked to being an athlete today in societies where sports are highly visible and culturally valued, and (2) the organization of today's high-performance sports, in which athletes must train full time at a level of intensity that precludes other commitments in their lives and makes them dependent on psychological, physiological, medical, and pharmacological support to be successful (Atry et al., 2013; Beamish, 2011; Brissoneau & Montez De Oca, 2018a, 2018b; Hoberman, 1992, 2005; Johnson, 2012; Maese, 2017; Ohl et al., 2015; Waddington and Smith, 2009). Because there are very few winners in high-performance sports means that deviant overconformity also occurs on teams and among athletes who will never win Olympic or World Cup medals, be ranked number 1, play in televised games, achieve public fame, receive college scholarships, or sign professional contracts.

One way to control deviant overconformity is to enable athletes to set limits when conforming to the norms of the sport ethic. However, this would not be viewed favorably by most coaches in elite sports. For example, when a fourteen-year-old gymnast is late for practice, her coach immediately sanctions her for violating team norms–a form of deviant underconformity. But when the same gymnast loses weight and becomes dangerously thin as she strives for distinction and pursues her sport dream, many coaches, parents, and judges don't see deviance as much as they see a dedicated athlete willing to suck it up and pay the price–that is, until stress fractures or anorexia interfere with competition, threaten her life, and put her in the hospital. Only then might they say that she went too far in conforming to the norms of the sport ethic. But they would seldom use the word *deviance* to describe her actions, because overconformity is seen as normal in elite gymnasts.

Fans also want athletes to exceed normative limits and put their bodies on the line. They see this as exciting and entertaining because it heightens the stakes associated with competition. When athletes do overconform to the norms of the sport ethic and play with concussions, broken bones, and torn ligaments, and refuse to quit, fans know that such actions are outside the limits off their acceptance. However, they often praise those athletes as heroes, especially if they play on their favorite team or for "their country."

To reduce deviant overconformity, sports would have to be organized primarily around the health and well-being of athletes, with limits set on the extent to which athletes conform to the norms of the sport ethic.

Although many people see sports as sites for supranormal achievements, this now requires that athletes train at a frequency and intensity that harms their bodies and requires dependence on technologies to keep them on the field and performing at optimum levels. Transforming high-performance sports into healthy activities is incompatible with how they are organized today, but it could happen if there were the will to do it. Without the will, many athletes will continue doing whatever it takes to stay in their sport and maintain their identity as an athlete.

RESEARCH ON DEVIANCE IN SPORTS

Media reports of deviance in sports and by people connected with sports have become daily occurrences. This raises sociological questions: Does deviance occur more regularly in sports than other spheres of life? What are the patterns of deviance in sports? Do athletes and people associated with sports have higher rates of deviance than others?

Most research focuses only on deviant underconformity among athletes–that is, deviance grounded in rejecting or ignoring team rules or civil and criminal laws. Deviant overconformity is ignored because it is seen as being entertaining and consistent with team cultures. Additionally, deviance among coaches, managers, team owners, and others in sports has seldom been studied because it is difficult to collect data from and about people in positions of power. These people have reasons and resources to keep secret the information needed to explain–or, in legal terms, *prove*–what they do. However, that does not mean that people in positions of power do not engage in deviance. Recent media coverage of scandals in high school and college sports generally involve coaches, and in professional and international sports they involve high profile members of organizations such as the International Olympic Committee, FIFA, National Olympic Committees (NOCs), and professional leagues and teams. This reminds us that deviance in sports is more common than most people want to admit because they generally see sports as a model of purity and goodness.

Character and greed may be related to deviance in sports, but there are important cultural and institutional factors as well, and they must be considered if we wish to understand this issue. These are identified in the following sections.

Deviance on the Field or Related to Sports

Sport-related deviance includes cheating, certain forms of gambling, fixing games or matches, harassment and abuse, hazing, institutional corruption, taking illegal performance-enhancing drugs, and other actions that violate criminal laws or rules in sports.

Cheating on the Field of Play Historical research indicates that cheating, dirty play, fighting, and the use of violence are less common today than in the days before television coverage and mega-salaries (Dunning, 1999; Elias, 1986; Guttmann, 2004; Scheinin, 1994). It also shows that sports today are more rule-governed than in the past and that on-the-field deviance is more likely to be punished and publicly criticized. However, comparing rates of on-the-field deviance among athletes from one time period to another is difficult because rules and enforcement standards change over time. Research shows that athletes in most sports interpret rules very loosely during games, and they create informal norms, which stretch or bend official rules. As one veteran athlete explains, "We players have our own justice system" (Player X, 2009). But this is not new.

Athletes in organized sports have traditionally "played to the level" permitted by umpires and referees–that is, they adjust their actions according to the way that referees enforce rules during a game. This means they will push the limits of rules as far as particular referees allow them to do so. Players also commit strategic fouls on the field to obtain an advantage over opponents, and players learn what rule violations are likely to be undetected by referees. But these actions are defined by players and fans alike as strategy rather than cheating.

Cheating, Corruption, and Harassment in Sport Organizations The perception that deviance has increased on and around the field is partly due to a combination of three factors. First, the constant addition of new rules creates new ways to be "deviant." Rulebooks in sport organizations such as the International Olympic Committee, international sport federations, and the National Collegiate Athletic Association (NCAA) have hundreds of rules and regulations today that didn't exist in the past, and every year more rules are added.

Second, the surveillance technologies used today increase detection of rule violations. For example, slow-motion instant replays enable referees to identify infractions they would have missed in the past. Even text messages, email evidence, photos, and videos from handheld devices have been used to identify deviance that previously would have remained undetected.

Third, personal stakes in the form of status and financial rewards associated with sports are so much higher today that players and others connected with sports have stronger incentives to cheat. This makes everyone concerned with sports more sensitive to the possibility that cheating will occur–and this leads to higher detection rates.

These factors have led to what seems to be an endless stream of cheating scandals in sports. The NCAA and its high-stakes Division I athletic programs provide classic examples of this. Most sport governing bodies, such as the NCAA, are self-policing. But the leaders of those organizations have always accepted the great sport myth to the point that they have not created effective rule enforcement divisions. They felt they didn't need them. Sports, they assumed, were essentially pure and good, and people in sports would regulate themselves because they shared in that purity and goodness. But this assumption is flawed, and it undermines the willingness of leaders to enforce rules and investigate suspected or reported infractions.

A second problem is that the officials in sport governing bodies often face inherent conflicts of interest in the process of policing themselves. So they create rules that make them look pure and good to outsiders, but they are ineffective when it comes to enforcement policies and procedures.

Third, the people who run sport organizations lack the experience that would prepare them to administer the systems of rule enforcement needed in today's high-stakes sport cultures. Like people in other spheres of life, people in sports have developed complex ways to cheat and skirt the rules. But the investigators don't have police powers and other investigative resources needed to consistently *prove* that cheating has occurred. This leads to bungled investigations and inconsistent and capricious punishments that weaken the legitimacy of the organizations themselves.

Finally, officials in sport organizations have generally been "groomed" for their positions in "good old boy" networks that have never been concerned about transparency and accountability in what they do. This applies to rule enforcement as well as budgets, travel expenses, hiring procedures, and the everyday business and personnel matters of an organization.

The lack of transparency and accountability creates problems that often escalate into long-term disasters now that billions of dollars flow through governing bodies such as the IOC and FIFA (Fédération Internationale de Football Association, the governing body of world soccer/football since 1904). This was recently seen in connection with sport mega-events such as the men's World Cup and the Olympic Games. Cost overruns, inside deals, bribes, kickbacks, and blatant corruption left large public debts in their wake. Corruption reportedly accounted for $30 billion of the $50 billion spent to host the winter Olympics in Sochi, Russia (Zirin, 2013). Tracking money trails in sports and sport events is difficult. Those who control sports organizations are able to hide and disguise financial transactions because they have not been investigated in the same ways that traditional businesses are investigated. Additionally, there is no global enforcement agency that has the power to fully investigate and hold accountable the people in these organizations when they engage in corrupt practices.

The takeaway point from this is that deviance in sports often takes the form of **institutional corruption**–that is, *established, widespread, and taken-for-granted processes and practices that, if publicly known, would be seen as immoral, unethical, or illegal to the point of destroying public trust in the organization and its leaders.*

Over the past three decades cases of institutional corruption have been relatively common. FIFA and the IOC appear to be organized in ways that lead to chronic cases of corruption (Bensinger, 2018; Blake & Calvert, 2015; Jennings, 1996; 2006, 2016; Jennings & Sambrook, 2000; O'Brien, 2017; Simson & Jennings, 1992; Sugden & Tomlinson, 2017). In the process, hundreds of millions of dollars have been banked by influential people in those organizations, a number of whom have recently been arrested and convicted of crimes, including fraud, money laundering, and bribery. Identifying institutional corruption is tedious and even dangerous, especially now that the financial stakes are so high, the incentives for self-policing are weak, and the opportunities for

(*Source:* YURI KADOBNOV/AFP/Getty Images)

FIFA President Gianni Infantino is with Russian President Vladimir Putin and Emir of Qatar, Sheikh Tamim bin Hamad Al-Thani, as the authority to host the 2022 Men's World Cup is symbolically transferred from Russia to Qatar with FIFA approval. An investigation of bribery allegations during the bidding processes won by Russia and Qatar led to the dismissal of more than half of the 22 FIFA executive committee members with disciplinary action taken against others (Robinson & Futterman, 2017). But there is little reason to conclude that institutional corruption has been eliminated from FIFA.

corruption are numerous and lucrative (Carmichael et al., 2017; Doidge, 2018; Smith & Willingham, 2015; Thamel and Wolff, 2013).

Research on institutional corruption is scarce given the extent to which it occurs in sports. Funding for such research is practically nonexistent, and there are career risks for any academic researcher who publishes evidence of corruption. The researcher will almost certainly be subjected to a smear campaign by representatives of any organizations implicated in the study, and these representatives often are influential and have more power than any scholars in the sociology of sport. So unless courageous investigative journalists backed by supportive media organizations do such investigations, corruption persists without consequences in certain sport organizations where people have consolidated power and use it to their advantage (Jennings, 2011).

When this occurs in an organization, it becomes a context in which harassment and exploitation are especially likely–again, without consequences for perpetrators. In the United States we saw this in the case of the athletic department at Penn State University, where a former assistant football coach was able to sexually abuse multiple boys for over a decade as he used the department's facilities without triggering any serious or sustained investigation. Other coaches, including the legendary football coach Joe Paterno, and athletic department and university officials were so concerned with maintaining the money- and status-generating football program that they shirked their legal obligations and overlooked the seriousness of the abuse occurring in their midst. It wasn't until investigative journalists exposed this situation that there was an official response to the deviance of the former coach (Hayes, 2012; Klarevas, 2011; McCarthy, 2012).

The Penn State case is one of many cases of illegal harassment and criminal abuse that have occurred in sport organizations, with administrators and coaches usually the perpetrators. The number of these cases being reported has increased dramatically since 2016 as current and former gymnasts associated with USA Gymnastics described how they were abused by the team doctor (Larry Nassar) and various coaches. This was followed by over a thousand other reported cases in other NGBs in the US, and at Michigan State University and the University of Southern California.

The processes involved in harassment and abuse have been studied meticulously since the 1990s by Celia Brackenridge from the United Kingdom, Kari Fasting from Norway, and their colleagues.[1] The dynamics of these processes vary from one situation to another, but they are most likely to occur in sport organizations where coaches and/or administrators have unquestioned power and control over the careers of athletes and are not held accountable for anything except sport outcomes. This will be discussed in Chapter 6, *Violence in Sports*.

[1]Brackenridge et al., 2008; Brackenridge and Fasting, 2009; Brackenridge et al., 2010a, 2010b; Brackenridge and Fasting et al., 2008; Fasting and Brackenridge, 2009; Fasting, Brackenridge, and Knorre, 2010; Fasting, Brackenridge, and Kjølberg, 2011.

The only way to break this potential cycle of cheating, corruption, harassment, and abuse is for sport organizations to abandon the practice of self-enforcement and voluntarily turn all enforcement matters over to an independent outside agency. This transfer would not be without problems, but it would make rule enforcement the job of people who don't have the conflicts of interest that exist when enforcement is handled internally (Donnelly & Kerr, 2018; Miller, 2012). Of course, the independent agency would require adequate funding, and its actions would have to be transparent and competent to establish trust. Additionally, specific forms of training are needed by most management-level people working in sport organizations to make them aware of their responsibilities to athletes and co-workers. Again, this training becomes increasingly effective when athletes and employees have independent authorities to whom they can go with questions and reports about harassment and abuse.

Sports Gambling, Match-Fixing, and Prop-Fixing

A United States Supreme Court decision in 2018 struck down the Professional and Amateur Sports Protection Act of 1992 (PASPA) that outlawed sports betting nationwide with exceptions for Nevada and four other states that already allowed it in 1992. This decision made it possible for other US states to join most countries of the world where sports betting is legal and regulated (Maese, 2018).

Gambling, once defined as a crime in many countries, is now among the top sports businesses in the world. When and where it was illegal, criminals became rich running betting operations, and where it is legal, it generates significant revenues for organizations that manage it and governments that tax it. The major sports leagues in the US have long opposed sports betting for fear that it would damage the integrity of competitive events by undermining faith in the validity of their outcomes. However, now that sports betting has become legal in a number of states, the leagues are trying to cash in on the revenues it generates–a topic that is discussed further in Chapter 11, *Sports and the Economy* and Chapter 12, *Sports and the Media*. In this chapter, we focus on forms of deviance associated with gambling: match-fixing and prop-fixing.

Match-fixing *occurs when one or more gamblers secretly pay athletes, referees, coaches or team officials to take actions that influence the final score of a match or game so the gamblers win their bets*. These actions could lead to an intentional loss or to a win in which the betting point spread is not covered by the favored athlete or team. For example, if an NBA team is favored to win a game by ten points, one or more players on the favored team could purposely miss shots or allow opponents to score points that cause the other team to win the game or lose by less than ten points. In this case, certain gamblers would win bets placed on the underdog team.

Prop-fixing *occurs when players are paid by a gambler to do something during a game or match that enables a gambler to win a proposition, or prop, bet.* Rather than focusing on the final score, a prop bet focuses on something happening during a game or match, such as which player or team will score first in an NBA game, who will win the second game in the third set of a tennis match, or will receive the first yellow card in a soccer match, and on and on. In some cases, one player can intentionally do something that would determine the winner of a prop bet without having an impact on the outcome of a game or match.

Sport federations and other sport governing bodies such as the NFL, the NCAA, and FIFA have explicit rules that prohibit athletes from betting on sports, especially their own sports and their own games or matches. Violating these rules brings severe sanctions, including lifetime bans on playing, coaching, or being formally connected with their sport in the future. This is to safeguard the legitimacy of competitive outcomes which must be trusted by players and spectators alike.

Prop bets don't usually involve large amounts of money and a clever player and gambler could work together to win them regularly, although bet-tracking software can aid in detecting such bets. Match-fixing scams often involve large bets and may involve multiple players and gamblers. They tend to occur in competitions where the players don't have multi-million-dollar contracts to risk if they are caught. This occurs mostly in lower division soccer matches, minor league hockey games, or any NCAA competition.

Match-fixing has become an international criminal activity with profits rivaling those for illegal weapons sales, prostitution, and drug trafficking. Global match-fixing syndicates are heavily involved (Hill and Longman, 2014). In 2013 investigators found evidence of match-fixing in more than 600 soccer matches worldwide, with hundreds of people involved across fifteen countries (Robinson, 2013). With organized crime involved, match-fixing is more difficult to investigate and control. Crime organizations operate globally, whereas police forces operate nationally with the exception of Interpol and Europol, which have limited powers and must work with national police forces. Additionally, organized crime doesn't merely bribe players and referees–it may also threaten them and their families with harm if they don't cooperate.

Gambling comes with problems that concern people who manage revenue-generating sports. But these people also realize that betting on sports is a "hook" that brings spectators to events and to media broadcasts and often keeps them there until the final minute of play. People who bet on sports also pay for expensive cable and satellite sports packages for their homes and regularly buy pay-per-view events in mixed martial arts and boxing. As bets are placed, people in sports organizations hope that match-fixing is effectively controlled and that spectators don't ever think they are watching rigged events.

Hazing: Deviance or Team Building? Hazing has long been an accepted practice as new members enter an established group or organization in which membership increases a person's status in a social world. It is more common in groups of males than groups of females, partly because men are more likely to assume that their groups are linked with high status.

Confusion about hazing often occurs because people don't distinguish between hazing and related processes, such as rites of passage, initiations, and bullying. A **rite of passage** *is an institutionalized cultural ritual that marks a transition from one status to another.* An **initiation** *is an expected, public, and formal ceremony that marks entry into a group or organization.* **Hazing** *is a secret, private, interpersonal process that reaffirms a hierarchical status difference between incoming and existing group members.* Finally, **bullying** *consists of aggressive acts that are meant to intimidate, exploit, or harm another person.* Of these four processes, hazing has been studied the least, mostly because it is private and secretive and involves experiences that people keep private because they are embarrassing.

There are times when hazing in sport teams involves clear cases of deviance, but research indicates that hazing processes are difficult to classify as deviant or as acceptable, for the following reasons (Eiserer, 2018):

(a) High school and college athletes are aware of hazing and often expect it when they become new members of a team.
(b) Most athletes who are hazed perceive their own hazing in positive terms or they are ambivalent about their experience and may not conclude that they have been hazed as others define it.
(c) Hazing often involves forms of humiliation, alcohol consumption, isolation, sleep deprivation, and sex acts that athletes keep private.

One way to make sense of these findings is to say that hazing has become normalized for most athletes, at least those who become members of high status teams. Additionally, certain hazing practices have become so normalized that those who experience them don't see them as "out of the ordinary," even though people in the larger community would disagree.

Research on hazing is scarce, but studies by Jennifer Waldron, Vicki Krane, and their colleagues (Waldron and Kowalski, 2009; Waldron et al., 2011) indicate that hazing contains dynamics that easily get out of hand and can seriously harm people. These dynamics exist largely because hazing is a private, secretive process that reproduces a hierarchical status and power distinction between senior and junior group members. For example, one of the ways to ensure secrecy is to force people to violate important social taboos in ways that they could not admit without being defined as deviant themselves.

In US culture such taboos often are related to sex, so there is a tendency in hazing processes to force people to engage in sexual activity defined as immoral, so they will keep it private (Editorial, 2017; Editors, 2018; Morse & St. George, 2018; Wixon & Riddle, 2017). Another guarantee of secrecy is to force people to drink so much that they will not clearly remember what they did or will not be believed if they tell someone about it. This is why hazing often involves forms drinking that put people in danger.

Due to its deviance and danger, hazing creates bonds and a form of vulnerability that coaches can use to control team members. This is why some coaches covertly approve of hazing–it gives them information that can be used to assert power over a team and to demand obedience without destroying team bonds.

My review of the evidence on hazing leads me to conclude that for high school and college students it should be replaced by initiation ceremonies in which new team members have public experiences that mark entry onto the team and signal their right to claim a new identity. In the case of professional teams, information about hazing suggests that it is more controlled and more focused on initiating rookies into a culture of respect for the players that have already "paid their dues" and shown that they deserve to be identified as athletes in this elite context.

After this litany of deviance in sports, the following conclusion may seem surprising: there are no historical studies showing that deviant underconformity on and around the field is more common now than in the past. However, cases of institutional corruption and the match-fixing side of gambling constitute significant problems that could jeopardize the future of some sports.

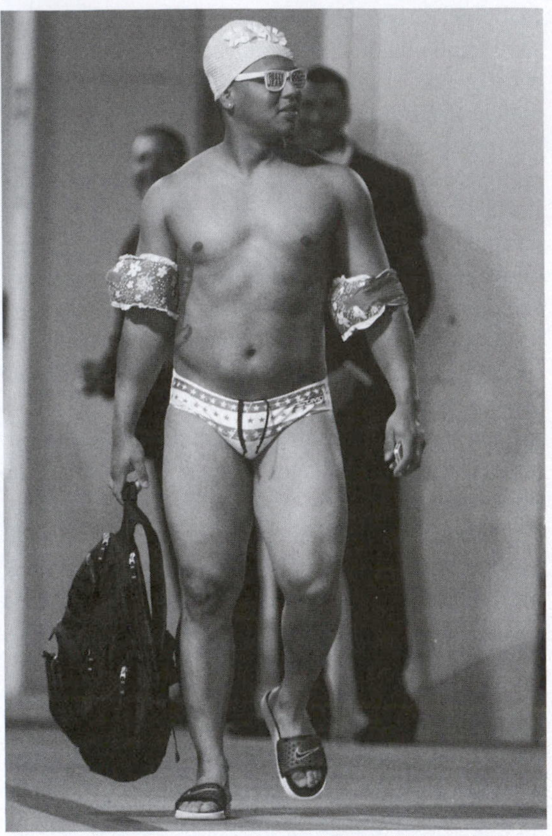

(*Source:* LM Otero/AP Photo)

Texas Rangers catcher Luis Martinez was forced by team veterans to wear a costume as part of rookie hazing as the team heads to the bus after a baseball game in Arlington, Texas.

Deviance Off the Field and Apart from Sports

Off-the-field deviance among athletes attracts widespread media attention. When athletes are arrested or linked to criminal activity, they make headlines and become lead stories on the evening news. However, research doesn't tell us if the rates of off-the-field deviance have gone up or down over time or if general rates are higher among athletes than their peers in the general population. The studies that deal with this have focused primarily on three topics: (1) crime rates and sport participation among high school students; (2) academic cheating and excessive alcohol use among high school and college athletes; and (3) particular felony rates among athletes.

Crime Rates Research on high school students shows that delinquency rates (i.e., crime rates for juveniles–under 18-years-old) among athletes often are lower than rates for other students from similar backgrounds. With a few exceptions, this finding applies for athletes in all sports, athletes in different societies, and both boys and girls from various racial and social-class backgrounds (Veliz and Shakib, 2012).

The problem with most of these studies is that they don't take into account three important factors: (1) students who have a criminal record are less likely than other students to try out and be selected for sport teams; (2) athletes may receive preferential treatment enabling them to avoid being charged for a crime after being arrested; and (3) deviance among high school athletes may be obscured by a "facade of conformity"–that is, athletes who conform to norms in public, but violate them only in private where detection is rare. This means that many studies may not have valid measures of criminal actions by athletes and, as a result, underestimate their juvenile delinquency rates. The point in this section is that some studies on sport participation and delinquency rates may overlook patterns of deviance among athletes or analyze data out of context so they can't explain why certain patterns exist.

Even when sport programs are designed as "interventions" for "at-risk youth," we lack a clear theory to explain how and why we might expect sport-based intervention programs to be effective in reducing criminal actions or producing other positive effects. Most of these programs have little effect because they do nothing to change the unemployment, poverty, racism, poor schools, and other delinquency-related factors that exist in most neighborhoods where sports for at-risk youth are offered.

We know from Chapter 3 (pp. 68–72) that we cannot make generalizations about athletes because experiences vary from one sports program to the next and because sport participation constitutes only one part of a person's experiences. Therefore, when someone says that "playing sports kept me out of trouble," we should investigate what that statement means in that person's life and then identify aspects of sport experiences that enable young people to see positive alternatives and make good choices in their lives. Until this research is done, our conclusion is that sport participation creates neither "saints nor sinners," although both may play sports.

Academic Cheating Despite highly publicized cases of college athletes having their coursework completed by "academic tutors," the charge that college athletes generally engage in academic cheating more often than other students, has not been studied systematically. If we compared athletes with other students, we might find comparable rates but different methods of cheating. An athlete may be more likely to hand in a paper written by an "academic tutor," whereas other students would obtain papers from files maintained at a fraternity house, from an online site, or from a professional writer hired by a parent. However, when a regular student is caught turning in a bogus paper, the case does not make national news, the student is not rebuked by people around the nation, and the reputation of the university is not questioned in the national media—as might occur if the cheater were an athlete.

Do athletes cheat more often because the stakes associated with making particular grades are higher for them than for other students, or do athletes cheat less because they are watched more closely and have more to lose if they are caught? We don't know the answer to this question, and we need studies comparing athletes with other students generally, with other students who would lose their scholarships or job opportunities if they did not maintain minimum grade point averages, and with other students who are members of tightly knit groups organized around nonacademic activities and identities. Only then will we be able to make definitive statements about academic cheating and sport participation.

Alcohol Use and Binge Drinking Underage and excessive alcohol consumption in high school and college is not limited to athletes. After reviewing dozens of studies on athletes and alcohol use, it is clear that the relationship between sport participation and patterns of use among athletes depends on factors such as team culture and the social activities that are a part of that culture. If athletes–male or female, high school or college–create a culture in which weekend parties are frequent, they will be more likely to drink and binge-drink than other athletes and students generally. Therefore, if being an athlete positions a young person in a culture where party attendance is encouraged or expected, drinking is more likely. However, some sports and teams may have cultures in which weekend social activities do not include parties and other social events at which alcohol may be present. So, the key factor is not so much the sport participation as the culture and social dynamics that come along with membership on a particular team (Donnelly, 2014; Fuchs, & Le Hénaff, 2014; Green, Nelson & Hartmann, 2014; Halldorsson, Thorlindsson & Sigfusdottir, 2014; Zhou, O'Brien & Heim, 2014).

Research on this topic is important because alcohol use and abuse is related to other forms of deviance. For example, we don't know if deviant overconformity that leads to cohesion and group dynamics among athletes contributes to alcohol use and binge drinking. Research is needed to see why, when, and how often this occurs.

Felony Rates Widely publicized cases of assault, hard-drug use, and driving under the influence (DUI) in which male athletes are the offenders have made it important to study these forms of deviance. At this point, research is scarce, and existing studies report mixed findings.

Another problem with studies of felony rates is that data on arrest rates for athletes are seldom compared with arrest rates in the general population or in populations comparable to the athletes in age, race/ethnicity, and socioeconomic background. For example, many people were shocked when a study of arrest rates from 2000–2013 indicated that rates for NFL players were lower than rates in the general US population for property crimes and public disturbance crimes, although they were higher for violent crimes in six of the 14 years covered in the study (Leal, Gertz & Piquero, 2015). A more recent study done by USA Today showed that the number of NFL player arrests and citations was cut in half between 2006 and 2018 (Schrotenboer, 2018).

However, when crime rates are compared it must be remembered that professional athletes may be treated differently than their peers in the general population. In some cases, their actions may be so visible that they are held more accountable than others engaging in the same actions. But in other cases, athletes may receive preferential treatment and avoid arrests for actions that would lead to an arrest of others.

Race also must be taken into account when discussing arrest rates for college and professional athletes. An investigation by *USA Today* (Schrotenboer, 2013) reports that when compared to white NFL players, black players are up to ten times more likely to be stopped by police while they are driving, and when they are stopped they are more likely to have their vehicles searched. Black players interviewed in the investigation said that when they are driving an expensive car in an area where an officer might think they don't belong, they are likely to be pulled over. If they object or give the impression that they are not fully cooperative, they are more likely than whites to be treated as a possible criminal.

This investigation does not prove that police are racist, but it certainly raises questions about the data on arrest rates among players when it comes to certain situations and possible crimes.

PERFORMANCE-ENHANCING SUBSTANCES: A CASE STUDY OF DEVIANT OVERCONFORMITY

The use of performance-enhancing substances remains a persistent issue in many sports (Fogel, 2017; Hruby, 2013; Hughes, 2013; King, 2014; King et al., 2014; Møller, Waddington & Hoberman, 2015; Ohl et al.,

2015; Panja, 2019; ProCon, 2016; Sefiha, 2012; Smith, 2015). Media stories about athletes using performance-enhancing substances are no longer shocking. However, most people don't know that drug and substance use in sports has a long history. For centuries athletes have taken a wide variety of everyday and exotic substances to aid their performances, and this has occurred at all levels of competition.

The use of performance-enhancing substances *predates* commercial sports and television, and it occurred regularly when so-called traditional values were widely accepted. Therefore, we must look beyond these factors to explain why athletes use performance-enhancing substances.

Research also suggests that substance use is not caused by defective socialization or a lack of moral character among athletes; in fact, it usually occurs among the most dedicated, committed, and hard-working athletes in sports (Coakley, 2015; Petrózi, 2007). At this point, it appears that most substance use and abuse is tied to an athlete's uncritical acceptance of the norms of the sport ethic. Therefore, it is grounded in overconformity–the same type of overconformity that occurs when distance runners continue training with serious stress fractures; when female gymnasts control weight by cutting their food consumption to dangerous levels; and when NFL players take injections of painkilling drugs so they can put their already injured bodies on the line week after painful week.

Sports provide powerful and memorable experiences, and many athletes are willing to "set no limits" in their quest to maintain participation and gain reaffirmation of their identities as members of a select group sharing lives characterized by intensity, challenge, and excitement (Smith, 2015). Athletes often refer to their desire to win when they are interviewed or when they talk with fans, but for most of them, winning is important because it enables them to continue playing the sport they love to play and to receive identity affirmation from other athletes. These dynamics encourage overconformity to the norms of the sport ethic, and they affect athletes at various levels of sports–from local gyms, where high school players work out, to the locker rooms of professional sport teams; they affect both women and men across many sports, from the 100 meter sprint to the marathon and from tennis to football.

The point here is that athletes use substances like HGH (human growth hormone) for reasons that differ greatly from the reasons that an alienated 25-year-old shoots heroin to get high and escape reality. The alienated 25-year-old rejects society's norms, whereas athletes using performance-enhancing substances accept society's norms about dedication, working hard, ignoring pain, and overcoming obstacles to reach goals. But as they uncritically overconform to these norms, they often go too far and accept without question the idea of using performance-enhancing technologies. This means that athletes don't use performance-enhancing substances (PESs) to escape reality as much as they use them to survive and succeed in elite sports. Additionally, full explanations of drug use in sports must put the user and the drug in the context of high-performance sports, the specific sport in which it occurs, and the team culture and relationships involved (Aubel et al., 2019; Coakley, 2015). Therefore, we need different explanations to understand why athletes use "drugs." The explanations and methods of control used to deal with people who reject norms and use heroin, cocaine, methamphetamines, cannabis, and other so-called recreational drugs are not relevant when trying to deal with the issue of PESs in sports.

Sport Careers and Performance-Enhancing Technologies

Our discussion in this section is an attempt to explain why the use of PESs persists in many sports despite drug-testing and anti-doping messages.

Studying the careers of athletes and the contexts in which they train and compete has been a long-term project of French sociologist Christophe Brissonneau. As a former elite cyclist, he has used his contacts in sports to collect data from athletes, trainers, coaches, and sport medicine professionals.

After analyzing data collected mostly through in-depth interviews with athletes in cycling, track and field, wrestling, weightlifting, and bodybuilding, Christophe and his colleagues at the University of Paris created a model that describes participation in elite sport as a three-part process in a multiphase sport career (Brissonneau and Ohl, 2010; Brissonneau & Montez De Oca, 2018a, 2018b; Ohl et al., 2015). An application of this model to careers in professional cycling is presented in Figure 5.4.

The model identifies five phases in the overall career of a professional cyclist. In each phase the cyclist experiences socialization in connection with (a) participation, (b) pharmacology, and (c) medical support.

Cyclists, like other athletes, begin their careers in the ordinary world as they discover cycling culture. During the first phase of the socialization process, they are amateurs and not concerned with using performance-related technologies or performance-enhancing substances; and medical support is provided by a general practitioner during routine checkups and general health assessments. These cyclists might race in local events, but their lives involve school and family. Cycling during this phase is focused on personal experiences rather than training and tracking performance; the goal is primarily to enjoy and learn more about cycling.

Cyclists enter the second phase of their sport careers if and when they decide to take racing more seriously and train with the goal of improving and possibly becoming a professional racer. Health and recovery from training and competition now become important, as does the need to be more

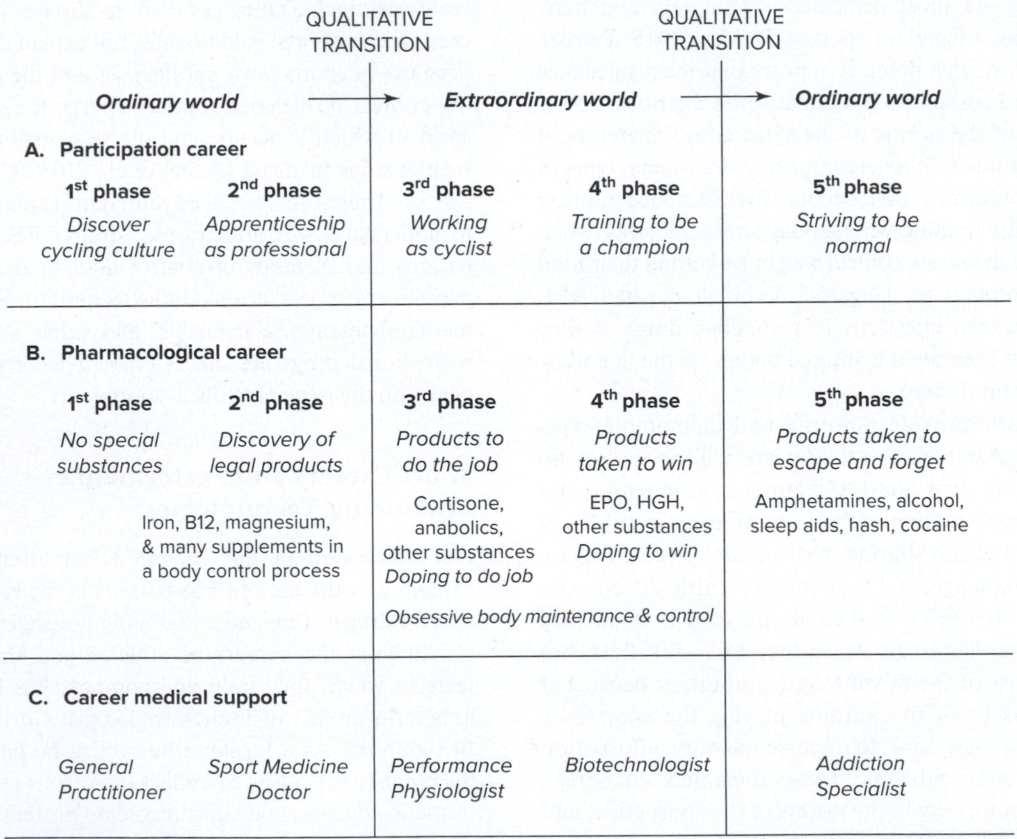

FIGURE 5.4 Brissonneau's model of a professional sport career.

rational and scientific in monitoring and controlling their bodies. Through their interaction with other cyclists, they discover legal supplements that can enhance their training and race performances. As they train, they begin to track and measure their physical attributes, from strength and muscle growth to endurance and the oxygen-carrying capacity of their circulatory systems (heart and lungs). Anything that enables them to train more intensely becomes attractive. If they see a need for injections of iron and vitamins C, B_6, and B_{12}, or other substances they learn how this is done. This marks the initiation of a pharmacological career that often is supported by sports medicine doctors, other athletes, and by many sources of technical and medical information in cycling culture.

Most cyclists (and other athletes) never move out of the second phase of a sport career, that is, they don't enter the extraordinary world of professional cycling. But for those who have the opportunity to move into the third phase and begin working as a cyclist–usually as a member of a team–there are significant qualitative changes in their lives. Now cycling becomes a job–sponsors are sought, athletes are paid, training and competition schedules are determined by others, and the pressure to improve performance becomes intense. Expectations, demands, and personal perspectives change dramatically. The cyclists' social world becomes increasingly exclusive and separated from the ordinary world, and their lives revolve around relationships with elite athletes, coaches, trainers, performance physiologists, team managers, and sponsors. All of these support people are concerned with the cyclist's performance above all else.

During this third phase, training is based on science and rationality. The duration and intensity of training increases and fatigue becomes the body's enemy. Over time the athletes realize that to succeed at the professional level, they must do things that push the normative boundaries that they accepted in the ordinary world. But they also know that for their bodies to function at full capacity, they must use technologies to help them recover from the physical damage done by their training and competition. To ignore these technologies means not doing their job and not being fit for competition. Pharmacological products offer assistance–*if* the athletes are willing to work at the level of intensity needed to take advantage of them. At this point, cyclists go beyond normal boundaries and use technologies and substances that enable them remain a professional athlete, even if they are illegal or banned.

The fourth phase of the cyclist's career involves an intensification of everything from the third phase. This involves a shift from doing the job to reaching the podium, winning stages in long races, and working with teammates to improve the team's record. At this point, a cyclist feels compelled to use all the performance-enhancing strategies provided by the biotechnologists who provide medical support and control most of their training.

Cyclists in this fourth phase of a sport career learn that overconforming to the norms of the sport ethic is normal–doing whatever it takes to continue performing at a supranormal level is the standard expectation that they have for themselves and that others have for them (Smith, 2017). Those unwilling to meet this expectation are seen as letting others down and violating the code that governs the lives of professional cyclists (and other pro athletes). Therefore, they train more obsessively and follow year-round training programs designed by personal trainers, nutritionists, and sport scientists. But to remain in their sport and continue to perform at the highest level, they must push their bodies beyond normal limits every day. When this is done for more than fifteen hours per week, their muscles begin to break down. Recovering from this, and from the injuries that are inevitable in training and competition, requires the use of various therapies, technologies, and substances. The harder cyclists train, the more they need these things to be competition ready and to sustain their careers.

During the fourth phase, medical support focuses on performance rather than overall health and wellbeing (Waddington, 2015). This involves using various combinations of substances, legal and/or illegal, to continue training and preparing the body to compete at the highest level. Strategies for doing this are learned from other cyclists, sport scientists and sport medicine experts hired by teams and sport federations. For cyclists to ignore these experts usually ends their professional careers, along with their team membership, sponsorships, income, relationships with elite peers, and their identity as an athlete. For those who have dedicated most of their lives to reaching this point in cycling, refusing to do whatever it takes is seldom a viable option. Some athletes refuse, but we seldom hear about them, because their careers languish or end quickly.

The training strategies during the fourth phase are extraordinary. To endure them and maximize the chances of winning, cyclists control everything that affects their ability to perform. This is when doping often becomes normalized as a training strategy. It enables them to train harder and longer than their opponents, and it becomes an integral part of the culture that is organized around achieving competitive success (Hruby, 2013). To refuse performance-enhancing substances under these conditions is especially difficult because now they represent teams, sport organizations, sponsors, and their communities or nations (Hoberman, 2005; Johnson, 2012). Additionally, cyclists begin to shift their priorities so that competitive success is more important than their long-term health. They also learn to hide their fatigue and injuries because they fear being replaced by younger and more durable teammates, and they want to avoid exposing weaknesses to opponents who will exploit them. In fact, cyclists who show weakness in a high-performance sport put in jeopardy their contract, endorsements, sponsorships, and even fan support.

During this fourth phase cycling is not something they do—*it is who they are.* Winning is important because it enables them to remain in elite sports, which at this point is the foundation of their lives and identities. To not win is to lose the basis for their primary identity, their relationships, experiences, and everyday routines. Therefore, when overconformity to the norms of the sport ethic is explained only in terms of a "win at all costs" mentality, it obscures the deeper personal meanings that are linked to being a cyclist at a time when that requires total dedication and commitment.

When a cyclist can no longer meet the expectations of sponsors, coaches, and team members it is time to exit the extraordinary world of professional cycling and rejoin the ordinary world. But this move from the fourth to the fifth phase in a sport career is often the toughest of all. Returning to normal after years of living an abnormal life in an extraordinary world requires serious social, psychological, and economic adjustments (Tinley, 2015, 2019). Routines are out of sync, and reasons for living seem fuzzy and uncertain. The pleasures of pushing the body to its limits are gone, as is the excitement of competition. The cyclists who have been sources of daily support are no longer there, and people in the ordinary world can't understand the difficulty involved in losing an identity as an elite athlete.

Striving to be normal involves renegotiating relationships with family and friends, if they are still available and willing to re-engage. But re-engaging is difficult when pre-sport identities are irrelevant and new identities don't yet exist. Feeling detached and seeing the ordinary world as boring compared to the extraordinary world of elite cycling can lead to the use of drugs and alcohol to get through the long days and nights. Seeking medical support from an addiction specialist, psychiatrist, or clinical psychologist often occurs at some point.

The seriousness of problems during this phase depends on many factors. But the difficulties of retirement from elite sports have become more common as the demands and expectations in high-performance sports have escalated since the mid-1980s. When sponsors and television entered the scene, and when training came to be based on rationality and science, expectations for elite athletes intensified. The "off-season" disappeared, there was no time for other jobs or education, and no excuses for poor performances.

Of course, not every cyclist or elite athlete fits perfectly into this model. There are differences by country, sport, gender, and the place of high-performance sports in specific cultures (Pitsch and

Emrich, 2012). But Brissonneau's model is based on 20 years of collecting data on the parts of a sport career that few of us ever see. In fact, popular conceptions of sport careers are based more on myth and wishful thinking than reality.

Additionally, elite cyclists and their peers in other sports know that if they disclosed everything that they experienced as they moved through the phases of their careers, people would be shocked and disappointed, other elite athletes would no longer support them, and their contracts might not be renewed. Therefore, they stick with a narrative that describes the first and second phases of the sport career model. This narrative stresses a connection between sports and health and the importance of values, hard work, and the purity and goodness of sports.

Sponsors embrace and promote this narrative because it reaffirms their business model as well as the beliefs of its executives, who often claim that their characters were shaped in positive ways back when they played sports. Media people who cover sports and those who work in sport organizations use this narrative to sustain the beliefs on which the popularity of sports has come to depend.

This means that deviance in sports is an economic issue as well as a health and cultural issue. What counts as deviance in sports is determined by what will sustain its popularity and support. This also shapes the sanctions and punishments handed out by sport leaders and rules committees. When athletes or low-level employees in sports do or say things that tarnish the perceived integrity of "the game" or allow people to see clearly into the extraordinary world of high-performance sports, they will be sanctioned.

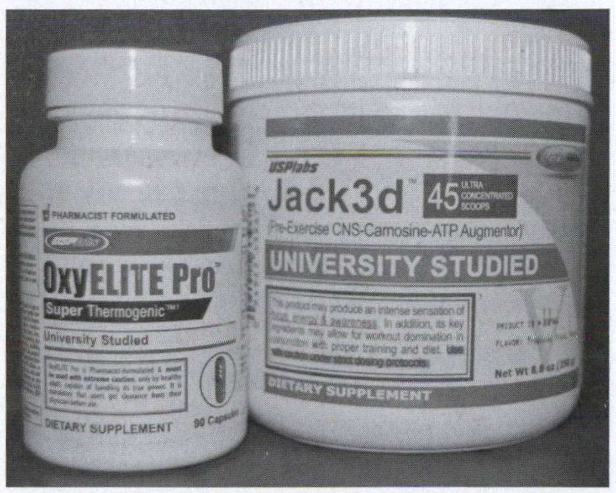

This product may produce an intense sensation of focus, energy & awareness. In addition, its key ingredients may allow for workout domination in conjunction with proper training and diet. Use with caution under strict dosing protocols.

(*Source:* Jay Coakley)

More than half of American adults use "nutritional supplements", spending over $31 billion annually on them (Coakley, 2020). Jack3d allegedly contains, a powerful stimulant, much like amphetamines. People claim that it enables them to work out longer and more intensely. OxyElite Pro warns that it should be used "only by healthy adults capable of handling its true power." Supplements are produced faster than drug-testing organizations can determine if they should be banned for athletes. This is partly because the United States does not require Federal Drug Agency approval of supplements before they are marketed and sold. Users of these products have reported harmful effects.

Doping from Inside High-Performance Sports

Controlling narratives about sports can be tricky. Elite athletes seldom give others a glimpse inside their extraordinary world. However, here are statements about drugs in which athletes do provide us with a brief look inside that world:

> It's professional sports. You do what you need to do to play and, at the end of the season, you get cleaned up [from all the drugs].
>
> –Ryan Zimmerman, MLB player (in White, 2012)

> A shot [of Toradol] in your butt cheek before a game (and you) feel like frickin' Superman when you walk on the field. Everything is numb. You feel great!.

After the game when you wake up, you feel like you got hit like a Mack truck because it hides everything. So what do you do? You go get another shot.[2]

—Matt McChesney, former University of Colorado and NFL player, 2015 (in Halsne & Koeberl, 2015)

My body was perpetually feeling bad, as were those of my teammates. Our training staff knew this and would encourage us to get a shot. We were told it would make us feel better. So we lined up for the needle.

—Nate Jackson, five-year NFL veteran (Jackson, 2011)

It's normal. You drop your pants . . . they give you a shot [of the painkiller Toradol], put the Band-Aid on, you go out and play. It may be stupid, it may be dumb, call me dumb and stupid then, because I want to be on the football field.

—Brian Urlacher, a thirteen-year NFL veteran (NFL Brief, 2012)

There's a certain point in your career where you're going through the pounding of the season and getting through that week of practice and trying to get to that next game day. Toradol is part of what gets you back to playing the way you normally can.

—Jim Kleinsasser, thirteen-year NFL veteran (Wiederer, 2012)

These statements are about a legal drug, and they come mostly from football players. Players seldom talk candidly in public about illegal or banned substances, but football players felt free to talk more openly about Toradol in 2011 after many had filed a class action suit against the NFL for allowing teams to administer it without following the warnings for the drug or discussing the side effects with players.

The statements also tell us that using drugs to enhance performance is a normal occurrence in the extraordinary world of high-performance sports. This conclusion has been supported in research by Evdoki Pappa and Eileen Kennedy (2013), who interviewed elite track-and-field athletes. They summarize their findings this way:

> The athletes give a clear indication that they see doping as a normalized phenomenon . . . Although sporting authorities have banned the use of PEDs, the athletes consider them necessary for their career and for competition at a high level. (pp. 289, 290)

This conclusion does not mean that all elite athletes use illegal substances. But it does mean that using such substances in the extraordinary world of high-performance sports is not seen by most athletes as an indication of moral corruption and weak character.

The War on Doping

Drug testing is relatively new in sports (Waddington and Smith, 2009). Prior to the mid-1980s, anti-doping policies existed largely to discourage athletes from dropping dead of overdoses, something that had become too common in certain sports as athletes experimented with a wide range of substances thought to boost training and performance. But as the money associated with sports has enabled athletes to hide their drug use, anti-doping agencies work to maintain an image of purity in sports. In fact, the stated rationale for the World Anti-Doping Code that guides Olympic sports and is enforced by the IOC, WADA, and USADA is that "doping is fundamentally contrary to the spirit of sport" (WADA, 2009). This rationale is grounded in an absolutist approach in which it is assumed that *any* use of banned performance-enhancing substances violates the ideals represented by sport and is therefore deviant.

The war on doping now being waged by WADA and USADA is supported by most people even if they are not sport fans. They feel that the essential purity and goodness of sports have been stained by

[2]The narcotic painkiller, Tramadol, has been given to athletes worldwide (especially cyclists) by their doctors and trainers. In the NFL and other collision sports, one of the drugs of choice is Toradol, an exceptionally strong nonsteroidal anti-inflammatory drug (NSAID); when it fails to cover the pain, opiates are prescribed, often indiscriminately and sometimes illegally by doctors who travel with teams. But each of these drugs has side effects more dangerous than many of the substances on the banned drugs list (King et al., 2014; Wertheim & Rodriguez, 2015).

performance-enhancing drugs and that any strategy that will purge them from sports should be supported. This approach also allows them to avoid critical questions, such as these:

1. Is it logical to praise athletes as warrior-heroes when they take injections of painkilling drugs to stay on the field, and then condemn them as cheaters when they take steroids, HGH, and other substances that help to heal injuries more quickly, rebuild muscles damaged by overtraining, or relax and recover after exhausting and tightly scheduled competitions?
2. Does it make sense to condemn athletes for failing to be positive role models for children, when we expect them to put their bodies on the line for the sake of our entertainment?
3. Why does drug testing focus on individual athletes rather than the culture of high-performance sports and the complex system in which people other than athletes develop, purchase, supply, administer, and study banned substances to determine how they can be taken without testing positive?
4. How can testing be justified by saying that it keeps athletes healthy and preserves fairness in sports, when it is clear that the sports most watched by fans are not good for a person's health and are not fair when some people have the resources to buy the best training and technology in the world and others don't even know it exists?
5. How can people in the United States, for example, say that athletes using a performance-enhancing substance are morally corrupt and should be banned from their careers, when they are part of a society in which appearance-enhancing, cognitive-enhancing, and performance-enhancing substances are consumed at rates unprecedented in human history?
6. Could the billions of dollars now spent on testing and police-like investigations of the urine, blood, and suspect actions of athletes be better spent on educating and working with athletes through their sport careers so they are fully informed and medically supported when they make choices about using available technologies to aid their training and competition?
7. Is it reasonable to condemn the use of so-called doping and at the same time support the Olympic motto "Faster, Higher, Stronger" and demand more record-setting performances, when athletes are now pushing the limits of human potential and damaging their bodies as they do so?

These and dozens of other critical questions about the current approach to doping control in sports make many people uncomfortable, so they are seldom asked. Therefore, the cat-and-mouse dynamics that have emerged with the current form of drug testing will continue. New technologies that improve vision, cognitive alertness, brain function, response time, strength, and speed are being developed at a record pace (Coakley, 2020; Epstein, 2011 Kotler & Wheal, 2018; Murray, 2018). Gene modification is close to being possible, if it has not already been done. This suggests that the most reasonable question to ask is this: How can these technologies (including drugs) be integrated into the lives of athletes (and the rest of us) without destroying our health and well-being?

Without asking these questions and changing the current approach to testing, doping scandals will continue to occur. Athletes will be caught, people will express their disgust and demand that the cheaters be punished, and then everyone (other than the punished athletes) will feel good until the next scandal occurs.

New Strategies for Doping Control

A central point in this chapter is that athletes use performance-enhancing substances not because they lack character or are victims of evil or exploitive coaches, but because they (1) uncritically accept and overconform to the norms of the sport ethic and (2) are part of a sport system in which therapies and supplements are needed to recover

(*Source:* Frederic A. Eyer)

"Don't worry, most of these are legal and the others won't show up on the drug tests!"

Most athletes today take multiple "nutritional supplements" (Mason and Lavallee, 2012). The industries that produce them are unregulated and often claim that certain products are performance-enhancing.

from intense training and competition schedules over which they have little control. This is why tougher rules and increased testing have not been effective.

Moral panics over drug use and oversimplified solutions will not change the reality of training and competition or the culture of high-performance sports, nor will it stop athletes from using substances that they see as necessary to maintain their identities and continue experiencing the joy and excitement of being an athlete.

The use of performance-enhancing substances and future forms of cognitive performance enhancement and gene modification cannot be effectively controlled in elite sport cultures as they are now organized. Effective control requires both cultural and structural changes in sports so that athletes are formally encouraged to set limits on how far they will go in conforming to the norms of the sport ethic and are given the information they need to understand the consequences of overconformity. Here are suggestions on where to begin these processes:

1. *Critically examine the deep hypocrisy involved in elite power and performance sports.* It isn't possible to effectively control the use of performance-enhancing substances when sport federations and teams encourage overconformity to the norms of the sport ethic. It makes no sense for people in sports to accept performance-enhancing strategies, such as injecting painkilling drugs and massive doses of vitamin B_{12} and to use medical devices and technologies that enable athletes to play with broken bones and injured joints and then punish athletes for using other substances that enable them to train and compete. When accepted practices in sport culture already permit the use of performance enhancing substances and technologies that push the limits of safety and common sense, it is not surprising that athletes use banned substances that also push those limits.
2. *Establish rules clearly indicating that certain risks to health will not be tolerated in sports.* When 16-year-old girls who compete with training-induced stress fractures in elite gymnastics are turned into national heroes and poster children for corporate sponsors, it promote deviant overconformity in sports. This sets up athletes for permanent injuries and disabilities. This is clearly a problem, and sport organizations should refocus on health over performance.
3. *Establish a "harm reduction" approach in which athletes are not allowed to play until certified as "well" (not simply "able to compete") by two independent physicians or medical personnel.* This approach differs from current practices in which trainers and medical personnel do what they can to return injured athletes to the game as quickly as possible. Trainers and physicians should be health advocates paid by someone other than team management. The focus of player health advocates would be protecting the long-term well-being of athletes. Therefore, instead of testing for drugs, athletes should be

tested to certify that they are healthy enough to participate. If drugs damage their health or make it dangerous for them to play, they would not be certified. Only when their health improves and meets established guidelines would they be allowed back on the field. This would be a major step in creating a new sport culture (Henning, 2017).

4. *Establish injury and health education programs for athletes.* This is a first step in establishing a sport culture in which *courage* is defined as recognizing limits to conformity and accepting the discipline necessary to accurately and responsibly acknowledge the consequences of deviant overconformity and sports injuries. Learning to be in tune with one's body rather than to deny pain and injury is important in controlling the use of potentially dangerous performance-enhancing substances.
5. *Establish a system of transparency and accountability for medical staff and sport scientists who work for athletes, teams, and sport federations.* Too many doctors, physiologists, psychologists, and trainers assist athletes as they overconform to the norms of the sport ethic, rather than helping them raise critical questions about the health risks that come with deviant overconformity. For example, sport psychology should be used to help athletes critically assess *why* they're doing what they're doing and *what* it means in their lives. Using science to enable athletes to give body and soul to their sports without asking these questions is to leave the door open for deviant overconformity, including the use of performance-enhancing substances.
6. *Make drug and substance education a key part of health education programs.* Parents, coaches, league administrators, managers, and trainers should participate with athletes in educational programs in which they consider and discuss the norms of the sport ethic and how to prevent deviant overconformity. Unless all these people understand their roles in reproducing a culture that supports substance use and abuse, the problems will continue.

We now face a future without clearly defined ideas about the meaning of achievement in sports. There are new financial incentives to succeed in sports, athlete identities have become more central in the lives of sport participants than ever before, and performance-enhancing technologies have become increasingly effective and available. As this occurs, the cost of drug testing has increased to a point that is not sustainable for organizations that do not have surplus money to spend. Therefore, we need *new* approaches and guidelines. Old approaches and guidelines combined with coercive methods of control are not effective. Trying to make sports into what we believe they were in the past is futile. We face new issues and challenges, and it will take new approaches to deal with them effectively.

Widespread participation is needed if sport cultures are to be successfully transformed. At present, both nation states and corporate sponsors have appropriated the culture of power and performance sports and used it to deliver messages that foster forms of deviant overconformity for the sake of national and corporate interests. There is no conspiracy underlying this, but it creates a challenge that can be met only through our collective awareness of what needs to be done, followed by collective efforts to do it. Even then changes will be incremental rather than revolutionary, but changes are possible if we work to create them in our sports, schools, and communities.

summary

IS DEVIANCE IN SPORTS OUT OF CONTROL?

The study of deviance in sports presents challenges due to four factors: (1) the diverse forms and causes of deviance in sports cannot be explained by a single theory; (2) the ideas, traits, and actions accepted in sports may be deviant in the rest of society at the same time that things accepted in society may be deviant in sports; (3) deviance in sports often involves accepting norms uncritically and without limits, rather than rejecting them; and (4) training in sports now involves so many new forms of science and technology that we lack norms to guide and evaluate the actions of athletes and others in sports.

People who assume that there are essential truths about right and wrong and good and evil use an absolutist approach to explain deviance. They believe that unchanging moral truths are the foundation for all norms. Therefore, every norm represents an ideal, and every action, trait, or idea that departs from that ideal is deviant, immoral, or evil. For example, if using banned substances is contrary to the ideal that sport is pure and good, any use of them at any time or place would be deviant, and if the substance use continued over time, it would eventually be defined as immoral or evil.

Sociologists generally use a constructionist approach to study and explain deviance in sports. This approach, based on a combination of cultural, interactionist, and structural theories, emphasizes that norms and normative boundaries are socially constructed through social interaction. This approach highlights a distinction between deviant underconformity and overconformity. This is important because some of the most serious forms of deviance in sports occur when athletes overconform to the norms of the sport ethic—a cluster of norms that emphasizes dedication to the game above all else, striving for distinction, taking risks and playing through pain and injury, and overcoming all obstacles in the pursuit of sport dreams. When limits are not set in the process of conforming to these norms, deviant overconformity occurs.

Most sociology of sport research has focused on the deviant underconformity of athletes. Research on deviance among coaches, managers, and others who control sports is relatively scarce, largely because people with power refuse to be studied in ways that might jeopardize their status and influence.

We don't know if cheating in sports is more prevalent today than in the past, but institutional corruption appears to be a growing problem in sport organizations, most of which lack formally enforced mandates to be transparent or accountable. Institutional corruption is accompanied by dynamics that foster harassment and abuse, including the sexual abuse of athletes.

The popularity of gambling on sports and the involvement of organized crime in the gambling business has increased the possibility of match-fixing in certain sports. For example, recent cases of match fixing in global soccer and other major sports have raised questions about the actions of players and referees who can influence game events and the final scores of matches and games.

Hazing new members of a sport team is a persistent problem because it occurs in secrecy. It can involve dangerous forms of deviance when it occurs among high school and college students who try to preserve secrecy by forcing new team members to violate strong social taboos.

Research indicates that athlete deviance off the field and away from sports continues to be a problem. However, the rates of deviance among athletes do not appear to be higher than rates among their peers who do not play organized sports. Possible exceptions to this involve drinking alcohol, binge drinking, and sexual assault.

The use and abuse of performance-enhancing substances is a common form of deviance among athletes, despite new rules, testing programs, and strong punishments for violators. Because so many people believe that sports are essentially pure and good, they use an absolutist approach when thinking about drugs in sports. Therefore, they see athletes who use banned substances as morally corrupt cheaters who must be purged from sports.

Brissonneau's model of a five-phase sports career is based on a constructionist approach, and it explains that substance use occurs in connection with the demands and expectations that require athletes to train in ways that are clearly "beyond normal" to meet them. Because the resulting fatigue, pain, and injuries take a toll on their bodies, athletes depend on specialized medical and pharmacological support to sustain their ability to perform. This normalizes the use of drugs and other technologies that enable them to perform.

Many athletes who are committed to doing whatever it takes to succeed and avoid being cut from their teams, view the use of performance-enhancing technologies as an integral part of training rather than a form of cheating, even though they know it violates rules. This mind-set also explains why athletes take injections of dangerous legal drugs such as Toradol and cortisone to mask pain and stay on the field.

The war on doping and current anti-doping policies involves testing athletes' urine and blood, and more recently the investigation of athletes' personal lives. This has created a cat-and-mouse dynamic in which athletes try to stay one step ahead of the testers. Even though this approach to "doping control" is costly and ineffective, it continues to be used because it serves the purposes of sponsors and sport organizations. When there are no positive tests, they can claim to be responsibly safeguarding the purity and goodness of sports, and when there are positive tests, they can express disgust and claim to be morally righteous as they punish the offending athletes.

New strategies for doping control involve asking critical questions about the current organization and culture of high-performance sports and honestly identifying their consequences for athletes. Instead of testing for drugs, a harm reduction approach could be used so that athletes are tested by qualified medical professionals to determine whether they are healthy enough to train and compete. If this were combined with education for athletes and for those who control sports, and if there was a system of transparency and accountability for medical staff and sport scientists who develop training programs for elite athletes, it might be more effective than drug testing as we face a future that will introduce many new forms of performance-enhancing technologies.

SUPPLEMENTAL READINGS

Reading 1. Using deviance to create commercial personas in sports
Reading 2. Deviant overconformity and underconformity: Is there a connection?
Reading 3. Is sport participation a cure for deviance?
Reading 4. Defining performance-enhancing substances
Reading 5. Why is the challenge of substance control so great in sports today?
Reading 6. Sport doping in recent history
Reading 7. Arguments for and against drug testing as a deterrent
Reading 8. Using the biological passport in doping control programs

SPORT MANAGEMENT ISSUES

- As a high school teacher and coach you hear that the veterans on the boys' wrestling team are planning to haze new members of their team. In the past, hazing by some of the teams has gotten out of hand, so you report your information to the principal and the athletic director. They ask you to create an alternative to hazing that will help team members bond in positive ways without engaging in demeaning or risky actions. Outline your plan and explain the differences between what you are proposing and hazing as it is defined in the chapter.
- You have an internship with a professional sport team. You love what you do, and on a few occasions you take modafinil, a cognitive enhancer, to stay up all night to meet project deadlines. Your supervisor is impressed and offers you a job that all the other interns wanted. You accept the job, pass the company's mandatory drug test, and have a successful first year on the job. Are you a cheater for taking this drug (which is on the WADA banned substance list)? Explain why or why not, in a way that is logical.
- You have been hired by the IOC to review and evaluate its current anti-doping approach and suggest alternatives, if appropriate. They have hired you because the current approach has not been well accepted or fully trusted by athletes around the world. Summarize the main points in your review and evaluation, and your suggestions, if any.

references

Atkinson, Michael & Kevin Young. 2008. *Deviance and social control in sport.* Champaign, IL: Human Kinetics.

Atry, Ashka, Mats G. Hansson & Ulrik Kihlbom. 2013. Cheating is the name of the game–conventional cheating arguments fail to articulate moral responses to doping. *Physical Culture and Sport. Studies and Research* 59: 21–32.

Aubel, Olivier, Lefèvre, Brice, Le Goff, Jean-Marie, Taverna, Natascia. 2019. The team effect on doping in professional male road cycling (2005–2016). *Scandinavian Journal of Medicine and Science in Sports* 29(4): 615–622.

Beamish, Rob. 2011. *Steroids: A new look at performance-enhancing drugs.* Santa Barbara, CA: Praeger.

Bensinger, Ken. 2018. *Red card: How the US blew the whistle on the world's biggest sports scandal.* New York NY: Simon & Schuster.

Berger, Jody. 2002. Pain game. *Rocky Mountain News* (February 23): 6S.

Blades, Nicole. 2005. Lucia Rijker. *ESPN, The Magazine* 8.11 (June 6): 96–97.

Blake, Heidi & Jonathan Calvert. 2015. *The ugly game: The corruption of FIFA and the Qatari plot to buy the World Cup.* New York NY: Scribner.

Bloodworth, Andrew, Mike McNamee & Jacinta Tan. 2017. Autonomy, eating disorders and elite gymnastics: Ethical and conceptual issues. *Sport, Education and Society* 22(8): 878–889.

Brackenridge, Celia & Kari Fasting. 2009. The grooming process in sport: Case studies of sexual harassment and abuse. In H. Humana (ed) *KINE 1000 Socio-Cultural Perspectives in Kinesiology*. Toronto: McGraw-Hill Ryerson Limited.

Brackenridge, Celia, D. Bishopp, S. Moussali & J. Tapp. 2008. The characteristics of sexual abuse in sport: A multidimensional scaling analysis of events described in media reports. *International Journal of Sport and Exercise Psychology* 16(4): 385–406.

Brackenridge, Celia, Kari Fasting, S. Kirby & Trisha Leahy, S. Parent & T. Svela Sand. 2010. *The place of sport in the UN Study on Violence against Children*. Florence, Italy: UNICEF Innocenti Research Centre, IRC Stock No. 595U, Innocenti Discussion Papers, IDP 2010-01.

Brackenridge, Celia, Kari Fasting, S. Kirby & Trisha Leahy. 2010. *Protecting Children from Violence in Sport: A review with a focus on industrialized countries*. Florence: United Nations Innocenti Research Centre Review.

Brennan, Christine. 2012.. Think Olympics are big now? Just wait. *USA Today* (September 14): http://www.usatoday.com/sports/olympics/story/2012/09/14/think-olympics-are-big-now-just-wait/57778012/1

Brissonneau, Christophe & Fabien Ohl. 2010. The genesis and effect of French anti-doping policies in cycling. *International Journal of Sport Policy* 2:173–187.

Brissonneau, Christophe & Jeffrey Montez de Oca. 2018a. *Doping in elite Sports: Voices of French sportspeople and Their doctors, 1950-2010*. New York/London: Routledge.

Brissonneau, Christophe & Jeffrey Montez de Oca. 2018b. The process of becoming a doper. *Engaging Sports* (January 18): https://thesocietypages.org/engagingsports/2018/01/18/the-process-of-becoming-a-doper/

Carmichael, Fiona, Giambattista Rossi & Denis Thomas. 2017. Production, efficiency, and corruption in Italian Serie A football. *Journal of Sports Economics* 18(1): 34–57.

Clifford, Stephanie, and Matt Apuzzo. 2015. After indicting 14 soccer officials, US vows to end graft in FIFA. *New York Times* (May 27): http://www.nytimes.com/2015/05/28/sports/soccer/fifa-officials-arrested-on-corruption-charges-blatter-isnt-among-them.html

Coakley, Jay. 2015. Drug use and deviant overconformity in sport: a sociological approach. In John Hoberman, Ivan Waddington & Verner Møller, (Eds.) *The Routledge handbook of drugs and sport* (pp. 379–392). London and New York: Routledge.

Coakley, Jay. 2020. The social construction of human enhancement: Implications for sports. In Katinka van de Ven, Kyle J. D. Mulrooney & Jim McVeigh, eds. *Human enhancement drugs* (pp. 40–53). London/New York: Routledge.

Coker-Cranney, Ashley, Jack C. Watson, Malayna Bernstein, Dana K. Volker & Jay Coakley. 2018. How far is too far? Understanding identity and overconformity in collegiate wrestlers. *Qualitative Research in Sport, Exercise and Health* 10(1): 92–116.

Doidge, Mark. 2018. "Either everyone was guilty or everyone was innocent": The Italian Power elite, neopatrimonialism, and the importance of social relations. *Journal of Sport and Social Issues* 42(2): 115–131.

Donnelly, Michele K. 2014. Drinking with the derby girls: Exploring the hidden ethnography in research of women's flat track roller derby. *International Review for the Sociology of Sport* 49(3–4): 346–366.

Donnelly, Peter & Kerr, Gretchen. 2018. *Revising Canada's policies on harassment and abuse in Sport: A position paper and recommendations.* Centre for Sport Policy Studies Position Papers. Toronto: Centre for Sport Policy Studies, Faculty of Kinesiology and Physical Education, University of Toronto.

Dunning, Eric. 1999. *Sport matters: Sociological studies of sport, violence and civilization*. London: Routledge.

Eden, Scott. 2019. The history if fixing isn't history. *ESPN Magazine* (March 4): 4.

Editorial. 2017. Sports hazing and bullying in high school is getting worse and demands action. *Dallas Morning News* (November 22): https://www.dallasnews.com/opinion/editorials/2017/11/21/sports-hazing-bullying-high-school-getting-worse-demands-action

Editors. 2018. Other views: The sordid truth about hazing. *The Washington Post* (November 11): http://www.timesonline.com/opinion/20181111/other-views-sordid-truth-about-hazing

Eiserer, Tanya. 2018. Hazing is a crime. Why aren't high schools doing more to stop it? *WFFA.com* (May 16): https://www.wfaa.com/article/news/local/investigates/hazing-is-a-crime-why-arent-high-schools-doing-more-to-stop-it/287-552762458

Elias, Norbert. 1986. An essay on sport and violence. Pp. 150–74 in N. Elias and E. Dunning (eds.), *Quest for excitement.* New York: Basil Blackwell.

Epstein, David. 2011. Sports medicine's new frontiers. *Sports Illustrated* 115 (5, August 8): 47–66.

Ewald, Keith & Robert M. Jiobu. 1985. Explaining positive deviance: Becker's model and the case of runners and bodybuilders. *Sociology of Sport Journal* 2, 2: 144–56.

Fasting, Kari, and Celia Brackenridge. 2009. Coaches, sexual harassment and education. *Sport, Education and Society* 14(1): 21–35. Online: http://bura.brunel.ac.uk/handle/2438/3207

Fasting, Kari, Celia Brackenridge & Gustav Kjølberg. 2013. Using court reports to enhance knowledge of sexual abuse in sport: A Norwegian case study. *Scandinavian Sport Studies Forum* 4(May): 49–67.

Fasting, Kari, Celia Brackenridge & Nada Knorre. 2010. Performance level and sexual harassment prevalence among female athletes in the Czech Republic. *Women in Sport and Physical Activity Journal* 19(1): 26-32. http://bura.brunel.ac.uk/handle/2438/3248 (retrieved 6/26/13)

Fogel, Bryan. 2017. *Icarus: Truth is the new banned substance.* A Netflix Film, online: https://www.netflix.com/title/80168079

Freeman, Mike. 1998. A cycle of violence, on the field and off. *New York Times,* section 8 (September 6): 1.

Fuchs, Jeremy. 2018. Fight back. *Sports Illustrated* 129(6, September 10): 68–77.

Fuchs, Julien & Yannick Le Hénaff. 2014. Alcohol consumption among women rugby players in

France: Uses of the "third half-time." *International Review for the Sociology of Sport* 49(3–4): 367–381.

George, Rachel. 2013. Snowmobile athletes defined risks. *USA Today* (January 30): 8C. Online: http://www.usatoday.com/story/sports/olympics /2013/01/29/snowmobile-athletes-x-games-caleb-moore-levi-lavallee/1875447/ (retrieved 6-21-2013)

Green, Kyle, Toben F Nelson & Douglas Hartmann. 2014. Binge drinking and sports participation in college: Patterns among athletes and former athletes. *International Review for the Sociology of Sport* 49(3–4): 417–434.

Guttmann, Allen. 2004. *Sports: The first five millennia.* Amherst: University of Massachusetts Press.

Halldorsson, Vidar, Thorolfur Thorlindsson, & Inga Dora Sigfusdottir. 2014. Adolescent sport participation and alcohol use: The importance of sport organization and the wider social context. *International Review for the Sociology of Sport* 49(3–4): 311–330.

Halsne, Chris & Chris Koeberl. 2015. Masking the pain: The trouble with Toradol in college sports.kdvr.com (May 13): https://kdvr.com/2015/05/13/masking-the-pain-toradol-in-college-sports/

Hayes, Chris. 2012. Wall Street, Penn State and institutional corruption. *MSNBC.com* (June 16): http://upwithchrishayes.msnbc.com/_news/2012/06/16/12255567-wall-street-penn-state-and-institutional-corruption (retrieved 6/26/13).

Heckert, Alex & Druann Heckert. 2002. A new typology of deviance: Integrating normative and reactivist definitions of deviance." *Deviant Behavior* 23: 449–479.

Henning, April. 2017. Challenges to promoting health for amateur athletes through anti-doping policy. *Drugs: Education, Prevention and Policy* 24(3): 306–313.

Hill, Declan and Jeré Longman. 2014. Fixed matches cast shadow over World Cup. *New York Times* (May 31): http://www.nytimes.com/2014/06/01/sports/soccer/fixed-matches-cast-shadow-over-world-cup.html

Hoberman, John M. 1992. *Mortal engines: The science of performance and the dehumanization of sport.* New York: Free Press.

Hoberman, John M. 2005. *Testosterone dreams: Rejuvenation, aphrodisia, doping.* Berkeley: University of California Press.

Hruby, Patrick. 2013. Why wouldn't NBA players use PEDs? *Sports on Earth* (February 15): http://www .sportsonearth.com/article/41666640

Hruby, Patrick. 2018. 'Junction Boys syndrome': How college football fatalities became normalized. *The Guardian* (August 19): https://www.theguardian.com/sport/2018/aug/19/college-football-deaths-offseason-workouts

Hughes, David. 2013. 'Organised crime and drugs in sport': Did they teach us about that in medical school? *British Journal of Sport Medicine* 47(11): 661–662.

Jackson, Nate. 2011. No pain, no gain? Not so fast. *New York Times* (December 13): http://www .nytimes .com/2011/12/14/opinion/painkillers-for-nfl-players-not-so-fast.html

Jennings, Andrew. 1996. *The new lords of the rings.* London: Pocket Books.

Jennings, Andrew. 2006. *Foul! The secret world of FIFA–bribes, vote rigging, and ticket scandals.* New York, NY: HarperSport.

Jennings, Andrew. 2011. Investigating corruption in corporate sport: The IOC and FIFA. *International Review for the Sociology of Sport* 46: 387–398.

Jennings, Andrew. 2016. *The dirty game: Uncovering the Scandal at FIFA.* New York NY: Random House.

Jennings, Andrew., and Clare Sambrook. 2000. *The great Olympic swindle: When the world wanted its games back*. New York, NY: Simon and Shuster.

Johnson, Mark. 2012. University of Texas professor explores cultural phenomenon of doping. *VeloNews. competitor.com* (November 16): http://velonews .competitor.com/2012/11/analysis/university-of -texas-professor-explores-cultural-phenomenon-of -doping_265230

Kimes, Mina. 2018. Aly Raisman takes the floor. *ESPN Magazine,* (July 30): 36–43.

King, Samantha. 2014. Beyond the war on drugs? Notes on prescription opioids and the NFL *Journal of Sport and Social Issues* 38(2): 184–193.

King, Samantha, R. Scott Carey, Naila Jinnah, Rob Millington, Andrea Phillipson, Carolyn Prouse & Matt Ventresca. 2014. When is a drug not a drug? Troubling silences and unsettling painkillers in the National Football League. *Sociology of Sport Journal* 31(3): 249–266.

Klarevas, Louis. 2011. Do the wrong thing: Why Penn State failed as an institution. *Huffington Post* (November 14): http://www.huffingtonpost.com/louis-klarevas/penn-state-scandal_b_1087603.html

Kotler, Steven & Jamie Wheal. 2018. *Stealing fire: How Silicon Valley, the Navy SEALs, and maverick scientists are revolutionizing the way we live and work*. New York NY: HarperCollins/Dey Street Books.

Longman, Jeré. 1996. Slow down, speed up. *New York Times* (May 1): B11.

Maese, Rick, 2017. NFL abuse of painkillers and other drugs described in court filings. *Washington Post* (March 9): https://www.washingtonpost.com/sports/redskins/nfl-abuse-of-painkillers-and-other-drugs-described-in-court-filings/2017/03/09/be1a71d8-035a-11e7-ad5b-d22680e18d10_story.html

Maese, Rick. 2018. Games within games. *Washington Post* (October 1): https://www.washingtonpost.com/graphics/2018/sports/gambling-fan-experience/

Mason, Bryan C., & Mark E. Lavallee. 2012. Emerging supplements in sports. *Sports Health: A Multidisciplinary Approach* 49(2):142–146.

McCarthy, Claudine. 2012. Law firm report finds institutional failures that led to Penn State scandal. *College Athletics and the Law* (September 14): http://www.collegeathleticslaw.com/sample-articles/law-firm-report-finds-institutional-failures-that-led-to-penn-state-scandal.aspx (retrieved 6/26/13)

Miller, Stephen A. 2012. The NCAA Needs to *Let Someone Else Enforce Its Rules. The Atlantic* (October 23): http://www.theatlantic.com/entertainment/archive/2012/10/the-ncaa-needs-to-let-someone-else-enforce-its-rules/264012/ (retrieved 6/26/13)

Møller, Verner, Ivan Waddington & John Hoberman, eds., 2015. *Routledge Handbook of Drugs and Sports*. London: Routledge.

Mooney, Chris. 2003. Teen herbicide. *Mother Jones* (May-June): 18–22.

Morse, Dan & Donna St. George. 2018. 'Stop, stop, stop': Police report describes alleged sex assaults in JV football locker room. *Washington Post* (November 6): https://www.washingtonpost.com/local/public-safety/stopstop-stop-police-report-describes-alleged-sex-assaults-in-jv-football-locker-room/2018/11/06/b7cfb75c-e1de-11e8-ab2c-b31dcd53ca6b_story.html

Murray, Thomas H. 2018. How gene doping will change sports. *Daily Beast* (February 7): https://www.thedailybeast.com/how-gene-doping-will-change-sports

NFL Brief. 2012. Urlacher admits use of painkillers. *Denver Post* (January 24): 6C.

O'Brien, Rebecca Davis. 2017. Two former FIFA officials convicted of corruption. *Wall Street Journal* (December 23): A7.

Ohl, Fabien, Bertrand Fincoeur, Vanessa Lentillon-Kaestner, Jacques Defrance & Christophe Brissonneau. 2015. The socialization of young cyclists and the culture of doping. *International Review for the Sociology of Sport* 50(7): 865–882.

Pappa, Evdokia & Eileen Kennedy. 2013. 'It was my thought . . . he made it a reality': Normalization and responsibility in athletes' accounts of performance-enhancing drug use. *International Review for the Sociology of Sport* 48(3): 277–294.

Petrózi, Andrea. 2007. Attitudes and doping: A structural equation analysis of the relationship between athletes' attitudes, sport orientation and doping behavior. *Substance Abuse Treatment, Prevention, and Policy* 2: 34.

Pitsch, Werner & Eike Emrich. 2012. The frequency of doping in elite sport: Results of a replication study. *International Review for the Sociology of Sport* 47(5): 559–580.

Platts, Chris & Andy Smith. 2016. Health, well-being and the `logic' of elite youth sports work. In Ken Green & Andy Smith, eds., *Routledge handbook of youth sport* (pp. 492–504). London/New York: Routledge.

Player X (Anonymous). 2009. Will a player die on the field one day? It's certainly possible. *ESPN The Magazine* 12.21 (October 19): 21.

Powell, Michael. 2019. The most honest man in college basketball is going to prison. *New York Times* (May 3): https://www.nytimes.com/2019/05/03/sports/college-basketball-trial.html

Panja. Tariq. 2019. Russia banned from Olympics and global sports for 4 years over doping. *New York Times* (December 9): https://www.nytimes.com/2019/12/09/sports/russia-doping-ban.html

ProCon. 2016. Historical timeline: History of performance enhancing drugs in sports. Retrieved from: https://sportsanddrugs.procon.org/view.timeline.php

Robinson, Joshua. 2013. Probe targets global match-fixing in soccer. *Wall Street Journal* (February 4): https://www.wsj.com/articles/SB10001424127887324445904578283501495637648

Robinson, Joshua & Matthew Futterman. 2017. FIFA releases secret report. *Wall Street Journal* (June 28): A14.

Scheinin, Richard. 1994. *Field of screams: The dark underside of America's national pastime*. New York: W. W. Norton & Company.

Schrotenboer, Brent. 2013. Arrests of black NFL players point to profiling. *USA Today* (November 29): 1-2A.

Schrotenboer, Brent. 2018. Fewer NFL players being arrested. *USA Today* (October 10): 1C.

Sefiha, Ophir. 2012. Bike racing, neutralization, and the social construction of performance-enhancing drug use. *Contemporary Drug Problems* 39 (Summer): 213–245.

Simson, Viv & Andrew Jennings. 1992. *The lords of the rings: Power, money and drugs in the modern Olympics*. London: Simon and Schuster.

Smith, Charlotte. 2017. Tour du dopage: Confessions of doping professional cyclists in a modern work environment. *International Review for the Sociology of Sport* 52(1): 97–111.

Smith, Jay M. & Mary Willingham. 2015. *Cheated: The UNC scandal, the education of athletes, and the future of big-time college sports*. University of Nebraska Press.

Sugden, John & Alan Tomlinson. 2017. *Football, corruption and lies: Revisiting 'Badfellas', the book FIFA tried to ban*. London/New York: Routledge.

Thamel, Pete & Alexamder Wolff. 2013. The institution has lost control. *Sports Illustrated* (June 17): 60–69.

Tinley, Scott. 2015. *Racing the sunset How athletes survive, thrive, or fail in life after sport.* New York: Skyhorse Publishing.

Tinley, Scott. 2015. *Racing the sunset How athletes survive, thrive, or fail in life after sport.* New York: Skyhorse Publishing.

Tinley, Scott. 2019. An enduring event: 20 years of one athlete's negotiation with pain at the Ironman Triathlon World Championships. In Kevin Young, ed. *The suffering body in sport: Shifting thresholds of pain, risk and injury. Research in the Sociology of Sport, Volume 12* (pp. 55–70). Bingley UK: Emerald Publishing Limited.

Tracy, Marc & Dan Barry. 2017. The rise, then shame, of Baylor Nation. *New York Times* (March 9): https://www.nytimes.com/2017/03/09/sports/baylor-football-sexual-assault.html

Veliz, Philip & Sohaila Shakib. 2012. Interscholastic sports participation and school based delinquency: Does participation in sport foster a positive high school environment? *Sociological Spectrum: Mid-South Sociological Association* 32(6): 558–580.

Waddington, Ivan. 2015. Towards an understanding of drug use in sport.: A medical sociological perspective. In John Hoberman, Ivan Waddington & Verner Møller, (Eds.) *The*

Routledge handbook of drugs and sport (pp. 405–417). London and New York: Routledge.

WADA. 2009. *World anti-doping code.* Montreal, Quebec, Canada: World Anti-Doping Agency. http://www.wada-ama.org/en/World-Anti-Doping-Program/Sports-and-Anti-Doping-Organizations/The-Code/ (retrieved 6/26/13).

Waddington, Ivan & Andy Smith. 2009. *An introduction to drugs in sport: Addicted to winning?* London and New York: Routledge.

Waldron, Jennifer J. & C. L. Kowalski. 2009. Crossing the line: Rites of passage, team aspects, and ambiguity of hazing. *Research Quarterly for Exercise and Sport* 80: 291–302.

Waldron, Jennifer J., Quinten Lynn & Vikki Krane. 2011. Duct tape, icy hot and paddles: narratives of initiation onto US male sport teams. *Sport, education and society* 16 (1): 111–125.

Watt, J. J. 2016. "Am I Done?" *The Players' Tribune* (November 22): http://www.theplayerstribune.com/jj-watt-am-i-done/

Wertheim, L. Jon & Ken Rodriguez. 2015. Smack epidemic: How pain killers are turning young athletes into heroin addicts. *Sports Illustrated* 122 (25, June 22): 66–71.

West, Brad. 2003. "Synergies in deviance: Revisiting the positive deviance debate." *Electronic Journal of Sociology* 7, 4 Online: www.sociology.org/content/vol7.4/west.html

White, Paul. 2012. Cortisone: Is it worth the shot? *USA Today* (October 9): 1–2C. Online: http://www.usatoday.com/story/sports/mlb/2012/10/08/mlb-cortisone-shots/1621781/

Wiederer, Dan. 2012. NFL and pain: League zeros in on one pain medication. *Minneapolis Star Tribune* (August 22): http://www.startribune.com/sports/vikings/166712256.html

Williams, Chelsea. 2018. Testimony in Lansing, Michigan. In our own words (January 17): online, https://inourownwords.us/2018/08/08/chelsea-williams/

Wixon, Matt & Greg Riddle. 2017. Special report: How culture of hazing, bullying in high school sports is only getting worse. *Dallas Morning News* (November 16): https://sportsday.dallasnews.com/high-school/high-schools/2017/11/16/special-report-culture-hazing-bullying-high-school-sports-getting-worse

Young, Kevin. 2019. *Sport, violence and society* (2nd edition). London and New York: Routledge.

Zhou, Jin, Kerry S O'Brien & Derek Heim. 2014. Alcohol consumption in sportspeople: The role of social cohesion, identity and happiness. *International Review for the Sociology of Sport* 49(3–4): 278–293.

Zirin, Dave. 2013. The ring and the rings: Vladimir Putin's mafia Olympics. *The Nation* (June 16): http://www.thenation.com/article/ring-and-rings-vladimir-putins-mafia-olympics/

(*Source:* Rob Carr/Staff/Getty Images)

chapter

6

VIOLENCE IN SPORTS

Who Suffers the Consequences

I DON'T WANT TO SOUND LIKE I'm bragging, because I'm not, but back [in the 1960s, when I played basketball] the violence was much more intense.

—Satch Sanders, former NBA player, 1999

IT'S THE MOST PERFECT feeling in the world to know you've hit a guy just right, that you've maximized the physical pain he can feel. . . . You feel the life just go out of him. You've taken all this man's energy and just dominated him.

—Michael Strahan, former NFL player (Layden, 2007)

If you're football, hockey or soccer the insurance business doesn't want you.

—Alex Fairly, CEO of the Fairly Group, a risk consulting firm (in Fainaru & Fainaru-Wada, 2019

We have to make sure we're not creating another Rome where there are gladiators dying on the field depending on whether Caesar gives a thumbs-up or thumbs-down.

—Tim Ridder, former college football player (Kelly, 2011)

Chapter Outline

Learning Objectives

- Define violence and distinguish it from related actions such as aggression and intimidation.
- Discuss historical trends for on-the-field and spectator violence.
- Explain the differences between the four major types of on-the-field violence in sports.
- Know the connections between violence in sports and deviant overconformity, commercialization, masculinity, and competition strategies.
- Understand when and how athletes learn to use violence as a strategy in sports.
- Describe the consequences of violence for athletes and understand the implications of brain trauma for athletes and for sports.
- Know the conditions under which athletes may learn to control their violent actions off the field and when their sport experiences may contribute to off-the-field violence, such as assault and sexual assault.
- Distinguish the various forms of spectator violence and identify the ones more common in North America than other parts of the world.
- Identify strategies that could be used to control venue and post-event violence.
- Discuss the incidence of terrorism at sport events and explain how and why terrorism influences sport events today.

Concussions and repeated head trauma experienced in football and other sports have recently been connected with serious long-term health problems such as dementia. The high school football team in Steubenville, Ohio, received national news coverage when two high-profile team members were found guilty of raping an unconscious young woman, whom they repeatedly and brutally dehumanized at parties attended by their teammates. A terrorist attack during the 2013 Boston Marathon killed three people and injured 264. And the most rapidly growing spectator sport in the United States in recent years is mixed martial arts, with its often-brutal fights staged in fenced cages.

These and many similar examples indicate that violence in sports an important topic to study and understand today. Therefore, the goal of this chapter is to use sociological research and theories to make sense of the origins and consequences of violence in sports. Chapter content focuses on six topics:

1. A practical definition of *violence*
2. A brief historical overview of violence in sports
3. The incidence and consequences of on-the-field violence
4. The relationship between on-the-field and off-the-field violence
5. Violence among sport spectators
6. The threat and incidence of terrorism at sport events

When there are research-based strategies for controlling violence, they will also be discussed.

WHAT IS VIOLENCE?

The meaning of violence is socially constructed. Definitions vary from one person and society to the next. In sociology, we try to define concepts in ways that reflect the times and places in which they will be used to identify and study particular aspects of social reality. For this reason, I use the definition developed by international experts at the World Health Organization (WHO). In their *World Report on Violence and Health,* they define violence as:

> *The intentional use of physical force or power, threatened or actual, against oneself, another person, or against a group or community, that either results in or has a high likelihood of resulting in injury, death, psychological harm, maldevelopment or deprivation* (Krug et al., 2002).

According to this definition, violence can be physical, sexual, psychological, or involve deprivation or neglect. In all cases, it consists of actions that cause or are likely to cause some form of harm to self or others, even when there is not an explicit intent to do harm. In most cases, violence involves actions taken to dominate, control, or intimidate others. When this occurs, it is connected with the dynamics of power in relationships between individuals, groups, or societies. This is why we refer to domestic violence between family members, gang violence between rival groups, and collective violence between large groups or countries seeking control over territory, material resources, or the lives of people defined as a threat.

We often think of violence as actions that are illegal or unsanctioned, but there are situations in which the use of violence is socially encouraged and approved. For instance, when violence is tied to a rejection of social norms, it is usually classified as illegal and punished. However, when violence occurs in connection with enforcing norms or protecting people and property, it often is approved and even lauded as necessary to preserve order, reaffirm social values, or achieve important goals. Therefore, violence may be tolerated or even glorified when police are perceived to be enforcing the law, when soldiers are protecting the homeland or when athletes are perceived to be pursuing victories in the name of others.

When violence occurs in connection with the widespread rejection of norms, it may be described as anarchy or lawlessness. When it occurs in connection with extreme methods of social control or extreme overconformity to norms, it may be defined as morally righteous, even when people are maimed or killed and property is destroyed.

In the case of sports, punching a referee who penalizes you is violence that involves a rejection of norms. It is defined as illegal and punished by teams and sport organizations. However, it is different when a football player delivers a punishing tackle, breaking the ribs or blowing out the knee of an opponent. Such violence helps to achieve a valued goal and is seen as acceptable, highlighted on video replays, and used by teammates and other players as a mark of one's status in football culture. Furthermore, in certain sports, an athlete's ability to do violence and endure it when perpetrated by others is used to affirm an athlete identity Sociologist Allan Johnson (2013) summarizes one of the major research findings about violence when he notes the following:

> *Violence is primarily about control. Violence works. It makes people do what they otherwise would not.*

People who enjoy playing or watching collision sports may not feel comfortable in admitting this, but the desire for control over others is a major reason for violence in sports, and it also is a reason that we don't often talk about it in explicit terms.

VIOLENCE IN SPORTS THROUGHOUT HISTORY

Violence is not new to sports (Dunning, 1999; Guttmann, 1998, 2004). Blood sports were popular among the ancient Greeks and throughout the Roman Empire. Deaths occurred regularly in connection with ritual games among the Mayans and Aztecs. Tournaments in medieval Europe were designed to train men for war and often resulted in death. Early forms of competitive sports were only loosely governed by rules, and they produced injuries and deaths at rates that would shock people today. Bearbaiting, cockfighting, dog fighting, bull fighting, and other "sporting" activities during those periods involved treatment of animals that many people today would define as criminal violenence.

Research indicates that, as part of an overall civilizing process in Europe and North America, modern sports were developed to be more rule-governed activities than the physical games in previous eras. As sports became formally organized, official rules prohibited certain forms of violence that had been common previously. Bloodshed decreased, and there was more emphasis on self-control to restrict the expression of violent impulses during competition (Dunning, 1999).

Social historians also point out that rates of violence in sports do not automatically decrease over time. In fact, as actions and emotional expressions have become more regulated and controlled in modern societies, players and spectators view "controlled" violence in sports as exciting. Furthermore, commercialization, professionalization, and globalization have given rise to forms of instrumental

(*Source:* Frederic A. Eyer)

"I want to thank my father who always said, 'Violence on the streetsis bad, but violence in sports is a natural expression of your manhood.'"

There are multiple reasons that people accept violence in sports but define it as criminal behavior off the field. Some believe that it is a natural expression of masculinity, and others believe that allowing it in sports will decrease a man's need to express violent impulses off the field. But evidence supports neither of these beliefs.

violence in many sports. This means that goal-oriented and entertainment-oriented violence have increased, at least temporarily, in many Western societies.

Sociologist Eric Dunning (1999) notes that violence remains a crucial social issue because the goal of modern sports is to create tension rather than eliminate it. Additionally, violent sports generally serve to reproduce an ideology that naturalizes the power of men over women. Overall, historical research shows that sports are given different meanings at different times and places and that we can understand violence in sports only when we analyze it in relation to the historical, social, and cultural contexts in which it occurs.

Serious sport has nothing to do with fair play. It is bound up with hatred, jealousy, boastfulness, disregard of all rules and sadistic pleasure in witnessing violence: in other words it is war minus the shooting. –Orwell, 1945

VIOLENCE ON THE FIELD

Violence in sports comes in multiple forms, and it is grounded in social and cultural factors related to the sport ethic, commercialization, ideas about masculinity, and strategies used in sports. Violence also has significant consequences for athletes and presents challenges for those who wish to control it. As we discuss these topics, it is useful to consider the different types of violence that occur in sports.

Types of Violence

The most frequently used typology of on-the-field violence among players was developed by the late Mike Smith (1983), a Canadian sociologist concerned about the consequences of hockey violence (1983; see Young, 2019). Smith identified four categories of violence in sports:

1. *Brutal body contact.* This includes actions common in certain sports and accepted by athletes as part of sport participation. Examples are collisions, hits, tackles, blocks, body checks, and other forms of forceful physical contact that can produce injuries. Most people in society define this forceful physical contact as dangerous, although they don't classify it as illegal or criminal. It may even be encouraged by coaches. For example, when asked about it, one coach explained: "We expect it, we demand it. . . . Our brand is a physical brand of football . . . you know, pound on these people until they give up" (Frontline, 2011).
2. *Borderline violence.* This includes actions that violate the rules of the game but are accepted by most players and coaches as consistent with the norms of the sport ethic and as useful competitive strategies. Examples are the "brushback" pitch in baseball, the forcefully placed elbow or knee in soccer and basketball, the strategic bump used by distance runners to put another runner off stride, the fistfight in ice hockey, and the forearm to the ribs of a quarterback in football. Although these actions are expected, they may provoke retaliation by other players. Official sanctions and fines are not usually severe for borderline violence. However, public pressure to increase the severity of sanctions has grown in recent years, and the severity of punishments has increased in some sports.
3. *Quasi-criminal violence.* This includes actions that violate the formal rules of the game, public laws, and even informal norms among players. Examples are cheap shots, late hits, sucker punches, and flagrant fouls that endanger players' bodies. Fines and suspensions are usually imposed on players who engage in this violence and most athletes condemn it as a rejection of the game norms.
4. *Criminal violence.* This includes actions that are clearly outside the law to the point that athletes condemn them and law enforcement officials prosecute them as crimes. Examples are assaults during games that appear to be premeditated and severe enough to kill or seriously maim a player. Criminal violence is relatively

rare, and when it occurs it is seldom prosecuted as a crime because sports are seen as special social contexts in which risks of physical harm are voluntarily accepted by athletes.

Sociologist Kevin Young (2019) has noted that this classification of sport violence is useful but that the lines separating the four types of violence shift over time as norms change in sports and societies. Furthermore, the classifications fail to address the origins of violence and the relationship of violent acts to the sport ethic, gender ideology, and the commercialization of sports. Despite these weaknesses, these four categories help us understand the distinctions that people make between various types of violence in sports.

Violence and Overconformity to the Norms of the Sport Ethic

In Pat Conroy's classic novel *The Prince of Tides* (1986), there is a scene in which a football coach in the United States addresses his team and describes the ideal football player. He uses words that many athletes in heavy-contact sports hear during their careers:

> Now a real hitter is a head-hunter who puts his head in the chest of his opponents and ain't happy if his opponent is still breathing after the play. A real hitter doesn't know what fear is except when he sees it in the eyes of a ball carrier he's about to split in half. A real hitter loves pain, loves the screaming and the sweating and the brawling and the hatred of life down in the trenches. He likes to be at the spot where the blood flows and the teeth get kicked out. That's what this sport's about, men. (p. 384)

Although coaches today dont use such vivid vocabulary athletes usually know what their coaches and teammates expect when it comes to being dedicated to the game and not letting the fear of injury reduce the physicality of their actions on the field. Even when they are concerned about the risks associated with brutal body contact and borderline violence, they generally accept and may use these forms of violence to enhance their status on a team, their identities as athletes, and their popularity among spectators. On the other hand, athletes who engage in quasi- and criminal violence are generally condemned by coaches, teammates, and spectators.

Violence involving overconformity to the norms of the sport ethic is partly related to the identity insecurities of athletes in high-performance sports. Athletes learn that "you're only as good as your last game," and they know that their identities and status as team members must be regularly reaffirmed through their actions on the field. Therefore, they often take extreme measures to prove themselves, even if it involves violence. Violence reinforces feelings of self-worth by eliciting acceptance from

(*Source:* Jay Coakley)

Violence is often connected with overconformity to the norms of the sport ethic. This high school rugby jacket presents violence as part of team culture. By associating violence with excellence, players learn what is expected on the field, even if they do not feel comfortable with brutal body contact and borderline violence.

other athletes. Willingly facing violence and playing in pain honors the importance of the game and expresses dedication to teammates and the culture of high-performance sport.

It is important to understand that such violent expressions of deviant overconformity to the norms of the sport ethic are not limited to men, even though they are more common among male than female athletes. Women also overconform to the norms of the sport ethic, and when they play contact sports, they face the challenge of drawing the line between assertive physicality and violence. For example, when sociologist Nancy Theberge (1999) spent a full season studying the experiences of women on an elite ice hockey team in Canada, she discovered that the women were drawn to the physicality of hockey, even though body checking was not allowed. As one woman said,

> I like a physical game. You get more fired up. I think when you get hit . . . like when you're fighting for a puck in the corner, when you're both fighting so you're both working hard and maybe the elbows are flying, that just makes you put more effort into it (Theberge, 1999, p. 147).

The experience of dealing with the physicality of contact sports and facing its consequences creates drama, excitement, strong emotions, and special interpersonal bonds among female athletes just as it does among males. Despite the risk and reality of pain and injuries, many women in contact sports find that the physical intensity and body contact in their sports make them feel alive and aware. Although many women are committed to controlling brutal body contact and more severe forms of violence, the love of their sport and the excitement of physicality can lead to violence on the field.

Commercialization and Violence in Sports

Some athletes in power and performance sports are paid well for their willingness and ability to do violence on the field. However, it would be inaccurate to identify money as the sole cause of violence in sports. Violent athletes in the past were paid very little, and athletes in high schools, colleges, and sport clubs today are paid nothing, yet they may engage in violence despite the pain and injuries associated with it (Van Valkenburg, 2012a).

Football players and athletes in other collision and contact sports engaged in violence on the field long before television coverage and the promise of big salaries. Players at all levels of organized football killed and maimed each other at rates that were far higher than the death and injury rates in football today. There are more injuries today because there are more players and this makes violence in certain sports a serious problem that must be addressed. But to say it is caused mainly by commercialization and money is a mistake.

This is an important point because many people who criticize sports claim that if athletes were true amateurs and played for love of the game instead of money, there would be less violence. But this conclusion contradicts research findings, and it distracts attention from the deep cultural and ideological roots of violence in particular sports and societies (Polychroniou, 2013). We could take money away from athletes tomorrow, but violence would be reduced only if there were changes in the culture in which athletes, especially male athletes, learn to value and do violence on the field.

Many people resist the notion that cultural changes are needed to control violence because it places the responsibility for change on all of us. It is easy to blame violence on wealthy and greedy team owners, athletes without moral character, and TV executives seeking higher viewer ratings, but it is more difficult to critically examine our culture and the normative and social organization of the sports that many people watch and enjoy. Similarly, it is difficult for people to critically examine the definitions of *masculinity* and the structure of gender relations that they have long accepted as part of the "natural" order of things. But such critiques are needed if we wish to understand and control violence in sports.

The point in this section is that commercialization has never been the *primary* cause of violence in sports. If violent sports are commercially successful in a community or society, it's because people want to play and watch them. For example, mixed martial arts (MMA) as represented by the UFC–Ultimate Fighting Championship–has become a rapidly growing media spectator sport in the United States because enough people are willing to participate in it and pay to watch it. UFC event tickets sell out, largely to an under-forty male crowd at an average of more than $200 per seat, and they also generate millions of dollars for pay-per-view subscriptions to events.

For some young men, MMA represents the same things that "boxing once did for their fathers and grandfathers: the ultimate measure of manhood, endurance and guts" (Quenqua, 2012). A father in New York explains that his ten-year-old son is an avid fan of UFC because the fighters "are the new superheroes for kids. It's just given them a whole new set of idols" (Quenqua, 2012). According to Joe Rogan, an MMA commentator, the UFC has become popular because people "enjoy violence, especially when it's in a controlled environment" (Bearak, 2011).

Similarly, violent images and words are often used to promote sport events because many marketing people believe that spectators are drawn to events involving violence–or at least the anticipation of it. This also is why some athletes create personas around narratives stressing their willingness to engage in brutal body contact and borderline violence. They want to attract fans who look up to athletes willing to put their bodies on the line for the sake of winning bouts, matches, or games.

Finally, for many athletes in heavy-contact sports, their participation involves a complex and intense mixture of passion, pleasure, violence, anxiety, fear, and pain that creates unique experiences for them. This intoxicating mixture of contradictory emotions is linked to the desire to dominate and control others and disrupt an opponent's desire to do the same (Pringle, 2009). Additionally, the process of doing and enduring violence for the sake of the game creates special bonds of mutual respect between athletes. These bonds anchor and reaffirm their identities and infuse special meaning into their lives.

The dynamics through which this occurs are difficult for athletes to explain and certainly difficult for "outsiders" to understand. For this reason, many athletes who play sports that are inherently violent say little about what they feel and why they enjoy what they do. They don't expect others to understand, because those of us outside this unique social world live mundane lives that don't involve the rush of pushing the envelope and living on the edge with peers who are the best at what they do.

To say that commercialization motivates violence among athletes is less accurate than to say that commercialization enables people–mostly men–to play sports in which these experiences are available. Of course, being paid to play a violent sport is not irrelevant, but money is seldom the primary factor that drives the participation of these athletes. For many of them, it may be the anticipation of violence that gives their lives significance.

Gender Ideology and Violence in Sports

Violence in sports is not limited to men. However, research indicates that if we want to understand violence in sports, we must understand gender ideology and issues of masculinity in culture. Sociologist Mike Messner explains:

> Young males come to sport with identities that lead them to define their athletic experience differently than females do. Despite the fact that few males truly enjoy hitting and being hit, and that one has to be socialized into participating in much of the violence commonplace in sport, males often view aggression, within the rule-bound structure of sport, as legitimate and "natural." (1992, p. 67)

In many societies, participation in power and performance sports has become an important way to prove masculinity. Boys discover that if they play these sports and others see them as being able to do violence, they can avoid social labels such as *pussy, girl, fag, wimp,* and *sissy*. This learning begins in youth sports, and by the time young men have become immersed in the social world of most power and performance sports, they accept brutal body contact and borderline violence as part of the game as it is played by "real" men.

(*Source:* Jeff Bottari/Zuffa LLC/Contributor/Getty Images)

Women's participation in Mixed Martial Arts cage fighting indicates that there is nothing in the genetic make-up of women that precludes participation in sports violence. However, women do not use their ability to do violence as a reaffirmation of their femininity or womanhood.

When women do violence in sports, it may be also seen as a sign of commitment or skill, but it is not seen as proof of femininity (Knapp, 2014; McCree, 2011; Young, 2019). Dominant gender ideology in many cultures links manhood with the ability to do violence, but there is no similar link between womanhood and violence. Therefore, female athletes who engage in violence do not receive the same support and rewards that men receive–unless they wrestle in the WWE, fight in mixed martial arts, or skate on a roller derby team where the sport personas of female athletes are constructed, in part, to shock or titillate spectators (Berra, 2005; Blumenthal, 2004). Boxing and mixed martial arts have recently provided a few female athletes with contexts in which they are rewarded for doing violence, but most women fighters do not feel that doing violence in their sport makes them more of a woman than females who are not fighters.

Despite the recent publicity given to a few women fighters, violent sports are viewed by many people as support for their belief that hierarchical distinctions between men and women are grounded in nature and cannot be altered (Fogel, 2011). Power and performance sports emphasize sex *difference* in terms of physical strength, *control* through domination, and *status* as a reward for physical conquests. The gender ideology formed around these ideas and beliefs has been central in many cultures. The stakes associated with preserving this ideology are so high that male boxers are paid millions of dollars for three to thirty-six minutes of brutalizing one another in the ring. Heavyweight boxers are among the highest-paid athletes in the world because they promote the idea two men facing each other in a violent confrontation is "nature in action," even though the combatants often lose millions of brain cells as they "prove" male superiority.

The irony in this approach is that, if a gender hierarchy were truly fixed in nature, there would be no need for sports to reaffirm "natural" differences between men and women. Gender would simply exist without spending so much time and effort teaching girls and boys how they should perform it. Power and performance sports are used as valuable aids in this teaching and learning process, and the men who play them serve as models of manhood in many countries.

When women participate in violent sports they disrupt the "logic" used to reaffirm traditional beliefs about gender. This leads some people to argue that women should not participate in these sports, and to treat the women who do as jokes, oddities, or freaks of nature.

The participation of women in violent sports often creates a dilemma for those of us who advocate progressive changes in gender ideology. Although participation contradicts the ideological belief that women are frail and vulnerable, it also reaffirms beliefs that have traditionally disadvantaged women through history. For this reason, some of us who support gender equity in sports hesitate to encourage girls and women to participate in violent sports.

The Institutionalization of Violence in Sports

Certain forms of violence are built into the culture and structure of particular sports. Athletes in these sports learn to use violence as a strategy, even though it may cause them pain and injury. Controlling institutionalized violence is difficult because it requires changing the culture and structure of particular sports–something that most people in governing bodies are hesitant to do.

Learning to Use Violence as a Strategy in Men's Contact Sports Athletes in heavy-contact sports often learn to use intimidation, aggression, and violence as strategies to achieve competitive success (Young, 2019). They routinely disapprove of quasi-criminal and criminal violence, but accept brutal body contact and borderline violence as long as it occurs within the rules of the game. They may not intend to hurt anyone, but this does not prevent them putting their bodies and the bodies of opponents in harm's way.

In boxing, football, ice hockey, rugby, and other heavy-contact sports, athletes also use their willingness to engage in violence to promote their careers, increase drama for spectators, and enhance publicity for themselves along with their sports and sponsors. Violence is also incorporated into game strategies when coaches use players as designated agents of intimidation and violence for their teams. These players are called "enforcers," "goons," and "hit men," and they are expected to protect teammates and strategically assist their teams by intimidating, provoking, fighting with, or injuring opponents. Their violent acts have been an accepted part of certain sports, especially ice hockey, but some athletes are beginning to challenge this aspect of sport culture because it may cause head trauma that could lead to CTE (chronic traumatic encephalitis) at a relatively young age.

Learning to Use Violence as a Strategy in Women's Contact Sports Information on violence among girls and women in contact sports remains scarce even though more women are participating in them (Young 2019). Participation in collision and heavy-contact sports creates the possibility for violence among female athletes, but few studies explore when and why it occurs.

Women's sports increasingly emphasize power and performance, and they have higher stakes associated with success. As women become increasingly immersed in the social world of elite power and performance sports, they become more tolerant of rule violations and aggressive actions on the playing field, but this pattern is less clear among women than it is among men.

As women compete at higher levels, they often become similar to men in how they embrace the sport ethic and use it to frame their identities as athletes. Like men, they are willing to dedicate themselves to the game, take risks, make sacrifices, pay the price, continue playing despite pain and injury, and overcome barriers in pursuit of their dreams. However, it is rare for them to link toughness, physicality, and aggression to what it means to be a woman in society. Similarly, coaches don't try to motivate female athletes by urging them to "go out and prove who the better woman is" on the field, even though they might urge women to play assertively. Therefore, at this time, women's contact sports are less violent than men's contact sports.

Consequences of Violence on the Field

Spectators often think about violence in sports in a paradoxical way: They accept brutal body contact and borderline violence, but the injuries caused by violence make them uneasy. They want violence without consequences–like the fictionalized violence they see in the media and video games in which characters engage in brutality without being seriously or permanently injured. However, sports violence is real, and it causes real pain, injury, disability, and death, although these negative consequences are usually hidden from spectators.

Research on pain and injury among athletes helps us understand that violence in sports has real consequences (Young, 2019). Rates of disabling injuries vary by sport, but they are high enough in many sports to constitute a public health issue. The "normal" brutal body contact and borderline violence in contact and collision sports regularly cause arthritis, concussions, brain trauma, bone fractures, torn ligaments, and other injuries many of which cause permanent damage that requires future medical attention because they affect health and well-being. In other words, the violence inherent in these sports takes a definite toll on athletes.

Concussions, Head Hits, and Brain Injuries Recent discussions of the consequences of violence on the field have focused primarily on football, although there also are concerns about ice hockey, soccer, lacrosse, boxing, and mixed martial arts. Most discussions have been in response to research showing a relationship between head trauma–including concussions and repetitive sub-concussive hits to the head–and the development of chronic traumatic encephalopathy (CTE) and other forms of brain damage (Fainaru-Wadaand and Fainaru, 2017; Goldman, 2018; Gordon, 2018; Tagge et al. 2018).

CTE is a neurodegenerative disease similar to early-onset dementia. Symptoms include cognitive impairment related to memory, reasoning, language and communication, problem solving, emotional control, and the ability to focus and pay attention. Evidence of CTE has been found in football players from high school through retired professional players as well as boxers, hockey players, and professional soccer players. Current studies are investigating the incidence and consequences of concussions in youth sports and football at all levels of participation (Armour, 2018; Gordon, 2018; Nowinski, 2014).

Although the brain is complex and there is much more to learn about head trauma and brain injury in sports, it is clear that the head hits that occur regularly in football can cause brain damage. This scientific fact has the potential to dramatically alter the sports landscape in the United States. Consequently, researchers are now investigating techniques for identifying brain damage among current athletes, the conditions under which damage is most likely to occur, who is the most susceptible to damage, the ways that damage can be minimized in various sports, and the best treatments for damage from past head trauma.

In the meantime, about 5000 former NFL players and family members sued the NFL in 2012 for failing to inform them of what the league knew about concussions and their impact on players' health (Fainaru-Wada and Fainaru, 2013; Frontline, 2013; Kenny, 2012). The NFL settled out of court with the plaintiffs in late-2013, agreeing to pay $765 million, an amount that will increase to an estimate $2 billion as additional claims are approved. In the agreement, the NFL admitted to no liability for players' problems and the league was allowed to keep secret all its research evidence on concussions. The National Hockey League (NHL) tried to avoid a similar settlement by offering 318 former players a $19 million settlement in late 2018, but many players, who suspect they suffer from CTE, chose to sue the NHL as individuals rather than joining a class action suit. League representatives have long insisted that there is no causal connection between CTE and the repeated head hits suffered during years of on-ice fighting and body checks–penalized and not penalized (Editor, 2019). But there is mounting evidence that brain damage has and continues to occur.

Between 2013 and 2020 over 100 lawsuits have been filed against the NCAA by individuals and groups of current and former college athletes seeking damages for brain injuries they attribute to head trauma experienced while playing college football and other sports. These suits claim that the NCAA failed to do one or more of the following: (1) recognize the problem and take actions that protected athletes from head trauma, (2) teach proper tackling techniques to avoid head trauma, (3) implement system-wide procedures for dealing with concussions on the field, and (4) educate "student-athletes" about head trauma and concussion issues.These legal issues are complex, and the NCAA has already paid out millions of dollars in out-of-court settlements.

Most important for the future of football is the fact that parents are increasingly concerned about the safety of their children. These concerns are associated with a significant recent decline in football participation among young people (San Francisco Chronicle, 2018; Solomon & Farrey, 2018b).

At the same time, school districts, college football conferences and athletic departments, and other sport organizations that sponsor football teams and programs are facing a major crisis as nearly all insurance companies are refusing to cover damages related to head injuries in collision sports. The risk analysts at the insurance companies have studied the research on these injuries and decided that the findings are valid and reliable. Therefore, the companies refuse to accept liability for future claims. As one insurance company executive stated, "If you're football, hockey or soccer, the insurance business doesn't want you" (Fainaru & Fainaru-Wada, 2019). At the same time, executives from sports organizations claim that organized sports cannot exist unless they have insurance protecting them from personal and organizational liability. More than any issue today, this could change the way sports are played in the United States initially, and then worldwide.

Growing awareness of research findings that identify the consequences of violence in sports has led the US Congress, about half of all state legislatures, and many sport organizations to develop regulations and protocols to protect young people who play sports–especially those in which there is a possibility for sustaining concussions and regular head trauma. These consist of rules about reporting concussions, dealing with them during events, and treating athletes who have experienced concussions.

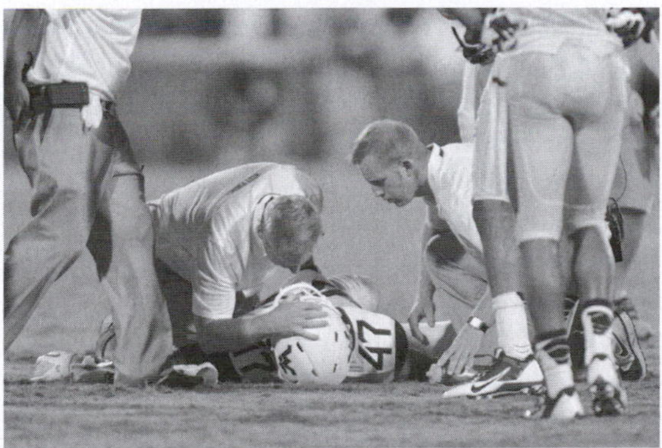

(*Source:* Jackson Laizure/Contributor/Getty Images)

Concussions receive publicity related to brain trauma in football. But emerging evidence suggests that repetitive subconcussive head hits are the most dangerous part of the game as it impacts brain health. Insurance companies know this and are withdrawing their coverage of brain damage in their policies with football programs at all age levels.

These rules and guidelines are certainly needed, but they are useful only if parents, coaches, and people in sport management know about and understand them and if concussions are either reported by players or diagnosed by qualified medical personnel (Kim et al., 2018; Sarmiento et al., 2019). However, parents and coaches often do not know about them or understand why they exist, and many athletes, especially males in power-and-performance sports, continue to take pride in not disclosing such injuries or they fear that if they do report them they won't be allowed to play a sport that is important to them (Dean, 2019).

At present it is difficult to accurately identify concussions on the sidelines. Youth, high school, and many college teams don't have the resources to hire neurologists with the training to do so. Sideline concussion tests are useful, although their reliability depends on the qualifications of those administering them and the cooperation of the athletes taking them. Additionally, there is no practical method for recognizing subconcussive head hits that over time may be causing more brain damage in some athletes than multiple concussions. If football players wore high tech helmets that recorded those hits, they would cost so much that only the NFL could afford them, and they may be afraid of what the data would indicate.

Research is under way to improve helmets used in certain sports and to develop other protective technologies. But the brain is difficult to protect whenever there is a forceful impact to or a violent twisting or snapping of the head. The brain is surrounded by fluid that prevents it from routinely coming into contact with the inside of the skull. Existing protective equipment may minimize damage to the skull in the case of a violent impact, but it cannot prevent the brain from slamming into the skull or rotating forcefully enough to damage brain cells. This is why some people argue that the brain cannot be protected and that new technologies give athletes the false impression that they can sustain violent impact to their heads without suffering negative health consequences. Until there is a technology that prevents the brain from moving inside the skull, using helmets to protect the outside of the skull will not prevent brain damage.

Controlling Violence on the Field

The roots of violence on the playing field are deep. They're grounded in overconformity to the sport ethic, commercialization, definitions of masculinity, and competition strategies.

Brutal body contact is the most difficult type of violence to control. It is grounded in the culture of power and performance sports and dominant gender ideology in a society. Unfortunately, about 90 percent of the serious injuries in these sports occur *within the rules* of the games and contests. This means that many men inevitably pay the price for their destructive definitions of *sports* and *masculinity.*

Efforts to control brutal body contact require changes in gender ideology and the cultures of certain sports. These changes won't occur without persistent and thoughtful strategies to document the dangers of the actions and the language that people use to reproduce violent sport cultures and the gender ideology that supports them. People should also calculate the cost of injuries due to brutal body contact and other types of violence in terms of medical expenses, lost work time and wages, school days missed, disability payments, family problems, and even reductions in life expectancy. Looking at these statistics will help us understand more fully the connections between sport participation and health.

The recent publicity about concussions and other serious physical and health problems experienced by athletes who play violent sports has initiated a number of moves to control violence on the field and its consequences. Representatives of football, hockey, boxing, and other sports now stress rule changes and tactics to promote safety rather than violence. Media commentators, players, and sport administrators think twice before using words and images that glorify violence on the field. They understand that the commercial success of particular sports is endangered if parents don't encourage children to play them or if young people decide that playing them is not worth the risk of serious injuries. At the state and community levels in the United States there are legislators seeking to ban tackle football for children under 13 years old and to ban heading the ball in soccer for players under 15 years old. Similar legislation is being considered in other countries.

Efforts to change contact sports to minimize violence have elicted strong responses from men who don't want to see collision sports "go soft." At the same time, the NFL has recently spent millions of dollars on commercial messages about their attempts to make football safer for players at all levels of competition (Montez de Oca et al., 2016). However, as with other sport organizations, it is difficult to determine whether these messages represent effective changes in their sports or if they are mostly public relations hype.

Rule changes can be helpful, but there is no way to reduce the violence in certain sports without making major structural changes in how the sports are played. For example, a sport like ice hockey can reduce hits to the head with rule changes, and youth programs can eliminate body checking altogether, but football presents a different set of challenges. Players cannot avoid head impacts as the game is now played. Head hits will occur regardless of advice on how to block, tackle or strengthen the neck to serve as a shock absorber.

Furthermore, people associated with football realize that the vitality and commercial success of their sport depends on recruiting boys and young men onto youth and school teams. If parents don't think the game is safe, they will encourage their children to engage in alternative sports. As with any sport, an inability to attract young people leads to a smaller pool of talent, which usually reduces spectator interest and the vitality of the sport as a part of popular culture.

Spectators have often used violence on the field as an indicator of player commitment and dedication–a sign of their willingness to put their bodies on the line for the sake of team pride and victory. For this reason, brutal body contact and borderline violence have been used by players and perceived by spectators as necessary for achieving victories and championships.

Violence on the Sidelines
Is Violence by Coaches Acceptable?

At one point during a game in the 2019 NCAA men's college basketball tournament, Tom Izzo,the well-known coach of Michigan State University, had to be restrained by one of his players. Izzo had called a time-out and was furious with a player–a 19-year-old first-year student from Indiana. He was screaming and pointing a finger into the player's chest. Izzo turned back to the team huddle but quickly returned to berating and humiliating the 19-year old. As he lunged toward the player, a team member came between them to protect his teammate.

This violent outburst occurred in front of a nearly full stadium with millions of people watching on television. But the players on the MSU team did not appear to be shocked, as if they had seen it before and come to accept it as Izzo just doing what he does. As Etan Thomas, aformer college and NBA basketball player watched this, he was reminded of a conversation he had with friends who had played at Indiana University when legendary Bobby Knight was the coach (Thomas, 2019).

These two players talked for 2 hours about "torment they both endured: the public and private humiliations, the degrading outbursts, the verbal abuse, the physical abuse, the cursing,the yelling, the screaming, the insults, the attempt to completely break them down" (Thomas, 2019). Each of them noted that they could not tell anyone about this abuse because everyone thought that Knight, with a notable winning record, was the perfect coach. Each of them also transferred to other universities and required therapy to come to terms with how Knight had damaged them. To make matters worse, they were criticized by people they didn't know for being too soft and weak to play for Knight.

Additional stories about Knight's physical and psychological violence directed to players and similar stories about other coaches begs a question: If parents treated their children and teachers treated their students this way, what

(*Source:* Jamie Squire/Staff/Getty Images)

Is psychological violence acceptable when coaches use it as part of their leadership approach? If not, why is it so widely accepted by people who should know better?

would happen to them? In many cases, they'd be reported to child protective services and fired from their teaching jobs. So how is this not defined as unacceptable violence when coaches do it? Is being violent considered an appropriate leadership method in sports? Does this apply only to coaches with impressive winning records? Is it because coaches who use violence also tell their players how much they care for them and treat them "as if they were their children"?

Research on this topic is scarce (Parent & Fortier, 2018). Players often are confused by coaches who are violent but kind; abusive, but supportive; and mean, but nurturing. Making sense of these contradictions in a sport setting seems to be difficult, although it has been done in domestic violence shelters and the recovery programs for domestic violence victims.

What do you think? Should coaches be sanctioned for such actions?

As we learn more about the damage done to the bodies and lives of athletes who engage in violence on the field, more people will raise moral questions about being entertained by actions that maim, cause lifelong chronic pain, and permanently disable the entertainers. But will people refuse to pay for tickets and media access to the point that football and other violent sports become cultural sideshows rather than part of mainstream US culture? At this point we don't know the answer to this question, but people ask it more frequently (Krattenmaker, 2013; Kroichick, 2018).

VIOLENCE OFF THE FIELD

When athletes in contact sports are arrested for violent crimes, people wonder if their violence off the field is related to the violent strategies they've learned on the field.

An NFL player raised this issue with the following comment:

> When you think about it, it is a strange thing that we do. During a game we want to kill each other. Then we're told to shake hands and drive home safely. Then a week later we try to kill each other again (Freeman, 1998, p. 1).

It is difficult to do good research on this topic. When people refer to statistical correlations that show a relationship between playing certain sports and high rates of violence off the field, it does not prove that playing violent sports causes people to be violent outside of sports. Two other issues must be considered before this conclusion can be made.

First, violent sports may attract people who already feel comfortable about doing violence on and off the field, regardless of what they may learn in their sport. *Second,* off the field violence among athletes may be due to unique situations encountered more often by athletes than other people. Athletes known for their toughness on the field may be encouraged, dared, or taunted by others to be tough on the streets. In some cases, they may be challenged to fight because of their reputations in sports. If trouble occurs and athletes are arrested for fighting in these circumstances, it is misleading to say that their actions were caused by what they learned in sports.

Control versus Carryover

Does playing sports teach people to control violent responses in the face of adversity, stress, defeat, hardship, and pain? Or does it create identities, personal orientations, and social dynamics that make violence off the field more likely?

French sociologist Loic Wacquant (1992, 1995) studied these issues for three years as he trained and gained the trust of the men who worked out at a traditional, highly structured, and reputable boxing gym in a Chicago neighborhood. During that time, he observed, interviewed, and documented the experiences and lives of more than fifty professional boxers. He not only learned the craft of boxing but also became immersed in the social world in which the boxers trained. He found that the social world encompassed by this gym was one in which the boxers learned to value their craft and dedicate themselves to the idea of being a professional boxer; they also learned to respect fellow boxers and accept the rules of sportsmanship that governed boxing as a profession. In a low-income neighborhood where poverty and hopelessness promoted intimidation and violence, these boxers accepted norms that disapproved of fighting outside the ring, they avoided street fights, and they internalized the controls necessary to follow a highly disciplined daily training schedule.

Only under very specific conditions would participation in a combat sport be associated with a reduction of off the field violence. For this to occur, participation would have to take place in a situation where there is an emphasis on self-control, respect for self and others, patience, responsibility, humility, and nonviolence away from the sport (Trulson, 1986). However, combat sports and heavy contact sports often emphasize hostility, physical domination, and a willingness to use one's body as a weapon. This is consistent with research showing that sport participation, especially for young men in contact sports, is associated with violence and fighting off the field (Beaver et al., 2016; Kreager, 2007; Wright and Fitzpatrick, 2006). Sociologist Derek Kreager analyzed data from a national sample of 6,397 seventh- to twelfth-graders and found that football players and wrestlers were over 40 percent more likely to be involved in fights than male peers who didn't play high school sports. Playing basketball and baseball were unrelated to fighting, and male tennis players had a 35 percent *lower* risk of fighting than male peers who didn't play sports. The likelihood of fighting also increased with the proportion of football players in a young man's friendship network.

In another national study, Wright and Fitzpatrick (2006) found that certain high school sports were associated with status dynamics that created or intensified ingroup versus outgroup differences among young people. Such differences may also account for more fighting.

More research is needed to understand the team cultures created in connection with particular sports, the meanings that athletes attach to their actions, and the place of violence in sport cultures more generally. Sport participation does not automatically teach people to control violence, nor does the violence used in certain sports inevitably carry over to other relationships and settings.

Sexual Violence in Sports

Between 2015 and the time I am writing this in early 2020, there have been uncounted allegations, reports, criminal charges, out of court settlements, trials, convictions, and major failures to address sexual violence and sexual assault issues in sport organizations. The cases have involved athletes, coaches, and team doctors. The victims have been child, teen, and adult athletes, and in most cases, females.

Research on the topic of sexual violence and assault has also increased during these years after nearly two decades of generally ignoring reports (Lavigne, 2018a, 2018b; Luther, 2016; McCray, 2015; Shortway, Oganesova & Vincent, 2018). In the following two sections I highlight this research and the most egregious cases.

Sexual Violence and Assault by Male Athletes Highly publicized cases in which male athletes are accused or convicted of assault, sexual assault, rape, and gang rape, create the impression that on-the-field violence influences off-the-field actions and relationships, especially relationships with women. Athletes are public figures and may be celebrities, so when they are accused and arrested, we hear and read about it multiple times. This repetition also creates the impression that male athletes are more violent and misogynist than other men.

The frequency and publicity given to sexual assault and violence by male athletes combined with the fact that the female victims of these assaults are often subject to character assassination and harassment indicates that there is a need for sport teams and organizations to directly and assertively address this issue. But there's also a need to understand the factors that influence violent off-the-field actions. Without this understanding, the preventive efforts of teams and organizations may not be effective. Obtaining valid and reliable data on sexual assault and sexual violence perpetrated by male athletes is a challenge. Efforts to collect statistics for professional and high school athletes are scarce, although there are stories and studies that have focused on specific cases. Colleges, however, have campus police and judicial affairs and Title IX offices that do collect data. The data don't account for underreporting and may not include actions that occur away from campus and local police.

The studies that have been done using the best available data consistently indicate that male college athletes are more often involved than other male students when there are reported charges of sexual misconduct, sexual assault, and sexual and domestic violence. The statistics for male athletes are similar to statistics for men in fraternities. There is some indication that this pattern prevails at colleges across all divisions and sizes, and it may also apply to men who play on all-male teams in certain intramural sports (Crosset, 1995, 1999; Luther, 2016; Shortaway, Oganesova & Vincent, 2018; Young et al., 2017).

Although each of the studies and literature reviews include factors that may explain this pattern, I feel comfortable hypothesizing that violence against women by male athletes is associated with a sport culture characterized by support for the following beliefs:

(a) that violence is an effective strategy for establishing manhood, achieving status as an athlete, and controlling women.
(b) that athletes should not be held to the same normative standards that apply to others in a community.

(c) that people outside the fraternity of elite athletes do not deserve the respect or concern that athletes reserve for each other.
(d) that most women are sexually attracted to athletes and can be sexually exploited without consequences.

Research on these factors will help us understand violence against women *in the full social and cultural contexts in which it occurs.*

The importance of being aware of the full context in which sexual assaults occur was seen in a Steubenville, Ohio, case. Two high-profile football team members were found guilty of raping an unconscious sixteen-year-old female student, whom they repeatedly and brutally dehumanized at parties with teammates in attendance. A video of young men at one of the parties contained such shocking and misogynist statements that it attracted nationwide attention and news coverage (Abad-Santos, 2013; Macur and Schweber, 2013; Murphy, 2013).

Although some people said that the culture of football was to blame, a closer look at the situation indicates that many factors were involved, including the place and meaning of high school football in Steubenville; the culture of the town itself; the prevailing local attitudes and beliefs about gender and women who are sexually assaulted; the characteristics and actions of the football coach and other school officials; the social organization of the high school; the separation between the football team and the rest of the community; the hubris, sense of privilege, and powerful group dynamics associated with the bonds between the football players; the use of alcohol by adolescents and a failure of young people at the parties to take responsibility for the safety of the young woman who had too much to drink; and the irresponsible choices of the two young men charged and found guilty in the case.

Future research may clarify the influence of these and other factors, and help to explain why none of the young people witnessing this and similar assaults was willing to step in and why men in certain all-male groups appear to lose concern and respect for women to the point of raping them and making fun of the rape. But research on male athletes should not obscure the fact that violence against women is not simply a "sport problem," that most of that violence is perpetrated by heterosexual men who do not play sports, and that our understanding of it must take into account factors in the larger culture (Crosset, 1995, 1999).

Assaults and Sexual Assaults by Coaches, Trainers, and Doctors

The focus on male athletes should not distract attention from other sport-related assault issues. For example, sexual assaults, including statutory rape, by coaches have a significant impact in sports and on people's lives (Brackenridge et al., 2008; Evans et al., 2018; Fasting et al., 2008; Moran, 2019; Reid, 2018a, 2018b).

Research by journalists at the *Seattle Times* found that 159 coaches in the state of Washington (where only 2 percent of the US population lives) were fired or reprimanded for sexual offenses between 1993 and 2003. Offenses ranged from harassment to rape, nearly all involved heterosexual male coaches victimizing girls, and about 60 percent of these coaches continued to coach or teach after the misconduct was known. Even though 159 coaches were fired or reprimanded, most reports of misconduct were neither investigated by school authorities nor reported to the police. Even when misconduct was admitted, the incidents were kept secret if the coaches agreed to leave their jobs. Sexual offenses in private sport clubs were especially problematic because clubs seldom regulate coaches' conduct, and most parents trust coaches even when evidence arouses suspicions of misconduct (Willmsen and O'Hagan, 2003).

This pattern has been repeated many times during the years after the report in the *Seattle Times*. In fact, apart from the standard male-dominated sports media, the biggest sports story in 2016–2018 was that hundreds of girls and young women were sexually assaulted over nearly 20 years by Larry Nassar, the sport medicine doctor who worked with athletes at

USA Gymnastics (USAG), the athletic department at Michigan State University (MSU), and other sport organizations (Lavigne & Murphy, 2019; Snider, 2018). This and related stories in other sports might never have been told without the persistent investigative reporting of journalists at the *Indianapolis Star* and the articles published by their colleagues at *USA Today* from early 2016 through the time I am writing this in early-2020.

It was with the support of *Indy Star* journalist Marisa Kwiatkowski that Rachael Denhollander, a former club level gymnast, came forward in 2016 and described in vivid detail how she had been sexually abused over multiple years by Nassar (Evans et al., 2018). Her disclosures led over 100 other gymnasts to come forward with their stories of how Nassar had sexually abused them under the guise of medical treatment. While this occurred over 20 years in gymnastics and the MSU athletic department, none of the leaders in those organization took reports of abuse seriously. They ignored, covered up, and filed away reports without following state law and reporting suspected abuse to the police or child protection officials in their communities.

Eventually, the heart-wrenching and tear-filled stories of women who had been exploited and abused culminated in lawsuits filed against USAG, the United States Olympic Committee (USOC), and MSU. The repercussions of over 500 reported cases of abuse by Nassar have been significant. They include the following:

- Larry Nassar was tried, convicted, and sentenced to 40–175 years in prison.
- The president of the USOC along with it's chief of sport performance and the president of USAG were fired or resigned in disgrace with possible criminal cases pending, and all members of the USAG Board of Directors were forced by the USOC to resign.
- USAG lost its corporate sponsors, was forced to declare bankruptcy and now faces a legal settlement in which it and the USOC agreed to pay up to $100 million in damages to 265 victims of the abuse they ignored.
- The MSU president was fired and charged with two felony counts, the athletic director was forced to resign, the university settled out of court with more than 300 victims for a sum of $500 million, the majority of which is scheduled to be paid by raising student fees and selling state bonds that Michigan taxpayers will eventually pay off.
- The USAG severed its relationship with the Karolyi Ranch where much of Nassar's abuse occurred. Run by Bela and Marta Karolyi, it had been the official training center for the national team, but national team athletes, including Simone Biles and others, refused to return to where they hade been assaulted.
- In 2018, the US Congress passed *The Protecting Young Athletes from Sexual Abuse and Safe Sport Authorization Act* which requires the national governing bodies (NGBs) for Olympic sports along with all amateur sports organizations to report all allegations of sex-abuse to law enforcement or child-welfare officials. It also authorized the United States Center for Safe Sport to ensure that US Olympic athletes can safely report allegations of abuse and that NGB officials follow strict standards for protecting athletes and detecting and reporting abuses (Moran, 2019).

As women came forward to report sex-abuse in gymnastics, a host of new and unresolved cases of sexual assault and abuse were also reported. The most significant involved USA Swimming "where the sexual abuse of underage swimmers by their coaches and others in positions of power within the sport was commonplace and even accepted by top officials and coaches" (Reid, 2018a). An investigation found that over the 20 year period between 1997 and 2017 at least 252 "swim coaches and officials [had] been arrested, charged by prosecutors, or disciplined by USAS for sexual abuse or misconduct against individuals under 18" (Reid,2018a). This involved at least 590 alleged victims of crimes, including statutory rape, rape, and child pornography. USAS also kept lists of dozens of coaches who had been arrested

(*Source:* Jay Coakley)

A 20-year history of ignoring reports of physical, emotional, and sexual abuse in developmental and national team programs indicate that the men in charge of the USOC are less interested in protecting athletes than in raising money and winning medals.

for abuse- related crimes but never banned them, so they now coach in other programs where parents and children do not know about their records. Additionally, some coaches banned by USAS and other NGBs have returned to coaching (PBS, 2018). During the same years that USAS was being investigated, it's executives spent nearly $80,000 to lobby against legislation that would make it easier for abuse victims to sue coaches and the sport organizations that employed them.

Additional investigations in the United States have documented or reviewed allegations of sexual abuse perpetrated by coaches and officials in NGBs including diving, taekwondo, figure skating, speed skating, weight lifting, equestrian sports, the Paralympics, and others (Reid, 2018b). Some of these remain ongoing (in 2020). Safe Sport, created in 2012, did nothing until 2016, and even then it was and remains slow to react, slow to investigate, and hesitant to impose punishments–an approach influenced by its close ties to the USOC and the reticence of the USOC and all 49 NGBs to police themselves. Additionally, the USOC has underfunded Safe Sport and presents it mostly as a brand to pacify parents so they would continue to pay for their children to participate in "USOC programs" (Moskovitz, 2018).

Sexual violence, assault, abuse, and exploitation cases are not limited to the United States. They have been and continue to be reported in other countries. They nearly always involve young female athletes whose lives and sport careers are controlled by male coaches under conditions where there is little or no transparency or accountability for their actions. The administrators in the sport organizations charged with enforcing rules and protecting athletes have generally ignored reports of athlete mistreatment, especially when violence is involved, for fear they will lose funding, sponsors, and their reputations if cases become public. For example, as the investigative reporters at the *Indianapolis Star* were uncovering and reporting Nassar's crimes at Michigan State

University, the NCAA did its own investigation and found no reason to take action. When asked about this in connection with the approaches taken by other countries to eliminate sexual abuse in sports, Celia Brackenridge, former director of the Centre for Youth Sport and Athlete Welfare in London and a highly respected expert on sexual, emotional, and physical abuse in sports, she said the following (in Sturtz, 2014):

> *I've been working on this topic since 1985, and we got through the denial in Europe, but the US is absolutely the most resistant of any country I've worked with. You are the only country without a national government agency for these children.*

She added that in some other countries, where there is less resistance to government involvement in sports, federal governments have created top-down national oversight systems to deal forcefully with these issues, and in most cases, they are at least a decade ahead of the United States in protecting young people in sports.

VIOLENCE AMONG SPECTATORS

Do sports incite violence among spectators? Or do some people use sports as sites for expressing themselves in violent ways? These are important questions because sports capture widespread public attention and spectators number in the billions. To answer these questions we must distinguish between watching sports on television and attending events in person. Further, we must study spectators in context if we wish to understand the emotional dynamics of identifying with teams and athletes, the meanings that spectators give to particular sporting events, and the varying circumstances under which people watch sports (Paradiso, 2009; Young, 2019).

Violence Among Media Viewers

Most people watch sports on television in their homes. They may express emotions and become angry at certain points, but we don't know much about when and why people express anger through violence directed at friends and family members at home. Nor do we know much about violence among people who watch televised sports in public settings such as bars, pubs, and around large video screens in public areas.

Most people who watch media sports outside the home restrict their emotional expressions to verbal comments. When they express anger, they nearly always direct it at the players, coaches, referees, or media commentators rather than fellow viewers. Even when emotional outbursts are defined as too loud or inappropriate, fellow viewers usually try to control the offender informally and peacefully. When fans from opposing teams watch an event at the same location, there often are sources of mutual identification that defuse differences and discourage physical violence, although verbal comments may become heated.

The belief that watching sports is associated with violence has led some people to wonder if watching sports–the Super Bowl, for example–is associated with temporary spikes in the rates of domestic violence in a community or the nation as a whole. To test the connection between the hours during which NFL games occurred and certain forms of criminal violence, Beth Adubato (2016) from the New York Institute of Technology worked with the Philadelphia police department and analyzed arrest records through the 2008-09 and 2009-10 NFL seasons. Her findings, based on a thorough statistical analysis, indicated that there was a significantly greater number of domestic violence arrests during the hours for which NFL games were televised than during the same hours on comparable non-sports Sundays. Domestic violence arrests were also higher on NFL game days than on game days in hockey, basketball, and baseball, including the World Series during those years. Overall, Adubato concluded that "the average football gameday is more dangerous to women–as victims of domestic violence–than the other days of the week" (p. 34).

Adubato's study was in one city and for two NFL seasons. Her findings suggest that the verbal and visual content of NFL games and the meaning they are given by some men may be a factor in some domestic violence cases. However, we need additional studies to substantiate this connection and determine its policy and policing implications. We know that the roots of domestic violence run deep, so we should not rush to judgment on NFL football broadcasts as a cause. Furthermore, we don't know enough about the ways that spectators integrate media sport content into their lives to say that watching sports does anything except provide emotionally focused social occasions.

Violence at Sport Venues

Historical Background Media reports of violent actions at sport events have increased our awareness of crowd violence. However, crowd violence is as old as spectator sports. Data documenting the actions of sport spectators through the ages are scarce, but research suggests that spectator violence occurred relatively often in the past and much of it would make crowd violence today seem rare and tame by comparison (Dunning, 1999; Guttmann, 1986, 1998; Scheinin, 1994; Young, 2019).

With the emergence of modern sports, violence among sport spectators decreased, but it remained common by today's standards. For example, a baseball game in 1900 was described by a journalist in this way:

> Thousands of gun slinging Chicago Cubs fans turned a Fourth of July doubleheader into a shoot-out at the OK Corral, endangering the lives of players and fellow spectators. Bullets sang, darted, and whizzed over players' heads as the rambunctious fans fired round after round whenever the Cubs scored against the gun-shy Philadelphia Phillies. The visiting team was so intimidated it lost both games . . . at Chicago's West Side Grounds (in Nash and Zullo, 1989, p. 133).

This newspaper account also reports that when the Cubs scored six runs in the sixth inning of the first game, guns were fired around the stadium to the point that gun smoke made it difficult to see the field. When the Cubs tied the score in the ninth inning, fans again fired guns, and hundreds of them shot holes in the roof of the grandstand, causing splinters to fly onto their heads. As the game remained tied during three extra innings, fans pounded the seats with the butts of their guns and fired in unison every time the Phillies' pitcher began his windup to throw a pitch. It rattled him so much that the Cubs scored on a wild pitch. After the score, a vocal and heavily armed Cubs fan stood up and shouted, "Load! Load at will! Fire!" Fans around the stadium emptied the rest of their ammunition in a final explosive volley.

Between 1900 and the early 1940s, crowd violence remained common: Bottles and other objects were thrown at players and umpires, and World Series games were disrupted by fans angered by umpires' calls or the actions of opposing players (Scheinin, 1994). Players feared being injured by spectators as much as they feared the "bean balls" thrown regularly at their heads by opposing pitchers.

During the 1950s and 1960s, high school basketball and football games in some US cities were sites for local youth gang wars. Gang members and a few students used chains, switchblade knives, brass knuckles, and tire irons to attack each other. During the late 1960s and early 1970s, some high school games in Chicago were closed to the public and played early on Saturday mornings because the regularly scheduled games had become occasions for crowd violence, much of it related to racial and ethnic tensions in the city.

These examples are mentioned here so we do not jump to the conclusion that violence is a bigger problem today than in the past, that coercive tactics should be used to control unruly fans, and that there is a general decline of civility among fans and in society as a whole. Some spectators are obnoxious and violent today, and they present law enforcement challenges and interfere with the enjoyment of other fans, but there is no systematic evidence that this is a problem out of control.

Violence at Sports Venues as a Social and Cultural Issue Violence that occurs in stadiums and arenas takes many forms. Spectators may verbally or physically attack opposing fans or spectators who represent an adversary outside the stadium, such as a rival gang. There may be invasions of a playing field to express outrage about a referee's decision or a play that is seen as unfair. Bigoted or racist spectators may attack members of a group they define as an enemy. Organized collections of spectators may engage in violent displays to support or oppose decisions made by team administrators, political officials, or other individuals or organizations.

Although scholars in England studied and developed theories about violence at sport events during the 1970s and 1980s, few studies have been published after 1990, and almost no systematic research has been published in the United States apart from work done by sociologist Jerry Lewis (2007). The research done in England provides valuable historical data and thoughtful analyses of the complex social processes in which particular forms of sport violence are located (Armstrong, 1998, 2007; Dunning, 1999; Dunning et al., 1988; Dunning et al., 2002; Young, 2007a, 2007b, 2019). In fact, it has been used as a guide to develop more effective policing strategies in connection with sport crowds worldwide.

For our purposes here, what we know is that sport events do not occur in social vacuums, and when tensions and conflicts are intense and widespread in a community or society, sport events may become sites for confrontations. For example, past spectator violence in the United States was grounded in racial tensions aggravated by highly publicized rivalries between high schools whose students come from different racial or ethnic backgrounds (Guttmann, 1986). In cities where housing segregation created heavily segregated schools, racial and ethnic conflicts contributed to confrontations before, during, and after games.

Research also indicates that nearly all crowd violence involves men. This suggests that ideas about manhood and the expression of masculinity influence crowd dynamics and the actions of spectators. Female fans may become involved in fights, but not nearly as often as men are. Crowd violence, therefore, is as much a gender issue as it is a racial, ethnic, or social-class issue, and controlling it effectively over the long run requires changes in gender ideology and ideas about masculinity as much as buying expensive surveillance systems and hiring additional police to patrol the sidelines at every event.

Venue Violence in North America Venue violence does occur in the United States and Canada, but not frequently enough or in patterns that constitute a significant threat to the safety and well-being of spectators. This is partly because North American sports events generally attract diversified crowds in which violent actions are voluntarily held in check most of the time for fear of injuring children or others defined as vulnerable. It also is due to the tendency among North American fans to see sport events as a realm that is separate from social and political realities outside the stadium. Finally, it is difficult for organized groups of fans sharing strong social or political attitudes to obtain unified blocks of tickets at a major event so they can express feelings through violent displays, as happens with some regularity in other parts of the world. For these reasons most spectators at North American sport venues limit their expressive actions to loud cheering, stomping feet to make noise, waving objects to show team loyalty, and verbally taunting referees, opposing players, and fans.

Of course, not all sport crowds in the North America are models of good behavior (Gallo, 2017; Wann et al., 2015; Young, 2019). Fights do occur, fans say nasty and sometimes hateful things to each other, referees, and players. Spectators have also thrown objects onto the playing surface to express their dissatisfaction with the poor play of their team or perceived bad calls by referees and umpires. But most cases of violence inside stadiums and arenas involve individuals or small groups of fans; they are not planned, politically motivated, or executed by large, organized collections of spectators with agendas unrelated to the event. Additionally, such violence would be difficult to initiate, given that spectators are closely "policed" when entering venues, making it rare for them to possess objects that could be used to destroy property or harm others.

(*Source:* Jay Coakley)

Thousands of diverse fans gathered around public video screens when the Rugby World Cup was hosted in Paris. These fans, mostly French, with large groups from England, Ireland, Australia, and New Zealand, were expressive, but violence was not observed by the author, who took this photo and talked with people in the crowd.

Venue Violence Worldwide As you know by now, making sense of what people think, do, and say requires that we understand the context in which people live and give meaning to the reality around them. Therefore, it is not surprising that people give different meanings to their identities as sport fans, the teams they support, and the purpose of attending games and matches (Wann and James, 2019). As a result, venue violence occurs in different forms and for different reasons from one country and cultural region to another (Dorsey, 2016, 2019; Kossakowski, 2017; Seabra, 2017; Wann & James, 2019; Wann et al., 2015, 2017). For example, in England during the 1970s and 1980s, young men who came from generations of loyal supporters of their local soccer clubs were alienated and angry when club administrators used new business models and made decisions that ignored the customs and preferences of fans. As they experienced high rates of unemployment and felt that the local and national governments were undermining their way of life, spectators used soccer matches as sites to express their feelings and confront opposing fans and the police in ways that they saw as reaffirming their identities as men. More recently, when so-called "hooligans" stand up against injustices and confront rival supporters, other spectators may understand their actions even though they morally object to their violence.

In a similar manner, soccer venues in parts of Europe, North Africa, Western Asia, and Latin America have become staging areas for young men to collectively express themselves, sometimes in violent and defiant ways. Their violence may express their general sense of alienation, objection to the commercialization of soccer and soccer clubs, nationalist and/or racist attitudes, special political agendas, dissatisfaction with ruling politicians–including powerful dictators, and their disdain for police that use brutality on the streets and, in many cases, enforce the interests of oppressive political regimes. Sport venues–usually soccer stadiums–for these men are places where they have more freedom and opportunities to express themselves collectively than they do on the streets (Dorsey,2016, 2017a, 2017b, 2018, 2019; Parkin, 2018; Smith, 2018). Additionally, the stadium, with the help of media coverage and the use of social media, enables them to be seen and heard so that the entire community or nation will know that they exist and are a force to be taken seriously.

It is difficult to make general descriptions or conclusions about venue violence worldwide. But web or YouTube searches for "football ultras," "ultras worldwide," "ultras-tifo," and "football pyro," will provide images of how fans express themselves around the world. In some cases you will see young men behaving badly as they engage in seriously dangerous pyro displays or express chauvinism, racism, sexism, and homophobia (Kossakowski, Antonowicz & Jakubowska, 2020). In other cases they will be standing up or chanting for justice in the face of repressive political regimes or delivering powerful political messages through card displays, chants, or orchestrated action (Doidge & Lieser, 2018). When these expressions are contrary to the social and political positions of other fans in the stadium or officials policing the events, it is difficult to avoid physical confrontations. Depending on the circumstances, these confrontations may involve or precipitate collective violence that can be deadly for people in the stadium. Examples of this have occurred recently in Serbia, Israel, Egypt, Pakistan, Russia, Turkey, and in North African countries where rebels have opposed the rule of oppressive political regimes.

Research in the sociology of sport indicates that fan cultures in certain regions are organized around nationalist affiliations and feelings, and these are regularly fused with various forms of racism, depending on which populations are perceived as threats or the cause of social and political problems. But nationalism and racism are never limited to stadium crowds alone. They are manifestations of realities in the larger community or society. Inside the stadium they become concentrated and magnified to the point that they cannot be dismissed or ignored. Of course, this is not a new phenomenon. Political leaders, patriots, sport team owners, and media commentators have used sports and sport venues to deliver political messages that support uncritical forms of nationalism capitalist expansion. As research continues, we will learn more about the complex and contentious forms of fan violence as they occur around the world.

Panics as Venue Violence By far, more people have died and been injured in panics and violent accidents than by any form of intentional spectator violence. The largest number of deaths in a sport-related panic occurred in Lima, Peru, in 1964 during an Argentina versus Peru soccer match to qualify for the 1964 Tokyo Olympic Games. When a well-known fan stormed the field to dispute a referee's call late in the game, he was beaten by police, which caused thousands to rush onto the field, with 300 to 320 people trampled to death in the process.

Similarly, a panic was incited in 2001 at a Premier League soccer match in Accra, Ghana, when police fired tear gas into an unruly crowd. Spectators rushed to exit doors, which had been locked, and 123 people were crushed to death by the force of the crowd (Langton, 2015). Most panics at sport venues follow this pattern: spectators are frightened and rush to limited or locked exits where many are trampled or crushed to death.

Whenever thousands of people gather together for an occasion intended to generate collective emotions and excitement, it's not surprising that crowd dynamics and circumstances influence their actions. This is especially true at sports events, where collective action is easily fueled by what social psychologists call *emotional contagion*–a process through which social norms are formed rapidly and are followed in a nearly spontaneous manner by large numbers of people. Although this does not always lead to violence, it increases the possibility of violent crowd movements as well as confrontations between collections of spectators and between spectators and agents of social control, such as the police. This also is a factor in post-event violence.

Remote and Post-Event Violence

In North America, the most destructive episodes of violence occur in riots after sports events or in fan gathering places outside a sport venue. This is most common at events for which the stakes are high, such as playoff and championship games. Celebratory riots occur among fans of victorious teams, whereas frustration riots occur among fans of teams suffering defeats. But both forms of riots are equally destructive to property, although loss of life is rare.

Celebratory Riots Oddly enough, some of the most dangerous and destructive crowd violence occurs during the celebrations that follow victories in important sport events (Lewis, 2007). Until recently, when middle-class, white college students in the US tore down goalposts after football victories or ransacked seats and threw seat pads and other objects onto the field, it was treated as displays of youthful exuberance and loyalty to the university. However, in the wake of injuries and mounting property damage associated with these incidents, stadium security officials now prevent fans from rushing onto the playing field when games end (Renfrow et al., 2016).

Cases of celebratory violence still occur, but new methods of social control have been reasonably successful in preventing them inside the stadium. But it is a slightly different story outside the stadium, where crowds gather in multiple locations. Local police usually anticipate celebratory crowds around a stadium, but effective control in an entire metro region depends on advance planning and having a requisite number of specially trained officers who can intervene without creating backlash in a crowd.

The use of social media by people in or around a collection of fans who engage in violence to celebrate a victory can aid in identifying and arresting perpetrators of violence, but research is needed to determine whether social media deter violence or fuel it among those who want digital evidence of their celebrations. In the meantime, some cities are using strategically placed surveillance cameras to capture images of perpetrators.

Research done by sociologist Jerry Lewis, author of the book *Sports Fan Violence in North America* (2007), indicates that most celebratory riots are associated with the following six general conditions:

- A natural urban gathering place for fans.
- The presence of a "cadre" of young, white men.
- Strong identification with the team.
- An event with high stakes such as a national or international championship.
- A key or deciding game or match in a playoff or championship series.
- A close, exciting contest.

Although there is no tested theory to explain involvement in a celebratory riot, young men might be seeking reaffirmation of their identification with a winning team and seeking status by engaging in actions that document their presence at a memorable occasion that they can discuss and brag about for the rest of their lives.

Frustration Riots Frustration riots are rare and less common than celebratory riots. Fans of teams that lose a deciding game or match in an important event are more likely to exit the scene of the loss and deal with their disappointment by themselves or with close friends. A notable exception to this pattern was a 2011 post-event riot in Vancouver, Canada, following the loss of the Vancouver Canucks to the Boston Bruins in the deciding game of the National Hockey League Stanley Cup championship series. Hundreds of young people started fires, turned over cars, and broke windows in a downtown area. Property damage was dramatic in terms of its apparent senselessness, and dozens of people were injured, primarily in confrontations with poorly prepared police officers. Unlike riots that occur in connection with political, labor, or civil rights demonstrations, this one was short-lived and people quickly exited the area as the police presence grew.

Police and political authorities initially described the rioters as thugs and professional anarchists with criminal intent, but videos showed that most of them were from local Vancouver families that strongly disapproved of their destructive actions (Mason, 2011). A classic example of this was captured in a photo of a young man trying to set fire to a rag stuffed in the fuel tank of a police car. The car did not blow up, but the young man was identified as a member of Canada's junior men's national water polo team and an academic all-star who had received an athletic scholarship to attend a US university at the end of the summer. After he turned himself in to police, he was suspended from the national team. Research on this event has not been published, but it appeared that this young man and others like him were mimicking what they perceived to be the culture of Canadian hockey as they displayed male rage, tore off their shirts, and yelled as if they were claiming domination through the destruction they caused (Zirin, 2011b).

Controlling Spectator Violence

A prerequisite for effective crowd control strategies is an awareness of factors associated with spectator violence. These include the following:

- Crowd size and the standing or seating patterns of spectators.
- Composition of the crowd in terms of age, sex, social class, and racial/ethnic mix.
- The importance and meaning of the event for spectators.
- The history of the relationship between the teams and among spectators.
- Crowd-control strategies used at the event (police, tear gas, attack dogs, surveillance cameras, or other security measures).
- Alcohol consumption by the spectators.
- Location of the event (neutral site or home site of one of the opponents).
- Spectators' reasons for attending the event and their expectations for outcomes.
- The importance of the team as a source of identity for spectators (class identity, ethnic or national identity, regional or local identity, club or gang identity).

Frederic A. Eyer

We need research on so-called celebratory riots. Research on other forms of collective action suggests that celebratory riots may not be as spontaneous and unplanned as many people think.

In other words, there is a combination of background and situational factors that influence the likelihood of spectator violence at a sports event. Over the past forty years, sociologists and law enforcement officials have done a good job of identifying those factors and developing social control strategies that take them into account. But additional things could be done. For example, we know that when spectators perceive violence on the field, they are more likely to engage in violence in the venue. Therefore, it is not wise to promote sports events as violent confrontations between hostile opponents.

Perceived hostility and violence might also be defused if players and coaches make public announcements emphasizing respect for the game and for opponents. The use of competent and professionally trained officials is also important, because when officials maintain control of a game and make calls the spectators define as fair, the likelihood of spectator violence decreases. Referees also could meet with both teams before the event and explain the need to leave hostilities in the locker rooms. Team officials could organize pregame unity rituals involving an exchange of team symbols and displays of respect between opponents. These rituals could be covered by the media so that fans could see that athletes do not view their opponents as enemies. But these strategies conflict with commercial media interests in hyping games as wars without weapons; therefore, we're faced with a choice: promote the safety of fans and players or boost media profits and gate receipts for team owners.

One of the most important preventive measures is to know and respect the needs and rights of spectators. This requires that crowd-control officials be trained to intervene in potentially disruptive situations without escalating the violence. Alcohol consumption should be regulated realistically, as done in many venues worldwide. Venues and the spaces around them should be safe and organized to enable spectators to move around while limiting contact between hostile fans of opposing teams. Exits should be accessible and clearly marked, and spectators should not be herded like animals before or after games. Encouraging attendance by families is important in lowering the incidence of violence.

Being aware of the historical, social, economic, and political issues that often underlie crowd violence is also important. Restrictive law-and-order responses to crowd violence may be temporarily effective, but they will not eliminate the underlying tensions and conflicts that often fuel violence. Policies dealing with oppressive forms of inequality, economic problems, unemployment, political marginalization, racism, bigotry, and distorted definitions of masculinity are needed. These factors often lead to tension, conflict, and violence.

When explaining a reduction of spectator violence at soccer venues in the United Kingdom, British sociologists Cleland and Cashmore (2016) report that it is due to more effective policing, improvement in stadium design, alcohol bans, the use of surveillance cameras, and increased ticket prices that limit attendance by spectators whose primary goal is to use violence to express anger and feelings of alienation. But the long term goal is to shape spectator norms and create effective and humane methods of social control.

Shaping norms can be difficult, but it's a more effective strategy than moving games to remote locations, hiring hundreds of security personnel, patrolling the stands, using surveillance cameras, scheduling games at times when crowds will be sparse, and recruiting police and soldiers to brandish automatic weapons. Of course, some of these tactics can be effective, but they should be last resorts or temporary measures used only during the time it takes to develop new spectator norms.

TERRORISM: PLANNED POLITICAL VIOLENCE AT SPORTS EVENTS

Terrorism and *terrorist* are words that create an emotional response. This is because **terrorism** *is a special form of violence designed to intimidate a target population of people for the purpose of achieving political or social goals.* It can occur anywhere, but it occurs most frequently in divided societies and situations where an oppressed population has an oppositional political agenda. In most cases, it is a strategic response to political repression and feelings of frustration, indignation, and anger (Turk, 2004).

Unlike most warfare, terrorism targets civilians to create pervasive fear in a target population. Therefore, terrorism is seldom random; it is strategically planned so that there will be maximum media coverage. The intent is that coverage will spread and sustain fear and make people feel that the very fabric of their social order is being torn apart. For example, the two terrorists directly responsible for the 2013 Boston Marathon bombings chose the event because it occurred on Patriots Day in Massachusetts and is symbolically linked with the beginning of the American Revolution and the formation of the United States. Also, the marathon is televised live and covered worldwide as a premier sports event. Therefore, news of a terrorist attack at the race would be communicated nationally and globally, and it would be linked to the very foundation of social order in the United States. The pressure cooker bombs used in Boston killed three people and injured 264, some seriously enough to require limb amputations. But the effects this terrorist act went far beyond Boston and marathons.

According to Bill Braniff, the executive director of START–the National Consortium for the Study of Terrorism and Responses to Terrorism, located at the University of Maryland–certain sports events are attractive targets for terrorism because of the following factors (Hruby, 2013c):

- The media are on location.
- The event is communal and seen as representing the values and spirit of a community or society.
- When people seek explanations for the attack, it provides the terrorists opportunity to deliver their political messages.
- The recurring media attention given to a special sports event serves as a regular reminder of the attack and perpetuates fears associated with it.

A marathon is a particularly soft target for terrorism because there is no central security checkpoint for spectators, who can access the race at many points along the 26.2-mile course. Despite this, a study done by START revealed that of the hundreds of marathons held worldwide in the twenty years preceding the 2013 Boston Marathon, only six had been sites for terrorist attacks (START, 2013). Three of these occurred in Northern Ireland (in 1998, 2003, and 2005) where political and social divisions between Protestants and Catholics have a long and violent history. But in each case, bombs were discovered and defused before they could explode.

Another "terrorist" (according to the START Report) attack occurred during a 1994 marathon in Bahrain (in the Persian Gulf) when a few runners were injured by men who allegedly objected to the proximity of the race course to the remains of a mosque and were offended by the shorts and tops worn by female runners. A terrorist attack also occurred in 2006 at a marathon in Lahore, Pakistan, where six buses were burned and four people were injured, including two police officers. The most recent terrorist incident at a marathon prior to the 2013 Boston Marathon was a 2008 suicide bomb attack in Colombo, Sri Lanka, that killed twelve runners and three spectators and injured about 100 others close to the starting line.

A suicide bomber attack in 2014 killed 57 spectators and injured over 50 others during the final minutes of a volleyball match in Eastern Afghanistan (Haidary, 2014). The victims included young men and boys along with police officers. Men's volleyball is popular with spectators in that part of the country. Finally, in late-2015 there was a failed suicide bomb attempt during a soccer game in Paris's Stade de France. When denied entry to the stadium, the three terrorists blew themselves up, but there were no other fatalities.

This record suggests that terrorists do not usually target sport events. Through the 110-year history of the Olympics there have been two terrorist attacks, one in 1972 when members of a Palestinian terrorist group called Black September entered the Olympic Village in Munich, Germany, went to rooms being occupied by Israeli athletes and coaches, shot and killed a wrestling coach and a weightlifter, and captured nine Israeli athletes. After a 21-hour standoff and a poorly planned rescue attempt, seventeen people were dead–ten Israeli athletes, one coach, one West German police officer, and five terrorists. The remaining terrorists were sought out and killed by Israeli commandos. The only other terrorist incident at the Olympics occurred at the 1996 Atlanta Games when a former US military explosives expert detonated several bombs that killed two people and injured over 100 to protest against abortion and the "global socialism" that he thought was destroying the United States.

The point of these examples is to show that terrorism has occurred at few sports events. In fact, until the 2013 Boston Marathon, the attack during the 1996 Atlanta Olympics was the only sport-related incident of terrorism in US history. But then came September 11, 2001, and the horrific attacks on the World Trade Center buildings in New York City, the Pentagon outside Washington, D.C., and a hijacked plane that ultimately crashed in Pennsylvania. Over 3000 people were killed and thousands were wounded on that day. The pervasive fear generated by 9/11 and the emerging narratives that imagined future terrorist attacks in vivid details have had a major impact on US culture and on major sport events.

When 9/11 occurred, Salt Lake City was preparing for the 2002 Winter Olympic Games. This led some people–all with different motives–to focus on the Salt Lake Games as the frontline for a possible global war on terror. Large security companies and other companies with security technologies to sell were influential in creating and promoting a new narrative of fear and the need for event organizers to provide comprehensive security no matter the cost (Giulianotti and Klauser, 2012; Hassan, 2012; McMichael, 2012; Schimmel, 2012; Sugden, 2012; Toohey and Taylor, 2012). As a result, the Salt Lake City Olympics and all subsequent Olympic Games have been assumed to be prime terrorist targets, leading organizers to spend increasing amounts of money for security. To question this assumption is nearly impossible in a climate of fear fueled in part by companies wanting to profit from the sales of high-priced security products (Graham, 2012). Most fans believe that sport venues are an inevitable target of terrorists, and they are willing to sacrifice personal privacy in order to feel safe at events (Cleland & Cashmore, 2018)

As shown in Table 6.1, security costs for the pre-9/11 Sydney Games were $180 million, or $12,500 per athlete (all data include Olympic and Paralympic athletes). But after 9/11, security costs for the much smaller winter games in Salt Lake City were $500 million, or $131,100 per athlete–a more than tenfold per athlete increase from two years earlier. This pattern has continued with Beijing spending $6.5 billion for security in 2008, or $430,000 per athlete. For London 2012, the security bill was an estimated $1.6 billion, or $114,300 per athlete.

Table 6.1 Olympic/Paralympic security costs, 2000–2020 (in US dollars)

Year	City	Security cost	Cost per athlete†
2000	Sydney	$180 million	$12,500
2002	Salt Lake City	$500 million	$131,100
2004	Athens	$1.5 billion	$103,000
2006	Turin	$1.4 billion	$350,500
2008	Beijing	$6.5 billion	$430,000
2010	Vancouver	$1.0 billion	$325,500
2012	London	$1.6 billion*	$114,300
2014	Sochi	NA	NA
2016	Brazil	$2.2 billion	195,800
2018	Pyeong-Chang	$19.6 million*	$6,640*
2020	Tokyo	NA	NA

Source: Canadian Broadcasting Company News.
*Estimates for London 2012 vary from $800 million to $1.6 billion. Pyeong-Chang ran out of money, but utilized 60,000 security forces and a host of security technologies to detect terrorist and cyber threats; the IOC also bought expensive liability and game cancellation insurance policies.
†The summer games have at least four-times more athletes than the winter games.

The cost for the 2016 Games in Rio de Janeiro was a staggering $2.2 billion, or nearly $196,000 per athlete (Zimbalist, 2017). Overall, security now constitutes about 12 to 20 percent of the total budget for the Olympics, and the worldwide security industry is now valued in the hundreds of billions of dollars.

Another factor that has boosted security expenses for the Olympics and other sports mega-events is that police and political officials in host cities use the fears of local citizens to buy and install security systems and employ a militaristic command-and-control approach to policing that most people would find unacceptable under other circumstances (McMichael, 2012; Schimmel, 2012). This supports the desire of developers and some politicians to gentrify the city, move the poor and homeless out, increase property values, and provide services for new urban elite residents seeking upscale housing, restaurants, and entertainment–all in a highly policed and secure environment. At the same time, the new narrative of fear leads people to seek security over privacy and accept a new high-tech approach to policing and social control.

Today, security strategies are part of the everyday routine at major sports venues. Spectators are scanned or searched when they enter venues, and there is strict enforcement of rules governing what may be brought into the venues. However, most security measures are discreet and take place behind the scenes in the form of bomb searches, electronic surveillance, and undercover tactics. When terrorist attacks don't occur, those who support high-tech social control say their system is working; and if a terrorist attack does occur, they argue that even more security technology is needed. In either case, those profiting from fear and uncertainty win. This, of course, makes it increasingly expensive to attend high-profile sport events at the same time that security costs are frequently paid with public money, meaning that the general population pays for the safety and comfort of those wealthy enough to buy tickets. The fear of terrorism has many consequences.

summary

DOES VIOLENCE IN SPORTS AFFECT OUR LIVES?

Violence is not new to sports. Athletes throughout history have engaged in actions and used strategies that cause or have the potential to cause injuries to themselves and others. Furthermore, spectators throughout history have regularly engaged in violent actions before, during, and after sports events. However, as people define violence in sports as controllable rather than a fact of life, they view it as a problem in need of a solution.

Violence on the field ranges from brutal body contact and borderline violence to quasi-criminal and criminal acts. It is linked with overconformity to the sport ethic, commercialization, cultural definitions of masculinity. It has become institutionalized in some sports as a strategy for competitive success, even though it causes injuries and permanent physical impairments among athletes. The use of enforcers is one example of institutionalized strategic violence in sports.

Controlling on the field violence is difficult, especially in men's contact sports, because it is often tied to players' identities as athletes and as men. Male athletes in contact sports learn to use violence and intimidation as strategic tools, but we don't know if the strategies learned in sports influence the expression of violence in relationships and situations that occur off the field.

Among males, learning to use violence as a tool within a sport is frequently tied to the reaffirmation of a form of masculinity that emphasizes a willingness to risk personal safety and intimidate others. If the boys and men who participate in certain sports learn to perceive this orientation as natural or appropriate, and receive support for it from sources inside sports and the general community, their participation in sports may contribute to violence off the field, including assault, sexual assault, and rape. However, such learning is not automatic, and men may, under certain circumstances, even learn to control anger and their expressions of violence when playing collision and contact sports.

The most important impact of violence in sports may be its reaffirmation of a gender ideology emphasizing that men are naturally superior to women. This ideology is based on the belief that an ability to do violence is an essential feature of manhood.

Female athletes in contact sports also engage in aggressive and violent acts, but little is known about the connections between these acts and the gender identities of girls and women at different levels of competition. Many women prefer an emphasis on supportive connections between teammates and opponents over an emphasis on physical domination. Therefore, aggression and violence do not occur in women's sports as often or through the same identity dynamics as they occur in men's sports.

Violence in sports has real consequences. Recent research on the incidence of brain damage caused by concussions and repetitive sub-concussive head hits has made many people aware of consequences that had been purposely hidden or had gone undiagnosed in the past. If further research indicates that permanent and severe damage can be caused by the violence inherent in certain sports, there will be significant changes in the popularity of those sports, especially football in the United States. In the meantime, violence in certain sports is connected with regular and sometimes severe injuries and long-term health problems.

The relationship between violence on the field and the actions of athletes off the field is difficult to untangle. In some cases–and under specific conditions–people may learn, even in violent sports, to control violent actions off the field. In other cases, players may have a difficult time drawing a line between "approved" violence on the field and appropriate actions off the field. Additionally, learning to use violence in a sport may not be as influential as the hubris, sense of entitlement, and all-male group dynamics that are associated with off the field violence among athletes. This may explain why athletes in certain sports seem to have higher sexual assault rates than their peers who don't play sports. But more research is needed on this possibility.

Violence occurs among spectators who view sports events through the media as well as those attending live events. Research is needed to explain the conditions under which violence occurs in crowds watching or listening to media representations of events. Studies at the sites of events indicate that venue violence is influenced by perceived violence on the field of play, crowd dynamics, the situation at the event itself, the overall historical and social contexts in which spectators give meaning to the event, and their relationships between spectators.

In some cases, venue violence may be planned to publicly oppose the policies of a political regime or the actions of police; it may be used to attract attention to political issues, injustice, or the existence of a population that seeks public recognition; or it may involve an expression of nationalism, racism, or bigotry directed against disliked groups of people. Venue violence is sometimes dramatic, especially in the case of crowd panics during which people are trampled or crushed to death.

Post-event celebratory riots are the most common form of spectator and fan violence in North America. Frustration riots are much less common, but both types of riots can be prevented or controlled through the use of trained police officers who know how to intervene in such situations without causing backlash and further fueling crowd violence. Controlling any form of spectator violence requires well-trained security and police forces.

Terrorism at sports events is rare, but the threat of terrorism and the politics of security alters policies, procedures, and the cost of hosting sport events, especially mega-events such as the Olympic Games. The terrorist attack at the 2013 Boston Marathon reminds us that global issues influence our lives, even when we attend our favorite sport events. Just as violence in sports affects our lives, the social conditions in which we live affect violence in sports. The challenge in providing security at sport events is that those responsible for the safety of spectators find that they must limit their security strategies to control costs or to protect personal privacy. In some cases, large expenditures on security technology are part of a larger effort to introduce coercive systems of social control and law enforcement.

SUPPLEMENTAL READINGS

Reading 1. Murderball: Violence in wheelchairs.
Reading 2. Violence and animal sports.
Reading 3. The social psychological dynamics of violence in sports.
Reading 4. Sport violence: More barbaric than you think.
Reading 5. Fan violence: Ultras in Italy as a case study.

SPORT MANAGEMENT ISSUES

- People in sport marketing and management have in the past endorsed the promotion of sports events in terms of anticipated violence on the field of play. Is this a viable strategy today? Explain why it is or is not.
- Controlling violence on the field presents a difficult challenge. Identify strategies for controlling various types of violence in US football or hockey in the NHL, and explain why you have chosen those strategies.
- You are a new program manager in a large public sports and recreation center. The director of the center tells you to design a program through which young people will learn to be less violent in the local neighborhood. Describe the program you would develop, and how it will be organized to meet your supervisor's expectations.
- You are the athletic director at a high school that is hosting an in-state rivalry game between your number-1-ranked football team and the number-2-ranked team in your division. Violence has occurred at past games with this team. Describe the measures you will take to control player and spectator violence in connection with the game.

references

Abad-Santos, Alexander. 2013. Everything you need to know about Steubenville High's football 'rape crew'. *The Atlantic Wire* (January 3): http://www.theatlanticwire.com/national/2013/01/steubenville-high-football-rape-crew/60554/ (retrieved 5-22-13).

Adubato, Beth.2016. The promise of violence: Televised, professional football games and domestic violence. *Journal of Sport and Social Issues* 40(1): 22–37. and recommendations for future study. *Trauma, Violence, & Abuse* 16(4): 438–443.

Armour, Nancy. 2018. One brain at a time. *USA Today* (August 28): 1A–2A.

Armstrong, Gary. 1998. *Football hooligans: Knowing the score.* Oxford: Berg.

Armstrong, Gary. 2007. Football hooliganism. In George Ritzer, ed. *Encyclopedia of sociology* (pp. 1767–1769). London/New York: Blackwell.

Bearak, Barry. 2011. U.F.C. Dips a toe into the mainstream. *New York Times* (November 11): http://www.nytimes.com/imagepages/2011/11/12/sports/12ufc1.html

Beaver, Kevin M.; J. C. Barnes & Brian B. Boutwell. 2016. Exploring the relationship between violent behavior and participation in football during adolescence: Findings from a sample of sibling pairs. *Youth & Society* 48(6): 786–809.

Berra, Lindsey. 2005. This is how they roll. *ESPN The Magazine* (December 5): 104–111.

Blumenthal, Ralph. 2004. Texas tough, in lipstick, fishnet and skates. *The New York Times*, Section 1 (August 1): 14.

Brackenridge, Celia; D. Bishopp, S. Moussali & J. Tapp. 2008. The characteristics of sexual abuse in sport: A multidimensional scaling analysis of events described in media reports. *International Journal of Sport and Exercise Psychology* 16(4): 385–406.

Cleland, Jamie & Ellis Cashmore. 2016. Football fans' views of violence in British football:

Evidence of a sanitized and gentrified culture. *Journal of Sport and Social Issues* 40(2): 124–142.

Cleland, Jamie & Ellis Cashmore. 2018. Nothing will be the same again after the Stade de France attack: Reflections of association football fans on terrorism, security and surveillance. *Journal of Sport and Social Issues* 42(6): 454–469.

Conroy, Pat. 1986. *The prince of tides.* Boston: Houghton Mifflin.

Crosset, Todd. 1995. *Outsiders in the clubhouse: The world of women's professional golf.* Albany, NY: State University of New York Press.

Crosset, Todd. 1999. Male athletes' violence against women: A critical assessment of the athletic affiliation, violence against women debate. *Quest* 52, 3: 244–257.

Daniels, Deborah J. (with Praedidium). 2017. *Report to USA Gymnastics on proposed policy and procedural changes for the protection of young athletes*. USAGym.org (June 26): https://usagym.org/PDFs/About%20USA%20Gymnastics/ddreport_062617.pdf

Dean, Nikolaus A. 2019. "Just Act Normal": Concussion and the (Re)negotiation of Athletic Identity. *Sociology of Sport Journal* 36(1): 22–31.

Doidge, Mark & Martin Lieser. 2018. The importance of research on the ultras: Introduction (to a special issue: *The Ultras - The global development of a fan phenomenon*. *Sport in Society* 21(6): 833–840.

Dorsey, James M. 2016. *The Turbulent World of Middle East Soccer*. New York: Oxford University Press.

Dorsey, James M. 2017a. Left with no choice: Egypt allows fans to attend international soccer matches. *The Turbulent World of Middle East Soccer* (July 7): https://mideastsoccer.blogspot.com/2017/07/left-with-no-choice-egypt-allows-fans.html

Dorsey, James M. 2017b. Soccer success has a price: Pressure builds to lift Egypt's stadium ban. *The Turbulent World of Middle East Soccer* (October 11): https://mideastsoccer.blogspot.com/2017/10/soccer-success-has-price-pressure.html

Dorsey, James M. 2018. The rise, fall, and rise again of the politics of Middle Eastern soccer. April 12): https://mideastsoccer.blogspot.com/2018/04/the-rise-fall-and-rise-again-of.html

Dorsey, James M. 2019. Once the backbone of Middle Eastern protests, ultras are down but not out. *The Turbulent World of Middle East Soccer* (March 2): http://mideastsoccer.blogspot.com/2019/03/once-backbone-of-middle-eastern.html

Dunning, Eric. 1999. *Sport matters: Sociological studies of sport, violence and civilization*. London: Routledge.

Dunning, Eric, Patrick Murphy, and John Williams. 1988. *The Roots of Football Hooliganism: An Historical and Sociological Study*. London: Routledge and Kegan Paul.

Dunning, Eric, Patrick Murphy, Ivan Waddington, and Antonios E. Astrinakis, eds. 2002. *Fighting fans: Football hooliganism as a world phenomenon*. Dublin: University College Dublin Press.

Evans, Tim, Joe Guillen, Gina Kaufman, Marisa Kwiatkowski, Matt Mencarini, & Mark Alesia. 2018. Larry Nassar: The making of a monster who abused gymnasts for decades. *USA Today Network* (March 9): https://www.usatoday.com/story/news/nation-now/2018/03/08/larry-nassar-sexually-abused-gymnasts-usa-gymnastics-michigan-state-university/406044002/

Fainaru, Steven & Mark Fainaru-Wada (with Greg Amante, Andrew Webber, & Adam Conway). 2019. For the NFL and all of football, a new threat: An evaporating insurance market. *Outside the Lines, ESPN.com* (January 17): http://www.espn.com/espn/story/_/id/25776964/insurance-market-football-evaporating-causing-major-threat-nfl-pop-warner-colleges-espn

Fainaru-Wada, Mark, and Steve Fainaru. 2013. *The NFL, concussions and the battle for truth.* New York: Crown Archetype.

Fainaru-Wada, Mark, and Steve Fainaru. 2017. NFL retakes control of brain research as touted alliance ends. *ESPN.com* (August 31): https://www.espn.com/espn/otl/story/_/id/20509977/nfl-takes-control-brain-research-100-million-donation-all-ending-partnerships-entities

Fasting, Kari, Celia Brackenridge, Katherine Miller, and Don Sabo. 2008. Participation in college sports and protection from sexual victimization. *International Journal of Sport and Exercise Psychology* 16(4): 427–441.

Fogel, Curtis. 2011. Sporting masculinity on the gridiron: Construction, characteristics, and consequences. *Canadian Social Science, 7*(2): 1–14.

Freeman, Mike. 1998. A cycle of violence, on the field and off. *New York Times,* section 8 (September 6): 1.

Frontline. 2011. Football high (video). *PBS.org* (April 12): http://video.pbs.org/video/1880045332/

Frontline. 2013. League of denial: The NFL's concussion crisis (video). *PBS.org* (October 8): http://video.pbs.org/video/2365093675/

Gallo, DJ. 2017. Unfriendly confines: The unsung history of America's low-key hooliganism. *The Guardian* (October 18): https://www.theguardian.com/sport/blog/2017/oct/18/unfriendly-confines-the-unsung-history-of-americas-low-key-hooliganism

Giulianotti, Richard, and Francisco Klauser. 2012. Sport mega-events and 'terrorism': A critical analysis. *International Review for the Sociology of Sport* 47(3): 307–323.

Goldman, Tom. 2018. Repeated head hits, not just concussions, may lead to a type of chronic brain damage. *National Public Radio, All Things Considered* (January 18): https://www.npr.org/sections/health-shots/2018/01/18/578355877/repeated-head-hits-not-concussions-may-be-behind-a-type-of-chronic-brain-damage

Gordon, Serena. 2018. Brain changes seen in MRIs of young football players. HealthDay News (November 26): https://health.usnews.com/health-care/articles/2018-11-26/brain-changes-seen-in-mris-of-young-football-players

Graham, Stephen. 22012. Olympics 2012 security: welcome to lockdown London. *The Guardian* (March 12): https://www.theguardian.com/sport/2012/mar/12/london-olympics-security-lockdown-london

Guttmann, Allen. 1986. *Sport spectators.* New York: Columbia University Press.

Guttmann, Allen. 1998. The appeal of violent sports. In J. Goldstein, ed., *Why we watch: The attractions of violent entertainment* (pp. 7–26). New York: Oxford University Press.

Guttmann, Allen. 2004. *Sports: The first five millennia.* Amherst: University of Massachusetts Press.

Haidary, Emal. 2014. Survivors tell of Afghan volleyball bombing that killed 57. Yahoo.com (November 24): https://news.yahoo.com/suicide-blast-afghan-volleyball-game-kills-around-50-154801930.html

Hassan, David. 2012. Sport and terrorism: Two of modern life's most prevalent themes. *International Review for the Sociology of Sport* 47: 263–267.

Hruby, Patrick. 2013. The NFL: Forever backward. *Sports on Earth* (February 8): http://www.patrickhruby.net/2013/02/subhead-here-drop-cap-here-suppose-you.html

Johnson, Allan. 2013. Fatal distraction: Manhood, guns, and violence. *Male Voice* (January 13): http://voicemalemagazine.org/fatal-distraction-manhood-guns-and-violence/#more-1143%27

Kelly, Jason. 2011. The damage done. *Notre Dame Magazine* (Autumn): http://magazine.nd.edu/news/25979-the-damage-done/

Kenny, Jeannine. 2012. *Plaintiffs' Master Administrative Long-Form Complaint* (In Re: National Football Players' Concussion Injury Litigation (United States District Curt, No. 2:12-md-02323-AB MDL No. 2323 (June 7): http://www.washingtonpost.com/wp-srv/sports/NFL-master-complaint.html (retrieved 5-25-13).

Kim, Sungwon, Daniel P. Connaughton, Robert F. Leeman & Jong Hoon Lee. 2018. Concussion knowledge of youth sport athletes, coaches, and parents: A review. *Journal of Amateur Sport* 4(1): 82–107.

Knapp, Bobbi A. 2014. Smash mouth football: Identity development and maintenance on a women's tackle football team. *Journal of Sport and Social Issues* 38(1): 51–74.

Kossakowski, Radosław. 2017. Where are the hooligans? Dimensions of football fandom in Poland. *International Review for the Sociology of Sport* 52(6): 693–711.

Kossakowski, Radosław, Dominik Antonowicz & Honorata Jakubowska. 2020. The reproduction of hegemonic masculinity in football fandom. An analysis of the performance of Polish ultras. In Magrath, Rory, Jamie Cleland & Eric Anderson, eds. *Palgrave handbook of masculinity and sport*. London: Palgrave Macmillan.

Krattenmaker, Tom. 2013. NFL violence a moral thorn for Christians. *USA Today* (October): http:// www.usatoday.com/story/opinion/2013/10/09/nfl -concussions-football-christians-column/2955997/

Kreager, Derek A. 2007. Unnecessary roughness? School sports, peer networks, and male adolescent violence. *American Sociological Review* 72(5): 705–724.

Kroichick, Ron. 2018 Tomorrow's game. *San Francisco Chronicle* (October 25): https://www.sfchronicle.com/sports/article/The-future-of-football-What-will-the-game-look-13319246.php

Krug, Etienne G., Linda L. Dahlberg, James A. Mercy, Anthony B. Zwi & Rafael Lozano. 2002. *World report on violence and health.* Geneva, Switzerland: World Health Organization.

Langton, Chris. 2015. Top 15 deadliest sports riots of all time. *TheSportster.com* (June 2): http://www.thesportster.com/entertain

Lavigne, Paula. 2018a. OTL: College athletes three times more likely to be named in Title IX sexual misconduct complaints. ESPN.com (November 2): http://www.espn.com/espn/otl/story/_/id/25149259/college-athletes-three-s-more-likely-named-title-ix-sexual-misconduct-complaints

Lavigne, Paula. 2018b. Baylor University settles Title IX lawsuit in which gang rape by up to 8 football players was alleged. ESPN.com (July 13): http://www.espn.com/college-football/story/_/id/24090683/baylor-university-settles-title-ix-lawsuit-which-gang-rape-8-football-players-was-alleged

Lavigne, Paula & Dan Murphy. 2019. Federal report cites Michigan State with systemic 'serious violations' of campus-safety law. *ESPN.com* (January 30): https://www.espn.com/espn/story/_/id/25885611/us-department-education-cites-michigan-state-university-clery-act-violations-espn-lines

Layden, Tim. 2007. The big hit. *Sports Illustrated* 107, 4 (July 30): 53–62.

Lewis, Jerry. 2007. *Sports fan violence in North America.* New York: Rowman & Littlefield.

Luther, Jessica. 2016. *Unsportsmanlike Conduct: College Football and the Politics of Rape*. Brooklyn, NY, NY: Akashic Books.

Macur, Juliet, and Nate Schweber. 2012. Rape case unfolds on web and splits city. *New York Times* (December 16): http://www.nytimes.com/2012/12/17/sports/high-school-football-rape-case-unfolds-online-and-divides-steubenville-ohio.html (retrieved 5-25-13).

Mason, Garu. 2011. The sad, painful truth about the Vancouver rioters' true identities. *Globe and Mail* (June 18): http://m.theglobeandmail.com/news/national/british-columbia/gary_mason/the-sad-painful-truth-about-the-vancouver-rioters-true-identities/article2066321/ (retrieved 5-30-13).

McCray, Kristy L. 2015. Intercollegiate athletes and sexual violence: A review of literature

McCree, Roy Dereck. 2011. The death of a female boxer: Media, sport, nationalism, and gender. *Journal of Sport and Social Issues* 35(4): 327–249.

McMichael, Christopher. 2012. Hosting the world. *City: analysis of urban trends, culture, theory, policy, action* 16:5, 519–534.

Messner, Michael A. 1992. *Power at play*. Beacon Press, Boston.

Montez de Oca, Jeffrey, Brandon Meyer & Jeffrey Scholes. 2016. Reaching the kids: NFL youth marketing and media. *Popular Communication* 14(1):3-11.

Moran, US Senator Jerry. 2019. US Olympic sexual abuse investigation. Washington DC: US Senate Commerce, Science, and Transportation Subcommittee on Consumer Protection, Product Safety, Insurance, and Data Security; online, https://www.moran.senate.gov/public/index.cfm/u-s-olympic-sexual-abuse-investigation

Moskovitz, Diana. 2018. Safe Sport, the USOC's attempt to stop child abuse, is set up to fail—just like it was supposed to. *Deadspin.com* (July 24): https://deadspin.com/safesport-the-usocs-attempt-to-stop-child-abuse-is-se-1826279217

Murphy, Wendy. 2013. CNN Steubenville coverage did more good than harm. *WeNews* (March 22): http://womensenews.org/story/rape/130321/cnn -steubenville-coverage-did-more-good-harm#. UUzznzfuwek (retrieved 5-25-13).

Nash, Bruce & Allan Zullo. 1989. *The baseball hall of shame(2)*. New York: Pocket Books.

Nowinski, Christopher. 2014. Head games: The global concussion crisis. Head Games–The Film, LLC.

Paradiso, Eugenio. 2009. The social, political, and economic causes of violence in Argentine soccer. *The Canadian Student Journal of Anthropology* 21(July): 65–79.

Parent, Sylvie & Kristine Fortier. 2018. Comprehensive overview of the problem of violence against athletes in sport. *Journal of Sport and Social Issues* 42(4): 227–246.

Parkin, Simon. 2018. The rise of Russia's neo-Nazi football hooligans. *The Guardian* (April 24): https://www.theguardian.com/news/2018/apr/24/russia-neo-nazi-football-hooligans-world-cup

PBS. 2018. Olympics executives' 'unconscionable' decision to hide Nassar sex abuse. *Pbs.org* (December 13): https://www.pbs.org/newshour/show/olympics-executives-engaged-in-unconscionable-concealment-of-nassar-sex-abuse

Polychroniou, D. J. 2013. Violence is deeply rooted in American culture: An interview with Henry A. Giroux. *Truth-Out* (January 17): http://truth-out.org/news/item/13982-violence-is-deeply-rooted-in-american-culture-interview-with-henry-a-giroux (retrieved 5-25-13).

Pringle, R. 2009. Defamiliarizing Heavy-Contact Sports: A Critical Examination of Rugby, Discipline, and Pleasure. *Sociology of Sport Journal* 26(2): 211–234.

Quenqua, Douglas. 2012. The fight club generation. *New York Times* (March 14): http://www.nytimes.com/2012/03/15/fashion/mixed-martial-arts-catches-on-with-the-internet-generation.html (retrieved 5-23-13).

Reid, Scott M. 2018a. 100s of USA swimmers were sexually abused for decades and the people in charge knew and ignored it, investigation finds. *Orange County Register* (February 16): https://www.ocregister.com/2018/02/16/investigation-usa-swimming-ignored-sexual-abuse-for-decades/

Reid, Scott M. 2018b. US Olympic sports' year of reckoning revealed 'ecosystem' that facilitated sexual abuse. *Orange County Register* (December 30): https://www.ocregister.com/2018/12/30/u-s-olympic-sports-year-of-reckoning-revealed-ecosystem-that-facilitated-sexual-abuse/

Renfrow, Daniel G., Terrence L. Wissick & Christopher M. Guard. 2016. (Re)Defining the situation when football fans rush the field. *Sociology of Sport Journal* 33(3): 250–261.

San Francisco Chronicle. 2018. The future of football. *San Francisco Chronicle* (October 25): https://www.sfchronicle.com/future-of-football/

San Francisco Chronicle. 2018. The future of football. *San Francisco Chronicle* (October 25): https://www.sfchronicle.com/future-of-football/

Sarmiento, Kelly; Zoe Donnell, Elizabeth Bell & Rosanne Hoffman. 2019. Barriers and opportunities for concussion communication and management in youth sports: A qualitative study, *Journal of Athlete Development and Experience* 1(3): Article 4, online, https://scholarworks.bgsu.edu/jade/vol1/iss3/4

Scheinin, Richard. 1994. *Field of screams: The dark underside of America's national pastime*. New York: W. W. Norton & Company

Schimmel, Kimberly S. 2012. Protecting the NFL/militarizing the homeland: Citizen soldiers and urban resilience in post-9/11 America.

International Review for the Sociology of Sport 47(3): 338–357.

Seabra, Daniel. 2017. Portoan Ultra Group members' social representation of Lisbon and Sport Lisboa and Benfica and its influence on the discourses and practices of the Portoan Ultra groups and their members. *Physical Culture and Sport Studies and Research* 73:5–14.

Shortway, Kendahl, Marina Oganesova & Andrew Vincent. 2018. Sexual assault on college campuses: What sport psychology practitioners need to know. *Journal of Clinical Sport Psychology*, Online first.

Smith, Michael. 1983. *Violence and sport.* Toronto: Butterworths.

Smith, Rory. 2018. Soccer fans in Buenos Aires turn their passion into something ugly. NYT (November 24): https://www.nytimes.com/2018/11/24/sports/boca-juniors-river-plate-copa-libertadores.html

Snider, Mike. 2018. Investigation by 'Indianapolis Star' hailed as proof of local journalism's impact. *USA Today* (January 25): https://www.usatoday.com/story/money/media/2018/01/25/investigation-indianapolis-star-hailed-proof-local-journalisms-impact/1066040001/

START. 2013. *Background report: Bombings at the Boston Marathon*. National Consortium for the Study of Terrorism and Responses to Terrorism, College Park, MD: University of Maryland.

Sturtz, Rachel. 2014. Unprotected. Outside Online: https://www.outsideonline.com/2162781/unprotected

Sugden, John. 2012. Watched by the Games: Surveillance and security at the Olympics. *International Review for the Sociology of Sport* 47(3): 414–429.

Tagge, Chad A. et al. (45 other authors), 2018. Concussion, microvascular injury, and early tauopathy in young athletes after impact head injury and an impact concussion mouse model. *Brain: A Journal of Neurology* 141(2): 422–458.

Theberge, Nancy. 1999. Being physical: Sources of pleasure and satisfaction in women's ice hockey. In Jay Coakley & Peter Donnelly, eds., *Inside Sports* (pp. 146–155). London: Routledge.

Thomas, Eton. 2019. Tom Izzo's abuse of Aaron Henry was the act of a bully and a coward. (April 6): https://www.theguardian.com/sport/2019/apr/06/tom-izzo-aaron-henry-abuse-michigan-state

Toohey, Kristine & Tracy Taylor. 2012. Surveillance and securitization: A forgotten Sydney Olympic legacy. *International Review for the Sociology of Sport* 47(3): 324–337.

Turk, Austin T. 2004. Sociology of terrorism. *Annual Review of Sociology* 30: 271–286.

Van Valkenburg, Kevin. 2012a. Games of chance. *ESPN.com* (August 30): http://espn.go.com/espn/otl/story/_/id/8307997/why-men-dave-coleman-jr-willing-risk-much-play-semi-pro-football (retrieved 2-20-13).

Wann, Daniel L. & Jeffrey D. James. 2019. Sport Fans: The Psychology and Social Impact of Fandom. New York/London: Routledge.

Wann, Daniel L., Paula J. Waddill, Danielle Bono, Holly Scheuchner & Kristen Ruga. 2017. Sport spectator verbal aggression: The impact of team identification and fan dysfunction on fans' abuse of opponents and officials. *Journal of Sport Behavior*, 4(4): 423–443.

Wann, Daniel L., Stephen Weaver, Brian Belva, Sagan Ladd & Sam Armstrong. 2015. Investigating the impact of team identification on the willingness to commit verbal and physical aggression by youth baseball spectators. *Journal of Amateur Sport* 1(1): 1–28.

Willmsen, Christine, and Maureen O'Hagan. 2003. Coaches continue working for schools and private teams after being caught for sexual misconduct. *Seattle Times*, 12/14, online at http://seattletimes.nwsource.com/news/local/coaches (retrieved June, 2005).

Wright, Darlene, and Kevin Fitzpatrick. 2006. Social capital and adolescent violent behavior correlates of fighting and weapon use among secondary school students. *Social Forces* 4: 1435–1453.

Young, Belinda-Rose, Sarah L. Desmarais, Julie A. Baldwin & Rasheeta Chandler. 2017. Sexual coercion practices among undergraduate male recreational athletes, intercollegiate athletes, and non-athletes. *Violence Against Women* 23(7) 795–812.

Young, Kevin. 2007a. Violence among athletes. In George Ritzer, ed. *Encyclopedia of sociology* (pp. 5199–5202). London/New York: Blackwell.

Young, Kevin. 2007b. Violence among spectators. In George Ritzer, ed. *Encyclopedia of sociology* (pp. 5202–5206). London/New York: Blackwell.

Young, Kevin. 2019. *Sport, violence and society.* London/New York: Routledge.

Zimbalist, Andrew. 2017. The economic legacy of Rio 2016. In Andrew Zimbalist (ed.) *Rio 2016: Olympic myths, hard realities.* Washington DC: Brookings Institution (pp. 207–237).

Zirin, Dave. 2011b. Understanding Vancouver's 'Hockey riot'. *The Nation* (June 16): http://www.thenation.com/article/understanding-vancouvers-hockey-riot/

chapter

7

(*Source*: Anna Gowthorpe/BPI/Shutterstock)

GENDER AND SPORTS

Is Equity Possible?

I played football growing up and I learned that, as a man, you kept things inside so you could use them as a weapon.

–Brian Barth, journalist (2018)

When you look at men's basketball, 99 percent of the jobs go to men, why shouldn't . . . 99 percent of the jobs in women's basketball go to women? We don't have enough female role models . . . We don't have enough women in power.

–Muffet McGraw, basketball coach, University of Notre Dame (in Whiteside, 2019)

Being gay, in sport, and in the closet, it has been a mental burden of not knowing how those around you will react. It was a perceived pressure that consumed me.

–Andy Brennan, professional soccer player in Australia (2019)

. . . absolutely fundamental to the fight for gender equality [is] the rejection of the definition of gender as the sum of our body parts. Feminism understands gender as a personal experience shaped by social, economic, and cultural forces.

–Jessica Stern (2019), Executive Director, OutRight Action International.

Chapter Outline

Learning Objectives

- Describe the two-sex classification system, and explain how it impacts the meaning and organization of sports as well as who participates in sports.
- Explain how orthodox gender ideology has influenced sports and how sports have influenced gender ideology.
- Understand the current approach to sex testing and how it is related to orthodox gender ideology.
- Identify reasons for the dramatic increase in sports participation rates among women of all ages since the mid-1970s.
- Identify existing gender inequities in sports and the barriers faced when trying to achieve equity.
- Understand what it means to say that sports and sports organizations today are male-dominated, male-identified, and male-centered.
- Explain how orthodox gender ideology influences lesbians, gay men, bisexuals, and transsexuals in sports today.
- Identify effective strategies to promote gender equity in sports and sports organizations.

> *I think that female athletes are completely accepted among both the guys and the girls. I mean I have played sports since I was 5 and I have never not been accepted by both the guys and the girls.*

This statement by a high school basketball player in the United States echoes the feelings of most girls and young women from relatively privileged backgrounds in wealthy nations. From their perspectives, gone are the days when many female athletes endured nasty comments and were taunted by peers. But gender remains important in sports, and gender-related forms of exclusion and discrimination continue to exist especially in patriarchal and many developing nations. This is why scholars in the sociology of sport regularly focus on gender and gender relations when they study sports as social phenomena.

This chapter focuses on complex relationships between sports and the way people think and feel about masculinity, femininity, homosexuality, heterosexuality, transsexuality and other aspects of gender in culture and society. The issues discussed are these:

- Why have most sports worldwide been defined as men's activities?
- How have girls and women been excluded or discouraged from playing sports?
- What accounts for recent increases in women's sport participation?
- Do gender inequities remain in sports?
- What barriers interfere with the achievement of gender equity?
- What strategies can produce more progress toward gender equity in sports?

CULTURAL ORIGINS OF GENDER INEQUITIES

In Chapter 1, we saw that **gender ideology** consists of *interrelated ideas and beliefs that are widely used to define masculinity and femininity, identify people in terms of sex and sexuality, evaluate forms of sexual expression, and organize social relationships.* The gender ideology that remains dominant in many societies is organized around three ideas and beliefs:

1. Human beings are biologically either female or male.
2. Heterosexuality is normal, and other expressions of sexual feelings, thoughts, and actions are seen as unnatural, abnormal, deviant, or immoral.
3. Men are physically stronger and more rational than women and more naturally suited to possess power and assume leadership positions in the public spheres of society.

Many people question or reject these conventional or orthodox ideas and beliefs today, but they continue to influence how people (a) think about and identify themselves and others, (b) form and evaluate relationships, (c) develop expectations for themselves and others, and (d) organize and distribute rewards in social worlds.

Even if we oppose orthodox gender ideology, it is so deeply rooted in our experiences and the organization of everyday life that we thoughtlessly use it as a cultural guide for making decisions about what we wear and how we talk, walk, present ourselves to others, choose college majors, and think about and plan for our future. In this sense, gender ideology leads us to police ourselves in addition to policing each other (Bergner, 2019).

Gender ideology varies from culture to culture, but most people use a gender ideology based on a simple binary (two-sex) classification system. Therefore, they assume that all humans can be classified into one of two biologically based **sex categories:** *male or female*. These categories are viewed in terms of physiological and psychological differences. This is why many people refer to males and females as "opposite" sexes, why they believe that the two sexes are naturally different, and why they expect males and females to differ in many ways.

These expectations based on the gender binary are the foundation for defining **gender,** or *what is considered to be masculine or feminine in a group or society.* In other words, sex is biological and gender is tied to social definitions used in social- and self-identification. In most societies, gender and gender distinctions are so deeply integrated into language systems, identities, and relationships that people cannot ignore them, even when they don't agree or identify with them. Additionally, gender distinctions are expressed in different ways across social classes, cultural settings, and sports.

The two-sex classification system is widely taken for granted. Most people use it as a basis for how they view the world and their place in it. Often they feel confused, uncomfortable, or even angry when they or others don't fit neatly into one of the two orthodox sex categories. This is why so many people find it difficult to think critically about gender and why they become defensive when others do so.

In this chapter, I use the term **orthodox gender ideology** *to represent the interrelated ideas and beliefs associated with this two-sex approach.* Using the word *orthodox* is meant to show that this view of gender represents a traditional and widely established way of thinking that many people view as unchanging "truth" linked to their religious beliefs or an overall sense of right and wrong.[1]

In societies where many people have access to science-based information about sex and gender and have personal experiences to support that information, there is a growing tendency to question all or part of orthodox gender ideology. As this occurs, some people form new perspectives on gender and what it means for how they see themselves, their relationships, and the organization of social worlds. This is happening mostly among young people whose expanding awareness of human and social variation leads them to feel uncomfortable with an inflexible two-sex classification system that has been used to marginalize and label those who don't "fit" into either category as immoral or unnatural. However, new ideas and beliefs about gender have not pulled together enough to form an identifiable and widely shared gender-inclusive ideology at this time. But an increasing number of people are moving in that direction, and this phenomenon is now being studied (Anderson and McCormack, 2018; Fink, LaVoi & Newhall, 2016; Gieseler, 2019; Jarvis, 2015; Koch, Scherer & Holt, 2018; Magrath, 2017; Rogers, 2019; Seagrave, 2016).

Even though many people worldwide cling to orthodox gender ideology, it is inconsistent with scientific evidence showing that anatomy, hormones, chromosomes, and secondary sex characteristics vary in complex ways that cannot be divided into two distinct, nonoverlapping sex categories. Noted scientists explain that sex is so biologically and culturally complex that it cannot be forced into two categories if we want to understand its implications in our lives (Fausto-Sterling, 2012; Jordan-Young and Karkazis, 2019).

Anne Fausto-Sterling, a biologist who has spent her life studying sex and the human body, notes, "There is no either/or; rather, there are shades of difference" (Fausto-Sterling, 2000a, p. 3). In other words, real bodies have hundreds of continuous physical traits that vary on a scale from low to high rather than falling neatly into two separate and opposite categories. Additionally, differences vary and overlap, so that the only way to conclude that there are only two sex categories is to arbitrarily decide what characteristics are most important and then fit them into two separate categories.

This means that the use of a two-category system for classifying all bodies is a reflection of social and cultural ideas rather than biological facts. But the categories have important effects regardless of their biological validity, because using them produces life-altering consequences for people. In fact, when people are born with physical traits that don't fit neatly into one sex category or the other, the gender ideology used by many physicians and parents in the past led them to surgically "fix" genitals and reproductive organs so that infants would appear to be more clearly male or female (Fausto-Sterling, 2000b; Harper, 2007; Quart, 2008). This approach is changing as people realize that bodies are more complex than a two-sex system leads us to believe, and that sex as well as gender is a social construction (Bergner, 2019; Laqueur, 1990). Today it is more customary for the parents of children with

[1]This choice of terms is inspired by the work of Eric Anderson (2009b, 2011b; Anderson & McCormack, 2018), who distinguishes orthodox masculinity from inclusive masculinity. His explanation for doing this can be extended to identify orthodox gender ideology and contrast it with inclusive gender ideology, which is increasingly used to think about gender in less rigid and dogmatic terms.

ambiguous anatomical characteristics to wait and let their children make their own decisions about surgeries or other medical treatments when they know how they want to identify themselves and understand the implications of sex identification in society (Travers, 2018).

Being Out of Gender Bounds

Orthodox gender ideology creates problems when it causes people to have rigid, unbending ideas and beliefs about the ways that males and females are supposed to look, think, feel, and act. Further, it leads to the assumption that heterosexuality is natural and normal. Therefore, those who appear or express feelings, thoughts, and actions that do not fit into the heterosexual male or female categories are unnatural, abnormal and, "out of bounds" in terms of gender (see Figure 7.1).

This approach marginalizes lesbians, gay men, bisexuals, transsexuals, queer, and intersex people (LGBTQs) and leads some people to view them as abnormal, unnatural, or immoral because they exist outside the two orthodox sex categories. This fosters **homophobia,** which is *a generalized fear or intolerance of anyone who isn't clearly classifiable as a heterosexual male or female* (Griffin, 1998). This fear or intolerance is created when people see others with an appearance or presentation of self that does not make sense to them in terms of the gender ideology they use. As long as the two-sex system is widely accepted, homophobia will exist in some form. For this reason, the achievement of full gender equity depends, in part, on transforming that system.

Orthodox Gender Ideology as a Tool to Maintain the Status Quo

Another important aspect of orthodox gender ideology is that it leads people to see males and females as different *and* unequal. For example, Figure 7.1 illustrates that males have greater access to higher levels of privilege, power, and influence than females have. Therefore, men occupy higher positions of power and influence in greater numbers than women do. Of course, this means that some men–*but not all men*–have a strong personal interest in preserving the two-sex system and the ideology it supports. This is why males are more likely than females to "self-police" gender boundaries and discourage all boys and men from pushing or crossing the line that separates "heterosexual men" from women and from anyone who is "out of gender bounds" in their view (Maor, 2019). Maintaining gender distinctions reaffirms orthodox gender ideology and legitimizes disproportionate male power in society.

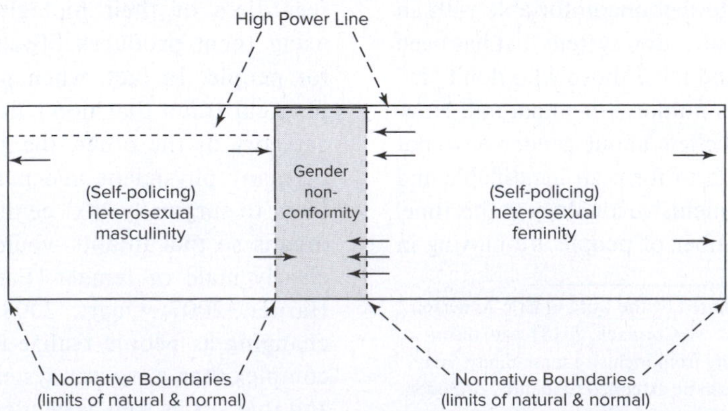

FIGURE 7.1 A two-category classification model: Identifying sex and defining gender in US culture.

When boys and men learn to accept orthodox gender ideology, they enforce restrictive normative boundaries for heterosexual masculinity. Additionally, to retain their greater access to positions of power and influence, they must also promote the belief that power and influence are legitimately linked with masculine characteristics and that existing gender boundaries are normal and natural. This is why males are generally more likely than females to intimidate or reject people who push gender boundaries or live outside them. When males push boundaries, they may be negatively labeled which can put them in a dangerous position among male peers who accept orthodox gender ideology. In a strange way, this is the price that most boys and men must pay to preserve an ideology that leads to the belief that it is natural for men to control sports along with nearly all major sources of wealth and political power in the world.

Women, on the other hand, have less to lose and more to gain in terms of power and influence if they *do* push and blur gender boundaries. This is why some–not all–girls and women take or are given more latitude or permission to exhibit a range of feelings, thoughts, and actions that is wider than the accepted range for boys and men (see Figure 7.1). Of course, heterosexual females do engage in self-policing that reaffirms normative boundaries not to be crossed without risking rejection. However, until girls enter mid-adolescence they often can be "tomboys" without being rejected (Daniels, 2009; Orenstein, 2008; Shuang, 2019).

For the past half century in the United States, orthodox gender ideology based on a two-sex classification system has fostered forms of socialization in which boys learn to limit their sense of personal possibilities more than girls learn to limit their possibilities across a wide range of options. For example, girls and women are more likely to play hockey or take boxing lessons than boys and men are to become figure skaters or take synchronized swimming lessons. This is partly because being female is devalued in mainstream US culture, and because some boys and men feel the need to reject any choices and actions associated with femininity. Therefore, they make choices that perpetuate the notion that men and women are different, with men being more naturally suited for positions involving power, leadership, and control.

Disrupting Orthodox Gender Ideology

Various aspects of orthodox gender ideology are widely challenged today. An increasing number of people worldwide now understand that certain ideas and beliefs produce and perpetuate gender inequalities that are arbitrary, restrictive, hurtful, and far too often brutal in their effects. In Figure 7.1 the arrows that push against the normative boundaries of the heterosexual male and female categories represent efforts to bend, extend, blur, and erase boundaries and escape their constraints. As boundary pushers and gender benders raise critical issues in society, they force others to either defend *or* critically assess prevailing beliefs about *masculinity* and *femininity* and the constraints and inequities created by those beliefs. Therefore, what we see today are cultural struggles between gender defenders and critical gender benders as they try to close or open up spaces in the gender order of society (MacArthur et al., 2017).

When gender defenders are dominant in these struggles, gender benders tend to be more cautious in their self-expression because the personal cost of gender-nonconforming can be very high–life itself, as reported in recent news. But when gender benders are more dominant in a society, people feel less constrained to be gender-conforming and they express a wider range of feelings, thoughts, and actions–which some people think is a good thing at the same time that others think it is a threat to the moral order in society. At this point, gender benders in most democratic societies have momentum on their side and people feel freer to challenge the constraints of orthodox gender ideology.

During these struggles most people find it difficult to give up ideas and beliefs that are central to how they make sense of the world, even when those ideas and beliefs sometimes put them at a disadvantage. For this reason, deeply held ideologies tend to slow the rate and extent of change in any society. For example, we see that many men and some women use their resources to defend and promote orthodox gender ideology because it supports their positions of privilege in the gender order. Therefore, they sponsor media programming, political candidates, community programs, laws, and informal norms that affirm the foundational ideas and beliefs on which that ideology rests—such as the views that women and men are different and suited for different tasks, and that anyone who is not a heterosexual is abnormal. But the legitimacy of their power and influence is not absolute, and it varies from one social world to another. That influence is being eroded by science, social action, and the everyday deeds of those who push gender boundaries in many places worldwide. But it also encourages homophobic people to threaten or physically attack LGBTQ people.

ORTHODOX GENDER IDEOLOGY AND SPORTS

When men created organized sports during the mid-nineteenth century, they were guided by gender ideology organized firmly around the three major beliefs that constitute the core of orthodox gender ideology today. This led them to select physical activities, develop rules, and establish governing bodies that reaffirmed those ideas and beliefs. This was not due to a conspiracy; they just never thought of alternatives. In their minds, sports were male territory and sites for establishing and proving heterosexual masculinity. Women were too weak and frail to participate. The preferred sports were those that involved physical contact, competition, and conquest.

The inclusion of women at the Olympic Games would be "impractical, uninteresting, unaesthetic, and incorrect." –Baron Pierre de Coubertin, 1912 (In Fitzgerald, 2016)

Although certain ideas and beliefs about gender have changed over time, the legacies of the men who established modern sports and shaped sport cultures remain influential today. For this reason, sports continue to be:

1. *Male-dominated,* so that ability and performance qualifications are associated with manhood and men; therefore, being "qualified" in sports means possessing masculine characteristics, or performing "like a man."
2. *Male-identified,* so that what men value is assumed to be valued in all sports, making sports a "man's world" that revolves around men and manhood; therefore, the femininity of female athletes may be questioned and women in coaching or positions of authority are seen by many as "out of place."
3. *Male-centered,* so that men and men's lives are the expected focus of attention; therefore, there are few women and women's sports represented in sports stories, history, legends, records, events, halls of fame, and media programming.

This helps us understand that sports are gendered social worlds in which competence is defined in connection with masculine traits, and female bodies and traits are viewed as athletically inferior. Therefore, when a female excels in sport, she might be described as "playing like a man," and a female coach, official, or administrator is considered capable when she does her job "like a man would do it." Despite the progress made by women in other spheres of life, sports remain *male-dominated social worlds.*

In *male-identified social worlds,* the values and experiences of men are assumed to be the standards for everyone. Therefore, female referees, athletic directors, team executives, and media broadcast commentators arouse suspicion about how they obtained their power and how they might use it in sports. If women attempt to reduce suspicions by "fitting in" or acting like men, they may be seen as phony or manipulative, and therefore undeserving of their position. This makes it easy to discredit women leaders in sports—people can say that they obtained their positions by unfairly gaining the favor of men or by being shrewd "stealth feminists" who don't like men and want to undermine traditional sport cultures. This seriously hinders the careers of women in coaching and administration.

In *male-centered social worlds,* people assume that men are the center of attention. The World Series, Super Bowl, Little League World Series, World Cup, and the Masters (golf tournament) are not labeled as "men's events," nor are pro football stadiums referred to as "men's sport centers," even though they're all about men and men's culture. Similarly, people refer to "athletes" when speaking about boys or men, and to "female athletes" when speaking about girls or women. In male-centered sports, men are the focus; women and their sports are secondary. Of course, this doesn't mean that women's sports are not important to the players and their supporters. But it does mean that on a general cultural level, they are seen as having less significance than men's sports.

Female Athletes as Invaders

Male-dominated/identified/centered sports and sports organizations have never been female-friendly. In the early 1900s, women struggled against tradition, male resistance, and legal prohibitions even to ride bicycles without being arrested and defined as immoral. In fact, the history of girls and women in sports during much of the twentieth century consists of individual and collective efforts to overcome exclusion and discrimination and to persistently claim spaces in which they could do sports (Claringbould & Adriaanse, 2015; Elsey & Nadel, 2019; Schiot, 2016; Schultz, 2014).

In the early twentieth century, women began to overcome some barriers and claim spaces in the "grace and beauty sports" of figure skating and gymnastics (Hart, 1981; Loy et al., 2009). These were considered artistic activities emphasizing coordination and attractive "body lines," so they conformed to emerging ideas and beliefs about femininity at that time in US history. Women also made their way into golf and tennis–individual sports played primarily by privileged white women who were careful to "act like ladies" on courses and courts. African American women overcame barriers and participated on some track-and-field teams at segregated high schools and the historically black colleges and universities in regions where black students were not admitted to "white" state schools. A few of the most talented made it onto US Olympic teams.

Myths That Discouraged Female Invaders Through much of the twentieth century, medical myths created anxieties about certain forms of sports participation. Girls and women were told that playing strenuous sports would damage the uterus, make child birth difficult, and produce unfeminine bodies. The exclusion of girls from Little League baseball was widely accepted through the 1950s due to the myth that being hit in the chest by a baseball or by an opponent sliding into a base could cause breast cancer later in life.

People believed these myths because they were consistent with orthodox gender ideology and the ideas that females were naturally weak and therefore vulnerable to injuries and overexhaustion in sports. Their sport participation was generally limited to activities involving solo performers (figure skating, gymnastics, and equestrian events) or competitions in which nets, lane dividers, and other barriers separated opponents (tennis, badminton, swimming, short running races, golf, archery, and fencing) and "protected" them from physical contact with each other. Basketball, field hockey, soccer, lacrosse, and other open-field or open-court team sports were labeled unladylike, which is why a women's *team* sport was not included in the Olympics until 1964–and it was volleyball. "Netless" team sports for women were added to the Olympics gradually: in 1976, basketball, team rowing, and team handball; in 1980, field hockey; in 1996, soccer and softball; and in 1998, ice hockey.

Because science has dispelled medical and overexhaustion myths, today's college students dismiss them. But those who lack access to current knowledge in biology and anatomy may still believe gender myths that discourage or exclude girls and women from sport participation. This is especially true in cultures where literacy rates are low and men control information, education, and sports.

(*Source:* Lisa Larsen/Time Life Pictures/Getty Images)

For most of the twentieth century, few schools sponsored competitive teams for girls and young women. Instead, they usually sponsored semi-annual "field days" or "sport nights" during which girls could compete in running races and other field events or give skills demonstrations to parents, as in this photo. Until the 1960s there were widely believed myths that vigorous sports would harm the female body and make it difficult for a woman to conceive, carry, and give birth to children.

In addition to myths, appeals to widely accepted values and norms also discouraged girls and women. Girls were told that cheering for boys in sports was more appropriate than playing sports. Women were told that the nation depended on them to focus on domestic activities and stay out of the man's world of sports. Those who challenged these restrictions during the late 1940s through the 1960s in the United States were widely perceived as invaders of male territory and made targets of ridicule and condemnation by both males and females who accepted orthodox gender ideology as "natural law."

Although girls and women have continued to push gender boundaries and have opened many sports to females, some people continue to believe that females should be banned from the "truly manly" sports of wrestling, football, boxing, and bull riding. Women who are serious about participating in those sports face significant challenges.

Ladies, Not Invaders To avoid being labeled as invaders, girls and women often chose to call themselves "ladies" when they played sports prior to the 1980s. This was done to let men know that they knew "their place" in sports and would not take resources away from the "real" sports played by men. This tradition continues today as female athletes and women's teams are regularly referred to as "ladies" (Arpina-Avsar et al., 2016; Dzikus, Smith & Evans, 2017).

A similar strategy to avoid being seen as invaders and gender nonconformers was for female athletes to dress and act like stereotypical "ladies" by wearing makeup, dresses, heels, nail polish, and engagement or wedding rings. During competitions, they wore skirts, bright hair ribbons, ponytails, and other "heterosexual femininity markers" to make sure they didn't push too hard against normative gender boundaries. The goal was to highlight stereotypical

(*Source:* Ted Soqui/Corbis/Getty Images)

If women play what is culturally defined as a "man's sport," and want people to watch them, they must dress appropriately so that no one mistakes them for seriously pushing gender boundaries. Lingerie football is an extreme example of this (Khomutova & Channon, 2015; Knapp, 2015). Would these women choose to play like this if there were other opportunities to play football seriously?

femininity *and* downplay any connection to masculinity by hiding their assertiveness and toughness. Even today there are men, a few women, and some sponsors who say that if women athletes want to attract spectators, they should hike up their shorts, tighten their shirts, and look like ladies.

Social science researchers referred to this self-presentation strategy as the "female apologetic" when it was used in the past (Adams et al., 2005; Krane et al., 2004). Female athletes today use a "reformed apologetic" that involves proudly expressing their assertiveness, toughness, and rightful place in sport at the same time that they communicate their femininity through clothes, makeup, accessories, and posing with and without clothes in magazines. In other words, they push gender boundaries to create more space to be female, but they don't want to erase the boundaries or transform dominant gender ideology.

Equipment and apparel companies use this reformed apologetic as a hook for marketing and selling products. There are bikinis in women's beach volleyball; "bunhuggers" (compression shorts) in running and volleyball; "cute" workout clothes; and the pervasive ponytails and bows worn by young white women on soccer and softball teams across the United States (where short haircuts are as rare as players without cleats). The most extreme examples of this are the lingerie leagues in basketball (https://www.facebook.com/pg/Lingerie-Basketball-132024553529886/photos/), hockey (now defunct), and football (Conn, 2015; Khomutova & Channon, 2015; Knapp, 2015; http://www.lflus.com/).

Exceptions to uncritical gender conformity are numerous as women worldwide challenge rules that require them to dress like females or rules that restrict participation in sports that involve combat or the kinds of physical contact that exist in the version of a game played by boys and men. For example, Serena Williams and other tennis players have challenged and changed rules related to female tennis attire, and Olympic boxers participating in the 2012 Olympics in London forced a rule change by refusing to wear skirts as demanded by the Amateur International Boxing Association (BBC, 2012a). One of the boxers explained that she was going forward into the ring, not backwards into a skirt.

Negotiating Entry and Claiming Space in the Male Preserve As explained in the previous sections, sports have long been a male preserve (Dunning, 1986; Theberge, 2012). This means that females have had to negotiate their way into sports and sport spaces and then negotiate further to obtain support and equity. This process continues today in all countries where women are free enough to consider playing sports (Kanemasu & Molnar, 2017).

Opportunities to participate in certain sports have increased significantly in societies where women's rights are respected, but access to spaces for playing sports is difficult to obtain in cases where male participants already compete for access to sports spaces. When access is contested, there may be official or legal mandates for gender equity, or girls and women must negotiate their way into those spaces. For example, when a girls' high school basketball team in the United States wants to use the school facilities for practices and games, there is a federal law that usually requires the school to give the girls' and boys' teams equal access. However, in many other societies, it would be difficult to even form a girls' team and even more difficult to find a court on which to practice and play.

When sports participation occurs outside of publicly supported organizations like schools and recreation programs, girls and women are usually "on their own" when it comes to negotiating access to spaces where participation occurs. This is the case in sports such as surfing, skateboarding, climbing, and other activities in which boys and men have previously claimed exclusive access. The frustrating thing for many girls and women is that they have to prove again and again that they have a right to claim access to the spaces they need to participate. Such negotiations are typical in nearly all sports in which boys and men have always had priority access, and they are especially challenging when participation in a sport is linked with being or becoming a man (Hertzog & Lev, 2019). Achieving gender equity under these circumstances is a major challenge.

Mixed Messages: The Burden of the Lady Legacy Social and cultural transformations take time and always face opposition. This has certainly been true in the quest to achieve gender equity in sports. As girls and women have entered sports, they have received mixed messages. Positive messages come from allies who support equitable opportunities for girls and women to play any and all sports, but other messages emphasize that sports participation should not undermine orthodox definitions of femininity. For example, as girls grow up they may be encouraged to play hard, but not rough; to be nice by sharing and taking turns; to avoid being bitchy or showing off; to be gracious competitors who maintain social relationships; and to pay attention to their physical appearance (Mutz & Meier, 2016; Tedesco, 2016; Zarrett, Cooky & Veliz, 2019). These mixed messages confuse some girls to the point that they shy away from competitive sports or don't take them seriously, especially during adolescence when they become more conscious of what it means to be female (Wallace, 2019).

Mixed messages were heard by Brandi Chastain in 1999 after she scored the winning penalty kick for the national US soccer team in the World Cup final game against the team from China. Most people cheered but others criticized Chastain for exuberantly screaming, ripping off her shirt, falling to her knees with fists clenched in triumph, and then running around the field in her sports bra. A journalist recently recounted that Chastain's celebration produced an unrelenting "outpouring of disgust" (Carmen, 2019). Another noted that her critics at the time referred to her actions as "a babe move" and wondered if she did it as a publicity stunt for Nike, the team sponsor (Sengupta, 2015). For months she was accused of flaunting her body, being ungracious and unladylike, and an embodiment of feminist definitions of gender. Her skills and accomplishments on the field were secondary or irrelevant to her critics.

Fast forward 20 years to 2019 when the women's national team defeated Thailand 13-0 in the opening round of the World Cup in France. Many people overlooked their inspired play and flawless teamwork and accused them of improperly running up the core and humiliating their opponents by expressing joy and support for each other after each score. But when men run up the score people are more likely to celebrate their prowess, as when the University of Michigan University football teams beat Rutgers 78-0 in 2016, when Oklahoma State trounced Savannah State 84-0 in 2012, and when other talented men's teams have won by similar lopsided scores. When the US national basketball team composed of top NBA players beat Angola 116-48 at the 1992 Olympics, it was hailed as "the dream team" and praised for having superior skills. Overall, most people don't think twice when a men's team dominates an opponent. That's what men are supposed to do. But it continues to be a different story for women.

MAINSTREAM SPORTS REAFFIRM ORTHODOX GENDER IDEOLOGY

Sports have long been sites for reaffirming beliefs about male-female *difference,* celebrating heterosexual masculinity, and legitimizing male power and dominance in nearly all spheres of social life (Paradis, 2012). When these beliefs are challenged, struggles result because the people who benefit from them don't want them changed. But challenges often raise questions that begin to erode traditional beliefs and create new ways of viewing sports and gender at all levels of competition. This is illustrated in the following sections.

Sports Reaffirm Male-Female Difference

Sports remain one of the only activities in contemporary liberal cultures in which sex segregation is expected, accepted, and mandatory in nearly all competitive events. Sex segregation continues because it is assumed that females are physically weaker and less capable than males and therefore must be protected from them.

Orthodox gender ideology discourages discussions about how and when sex segregation should be eliminated in sports. This contributes to ambivalence, mixed messages, and confusion about female athletes, the realities of biological sex, and the lived experiences of people for whom gender conformity is not an option.

Using Sex Tests to Maintain the Two-Sex System Of all the physical differences that exist among humans, people have chosen to organize all but a few of them around only one of them: sex. Not height, weight, muscle mass, skin color, or body type; just biological sex. The assumption that men are naturally superior to women in sports makes it necessary to separate male from female competitors, and the fear that a male may masquerade as a female has led to the creation of tests to make sure that competitors claiming to be female are female. But the necessity, validity, and reliability of these tests have become major sources of controversy in a number of sports. A brief review of the tests that have been used and how tests are being applied today shows why they are controversial.

Until the late-1960s, female athletes were regularly subjected to exams by medical professionals who would check their genitalia and secondary sex characteristics to document that they were females before they could compete in certain international events (Donnelly and Donnelly, 2013; Padawer, 2016). Female athletes emphatically objected to this. The test never identified a single gender imposter, but it did lead to unfair disqualification of women who looked too unfeminine to the judges (Huening, 2009; Karkazis et al., 2012; Kidd, 2019; Moskovitz, 2019; Padawer, 2016; Simpson et al., 2000). As a result, the international track and field federation as well as the Pan American Games and the Commonwealth Games abandoned such exams in 1967.

In late-1967, the IOC and other sport organizations replaced the exams with a chromosome test that involved scraping cells from the inside of a woman's cheek and analyzing them to identify "Barr bodies" associated with the XX sex chromosomes typical for females. But human bodies are diverse in terms of sex chromosome characteristics

(*Source:* Ian MacNicol/Getty Images)

Caster Semenya (second from left) has been told by the officials in international track and field to take hormone suppressing drugs to lower her natural testosterone levels so that women's sports in her events will be fair. Semenya has won two Olympic medals, one gold (2016) and one bronze (2012). Michael Phelps, the US swimmer who has won 23 Olympic gold medals, 5 bronze and silvers, and dominated world championships for two decades–winning seven gold medals at just one world event–has an abnormally long wingspan to generate force in the water, double jointed ankles that boost his kicking power, and he produces half the lactic acid of other swimmers which increases his endurance (Hesse, 2019), But swimming officials did not say that he looked suspicious, that he should have corrective surgery on his ankles, or that he should take drugs to boost his lactic acid production so that swimming would be more fair. His total domination was celebrated. Semenya wins a few races and her body is criticized and policed for over 10 years.

as well as genetic, cellular, hormonal, and anatomical characteristics.[2] Therefore, this "Barr body"/chromosome test was clearly invalid and unreliable, but it was used for over 30 years and led to the mistaken disqualification of many women who had no unfair biological advantage in their sports (Huening, 2009; Karkazis et al., 2012; Padawer, 2016).

By 1991, there was clear consensus among scientists that human bodies do not fit neatly into the two distinct sex categories around which sports were organized. Therefore, choosing one or more traits to determine if an athlete is a *female* would always be arbitrary, subjective, and unfair to some women. Finally, in 1999, the IOC abandoned sex testing and verification. However,

[2]Each cell in a human body contains 46 chromosomes, or 23 pairs. The configuration of the 23rd pair determines biological sex with females usually having two X chromosomes and males usually having one X and one Y chromosome. However, chromosome variations do occur in some males and some females. The term *Differences of Sex Development* (DSD) is often used when a person's genetics, hormones, internal organs, or external genitalia do not match the typical female or male pattern.

the organizers of the 2008 Olympic Games in Beijing set up an "unofficial" gender test lab where they drew blood samples from female athletes who were identified as having a "suspicious" appearance. This received little attention and failed to identify anyone as a gender fraud (Boylan, 2008; Thomas, 2008b). In fact, all the testing over the previous 40 years had identified only one case of gender fraud.

Caster Semenya and New Tests The sex testing and verification policy of the IOC and other sport governing bodies changed in 2012 in response to a 2009 case involving Mokgadi Caster Semenya, an eighteen-year-old woman from South Africa. Semenya was born and raised as a female, always identified herself as female, changed clothes and showered with female teammates, and was treated as female by everyone she knew. But when she ran a surprisingly good time and won a gold medal in the 2009 800-meter finals of the World Championships, some of her opponents and officials from other nations questioned her classification as a female. According to their (cultural) standards, she didn't appear feminine, and they accused her of not being a "real" female.

Complicating matters was that Semenya is a black African from a family and community with few resources and certainly no professional medical providers, whereas those who questioned her sex were mostly whites from wealthy nations. Many black Africans believed that questions about Semenya were based on a combination of racism and white ignorance about people of color, whose beliefs about gender were not shaped by the global fashion industry and the women it used to represent the feminine ideal (Meyers, 2019; Moyo, 2009; SAPA, 2009; Smith, 2009; see also Cooky et al., 2013).

Semenya's time of 1:55:45 when she won the 800-meter race was fast, but prior to 2009, 12 women from nine nations had posted twenty-five times that were faster (http://www.alltime-athletics.com/w_800ok.htm). But according to some people who viewed the world through the distorting filters of orthodox gender ideology in North America and Europe, she looked "too masculine." Even 10 years later in 2019 Semenya's personal best of 1:54.25 is a second slower than the world record; it is the third best time in history, so it is a stretch to say it is abnormal.

Unlike many 18-year-old women in wealthy nations, Semenya did not come from a culture where body management practices involve styling hair, using makeup, whitening teeth, removing most facial and body hair, raising voice pitch, adopting particular gestures and speech styles, wearing "cute" clothing, and having cosmetic surgeries to *appear* feminine. So in 2009 the International Association of Athletics Federations (IAAF), the governing body for track and field, demanded that she have multiple examinations and tests to identify her "true" sex.

Nearly a year later the officials in the governing body announced that Semenya was who she knew herself to be, and they allowed her to compete again in IAAF events for women. But the controversy that swirled around this young woman and information about her supposedly private test results attracted global media attention that severely humiliated her and pushed her into depression (Levy, 2009; Vannini and Fornssler, 2011). Fortunately, her support system was strong and she made a comeback to run in 2011 and at the Olympics in 2012.

The "female fairness" policy that the IOC and other sport organizations developed in response to Semenya's case was put into use in 2011 and 2012. It involved testing only women who "arouse suspicion" and appeared "too masculine" to compete fairly in women's sport events, which wasn't a new approach. What was new was that "suspicious women" were not eligible to compete until they submitted to a test for ***hyperandrogenism,*** a condition that exists when women have *naturally* elevated androgens (i.e., hormones produced by glands in the human body's endocrine system; testosterone and androstenedione are the two primary androgens). Although both female and male bodies produce androgens, people mistakenly refer to them as "male hormones" because, among other things, they stimulate the development of secondary sex traits during puberty (deepening of the voice, growth of pubic and facial hair, and muscle and bone growth).

The IOC, with advice from a panel of scientists, decided that it would use testosterone level as *the single biological indicator* of "femaleness" in high-performance sports. Testosterone is naturally produced mainly by the testes and adrenal glands in men, but it is also produced by the ovaries and adrenal glands in women. Therefore, it is *naturally* present in nearly all female bodies, just as estrogens, which aid in protein synthesis, are *naturally* present in all male bodies, even though people mistakenly refer to estrogens as "female hormones."

The IOC and the IAAF ruled that women with hyperandrogenism were eligible to compete only if their testosterone level was below "the normal male range" of 10-nanomoles-per-liter of blood (IAAF, 2011, p. 12). They also ruled that if a woman's testosterone level was found to be in the normal male range, she could compete *only* if additional tests proved that her body is "androgen insensitive," meaning that it does not process or utilize any amount of testosterone (which could actually put her at a disadvantage in many events). But *if* the tests indicated she is *not* androgen insensitive, she could not compete as a woman until she had drug treatments to suppress her natural production of testosterone to the point that her testosterone level was well below that of a normal man, which made her a woman in the eyes of the IOC and international sport federations.

Unsurprisingly, access to tests and drug treatments under the supervision of a trusted and experienced physician is not equally available to female athletes worldwide. But the IOC and other sport organizations did not see this as being unfair enough to alter their new "female fairness" policy. According to scientists who didn't work for or advise the IOC and other sport organizations, there were many problems with the policy (Karkazis et al., 2012; Robson, 2010; Sailors et al., 2012; Shani and Barilan, 2012; Sullivan, 2012; Viloria and Martinez-Patino, 2012; Wahlert and Fiester, 2012). Among them are the following:

1. Policing femininity is neither easy nor fair because human bodies cannot be divided into two nonoverlapping categories.
2. Basing women's eligibility on appearance invites discrimination, discourages females from participating in elite sports, and encourages women to use makeover strategies to look "feminine" as defined in "Western" cultures.
3. The testing and treatment requirements are unfair to women who lack resources or who live in places where "Western" medicine is scarce or unavailable.
4. The policy can have harmful psychological consequences for women who are told they are not "woman enough" to compete in high-performance sports for women.
5. The policy assumes that testosterone is the only factor that identifies sex, and that a high level of testosterone creates unfairness in women's events. There are more than 200 *biological* factors that influence sport performance, and research has not shown that testosterone is the only factor that makes a difference (Jordan-Young and Karkazis, 2019; Karkazis, 2019; Pielke, Tucker & Boye, 2019).
6. The policy claims to be about fairness, but it ignores unfair differences in access to training, quality coaching, equipment, technology, sport medicine, and nutritional foods–which also influence performance in women's events.
7. The policy creates a context of suspicion based solely on selective gender-based appearance norms.
8. The policy ignores biological factors as a source of unfairness in men's events, even though hormonal and genetic variations influence the athletic performances of men.

While these rules were in effect, a number of women were disqualified from participation as females. The most highly publicized case was Dutee Chand, a slender 5-foot tall 18-year old sprinter from a rural village in India. After she won gold medals in the 200-meter sprint and the 4 × 400-meter relay at the 2014 Asian Junior Athletics Championships, some people complained that her muscles looked like men's muscles and her running stride was too long for her to be a real female. Chand had never heard of a sex verification test, but the IAAF made her undergo a chromosome analysis, an M.R.I., and a gynecological exam in which doctors measured and pulsated her clitoris, vagina, and labia, and then measuring her breast size and her pubic hair region to see where she fit on a five-grade scale that was depicted in illustrations. All of this was part of the IAAF protocol to determine if her "chromosomes, hormones, genitalia, reproductive organs, and secondary sex characteristics" were typical for a "real female." Chand failed the test and was disqualified because her testosterone was too high. A few other young women athletes were subjected to the same routine and the doctors recommended that they have surgeries to make them "more normal" (Padawer, 2016).

The IAAF, IOC, and other international sport federations were concerned that intersex athletes were competing as females. Intersex manifests in a number of ways, but there are three major manifestations for intersex women:

1. Having XX chromosomes and ovaries plus ambiguous genitalia that are neither male nor female due to a unique genetic variation before birth.
2. Having XY chromosomes and undescended testes that usually causes the female to develop a deeper voice, a large clitoris, and more well-defined muscles during puberty.
3. Having XY chromosomes and internal testes, developing in a normal pattern as a female, and being insensitive to what may often be higher than normal testosterone levels.

This officially made all intersex female athletes suspect in the eyes of those who controlled women's sports, because it may lead these women to have an advantage in certain events.

What is a female? The testing continues Chand, with the help of experts who thought that this approach to eligibility as a female athlete was based on faulty science and unfair, filed a complaint with the International Court of Arbitration for Sport (CAS). The Court suspended the IAAF regulation for 2 years saying that the evidence was weak or flawed. This encouraged the IAAF and IOC to seek more evidence that would justify a permanent exclusionary policy. This meant that Chand and Semenya could participate in the 2016 Olympic Games in Rio de Janeiro. Dutee Chand failed to qualify for the finals in the 200-meter sprint and Caster Semenya won the gold medal in the 800-meter run with a personal best time of 1:55:28.

After the Olympics, Sebastian Coe, the IAAF president, commissioned a study that led the IAAF to institute new rules saying that female athletes must have a testosterone level of 5 nanomoles-per-liter of blood or less and maintain their levels under that threshold for at least 6 months before competing in running races between 400-meters and a mile. The rule applied to women with "46 XY DSD," that is females with XY chromosomes plus testosterone levels in the male range (i.e., 7.7–29.4 nanomoles per liter). Semenya challenged the new rule in early 2019 and in May the Court of Arbitration for Sport ruled that the rule was discriminatory but its positive outcome outweighed its negative outcome: that is, maintaining "fair competition" in certain women's track events is more important than requiring Semenya (and all 46 XY DSD athletes) to take hormone reducing drugs or have the source (e.g., undescended testes) of testosterone surgically removed, both of which involve health risks.

Semenya immediately filed an appeal with a Swiss federal court (because CAS is in Switzerland), and the federal court ruled in late-May that the IAAF could *not* implement its new rules until a full decision was made by the Swiss Federal Tribunal (the Swiss "supreme court"). In July 2019, the Tribunal revoked the ban on the regulations. This made Chand, Semenya, and others ineligible to participate in their events at the 2020 Olympic games in Tokyo.

Natural physical traits have always contributed to an athlete's ability and performance, but when they are viewed through the lens of of orthodox gender ideology women with unique anatomical, mutational, or biochemical advantages, are seen as deviant and freaks of nature, whereas men are seen as wonders of nature and super athletes who inspire our sense of human potential. As an African woman, Caster Semenya understands this. According to sociologist Anima Adjepong, Semenya's unapologetic embrace of masculine traits represents an affirmation of gender non-conforming African women "whose strength and physical prowess subject them to the invasive scrutiny of sporting bodies such as the IOC and IAAF, and for all of us who resist a gender binary that constructs women as inferior to men" (Adjepong, 2019)

Sports Celebrate Masculinity

Gender is not fixed in nature. Ideas and beliefs about masculinity and femininity are changeable. For these reasons, it takes never-ending "culture work" to preserve a particular way of thinking about gender and what it means to be a man or woman. This work involves being aware of gender boundaries, maintaining them through myths and rituals, and "doing" or "performing" gender in conformity with the prevailing gender ideology. It also involves policing gender boundaries by sanctioning (teasing, bullying, or marginalizing) those who push or ignore the boundaries.

Pushing gender boundaries is risky because the two-sex system usually becomes an embodied aspect of self for most people and influences how they experience the world and identify themselves and others. This makes sports culturally important in many societies, because sports consist of body movements, norms, thinking processes, and organizational structures that reproduce a form of masculinity revolving around strength, power, and conquest. In the social sciences we often refer to this as **hegemonic masculinity**–that is, the form of masculinity that is dominant or has the most clout in society. As a result, sports are a primary site where boys learn the language and meanings of manhood in their social worlds and use them as reference points for their identities and everyday "manhood acts" that signify heterosexual masculine selves (Matthews, 2016; Maor, 2019; Thangaraj, 2016; Wellard, 2012; Vaccaro & Swauger, 2015).

The celebration of masculinity is vividly presented through the bodily performances of popular male athletes. In many societies today, "male athletes have displaced soldiers as the masculine ideal" (Kuper, 2012, p. 14). For example, male athletes who train and sacrifice their bodies for the sake of victory are described as "warriors," and their achievements in power and performance sports are used in everyday life as evidence of men's aggressive nature, their superiority over women, and their right to claim social and physical space in social worlds.

This is why many men resist changes in rules that would "sissify" their sport by restricting violence or reducing injuries, although the incidence of brain injuries is leading some men to rethink their commitment to this form of masculinity.

Sports Legitimize Male Power and Dominance

The Stronger Women Get, the More Men Love Football. This is the title of a 1994 book by Mariah Burton Nelson. Her point was that strong women, including strong female athletes, challenge the widely accepted belief that men are stronger and more effective leaders than women. In the face of this challenge, those who uncritically accept dominant gender ideology turn to football and men's heavy contact sports to reaffirm their beliefs about male superiority (Herzog & Lev, 2019). Interestingly, football in the United States has become increasingly popular since 1994 when Nelson wrote her book. At the same time, women who play football or other heavy contact sports are regularly challenged, demeaned and ridiculed (Adams & Leavitt, 2018; DiCarlo, 2016; Matthews, 2016; Tjønndal, 2019).

This also is why some people pay high prices to see championship boxing bouts between men, and why male boxers are the world's highest-paid athletes in terms of single-event pay and pay per minute of active competition or game time. In fact, no athletes come close to the boxers' pay per minute. For example, during the 2017–18 season the combined salaries and endorsements of LeBron James, Cristiano Ronaldo, and Lionel Messi totaled $259 million. But on August 26, 2017 boxer Floyd Mayweather made $275 as he defeated Conor McGregor in a 10-round fight ending in a Technical Knockout (Badenhausen, 2018). LeBron, Cristiano, and Messi played about 11,000 minutes, making about $20,000 per minute. Mayweather boxed

(*Source:* Jay Coakley)

Orthodox gender ideology is reproduced in many men's sports. Some of those sports provide a vocabulary and a set of symbols and stories that erase diverse and inclusive masculinities and present a homogenized manhood in which the heroic warrior is the model of a real man. For boys this can inspire fantasies in which playing the role of warrior and superhero is the substance of being a man.

for 30 minutes and made over $9 million per minute, or 45 times more per minute than the three stars combined. Additionally, Mayweather was the highest paid athlete in the world four times from 2011–2017.

Although playing sports empowers many girls and women as individuals, sport as an institution remains gendered in ways that reaffirm heterosexual male power (McDonald, 2015). A clear example of this is that men control much of the power in women's sports, whereas women control practically no power in men's sports. Girls and women have participation opportunities, but they play sports in contexts where it appears that men are better than women when it comes to being leaders and wielding power. Even in unstructured sport settings, boys and men claim physical space and leadership roles as girls and women almost always resign themselves to being followers rather than leaders (Carr, 2017; Comley, 2016; Heinecken, 2020; Matthews, 2016; Sisjord, 2019). Until this gendered form of organization is changed, women will not have equal access to power in business, politics, and other spheres of life.

PROGRESS TOWARD GENDER EQUITY

The single most dramatic change in sports over the past two generations has been increased participation among girls and women. This phenomenon has occurred mostly in wealthy postindustrial nations, but there also have been increases in many developing nations. To remind people in the United States that this change is recent, President Obama noted in 2012 that "it wasn't so long ago that something like pursuing varsity sports was an unlikely dream for young women in America. Their teams often made do with second rate facilities, hand-me-down uniforms, and next to no funding" (Obama, 2012, p. 11).

Progress toward gender equity was evident during the 2012 Olympics in London, where for the first time in Olympic history:

- There were no male-only sports (boxing was the last all-male sport).
- Every nation's athletes included women.
- The US team had more women than men.
- An African American woman won a gold medal in all-around gymnastics.
- A female Saudi athlete wore a hijab in judo.

There is arguably no piece of progressive legislation that's touched more people's lives than Title IX, which allowed young women equal opportunity in education and sports.

–Dave Zirin, sport journalist (2012)

These and other forms of recent progress have resulted from the following factors:

- New opportunities
- Government legislation mandating equal rights
- The global women's rights movement
- The health and fitness movement
- Increased media coverage of women in sports

New Opportunities

New opportunities account for most of the increased sports participation among girls and women since the mid-1970s. Prior to that time, many girls and women did not play sports simply because there were no teams and programs for them. Today, access to sports participation varies, with white girls and women in middle- and upper-income families having greater access than their peers who are less well-off and living in predominantly ethnic minority neighborhoods. Despite this variation, new teams and programs have inspired and supported interests that were ignored in the past.

Government Legislation Mandating Equal Rights

Many girls and women would not be playing sports today if it weren't for local and national legislation mandating equal rights. Policies and rules requiring equal opportunities and treatment for females are primarily the result of persistent political actions advocating gender equality. For example, the US Congress passed Title IX of the Educational Amendments in 1972 after years of lobbying by feminists and other concerned citizens. Title IX law declared that *no person in the United States shall, on the basis of sex, be excluded from participation in, be denied the benefits of, or be subjected to discrimination under any educational program or activity receiving federal financial assistance.* The penalty for not following this law is that an educational institution could lose some or all of the funds it receives from the federal government. See Reflect on Sport, "Title IX Compliance" for an explanation of gender equity.

This law made sense to most people when it was applied to education in the classroom, but when it was applied to sports, many people, mostly men, criticized and resisted it. The men who controlled athletic programs in high schools and colleges thought that sharing half of all sport resources with women was outrageous and subversive. Their resistance delayed the enforcement of Title IX for 7 years and undermined enforcement of the law through much of the 1980s and between 2005 and 2009. Even today, opposition to Title IX remains strong, but after nearly 50 years, all court decisions have upheld its legality and most of its enforcement guidelines (Brown, 2019).

Initially, those objecting to the law claimed that mandating equity was unfair because boys and men were naturally suited for sports, whereas girls and women were not. In fact, in 1971, there were 3.7 million boys and only 295,000 girls playing high school sports–that is, boys outnumbered girls on teams by 12.5 to 1. Similarly, out of every dollar spent on high school sports, boys received 99 cents and girls received a penny. Overall, the men who ran these programs assumed that these differences actually proved their orthodox ideas about gender and demonstrated that Title IX contradicted the laws of nature.

At the college level, it was much the same. In 1971, there were 180,000 men and 32,000 women on intercollegiate teams; 1 of every 10 male college students and 1 of every 100 female students played intercollegiate sports. Women's sport programs received only 1 percent of university athletic budgets, even though student fees and state taxes paid by women were used to fund intercollegiate athletic programs. For many years women subsidized men's college sports with no benefit for themselves.

The impact of Title IX in school sports is clear. Between 1971 and 2019, the number of girls playing varsity high school sports increased from 295,000 to more than 3.4 million–an increase of more than 1000 percent! Instead of 1 of every 27 high school girls playing on teams, today 1 in 3 play on teams. Similarly, the number of women on college teams increased from 32,000 to over 216,400–an increase of more than 600 percent! Today, about 5 percent of all female college students play intercollegiate sports.

As opportunities for girls and women have increased, the number of boys on high school teams increased from 3.7 million to 4.5 million, and the number of men on college teams increased from 180,000 to 282,600. Another important outcome of Title IX is that many boys and men have learned to see and respect women as athletes–something that rarely occurred prior to the 1990s.[3]

The Global Women's Rights Movement

The global women's rights movement over the past half century has emphasized that girls and women are enhanced as human beings when they develop their intellectual *and* physical abilities. This idea has inspired a much sports participation, even among girls and women who in the past never would have thought of playing sports (Staurowsky et al., 2020).

The global women's movement has also influenced changes in the occupational and family roles of women and enabled some of them to acquire the time and resources they need to play sports. When women's rights expand and male control over women's lives and bodies is weakened, more girls and women choose to play sports. Additional changes are needed, especially in poor nations and among low-income women in wealthy nations, but participation opportunities today are far less restricted than they were two generations ago.

The Health and Fitness Movement

Since the mid-1970s, research has made people more aware of the health benefits of physical activity (CDC, 2011; World Health Organization, 2013). This has encouraged girls and women to seek opportunities to play sports. Although much of the publicity associated with health and fitness campaigns is tied to the prevailing feminine ideal of being thin and heterosexually attractive, there have also been campaigns promoting *development of physical strength and competence.*

Within ever-shifting cultural limits, well-defined muscles are increasingly accepted as appropriate for women of all ages (Reid, 2018). Traditional ideas about body image remain strong, as illustrated by fitness fashions and marketing images of women's fitness, but many women today reject or temporarily ignore those ideas and focus on physical strength and competence in sports rather than aspiring to look like airbrushed and "photoshopped-to-be-thin" models.

Overall, the health and fitness movement has made many people more aware of the tensions between public health and the companies that produce sporting goods and apparel. Although more girls and women are aware that these companies use insecurity and dissatisfaction with self to promote consumption, they are constantly bombarded with messages and images that stress gender differences and use unreal body images to market products. This often creates mixed message for girls and women: they are encouraged to participate in sports, but many of these messages reproduce aspects of orthodox gender ideology that have created past and current inequities in sports. Of course, parents, teachers, physical educators, and those who promote public health offer alternatives to

---

[3]The participation data in this section come from the National Federation of High Schools (NFHS) and the National Collegiate Athletic Association (NCAA). Therefore, participants in schools not affiliated with these two organizations are not counted.

reflect on SPORTS

Title IX Compliance
What Counts as Equity?

Title IX compliance requires that a school meet any one of three equity tests:

1. *Proportional participation test*–meaning that the proportion of women on sports teams is similar to the proportion of women enrolled as full-time undergraduate students.
2. *History of progress test*–meaning that a school can document that it has a clear history and continuing practice of expanding its sports program for female athletes.
3. *Accommodation of interest test*–meaning that a school can prove that it has fully and effectively accommodated the sports participation interests of female students currently enrolled and potential future students in nearby high schools.

Tests 2 and 3 were often used to comply during the early years of enforcing Title IX. But eventually schools had to present concrete numbers to pass test 1 or have exceptional reasons for continuing to claim compliance under tests 2 and 3.

National sports participation numbers for 2019 showed that there were 1.15 million fewer girls than boys playing on high school sport teams (http://www.nfhs.org/ParticipationStatistics/ParticipationStatistics). In NCAA universities, there were 62,236 fewer women than men on teams. In 2018, 44 percent of NCAA athletes were women and 56 percent of NCAA athletes were men.

Participation inequity in universities has become an increasingly contentious matter, as the average student body is now 57 percent female and 43 percent male. In 2005, the George W. Bush administration altered the criteria for complying with the *accommodation of interest test* to appease those who continued to believe that the *proportional participation test* was unfair to men. Instead of demanding multiple indicators to prove that a school met the interests of its female students, the new criteria required only that an email or web-based survey be conducted to identify interests in playing sports. Proponents of Title IX objected to this change, and the Obama administration reversed course and went back to demanding multiple indicators to show that interests were being met (Brake, 2010; Lederman, 2010). Currently, the Trump administration and Betsy De Vos, his Education Secretary, have little interest in enforcing this aspect of Title IX law.

commercially driven messages and images. As these alternatives have influenced the everyday lives of girls and women, sport participation has increased.

Increased Media Coverage of Women in Sports

Women's sports are covered far less often and in less detail than men's sports, but social media and expansion of traditional media channels now enable girls and women to see and read about the achievements of female athletes in a range of sports. For example, *espnW* (http://espn.go.com/espnw/) isn't a heavily promoted website, but for those seeking information about women in sport it provides a full range of news, stories, images, and videos. Such exposure encourages girls and women by publicly legitimizing their participation and providing alternatives to media content that portrays women in powerless or sexually objectified terms. When girls see women who are physically strong and competent athletes, it becomes easier for them to envision themselves as athletes and define sports as human activities rather than male-only activities. However, we need research that identifies the conditions under which this occurs.

The people who make sports programming decisions in traditional media seldom decide to cover women's sports. Only about 4 percent of all sports coverage is dedicated to women's events, and nearly 90 percent of the on-air people who

(*Source:* Rick Loomis/Los Angeles Times/Getty Images)

Although more girls and women are playing sports, there are regions where they are discouraged or even punished for doing so. When sociology of sport scholars studied girls skating in Afghanistan and considered posting photos online, one of the girls told them, " Once my relatives see me on social media . . . It will be something very bad for my family" (Thorpe, Hayhurst, & Chawansky, 2018).

cover sports are men; and this pattern is characteristic worldwide (UNESCO, 2018). However, viewer ratings for women's events are increasing and occasionally surpassing the ratings for men's events (Strauss, 2019a, 2019b). Important today are new media that increasingly enable girls and women to create their own coverage by posting stories and images online. However, blogs and twitter coverage communicate mostly to relatively small populations of people with strong connections with women's sports, especially when they are published by female athletes. At this point, little is known about the role of new media in attracting girls and women to participate in sports.

GENDER INEQUITIES REMAIN

Anti-discrimination laws combined with the women's rights movement and other factors have produced dramatic increases in sports participation among girls and women. But equity is far from being achieved in the United States and worldwide. The primary areas in which inequalities remain are participation, support for athletes, and access to positions of power.

Participation Inequities

Today most people in the United States and many other nations agree that girls and women should have opportunities to play sports. But they don't always agree when considering the sports they should play and the funding and other resources that should support their participation. For example, FIFA awarded $4 million to the winners of the 2019 Women's World Cup and $38 million to the French team that won the Men's World Cup in 2018. All the women's teams shared $30 million, whereas the men's teams shared $400 million. This pattern is related to the media rights fees paid to cover the events but its also due to the failure of FIFA to invest in marketing and building the value of women's soccer (Allison, 2018). Despite increases in participation opportunities over the past two generations, female athletes remain underrepresented in nearly all sports worldwide at all levels of competition.

High School and College Sports in the United States Due to Title IX, the United States has been a leader in the provision of sports participation opportunities for girls and women in school-sponsored sports. However, gender inequities remain in many high schools and colleges, and it will be difficult to achieve equity in the near future. The Office for Civil Rights (OCR) is charged with enforcing Title IX, but it also handles, for the entire United States, all cases of discrimination related to age, race, and disability. Therefore, it lacks resources to investigate more than a few Title IX complaints about gender inequities in sports. Even though reported Title IX violations have been widespread over the past four decades, not one school has lost federal funding for violating the law. Noncompliant schools are usually asked to monitor themselves and report back to the OCR, but this process is slow and produces mixed results, with some schools making changes and others resisting or delaying changes for years or indefinitely.

Universities face compliance challenges, but budget crises provide a convenient excuse for not changing athletic programs in ways that would be met with strong protests from those who have a vested interest in men's sports. For example, over the past 20 years, men in athletic departments have manipulated sports participation data to avoid OCR investigations. Coaches and school officials have double- and triple-counted female athletes by listing them on rosters for multiple teams, even though teams were the same, such as indoor and outdoor track. Officials have also listed on rosters women who had never tried out for teams or were cut before seasons began. Some universities have even counted as women the men who practiced with women's basketball and volleyball teams.

High schools are seldom investigated for gender inequities in sports participation, even though there have been thousands of Title IX complaints filed with the OCR over the past decade. However, budget shortages and a lack of will among federal officials have led the OCR to dismiss nearly all those complaints without investigations.

Professional Sports The most glaring gender inequality occurs at the professional level, where women's sports struggle to exist. The WNBA, founded in 1996, is the most successful professional team league for women in the United States, but it is floundering financially. The league has never been profitable, and six of the twelve teams were owned and supported by NBA teams as 2019 drew to a close. Although the players and owners of WNBA teams signed a new eight-year collective bargaining agreement in early-2020, the previous the average salaries of players was $75,000, whereas the average salary of NBA players was $6,400,000. This means that WNBA players made $2,143 per game for 35 games, whereas NBA players made $78,000 per game for 82 games, or 36 times more per game than WNBA players. This means that many WNBA players also play on teams in other countries to sustain their careers. Importantly, the WNBA loses about $10 million per year and is losing game attendance, whereas the NBA has had an expanding audience and $7.4 billion in annual revenue.

In soccer worldwide, women earn a fraction of what men earn and there are far fewer women playing professionally. In the United States, there are only nine teams in the National Women's Soccer League (NWSL), despite the popularity of the women's national team. The average NWSL salary in 2019 was about $20,000 per year, the maximum salary was $46,200, and the league had no television contract. This meant that top players often signed contracts with teams in wealthy European countries, plus they may also play on the women's

Face Off with Football

Many high schools and colleges in the United States fail to meet equity goals primarily due to the size and cost of football teams. For example, when a men's Division I football team has 80 to 120 members, awards eighty-five scholarships, employs up to eleven coaches, and has high operational costs, there is little chance for a women's sports program to match the men's program in terms of budget and number of athletes. Despite this, university officials resist cutting the size and budgets of football teams–even though at least 70 percent of all Division I (i.e., "big-time") football programs have more expenses than revenues each year.

This management decision puts many athletic directors in a position where they must save money by dropping men's teams such as wrestling, gymnastics, and diving. When men on these teams become angry, they blame Title IX rather than the management priorities that make football untouchable. But these men don't challenge football, because the culture and structure of the entire athletic department often revolves around it. Therefore, defining the loss of men's teams in terms of a men-versus-women conflict makes more sense to many men than challenging the sport (football) that reproduces the gender ideology that many of them have used to form their identities and achieve social status since they were young boys.

When football is the "cultural and structural centerpiece" in schools and communities, gender equity is chronically out of reach. Ironically, some of the best-funded intercollegiate women's sport programs exist in the few dozen universities where big-time football teams enjoy large payouts from bowl games and media rights revenues. The other universities–over 400 of them–have football teams that don't play in lucrative bowl games or receive significant money from selling media rights. These teams incur major financial losses and depend on support from boosters whose identities are connected with football and the ideologies it reproduces. But these ideologies aren't compatible with achieving gender equity, and it is important to understand their impact on the distribution of power and resources in sports.

The point here is that until the status and organization of football is changed, most high schools and universities will fail to meet gender equity requirements for participation expenditures, and the employment of women in coaching and administrative positions.

national team (USWNT) and are paid per game as determined by the US Soccer Federation (USSF).

The US national women's soccer team (USWNT) is currently suing the US Soccer Federation contending that it violates the Equal Pay Act by paying the women only 38 percent of what it pays players on the men's national team and by providing less support for travel and training. The members of the women's team have noted that they've been much more successful than the men's team and are regularly ranked number 1 in the world. The USSF claims that the pay gap is justified because the men's team generates more money due to more lucrative media contracts and other revenues, although this has been challenged by the women's team. As I write this, the USSF and the USWNT failed to resolve their differences in a mediation and the players are seeking a jury trial in their pay-equity case.

Ice hockey is another team sport in which women cannot earn a living wage. The Canadian Women's Hockey League (NWHL) discontinued operations in 2019 and the 200 players associated with the National Women's Hockey League in the United States have refused to play until working conditions improve. Players in the NWHL were paid salaries ranging from $2000 to $10,000 per year and only 18 percent of the USA Hockey board of directors are women (Berkman, 2019). There are "semiprofessional" women's leagues in volleyball, football, and other sports, but most lose money or operate as nonprofits, and players seldom are paid unless there are cash prizes for winning well-sponsored tournaments.

The Ladies Professional Golf Association (LPGA) and the Women's Tennis Association (WTA) are long-standing professional organizations. They sponsor tournaments worldwide, but their total annual prize money is considerably smaller than for men's golf and tennis. Interest in these tournaments declined recently among US spectators and corporations because only three of the top 25 golfers in the world were from the United States (in mid-2019), whereas 18 of the top 25 golfers in the world in mid-2019 were from Japan, South Korea, China, and Taiwan; and because there were only three US tennis players ranked in the top 25 in the world.

Olympic and Paralympic Sports The data in Figure 7.2 and Table 7.1 illustrate that women in the modern Olympic Games have always had fewer events and participants than men have had. Additionally, the International Olympic Committee (IOC) had no women members from 1896 to 1981 (85 years), and did not approve a 1500-meter run for women until the 1972 Games in Munich. It was not until 1984 in Los Angeles that women were allowed to run the marathon. Women waited until 1988 and 1996 to run the 10,000- and 5000-meter races, respectively. Wrestling and boxing were not approved until 2004 and 2012, respectively. Women comprised 45 percent of all athletes at the 2016 Olympic Games in Rio, and 53 percent of the athletes in the US delegation.

The Paralympic Games have an even more dismal record on gender, although progress towards equity has occurred recently. Table 7.2 shows that in the Paralympic Games male athletes outnumbered female athletes by 4:1 in 2006, but only by 6:4 in 2016. The US delegation in 2016 was close to 50:50, which is a major improvement on past games. This issue is discussed more fully in Chapter 10.

Informal and Alternative Sports Informal games and alternative sports often have gender dynamics that create access challenges for most girls and women. These activities are nearly always male-dominated/identified/centered. Boys and men usually control the spaces in which they occur and the norms used to acknowledge the identity claims of participants. This discourages girls and women, who must have exceptional skills to be given a chance to participate and be accepted as an athlete by their male peers. In

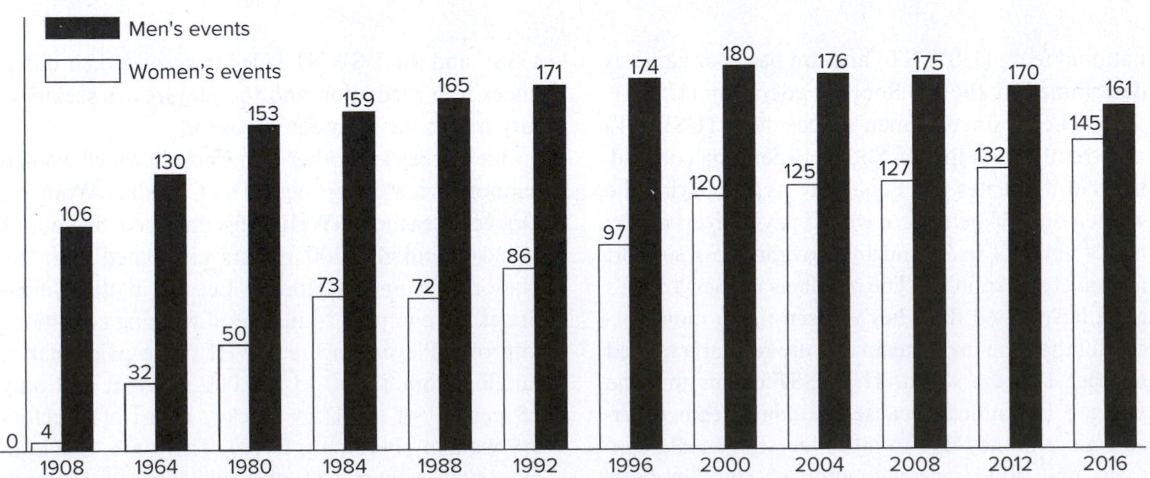

FIGURE 7.2 Number of women's and men's events in selected Summer Olympic Games, 1908–2016.

Table 7.1 Male and female athletes in the modern Summer Olympic Games, 1896–2016

Year	Place	Countries Represented	Male Athletes	Female Athletes	Percent Female
1896	Athens	14	241	0	0.0
1900	Paris	24	975	22	2.2
1904	St. Louis	12	645	6	0.9
1908	London	22	1971	37	1.8
1912	Stockholm	28	2359	48	2.0
1916	Olympics scheduled for Berlin canceled because of World War I.				
1920	Antwerp	29	2561	63	2.5
1924	Paris	44	2954	135	4.4
1928	Amsterdam	46	2606	277	9.6
1932	Los Angeles	37	1206	126	9.5
1936	Berlin	49	3632	331	8.4
1940	Olympics scheduled for Tokyo canceled because of World War II.				
1944	Olympics canceled because of World War II.				
1948	London	59	3714	390	9.5
1952	Helsinki	69	4436	519	10.5
1956	Melbourne	72	2938	376	11.3
1960	Rome	83	4727	611	11.4
1964	Tokyo	93	4473	678	13.2
1968	Mexico City	112	4735	781	14.2
1972	Munich	122	6075	1059	14.8
1976	Montreal	92	4824	1260	20.7
1980	Moscow	81	4064	1115	21.5
1984	Los Angeles	140	5263	1566	22.9
1988	Seoul	159	6197	2194	26.1
1992	Barcelona	169	6652	2704	28.9
1996	Atlanta	197	6806	3512	34.0*
2000	Sydney	199	6582	4069	38.2
2004	Athens	201	6262	4329	40.9
2008	Beijing	205	6450	4746	42.4
2012	London	205	6098	4362	41.7
2016	Rio de Janeiro	206	6178	5059	45.0

Source: http://www.mapsofworld.com/olympics/trivia/number-of-participants.html

*Twenty-six countries sent only male athletes to the 1996 Summer Games.

Note: These data show 120 years of gradual progress toward gender equity. At this rate, the 2020 Summer Games may have equal numbers of men and women. The number of athletes participating in 1976, 1980, and 1984 was lower than expected, due to boycotts.

Table 7.2 Female and male athletes at recent Paralympic Games, all nations and US delegation 2006–2016

Recent Paralympic Games*	Number of Females (%)	Number of Males (%)	Total Number of Athletes
2016 Rio de Janeiro	1670 (39%)	2663 (61%)	4333
2012 Summer Games–London 164 nations	1513 (35%)	2756 (65%)	4269
2010 Winter Games–Vancouver 44 nations	121 (24%)	381 (76%)	502
2006 Winter Games–Turin, Italy 39 nations	99 (21%)	375 (79%)	384
2016 Rio de Janeiro	121 (46%)	146 (54%)	267
2012 Summer Games–London US delegation	94 (41%)	133 (59%)	227
2010 Winter Games–Vancouver US delegation	13 (26%)	37 (74%)	50
2006 Winter Games–Turin, Italy US delegation	11 (20%)	45 (80%)	56

Source: Smith and Wrynn, 2010; International Paralympic Committee; www.teamusa.org
*Data for China are unavailable

some cases, entry into these activities is "sponsored" by influential male participants who convince others that a particular girl or woman should have a chance to demonstrate her skills as an athlete.

Compared to men, access to sports participation opportunities for girls and women is also limited by the time constraints associated with household chores, child care, and other family responsibilities. Men are more likely than women to compartmentalize their lives, put job and family issues on hold, and take time to work out or play sports. In the case of married couples, even when both people work full time, women often "subsidize" the sport participation of their male partners by dedicating more of their time to household and family responsibilities.

Title IX law does not apply to informal activities, which means there is no legal pressure to change. But female participants have formed activist groups that are becoming more proactive in pushing for recognition and inclusion. Additionally, there are new organizations worldwide that advocate for the inclusion of girls and women in a range of alternative sports, especially skateboarding (Atencio et al., 2018). At the same time, some boys and men pushback as they assume that they should have priority when using spaces, facilities, or resources for sports.

Research also shows that alternative sports are organized around the values and experiences of boys and young men (Carr, 2017; Comley, 2016; Matthews, 2016; Wheaton & Thorpe, 2018). Observing nearly any skateboard park reaffirms this point. Girls and young women are usually spectators–bystanders with boards, or they're cautiously assertive participants who must work harder than male peers to be taken seriously as skaters. Additionally, when females do claim space for themselves in bowls or ramp areas, they usually do so on terms set by the males.

Many action and "extreme" sports focus on facing one's fears, taking risks, and pushing normative limits. The boys and young men in these sports say that recognition and inclusion is based on skill, guts, and aggressiveness, not gender. However, the vocabulary used in these activities highlights the need to possess "big *cahones*" and the willingness to go "balls to the wall" to be accepted. Therefore, females must "have balls"–that is, enough skill and guts to attempt and occasionally accomplish creative and dangerous tricks that boys and men deem to be crucial in the identity-claiming process. This vocabulary and the norms in the sports privilege males and put females at a disadvantage.

The consequences of the male-dominated/identified/centered culture and organization of alternative and action sports are also seen in media-created, corporate-sponsored versions such as the X Games, Street League Skateboarding Pro Tour, the Maloof Money Cup, and the Dew Tour. Patterns vary from one sport to another, but including women is not usually a high-priority goal in most extreme sports.

In response to the masculinized cultures in most alternative sports, some women have created new sports or revised others so they are organized around their own experiences and goals. A good example of this is the rapidly growing flat-track roller derby. The Women's Flat Track Derby Association (WFTDA) in 2019 had 463 member leagues on six continents (https://wftda.com/wftda-leagues/). As one participant–a young lawyer from Houston–described it,

> *The roller derby of today is . . . an empowering sport for female athletes. It's also a sisterhood. This is not a sport for dainty girls. Most of the girls are extremely muscular and have some heft to prevent them from being knocked down. . . .* (Murphy, 2012)

Roller derby team cultures are organized around the values and experiences of women (Beaver, 2016; Breeze, 2015; Donnelly, 2014; Gieseler, 2014; Liu, Baghurst & Bradley, 2018; Murphy, 2012; Pavlidis and Fullagar, 2013, 2014, 2015; Pavlidis & Connor, 2016;

(*Source:* Bryan Winter/Sports Illustrated/Getty Images)

Roller derby teams are becoming widespread as women seek new sports experiences and form new sports cultures. The athletes on these teams embrace a wide array of ideas and beliefs about femininity; most reject orthodox gender ideology. Derby bouts are sites where alternative definitions of femininity are presented to spectators.

Pavlidis & O'Brien, 2017). They emphasize inclusion and bring diverse women together in supportive relationships. They also provide spaces in which women can present an array of sexualities through personas constructed to express individual approaches to gender that would be perceived as "out of the ordinary" in mainstream contexts. At the same time, being able to present these personas (or selves) in derby enables women to feel more comfortable with them, at least among themselves and most derby spectators. Additionally, spectators are treated to a rainbow of sexuality possibilities that disrupt dominant gender ideology at the same time that they are entertaining.

Support for Athletes

Female athletes in many US high schools and colleges receive less sport-related support than boys and men receive. This pattern also exists in sport-sponsoring organizations worldwide. Historically, inequities have existed in the following areas:

- Access to facilities
- Quality of facilities (playing surfaces, weight training, locker rooms, showers, and so on)
- Availability of scholarships*
- Program operating expenses
- Provision and maintenance of equipment and supplies
- Recruiting budgets*
- Scheduling of games and practice times
- Travel and per diem expenses
- Opportunity to receive academic tutoring*
- Numbers of coaches assigned to teams
- Salaries for administrators, coaches, trainers, and other staff
- Provision of medical and training services and facilities
- Publicity and media coverage for women's teams and events

Inequities in some of these areas remain in many schools, but they are a greater problem in community programs, where they often go undetected unless someone digs through data from many sources to identify them.

**These apply primarily to US colleges and universities.*

Most people today realize that a lack of support subverts sports participation among girls and women. For well over a century, men built their programs, shaped them to fit their interests and values, generated interest in participation, marketed them to spectators, and sold them to sponsors. During this time, public funds and facilities, student fees, and private sponsorships were used to fund, promote, and expand programs for boys and men. Few sports for girls and women have enjoyed the support received in the past by sports for boys and men (Allison, 2018). As publicly funded, neighborhood-based sport programs have nearly disappeared, girls and women today are missing the publicly supported participation opportunities that boys and men enjoyed from the 1950s through the early 1980s. In this sense, girls and women have been historically shortchanged compared to their male peers. The historical support that boys and men received has been crucial in building talent pools and spectator interests that drive the success of men's high school, college, and professional sports today. If girls and women had the same support during those four decades, today's inequities might be less significant.

Access to Positions of Power

Gender inequality is most glaring when it comes to who holds positions of power in sports. As the visibility and importance of sports for girls and women has increased, most of the positions of power in those sports have been given to and taken by men. At the same time, almost none of the power positions in men's sports are held by women. Data at all levels of competition show that women are severely underrepresented in coaching and administration jobs, especially at the highest levels of power in sports (Fasting, Sisjord & Sand, 2017; Houghton, Pieper & Smith, 2017; Norman, Rankin-Wright & Allison, 2018; Zarrett, Cooky & Veliz, 2019).

Men today coach the majority of women's teams, they occupy the top positions of power in women's sports programs, and they make most of the decisions that impact girls and women in sports. At the same time, women have no noticeable power in men's sports and struggle to gain access to power in women's sports. Data collected since 1972 in the United States documents these gender trends for college coaching and administration positions in NCAA institutions (Acosta & Carpenter, 2015; Lapchick, 2019; LaVoi, 2019):

- When Title IX became law in 1972, women coached 90 percent of women's teams in the NCAA; by 1978 the proportion dropped to 58 percent; in 2019 it was about 42 percent.
- In 1998, there were 188 woman serving as athletic directors (ADs) in NCAA institutions (19 percent of all ADs); in 2018 women held 10.5 percent of the AD positions in Division I, 18 percent in DII, and 32 percent in DIII.
- The athletic departments that have had female athletic directors over the years have also had higher proportions of women coaches, and the proportion of female coaches and administrators has always been lowest in NCAA Division I and highest in Division III.
- Less than 13 percent of all NCAA institutions had a female full-time sports information director in 2018, and for nearly all previous years it has been at 10 percent or less.
- Very few women are head coaches for men's or gender-combined teams in swimming, cross-country, or tennis in 2018, 4 percent of those jobs were held by women in DI and DII, and 6.8 percent in DIII, and less than 1 percent of men have ever had a female coach on a school team.

If 80 percent of the administrators and head coaches of all NCAA athletic departments and intercollegiate teams were women, men would be outraged. They would immediately demand affirmative action programs, and file lawsuits. Up until now, women have been far less demanding as they have faced limited access to power positions in sports.

The exclusion and underrepresentation of women in coaching and administration exists worldwide. For example, at the last four Olympic Games (Vancouver, London, Sochi, and Rio de Janeiro), 90 percent of all accredited coaches from all countries were men (https://www.olympic.org/women-in-sport/background/statistics). In the top 5 men's leagues in the US—NBA, NFL, NHL, MLB, & MLS–there are about 2600 coaches, and the total number of female coaches is six (Struby, 2019). The IOC, the world's most powerful sport organization, had *no* women members for 85 years (1896 to 1981) and it has never had a female president. In 1996, the IOC promised that in the Olympic movement, women would make up 20 percent of its decision-making boards by 2005. They missed that target date by a decade, but in 2019 women made up one-third of the IOC members and 31 percent of executive board members. Additionally, 43 percent of the IOC Commissions were chaired by women in 2019.

Coaching numbers worldwide show that few women coach women's or men's national teams, and women coaches are very rare in professional leagues outside of North America.

The major reasons for the underrepresentation of women in coaching and administrative positions include the following (Adriaanse, 2019; Henry and Robison, 2010; Norman, Rankin-Wright & Allison, 2018):

- Women are not considered for half of all coaching and administration jobs–that is, coaching or managing men's teams and programs.
- Compared to men, women have fewer influential sport-related social connections to help them obtain jobs in women's or men's sports.
- Job search committees are often dominated by men who perceive female applicants as being less qualified than male applicants.
- Many women have not had career-related support systems and development opportunities that many men have had when they apply for jobs.
- Women working in male-dominated/identified/centered sports programs are more likely than their male peers to experience sexual harassment, which sets them up to fail or discourages them from remaining in coaching and administration jobs.

These factors affect opportunities *and* aspirations. They influence who applies for jobs, how applicants fare during the hiring process, how coaches and administrators are evaluated, who enjoys coaching, and who is promoted into higher-paying jobs with more responsibility and power.

People on job search committees seek, interview, evaluate, and hire candidates that they think will succeed in male-dominated/identified/centered organizations. After assessing objective qualifications, such as years of experience and win–loss records, search committee members subjectively assess such things as a candidate's abilities to recruit and motivate players, raise money, command respect in the community (among boosters, fans, sports reporters who are mostly white men), build toughness and character among players, maintain team discipline, and "fit into" the athletic department or sports organization.

None of these assessments occurs in a vacuum, and some are influenced by gender ideology in addition to past-performance records. Although people on search committees do not agree on all things, many think in terms that favor men over women. This is because coaching and other forms of leadership often are seen as consistent with traditional ideas about masculinity: a good coach is one who "coaches like a man"–a taken-for-granted principle in male-dominated and male-identified sports cultures.

Under these conditions, women are hired only when they present compelling evidence that they can do things as men have done them in the past. When women are hired, they are less likely than men to feel welcome and fully included in sports organizations. Therefore, they often have lower levels of job satisfaction and higher rates of job turnover. This causes some people to conclude that women simply don't have what it takes to survive in sports. But this conclusion ignores the fact that job expectations in sports have been developed over the years by men who have had wives to raise their children, provide emotional support to them and their teams, host social events for teams and boosters, coordinate their social schedules, handle household finances and maintenance, make sure they're not distracted by family and household issues, and faithfully attend games season after season. If female coaches and administrators had an opportunity to build programs and coach teams under similar conditions, job satisfaction would be higher and turnover would be lower.

Finally, some sports organizations have records of being negligent in controlling sexual harassment and responding to complaints from women who wish to be taken seriously in the structure and culture of sports organizations and programs. This means that people in the programs must critically assess the impact of male-dominated/identified/centered forms of social organization on both males and females. Unless this assessment takes place and changes are made, gender equity will never be achieved in coaching and administration.

BARRIERS TO EQUITY

Progress toward gender equity has been significant, but there continue to be inequities in several important spheres. As strategies are developed to eliminate inequities, it is essential to be aware of barriers that will be encountered along the way. These include the following:

1. Budget cuts and privatization of sports programs
2. Few models of women in positions of power
3. A cultural emphasis on "cosmetic fitness" for women
4. Trivialization of women's sports
5. Resistance in male-dominated/identified/centered sports organizations

Budget Cuts and the Privatization of Sports

Gender equity is often subverted by budget cuts. Compared with programs for boys and men, programs for girls and women are more vulnerable to cuts because they are less well-established and have less market presence and revenue-generating potential, and less administrative, corporate, community, and institutional support. Therefore, to cut funds equally from sports teams and programs for everyone has a greater negative impact on programs for girls and women. Programs for boys and men are less vulnerable because they've had more than a century to develop legitimacy, institutional support, loyal fans, and sponsors.

As public, tax-supported sport programs are cut, opportunities to play sports become privatized, which also has a disproportionately negative impact on girls and women, especially in low-income areas. Public programs are accountable to voters and regulated by government rules mandating equal rights and opportunities. But private programs are accountable to the market, meaning that they respond to the needs of dues-paying participants and private sponsors rather than a commitment to gender equity. "Free-enterprise sports" are great for people with money. But they are neither "free" nor "enterprising" when it comes to providing opportunities for girls and women with few financial resources. Commercial programs serve only those who can buy what's for sale, so they are rare in low-income and many ethnic minority areas.

When sports programs are cut in public schools, booster organizations are more likely to step up and provide funds and facilities for boys' sports, such as football, than for girls' sports. Neither boosters nor private providers are required to follow Title IX law, because they receive no support from the federal government. When these resource providers are not committed to gender equity, girls and women lose opportunities.

Budget cuts and privatization affect sports programs worldwide. In wealthy democratic nations there generally is cultural pressure and official commitments to gender equity, especially related to participation opportunities. Girls and women in poor and developing nations usually have little access to participation unless it is provided by a national government. In patriarchal cultures and societies, females often are discouraged from playing sports or forced to play under restricted conditions. This means that progress toward gender equity is uneven with most international competitions for women being dominated by the wealthy nations.

Few Models of Women in Positions of Power

As women's sports have become more visible and important they have been folded into men's programs and men have moved into coaching, managerial, and administrative positions. During this process, women have often lost their jobs to men who were less likely than women to mentor, recruit, and support women seeking jobs in sports. And women coaches often felt pressure to hire male assistant coaches to avoid the perception that they preferred women and disliked men.

As young female athletes see that men occupy most of the positions of power and leadership in sports organizations, they are less likely to envision themselves as future leaders in sports. In their minds, positions of power automatically go to men and the abilities and contributions of women are valued less than those of men. Nicole LaVoi (2018), co-director of the Tucker Center for Research on Girls and Women in Sport notes that female athletes benefit when they have female role models. This shows them that coaching and sports administration are realistic career goals and that they don't have to depend solely on men for support if they chose a sports career. Additionally, it is important for boys and men to see women as capable leaders in sports and to learn from them if they chose a sports career. If and when more women coach and manage men's teams and programs it will push the normative boundaries of sports cultures, expand the perspectives used in governing sports, and affirm a commitment to inclusion.

Cultural Emphasis on "Cosmetic Fitness"

Girls and women receive mixed and confusing cultural messages about body image and sports participation. Although they see powerful female athletes, they cannot escape media images of celebrities and models whose bodies are shaped by food deprivation, cosmetic surgery, and digital manipulations. They hear that physical power and competence are important, but they see rewards going to women who appear young, vulnerable, and nonathletic. They are advised to be strong but thin, fit but feminine, in shape *and* shapely. They see attractive athletes packaged and presented as fashion models rather than strong, skilled performers. And they often conclude that even when you're a good athlete, being hot is what really matters (Mutz & Meier, 2016).

Cultural messages promoting appearance and beauty clearly outnumber those promoting the pleasure of playing sports. People in marketing departments know that females consume more products when they are insecure about their appearance. Therefore, even ads that show women doing sports are carefully staged to make female consumers feel insecure rather than confident about their bodies. This marketing strategy is so powerful that some females avoid sports until they are thin enough to look "good" and wear "cute" clothes; others combine their sport participation with pathogenic weight-control strategies to become dangerously thin or undernourished.

Overall, the tensions between cosmetic fitness and being physically strong and skilled keep a significant segment of girls and women out of sports (Zarrett, Cooky & Veliz, 2019). Additionally, young women seeking cosmetic fitness sometimes drop out of sports if they gain weight while they train, and others drop out after achieving weight-loss goals. Cultural messages about cosmetic fitness are here to stay, and they continue to be a barrier to gender equity in sports–unless they are critically assessed as subversive tools that foster insecurity and drive consumption.

Trivialization of Women's Sports

The most visible and popular sports in society are based on the values and experiences of men. They often emphasize skills and evaluative standards that disadvantage women, especially at the elite level. For example, women play soccer, but they don't kick with the same force as men do. They play basketball, but they don't dunk like men. They play hockey, but they don't check or fight like men. They do sports, but they don't do them like men do them. For example, as ice hockey leagues for girls have been established in Canada, it has been difficult for some of them to obtain ice time because their leagues are perceived as second class by those who control hockey and the ice rinks (Adams & Leavitt, 2018). By trivializing girls' hockey, the boys and men are able to preserve their privileged access to the ice.

This leads some people to see women's sports as inferior and not take them as seriously as they take men's sports. This undermines the possibility of achieving gender equity.

A classic example of women's sports being trivialized occurred in 2019 in connection with the FIFA Women's World Cup that is held every 4 years. Over the past 28 years, this international competition has become the premier global event in women's sports. It attracts a global audience and is used by the 24 qualifying national teams as a showcase for soccer in their countries and to grow women's soccer worldwide. FIFA, the organization that controls all major soccer tournaments worldwide, announced on September 28, 2017, that the Women's World Cup would begin on June 7, 2019, with the final match to be played on July 7.

Nearly a year later, two of the six continental confederations in FIFA–CONCACAF, the governing body for soccer in North and Central America and the Caribbean, and CONMEBOL, the governing body for soccer in South America–announced that their competitions for men's national teams would begin in June 2019, with their final games to be played on July 7. This announcement sent a shockwave through the women's soccer world. The men who manage FIFA and its confederations had forgotten or never thought about the Women's World Cup and scheduled their competitions during the same month with their championships on the same day as the women's final. This had a major negative impact on women's matches, especially the championship match. Advertising revenues and viewer ratings were reduced as the men's tournaments that are held every 2 to 3 years undermined the publicity that was expected to boost participation by girls and the popularity of women's soccer matches worldwide. This mistake was made because the men who run global soccer had trivialized women's soccer to the point that they forgot or simply ignored the dates for the Women's World Cup tournament and its final game (Smith, 2019). With support like that from the world's most powerful sport organization, it is difficult to overcome the barriers to gender equity.

Male-Dominated/Identified/Centered Sport Organizations

Sports remain closely linked with orthodox forms of masculinity. Males have long used sports as sites to establish their identities as men and gain status in the larger community. The cultures created around sports programs and teams were created to nurture and reaffirm a shared sense of manhood. This gave boys and men a sense of agency–that is, a feeling that they had control over who they were and how others perceived them.

When girls and women finally had opportunities to play sports, the number of participants grew exponentially. But their participation has not yet matched male participation rates. The standard explanation for this persistent difference is that girls and women "just aren't as interested in sports as much as boys and men are." But a more accurate statement would be this: *Compared to boys and men, girls and women experience fewer positive vibes and less support in sports and sport cultures that have been created by and for men for the sake of learning about masculinity and reaffirming a shared sense of manhood associated with feelings of power and control.*

The point here is that persistent gender inequities are not due to a lack of interest among girls and women as much as they are due to sports and sports organizations that do not directly reflect girls' and women's lived experiences in the same way that they reflect and reaffirm the lived experiences of boys and men (Zarrett, Cooky & Veliz, 2019).

Research shows that when programs and teams are organized to enable girls and women to control and claim ownership of sports on an organizational and institutional level, gender equity becomes more achievable (Cooky, 2004, 2009). This reminds us that in addition to influencing identity, cultural expectations, and social interaction, gender is embedded in the logic of organizations and institutions (Adriaanse, 2019; Messner, 2011; Risman and Davis, 2013). It is this organizational and institutional dimension of gender that now slows progress toward equity in sports. In other words, we can change our attitudes and personal relationships to be more inclusive and less constrained by orthodox gender ideology, but until we change the taken-for-granted gender logic that structures so much of sports and sports organizations, full gender equity will not be achieved. When the logic of gender that shapes cultural and organizational processes in sports is based exclusively on the values and experiences of men, these processes privilege men more than women and lead women to feel less welcome and less personally accepted in all aspects of sports than their male peers feel.

GENDER EQUITY AND SEXUALITY

Sports have long been associated with male heterosexuality and have been sites for the expression of homophobia and the performance of heterosexual masculinity as a cultural ideal. The history and sociology of sport have clearly documented these patterns and how they have impacted the lives of lesbians, gay men, bisexuals, transsexuals, and intersex persons (LGBTQs). However, in certain regions of the world, including much of northern and western Europe, Australia, New Zealand, and North America, a growing number of men have adopted a more inclusive definition of masculinity, a definition that accepts variations that were and continue to be rejected by those who see the world through the lens of orthodox gender ideology (Pew Global Attitudes Project, 2013). As a result,

(*Source:* John Crouch/Icon Sportswire/Getty Images)

When women are included in men's sports it usually has more to do with physical appearance than athletic skills. The Colorado Avalanche in the National Hockey League uses women to clean the ice. Their clothing was chosen for aesthetic rather than functional reasons. This is not the form of inclusion that advances gender equity in ice hockey.

sports have become a less supportive context for homophobia. Examples include the following:

- Players using homophobic slurs have been criticized by other players, reprimanded by team and league officials, and portrayed negatively in mainstream media.
- Both male and female athletes have publicly supported LGBTQ rights and marriage equality, and have occasionally been among the most vocal and visible supporters of LGBTQ rights.
- Sports organizations, groups of athletes, and Outsports.com have discussed strategies that might be used by athletes if and when they decide to come out.
- The National Hockey League (NHL) and its Players' Association (NHLPA) in early 2013 became the first major men's sports organization to issue a formal statement condemning anti-LGBTQ bigotry and promising support for players who come out.
- Major League Soccer has suspended and fined players for using homophobic slurs.
- The Ultimate Fighting Championship (UFC) suspended a mixed martial arts fighter and mandated that he do community service for the LGBTQ community as a result of his transphobic comments about a fighter who had undergone male-to-female gender reassignment surgery.
- The coverage of and response to gay male athletes who have come out in recent years has been largely supportive.
- Nineteen US states now have rules to enable transgender students in high school to compete on teams that correspond with their gender

identities rather than the sex designation listed in their school records. The NCAA has a policy supportive of transgender participation, and other sports organizations, including the IOC, LPGA, USGA, and many Olympic sports federations, now have policies that specify the conditions under which transgendered athletes may participate.

- The high-profile women athletes who have come out recently have received little news coverage because it has been 40 years since tennis player Martina Navratilova came out in 1981, and coming out today is accepted to the point that it is no longer a major news story.

This list should not be taken to mean that LGBTQs face no challenges or live free of the sting of homophobia and significant forms of discrimination. Men in elite sports are not knocking the door down coming out, and fears about the negative consequences of coming out remain strong in both men's and women's sports. More serious fears are felt by bisexuals and transgender people; and people with intersex characteristics are not making public announcements about their sexuality. The participation of male-to-female transgender athletes is being contested at both the high school and college levels in the United States. Eligibility and the conditions under which eligibility is granted are discussed and debated worldwide as people impose a two sex sport system on everyone who participates (BettingOffers, 2019).

Homophobia continues to exist. It is based on the notion that homosexuality is abnormal, deviant, or immoral–out of normative boundaries according to orthodox gender ideology. Along with transphobia, it fuels prejudice, discrimination, harassment, and violence directed toward those identified or believed to have identities or sexual orientations that are something other than heterosexual.

When LGBTQs play sports, many remain careful to keep their sexual identities private or disclosed only to select friends and family members. They either have mixed or confused feelings about themselves or they fear possible negative responses from others. But as more people come out publicly, it normalizes gender nonconforming identities. Still, the anticipated challenges of coming out can be overwhelming, so most LGBTQ athletes remain closeted, pass as heterosexual, selectively reveal their identity only to trustworthy others, or choose sports in which they are less likely to confront homophobia (Kopycinski, 2018).

Lesbians in Sports

Acceptance of gender-nonconforming athletes is greater in women's than in men's sports. But even today, homophobia discourages some females from playing certain sports and from appearing "too masculine" or "too unfeminine" if they do play sports. Additionally, it still causes some parents to steer daughters away from teams, programs, and sports that they believe attract lesbians or have lesbian coaches.

When girls and women fear the label of *lesbian* or fear being associated with lesbians, they may avoid certain sports, limit their commitment to sports, de-emphasize their athletic identities, or emphasize a "presentation of self" that explicitly portrays heterosexuality. For example, some young women in the United States avoid cutting their hair short because it could elicit "homophobic teasing" from peers. At the same time, homophobia prompts lesbian athletes to keep their identity secret even though it limits their relationships with teammates and leads to loneliness and isolation.

Pat Griffin's groundbreaking book *Strong Women, Deep Closets: Lesbians and Homophobia in Sports* (1998) provides clear evidence that "sports and lesbians have always gone together" (p. ix). She notes that this evidence has been ignored in the popular consciousness, largely because of cultural myths about lesbians. Although most myths have been challenged and discredited, some people continue to believe them. For example, some think that lesbians are predatory and want to "convert" others to their "way of life," which is judged to be immoral and depressing. When lesbian athletes, coaches, and administrators perceive that people think this way, they often feel undervalued and experience a sense of isolation. When heterosexual peers believe these myths or even wonder about their veracity, they fear or avoid lesbian athletes and coaches; when coaches and administrators believe them, they're less likely to hire and promote lesbians in coaching and sport management.

The homophobic statement "No bow, Lesbo" is still used on some women's teams and accounts for what has become a standard practice of girls and young women wearing cute bows with their ponytails when they play games. In college sports there are still heterosexual coaches who describe their teams as "wholesome" and being grounded in "family values" to indicate that they are anti-lesbian; and they may infer that competing programs don't have the same values–implying that their coaches or some players are lesbian. Such expressions of homophobia have discouraged some young women from pursuing careers in coaching, especially at the college level where recruitment competition can be intense.

Some women's sports and teams are characterized by a "don't ask, don't tell" culture in which lesbians hide their identity to play the sports they love without being harassed or marginalized. However, this strategy has costs, and it slows changes that might defuse or erase homophobia. Overall, a "don't ask, don't tell" approach affects both heterosexual women and lesbians, all of whom restrain their actions to avoid suspicions or being labeled as lesbians.

Pat Griffin encourages people to be open and truthful about sexual identity, but she explains that lesbians must be prepared to handle everything from hostility to cautious acceptance when they come out. She points out that handling challenges is easier (a) when friends, teammates, and coaches provide support; (b) when there are local organizations that challenge homophobia and advocate tolerance; and (c) when there is institutionalized legal protection and support for gays and lesbians in organizations, communities, and society.

The points made in this section apply primarily to the United States. Although there are a few societies in which lesbians are more widely accepted than they are in the US, there are many others where being a known or suspected lesbian puts a person's life in danger. For example, in South Africa where homophobia permeates the culture as well as sports organizations, "black queer women athletes are brutalised, sexualised, or made invisible" (Engh & Potgieter, 2018). In practical terms, the combination of misogyny and homophobia serve to silence all voices but for those of heterosexual males.

(*Source:* Molly Darlington - AMA/Getty Images)

Megan Rapinoe, a popular American soccer player, is an out lesbian. This, along with her advocacy of LGBTQ issues, does not appear to affect her relationships with teammates or fans. In most women's sports, lesbians are accepted by teammates, integrated into team relationships, and accepted by fans, especially younger ones.

Gay Men in Sports

Changes related to attitudes about homosexuality have not been as significant in men's sports as in women's sports. The culture of many men's sports continues to support a vocabulary of homophobia. However, heterosexual male athletes have in recent years been generally supportive of teammates who come out to them. This has led sociologist Eric Anderson and others (Anderson & McCormack, 2018; Magrath, Cleland & Anderson, 2020) to conclude that there is a more inclusive form of masculinity emerging among young men, a form that rejects the rigidity of orthodox gender ideology. But Anderson and others note that homophobia remains a serious threat in men's sports and discourages nearly all gay athletes, coaches, and administrators from coming out, especially in highly visible elite sports where it would attract widespread media attention and could seriously disrupt the person's life and interfere with meeting expectations as a player or manager.

Playing certain sports remains a rite of passage for boys to become men. Male athletes in power and performance sports remain models of heterosexual manhood in most societies today. Therefore, there is much at stake in maintaining silence about gay men in sports, discouraging them from revealing their identities, and policing gender boundaries in and through men's sports. This preserves the integrity of existing normative gender boundaries, the glorified status of male athletes, and male access to power and influence in society.

A seldom discussed consequence of homophobia is that it creates a context in which boys and men resist or feel ashamed of their feelings of affection toward other men. When this occurs, they may mimic violent caricatures of masculinity to express their manhood–or it may force male athletes to express their connections with each other through head-butts, belly bashers, arm punches, forearm crosses, fist bumping, and other ritualistic actions that disguise intimacy. These "bro gestures" may make boys and men feel good, but they also keep them in the "act like a man box," which limits possibilities in their lives.

Intersex and Transgender Persons in Sports

What happens to people born with a combination of male and female sex traits or those who have a gender identity or behavior that falls outside stereotypical norms (e.g., transgender) or does not match the gender they were assigned at birth (e.g., transsexual)? This population consists of an estimated 120 million intersex people worldwide and many times that number who identify themselves as "trans" in some way (Fausto-Sterling, 2000b). Where do they fit in sports organized around a rigid two-sex system?

Although intersex and "trans" women and men have been ignored or routinely excluded from nearly all organized sports, recent policy changes have allowed transsexuals to participate in sports if they meet certain conditions related to standard medical practices and hormone therapy.

The IOC policy approved in 2004 stated that trans women athletes may compete if they had undergone sex-reassignment surgery, if they were legally classified as a female, and if they underwent 2 years of approved medically supervised testosterone suppression. In 2015 the IOC deleted the surgery requirement and specified that athletes must maintain a testosterone level under 10 nanomoles per liter of blood for 12 months prior to a competition. In 2019 the allowable testosterone level was lowered to 5 nonomoles–a rule that is being appealed as I write this. However, in the years since 2004, out of over 50,000 Olympians there has not been one openly transgender athlete to compete in an event. Trans men may compete in any event as long as they have undergone testosterone supplementation under an approved doctor's care.

The IOC policy is relatively restrictive compared to the NCAA policy, which does not require surgery because it is prohibitively expensive for college students and sometimes takes a few years to complete–and genitalia have no influence on sport performance. Additionally, NCAA policy states that only 1 year of testosterone suppression is needed for trans women to be eligible to compete in women's sports; and trans men have a medical exemption to take testosterone under approved medical supervision so they can compete with men without violating drug rules, but they are not eligible to compete in women's sports.

Trans athletes push gender boundaries, but intersex people born with "a reproductive or sexual anatomy and/or chromosome pattern that doesn't fit typical definitions of male or female" create confusion for those using orthodox gender ideology as noted in the discussion of Caster Semenya and the refusal of the international track and field federation to accept natural variations in the traits of females.

These policies illustrate how difficult it is to develop regulations so that human bodies fit into sports organized around a rigid two-sex classification system. Even more difficult, is renegotiating the meaning of sex to eliminate the traditional normative boundaries that separate females and males into nonoverlapping categories. Gender activists refer to "the queering of sport" as the process of renegotiating or eliminating the two-sex system and becoming fully gender-inclusive.

The dynamics of this queering of sport process have been studied by Ann Travers and her colleagues at Simon Fraser University in British Columbia (Travers, 2006, 2013b; Travers and Deri, 2011). Travers spent over 4 years observing and interviewing participants in lesbian softball leagues throughout North America. In the process, she investigated tensions around the inclusion of transgender and transsexual persons on teams. Initially she found that many players in the leagues used the two-sex system to identify themselves and others, even though nearly all of them rejected parts of orthodox gender ideology. Therefore, many were uncertain or uncomfortable about allowing a person to play in a "lesbian-women's league" if that person could not be clearly classified as female. In particular, this affected those just beginning the transition from male to female and those close to completing the transition from female to male.

Most players in the league used a hormone-centered perspective to determine if a person was female enough to play without raising questions about fairness. As a person's testosterone and strength declined, she was accepted in the league, but as testosterone and strength increased it was difficult to know when a person should drop out and play on a men's team. When players were making a female to male transition, some others were upset that the person had chosen to identify and live as a man instead of remaining a lesbian, and those making the transition felt unfairly abandoned after they had spent much of their lives working for lesbian rights and sustaining supportive lesbian communities and networks.

As Travers and Deri (2011) observed and analyzed these dynamics, they noted "how deeply complicated it is to attempt to re-negotiate sexed boundaries." But they also noted that it was possible to shift away from organizing sport around a rigid two-sex system. This shift is a work in process, and whether or how it will continue is uncertain. The next challenge for the softball league might be how to include those who reject gender as an identity category because it imposes unnecessary limits on who they can be, how others treat them, and how they live their lives.

STRATEGIES TO ACHIEVE EQUITY

Achieving gender equity requires action by people possessing the critical awareness needed to transform gender ideology and how we do sports, so that participation is accessible and meaningful regardless of gender. This is a complex and challenging task. There are practical and effective ways to accomplish it, but they involve both women and men and a willingness to critically assess how we do sports today.

Using the Law and Engaging in Grassroots Activism

In societies where laws mandate equal gender opportunities, as in the case of Title IX in the United States, those laws must be consistently enforced over time. If this does not occur, backsliding into past inequities is likely, due to the continuing male-dominated power structure in most sports organizations. Even though nearly everyone in the United States supports the idea of gender equity, those who control sports organizations often resist changes because they are likely to lose some power in the process. Additionally, many head coaches who have grown up in the post–Title IX era have little understanding of the meaning of gender equity, how to achieve it, and how it relates to their jobs (Staurowsky and Weight, 2011). This means that legal action is one strategy, but certainly not the only or most important strategy, for achieving gender equity.

Most effective in the quest for gender equity are grassroots actions that identify inequities and support needed changes. These grassroots actions include the following:

- *Confront discriminatory practices* in your athletic department and become an advocate for female athletes, coaches, and administrators.
- *Insist on fair and open employment practices* in the entire organization, including the athletic department.
- *Keep a record of equity data* and have an independent group issue a public "gender equity report card" every 3–4 years for your athletic department or sport program.
- *Learn and educate others* about the history of gender discrimination in sports and how to recognize the subtle forms of discrimination that operate in sport worlds that are male-dominated, male-identified, and male-centered.
- *Object* to practices and policies that decrease opportunities for women in sports, *and inform* the media of them.
- *Package and promote women's sports* as revenue producers, so there will be financial incentives to increase participation opportunities for women.
- *Recruit female athletes into coaching* by establishing internships and training programs.
- *Use women's hiring networks* when seeking coaches and administrators in sports programs.
- *Create a supportive work climate* for women and establish policies to eliminate sexual harassment in the athletic department.

These actions involve a combination of research, public relations, advocacy, political participation, and education. They're based on the assumption that equity will be achieved only through persistent struggle, effective political organization, and changes that enable girls and women to play sports on their own terms rather than exclusively on terms that have been set by boys and men with power and influence.

Boys and Men Benefit from Gender Equity

When discussing gender, people often focus on girls and women and overlook the fact that ideas and beliefs about gender have major relevance for boys and men, whose lives may be negatively affected by hegemonic masculinity. This is true in sports, the military, work, and on the streets, where men are killed, seriously injured, and put in situations that damage their health and well-being more often than is the case for women.

Gender equity in sports is not just a woman's issue. It also involves creating options for boys and men to play sports based on pleasure and participation more than power and performance. The widely accepted belief that the actions of boys and men are driven by testosterone, innate aggressive tendencies, and a need to dominate others creates havoc in everyday life, and it promotes heavy-contact and collision sports as primary molders of manhood. But those sports don't fit the interests and body types of most boys and young men. In fact, most adult males don't play those sports, primarily because they know it is not healthy to do so.

Sports currently privilege men over women, but they also privilege some men over other men. When men realize that certain sports perpetuate attitudes and orientations that often undermine their relationships with one another and with women, they are more inclined to view sports critically and become agents of change. Men who want to move beyond expressing their fondness for each other by teasing, pranking, hazing, mock fighting, and getting memorably drunk at the next football game have good reason

(*Source*: Photo courtesy of The Hunger Project; www.thp.org)

Developing physical skills often improves health and provides girls and women with a sense of empowerment. This is true for Reshma, a 7-year-old in Dhaka, Bangladesh. However, if the culture and social structure in Bangladesh are organized to systematically prevent females from gaining power in society, Reshma's joy and sense of empowerment from winning this race will be temporary and difficult to convert into the power to make needed institutional changes as an adult (see Musto, 2013).

to join with women concerned who critically assess dominant sport forms in their societies. In the process they will learn how to work, play sports, and live with men and women in mutually supportive relationships. The alternative is to remain stuck in the mud of hegemonic masculinity, blame women for problems, and seek refuge by watching bigger, stronger, faster men play sports in which they hurt each other.

Research indicates that growing numbers of young men today, including those who play sports, are more critical of hegemonic masculinity than was common in previous generations. Studies by Eric Anderson (2015), Brian Barth (2018), Carly Gieseler (2019), Nigel Jarvis (2015), B. Michael (2015); Nick Rogers (2019), and Adam White (2017) each found that there are growing numbers of male athletes who use "alternative," "ambivalent," "inclusive," and "moderated" masculinities, to identify and assess themselves and male peers. Although this often occurs as an individual or small group/team phenomenon, these young men did not view themselves or others through the lens of orthodox gender ideology. Instead, they avoided violence, expressed their emotions, demonstrated compassion, and nurtured relationships on and off the field that blurred rigid divisions between masculine and feminine. As more boys and men do this, there will be more social and cultural space for inclusive masculinity as well as various forms of gender-inclusive ideology. This makes gender equity more achievable, and opens up possibilities to create sports that provide people of all ages and abilities with more welcoming and satisfying experiences.

Empowering Girls and Women Through Sports

Sports participation offers girls and women opportunities to connect with the power of their bodies and reject notions that females are naturally weak, dependent, and powerless. It helps them overcome the feeling that their bodies are objects to be viewed, evaluated, and consumed. The physical skills and strength often gained through sports participation help some girls and women feel less vulnerable, more competent and independent, and more in control of their physical safety and psychological well-being.

However, empowerment does not occur automatically when a girl or woman plays sports, nor does a sense of personal empowerment always lead to actions that push the normative boundaries of heterosexual femininity or promote gender equity in sports or other spheres of life. Feeling competent as athletes does not guarantee that women will critically assess gender ideology and gender relations or work for equity in sports or society. Those who play at elite levels often avoid becoming "boat rockers" critical of the gender order for fear that they might alienate friends and fans and jeopardize their endorsement contracts.

This has also been the case for some women hired and promoted into leadership positions in major sports organizations. Women in those positions are expected to promote power and performance sports in society. The men who control sports organizations seldom hire women who put *women's issues* on the same level as *sport issues.* Of course, not all female leaders become uncritical cheerleaders for power and performance sports, but it takes effort and courage to critically analyze sports and use one's power to change them.

Changing the Way We Do Sports

Gender equity involves more than just pushing boundaries to make space for new ways to define and perform masculinity and femininity. It also requires erasing normative boundaries so that sports are fully gender-inclusive–for LGBTQs *and* heterosexual males and females. This process has begun, but much more needs to be done before it is achieved.

When people talk about gender equity, they usually focus on how to increase opportunities for girls and women to play competitive sports in the same ways that boys and men play them. The standard policy position is that the best way to serve girls and women is to provide the same programs and opportunities that boys and men have. But this approach does not always attract females or keep them involved.

The reasons for this are many. First, compared with boys, girls are less likely to see themselves as having sport skills, so they are less likely to take advantage of sport participation opportunities.

Second, the discourse that pervades competitive sports at nearly all levels is and always has been heavily masculinized and is full of military terms and metaphors that appeal more to boys than girls.

Third, men are more likely than women to be coaches and managers in these programs, which leads girls and women to question who is really valued in sports. Additionally, many girls see during their first competitive sport experiences that "Dad knows sports" and "Mom knows how to pack a lunch."

Fourth, sports are so sex-segregated that many females see them as representing ideas and beliefs that sustain aspects of orthodox gender ideology that are questioned outside of sports. When high schools and colleges fail to sponsor sex-integrated sports, they miss an opportunity to challenge those ideas and beliefs.

Fifth, when males and females play together, males usually assume leadership roles even when they may not be the best leaders. This might make boys and men feel good, but it doesn't make playing sports much fun for girls and women.

Of course, there are notable exceptions to each of these points, and that is partly why many girls and women *do* play sports today. But equity isn't achieved through "exceptions." Nor is it sustainable when sport providers say that "girls just aren't interested" when girls fail to show up for or stay involved in sports that are just like the sports that the boys play. It takes work to critically assess sports programs in terms of gender equity and look beyond the girls and women who learned to love sports and remain in them because they overlook, passively accept, or actively endorse the hypermasculinized discourse, organization, and culture that often characterize them. When sports reproduce orthodox gender ideology, and when orthodox gender ideology is embedded in the logic and structure of sports and sports organizations, those who feel constrained by that ideology will not feel welcome.

From a practical (and pragmatic) standpoint this means that there is a need for new and creative sport programs, discourses, and images that enable more people to see space for themselves as participants (Magrath, 2017b). In the long run, achieving gender equity requires a dual approach: creating new and different sports as well as expanding opportunities and creating for women and gender nonconformers access to power positions in established sports. Changes are more likely if people currently in positions of power can envision and create alternatives for the future, and if those who already envision new forms of sport gain access to power and resources so they can make their visions a reality.

All of us contribute to achieving gender equity when we critically assess how we talk about and do sports (Bergesen, 2017; Magrath, 2017b). After all, there is no need for all sports to represent the perspectives of men who are fascinated by domination and conquest. Full equity means that all people have a wide range of choices when it comes to organizing, playing, and giving meaning to sports.

summary

IS EQUITY POSSIBLE?

Gender equity in sports is integrally tied to ideology, power, and structural issues. Although ideas and beliefs about masculinity and femininity are fluid and subject to change, the prevailing gender ideology in many societies remains organized around the assumption that there are essential differences between females and males, that exceptions to heterosexuality are abnormal, and that men are physically stronger and more rational than women. This orthodox ideology is questioned today, but it has shaped the current culture and organization of sport.

Sports today are sites at which this gender ideology is reaffirmed *and* resisted. However, because most sports are based on a two-sex model, the impact of resistance is limited. Even when women achieve excellence in sports, it occurs in a context in which ideas and beliefs about male–female differences and the "natural" physical superiority of men over women are reaffirmed. Gender inequities persist because sports have traditionally been organized to be male-dominated, male-identified, and male-centered. This makes them very difficult to change, and at the same time they provide a less welcoming context for girls and women than for boys and men.

Orthodox gender ideology also leads to the marginalization of lesbians, gay men, bisexuals, transgender, queer, and intersex persons in sports. The culture and organization of sports celebrate primarily a form of masculinity that leaves little space for gender nonconformity. This means that sports often are sites where people must push gender boundaries to increase normative spaces for themselves and to be acknowledged as athletes.

Despite orthodox gender ideology, sport participation among girls and women has increased dramatically since the late 1970s. This change is the result of new opportunities, equal rights legislation, the women's movement, the health and fitness movement, and increased publicity given to female athletes. But full gender equity is far from being achieved, and future increases in participation rates will not be automatic.

The reasons to be cautious when anticipating more changes in the future include budget cuts, the privatization of sports participation opportunities, a relative lack of female coaches and administrators, a cultural emphasis on cosmetic fitness among women, the trivialization of women's sports, and the existence of homophobia.

More women than ever are playing sports and working in sports organizations, but gender inequities continue to exist in participation opportunities, support for athletes, jobs for women in coaching and administration, and informal and alternative sports. Even when sports participation gives women a feeling of personal empowerment, the achievement of full gender equity is impossible without a critical analysis of the gender ideology used in sports and society. Critical analysis is important because it guides efforts to achieve equity and it shows that there are reasons for men to join women in trying to achieve equity.

Historically, gender ideology and sports have been organized around the values and experiences of heterosexual men. Real and lasting gender equity depends on changing the dominant definitions of masculinity and femininity and the way we do sports. Useful strategies include developing new sports and sport organizations and changing existing sports. Changes also depend on using new ways to talk about sports. Until there are significant changes in gender ideology and the logic embedded in sports and sport organizations, full gender equity will not be achieved.

SUPPLEMENTAL READINGS

Reading 1. Definition and explanation of sexual terms used in Chapter 7
Reading 2. A continuing struggle: Women's professional basketball in the United States
Reading 3. Reasons for men to police gender boundaries: Preserving access to power
Reading 4. Using myths to exclude women from sports
Reading 5. Links to newspaper coverage of Caster Semenya and IOC/IAAF rules for intersex athletes
Reading 6. "The stronger women get, the more men love football"
Reading 7. History, impact, and current status of Title IX
Reading 8. Building muscles: Pushing boundaries of femininity?
Reading 9. Lost between two categories: The girl who didn't fit

SPORT MANAGEMENT ISSUES

- You've been asked to address the directors of international federations for Olympic sports. They want you to identify for them the major areas in which gender equity has not been achieved and how they might move more quickly toward the achievement of equity. List the main points you would include in your address.
- You have just been appointed chairperson of a special committee charged with studying gender equity in your university's sport programs. You must develop a research design and present it to the rest of the committee members. Outline the types of data you will collect to assess whether equity has been achieved. What do you expect to find at your university?
- As an assistant athletic director you have been asked to recommend changes to produce full gender inclusion in athletic department culture. The existing culture has been created by heterosexual men over the years as they occupied positions of power and made all major decisions about the organization of the department. Discuss the major issues that will be covered in your recommendations and the major strategies to creating full inclusion.
- You are a management consultant for a number of international sports federations. At their upcoming conference you are giving a presentation on the eligibility of trans and intersex athletes. They want to know if you prefer the rules of the IOC over the rules of the NCAA. Explain your preference and why you have chosen one over the other.

references

Acosta, Vivien & Linda Carpenter. 2015. *Women in intercollegiate sport: A longitudinal, national study, thirty-seven year update, 1977-2014*. Online, www.acostacarpenter.org

Adams, Carly & Stacey Leavitt. 2018. 'It's just girls' hockey': Troubling progress narratives in girls' and women's sport. *International Review for the Sociology of Sport* 53(2): 152-172.

Adams, N., A. Schmitke, A. & A. Franklin. 2005. Tomboys, dykes, and girly girls: Interrogating the subjectivities of adolescent female athletes. *Women's Studies Quarterly* 33(1/2): 17-34.

Adjepong, Anima. 2019. Voetsek! Get[ting] lost: African sportswomen in 'the sporting black diaspora.' *International Review for the Sociology of Sport* Article first published online, March 24.

Adriaanse, Johanna A. 2019. The influence of gendered emotional relations on gender equality in sport governance. *Journal of Sociology* Apr 17, 2019, OnlineFirst.

Adriaanse, Johanna A & Inge Claringbould. 2016. Gender equality in sport leadership: From the Brighton Declaration to the Sydney Scoreboard. *International Review for the Sociology of Sport* 51(5): 547-566.

Allison, Rachel. 2018. *Kicking center.* New Brunswick, NJ: Rutgers University Press.

Anderson, Eric & Mark McCormack. 2018. Inclusive masculinity theory: Overview, reflection and refinement. *Journal of Gender Studies* 27(5): 547-561.

Anderson, Eric, and Mark McCormack. 2015. Cuddling and spooning: Heteromasculinity and homosocial tactility among student-athletes. *Men and Masculinities* 18(2): 214-230.

Anderson, Eric. 2009. *Inclusive masculinity: The changing nature of masculinities.* New York: Routledge.

Anderson, Eric. 2011. Masculinities and sexualities in sports and physical cultures: Three decades of evolving research. *Journal of Homosexuality* 58(5): 565-578.

Anderson, Eric. 2015. *21st century jocks: Sporting men and contemporary heterosexuality*. Palgrave Macmillan.

Arpinar-Avsar, Pinar; Serkan Girgin & Nefise Bulgu. 2016. Lady or woman? The debate on lexical choice for describing females in sport in the Turkish language. *International Review for the Sociology of Sport* 51(2): 178-200.

Atencio, Matthew, Becky Beal, E. Missy Wright, and ZáNean McClain. 2018. *Moving borders: Skateboarding and the changing landscape of urban youth sports.* Fayetteville, AK: The University of Arkansas Press.

Badenhausen, Kurt. 2018. How Floyd Mayweather made a record $275 million for one night of work. *Forbes.com* (June 5): https://www.forbes.com/sites/kurtbadenhausen/2018/06/05/how-floyd-mayweather-earned-275-million-for-one-night-of-work/#505b0e4b6e4d

Barth, Brian. 2018. The good men: Inside the all-male group taking on modern masculinity. *The Guardian* (June 18): https://www.theguardian.com/world/2018/jun/18/the-good-men-inside-the-all-male-group-taking-on-modern-masculinity

BBC. 2012. London 2012: Olympics women's boxing skirts issue to be decided. *BBC.co.uk* (January 24): http://news.bbc.co.uk/sport2/hi/boxing/16608826.stm

Beaver, Travis D. 2016. Roller derby uniforms: The pleasures and dilemmas of sexualized attire. *International Review for the Sociology of Sport* 52(6): 639-657.

Bergesen, Sally. 2017. We must change the narrative around women's sports. *OutsideOnline.com* (August 23): https://www.outsideonline.com/2234521/we-must -change-narrative-around-womens-sports

Bergner, Daniel. 2019. The struggles of rejecting the gender binary. *New York Times Magazine* (June 4): https://www.nytimes.com/2019/06/04/magazine/gender-nonbinary.html

Berkman, Seth. 2019. N.W.H.L. moves to unify pro women's hockey as its rival fades away. *New*

York Times (April 2): https://www.nytimes.com/2019/04/02/sports/nwhl-nhl.html

BettingOffers. 2019. Do transgender athletes have an unfair advantage? BettingOffers.com (March 4): https://www.betting-offers.com/2019/03/do-transgender-athletes-have-an-unfair-advantage/

Boylan, Jennifer Finney. 2008. The XY games. *The New York Times* (August 3). Online: http://www.nytimes.com/2008/08/03/opinion/03boylan.html

Breeze, Maddie. 2015. *Seriousness and women's roller derby: Gender, organization, and ambivalence.* New York: Palgrave Macmillan.

Brennan, Andy. 2019. It's taken me years to get comfortable saying this: "I'm a gay footballer." *The Guardian* (May 14): https://www.theguardian.com/football/2019/may/15/its-taken-me-years-to-get-comfortable-saying-this-im-a-gay-footballer

Brown, Sarah. 2019. Title IX will remain a battleground. *TCHE* (February 18): https://www.chronicle.com/interactives/horizon

Carman, Diane. 2019. Remember, girls, losers don't have to worry about celebrating too much. *Colorado Sun* (June 23): https://coloradosun.com/2019/06/23/world-cup-soccer-women-athletics-opinion/

Carr, John N. 2017. Skateboarding in dude space: The roles of space and sport in constructing gender among adult skateboarders. *Sociology of Sport Journal* 34(1): 25–34.

Claringbould, Inge & Johanna Adriaanse. 2015. 'Silver cups versus ice creams': Parental involvement with the construction of gender in the field of their son's soccer. *Sociology of Sport Journal* 32(2): 201–219.

Comley, Cassie. 2016. "We have to establish our territory": How women surfers 'carve out' gendered spaces within surfing. *Sport in Society* 19(8/9): 1289–1298.

Conn, Jordan Ritter. 2015. The lingerie football trap. *Grantland.com* (July 23): http://grantland.com /features/legends-football-league-womens-lingerie-football-league-mitchell-mortaza/

Cooky, Cheryl. 2004. Raising the bar? Urban girls' negotiations of structural barriers in recreational sports. Paper presented at the annual conference of the American Sociological Society, San Francisco (August).

Cooky, Cheryl. 2009. "Girls just aren't interested": The social construction of interest in girls' sport. *Sociological Perspectives* 52(2): 259–284.

Cooky, Cheryl; Ranissa Dycus and Shari L. Dworkin. 2013. "What makes a woman a woman?" Versus "Our first lady of sport": A comparative analysis of the United States and the South African media coverage of Caster Semenya. *Journal of Sport and Social Issues* 37(1): 31–56.

Daniels, Dayna B. 2009. *Polygendered and ponytailed: The dilemma of femininity and the female athlete.* Toronto, ON: Women's Press.

DiCarlo, Danielle. 2016. Playing like a girl? The negotiation of gender and sexual identity among female ice hockey athletes on male teams. *Sport in Society* 19(8/9): 1363–1373.

Donnelly, Michele K. 2014. Drinking with the derby girls: Exploring the hidden ethnography in research of women's flat track roller derby. *International Review for the Sociology of Sport* 49(3/4): 346–366.

Donnelly, Peter & Donnelly, Michele K. 2013. *The London 2012 Olympics: A gender equality audit.* Centre for Sport Policy Studies Research Report. Toronto: Centre for Sport Policy Studies, Faculty of Kinesiology and Physical Education, University of Toronto.

Donnelly, Peter, Mark Norman &Bruce Kidd. 2017. *Gender Equity in Canadian Interuniversity Sport 2014–2015: A Biennial Report (No. 3).* Toronto, ON: University of Toronto Centre for Sport Policy Studies.

Dunning, Eric. 1986. Sport as a male preserve: Notes on the social sources of masculine identity and its transformations. *Theory, Culture and Society* 3(1): 79–90.

Dzikus, Lars; Allison B. Smith & Jonathan Evans. 2017. "What it means to be a 'Lady'":

Defending the "Lady Vols" nickname and logo. *Sociology of Sport Journal* 34(1): 35–45.

Elsey, Brenda & Joshua Nadel. 2019. *Futbolera: A history of women and sports in Latin America*. Austin TX: University of Texas Press.

Engh, Mari Haugaa & Cheryl Potgieter. 2018. Hetero-sexing the athlete: Public and popular discourses on sexuality and women's sport in South Africa. *Acta Academica* 50(2): 34–51.

Fasting, Kari; Mari Kristin Sisjord & Trond Svela Sand. 2017. Norwegian elite-level coaches: Who are they? *Scandinavian Sport Studies Forum* 8: 29–47.

Fausto-Sterling, Anne, 2012. *Sex/gender: Biology in a social world*. London/New York: Routledge.

Fausto-Sterling, Anne. 2000. *Sexing the body: Gender politics and the construction of sexuality*. New York: Basic Books.

Fausto-Sterling, Anne. 2000. The five sexes, revisited. *Sciences* 40(4): 18–23.

Fitzgerald, Elizabeth. 2016. Women & the Olympic Games: "uninteresting, unaesthetic, incorrect." *SBS.com.au* (May 3): https://www.sbs.com.au/topics/zela/article/2016/05/03/women-olympic-games-uninteresting-unaesthetic-incorrect

Gieseler, Carly. 2014. Derby drag: Parodying sexualities in the sport of roller derby. *Sexualities* 17(5–6): 758–776.

Gieseler, Carly. 2019. Learning to fail: Adolescent resistance in extreme sports. *Journal of Sport and Social Issues* 43(4): 276–295.

Griffin, Pat. 1998. *Strong women, deep closets: Lesbians and homophobia in sport.* Champaign, IL: Human Kinetics.

Harper, Catherine. 2007. *Intersex.* New York: Berg.

Hart, M. Marie. 1981. On being female in sport. In M. M. Hart & S. Birrell, eds, *Sport in the socio-cultural process* (pp. 291–301). Dubuque, Iowa: William C. Brown.

Heinecken, Dawn. 2020.The heart of the game: Girls, sports and the limits of "empowerment." *Journal of Sport and Social Issues* Online first, January 11.

Henry, Ian & Leigh Robinson. 2010. *Gender equality and leadership in Olympic bodies.* Lausanne, Switzerland: International Olympic Committee.

Hertzog, Esther & Assaf Lev. 2019. Male dominance under threat: Machoism confronts female defiance in Israeli gyms. *Journal of Contemporary Ethnography*. Online first, March 6.

Hesse, Monica. 2019. We celebrated Michael Phelps's genetic differences. Why punish Caster Semenya for hers? *Washington Post* (May 2): https://www.washingtonpost.com/lifestyle/style/we-celebrated-michael-phelpss-genetic-differences-why-punish-caster-semenya-for-hers/2019/05/02/93d08c8c-6c2b-11e9-be3a-33217240a539_story.html

Houghton, E.J., L.P. Pieper & M.M. Smith. 2017. *Women in the 2016 Olympic and Paralympic Games: An analysis of participation, leadership, and media coverage.* East Meadow, NY: Women's Sports Foundation.https://www.womenssportsfoundation.org/wp-content/uploads/2017/11/wsf-2016-olympic_paralympic-report-final.pdf

Huening, Drew. 2009. Olympic gender testing: A historic review of gender testing and its influence on current IOC policy. *drewhuening.com*: http:// drewhuening.com/PDFs/drew_huening_olympic.pdf

IAAF. 2011. IAAF regulations governing eligibility of females with hyperandrogenism to compete in women's competitions (In force as from 1st May 2011). Online: http://www.iaaf.org/about-iaaf/documents /medical

Jarvis, Nigel. 2015. The inclusive masculinities of heterosexual men within UK gay sport clubs. *International Review for the Sociology of Sport*. 50(3): 283–300.

Kanemasu, Yoko & Gyozo Molnar. 2017. Double-trouble: Negotiating gender and sexuality in post-colonial women's rugby in Fiji. *International Review for the Sociology of Sport* 52(4): 430–446.

Karkazis, Katrina, Rebecca Jordan-Young, Georgiann Davis, and Silvia Camporesi. 2012. Out of bounds? A critique of the new policies on hyperandrogenism in elite female athletes. *The American Journal of Bioethics* 12(7): 3–16.

Karkazis, Katrina. 2019. Stop talking about testosterone – there's no such thing as a 'true sex.' *The Guardian* (March 6): https://www.theguardian.com/commentisfree/2019/mar/06/testosterone-biological-sex-sports-bodies

Khomutova, Anastasiya & Alex Channon. 2015. 'Legends' in 'lingerie': Sexuality and athleticism in the 2013 Legends Football League US Season. *Sociology of Sport Journal* 32(2): 161–182.

Knapp, Bobbi A. 2015. Garters on the gridiron: A critical reading of the lingerie football league. *International Review for the Sociology of Sport* 50(2):141–160.

Koch, Jordan, Jay Scherer & Nicholas Holt, 2018. Slap shot! Sport, masculinities, and homelessness in the downtown core of a divided Western Canadian inner city. *Journal of Sport and Social Issues* 42(4): 270–294.

Kopycinski, Gary. 2018. Survey finds teen LGBTQ student-athletes overwhelmingly remain closeted. (July 9): https://www.enewspf.com/latest-news/schools/survey-finds-teen-lgbtq-student-athletes-overwhelmingly-remain-closeted/

Krane, Vicki., Pricilla Y.L. Choi, Shannon M. Baird, Christine M. Aimar, and Kerrie J. Kauer. 2004. Living the paradox: Female athletes negotiate femininity and muscularity. *Sex Roles* 50(5/6): 315–329.

Kuper, Simon. 2012. Gold rush. *The Financial Times* (July 7): Life & Arts, p. 14.

Lapchick, Richard. 2019. The 2018 racial and gender report card: College sport. The Institute for Diversity and Ethics in Sport, University of Central florida.

Laqueur, Thomas. 1990. *Making sex.* Cambridge, MA: Harvard University Press.

LaVoi, Nicole M. 2019. *Head coaches of women's collegiate teams: A report on seven select NCAA Division-I institutions, 2018–19.* Minneapolis: The Tucker Center for Research on Girls & Women in Sport.

LaVoi, Nicole M. 2018. 8 reasons why women coaches matter. *SwimSwam.com* (September 1): https://swimswam.com/8-reasons-why-women-coaches-matter/

Levy, Ariel. 2009. Either/Or: Sports, sex, and the case of Caster Semenya. *The New Yorker* (November 30): http://www.newyorker.com/reporting /2009/11/30/091130fa_fact_levy

Liu, Hung-Ling, Timothy Baghurst & Michael Bradley. 2018. Female roller derby athletes' athletic identity and systematic pursuit of leisure. *Journal of Amateur Sport* 4(1): 108–128.

Loy, John W.; Fiona McLachlan & Douglas Booth. 2009. Connotations of female movement and meaning: The development of women's participation in the Olympic Games. *Olympika* 18: 1–24.

Magrath, Rory, Jamie Cleland & Eric Anderson, eds. 2020. *Palgrave Handbook of Masculinity and Sport.* London: Palgrave Macmillan.

Magrath, Rory. 2017a. The intersection of race, religion and homophobia in British football. *International Review for the Sociology of Sport* 2(4): 411–429.

Magrath, Rory. 2017b. 'To try and gain an advantage for my team': Homophobic and homosexually themed chanting among English football fans. *Sociology* 52(4): 709–726.

Maor, Maya. 2019. Masculinities in the middle: Policing of masculinity, and the central and marginal roles of adolescent boys in adult martial art groups. *Sociology of Sport Journal* 36(1): 97–105.

Matthews, Christopher R. 2016. The tyranny of the male preserve. *Gender & Society* 30(2): 312–333.

McDonald, Mary. 2015. Imagining neoliberal feminisms? Thinking critically about the US diplomacy campaign, 'Empowering women and girls through sports.' *Sport in Society: Cultures, Commerce, Media, Politics* 18(8): 909–922.

Messner, Michael A. 2011. Gender ideologies, youth sports, and the production of soft essentialism. *Sociology of Sport Journal* 28(2): 151–170.

Meyers, Dvora. 2019. The obsession with Caster Semeya's body was racist from the very beginning. *Deadspin.com* (May 4): https://deadspin.com/the-obsession-with-caster-semenyas-body-was-racist-from-1832994493

Michael, B. 'Just don't hit on me and I'm fine': Mapping high school wrestlers' relationship to inclusive masculinity and heterosexual recuperation. *International Review for the Sociology of Sport* 50(8): 912–928.

Moskovitz, Diana. 2019. One of the top voices for women in sports doesn't think Caster Semeya is a woman. *Deadspin.com* (May 8): https://deadspin.com/one-of-the-top-voices-for-women-in-sports-doesnt-think-1834585212

Moyo, Phatisani. 2009. She's a lady, man. *Mail and Guardian* (August 21): http://mg.co.za/article/2009-08-21-shes-a-lady-man

Murphy, Jean. 2012. Getting 'whipped' into shape. *Wall Street Journal* (January 3): D2. http://online.wsj.com/article/SB10001424052970203479104577124573567538192.html

Musto, Michela. 2014. Athletes in the pool, girls and boys on deck: The contextual construction of gender in coed youth swimming. *Gender & Society* 28(3): 359–380.

Mutz, Michael & Henk Erik Meier. 2016. Successful, sexy, popular: Athletic performance and physical attractiveness as determinants of public interest in male and female soccer players. *International Review for the Sociology of Sport* 51(5): 567–580.

Nelson, Mariah Burton. 1994. *The stronger women get, the more men love football.* New York: Harcourt Brace and Company.

Norman, Leanne, Alexandra J. Rankin-Wright & Wayne Allison. 2018. "It's a concrete ceiling; it's not even glass": Understanding tenets of organizational culture that supports the progression of women as coaches and coach developers. *Journal of Sport and Social Issues.* 42(5): 393–414.

Padawer, Ruth. 2016. The humiliating practice of sex-testing female athletes. *New York Times Magazine* (June 28): https://www.nytimes.com/2016/07/03/magazine/the-humiliating-practice-of-sex-testing-female-athletes.html

Orenstein, Peggy. 2008. The way we live now: Girls will be girls. *New York Times Magazine* (February 10): http://www.nytimes.com/2008/02/10 /magazine/10wwln-lede-t.html

Obama, Barack. 2012. Entitled to a fair shot: The president reflects on the impact of Title IX. *Newsweek* 160(1 & 2, July 2 & 9): 10–11.

Paradis, Elise. 2012. Boxers, briefs or bras? Bodies, gender and change in the boxing gym. *Body and Society* 18(2): 82–109.

Pavlidis, Adele & Wendy O'Brien. 2017. Sport and feminism in China: On the possibilities of conceiving roller derby as a feminist intervention. *Journal of Sociology*, First Published July 29, 2017.

Pavlidis, Adele & James Connor. 2016. Men in a "women only" sport? Contesting gender relations and sex integration in roller derby. *Sport in Society* 19(8/9): 1349–1362.

Pavlidis, Adele & Simone Fullagar. 2013. Becoming roller derby grrrls: Exploring the gendered play of affect in mediated sport cultures. *International Review for the Sociology of Sport* 48.

Pavlidis, Adele & Simone Fullagar. 2013. Becoming roller derby grrrls: Exploring the gendered play of affect in mediated sport cultures. *International Review for the Sociology of Sport* 48(6): 673–688.

Pavlidis, Adele & Simone Fullagar. 2014. Sport, Gender and Power: The rise of roller derby. London/New York: Routledge.

Pavlidis, Adele & Simone Fullagar. 2015. The pain and pleasure of roller derby: Thinking through affect and subjectification. *International Journal of Cultural Studies* 18(5): 483–499.

Pew Global Attitudes Project. 2013. *The global divide on homosexuality*. Pew Research Center June 4): http://www.pewglobal.org/files/2013/06/Pew-Global-Attitudes-Homosexuality-Report-FINAL-JUNE-4-20131.pdf

Pielke, Roger, Jr., Ross Tucker & Erik Boye. 2019. Scientific integrity and the IAAF testosterone regulations. *The International Sports Law Journal.* https://link.springer.com/article/10.1007/s40318-019-00143-w

Quart, Alissa. 2008. When girls will be boys. *New York Times* (March 16): http://www.nytimes.com/2008/03/16/magazine/16students-t.html

Reid, Morgan. 2018. Anatomy of a student-athlete. *The Players' Tribune* (January 25): https://www.theplayerstribune.com/en-us/articles/morgan-reid-duke-soccer-nwsl/

Risman, Barbara J., and Georgiann Davis. 2013. From sex roles to gender structure. *Current Sociology* 61(5/6): 733–755.

Robson, Douglas. 2010. Gender issues in sport, court. *USA Today* (November 30): 1-2C.

Rogers, Nick. 2019. Holding court: The social regulation of masculinity in university pickup basketball. *Journal of Contemporary Ethnography*. First Published February 10, 2019

Sailors, Pam R., Sarah Teetzel, and Charlene Weaving. 2012. The complexities of sport, gender, and drug testing. *The American Journal of Bioethics* 12(7): 23–25.

SAPA (South African Press Association). 2009. SA lashes out at 'racist' world athletics body. *Mail and Guardian* (August 20): http://www.mg.co.za/article/2009-08-20-sa-lashes-out-at-racist-world-athletics-body

Schiot, Molly. 2016. *Game changers: The unsung heroines of sports history*. New York: Simon & Schuster

Schultz, Jamie. *Qualifying times: Points of change in US women's sport.* Champaign, IL: University of Illinois Press

Segrave, Jeffrey O. 2016. Challenging the gender binary: The fictive and real world of quidditch. *Sport in Society* 19(8/9): 1299–1315.

Sengupta, Debjan. 2015. Brandi Chastain: The woman who turned the world toward women's football. *Goaldentimes.org* (July 3): HYPERLINK "http://www.goaldentimes.org%2Fbrandi-chastain-the-woman-who-turned-the-world-toward-womens-football%2F" www.goaldentimes.org%2Fbrandi-chastain-the-woman-who-turned-the-world-toward-womens-football%2F

Shani, Roi, and Yechiel Michael Barilan. 2012. Excellence, deviance, and gender: Lessons from the XYY Episode. *The American Journal of Bioethics* 12(7): 27–30.

Shuang, Wang. 2019. On the pitch, you are never alone. *The Players' Tribune* (June 7): https://www.theplayerstribune.com/en-us/articles/wang-shuang-china-world-cup

Simpson, Joe Leigh et al. 2000. Gender verification in the Olympics. *JAMA* 284(12): 1568–1569; http://jama.jamanetwork.com/article.aspx?articleid=193101

Sisjord, Mari Kristin. 2019. Gender, sexuality, and sports: Shifting attitudes in snowboarding culture. In Joseph Maguire, et al., eds., *The business and culture of sports: Society, politics, economy, environment*, vol. 1: Foundations, Macmillan Reference USA (pp. 321–338). *Gale Virtual Reference Library*, https://link.gale.com/apps/doc/CX7631400006/GVRL?u=bcsdemo&sid=GVRL&xid=10bb68c5 Accessed 8 June 2019.

Smith, Dorothy E. 2009. Categories are not enough. *Gender & Society* 23(1): 76–80.

Smith, Maureen & Alison M. Wrynn. 2010. *Women in the 2010 Olympic and Paralympic Games: An Analysis of Participation, Leadership and Media Opportunities*. East Meadow, NY: Women's Sports Foundation; http://www.womenssportsfoundation.org/home/research/articles-and-reports/athletes/2010-olympic-report

Smith, Rory. 2019. Women's soccer's big moment, big-footed by indifference and a 'clerical error.' *New York Times* (June 7): https://www.nytimes.com/2019/06/07/sports/womens-world-cup-preview.html

Staurowsky, Ellen J. & Erianne A. Weight. 2011. Title IX literacy: What coaches don't know and need to find out. *Journal of Intercollegiate Sport* 4(2): 190–209.

Staurowsky, Ellen J., Nicholas Watanabe, Josweph Cooper, Cheryl Cooky, Nancy Lough, Amanda Paule-Koba, Jennifer Pharr, Sarah Williams,

Sarah Cummings, Karen Issokson-Silver, & Marjorie Snyder. 2020. *Chasing Equity: The Triumphs, Challenges, and Opportunities in Sports for Girls and Women.* New York, NY: Women's Sports Foundation.

Stern, Jessica. 2019. Transphobia and the anti-gender movement. *WeNews* (May 16): https://womensenews.org/2019/05/transphobia-and-the-anti-gender-movement/

Strauss, Ben. 2019a. For broadcasters, Women's World Cup rallies record audiences with an event and a cause. *Washington Post* (June 27): https://www.washingtonpost.com/sports/2019/06/27/womens-world-cup-ratings-record-audiences-thrill-broadcasters/

Strauss, Ben. 2019b. Women's World Cup final delivers viewers for Fox, despite early start time. *Washington Post* (July 8): https://www.washingtonpost.com/sports/2019/07/08/womens-world-cup-final-delivers-viewers-fox-despite-early-start-time/

Struby, Tim. 2018. The glass sideline. *SBNation.com* (November 27): https://www.sbnation.com/2018/11/27/18096989/women-coaching-men-professional-sports-nfl-glass-sideline

Sullivan, Claire F. 2011. Gender verification and gender policies in elite sport: Eligibility and "fair play." *Journal of Sport and Social Issues* 35(4): 400–419.

Tedesco, Carina. 2016. Makeup boosts confidence, performance for these female teen athletes. *womensenews.org* (December 22): http://womensenews.org/2016/12/makeup-boosts-confidence-performance-for-these-female-teen-athletes/

Thangaraj, Stanley I. 2016. *Desi hoop dreams: Pickup basketball and the making of Asian American masculinity*. New York, NY: New York University Press.

Theberge, Nancy. 2012. Toward a feminist alternative to sport as a male preserve. *Quest* 37(2): 193–202.

Thomas, Katie. 2008. A lab is set to test the gender of some female athletes. *New York Times* (July 30): http://www.nytimes.com/2008/07/30/sports/olympics /30gender.html

Thomas, Katie. 2011. College teams, relying on deception, undermine gender equity. *New York Times* (April 25): http://www.nytimes.com/2011/04/26/sports/26titleix.html

Thorpe, Holly, Lyndsay Hayhurst & Megan Chawansky. 2018. `Once my relatives see me on social media…it will be something very bad for my family': The ethics and risks of organizational representations of sporting girls from the global south. *Sociology of Sport Journal* 35(3): 226–237.

Tjønndal, Anne. 2019. "Girls are not made of glass!": Barriers experienced by women in Norwegian Olympic Boxing. *Sociology of Sport Journal* 36(1): 87–96.

Travers, Ann, & Jillian Deri. 2011. Transgender inclusion and the changing face of lesbian softball leagues. *International Review for the Sociology of Sport.* 46(4):488–507.

Travers, Ann. 2006. Queering sport: Lesbian softball leagues and the transgender challenge. *International Review for the Sociology of Sport* 41(3/4): 431–446.

Travers, Ann. 2013. Transformative sporting visions. *Journal of Sport and Social Issues* 37(1): 3–7.

Travers, Ann. 2018. *The trans generation: How trans kids (and their parents) are creating a gender revolution.* New York: New York University Press.

UNESCO. 2018. Fairer media coverage of sportswomen. *UNESCO.org* (February 8): https://en.unesco.org/news/unesco-calls-fairer-media-coverage-sportswomen

Vaccaro, Christian A. & Melissa L. Swauger. 2015. *Unleashing manhood in the cage: Masculinity and mixed martial arts.* Lanham, MD: Lexington Books.

Vannini, April & Barbara Fornssler. 2011. Girl, interrupted: Interpreting Semenya's body, gender verification testing, and public discourse. *Cultural Studies–Critical Methodologies* 11(3): 243–257.

Viloria, Hida Patricia, and Maria Jose Martinez-Patino. 2012. Reexamining rationales of "fairness": An athlete and insider's perspective on the new policies on hyperandrogenism in elite female athletes. *The American Journal of Bioethics* 12(7): 17-19.

Wahlert, Lance, and Autumn Fiester. 2012. Gender transports: Privileging the "natural" in gender testing debates for intersex and transgender athletes. *The American Journal of Bioethics* 12(7): 19-21.

Wallace, Jennifer, 2019. Teaching girls to be great competitors. *Wall Street Journal* (April 13): C3.

Wellard, Ian. 2012. *Sport, masculinities and the body*. London: Routledge.

Wheaton, Belinda & Holly Thorpe. 2018. Action sports, the Olympic Games, and the opportunities and challenges for gender equity: The cases of surfing and skateboarding. *Journal of Sport and Social Issues* 42(5): 315-342.

White, Adam. 2017. Inclusive masculinities in contemporary football: Men in the beautiful game. *Sociology of Sport Journal* 34(4): 364-366.

Whiteside, Kelly. 2019. At Final Four, Muffet McGraw makes a forceful case for women in power. NYT (April 4): https://www.nytimes.com/2019/04/04/sports/womens-final-four-muffet-mcgraw.html

World Health Organization, 2013. *Research for universal health coverage: World health report 2013.* Geneva, Switzerland: Who Press.

Zarrett, Nicole, Cheryl Cooky & Philip Veliz. 2019. *Coaching through a Gender Lens: Maximizing Girls' Play and Potential.* New York, NY: Women's Sports Foundation.

chapter

8

(*Source:* Michael Boyd, Irish Football Association)

RACE AND ETHNICITY

Are They Important in Sports?

[As a white person discussing race], you've got to be comfortable with being uncomfortable. Once you're able to do that, you have this whole new set of lenses and eyes for what is going on in our country today.

–Kyle Korver, NBA player, Utah Jazz (Youtube, 2019)

Racism is a dark cloud that lingers heavily over European football. The beautiful game should not be known to others for divisiveness, but instead for passion, joy and togetherness.

–Mathew Reed, journalist, TheShadowLeague (2019)

. . . it's very subtle in the way race plays a factor in how people are viewed and the stories, perceptions and all the subconscious bias that can go on. That's a very real thing to me now.

–Jeremy Lin, NBA player, Toronto Raptors (in Chow, 2019)

It's tough because . . . we grew up in [the United States] and yet our last names are . . . Morales or Gomez or whatever. And so, Americans don't view us as fully Americans, even though we were born here.

–ESPN reporter Pedro Gomez (in Morales, 2016)

Chapter Outline

Learning Objectives

- Understand the concepts of race, ethnicity, and minority group, and distinguish between them.
- Explain why race is a social construction and how racial categories are based on social meanings rather than a valid biological classification system.
- Explain how and why race and racial ideology have been linked with sports in the United States.
- Explain why scientists and others have searched for sports performance genes in bodies with dark skin and why this is a misleading and futile exercise.
- Explain the author's sociological explanation of the relationship between skin color and athletic performance.
- Identify factors that have influenced sports participation among African Americans, Native Americans, Latinos and Latinas, and Asian Pacific Americans.
- Explain why the use of Native American images for team names, logos, and mascots has been a contentious issue in the United States.
- Understand the expressions of racism and bigotry in European sports and the factors that currently influence those expressions.
- Identify the major challenges related to race and ethnic relations in sports today, and explain how they are different from the challenges faced throughout most of the twentieth century.

Sports involve complex racial and ethnic issues, and their relevance has increased as global migration and political changes bring together people from diverse racial and ethnic backgrounds. The challenges created by racial and ethnic diversity are among the most important ones that we face as we live, work, and play together in the twenty-first century (Edwards, 2000).

Ideas and beliefs about race and ethnicity traditionally influence self-perceptions, social relationships, and the organization of social life. Sports reflect this influence and are sites where people challenge or reproduce racial ideologies and existing patterns of racial and ethnic relations in society. As people make sense of sports and give meaning to their experiences and observations, they often take into account their beliefs about skin color and ethnicity. The once-popular statement, "White men can't jump," is an example of this.

Not surprisingly, the social meanings and experiences associated with skin color and ethnic background influence access to sports participation, decisions about playing sports, the ways that people integrate sports into their lives, and the organization and sponsorship of sports. Some people in racial and ethnic groups use participation to express their cultural identity and others use it to assimilate into a another culture. In some cases, people are identified and evaluated as athletes, coaches, or media commentators based on the meanings given to their skin color or ethnic background. Sports also are cultural sites where people formulate or change ideas and beliefs about skin color and ethnic heritage.

This means that sports are more than mere reflections of racial and ethnic relations in society: they're sites where racial and ethnic relations are perpetuated and changed. Therefore, the depth of our understanding of sports in society depends on what we know about race and ethnicity in various social worlds.

This chapter focuses on the following topics:

1. Definitions of *race* and *ethnicity,* as well as the origins of current ideas about race.
2. Racial classification systems and the influence of racial ideology in sports.
3. Sports participation patterns among racial and ethnic minorities in the United States.
4. The dynamics of racial and ethnic relations in sports worldwide and in sports cultures.

DEFINING *RACE* AND *ETHNICITY*

Discussions about race and ethnicity are confusing when people don't define their terms. In this chapter, **race** refers to *a population of people who are believed to be naturally or biologically distinct from other populations.* Race exists only when people use a classification system that divides all human beings into distinct categories, which are believed to share genetically based physical traits passed from one generation to the next. Racial categories are developed around the meanings that people give to real or assumed physical traits that they use to characterize a racial population.

Ethnicity is different from race in that it refers to *a cultural heritage that people use to identify a particular population.* Ethnicity is not based on biology or genetically determined traits; instead, it is based on cultural traditions and history. This means that an **ethnic population** is *a category of people regarded as socially distinct because they share a way of life, a collective history, and a sense of themselves as a unique population.*

Confusion sometimes occurs when people use the term *minority* as they talk about racial or ethnic populations. In sociological terms, a **minority** is *a socially identified population that suffers disadvantages due to systematic discrimination and has a strong sense of social togetherness based on shared experiences of past and current discrimination.* Therefore, *not all* minorities are racial or ethnic populations, and *not all* racial or ethnic populations are minorities. For example, whites in the United States often are identified as a race, but they would not be a minority unless another racial or ethnic population had the power to subject them to systematic discrimination that would collectively disadvantage whites as a population category in American society. Similarly, Polish people in Chicago are considered an ethnic population, but not a minority. Mexican Americans, on the other hand, are an ethnic population that is a minority because of past and current discrimination experienced by people with Mexican heritage.

African Americans often are referred to as a race because of the meanings that people have given to skin color in the United States; additionally, they are referred to as an ethnic group because of their shared cultural heritage. This has led many people to use *race* and *ethnicity* interchangeably without acknowledging that one is based on a *classification of physical traits* and the other on *the existence of a shared culture.*

Sociologists attempt to avoid this conceptual confusion by using the term "race" only when they refer to the social meanings that people have given to physical traits such as skin color, hair texture, facial characteristics, stature, and others. These meanings, they say, have been so influential in society that shared ways of life have been developed around them. Therefore, many sociologists today focus on ethnicity rather than race, except when they study the social consequences of widespread ideas and beliefs about skin color in particular.

This information about race confuses many people who have been socialized to take for granted that race is a biological reality. To be told that race is not a biological fact but a social creation based on the meanings given to skin color is difficult to accept. But it begins to make sense when we learn why the concept of race was created and how ideas and beliefs about race were used to gain political and economic power around the world.

CREATING RACE AND RACIAL IDEOLOGIES

Physical and cultural diversity is a fact of life, and people throughout history have categorized one another, often using physical appearance and cultural characteristics to do so (AAA, 2006a, 2006b, 2006c). However, the idea that there are distinct, identifiable races did not exist until. Europeans developed it during the seventeenth century as they explored the world and encountered people who looked and lived unlike anything they'd ever known. As they colonized regions on nearly every continent, Europeans created classification systems to distinguish the populations they encountered. They used the term *race* very loosely to refer to people with particular religious beliefs (Hindus), language or ethnic traditions (the Basque people in Spain), histories (indigenous peoples such as New World "Indians" and "Aborigines"), national origins (Chinese), and social status (chronically poor people, such as Gypsies in Europe or the Untouchables in India).

More specific ideas about race emerged during the eighteenth century in connection with religious beliefs, scientific theories, and a combination of political and economic processes (Fredrickson, 2003; HoSang et al., 2012; Omi and Winant, 1994, Roberts, 2011; Saini, 2019; Science vs, 2019; Winant, 2015). Over time, people in many societies came to use the term *race* to identify and rank populations they believed were naturally or biologically distinct from other populations. This shift from a descriptive to a biology-based notion of race was also linked with efforts to rank races from superior to inferior and civilized to uncivilized. Unsurprisingly, light-skinned people put themselves at the top of the rankings, a decision that people from northern Europe used to justify colonizing and exercising power over people of color around the world.

Intellectuals and scientists in the seventeenth though twentieth centuries facilitated this shift by developing appearance-based racial classification frameworks that enabled them to "discover" dozens of races, subraces, collateral races, and collateral subraces–terms that many scientists used as they analyzed the physical variations of people in colonized territories and other regions of the world (see http://www.understandingrace.org/history/science/early_class.html).

Faulty "scientific" analyses combined with the observations and anecdotal stories told by explorers led to the development of **racial ideologies**–*interrelated ideas and beliefs that are widely used to classify human beings in categories assumed to be biological and related to attributes such as intelligence, temperament, and physical abilities.* The racial classification models developed in Europe were based on the assumption that the appearance and actions of white Europeans were normal and that all deviations from European standards were strange, exotic, primitive, or immoral (Carrington, 2007; Roberts, 2011; Saini, 2019; Science vs, 2019). In fact, Europeans captured dark-skinned people to put them in exhibitions at which they were displayed to demonstrate that they were naturally inferior to light-skinned Europeans (AAA, 2006c). In this way, the "whiteness" of northern Europeans became a standard against which the appearance and actions of *others* ("*those* people") were measured and evaluated. In other words, the regions that were white-dominated also became white-identified and white-centered in a social and cultural sense.

From the eighteenth through much of the twentieth century, people from northern and western Europe used these racial ideologies to conclude that people of color around the world were primitive beings driven by brawn rather than brains, instincts rather than moral codes, and impulse rather than rationality. This way of thinking, they believed, gave them "moral permission" to colonize and subsequently exploit, subjugate, enslave, and even murder dark-skinned peoples without guilt or sin in religious terms (Carrington, 2007; Fredrickson, 2003; Hoberman, 1992; PBS, 2006; Roberts, 2011; Saini, 2019; Smedley, 1997, 1999, 2003; Winant, 2001, 2004, 2006). Some also used racial ideology to define people of color as pagans in need of spiritual salvation. These people worked to "civilize" and save the souls of dark-skinned "others" to the point that white historians identified people of color as "the white man's burden."

Over time, these racial ideologies became widely accepted, and white people used them to connect skin color with other traits including intelligence, moral character, physical characteristics and skills. This also occurred in the United States, although the racial ranking system used by Americans was the only one to assert that Anglo (that is, "English-speaking") whiteness was supreme by nature and divine law and that all others were less than fully human (Treitler, 2016). This, in turn, justified stripping humanity from "black, red, brown, and yellow" people.

Racial Ideology in the United States

Racial ideology in the United States is unique. It emerged during the seventeenth and eighteenth centuries as proslavery colonists developed moral justifications for enslaving Africans and treating them inhumanely. By the early nineteenth century, many white people believed that race, represented primarily by skin color, was a mark of a person's humanity and moral worth. Africans and Indians, they concluded, were subhuman and incapable of being civilized. By nature, these "colored peoples" were socially, intellectually, and morally inferior to light-skinned Europeans–a fact that was accepted without question by most light-skinned Euro-Americans (Morgan, 1993; PBS, 2006; Smedley, 1997). This ideology came to be widely shared for three reasons.

First, as the need for political expansion became important to the newly formed United States, the (white) citizens and government officials who promoted westward territorial expansion used racial ideology to justify killing, capturing, and confining "Indians" to reservations.

Second, after the abolition of slavery, white Southerners used the "accepted fact" of black inferiority to justify hundreds of new laws that restricted the lives of "Negroes" and enforced racial segregation in all public settings; these were called Jim Crow laws (DuBois, 1935).

Third, scientists at prestigious universities, including Harvard, did research on race and published influential books and articles claiming to "prove" the existence of race, the "natural superiority" of white people, and the "natural inferiority" of blacks and other people of color (St. Louis, 2010).

The acceptance of this ideology was so pervasive that the US government established policies to remove Native Americans from valued lands, and in 1896, the US Supreme Court ruled to legalize the segregation of people defined as "Negroes." The opinion of the court was that "if one race be inferior to the other socially, the Constitution of the United States cannot put them on the same plane" (US Supreme Court, *Plessy* v. *Ferguson,* 1896). This ruling, even more than slavery, influenced race relations from 1896 until today because it legitimized hundreds of laws, political policies, and patterns of racial segregation that connected whiteness with privilege, full citizenship, voting rights, and social-intellectual-moral superiority over people of color in the United States (Nobles, 2000).

As patterns of immigration changed between 1840 and 1920, people came to the United States from Ireland, southern Europe (Italy, Greece, and Sicily), China, Japan, and Israel. At the same time, racial ideology was used to link whiteness with one's identity as an American. Therefore, the question of who counted as white was often hotly debated as immigrant populations tried to claim American identities.

(*Source:* FRANCK ROBICHON/EPA-EFE/Shutterstock)

US figure skaters, Vincent Zhou (left) and Nathan Chen, won the bronze and gold medals in the 2019 World Figure Skating Championships. Despite being born in the United States, they and others with Asian ancestry deal with being perceived as "forever foreign" in their homeland. Racial ideology in the United States is based on the assumption that being American is synonymous with being a white Euro-American. Therefore, Zhou and Chen are regularly asked, "Where are you from?" Their answers, "San Jose, California" and "Salt Lake City, Utah," are not the answers that other Americans seek.

Through the late 1800s and early 1900s, Irish, Jewish, Italian, Japanese, Chinese, and all Eastern European and Western Asian populations were considered to be nonwhite and, therefore, unqualified for US citizenship or running for a federal political office. As some members of these ethnic populations objected to being classified as "colored" and denied citizenship, they took legal cases all the way to the Supreme Court to prove that they had ancestral links to "real" white people. It took some of these people many years to establish or prove their whiteness because whites with Western and northern European backgrounds carefully maintained racial ideology to preserve their privilege in US culture and society.

These cases confused the Supreme Court because the justices differed on how to define "white." For example, in one case the court ruled that even though a Japanese man was light-skinned, he was not a true Caucasian, so he could not become a citizen. But in another case the court ruled that even though a man had Caucasian ancestors from the Caucasus region, his dark skin disqualified him for citizenship (Dewan, 2013).

Today we are witnessing changes in the form of white and black racial categories as the idea of race is modified in connection with (a) new patterns of immigration from Asia, Latin America, and the Caribbean; (b) new expressions of anti-immigrant attitudes; and (c) the racialization of Latino and new Asian immigrant populations. But this has not changed the traditional belief that whiteness is a pure and innately special racial category and this has, through recent history, created a deep cultural acceptance of racial segregation and inequality and strong political resistance to policies addressing the racial and ethnic inequities that remain part of American society.

The Problem with Race and Racial Ideology

Research since the 1950s has produced overwhelming evidence that the concept of *race* is not biologically valid (Fox, 2012; PBS, 2006; Roberts, 2011; Saini, 2019; Science vs, 2019; Smith, 2013). This point has received powerful support from the Human Genome Project, which demonstrates that external traits such as skin color, hair texture, and eye shape are not genetically linked with patterns of internal differences among human beings. We now know that there is more biological diversity within any so-called racial population than there is between any two racial populations, no matter how different they may seem on the surface (AAA, 1998; PBS, 2006; Saini, 2019; Williams, 2005).

Noted anthropologist Audrey Smedley (2003), explains that the idea of race has had a powerful impact on history and society, but it has little to do with real biological diversity among human beings. This is because the concept of *race* identifies categories and classifications that people use to explain the existence of social differences and inequalities in social worlds. In this sense, race is a myth based on socially created ideas about variations in human potential and abilities that are assumed to be biological.

This conclusion is surprising to most people in the United States because they've learned to "see" race as a fact of nature and use it to sort people into what they believe are biology-based categories. They've also used ideas and beliefs about race to make sense of the world and the experiences of various people. Racial ideology is so deeply rooted in US culture that many people see race as an unchangeable fact of nature that cannot be ignored when it comes to understanding human beings, forming social relationships, and organizing social worlds (Song, 2018; Treitler, 2016).

To put biological notions of race aside requires a major shift in thinking for many people. This complicates the world and changes our sense of how it is organized and how it operates. But when we move beyond traditional racial ideology in the United States, we see that definitions of race and approaches to racial classification vary widely across cultures and over time. Thus, a person classified as black in the United States may not be considered "black" in Brazil, Haiti, Egypt, or South Africa, where approaches to racial classification have been created under different social, cultural, and historical circumstances. For instance, golfer Tiger Woods is classified as a black person in the United States, Asian in Japan, and Thai in Thailand where his mother was born.[1]

Definitions of race have also varied from one US state to another through much of the twentieth century. This created confusion because people could be legally classified as black in one state but white in another. To add more confusion, definitions within states changed over time as social norms changed (Davis, 2001). These cultural and historical variations indicate that race is a social construction instead of a biological fact.

Another problem with *race* is that racial classification models systems force people to make clear racial distinctions on the basis of *continuous traits* such as skin color and other physical traits attributes possessed to some degree by all human beings. Height is an example of a continuous physical trait: All humans have some height, although height measurements vary along a continuum from the shortest person in the world to the tallest. If we wanted to classify all human beings into particular height categories, we would have to decide where and how many lines we should draw along the height continuum. This could be done only if the people in charge of drawing the lines could come to an agreement about the meanings associated with various heights. But agreements made in one part of

[1]Terminology can be confusing when discussing race and ethnicity. In this chapter, I use the term, "black," as a generic description of race; it includes people from many cultural backgrounds, primarily in Africa and the Caribbean. "African American" refers to people born in the US with African ancestry. "People of color" is a general term referring to all "non-white" racial and ethnic populations (Brown, 2019).

Snow white | Midnight black

Skin color continuum

Skin color is a continuous trait that varies from snow white to midnight black with an infinite number of skin tones in between. As with any continuous trait,* we can draw as many "racial category lines" as we choose and locate them anywhere on the skin color continuum. We could draw two lines or 30, depending on our ideas about "race." Our decisions about the number and location of lines are determined by social agreements, not biological facts. Over the past four centuries, some people have drawn many lines; others have drawn few; and scientists today draw none, because they no longer try to classify human beings into distinct races.

*Continuous traits are such things as height, weight, nose width or length, leg length or leg length to body height ratio, number of fast or slow twitch muscle fibers, brain size or weight–any trait that varies continuously from low to high or from a few to many.

FIGURE 8.1 Racial ideology: Drawing lines and creating categories.

the world would likely vary from agreements made in other parts of the world, depending on social and cultural factors that influenced the relevance of height. Therefore, in some societies a 5-foot, 10-inch-tall man would be classified as tall, whereas other societies might define "tall" as 6 feet, 5 inches or more. To make classification matters more complicated, people sometimes change their ideas about what they consider to be short or tall. Additionally, evidence clearly shows that the average height of people in different societies changes over time as diets, lifestyles, and height preferences change, even though height is a physical, genetically based trait (Bilger, 2004). This is why the Japanese now have an average height nearly the same as Americans, and northern Europeans have surpassed Americans in average height (Komlos and Lauderdale, 2007).

Like height, skin color also is a continuous physical trait. As illustrated in Figure 8.1, it varies from *snow white* at one end of the spectrum to *midnight black* on the other, with an infinite array of shades in between. When skin color is used to identify racial categories, the lines drawn to identify different races are based on the meanings given to skin color by the people doing the classifying. Therefore, the identification of races is based on social agreements about where and how many racial dividing lines to draw; it is not based on objectively identifiable biological division points.

Racial classification in the United States was traditionally based on the "one-drop rule." This meant that any person with a black ancestor was classified as "Negro" (black) and could not be considered a white person in legal terms even if he or she appeared to be white, although some people with black ancestors "passed" as white. This approach to racial classification was based on decisions that white people made in an effort to perpetuate slavery, maintain the "purity" of the "white race," discourage white women from forming sexual relationships and having children with black men, deny interracial children legal ownership of a white parent's property, and guarantee that white men would retain power and property in society (Davis, 2001). The uniquely American one-drop rule was based on a social agreement among white men, not on any deep biological significance of "black blood" or "white blood." However, widespread agreement among white men in the United States has often become the foundation for laws and cultural "truths." For example, the "one-drop rule" (that is, the *rule of hypodescent*) continues to influence the identities and the classification of children having one black parent (Ho, Kteily & Chen, 2017)

The problem with using the one-drop rule to define race is that "mixed-race" people are erased in history (and sports). It also creates social and identity confusion. For example, when golfer Tiger Woods was identified as "black," he declared that he was *Cablinasian*–a term he invented to represent that he is one-fourth Thai, one-fourth Chinese, one-fourth African American, one-eighth Native American, and one-eighth white European (Ca-bl-in-asian = *Ca*ucasian + *Bl*ack + *In*dian + *Asian*). However, when people use the one-drop rule, they ignore diverse ancestry and identify people as black if they are not "pure" white. This is why mixed-race persons in sports are described as black, even though a parent or multiple grandparents are white, Asian, and/or Latinx (Middleton, 2008).

To say that race is a social construction does not deny the existence of physical variations between human populations. These variations are real and some are meaningful, such as those having medical implications, but they don't correspond with the skin-color–based racial classification system widely used in the United States. Additionally, scientists now know that physiological traits, including particular genetic patterns, are influenced by the experiences of individuals and the long-term, collective experiences of specific populations. Therefore, a population that has lived for centuries in a certain mountainous region in Africa may have more or less of a specific trait than a population that has lived for centuries in Norway, but this does not justify classifying these populations as different races due to skin color.

Even though race is not a valid biological concept, its social significance has profoundly influenced the lives of billions of people for three centuries. As people have developed ideas and beliefs around skin color, the resulting racial ideologies have become deeply embedded in many cultures. These ideologies change over time, but they continue to exert a powerful influence on people's lives (Saini, 2019; Song, 2018).

The primary problem with *race* and racial ideologies is that they have been used for three centuries to justify the oppression and exploitation of one population by another. Therefore, they've fueled and supported **racism,** defined as *attitudes, actions, and policies based on the belief that people in one racial category are inherently superior to people in one or more other categories.* In extreme cases, racial ideology has supported beliefs that people in certain populations are (1) childlike beings in need of external control; (2) subhuman beings that can be exploited without guilt; (3) forms of property that can be bought and sold; or (4) evil beings that should be eliminated through **genocide,** that is, *the systematic killing of an identifiable population.*

Another problem with race and racial ideologies is that they foster the use of **racial stereotypes,** or *generalizations used to define and judge all individuals who are classified in a particular racial category.* Because stereotypes provide ready-made evaluative frameworks for making quick judgments and conclusions about others, they're widely used by people who don't have the opportunity or aren't willing to learn about those who have experiences influenced by popular beliefs about skin color. Knowledge, when used critically, undermines racial stereotypes and gradually erodes the ideologies that support them and the racism that often accompanies them.

Race, Racial Ideology, and Sports

None of us is born with a racial ideology. We acquire it over time as we interact with others and learn to give meanings to physical characteristics such as skin color, eye shape, the color and texture of hair, or even specific bodily movements. These meanings become the basis for classifying people into racial categories and associating categories with particular psychological and emotional characteristics, intellectual and physical abilities, and even patterns of action and lifestyles.

This process of creating and using racial meanings is built into the cultural fabric of many societies, including the United States. It occurs as we interact with family members, friends, neighbors, peers, teachers, and people we meet in our everyday lives. And it is reproduced in connection with

(*Source:* David Cannon/ALLSPORT/Getty Images)

Tiger Woods is only one-fourth African American, yet he is often identified as black because of the one-drop rule used in the United States. His mother, Kultida Woods, shown here in a 1998 family photo, is half Thai and half Chinese; his father, Earl (now deceased) was half African American, one-fourth Native American, and one-fourth Caucasian.

general cultural perspectives as well as images and stories in children's books, textbooks, popular films, television programs, video games, song lyrics, and other media content. We incorporate these perspectives, images, and stories into our lives to the extent that we perceive them to be compatible with our experiences. In this sense, race is much like gender: it consists of meaning, performance, and organization (see Chapter 2, pp. 42–43).

The influence of race and racial ideologies in sports has been and continues to be significant in the United States (Benson, 2017; Bimper, 2015, 2017; Bryant, 2018; Cooper, 2019; Edwards, 2017; Harper, 2018; Hartmann, 2016; Hylton & Lawrence, 2016; Korver, 2019; Leonard, 2017; Love, Gonzalez-Sobrino & Hughey, 2017; Runstedtler, 2018; Siler, 2019). Through the nineteenth and much of the twentieth century when African Americans engaged in clearly courageous acts, many whites used racial ideology to conclude that such acts among blacks were based on ignorance and desperation rather than *real* character. Some white people went so far as to say that black people, including black athletes, did not feel pain in the same way that white people did and this permitted black people to engage in superhuman physical feats and endure physical beatings, as in the case of boxers (Mead, 1985).

Many white people concluded that the success of black athletes was meaningless because blacks were driven by simple animal instincts instead of the heroic and moral character that accounted for the achievements of white athletes. For example, when legendary boxer Joe Louis defeated a "white" Italian for the heavyweight championship of the world in 1935, the wire service story that went around the world began with these words:

> Something sly and sinister and perhaps not quite human came out of the African jungle last night to strike down [its opponent] . . . (in Mead, 1985, p. 91)

Few people today would use such blatantly racist language in public, but traditional ideas about race continue to exist and there is ample evidence of racist feelings in online comments and tweets. Therefore, when eight black athletes line up in the Olympic finals of the 100-m dash or play in an NBA All-Star game, many people talk about "natural speed and jumping abilities," and some scientists study dark-skinned bodies as they look for the internal physical traits that will explain why they outperform white athletes in certain sports.

On the other hand, when white athletes do extraordinary physical things, dominant racial ideology leads people to conclude that it is either expected or a result of fortitude, intelligence, moral character, strategic preparation, coachability, and good organization. Therefore, few people want to study white-skinned bodies when all the finalists in multiple Olympic Nordic (cross-country skiing) events are "white." When white skiers from Austria and Switzerland—countries half the size of Colorado, with one-twentieth the population the United States—win World Cup championships year after year, people don't say that they succeed because their white skin is a sign of genetic advantages. Everyone already knows why the Austrians and Swiss are such good skiers: They live in the Alps, they learn to ski before they go to preschool, they grow up in a culture in which skiing is

"Jumping Genes" in Black Bodies

Why Do People Look for Them, and What Will It Mean If They Find Them?

When people seek genetic explanations for the achievements of black athletes, sociologists raise questions about the validity and purpose of the research. Let's use the search for "jumping genes" to explore whether these questions are justified. Our questions about research on this issue are based on two factors: (1) many current ideas about the operation and effects of genes are oversimplified and misleading and (2) jumping is much more than a simple physical activity.

OVERSIMPLIFIED AND MISLEADING IDEAS ABOUT GENES

Most people have great hopes for genetic research. They see genes as the building blocks of life that will enable us to explain and control everything from food supplies to human feelings, thoughts, and actions. These hopes have inspired studies seeking genes for violence and intelligence as well as genes that enable people to sprint fast, run record-setting marathons, and jump high. Genes, in the minds of many people, constitute the "magic bullets" that will enable us to understand the world and everyone in it.

According to Robert Sapolsky (2000), a professor of biology and neurology at Stanford University, this notion of the "primacy of the gene" fosters deterministic and reductionist views of human actions and social problems. The actions of human beings, he explains, cannot be reduced to particular genetic factors. Even though genes are important, they do not work independently of the environment. Research shows that genes are activated and suppressed by many environmental factors; furthermore, even the *effects* of genes inside the human body are influenced by numerous environmental factors, including the body itself (Cloud, 2010; Epstein, 2013).

Genes are neither autonomous nor the sole causes of important, real-life outcomes associated with our bodies and what they do. The influence of genes is regulated by chemicals that exist in cells as well as chemicals, such as hormones, that come from other parts of the body. These chemicals and hormones are influenced, in turn, by a wide range of external environmental factors. For example, when a mother rat licks and grooms her infant, her actions initiate biochemical processes that activate genes regulating the physical growth of the infant rat. Therefore, geneticists have concluded that the operation and effects of genes cannot be separated from the environment that switches them on and off and influences their effects in the body (Davids et al., 2007).

The point is this: Genes do not exist and operate in environmental vacuums. This is true for genes related to diseases and genes related to jumping. Furthermore, we know that physical actions such as jumping, running, and shooting a basketball all involve one or more clusters of multiple genes. To explain overall success in a sport such as basketball or soccer requires an investigation of "at least 124 genes and thousands, perhaps millions, of combinations of those genes," and this would provide only part of an explanation (Farrey, 2005). The rest would involve research on why people choose to do certain sports, why they're motivated to practice and excel, how they're recognized and identified by coaches and sponsors, and how they're able to perform under particular conditions.

This means that discovering "jumping genes" would be exciting, but it would *not* explain why one person jumps higher than another, *nor* would it explain why people from one population jump, on average, higher than people from other populations. Furthermore, no evidence shows that particular genes related to jumping or other complex sport performances vary systematically with skin color or any socially constructed ideas about race and racial classifications (PBS, 2006, episode 1).

JUMPING IS MORE THAN A PHYSICAL ACTIVITY

Jumping is much more than a mechanical, springlike action initiated by a few leg muscles. It is a total body movement involving neck, shoulders, arms, wrists, hands, torso, waist, hips, thighs, knees, calves, ankles, feet, and toes. Jumping also involves a timed coordination of the upper and lower body, a particular type of flexibility, a "kinesthetic feel," and a total body rhythm. It is an act of grace as much as power, a rhythmic act as much as a sudden muscular burst, an individual expression as much as an exertion, and it is tied to a sense of the body in harmony with space as much as overcoming gravity through physical force.

(*Source:* Frederic A. Eyer)

"Of course, white folks are good at this. After 500 years of colonizing the world by sea, they've been bred to have exceptional sailing genes!"

This statement is laughable when made about whites. However, similar statements about blacks have been used by scientists as a basis for hundreds of studies over the last century. As a result, racial ideology has influenced the process of knowledge production as well as everyday explanations of social worlds and the actions of individuals.

Athletes in different sports jump in different ways. Gymnasts, volleyball players, figure skaters, skateboarders, mogul skiers, BMX bikers, wakeboarders, basketball players, ski jumpers, high jumpers, long jumpers, triple-jumpers, and steeple-chase runners all jump, but their techniques and styles vary greatly from sport to sport and person to person. The act of jumping among people whose skin color and ethnic heritage have been given important social meanings is especially complex because race and ethnicity are types of performances in their own ways (Clammer, 2015). In other words, performing race and ethnicity often involves physical expressions and body movements that are grounded in the cultural-kinesthetic histories of particular populations and stereotypes about them.

Noted scholar Gerald Early (1998) explains that playing sports is an *ethnic performance* because the relevance and meaning of bodily movements vary from one cultural context to another. For example, jumping is irrelevant to the performances of world leaders, CEOs of major corporations, sport team owners, coaches, doctors, and college professors. The power, influence, and resources that these people possess do *not* depend on their jumping abilities. The statement that "white men can't jump" isn't defined as a racial slur by most whites, because jumping deficiencies have not stopped them from dominating the seats of power worldwide (Myers, 2000). Outside of a few sports, jumping ability has nothing to do with success, power, or wealth. As Public Enemy rapped in the 1998 film, *He Got Game,* "White men in suits don't *have* to jump."

To study the physical aspects of jumping, sprinting, and distance running is important because it helps us understand human biology more fully. But this research will not explain why people in some social and cultural populations jump high in certain sports and not others, or don't jump at all. Such explanations must take into account the historical, cultural, and social circumstances that make jumping and running important in some people's lives and why some people work hard to develop jumping and running abilities. There certainly are genes related to jumping, but it's wrong to assume that they operate independent of environmental factors, are connected with skin color in physical terms, or correspond with the racial categories that people have constructed for social and political purposes. Knowledge about genes is important, but it will never explain the complex physical and cultural performance of slam dunks choreographed by NBA players with varying skin color from 138 countries and territories (in the 2019–20 season). Nor will it explain the amazing vertical leaps and hang times of European, Brazilian, Chinese, and Japanese volleyball players who have won so many international events. Nor will it tell us why whites always win America's Cup yacht races and nearly every "big air" event in action sports. But when people see the world through a racialized lens, they miss most of what they don't expect to see.

highly valued, they have many opportunities to ski, all their friends ski and talk about skiing, they see fellow Austrian and Swiss skiers winning races and making money in highly publicized (in Europe) World Cup competitions, and their cultural heroes are skiers. But this is a cultural explanation, not a biological one.

When athletes are white, racial ideology focuses attention on *social* and *cultural* factors rather than biological and genetic factors. This is why scientists don't do studies to identify hockey genes among white Canadians, weight-lifting genes among white Bulgarians, or swimming genes among white Americans. Dominant racial ideology prevents people from seeing "whiteness" as an issue in these cases because it is the taken-for-granted "normal," standard against which "others" are viewed. When dominant racial ideology serves as the cultural foundation of a white-dominated, white-identified, and white-centered society, the success of white athletes is the benchmark against which the actions and achievements of others are assessed and interpreted. At the same time, the success of black athletes is seen as an invasion or a takeover–a "problem" in need of an explanation focused on dark-skinned bodies.

When scholars don't ask critical questions about their own ways of viewing race and ethnicity, racial ideology will influence the process of producing knowledge. This is highlighted in the box "'Jumping Genes' in Black Bodies" on pages 266–267.

Racial Ideology and a Sense of Athletic Destiny Among African American Men Does racial ideology influence the ways that African Americans interpret their own physical abilities and potential as athletes? This is a controversial question. Research combined with statements by athletes and coaches suggests that many young African Americans, especially men, grow up believing that the black body is superior when it comes to physical abilities in certain sports (May, 2008; Steele, 2010). This belief inspires some young people to believe it is their biological and cultural destiny to play certain sports and play them better than others. This inspiration is intensified when young black men and women feel that their chances of gaining respect and material success are dismal in any realm other than a few sports (Bimper and Harrison, 2011; Cooper, 2018, 2019; Harrison et al., 2011; May, 2008, 2009b; Shakib and Veliz, 2012; Singer and May, 2011; Smith, 2007).

Figure 8.2 outlines a sociological explanation of the athletic achievements of African American male athletes. The top section of the figure shows that racial stereotypes about the innate physical abilities of black people have been a part of US history and culture. When these stereotypes are combined with restricted opportunities in mainstream occupations and heavily sponsored opportunities to develop skills in certain sports, many black youngsters are motivated to play those sports. Over time they come to believe that it is their destiny to excel in those sports, especially relative to whites (see the middle section of Figure 8.2). This sense of destiny is based largely on misinformation about opportunity structures and the odds of achieving success in various occupations, but it is widely believed (Cooper, 2019). As a result, it creates a context in which young black men work hard to develop their skills and frame their achievements in terms of race as well as personal motivation (see the bottom section of Figure 8.2).

Does this sociological approach explain the notable achievements of African American men in basketball, football, track, and boxing? This is a difficult question to answer, but historical evidence indicates that a perceived collective sense of biological or cultural destiny to succeed in a specific venture can dramatically influence the achievements of an entire population. Three centuries ago, white men from the small island nation of England felt that it was their biological and cultural destiny to colonize and rule other parts of the world. This belief was so powerful that it led them to conquer over one-half the world as they formed the British Empire! This dwarfs the achievements of blacks in certain sports today. Further, it is clear that British colonization was driven by a combination of historical, cultural, and social factors; it was not due to British genes. Overall, when social worlds are organized to foster a sense of destiny among particular people, it

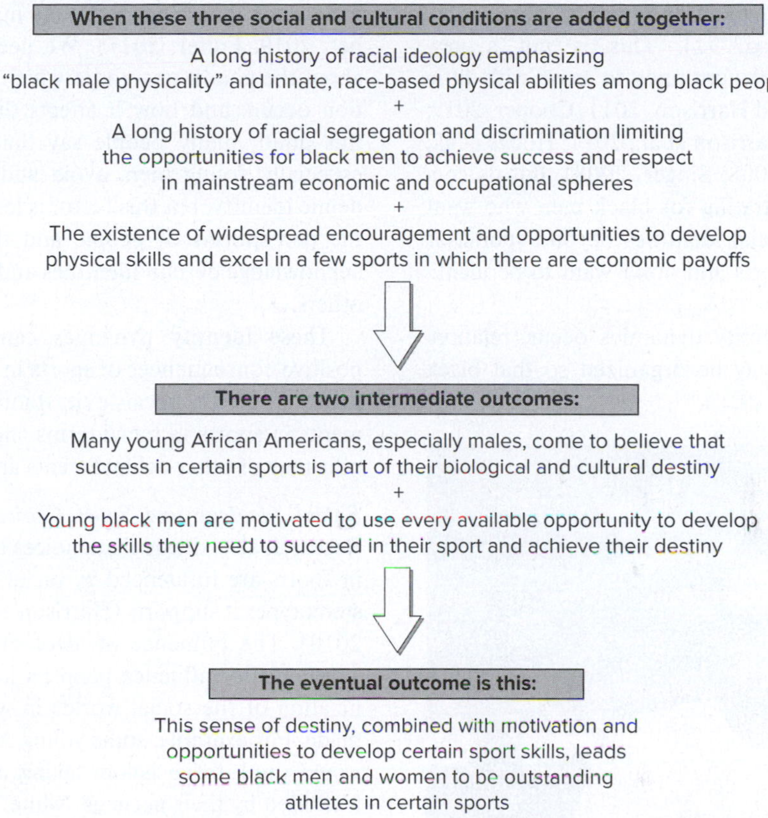

When these three social and cultural conditions are added together:

A long history of racial ideology emphasizing "black male physicality" and innate, race-based physical abilities among black people

+

A long history of racial segregation and discrimination limiting the opportunities for black men to achieve success and respect in mainstream economic and occupational spheres

+

The existence of widespread encouragement and opportunities to develop physical skills and excel in a few sports in which there are economic payoffs

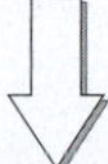

There are two intermediate outcomes:

Many young African Americans, especially males, come to believe that success in certain sports is part of their biological and cultural destiny

+

Young black men are motivated to use every available opportunity to develop the skills they need to succeed in their sport and achieve their destiny

The eventual outcome is this:

This sense of destiny, combined with motivation and opportunities to develop certain sport skills, leads some black men and women to be outstanding athletes in certain sports

FIGURE 8.2 A sociological explanation of the achievements of African American male athletes.

shouldn't be surprising when those people achieve notable things in pursuit of what they believe they can accomplish.

The Challenge of Escaping Racial Ideology in Sports The most effective way to defuse racial ideology is for people to understand each other's history and heritage and to depend on each other to achieve their goals. However, when ethnic segregation exists, as it does in US housing and schools, there is a tendency for black males to be "tagged" in ways that subvert their success in claiming identities that don't fit expectations based on racial ideology. For instance, if black high school students play on sports teams and participate in the school's honors program, other students and teachers are more likely to identify the black males as athletes rather than honors students, whereas black females are identified in connection with both statuses. At the same time, if Asian and white students (male and female) are in the honors program and on school sports teams, they are more likely to be identified as honors students rather than athletes. This tendency to differentially identify students in connection with race has been consistently documented in research (Cooper, 2018, 2019; Evans et al., 2011; Fuller, 2017; Fuller, Harrison & Bukstein, 2017; May, 2008, 2009; Shakib and Veliz, 2012; Withycombe, 2011).

As two black male college athletes noted, "Everyone around perceives us being [on campus] only for our physical talents," and "Everything is white [on campus], only sports [are] for blacks" (Harrison, 1998, p. 72). This is not a new phenomenon and it continues to exist with little change (Bimper and Harrison, 2011; Cooper, 2019; el-Khoury, 2012; Harrison et al., 2011; Hodge et al., 2008; Melendez, 2008; Singer, 2008). But its consequences are frustrating for black men who want to expand their social identities beyond sports, or who don't play sports and don't want to be identified with them.

When these identity dynamics occur, relationships in schools may be organized so that black male students are academically marginalized (Cooper, 2019; Fuller, 2017). We need to know more about the conditions under which this marginalization occurs and how it affects those involved. At this point, many people say that black students, especially young men, avoid and devalue an academic identity, but this factor is less important than the perceptions of people and their tendency to acknowledge certain identities and skills and ignore others.

(*Source:* Jay Coakley)

Many African American men grow up taking sports, especially basketball and football, very seriously. By age 11 this boy has learned not to smile when presenting himself as an athlete. His father reminded him to look serious and tough for this photo because it represented an identity that should be taken seriously.

These identity dynamics can undermine the positive consequences of sports in the lives of many black students, because it frames their achievements in sports in racial terms and reduces the significance of other achievements and potential.

Racial Ideology and Sport Choices Among Whites Research also shows that choices and achievements in sports are influenced by racial ideology and the stereotypes it supports (Harrison et al., 2011; Steele, 2010). The influence of ideology is subtle, but it continues to influence people's lives and the organization of the social worlds in which choices are made. For example, some young African Americans would think twice before taking up a sport that is identified by their peers as "white," for fear of being labeled a "wannabe white." Similarly, white girls and boys in certain areas might choose to play soccer or lacrosse because the school football and basketball teams have mostly black players.

Research is needed to determine the conditions under which sports participation choices are influenced by racial ideology, but doing this research can be tricky because these choices quickly become taken for granted and built into social and physical environments. As a result, people are more likely to see them as "personal preferences" rather than as reflections of a pervasive racial ideology that shapes the social and physical environment that influences people's choices.

Racial Ideology, Gender, and Social Class

Racial and gender ideologies are interconnected in US sports. For example, the implications of racial ideology for black men are different from those for

(*Source:* Pat Miller)

Racial ideology operates in diverse ways. In some cases, it influences whites to avoid the sports in which blacks have a record of excellence. This way of thinking did not influence the white teen on this team, nor does it influence whites in Europe and Australia where racial ideology does not discourage them from playing basketball and learning to run and jump as NBA players do.

black women. This is partly because the bodies of black men have been viewed and socially defined differently in US culture than the bodies of black women.

Over the past three centuries many whites in the United States grew up fearing the power of black male bodies, feeling anxious about their sexual capacities and being fascinated by their physical movements. Ironically, this consequence of racial ideology has enabled some black men to use their bodies as entertainment commodities, first on stage in music and vaudeville theater and later on athletic fields. Black female bodies, on the other hand, were seen in sexualized terms or as the nurturing nanny—neither of which made them valuable entertainment commodities in sports (Collins, 2005; Corbett and Johnson, 2000).

This means that racial and gender ideology create slightly different challenges for black female athletes. For example, Donna Daniels, an African

American studies scholar, suggests that the norms for physical appearance among females in predominantly white cultures have been racialized so that black female athletes exist in a realm outside the normal range of acceptance. To gain acceptance, they must carefully "monitor and strategize about how they are seen and understood by people who are not accustomed to their physical presence or intellect, whether on the court, field, or peddling a product" (2000, p. 26). If they're not careful, there's a danger that people will interpret their confidence and intelligence as arrogance and cockiness or as an indication that they are "too black." Therefore, some black women learn to present themselves to others in ways that tone down their toughness and make them appear amicable and nonthreatening–much like Oprah Winfrey–lest they face chronic marginalization in the cultural mainstream (Houston, 2019; Kent et al., 2018; O'Neal, 2018; Jones, 2018).

This point was poignantly illustrated when radio and talk show host Don Imus saw the strength and toughness of the black women on the Rutgers University basketball team and could find no other words to describe them except "some rough girls from Rutgers . . . some nappy-headed ho's." As for Rutgers' opponents, Imus said, "The girls from Tennessee–they all looked cute." Then the show's executive producer said that the game pitted "the jigaboos versus the wannabes." To Imus and his producer, both of whom were fired for their on-air conversation, the appearance of the women from the Rutgers team was "too black" and outside of their range of acceptance.

This was reminiscent of ways that the media in the 1990s pathologized the bodies of Venus and Serena Williams as exotic yet repulsive, animalistic yet supremely athletic, unfeminine yet erotic. These stories are put into a historical context in the Reflect on Sports box, "Vénus Noire."

Studies of black women playing sports or coaching in college suggest that they often feel a special sense of isolation on predominantly white campuses (Bernard, 2014; Borland and Bruening, 2010; Carter and Hart, 2010; Houston, 2019). This is primarily due to dealing with the double jeopardy of racial and gender ideology. Compared with their male peers, black females are more likely to be patronized, lack access to power and the people who wield power in athletic departments, and have fewer mentors and sources of social support in the schools or departments in which they play or work. As a result, they often depend heavily on their families for guidance and support (Carter and Hart, 2010)–and it may be that black families are more likely to offer and provide this support for their daughters than for their sons. When all these factors are combined, black female athletes and coaches face formidable challenges as they negotiate their way in sports, especially on predominantly white US campuses.

SPORTS PARTICIPATION AMONG ETHNIC MINORITIES IN THE UNITED STATES

Sports in the United States have long histories of racial and ethnic exclusion. Men and women in all ethnic minorities traditionally have been underrepresented at all levels of competition and management in most competitive sports, even in high schools and community programs. Prior to the 1950s, the organizations that sponsored sports teams and events seldom opened their doors fully to African Americans, Latinxs, Native Americans, or Asian Americans. When members of ethnic minority groups played sports, they usually played among themselves in games and events segregated by choice or by necessity (Giles, 2004; Miller and Wiggins, 2003; Niiya, 2000; Powers-Beck, 2004; Ruck, 1987).

Sports Participation Among African Americans

Throughout much of the twentieth century, white people in the United States consistently avoided playing with and against black people. Black people of all ages were systematically excluded from participation

Vénus Noire

A Legacy of Racism After 200 Years

The legacy of past racist beliefs about the black female body was resurrected again in December 2012 when Danish tennis player Caroline Wozniacki stuffed bulky towels over her sports bra and into the back of her tennis skirt to portray her caricature of Serena Williams during a match with Maria Sharapova in Brazil. Wozniacki probably did not know what that meant for her friends, Serena and Venus Williams. For them it was a naïve act of racism and a reminder of how they have been compared to "Hottentot Venus," a South African woman whose real name was Saartjie Baartman.

Baartman was captured by British colonizers in 1810, brought to Europe, and displayed in exhibitions, World Fairs, and "freak shows" as an example of the primitive character of black Africans (AAA, 2006c; Hobson, 2005; Holmes, 2007; Kechiche, 2005; A. Little, 2012; Martin, 2009; Maseko, 1998; Webster, 2000).

Baartman was a member of the Hottentot people, who had a genetic trait causing them to retain fat cells in their breasts and buttocks. Through the rest of her life Baartman was exhibited to whites as an animal-like creature. Her genital region evoked special curiosity because white people at that time were fascinated by what they believed to be the innate hypersexuality of the black female body.

After Baartman died, the anthropologist who had sold her to a carnival showman years before repossessed her body for an inhumane postmortem in which he removed her brain and cut off, dissected, and examined her genitals in hopes of contributing to white knowledge about black female bodies, brains, and sexuality.

(*Source:* Andre Penner/AP Photo)

(*Source:* City of Westminster Archives Centre)

When Caroline Wozniacki mimicked Serena Williams in public she unwittingly revived a global legacy of racist beliefs about black female sexuality. For those who know racial history, this stunt was reminiscent of what happened to Saartjie Baartman, who is caricatured in this racist image that is 200 years old.

Continued

Vénus Noire (*continued*)

This widespread fascination with Baartman's assumed hypersexuality marked an early chapter in a continuing 200-year-old story of the beliefs that white people have had about the black female body (see Burton, 2012). Throughout much of the story, those beliefs were emotionally charged with a complex combination of desire and repulsion grounded in the racism of the day (Hobson, 2005).

To illustrate the indirect impact of that story we can go back to the mid-nineteenth century, when beliefs about Baartman's body reaffirmed the use of a bustle and corset to accentuate the buttocks ("booty" today) and breasts while thinning the waist. In England and other parts of Western Europe, this "look" represented idealized female sexual identity–a way to be sexy while covering every inch of the body with layers of Victoria Era clothing. Anyone who has watched Disney's animated "princess" films depicting women of this era is familiar with this "bustle and corset look."

Of course, history books have told only the racially censored white interpretation of the "bustle and corset" fashion. But Venus and Serena Williams know the African interpretation–as did Nelson Mandela, who, as the globally respected former president of South Africa, finally in 2002, succeeded in convincing the French government to return Baartman's body to her homeland to be buried there.

White journalists covering the match in which Caroline Wozniacki pulled her stunt represented it as "fun and games." Anita Little, a young journalist writing for *Ms.* magazine called it a case of "accidental racism." But as an African American woman, Little knows that such accidents damage black women and reinforce a 200-year-old story about white superiority and black inferiority that has shaped recent human history. For Serena Williams, this accidental racism was probably interpreted in terms of that longer story combined with the 25 years of nasty and racist comments about her body–comments naively reaffirmed by someone she considered a friend (Newman, 2018).

Now that you know a small part of one chapter in that 200-year-old history, what would you tell Caroline Wozniacki to do the next time she sees Serena Williams in private? *In sociological terms, why have the bodies and general physical appearance of Venus and Serena Williams been picked apart so much over the past 25 years?*

in white-controlled sports programs and organizations because many white people believed that they didn't have the character or fortitude to compete with them. This meant that participation opportunities for young black girls and boys were limited to only a few sports–usually those that their segregated schools and communities could afford to provide. Even today, 48 million black or African Americans are underrepresented in or absent from most sports at most levels of competition. This fact is often overlooked because a few of the most popular spectator sports involve high proportions of black athletes. People see this and don't realize that black men and women are absent or nearly absent in thirty-nine of forty-four men's and women's sports played in US colleges, most of the dozens of sports played at the international amateur level, and all but five of the dozens of professional sports in the United States. There is a similar pattern in Canada and in European countries with strong sporting traditions.

The exceptions to this pattern of exclusion stand out because they *are* exceptions. The underrepresentation of blacks in most sports is much greater than the underrepresentation of whites in basketball, football, and track and field. Additionally, there are proportionately many more white students who play basketball and football in high school and college than there are black students who play tennis or golf at those levels. Finding black drivers at an Indy-car or NASCAR race is difficult or impossible; drivers, support personnel, and nearly 100 percent of the spectators are white.

In a *white-centered* cultural setting where the lives of white people are the expected focus of attention,

(*Source:* Library of Congress)

Black athletes were not taken seriously by most white people through much of the twentieth century. To earn a living playing sports, they often had to present themselves in ways that fit the racial (and racist) stereotypes held by white people. The Indianapolis Clowns baseball team and the Harlem Globetrotters basketball team joked around and behaved in childlike ways so that white people would pay to watch them. Racism restricted cultural space for black men and women to be entertainers, and they faced near-total exclusion in other spheres of social life, including mainstream sports.

they don't think about the whiteness of these sports; for them, it is simply normal and not even noticed. And in *white-dominated, white-identified* settings where the characteristics of white people are used as the standards for judging qualifications, most white people never think that they might have an advantage when it comes to fitting in or being hired and promoted. At the same time, blacks and other ethnic minorities must be careful not to be too black or too ethnic if they wish to succeed in these settings.

Throughout US sports history, the participation of black females has been severely limited and has received little attention, apart from that given to occasional Olympic medal winners in track events. As noted previously, research shows that black women are keenly aware of the need to "tone down" their toughness and confidence lest they "threaten" white people who don't know them or understand race relations in the United States.

In the case of black girls, a study by ethnomusicologist Kyra Gaunt (2006) shows that games in urban girl culture traditionally combine songs, chants, handclapping, footstomping, and rhythmic movement–a combination that doesn't fit with widely used definitions of sport (Cole, 2006). Many of these games, including traditional double-dutch, involve complex physical challenges combined with a body-conscious physicality and embodied musicality traceable to African origins.

Overall, rates of sport participation in middle- and upper-middle-income white communities in the United States are much higher than those in most predominantly black communities, especially where resources are scarce. Racial ideology causes many white people to overlook this fact. They see only the black men who make high salaries in high-profile sports and assume that blacks have "taken over" sports, that racial discrimination no longer exists, and that the nation is now color blind. Overall, this is how dominant racial ideology erases people and problems that cause discomfort for the racially privileged (Leonard, 2017).

Sports Participation Among Native Americans

There are 6.9 million "American Indian and Alaska Natives" in the United States and about 2.2 million live on or very close to 324 federally recognized reservations. Although the US census counts Native Americans as a single demographic category, they comprise dozens of diverse cultural populations and come from 566 federally recognized "Indian tribes," according to the Bureau of Indian Affairs. The differences between many of these populations are socially significant. However, most non-Native Americans tend to erase these differences by referring generally to "Indians" and envisioning stereotypical habits and dress–long hair, feathers, buckskin, moccasins, bows and arrows, horseback riding, war-whooping, tomahawk-chopping, and half-naked, even in cold northern states.

Native American sports participation patterns are diverse. They vary with cultural traditions, socioeconomic status, and whether people live on or off reservations. For example, participation patterns are heavily affected by a poverty rate of 26 percent and up to 50 percent on reservations–over twice the poverty rate in the United States as a whole (about 12.3 percent in 2018).

If you want [your mascot] to be a savage–use your own picture. . . . How would you feel if the team was called the Washington Darkies?

–Former Colorado senator Ben Nighthorse Campbell, the only Native American senator in US history (in Zirin, 2013)

Many sports in traditional Native American cultures combine physical activities with ritual and ceremony. Although individual Native American athletes have done well and set records over the past century, public recognition has often been limited to those few standouts on the football and baseball teams from reservation schools. For example, when Jim Thorpe and his teammates at the Carlisle School, a segregated government training school, defeated outstanding college teams in 1911 and 1912, they attracted considerable attention (Bloom, 2000; Oxendine, 1988). But apart from a few teams and individual athletes in segregated government schools, Native American sports participation has been limited by high rates of poverty and poor health, few accessible opportunities, a lack of equipment and facilities, and little support from those who control sports.

Native Americans who can play intercollegiate sports often fear being cut off from their cultural roots and support systems. For those who grow up learning their culture, there often is tension between the larger US or Canadian culture and their way of life. These tensions increase when they encounter negative representations of their culture in the form of teams named Indians, Redskins, Redmen, and Savages and mascots and logos that mimic stereotypes of "Indians." Watching or playing sports under such conditions involves losing control of one's identity (King, 2016). It is depressing to see a distorted or historically inappropriate caricature of a Native American on the gym wall or floor (!) of a school where students have no knowledge of local or regional native cultures and histories. For Native Americans this means that they must (1) swallow cultural pride; (2) repress anger against insensitive, historically ignorant non-Native Americans; and (3) suspend hope of being understood in terms of their identity and cultural heritage. Reflect on Sports, "Identity Theft," on pages 278–279 discusses this issue.

Native American athletes also face the challenge of preserving their cultural identities when their orientations don't fit with the culture of the power and performance sports sponsored by most schools. Through the years, some white coaches who have worked in reservation schools have tried to strip Native American students of cultural traditions that emphasize cooperation and replace them with Euro-American orientations that stress competition. When the students don't give up their cultural souls voluntarily, coaches simply avoid recruiting them. This is a problem that affects many Native American high school students who play basketball, a popular sport on reservations and one in which young Native Americans often excel (Klein, 2018; Longman, 2013).

Fortunately, Native American sports experiences do not always involve dramatic cultural compromises. Some Native Americans play sports in contexts in which their identities are respected and supported by others. In these cases, sports provide opportunities for students to learn about the cultural backgrounds of others. In other cases,

Native Americans adopt Euro-American ways and play sports without expressing any evidence of their cultural heritage; that is, they "go along with" the dominant culture, even if they don't agree with or accept all of it. And there are cases in which Native Americans redefine sports participation to fit their experiences and cultural beliefs–a strategy used by many ethnic minorities who play sports developed by and for people in the dominant culture (Dubnewick et al., 2018; Klein, 2018; Norman, Hart & Petherick, 2019; Thangaraj, 2016).

Sports Participation Among Latinos and Latinas

The 60 million Latinxs in the United States (18.3 percent of the population) include people from diverse cultures.[2] They may share language, colonial history, or Catholic religious beliefs, but their cultures, histories, and migration patterns vary greatly. Mexican Americans constitute the largest Latinx group (63 percent), followed by Puerto Ricans (10 percent), Cubans (4 percent), Central and South Americans (15 percent), and other Hispanic people (9 percent).

When dealing with sports in the United States, it's useful to distinguish between three categories of Latinxs: (1) US born and naturalized citizens; (2) Latin Americans working as athletes in the United States; and (3) workers or their family members who are in the United States without legal approval. The role of sports varies greatly in the everyday lives of people in each of these three categories.

Native-Born and Naturalized Citizens with Latinx Heritage Because much of the southwestern United States (California, Texas, Nevada, Utah, most of Arizona and New Mexico, and parts of Colorado and Wyoming) was part of Mexico prior to the mid-nineteenth century, the ancestors of Latinxs were living in this region long before 1620 when European pilgrims docked the *Mayflower* in Plymouth Harbor. Therefore, Latinx people have played major roles in establishing communities, schools, businesses, churches, hospitals, and sports programs in the Southwest, which is home to 25 percent of the total US population. Unsurprisingly, they've also played and been successful in the same sports as others in the Southwest (Mendoza, 2007).

The exceptions to this pattern involve people who emigrated from Mexico and other parts of Latin America during the twentieth century to work in low-status jobs in US industry and agriculture. Many people in this category are naturalized citizens or children who were born in the United States. They frequently maintain family connections in Mexico and generally experience various forms of ethnic discrimination. Work patterns, poverty, segregation, discrimination, and cultural traditions have influenced their sports involvement. Scarce time and resources, and little access to facilities and teams have restricted participation (Swanson et al., 2013). These patterns are similar to the ones that exist among Latinxs and Afro-Caribbeans in Canada (Joseph, 2012, 2014).

When anthropologist Doug Foley (1990a, 1990b, 1999b) studied "Mexicano-Anglo relations" associated with high school football in a small Texas town, he found that working-class Mexican males (*vatos*) rejected sports participation but used Friday night football games as occasions for publicly displaying their Mexican identities and establishing social reputations in the community. Foley

---

[2]What is the appropriate word to use when referring to a diverse population of people from Spanish-speaking regions of the world? *Spanish* was initially used but it referred too directly to Spain and excluded people who spoke Spanish but had no connection with Spain. *Hispanic* is a demographic term invented by the US Census Bureau to refer to people of any race who have "Spanish/Hispanic/Latino origin." *Chicano/Chicana* are identity terms used mostly by Mexicans in the United States who see themselves connected with pre-Columbian "Indian" tribes (Aztecs, for example). *Mexicano* and *Mexicana* are terms linking one's heritage and identity to the state of Mexico. *Latino/Latina* are used as more inclusive terms for men and women from Latin America. Most recently, in an attempt to avoid the gendered Spanish words (Latino for male, Latina for female), some people now use Latinx ("La-TEEN-ex") and Latinxs when referring to gender-mixed populations that include those who don't identify as male or female.

Identity Theft?
Using Native American Names and Images in Sports

Using stereotypes to characterize Native Americans is so common that most people don't realize they do it. When people take Native American images and names, claim ownership of them, and then use them for team names, mascots, and logos, sports perpetuate an ideology that trivializes and distorts the diverse histories and traditions of native cultures. No other ethnic population is subject to this form of cultural identity theft. As sportswriter Jon Saraceno (2005) exclaims, "Can you imagine the reaction if any school dressed a mascot in an Afro wig and a dashiki? Or encouraged fans to show up in blackface?" (p. 10C).

To understand this issue, consider this story told by the group, Concerned American Indian Parents:

> An American Indian student attended his school's pep rally in preparation for a football game against a rival school. The rival school's mascot was an American Indian. The pep rally included the burning of an Indian in effigy along with posters and banners labeled "Scalp the Indians," "Kill the Indians," and "Let's burn the Indians at the stake." The student, hurt and embarrassed, tore the banners down. His fellow students couldn't understand his hurt and pain.

This incident occurred in a public school in 1988, 20 years after the National Congress of American Indians initiated a campaign to eliminate stereotypes of "Indians" in US culture. In 1970, over 3000 schools were using Native American images, names, logos, and mascots for their sport teams. Many of these changed their names and mascots when they realized that it wasn't right to use the identities of other human beings to represent and promote themselves. However, a number of schools and a few professional teams still engage in this form of identity theft as they call themselves "Indians," "Savages," "Warriors," "Chiefs," "Braves," "Redskins," "Red Raiders," and "Redmen" and have mascots that cross-dress as Indians by donning war bonnets and paint, brandishing spears and tomahawks, pounding tom-toms, intoning rhythmic chants, and mimicking religious and cultural dances.

Some schools continue to display "*their* Indian" on gym walls and floors, scoreboards, and products they sell for a profit. They say that they're engaging in a "harmless" tradition that "honors" the "Indians" from whom they've taken images and identities. But many Native Americans point out that they are not honored by people who don't listen to them or respect their cultures.

(*Source:* Jay Coakley)

Many high schools in the United States continue to cling to ownership of "their" Indian names, logos, and mascots, despite objections from Native Americans. Some school officials, coaches, parents, and students say that their intent is to "honor their Indian," but they put his caricatured image on their gym floors and benches where people step and sit on them–actions unlikely to be accepted when honoring culturally important historical figures, such as Abraham Lincoln or Ronald Reagan. This [cartoon] image is used by a public high school in Colorado calling themselves the "Fightin' Reds."

What if the San Diego Padres' mascot were a fearsome black-robed missionary who walked the sidelines swinging an 8-foot-long rosary and carrying a 9-foot-long plastic crucifix? And what if he led fans in a hip-hop version of the sacred Gregorian chant as spectators waved little crucifixes and rapped the lyrics of their chant? People would be outraged because they know the history and meaning of Christian beliefs, objects, and rituals.

If more Americans knew the histories, cultural traditions, and religious rituals of the 566 Native American tribes and nations in the United States today, would they be as likely to use Native American team names and allow naïve students to dress in costumes made of items defined as sacred in the religious traditions of many Native Americans? Would they allow fans to mimic sacred chants and perform war-whooping, tomahawk-chopping cheers based on racist images from old "cowboy and Indian" movies?

Most public school officials and state legislators now realize that it's cruel and inconsiderate to misrepresent people whose ancestors were massacred, ordered off their lands at gunpoint, and confined to reservations by US government agents. They also realize that romanticizing a distorted version of the past by taking the names and images of people who currently experience discrimination, poverty, and the negative effects of stereotypes is a careless act of white privilege and hypocrisy. Therefore, some states and school districts now have policies banning such practices.

In 2003, the National Collegiate Athletic Association (NCAA) recommended that all universities using American Indian names, mascots, or logos review their practices and determine if they undermined the NCAA's commitment to cultural diversity. In 2005, the NCAA banned the display of Native American names, logos, and mascots on uniforms and other clothing and at NCAA playoff games and championships. But NCAA officials made an exception for Florida State University (FSU), whose officials claimed they had permission from the Seminole Tribe in Florida (but not the Seminole Nation of Oklahoma) to use the Seminole name and logo image in an honorable way (Staurowsky, 2007). "Honorable" for FSU means having a white European American student paint his face, put on a headband and a colorful shirt, carry a feather-covered spear, and ride into the football stadium on a horse named Seminole. And fans can honor *their* "Nole," as they call "their Indian," by buying products adorned with the painted and feathered "Seminole face." These products include floor mats, welcome mats, stadium seats, paper plates, and other things that fans use to sit, stand, and wipe their feet on. This is a strange way to show honor, but it makes money for the university and keeps the wealthy white boosters happy, even if it mocks the courses in their history department and makes the FSU diversity policy a symbol of hypocrisy.

The insensitivity of people at FSU is not an isolated case (Davis-Delano, 2007; Endres, 2015; Gallant, 2017; King, 2016; Leonard, 2017; Williams, 2007). For example, in 1999, a panel in the US Patent and Trademark Office ruled that "Redskins," "Redskin-ettes," and the logo of a feathered "Redskin" man as used by Washington, DC's NFL team "disparaged" Native Americans. The panel canceled six exclusive trademarks, ending the NFL's exclusive ownership of the "Redskins" name and logo. But in 2003, a federal district court judge overturned the panel's ruling because Native Americans had not objected back in 1967 when all NFL trademarks were registered. At this point the NFL still controls its "Redskins"–located in the capital city of the government that broke all but 1 of over 400 treaties with Native Americans (Dorgan, 2013). This case symbolizes the history of oppression endured by Native Americans.

In 2013, there were additional efforts to convince the owner of the Washington team to change its name, but he said he would NEVER do so. In 2014, forty-nine members of the US Senate signed a letter to NFL commissioner Roger Goodell asking the league to change the name of the team so the league would be on the "right side of history" by not endorsing "slurs against Native Americans" (https://www.nytimes.com/interactive/2014/05/22/sports/football/22redskins-letter.html).

What do you think? Is it honorific or identity theft?

also described how the Mexicans protested a high school homecoming ceremony that marginalized Mexicans and gave center stage to Anglos (that is, white people with European ancestry). Additionally, the Mexican-American football coach resigned in frustration when faced with the bigotry and contradictory expectations of powerful Anglo boosters and school board members.

Foley concluded that despite being a site for resistance against prevailing Anglo ways of doing things in the town, high school football ultimately perpetuated the power and privilege of the local Anglos. As long as Mexicanos saw and did things the Anglo way, they were accepted. But when they raised ethnic issues they were ignored, opposed, or marginalized.

There's a need to update Foley's work and to do research in urban areas as well as smaller towns. We know little about sports in the lives of young people who are first-, second-, and third-generation Latinxs in the United States. There are anecdotal accounts of young people who overcome barriers to play on school teams or at the professional level, but in-depth, community-based research is lacking (Aldama & González, 2014).

Similarly, there's been little research on Puerto Ricans in northeastern states, especially New York, and Cubans in southeastern states, especially Florida. Among those who are second- or third-generation residents of the United States, sport participation patterns match the patterns of those with similar family incomes and levels of education. For example, relatively poor Puerto Ricans in New York City and other urban areas on the eastern seaboard have sports participation patterns matching other populations with scarce resources. Boxing, baseball, and soccer are among the most popular sports. The relatively wealthy Cubans who came to the United States after Fidel Castro and the communist party came to power in 1959 have participation patterns that match their socioeconomic counterparts. More recent Cuban immigrants have patterns closer to those of recent immigrants from Mexico—boxing, soccer, and baseball among the men and softball and basketball among the women.

(*Source:* Debby Wong/Shutterstock)

Laurie Hernandez, a Latina from New Jersey, was a multi-medal winning gymnast for Team USA in the 2016 Olympic Games in Rio de Janeiro. Then she became the youngest-ever winner on the reality TV show, Dancing with the Stars. As she trains for the 2020 Olympics she has written two books. This one is directed at girls like her and how they should embrace the challenges of sports participation.

Research on Latinas in the United States indicates that ethnic traditions and gender norms influence their sports participation (Darvin, Cintron & Hancock, 2017; Jamieson, 2005, 2007; Lopez, 2019; Sylwester, 2005a, 2005b, 2005c). First-generation Latinas often lack parental support to play sports. Parents control their daughters more strictly than they control their sons, and daughters are expected to do household tasks such as caring for siblings, assisting with meal preparation, and cleaning house—all of which interfere with playing sports in families where meeting expenses is a struggle and transportation to practices and games is unavailable or costly.

Second- and third-generation Latinas face fewer parental constraints, and some parents are willing to use family resources to fund their daughters' sports participation. However, rates of participation remain relatively low as girls see fewer benefits than costs associated with being an athlete and subjecting themselves to teasing and homophobia, mostly from boys (Darvin, Cintron & Hancock, 2017; Lopez, 2019). Even talented high school players may be hesitant to play intercollegiate sports if it means going to a college far from home where there is little support for their Latina identities and traditions. Katherine Jamieson's (2005, 2007) research describes the unique identity management experiences of Latina intercollegiate athletes who must bridge a cultural divide as they live, study, and play with others who know little about merging cultural identities and managing relationships in two cultural spheres. But this research also needs to be updated, because ethnic relations are constantly emerging social phenomena.

Young Latinas today are more likely than their peers in past generations to see athletes who look like them. There's some media coverage showing Latinas in golf, softball, and soccer, but most inspiration comes from older sisters and neighbor girls who play sports. Research on the experiences of Latinas is important because it helps us understand the dynamics faced by young women caught up in the experience of immigration and making their way in a new society. At this point, we know little about the experiences of younger Latinas as they combine family life with school, sports, and jobs, and about adult Latinas who play sports in local leagues. Women playing in local leagues often use their participation to maintain regular contact with relatives and friends in the United States and Mexico, which makes soccer and softball especially important in their lives.

Latin Americans Working as Athletes in US Sports For well over a century boys and young men from poor families in Cuba, Puerto Rico, the Dominican Republic, Mexico, and Venezuela have dreamed about playing professional baseball in their home countries or the United States (Burgos, 2007; Regalado, 2008).

Between 1880 and the late 1930s, players from Latin America–often from Cuba–played on white US professional teams and Negro League teams. Although they faced strong discrimination on white teams, they learned that they could negotiate team membership by using their Spanish names to claim they were Latino, not "black." White players and management often accepted this in the interest of including highly skilled players on their teams, even when the Latino players were dark-skinned. Therefore, Latino players quietly passed through "the color line" and disrupted the "one-drop" racial classification system used in Major League Baseball (MLB). Additionally, many white, black, and Latino players had played in ethnically mixed Latin American leagues in the decades prior to the desegregation of MLB (Burgos, 2007).

These factors, according to historian Adrian Burgos (2007), helped erode resistance to desegregation and made it easier for Branch Rickey to convince his co-owners of the Brooklyn Dodgers to make Jackie Robinson, an African American a team member in 1947. This means that breaking the color line in baseball was a multi-ethnic process rather than a single event in black-white relations (Lapchick, 2010). Latino players had long been involved in weakening the color line and demonstrating that the US definition of race was arbitrary and inconsistent. In fact, during the early twentieth century, some African Americans were known to learn Spanish and take Spanish names so they could pass as Cubans or Dominicans and play on racially segregated teams.

Latinos constitute 27.4 percent of the players in MLB today and about 40 percent of all minor league players; 85 percent of Major League players born outside the United States come from Latin America. This is part of a century-long process through which players learned skills in community and professional leagues in Latin America, and more recently, in baseball training academies, mostly in the Dominican Republic (Klein, 2006; Passan, 2018). Baseball has long been seen as the ticket to take a young man out of poverty, enabling him to support his extended family and make contributions to his local community.

When scouts for MLB (Major League Baseball) teams realized that there was so much baseball talent in the Dominican Republic, they built training academies to gain access to the young players and then assess, develop, and control them. This began in the 1970s and continues today, although Dominicans with ties to their communities have now developed their own academies so they can "broker" players to academies sponsored by MLB teams (Klein, 2006; Passan, 2018). In this way, the Dominicans have regained partial control over their own talent so that Major League teams don't just take the best players and, as they do so, destroy local leagues and teams.

The academies are businesses, and working and living conditions for players, often as young as 10-years old, are substandard, if not deplorable (Passan, 2018). However, the dream of being a professional player influences the choices of boys who see no other options in their lives. The academies, despite management corruption and the exploitation of boys, are the only pipeline to the major leagues. For example, 90 Dominicans currently play on MLB teams (Anzil, 2019). In fact, over the years, seventy MLB players have come from San Pedro de Macorís, a Dominican city of 200,000 people, and in 1990 it was the birthplace of five of the twenty-six starting shortstops in MLB (Dannheisser, 2008).

Once Latin American players sign contracts with MLB teams, they face significant cultural adjustments and language problems and the strain of living in a society where few people understand their cultural backgrounds (Bretón and Villegas, 1999; Burgos, 2007; Klein, 1991, 2006). This is partly why 90 to 95 percent of Latino players who sign contracts never make it beyond the minor leagues. Even those lucky enough to make minor league teams often are cut after a year or two, and rather than return home as "failures," they often find ways to remain in the United States as undocumented workers at low-wage jobs. Overall, this is a typical pattern in the lives of young men recruited by teams seeking relatively cheap baseball talent from Latin America and the Caribbean (Breton, 2000, p. 15), but their stories remain untold in the United States and Canadian media.

Since the 1970s, the proportion of Latin American players has increased in US professional leagues because they constituted a pool of cheap baseball labor. Established Latino stars are well paid, but young players have signed for a fraction of the money paid to new players born and trained in the United States. For example, a vice president of a MLB team said that it costs less to sign five Latin American players than one player from the United States. This "boatload approach" to signing these players has begun to change now that Latino "agents" are advocating the interests of many new players and as MLB teams have fewer visas they can give to non-citizen players because of new immigration and homeland security policies.

One of the problems now faced by Latino players is that they are more likely to test positive for drugs than players raised in the United States (Gordon, 2007; Passan, 2018). Since 2005 when MLB initiated its new drug-testing policy, most of the Latinos who have tested positive have spoken little English; have not known all the substances on the banned substance list; and have come from countries where medical care is scarce and taking vitamins, supplements, and over-the-counter drugs is common (Gordon, 2007; Jenkins, 2005; LeBatard, 2005). Many drugs are less regulated in Latin America than in the United States, and some, including anabolic steroids, are available over the counter. The cheapest and most accessible steroids are those used by ranchers and farmers to increase the growth of their animals. Therefore, when young baseball players are desperate to escape poverty and hunger, they may take these drugs despite risks to their health. Additionally, there are cases of steroids being given to unsuspecting boys at the academies in an effort to increase their strength and attract attention from MLB scouts.

On the positive side of things, Latino players today enjoy the benefits of a visible and growing Latino culture in the United States, a growing Spanish-language media, a shared identity with many other players, and increased salaries that give them financial leverage that players in previous eras never had. Stereotypes continue to exist, but they are not as widely held as in the past, and when they are used in public, they are more likely to be challenged.

Undocumented Workers and Their Family Members

We know little about sports in the lives of undocumented Latinx workers and their families, who number in the millions. Sport involvement patterns are likely to vary with their income, education, and the number of years they've been in the United States. In some cases, sports are used as a means of assimilating into and expressing familiarity with US culture and developing relationships with non-Latinxs. In other cases, workers and their families often use weekend soccer, baseball, and softball games to come together and exchange information about jobs, friends, and family in Latin America, transferring money home, obtaining medical care and housing, and other things crucial to survival and maintaining support that can be helpful when a crisis strikes–a regular occurrence for many of these workers and their families.

A Need for Research Knowledge about the sport experiences of Latinxs is important because they are the fastest-growing ethnic population in the United States. Physical educators, coaches, and sports administrators need research that helps them provide services and opportunities that meet the needs of Latinxs. For example, the economic success of professional soccer in much of the United States depends on being sensitive to the interests and orientations of Latinx athletes and spectators. Latinxs are eager to have their cultural heritage recognized and incorporated into sports and sports experiences in the United States and into the awareness of their fellow citizens. In the public sector, there's a growing need for inclusive programs that provide participants from diverse backgrounds with opportunities to learn about the heritage, personal orientations, and experiences of their Latinx peers.

Sports Participation Among Asian Pacific Americans[3]

There are over 16 million Asian Pacific Americans (APAs) in the United States. The legacy of wars and the global migration of labor has brought people from many Asian Pacific cultures to the United States. Many live on the West Coast and in cities where particular jobs have been plentiful. However, the heritage and histories of APAs are very diverse, representing at least twenty nations and dozens of cultures. This diversity is often ignored in media coverage and research that focuses on "Asians."

Although people with Chinese and Japanese ancestry have long played sports in their own communities (Chen, 2012; Nakamura, 2016; Niiya, 2000; Thangaraj, Arnaldo & Chin, 2016; Yep, 2009, 2010, 2012), the recent success and popularity of APA athletes has raised important issues about ethnic dynamics in sports. For example, the popularity of Jeremy Lin (Taiwanese/Chinese) in the NBA; Japanese and Korean baseball players, and Samoan, Tongan, and Hawaiian players in the NFL; along with golfers Tiger Woods (Chinese and Thai) and Sung Hyun Park (Korean); speed skater Apolo Anton Ohno; and figure skaters Nathan Chen and Alysa Liu (each a 2019 national champion), and Maia and Alex Shibutani (who won the bronze medal at the 2018 Winter Olympic Games), highlights the extent to which many Asians and Asian Americans have embraced sports played in the United States.

The popular all-star baseball player Ichiro Suzuki (now retired) attracted so many Japanese spectators to Safeco Field in Seattle that signs in the stadium were posted in both Japanese and English. However, we don't have good information on the impact of Suzuki and other APA players on ethnic relations in the stadiums and communities where they play and live.

Historical research shows that certain sports have provided APAs with opportunities to challenge and discredit stereotypes about their lack of height and strength, their introverted "nature," and their singular dedication to intellectual development (Chin, 2015, 2016; Thangaraj, 2016; Thangaraj, Arnaldo & Chin, 2016; Yep, 2009, 2010, 2012). Yun-Oh Whang, a native Korean and a professor of sports marketing, acknowledged this point when he said:

> Asian Americans put huge value on education. [Therefore, it] is common that coaches and teachers at schools presume that an Asian American kid belongs in the science lab, not on the football field.

---

[3]At this point in time, the literature related to North America focuses primarily on Asians whose ancestry is from Pacific Rim nations and cultures. This excludes people from countries in South Asia, including India, and in Western Asia, including Persian Gulf countries and cultures (or "The Middle East" from a British geographical standpoint). The literature in Europe, especially research done in Britain, focuses more on ethnic populations from South and Western Asia (Fleming, 2007; Fleming and Tomlinson, 2007; Long et al., 2007).

> This is why it is so important that Asian American athletes have to rise to the top and show the general public that Asian Americans can also achieve excellence in sports (in Lapchick, 2007).

Playing sports also has been a way for some APAs to gain greater acceptance in schools and local communities. This is especially true for recent immigrants who seek assimilation. However, sociologist Christina Chin (2015, 2016) found that third- and fourth-generation Japanese-American parents have used Japanese youth sport leagues to network and build relationships with other Japanese families. The league provides a context in which their children can meet and befriend Japanese-American peers, including cousins and members of their extended family. The lack of recent immigrants from Japan and the current tendency of many families to choose housing to be close to jobs or good schools, means that children who are recent immigrants have had few opportunities to meet peers from Japanese families. This hasn't bothered the children as much as it does their parents, who value preserving important aspects of Japanese culture and passing them on to the next generation.

(*Source:* Vaughn Ridley/Getty Images)

When Jeremy Lin led the New York Knicks to a successful 2011-2012 season, his accomplishments created a "Linsanity" among basketball fans worldwide, especially in Taiwan and China, each of which claimed him as a native son because his mother and father are from Taiwan but his paternal grandparents are from mainland China (Chiang and Chen, 2013). Lin, who went on to play for other NBA teams before joining the Toronto Raptors in 2018, initiated a socially important national discussion about Asian Americans and their contributions to US culture and society.

One of the league's founders explained that he started the sport program to provide an activity through which children could meet "other Japanese and give them the opportunity to eventually someday marry if they want to. . . . We weren't trying to say you have to marry Japanese, like some parents. I just wanted to expose them . . . to other Japanese" (Chin, 2016, p. 1080). In addition to the matchmaking possibilities, the league also provides parents with a setting in which they can join with their Japanese American peers to become involved in their local communities. So they use the youth sports leagues to solidify relationships with other Japanese-American families, perpetuate cultural values among their children, and form networks to support their involvement in the larger community.

Christina Chin's research shows that the experiences and sports participation patterns of APAs often vary depending on their immigration histories. Chinese Americans and Japanese Americans whose families have lived in the United States for four or more generations have different experiences from those of first- and second-generation APAs from Vietnam, Thailand, Cambodia, Laos, the Philippines, Malaysia, and Indonesia. Researchers must be sensitive to these differences and the ways that they influence sports participation patterns and experiences. Gender and social-class variations among APAs also are important areas for study.

A relatively exceptional pattern exists in the case of young men from the Samoan Islands (American Samoa and Western Samoa, including Tonga) who come to the United States to play football (Feldman, 2007; Garber, 2007a, 2007b; Miller, 2007). With a population the size of Anchorage, Alaska (260,000 people), these islands are the birthplace of 30 NFL players in 2015, plus more than 200 college football players. Universities also recruit many players from neighboring Tonga

Island, which has a population the size of Peoria, Illinois (115,000). The sport traditions on all of these islands tend to involve rugby and cricket more than American sports, but young men from low-income families have defined football as their ticket to upward mobility, much as the young men from the Dominican Republic see baseball. At this point, research is needed on the conditions under which this and other patterns occur.

Currently, we also need to know more about the ways in which images of Asian and Asian American athletes are taken up and represented in US media and in the minds of Americans. Research is also needed on the dramatic rise in popularity of various martial arts in the United States. Karate, judo, taekwondo, and other sports with Asian origins have become especially popular among children, but we don't know if participation in these martial arts has increased children's knowledge and awareness of Asian cultures, influenced ethnic relations in elementary schools, or discredited anti-Asian stereotypes among children and others who participate in these sports. It may be that these sport forms become so Americanized that their Asian roots are lost or ignored by participants–but we don't know.

Summary

The previous four sections on sports participation among ethnic minorities focused on the United States. However, research from a number of countries indicates that sports can be used by individual athletes and by racial and ethnic groups in the following three ways:

1. To break down social and cultural barriers, discredit stereotypes, and facilitate inclusion.
2. To preserve and extend ingroup relationships that support racial and ethnic identities and make it possible to retain a connection with their native culture as they navigate the dominant culture of a country.

Additionally, there are cases where sports are so deeply segregated by race and ethnicity in a society that they prevent people from gaining the experiences and knowledge that could lead to intergroup understanding, tolerance, and cooperation.

Sports can bring people together, but they also may be organized in ways that segregate participants by race or ethnicity. When teams come to represent particular racial and ethnic groups, competitions can be sites at which bigotry is expressed and negative intergroup feelings are intensified.

Using sports to bring people together *and* create positive relationships that carryover and influence the larger community is a challenge. Even carefully planned strategies may not work when racial or ethnic animosities are strong or when participants don't have enough power to influence what occurs in the larger community (Meir & Fletcher, 2019). These issues are discussed in the following sections of the chapter.

RACE, ETHNICITY, AND SPORT IN A GLOBAL PERSPECTIVE

Sociologist Mauro Valeri, director of Italy's Observatory on Racism and Anti-Racism in Football (Soccer), collected data on racist incidents in Italian soccer from 2000 to 2009. After analyzing the data, he concluded that racism has become part of the structure of soccer in Italy. Although his research focuses on one country, his conclusion applies to many and remains applicable today as racist incidents have increased globally since 2009 (Mohdin, 2019; Smith, 2019). As global migration changes the demographic profiles of cities and nations, and as soccer teams and fans become more racially and ethnically diverse, the stereotypes and racism that have been dormant are renewed as people encounter others with unfamiliar customs and cultures.

Valeri's (2010) analysis led him to identify three primary expressions of racism in soccer:

1. **Direct racism** in which fans insult players for ethnic, racial, or religious reasons. Examples of this include spectators who throw bananas and make monkey sounds when players with African ancestry take the field. In some cases, this racism is even directed at players on the home team, as spectators have always seen

their club and team as direct representations of their local or national culture, which for them is tied to ideas about race and ethnicity. Racist chants and songs sung by groups of fans are so offensive that black players and their teammates have walked off the field to forfeit matches in protest, and referees have threatened to penalize the home team if officials do not control the racist expressions of spectators.

2. **Indirect racism** in which fans use chants or banners that promote a bigoted or discriminatory political agenda having no direct connection with soccer or players. These agendas often call for restricting immigration from certain countries, policing certain immigrant groups, or prohibiting ethnic forms of clothing or customs in public.
3. **Racism on the field** in which negative racial, ethnic, or religious comments are made by and to players, coaches, and referees. An example of this is players using bigoted slurs to demean opponents or referees. As these slurs have become public, soccer officials have created new anti-racist policies and fined players and referees who violate them. But the slurs continue and some fans cheer the players who make them.

Valeri found that each of these forms of racism increased significantly over the decade he collected data and they continue today.

This pattern of expressing racist ideas and beliefs at sport events has become a persistent problem in many countries, especially in Europe where immigration policies are less strict than in other parts of the world. Although these policies reflect a desire to have access to cheap immigrant labor, many citizens see the immigrants as a threat to their cultural values, quality of life, and the political stability of their cities and country. In response, there has also been a turn to right-wing populist political candidates whose campaigns and policy positions include inflammatory rhetoric about certain racial, ethnic, or religious populations.

Because sports teams are sponsored by clubs with members from the local population, sports events often become sites for the expression of this rhetoric. This differs from North America, where fans don't identify so closely with the management of teams, don't see stadiums as sites for overt political expression, and are more controlled in the public expression of racist and bigoted comments.

As people around the world respond to changing global forces and conditions that push them away from certain geographical regions and pull them toward others, racial and ethnic relations become important social, political, and economic issues. When people have not had to deal with social and cultural diversity as a regular fact of life, they often resist coming to terms with rapidly growing immigrant populations that have unfamiliar customs and cultures that they see as strange, disruptive, or immoral. At the same time, the new immigrants often find it difficult to adjust to local customs and culture and resent the discrimination they face as they try to make a living. There is no end in sight for these migration processes as regional economies and job opportunities go through boom-and-bust cycles and as communications and transportation technologies make it easier for people to move around the globe in the hope of supporting themselves and their families.

Sports are clearly involved in these global push-and-pull processes. Teams and athletes regularly vacate locations where they cannot survive or meet expectations for success; at the same time, they are attracted to locations where success is more likely, even when the spectators are of a different ethnicity. Teams now recruit athletes and coaches worldwide, elite athletes move wherever they have the best opportunity to make a living, and coaches and managers follow opportunities without giving much thought to national borders–unless visa requirements create barriers they cannot overcome. Wealthy individuals and corporations that have made huge profits from global expansion and financial deals now shop for professional teams worldwide and may own teams in three or four different countries across multiple sports. Additionally, nations now bid to host global sport events so they can increase tourism and investments among diverse noncitizens.

Soccer players in Africa and parts of Latin America now look to European leagues and clubs for professional contracts, just as Latin American and some East Asian baseball players look to the United States. The United States is also a priority global destination for young people seeking high school and college athletic scholarships so they can attend school as they develop sport skills and earn degrees that will enable them to survive in a global economy.

(*Source:* Michael Boyd, Irish Football Association)

The Irish Football Association (IFA) in Northern Ireland was a pioneer in using sports to strategically intervene in the lives of young people to bridge social divisions related to race, ethnicity, and religion. They began in the early 1990s and have revised their approach as they learned what succeeded and what didn't. Their success is due to the continuity of leadership and IFA support–things that similar efforts in other countries often lack. In response to increased racial incidents in recent years, many anti-racism organizations now exist in Europe but they are not very effective.

These global processes now force people to deal with racial and ethnic issues for which they are unprepared and which they are often unwilling to consider. Sports are regularly described as sites for creating social integration, but it is clear that this does not occur automatically; in fact, the opposite often occurs when sports become sites for the expression of racial, ethnic, and religious conflict and prejudices. This has led to efforts among some people–in and outside of sports–to create programs designed to defuse racial and ethnic conflict and make sport venues "racist-free zones" in their communities and in sport leagues that cross national borders.

There also is a need for teams and leagues to sponsor programs that facilitate more tolerant forms of racial and ethnic relations. In some cases, diversity courses are needed for everyone from owners to athletes. To work in sports today and have positive experiences, people must do their homework and learn about the cultural perspectives of players, coaches, spectators, and even club and team owners from unfamiliar ethnic backgrounds. In this sense, as people in sports become more effective in facilitating amicable racial and ethnic relations, the better off their lives, teams, organizations, and communities will be.

From a sociological perspective, it is interesting that as global migration creates a need for teams and sport organizations to become more ethnically and culturally inclusive, the growing inequality in many nations is leading to the creation of local sports and sports organizations that are more ethnically and culturally homogeneous. However, it is naïve for people in these homogeneous programs to assume that they can avoid facing the racial and ethnic issues that exist in the rest of the world.

Regardless of where they grow up, nearly all aspiring athletes will be required to deal constructively with ethnic differences on their teams and in their sports organizations. Coaches and team officials now must go beyond simply dealing with ethnic diversity and turn it into a competitive advantage if they wish to keep their jobs. Cultural and language issues present never ending challenges that call for creative solutions to bring athletes and other personnel together in ways that help teams succeed.

THE DYNAMICS OF RACIAL AND ETHNIC RELATIONS IN SPORTS

Racial and ethnic relations are dynamic phenomena. The challenges they present today are different from the ones faced 20 years ago, and when current challenges are met, new social situations are created in which new challenges emerge. For example, once racial and ethnic segregation is eliminated and people come together, they must learn to live, work, and play with each other despite diverse experiences and cultural perspectives. Meeting this challenge requires a commitment to equal treatment, *plus* learning about the perspectives of others, and then determining how to form and maintain relationships while respecting differences, making compromises, and supporting one another in the pursuit of goals that may not always be shared in the same ways. None of this is easy, and challenges are never met once and for all time.

Many people think in unrealistic terms when it comes to racial and ethnic relations. They believe that opening a door so that others may enter a social world is all that's needed to achieve racial and ethnic harmony (Ekholm, 2019). However, this is merely a first step in a never-ending process of nurturing relationships, producing an inclusive society, and sharing power with others. Racial and ethnic diversity brings potential vitality and creativity to a team, organization, or society, but this potential does not automatically become reality. It requires constant awareness, commitment, and work to achieve and maintain it.

The following sections deal with three major challenges related to racial and ethnic relations in sports today: (1) eliminating racial and ethnic exclusion in sports participation; (2) dealing with and managing racial and ethnic diversity by creating an inclusive culture on teams and in organizations; and (3) integrating positions of power in organizations.

Eliminating Racial and Ethnic Exclusion in Sports

Racial and ethnic diversity is most likely to exist in sports under the following six conditions:

1. When those who control teams personally benefit if they recruit and play the best players regardless of skin color or ethnicity.
2. When athlete performance can be measured in concrete, objective terms so that racism and prejudice are less likely to influence judgments about skills.
3. When an entire team benefits from a good performance by a teammate, regardless of the teammate's skin color or ethnicity.
4. When friendships and off-the-field social relationships between teammates are not required for team success.

These four characteristics limit the threats that cause fear and create resistance to racial and ethnic desegregation. Therefore, when the white men who controlled professional teams and revenue-producing college teams in the United States realized that they could benefit financially from recruiting ethnic minority players without giving up power and control and without disrupting the existing structure and relationships in their sports, they began to do so.

Desegregation occurs more slowly in sports that lack the characteristics listed above. Golf, tennis, swimming, and other sports played in private clubs where social interaction is much more personal and often involves male–female relationships have been slow to accept racial and ethnic diversity. As social contacts become increasingly personal, people are more likely to enforce various forms of exclusion. This is why informal forms of racial and ethnic exclusion still exist in many private sports clubs and why there are so few African Americans, Latinos, and Asian Pacific Americans in professional golf and tennis or in club-based sports such as lacrosse and swimming.

The most significant forms of racial and ethnic exclusion today occur at the community level where they are hidden behind the fees and other resources required for sport participation. People can claim to have ethnically open sport programs when in reality their location, fees, and lack of public transportation preclude ethnically inclusive participation.

As public programs are dropped and sports are offered primarily by commercial providers, patterns of exclusion reflect race and ethnicity to the extent that race and ethnicity influence residential location and income. This type of exclusion occurs regularly in the United States and is difficult to eliminate because market forces do the dirty work of segregation without race or ethnicity even being mentioned. Developing strategies to undermine these dynamics and make sports more inclusive is one of the most difficult challenges we now face worldwide.

Dealing With and Managing Racial and Ethnic Diversity in Sports

History shows that when Branch Rickey signed black player Jackie Robinson to a contract with the Brooklyn Dodgers in 1946, many new challenges confronted Rickey, Robinson, the Dodgers organization, players throughout the league, other baseball teams in the National League, and spectators attending baseball games. Rickey had to convince his partners in the Dodgers organization and other team owners that it was in their interest to abandon their practice of segregation. Robinson had to endure unspeakable racism from opponents, spectators, and others. To control his anger and depression, he needed support from Rickey, his coach, teammates, and his wife, Rachel.

As thousands of African American fans wanted to see Robinson, the Dodgers and other teams had to change their policies of racial exclusion and

(*Source:* Library of Congress #LC-USZ62-119883)

Eliminating racial barriers to sport participation is as important today as it was when Jackie Robinson joined the Brooklyn Dodgers in 1947. After the desegregation of Major League Baseball, there were new challenges associated with managing intergroup relations on teams and integrating positions of power in sport organizations. These challenges continue to exist.

segregation in their stadiums. Teammates on the Dodgers were forced to decide if and how they would support Robinson on and off the field. The team's coach had to manage interracial dynamics he knew nothing about: Who would be Robinson's roommate on road trips, where would the team stay and eat in cities where hotels and restaurants excluded blacks, and what would he say to players who made racist comments that could destroy team morale? These questions had never been asked in the past because Major League Baseball had excluded black players.

White baseball fans who had never met a black person now faced the prospect of sitting next to one if they wanted to attend a game. Black fans, who were uncomfortable with white people, faced a similar challenge. Stadium managers faced the challenge of serving food to people with different tastes and traditions; white, working-class service workers had to serve black customers–a totally new experience for them. Journalists and radio announcers had to decide how they would represent Robinson's experiences in their coverage–would they talk about racism on the field and in the clubhouse and about the way Robinson handled it, or would they ignore race, even though it was relevant to the game?

These are just a few of the new challenges created when MLB was desegregated. And as these challenges were met, new ones emerged. For example, as other black players were signed to teams, players began to racially segregate themselves in locker rooms. Black players could not buy homes in segregated white areas of the cities where they played, and when they challenged records set by whites, they received death threats. Stadium security became an issue, some teams became racially divided, and black players often felt marginalized because coaches, managers, trainers, and owners were white men.

Even the positions of black and white players fit patterns shaped by racial ideology. Black-players, expected to be fast and physically gifted, were assigned to the outfield in baseball and wide receiver and defensive and running back in football–positions believed to call for speed and quick reactions–whereas white players, expected to be smart, played positions believed to require intelligence, leadership, and decision-making skills, such as pitcher and catcher in baseball and quarterback and offensive guard in football. These position placements, or *stacking patterns*, as they've been called in the sociology of sport, have prevented most blacks from playing the positions at which they would be identified as good candidates for coaching jobs after they retired (Siler, 2019). This is related to a challenge that has become chronic in most sports worldwide: the lack of black CEOs, general managers, and head coaches (Bradbury, van Sterkenburg & Mignon, 2018).

This example illustrates that challenges related to race and ethnicity are an ever-present part of our lives; they will exist as long as skin color and ethnicity influence people's lives and are viewed as socially important. This is not new, nor is it unique to sports. Managers and coaches must now be ready and able to work effectively with players from multiple cultural and national backgrounds, meld them into a team, defuse and debunk players' racial and ethnic stereotypes, and facilitate respect for customs and lifestyles they've not seen before. Even determining the food to be served in pregame meals now requires creative management strategies.

Athletes and coaches must learn new ways to communicate effectively on ethnically diverse teams, and marketing people must learn how to promote racially and ethnically diverse teams to predominantly white, Euro-American fans. Ethnic issues enter into sponsorship considerations and products sold at games, and ethnic awareness is now an important qualification for those who handle advertising and sponsorship deals. For example, the success of professional soccer in the United States depends partly on attracting ethnic spectators to games and television broadcasts. Spanish-speaking announcers are crucial, and deals must be made with radio and television stations that broadcast in Spanish.

Teams in the NFL and NBA now face situations in which 70 to 80 percent of their players are black, whereas 90 to 95 percent of their season ticket holders are white. Many people are aware of this issue, but it's rarely discussed because Americans have a "civic etiquette" that keeps these issues "off the table" in public settings (Eliasoph, 1999). But if the challenges related to race and ethnicity in sports are to be met, changes in this etiquette are needed so that open and honest discussions can occur.

Integrating Positions of Power in Sport Organizations

Despite progressive changes in many sports, positions of power and control are held primarily by white, non-Latinx men. There are exceptions to this pattern, but they do not eliminate pervasive and persistent racial and ethnic inequalities related to power and control in sports (Belson, 2019, 2020).

Data on who holds positions of power change every year, and it is difficult to obtain consistent information from sport teams and organizations. Fortunately, Richard Lapchick, director of The Institute for Diversity and Ethics in Sport (TIDES) and his colleagues at the University of Central Florida, regularly publish *Racial and Gender Report Cards* for the NCAA and many professional sports. They contain data on the racial and ethnic composition of players in major professional team sports and an analysis of the number and types of jobs held by women and people of color in major professional and university sports organizations. The report cards cover everyone from owners and athletic directors to office staff, athletic trainers, and radio and television announcers.

The recent report cards on professional leagues and teams show that white men are overrepresented in the top power positions in the major professional sports played in the United States. Blacks are overrepresented among players in a few sports, but they generally play under the control and management of white men.

Patterns are similar in most sport organizations at nearly all levels of competition (Lapchick, 2019). Overall, data suggest that full inclusion in terms of sharing power is far from being achieved. In fact, the movement of women and ethnic minority persons into power positions in sports has stalled recently. Without constant attention and effective strategies, power remains in the hands of white men whose backgrounds position them to obtain leadership roles.

Overall, people do not give up racial and ethnic beliefs easily, especially when they come in the form of well-established ideologies rooted deeply in their cultures. Those who benefit from dominant racial ideology generally resist changes in the relationships and social structures that reproduce it. This is why certain racial and ethnic inequities remain part of sports.

Sports may bring people together, but they do not automatically lead them to adopt tolerant attitudes or change long-standing practices of exclusion in the rest of their lives (Ekholm, 2019). For example, white team owners, general managers, and athletic directors in the United States worked with black athletes for many years before they ever hired black coaches or administrators. It often requires social and legal pressures to force people in positions of power to act more affirmatively in their hiring practices. In the meantime, blacks and other ethnic minorities remain underrepresented in coaching and administration.

Although there is resistance to certain types of changes in sports, some sports organizations are more progressive than others when it comes to improving racial and ethnic relations. However, good things do not happen automatically, nor do changes in people's attitudes automatically translate into changes in the overall organization of sports. Challenging the negative beliefs and attitudes of individuals is one thing; changing the relationships and social structures that have been built on those beliefs and attitudes is another. Both changes are needed, but neither will occur automatically just because sports bring people together in the same locker rooms and stadiums.

The reports cards published by Lapchick and TIDES on hiring practices have kept a bright light shining on the racial and ethnic composition of major sports organizations in the United States. This light creates heat that makes decision makers uncomfortable if they are not making progress toward full racial and ethnic inclusion. Public scrutiny is an effective strategy because progress comes only when those in power work to bring about change. It has never been easy for people to deal with racial and ethnic issues, but if it is done in sports, it attracts public attention that can inspire changes in other spheres of life.

The racial and ethnic diversity training sessions used over the past two decades have produced some changes, but promoting positive changes in ethnic relations today requires leaders who are trained specifically to create more inclusive cultures and power structures in sports organizations. This means that training must go beyond athletes and include everyone from team owners and athletic directors to mid-level management, coaches, and people in marketing, media, and public information. When training programs are directed primarily toward employees, the employees won't take them seriously if they don't see their superiors making a personal commitment to them.

Even people who are sensitive to ethnic diversity issues require regular opportunities to renew and extend their knowledge of the experiences and perspectives of others who have different vantage points in social worlds. This means that effective training requires information and approaches organized around the perspectives of underrepresented ethnic populations. This is crucial because progressive change takes into account the interests of those least likely to be heard or to hold positions of power.

summary

ARE RACE AND ETHNICITY IMPORTANT IN SPORTS?

Racial and ethnic issues exist in sports, just as they exist in other spheres of social life. As people watch, play, and talk about sports, they often take into account ideas about skin color and ethnicity. The meanings given to skin color and ethnic background influence access to sport participation and the decisions that people make about sports in their lives.

Race refers to a category of people identified through a classification system based on meanings given to physical traits among humans; *ethnicity* refers to collections of people identified in terms of their shared cultural heritage. Racial and ethnic *minorities* are populations that have endured systematic forms of discrimination in a society.

The idea of race has a complex history, and it serves as the foundation for racial ideology, which people use to identify and make sense of "racial" characteristics and differences. Racial ideology, like other social constructions, changes over time as ideas and relationships change. However, over the past century in the United States, dominant racial ideology has supported the notion that there are important biological and cognitive differences between people classified as "black" as opposed to "white," and that these differences explain the success of black athletes in certain sports and sport positions.

Racial ideology influences the ways that many people connect skin color with athletic performance. At the same time, it influences participation decisions and achievement patterns in sports. Race, gender, and class relations in American society combine to create a context in which black males emphasize a stylized persona that adds to the commodity value of the black male body in sports and enables some black athletes to use widely accepted ideas about race to intimidate white opponents in sports.

Sports participation patterns among African Americans, Native Americans, Latinx Americans, and Asian Pacific Americans each have unique histories. Combinations of cultural, social, economic, and political factors have influenced those histories. However, sports participation in ethnic minority populations usually occurs under terms set by the dominant ethnic population in a community or society. Minority populations are seldom able to use sports to challenge the power and privilege of the dominant group, even though particular individuals may experience great personal success in sports.

Racial and ethnic issues affect sports worldwide. Europe currently faces challenges as increased migration has created tensions between native-born citizens and immigrants. As a result, previously dormant racist attitudes are now being expressed in connection with sports, especially soccer. This has created new challenges for sports teams and organizations worldwide. Racist and bigoted actions by spectators, athletes, coaches, and referees have increased since the beginning of this century and now are a significant problem for which there must be local and sport-related solutions.

The fact that some sports have histories of racially and ethnically mixed participation does not mean that problems have been eliminated. Harmonious racial and ethnic relations never occur automatically, and ethnic harmony is never established once and for all time. As current problems are solved, new relationships and new challenges are created. This means that racial and ethnic issues require regular attention if challenges are to be anticipated accurately and dealt with successfully. Success also depends on whether members of the dominant ethnic population see value in racial and ethnic diversity and commit themselves to dealing with diversity issues alongside those with different ethnic backgrounds.

Sports continue to be sites for racial and ethnic tensions and problems. But despite this, they also can be sites for challenging racial ideology and transforming ethnic relations. This happens only when people in sports plan strategies to encourage critical awareness of ethnic prejudices, racist ideas, and forms of discrimination built into the culture and structure of sports organizations. This awareness is required to increase ethnic inclusion, deal with and manage ethnic diversity, and integrate ethnic minorities into the power structures of organizations. Without this awareness, ethnic relations often become volatile and lead to overt forms of hostility.

SUPPLEMENTAL READINGS

Reading 1. Knowledge about race today (from PBS, "Race: The Power of an Illusion")
Reading 2. Media coverage of Joe Louis
Reading 3. Racial ideology in sports
Reading 4. Native Americans and team mascots
Reading 5. Samoan men in college and professional football
Reading 6. Profit motives and desegregating sports
Reading 7. Sports as sites for transforming racial attitudes
Reading 8. Why aren't all sports racially and ethnically desegregated?

SPORT MANAGEMENT ISSUES

- The athletic department in your predominantly white university has asked you to develop a campaign for the campus and community that will make it possible for African American students, especially young men, to be seen by teachers and students as students who take their education seriously. The ultimate goal is to change campus culture to support the student identity of African American students, especially those on sport teams. Where would you begin and what would be the focus of your program?
- You have been hired as the athletic director for a school district in Colorado. One of the high schools in the district has the nickname "Redmen," and the school's mascot is a caricature of a male Indian who dances and chants on the sidelines holding and waving a plastic tomahawk. A group of Native Americans from the local area tells you they are offended and asks you to convince people at the school to drop the name, the mascot, and team cheers that mimic Indian religious chants. Explain what you will do to respond to the group and to facilitate an educational solution for this issue.
- Your town has recently had a large influx of immigrants from Mexico and a few Asian countries. The editor of your local newspaper writes an editorial in which he suggests that the high school's varsity sport program is an effective tool for establishing good intergroup relations in the town. You read it and conclude that he has not thought of the challenges faced when trying to use sports in this way. You write a letter to the editor in which you explain these things to the readers of the paper. What does your letter say?

- Data clearly suggest that it is difficult to integrate positions of power in sport organizations. As a sport management consultant you have been hired to offer recommendations to enhance racial and ethnic diversity in a suburban school district on the West Coast. Describe your three primary recommendations, and explain why you made them.
- Major League Soccer has become increasingly popular in the United States. You have been hired as the community relations director for a new team in an area of southern California with a large and diverse population of people from Latin American countries. The financial success of your team depends on attracting fans and season ticket holders from this population. List the first five things you would do to meet this goal, and explain why you chose these five strategies over other possibilities.

references

AAA. 1998. Statement on "Race." Washington, DC: American Anthropological Association. www.aaanet.org/stmts/racepp.htm (retrieved June, 2005).

AAA. 2006a. Science: 1680s–1800s: Early classification of nature. (http://www.understandingrace.org/history/science/early_class .html). In American Anthropological Association. *Race: Are we so different.* Online: http://www.understandingrace.org/about/index.html

AAA. 2006b. 1770s–1850s: One race or several species. (http://www.understandingrace.org/history/science /one_race.html). In American Anthropological Association. *Race: Are we so different.* Online: http://www.understandingrace.org/about/index.html

AAA. 2006c. 1830s–1890s: Race science exhibitions. (http://www.understandingrace.org/history /science/race_science_exhibit.html). In American Anthropological Association. *Race: Are we so different.* Online: http://www.understandingrace.org /about/index.html

Aldama, Frederick Luis & Christpher González. 2014. *Latinos in the end zone: Conversations on the brown color line in the NFL.* New York NY: Palgrave Macmillan.

Anzil, Federico. 2019. The rise of Latinos in Major League Baseball. Visme.co; online,

Belson, Ken. 2020. In competition for top jobs, in the N.F.L. and beyond, it pays to be a white man. *New York Times* (January 12): https://www.nytimes.com/2020/01/12/sports/football/rooney-rule-nfl-coach-diversity.html

Belson, Ken. 2019. Only three N.F.L. head coaches are black. 'It's embarrassing.' *New York Times* (December 31): https://www.nytimes.com/2019/12/31/sports/football/nfl-coach-diversity.html

Benson, Peter. 2017. Big football: Corporate social responsibility and the culture and color of injury in America's most popular sport. *Journal of Sport and Social Issues* 41 (4): 307–334.

Bernard, Laura M. 2014. "Nowhere for me to go:" Black female student-athletes experiences on a predominantly White campus. *Journal for the Study of Sports and Athletes in Education* 8(2): 67–76.

Bimper, Albert Y. Jr. 2017. Mentorship of Black student-athletes at a predominately White American university: Critical race theory perspective on student-athlete development. *Sport, Education and Society* 22(2):175–193.

Bimper, Albert Y. 2015. Lifting the veil: Exploring colorblind racism in black student-athlete experiences. *Journal of Sport and Social Issues* 39(3): 225–243.

Bimper, Albert Y., Jr., and Louis Harrison, Jr. 2011. Meet me at the crossroads: African American athletic and racial identity. *Quest* 63(3): 275–288.

Bloom, John. 2000. *To show what an Indian can do: Sports at Native American boarding schools.* Minneapolis, MN: University of Minnesota Press.

Borland, John F. & Jennifer E. Bruening 2010. Navigating barriers: A qualitative examination of the underrepresentation of Black females as head coaches in collegiate basketball. *Sport Management Review* 13: 407–420.

Bradbury, Steven, Jacco van Sterkenburg & Patrick Mignon. 2018. The under-representation and experiences of elite level minority coaches in professional football in England, France and the Netherlands. *International Review for the Sociology of Sport* 53(3): 313–334.

Bretón, Marcos & José Luis Villegas. 1999. *Away games: The life and times of a Latin baseball player*. Albuquerque, NM: University of New Mexico Press.

Bretón, Marcos. 2000. Field of broken dreams: Latinos and baseball. *ColorLines* 3(1): 13–17.

Brown, Stacy M. 2019. "Black" or "African American?" *blackpressusa.com* (June 2): https://www.blackpressusa.com/commentary-black-or-african-american/

Bryant, Howard. 2018. *The heritage: Black athletes, a divided America, and the politics of patriotism*. Boston: Beacon Press.

Burgos, Adrian. 2007. *Playing America's game: Baseball, Latinos, and the color line*. Berkeley: University of California Press.

Burton, Nsenga. 2012. "N–ger Cake" fl ap: Hottentot Venus 2.0. *The Root* (April 17): http://www.theroot .com/buzz/liljeroths-nger-cake-hottentot-venus-20

Carrington, Ben. 2007. Sport, masculinity and black cultural resistance. In Alan Tomlinson, ed. *The sport studies reader* (pp. 298–303). London/New York: Routledge.

Carter, Akilah R. & Algerian Hart. 2010. Perspectives of mentoring: The Black female student-athlete. *Sport Management Review* 13: 382–394.

Chen, Tzu-Hsuan. 2012. From the "Taiwan Yankees" to the New York Yankees: The glocal narratives of baseball. *Sociology of Sport Journal* 29(4): 546–558.

Chiang, Ying, and Tzu-Hsuan Chen. 2013. Adopting the diasporic son: Jeremy Lin and Taiwan sport nationalism. *International Review for the Sociology of Sport* 50(6): 705–721.

Chin, Christina B. 2015. "'Aren't you a little short to play ball?': Japanese American youth and racial microaggressions in basketball leagues." *Amerasia Journal* 41(2): 47–65.

Chin, Christina B. 2016. 'We've got team spirit!': Ethnic community building and Japanese American youth basketball leagues. *Ethnic and Racial Studies* 39(6): 1070–1088.

Chow, Gary. 2019. Jeremy Lin: 'There's definitely some bittersweetness to my career' (February 22): https://theundefeated.com/features/jeremy-lin-on-being-the-only-asian-american-in-the-nba-at-times-it-kind-of-sucks/

Clammer, John. 2015. Performing ethnicity: Performance, gender, body and belief in the construction and signaling of identity. *Ethnic and Racial Studies* 38(13): 2159–2166.

Cloud, John. 2010. Why genes aren't destiny. *Time* 175, 2 (January 18): 49–53; online, http://www.time.com/time/health/article/0,8599,1951968,00.html

Cole, CL. 2006. Nicole Franklin's double dutch. *Journal of Sport and Social Issues* 30, 2: 119–121.

Collins, Patricia Hill. 2005. *Black sexual politics: African Americans, Gender, and the new racism*. New York/London: Routledge.

Cooper, Joseph. 2018. Dangerous stereotypes stalk black college athletes. *TheConversation.com* (August 20): https://theconversation.com/dangerous-stereotypes-stalk-black-college-athletes-101655

Cooper, Joseph. 2019. *From exploitation back to empowerment*. New York: Peter Lang Publishing, Inc.

Corbett, Doris, and William Johnson. 2000. The African American female in collegiate sport: Sexism and racism. In Dana Brooks & Ronald Althouse, eds. *Racism in college athletics: The African American athlete's experience* (pp. 199–226). Morgantown, WV: Fitness Information Technology, Inc.

Daniels, Donna. 2000. Gazing at the new black woman athlete. *ColorLines* 3, 1: 25–26.

Darvin, Lindsey, Alicia Cintron & Meg Hancock. 2017. ¿Por qué jugar? Sport socialization among Hispanic/Latina female NCAA division I student-athletes. *Journal of Amateur Sport* 3(2): 27–54.

Davids, Keith, and Joseph Baker. 2007. Genes, environment and sport performance: Why the nature-nurture dualism is no longer relevant. *Sports Medicine* 37(11): 961–980.

Davis, F. James. 2001. *Who is black: One nation's definition*. University Park, PA: Penn State University Press.

Davis-Delano, Laurel R 2017. R*dskins: Insult and brand. *Sociology of Sport Journal* 34(1): 94–95.

Dewan, Shaila. 2013. Has 'Caucasian' lost its meaning? *New York Times* (July 6): http://www.nytimes .com/2013/07/07/sunday-review/has-caucasian-lost-its-meaning.html

Dorgan, Byron. 2013. Broken promises. *New York Times* (July 10): http://www.nytimes.com/2013/07/11/opinion/broken-promises.html

Dubnewick, Michael, Tristan Hopper, John C. Spence & Tara-Leigh F. McHugh. 2018. "There's a cultural pride through our games": Enhancing the sport experiences of indigenous youth in Canada through participation in traditional games. *Journal of Sport and Social Issues* 42(4): 207–226.

DuBois, William Edward Burghardt.1935. *Black reconstruction in America*. New York: Harcourt, Brace.

Early, Gerald. 1998. Performance and reality: Race, sports and the modern world. *The Nation* 267(5): 11–20.

Edwards, Harry. 2000. The decline of the black athlete (as interviewed by D. Leonard). *ColorLines* 3(3): 29–24.

Edwards, Harry. 2017. *The revolt of the black athlete*. Urbana IL: University of Illinois Press.

Ekholm, David. 2019. Sport as a means of governing social integration: Discourses on bridging and bonding social relations. *Sociology of Sport Journal* 36(2): 152–161.

el-Khoury, Laura J. 2012. 'Being while black': Resistance and the management of the self. *Social Identities* 18(1): 85–100.

Endres, Danielle. 2015. American Indian permission for mascots: Resistance or complicity within rhetorical colonialism? *Rhetoric & Public Affairs* 18(4): 649–690.

Epstein, David. 2013. *The sports gene.* New York: Penguin Group.

Evans, Ashley B.; Kristine E. Copping, Stephanie J. Rowley & Beth Kurtz-Costes. 2011. Academic self-concept in black adolescents: Do race and gender stereotypes matter? *Self and Identity* 10(2): 263–277.

Farrey, Tom. 2005. Baby you're the greatest: Genetic testing for athletic traits. *ESPN The Magazine* 8.03 (February 14): 80–87 (http://sports.espn.go.com/espn/news/story?id=2022781).

Feldman, Bruce. 2007. A recruiting pitch of another kind. *ESPN The Magazine* (May 28): http://espn.go.com/gen/s/2002/0527/1387550.html

Fleming, Scott, and Alan Tomlinson. 2007. Racism and xenophobia in English football. In Alan Tomlinson, ed., *The sport studies reader* (pp. 304–315). London/ New York: Routledge.

Fleming, Scott. 2007. Sport and South Asian youth: The perils of 'false universalism" and stereotyping. In Alan Tomlinson, ed. *The sport studies reader* (pp. 289–297). London/New York: Routledge.

Foley, Douglas E. 1990a. *Learning capitalist culture.* Philadelphia: University of Pennsylvania Press.

Foley, Douglas E. 1990b. The great American football ritual: Reproducing race, class, and gender inequality. *Sociology of Sport Journal* 7, 2: 111–35.

Foley, Douglas E. 1999c. High school football: Deep in the heart of south Tejas. In Jay Coakley & Peter Donnelly, eds., *Inside Sports* (pp. 133–138). London: Routledge

Fox, Claudia K.; Daheia Barr-Anderson, Dianne Neumark-Sztainer & Melanie Wall. 2010. Physical activity and sports team participation: Association with academic outcomes in middle school and high school students. *Journal of School Health* 80: 31–37.

Fredrickson, George M. 2003. *Racism: A short history.* Princeton, NJ: Princeton University Press.

Fuller, Rhema D. 2017. Perception or reality: The relationship between stereotypes, discrimination, and the academic outcomes of African American male college athletes. *Journal of Sport and Social Issues* 41(5): 402–424.

Fuller, Rhema D., C. Keith Harrison & Scott J. Bukstein. 2017. A study of significance of racial and athletic identification on educational perceptions among African American male college athletes. *Race Ethnicity and Education* 20(5): 711–722.

Garber, Greg. 2007a. The Dominican Republic of the NFL. *ESPN The Magazine* (May 28): http://espn .go.com/gen/s/2002/0527/1387626 .html

Garber, Greg. 2007b. They might be giants. *ESPN The Magazine* (May 28): http://espn.go.com /gen/s /2002/0527/1387627.html

Gaunt, Kyra D. 2006. *The games black girls play.* New York: New York University Press.

Giles, Audrey. 2004. Kevlar®, Crisco®, and Menstruation: "Tradition" and Dene Games. *Sociology of Sport Journal* 21, 1: 18–35.

Gordon, Ian. 2007. Caught looking. *ESPN The Magazine* 10.11 (June 4): 100–104.

Harper, Shaun. 2018. Black male student-athletes and racial inequities in NCAA Division 1 college sports. 2018 edition. Los Angeles: University of Southern California, Race and Equity Center; online, https://race.usc.edu /wp-content/uploads/2018/03/2018_Sports _Report.pdf

Harrison, C. Keith. 1998. Themes that thread through society: Racism and athletic manifestation in the African-American community. *Race, Ethnicity and Education* 1(1): 63–74.

Harrison, C. Keith; Suzanne Malia Lawrence & Scott J. Bukstein. 2011. White College Students' Explanations of White (and Black) Athletic Performance: A Qualitative Investigation of White College Students. *Sociology of Sport Journal* 28(3): 347–361.

Hartmann, Douglas. 2016. *Midnight Basketball: Race, sports, and neoliberal social policy*. Chicago: University of Chicago Press.

Ho, Arnold K., Nour S. Kteily & Jacqueline M. Chen. 2017. "You're one of us": Black Americans' use of hypodescent and its association with egalitarianism. *Journal of Personality and Social Psychology 113(5):* 753–768.

Hoberman, John M. 1992. *Mortal engines: The science of performance and the dehumanization of sport.* New York: Free Press.

Hobson, Janell. 2005. The "batty" politic: Toward an aesthetic of the black female body. *AfricanAmerica. org* (March 15): http:// www.africanamerica.org/topic/serena-and -hottentot-venus

Hodge, S.R., F.M. Kozub, A.D. Dixson, J.L. Moore, III., and K. Kambon. 2008. A comparison of high school students' stereotypic beliefs about intelligence and athleticism. *Educational Foundations* 22(1/2): 99–119.

Holmes, Rachel. 2007. *African queen: The real life of the Hottentot Venus.* New York: Random House.

HoSang, Daniel Martinez, Oneka LaBennett, and Laura Pulido, eds. 2012. *Racial formation in the twenty-first century.* Berkeley, CA: University of California Press.

Houston Beau Manierre. 2019. *Exceptional recruiting: Identity intersections' impact of decision making for young black women athletes during the NCAA recruiting process.* A dissertation submitted to the Graduate Faculty, University of Colorado, Colorado Springs.

Hylton, Kevin & Stefan Lawrence. 2016. 'For your ears only!' Donald Sterling and backstage racism in sport. *Ethnic and Racial Studies*. 39(15): 2740–2757.

Jamieson, Katherine M. 2007. Advance at your own risk: Latinas, families, and collegiate softball. In Jorge Iber & Samuel O. Regalado, eds., *Mexican Americans and sports: A reader on athletics and barrio life* (pp. 213–232). College Station: Texas A&M University Press.

Jamieson, Katherine. 2005. "All my hopes and dreams": Families, schools, and subjectivities in collegiate softball. *Journal of Sport and Social Issues* 29(2): 133–147.

Jenkins, Chris. 2005. Steroid policy hits Latin Americans. *USA Today* (May 6): 7C.

Jones, Maya. 2018. New study examines history of black women fighting to be respected as athletes. *TheUndefeated.com* (June 25): https://theundefeated.com/features/morgan-state-university-study-examines-history-of-black-women-fighting-to-be-respected-as-athletes/

Joseph, Janelle. 2012a. The practice of capoeira: Diasporic black culture in Canada. *Ethnic and Racial Studies* 35(6): 1078–1095.

Joseph, Janelle. 2014. Culture, community, consciousness: The Caribbean sporting diaspora. *International Review for the Sociology of Sport* 49(6): 669–687.

Kechiche, Abdellatif. 2005. *Back Venus* (*Vénus noire*). Paris: MK2 Productions (film released, 2010). Online: http://www.youtube.com/watch?feature=player_embedded&v=_PD5aAd7HPc#at=33

Kent, Milton, Edward Robinson, Ron Taylor & Tonyaa Weathersbee. 2018. *Beating opponents, battling belittlement: How African-American female athletes use community to navigate negative images.* School of Global Journalism & Communication, Morgan State University.

King, C. Richard. 2016. *Redskins: Insult and brand.* Lincoln, NE: University of Nebraska Press.

Klein, Alan. 1991. *Sugarball: The American game, the Dominican dream.* New Haven, CT: Yale University Press.

Klein, Alan. 2006. *Growing the game: The globalization of major league baseball.* New Haven, CT: Yale University Press.

Klein. Alan. 2018. Engaging acrimony: Performing Lakota basketball in South Dakota. *Sociology of Sport Journal* 35(1): 58–65.

Komlos, John, and Benjamin E. Lauderdale. 2007. Underperformance in affluence: The remarkable relative decline in US heights in the second half of the 20th century. *Social Science Quarterly* 88(2): 283–305.

Korver, Kyle. 2019. Privileged. *The Players' Tribune* (April 8): https://www.theplayerstribune.com/en-us/articles/kyle-korver-utah-jazz-nba

Lapchick, Richard E. 2007. Asian American athletes: Past, present and future. *ESPN The Magazine* (May 1): http://espn.go.com/gen/s/2002/0430/1376346.html

Lapchick, Richard E. 2010. *100 campeones: Latino groundbreakers who paved the way in sport.* Morgantown: Fitness Information Technology.

Richard Lapchick. 2019. College sports continue to fall short when it comes to hiring diversely. ESPN.com (December 18): https://www.espn.com/college-football/story/_/id/28325924/college-sports-continue-fall-short-comes-hiring-diversely

Le Batard, Dan. 2005. Open look: Is it cheating if you don't understand the rules? *Es posible. ESPN The Magazine* 8.10 (May 23): 14.

Leonard, David J. 2017. *Playing while white: Privilege and power on and off the field.* Seattle WA: University of Washington Press.

Little, Anita. 2012. Serena Williams, the Hottentot Venus and accidental racism. *Ms Magazine* (December 15): http://msmagazine.com/blog/2012/12/15/serena-williams-the-hottentot-venus-and-accidental-racism/

Long, Jonathan, Ben Carrington, and Karl Spracklin. 2007. 'Asians cannot wear turbans in the scrum': Explorations of racist discourse within professional rugby league. In Alan Tomlinson, ed., *The sport studies reader* (pp. 283–288). London/New York: Routledge.

Longman, Jeré. 2013. Far from reservation, sisters lead Louisville. *New York Times* (April 6): http://www .nytimes.com/2013/04/07/sports/ncaabasketball /final-four-for-louisville-american-indian-sisters-inspire.html

Lopez, Vera. 2019. No Latina girls allowed: Gender-based teasing within school sports and physical activity contexts. *Youth and Society* 51(3): 377–393.

Love, Adam; Bianca Gonzalez-Sobrino & Matthew W. Hughey. 2017. Excessive celebration? The racialization of recruiting commitments on college football message boards. *Sociology of Sport Journal* 34(3): 235–247.

Martin, Renee. 2009. Is Serena Williams the new Sarah Baartman? *Global Comment* (July 8): http://globalcomment.com/is-serena-williams-the-new-sarah-baartman/

Maseko, Zola. 1998. *The life and times of Sara Baartman: "The Hottentot Venus."* Brooklyn, NY: Icarus Films.

May, Reuben A. Buford. 2008. *Living through the hoop: High school basketball, race, and the American dream.* New York: New York University Press.

May, Ruben A. B. 2009. The good and bad of it all: Professional Black male basketball players as role models for young Black male basketball players. *Sociology of Sport Journal* 26(3): 443–461.

Mead, Chris. 1985. *Champion Joe Louis: Black hero in white America.* New York: Charles Scribner's Sons.

Meir, David & Thomas Fletcher. 2019. The transformative potential of using participatory community sport initiatives to promote social cohesion in divided community contexts. *International Review for the sociology of Sport* 54(2): 218–238.

Melendez, Mickey C. 2008. Black football players on a predominantly white college campus: Psychosocial and emotional realities of the Black college athlete experience. *The Journal of Black Psychology* 34(4): 423–451.

Mendoza, Alexander. 2007. Beating the odds: Mexican American distance runners in Texas, 1950–1995. In Jorge Iber & Samuel O. Regalado, eds., *Mexican Americans and sports: A reader on athletics and barrio life* (pp. 188–191). College Station: Texas A&M University Press.

Middleton, Richard T. 2008. Institutions, inculcation, and black racial identity: Pigmentocracy vs. the rule of hypodescent. *Social Identities* 14(5): 567–585.

Miller, Patrick B. & David K. Wiggins, eds. 2003. *Sport and the color line: Black athletes and race relations in twentieth-century America*. London/New York: Routledge.

Miller, Ted. 2007. American football, Samoan style. *ESPN The Magazine* (May 28): http://espn.go.com /gen/s/2002/0527/1387562.html

Mohdin, Aamna. 2019. Football must do more to tackle racism, says Downing Street. *The Guardian* (December 23): https://www.theguardian.com/world/2019/dec/23/pfa-calls-for-uk-government-inquiry-into-racism-in-football

Morales, Sarina. 2016. Laurie Hernandez is Puerto Rican whether anyone agrees or not. *TheUndefeated.com* (September 14): https://theundefeated.com/features/laurie-hernandez-is-puerto-rican-whether-anyone-agrees-or-not/

Morgan, Robert. 1993. The 'Great Emancipator' and the issue of race. *The Journal for Historical Review* 13(5): 4. Online: http://www.ihr.org/jhr/v13 /v13n5p-4_Morgan.html

Myers, J. 2000. *Afraid of the dark: What whites and blacks need to know about each other.* Chicago: Lawrence Hill Books.

Nakamura, Yuka. 2016. Rethinking identity politics: The multiple attachments of an 'exclusive' sport organization. *Sociology of Sport Journal* 33(2): 146–155.

Newman, Brooke. 2018. The long history behind the racist attacks on Serena Williams. *Washington Post* (September 11): https://www.washingtonpost.com/outlook/2018/09/11/long-history-behind-racist-attacks-serena-williams./

Niiya, Brian, ed. 2000. *More than a game: Sport in the Japanese American community.* Los Angeles: Japanese American National Museum.

Nobles, Melissa. 2000. *Shades of citizenship: Race and the census in modern politics.* Stanford, CA: Stanford University Press.

Norman, Moss E., Michael Hart & LeAnne Petherick. 2019. Indigenous gender reformations: physical culture, settler colonialism and the politics of containment. *Sociology of Sport Journal* 36(2): 113–123

Omi, Michael & Howard Winant. 1994. *Racial formation in the United States*. New York/London: Routledge.

O'Neal, Lonnae. 2018. The struggle is real: The unrelenting weight of being a black, female athlete. *TheUndefeated.com* (June 25): https://

theundefeated.com/features/the-struggle-is-real-the-unrelenting-weight-of-being-a-black-female-athlete/

Oxendine, Joseph B. 1988. *American Indian sports heritage.* Champaign, IL: Human Kinetics.

Passan, Jeff. 2018. How a child-molesting trainer and teenage steroid use has come to define Latin American baseball. *Yahoo Sports* (July 9): https://sports.yahoo.com/child-molesting-trainer-teenage-steroid-use-come-define-latin-american-baseball-010517552.html

PBS. 2006. *Race–The power of an illusion* (transcripts of Episodes I, II, III). Online: http://www.newsreel .org/nav/title .asp?tc=CN0149

Powers-Beck, Jeffrey P. 2004. *The American Indian integration of baseball.* Lincoln: University of Nebraska Press.

Reed, Matthew. 2019. Moise Kean & Mario Balotelli, the Black Italians. TheShadowLeague .com (May 8): https://theshadowleague.com /moise-kean-mario-balotelli-the-black-italians/

Regalado, Samuel O. 2008. *Viva Baseball! Latin major leaguers and their special hunger.* Urbana: University of Illinois Press.

Roberts, Dorothy. 2011. *Fatal invention: How science, politics, and big business re-create race in the twenty-first century.* New York NY: The New Press.

Ruck, Rob. 1987. *Sandlot seasons: Sport in black Pittsburgh.* Urbana, IL: University of Illinois Press.

Runstedtler, Theresa. 2018. More than just play: Unmasking black child labor in the athletic industrial complex. *Journal of Sport and Social Issues* 42(3): 152–169.

Saini, Angela. 2019. *Superior: The return of race science*. Boston MA: Beacon Press

Sapolsky, Robert M. 2000. Genetic hyping. *The Sciences* 40(2): http://www.panix.com /userdirs/jwinters/thesciences/Sapolsky _MA00/SapolskyFrame.html

Saraceno, Jon. 2005. Native Americans aren't fair game for nicknames. *USA Today* (June 1): 10C.

Science vs. 2019. Race: Can we see it in our DNA? *GimletMedia.com* (April 19): https:// gimletmedia.com/shows/science-vs/6nhgxk /race-can-we-see-it-in-our-dna

Shakib, Sohaila & Philip Veliz. 2013. Race, sport and social support: A comparison between African American and White youths' perceptions of social support for sport participation. *International Review for the Sociology of Sport* 48(3): 295–317.

Siler, Kyle. 2019. Pipelines on the gridiron: Player backgrounds, opportunity structures and racial stratification in American college football. *Sociology of Sport Journal* 36(1): 57–76.

Singer, John N. & Reuben A. Buford May. 2011. The career trajectory of a Black male high school basketball player: A social reproduction perspective. *International Review for the Sociology of Sport* 46(3): 299–314.

Singer, John N. 2008. Benefits and detriments of African American male athletes' participation in a big time college football program. *International Review for the Sociology of Sport* 43(4): 399–408.

Smedley, Audrey. 1997. Origin of the idea of race. *Anthropology Newsletter*, November; online at www.pbs.org/race/000_About/002_04 -background-02-09.htm (retrieved October 15, 2005).

Smedley, Audrey. 1999. Review of Theodore Allen, *The Invention of the White Race, vol. 2. Journal of World History* 10, 1 (Spring): 234–237.

Smedley, Audrey. 2003. PBS interview for the series, *Race - The power of an illusion*. www .pbs.org/race/000_About/002_04 -background-02-06.htm (retrieved June, 2005).

Smith, Earl. 2007. *Race, sport and the American dream.* Durham, NC: Carolina Academic Press.

Smith, Rory. 2019. Italian soccer's anti-racism campaign features paintings of monkeys. *New York Times* (December 16): https://www .nytimes.com/2019/12/16/sports/soccer/italy -soccer-racism.html

Smith, Justin E.H. 2013. The Enlightenment's 'race' problem, and ours. *New York Times* (February 10): http://opinionator

.blogs. nytimes.com/2013/02/10/ why -has-race-survived/

Song, Miri. 2018. Why we still need to talk about race, *Ethnic and Racial Studies* 41(6): 1131–1145.

St. Louis, Brett. 2010. Sport, genetics and the `natural athlete': The resurgence of racial science. *Body & Society* 9, 2: 75–95.

Staurowsky, Ellen J. 2007. "You know, we are all Indian": Exploring white power and privilege in reactions to the NCAA Native American Mascot Policy. *Journal of Sport and Social Issues* 31(1): 61–76.

Steele, Claude M. 2010. *Whisting Vivaldi and other clues to how stereotype affect us*. New York: W.W. Norton & Company.

Swanson, Jennifer; Amelie Ramirez & Kipling J. Gallion. 2013. Salud America! "Active Spaces for Latino Kids. Princeton, NJ: The Robert Woods Johnson Foundation.

Sylwester, MaryJo. 2005a. Girls following in Ochoa's, Fernandez's sports cleats. *USA Today* (March 29): 4C.

Sylwester, MaryJo. 2005b. Hispanic girls in sports held back by tradition. *USA Today* (March 29): 1A–2A.

Sylwester, MaryJo. 2005c. Sky's the limit for Hispanic teen. *USA Today* (March 29): 4C.

Thangaraj, Stanley I. 2016. *Desi hoop dreams: Pickup basketball and the making of Asian American masculinity*. New York NY: New York University Press.

Thangaraj, Stanley I., Constancio Arnaldo & Christina B. Chin, eds. 2016. *Asian American Sporting Cultures. New York NY: New York University Press.*

Treitler, Vilna Bashi. 2016. Racialization and its paradigms: From Ireland to North America *Current Sociology* 64(2): 213–227.

Valeri, Mauro. 2010. *What a cheer: Ten years of racism in Italian football* (*Che Razza di Tifo*). Donzelli, Italy.

Webster, Paul. 2000. France keeps a hold on Black Venus. *The Observer* (April 2): http://www .guardian.co.uk/world/2000/apr/02/paulwebster .theobserver1

Williams, Dana. 2007. Where's the honor? Attitudes toward the "Fighting Sioux" nickname and logo. *Sociology of Sport Journal* 24(4): 437–456.

Williams, Patricia J. 2005. Genetically speaking. *The Nation* 280(24): 10.

Winant, Howard. 2001. *The world is a ghetto: Race and democracy since World War II*. New York: Basic Books.

Winant, Howard. 2004. *The new politics of race: Globalism, difference, justice.* Minneapolis: University of Minnesota Press.

Winant, Howard. 2006. Race and racism: Towards a global future. *Ethnic and Racial Studies* 29(5): 986–1003.

Winant, Howard. 2015. Race, ethnicity and social science. *Ethnic and Racial Studies* 38(13): 2176–2185.

Withycombe, Jenny Lind. 2011. Intersecting selves: African American female athletes' experiences of sport. *Sociology of Sport Journal* 28(4): 478–493.

Yep, Kathleen S. 2009. *Outside the paint: When basketball ruled at the Chinese playground.* Temple University Press.

Yep, Kathleen S. 2010. Playing rough and tough: Chinese American women basketball players in the 1930s and 1940s. *Frontiers: A Journal of Women's Studies* 31(1): 123–141.

Yep, Kathleen S. 2012. Peddling sport: Liberal multiculturalism and the racial triangularization of blackness, Chineseness, and Native American-ness in professional basketball. *Ethnic and Racial Studies* 35(6): 971–987.

YouTube. 2019. Kyle Korver and his Utah Jazz teammates talk racism and the NBA. Youtube .com (April 80): https://www.youtube.com /watch?v=rn6CVpmmrno

Zirin, Dave. 2013. Redskins: The clock is now ticking on changing the name. *The Nation* (February 11): http://www.thenation.com/blog/172806 /redskins-clock-now-tickingchanging-name

chapter

9

(*Source:* Elizabeth Pike)

SOCIAL CLASS

Do Money and Power Matter in Sports?

The system is totally rigged against poor people. The way we're funding these sports today, if you're in the bottom half economically, you're going to struggle, and if you're in the bottom 20 percent, you're pretty much out of it.

–Clark Power, Founder, Play Like a Champion Today (Temple, 2019)

The decline of youth sports participation is . . . tailored to exacerbate fears about the state of American childhood. . . . But dig into the numbers, and a more complex, two-track story emerges. . . . This isn't a story about American childhood; it's about American inequality.

– Derek Thompson, journalist, 2018

"Football is the answer in the middle of poverty, in the middle of crime, and in the middle of a water crisis because it takes away all your excuses, and it tells you to be better no matter how good or great you are."

–High School student, Flint MI (*Football Town*, episode 7, 2019)

The focus on individualism and declining notions of shared responsibility have led to social segregation by social class in the United States . . . In the 1950s there was an emphasis on "our community" whereas today the emphasis is on "my kids." If they are someone else's kids, let them take care of them; it's not my responsibility.

–Robert Putnam, Professor of Public Policy, Harvard University (2016)

Chapter Outline

Learning Objectives

- Define social class, class ideology, and class relations, and explain how they are related to sports today.
- Identify who has power in sports today, and the interests that are served by that power.
- Critically assess the argument that professional sports arenas and stadia benefit everyone and create jobs in a city.
- Explain how class, gender, race, and ethnic relations intersect and influence sport participation patterns in society.
- Explain why sports in the future are likely to be less diverse in terms of ethnicity and social class.
- Describe the ways in which social class impacts sport spectators today.
- Outline the economic and career opportunities that exist in sports today, especially for women and ethnic minorities.
- Identify the conditions under which sport participation is most likely and least likely to lead to upward mobility and occupational success.
- Understand the reality of college scholarships today and how they may be related to occupational success.

People like to think that sport is the great equalizer, that it transcends issues of money, power, and economic inequalities. They see sports as open activities in which success comes only through individual ability and hard work. However, all organized sports depend on material resources, and those resources must come from somewhere. Therefore, playing, watching, and excelling in sports depend on resources supplied by individuals, families, governments, or private organizations.

More than ever before, it takes money to play sports and develop sport skills. Tickets are expensive, and spectators often are divided by social class in the stadium: The wealthy and well connected sit in luxury suites and club seats, whereas fans who are less well off sit in other sections, depending on their ability to pay for premium tickets or buy season tickets.

Today, it takes money to watch sports on television as satellite and cable connections come with ever-increasing monthly subscriber fees, expensive sport packages, and pay-per-view costs. This means that sports and sports participation are closely linked with the distribution of economic resources in society.

Many people believe that sports are a path to economic success for people from all social classes. When people talk about athletes, they often mention particular rags-to-riches stories. However, these beliefs and stories distract attention from the ways in which sports reflect and perpetuate economic inequalities.

This chapter deals with matters of money and wealth, as well as larger sociological issues related to social class and socioeconomic mobility. Our discussion focuses on the following questions:

1. What is meant by *social class* and *class relations?*
2. How do social class and class relations influence sports and sport participation?
3. Are sports open and democratic in the provision of economic and career opportunities?
4. Does playing sports contribute to occupational success and social mobility among former athletes?

SOCIAL CLASS AND CLASS RELATIONS

Understanding social class and the related concepts of social stratification, socioeconomic status, and life chances is important when studying social worlds. Economic resources are related to power in society, and economic inequalities influence many aspects of people's lives.

Social class refers to *categories of people who share an economic position in society based on their income, wealth (savings and assets), education, occupation, and social connections.* People in a particular social class also share similar **life chances**–that is, *similar odds for achieving economic success and power in society.* Social classes exist in all contemporary societies because life chances are not equally distributed across all people.

Social stratification refers to *structured forms of economic inequalities that are part of the organization of everyday social life.* In other words, in comparison with people from upper social classes, people from lower social classes have fewer opportunities to achieve economic success and power. Children born into wealthy, powerful, and well-connected families are in better positions to become wealthy, powerful, and well-connected adults than are children born into poor families that lack influence and social networks connecting them with educational and career opportunities.

Most of us are aware of economic inequalities in society. We see them all around us. We know they exist and influence people's lives, but there are few public discussions about the impact of social class on our views of ourselves and others, our social relationships, and our everyday lives. In other words, we don't discuss **class relations**–the *ways that social class is incorporated into the organization of our everyday lives.* We often hear about the importance of equal opportunities in society, but there are few discussions about the ways that people in upper socioeconomic classes use their income, wealth, and power to maintain their positions of advantage in society and pass that advantage from one generation to the next. Instead, we hear "rags-to-riches" stories about individuals who overcame poverty or a lower-class background to become wealthy, stories about "millionaires next door," and stories about CEOs who are "regular guys" with annual incomes of $10 million or more.

Ignored in the media and popular discourse are the oppressive effects of poverty and the limited opportunities available to those who lack economic resources, access to good education, and well-placed social connections. Those stories are too depressing to put in the news, claim executives for the commercial media–people don't like to hear about them, and they lower audience ratings. However, social-class differences in the form of socioeconomic inequalities are real; they have real consequences for life chances, they affect nearly every facet of people's lives, and all of this is clearly documented by valid and reliable data (Erikson, 2015; Frank, 2017; Payne, 2017; Pew Research Center, 2019; Piketty, 2014).

People in the United States often shy away from critical discussions of social class and class relations because they're uneasy about acknowledging that equality of opportunity is largely a myth in their society (Frank, 2017). This is especially true in regard to sports and sports participation–a sphere of life in which most people believe that money and class-based advantages don't matter (Buchanan, Odenheimer & Prewitt-White, 2016; Thompson, 2018).

The discussion of social class and class relations in this chapter is grounded in a critical approach that identifies who benefits from and who is disadvantaged by the ways that sports are organized and played. The focus is on economic inequality, the processes through which inequality is reproduced, how it benefits wealthy and powerful people, and how it affects sports and the lives of people associated with sports.

SPORTS AND ECONOMIC INEQUALITY

Money and economic power exert significant influence on the goals, purpose, and organization of sports in society. Many people believe that sports and sports participation are open to all people and that inequalities related to money, position, and influence have no effect on the organized games we play and watch. However, formally organized sports could not be developed, scheduled, or maintained without economic resources. Those who control money and economic power use them to organize and sponsor sports. As they do so, they give preference to sport forms that reflect and maintain their values and interests. As a result, sports emerge out of a context in which inequality shapes decisions and the allocation of resources. In the process, sports reproduce the very inequalities that so many people think are absent in them.

The wealthy aristocrats who developed the modern Olympic Games even used their power to establish a definition of *amateur* that favored athletes from wealthy backgrounds. This definition, which excluded athletes who used their sport skills to earn a living, has been revised over the years so the Olympics now include those who are not independently wealthy. However, the NCAA continues to use a definition of amateur that prohibits athletes from being paid beyond the cost of their education, even if they are part of a multi-billion dollar business in which others can make millions of dollars annually. Throughout most organized sports, money and economic power now operate in complex ways as elite-level training has become privatized and costly in many countries.

Elite and powerful people have considerable influence over what "counts as sport" and how sports are organized and played in mainstream social worlds. Even when grassroots games and physical activities become formally organized as sports, they don't become popular unless they can be used to reaffirm the interests and ideologies of sponsors with resources. For example, ESPN organized and televised the X Games to fit the needs of corporate sponsors that buy advertising time to promote their products to young males.

Even informal games require facilities, equipment, and safe play spaces–all of which are more plentiful in upper- and upper-middle-income neighborhoods. Low-income neighborhoods generally lack what is needed to initiate and sustain informal activities; families don't have large lawns at their homes, they don't live on safe cul-de-sacs without traffic, and there is a short supply of well-maintained neighborhood parks. This is why social class and class relations must be taken into account when we study sports in society and try to explain the patterns of sport participation we see around us.

The Dynamics of Class Relations

To understand the dynamics of class relations, think about the ways that age relations operate in sports. Even though young people are capable of creating and playing games on their own, adults intervene and create organized youth sport programs. These programs emphasize things that adults think are best for their children. As noted in Chapter 4, *Organized Youth Sports*, adults have the resources to develop, schedule, and maintain organized sports that reflect their ideas of what children should be doing and learning. Children often enjoy these adult-controlled sports, but their participation occurs in a framework that is determined by adults and organized to legitimize and reproduce adult control over their lives.

Age relations are especially apparent in youth sports when participants don't meet adult expectations or when they violate the rules developed by adults. The adults use their power to define deviance, identify when it occurs, and demand that children comply with rules and expectations. Overall, adults use their superior resources to convince young people that "the adults' way" is "the right way" to play sports. When young people comply with adults' rules and meet adults' expectations, they're rewarded and told that they have "character." This is why many adults are fond of college and professional coaches who are autocratic and controlling. These coaches reaffirm the beliefs that it is normal and necessary for adults to control young people and that young people must learn to accept that control. In this way, sports reproduce a hierarchical form of age relations, with adult power and privilege defined as normal and necessary aspects of social worlds.

Class relations work in similar ways. People with resources sponsor sports that support their ideas about "good character," individual responsibility, competition, excellence, achievement, and proper social organization. In fact, whenever people obtain power in a social world, they define "character" in a way that promotes their interests. For example, when wealthy and powerful people play sports in exclusive clubs, such as Augusta National (golf club) in Georgia, they use a class ideology that legitimizes their right to do so and establishes their membership in such a club as a privilege they deserve for being winners in society. This also is reflected in the compensation received by CEOs of large corporations: In 1965 they received about eighteen times more than typical workers that year. In 1978 it was 27 times more, in 1995 it was 135 times more, and in 2018 it was over 361 times more (Hembree, 2018; Mishel and Schieder, 2017). As top executives took more pay for themselves, the pay for typical workers remained stuck at 1980 levels. This illustrates how power and position often influence class relations.

Over those same years corporate sponsorship of sports has increased exponentially. This, too, is linked to class relations because CEOs seek to sponsor sports that can be presented in ways that reaffirm the existing class structure in society and the ideology that supports it. This is partly why popular spectator sports worldwide emphasize competition, individualism, highly specialized skills, the use of technology, and dominance over opponents. When these values and cultural practices are widely accepted, average people are more likely to believe that the status and privilege of the wealthy and powerful are legitimate and deserved.

Sports that emphasize partnership, sharing, open participation, nurturance, and mutual support are seldom sponsored because people with power don't want to promote values that reaffirm equality and horizontal forms of social organization in society.

As the globalization of money, commercial trade, and financing opened up in the late 1970s, class relations in many societies changed to increase the income, wealth, and consumption gaps between the

(*Source:* Jay Coakley)

The belief that wealth and power are achieved through competitive success implies that being wealthy and powerful is proof of one's abilities, qualifications, and overall moral worth. Exclusive sports clubs reaffirm this belief and reinforce the idea that the class privileges enjoyed by wealthy and powerful people are deserved; and the clubs are sites for establishing relationships used to perpetuate mutually beneficial privileged status.

poor and the powerful. These economic changes enabled those who were connected with the flow of capital around the world to increase their power and wealth (Piketty, 2014; Stiglitz, 2012). As a result, the gap between the rich and the poor expanded in terms of income, wealth, and political influence.

Class Ideology in the United States

Sociologists define **class ideology** as *interrelated ideas and beliefs that people use to understand economic inequalities, identify their class position, and evaluate the impact of economic inequalities on the organization of social worlds.* Dominant class ideology in the United States has long been organized around two themes: the American Dream and a belief that the United States is a meritocracy.

The **American Dream** is *a hopeful vision of boundless opportunities for individuals to succeed economically and live a happy life based on hard work and consumption.* It focuses attention on individual aspirations and often blurs an awareness of social class differences in material living conditions and differential life chances among categories of people. The uniquely American belief that "you can be anything you want to be" never acknowledges that a person's class position influences life chances or that life chances influence patterns of social and economic mobility in all social classes. Therefore, Americans often dream about what they hope to be in the future rather than critically examining their current economic circumstances and the ways that class relations affect their lives. The belief that "you can be anything" also discredits poor and low-income people by associating poverty with individual failure, laziness, and weakness of character.

The American Dream is usually connected with a belief that the United States is a **meritocracy**—*a social world in which rewards go to people who deserve them due to their abilities, qualifications, and recognized achievements*. Believing that the United States is a meritocracy helps people explain and justify economic inequalities. It supports the assumption that success is rightfully earned and failure is caused by poor choices and a lack of ambition.

Sustaining a belief that the United States is a meritocracy depends on related beliefs that individual ability, qualifications, and character are objectively proven through competitive success; that humans are naturally competitive; and that competition is the only fair way to allocate rewards in a society. This is why people with money and power like to use sports as a metaphor for life—it identifies winners like them as deserving individuals who have outperformed others in a natural process of individual competition and achievement.

Figure 9.1 shows that class ideology in the United States consists of interrelated ideas and beliefs about the American Dream, meritocracy, and competition; it illustrates that inequality is a result of people receiving what they deserve; it emphasizes that opportunities exist and that success is achieved only when people develop abilities and work hard; and it justifies inequality as a natural result of competition in a society where merit counts.

One of the outcomes of such an ideology is that competitive success comes to be linked with moral worth. The belief that "you get what you deserve, and you deserve what you get" works to the advantage of people with wealth, because it implies that they deserve what they have and that inequality is a fair and natural outcome of competitive processes. A related belief is that as long as competition is free and unregulated, only the best will succeed and only the lazy and unqualified will fail.

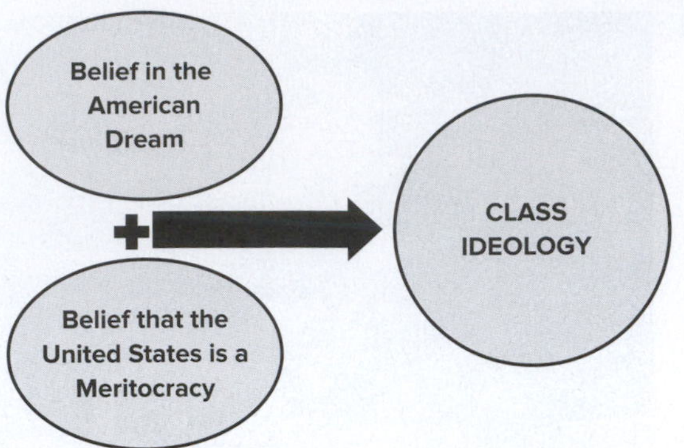

FIGURE 9.1 The two primary beliefs that inform and support class ideology in the United States.

Promoting this ideology is difficult when it conflicts with the real experiences of many Americans who work hard and haven't achieved success in the form of the American Dream or have seen their success disappear due to factors beyond their control. Therefore, people in the upper classes are most likely to retain their position and status *if* they can create and perpetuate widespread agreement that competition is a natural and fair way to allocate rewards and that the winners in competitive processes deserve the rewards they receive. This, of course, is how sports come to be connected with class relations in society. Sports offer "proof" that inequalities are based on merit, that competition identifies winners, and that losers should work harder or change themselves if they want to be winners, or simply try and try again. Most important, sports provides a metaphor for society that portrays social class as a characteristic of individuals rather than an economic structure that influences life chances and the distribution of resources in society (Falcous and McLeod, 2012).

Alan Tomlinson, a British sociologist who has studied power and social class for decades, has noted that sports, as they are sponsored and played today, ultimately "reproduce social and economic distinctions and preserve the power and influence of those who control resources in society." As a result, he says, sports today "cannot be fully understood unless this key influence and core dynamic is fully recognized" (2007, p. 4695).

Class Relations and Who Has Power in Sports

Decisions that affect the meaning, purpose, and organization of sports are made at many levels–from neighborhood youth sport programs to the International Olympic Committee. Although scholars who study sports in society identify people who exercise power in various settings, they usually don't rank those with power in and over sports. But this was done in 2018 by the *Sport Business Journal* (King, 2018). Their list of the 20 most powerful people in sports business is shown in Table 9.1.

There are no coaches and only one athlete on the list because they are simply hired hands–workers who serve at the discretion of those who run the business of sport. Therefore, the journalists who did the selecting and ranking focused on who could make decisions that would have a profound influence on the organization and culture of sports in the United States. Among the top twenty are eight CEOs in major sport organizations, including two NFL teams. There are eight CEOs of media and media marketing companies and two owners of sport teams (in the NFL). Rounding out the top 20 are LeBron James, who was new to Los Angeles when this list was compiled, and the American Sport Gambler, that became powerful when the US Supreme Court ruled that states could permit

Table 9.1 Top 20 most influential people in sports business*

Rank	Name	Position
1.	American Sport Gambler	(will influence media ratings for mainstream sports)
2.	Adam Silver	Commissioner, National Basketball Association
3.	Roger Goodell	Commissioner, National Football League
4.	Eric Shanks	CEO & Executive Producer, Fox Sports
5.	Rob Manford	Commissioner, Major League Baseball
6.	David Levy	President, Turner Broadcasting
7.	Casey Wasserman	Chairman & CEO, Wasserman, Chairman, LA 2028
8.	Mark Parker	Chairman, President & CEO, Nike
9.	Joe Jacob / Peter Gruber	Owners, Golden State Warriors
10.	Gary Bettman	Commissioner, National Hockey League
11.	Mark Lazarus	Chairman, NBC Broadcasting & Sports, NBCUniversal
12.	Ari Emanual / Patrick Whitesell	CEO, Endeavor / Executive Chairman, Endeavor
13.	Jerry Jones	Owner, Dallas Cowboys
14.	Robert Kraft	Chairman & CEO, The Kraft Group
15.	LeBron James	All-star, Activist & Entrepreneur, Los Angeles Lakers
16.	Don Garber	Commissioner, Major League Soccer
17.	Sean McManus / David Berson	Chairman, CBS Sports / President, CBS Sports
18.	Michael Levine / Howard Nuchow	Coheads, Creative Artists Agency (athletes are clients)
19.	Phil Anschutz	Chairman & CEO, Anschutz Entertainment Group
20.	Ted Leonsis	Owner & CEO, Monumental Sports & Entertainment

**Source: Sports Business Journal* (King, 2018). This list reflects rankings in the context of the United States in 2018; a global influence list would be much different.

gambling on sports events. As up to 100 million Americans place legal bets on sports it will impact the way people watch sports, the content of sports media programming, and the organization of sport venues when it is possible to bet on the game at the game. There will be additional changes as each state makes decisions on the legality of sports betting and as they compete with each other for a piece of what will quickly become a $6 billion business with a great potential for growth.

Finally, all 20 of the people on the list are men–although women are among the American gamblers–and eighteen of the twenty are white men. It is clear that white men hold nearly 100 percent of the major power positions in elite sports today. These men have much in common with other economic elites in the United States. Collectively, they benefit from a class ideology that legitimizes the existing status and power hierarchy in American society and supports the idea that the current level of economic inequality, even though it is greater than it has been for a century, is good for the country. This is why they are sincerely committed to a form of sport–elite men's sports–in which competition, conquest, individualism, authority, and consumption are highlighted in everything from media coverage and stadium design to team logos and ads for upcoming games and contests.

Although the power wielded by these and other powerful people in sports does not ignore the interests of common folk in the United States and worldwide, it clearly focuses on the expansion and profitability of the organizations represented by the power holders. Therefore, sports are sponsored and presented to highlight the meanings and orientations valued by economic elites at the same time that they provide exciting and enjoyable experiences to people like you and me.

This relationship between sports and social class explains why many of us in the sociology of sport use a combination of structural and cultural theories to help us understand sports in society. For example, Antonio Gramsci, an Italian political theorist, developed a theory stating that members of the "ruling class" in contemporary societies maintain their power to the extent that they can develop creative ways to convince most people that their society is organized as fairly and efficiently as possible under current social and economic conditions. One of the strategies for doing this is to become the primary providers of popular pleasure and entertainment so that people see the ruling class as sponsors of their joy and excitement. This strategy is especially effective if the ruling class can use entertaining events to promote particular ideas and beliefs about what should be important in people's lives. In this way, sports and other forms of exciting entertainment become cultural vehicles for establishing "ideological outposts" in the minds of people who are ruled. These outposts can then be used to send other messages into the popular consciousness–messages from sponsors and media commentators who reaffirm a class ideology legitimizing current forms of class inequality in society. Additionally, at this point in time, the "ruling class" also makes billions of dollars as they perpetuate this ideology–an outcome that further solidifies their status and power. This critical theoretical approach helps us see the dynamics of class relations and the process of hegemony at work in sports and other spheres of our lives.

SOCIAL CLASS AND SPORT PARTICIPATION PATTERNS

In all societies, social class and class relations influence who plays, who watches, who consumes information about sports, and what information about sports is available in mainstream media. Patterns of sport participation and consumption are closely associated with money, power, and privilege. At a basic level, organized sports are a luxury item in the economies of many nations, and they are most prevalent in wealthy nations where people have discretionary money and time.

Active sport participation, attendance at events, and consuming media sports are positively correlated with a person's income, education, and occupational status. Training at the elite level of sports requires considerable resources. Some costs may be covered by sponsors for those lucky enough to have them, but others must be covered by personal funds. For example, when the record-setting swimmer Dara Torres trained for the 2008 Olympics, she spent about $100,000 per year for her support staff, including a pool coach, a strength and conditioning coach who also is her dietician, two full-time people who stretch her muscles, a physical therapist, a masseuse, and a nanny to care for her daughter (Crouse, 2007). Torres was 41 years old, but she represents a widely accepted approach to training for elite athletes of any age.

Most elite sports require expensive equipment and training. For example, in any form of motor racing the costs can reach $200,000 per year, *plus* private driving coaches at $5000 per weekend (Cacciola, 2012). Clearly, this influences who can become seriously involved and successful in these sports.

Even the health and fitness movement, often described as a grassroots phenomenon in North America, involves mostly people who have higher-than-average incomes and education and work in professional or managerial occupations (Ingraham, 2018). For the most part, people in low-income jobs don't run, bicycle, or swim as often as their high-income counterparts. Nor do they play as many organized sports on their lunch hours, after work, on weekends, or during vacations. This pattern holds true throughout the life course, for younger and older people, men and women,

(*Source:* Basia Borzecka)

Young people in low-income families usually play sports at public parks and schools. These activities often are creatively arranged, as shown by these slackliners. But they lack the support and consistency characterized by organized sports. Young people in upper- and upper-middle-class families have resources to purchase access to privately owned sport facilities and spaces. This results in different sports experiences and different sports participation patterns from one social class to another.

racial and ethnic populations, and people with disabilities: *Social class is related strongly to participation among all categories of people* (Allison, 2018; Allison, Davis & Barranco, 2018; Andersen and Bakken, 2019; Buchanan, Odenheimer & Prewitt-White, 2016; Cairney et al., 2015; Coalter, 2013; Eckstein, 2019; Farrey, 2017; Kim et al., 2016; Moret and Ohl, 2019; Stuij, 2015; Vandermeerschen, Vos & Scheerder, 2016; White and McTeer, 2012).

Over time, economic inequality in society leads to the formation of class-based lifestyles that involve particular forms of sports (Bourdieu, 1986a, 1986b; Ceron-Anaya, 2017; Clarey, 2019; DeLuca, 2013; McLaughlin, 2018; Stuij, 2015). For the most part, sport participation in various lifestyles reflects patterns of sponsorship and access to participation opportunities. For example, the lifestyles of wealthy people routinely include golf, tennis, skiing, swimming, sailing, and other sports that are self-funded and played at exclusive clubs and resorts. These sports often involve expensive facilities, equipment, and/or clothing, and generally require that people have jobs and/or lives in which they have the control, freedom, and time needed to participate; some people also combine sport participation with their jobs by using facilities that their business associates also use. This has interesting implications in the United States, where companies pay the club memberships of their top executives and then classify most club expenses as "business deductions" on the corporation's tax returns. Taking these deductions reduces the company's taxes and reduces the tax revenues that fund public sport programs for people who cannot afford golf, tennis, or elite health club memberships. At the same time, executives and their friends and relatives enjoy free perks worth untold billions of dollars, which they refer to as "development investments" rather than "welfare for the rich."

The lifestyles of middle-income and working-class people, on the other hand, tend to include sports that by tradition are free and open to the public, sponsored by public funds, or available through public schools. When these sports involve the use of expensive equipment or clothing, participation occurs in connection with various forms of financial sacrifice. For instance, buying a motocross bike so his child can ride and race means that a father must work overtime, cancel the family vacation, and organize family leisure around motocross races.

The lifestyles of low-income people and those living under the poverty line seldom involve regular sports participation, unless a shoe company identifies young potential stars and sponsors their participation. When people struggle to stretch the family budget, they seldom can maintain a lifestyle that includes regular sport participation. Spending money to play or watch sports in person is a luxury that most low-income people can't afford. Despite this most people in wealthy nations continue to believe that sports are a meritocracy in which everyone has an equal chance to play and succeed (Wiecek, 2018).

Homemaking, Child Rearing, and Earning a Living: Class and Gender Relations in Women's Lives

The impact of social class on sports participation often varies by age, gender, race and ethnicity, and geographic location. For example, married women with children are less likely than their male counterparts to have the time and resources to play sports (Taniguchi and Shupe, 2012). To join a soccer team that schedules practices late in the afternoon and plays games in the evening or on weekends is all but impossible when you're the family cook, shopper, chauffeur, housekeeper, and homework supervisor.

On the other hand, married men with children are less likely to feel such constraints (Taniguchi and Shupe, 2012). When they play softball or soccer after work, their wives may delay family dinners or keep dinner warm until they arrive home. When they schedule a golf game on a Saturday morning, their wives make breakfast for the children and then chauffeur one or more children to their youth sports games.

Women in middle- and lower-income families are most constrained by homemaking and child rearing responsibilities. Unable to pay for child care, domestic help, and sports participation fees, these women have few opportunities to play sports. They also lack time, transportation to and from sport facilities, access to gyms and playing fields in their neighborhoods, and the sense of physical safety that enables them to feel secure enough to leave home and travel to places where they can play sports.

When playing a sport requires multiple participants, the lack of resources among some women affects others, because it reduces their prospects for assembling the requisite number of players. This is also true for men, but women from middle- and lower-income families are more likely than their male counterparts to lack the network of relationships out of which sports interests and participation emerge and are sustained over time.

Women from upper-income families, on the other hand, usually face few constraints on sport participation. They can afford child care, domestic help, carryout dinners, and sport fees. They participate by themselves and with friends and family members. Their social networks include other women who also have resources to play sports. Girls and young women who grow up in these families play sports during their childhoods and attend schools with well-funded sport programs. They seldom experience the same constraints as their lower-income counterparts, even though their opportunities may not equal those of their upper-income male peers.

The sports participation of girls and young women also is limited when they're expected to shoulder responsibilities at home. For example, in low-income families, especially single-parent and immigrant families, teenage daughters often are expected to care for younger siblings after school until evening when parents return from work. But schools and teams rarely sponsor and organize cooperative child care for students who care for siblings. Such cooperative strategies are foreign to individualistically oriented people in the United States and might be rejected as being "socialist." But without arrangements that help them with their child-care responsibilities, such students will typically drop out of sports or never try out.

Boys and girls from higher-income families seldom have household responsibilities that force them to drop out of sports. Instead, their parents drive them to practices, lessons, and games; make sure they are well-fed; have equipment they need; and provide access to cars when they are old enough to drive themselves to practices and games.

The implications of social-class dynamics become very serious when health and obesity issues are considered. Limited opportunities to exercise safely and play sports are among the factors contributing to high rates of obesity, diabetes, and heart disease, especially among girls and women from low-income households. The availability of facilities, safe spaces, transportation, and sports programs all vary by social class, and girls and women in low-income households experience the effects of social class in different and more profoundly negative ways when it comes to involvement in physical activities and sports (Kelley and Carchia, 2013; NPR et al., 2015).

Being Respected and Becoming a Man: Class and Gender Relations in Men's Lives

Many boys and young men use sports to establish a masculine identity, but the dynamics of this process vary by social class. For example, in a qualitative analysis of essays written about sports by 15- and 16-year-old French Canadian boys in the Montreal area, Suzanne Laberge and Mathieu Albert (1999) discovered that *upper-class boys* connected their sports participation with masculinity because playing sports, they said, taught them leadership skills, and being a leader was central to their definition of masculinity. *Middle-class boys* said that playing sports provided them with opportunities to be with peers and gain acceptance in male groups, which fit their ideas of what they needed to do to establish identities as young men. According to *working-class boys*, playing sports enabled them to display toughness and develop the rugged personas that matched their ideas of manhood. In this sense, social class influenced the ways that sports and sport experiences were integrated into the lives of these young men.

Public Money and Private Profits
When Do Sports Perpetuate Social Inequality?

The dynamics of class relations sometimes have ironic twists. This is certainly true when public money is used to build stadiums and arenas that are then used by wealthy individuals who own professional sport teams that often bring them large profits. Billions of dollars of public money in the United States is spent to build these facilities that add to the wealth of powerful individuals and corporations and then subsidize their real estate developments in the area immediately around the facilities.

Furthermore, wealthy investors often purchase the tax-free municipal bonds that cities sell to obtain the cash to build these facilities. This means that while city and/or state taxes are collected from the general population to pay off the bonds, wealthy investors receive tax-free returns, and team owners use the facilities built by taxpayers to make large amounts of money for themselves. When sales taxes are used to pay off bonds, people in low- and middle-income households pay a higher percentage of their annual incomes to build the stadiums than people in higher-income households. This amounts to a case of the poor subsidizing the rich with government approval for the financial benefit of billionaire sport team owners.

Ironically, the average residents whose taxes build stadiums and arenas usually can't afford to buy tickets to sports events in these venues. One reason for high ticket prices is that corporate accounts are used to buy so many tickets to games that the team owners raise ticket prices to match the demand. Higher prices seldom discourage corporate executives because until 2018 they could claim a portion of the ticket costs as a business deduction, thereby reducing their taxes by 18–35 percent. As a result, tax revenues decline and the government has less money to fund sport programs for average taxpayers, and most of those taxpayers can't afford the expensive tickets. This means that stadiums today seldom are places where social classes mix as they cheer for the same team. In fact, when corporate credit cards are used to purchase blocks of season tickets, as they

(*Source:* Frederic A. Eyer)

"I thought they said 'Sport brings everyone together' when they used our tax money to build this place!"

Many stadiums today have policies that create the equivalent of "gated neighborhoods" for high rollers with premium tickets. Stadiums may be built with public money, but they are full of no-trespassing areas for the public. Who benefits from this example of class relations in action?

Boys in US culture are more likely to make commitments to athletic careers at a young age when they perceive limited options for other careers and when their family situation is financially insecure (Gregory, 2013; May, 2009). This means that the personal stakes associated with playing sports are different and often greater for boys from low-income households than they are for boys from higher-income households. Similarly, male athletes from poor and working-class households often use sports are in most venues, the only mixing of social classes is between "the haves" and "the have-mores." Meanwhile, team owners misleadingly blame players' salaries for escalating ticket prices.

The dynamics of class relations do not stop here. After contributing public money to build stadiums and arenas, local and state governments often give discounted property tax rates to team owners and their real estate partners who develop areas around the new venues. Property taxes are the main source of revenues for public schools, so urban public schools often have less money as team owners and developers increase their wealth. Meanwhile, professional teams sponsor a few charity programs for "inner-city kids" and occasionally send players to speak at urban schools—all of which garner press coverage that describes team owners and athletes as great public servants! As school systems fail due to poor funding and teachers complain about this scam, local editorials and letters to the editor accuse educators of wasting public money and demand that they become more frugal.

This method of transferring public money into the private pockets of wealthy individuals has occurred as social services for the unemployed, the working poor, children, and people with disabilities are being cut.

WHAT ABOUT JOBS CREATED BY SPORTS?

Jobs are created whenever hundreds of millions of dollars are spent in a city. But those jobs also would be created if the arenas and stadiums were privately financed. Furthermore, when cities spend public money to build stadiums for professional teams, they create far fewer jobs than could be created by other forms of economic development. Measuring the true cost of job creation is tricky. The type of job created and the economic conditions at the time and place that the job is created all influence costs. However, for the money spent to build a major sport facility, the returns in the form of new jobs are relatively low. The facilities employ relatively few people, they are closed much of the time, and most of the jobs are seasonal and low paying. Therefore, after reading reports of studies done by independent economists, it appears to me that for each job created by a new stadium, between 10 and 20 new jobs could have been created if the same amount of public money had been invested in more strategically chosen development projects. This means that stadiums and large arenas are lousy job creators for the public money spent on them.

WHO ELSE BENEFITS?

Sport team owners are not the only wealthy and powerful people who benefit when stadiums and arenas are built with public money. New publicly financed sport facilities increase property values in urban areas in which major investors and developers can initiate profitable projects. Others also may benefit as money trickles down to the rest of the community, but the average taxpayers who fund the facilities will never see the benefits enjoyed by the wealthy few. Additionally, these developments often require the displacement of low-income housing that is seldom replaced. As a result, many of these sports venues fuel gentrification.

Publicly financed sport venues may provide the illusion of unity and development in a city, but they are mostly vehicles for transferring public money to wealthy individuals and corporations. Behind the illusion often exists disunity and economic inequality.

participation to obtain "respect" in a society where they often lack other means to do so.

Because young men from low-income households often have more at stake when it comes to playing sports, they face more personal pressure than wealthier peers, because they often lack the material resources required to train, develop skills, and be noticed by people who can serve as their advocates. Unless public school athletic programs and coaches can provide these things, these young people—boys and girls alike—have fewer opportunities for moving up to higher levels of competition than their upper-income peers have. The last remaining exceptions to this social-class discrepancy in the US are in football, basketball, and track, which are usually funded in public schools with qualified coaches and enough visibility for some players to be seen by potential mentors and advocates.

Young people from upper-income households often have so many opportunities that they seldom see sports as high-stakes, career-related activities in their lives. For a young person with a car, nice clothes, money for college tuition, and good career contacts for the future, playing sports can be fun, but it's not perceived as necessary for economic survival, gaining respect, or establishing an identity. Therefore, young men from middle- and upper-income backgrounds often disengage gradually from childhood dreams of becoming professional athletes and develop new visions for their futures. For them, playing sports does not hold the same life significance as it does for their peers from working-class and low-income households (NPR et al., 2015).

Fighting to Survive: Class, Gender, and Ethnic Relations Among Boxers

Chris Dundee, a famous boxing promoter, once said, "Any man with a good trade isn't about to get himself knocked on his butt to make a dollar" (in Messner, 1992, p. 82). What he meant was that middle- and upper-class boys and men have no reason to play a

(*Source:* JOHN GURZINSKI/AFP/Getty Images)

Boxing has long been a sport for men from low-income groups. As a long-time boxing coach says, "If you want to know who's at d' bottom of society, all you gotta to do is look at who's boxin" (in Wacquant, 2004, p. 42).

sport that destroys brain cells, that boxers always come from the lowest and most economically desperate income groups in society, and that boxing gyms are located in neighborhoods where desperation is most intense and life-piercing (Wacquant, 2004).

The dynamics of becoming and staying involved in boxing have been studied and described by French sociologist Loïc Wacquant` (1992, 1995a, 1995b, 2004). Wacquant spent over 3 years training and hanging out at a boxing gym in a low-income Chicago neighborhood. During that time, he documented the life experiences of fifty professional boxers, most of whom were African Americans. His analysis shows that deciding to dedicate oneself to boxing in the United States is related to a combination of class, race, and gender relations.

The alternative to boxing for these young men often was the violence of the streets. When Wacquant asked one boxer where he'd be today if he hadn't started boxing, he said,

> If it wasn't for boxin,' I don't know where I'd be . . . Prob'ly in prison or dead somewhere, you never know. I grew up in a tough neighbo'hood, so it's good for me, at least, to think 'bout what I do before I do it. To keep me outa the street, you know. The gym is a good place for me to be every day. Because when you're in d'gym, you . . . don' have to worry about getting' into trouble or getting shot at (in Wacquant, 2004, p. 239).

Wacquant explains that most boxers know they would not be boxing if they had been born in households where resources and other career opportunities existed. "Don't nobody be out there fightin' with an MBA," observed a trainer-coach at the gym (in Wacquant, 1995a, p. 521). Wacquant notes that these men see boxing as a "coerced affection, a captive love, one ultimately born of racial and class necessity" (1995a, p. 521). When he asked one boxer what he would change in his life, the answer represented the feelings of many men at the gym:

> I wish I was born taller, I wish I was born in a rich family, I . . . wish I was smart, an' I had the brains to go to school an' really become somebody real important. For me I mean I can't stand the sport, I hate the sport, [but] it's carved inside of me so I can't let it go (in Wacquant, 1995a, p. 521).

Overall, these men were simultaneously committed to and repulsed by their trade, and their participation was clearly connected with the dynamics of social class in their lives. Boxing and the gym provided a refuge from the violence, hopelessness, and indignity of the racism and poverty that framed their lives since birth. They excelled at the sport because being a young, poor, black man in America "is no bed of roses" (Wacquant, 2004, p. 238).

This case of boxing shows that all sports participation is embedded in particular social and cultural contexts. For young people from resource-deprived areas and families, sports participation may help them cope with or survive the immediate circumstances of their lives, but it does not automatically provide "lifelines" or "hookups" that connect them with other social worlds in which opportunities are available. Philosopher-boxer Joseph Lewandowski (2007, 2008) points this out in his research on boxing in communities characterized by "social poverty"—an absence of *vertical social capital* that connects young persons to people at higher levels of social stratification and real opportunities to move "up and out" of their immediate circumstances, or even to change them. In other words, playing a sport may earn a person respect in the local neighborhood, but this respect comes in the form of horizontal social capital, that is, relationships at the same level of social stratification. This may be useful for managing current circumstances where they live, but sports participation rarely leads to upward social mobility unless it enables a young person to earn vertical social capital that opens doors to real opportunities.

Class Relations in Action: Changing Patterns in Sport Participation Opportunities

Publicly funded youth sports programs have been reduced or eliminated in many US communities, and varsity teams in low-income school districts are being eliminated (Kelley and Carchia, 2013;

Veklerov, 2018). When this occurs, fewer young people from low-income neighborhoods have opportunities to play sports, especially those requiring large fields and safe, functional facilities. This is why basketball remains a primary focus among low-income boys and girls; public schools usually can offer basketball teams and coaches if they have a usable gym that has not been converted into a permanent lunchroom or classroom.

School sports programs in middle- and upper-income areas also may be threatened by financial problems, but they're maintained by "participation fees" paid by athletes' parents. These fees, as high as $500 or more per sport, guarantee that teams across many sports are available for young people lucky enough to be born into well-to-do households. Additionally, when school teams don't meet the expectations of well-to-do parents, they either vote to raise more public funds or use private funds to build new fields and facilities, hire coaches, and run high-profile tournaments that often attract college coaches who recruit athletes by giving them scholarships. Therefore, when tax revolts and political decisions cause public programs to disappear, well-to-do people simply buy private sport participation opportunities for their children.

This highlights the influence of social class in sports. In fact, when it comes to sports participation today, the socioeconomic status of an athlete's family has never been more important. Participation now depends almost exclusively on family resources. This point was made more generally by Robert Putnam, a respected public policy professor at Harvard, when he noted the following:

> We're moving toward an America that none of us have ever lived in, in which being affluent or being poor is inherited. . . . The most important decision any kid makes [today] is choosing their parents (in Rinaldi, 2015).

Therefore, we can expect that sports participation, the development of sports skills, and rewards for sports performance will increasingly go to people in households with above-average income and wealth.

When we compare the availability and quality of school and club sport programs by social class, we see that economic inequalities have a major impact on opportunities for sports participation today. With funds being cut and coaches laid off, schools in poor neighborhoods struggle to maintain sports programs while looking for new funding from corporations. But corporations usually sponsor only the sports that promote their brand and products. For example, a shoe company will support basketball because it fits with its marketing and advertising programs. Corporate funders support individuals, teams, and sports that generate product visibility through media coverage and high-profile state and national tournaments. This keeps certain sports alive, but only on terms that continue to meet corporate interests.

Tables 9.2 and 9.3 show that the socioeconomic playing field is not level when it comes to race and ethnicity. Black and Latinx households are at a significant disadvantage when it comes to financial resources that could be spent on sports and sports participation. In terms of annual income, Latinx and black households, respectively, have incomes that are $17,660 and $22,600 *less* than the annual incomes of white households. Over the course of a 40 year work life, this amounts to a deficit of over $706,000 for Latinx households and $904,000 for black households.

The racial and ethnic wealth gaps as shown in Table 9.3 are even more influential when it comes to making financial decisions in a family. When compared with white households, black households possess $146,470 less wealth, and Latinx households possess $141,410 less wealth. Wealth serves as a cushion that provides stability in a household, and it certainly has an impact on family decisions about spending money for sports participation. These income and wealth gaps will influence who has opportunities to develop elite sports skills, receive athletic scholarships, and play sports at elite levels.

Class Relations in Action: The Cost of Attending Sport Events

It remains possible to attend some sports events for free. High school and many college games and

Table 9.2 Median household income in United States by race and Hispanic origin, 2017

Category	Income
All categories	$61,372
Asian households	$82,331
White households (not Hispanic)	$68,145
Latino households (any race)	$50,486
Black households	$40,258

Source: US Census Bureau, Income and Poverty in the United States: 2017, September 2018.

Table 9.3 Median household wealth in United States by race and ethnicity, 2017

Category	Median wealth*
White households	$162,770
Latino households (any race)	$21,360
Black households	$16,300

Source: Board of Governors of the Federal Reserve System, 2016 Survey of Consumer Finances, September 2017.
*Household **wealth** consists of all assets in the form of money in the bank; equity in a home, car, or other appraised possessions; and retirement funds in investments or savings.

meets in the United States are affordable for most people, and in some communities the tickets for minor league sports are reasonably priced. But tickets to most major intercollegiate and professional games are beyond the means of most people, even those whose taxes were used to build the venues in which the games are played. The cost of attending these events has increased much more rapidly than the rate of inflation over the past thirty years.

Table 9.4 shows that the inflation rate between 1991 and 2019 was 87 percent, whereas average ticket prices for MLB, the NFL, the NBA, and the NHL increased 196 percent, 255 percent, 196 percent, and 141 percent, respectively, during the same period. Therefore, ticket prices have increased three to four times the rate of inflation—partly due to increased costs at new stadiums and arenas, but mostly due to team owners wanting to attract people who have money to spend on food, drinks, apparel, and everything else they sell. This is why new facilities resemble giant circular shopping malls built around a central entertainment stage. They house

Table 9.4 Fan cost index versus inflation in the United States, 1991–2019

	FAN COST INDEX*				1991–2019
	1991 ($)	2001 ($)	2011 ($)	2019 ($)	Increase (%)
Major League Baseball	79	141	198	234	196
National Football League	151	303	427	536	255
National Basketball Association	142	277	301	421	196
National Hockey League	150	275	329	362	141
			US cost of living increase, 1991 to 2019 = 87%§		

Source: Adapted from data in Team Marketing Report, www.teammarketing.com
**Fan Cost Index* is the cost for a family of four to attend a game; it includes prices for four tickets, four small drinks, two small beers, four hot dogs, two programs, two adult-size caps, and parking. Data for the NBA and NHL for 2004–2019 do not include premium ticket costs in the average, and this makes it difficult to do precise long-term comparisons.
§Represents the official cost of living increase as determined by the American Institute for Economic Research, https://www.aier.org/cost-living-calculator

(*Source:* Jay Coakley)

Children in middle-class suburban areas often have safe streets on which to play. The boys in this cul-de-sac have multiple portable basketball goals, and they occasionally play full-court games in the street. They have many sport participation options in their lives, which their families often use as opportunities for sociability.

expensive luxury suites and separate club seating, where high-income spectators have special services available—waitstaff, hot food menus, private restrooms, televisions, refrigerators, lounge chairs, temperature controls, private entrances with no waiting lines or turnstiles, and special parking areas—so that attending a game is no different from going to an exclusive private club.

As tickets become more expensive and spectators are increasingly segregated according to their ability to pay, social class and class relations become more evident in the stands. Spectators may cheer at the same times and experience similar emotions, but this is the extent to which social-class differences are transcended at the events, and the reality of social class and inequality returns as soon as people leave the stadium.

Efforts by some fans wanting to reduce ticket prices seldom develop traction because people in luxury boxes, club seats, and other premium seats don't want to join or be identified with spectators who can't afford high-priced tickets and concessions. Expensive tickets are status symbols for wealthy spectators; they *want* class distinctions to be part of the sport experience, and they are willing to pay—or have their corporations pay high prices so they can conspicuously display their status and have an experience with other wealthy people.

Attendance and seating at many events, from the opening ceremonies at the Olympics to the NFL Super Bowl, are now tied to conspicuous displays of wealth, status, influence, and corporate power. After observing a recent Super Bowl and the events leading up to the game, journalist Dave Zirin (2008) concluded that "Before it is anything else, before it's even a football game, the Super Bowl is . . . a 2-week entertainment festival for the rich and shameless." Although ticket prices vary year to year depending on the teams involved, they range from about $3,000 to $5,500 (resale) per seat. Live attendance at the Super Bowl and other sports mega-events is priced at a level that few individuals can afford unless they are using company credit cards to buy them.

GLOBAL INEQUALITIES AND SPORTS

When we discuss social class and sports, it is essential to think beyond our own society. Inequalities exist at all levels of social organization—in families, groups, organizations, communities, societies, and the world.

Global inequalities related to per capita income, living standards, and access to developmental resources cause many of the most serious problems that we face today. Research shows that even though the number of people living in extreme poverty has declined over the past two decades, the gap between the richest and poorest people worldwide is growing wider. Close to 3.5 billion people, about 46 percent of the world population, lives on less than $5.50 per day as they struggle to maintain stability in their lives (Alvaredo et al., 2018; World Bank, 2018).

The meanings given to the global gap between the wealthy and poor differ depending on the ideologies that people use to guide their understanding of world affairs. But apart from ideological interpretations, it is clear that about 40 percent of all people in the world have few resources to use on anything beyond basic survival. They may play games, but they seldom have the resources needed to organize and play sports as we know them. For these people, the sports played in the United States and other post-industrial nations are clearly out of reach. They can't understand how or why boxer Floyd Mayweather made $285 million in 2018, an amount equivalent to the annual living expenses of about 600,000 people in certain regions of the world. Similarly, workers who make less than $3 a day producing the balls, shoes, and other equipment and clothing used by most people in wealthy nations, would question the fairness of such inequality.

The Olympic Games provide a clear example of the impact of global inequality in sports. Those who follow the Summer or Winter Olympics through mainstream media hear and read that these are celebrations of athlete commitment, dedication, hard work, and sacrifice. Absent in the coverage is recognition that the Games are also a celebration of wealth and inequality. For example, prior to the 2020 Olympic Games in Tokyo, 78 of the approximately 204 nations that have participated in the Olympics have never won a medal and another 62 countries have won 5 or fewer medals in Olympic history. Many nations have not won a medal for at least 40 years. The United States, on the other hand, with its combination of wealth and population size, have won 2,827 medals—over 1069 more than any other nation.

Even in wealthy countries, a disproportionate share of medals has always been won by athletes with support from families. Exceptions to this pattern are few. The former Soviet Union, German Democratic Republic (East Germany), China, and Cuba have experienced considerable success. But in these communist countries, central state planners used public money to train and support an impressive number of medal winners.

(*Source:* Jay Coakley)

Since 2003, the annual Homeless World Cup has been held in different cities where national teams comprised of homeless people, mostly men, compete during a three-day tournament. This event was initiated by two editors of newspapers that serve homeless people. Their readers sometimes played informal soccer games, so they recruited sponsors and have organized the event each year. In 2019, teams from more than 50 countries competed in Cardiff (Wales). In addition to being a sports event, the tournament is a site for initiating and sustaining political strategies advocating the rights of homeless people worldwide.

Other exceptions are individual athletes who have wealthy corporate sponsors. For example, US hurdler, Lolo Jones, was able to use her talent, face, and physique to attract corporations that wanted to capitalize on the media attention she receives (Longman, 2012). But even Red Bull, her major sponsor, hedged its investment in Jones by hiring twenty-two scientists and technicians to work with her exclusively from 2005 through 2012. These performance specialists monitored her training runs with 40 motion-capture cameras. An Optojump system replicated her feet hitting the track surface on every stride during 110 meters of hurdling. The Phantom Flex high-speed camera moved astride her and recorded 1500 frames per second as she ran. The resulting analyses of these data and input from other specialists were then used to customize daily training for Jones (McClusky, 2012). Today, in wealthy nations, there are a number of well supported athletes who have access to these training technologies, which makes the idea of a "level playing field" laughable, despite claims by the IOC and media commentators that the competitions are fair.

Because athletes are now pushing the performance limits of the human body, they increasingly seek technologies that will bring them success (Hurley, 2018). But these technologies are expensive, especially when they are delivered and managed by physiologists, biomechanists, medical experts, biochemists, strength coaches, virtual reality trainers, nutritionists, psychologists, recovery experts, video and statistical analysts –all of whom work with coaches to turn scientific findings into training programs. Access to this training is restricted to a small proportion of athletes that compete at a national or international level. Fairness and a level playing field are undermined by this inequality.

Patterns are similar for the Paralympics, where GDP–*gross domestic product,* or the monetary value of all goods and services produced annually–along with the population size of a country are highly correlated with the number of medals won by athletes (Buts et al., 2013). Traveling to the Paralympics is especially costly for Paralympians because they often must bring with them prostheses, wheelchairs, and a person to help them navigate unanticipated barriers. This is why athletes from the nation that hosts the Paralympics win 80 percent more medals than it's athletes won in the previous Paralympic Games. Travel is not a major issue for them, and they know what to anticipate while in the host city. Additionally, host cities and nations make special efforts to make sure that their athletes confront as few barriers as possible.

Athletes from nations with relatively low GDP are extremely unlikely to have access to the training and support required to qualify for and travel to the Paralympics. In countries where poverty rates are high, people with physical or intellectual impairments have little or no opportunity to participate and train in sports.

ECONOMIC AND CAREER OPPORTUNITIES IN SPORTS

Many people in the United States see sports as a sphere in which people from low-income and poor backgrounds can experience upward social mobility–an affirmation of the American Dream (Green and Hartmann, 2012). **Social mobility** is a term used by sociologists to refer to *changes in wealth, education, and occupation over a person's lifetime or from one generation to the next in families.* Social mobility can occur in downward or upward directions.

On a general level, career and mobility opportunities exist in sports and sport organizations. However, as we consider the impact of sports on mobility in the United States, it is useful to know the following things about sport-related opportunities:

1. The number of paid career opportunities in sports is limited, and the playing careers of most professional athletes are short term.
2. Professional opportunities for women are growing but remain limited on and off the field relative to men.
3. Professional opportunities for ethnic minorities are growing but remain limited on and off the field relative to whites with European heritage.

These points are discussed in the following sections.

Career Opportunities Are Limited

Young athletes often have visions of playing professional sports, and their parents may have similar visions. But the chances of turning these visions into realities are remote. The odds or chances for a person to become a college or professional athlete are difficult to calculate, and many different methods have been used. For example, the calculations could be based on the number of players in the top league in a sport, such as the National Hockey League in North America, or they could be based on the number of professional hockey players in all major and minor league teams worldwide. The fact that about 80 percent of the players in the NHL and one-fourth of all college hockey players come from outside the United States means that it is meaningless to calculate the odds of a US high school hockey player making it to a college team or the NHL without taking this into account. This is the case for other sports as well. For example, nearly one-third of all college tennis players come from outside the United States. The point here is that all calculations must be qualified, and many estimates reported in the media are inaccurate.

Additionally, professional sports opportunities are short term, averaging 3–5 years in team sports and three to 12 years in individual sports. This means that, after playing careers end, there are about *forty additional years* in a person's work life. Unfortunately, many people, including athletes, coaches, and parents, ignore this aspect of reality.

Media coverage focuses on the best athletes in the most popular sports, and they often have longer and more lucrative playing careers than others. Little coverage is given to the more typical cases—that is, those who play for one or two seasons before being cut or forced to quit for other reasons, especially injuries or lack of resources to pay for training. We hear about the long careers of popular NFL quarterbacks, but little about the many players whose 1-year contracts are not renewed after their first season. The average age of players on the *oldest* NFL team in 2018 was 27 years old and 16 of the 32 NFL teams had an average age of less than 26 years old. (Kempski, 2018). With the average career length being just over three years long, many players say that NFL stands for "Not For Long" (Schultz, 2017). This means that few players older than 30 are still in the league. Much more typical than 30-year-old players contemplating another season are 24-year-olds facing the end of their professional sport careers (Belson, 2018).

Finally, many professional athletes at the minor league level make less than workers in nonsport occupations. For example, most players in minor league baseball make less than minimum wage in the US when their hours of training, competition, and traveling are totaled (Eibeler, 2018). Their season is over 5 months long, they play 140 games, and most players are paid less than $55 per game, or about $7,500 for the season. Elementary school teachers have much higher salaries than these players, better working conditions, greater financial stability, and a pension plan.

(*Source:* Frederic A. Eyer)

"Ah, the glamorous life of a spoiled, overpaid professional athlete!"

Only a few professional athletes achieve fame and fortune. Thousands of others play in minor and semipro leagues in which salaries are low and working conditions are poor.

Opportunities for Women Are Growing but Remain Limited

Career opportunities for female athletes are limited relative to opportunities for men. Tennis and golf provide opportunities, but the professional tours for these sports draw athletes worldwide. For women in the United States, this means that the competition to make a living in these sports is great. About 2,500 players representing 100 nations competed in Women's Tennis Association (WTA) tournaments during 2019, but only the top 200 players won enough money to fully pay for their expenses on the tour. Of those, only twenty-one were from the United States. In fact, most US players are among the 1300 that had made less than $5000 during the year.

In the Ladies Professional Golf Association (LPGA), fewer than 40 golfers out of the approximately 95 million adult women in the United States make enough prize money to cover their expenses during a season of tournaments.

There are opportunities in professional basketball, volleyball, soccer, figure skating, bowling, skiing, bicycling, track and field, and rodeo, but the number of professional female athletes in these sports remains low, and only a few women make over $100,000 annually. For example, when Forbes magazine ranked the top 100 moneymaking athletes worldwide during 2018, Serena Williams was the only woman on the list.

Professional leagues for women now exist in basketball and beach volleyball, but they have provided career opportunities for fewer than 400 athletes in any given recent year. The National Women's

Soccer League was established in April 2013 as the third attempt to make women's professional soccer a spectator sport. In 2019 there were nine teams and 282 players, although only 190 of those players were mainstays on the nine teams. Each team had a $421,500 salary cap for the year with the minimum salary being $16,538 and the maximum salary being a $46,200. To assist the league, the soccer federations from the United States, Canada, and Mexico paid the salaries of players on their national teams–about fifty players in all.

In the WNBA, the pay is a fraction of what men in the NBA make–an average of about $79,000 in 2019, with a league minimum salary of about $41,000. None of the 144 players is allowed to make more than $113,500 for the season. The total salaries for all WNBA players amounted to about $11.4 million, which was only one-third of the salary paid to LeBron James for the 2018-19 season. Another way to compare is to say that for every salary dollar that an NBA player makes, a WNBA player makes about 1.3-cents. To be fair, there are 48 more games in an NBA versus a WNBA season, so WNBA players really earn almost 4-cents for every dollar earned by an NBA player.

There are opportunities for some of the top women athletes to play professional sports in other parts of the world. For example, US national soccer team star Megan Rapinoe has played for a professional team in France, where she made $14,000 a month. Most of the top WNBA players also play on teams in Europe where they often make more than during their seasons in the United States.

What about other careers in sports? There are jobs for women in coaching, training, officiating, sports medicine, sports information, public relations, marketing, and administration. As noted in Chapter 7, most of the jobs in women's sports continue to be held by men, and women seldom are hired for jobs in men's programs, except in peripheral support positions. In the United States, when men's and women's high school or college athletic programs are combined, men become the athletic directors in about 80 percent of the cases. Women in most post-industrial nations have challenged the legacy of traditional gender ideology, and progress has been made in some sports organizations. However, a heavily gendered division of labor continues to exist in nearly all organizations. In traditional and developing nations, the record of progress is negligible, and very few women hold positions of power in any sports organizations.

Job opportunities for women have not increased as rapidly as women's programs have grown. This is partly due to the persistence of orthodox gender ideology and the fact that Title IX does not have precise enforcement procedures when it comes to equity in coaching and administration. Title IX enforcement focuses almost exclusively on athletes, and has had little impact in other aspects of school sports and no direct impact on sports outside of schools that receive money from the federal government. Therefore, a pattern of female underrepresentation exists in nearly all job categories and nearly all sports organizations. This pattern exists worldwide.

Opportunities for women in sports will continue to shift toward equity, but many people resist making the structural and ideological changes that would produce full equity. In the meantime, there may be gradual increases in the number of women coaches, sports broadcasters, athletic trainers, administrators, and referees. Changes will occur more rapidly in certain sport industries that target women as consumers and need women employees to increase their sales and profits. But the gender ideology used by influential decision makers *inside* many sports organizations will continue to privilege those perceived as tough, strong, competitive, and aggressive–and men are more likely to be perceived in such terms.

Many women who work in sports organizations continue to deal with organizational cultures that are primarily based on the values and experiences of men. This contributes to low job satisfaction and high job turnover among women. Professional development programs, workshops, and coaching clinics have been developed since the late 1990s to assist women as they work in and try to change these cultures and make them more inclusive. However, full equity won't occur until more men in sports organizations change their ideas about gender and its connection with sports and leadership.

Opportunities for African Americans and Other Ethnic Minorities Are Growing but Remain Limited

The visibility of black athletes in certain spectator sports often leads people to conclude that sports offer abundant career opportunities for African Americans. Anecdotal support for this conclusion is provided by successful black athletes who attribute their wealth and fame to sports. However, the extent to which job opportunities for blacks exist in sports has been greatly overstated. Very little publicity is given to the actual number and proportion of blacks who play sports for a living or make a living working in sports organizations. Also ignored is the fact that sports provide very few career opportunities for black women.

African-American athletes are involved almost exclusively in five professional spectator sports: boxing, basketball, football, baseball, and track. At the same time, some of the most lucrative sports for athletes are almost exclusively white–tennis, golf, hockey, and motor racing are examples. My best guess is that fewer than 6000 African Americans, or about 1 of every 6660 African Americans, currently make significant incomes as professional athletes in the United States.

This indicates that sports don't provide exceptional upward mobility opportunities and that there are better career opportunities outside of sports–if there are educational opportunities to take advantage of them. Of course, these facts are distorted in media content that presents disproportionately more images of successful black athletes than blacks in other positive roles. If young African Americans use media images as a basis for making choices and envisioning their future, their choices will be based on faulty information.

Employment Barriers for Black Athletes When sports were first desegregated in the United States, blacks faced *entry barriers*–that is, unless they had exceptional skills and exemplary personal characteristics they were not recruited or given professional contracts. Racial prejudice was strong and team owners assumed that white players, coaches, and spectators would not accept black players unless they made immediate and significant contributions to a team. Black athletes without exceptional skills were passed by. Therefore, the performance statistics for black athletes surpassed those of white athletes, a fact that many white people used to reinforce their stereotypes about the "natural" physicality of black people with African ancestry.

As entry barriers declined between 1960 and the late 1970s, new barriers related to retention took their place. *Retention barriers* existed when contracts for experienced black players were not renewed unless the players had significantly better performance records than white players at the same career stage. This pattern existed through the early 1990s, but it has faded with time.

Race-based salary discrimination existed in most sports immediately following desegregation, but evidence suggests that it is not a chronic issue in major team sports. This is because performance can be objectively measured, tracked, and compared to the performances of other players. Statistics are now kept on nearly every conceivable dimension of an athlete's skill. Players' agents use these statistics during salary negotiations, and they have an incentive to do so because they receive a percentage of players' salaries and don't want racial discrimination to decrease their incomes.

Employment Barriers in Coaching and Off-the-Field Jobs During the 1980s and 1990s, many college and professional sport teams had plantation-like hiring practices–they employed black workers but hired only white managers. Since the mid-1990s, the rate at which blacks have been hired in managerial positions has varied by sport. There's been slow progress in some sports organizations, especially those associated with college and professional football (Harrison & Bukstein, 2018; Lapchick, 2018).

To rectify the lack of black coaches, legal pressures forced the NFL in 2003 to adopt the "Rooney

(*Source:* Ronald Cortes/Getty Images)

After a successful playing career, Becky Hammon joined the NBA's San Antonio Spurs in 2014 as an assistant coach and is now the top assistant for head coach Greg Popovich. Popovich says, "She's been perfect" and the players respect her (in Gaines, 2017). When her name was mentioned for a head coaching job, all-star Pau Gasol said, "To me, it would be strange if NBA teams were not interested in her as a head coach. . . . Becky Hammon can coach NBA basketball. Period" (in Gasol, 2018). Now the question becomes: why are women overlooked as coaches of men's teams?

Rule," which required teams to interview minority candidates for open coaching positions. Although the impact of this affirmative action policy is not clear, only four of the 32 NFL teams had black head coaches during the 2019–20 season. With 70 percent of the players being black men, 88 percent of the head coaches are white men.

Discriminatory hiring patterns have also been troubling in big-time college football. Although the NCAA claims a commitment to diversity, their progress in achieving it has been slow (LaFave, Nelson & Doherty, 2018). In 2007, Keith Harrison, a scholar at the University of Central Florida, completed a thorough study of NCAA hiring practices and concluded that the head football coach position "is the most segregated position in all college sports" (Harrison, 2007). At the start of the 2019–2020 season, there were only 14 African-American head football coaches in the 130 Football Bowl Subdivision (FBS), down from 21 during the 2013–2014 season; 85 percent of the head coaches were white men. The percentage of black head coaches across all men's and women's sports in NCAA Divisions I, II, and III hovers around 5 percent (excluding HBCUs, Historically Black Colleges and Universities). Overall, black men and women make up less than 5 percent of the athletic directors at more than 1200 NCAA universities, and in the 30 Division I conferences there is only one black commissioner.

Research indicates that when chief executive officers (CEOs) recruit candidates for top management positions, they favor people with backgrounds and orientations similar to their own, and they often hire people they know or have worked with in the past (Belson, 2020; Day, 2018; Harrison & Bukstein, 2018). Familiar people are "known quantities" and perceived to be predictable and trustworthy. Therefore, if a team owner or university athletic director is a white male, which is true in about 80 percent of all cases, he may wonder about the qualifications of ethnic minority candidates, especially if he lacks exposure to diversity (Roberts, 2007). He may wonder if he can trust them to be supportive and fit in with his managerial style and approach. If he has doubts, he'll choose the candidate he believes is most like himself. Additionally, black head coaches in professional and big-time college sports appear to be assessed more critically than white head coaches, and when they are fired, they are less likely to be rehired at the same level (Bell, 2013).

These dynamics, which are seldom identified as "racial" or "ethnic," often exist in sports and other organizations. However, they continually reproduce an organizational culture and operating procedures that cause minority men and all women to be underrepresented in positions of power and responsibility.

Opportunities for Ethnic Minorities The dynamics of ethnic relations in every culture are unique. Making generalizations about ethnic relations and opportunities in sports is difficult. However, dominant sport forms in any culture tend to reproduce cultural values and the social structures supported by those values. This means three things:

1. Members of the dominant social class in a society may exclude or define as unqualified job candidates with characteristics and cultural backgrounds different from their own.
2. Ethnic minorities often must adopt the values and orientations of the dominant social class if they want to be hired and promoted in sport organizations.
3. The values, orientations, and experiences of ethnic minorities are seldom represented in the culture of sport organizations.

Latin Americans, Asian Pacific Americans, and Native Americans are clearly underrepresented in most sports and sports organizations in the United States (Lapchick, 2018). Many Euro-Americans feel uncomfortable with ethnic diversity in situations in which they must trust and work closely with coworkers. Most often, this feeling is caused by a lack of knowledge about the heritage and customs of others and little exposure to ethnic diversity involving meaningful communication. Exceptions to this are found in Major League Baseball and Major League Soccer teams that have many Latino players and a fair representation of Latinos in management. However, neither Asian Pacific Americans nor Native Americans fare very well in any US sports organizations, partly because they are perceived as having little sports knowledge and experience, regardless of the reality of their lives.

SPORT PARTICIPATION AND OCCUPATIONAL CAREERS AMONG FORMER ATHLETES

What happens in the occupational careers of former athletes? Are their career patterns different from the patterns of others? Is sport participation a stepping-stone to future occupational success and upward social mobility? Does playing sports have economic payoffs after active participation is over?

Research findings on this topic are tricky to interpret. For example, young people who play on school sport teams generally come from families that have higher incomes and more wealth than the families of other students. Therefore, if they have more successful occupational careers, how do we know if this is due to family-related socioeconomic advantages or to their experiences in sports?

In cases where researchers have controlled for the influence of family income and wealth, it appears that athletes may have a slight advantage over comparable peers if playing on a sport team does one or more of the following things:

1. Increases opportunities for a young person to complete academic degrees, develop job-related skills, and/or extend one's knowledge about the world outside of sports.
2. Increases support from significant others for *overall* growth and development, not just sport development.
3. Provides opportunities to develop social networks that are connected with career possibilities outside of sports and sports organizations.
4. Expands experiences, identities, and abilities *unrelated* to sports.

When sports teams are organized to foster one or more of these four developmental outcomes, athletes are more likely to have career-related advantages due to their sport participation. However, sport teams are seldom organized to do these four thing. Coaches often want to separate athletes from experiences and relationships unrelated to their sport. They define dedication in terms of focusing exclusively on improving sport performance and winning competitions. When this is how sport participation is organized, overall development among athletes is constricted rather than expanded, and athletes may be at a disadvantage when it comes to career success.

Overall, sport participation does not automatically confer developmental advantages on athletes. Those advantages depend on how sport programs and teams are organized. When playing sports expands developmental opportunities for young people, it is more likely to be associated with future occupational success. When playing sports constricts developmental opportunities, future success is less likely.

Highly Paid Athletes and Career Success After Playing Sports

Conclusions about sport participation, career success, and social mobility must be qualified in light of the following recent changes related to elite and professional sports in the United States and other wealthy societies:

- An increase in salaries that began in the mid-1970s has enabled some professional athletes to save and invest money that can be used to create future career opportunities.
- An increase in the media coverage and overall visibility of sports has created greater name recognition than past athletes enjoyed; therefore, athletes today can convert themselves into a "brand" that may lead to career opportunities and success.
- Athletes have become more aware that they must carefully manage their resources to maximize future opportunities.

Of course, most professional athletes have short careers or play at levels at which they do not make much money. When they retire, they face the same career challenges encountered by their age peers, and they experience patterns of success and failure similar to patterns among comparable peers who didn't play sports. This means that playing sports neither ensures nor boosts one's chances of career success.

In Chapter 3, *Sports and Socialization,* it was explained that retirement from sports is best described as a process rather than a single event, and most athletes don't retire from sports on a moment's notice–they disengage gradually and revise their priorities as they disengage. Although many athletes handle this process smoothly, develop other interests, and move into relatively satisfying occupations, others experience short- or long-term adjustment problems that interfere with occupational success and overall life satisfaction.

The four challenges that retiring athletes face are to (1) reaffirm or reconstruct identities in terms of activities, abilities, and relationships that are not directly related to sport participation; (2) nurture or renegotiate relationships with family and friends so that new identities can be established and reaffirmed; (3) re-engage with the normal, everyday world in ways that provide a personal sense of meaning; and (4) come to terms with the totality of their life in sports. Meeting these challenges successfully may take time, and it always involves relationships that support nonsport identities (Tinley, 2015a).

The fact that athletes today have had to make such a complete commitment to their sports from an early age has often cut them off from the very experiences and relationships they need when they must adjust to life after they stop competing. They have never had an "off season" as athletes had in the past, nor have they had the time or energy to focus on personal development away from the intense seven-day-a-week training and competition schedule. The longer athletes are cut off from non-sport relationships and experiences, and the more central and salient their athlete identity, the more difficulty they will have when making the transition out of sport and into non-sport-related social worlds.

Studies also show that adjustment problems are most likely when injuries force an athlete to retire without notice (Smith and Hardin, 2018; Tinley, 2015a; Turner, 2018). Injuries link retirement with larger issues of health and self-esteem and propel a person into life-changing transitions before they're expected. When this occurs, athletes often need career-transition counseling and other support.

When athletes encounter problems transitioning out of sports into careers and other activities, support should be and occasionally is provided by the sports organizations that benefited from their labor. Some organizations, including universities and national governing bodies for Olympic sports do this through transition programs focusing on career self-assessments, life skills training, career planning, résumé writing, job search strategies, interviewing skills, career placement contacts, and psychological counseling. Retiring athletes often find it helpful to receive guidance in identifying the skills they learned in sports and how those skills can be transferred to subsequent careers.

Athletic Scholarships and Occupational Success

The United States is the only country in the world where some colleges and universities provide scholarships to athletes who play on their sports teams. These scholarships provide financial support to pay for some or all tuition and other education-related expenses. As the cost of higher education has increased far beyond the rate of inflation and income growth, the value of athletic scholarships has increased. As a result, many parents see the possibility of a financial payoff if one or more of their children excels in a sport and is offered a scholarship.

Unfortunately, there is much misinformation about the number and value of athletic scholarships in the United States. Most people believe that they are more numerous and valuable than they actually are. As far as I can tell, this belief exists for the following reasons:

1. When high school athletes receive standard recruiting letters from university coaches they often tell people that they are anticipating *full* scholarships when in fact they subsequently receive only partial aid or no aid at all. When they don't disclose this disappointing outcome many people continue to believe that the scholarship was actually received.
2. Athletes who receive partial tuition waivers or other forms of partial athletic aid sometimes lead people to believe that they have full scholarships.
3. Many people assume that everyone who makes a college team, especially at large universities, has a scholarship, but this is not true.

There were over 20 million undergraduate students in 2018–2019. Table 9.5 shows that 500,733 (about 2.5 percent) of these students were on intercollegiate teams. Approximately 177,559 athletic scholarships were available for those team members. Some received full scholarships covering tuition, room, meals, and fees, but most received partial scholarships amounting to a fraction of a full scholarship as determined by the team coach. The average amount of a scholarship in NCAA Division I schools was about $14,270 for men and $15,162 for women in 2013, but these dollar amounts were much lower for athletes in NCAA Division II, NAIA, and NJCAA schools.

When parents and athletes discover that full scholarships are available to only one-third of the athletes on college teams, they are shocked. Their shock may turn into disbelief when they remember that they spent $5000 or more a year to keep their son or daughter in a sport from age six to seventeen–a minimum "investment" of $60,000, to say nothing of the time, energy, and long weekends spent driving to and sitting at practices, games, and tournaments–and eating fast food. Even if their son or daughter does receive a scholarship in an NCAA Division I school, he or she will work very hard for 35 to 40 hours per week for all or nearly all of the academic year. Scholarships may be lost due to injuries or coach decisions, and some athletes may quit teams because they don't feel that the scholarship is worth the effort. Additionally, the dollar value of an average scholarship is often far less than parents have "invested" into their child's sport career. This means that spending money to develop a child's sport skills in the hope of seeing a net benefit in the form of a college scholarship makes no financial sense.

Table 9.5 Number of college athletes and maximum number of scholarships available, 2018–2019

	Total	Men	Women
Total number of college athletes*	500,733	281,928	218,805
Maximum number of athletic scholarships**	177,559	92,658	84,901
Average value of athletic scholarship per athlete in			
NCAA Division I		$14,270	$15,162
NCAA Division II		$5,548	$6,814
NAIA		$6,603	$6,964
NJCAA		$2,069	$2,810

Source: http://www.scholarshipstats.com/ncaalimits.html (retrieved, 7-10-19)

*Includes athletes in all three divisions of the NCAA and athletes in schools aligned with the National Association of Intercollegiate Athletics (NAIA) and the National Junior College Athletic Association (NJCAA).

**Each college team has a maximum number of scholarships that can be awarded in any year. However, the actual number of scholarships awarded is less than the maximum due to budget constraints and decisions by athletic directors and coaches.

Another way to make sense of the data in Table 9.5 is to say that among all full-time undergraduate students less than 2 percent receive some form of athletic aid. In fact, *academic* scholarships amount to many millions of dollars more than the total amount of *athletic* scholarships, even though many high school students and their parents don't know this.

Class, gender, and race dynamics are strongly connected with athletic scholarships. First, young people in upper-middle-class families (with household incomes of $100,000 per year or more) have resources to develop skills in highly privatized sports such as lacrosse, soccer, volleyball, rowing, swimming, water polo, field hockey, softball, and ice hockey. As a result, they are more likely than athletes in middle- and lower-income families to receive athletic scholarships, although most could afford college without athletic aid.

When Tom Farrey (2008), then an Emmy-Award-winning journalist at ESPN, investigated this issue he concluded that "college athletics in general are more the province of the privileged than the poor" (p. 145).

In a follow-up investigation in 2017, Farrey found that this pattern persisted and even carried over to basketball. He concluded the following:

> *Indeed, most athletic scholarships are going to middle-class kids with college-educated parents, not to kids from poor families who need a scholarship to get anywhere close to a university campus. . . . Simply put, NCAA sports have been gentrified.* (Farrey, 2017)

Farrey's observation is supported by recent studies. Amanda Paule's (2012) study of the recruiting strategies of college coaches showed that they looked for athletes from upper-income backgrounds who could afford to take a partial scholarship and pay the rest of their expenses, or athletes from very low-income backgrounds who could qualify for need-based aid that came from outside the athletic department. Additionally, because many coaches had small recruiting budgets, they sometimes limited their scouting to camps and tournaments at which young people from middle- and upper-income families were usually overrepresented.

A study investigating the social class and family backgrounds of NBA players led Joshua Dubrow and Jimi Adams (2012) to conclude that white athletes from low-income backgrounds were 75 percent less likely to play in the NBA than athletes from families that were better off. Among black athletes, those from low-income families were 37 percent less likely to become NBA players than their peers from well-off families.

Second, the college sports that offer high school seniors the best odds for a scholarship include rowing, golf, equestrian events, gymnastics, lacrosse, swimming, fencing, and water polo—all of which are dominated by upper-middle-class, white participants (Farrey, 2008).

Despite these studies and what we now know about social class and sport participation, people in the media regularly feature stories that highlight young people who rise from poverty to achieve fame and financial security. This recycles the myth that sports are a path to a better life at the same time that it reaffirms the American Dream, reinforces the image of the United States as a true meritocracy, and promulgates the class ideology supported by those beliefs.

"Beneath the thin layer of sport entertainment that makes its way onto television are the bulk of college athletes: Well-off and white." –Tom Farrey, ESPN journalist (2008)

Third, the only college sports that consistently generate revenues are those in which the majority of players are black men: Division I football and men's basketball. On average, these men come from households with less wealth and income than the households from which most other Division I athletes come (Allison, Davis & Barranco, 2018). This creates an interesting class- and race-based scenario: Black men work in their sports to generate revenues that provide scholarships to white athletes from households generally having far greater wealth. White parents, students, and athletes don't think about this pattern of resource distribution, but black football and basketball players are well aware of it.

Overall, when athletic scholarships go to financially needy young people who focus on learning and earn their degrees, participation in college sports increases their chances for career success. But this is far more the exception than the rule.

summary

DO MONEY AND POWER MATTER IN SPORTS?

Social class and class relations are integrally involved in sports. Organized sports depend on resources, and those who provide them do so in ways that support their interests by establishing economic arrangements that work to their advantage. This is why dominant sport forms in the United States and other nations with market economies promote an ideology based on a belief in meritocracy and the idea that people always get what they deserve, and deserve what they get.

In the United States this belief combined with belief in the American Dream constitutes a class ideology that promotes favorable conclusions about the character and qualifications of wealthy and powerful people at the same time that it disadvantages the poor and powerless. Furthermore, it leads to the conclusion that economic inequality, even when it is extreme and oppressive, is natural and beneficial for society as a whole.

Class relations also are tied to patterns of sport team ownership, event sponsorship, and media coverage of sports. As public funds are used to build stadiums and arenas, wealthy team owners receive subsidies that expand their income and power. At the same time, economic and political elites, including powerful transnational corporations, sponsor the teams, events, and media coverage that bring people pleasure and excitement. Although fans don't always give sports the meaning that sponsors would like them to, they seldom subject sports to critical analysis and usually don't see sports as perpetuating a class ideology that justifies inequality and public policies that foster inequality. But this is part of what makes sports useful tools for influencing popular assumptions about how the world works.

Sport participation patterns worldwide are connected with social class and the distribution of material resources. Organized sports are a luxury that people in many regions of the world cannot afford. Even in wealthy societies, sport participation is most common among those in the middle and upper classes, and class-based lifestyles often go hand-in-hand with staging and participating in certain sports.

Sports participation patterns also are connected with the intersection of class, gender, race, and ethnicity in people's lives. This is seen in the case of girls and women who have low participation rates when resources are scarce and among men who see sports as a means of obtaining respect when they are living on the social and economic margins of society. Boxing provides an example of a sport in which class, gender, race, and ethnicity intersect in a powerful combination. As a result, the boxing gym often becomes a safe space that offers temporary refuge for minority men who live in neighborhoods where poverty, racism, and despair spawn desperate acts of violence among their peers.

The same social forces that bring ethnic minority men to boxing also fuel many variations of *hoop dreams* that captivate the attention of young ethnic minorities, especially black males. These dreams are sources of hope but they seldom come to fruition amid the reality of school and gym closings, school teams being dropped, and a lack of access to the resources required for training and the development of elite sport skills.

Patterns of watching sports also are connected with social class and class relations. This is demonstrated by the increased segregation of fans in stadiums and arenas. Luxury suites, club seating, and patterns of season-ticket allocations separate people by a combination of wealth, power, and access to resources. In the process, inequality becomes increasingly normalized to the point that people are less likely to object to policies that privilege those with the money to buy a spot at the front of the line, or to establish their own line-free VIP entrance to the luxury suites.

Opportunities for careers that hold the hope of upward social mobility exist for some people in sports. For athletes, these opportunities often are scarce and short-lived, and they reflect patterns of class, gender, and ethnic relations in society. These patterns take various forms with regard to careers in sport organizations. Although opportunities in some of these jobs have increased, white men still hold nearly all power positions in sports organizations. This will change only when the organizational cultures of sports teams and athletic departments become more inclusive and provide new ways for women and ethnic minorities to participate fully in shaping the policies and norms used to determine qualifications in sports and organize social relations shape culture at the workplace.

Research generally indicates that people who use sports participation to expand their social and cultural capital often have an advantage when seeking occupational careers apart from sports. However, when sports participation constricts social and cultural capital, it's likely to have a negative effect on later career success. The relevance of this pattern varies by sport and is affected by the resources that athletes can accumulate during their playing careers.

Ending athletic careers may create stress and personal challenges, but many athletes move through the retirement process without experiencing excessive trauma or difficulty. Problems are most likely when identities and relationships have been built exclusively in connection with sports. Then professional help may be needed to successfully transition into satisfying careers and relationships in which mutual support encourages growth and the development of new identities. Otherwise, it is possible to become stuck in the "glory days" of being an athlete instead of facing the challenges presented in life after sports.

Athletic scholarships help some young people further their educations and possibly achieve career success, but athletic aid is relatively scarce compared with other scholarships and forms of financial assistance. Furthermore, athletic scholarships do not always change the future career patterns of young people unless they are used to expand identities, relationships, and experiences.

In conclusion, sports are clearly tied to patterns of class, class relations, and social inequality in society. Money and economic power do matter, and they matter in ways that often reproduce existing patterns of social class and life chances.

SUPPLEMENTAL READINGS

Reading 1. Social class and the future of high school sports

Reading 2. Home countries of the 100 highest-paid athletes

Reading 3. Year round sports participation and future career options

Reading 4. Professional football players and poverty rates by state

Reading 5. The World Cup and the Olympics: Who received benefits in Brazil?

SPORT MANAGEMENT ISSUES

- You have a job with a multi-state youth soccer organization. One of your assignments is to prepare a "Guide for Parents" in which, among other things, you tell parents what they can expect for their children. You include a realistic discussion of the probability that a son or daughter would receive a scholarship. However, the head of the organization tells you to take it out of the guide. Explain what you initially wrote to parents, and also explain why the head of the organization told you to eliminate it from the guide.
- Your soccer coach tells you and everyone else on the university lacrosse team that sports are uniquely American activities because they embody the American Dream and are organized so that money has no influence on performance. He also says that sports are the best way for young people from "disadvantaged" backgrounds to get ahead in life. One of your teammates doubts the truth of what the coach said and asks you to critique his comments. Explain what you would tell your teammate.
- One of your classmates is an international student from Brazil. When she learns you're taking a course on sports, she tells you that sports are luxury items that distract people from political realities in their lives and use valuable resources that should be spent on meeting basic human needs. She wants to know what you think. List and explain at least five points that you will make in your response.
- You have been hired by the NCAA to create guidelines that coaches can use to expand the overall developmental opportunities for their athletes. One of the goals is to help athletes maximize their career success. List the top five guidelines in your report and explain why each is important to the overall development of athletes.

references

Allison, Rachel. 2018. Assessing the patterns: Race, social class, and opportunities in American football. *The Society Pages* (January 11): https://thesocietypages.org/engagingsports/2018/01/11/assessing-the-patterns-race-class-and-opportunities-in-american-football/

Allison, Rachel, Adriene Davis & Raymond Barranco. 2018. A comparison of hometown socioeconomics and demographics for black and white elite football players in the US *International Review for the Sociology of Sport* 534(5): 615–629.

Alvaredo, Facundo, Lucas Chancel, Thomas Piketty, Emmanuel Saez & Gabriel Zucman. 2018. *World inequality report 2018*. World Inequality Lab, Paris School of Economics. Online, https://wir2018.wid.world/

Andersen, Patrick Lie & Anders Bakken. 2019. Social class differences in youths' participation in organized sports: What are the mechanisms? *International Review for the Sociology of Sport* 54(8): 921–937.

Bell, Jarrett. 2013. Diversity study: Black head coaches rarely get second chances. *USA Today* (May 1): http://www.usatoday.com/story/sports /nfl/2013/05/01/coaching-diversity-rooney-rule -central-florida-keith-harrison/2127051/

Belson, Ken. 2018. Life in N.F.L. purgatory. *New York Times* (November 15): https://www.nytimes.com/2018/11/15/sports/football/nfl-free-agents.html

Belson, Ken. 2020. In competition for top jobs, in the N.F.L. and beyond, it pays to be a white man. *New York Times* (January 12): https://www.nytimes.com/2020/01/12/sports/football/rooney-rule-nfl-coach-diversity.html

Bourdieu, Pierre. 1986a. *Distinction: A social critique of the judgment of taste*. London: Routledge.

Bourdieu, Pierre. 1986b. The forms of capital. In J. G. Richards, ed., *Handbook of Theory and*

Research for the Sociology of Education (pp. 242–258). New York: Greenwood Press.

Buchanan, Rebecca R., Eleanor F. Odenheimer, Tanya R. Prewitt-White. 2016. An examination of equal access in athletic programs throughout public high schools in the United States. *Journal of Amateur Sport* 2(1): 99–118.

Buts, Caroline; Cindy Du Bois, Bruno Heyndels & Marc Jegers. 2013. Socioeconomic determinants of success at the Summer Paralympics. *Journal of Sports Economics* 14:133–147.

Cacciola, Scott. 2012. The long, arduous road to Indy. *Wall Street Journal* (May 25): D10.

Cairney, John, Divya Joshi, Matthew Kwan, John Hay & Brent Faught. 2015. Children's participation in organized sport and physical activities and active free play: Exploring the impact of time, gender and neighbourhood household income using longitudinal data. *Sociology of Sport Journal* 32(3): 266–283.

Ceron-Anaya, Hugo. 2017. Not everybody is a golfer: Bourdieu and affluent bodies in Mexico. *Journal of Contemporary Ethnography* 46(3): 285–309.

Clarey, Christopher. 2019. At Shiffrin's alma mater, future ski champions for $58,000 a year. *NYT* (February 13): https://www.nytimes.com/2019/02/13/sports/mikaela-shiffrin-burke-mountain-academy.html

Coalter, Fred. 2013. Game Plan and The Spirit Level: the class ceiling and the limits of sports policy? *International Journal of Sport Policy and Politics* 5(1): 3–19.

Crouse, Karen. 2007. Torres is getting older, but swimming faster. *The New York Times* (November 18): http://www.nytimes.com/2007/11/18/sports/othersports/18torres.html" www.nytimes.com/2007/11/18/sports/othersports/18torres.html

Day, Jacob. 2018. "Climbing the ladder or getting stuck: An optimal matching analysis of racial differences in college football coaches' job-level career patterns." *Research in Social Stratification and Mobility* 53: 1–15.

DeLuca, Jaime R. 2013. Submersed in social segregation: The (re)production of social capital through swim club membership. *Journal of Sport and Social Issues* 37(4): 340–363.

Dubrow, Joshua Kjerulf, and Jimi Adams. 2012. Hoop inequalities: Race, class and family structure background and the odds of playing in the National Basketball Association. *International Review for the Sociology of Sport* 47(1): 43–59.

Eckstein, Rick, 2019. College admission scandal grew out of a system that was ripe for corruption. *The Conversation* (March 13): https://theconversation.com/college-admission-scandal-grew-out-of-a-system-that-was-ripe-for-corruption-113439

Eibeler, Smith. 2018. Congress passes the "Save America's Pastime Act" to screw minor league baseball players out of minimum wage and overtime pay. *New Jersey Employment Blog* (March 30): https://www.newjerseyemploymentlawyersblog.com/2018/03/congress-passes-save-americas-pastime-act-screw-minor-league-baseball-players-minimum-wage-overtime-pay.html

Erickson, Megan. 2015. *Class war: The privatization of childhood*. Brooklyn NY: Verso.

Falcous, Mark & Christopher McLeod. 2012. Anyone for tennis? Sport, class and status in New Zealand. *New Zealand Sociology* 27(1): 13–30.

Farrey, Tom, 2008. *Game on: The All-American race to make champions of our children*. New York: ESPN Books.

Farrey, Tom. 2017. The gentrification of college hoops. *Theundefeated.com* (March): https://theundefeated.com/features/gentrification-of-ncaa-division-1-college-basketball/

Football Town (Episode 7): Flint MI. Video: https://www.facebook.com/watch/?v=2278987532171176

Frank, Robert H. 2017. *Success and luck: Good fortune and the myth of meritocracy*. Princeton NJ: Princeton University Press.

Gaines, Cork. 2017. Gregg Popovich compared Becky Hammon to Steve Kerr and says she has what it takes to be an NBA coach.

Business Insider (March 29): https://www.businessinsider.com/gregg-popovich-becky-hammon-nba-coach-2017-3

Gasol, Pau. 2018 An open letter about female coaches. *The Players' Tribune* (May 11): https://www.theplayerstribune.com/en-us/articles/pau-gasol-becky-hammon

Green, Kyle & Doug Hartmann. 2012. Politics and sports: Strange, secret bedfellows. *The Society Pages* (Feb 3): http://thesocietypages.org/papers/politics-and-sport/

Gregory, Sean. 2013. Should this kid be making $225,047 a year for playing college football? *Time* 182(12, September 16): 36–42.

Harrison, C. Keith (with Sharon Yee). 2007. *The big game in sport management and higher education: The hiring practices of Division IA and IAA head football coaches.* Indianapolis: Black Coaches and Administrators.

Harrison, C. Keith & Scott Bukstein. 2018. Occupational mobility patterns: An examination of leadership, access, opportunity, social capital and the reshuffling effect within the National Football League (Volume VII). A report presented by the National Football League Online, http://www.coachingmobilityreport.com

Hembree, Diana. 2018. CEO pay skyrockets to 361 times that of the average worker. *Forbes.com* (May 22): https://www.forbes.com/sites/dianahembree/2018/05/22/ceo-pay-skyrockets-to-361-times-that-of-the-average-worker/#1b1836c6776d

Hurley, Olivia A. 2018. *Sport cyberpsychology*. London/New York: Routledge.

Ingraham, Christopher. 2018. More money, more fitness: Why people in the wealthiest states get more exercise. *Washington Post* (July 3): https://www.washingtonpost.com/news/wonk/wp/2018/07/03/more-money-more-fitness-why-people-in-the-wealthiest-states-get-more-exercise/

Kelley, Bruce, and Carl Carchia. 2013. "Hey, data data–swing!" The hidden demographics of youth sports. *ESPN The Magazine* (July 11): http://espn.go.com/espn/story/_/id/9469252/hidden-demographics-youth-sports-espn-magazine

Kempski, Jimmy. 2018. Ranking NFL teams by age after 53-man cutdowns: 2018 edition. *Philly Voice* (September 1): https://www.phillyvoice.com/ranking-nfl-teams-age-after-53-man-cutdowns-2018-edition/

Kim, Amy Chan Hyung, Christopher Coutts, Joshua I. Newman, Simon Brandon-Lai & Minjung Kim. 2016. Social geographies at play: Mapping the spatial politics of community-based youth sport participation. *Journal of Amateur Sport* 2(1): 39–72.

King, Bill. 2018. Top 50 most influential people in sports business. *Sports Business Journal* (December 17): https://www.sportsbusinessdaily.com/Journal/Issues/2018/12/17/Most-Influential.aspx

Laberge, Suzanne, and Mathieu Albert. 1999. Conceptions of masculinity and of gender transgressions in sport among adolescent boys: Hegemony, contestation, and social class dynamic. *Men and Masculinities* 1(3): 243–267.

LaFave, Daniel; Randy Nelson & Michael Doherty. 2018. Race and retention in a competitive labor market: The role of historically black colleges and universities in NCAA basketball. *Journal of Sports Economics* 19(3): 417–451.

Lewandowski, Joseph. 2007. Boxing: The sweet science of constraints. *Journal of the Philosophy of Sport* 34(1): 26–38.

Lewandowski, Joseph. 2008. On social poverty: Human development and the distribution of social capital. *Journal of Poverty* 12(1): 27–48.

Longman, Jeré. 2012. For Lolo Jones, everything is image. *New York Times* (August 4): http://www.nytimes.com/2012/08/05/sports/olympics/olympian-lolo-jones-draws-attention-to-beauty-not-achievement.html

May, Ruben A. B. 2009. The good and bad of it all: Professional Black male basketball players as role models for young Black male basketball players. *Sociology of Sport Journal* 26(3): 443–461.

McClusky, Mark. 2012. One one-hundredth of a second faster: Building better Olympic athletes. *Wired.com* (July 25): http://www.wired.com/playbook/2012/06 /ff_superhumans/all/

McLaughlin, Katy. 2018. Wealthy parents help child athletes go pro in their own backyards. *Wall Street Journal* (August 16): https://www.wsj.com/articles/wealthy-parents-help-child-athletes-go-pro-in-their-own-backyards-1534429841

Messner, Michael A. 1992. *Power at play*. Beacon Press, Boston.

Mishel, Lawrence & Jessica Schieder. 2017. *CEO pay remains high relative to the pay of typical workers and high-wage earners*. Washington DC: Economic Policy Institute. Online, https://www.epi.org/publication/ceo-pay-remains-high-relative-to-the-pay-of-typical-workers-and-high-wage-earners/

Moret, Orlan & Fabien Ohl. 2018. Social class, the elite hockey player career and educational paths. *International Review for the Sociology of Sport* Online first, March 29.

NPR et al. 2015. *Sports and health in America.* A national poll sponsored by NPR, Robert Wood Johnson Foundation, and Harvard T.H. Chan School of Public Health. Online, http://www.rwjf.org/en/library/research/2015/06/sports-and-health-in-america.html

Paule, Amanda. 2012. Recruiting high caliber athletes during difficult financial times: Coaches' perceptions of the recruitment process and the role of socioeconomic status. Unpublished paper, Bowling Green State University, School of Human Movement, Sport and Leisure Studies.

Payne, Keith. 2017. *The broken ladder: How inequality affects the way we think, live, and die*. New York NY: Penguin Random House.

Pew Research Center. 2019. *Income inequality*. Washington DC: Pew Research Center https://www.pewresearch.org/topics/income-inequality/

Piketty, Thomas. 2014. *Capital in the twenty-first century*. Cambridge MA: Harvard University Press.

Putnam, Robert. 2016. *Our kids: The American dream in crisis*. New York NY: Simon & Schuster.

Rinaldi, Ray Mark. 2015. At Aspen Ideas Festival 2015: Dwelling on the decline of America. *Denver Post* (July 3): http://www.denverpost.com/news/ci_28429223/at-aspen-ideas-festival-2015-dwelling-decline-america

Roberts, Selena. 2007. College booster bias is delaying minority hiring. *New York Times* (January 28): Roberts, Selena. 2007a. College booster bias is delaying minority hiring. *New York Times* (January 28): http://select.nytimes.com/2007/01/28/sports/ncaafootball/28roberts.html

Schultz, Jordan. 2017. The average NFL career lasts just 3 years. This player is focused on what happens next. *Huffington Post* (March 28): http://www.huffingtonpost.com/entry/ricky-jean-francois-after-nfl-career_us_5888e484e4b0024605fd23d1

Smith, Allison B. & Robin Hardin. 2018. Female student-athletes' transition out of collegiate competition. *Journal of Amateur Sport* 4(3): 61–86.

Stiglitz, Joseph. 2012. *The price of inequality*. New York: W. W. Norton & Company.

Stuij, Mirjam. 2015. Habitus and social class: A case study on socialisation into sports and exercise. *Sport, Education and Society* 20(6): 780–798.

Taniguchi, Hiromi & Frances L Shupe. 2014. Gender and family status differences in leisure-time sports/fitness participation. *International Review for the Sociology of Sport* 49(1): 65–84.

Temple, Kerry. 2019. Playing for keeps. *Notre Dame Magazine* 48(2): 23–27.

Thompson, Derek. 2018. American meritocracy is killing youth sports. *The Atlantic* https://www.theatlantic.com/ideas/archive/2018/11/income-inequality-explains-decline-youth-sports/574975/

Tinley, Scott. 2015. *Racing the sunset How athletes survive, thrive, or fail in life after sport.* New York: Skyhorse Publishing.

Tomlinson, Alan. 2007. Sport and social class. In George Ritzer, ed., *Encyclopedia of sociology* (pp. 4695–4699). London/New York: Blackwell.

Turner, Robert W. 2018. *Not for long: The life and career of the NFL athlete*. New York/London: Oxford University Press.

Vandermeerschen, Hanne; Steven Vos & Jeroen Scheerder. 2016. Towards level playing fields? A time trend analysis of young people's participation in club-organised sports. *International Review for the Sociology of Sport* 51(4): 468–484.

Veklerov, Kimberly. 2018. Half the sports are gone at Oakland high schools and girls take brunt of cuts. SanFrancisco Chronicle (August 24): https://www.sfchronicle.com/bayarea/article/Oakland-high-schools-back-in-session-but-half-of-13181374.php

Wacquant, Loïc J. D. 1992. The social logic of boxing in Black Chicago: Toward a sociology of pugilism. *Sociology of Sport Journal* 9, 3: 221–54.

Wacquant, Loïc J. D. 1995a. The pugilistic point of view: How boxers think and feel about their trade. *Theory and Society* 24: 489–535.

Wacquant, Loïc J. D. 1995b. Pugs at work: Bodily capital and bodily labour among professional boxers. *Body & Society* 1, 1: 65–93.

Wacquant, Loïc. 2004. *Body and soul: Notebooks of an apprentice boxer*. Oxford/New York: Oxford University Press.

White, Philip, &William McTeer. 2012. Socioeconomic status and sport participation at different developmental stages during childhood and youth: Multivariate analyses using Canadian national survey data. *Sociology of Sport Journal* 29(2): 186–209.

Wiecek, Paul. 2018. Gap between haves and have-nots widening in kids' sports. (August 20): https://www.winnipegfreepress.com/sports/gap-between-haves-and-have-nots-widening-in-sports-kids-sports-491292281.html

World Bank. 2018. Nearly half the world lives on less than $5.50 a day. Washington DC: World Bank. Online, https://www.worldbank.org/en/news/press-release/2018/10/17/nearly-half-the-world-lives-on-less-than-550-a-day

Zirin, Dave. 2008. Calling sports sociology off the bench. *Contexts*, 7:28–31.

10

AGE AND ABILITY*

Barriers to Participation and Inclusion

chapter

10

(*Source:* Rich Cruse/Photo courtesy of the Challenged Athletes Foundation, http://www.challengedathletes.org)

AGE AND ABILITY*

Barriers to Participation and Inclusion?

. . . age, disease, and accident mean that all able-bodiedness is a temporary state. Even able-bodied people can "die in the woods" alone—they, too, are dependent upon society.

—Joshua Rothman, journalist (2017)

. . . we must demolish the false dividing line between 'normal' and 'disabled' [meaning impaired] and attack the whole concept of physical normality. We have to recognise that disablement [impairment] is not merely the physical state of a small minority of people. It is the normal condition of humanity.

—Allan Sutherland, British author, performer, and activist (1981)

I am a disabled woman interested in sport and I do not know of one disabled athlete who has made a difference in the lives of the people who are disabled in my circle of disabled friends.

—Esther, Disability Rights activist (Braye et al., 2013)

My life was transformed by my new arm. Everything got easier. . . . I noticed that it also changed how others perceive me. No longer did I get looks of pity when walking in public. Instead, the looks I got changed to genuine curiosity at this robotic device.

—Patrick Kane (2018)

*Coauthored with Elizabeth Pike

Chapter Outline

Learning Objectives

- Know the meaning and consequences of ableist ideology, ageism, and ableism.
- Explain the relationship between age and sports participation patterns and why older people are playing sports more frequently today.
- Distinguish between impairments and disabilities, and give examples of each.
- Understand the differences between the medical and social models of disability.
- Describe what it means to live in "the empire of the normal" for those who have a disability and want to play sports.
- Explain how the media and gender are involved in the social construction of disability.
- Identify four barriers that impact the sports participation of people with disabilities.
- Understand the dynamics of exclusion and inclusion processes involving sports and people with disabilities.
- Describe the major challenges facing disability sports, especially the Paralympics and Special Olympics.
- From the perspective most people with a disability, explain the pros and cons associated with the use of new technologies in the Paralympic Games.

Are you able-bodied? If so, what makes you so? If not, why not? Will you always be this way, regardless of your age or circumstances?

How *able* must you be to think of yourself as able-bodied? Which abilities matter the most? If you wear contacts to see more clearly, are you able-bodied or merely "passing" as such? Are you disabled if you have a prosthetic knee or hip replacement? What if your legs are amputated below the knees and you can use prosthetic legs to run faster than most of your peers with legs of flesh and bones?

Trying to answer these questions helps us realize that abilities are variable and impermanent. They change over time, sometimes increasing, sometimes declining. Some abilities may be very important in some situations but irrelevant in others. This means that being able-bodied is a temporary and variable condition.

Does age affect how you assess your ability? If at age 20 you are physically stronger, faster, and more coordinated than a 4-year-old or a 44-year-old, would you consider them disabled? If strength, speed, and coordination have nothing to do with accomplishing a task, what does it mean to be able-bodied?

These questions force us to consider how ability is defined and who defines it. For example, we might ask a person born without sight to talk about ability and learn how she understands it from her perspective. We could compare her ideas and perceptions with those who have 20/20 vision and with those who must wear glasses or contacts to see properly. Similarly, we could ask people who are 10, 20, 50, and 80-years-old to do the same. This would provide a good starting point for discussing the meaning of ability and the extent to which meanings vary from one perspective to another.

Fortunately, others have already done this and given us a basis for discussing age, ability, and sports participation. We will use their research to explore four questions in this chapter:

1. What counts as ability, who decides this, and how do ideologies related to age and ability influence the meaning of disability in sports?
2. How do ideas and beliefs about age and ability influence physical activity and sports participation?
3. What issues do people who are defined as "disabled" face when they seek or take advantage of opportunities to play sports?
4. What are the connections between human beings, technology, and ability in sports?

WHAT COUNTS AS ABILITY?

A primary theme in this book is that our lives and the social worlds in which we live are influenced by **ideologies**—the ideas and beliefs commonly used to give meaning to the world and make sense of experiences. In this chapter, we consider the ways that socially accepted ideas and beliefs about *age* and *ability* are related to sports participation. This is partly because the body is central to our sense of self and our social identity (Thualagant, 2012). From an early age we learn norms for evaluating and classifying bodies—whether they are tall, short, fit, frail, thin, fat, attractive, unattractive, young, old, athletic, awkward, disabled, and so on. As we learn these norms, most of us maintain, modify, and fashion our bodies as part of a self-identity project.

When sports were formally organized during the late 1800s and early 1900s, an emerging social psychological theory at that time stressed that proper physical and character development required young people to participate in organized physical activities. At the same time, it was widely believed that people older than 40 should avoid vigorous activities, including strenuous sports, and not overstress themselves, because they had passed their prime and were facing inevitable and unavoidable physical decline.

Similarly, people with particular physical and intellectual impairments were denied access to sports participation because it was believed that vigorous activity would overexcite them and be dangerous for them and people around them. As a result, anyone defined as *old* or *disabled* according to standards used at the time were marginalized or excluded from physical activities and sports.

Unfortunately, the legacies of these historical practices and standards remain with us. They exist in the form of **ableist ideology** consisting of *interrelated ideas and beliefs that are widely used to identify people as physically or intellectually disabled, to justify treating them as inferior, and to organize social worlds and physical spaces without taking them into account.*

This ideology is common in meritocracies where people are compared and ranked in terms of abilities, qualifications, and recognized achievements. As it informs everyday social interaction, people tend to patronize, pity, pathologize, demean, and sometimes dehumanize those perceived to be incapable of meeting particular standards of physical or intellectual performance. Over time, ableist ideology leads to forms of social organization in which older and disabled people are marginalized and segregated from mainstream settings and activities, especially organized, competitive sports.

Ableist ideology is based on a rejection of physical and intellectual variation as a natural and normal part of human existence. It also ignores the fact that the meanings given to different abilities change from one situation to another and that everyone's abilities vary over time and can change suddenly as a result of injury or disease. For example, when I was playing college basketball at 18-years-old, my physical quickness and vertical jumping ability were important in my life. But as a 75-year-old family member, friend, and sociologist, other abilities have replaced physical quickness and vertical jumping ability in my life. Additionally, when I was diagnosed with multiple sclerosis at 49-years-old, my primary physical goal was to continue walking–an ability I'd always taken for granted. These changes in the meanings given to abilities are not unique to me; they happen with everyone, sometimes gradually, sometimes in an instant.

An irony associated with ableist ideology is that those who use it to categorize others as disabled overlook the temporary nature of their own abilities. When people use gender, racial, or class ideologies to claim superiority over others, they usually escape being negatively evaluated by others who use them. But this is not the case with ableist ideology, because others will use it to negatively evaluate those who used it earlier in their lives (Harpur, 2012). In other words, using it today will disadvantage you tomorrow.

Ableist ideology is also based on the assumption that impairments are abnormalities, disregarding the fact that no mind or body works perfectly in all situations and at all times. We might have an ideal image of a human being without any impairments, but such a person does not exist. Each of us is impaired in some way. This is simply part of the human condition. If we are lucky, we live our lives around our impairments without major inconvenience, we are appreciated for the abilities we have, and we avoid being labeled by others as *sub*normal and *dis*abled. When we think of our future, we hope to avoid profound impairments that prevent us from being who we want to be and doing what we want to do.

So if none of us is perfect and everyone who lives long enough will be limited by impairments at some point during the lifecourse, how is it possible to divide people into two categories: *able-bodied* and *disabled?* Who decides which impairments count when classifying people as *dis*abled–a term that implies a condition worse than "unable." For example, if a 10-year-old with an impaired left arm and hand uses an adapted ski pole and skis faster and with more control than her friends, should she be classified as disabled? Who makes that decision and for what reason? Likewise, if the same 10-year-old wears a brace on her left ankle and calf and cannot do cartwheels and backflips like her best friend but can tie her shoes one-handed and run a 5-km race faster than her friend, is it appropriate to say she is a disabled runner?

These questions are meant to encourage critical thinking about the meaning of ability and disability and how we distinguish between able-bodied and disabled. They are *not* meant to dismiss or understate the real challenges faced by people with

(*Source:* Paul Harvey IV)

Ageism affects relationships in many cultures, especially those in which youth is valued over experience. This leads to age segregation, especially in physical activities and sports. As a result, older people choose to participate in the Senior Games or Masters events; they seldom engage in sports or physical activities with younger people outside of their families.

impairments that force them to make substantial and often difficult adjustments in their lives. Some of these challenges may also influence their opportunities and choices, especially when others take a visible impairment to be a defining mark of general inability. But when and under what conditions does a particular impairment become a disability?

To answer these questions and understand the meaning of ability and disability in sports, it is important to know about the two "isms" that form the foundation for ableist ideology. These are *ageism* and *ableism.*

Ageism

The term *ageism* was first used in 1969 by Robert Butler, a physician and psychiatrist who was inspired to study how older people were treated in society when his medical school teachers used rude and sarcastic terms as they talked about older patients and their medical conditions. He grew up with his grandparents, and he was angered by this. As he learned more about the negative attitudes and stereotypes that shaped the treatment of older people in the United States, he defined **ageism** as *an evaluative perspective that favors one age group–usually younger people–over others and justifies discrimination against particular age groups that are assumed to be incapable of full participation in valued social and cultural activities.* According to Butler, this perspective distorted relationships with older people and denied their abilities, both physical and intellectual.

The perspective of ageism rests on the belief that younger people are more capable than and superior to those who have passed through middle age and become old. This belief is so widespread in some cultures that most people take it for granted, make jokes about being old, and develop a general fear of their own aging. This belief also accounts for much of the age discrimination that has become one of the most frequently reported forms of workplace discrimination in many countries today. Reported cases of age discrimination in US workplaces outnumber race or sex discrimination cases by three to one (AARP Research, 2018; EEOC, 2013). The irony of this in the United States is that when people in the baby-boom generation, born between 1946 and 1964, were young, they were guilty of negatively stereotyping older people, and now that they are in their sixties and seventies, they are fighting against ageism and age discrimination.

Although people in the baby-boom generation saw many of their parents passively accept age discrimination in employment and other spheres of life and even internalize aspects of ageism, many of them now defy ageist stereotypes and blur the normative boundaries that limited their parents' lives (Jenkins, 2018). One strategy is to critique the words that others use to describe them. For example, "the elderly," "golden agers," "seniors," "senior citizens," "the aged," and "dear" or "honey"–terms commonly used in the past and occasionally used today–are now seen as patronizing, inaccurate, or based on ageist stereotypes (Gullette, 2018).

Older people is the age identification term preferred by older people today, because it locates age on a continuum along which people are identified as "younger" or "older," depending on the point of reference. This approach challenges ableist ideology and recognizes that aging is a natural process and that everyone remains a *person* at every point along the way. This and other strategies have been effective to the point that attitudes about aging and older people are changing.

Ableism

Ableist ideology, or **ableism**, *is an evaluative perspective in which the label of disability marks a person as inferior and incapable of full participation in mainstream activities.* People using this perspective tend to patronize, pathologize, or pity those who cannot meet particular standards of physical or intellectual ability due to a visible or inferred **impairment**–which is *a physical, sensory or intellectual condition that potentially limits a person's full participation in certain social or physical environments.*

Over time, ableism leads to forms of social organization in which people with disabilities are marginalized and segregated from settings and activities created by those who don't currently have a visible impairment that could mark them as **disabled**, that is, as *a person with an impairment that is determined by an influential person or official agency to cause significant functional limitations.*

Thomas Hehir, director of the School Leadership Program at Harvard University, explains that when ableism shapes our decisions, it usually leads us to make "the world unwelcoming and inaccessible for people with disabilities" (Hehir, 2002, p. 13). In the case of schools, says Hehir, ableism leads people, including parents and teachers, to assume that "it is preferable for a child to read print rather than Braille, walk rather than use a wheelchair, spell independently rather than use a spell-checker, read written text rather than listen to a book on tape, and hang out with non-disabled kids rather than with other disabled kids" (Hehir, 2005, p. 13).

In this way, ableism leads people to forget that variations in ability are a normal part of human existence; they occur over time for each of us, and exist across multiple ability dimensions. Similarly, it leads people to overlook the possibility that able-bodied persons could become disabled tomorrow due to injury, disease, or other events in their lives. This means that being able-bodied is a temporary condition, and to classify people as *disabled* and *able-bodied* tells us little about people's lives, even though it may be useful for political purposes and to identify special service and support needs for particular people. We know that there are many types of abilities used for many purposes, and even though it might be possible to rank people from low to high on a particular ability in a particular situation or in reference to a specific task, it is impossible to have one ability-based ranking system that is meaningful across all situations and tasks, or across all sports.

So how do we decide when to use a "disability vocabulary" and what are the implications of doing so? This question will be answered in the following sections.

CONSTRUCTING THE MEANING OF *AGE*

Ideas and beliefs about age vary over time and from one culture to another. They even vary from one situation to another, depending on the activities and attributes valued in particular social worlds. In societies characterized by high rates of change, youth is generally valued over age. Being "old" in such societies is associated with being inflexible, out of touch, resistant to change, and possessing outdated knowledge. When this view is combined with beliefs that aging involves physical and intellectual decline, many people develop negative attitudes about becoming older. These attitudes may then become stereotypes of the experience of being older. For example, children in North America often learn that ability is associated with youth, and inability is associated with being old. Therefore, a five-year-old girl may describe her grandfather as *old* if he has health-related impairments and does not play with her in physically active ways as he did in the past. At the same time, she may describe her grandmother of the same age as *young*—or *not old*—because she enjoys physical activities and plays soccer with her in the park. Through her relationships and experiences, this five-year-old has learned to equate old age with inactivity and a lack of physical abilities. For her, being physically able and active is a sign of youth.

When this perception of age is widely accepted and incorporated into the general narratives and stories about aging in a culture, it perpetuates negative beliefs about becoming and being old (Pike, 2015). This leads people to reduce physical activity as they age, and it supports the notion that communities should not be concerned about providing publicly funded opportunities for older people to be active and play sports. Under these conditions, those who wish to be active have little social support and few opportunities to play active sports (Kerr et al., 2018; Pike, 2015; Tulle, 2008a, 2008b, 2008c).

We don't stop playing because we grow old; we grow old because we stop playing. —George Bernard Shaw

Until recently, older people in many parts of the world were expected to withdraw from everyday work routines due to their frailty and weakness, or as a reward for many years of hard work. During most of the twentieth century, older people were often told to take it easy, preserve their energy and strength, and make sure they had enough rest on a daily basis. Even doctors in North America and much of Europe advised older patients, especially women, to avoid depleting their energy by "doing too much." Therefore, older people have traditionally avoided strenuous physical activity and even feared it as a threat to their health and well-being. For them, playing sports was out of the question because it would put too much strain on their hearts and create shoulder, back, hip, and knee problems. "Acting your age" meant being inactive for older people, although the age at which a person is defined as old varies widely by ethnicity, social class, and gender both within and between societies (Peterson & Ralston, 2017).

The legacy of this approach for older people remains influential, even in societies where research has shown that physical exercise will not harm them unless they have certain chronic conditions or are not physically prepared to engage in activities requiring certain levels of strength and flexibility. But we may still hear older people say, "I'm too old to do that"—when they really mean that they are not physically prepared to do it, or they doesn't want to show that they can't do it as well as they did it in the past.

Aging as a Social and Political Issue

People over 60-years-old are the fastest growing segment of the population in many societies. This is due to improved access to health care and rising literacy rates. In 2018, the average life expectancy worldwide was 74 for females and seventy for males. A growing number of countries have an average life expectancy over eighty years old. While many people celebrate longer life expectancy, others are concerned that it will make health care and social services unsustainable at current levels.

These concerns are intensified by ageist assumptions that older people make no contributions to society and ultimately are a burden that younger people must bear (Pike, 2011). To make matters worse, these assumptions further marginalize older people, encourage them to be physically inactive, separate them from contexts in which they can make contributions, and deny them opportunities to participate in continuing education and professional development needed to maintain their contributions. Also, when ageism and ableist ideology are pervasive in a society, older people often internalize these assumptions and voluntarily withdraw from activities, ceasing to be vital members of their communities and society. As a result, ageism becomes a self-fulfilling prophecy.

Another social and political issue that has emerged in recent years is grounded in the belief that rigorous exercise enables people to stay youthful because it delays and minimizes natural decremental changes that occur with aging (Marshall & Rahman, 2015). Although we still have much to learn about the effects of various forms and intensity of physical activity on the overall well-being of older people, there are sport scientists and medical practitioners who confidently assert that being physically active is always a good thing–that it will extend and improve the quality of people's lives and help them avoid the illnesses and diseases that older people often experience. But they don't talk about the frequency of sports injuries and the heavy dependence on health care among older athletes who need medical assistance to continue training and competing.

This leads people to believe that if older people do become ill or have a disease, it is due to their personal choice not to take care of themselves properly. Evidence shows that this is *not* true (Tulle, 2008c). But if policy makers believe it, they are unlikely to recommend services and medical care for older people, because only "lazy and irresponsible" older people need them. This creates a political situation in which there is little concern about national and community-based programs for older people. In this way, people who think that physical activity and sports are the answer to numerous social and health problems provide support for a neoliberal political and cultural ideology stressing that when people take personal responsibility for their own lives, most problems will be solved (Collinet and Delalandre, 2015). In connection with aging, this is one way that sports and sports science can influence political decisions that impact people's lives.

Age, Sports, and Ability

Most social gerontologists today point out that while aging is an intrinsically physical process of irreversible decline, the social significance given to this process is important. In particular, their research seeks to address an imbalance in sociological research, which has been dominated by studies of youth as the future producers and consumers in society. At the same time, older people are overlooked because they're seen as having few productive and consumptive capacities. The research of social gerontologists also helps us in the sociology of sport to develop our own studies of age, sports, and ability, and the meanings given to sports participation at different points during the life span.

There are innumerable studies of the developmental implications of youth sports participation, and we have learned much about age-appropriate physical activity involvement from early childhood through adolescence (Dorsch et al., forthcoming). But studies of the implication and dynamics of sports participation among older people are rare. This is partly because older people are assumed to be "grown up"–that is, their growth and development are complete, so there is little reason to study physical activities and sports in their lives.

This approach is shortsighted and ignores the reality of aging populations in many societies. Additionally, as the cohorts of people turning fifty years old and older now see themselves as capable of engaging in sports and related vigorous physical

(*Source:* Divyakant Solanki/EPA/Shutterstock)

Fauja Singh, a 101-year-old British amateur runner, currently holds the record for the oldest runner to complete a marathon. Here, at the Standard Chartered Mumbai Marathon 2013 in Mumbai, India, he participates in a 4.3-km run for older people.

activities, there is a need to understand the full implications of their participation. Historically, public policies and private sector funding has focused on providing young people with opportunities and encouragement to participate in sports but the provision of opportunities and encouragement for older people has largely been ignored.

Unsurprisingly, popular sports worldwide celebrate youth and youthfulness. They often are viewed as stages on which "the future" of societies is exhibited. Sports played by older people are given little attention. Apart from seniors golf tournaments used by corporate sponsors to market products and services to wealthy, influential older men who make product choices for large corporations, there is no consistent coverage of sports involving older athletes. The exception is coverage in which older people make the news as novelties by being the oldest person to run a marathon or the first eighty-year-old to climb a mountain or swim across a local lake.

With this said, many of us have noticed that some elite athletes now play to older ages than in the past. Advances in sports science have improved nutrition and training so that athletes have shorter recovery time as they continue to train intensely. Commentators now refer to the longevity of older players, and sponsors that want to sell products to older consumers sign endorsement contracts with older athletes who retain their celebrity personas and their ability to sell products.

Emerging Ideas About Aging and Sports

The baby-boom generation, born between 1946 and 1964 in the United States, most of Europe, and Russia, has until recently been the largest age-based segment of the population in countries where there was a strong sense of hope and possibility after World War II ended. This positive outlook led couples to have many children over that eighteen-year period, and demographers labeled them the Baby Boom Generation.

Over the years, baby boomers have had a strong influence on everything from the rise of popular culture to the expansion of science and higher education. Compared with previous generations they also grew up with more access to youth sports, and they attended high school and college at higher rates. Now they are past sixty years old and are more physically active than older people were in the past. As a result, they are challenging ageist beliefs and when they receive media coverage, it is likely to describe them as part of a trend rather than novelties.

On average, baby boomers are healthier than previous generations of older people and they have more resources to continue their physical activities and sports participation. They also have been privileged to live during a period of economic expansion and were children during a time of widespread public support for sports programs. Additionally, the youngest women in this generation were the first in the United States to benefit from the opportunities created by Title IX and similar gender equity laws in other countries. As these factors merged together, many baby boomers made sports participation a total family activity–something that was rare in the past. As a result, they now have more support from family and friends for continuing or initiating participation than any previous older generation.

This generational shift in ideas and beliefs about age and physical activity does not mean that all older people today are physically active. In fact, the rates of physical inactivity, obesity, and related health problems are disappointingly high. Additionally, some baby boomers accept ableist ideology and deny their own aging, whereas others succumb to ageist stereotypes and attempt to hide their aging with hair dye, diet regimes, cosmetic surgery, drugs, and other enhancement procedures. Some, of course, use sports participation and exercise routines in the hope of looking younger longer–hope fostered through billions of dollars of advertising by the appearance enhancement industry.

The point here is that the sheer size of the baby-boom generation, along with its access to resources, has enabled it to have a high degree of cultural clout. And many boomers approach older adulthood with the expectation that if they wish to be active, there should be opportunities for them to do so, or else they will create those opportunities on their own. In this sense they are challenging the prevailing ableist ideology and popular ideas about what is natural and normal for older people (Collinet and Delalandre, 2015; O'Connor, 2018; Willing et al., 2019).

At the same time, older people today are challenging the ways in which sports are organized. Many of them engage in traditional and new forms of lifestyle sports (Wheaton, 2013). This provides space for people with differing interests: some focus on results, personal bests, and other aspects of achievement, and others seek social experiences in settings where people are interested in doing physical things for the joy of it.

Older People Only: Age-Segregated Sports

For various reasons, some older people prefer to participate in age-segregated sports. Long-time sports participants may seek events involving peers who share their age-related interests and experiences, whereas new participants often avoid events involving younger people, who may not be sensitive to the concerns of older athletes.

A number of individual sports now sponsor masters and veterans competitions. Cycling, dance, skiing, table tennis, tennis, and triathlon are examples. Swimming and track and field (athletics) have the longest histories of masters-level events. The first World Masters Swimming Championships were held in Tokyo in 1986, and the same event held in Budapest in 2017 attracted over 10,000 competitors from more than eighty affiliated national federations.

The World Masters Games is a multi-sport event held every four years since 1995 for competitors over thirty-five years old. It is recognized by the International Olympic Committee and partners with the International Paralympic Committee to support the Olympic Movement and the sport-for-all philosophy of the Olympic Charter. The 2018 Games in Malaga (Spain) brought together over 8000 athletes representing 100 nations to compete in thirty core sports. These games present themselves as inclusive events that focus on the health advantages of lifelong sports participation.

Studies of middle-age and older people who participate in masters events are now helping us understand more about the role of sports participation in the aging process (Drummond, 2020; Gayman et al., 2017; Horton et al., 2018). Data from these studies indicate that in most cases, continuing sports participation helps people negotiate the

(*Source:* Nancy Coakley)

This is one of many three-generation entries into the 5- and 10-km Human Race in Fort Collins, Colorado, during the summer of 2013. These family members–ages 69, 44, 16, and 14–regularly run races together.

process of getting older. As they move from middle age to later life, they recognize and accept that the level of their performance in sports will decline, although competition remains exciting for them. Some constantly push themselves to excel; others might do so mostly when they enter a new age category and have a chance to place high in their age group in a particular event.

When these athletes talk about sports in their lives, it appears that they use them "to simultaneously resist and accept the aging process" (Dionigi et al., 2013, p. 385). They experience stress, illness, and acute injuries, but staying in sports enables them to maintain their sense of physical competence, experience social and mental stimulation, and feel resilient in the face of advancing age. They don't want age to define them and are pleased when others do not define them in terms of age and think they look younger than they are.

Unfortunately, most of the existing research focuses on white, middle-class people, who often use a particular fitness discourse when they talk about sports participation. At this time we know little about the participation of people of color or people who lack material resources. It is likely that their participation rates are relatively low, but for those who are involved in Masters and other events, it would be useful to know the meanings they give to their experiences and how those meanings change in connection with aging and shifting life circumstances.

There is little doubt that veterans and masters sports programs will increase as a growing population of older people demand them and as people see them as a way to create careers and make money. Economic development officials in cities worldwide now see sports events for older people as a way to increase tourism and bring into the city people who are likely to have money to spend on hotels, restaurants, and local tourist attractions.

Active older people are also attracted to events in which they can compete without feeling the pressure to constantly improve their performance. Instead of focusing on progressive improvement, they emphasize maintaining their physical abilities so they can remain active as they become older. For this reason, older people often avoid sports with high injury rates. Research in Europe has recently found that the participation histories reported by 1739 people over fifty years old involved progressively less competition and more diversity in terms of how sports were organized (Klostermann and Nagel, 2012).

It is difficult to track changes in how people integrate sports participation into their lives as they age, but from what we know at this time, it appears that as people age, they prefer lifestyle sports and modified versions of competitive activities that are organized to emphasize the pleasure of movement, social experiences, and controlled challenges. Many older people also choose to engage in walking, swimming, strength training, yoga, tai chi, and similar activities that involve no competition. They take these activities seriously at the same time that they focus on health, fitness, social experiences, and the overall pleasure of participation. Evidence also indicates that some older people now choose to play physically active video games so they can exercise in the safety and comfort of their homes (DeSchutter & Brown, 2016; Osmanovic & Pecchioni, 2016; Sayago et al., 2016; Schell et al., 2016).

Overall it is likely that images of older people who are active, fit, healthy, and accomplished athletes will become more visible over time. This might inspire others to be active in ways that challenge the credibility of those who use ageism and ableism to mark older people as incapable and inferior. On the other hand, the images could be used by people with a political agenda based on ableist ideology to argue that older people who don't meet exercise expectations should not receive public support because they lack moral worth. This means that as older people become more physically active, the meanings given to age and ability can vary significantly in connection with social and economic policy agendas.

Age, Ability, and Context

As we grow older, our age intersects with other social factors such as gender, race/ethnicity, and socioeconomic status, and this influences our experiences of sports in later life. For example, older white men's experiences and opportunities are very different from those of older black women; and wealthier people have more choices than people with few material resources. Additionally, social definitions of age and gender often create a "double jeopardy," for older women who are discouraged from taking sports participation and physical activity as a serious part of their lives.

Women have longer life expectancies than men in nearly all societies, a social condition described as the "feminization of aging". However, statistics indicate that women are less physically active than men throughout the life span and their activity levels decline significantly in later life. This is due, in part, to their continued domestic responsibilities in later life as they maintain their role as caregivers for grandchildren and their own parents.

Although many sports remain male-dominated, an increasing number of women in some sectors of society see physical activity and sports participation as part of an overall program to maintain their health, strength, and flexibility as they age. The pace and extent of this trend varies greatly from one society and population to another, depending on patterns of gender relations, the popularity and accessibility of personal enhancement technologies, and the experiences and perspectives of older women (Horton et al., 2018).

Women sometimes exercise to delay the appearance of aging, which reaffirms ageist ideology at the same time that it may support personal health. Older women, particularly those with high socioeconomic status, can engage in sports activities and belong to leisure clubs as a way to embrace and negotiate the aging process or as a way to fight it (Dionigi et al., 2013). This raises interesting research questions: Do those who use physical activity to fight or "delay" the aging process benefit more or less, and do they drop out more or less often, than those who exercise or play sports for other reasons?

Age and gender also intersect with ethnicity and social class in connection with physical activity and sports participation. Ethnicity issues are complex in countries where immigrants come from a wide array of cultures and have migration patterns that span multiple generations. Patterns in the United States for first-generation immigrants from China are likely different than patterns among fifth-generation or later Chinese Americans who have ideas and beliefs about age and ability that are based on their experiences in the United States. Similarly, patterns among first- and later-generation people with Mexican ancestry will differ with their unique experiences. For the most part, research indicates that the longer an immigrant population lives in the United States, the more likely it is that their lifestyles will match those of their status peers in US culture.

As noted in Chapter 9, socioeconomic status is strongly related to patterns of physical activity and sports participation. Participation is perceived as a personal choice, but choices expand with a person's financial resources. Therefore, older people who are able to maintain their lifestyles will continue with their previous physical activity habits to the extent that their health and general social situation permit.

Most media images of active older people portray those who are well-off and healthy (Marshall and Rahman, 2015). The images are primarily in commercial ads promoting the "ideal" way to live as retired people, and that life involves cruising and jetting off to attractive tourist destinations and joining friends engaged in never-ending consumption of goods, services and a combination of supplements and prescription drugs. However, more than 90 percent of older people worldwide cannot live such a consumption-oriented lifestyle. Their life choices are based on limited financial resources and the accessibility of opportunities

(*Source:* Paul Harvey IV)

These men are running in an age division race; they compete only with age peers. However, various sports events, such as the 100-meter sprint, could be organized so that "handicaps" could be calculated for each runner on the basis of past performances. Therefore, a 68-year-old runner might have a starting line 7-yards ahead of a 17-year old runner. This would allow men and women of all ages to compete with each other in the same event.

to engage in physical activities with friends. Cost, accessibility, and sociability matter the most in their choices about physical activity participation (Pike, 2012). For most older people living primarily on social security, pensions, and limited savings, choices outside the home are scarce or nonexistent. Research is needed on this topic.

CONSTRUCTING THE MEANING OF *ABILITY*

"Ability" is a loaded concept. Different people see various abilities as essential as they view the world from their vantage point. Ask an engineer about ability, and the response will be different from what an artist or auto mechanic might say. On average, men will describe ability in terms that don't match up with what women say, and the same goes for older and younger people, African Americans and Euro-Americans, people in ethnic minority and majority populations, the wealthy and the poor. Variations also occur from one culture and situation to another.

You get the point: Ability is a complex phenomenon, and its meaning shifts depending on the situation and a person's vantage point and experiences. The same goes for ability's often misunderstood sibling: *disability*. This point is emphasized by Damon Rose, one of the directors of the disability website *Ouch!* (https://www.bbc.co.uk/programmes/p02r6yqw). Rose is registered as blind and understands how people with disabilities respond to the words used to identify them (Rose, 2004). For example, *handicapped* is an offensive designation. For most people with a disability, **handicapped** means *being held back, weighed down, and marked as inferior due to perceived physical or intellectual impairments.* The word is based on the perspective of non-disabled people who decided that particular impairments should define the identities of those who live with them.

Rose realizes that words have power and may be used to discredit people with certain attributes and perpetuate the barriers that disrupt and influence their lives. This means that as we work to understand the meaning of *dis*ability in sports, it is important that we use terminology that does not unwittingly disadvantage those who already face the challenge of living with and around their physical or intellectual impairments.

The definition of the term "*dis*ability" has been debated for many years by health and medical professionals, government officials, school administrators, physiologists, psychologists, social scientists, and those who live with physical or intellectual impairments (Harpur, 2012). This is because official definitions are used to determine who qualifies for public assistance in schools and government programs, who is protected by antidiscrimination laws, who may park in reserved areas and use designated facilities, who may or may not participate in mainstream or "disability sports," and so on.

According to the World Health Organization, definitions should be taken seriously because disability "is a complex phenomenon, reflecting the interaction between features of a person's body and features of the society in which he or she lives" (WHO, 2011). This is relevant in connection with sports, because disability is nearly a universal aspect of experience. With rare exceptions, each of us will be impaired at some point in time in a way that limits how we function in everyday life–and the likelihood of this being permanent rather than temporary increases with age. The challenges we face when this occurs are many, and they usually exist in the form of barriers that are common features of our everyday social and physical environments. This makes it a matter of self-interest to support interventions to remove barriers that limit and restrict activities and participation among people with varying abilities. These barriers are present in (a) physical environments designed solely for people without movement impairments; (b) social norms and organizational structures that ignore, marginalize, or exclude people with certain impairments; and (c) personal attitudes and vocabulary that link disability with inferiority.

None of us is physically or mentally perfect, and we regularly make personal adjustments to reduce the impact of our own weaknesses and lack of ability. If we are lucky, we have access to support systems and assistive devices that make those adjustments more effective and less disruptive. Those of us with corrective lenses, for instance, may take clear vision for granted, but only because an assistive device reduces the impact of our sight impairment in our lives.

It is also important to avoid arbitrary barriers that turn our impairments into disabilities. For example, prior to the late 1990s, if your leg was amputated below the knee, you could not have been a member of your national powerlifting team, because the rules of the International Powerlifting Federation (IPF) stated that to be eligible for official events, a competitor doing a bench press and other compulsory lifts must have two feet in contact with the floor–and a prosthetic foot did not qualify as a "real" foot. This meant that you would have been "*dis*'d" by the IPF–that is, *dis*qualified due to *dis*ability. After a few *dis*'d athletes legally challenged this rule, it was changed so that a prosthetic leg and foot were permitted as replacements for a flesh-and-bones leg and foot.

In this example, the original IPF rule had converted an impairment into disability. The revised rule eliminated disability by removing the barrier that restricted participation. However, the connection between impairments and abilities is often more complex than this. We saw this with Oscar Pistorius, the 100- and 200-m sprinter from South Africa, who fought a long legal and scientific "classification" battle to qualify for participation in the 2012 Olympics as a runner with two below-the-knee prostheses. The prostheses that Pistorius wore were Flex-Foot Cheetah blades. As he set records in the Paralympics and won a world championship in track and field (athletics), Pistorius was nicknamed "the blade runner" and "the fastest man on no legs." But he was "*dis*'d" when the IOC and the IAAF ruled that he could not participate in the Olympic Games because his prostheses gave him an "unfair advantage" over other Olympic runners in the 100- and 200-meter sprints. After reviewing considerable research evidence and deliberating for nearly a year, the Court of Arbitration for Sport concluded that the carbon-fiber devices used by Pistorius did not give him a net advantage in his events.

The Pistorius case attracted massive media coverage, and it raised many issues about the meaning of ability and disability in sports. These issues are important, but most people with physical impairments are concerned with more basic and practical matters, such as access to sports participation opportunities, adaptive sports equipment, knowledgeable coaches, barrier-free facilities, transportation to and from practice and competitions, and basic support for training.

The Emerging Meaning of *Dis*ability

The discussion of ability in this chapter is based on the hope that we will gradually replace the current language of disability with a new language of ability that focuses on making sure that no one is denied human rights due to their physical or intellectual abilities. At the same time, it also is important to know that the terms *disability* and *disabled* were first used by people who wanted to replace widely used negative terms such as *freak, deformed, invalid, cripple, gimp, lame, spaz, spastic,* and *handicapped* in reference to people with physical impairments, and *imbecile, idiot, lunatic, demented, retarded, retard,* and *feebleminded* in reference to people with intellectual impairments.

During most of the twentieth century people believed that impairment and disability were same thing. This belief was consistent with the medical model that was and continues to be used to understand physical and intellectual impairments and how to deal with them. This model was challenged during the 1960s as people with disabilities and their advocates promoted a social model of disability that has become increasingly popular in the years since then. The approaches used in each of these two models of disability are explained in Table 10.1.

According to the medical model of disability the goal is to diagnose the origin of a physical or intellectual impairment and then use medical or other

Table 10.1 The medical model and social model: two approaches to disability

Medical Model	Social Model
Personal impairment is the problem	Lack of accommodations is the problem
Physical impairment, lack of sensory function, or intellectual deficit is the problem	are the problem
Disability is caused by physical and intellectual defects that prevent full participation in social and physical environments.	Disability is caused by prejudice, stereotypes, physical barriers, and lack of knowledge about physical and intellectual impairments and how they can be accommodated
Disability is cured by fixing impairments through medical treatment, therapy, or rehabilitation.	Disability is eliminated through accommodations that increase choices and control for people with impairments
A cure depends on access to professionals who use surgery, therapy, and rehabilitation to "normalize" the impaired person	A solution depends on taking political action to eliminate barriers and create accommodations
The effectiveness of a cure depends on the expertise of professionals and the quality of assistive devises and technologies	An effective solution depends on recruiting and organizing allies and executing strategies to influence decision-makers
When having an impairment fixed, the person submits to surgery, therapy, or rehabilitation	In taking political action, the person invests time, energy, other personal resources
Ultimately, people with a disability are responsible for seeking out treatments, therapies, and technologies that will fix their defects and improve their abilities	Ultimately, the community is responsible for facilitating and mandating the elimination of social and physical barriers that disable people with impairments

Explanation for Table 10.1: The medical and social models are based on different conceptions of disability and how to deal with impairments that affect people's lives. This has led people in and working with the disability community along with scholars doing research on disability issues to debate the merits of each model. These debates have clarified the details of each model so that people can make informed choices about when and how to use each of them. Although some people have chosen to accept one model and reject the other, there are times when one or both are appropriate to use; it's not always an either/or choice.

treatments to fix it. If successful, the body or mind is "normalized" and the person becomes able to join or rejoin mainstream society. If not successful, the next alternative was a rehabilitation program to help the person overcome his or her flawed condition to an extent that would permit at least partial participation in society. These medical, therapeutic, and rehabilitative treatments were identified and performed by professionals in their fields, and people with disabilities were passive recipients throughout the process.

The medical model has remained popular for two reasons. First, many people continue to accept ableist ideology and see disability as an individual condition in need of expert diagnosis and treatment. Second, a massive industry has been built around this approach, and it prospers when the primary goal is to fix or rehabilitate bodies and minds. According to the social model, both these reasons ignore the fact that variations in physical and intellectual characteristics and abilities are a natural and normal part of the human condition and that they are converted into disabilities by a combination of negative attitudes, stereotypes, and barrier-filled social arrangements and built environments.

During the 1960s, Mike Oliver, a disability studies scholar in England, joined with disability rights activists to introduce and advocate the use of a social model to conceptualize and understand disability (see Table 10.1). Oliver argued that the experience of being disabled was actually a product of social oppression rather than personal defects that had to be "fixed" for a person to become "normal" (Oliver, 1983, 1990).

Many people with disabilities already considered themselves to be normal and resented being seen as flawed and inferior. From their perspective, impairment was a fact of life but their *dis*ability was caused by the social and cultural responses to their impairments. Therefore, disability became a social issue in need of a political solution more than a personal trouble in need of medical or psychological treatment. The focus on treatment, therapy, and rehabilitation shifted to a focus on political actions that confronted barriers created by negative attitudes, poorly organized and managed social arrangements, and thoughtlessly designed physical environments. The goal implied by the social model was cultural and environmental transformation instead of medical and pharmacological fixes for individuals.

Embracing the social model of disability did not mean that individuals no longer sought medical assistance and treatment to ameliorate the pain or inconvenience caused by impairments. But it did mean that problems caused by disability were seen to be most effectively solved through social and cultural change (Couser, 2009; Oliver, 1983, 1990).

The social model identified barriers as the problem and removing them as the goal. In the decades following the 1960s, this approach unified people in the disability community who shared common experiences of oppression and misrepresentation across all disability categories (Beauchamp-Pryor, 2011; Shakespeare and Watson, 2002). As a result, the social model inspired changes worldwide. Locating disability in culture and society rather than the bodies and minds of individuals shifted the focus from rehabilitation to accessibility, from charity to opportunity, and from risky surgeries to dependable support systems.

As people learned more about disabling barriers built into the structure of everyday life, they called for changes that acknowledged normal variations in human abilities. They realized that they could not eliminate the paralysis caused by a spinal cord injury, but that it was possible to provide physical environments designed to accommodate wheelchairs.

The political activism fueled by the social model was liberating and empowering for people with impairments. To focus on social oppression rather than their own bodies as *the problem* served to legitimize previously repressed anger and boost their sense of self-worth. It was personally fulfilling to fight for rights rather than depending on charity. Most important, their actions led to the passage of new laws mandating accessibility and prohibiting ableism and discrimination. In the United States, the Americans with Disabilities Act (ADA) is a primary example of such a law.

The ADA was passed and signed into law by President George Bush in 1990. It stated that all programs and facilities that are open to everyone must also be open to people with disabilities unless such access creates direct threats to the health and safety of the people involved. When applied to sports this means that people with disabilities must be allowed to participate in programs open to everyone as long as they and the accommodations they require do not threaten the health and safety of other players, cause "undue burden" for the sponsoring organization, or fundamentally change the sport being played (Block, 1995).

Threats to health and safety in sports and other activities must be real, based on objective information, and unavoidable, even after reasonable efforts have been made to eliminate them. For example, if a child wears a metal brace to stabilize a leg impaired by cerebral palsy, she must be allowed to play in a youth soccer league if the brace is designed so it will not hurt anyone and if the league does not have to make burdensome changes or fundamentally alter its game rules to accommodate her participation. Additionally, if tryouts are required for everyone wanting to play in a program, the girl with the brace may not be prohibited from trying out because of her impairment. However, she may be cut if she does not meet the physical skills standards applied to everyone being assessed. The coach may *not* require that all players on the team must run the same way, but she may say that being able and willing to run at a reasonable pace is a standard requirement for team membership.

Unfortunately, the fiscal austerity policy approach that has become common in many countries has undermined many of the hard-won changes inspired by the social model. This situation and criticisms of the model have fragmented the disability community and enabled people with neoliberal political agendas to revive the medical model and its emphasis on the need for people to be personally responsible for making and keeping themselves well. As a result, programs for people with disabilities have been severely cut or eliminated. Even military veterans with severe impairments caused by injuries sustained in recent wars have seen their programs downsized or eliminated. As this continues there are renewed calls for a revival of political action based on the social model (Oliver, 2013; Oliver and Barnes, 2012).

The Meaning of Ability Differences

Before reading this book, what would have happened if you were asked to close your eyes and picture five different sport scenes? Would any of those scenes involved athletes with a disability? Unless you have played disability sports or seen them played by friends or family members, it is unlikely.

This imagination exercise is *not* meant to evoke guilt. Our views of the world are based on personal experiences; and our experiences are influenced by the meanings given to age, gender, race, ethnicity, social class, sexuality, disability, and other socially significant characteristics in our culture. Neither culture nor society forces us to think or do certain things, but the only way to mute their influence is to critically examine them and learn the ways in which cultural meanings and social organization create constraints *and* opportunities in people's lives, including people with a disability. Once we know these things, strategies for disrupting them can be created.

Consider the case of Danny: At the age of 21 he was a popular and highly skilled rugby player. Then came the accident, the amputation of his right arm just below the shoulder, the therapy, and eventually, getting back with friends. But reconnecting with friends after suddenly becoming impaired was not easy. Danny described his experience with these words: "A lot of them found it very difficult . . . to come to terms with it . . . And they found it hard to be around me, friends that I'd had for years" (Brittain, 2004, p. 437; see also Smith, 2013).

Chris, an athlete with cerebral palsy and one of Danny's teammates on the British Paralympic Team, explains why his friends felt uncomfortable: "They have very little knowledge of people with a disability, and they think that if they leave me alone, don't come in contact with me, and don't get involved, its not their problem" (Brittain, 2004, p. 437).

Chris raises a recurring issue in the history of disability: What happens when people define physical or intellectual impairments as "differences" and use them to create a category of "others" who are distinguished from "us normals" in social worlds?

Throughout history, people with disabilities have been described by words that connote revulsion, resentment, dread, shame, and limitations. In Europe and North America, it took World War II and thousands of returning soldiers impaired by injuries to raise widespread concerns about the words used to describe people with disabilities. Language changed. Today, people with intellectual disabilities now have the Special Olympics as a participation option. Elite athletes with physical disabilities may qualify for the Paralympics ("para" meaning *parallel with,* not *paraplegic*). Words like *retard, spaz* (spastic), *cripple, freak, deaf and dumb, handicapped,* and *deformed* have been driven out of favor. But comments such as "She's a quad," "They're amputees," and "What a retard!" can still be heard on occasion.

Improvements have occurred, but when people with a disability are defined as "others," encountering

Living in the Empire of the Normal

Mainstream media images of bodies in contemporary cultures highlight healthy, fit, and traditionally attractive models with no visible impairments. Images of impaired bodies are rare, except in notices for fund-raising events to "help the disabled." Only recently have a few people with physical impairments been positively represented in popular media, and most have been skilled athletes. But this is a typical pattern in the "Empire of the Normal," where people with impaired bodies or minds are exiled to the margins of the Empire and controlled by medical experts and "rehab" programs (Couser, 2000, 2009; Goffman, 1961, 1963).

When residents of the Empire see a person with a visible impairment, they either shy away or ask the person: What happened to you? Why are you this way? [Meaning: Why are you not like me and everyone else in the Empire of the Normal?] Answering these questions is the price of admission into the Empire. Knowing this, people with visible impairments develop "body stories"–narratives that they use to account for their impairment in a manner that prevents them from being exiled before they complete their business in the Empire. But completing business often is difficult because the story must be told again and again and again. As a result, their identity may come to be shaped around their impairment rather than their abilities and other traits (Thomson, 2000, 2009).

When people with visible impairments play sports in the Empire, it is usually on the invitation of an established resident, or on the recommendations of a medical expert–physical therapist, doctor, psychiatrist, or psychologist. In fact, the first version of what we now call Paralympic sports was created in a British medical center for war veterans with spinal cord injuries. Ludwig Guttmann, the neurosurgeon who founded the center, felt that playing sports was effective rehabilitation therapy for patients. When he scheduled these events to be played publicly at the same time that the 1948 Olympic Games were being staged in London, he was described as a radical. His action had disrupted the Empire of the Normal and forced its residents to encounter bodies with serious physical impairments. This violated the Empire norm regarding people with

them often forces people to deal with their own vulnerability, aging, and mortality. And when it challenges their faulty assumptions about normalcy around which they have constructed their identities, it can be very upsetting. Therefore, those who identify themselves as physically and intellectually "normal" often ignore, avoid, or patronize people with a disability. This reproduces ableism and undermines the possibility of abandoning ableist ideology.

The fear of "otherness" is powerful, and people in many cultures traditionally restrict and manage their contact with "others" by enlisting the services of experts as explained in connection with the medical model of disability. These include doctors, mental health workers, psychiatrists, healers, shamans, witch doctors, priests, exorcists, and all professionals whose assumed competence gives them the right to examine, test, classify, and prescribe "normalizing treatments" for "impaired others." Therefore, the history of disability is also the history of giving meaning to difference, creating "others," and using current and limited knowledge to treat "otherness" (Foucault, 1961/1967; Goffman, 1961, 1963).

Disability activist and writer Thomas Couser points out that by defining people with physical and intellectual impairments as *others*, we marginalize them and create for ourselves the illusion that we live in a normal reality. The implications of this are explored in the Reflect on Sports box "Living in the Empire of the Normal."

Media Constructions of *Dis*Ability

Disability sports receive little media coverage apart from the Paralympic Games, which may receive limited coverage in newspapers and television programming. World championships and other major events receive no mainstream media coverage a disability. The norm, "Out of sight, out of mind," had always been respected in the past (Brittain, 2012).

It is rare for people with physical or intellectual impairments to play sports in the Empire because there is a shortage of accessible opportunities, resources for transportation, adapted equipment, knowledgeable coaches, and programs designed to support their achievement and success. Even when opportunities are available, decisions to participate are influenced by responses anticipated from residents of the Empire: How will they define my body? Will they treat me as an athlete or patronize me as a courageous cripple?

Research indicates that people identified as *disabled* define and give meaning to their sports participation as they integrate sports experiences into their lives. When their participation is treated by people from the Empire as trivial or "second class," they may develop self-doubt and a sense of inferiority. Patronizing and artificial praise create anger, disappointment, and loneliness. But when people are genuinely supportive, take players' participation seriously, and appreciate their skills, it builds confidence and confirms a sense of normalcy, which usually is fragile and unstable in the confines of the Empire.

Athletes with physical impairments often are discouraged from playing with or alongside athletes residing in the Empire. Instead, they play in "special" programs with others like them, and this influences the meanings they give to their experiences.

In recent years, athletes with physical or intellectual disabilities have seen their sports as sites for challenging dominant body images and expectations in the Empire of the Normal. Developing sport skills, many hope, is a way to break through the walls of the Empire and discredit residents who accept ableist ideology and believe that until impaired bodies are fixed and made normal they should not play in the Empire (Thomson, 2002).

At this point in time, it is difficult to say that residents of the Empire will abandon arrangements that privilege them in a manner they've come to expect. So what will it take for the Empire to pull down its walls and work to achieve inclusion? *What do you think?*

(Brown & Pappous, 2018). People who make programming decisions for commercial media assume that covering disability sports is a money-losing proposition. Additionally, most media people have never played or even seen disability sports, and they lack the words and experiences that would enable them to provide coverage that might build a media audience. This creates a situation in which there is tension between commercial interests that prefer a "super-crip" approach and the athletes who prefer an ability-based approach (Purdue, 2013; Purdue & Howe, 2015).

Research shows that when disability sports have been covered in mainstream media, athletes often are portrayed as "courageous victims" or "heroic supercrips" who engage in *inspiring* athletic performances (Rival, 2015; Pullen et al., 2019; Schantz and Gilbert, 2012; Silva and Howe, 2012; Tynedal and Wolbring, 2013). Sociologist Ian Brittain (2004) analyzed this coverage and found that media images and narratives usually fell into one of the following categories:

Patronizing: "Aren't they marvelous!"
Curiosity: "Do you think she can really do that?"
Tragedy: "On that fateful day, his life was changed forever."
Inspiration: "She's a true hero and a model for all of us."
Mystification: "I can't believe he just did that!"
Pity: "Give her a hand for trying so hard."
Surprise: "Stay tuned to see physical feats you've never imagined!"

Images and narratives organized around these themes construct disability in terms of the medical model. They focus on personal impairments that must be overcome. This leads people to ignore *why* particular social meanings are given to disabilities and *how* they shape the lives of people with specific impairments (Bartsch et al., 2018). As a result, media coverage often perpetuates the ableist belief that disabilities are abnormalities.

Media coverage of the 2012 Paralympics in London highlighted certain technologies used by athletes (Wolbring, 2012b). Artificial "running legs" and the athletes who used them were covered as if they were new models of race cars and drivers. But wheelchairs received less coverage and the athletes using them were regularly described as "wheelchair *bound*" rather than wheelchair users. The inference in this coverage was that wheelchairs were confining, whereas the artificial legs were liberating, even transforming. For the commentators viewing these devices from their vantage point in the empire of the normal, this is not surprising. Sleek, efficient legs were for them supernormalizing, whereas the wheelchair, even a $10,000 racing chair, remained an indicator of disability through ableist eyes.

Carla Silva and David Howe at Loughborough University in England were led to similar conclusions by their research (Silva and Howe, 2012). They found that media coverage of Paralympic athletes often represented them as "supercrips" who have overcome astonishing odds to do what they do. This was also true in two promotional media campaigns they analyzed–one in Portugal and one in the United Kingdom. The former focused on Portuguese *Superatleta*–"super athletes"–and used a Superman "S" in the campaign logo. Media ads depicted a person in a wheelchair negotiating his way around an illegally parked car that blocked sidewalk access–as if disability mysteriously infused power into his body. The UK campaign was titled *Freaks of Nature,* and it was launched by a major commercial television company wanting to hype the "staggering ability" of Paralympic athletes at the upcoming 2012 Paralympic Games.

Both campaigns created controversies. Silva and Howe explain that this wasn't surprising, because there is little consensus on how to represent disability in sport events. In the absence of public discourse about the meaning of disability and the experiences of people who face disability in their everyday lives, media people did not know how to talk about it, much less present it to a commercial television audience seeking entertainment.

Silva and Howe fear that the supercrip narratives currently used when covering the Paralympics may reaffirm the neoliberal ableist idea that it is up to people with disabilities to overcome them on their own so they can live normal lives like "the rest of us." Alternatively, Silva and Howe hope that future coverage will represent Paralympic athletes with a narrative emphasizing that physical difference is a naturally occurring phenomenon that creates for each of us an opportunity to accommodate those differences in ways that make our families, schools, communities, and societies more humane and inclusive.

The Special Olympics for people with intellectual disabilities presents a slightly different challenge to journalists and commentators, because events are organized as competitive at the same time that they emphasize the importance of participation over winning. For example, a study of the television news coverage of the 2009 National Special Olympics in Great Britain found that commentators used complex and "mixed" messages in their representations of the event (Carter and Williams, 2012). They sustained a relentlessly "positive" tone in their comments, focused on human interest stories, ignored larger social and political issues related to disabilities, and tended to become emotional and use words like *courageous* and *inspirational* when they interviewed family members of the athletes. However, the researchers stated that the commentators did a reasonably good job, given that they had little experience or training preparing them to discuss learning disability issues or to interview people with varying intellectual abilities.

Despite misguided media representations, most athletes with a disability will accept coverage containing misrepresentations over no coverage. Like other athletes, they want to be acknowledged for their physical competence. But they also hope that their visibility and accomplishments will challenge traditional stereotypes and make people aware of issues related to ableism and the need for inclusion in all spheres of society. For this to occur, and to avoid replacing negative stereotypes with a similarly unrealistic supercrip stereotype, people in the media need guidance to provide coverage that accurately represents the lives of participants.

Gendering *Dis*Ability

In cultures where femininity is associated with physical attractiveness and sexual desirability, and masculinity is associated with power and strength, gender shapes the ways people negotiate the meaning of physical disabilities in their lives (Richard et al., 2017; Thompson & Langendoerfer, 2016). This is illustrated in the following stories about Anna, Nick, and Mark, all of whom have participated in research projects on disability.

Anna was born with underdeveloped arms and feet. Despite encouragement and support from a close friend, she resisted going to the gym and becoming involved in sports. She explained her resistance in the following way:

> I really wanted to go–inside, I was dying to be physical, to have a go at "pumping iron"... But at the time I just couldn't say yes . . . I was too ashamed of my body. . . . It was the same thing with swimming. I just couldn't bear the thought of people looking at me. I felt really vulnerable (Hargreaves, 2000, p. 187).

Anna's fear of her body being seen and judged is not unique. Negotiating the meanings that we and others give to our bodies is a complex and challenging process. Women who accept dominant gender ideology often make choices that reduce sports participation. For example, a young woman with an amputated leg might choose a prosthesis that is natural looking, rather than one that is more functional and better suited to playing sports. As one woman explained, "It's one thing to see a man with a Terminator leg . . . . It may inspire people to say, 'Cool.' But body image for women in this country is model thin and long sexy legs" (Marriott, 2005).[1]

Nick, a 20-year-old American college student whose legs had to be amputated after he contracted a rare bacterial disease when he was fourteen, agrees with this explanation. He wears Terminator legs and loves them. He points out that whenever his legs run short on their charge, he doesn't hesitate to plug them into the nearest electrical outlet.

Even though Nick has no problem with people seeing his "Terminator legs," he and other men with a disability face a challenge when negotiating the meaning of masculinity in the face of a disabling physical impairment. This is especially true in the case of men who accept a gender ideology that ties masculinity to physical strength and the ability to outperform or dominate others. An example is provided by Mark.

As a young man whose legs were paralyzed by an accident, Mark explains that his ideas about masculinity make dealing with his impairment especially difficult. For example, after filling his car with fuel and putting his wheelchair in the back, his car had an ignition problem and Mark could not start the engine. A man waiting for the pump impatiently honked his horn and shouted obscenities out his window. Mark said that before his accident he would have turned around, walked back, and "laid him out." Being unable to do so led him to say, "Now I'm useless . . . my manhood has been shattered" (Sparkes and Smith, 2002, p. 269).

Although Mark did not use the same words that Anna used, each felt vulnerable due to cultural definitions of gender. Some men with a disability who feel vulnerable might, like Anna, avoid participating in sports, whereas others might view sports as sites for asserting or reaffirming their masculinity.

Sociologists Smith and Sparkes (2002) point out that people create their identities, including

[1]"Terminator leg" is how some people refer to the cyborg-like appearance of hi-tech, battery-powered prosthetic legs that have *not* been disguised to look like flesh and bone, so-called after the cybernetic character played by Arnold Schwarzenegger in the 1984 film *The Terminator* and its many sequels.

gender identities, through narratives–that is, the stories that show and tell others about themselves. Their research indicates that playing power and performance sports is consistent with a narrative in which manhood is constructed through physical accomplishments and dominance over other men (Rugoho, 2020).

(*Source:* Courtesy of the Challenged Athletes Foundation, http://www.challengedathletes.org)

A visible impairment often arouses curiosity and leads others to ask, "What happened [to you to make you different from 'normal' people]?" People with physical impairments answer this question with a story that explains "why my body is different from your body." If this occurs regularly, identity may become linked with impairment and it becomes difficult to be recognized for more meaningful and important dimensions of self. To be known primarily in connection with impairment creates limitations and loneliness–it is *disabling*. Having older role models helps deal with this issue.

When traditional gender narratives are not critically assessed, and when alternative or oppositional narratives are not available, both women and men with certain physical impairments will experience challenges related to ability and participation in sports. Women might avoid participation for fear that their bodies will be seen as unfeminine, and men might avoid participation for fear that they will not be able to assert themselves and overpower other men. Therefore, anyone dealing with physical impairment and disability benefits by having access to counter-narratives that construct gender in more inclusive terms.

When there are multiple ways to be a woman or a man, people with visible disabilities have more options for negotiating the meanings that they and others give to their bodies (Sparkes et al., 2018). This was documented in a study of women wheelchair users playing sledge hockey, wheelchair basketball, and table tennis (Apelmo, 2012). The women challenged stereotypical notions of gender in sport by displaying determination, strength, and risk taking, while simultaneously embodying a more traditional femininity in resisting the widespread view of disabled women as non-gendered and asexual. Such an approach might enable women like Anna to become more physical and have a go at pumping iron, and it might enable Mark to accept help without feeling that he is sacrificing his manhood in the process.

SPORTS AND ABILITY

Sports are often at the center of inclusion battles involving people with impairments. As highly visible and culturally valued activities, participation in sports can be self-affirming and a means of gaining social acceptance with peers and in society generally. Because people usually see participation as a character-building experience, it is especially important for people with a disability because their character is often questioned as people see physical and intellectual impairments as marks of "flawed individuals." But sports are usually organized to be ability exclusive, so people with a disability are pushed to the sidelines without opportunities to discover, nurture, and extend their abilities through a potentially confidence-building activity.

Activists have worked at regional, national, and global levels for a number of years to make sport participation a right for all people, including those with a disability (Berghs et al., 2020). This influenced passage of the 2006 UN Convention on the Rights of Persons with Disabilities, which placed sports among the usual activities of citizenship and led to calls for accessibility in sports venues, increased funding, supportive policies, appropriate programs, effective disability organizations, and the involvement of people with a disability in positions of power and influence in sports organizations.

Despite the pronouncements of the UN and other international organizations, progress has been slow and the barriers to overcome many. For example, there are few opportunities for people to learn how to teach physical skills development that is age- and ability-appropriate for children and teens with various physical impairments. Few gyms and other sports facilities are fully accessible, and the public transportation to and from those venues may not be convenient for people with impaired mobility. Overprotective family members and a lack of family resources also discourage participation.

Even though there are public concerns about opportunities for people with disabilities, there are few advocates with the power and influence to mandate the elimination of barriers and create programs that are welcoming and staffed with experts trained to facilitate sport participation among people with a range of different impairments. At this time, there are one-time opportunities in many communities, but these have little impact unless they are followed up with regularly scheduled programs.

These barriers are common worldwide, but they are especially prominent in developing countries where resources are scarce and few people listen to the voices of people with impairments (Bickenbach, 2011; WHO, 2011). As disability rights activists have won incremental success in wealthy, democratic countries, there is a widening gap between the life chances of disabled people in poor versus wealthy countries. Physical education and sport-for-all programs are luxuries that can seldom be afforded in much of the world, where access isn't even an issue because sport facilities and programs don't exist. Additionally, most people with physical or intellectual impairments in poor countries must focus all their personal energy and time on survival.

Religion, culture, language, and the lingering influence of colonialism may also create barriers in many parts of the world. At this point there is limited research investigating the dynamics of disability in regions where poverty, political instability, and wars have undermined possibilities for organized sports, including disability sports. However, in those areas sports may exist sporadically in spaces created by sport for development programs or local collections of people, mostly boys or men seeking opportunities to play (see http://archive.noorimages.com/series/1.34; see also, Berghs et al., 2020).

Exclusion and Inclusion

From a sociological perspective, processes of exclusion and inclusion always involve power relations. The situations in which these processes occur are organized around norms and traditions that influence or determine who is welcome and who is not. Norms and power relations also influence interaction between those who are included, and the conditions under which they can participate.

Exclusion and inclusion can occur formally or informally. For example, students in wheelchairs in US high schools know that they are excluded from tryouts for the school basketball team just as they have been informally excluded by their peers who play intramurals and pickup games after school. Norms and expectations have been developed by officials in schools located in the Empire of the Normal. For them, sports for students with a disability are an "extra"—something out of the ordinary, something that would disrupt the schedules of "normal" students and require coaches to have specialized knowledge that they currently lack.

For these reasons, only a handful of US secondary schools and universities have sports for students using wheelchairs or in need of adaptive equipment. Although the National Federation of State High School Associations (NFHS) and the National Collegiate Athletic Association (NCAA) give token recognition to sports for athletes with a disability, the exclusion of disabled students from school sports is systemic, pervasive, and often illegal.

Young people with a disability generally have only two options if they wish to play sports: find an organized adapted sports program, or play informal games in which peers are willing and able to develop adaptations. Few communities have adapted youth sport programs, and informal games seldom include young people with the skills needed to make accommodations for a peer with a disability. The dilemma this presents was noted by a ten-year-old boy with cerebral palsy when he said that other kids like him, "but . . . if I'm trying to get in a game without a friend, it's kind of hard" (in Taub and Greer, 2000, p. 406). In other words, without a friend who has enough power with peers and enough experience with physical or intellectual impairments to facilitate a process of adaptation and inclusion, this ten-year-old does not play sports.

Unless these opportunities occur, children with a disability miss opportunities to make friends and participate in activities that have "normalizing" effects in cultures where sports are contexts for gaining social acceptance and self-validation. A young person with cerebral palsy expressed the importance of these opportunities in this way (in Taub and Greer, 2000, pp. 406, 408):

> [Playing games] makes me feel good 'cause I get to be with everybody . . . [We can] talk about how our day was in school while we play. Playing basketball is something that I can do with my friends that I never thought I could do [with them], but I can, I can!

Responses to Exclusion When people lack power, they usually respond to systemic and pervasive exclusion with resignation or by seeking contexts in which they feel welcome. Sometimes they find support by aligning themselves with others who have been excluded, or they might accept isolation and the self-doubts that accompany it. Over time, those who are excluded become invisible. In the case of students with a disability, this occurs regularly.

(*Source:* Claudio Echeverria)

Disability and being defined as physically or intellectually different are not the same thing. Achondroplasia, or dwarfism, occurs when a child is born with one dwarfism gene and one non-dwarfism gene. Some people in the little peoples' community say that dwarfism is a disability because it often involves spinal cord impairments and because discrimination is so pervasive. Others say that simply having a short stature should not be considered a disability. However, because they are routinely excluded, little people (LP) have formed their own sport programs and championships so they will have opportunities to participate such as this 5-on-5 indoor soccer tournament.

Students with a disability seldom see themselves participating in school sports. For example, when Bob Szyman left his position as secretary general of the International Wheelchair Basketball Federation (IWBF) to teach special education and physical education in Chicago, his goal was to establish a wheelchair basketball league for city high schools. But his biggest challenge was finding students and parents who were excited about such a league. Students with disabilities had no expectations, and there was no wheelchair sport culture in the schools. Additionally, there were no administrators, teachers, or coaches asking why there were no "paravarsity teams" in their district or schools. When Szyman, who now teaches at Chicago State University, organized wheelchair sports camps and competitions, the participants went out of their way to thank him, but they didn't ask why their schools had no sports programs for them. They were so accustomed to exclusion that they had no expectations to be included. Szyman has had some success in establishing adaptive sport opportunities, but an official high school league has not been organized.

Another way of responding to exclusion is illustrated by Tatiana McFadden, who has won 16 Paralympic medals in wheelchair racing and one in a sprint sitting cross-country skiing event. She has won the wheelchair division in 24 marathons, including those in London, New York, Chicago, and Boston—even winning all four of those major marathons in the same year (2013). She adds those accomplishments to her twenty World Championship medals (McCoy, 2019).

McFadden was born in Russia. Both of her legs were paralyzed due to spina bifida, and her mother, who had no means of caring for Tatiana, left her in an orphanage, where she used only her hands to scoot around for the first six years of her life. Near death, Tatiana was noticed by Deborah McFadden, a US Department of Health official who was visiting Russian facilities. McFadden adopted her and used sports to help strengthen her. At eight years old, Tatiana began racing in her wheelchair. But when she went to high school, she was told she could not participate on the track team because her chair gave her an advantage over other runners and was a danger to them as they raced. This left her to train and race alone in "special competitions"— experiences that were meaningless and embarrassing.

Tatiana knew her rights, and she sued the school district and won the right to race on the track with runners, although her time did not count for her team. When she graduated, she went to the University of Illinois at Urbana-Champaign, where she could train in a disability sports program—among the best of only a few university programs. Today she is known as the top woman wheelchair distance racer in the world as well as an activist who fights for disability rights in sports.

The Emerging Meaning of Inclusion *Inclusion* is the new buzzword today in organizations and communities where various forms of diversity are common. However, people often use the term without knowing that it means other than simply removing a few obvious barriers. They don't understand that hanging up a "Now Open to All" sign after years of systemic exclusion will not bring about real inclusion.

Social inclusion is a complex process involving the following actions (Donnelly and Coakley, 2002):

- Investments and strategies that create the conditions for inclusion by closing physical and social distances and resource gaps that lead people to think in terms of *us* and *them*
- Creating contexts in which previously excluded people can see that they are valued, respected, and contributing members of a group or community
- A proactive, developmental approach to social well-being in which people are supported in connection with their needs
- Recognition of the reality of diversity as well as the commonality of people's lived experiences and shared aspirations

This means that achieving and sustaining inclusion requires sensitivity, knowledge, experience, and hard work. It is an ongoing process rather than a goal to be achieved once and for all time. When people forget to sustain the process, backsliding to previous forms of exclusion is likely.

Inclusion of people with disabilities is mandated in the United States by the 1973 Rehabilitation Act. Similar to the mandate for gender equity brought about by Title IX (see Chapter 7), this Act applied to all programs receiving federal aid and stated that people with disabilities could not be denied benefits or opportunities received by other citizens. As with Title IX, it was not fully enforced because officials in schools and agencies claimed that they didn't understand it. This led to the passage in 1990 of the ADA, which mandated access and equity in more specific terms and applied to private as well as public facilities. For example, access was an issue when a building had stairs but no elevator, when streets had curbs that prevented wheelchair mobility, when there were no ramps to doorways and walkways, and when restrooms and toilets were clearly impossible to use by people using a wheelchair. "Access" issues were usually easy to see, but equity was another matter. Those who objected to making changes continued to claim they didn't know what "equity" meant.

After the US Government Accountability Office issued a research report showing that students with a disability were generally denied an equal opportunity to participate in school sports programs and therefore denied the health and social benefits of athletic participation, US Education Secretary Arne Duncan issued an equity "guideline" letter in January 2013 (Duncan, 2013; Resmovits, 2013). It told all school officials that because "sports can provide invaluable lessons in discipline, selflessness, passion, and courage," they must make sure that "students with disabilities have an equal opportunity to benefit from the life lessons they can learn on the playing field or on the court" (see Galanter, 2013). Secretary Duncan also provided specific examples of the types of "reasonable modifications" that officials must consider in connection with "existing policies, practices, or procedures for students with intellectual, developmental, physical, or any other type of disability." Examples included the following:

- Using a visual cue in addition to a starter pistol so that students with a hearing impairment who are who make the track team can compete.
- Waiving a rule requiring a "two-hand-touch" finish in swim events so that a one-armed swimmer with the requisite ability can participate at swim meets.

This letter created panic among officials who saw nothing but problems in making such accommodations. But it gave hope to students previously excluded from sports because they had a physical or intellectual impairment. Therefore, a process of inclusion that began in 1973 is taken slightly more seriously today, after more than four decades of resistance to change.

Education is only one sphere in which inclusion is an issue. Community officials must also consider what inclusion means for their park and recreation programs. Officials in youth sports have seldom thought about these issues and many of them continue to struggle with the meaning of inclusion for their policies and programs.

DISABILITY SPORTS

When disability is viewed as a weaknesses or defect that makes a person inferior to others, it is important to have a strategy to normalize one's body in the eyes of others. For example, it does not take long for children with a visible impairment to realize that others see them as different. Over time they learn that it is difficult to predict how people, including their age peers, will perceive and treat them. If they have a supportive family and friends they will learn to see themselves in terms of their abilities rather than their impairment. Their impairment doesn't become irrelevant but they learn to live with and around it.

Research by Higgins et al. (2002) found that individuals who underwent this transformation process were more likely to accept themselves in ways that enabled them to move ahead with other forms of development. However, not all people with an impairment experience this transformation.

When Ben Quilter was seven years old, he took up judo in order to take part in the same sport as his brother. By the time he was twelve he was competing in regional and national competitions. But then Ben's eyesight began to deteriorate, and at age 16 he was categorized as a visually impaired competitor. The rules of judo are adapted for visually impaired participants so that they start bouts "gripped up" with their opponent, and there are some changes to the judo ring. However, Ben explains that these changes are sufficiently minor to allow visually impaired and sighted athletes to train and compete with each other. Also, the organization and funding of judo is similar for sighted and visually impaired athletes. In 2008, Ben was selected for the Paralympic Team for the Beijing Games, and the team was announced at the same press launch as the judo team for the Olympic Games. Ben won a bronze medal in the London 2012 Paralympic Games and said that in judo "everything's the same, just train full time with the guys, I'm treated like everyone else really, you wouldn't even know that I had a visual problem."

Ben's experience in judo is an example of how sports can be organized so that people with disabilities are treated on equal terms with other athletes. A related example is the Disability Sports Events (DSE), established in 1961. Based in England, the DSE sponsors competitions in a range of sports for people with any impairment at any age It also hosts a "mini games" multi-sport event for children six to 12 years old. The events include a series of inclusive sports and games to encourage young people with various impairments to become involved in sports. Other young people and volunteers are available to assist athletes if the need arises. One of the sports included is Zonal Tag Rugby, an adapted form of rugby in which participants with various impairments participate and compete in a safe and challenging sporting competition. However, DSE receives no government funding, and its future is not certain.

The kind of idealism seen in these examples is heartening to those who know young people who seek sports programs that are organized to be inclusive. It is also heartening to the thousands of veterans returning from battlefields with amputated limbs, sight and hearing impairments, and injuries that impede or prohibit walking. Making sports accessible to them would seem to be a no-brainer, even among those who lack idealism. As veterans return to communities, universities, gyms, parks, and workplaces, idealism combined with creative accommodations are essential if barriers are to be eliminated.

Paralympics: Sports for People with Physical Disabilities

Today's Paralympic Games were first conceived by Ludwig Guttmann, a neurosurgeon and director of Stoke Mandeville, a British medical center for war veterans with spinal cord injuries. When he first came to the center in 1943, he was horrified by the way military veterans were treated. With severe paralysis due to war-related spinal cord injuries, they were merely kept alive without movement or hope. Guttmann came up with the idea that sports could be used as a form of therapy that would enhance the quality of life for his patients.

Guttmann was a strong advocate for his patients and felt that they had been pushed to the periphery of the empire of the normal so that people could avoid facing the reality of their impaired bodies. When the 1948 Olympic Games were scheduled to open in London, Guttmann decided that he could bring recognition to his patients and to the success of his therapeutic approach by scheduling a public display of wheelchair archery and the javelin throw on the same day as the opening of the Olympics. Sixteen people with spinal cord injuries participated.

Guttmann's event received no publicity, but he was energized by its impact on the veterans and he foresaw a time when athletes with disabilities would compete alongside Olympic athletes. He hosted nine "annual" Stoke Mandeville Games, which in 1952 began to attract a few veterans from outside of England. In 1960 during the week after the Olympic Games were held in Rome, Guttmann and others hosted 400 competitors in Rome at the first *Parallel Olympics.* Most of the athletes, who competed in eight different events, were military veterans with spinal cord injuries (Brittain, 2012a).

Following the event in Rome, the Parallel Olympics was renamed the *Paralympic Games,* which have been held every four years after 1960, with the first Winter Paralympics held in Sweden in 1976. The Summer and Winter Paralympic Games have grown in scope and popularity, largely due to efforts of people who have worked to nurture and sustain them through significant financial and political challenges.

The mission of the Paralympics is to enable athletes with disabilities to achieve sporting excellence and to inspire and excite the world. Additionally, the hope is to make a better world for all people with physical impairments by challenging the negative attitudes and stereotypes that are significant barriers to the full inclusion of people with disabilities in all spheres of society.

Despite intertwined histories and some shared values, the relationship between the Olympic and Paralympic movements has been complicated and tension-filled. For example, in 1983 IOC president Juan Antonio Samaranch told representatives of Paralympic athletes and disability sport organizations that they could no longer use Olympic images, including the "Olympic rings," at any of their events. The Olympics, explained Samaranch, was a global brand with its own commercial interests and goals, and this meant that the IOC would take legal action against anyone using its logo and other symbols. Even the Olympic flag, he told them, was a licensed logo, and it could be used only by those who paid for the right to do so (Jennings, 1996a).

Disability sports organizations and their athletes did not want to split from the IOC, so they focused on organizing the Paralympic Games that would follow the 1984 Olympics in Los Angeles. But neither the Los Angeles Olympic Organizing Committee nor the US Olympic Committee (USOC) would support them and their event. So they were forced to hold smaller simultaneous events in New York and Stoke Mandeville, England. At the same time, they formed the International Coordinating Committee of World Organizations for the Disabled (ICC) and made it the governing body for the Paralympic Games.

Dr. Jens Bromann, who had once competed in sports for blind athletes, guided disability sports through this challenging period and was elected president of the new ICC. His efforts, along with support from Korean Olympic officials, made the 1988 Paralympic Games a huge success. Held after the 1988 Olympics in Seoul, Korea, the Paralympics brought together more than 3000 athletes from sixty-one nations. At the opening ceremonies, the Korean organizers presented Bromann a flag they had designed specifically for the Korean Paralympic Games. It was white and had five *tae geuks,* or traditional Korean line symbols, that resembled teardrops in the same positions and colors as the five interlocking rings on the Olympic flag (see image A in Figure 10.2). This design was used to show the connection between the Paralympics and the Olympic movement, and that Paralympic athletes train and compete as Olympic athletes do.

The new Paralympic logo and flag infuriated executives at the IOC because they thought it infringed on their five-rings logo. To appease the IOC, a new logo was launched at the 1994 IPC World Championships (see image B in Figure 10.2). The tae geuks again appeared as teardrops, but officials explained that they now represented the Paralympic motto: "Mind, Body, and Spirit." This flag was used through the 2004 Paralympic Games in Athens. In 2008, after the IPC and IOC resolved many of their differences and agreed to hold events in the same host cities, the IPC adopted a new symbol and flag to represent the unique purpose and identity of the Paralympic Games (see image C in Figure 10.2). It consisted of three elements in red, blue, and green—the colors most often used in national flags. The elements are known as *Agitos* (a Latin word meaning, *I move*), and they appear to be in motion around a central point, representing a dynamic, global "Spirit in Motion"—the new motto of the Paralympics.

The Spirit in Motion flag was first used at the 2008 Paralympics in Beijing, and the IOC did not object. At this point, the "one bid, one city" agreement has been successful, but tensions remain between the two organizations as they compete for sponsors, funding, and media coverage.

Today the IPC uses a commercial approach similar to the one used by the IOC. Its flag is now a licensed logo—like the IOC flag. But this change raises questions about who will benefit from and be hurt by the commercialization of elite disability sports. Athletes who can attract spectators and sponsors will certainly benefit, but will a focus on these top performers inspire sports participation among people with a disability or will it turn them into spectators? Will people

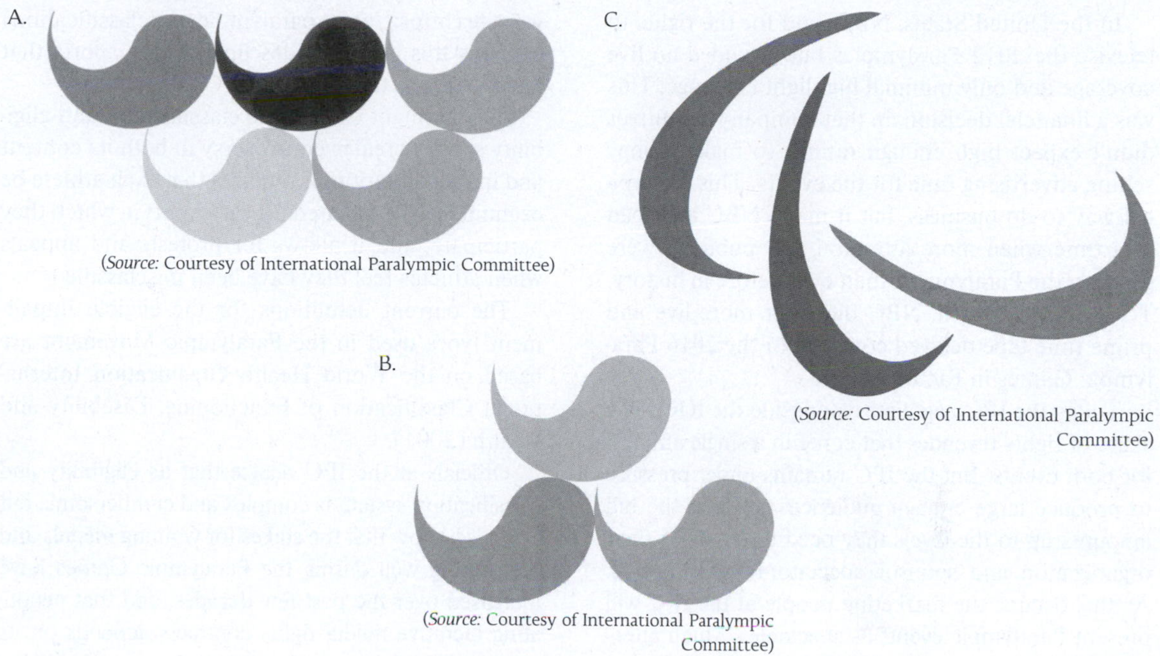

(*Source:* Courtesy of International Paralympic Committee)

(*Source:* Courtesy of International Paralympic Committee)

(*Source:* Courtesy of International Paralympic Committee)

FIGURE 10.1 Logos used on Paralympic flags in 1988 (A), 1994 (B), and today (C). These three logos have been used by the Paralympics in response to IOC demands that they not use any image that could be compared to the five-rings Olympic logo and flag. The five-teardrops flag and logo (A) was used in Seoul, Korea in 1988; the three-teardrops flag and logo (B) was used from 1994 through 2004, and the Spirit in Motion flag and logo (C) was used at the Beijing Paralympic Games in 2008.

be inclined to donate money to support only elite athletes, or will the Paralympics open doors so that people with a disability are seen as deserving the same opportunities received by others? Research on the impact of media coverage of the Paralympic Games provides answers to these and related questions.

Media Coverage of the Paralympic Games Now that the IPC has adopted a commercial model, its survival depends heavily on the sale of media rights to events. As we will see in Chapter 11, this shifts the focus from the athletes to spectators and sponsors, and it alters the orientations of those who plan, program, and manage events. Storylines are needed to attract spectators. Individual athletes must be highlighted to keep people interested in who they are and how they perform. The drama and excitement of particular events is crucial, and this must be the focus of marketing.

The Paralympics have never been a highly rated media event and have received little media attention in the past. However, there was a concerted attempt to change this with the 2012 games in London. The media in the United Kingdom covered the Paralympics at an unprecedented level, devoting to it over 150 hours of live television coverage on a primary channel with additional coverage on three cable channels and two major radio channels. The Australian Broadcasting Company provided 100 hours of live coverage, including the opening and closing ceremonies. Media companies in Canada provided nearly 600 hours of live coverage through four online streams along with a daily one-hour highlight program on major English- and French-language channels.

In the United States, NBC paid for the rights to televise the 2012 Paralympics but provided no live coverage and only minimal highlight coverage. This was a financial decision, in that company executives didn't expect high enough ratings to make money selling advertising time for the events. This is a typical way to do business, but it made NBC look bad at a time when more attention and publicity were given to the Paralympics than ever before in history. To regain good will, NBC did offer more live and prime time tape delayed coverage of the 2016 Paralympic Games in Rio de Janeiro.

Today the IPC negotiates alongside the IOC for a share of rights revenues that come in a single amount for both events. But the IPC remains under pressure to produce large enough audiences to drive the bid amounts up to the levels they need to maintain their organization and sponsor spectator-friendly events. As this occurs, the marketing people at the IPC will present Paralympic events as spectacles. Much attention will be given to popular athletes, high-tech prostheses such as the carbon-fiber legs worn by runners, events where athletes will inspire awe and amazement, and medal counts for countries.

Attempts to market the Paralympics as a spectacle are met with widespread criticism (Howe & Silva, 2018). Many people object to commercialization and what it means for disability sports. Market forces determine who is funded, which countries win medals, and specific aspects of media coverage. Media companies that buy the rights to the Paralympics and to world championships may hype "bionic athletes" and high-tech prostheses that will catch the attention of spectators. At the same time, the IPC faces the challenge of revising its classification and eligibility system so that fair competitions are guaranteed.

Classification Issues Creating fair competition has always been a primary challenge for those who organize disability sports. Variations in physical impairments are nearly infinite, and the full impact of impairments is unique to each individual competitor. This means that each sport has its own rules for determining how athletes are classified and grouped into competition categories. The IPC Classification website (https://www.paralympic.org/classification) explains this and provides links to the sports that have events in the Paralympic Games.

As you might expect, the classification and eligibility system creates controversy in both its content and implementation. It requires that each athlete be examined and evaluated for each sport in which they participate, and it allows for protests and appeals when athletes feel they have been misclassified.

The current definitions for the eligible impairment types used in the Paralympic Movement are based on the World Health Organization International Classification of Functioning, Disability and Health (2001).

Officials at the IPC realize that its eligibility and classification system is complex and cumbersome, but they also know that the stakes for winning medals and performing well during the Paralympic Games have increased over the past few decades, and that negotiating lucrative media rights contracts depends on its ability to stage events that are understandable for a global audience.

The biggest problem with any eligibility and classification system that might be used by the IPC is that it will always favor athletes in wealthier nations. Participation in disability sports is especially expensive because it often requires special transportation arrangements, adaptive equipment, and specialized coaches, trainers, medical personnel, and training venues. Therefore, medal counts will always reflect average per capita income for participants' countries–a pattern more pronounced in the Paralympics than in the Olympic Games.

Special Olympics: Sports for People with Intellectual Disabilities

In 1968 the International Olympic Committee granted Eunice Kennedy Shriver permission to use the word "Olympics" for a sporting event that would offer adults and children with an intellectual disability year-round training and competitions in Olympic-type sports (Foote and Collins, 2011). Today the Special Olympics is a multifaceted global organization that sponsors research, builds support

(*Source:* Paul Harvey IV)

Special Olympics provides opportunities for people who are intellectually disabled. Participants range in age and they often befriend volunteers at the events. The challenge for Special Olympics is to create strategies for sustaining those relationships so they carry over to other community settings. This is why they created Unified Sports, an inclusive program in which teams consist of relatively equal numbers of participants with and without intellectual disability. The goal is to create relationships and mentoring that occur outside of the events.

communities, and offers health education programs. But its primary purpose is to offer people with an intellectual disability "continuing opportunities to develop physical fitness, demonstrate courage, experience joy and participate in a sharing of gifts, skills and friendship with their families, other Special Olympics athletes and the community" (https://www.specialolympics.org/about/our-mission).

Some local groups and organizations sponsor and manage sport programs for people with an intellectual disability, but the Special Olympics stands out in terms of its size and influence. It sponsors 50,000 competitions a year—136 each day—around the world. About 7500 athletes from 190 nations participated in 24 sports during the 2019 World Summer Games in Abu Dhabi and Dubai (United Arab Emirates). The Special Olympics World Games are held every two years, alternating with summer and winter events.

As an organization, the Special Olympics raises funds and organizes events more efficiently than most NGOs in the world. But it has been criticized for organizing its programs in ways that reinforce negative stereotypes and ableist ideology (Storey, 2004, 2008). Participants in the programs don't learn functional skills that are transferable to their lives in the community, they are treated in paternalistic ways by volunteers and spectators, they are not connected with people who can advocate their interests or be their friends after events are over, and there is no evidence that their lives are changed in any significant ways because of their participation.

In response to these criticisms, people managing the Special Olympics recently developed Unified Sports, a global program in which people with an intellectual disability are paired with teammates from the general community in competitive, developmental, or recreational sports, depending on their interests. The program is designed to facilitate friendships and inclusion in the larger community and enable individuals with impairments to engage with others on the basis of their abilities. The Unified Sports program is based

(*Source:* Jay Coakley)

This is one of the Unified teams at a high school in Colorado. A small but growing number of school districts in the United States are using the Unified sports model from the Special Olympics to organize their own teams across one or more sports. This team is successful in that relationships formed between teammates do carry over into the school. But carryover to realms outside of the school is rare.

on research and theory, and it is revised as evaluation research identifies weaknesses and strengths.

When it was created in 1968, the goal of Special Olympics was to provide dedicated spaces and activities for people who at that time were feared, ridiculed, mistreated, and usually cut off from the empire of the normal. It managed to accomplish this goal, but it had no strategy for systematically engaging participants in the larger community or preparing the community to include people with an intellectual disability into everyday activities so they could live more independently.

Today the organization is actively addressing these oversights while retaining its traditional programs for people who need more direct support and assistance. However, most people in the empire of the normal have no experience interacting with intellectually impaired people who have not had opportunities to participate in everyday activities. To create those opportunities in sports requires a level of awareness and support that remains rare in most social worlds. In the meantime, people with an intellectual disability seek opportunities to play sports in supportive environments that positively connect them with peers and the larger community.

Disability Sport Legacies

The legacy goals of disability sports vary with the organizations that sponsor them. As with sports generally, intended legacies often differ from reality. Until recently people in disability sports organizations had not thought of doing systematic evaluation research that would critically assess whether their goals were being achieved. Of course, different organizations have different goals. In some cases, the primary goal is to give people with particular characteristics or impairments opportunities to play sports with peers under conditions that they control. After being excluded so completely from sports in the past, they have established their own sports and sport events in which they don't have to deal with negative attitudes, curiosity and staring, and feeling like they are oddities. In other cases, the goal is for sports programs and events is to empower people with a disability, foster positive public attitudes, and enable people to fully participate in the general community (Brittain, 2012b; Wedgwood, 2013).

Although research on the impact of disability sports is scarce, a few recent studies provide basic assessments of what may or may not be occurring. Interviews with Paralympic stakeholders–people personally associated with the organization–indicated that the athletes were perceived to be personally empowered by their involvement, but other positive outcomes were few (Purdue and Howe, 2012, 2015). In fact, the athletes were not perceived as models that inspired people with a disability, because they did not describe themselves as *disabled* and were never shown dealing with everyday issues that others face. Similarly, other research indicates that the physical activity and recreational sport participation rates among people with a disability had not increased with the growing popularity of the Paralympics because structural barriers continued to exist in societies (Brown & Pappous, 2018;

(*Source:* Ben Hoskins/Getty Images)

Wheelchair rugby–formerly described as "quad rugby" and "murderball"–is played in the Paralympics and in national and world championships. Some rugby players use a highly masculinized vocabulary to describe the intimidation and violence that occur in their sport. Although wheelchair rugby challenges stereotypes about people with a disability, it reaffirms a gender ideology in which manhood is defined in terms of the ability to do violence.

Pullen et al., 2019). Being inspired by Paralympic athletes did nothing to eliminate negative attitudes, increase funding for disability sports, improve accessibility to venues, provide convenient transportation, or create knowledgeable and experienced coaches and support staff (Wilson and Khoob, 2013).

Observations made by disability rights activists support these findings (Ahmed, 2013; Braye et al., 2012). Watching athletes run on $20,000 prostheses or play rugby and race in $7000 wheelchairs did not make disability "cool" or change the reality of dealing with impairments. Also, the dozens of impairment classification categories used to sort competitors seemed irrelevant to many activists, who felt that people could not see themselves in categories created by the IPC. Additionally, individual needs continued to be unmet after the Paralympics. It is true that a few people in the empire of the normal saw athletes perform during the Paralympics, but seeing them did not motivate those people to support local disability programs or vote for legislation to bring about equity. In fact, the activists worried that the opposite was more likely: after seeing the ability of the athletes, people would conclude that disability was not an issue, thereby reproducing ableist ideology and ableist attitudes (Brittain & Beacom, 2016; Brown & Pappous, 2018; Rival, 2015).

Finally, males are disproportionately overrepresented among athletes in disability sports. This is partly because more boys and men engage in risky actions that can cause physical impairments, and girls and women with physical or intellectual impairments may be more protected by family members and not encouraged to seek sports participation opportunities. In any case, the culture of disability sports is heavily masculine and this may lead females to feel unwelcome. There may also be subtle sexism in the referral process that moves people from rehabilitation programs into sports programs. If doctors and therapists don't encourage girls and women to move into sports as much as they encourage boys and men, it would reproduce an already male-dominated, male-centered, and male-identified sport culture. The visibility and popularity of wheelchair rugby, or "murderball" as it is known by men in disability sports, reaffirms this point.

TECHNOLOGY AND ABILITY

When athletes use technologies to adapt their bodies to the physical challenges presented by sports, they blur the line between body and machine. Of course, this is neither new nor unique to disability sports. Specialized equipment and technologies (such as climbing shoes or special rowing blades) have long been used in all sports. Similar to the wheelchairs, crutches, and prostheses used by people with physical impairments, they help them move more efficiently (Apelmo, 2012; Black, 2014).

Various forms of "assistive" performance enhancements are used in most sports. Tennis and baseball players have "assistive" elbow and knee reconstructions using super strong synthetic ligaments or stronger ligaments taken from other parts of their bodies. Endurance athletes sleep in "assistive" hyperbaric chambers to increase endurance by boosting the oxygen-carrying capacity of their red blood cells. Lionel Messi, reputedly the best soccer player in the world today, took growth hormones that added inches to his unusually short stature, and dozens of baseball players and golfers have had Lasik eye surgery to obtain 20/15 vision and the ability to see a baseball or golf ball more distinctly. These athletes don't think of themselves as disabled nor do they see the use of such "assistive" and performance-enhancing procedures as compensation for weakness or as cheating, and it is certain that none of them ever thought of participating in the Paralympics.

In the 1980s, biologist Haraway (1985) made the case that many people could be described as cyborgs because they depended on machines and communication technologies to navigate their way through everyday life, and this was well before smartphones appeared as fixed appendages of human hands. But the most intense and complex example of this cyborg hybridization is probably experienced by severely impaired people who merge technologies with their own bodies to claim and sustain their humanity (Tamari, 2017).

Oscar Pistorius, the South African sprinter, has recently been the most visible sporting cyborg.

Identified as "Blade Runner" or "the fastest man on no legs," he was born with no fibula bones in his legs. Oscar's parents decided when he was eleven months old that below-the-knee prosthetic legs and feet would enable him to move more freely, and the surgery was completed in 1987.

As an active, athletic boy, Oscar dreamed of playing elite rugby. Never having experienced a body without prosthetic legs, he did everything his friends did. Through middle school and high school he wrestled and played cricket, rugby, water polo, and tennis. But after he shattered his knee playing rugby in late 2003, his doctor prescribed running as physical therapy. In January 2004 at the age of seventeen he began to train as a sprinter. Two months later he competed in his first 100-meter race, winning a gold medal and setting a world record time of 11.51 seconds in two Paralympic categories: the T44 class for athletes with a "single leg *below knee amputation*" and the T43 class for "double leg *below knee amputation.*"

His success in these races led to his competing in the 2004 Paralympic Games in Athens, Greece, where he won a silver medal in the 100-meter and a gold medal in the 200-meter sprint. Overall, he set four world records at those games, and went on to compete and win in the 2008 and 2012 Paralympic Games.

Team OSSUR has sponsored Pistorius and other record-setting Paralympic sprinters who wear Ossur's carbon-fiber Flex-Foot Cheetah prosthesis. The Flex-Foot replicates the hind leg of a cat, with a small-profile foot that extends and reaches out to contact the ground while the large thigh muscles pull the body forward. These prosthetic legs return about 95 percent of the energy put into them by the runners' upper legs. A human lower leg returns about 200 percent of the energy put into them, which OSSUR researchers have taken as a challenge to duplicate the running power of a human leg, a goal that will take some time to achieve.

The goal for many amputees is no longer to reach a "natural" level of ability but to exceed it, using whatever cutting-edge technology is available. As this new generation sees it, our tools are evolving faster than the human body, so why obey the limits of mere nature?

—Daniel H Wilson, robotics engineer, 2012.

In 2007, Pistorius began training like an Olympic sprinter in a quest to qualify for the 2008 Olympics in Beijing. However, his quest was foiled when the IAAF, the global governing body for track and field, disqualified him. After reviewing research they had commissioned, the IAAF executive committee concluded that his prosthetic legs gave him an advantage over Olympic runners (IPC, 2008). In a sense, Pistorius was "*dis*'ed" by the IAAF for being abnormally able.

Pistorius appealed the IAAF decision and asked the International Court of Arbitration for Sport to consider other studies that went beyond the IAAF laboratory tests, which did not assess the carbon-fiber leg in a running situation. He knew from experience that the bladelike legs slowed him at the start of a race, provided poor traction on a wet track, produced rotational forces that were difficult to control, and supplied none of the maneuverability and control supplied by the human leg, ankle, and foot (Longman, 2007).

After independent researchers conducted further studies, and the international court reviewed the data, the IAAF overturned its ban in May 2008 and ruled that Pistorius was eligible to qualify for the Olympics and participate in other international events. Although he failed to qualify for the 2008 Olympics in Beijing, Pistorius continued training and qualified to compete in the 2012 Olympic Games in London. He was neither the first athlete with a physical impairment to compete in the Olympics, nor the first to use a prosthetic limb, but his story resonated with people as they followed it through global media coverage.

Virtual Bodies and Cyborg Identities

The issues raised by Pistorius and his carbon-fiber legs received massive attention. The image of cyborg athletes, as informed by science fiction

(*Source:* Rich Cruse/Photo courtesy of the Challenged Athletes Foundation, http://www.challengedathletes.org)

Normal, enhanced, or disabled? The lines between these categories are becoming increasingly blurred. This is creating ethical and practical dilemmas in sports organizations, because it is difficult to preserve a level playing field when engineered enhancements are used. People in Paralympic and related organizations may be ahead of others in dealing with this, because they have already confronted enhancements and developed a classification code that takes them into account.

action films featuring mechanically and genetically engineered bodies, created moral panic among people worried about altering human nature. At the same time, others used the medical model to imagine the liberating possibilities of bionic body parts that could fix physical impairments, make people better than normal, and be improved over time to even negate the effects of aging.

A visible spokesperson for the bionic dreamers has been Hugh Herr, director of the Biomechatronics Research Group at MIT. Herr became a bilateral amputee at seventeen years old, and his dissatisfaction with painful and poorly designed prosthetics inspired him to obtain a PhD in engineering as he developed innovative prostheses, including for his own lower leg, ankle, and foot. Herr predicts that there will be "extreme interfaces" between soft and hard materials integrated with skin, bone, muscle, and nerves, making prosthetic body parts move naturally with messages delivered from the brain through synthetic nerves (Moss, 2011; Rago, 2013). This prediction aligns Herr with others described as transhumanists, a collection of dreamers and scientists described in the Reflect on Sport box "Nobody's Perfect: Does That Mean I'm Impaired?"

Sport philosophers and others present arguments for banning prosthetics in sports. They say that the precise contribution of prosthetics to performance may never be known, which may put athletes with a disability at an unfair advantage over those who do not or cannot use such technology. Also, the impact of technology on the design of prostheses is likely to affect athletes' abilities and unfairly advantage those with the resources to access the most recent innovations.

The proponents of banning prostheses are up against powerful corporations that will showcase and market their new performance-enhancing technologies through the bodies of athletes in the Paralympics and other disability sports events (Goffette, 2018; Roduit & Gaehwiler, 2018; Wolbring, 2012a, 2012c). In turn, this will be attractive to amputees who see a possibility for exceeding natural limits and "evolving faster than the human body" (Wilson, 2012). Popular culture has already introduced this idea in the form of "iron man" exoskeletons that permit unnatural physical feats.

Access to Technology

We occasionally hear heartening stories about people using assistive devices made of Kevlar, carbon-fiber

Nobody's Perfect
Does That Mean I'm Impaired?

Ableism leads people in different directions. One of the emerging pathways is being charted by transhumanists, who use the medical model as a lens for imagining the future of human bodies.

Transhumanists believe that all bodies can be improved so that people can achieve goals currently out of reach. They claim that we have not taken full advantage of available enhancement procedures and technologies because we cling to outdated beliefs based on religion and cultural traditions–beliefs no longer in sync with twenty-first-century knowledge.

In the case of sports, transhumanists predict that athletes will seek and use various forms of body- and performance-enhancing technologies that are undetectable without monitoring, scanning, and controlling bodies from birth onward. As athletes demonstrate what is possible by using innovative enhancements, they will expand our sense of what is possible in our relationship with the physical world. This process is already under way with corrective lenses for eyes, joint replacements, ligament transfers and replacements, muscle generation, bone grafts, stem cell therapies, and a wide array of surgeries that enable athletes to return to their sports more quickly than ever before and train themselves back to 100 percent. The goal of transhumanists is for the athlete to return better than 100 percent.

The credibility of transhumanists is challenged by critics of ableist ideology, by people panicked about turning humans into cyborgs, and by skeptics who say that transhumanists are opportunists who profit by intensifying people's insecurities about their bodies and then selling them expensive enhancement procedures or technologies.

As you consider the pros and cons of transhumanism, imagine this: You are a top college basketball player looking forward to signing a professional contract, but during your junior year you rupture your ACL during the final minutes of the NCAA finals. Your orthopedic surgeon says she can repair it to provide stability for walking but not for playing competitive basketball, or she can surgically insert a newly developed synthetic ligament that is stronger than the original and better suited for enduring the physical stress of NBA basketball. Your insurance will cover either surgery. Which one would you choose?

If you choose the synthetic ligament, what would prevent others from having similar surgeries so they could do more intense muscle conditioning to improve their speed and vertical jumping ability? Where and for whom would you draw the line when it comes to such body enhancements? We may find this form of transhumanism to be troubling, but we cannot escape these questions as new technologies are being developed. *What will happen if no lines are drawn or if we cannot determine when lines have been crossed?*

---

biologics, and other high-tech materials. For people who compete in the Paralympics, these materials are now used to make light and fast racing wheelchairs, revolutionary running prostheses, racing mono-skis to maneuver down steep mountain slopes, and other assistive devices that extend skills and broaden the experiences through which people can feel joy and accomplishment.

This technology is often seductive when we see it for the first time–so seductive that we may focus on the device and overlook those who might benefit from it. However, as most athletes know, technologies are only as good as the people who use them. And most people with disabilities know that adaptive technologies for sports are prohibitively expensive.

American athlete Diane Cabrera discovered this when cancer took her leg in 2001. A new prosthesis enabled her to walk, but it cost $11,000 and her medical insurance covered only $4000 per year. She spread payments over 2 years and struggled to find $2200 for additional payments related to diagnostics, fitting, tuning, and maintaining the device. When she needed a new leg socket in 2005, she put it off due to cost.

That's what many people do today when they need prostheses. Whereas standard prostheses may be partially covered by insurance, prosthetic limbs and adaptive devices for sports involve additional costs that must be paid by individuals in nearly all cases. Sport prosthetics require replacement every year or two, and other prosthetic limbs should be replaced every four to six years. Racing wheelchairs can cost $5000 or more, and Kevlar wheels push the cost higher. When they are customized for rugby, add another $1600. Although top Paralympic sprinters may have sponsors that pay for their Flex-Foot Cheetah prostheses, the cost is about $20,000 for each leg, and they must be replaced or refurbished regularly when training full time. How do unsponsored runners pay for these and even more expensive full leg prostheses?

The cost of adaptive equipment is a significant barrier to sports participation for many people with physical impairments. For example, US data for 2017 indicate that among adults having an ambulatory disability, the following is true:[2]

- only 35 percent had a high school diploma or equivalent
- only 25 percent were employed, and only 16 percent were employed full-time/full-year.
- they live in households with a median income of $39,100, and 29 percent live below the poverty line

People with disabilities also have higher expenses for daily living and required care. These are the realities of social class and disability in the United States. These realities may be slightly better in a few countries but they are much worse in most (Mojtahedi & Katsui, 2018). This means that in global terms, nearly all people face formidable barriers in terms of accessing assistive technologies and regularly participating in sports at any level (Berghs et al., 2020).

[2] US Department of Labor, 2017; http://disabilitystatistics.org/reports/acs.cfm; see also, Maroto, Pettinicchio & Patterson (2019).

summary

ARE AGE AND ABILITY BARRIERS TO PARTICIPATION?

Sports and sports participation are closely tied to culturally based ideas and beliefs about ability and the body. These ideas and beliefs impact each of us, because they serve as a baseline for our own definition of "normal." We experience this impact to different degrees as our abilities and bodies change over time due to aging and impairments caused by injuries, illness, or chronic disease. Because ability and the body are involved in sports and physical activities, these ideas and beliefs affect rates of sports participation and a society's provision of opportunities to participate in sports.

Ableist ideology, ageism, and ableism negatively impact sports and physical activity participation among people whose abilities and bodies do not measure up to prevailing or dominant social conceptions of *normal.* This occurs despite natural physical and intellectual variations among human beings. This is similar to the dynamics of sexism and racism, except that ableist ideology, ageism, and ableism will eventually impact everyone, even those who previously used it to marginalize or disadvantage others.

Ageism accounts for various manifestations of age discrimination. In the case of sports, ageism leads to age-segregated patterns of participation and provision of participation opportunities. This affects older people negatively because of the widespread belief that playing sports is not developmentally important for people who are "grown up."

Ableism accounts for the creation of a *dis*ability category in society and in sports. People are assigned to this category due to visible or functional impairments. This locates them outside of the realm of "normal" and leads them to be seen by many people as flawed and inferior.

Ideas and beliefs about aging vary over time and from one social world to another, but in societies characterized by rapid social and technological change, being younger is valued over being older. This has turned age into a social and political issue in many societies, especially those in which the average age of the population is increasing and older people are becoming increasingly powerful in political terms. This is occurring in the United States and other societies in which numerically large cohorts of people born in the years after World War II are in their fifties and sixties and seventies.

Because older people have used a disproportionate share of medical care resources in many societies, sports and physical activities have been identified in neoliberal societies as tools that older people must use to stay healthy and cut medical costs. This new focus raises issues related to gender, ethnicity, and social class, because women, first-generation ethnic immigrants, and people with lower income and education often have very low rates of sports participation. Additionally, the cost of participation in private, for-profit programs puts membership out of reach for nearly all people in these categories.

The meaning of ability varies by situation, but it has been defined in many societies in a way that "*dis*'s"—or classifies as *dis*abled—people perceived as incapable of fully participating in mainstream social and economic life. This turns *disability* into a social and political category that has significant implications for many people.

The meaning of disability differs depending on the assumptions used when defining it. When assumptions are based on the medical model, impairments are the problem, and "fixing" them through treatment and rehabilitation is the solution. When assumptions are based on the social model, problems rest in a world full of physical and social barriers that could be minimized by responsive designs, education, and cultural change.

Many people with impairments prefer the social model because it provides them with a strategy for challenging the power of the empire of the normal, where they are seen as subnormal outsiders due to their physical or intellectual attributes. The media generally reproduce the norms of the empire as they portray athletes with disabilities as courageous victims or heroic supercrips. Such portrayals are based on misinformation and will change only when media personnel develop the vocabulary that takes them beyond disabilities into the realm of abilities.

Because of their visibility and cultural importance, sports have become sites at which disability issues are confronted and contested. Processes of ability-related exclusion and inclusion in sports have become a focus of many governmental and nongovernmental organizations and officials from international to local levels. Belief in the great sport myth has led to policies that foster inclusion based on the assumption that sports participation will change the lives of people with disabilities. Although this has led to new programs it has not eliminated the social and structural barriers that interfere with a wide range of participation opportunities.

In the face of exclusion or poorly managed and inconvenient sports programs, people with particular disabilities have created their own sports organizations and events to meet their needs and expectations. In other cases, individuals or groups of people have challenged traditions of exclusion through protests and legal actions. As this occurs, the meaning of inclusion has changed and come closer to involving full equity of opportunities. But there is much left to be done.

Disability sports have traditionally been viewed through the lens of the medical model and seen as forms of physical therapy and rehabilitation. As elite athletes with a disability have attempted to change this approach and be treated like other elite athletes, they have faced resistance from established sports organizations. The IPC, for example, has faced resistance from the IOC, and disability events such as the Paralympics receive little support or media coverage compared to other sports events. At the same time, disability sports organizations face their own challenges related to eligibility issues and competition classifications based on impairment and potential ability.

The Special Olympics have become a significant global nonprofit organization. With annual revenues approaching $100 million, it provides training and competition opportunities in 190 nations for over 4 million people with an intellectual disability. Because research has indicated that Special Olympics programs have not achieved their goal of integrating people with an intellectual disability into mainstream society, the organization has created new programs to emphasize social integration and equity.

The overall legacy of disability sports is now being questioned, because the publicity given to the Paralympics and other elite events has not led to structural changes and new programs benefiting the vast majority of people with disabilities. In fact, much of the attention in elite events focuses on technologies used by athletes with amputations—a classic example being the carbon-fiber Flex-Foot Cheetah prostheses used by Oscar Pistorius and other record-setting runners.

These technologies have led to discussions and heated debates about physically engineered bodies and turning athletes into cyborgs. The influence of ableist ideology and ableism has led some people to promote transhumanism, which assumes that all human bodies can and should be improved with technology—a position that incites moral panic among people who fear that this will eventually dehumanize individuals and disrupt the social order.

These debates cool down once people realize the cost of the technologies being used in the Paralympics today and the estimated costs of future technologies. Due to the practical issue of cost, most people with a disability are not concerned about futuristic prostheses. They don't see themselves buying exoskeletons so they can perform superhuman feats. More realistically, they hope to see restrooms designed so that they can use toilets without performing gymnastics routines and miraculous wheelchair moves.

SUPPLEMENTAL READINGS

Reading 1. We're not handicapped: We just can't hear
Reading 2. How can I wear shoes if I don't have feet?
Reading 3. The hit isn't real unless it bends steel: Men and murderball
Reading 4. Paying the price: The cost of sport prostheses
Reading 5. Tensions in the Olympic family: Siblings with disabilities
Reading 6. "One of God's favorites": Religion and disability

SPORT MANAGEMENT ISSUES

- As the new manager of a community sport center in a region with many middle- and working-class older people, your success depends on programming that attracts older people. Identify the issues you will discuss with your new programming and management staff during a two-day training session with them.
- You are the assistant athletic director in a major urban public school district, and you are responsible for compliance with the new US Department of Education's guidelines on sports for students with disabilities. Outline two different program proposals that you will present to the district school board when they make decisions about how the district will allocate funds to comply with federal guidelines.
- As a sport management student you have been asked by students in special education to work with them in developing a sport and physical activity program for people with disabilities in the surrounding community. The first brainstorming session is soon, and you are preparing the list of issues you will bring to the session. Identify and explain the five most important issues you want the group to consider.
- You are an education consultant to the Department of Education in your society. Given what the research indicates about the kinds of sports that adults prefer, what recommendations do you have for the kinds of sports and physical activities that should be included in the typical high school physical education curriculum? In other words, what sports and physical activities should young people be learning during their teen years that will help them to stay physically active and healthy through their adult lives? List three of them and give reasons for why you have chosen them.

references

AARP Research. 2018 The value of experience: AARP multicultural work and jobs study. AARP (formerly American Association od Retired Persons), online, https://www.aarp.org/content/dam/aarp/research/surveys_statistics/econ/2018/value-of-experience-chartbook.doi.10.26419-2Fres.00177.003.pdf

Ahmed, Nadia. 2013. Paralympics 2012 legacy: Accessible housing and disability equality or inequality? *Disability & Society* 28(1): 129–133.

Apelmo, Elisabet. 2012. Falling in love with a wheelchair: Enabling/disabling technologies. *Sport in Society* 15(3): 399–408.

Bartsch, Anne; Mary Beth Oliver, Cordula Nitsch & Sebastian Scherr. 2018. Inspired by the Paralympics: Effects of empathy on audience interest in para-sports and on the destigmatization of persons with disabilities. *Communication Research* 45(4): 525–553.

Beauchamp-Pryor, Karen. 2011. Impairment, cure and identity: 'Where do I fit in?' *Disability & Society* 26(1): 5–17.

Berghs, Maria, Tsitsi Chataika, Yahya El-Lahib & Kudakwashe Dube, eds. 2020. *The Routledge handbook of disability activism*. London/New York: Routledge.

Bickenbach, Jerome. 2011. The world report on disability. *Disability & Society* 26(5): 655–658.

Black, Daniel. 2014. Where bodies end and artefacts begin: Tools, machines and interfaces. *Body & Society* 20(1): 31–60.

Block, Martin E. 1995. Americans with Disability Act: Its impact on youth sports. *Journal of Health, Physical Education, Recreation and Dance* 66(1): 28–32.

Braye, S., Gibbons, T. and Dixon, K. 2013. 'Disability 'rights' or 'wrongs'? The claims of the International Paralympic Committee, the London 2012 Paralympics and disability rights in the UK', *Sociological Research Online*, 18(3), 16.

Braye, Stuart; Kevin Dixon & Tom Gibbons. 2013. 'A mockery of equality': an exploratory investigation into disabled activists' views of the Paralympic Games. *Disability & Society* 28(7): 984–996.

Brittain, Ian. 2004. Perceptions of disability and their impact upon involvement in sport for people with disabilities at all levels. *Journal of Sport and Social Issues* 28(4): 429–452.

Brittain, Ian. 2004. The role of schools in constructing self-perceptions of sport and physical education in relation to people with disabilities. *Sport, Education and Society* 9(1): 75–94.

Brittain, Ian. 2012. *From Stoke Mandeville to Stratford: A history of the Summer Paralympic Games.* Champaign IL: Common Ground Publishing (Sport and Society).

Brittain Ian & A. Beacom. 2016. Leveraging the London 2012 Paralympic Games: What legacy for disabled people? *Journal of Sport and Social Issues* 40(6): 499–521.

Brown, Christopher & Athanasios (Sakis) Pappous. 2018. "The Legacy Element . . . It Just Felt More Woolly": Exploring the Reasons for the Decline in People With Disabilities' Sport Participation in England 5 Years After the London 2012 Paralympic Games. Journal of Sport and Social Issues 42(5): 343–368.

Carter, Neil & John Williams. 2012. 'A genuinely emotional week': Learning disability, sport and television–notes on the Special Olympics GB National Summer Games 2009. *Media Culture & Society* 34(2): 211–227.

Collinet, Cécile & Matthieu Delalandre. 2017. Physical and sports activities, and healthy and active ageing: Establishing a frame of reference for public action. *International Review for the Sociology of Sport* 52(5): 570–583.

Couser, G. Thomas. 2000. The empire of the "normal": A forum on disability and self-representation-introduction. *American Quarterly* 52, 2: 305–310.

Couser, G. Thomas. 2009. *Signifying bodies: Disability in contemporary life writing*. Ann Arbor: University of Michigan Press.

De Schutter, Bob & Julie A. Brown. 2016. Digital games as a source of enjoyment in later life. *Games and Culture* 11(1/2): 28–52.

Dionigi, Rylee A., Sean Horton & Joseph Baker. 2013. Negotiations of the ageing process: Older adults' stories of sports participation. *Sport, Education and Society* 18(3): 370–387.

Donnelly, Peter, and Jay Coakley. 2003. *The role of recreation in promoting social inclusion*. Monograph in the Working Paper Series on Social Inclusion published by the Laidlaw Foundation, Toronto, Ontario.

Dorsch, Travis E., Alan L. Smith, Jordan A. Blazo, Jay Coakley, Jean Côté, Christopher R. D. Wagstaff, Stacy Warner, & Michael Q. King. Forthcoming. Toward an integrated theory of the youth sport system. Under review.

Drummond, Murray. 2020. I have no idea what my body is now capable of, or should I say 'not capable of': The ageing male body in sport: To midlife and beyond. In Magrath, Rory, Jamie Cleland & Eric Anderson, eds. *Palgrave handbook of masculinity and sport*. London: Palgrave Macmillan.

Duncan, Arne. 2013. We must provide equal opportunity in sports to students with disabilities. *US Department of Education* (January 25): http://www.ed.gov/blog/2013/01/we-must-provide-equal-opportunity-in-sports-to-students-with-disabilities/

EEOC. 2013. Nearly 100,000 job bias charges in fiscal year 2012. *Equal Employment Opportunity Commission* (January 28): http://www.eeoc.gov/eeoc/newsroom/release/1-28-13.cfm

Foote, Chandra J. & Bill Collins. 2011. You know, Eunice, the world will never be the same after this. *International Journal of Special Education* 26(3): 285–295.

Foucault, Michel. 1961/1967. *Madness and civilization*. London: Travistock.

Galanter, Seth M. 2013. "Dear Colleague" letter. Washington, DC: United States Department of Education, Office for Civil Rights.

Gayman, Amy M.; Jessica Fraser-Thomas, Rylee A. Dionigi, Sean Horton & Joseph Baker. 2017. Is sport good for older adults? A systematic review of psychosocial outcomes of older adults' sport participation. *International Review of Sport and Exercise Psychology* 10(1):164–185.

Goffette, Jérôme. 2018. Prosthetic dreams: "Wow Effect", mechanical paradigm and modular body–prospects on prosthetics. *Sport in Society* 21(4): 705–712.

Goffman, Erving. 1961. *Asylums: Essays on the social situation of mental patients and other inmates.* Garden City, NY: Anchor Books.

Goffman, Erving. 1963. *Stigma: Notes on the management of spoiled identities*. Englewodd Cliffs, NJ: Prentice-Hall, Inc.

Gullette, Margaret Morganroth. 2018. Against 'aging'–How to talk about growing older. *Theory, Culture & Society* 35(7/8): 251–270.

Haraway, Donna. 1991. *A cyborg manifesto: Science, technology, and socialist-feminism in the late twentieth century*. Published online (retrieved 11 December, 2013): http://www.egs.edu/faculty/donna-haraway/articles/donna-haraway-a-cyborg-manifesto/

Hargreaves, Jennifer. 2000. *Heroines of sport: The politics of difference and identity*. London: Routledge.

Harpur, Paul. 2012. From disability to ability: changing the phrasing of the debate. *Disability and Society* 27(3): 325–337.

Hehir, Thomas. 2002. Eliminating ableism in education. *The Harvard Educational Review* 72(1): 1–32.

Hehir, Thomas. 2005. *New directions in special education: Eliminating ableism in policy and practice*. Cambridge MA: Harvard Education Press

Higgins, Eleanor L, Marshall H. Rashkind, Roberta J. Goldberg, and Kenneth L. Herman. 2002. Stages of acceptance of a learning disability: The impact of labeling. *Learning Disabilities Quarterly* 25(1): 3–18.

Horton, Sean, Rylee A. Dionigi, Michael Gard, Joseph Baker & Patricia Weir. 2018. "Don't sit back with the geraniums, get out": The complexity of older women's stories of sport participation. *Journal of Amateur Sport* 4(1): 24–51.

Howe, P. David & Carla Filomena Silva. 2018. The fiddle of using the Paralympic Games as a vehicle for expanding [dis]ability sport participation. *Sport in Society* 21(1): 125–136.

Jenkins, Jo Ann. *2018. Disrupt aging*. New York: Public Affairs.

Jennings, Andrew. 1996. *The new lords of the rings.* London: Pocket Books.

Kane, Patrick. 2018. Being bionic: how technology transformed my life. *The Guardian* (November 15): https://www.theguardian.com/technology/2018/nov/15/being-bionic-how-technology-transformed-my-life-prosthetic-limbs

Kerr, Roslyn, Natalie Barker-Ruchti, Myrian Nunomura, Georgia Cervin & Astrid Schubring. 2018. The role of setting in the field: The positioning of older bodies in the field of elite women's gymnastics. *Sociology* 52(4): 727–743.

Klostermann, Claudia & Siegfried Nagel. 2014. Changes in German sport participation: Historical trends in individual sports. *International Review for the Sociology of Sport* 49(5): 609–634.

Longman, Jeré. 2007a. An amputee sprinter: Is he disabled or too-abled? *New York Times* (May 15): http://www.nytimes.com/2007/05/15/sports /othersports/15runner.html

Maroto, Michelle, David Pettinicchio & Drew C. Patterson. 2019. Hierarchies of categorical disadvantage: Economic insecurity at the intersection of disability, gender, and race. Gender & Society 33(1): 64–93.

Marriott, Michael. 2005. Cyberbodies: Robo-legs. *The New York Times*, June 20: F1.

Marshall, Barbara L. & Momin Rahman. 2015. Celebrity, ageing and the construction of 'third age' identities. *International Journal of Cultural Studies* 18(6): 577–593.

McCoy, Jenny. 2019. 17-time Paralympic medalist Tatyana McFadden on fighting for the rights of athletes with disabilities. Self.com (May 14): https://www.self.com/story/paralympic-medalist-tatyana-mcfadden-on-fighting-for-equal-rights

Mojtahedi, Mina C. & Hisayo Katsui. 2018. Making the right real! A case study on the implementation of the right to sport for persons with disabilities in Ethiopia. *Sport in Society* 21(1): 40–49.

Moss, Frank. 2011. *The Sorcerers and their apprentices: How the digital magicians of the MIT Media Lab are creating the innovative technologies that will change our lives.* New York: Crown Business.

Oliver, Mike & C. Barnes. 2012. The *new politics of disablement*. Basingstoke: Palgrave.

Oliver, Mike. 1983. *Social work with disabled people*. Basingstoke: Macmillan.

Oliver, Mike. 1990. The *politics of disablement*. Basingstoke: Macmillan.

Oliver, Mike. 2013. The social model of disability: Thirty years on. *Disability & Society* 28(7): 1024–1026.

Osmanovic, Sanela & Loretta Pecchioni. 2016. Beyond entertainment: Motivations and outcomes of video game playing by older adults and their younger family members. *Games and Culture* 11(1/2): 130–149.

O'Connor, Paul. 2018. Beyond the youth culture: Understanding middle-aged skateboarder through temporal capital. *International Review for the Sociology of Sport* 53(8): 924–943.

Peterson, Lindsey & Margaret Ralston. 2017. Valued elders or societal burden: Cross-national attitudes toward older adults. *International Sociology* 32(6): 731–754.

Pike, Elizabeth C.J. 2011. The Active Ageing agenda, old folk devils and a new moral panic. *Sociology of Sport Journal* 28(2): 209–225.

Pike, Elizabeth C.J. 2012. Aquatic antiques: Swimming off this mortal coil? *International Review for the Sociology of Sport* 47(4): 492–510.

Pike, Elizabeth CJ. 2015. Assessing the sociology of sport: On age and ability. International Review for the Sociology of Sport 50(4-5): 570–574.

Pullen, Emma, Daniel Jackson, Michael Silk & Richard Scullion. 2019. Re-presenting the Paralympics: (contested) philosophies, production practices and the hypervisibility of disability. *Media, Culture & Society* 41(4): 465–481.

Purdue, David E.J. & P. David Howe. 2012. Empower, inspire, achieve: (Dis)empowerment and the Paralympic Games. *Disability & Society* 27(7): 903–916.

Purdue, David E. J. 2013. An (in)convenient truce? Paralympic stakeholders' reflections on the Olympic–Paralympic relationship. *Journal of Sport and Social Issues* 37(4): 384–402.

Purdue, David E.J. & P. David Howe. 2015. Plotting a Paralympic field: An elite disability sport competition viewed through Bourdieu's sociological lens. *International Review for the Sociology of Sport* 50(1): 83–97.

Rago, Joseph. 2013. The liberating age of bionics. *Wall Street Journal* (July 17): A11.

Resmovits, Joy. 2013. Students with disabilities have right to play school sports, Obama administration tells schools. *Huffington Post* (January 24): http://www.huffingtonpost.com/2013/01/24/students-disabilities-school-sports-obama_n_2546057.html

Richard, Rémi; Helene Joncheray & Eric Dugas. 2017. Disabled sportswomen and gender construction in powerchair football. *International Review for the Sociology of Sport* 52(1): 61–81.

Rival, Deborah L. 2015. Athletes with disabilities: Where does empowerment end and disempowerment begin? *The International Journal of Sport and Society: Annual Review* 5:1–10.

Roduit, Johann A. R. & Roman Gaehwiler, 2018. Ethics and enhancement in sport: becoming the fastest (human?) being, *Sport in Society*, 21(4): 713–719.

Rose, Damon. 2004. Don't call me handicapped. *BBC News* (October 4): http://news.bbc.co.uk/2/hi/uk_news/magazine/3708576.stm

Rothman, Joshua. 2017. Are disability rights and animal rights connected? *The New Yorker* (June 5): http://www.newyorker.com/culture/persons-of-interest/are-disability-rights-and-animal-rights-connected

Rugoho, Tafadzxa. 2020. My disability, my ammunition, my asset in advocacy work. In Maria Berghs, Tsitsi Chataika, Yahya El-Lahib, Kudakwashe Dube, eds. *The Routledge handbook of disability activism* (pp. 144–154). London/New York: Routledge.

Sayago, Sergio; Andrea Rosales, Valeria Righi, Susan M. Ferreira, Graeme W. Coleman & Josep Blat. 2016. On the conceptualization, design, and evaluation of appealing, meaningful, and playable digital games for older people. *Games and Culture* 11(1/2): 53–80.

Schantz, Otto J. & Keith Gilbert. 2012. *Heroes or zeros? – The media's perceptions of Paralympic sport*. Champaign IL: Common Ground Publishing (Sport and Society).

Schell, Robyn; Simone Hausknecht, Fan Zhang & David Kaufman. 2016. Social benefits of playing Wii bowling for older adults. *Games and Culture* 11(1/2): 81–103.

Shakespeare, Tom & Nicholas Watson. 2002. The social model of disability: an outdated ideology? *Research in Social Science and Disability* 2(1): 9–28.

Silva, Carla Filomena, & P. David Howe. 2012. The (in)validity of supercrip representation of Paralympian athletes. *Journal of Sport and Social Issues* 36(2): 174–194.

Smith, Brett, and Andrew Sparkes. 2002. Men, sport spinal cord injury and the construction of coherence: Narrative practice in action. *Qualitative Research* 2(2): 143–171.

Smith, Brett. 2013. Sporting spinal cord injuries, social relations, and rehabilitation narratives: An ethnographic creative non-fiction of becoming disabled through sport. *Sociology of Sport Journal* 30(2): 132–152.

Sparkes, Andrew & Brett Smith. 2002. Sport, spinal cord injury, embodied masculinities, and the dilemmas of narrative identity. *Men and Masculinities* 4, 3: 258–285.

Sparkes, Andrew C.; James Brighton & Kay Inckle. 2018. Imperfect perfection and wheelchair bodybuilding: Challenging ableism or reproducing normalcy? *Sociology* 52(6): 1307–1323.

Storey, Keith. 2008. The more things change, the more they are the same: Continuing concerns with the Special Olympics. *Research and Practice for Persons with Severe Disabilities* 33(3): 134–142.

Storey, Keith. 2004. The case against Special Olympics. *Journal of Disability Policy Studies* 15: 35–42.

Sutherland, Allan. 1981. *Disabled we stand.* Bloomington, IN: Indiana University Press.

Tamari, Tomoko. 2017. Body image and prosthetic aesthetics: Disability, technology and Paralympic culture. *Body & Society* 23(2): 25–56.

Taub, Diane E. & Kimberly R. Greer. 2000. Physical activity as a normalizing experience for school-age children with physical disabilities: Implications for legitimating of social identity and enhancement of social ties. *Journal of Sport and Social Issues* 24(4): 395–414.

Thomson, Rosemarie Garland. 2000. Staring back: Self-representations of disabled performance artists. *American Quarterly* 52, 2 (June): 334-338.

Thomson, Rosemarie Garland. 2002. Integrating disability, transforming feminist theory *National Women's Studies Association Journal* 14, 3: 1–32.

Thomson, Rosemarie Garland. 2002. Integrating disability, transforming feminist theory *National Women's Studies Association Journal* 14, 3: 1–32.

Thomson, Rosemarie Garland. 2009. *Staring: How we look*. New York: Oxford University Press.

Thualagant, Nicole. 2012. The conceptualization of fitness doping and its limitations, *Sport in Society* 15(3): 409–419.

Tulle, Emmanuelle. 2008. Acting your age? Sports science and the ageing body. *Journal of Aging Studies* 22(4): 340–347.

Tulle, Emmanuelle. 2008. *Ageing, The body and social change.* Basingstoke: Palgrave MacMillan.

Tulle, Emmanuelle. 2008. The ageing body and the ontology of ageing: Athletic competence in later life. *Body and Society*14, 3:1–19.

Tynedal, Jeremy & Gregor Wolbring. 2013. Paralympics and its athletes through the lens of the New York Times. *Sports* 1(1):13–36.

Wedgwood, Nikki. 2013. Hahn versus Guttmann: Revisiting 'Sports and the Political Movement of Disabled Persons.' *Disability & Society* 29(1): 129–142.

Wheaton, Belinda. 2013. *The cultural politics of lifestyle sports*. London: Routledge.

WHO. 2011. *World report on disability.* Geneva, Switzerland: World Health Organization.

WHO. 2001. *International classification of functioning, disability and health*. Geneva, Switzerland: World Health Organization. Online, https://unstats.un.org/unsd/disability/pdfs/ac.81-b4.pdf

Willing, Indigo, Andy Bennett, Mikko Piispa & Ben Green. 2019. Skateboarding and the 'tired generation': Ageing in youth cultures and lifestyle sports. *Sociology* 53(3): 503–518.

Wilson, Brian. 2012. *Sport and peace: A sociological perspective*. New York: Oxford.

Wilson, Noela C. & Selina Khoob. 2013. Benefits and barriers to sports participation for athletes with disabilities: The case of Malaysia. *Disability & Society* 28(8): 1132–1145.

Wolbring, Gregor. 2012a. Paralympians outperforming Olympians: An increasing challenge for Olympism and the Paralympic and Olympic Movement. Sport, Ethics and Philosophy 6(2): 251–266.

Wolbring, Gregor. 2012b. Leg-ism leaves some Paralympic stars out on a limb. *TheConversation.com* (29 August): https://theconversation.com/leg-ism-leaves-some-paralympic-stars-out-on-a-limb-9008

Wolbring, Gregor. 2012c. Superhip to supercrip: the 'trickle-down' effect of the Paralympics. *TheConversation.com* (August 31): https://theconversation.com/superhip-to-supercrip-the-trickle-down-effect-of-the-paralympics-9009

chapter

11

(*Source:* Kyodo/AP Images)

SPORTS AND THE ECONOMY

What Are the Characteristics of Commercial Sports?

. . . the men and women who play sports did not choose to give up the basic human rights that we would want for every worker.

–DeMaurice Smith, Executive director, NFL Players Association, (in Whyno, 2017)

The shining city on a hill for [US] teams and their TV partners . . . is online gambling. Even the most boring or blowout contest might still be riveting to viewers if allowed to place bet by smartphone on every pitch, putt, or free throw.

–Homan W. Jenkins, Jr., Wall Street Journal business journalist (2019)

Sport must now be run in partnership with the players and sport must act proactively to prevent and minimize and address any adverse human rights impacts.

–Brandon Schwab, Executive director, World Players Association (in Whyno, 2017)

There's something inherently wrong about its costing a family of four $500 to take in a baseball game–even something . . . unAmerican.

–Joseph Epstein, author and former editor of the *American Scholar* (2018)

Chapter Outline

Emergence and Growth of Commercial Sports
Commercialization and Changes in Sports
The Organization of Professional Sports in North America
The Organization of Amateur Sports in North America
Legal Status and Incomes of Athletes in Commercial Sports
Summary: What Are the Characteristics of Commercial Sports?

Learning Objectives

- Identify the conditions under which commercial sports emerge and grow in a society.
- Identify economic and ideological reasons why sports have become so popular in society today.
- Explain how the corporate branding of sports is related to the establishment of ideological outposts around the world today.
- Discuss how commercialization affects the rules, culture, and organization of sports.
- Distinguish differences between aesthetic orientations and heroic orientations, and explain how they are influenced by the commercialization of sports.
- Explain how the owners of the major professional sports have benefited from being allowed to establish cartels, monopolies, and monopsonies.
- Identify the major forms of public assistance received by professional sport franchises and leagues in the United States.
- Identify differences in the legal status of professional and amateur athletes in both individual and team sports.
- Describe the patterns of income received by professional and amateur athletes, and explain why the range of incomes received by athletes is so great today.

Sports have been used as public entertainment through history. However, they've never been so thoroughly commercialized as they are today. Never before have economic factors so totally dominated decisions about sports, and never before have economic organizations and corporate interests had so much power and control over the meaning, purpose, and organization of sports.

The economic stakes for athletes and sponsors have never been higher than they are today. The bottom line has replaced the goal line. Sports are now evaluated by gate receipts, concessions and merchandise sales, licensing fees, media rights contracts, and social media followers. Games and events are evaluated using media criteria such as market share, ratings points, and the cost of commercial time. Athletes are evaluated by their entertainment value as well as physical skills. Stadiums, teams, and events are named after corporations and linked to corporate logos instead of people and places that have local historical meaning.

Corporate interests influence team colors, uniform designs, event schedules, media coverage, and the comments of announcers during games and matches. Media companies and other corporations sponsor and plan events, and they own a growing number of sport teams. Many sports are corporate enterprises, tied to marketing concerns and processes of global capitalist expansion. The mergers of major corporate conglomerates that began in the 1990s and now continue in the twenty-first century have connected sport teams and events with media and entertainment companies. The names of transnational corporations are now synonymous with the athletes, events, and sports that bring pleasure to the lives of millions of people.

Because economic factors are so important in sports, this chapter focuses on the following questions:

1. Under what conditions do commercial sports emerge and prosper in a society?
2. What changes occur in the meaning, purpose, and organization of sports when they become commercial activities?
3. Who owns, sponsors, and promotes sports, and what are their interests?
4. What is the legal and financial status of athletes in commercial sports?

EMERGENCE AND GROWTH OF COMMERCIAL SPORTS

Commercial sports are organized and played for profit. Their success depends on gate receipts, concessions, sponsorships, the sale of media broadcasting rights, and other revenue streams associated with sport images and personalities. Therefore, commercial sports grow and prosper best under five social and economic conditions.

First, they are most prevalent in market economies where material rewards are highly valued by athletes, team owners, event sponsors, and spectators.

Second, they usually exist in societies that have large, densely populated cities with high concentrations of potential spectators. Although some forms of commercial sports can be maintained in rural, agricultural societies, their revenues would not support full-time professional athletes or sport promoters.

Third, commercial sports are a luxury, and they prosper only when the standard of living is high enough that people have time and resources to play and watch events that have no tangible products required for survival. Transportation and communications technologies must exist for sponsors to make money. Therefore, commercial sports are common in wealthy, urban, and industrial or post-industrial societies; they seldom exist in labor-intensive, poor societies where people must use all their resources to survive.

Fourth, commercial sports require large amounts of capital (money or credit) to build and maintain stadiums and arenas in which events can be played and watched. Capital can be accumulated in the public or private sector, but in either case, the willingness to invest in sports depends on anticipated payoffs in the form of publicity, profits, or power.

(*Source:* Onur Coban/Anadolu Agency/Getty Images)

Sports are played in nearly all cultures, but professional sports seldom exist in labor-intensive, poor nations. The Afghan horsemen here are playing buzkashi, a popular sport in their country, but Afghanistan lacks the general conditions needed to sustain buzkashi as a professional sport with fulltime paid athletes and paying fans.

Private investment in sports occurs when investors expect financial profits; *public* investment occurs when political leaders believe that commercial sports serve their personal interests, the interests of "the public," or a combination of both.

Fifth, commercial sports flourish in cultures where lifestyles emphasize consumption and material status symbols. This enables everything associated with sports to be marketed and sold: athletes (including their names, autographs, and images), merchandise, team names, and logos. When people express their identities through clothing, other possessions, and their associations with status symbols and celebrities, they will spend money on sports that have meaning in their social world. The success of commercial sports depends on selling symbols and emotional experiences to audiences, and then selling audiences to sponsors and the media.

Class Relations and Commercial Sports

Sports most likely to be commercialized are those watched, played, or used for profit by people who control economic resources in society. For example, golf is a major commercial sport, even though it does not lend itself to commercial presentation. It's inconvenient to stage a golf event for a live audience or to televise it. Camera placement and media commentary are difficult to arrange, and live spectators see only a small portion of the action. Golf does not involve vigorous action or head-to-head competition, except in rare cases of match play. Usually, if you don't play golf or know the players, you have little or no reason to watch it.

But golf is popular among wealthy and powerful men, who are important to sponsors and advertisers because they make consumption decisions for themselves, their families, their businesses, and thousands of employees who work under their supervision. They buy luxury cars and other high-end products for themselves, but more important to advertisers is that they buy thousands of company cars and computers for employees and make large investment decisions related to pensions and company capital.

This collection of golf supporters has economic clout that goes far beyond personal and family lives. This makes golf an attractive sport for corporations that have images and products that appeal to consumers with money and influence. This is why auto companies with high-priced cars sponsor and advertise on the PGA, LPGA, and Champions (Senior) PGA tours. This also is why major television networks cover golf tournaments: They can sell commercial time at a high rate per minute because those watching golf have money to spend—their money *and* the money of the companies they control. The converse of this is also true: Sports attracting low- and middle-income audiences are ignored by television or covered only under special circumstances. If wealthy executives bowled, we would see more bowling on commercial television and more bowling facilities on prime real estate in cities; but wealthy people seldom bowl, so bowling receives little coverage.

Market economies always privilege the interests of those who have the power and resources to select sports for promotion and coverage. Unless those people want to play, sponsor, or watch a sport, it won't be commercialized on a large scale, nor will it be given cultural significance in society. A sport won't become a "national pastime" or be associated with "character," community spirit, civic unity, and political loyalty unless it's favored by people with resources.

This is why football is now known as "America's game"—it celebrates and privileges the values and experiences of the men who control and benefit from corporate wealth and power in North America. This is why men pay thousands of dollars to buy expensive season tickets to college and professional football games, why male executives use corporation money to buy expensive blocks of "company tickets" to football games, and why corporation presidents write hundred-thousand-dollar checks to pay for luxury boxes and club seats for themselves, friends, and clients. They enjoy football, but most important, it reproduces an ideology that fosters their interests.

Women who want to be a part of the power structure in the United States often find that they must learn to "talk football" so they can communicate with the men who have created organizational cultures and control women's careers. If female executives don't go to the next big football game and take clients with them, they risk being excluded from the "masculinity loop" that is central to corporate culture and communication (Gregory, 2009). When they go to work every Monday during the fall, they know that their ability to "talk football" can keep them in touch with male co-workers.

The Creation of Spectator Interest

Sport spectators are likely to be plentiful in societies where there's a general quest for excitement, an ideological emphasis on material success, childhood experiences with sports, and easy access to sports through the media.

The Quest for Excitement When social life is highly controlled and organized, everyday routines often cause people to feel emotionally constrained. This fosters a search for activities that offer tension-excitement and emotional arousal. According to sociologists Eric Dunning and Norbert Elias, historical evidence suggests that this is common in modern societies. Sports, they contend, provide activities in which rules and norms can be shaped to foster emotional arousal and exciting actions, thereby eliminating boredom without disrupting social order in society (Dunning, 1999; Elias and Dunning, 1986).

Sports generally involve a tension between order and disruption. To manage this tension, norms and rules in sports must be loose enough to allow exciting action, but not so loose that they permit uncontrolled violence or other forms of destructive actions. When norms and rules are too constraining, sports are boring and people lose interest; when they are too loose, sports become sites for reckless and dangerous actions that jeopardize health and social order. The challenge is to find and maintain a balance.

This explanation of spectator interest raises the question, "Why do so many people give priority to sports over other activities in their quest for excitement?" Cultural theorists suggest that answers can be found by looking at the connection between ideology and cultural practices. This leads us to consider the following factors.

Social Class Ideology and Spectator Interest Spectator interest in sports is highest among those who believe in a meritocratic ideal: the idea that success is always based on skill and hard work, and skill and hard work always lead to success. This belief supports a widely held class ideology in societies with capitalist economies. Those who hold it often use sports as a model for how the social world should operate. When sports promote the idea that success is achieved through hard work and skill, their ideology is reaffirmed, and they become more secure in their beliefs. This is why sports media commentators emphasize that athletes and teams succeed when they work hard and have talent. This also is why corporations use the bodies of elite athletes to represent their public relations and marketing images—the finely tuned bodies of athletes are concrete examples of skill, power, and success as well as the use of science and technology (Hoberman, 1994). When high-profile athletes can deliver this message for corporations, lucrative endorsements come their way.

Youth Sport Programs and Spectator Interest Spectator interest often is initiated during childhood sports experiences. When organized youth sports programs emphasize skills, competition, and success, participants are likely to grow up wanting to watch elite athletes. For young people who continue to play sports, watching elite athletes provides them with models for playing and improving skills; for those who discontinue active participation, watching elite athletes provides continuous connections with the images and experiences of success that they learned while playing organized youth sports.

NFL executives understand the importance of this connection between youth sports and spectator interest. For example, as parents learn more about the dangers of brain injuries in football, the NFL has joined with USA Football to conduct a major public relations campaign to convince parents that football is being made safer and that they should encourage their sons to play the game (Montez de Oca & Cotner, 2020; Montez de Oca, Meyer & Scholes, 2016; Rugg, 2019). If youth football programs decline, so does the number of future players, season ticket purchasers, and media consumers of football.

Media Coverage and Spectator Interest Media promote the commercialization of sports by publicizing and covering events in ways that sustain spectator interest. Television increases spectator access to events and athletes worldwide and provides unique representations of sports. Camera coverage enables viewers to focus on the action and view replays in slow motion as they listen to the "insider" comments of announcers—all of which further immerses spectators into vicarious and potentially exciting sport experiences.

On-air commentators serve the media audience as fellow spectators who embellish the action and heighten identification with athletes and teams.

(*Source:* Jay Coakley)

Football is the most widely watched sport in the United States. It offers excitement in the form of rule-governed violence, and it reaffirms the notion that success is achieved through competition and dominating opponents. Youth football teams are very popular, and more young men play high school football than any other high school sport. Football lends itself to media coverage during which replays, slow motion, and expert commentary are used to dissect plays and game plans.

Commentators provide inside stories, analyze strategies, describe athletes as personalities, and magnify the importance an excitement of events.

Television recruits new spectators by teaching newcomers the rules and strategies of a sport at home with family and friends without purchasing expensive tickets. This is a painless way to be socialized into a spectator role, and it increases the number of people who will eventually buy tickets, watch televised games, pay for cable and satellite sports programming, and even become pay-per-view customers in the future.

Economic Factors and the Globalization of Commercial Sports

Commercial sports are now global in scope (Giulianotti & Numerato, 2018). Globalization has occurred because (1) those who control, sponsor, and promote sports seek new ways to expand markets and maximize profits, and (2) transnational corporations use sports as vehicles for introducing their products and services around the world. This makes sports a form of global cultural trade that is exported and imported in a manner similar to other products.

Sports Organizations Look for Global Markets Commercial sports organizations are businesses, and their goal is to expand into as many markets as possible. In fact, future profits for major professional sports depend on selling media rights and consumer merchandise. Most leagues now market themselves outside their home countries and use various strategies to develop identification with their sport, teams, and players. In this way, sports organizations become exporters of culture as well as products to be consumed.

The desire for global expansion is the main reason why the NBA has played 73 preseason and 30 regular season games outside North America since the early 1990s. Additionally, the league has a history of sending teams to Europe to play local clubs and to other parts of the world to play exhibition games. This exposure helped market NBA broadcasting rights and official NBA products worldwide. Today, the NBA finals and the NBA All-Star games are televised annually in 215 countries in 50 languages and there were 108 international players from 42 countries playing in the league during the 2018–19 season. Outside the United States, China constitutes the largest NBA market and player development focus. More than 50,000 stores in China sell NBA merchandise, about 30 percent of all visitors to NBA.com enter through the Mandarin language portal at the site, and over 25 million people watch weekly NBA games televised in China. Additionally, the NBA and FIBA, the international basketball federation, launched a league in Africa in 2020 to give the game a more global footprint (Weiner, 2018; Zillgitt, 2019).

The desire for global expansion has led NFL, NBA, NHL, and MLB teams to play exhibition and regular season games in Mexico, China, Japan, England, France, Germany, and Australia and to subsidize leagues and outreach programs for marketing purposes. This spirit of globalization is neither new nor limited to North American sports organizations. The International Olympic Committee (IOC) has incorporated national Olympic committees from every nation worldwide and has turned the Olympic Games into the most successful and financially lucrative media sport events in history. Furthermore, the IOC, like some other sports organizations, has turned itself and the Olympics into a global brand.

The sport with the longest history of global expansion is soccer, which is governed by FIFA—the Fédération Internationale de Football Association. The top soccer clubs in Europe have used multiple strategies to expand their global marketing reach. The best current example is Real Madrid Football Club (FC) in the Liga Nacional de Fútbol Profesional, or La Liga, the premier twenty-team league in Spain. It was valued at $4.4 billion in 2019 and is owned by about 60,000 club members. It has over 207 million social media followers and is rated as one of the twenty most recognizable brands in the world.

Two other sport teams with similar global recognition and value are Manchester United FC in England's Premier League and Barcelona FC in La Liga with Real Madrid. Barcelona, long known as a football club of the working class, has 193 million social media followers worldwide and may be the most recognizable sport brand in the world because of its working-class identification.

As a point of comparison, the New York Yankees and the Dallas Cowboys are valued at $4.6 and $5 billion respectively, but they have fewer than 30 million social media followers between them. Barcelona FC has ten times more followers than the Dallas Cowboys, and about the same number of followers as all thirty-two NFL teams combined. The only US team with a strong global profile is the Los Angeles Lakers, with nearly 30 million social media followers and high brand recognition. These data have attracted the attention of the leaders of US sport leagues because they indicate that there is much room for global expansion.

Corporations Use Sports as Vehicles for Global Expansion Because certain sports capture the attention, emotions, and allegiance of so many people worldwide, corporations are eager to sponsor them. Corporations need symbols of success and productivity that they can use as "marketing hooks" for products and as representations of their images. For example, people around the world still associate Michael Jordan with the "Air Jordan" trademark copyrighted by Nike; and many people now assume a connection between the Olympics and both McDonald's and Coca-Cola.

By unrolling the red carpet to the advertising and marketing of junk-food giants, the IOC is setting a toxic trap to hundreds of millions of parents and kids.

–Monika Kosinska, European Public Health Alliance (in Jack, 2012)

In the United States, the "gold medal" achievement for a corporation is to convert the company into a brand that can be associated with various forms of status and identity. Sports serve as effective sites for doing this as sport images and products can be used to represent people's identities at the same time that they can represent other things that give them status in particular social worlds. This dynamic drives consumption and corporate profits. As a result, most people inadvertently boost brand power by wearing clothes that prominently display corporate or team logos. But corporations have convinced them that this is part of personal identity construction rather than free advertising for a company that cares nothing about them personally.

Companies whose profits depend on selling alcohol, tobacco, fossil fuels, fast food, soft drinks, and candy are especially eager to have their products associated with sports. This enables them to defuse negative publicity about unhealthy and negative aspects of their products and production processes. They want people to think that "if the sports we love are brought to us by beer, cigarettes, liquor, soft drinks, beef burgers, deep-fried foods, candy bars, and fossil fuels, these things must have some redeeming qualities."

We now live in an era of transnational corporations (TNCs) that influence economic activity worldwide, affecting who has jobs, the kinds of work people do, salaries and working conditions, the products that people can buy, where they can buy them, and what they cost. When these corporations sponsor sports, they negotiate deals that promote their interests, increase their power, and create positive images of themselves as "global citizens and leaders." This is worth an investment of billions of dollars each year. For example, eleven global corporations, including Coca-Cola and McDonald's each paid $100 million just for the rights to advertise in connection with the recent Olympic Games; and Anheuser-Busch (Budweiser) spent nearly $500 million for commercial time during Super Bowls between 2003 and 2019. Like other multinational corporations, these companies buy commercial time during sport events to promote the belief that pleasure and excitement in people's everyday lives depend on them. They use this belief as an ideological outpost in the minds of people worldwide, and as information is filtered through these outposts, corporate executives hope to defuse opposition to the products and operational practices of their companies. When successful, this strategy boosts their legitimacy and contributes to corporate hegemony worldwide.

The success of this strategy led a Coca-Cola executive to tell IOC officials that they owed loyalty to Coke. He explained that

> Just as sponsors have the responsibility to preserve the integrity of the sport, enhance its image, help grow its prestige and its attendance, so too, do you [in sports] have responsibility and accountability to the sponsor (cited in Reid, 1996, p. 4BB).

IOC officials know that drinking cola does not meet the nutritional needs of elite athletes or the health goals of the Olympic movement, but they respond supportively to this executive's message. Coca-Cola has worked for nearly a century to colonize their minds and establish the outposts through which this message has been transmitted. This is why past official program brochures for the Olympics contains these words:

> Without sponsors, there would be no Olympic Games. Without the Olympic Games, there would be no dreams. Without dreams, there would be nothing (cited in Horne, 2007).

Of course, the sponsors themselves could not have written a statement better suited to their purposes. They want people to focus on dreams rather than the realities related to consumption and global corporate expansion; the Olympic Games continue to be awash in Coca-Cola imagery as outposts continue to be established in the minds of billions of potential consumers of soft drinks.

Outposts in Action: Branding Sports When ranchers want to show ownership of animals, they burn their logos into the animals' hides. The brand is their mark of ownership. And in the realm of sports, nearly all major stadiums and arenas in North America now display the brands of airlines, banks, brewers, and a gang of companies selling cars, oil, auto parts, energy, soft drinks, and communications services and products. For the venues in which NFL, NBA, and MLB teams play, these branding or naming rights sell for $3 million to $23 million per year. Deals usually are for 10–30 years and often include signage in and around the venue, the use of luxury boxes and club seats, promotional rights for events, and exclusive concession rights (e.g., the four Pepsi Centers in the United States sell only Pepsi products to fans). This benefits corporations, especially in major cities where four large billboards can cost up to $100,000 a month ($1.2 million per year). Having multiple billboard-like surfaces inside and outside a stadium is viewed as a good investment by corporate executives, especially when the name of their company is used in everyday conversations and they receive "sport perks" for themselves, customers, and friends.

The branding of sports also is apparent inside stadiums, where nearly every available surface is sold for corporate displays. Surfaces without corporate messages are now defined as wasted space, even in publicly owned facilities. This occurs at all levels of sports. For instance, many corporations desperately want to establish outposts in the minds of high school students who are in the process of forming lifelong preferences for products such as soft drinks. David Carter from the Sports Marketing Company in California knows that high school sports need revenues, so he predicts that "commercialism is coming to a school near you: the high school cheerleaders will be brought to you by Gatorade, and the football team will be presented by Outback [Steakhouse]" (in Pennington, 2004, p. 1).

As corporations brand public spaces, community identities often come to be linked with brands, thereby converting the physical embodiments of local traditions and histories into highly visible signs that promote consumption and identify corporations as providers of pleasure and excitement. In the process, the public good is replaced by the corporate good, even in spaces paid for and owned by citizen-taxpayers.

Sport events also are branded. College football fans in the United States watch everything from the Playstation Fiesta Bowl to the Chick-fil-A Peach Bowl during December and early January. College football is clearly branded, as are the athletes who wear corporate logos on their shirts, shoes, helmets, and warm-up clothing.

NASCAR auto and truck racing has always been heavily branded. Although they have changed their branding strategies recently, they still have branded races such as Coca Cola 600, Coke Zero Sugar 400, Food City 500, Hollywood Casino 400, and Big Machine Vodka 400 at the Brickyard. Additionally, racecars are billboards with surface spaces purchased by companies selling products that often cannot be advertised on network television, such as hard liquor and tobacco. This is why it was so important for NASCAR to be nationally televised–the liquor and tobacco companies wanted their brand names in front of a national audience for 250 to 600 laps during races.

Professional events in golf, tennis, beach volleyball, skiing, ice skating, and most other sports are now named after global corporations that want their names and products to be recognized worldwide. Corporations also brand teams in cycling, soccer, rugby, and many other sports. Professional baseball teams in Japan are named after corporations, not cities. Players and even referees in most sports wear the corporate logos of sponsors on their uniforms. Because European soccer was televised for many years by

(*Source:* Frederic A. Eyer. All rights reserved. Used with permission)

"This is Pepsi McDonald at Mad Max Fury Road Park where the Microsoft Raiders will battle the Wal-Mart Titans. Team captains, Nike Jones and Budweiser Williams, prepare for the Franklin Mint Coin Toss, right after this message from our sponsor, Ford trucks—giving you power on demand!"

Televised versions of commercial sports have become inseparable from the logos and products of corporate sponsors.

public TV stations that had no commercials, corporations put their logos on the players themselves and around the walls of the playing fields so that spectators would see them constantly. This tradition continues even though commercial media now own the rights to televise most sport events worldwide.

Corporate branders now give priority to sports that appeal to young males, a demographic category defined as "hard to reach." So there are the X Games, Dew Tour, numerous events sponsored by Red Bull Energy Drink, Van's Triple Crown (surfing, skateboarding, snowboarding), McDonald's All-American High School Basketball Games, Monster Energy AMA Supercross, GoPro Mountain Games, and the Nike Hoop Summit.

Sports agents today tell athletes that they can be brands and their goal should be to merge with other commercial entities rather than simply endorse a company's products. Michael Jordan was the first to do this. He initially endorsed Nike products but gradually became a brand in his own right. Today he has his own line of products in addition to "Air Jordan." Tony Hawk has done this with his own line of skateboards and other products. However, this strategy is possible only for athletes whose celebrity is great enough to be converted into a brand.

In all other cases, it is corporations who choose who and what they wish to brand. For example, some athletes as young as 12 years old may be known as Nike, Adidas, or Under Armour athletes. Corporate executives now try to brand athletes as early as possible so that they can socialize the athletes to develop marketable personas that can be used to effectively promote corporate interests.

The Super Bowl, far too expensive for any single corporation to brand on its own, is known as much for its ads as for the game itself. Corporate sponsors of the 2020 Super Bowl paid about $5.5 million for thirty-second commercial spots during the telecast of the game–that's over $183,000 per second! Corporate sponsors pay this rate because their ads are seen live by viewers who can't "fast forward" through commercials and they receive exposure beyond the game itself–in terms of previews, summaries, highlights, evaluations, and rankings in other media coverage–and they will be available for years on the Internet where people can see every ad starting with the 1969 Super Bowl. Corporations have branded the Super Bowl to such an extent that it has been described as a program where the commercials are the entertainment, and the game may or may not be entertaining.

Future forms of corporate branding are difficult to predict because it's hard to say where people will draw the line and prevent corporations from colonizing their lives. Ads during television coverage are now inserted digitally on the field, court, and other surfaces of arenas and stadiums so that viewers cannot escape them even when they record events and delete commercials. Corporations spend more of their advertising money today to purchase brand-placement rights, so their names, logos, and products appear directly in the content of sports. This maximizes the branding of playing fields/spaces, uniforms, and athletes' bodies.

The Limits of Corporate Branding Can corporations go too far in their branding of sports? People

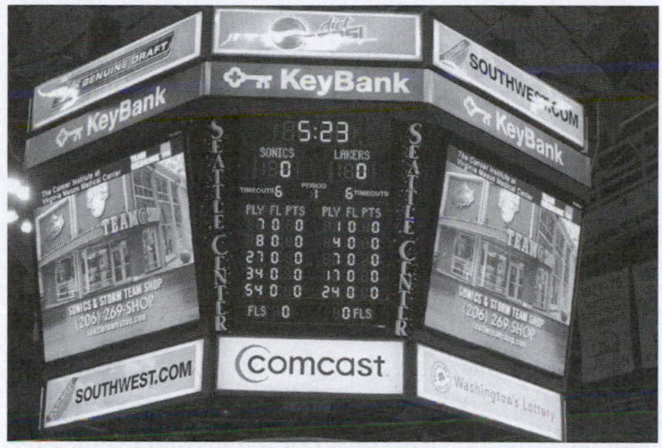

(*Source:* Jay Coakley)

The goal of branding is to establish outposts in people's heads by connecting personal pleasure and excitement with corporations and their products. This is why sport venues are filled with corporate logos and messages.

in New Jersey didn't resist when a local elementary school sold naming rights for its gym to ShopRite, a supermarket chain. Most high school and college sports programs have not resisted. Football fans don't object when McDonald's is touted as the NFL's Official Fast-Food Sponsor, and Olympic officials, who claim to be dedicated to health and fitness, have long accepted McDonald's and Coca-Cola as official sponsors of the Olympic Games. Despite a handful of cases where people objected to ads located on the actual field of play, sports are for sale, and corporations are willing buyers when deals boost their power and profits and promote consumption as a lifestyle.

In less than a generation, sports have been so thoroughly branded that many people, especially those younger than 30 years old, see this situation as "normal"–as the way it is and should be. Does this mean that corporations have established ideological outposts in their heads to the point that they accept corporate power as inevitable and even desirable? If so, corporate hegemony is deeply entrenched, even if some people resist and argue that the control of sports should not rest in the hands of corporate entities accountable only to market forces. If so, commercial sports are a site where people with political and financial resources can package their values and ideas and present them in a form that most people see as normal, acceptable, and even entertaining.

COMMERCIALIZATION AND CHANGES IN SPORTS

What happens to sports as they shift from being activities organized for players to activities organized for paying spectators and sponsors? Do they change? If so, in what ways?

When a sport is converted into commercial entertainment, its success depends solely on spectator appeal. Although spectators watch sports for many reasons, their interest is tied to a combination of four factors (Cox, 2018; Lee, 2018):

- Attachment to those involved ("Do I know, like, or strongly identify with players and/or teams?")
- The uncertainty of an event's outcome ("Will it be a close contest?" and "Who might win?")
- The stakes associated with an event ("How much money, status, or danger is involved in the contest?")
- The anticipated display of excellence, heroics, or dramatic expression by the athletes ("Are the players and/or teams skilled and entertaining?" and "Might they set a record?" or "be the best team/athlete ever?")

When spectators say they saw "a good game," they usually mean that it was one in which (1) they were attached personally or emotionally to an athlete or a team; (2) the outcome was in doubt until the last minutes or seconds; (3) the stakes were so high that players were totally committed to and engrossed in the action; or (4) there were skilled and dramatic performances. Events containing all four of these factors are remembered and discussed for many years.

Because attachment, uncertainty, high stakes, and performance attract spectators, successful commercial sports are organized to maximize the probability that all four factors will exist in an event. To understand how this affects sports, we will consider the impact of commercialization on the following three aspects of sports:

1. The internal structure and goals of sports
2. The orientations of athletes, coaches, and sponsors
3. The people and organizations that control sports

Internal Structure and Goals of Sports

Commercialization influences the internal structure and goals of newly developed sports, but it has less influence on long-established sports. New sports developed explicitly for commercial purposes are organized to maximize what a target audience will find entertaining. This is not the only factor that influences the internal structure and goals of new sports, but it is the *primary* one. It is apparent in indoor soccer, indoor lacrosse, arena football, beach volleyball, American Ninja Warrior, and commercialized action sports. Therefore, rules in the X Games maximize "big air," dangerous and spectacular moves, and the technical aspects of equipment, often manufactured by event sponsors. And when mixed martial arts was commercialized in the form of the Ultimate Fighting Championship (UFC), holding the fights in a cage was clearly an entertainment strategy–and it has been successful!

Commercialization also forces more established sports to make action more exciting and understandable for spectators, but the changes seldom alter the basic internal organization and goals of the sports. For example, rules in the NFL have been changed to protect quarterbacks, increase passing as an offensive strategy, discourage field goals, protect players from career-ending injuries, establish "television/commercial time-outs," and set game schedules to fit the interests of commercial sponsors. But the basic organization and goals of the game have remained the same.

Changes in commercialized spectator sports usually do a combination of these six things: (1) speed up the action; (2) increase scoring; (3) balance competition; (4) maximize drama; (5) heighten attachment to players and teams; and (6) provide "commercial time-outs." A review of rule changes in many sports shows the importance of these factors. For example, the designated hitter position in baseball's American League was added to increase scoring opportunities and heighten dramatic action. Soccer rules were changed to prevent matches from ending in ties. Tennis scoring was changed to meet the time requirements of television networks. Golf tournaments now involve total stroke counts rather than match play, so that big-name players aren't eliminated in an early round of a televised event. Free throws were minimized in basketball to speed up action. A sudden-death overtime period followed by a player versus goalie shootout (if needed) is now used by the National Hockey League to eliminate tie games and provide spectators with exciting action.

Although these changes are grounded in commercialization, they haven't altered the internal structure and goals of long-established sports. Teams remain the same size with similar positions, and outscoring opponents remains the primary goal. But games and matches are presented as *total entertainment experiences.* There's loud music, rapidly changing video displays, light displays, cheerleaders and mascots that present entertaining performances, and announcers that heighten drama with excited and colorful descriptions of the action. This entertainment package represents a change, but it affects the context surrounding a game or match rather than the structure and goals of the sport itself.

Orientations of Athletes, Coaches, and Sponsors

Commercial sports occur within a promotional culture created to sell athletic performances to audiences and sell audiences to sponsors. These sports are promoted through marketing hype based on stories, myths, and images created around players, teams, and even stadiums or arenas. Athletes become entertainers, and the orientations of nearly everyone in sports shift toward an emphasis on heroic action and away from aesthetic action.

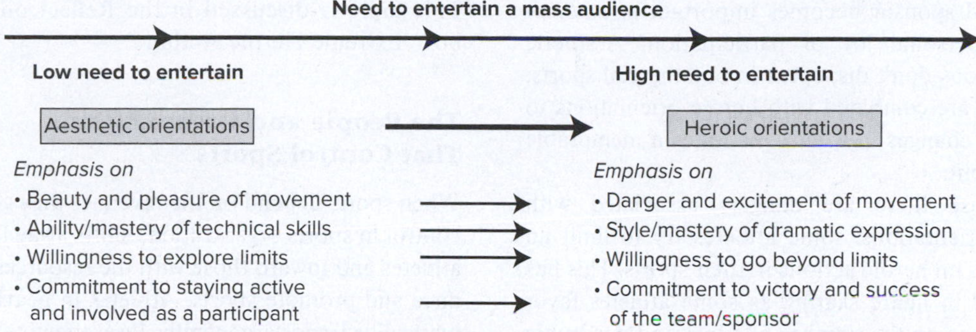

Note: The orientations associated with commercial spectator sports involve a shift from aesthetics to heroics–from skills to spectacle. Spectators need technical knowledge about a sport to be entertained by aesthetic action; when spectators lack this knowledge, they seek and focus on heroic action. Therefore, athletes and others associated with the game emphasize heroic orientations in their performances. "Heroic," as used here, refers to those who "play to the crowd" with entertaining forms of dramatic expression. The extreme version of this occurs in professional wrestling where stereotypical heroes and villains engage in heroic, dramatic, spectacular, and dangerous performances in the ring. Concerns about beauty, mastery, reasoned engagement, and athlete well-being are not the stuff of mass entertainment sports.

FIGURE 11.1 Shifting orientations: What happens when there is a need to entertain a mass audience.

As illustrated in Figure 11.1, this shift is designed to attract a mass audience.

Because many people in a *mass* audience lack technical knowledge about the sport they watch, they are entertained mostly by intense action, danger, the dramatic expressions of athletes and coaches, and manifestations of commitment to victory. These things are easily understood by spectators who don't know enough about the sport to be captivated by precise physical skills and subtle strategies.

When spectators lack technical knowledge about football, for example, they are entertained more by a running back's end-zone antics after a touchdown than by the lineman's block that enabled the running back to score the touchdown. Those who know little about the technical aspects of ice skating are entertained more by triple and quadruple jumps than routines that are carefully choreographed and flawlessly executed. Without dangerous jumps, naïve spectators become bored because they don't recognize subtle differences in the skills and routines of skaters. Those who lack technical knowledge about basketball are more impressed by slam dunks than a well-coordinated defensive strategy that wins a game.

Players realize what a mass audience wants and often "play to the crowd" with heroic displays and exciting or controversial personas. They may even refer to games as "showtime." In commercial terms, a player's style and persona often are as valuable as technical skills. This is why announcers and journalists focus on athletes who can make the big plays and are willing to talk in dramatic terms about their performances. A mass audience is thrilled by long touchdown passes, home runs, and athletes who collapse as they surpass their physical limits.

Overall, commercialization involves a shift in orientations so that the danger of movement becomes important *in addition to* the beauty of movement; style and dramatic expression become important *in addition to* skills; pushing beyond personal limits becomes important *in addition to* exploring limits; and commitment to victory for the team and sponsor becomes important *in addition to* the personal joy of participation. Aesthetic orientations don't disappear in commercial sports, but they are combined with heroic orientations to produce changes in what constitutes a memorable sport event.

Because there are dangers associated with heroic orientations, some athletes try to limit an emphasis on heroic actions in their sports. This has occurred in figure skating as some athletes favor restrictions on the number of triple and quadruple jumps required in skating programs. They worry that the quest for commercial success jeopardizes their bodies. Other skaters, however, adopt heroic orientations to please audiences and conform to shifts in the orientations of judges, coaches, and other skaters. As a result, they train to successfully land a succession of triple jumps along with quad jumps without breaking bones or destroying the continuity of their skating programs. Aesthetic orientations still exist, but heroic orientations have been woven into popular definitions of "quality" in skating performances.

As heroic orientations become more important, so do concerns about athletes becoming entertainers and sports turning into circus spectacles. For example, as accidents in NASCAR races have been linked to issues of revenge between drivers and strategies to prevent certain drivers from winning series championships, some people wonder if the sport is turning into a weekly circus act (Gluck, 2015). The challenge facing NASCAR executives is to decide whether the races are a form of honest competition or spectacles that pit drivers against each other in demolition derbies.

This issue is not limited to NASCAR. Those who control commercial sports must eventually deal with similar questions. For example, what happens to a sport when heroic orientations are pushed to extremes? Are spectators willing to have aesthetic orientations abandoned in favor of the heroic? What would events be like if this happened? One way to answer this question is to study professional wrestling–a sport turned into heroic spectacle in a quest to be entertaining. This topic is discussed in the Reflect on Sports box "Extreme Heroic Action."

The People and Organizations That Control Sports

When sports depend on the revenues they generate, control in sports organizations shifts away from the athletes and toward those with the resources to produce and promote sports. Athletes in heavily commercialized sports generally lose effective control over the conditions of their own sport participation. These conditions are controlled by a combination of general managers, team owners, corporate sponsors, advertisers, media personnel, marketing and publicity staff, professional management staff, accountants, and agents.

The organizations that control commercial sports are designed to maximize profits. Decision making promotes economic interests and defines athletes as commodities to be managed. Therefore, athletes in commercial sports usually are cut out of decision-making processes, even when the decisions affect their health and the rewards they receive for playing. This leads them to develop strategies to represent their interests relative to the interests of team owners, agents, advertising executives, media people, and corporate sponsors. For example, athletes in ESPN's X Games constantly struggle to maintain the "alternative" spirit and norms of their sport cultures as they participate under conditions controlled by ESPN and corporate sponsors.

Like many athletes before them, the athletes in action sports find it difficult to oppose the power of the media and corporate sponsors. If they want the rewards offered in commercial sports, they answer first to the sponsors. This isn't new; sponsors traditionally define the conditions of sport participation. But some people view the power shifts that come with commercialization in critical terms, assessing carefully the pros and cons of a commercial model in which corporations set the terms and conditions of playing sports. Commercialization may not significantly change the structure and goals of some sports, but it does come with major changes in

Extreme Heroic Action: *Professional Wrestling as "Sportainment"*

Professional wrestling is commercialization pushed to an extreme. It isolates elements of commercial sports and dramatizes them through parody and caricature (Barnett, 2017; Sammond, 2005; Schiesel, 2007a; Smith, 2008). In the process, it abandons aesthetic orientations and highlights the heroic.

Starting in the late 1990s, professional wrestling captured widespread spectator interest and was a smashing commercial success. It bodyslammed its way into popular culture worldwide. It featured events in sold out stadiums nearly every night in North American cities. *Raw Is War* and *Smackdown!* were top-ranked programs on ad-supported cable television. Pay-per-view events often subscribed over half a million viewers at $30 per month and up to $50 for special events. Matches were televised in nine languages in 120 countries, wrestling videos were the best-selling "sports videos" in the world, and wrestling action figures outsold all other characters in popular culture.

Branded as World Wrestling Entertainment, professional wrestling events remain among the highest-rated programs on television worldwide. More than 8000 hours of WWE programming is available in

(*Source:* carol moir/Alamy Stock Photo)

Professional wrestling turns sport into spectacle. Popular worldwide, it is organized around heroic orientations. In Spanish-speaking countries, pro wrestling is known as Lucha Libre–open wrestling in which masks are worn, with the exception of Cassandro, "Queen of the Ring" and the first openly gay celebrity wrestler (Brody, 2019). Most matches are representations of battles between what fans perceive as good and evil.

Continued

Extreme Heroic Action (*continued*)

180 countries and 28 languages, and the WWE Network now provides historical as well as current coverage and commentary of wrestling matches dating back to 1993.

For over 20 years, *Monday Nitro* and *Monday Night Raw* have cut into the audience for Monday Night Football and the finals of the NCAA men's basketball tournament. *Raw, Smackdown!,* and *WWE Main Event* have had viewer ratings consistently higher than mainstream sport events, and WWE pay-per-view events often generate impressive revenues. *Monday Night Raw* and SmackDown Live are the two longest running weekly episodic programs in US primetime history, and Total Divas, a reality series about women wrestlers, is running in its ninth season.

The popularity of professional wrestling is grounded in the heroic actions of performers combined with story lines and personas that engage spectators' concerns with issues related to social class, gender, ethnicity, job security, and national identity. In most cases, story lines and personas are performed by hypermasculine, heterosexual, and homophobic strong men who are arbitrarily victimized or privileged by greedy, underhanded corporate bosses or random, unpredictable events. The men are either supported or undermined by women, represented as alluring and vulnerable sex objects or exotic and heavily muscled sadomasochists. Overall, events are staged to represent male fantasies and fears about sex and power, and their concerns about work in a world where men feel they are losing control.

As cultural ideas about gender changed and women rejected the norm of "stand by your man no matter what," and claimed control over their bodies, careers, and presentation of self, WWE brought them into the ring to fight it out. Wrestling fans responded as headliners Ronda Rousey, Charlotte Flair, and Becky Lynch attracted a sellout crowd of over 82,000 to a 2019 WrestleMania event in Met Life Stadium (New Jersey). Instead of fighting over a man, these women displayed attitude and aspiration as they performed as individuals striving for success.

Sociologist Brendan Maguire used structural theory to hypothesize that pro wrestling is popular because it "addresses the anxiety and angst associated with community breakdown, social disenchantment, and political correctness" (2005, p. 174). He explained that when community ties are strong and social satisfaction is high and social control is not overly constraining, people have little anxiety and little need to be entertained by dramatic parodies of heroic wrestling action.

Cultural theories, on the other hand, lead to other hypotheses based on past evidence that the popularity of any cultural practice, including professional wrestling, depends on the extent to which it reaffirms the ideologies that people use to make sense of their lives and the world around them. Therefore, the goal of those who produce sport entertainment is to provide spectators with pleasure and excitement that occurs within the boundaries of the ring, court, and playing field. Spectators enjoy the action and the power structure of sport remains intact.

power relations and the organizational contexts in which sports are played.

Responses to Commercialization: Athletes and Fans

The progressive commercialization of certain sports has increased profits for team owners, league officials, media companies, and corporate sponsors. It has also provided some athletes with higher salaries and the general public with more media access to sports events. At the same time, it has marginalized or excluded athletes and fans from decision-making processes related to how sports are organized, played, and watched. When decisions driven by commercial interests conflict with the interests of athletes and fans, they have occasionally resisted the power brokers in the sports industrial complex and tried to force a showdown to have their voices heard.

Athletes in some leagues have formed players associations to compel officials and team owners to recognize their interests in decision-making processes. This strategy has succeeded in some professional leagues, but most athletes don't have access to such associations, so they remain excluded from decision-making that impacts their health and careers (Bachman, 2019).

In the face of this situation, representatives of over 100 athlete organizations met in Switzerland in 2011 to explore how they could create an independent voice for athletes worldwide (Whyno, 2017). This led to the formation of the UNI World Athletes in 2014 which quickly morphed into the World Players Association (WPA) that now has 85,000 professional athletes as members and is formally connected with over 100 athlete organizations in 60 countries.

The WPA gives players a forum for connecting with each other and sharing information about experiences, working conditions, and labor relations. It also works directly with local athlete organizations. For example, WPA officials met with athletes and officials from the European Basketball Player Associations in Italy during 2019 to strengthen social dialogue and the bargaining power among professional players from France, Spain, and Italy (EUAthletes, 2017). Annual WPA conferences are organized around seminars and education programs for athletes at all points in their careers and around political issues related to working conditions and human rights (the 2021 conference to be held in the USA).

The WPA has also teamed up with other organizations concerned with human rights and working conditions to influence the governance and policies of the IOC, FIFA, and other international and national sports governing bodies. A major effort in 2017 led to the announcement of a Universal Declaration of Player Rights that addressed "persistent, systemic and long-standing violations of players' fundamental rights throughout world sport" (EUAthletes, 2018). This was important because it was the first time that an international document articulated the "human and labor rights" of players worldwide. According to Brendan Schwab, director of the WPA, the declaration filled a glaring gap because in the thousands of pages of sport rule books worldwide there was not one statement about the personal, labor, or legal rights of athletes (Schwab, 2018). Due to player support for the WPA, it is likely that it will advance a long-term process of making athletes' voices heard on issues related to the humanity of sports–issues rarely addressed by commercial sports organizations seeking to increase revenues.

Like athletes, fans also are excluded in the decision-making processes of commercial sports. In cases where teams are sponsored through a club system in which members historically participated in decision-making related to club affairs, these members and the larger fan groups to which they belong have recently protested the decisions of team owners and management and called for fan voices to be heard on a range of issues (Androus & Giudici, 2018; Gaffney, 2015; Hill, Canniford & Millward, 2018; Hognestad, 2015; Numerato, 2015; Putra, 2019; Scherer, 2016).

As professional club teams generated more revenues, especially from sponsors and the sales of media rights, they depended less and less on the support of local communities, especially segments of those communities that had been long-time, working-class supporters of local clubs. Stadiums were renovated or constructed in new locations with the intent of attracting wealthier and less rowdy spectators who would pay higher prices for tickets in venues where all their experiences were commodified. In the process, male working-class fans were treated as consumers to be regulated and controlled and then marginalized to the point that they felt disconnected with the teams around which their identities had been formed for generations. Combined with feelings of powerlessness in other aspects of their lives, this led some fans to use football/soccer as a context in which to voice their resistance to neo-liberal trends driven by commercial interests.

Fan organizations, such as *Against Modern Football, Anti-Modern Football*, *Stand Against Modern Football,* and the *Football Supporters Federation* (in the UK) were formed over the past 20 years to protest the commercialization of football in European and Latin American countries. Although these organizations enabled people to express their dissatisfaction with being pushed aside in decision-making processes and having local traditions ignored as football was commodified, few of them have had long term impact. Their members were vocal in protesting commercialization but they seldom had strategies for change or even a clear vision for what they wanted football to be (Cloake, 2013). As a result, they were rarely taken seriously by new club owners whose power and wealth enabled them to ignore the protests or solicit the support of local police to quiet the fans. Only in a few cases, mostly at local levels, have organizations had enough power to be consulted by club officials on certain policies.

The two major fan organizations in the United States are the *League of Fans* (LOF) and the *Sports Fans Coalition* (SFC), formed in the 1970s and 2009, respectively. SFC is self-described as "a grassroots, sports fans advocacy organization . . . made up of sports fans who want to have a say in how the sports industry works, and to put fans first" (https://www.sportsfans.org/). The LOF, on the other hand, is "a sports reform project founded by long-time social and political activist, Ralph Nader, to fight for the higher principles of justice, fair play, equal opportunity and civil rights in sports; and to encourage safety and civic responsibility in sports industry and culture" (Reed, 2015; https://www.leagueoffans.org).

These organizations both work to inform the public and policy-makers about issues that negatively impact fans and athletes. SFC focuses more on the interests of fans and sports governance issues, and it tends to use a legal-political approach as it deals with these issues. The LOF is more of a think tank focusing on social justice, public policy, and general reform issues; it tends to use a public information and social influence approach. Two of the current projects for the SFC (as of mid-2019) were (1) creating legal agreements in which the public funding of stadiums is tied together with guaranteed benefits for fans and the local community and (2) soliciting public support for a Sports Bettors' Bill of Rights to protect fans as sports betting becomes legal in more states. At the same time, LOF was working on (1) head injuries and brain trauma suffered by athletes and (2) promoting cardio-based physical education and sport-for-all programs in schools as opposed to the current emphasis on exclusive varsity sports.

Most sports fans in the United States have never heard of these organizations. Their identities are connected with teams and athletes and they are not actively concerned about social and labor issues in sports. If they seek a feeling of power as fans, they often participate in fantasy sports where they create their own fantasy teams to manage. The major sport leagues own and promote fantasy sports because it increases fan engagement and league income and leads fans to feel that they are in control even though they have no real power.

THE ORGANIZATION OF PROFESSIONAL SPORTS IN NORTH AMERICA

Professional sports in North America are privately owned by individuals, partnerships, or corporations. The wealth and power of owners is greatest at the top levels of professional sports and less so in minor leagues and sports with relatively small audiences. Similarly, sponsors and event promoters range from individuals to large transnational corporations, depending on the size of events.

The Owners of Sport Teams

Most of the individuals or companies that own minor-league teams in North America don't make much money. Many are happy to break even and avoid the losses that are commonplace at this level of sports ownership. Also, many teams, leagues, and events have been financial disasters over the past 50 years. Five football leagues, a hockey league, a few soccer leagues, a volleyball league, four men's and five women's basketball leagues, a team tennis league, and a number of basketball and soccer teams have gone out of business, leaving many owners, sponsors, and promoters in debt. This list covers only the United States and doesn't include all those who have lost money on tournaments and special events.

The owners of major men's professional sport franchises in North America are very different from owners at other levels of commercial sports. Teams or franchises in the NFL, NBA, NHL, and MLB in 2019 were valued from about $290 million (Arizona Coyotes in the NHL) to about $5 billion (Dallas Cowboys in the NFL). Therefore, the owners of teams in these leagues are large corporations and a few very wealthy individuals with assets ranging from hundreds of millions to billions of dollars. Each of these four major men's leagues is organized as a monopoly. Most teams in these leagues play in publicly subsidized facilities, owners make good to excellent returns on their investments, and support from media companies and corporate sponsors almost guarantees continued financial success at this level of ownership.

Similarly, the large corporations that sponsor particular events, from major golf and tennis tournaments to NASCAR and Grand Prix races, know the costs and benefits involved. Their association with top events provides them with advertising platforms and connects them with clearly identified categories of consumers. Media companies also sponsor events so they can control their own programming, as in the case of ESPN's X Games, Red Bull sports, and others.

Major sport sponsorships enable companies that sell tobacco, alcohol, and junk food to link their products and logos with popular activities. Executives at these companies know that people associate sports with strong, healthy bodies instead of cancer, heart disease, diabetes, obesity, tooth decay, and other forms of poor health associated with their products. Their hope is to use sports to increase their legitimacy as "corporate citizens" and defuse resistance to their policies and products.

Investments in sports and sport events are motivated by many factors. In some cases, investors are wealthy fans looking to satisfy lifelong fantasies, build their egos, or socialize with celebrity athletes. Buying a team or sponsoring major events gives them more enjoyment and prestige than other business ventures, often making them instant celebrities in an exclusive business club that plays by less restrictive rules than other businesses (Schrotenboer, 2019).

Those who invest in sports enjoy their status, but they don't allow fun and fantasy to interfere with business and the growth of their capital. They don't enjoy losing money or sharing power. They may look at their athletes as heroes, but they want to control them and maximize investment returns. They may be civic boosters and supporters of public projects, but they define the "public good" in terms that emphasize capitalist expansion and their own business interests, usually to the exclusion of other definitions. They may not agree with fellow owners and sponsors on all issues, but they do agree that their investments must be protected and their profits maximized.

Team Owners and Sport Leagues as Cartels

The tendency to think alike has been especially strong among the owners of teams in the major North American sport leagues. Unity among owners has led to the formation of effective cartels. A **cartel** is *a centralized group that coordinates the actions of a selected collection of people or businesses.* Therefore, even though each sport franchise in each league is usually a separate business, the team owners in each sport come together to form a cartel representing their collective interests. The cartel is used to control inter-team competition for players, fans, media revenues, and sales of licensed merchandise. Additionally, it's used to eliminate competition from others who might form teams and leagues in the same sports. When a cartel succeeds, as it has in each of the major men's professional team sports, it becomes a **monopoly**–*the one and only provider of a particular product or service.*

Each league–the NBA, NFL, NHL, and MLB–is also a **monopsony,** or *a single buyer of a product or service*–in this case, elite athletic labor in a particular

(*Source:* Frederic A. Eyer. All rights reserved. Used with permission)

"Winning is easy when you form a cartel, prevent others from playing, and maintain exclusive control over a highly desired product."

The growth and profitability of commercial sports worldwide have little to do with athletes. Owners, sponsors, and media executives control sports today, and they make money when governments allow them to operate as cartels and keep competitors out of the game.

sport. This means that if a college football player wants to play professional football in the United States, he has one choice: the NFL. And the NFL, like other monopsony leagues, has developed a system to force new players to negotiate contracts only with the team that drafts them. This enables owners to sign new players to contracts without bidding against other teams, which might be willing to pay particular players more money.

As a cartel, the owners prevent new leagues from being established and competing with them for players, and they also prevent new teams from entering their league without their permission. When permission is given, it involves conditions set by the cartel. For example, the new team owner is charged an entry fee to become a part of the league and must give back to the cartel some of the team's profits for a certain number of years. Furthermore, a new owner can locate only in a city approved by the cartel, and no current owner can move a team to another city without cartel approval.

Being part of a legal cartel enables most team owners to make impressive sums of money. During the mid-1960s, NFL teams were bought and sold for about $10 million; in 2020 the average franchise value was close to $3 billion. That amounts to an average *annual* return of over $50 million on an original investment of $10 million. This is what a cartel does: it limits the supply of teams and drives up the value of existing teams. Of course, team owners do not include capital gains (in the team value) when they announce that annual profits are low and they must raise ticket prices and have a new stadium so they can be "competitive" with other teams. When you are in a cartel, you can get away with this deception and commercial blackmail without going to jail. Additionally, team owners use their power to influence the rule makers who set the rules that govern them.

Each league also has unique internal agreements regulating how teams can negotiate the sale of local broadcasting rights to their games. The NFL does not allow teams to sign independent television or radio contracts for local broadcasts of their games, but MLB does. This creates significant disparities in the incomes of baseball teams, because the New York Yankees can negotiate a local media rights deal that may be a hundred times higher than what the Kansas City Royals can negotiate in a much smaller media market.

The biggest differences between the major men's sport leagues are related to their contractual agreements with the players' association in each league. Although each league gives players as few rights and as little money as possible, athletes have negotiated over the last five decades to gain control over their careers, regulate the conditions of their sport participation, and increase their salaries. This topic is discussed in the section on page 404, titled "Legal Status and Incomes of Athletes in Commercial Sports."

Team Owners and Public Assistance

The belief that cities cannot have "major league status" unless they have professional sports teams and sports megaevents has enabled sports team owners and promoters to receive public money. Most common is the use of public funds to build arenas and stadiums. As noted in Chapter 9 (pp. 310–311), this "stadium socialism" enables wealthy and powerful capitalists to use public money for personal gain, but when the media discuss this transfer of funds, it is usually described as "economic development" rather than "welfare for the rich."

The use of public assistance to subsidize stadiums and arenas for team owners is based on a belief that these venues benefit the entire community in the following five ways:

1. A stadium and pro team create jobs; those who hold the jobs spend money and pay taxes in the city so that everyone benefits.
2. Stadium construction infuses money into the local economy; this money is spent over and over and generates tax revenues as it circulates.
3. The team attracts businesses to the city, and this increases local revenues.
4. The team attracts regional and national media attention, which boosts tourism and contributes to overall economic development.
5. The team creates positive psychic and social benefits, boosting social unity and feelings of pride and well-being in the local population.

Despite these claims made by owners and their allies, impact studies done by *independent* researchers generally reach the following conclusions:[1]

1. Teams and stadiums create jobs, but apart from highly paid athletes and team executives, these jobs are low paid, part-time, and seasonal. Additionally, many athletes on the team don't live in the city or spend their money there.
2. The companies that design and build stadiums are seldom local, and construction materials and workers on major projects often come from outside the region or even from outside the country. Therefore, much of the money spent on a stadium or arena does not circulate as stadium boosters predict.
3. Stadiums attract other businesses, but most are restaurant and entertainment franchises headquartered in other cities. These franchises often have enough cash to undercut and drive out locally owned businesses. Out-of-town people do attend games, but most people who buy tickets live close enough to make day trips to games, and their purchases inside the stadium don't benefit businesses outside the stadium gates.
4. Stadiums and teams generate public relations for the city, but this has mixed results for tourism because fans who spend money in and around the stadium have fewer dollars to spend in their own neighborhoods. A stadium often helps nearby businesses, but it often hurts outlying businesses. When a family of four spends $13,000 for average NBA season tickets, and another $5000 for meals and parking for 41 home games, it will spend less money on dinners and entertainment close to home–if they have any money left!
5. A pro sport team can make some people feel good and may enhance general perceptions of a city, but this is difficult to measure and little is known about its consequences for the city as a whole. Additionally, the feelings of fans often vary with the success of a team, and the feelings of those who are not fans may not be improved by a men's sport team that reaffirms traditional masculinity and values emphasizing domination and conquest.

Independent researchers explain that positive effects are bound to occur when a city spends $500 million to a billion dollars of public money on a project. However, they also point out that the public good might be better served if tax money were spent on things other than a stadium. For example, during the mid-1990s, the city of Cleveland spent nearly a billion dollars of public money to build three

[1] Independent studies of this issue are numerous and all of them come to the conclusion that investing pubic money in stadiums and arenas does not provide the benefits that owners claim: see Bagli, 2019; Bandow (2003); Brown et al., (2004); Chan (2018); Curry et al., (2004); Delaney and Eckstein (2003); deMause and Cagan (2008); Farren (2017); Friedman and Andrews, 2011; Friedman et al., (2004); Gayer, Drukker & Gold (2016); Lewis (2010); Povich (2016); Propheter, 2017; Ritholtz (2018); Rossi (2018); Silk (2004); Smith and Ingham (2003); Staff (2018).

(*Source:* Rich Graessle/Icon Sportswire/Getty Images)

US Bank Stadium, home of the NFL's Minnesota Vikings, opened in mid-2016. The Vikings are owned primarily by multi-billionaire Zygmunt Wilf. The stadium cost was $1.1 billion, and it was funded through the largest public-private partnership in Minnesota history. The public–that is, taxpayers in Minneapolis and Minnesota–took on a debt obligation of over $500 million, which amounts to nearly $1 billion including interest over three decades, and the team owners owe $530 million. As construction of the stadium began in late-2013, the value of the Vikings was $1 billion; when the stadium opened in 2016, the value of the team was $2.2 billion, an increase of $1.2 billion over 30 months, and a net gain of over $600 million for the billionaire owners of the team. *Conclusion*: in this "partnership," the owners profited greatly and the taxpayers will be paying for the stadium and stadium maintenance through 2046.

sport facilities and related infrastructure. Inner-city residents during the same years pleaded with the city to install a drinking fountain in a park in a working-class neighborhood, and teachers held classes in renovated shower rooms in local public schools because there was no money to fund new educational facilities for inner-city students. At the same time, the owners of the three sport teams received a fifty-year exemption on taxes related to their teams and facilities, and $120 million in tax abatements on other real estate development in the area around the stadiums. This means that the city annually forfeited about $50 million in city and county tax revenues at a time when there were desperate needs among residents. In the meantime, the franchise values for the NFL, NBA, and MLB teams in Cleveland increased dramatically, giving multimillion-dollar capital gains to each of the wealthy owners.

Sociologists Kevin Delaney and Rick Eckstein (2003) studied the Cleveland case along with eight other cities where public money was used to build stadiums for private use. They concluded that the results in Cleveland were better than in the other cities. However, they found no evidence that the three stadiums fostered a downtown rejuvenation, as stadium proponents had predicted. Neither the number of businesses nor job creation rates increased, and in the three years following the construction, the cost for each new job created was $231,000, nearly twenty times higher than the cost to develop jobs with public programs. The new sport facilities failed to lower poverty rates, improve schools, or increase the availability of safe, low-cost housing (deMause and Cagan, 2008), but they did force poor people to move to other areas of town which gave developers cheap access to land on which they could build.

The people who object to stadium subsidies seldom have resources to oppose the well-financed, professionally packaged proposals developed by the consultants hired by team owners. The social activists who might lead the opposition already deal full time with problems related to unemployment, underfunded schools, homelessness, poor health, and the lack of needed social services in cities. They cannot abandon these tasks to lobby against using public money to benefit billionaire team owners and millionaire celebrity athletes. At the same time, local people are persuaded to think that team owners will abandon their city if they don't pony up public money to build a new facility with the requisite number of luxury suites and club seats.

When thinking about public subsidies to sport teams, it's helpful to consider alternative uses of public funds. For example, my former hometown of Colorado Springs used $6 million of public money in 2000 to construct a youth sport complex consisting of 12 baseball, softball, and T-ball fields of various sizes with bleacher seating; ten soccer/football fields; six volleyball courts; an in-line skating rink; a batting cage (for baseball hitting practice); and multiple basketball courts. At the same time, $300 million of tax money from six Denver metro counties was used to build a new stadium for Pat Bowlen, the wealthy owner of the Denver Broncos. Instead of doing this, the counties could have done what Colorado Springs did and used the $300 million to build 600 baseball, softball, and T-ball fields; 500 soccer/football fields; 300 volleyball courts; 50 in-line skating rinks; 50 batting cages; and 250 basketball courts around the metro area.

Which of these two alternatives would have had the most positive impact on the overall quality of life in the Denver metro area? If the money had been spent on local recreation facilities, individuals and families in the region would now have easy access to one or more of them seven days a week for a nominal cost. Maybe people in the region would be more physically active and healthier. Instead, the region has a 72,000-seat stadium used by the Denver Broncos ten times a year, or thirteen times if they make the playoffs with home-field advantage and win all games leading up to the Super Bowl. Since the stadium was built, the team has played fewer than eleven home games per season except in 2015, and spectators have paid an average of over $85 a seat for 210 home games from 2001 through 2018. This amounts to about $1.3 billion; and with parking and concessions expenditures, people have paid about $1.6 billion to attend games in a stadium subsidized by their taxes.

Most of this money has gone into the pockets of team owners, executives, and players, who spend part of it in Denver but much of it elsewhere. Also, the owners keep half of the stadium naming-rights money and the other half goes into the public fund to pay maintenance costs for the stadium, which is the responsibility of the taxpayers. Many of the stay-at-home fans of the team pay larger cable and satellite costs to see games and spend at least fifty hours a year sitting down watching Bronco games and consuming food and drinks at home or in bars. They become emotionally invested in the team, players, and outcomes of games and seasons, and they have fun with family and friends when watching and talking about things related to "their" team.

Some people prefer the NFL stadium, but many others might prefer an abundance of local recreation facilities, if they had a choice. Among those preferring the stadium are people with the power and resources to obtain what they want. And they want new stadiums and access to the revenue streams that a stadium generates. They have memberships in athletic and fitness clubs and don't care about building public recreation centers. Even their children play sports in private clubs and on teams that use private facilities. Additionally, they have mini fitness centers in their homes.

This is how power and social class shape local cultures, access to particular kinds of sport facilities, and priorities for spending public money related to sports.

Sources of Income for Team Owners

The owners of top pro teams in the major men's sports make money from four primary sources: (1) media rights, (2) gate receipts, (3) sponsors, and (4) merchandising. The amounts and proportions of each of these revenue sources vary from league to league and team to team.

The continuing wave of new stadium construction and renovation is the result of owners demanding venues that generate new revenue streams. This is why these stadiums resemble shopping malls built around playing fields. Sociologist George Ritzer (2005) describes them as "cathedrals of consumption" designed so that consumption is seamlessly included in spectator experiences. Owners see this as important because it enables them to capture a greater share of the entertainment dollar in a highly competitive urban entertainment market. Their revenue generating strategy is to use as much public money as possible to build new venues that contain more luxury boxes and fewer "cheap seats." Then they increase the price of tickets and concessions, and use the same strategy again when another new venue will increase their revenues even more.

When a new stadium is built, the value of the team that plays there increases at least 25 percent. This means that if a city builds a $700 million stadium for an NFL team that is valued at $4 billion, the franchise value will increase about $1 billion. This increase goes directly to the owners as team value.

To prevent people from realizing how public money is used to subsidize their wealth, the owners make sure that announcers describe *their* teams as *your* New York Giants, Cleveland Cavaliers, Detroit Red Wings, or Colorado Rockies. The owners are happy to support the illusion that their teams belong to the community, as long as they collect the revenues and capital gains while taxpayers take the risks and receive little benefit apart from the emotional perks that come from living in a region that has a professional men's sport team located there.

The Promise of Gambling Revenues

The people who profit from commercial sports always have their eyes open to the existence of new revenue streams. As noted in Chapter 5, *Deviance in Sports*, a 2018 US Supreme Court decision allowed states to approve sports betting. As state officials realize that it is easier to control corruption in connection with legalized gambling than with illegal gambling, they are cautiously moving in that direction (Minton, 2018; Rogers & Hjelmgaard, 2018). As of 2020, twenty-one states have approved sports betting in some form and all but six of the other twenty-nine states have voted down bills to allow it, but other bills will be brought to many of those states in the near future as attitudes against gambling continue to soften and as legislators seek new tax revenues.

According to the projections of a research firm that studies gaming, the revenue made by legal sports betting operations in the United States during 2019 will top $800 million. That would increase to $17.3 billion if sports betting were legal in all 50 states, and the total projected amount of money that would be bet each year on sports if it were legal in all 50 states would be well over $250 billion with three-fourths of all bets placed online (Burnsed, 2019; Gray, 2019). Under these conditions, the potential revenue increases for major men's sports leagues and teams are significant (American Gaming Association, 2018).

Although the official position of people in major commercial sports organizations has been anti-gambling, most of them had a quick change of heart as they identified ways to increase revenues in connection with sports betting (Maese, 2018). For example, the top professional men's leagues asked states to give them a share of gambling revenues for overseeing "the integrity of games," and providing the game data that made bets possibles. The states denied these requests which led the leagues to partner with casinos and sports betting operations in sponsorship and partnership deals. NBA officials were among the first to work with US and international sportsbooks, including MGM Resorts (and casinos) to sell them advertising opportunities as well as official NBA and WNBA game data that is used to calculate the odds for in-game betting (Broughton, 2018; Purdum, 2018).

The National Hockey League, a long-time opponent of sports betting signed partnership deals with William Hill, part of the world's largest gaming organization; with FanDuel, the daily fantasy sports organization that is now an official sports betting operation; and with El Dorado Resorts that have gambling operations directly connected with NHL teams located in states where sports betting is or will soon be legal (O'Malley, 2019; Ramsey, 2018). In fact, the FanDuel Sportsbook will have its logo embedded in the ice as the New Jersey Devils play their games in the Prudential Center arena. Strangely, the NHL is also partners with DraftKings, a competitor of FanDuel, and has even invested in the company as it moves into the sports betting business.

Despite being shut out of direct gambling-related revenues, team owners and league officials know that media companies will benefit from increased sports betting because people who bet on sports are highly engaged fans who often consume televised sports obsessively, buy expensive cable and pay-per-view packages, and seek media content that they use to inform their bets (Drape, 2019; Jenkins, 2019; PwC, 2018; Schoenfeld, 2019). When media revenues increase, sport leagues and teams seek more money when they sell the rights to broadcast their games.

Unlike the professional leagues, the NCAA has not been eager to endorse sports betting (Burnsed, 2019; NCAA, 2019; Rodenberg, 2019). Professional players generally make too much money to risk participating in match- or prop-fixing (see Chapter 5), but college players are not paid and are more likely candidates for cooperating with corrupt gamblers for a share of payouts on "fixed" bets. To discourage this and to warn players of the dangers of betting on sports, the NCAA plans anti-gambling education and enforcement programs for all athletes, especially the men on high profile football and basketball teams. In the meantime, Division I universities, the high-profile conferences, and the NCAA will benefit from sports betting if they can demand more rights fees from media companies. Again, the more people bet on sports, the more they consume sports through media.

Worldwide, sports betting is a multibillion-dollar business. It has for some time been legal in most of Europe and parts of Asia, although it is regulated by national governments. International sports betting is estimated to be a $250 billion business and the United States already accounts for about $70 billion of that amount with most of that amount being wagered illegally (Gray, 2019). Legalization will certainly increase that betting activity.

THE ORGANIZATION OF AMATEUR SPORTS IN NORTH AMERICA

So-called amateur sports don't have owners, but they do have commercial sponsors and governing bodies that control events and athletes. Generally, the sponsors in the United States are corporations interested in using amateur sports for publicity and advertising purposes. The governing bodies of amateur sports operate on a nonprofit basis, although they use revenues from events to maintain their organizations and exert control over amateur sports. They generally hire for-profit companies to organize, publicize, and administer the events for them.

Centralized state-sponsored sport authorities administer amateur sports in nearly all countries except the United States. They work with the national governing bodies (NGBs) of individual sports, and together they control events, athletes, and revenues. Sport Canada and the Canadian Olympic Association are examples of such centralized authorities; they develop the policies that govern the various national sport organizations in Canada, from youth sports to national teams.

In the United States, the organization and control of amateur sports is much less centralized. Policies, rules, fund-raising strategies, and methods of operating vary from one organization to the next. For example, the major governing body in intercollegiate sports is the National Collegiate Athletic Association (NCAA). For amateur sports not connected with universities, the major controlling organization is the United States Olympic and Paralympic Committee (USOPC). However, within the USOPC, each of the 47 separate NGBs regulate and control a particular amateur sport. NGBs raise most of their own funds through corporate and individual sponsors, and each one sets its own policies to supplement the rules and policies of the USOPC and IOC. The USOPC has long tried to establish continuity in American amateur sports, but the NGBs and other organizations are very protective of their own turf, and they seldom give up power; instead, they fight to maintain exclusive control over rules, revenues, and athletes. This has caused many political battles in and among organizations.

(*Source:* Frederic A. Eyer. All rights reserved. Used with permission)

Recently built stadiums resemble shopping malls, and some fans see attendance as a shopping opportunity. They're a captive audience, and team owners want to capture as many of their entertainment dollars as possible. This fan has taken the consumption bait and is less interested in the game than buying products to prove he was there.

All amateur sports organizations share an interest in two things: (1) controlling the athletes in their sports and (2) controlling the money generated from sponsorships and competitive events. Sponsorship patterns in amateur sports take many forms. Universities, for example, "sell" their athletic departments, allowing corporations to brand their athletic teams and the bodies of athletes in exchange for money, scholarships, equipment, and apparel. Corporations and universities usually enter these agreements outside of any democratic processes involving votes by students, athletes, or the citizens whose taxes fund the universities.

The NGBs of US amateur sports depend on corporate sponsorships to pay for athlete training, operating expenses, and competitive events. Corporate logos appear on the clothing and equipment of amateur athletes. A few top athletes may sign endorsement deals as individuals, but they cannot do so when the deals conflict with the interests of NGB sponsors.

When this model of corporate sponsorship is used, the economics of sports are linked to the fluctuations of market economies and the profits of large corporations. Corporations sponsor only those sports that foster their interests, and economic conditions influence their ability and willingness to maintain sponsorships. For example, when the Women's United Soccer Association (WUSA) and its 180 professional athletes needed $20 million in 2003 to survive another year, Nike could have reduced the $450-million deal they made with Manchester United, a men's soccer team in England, so it could support WUSA, but it didn't because corporations are about profits, and women's soccer didn't fit into their business plans.

LEGAL STATUS AND INCOMES OF ATHLETES IN COMMERCIAL SPORTS

When sports are commercialized, athletes are entertainers. This is obvious at the professional level, but it's also true in other commercial sports such as big-time college football and basketball. Professional athletes are paid for their efforts, whereas amateur athletes receive rewards within limits set by the organizations that govern their lives. This raises these two questions:

1. What is the legal status of the athlete-entertainers in sports?
2. How are athlete-entertainers rewarded for their work?

Many people don't think of athletes as workers, and they overlook owner–player relations in professional sports as a form of labor relations. Most people associate sports with play, and they see athletes as having fun rather than working. However, when sports are businesses, players are workers, even though they may have fun on the job. This isn't unique; many workers enjoy their jobs. But regardless of enjoyment, issues of legal status and fair rewards for work are important.

This section focuses on the United States and does not consider all the sports that collect gate receipts but never make enough money to pay for anything but basic expenses, if that. Therefore, we don't discuss high school sports, non-revenue-producing college sports, or other nonprofit local sports in which teams sell tickets to events.

> **The NFL is a machine. The operators of the machine pull its levers more frantically every season, pushing it past its breaking point. So the league has stockpiled interchangeable spare parts. The broken ones are seamlessly replaced and the machine keeps rolling.**
>
> –Nate Jackson, former NFL player (2011)

Professional Athletes

The legal status of athletes has always been the most controversial issue in professional team sports.

Legal Status: Team Sports Until the mid-1970s, professional athletes in the major sport leagues had little or no legal power to control their careers. They could play only for the team that drafted and owned them. They could not control when and to whom they might be traded during their careers, even when their contracts expired or were revoked by owners. Furthermore, they were obliged to sign standard contracts saying that they agreed to forfeit to their owners all rights over their careers. Basically, they were bought and sold like property and seldom consulted about their wishes. They were at the mercy of team owners, managers, and coaches.

In all sports, this form of employee restriction was called the **reserve system** because it was *a set of practices that enabled team owners to reserve the labor of athletes for themselves and control the movement of athletes from team to team in their sport.*

As long as the reserve system was legal, owners could maintain low salaries and near-total control over the conditions under which athletes played their sports. Parts of the reserve system continue to exist in professional sports, but players' associations (that is, unions) in each of the major professional leagues for men have challenged the system in court and forced significant changes that increased their rights as workers so they could negotiate with owners to control conditions of their work and establish guidelines for their salaries.

In any other business, a reserve system of the type used in men's professional sports would violate antitrust laws. Companies cannot control employee movement from firm to firm, and they certainly cannot draft employees so that no other company can hire them, nor can they trade them at will to another company. But this type of reserve system, with modifications since the 1970s, has been defined by the US Congress as legal in sports, and owners use it with minimal interference from any government agency.

Team owners justify the reserve system by saying that it's needed to maintain competitive balance between teams in their leagues. They argue that, if athletes could play with any team, the wealthiest owners in the biggest cities and TV markets would buy all the good athletes and prevent teams in smaller cities and TV markets from being winners.

The irony of this argument is that team owners are free-market capitalists who argue that free-market processes would destroy their business! They embrace regulation and "sport socialism" because it protects their power and wealth; they form cartels to restrict athletes' rights and salaries, *but* they advocate deregulation in the economy as a whole. Their positions are ideologically inconsistent, but profitable for them.

Professional athletes always have objected to the reserve system, but it wasn't until 1976 that court rulings gave professional athletes the right to become *free agents* under certain conditions. The meaning of free agency varies, but in all leagues it allows some players whose contracts have expired to seek contracts with other teams that bid for their services. This change has had a dramatic effect on the salaries of top professional athletes from the late 1970s to the present. Table 11.1 lists average salaries in major sport leagues from 1950 to 2019, and the data show the dramatic increases that occurred after the mid-1970s.

Prior to the mid-1970s pro athletes made two to four times more than median family income in the United States. After free agency was allowed in the 1970s, salaries skyrocketed. With rising revenues from gate receipts and media rights, salaries increased rapidly as teams competed for players and negotiated new Collective Bargaining Agreements (CBAs) with players' unions. In 2019, the ratio of average salaries relative to median family income was 104:1 for the NBA; 60:1 for MLB; 37:1 for the NHL; 39:1 for the NFL; 5:1 for the MLS, 1:1 for the WNBA and .3:1 for the NWSL.

Owner–athlete relations change every time a new CBA is negotiated and signed. Although team owners, league officials, and some fans dislike the players' unions, these organizations have enabled players to gain more control over their salaries and working conditions. Labor negotiations and players'

Table 11.1 Average salaries in major US professional leagues, compared with median family income, 1950–2019*

	SPORT LEAGUE							Median
Year	**NFL**	**NBA**	**WNBA**	**NHL**	**MLB**	**MLS**	**NWSL**	**US Family Income†**
1950	15,000	5,100	NA	5,000	13,300	NA	NA	4,000
1960	17,100	13,000	NA	14,100	19,000	NA	NA	5,620
1970	23,000	40,000	NA	25,000	29,300	NA	NA	9,867
1980	79,000	190,000	NA	110,000	143,000	NA	NA	21,023
1990	395,400	824,000	NA	247,000	598,000	NA	NA	35,353
2000	1,116,100	3,600,000	60,000‡	1,050,000	1,988,034	100,000	NA	50,732
2010	1,900,000	5,150,000	52,000‡	2,400,000	3,298,000	140,000	NA	60,236
2019	2,910,000	7,770,000	79,000	2,780,000	4,510,000	380,000	20,000**	75,500

*Data on players' salaries come from many sources, but I try to be accurate and consistent. Average salaries before 1971 are estimates because players' associations did not exist and teams had notoriously unreliable payroll data.

†This is median annual income for families–that is, households consisting of parents and children. Half of all families fall above the median, and half fall below it. Data are from the US Census.

‡Estimate based on the salary cap and stated salaries based on years in the league and the round in which players were drafted.

**The National Women's Soccer League played its first game in 2013. The salary money available to each team in 2019 was $421,500 and rosters consisted of 20–22 players; this means that the average salary was about $21,000, although the salaries of national team players were usually paid by their national federations.

strikes in professional team sports have focused primarily on issues of freedom and control over careers, rather than money, although money has certainly been an issue. As a result, free agency now exists for all players after they've been under contract for a certain number of years, and owners no longer have absolute control over players' careers.

Although it's been a struggle for professional team athletes to maintain their unions, they realize that crucial labor issues must be negotiated every time they renew their CBA with the owners' cartel. At this time, the main issues negotiated in CBAs are the following:

1. The definition of league revenues, and the percentage of those revenues that the team owners must allocate to players' salaries and benefits.
2. The extent to which owners can share revenues with one another (and thereby reduce incentives to win and to pay large salaries to players who would help the team to win).
3. Salary limits for rookies signing their first pro contract, salary restrictions for veteran players, and minimum salary levels for all players.
4. The conditions under which players can become free agents and the rights of players who are free agents.
5. A salary cap that sets the maximum player payroll for teams and a formula determining the fines that an owner must pay if the team's payroll exceeds the cap.
6. A total team salary floor that sets the minimum payroll for each team in a league.
7. The conditions under which players or teams can request an outside arbitrator to determine the fairness of an existing or proposed contract.
8. Changes in the rules of the game.

Each of these issues can be contentious in CBA negotiations, or even before a CBA is up for renewal. If owners don't like the terms of a current CBA and the players' association refuses to talk with them about changes, the owners may use a **lockout**, or *an employer-imposed work stoppage* that, in the case of professional sports, suspends all games and practices until the dispute is resolved and the CBA is revised to the owners' satisfaction. If players don't like the terms of a current CBA and the owners refuse to talk with them, the players may call a **strike**, which is *a work stoppage in which employees refuse to work until a labor dispute is resolved,* and players agree to sign a new CBA.

Strikes or lockouts occur in either of two situations: (a) when business conditions change to the point that owners or players decide that the existing CBA is no longer fair or reasonable, and (b) when a CBA has expired and the owners and players cannot come to an agreement. Back when players had low salaries and little control over working conditions in their sport, strikes were more likely than lockouts. But now that players have legal leverage as they negotiate their salaries and have been able to control important aspects of their working conditions through CBAs, strikes are less common and lockouts are more common.

At the same time, as corporations and outside investors have become team owners, they seek high investment returns and predictability in their financial projections and feel that they must have more control over players' salaries and benefits. Additionally, they generally detest players' associations because they are basically labor unions. One owners' strategy to gain more control has been to request that certain parts of an existing CBA be renegotiated because there are new issues that they face. But if players are happy with the existing CBA, they are not interested in talking about anything with owners. The result of this situation is that owners have imposed lockouts on players, which means that there are no more games or practices, and players receive no paychecks. NHL owners locked out players in 2004–2005 and 2012–2013; NBA owners locked out players in 2011, as did NFL owners.

The owners know that they can outlast the players through a work stoppage. They are independently wealthy and will take short-term losses for long-term gains. The players, on the other hand, have short careers and must take advantage of their youth while they have it. A season-long lockout could mean a 15 to 33 percent loss of sport career lifetime income for each player; for the owners, it's a minor blip in their investment portfolios. Additionally, the owners know that younger, lower-paid players have different contract concerns than highly paid stars, and this difference will eventually erode unity among the players. Then the owners can make a deal that favors themselves.

The issues in each of the owner-imposed lockouts over the recent past have been different, but in each case the owners wanted to keep a larger share of revenues and give players less. They also wanted lower "caps," or payroll limits for each team so they could pay players less and give teams in the smaller markets a better chance to compete more successfully with wealthier teams in larger markets. The owners also wanted to limit when and how players become free agents, because free agency forces them to compete with each other when trying to sign good players to contracts. Unregulated free agency gives leverage to the players, and owners don't like that kind of "free-market" situation. Finally, the owners usually want the CBA to contain limits on what they pay top players on their teams. This makes it easier for them to negotiate deals without paying what the players might receive from other teams.

In general, the owners don't want to spend more than 40 to 50 percent of total revenues on players' salaries and benefits. Ideally, they'd like to keep 60 percent or more of all revenues so there would be plenty of money left over for them after they pay all the bills. At this point, most players in the big spectator sports think they should be entitled to at least 50 cents of every dollar of revenue that is collected by the league and teams. Through the recent lockouts the owners have succeeded in pushing the players' percentage lower. Future lockouts will indicate how low they can force the share of revenues going to players.

As opposed to athletes in high-revenue sports, athletes in most minor leagues and lower-revenue sports have few rights and little control over their careers. The players at this level far outnumber players in the top levels of professional sports, and they often work for low pay under uncertain conditions, and with few rights. Owners almost always have the last word in these sports, although most owners at this level don't usually make large amounts of money.

Legal Status: Individual Sports The legal status of professional athletes in individual sports varies greatly from sport to sport and even from one athlete to another. Although there are important differences between boxing, bowling, golf, tennis, auto racing, rodeo, horse racing, track-and-field, skiing, biking, and a number of recently professionalized action sports, a few generalizations can be made.

The legal status of athletes in individual sports largely depends on what athletes must do to train and qualify for competitions. For example, few athletes can afford to pay for all the training needed to develop professional-level skills in a sport. Furthermore, they don't have the knowledge or connections to meet the formal requirements to become an official competitor in their sport, which may include having a recognized agent or manager (as in boxing), being formally accepted by other participants (as in most auto racing), obtaining membership in a professional organization (as in most bowling, golf, and tennis tournaments), or gaining a special invitation through an official selection group (as in professional track-and-field meets).

Whenever athletes need sponsors to pay for training or agents to help them meet participation requirements, their legal status is shaped by the contracts they sign with these people and then with the organizations that regulate participation. This is why the legal status of athletes in individual sports varies so widely.

Let's use boxing as an example. Because many boxers come from low-income backgrounds, they lack the resources to develop high-level boxing skills and arrange official bouts with other boxers. They must have trainers, managers, and sponsors, and the support of these people always comes with conditions that are written in formal contracts or based on informal agreements. In either case, boxers must forfeit control over much of their lives and a portion of the rewards they may earn in future bouts. This means that few boxers have much control over their careers, even when they win large amounts of prize money.

They are forced to trade control over their bodies and careers for the opportunity to continue boxing. This is an example of how class relations operate in sports: when people lack resources, they are limited in the ways they can negotiate the conditions under which their sport careers occur.

The legal status of athletes in certain individual sports is defined in the bylaws of professional organizations such as the Professional Golf Association (PGA), the Ladies' Professional Golf Association (LPGA), the Association of Tennis Professionals (ATP), and the Professional Rodeo Cowboys Association (PRCA). When athletes play a role in controlling these organizations, the policies support athletes' rights and enable them to manage some of the conditions under which they compete. Without such organizations, athletes in these sports would have few rights as workers.

(*Source:* JOHANNES EISELE/AFP/Getty Images)

Individuals and teams in esports are now being paid by team owners, they win cash prizes, and sign endorsement deals, all with few legal guidelines and protection. The winner of this *Fortnite World Cup* held in New York in July 2019 was a 16-year-old boy from the United States His $3 million first-place prize was more than winners received in recent events such as the Wimbledon Tennis Championship and the Indy 500, and more than the combined winners of The Masters, the Tour de France, the Hawaii Ironman, and the New York Marathon received in 2019 (Richter, 2019). Epic Games, the owner of Fortnite gave $100 million to their tournament winners during 2018 and 2019.

Income: Team Sports Despite publicity given to the supercontracts of some athletes in the top professional leagues, salaries vary widely across the levels and divisions of professional team sports. For example, in 2019 there were about 6,500 minor league baseball players on 244 teams in North America. The teams exploit "the dream" that these young men have of playing on a Major League team, so the basic salary is $1,160 per month in a 5-month season. This amounts to $7.25 per hour for a 40-hour work week. However, most players work 50-70 hour weeks and are not paid for spring training or for any conditioning time during the off season. To make matters worse, the US Congress passed the Save America's Pastime Act in 2019 to exempt teams from federal fair labor laws so they are not required to pay overtime after 40 hours of work in a week.

Players in the NBA G League make $35,000 per year plus a few benefits, although a few "select" players can make up to $125,000–a concession made by the NBA to keep top players from seeking contracts with teams in other countries. The players in the highest level of minor league hockey make a minimum of $47,500 per year plus some benefits, and some players have six-figure salaries when they are on-call to move up to the NHL. The minimum salary for rookies in a minor hockey league is $1840 per month, about $700 per month more than the baseball players make.

In most cases, being a professional athlete in all but the top men's team sports continues to be a seasonal job with few benefits and little or no career security. The leagues struggle to survive, players often do not make a living wage, they have little control over where they live, and job security is nonexistent. The players are motivated by the love of the game or by the myth that you can be anything you want to be if you work hard enough.

To understand the range of incomes in top level men's team sports, consider that in recent seasons the total salaries of 15 percent of MLB players have been about the same as the total salaries of the other 85 percent of players. This is why the average–or *mean*–salary in Major League Baseball was about $4.38 million in 2019, whereas the median salary is less than one-third that amount at $1.4 million per year.

The big salaries for a few players drive up the average for the entire league.

Mega-salaries in men's professional team sports did not exist before the 1980s. The data in Table 11.1 show that players' average salaries have grown far beyond median family income in the United States. For example, players in 1950 had salaries not much higher than median family income at that time. In 2018–19, the average NBA salary was more than 100 times greater than the median family income!

The dramatic increase in salaries at the top level of pro sports since 1980 can be attributed to two factors: (1) changes in the legal status and rights of players, which have led to free agency and the use of a salary arbitration process and (2) increased revenues, especially through the sale of media rights, flowing to leagues and owners (see Chapter 12). Data in Table 11.1 show that the increases in player salaries correspond closely with court decisions and labor agreements that changed the legal status of athletes and gave them bargaining power in contract negotiations with team owners.

Income: Individual Sports As with team sports, publicity is given to the highest-paid athletes in individual sports. However, the reality is that many players in these sports don't make enough money from tournament winnings to pay all their expenses and support themselves comfortably. Many golfers, tennis players, bowlers, track-and-field athletes, auto and motorcycle racers, rodeo riders, figure skaters, and others must carefully manage their money so that they don't spend more than they win as they travel from event to event. When tournament winnings are listed in the newspaper, nothing is said about the expenses for hotels, food, and transportation or about other expenses for coaches, agents, managers, and various support people. The top money winners don't worry about these expenses, but most athletes in individual sports are not big money winners.

The majority of men and women playing professional tennis, golf, and other individual sports do not make enough prize money to pay their training and travel expenses each year, although many have sponsors that subsidize them. Some athletes with sponsors may be under contract to share their winnings with them. The sponsors/investors cover expenses during the lean years but then take a percentage of prize money if and when the athletes win matches or tournaments.

Sponsorship agreements cause problems for professional athletes in many individual sports. Being contractually tied, for example, to an equipment manufacturer or another sponsor often puts athletes in a state of dependency. They may not have the freedom to choose when or how often they will compete, and sponsors may require them to attend social functions, at which they talk with fan-consumers, sign autographs, and promote products.

Overall, a few athletes in individual sports have large incomes, whereas most others struggle to cover expenses. Only when sport events are broadcast on television can athletes compete for major prize money and earn large incomes, unless they are amateurs or have not bargained for their rights as workers.

Amateur Athletes in Commercial Sports

The term, **amateur**, can mean many things, but it is used here to refer to *athletes whose participation eligibility requires that they make no money from their athletic performances or in connection with their status as an athlete*. Prior to 1971, the IOC and the NGBs of many sports required all competitors to be amateurs. But this became increasingly impractical as national and international athletes trained full time. Keeping the amateur requirement would exclude anyone who didn't come from a wealthy background. So the IOC and other sports organizations changed their rules and changed them again to allow established professional athletes to participate.

The only amateur athletes in the Olympics today are boxers and wrestlers. Allowing professionals to compete in these two sports is seen as a safety issue, so the amateur requirement has been retained. All other Olympic athletes may compete for prize money and work in sports, which had been prohibited for most of the twentieth century.

Apart from sport governing bodies like the US Golf Association and the US Tennis Association that continue to sponsor official tournaments for amateurs, the only sport governing bodies that use an amateur status eligibility requirement are the Amateur Athletic Association (AAU) and the National Collegiate Athletic Association (NCAA).

The AAU has a long history of sport sponsorship, but today it focuses mostly on youth sports. It continues to exist only because it signed in 1994 a 30-year cooperative deal with Walt Disney World Resort. The deal specified that the AAU would hold most of its national championships in over 25 different youth sports at the Wide World of Sports facilities in Lake Buena Vista, Florida. These facilities are located next to Disney World, which meant that as tens of thousands of young athletes came to national AAU tournaments, they would be escorted by families that would turn the trip into a vacation and spend extra days and much money at Disney World. When Disney merged with Capital Cities/ABC in 1995 and acquired the upstart ESPN in the deal, the AAU gained an influential media partner.

This symbiotic relationship between the non-profit AAU and the for-profit Walt Disney Company (and ESPN) was a major marketing triumph for both organizations. The AAU relocated its headquarters to Lake Buena Vista and now holds over 40 national tournaments at the ESPN Wide World of Sports complex. This provided programing opportunities for ESPN. It also enabled them to track young athletes and develop storylines for those who might be successful in the future, and it gave them a golden opportunity to recruit new ESPN viewers/subscribers at a young age.

Disney World benefitted from the tourism generated by the tournaments and the AAU leaders had new headquarters, an attractive marketing position, and financial security. As they have recruited young athletes and youth sport teams into their organization, families have spent untold millions of dollars as their children have played in what are hyped as national championships year after year after year. For example, when the AAU held its 12-day Junior National Volleyball Championships in June 2019, they brought 2,800 teams and 45,000 participants from around the world to Orlando. With them came family members, 9,000 team coaches, and 700 college coaches wanting to scout and recruit players. A total of over 120,000 "volleyball people" had an estimated economic impact of 91 million dollars for the Orlando/Central Florida area. This, of course, is a new monetized version of amateurism in which people can generate massive revenues under the cover of non-profit organizations that operate with and like businesses. This has converted youth sports into a massive industry.

Like the AAU, the NCAA also requires amateur status to participate in college sports. This generally means that athletes cannot have played any sport in which they received cash or in-kind rewards and they cannot have worked in a job where they were hired for their sport skills. However, the NCAA has changed the meaning of amateur many times in its history, especially as it applies to athletes in the Division I revenue-producing sports of football, men's basketball (Schneider, 2011; Zimbalist and Sack, 2013). These changes have been justified in various and sometimes contradictory terms, but they have been made primarily to retain control over athletes while avoiding the charge that big-time college sport programs are using a professional business model and, therefore, should pay players cash salaries and pay taxes on the income made by profit-generating teams (Huma and Staurowsky, 2011, 2012). In fact, it takes 40 bylaws to define "amateur status" in the NCAA rule book, because it is difficult to make sense of amateurism in connection with teams and athletic programs operated as businesses but described as non-profit educational activities.

College athletes lack power to negotiate the conditions of their sport participation. Even in revenue-producing college sports, they have few rights and no meaningful way of filing complaints when they've been treated unfairly or denied the right to play their sports. The athletes are not allowed to share the revenues that they may generate or benefit when universities and the NCAA use their names and images in marketing campaigns.

Many college athletes recognize that they lack rights, but it has been difficult for them to lobby for changes. Challenging universities or the NCAA in court is expensive and would take far longer than the 4–5 years that athletes spend in a college sport career. Forming an athletes' organization might make it possible to bargain for rights, but bringing together athletes from many campuses and sports would require resources that athletes don't have. As a result many college athletes are in a dependent status and under the control of their coaches and athletic departments.

Although the NCAA now allows its Division I member institutions to award multiple year scholarships and adjust scholarship amounts to cover the full cost of attending a particular university, it continues to require that athletes remain amateurs. However, as more people have seen the hypocrisy of this, the NCAA is, as I write this, being pressured to revise its definition of amateur to allow athletes to profit from using their names under certain conditions. At the same time, the NCAA resists defining college athletes as employees, which would change the entire landscape of college sports in the United States.

summary

WHAT ARE THE CHARACTERISTICS OF COMMERCIAL SPORTS?

Commercial sports are visible parts of many societies today. They grow and prosper best in urban, industrial, and post-industrial nations with relatively efficient transportation and communications systems, a standard of living that allows people the time and money to play and watch sports, and a culture that emphasizes consumption and material status symbols.

Spectator interest in commercial sports is based on a combination of a quest for excitement, ideologies emphasizing success, the existence of youth sport programs, and media coverage that introduces people to the rules of sports and the athletes who play them.

The recent worldwide growth of commercial sports has been fueled by sport organizations seeking global markets and corporations using sports as vehicles for global capitalist expansion. This growth will continue as long as it serves the interests of multinational corporations. As it does, sports, sports facilities, events, and athletes are branded with corporate logos and ideological messages promoting consumption and dependence on corporations for excitement and pleasure.

Commercialization leads to changes in the internal structure and goals of certain sports, the orientations of people involved in sports, and the people and organizations that control sports. Rules are changed to make events more fan-friendly and more profitable. People in sports, especially athletes, emphasize heroic orientations over aesthetic orientations and use style and dramatic expression to impress mass audiences. Overall, commercial sports are packaged as total entertainment experiences for spectators, mostly for the benefit of people who lack technical knowledge about the games or events they're watching.

Commercial sports are unique businesses. At the minor league level, they generate modest revenues for owners and sponsors. However, team owners at the top levels of professional sports have formed cartels to generate significant revenues. Like event sponsors and promoters, team owners are involved with commercial sports to make money while having fun and establishing good public images for themselves or their corporations and corporate products and policies. Their cartels enable them to control costs, stifle competition, and increase revenues, especially those coming from the sale of broadcasting rights to media companies. Profits also are enhanced by public support and subsidies, often associated with tax breaks and the construction and operation of stadiums and arenas. Now that states are beginning to approve sports betting, the cartels will also benefit from increased media rights sales.

It is ironic that North American professional sports often are used as models of democracy and free enterprise when, in fact, their success has been built on carefully planned autocratic control and monopolistic business practices. In practical terms, these team owners have effectively eliminated free-market competition in their sport businesses and used public money and facilities to increase their wealth and power. In response, athletes and fans have formed groups and organizations to oppose the consequences of commercialization that impact them negatively.

The administration and control of amateur commercial sports rest in the hands of numerous sports organizations. Although these organizations exist to support the training and competition of amateur athletes, their primary goal is to control both athletes and revenues generated through membership fees, tournaments, sponsorships, and donations. Those with the most money and influence usually win the power struggles in amateur sports, and athletes and fans seldom have the resources to promote their interests in these struggles. Corporate sponsors are now a major force in amateur sports, and their goals strongly influence what happens in them.

Commercialization transforms athletes into entertainers. Because athletes generate revenues through their performances, issues related to players' rights and their fair share of revenues generated by their performances are very important. As rights and revenues have increased, so have players' incomes. Media coverage and the rights fees paid by media companies have been key in this process.

Most athletes in professional sports do not make vast sums of money. Players outside the top men's sports and golf and tennis for women have incomes that are surprisingly low. Income among amateur athletes is limited by the rules of governing bodies in particular sports.

Intercollegiate athletes in the United States have what amounts to a regulated maximum wage in the form of athletic scholarships, which many people see as unfair when some athletes generate millions of dollars of revenue for their universities. In other amateur sports, athletes may receive direct cash payments for performances and endorsements, and some receive support from the organizations to which they belong, but relatively few make large amounts of money.

The structure and dynamics of commercial sports vary from nation to nation. Commercial sports in most of the world have not generated the massive revenues associated with a few high-profile, heavily televised sports in North America, Australia, Western Europe, and parts of Latin America and eastern Asia. Profits for owners and promoters around the world depend on supportive relationships with the media, large corporations, and governments. These relationships have shaped the character of all commercial sports, professional and amateur.

The commercial model of sports is not the only one that might provide athletes and spectators with enjoyable and satisfying experiences. However, because most people are unaware of alternative models, they continue to express a desire for what they get, even when it is largely determined by the interests of people with wealth and power. Therefore, changes will occur only when spectators and people in sports develop visions for what sports could and should look like if they were not shaped so much by the economic interests of wealthy and powerful people and people hoping to become wealthy and powerful.

SUPPLEMENTAL READINGS

Reading 1. Women's professional team sports can't get traction
Reading 2. Turning spectacle into sport: Mixed martial arts
Reading 3. Red Bull and high-energy sports
Reading 4. Why business and political leaders love new stadiums
Reading 5. Franchise values and making money in professional sports
Reading 6. A tale of two hockey lockouts
Reading 7. Fantasy sports & esports: New commercial frontiers

SPORT MANAGEMENT ISSUES

- You are in a sport studies course that has students from multiple countries. They ask you what is needed to develop successful commercial sports in a country. Outline the major points that you will make when talking with them, and explain those points in a way that will make sense to people from social and cultural backgrounds that are different than your background.

- Powerful and wealthy people in a country undergoing economic expansion want to create a high level of spectator interest in sports throughout their society. They hire you to survey the sociology of sport to discover how to create spectator interests. Using material in this chapter, what do you tell them?
- You live in a large city that has been undergoing a steady process of social and economic decline. The state has made $300 million available to build a new arena for the professional hockey team in the city. You have been asked to discuss whether this is a good use of public money. City leaders say that a new arena and a successful hockey team will revitalize the city and create a supportive context for development. You are asked to agree or disagree and to explain your answer.
- You are the athletic director for a large private high school in your community. The school is facing a budget crisis that affects your sports programs. The local soft-drink distributor tells you that his company will give you $50,000 a year if he can put his drink logo on the scoreboard and in a dozen other places in the sport facilities and put soft-drink machines in the locker rooms. He also wants you and the coaches to do a local commercial for his company. The principal and parent board say it is your decision. Now you must explain to them what you've decided. Outline the points you will make to them.

references

American Gaming Association. 2018. How much to leagues stand to gain from legal sports betting? A report by Nielsen Research. *AmericanGaming.org* (September): https://www.americangaming.org/wp-content/uploads/2018/10/Nielsen-Research-All-4-Leagues-FINAL.pdf

Androus, Zachary & Lorenzo Giudici. 2018. The de-professionalization of football: The people's football movement in Italy. *Journal of Sport and Social Issues* 42(3): 170–183.

Bachman, Rachel. 2019. Olympic athletes consider a union. *Wall Street Journal* (February 17): A14.

Bagli, Charles V. 2019. So many seats, so many tax breaks. *New York Times* (July 11): https://www.nytimes.com/2018/07/11/nyregion/stadiums-arenas-funding-nyc.html

Bandow, Doug. 2003. *Surprise: Stadiums don't pay after all!* Cato Institute Report (October 19). Washington, DC: Cato Institute.

Barnett, Josh. 2017. From mat to ring, WWE's amateur and pro wrestling connection. *USA Today* (May 2): https://www.usatoday.com/story/sports/2017/05/02/wwe-olympic-wrestling-ncaa-kurt-angle-brock-lesnar-chad-gable-jason-jordan/100825750/

Brody, Richard. 2019. "Cassandro, the Exotico!," Reviewed: An intimate portrait of a Lucha-Libre star. The New Yorker (July 19): https://www.newyorker.com/culture/the-front-row/cassandro-the-exotico-reviewed-an-intimate-portrait-of-a-lucha-libre-star

Broughton, David. 2018. Media, gambling, new stadiums to push North American sports market to $80 billion. *SportsBusinessDaily.com* (November 5): https://www.sportsbusinessdaily.com/Journal/Issues/2018/11/05/Media/PwC.aspx

Brown, Matthew, Mark Nagell, Chad McEvoy & Daniel Rascher. 2004. Revenue and wealth maximization in the National Football League: The impact of stadia. *Sport Marketing Quarterly* 13(4): 227–236.

Burnsed, Brian. 2019. Doubling down. *Champion Magazine* 12(3): 32–41. Online, http://www.ncaa.org/static/champion/doubling-down/

Chan, Justin. 2018. The hypocrisy of publicly funded stadiums. *71Republic.com* (February 4): https://71republic.com/2018/02/04/hypocrisy-public-stadiums/

Cloake, Martin. 2013. Why stand against modern football? *NewStatesman.com* (August 23): https://www.newstatesman.com/business/2013/08/why-stand-against-modern-football

Cox, Adam. 2018. Spectator demand, uncertainty of results, and public interest: Evidence from the English Premier League. *Journal of Sports Economics* 19(1): 3–30.

Curry, Timothy J., Kent P. Schwirian, and Rachael Woldoff. 2004. *High stakes: Big time sports and downtown redevelopment.* Columbus: Ohio State University Press.

Delaney, Kevin J., and Rick Eckstein. 2003. The devil is in the details: Neutralizing critical studies of publicly subsidized stadiums. *Critical Sociology* 29(2): 189–210.

deMause, Neil, and Joanna Cagan. 2008. *Field of schemes: How the great stadium swindle turns public money into private profit* (revised/expanded edition). Lincoln: University of Nebraska Press.

Drape, Joe. 2019. New Jersey embraces sports gambling, and a billion-dollar business is born. (January 29): https://www.nytimes.com/2019/01/29/sports/sports-gambling-new-jersey.html

Dunning, Eric. 1999. *Sport matters: Sociological studies of sport, violence and civilization*. London: Routledge.

Elias, Norbert & Eric Dunning. 1986. *Quest for excitement.* New York: Basil Blackwell.

Epstein, Joseph. 2018. Don't take me out to the ballgame–I can't afford it. *Wall Street Journal* (July 12): https://www.wsj.com/articles/dont-take-me-out-to-the-ballgamei-cant-afford-it-1531435684

EUAthletes. 2017. World Players Association launches the Universal Declaration of Player Rights. EUAthletes.org (December 14): https://www.euathletes.org/category/world-players-association/

Farren, Michael. 2017. Priciest national pastime: Sports subsidies aren't worth the cost to taxpayers. *USNews.com* (July 3): https://www.usnews.com/opinion/economic-intelligence/articles/2017-07-03/sport-subsidies-are-a-terrible-deal-for-american-taxpayers

Friedman, Michael T., and David L. Andrews. 2011. The built sport spectacle and the opacity of democracy. *International Review for the Sociology of Sport* 46(2): 181–204.

Friedman, Michael T., David L. Andrews, and Michael L. Silk. 2004. Sport and the façade of redevelopment in the postindustrial city. *Sociology of Sport Journal* 21(2): 119–139.

Gaffney, Christopher. 2015. Virando o jogo: The challenges and possibilities for social mobilization in Brazilian football. *Journal of Sport and Social Issues* 39(2): 155–174.

Gayer, Ted, Austin J. Drukker & Alexander K. Gold. 2016. Tax-exempt municipal bonds and the financing of professional sports stadiums. *Economic Studies at Brookings* (September): https://www.brookings.edu/wp-content/uploads/2016/09/gayerdrukkergold_stadiumsubsidies_090816.pdf

Giulianotti, Richard & Dino Numerato. 2018. Global sport and consumer culture: An introduction. *Journal of Consumer Culture* 18(2): 229–240.

Gluck, Jeff. 2015. Real sport or circus sideshow? *USA Today* (November 2): 7C.

Gray, Aaron. 2019. The size and increase of the global sports betting market. SportsBettingDime.com (January 25): https://www.sportsbettingdime.com/guides/finance/global-sports-betting-market/

Gregory, Michele Rene. 2009. Inside the locker room: Homosociability in the advertising industry. *Gender, Work and Organization* 16(3): 323–347.

Hill, Tim, Robin Canniford & Peter Millward. 2018. Against modern football: Mobilising protest movements in social media. *Sociology* 52(4): 688–708.

Hoberman, John M. 1994. The sportive-dynamic body as a symbol of productivity. In T. Siebers, ed., *Heterotopia: Postmodern utopia and the body politic* (pp. 199–228). Ann Arbor: University of Michigan Press.

Hognestad, Hans Kristian. 2015. "Rimi Bowl" and the quest for authenticity: Fan autonomy and commodification in Norwegian football. *Journal of Sport and Social Issues* 39(2): 139–154.

Holman, Kohan, Rafi. 2017. *The arena: Inside the tailgating, ticket-scalping, mascot-racing, dubiously funded, and possibly haunted monuments of American sport*. New York NY: Liveright.

Horne, John D. 2007. The four 'knowns' of sports mega-events. *Leisure Studies* 26(1): 81–96. https://www.pwc.com/us/en/industry/entertainment-media/assets/2018-sports-outlook.pdf

Huma, Ramogi, and Ellen J. Staurowsky. 2011. *The price of poverty in big-time college sports.* National College Players Association and Drexel University. Online: http://assets.usw.org/ncpa/The-Price-of- Poverty-in-Big-Time-College-Sport.pdf

Huma, Ramogi, and Ellen J. Staurowsky. 2012. *The $6 billion heist: Robbing college athletes under the guise of amateurism.* A report collaboratively produced by the National College Players Association and Drexel University Sport Management. Online: http://www.ncpanow.org

Jack, Andrew. 2012. Lifestyle conditions increase the pain for medical systems. *Financial Times* (July 31): https://www.ft.com/content/178497aa-d276-11e1-abe7-00144feabdc0

Jackson, Nate. 2011. No pain, no gain? Not so fast. *New York Times* (December 13): http://www.nytimes.com/2011/12/14/opinion/painkillers-for-nfl-players-not-so-fast.html

Jenkins, Holman W., Jr., 2019. Gambling will take over TV sports. *Wall Street Journal* (April 20): A15.

Lee, Young H. 2018. Common factors in Major League Baseball game attendance. *Journal of Sports Economics* 19(4): 583–598.

Lewis, Frank W. 2010. In Cleveland, sports fans cheer until it hurts. *New York Times* (May 14): http://www.nytimes.com/2010/05/15/sports/basketball/15cleveland.html

Maese, Rick. 2018. Games within games. *Washington Post* (October 1): https://www.washingtonpost.com/graphics/2018/sports/gambling-fan-experience/

Maguire, Brendan. 2005. American professional wrestling: Evolution, content, and popular appeal. *Sociological Spectrum* 25, 2: 155–176.

Minton, Michelle. 2018. Legalizing sports betting in the United States. *Competitive Enterprise Institute*, No. 243 (March 15): Online, https://cei.org/sites/default/files/Michelle%20Minton%20-%20Legalizing%20Sports%20Betting%20in%20the%20United%20States.pdf

Montez de Oca, Jeffrey & Molly Cotner. 2020. "Killing the football widow and creating new fans: NFL Marketing beyond 'pink it & shrink it'." In Holly Thorpe, Kim Toffoletti & Jessica Francombe-Webb, eds. *New Sporting Femininities: Embodied Politics in Postfeminist Times.* London: Palgrave.

Montez de Oca, Jeffrey, Brandon Meyer, and Jeffrey Scholes. 2016. "Reaching the kids: How the NFL markets to youth." *Popular Communication* 14(1): 3–11.https://www.tandfonline.com/doi/full/10.1080/15405702.2015.1084623

NCAA. 2019. Sports wagering. National Collegiate Athletic Association, Indianapolis IN. Online, http://www.ncaa.org/themes-topics/sports-wagering

Numerato, Dino. 2015. Who says "no to modern football?" Italian supporters, reflexivity, and neo-liberalism. *Journal of Sport and Social Issues* 39(2): 120–138.

O'Malley, Andrew. 2019. NHL signs deal with William Hill as sports betting partner. *VegasSlotsOnline.com* (March 29): https://www.vegasslotsonline.com/news/2019/03/29/nhl-signs-deal-william-hill-sports-betting-partner/

Pennington, Bill. 2004. Reading, Writing and Corporate Sponsorships. *The New York Times*, Section A (October 18): 1.

Povich, Elaine. Why should public money be used to build sports stadiums? *PBS NewsHour*

(July13): https://www.pbs.org/newshour/nation/public-money-used-build-sports stadiums

Propheter, Geoffrey. 2017. Subsidies and stadia' opulence. *Journal of Sports Economics* 18(1): 3–18.

Purdum, David. 2018. NBA to distribute real-time data for betting odds. ESPN http://www.espn.com/chalk/story/_/id/25398501/sportsbooks-begin-using-real-official-nba-data-game-betting-odds

Putra, Linggar Rama Dian. 2019. "Your neighbors walk alone (YNWA)": Urban regeneration and the predicament of being local fans in the commercialized English Football League. *Journal of Sport and Social Issues* 43(1): 44–68.

PwC. 2018. At the gate and beyond: Outlook for the sports market in North America through 2022. PwC Sports Outlook (October):

Ramsey, Eric. 2018. FanDuel becomes official DFS, sports betting partner for NHL. *LegalSportsReport.com* (November 5): https://www.legalsportsreport.com/25544/fanduel-nhl-sports-betting/

Reed, Ken. 2015. *How we can save sports: A game plan.* Lanham MD: Rowman & Littlefield.

Reid, S. M. 1996. The selling of the Games. *The Denver Post* (July 21) 4BB.

Richter, Felix, 2019. Fortnite world champion bags $3 million prize. *Statista.com* (July 29): https://www.statista.com/chart/17607/fortnite-world-cup-prize-money-in-perspective/

Ritholtz, Barry. 2018. Four reasons taxpayers should never subsidize stadiums. *Bloomberg.com* (July 16): https://www.bloomberg.com/opinion/articles/2018-07-16/four-reasons-taxpayers-should-never-subsidize-stadiums

Ritzer, George. 2005. *Enchanting a disenchanted world: Revolutionizing the means of consumption* (2nd edition). Thousand Oaks, CA: Pine Forge Press.

Rodenberg, Ryan, 2019. NCAA pivots to address sports betting integrity. ESPN.com (March 11): https://www.espn.com/chalk/story/_/id/26229344/how-ncaa-pivoting-address-sports-betting-integrity

Rogers, Martin & Kim Hjelmgaard, 2018. What the US can learn about legalized sports betting from the U.K. *USA Today* (June 6): https://www.usatoday.com/story/sports/2018/06/06/sports-betting-what-u-s-can-learn-legalization-u-k/664382002/

Rossi, Jason. 2018. The 15 cities where your tax dollars paid for billion-dollar stadiums. *Cheatsheet.com* (April 30): https://www.cheatsheet.com/culture/taxpayer-money-billion-dollar-stadiums.html/

Rugg, Adam. 2019. Working out their future: The NFL's Play 60 campaign and the production of adolescent fans and players. *Journal of Sport and Social Issues* 43(1): 69–88.

Sammond, Nicholas, ed. 2005. *Steel chair to the head: The pleasure and pain of professional wrestling.* Durham, NC: Duke University Press.

Scherer, Jay. 2016. Resisting the world-class city: Community opposition and the politics of a local arena development. *Sociology of Sport Journal* 33(1): 39–53.

Schiesel, Seth. 2007b. With famed players, game takes on Madden's turf. *New York Times* (September 17): http://www.nytimes.com/2007/09/17/technology/17game.html

Schoenfeld, Bruce. 2019. Will sports betting transform how games are watched, and even played? *New York Times Magazine* (January 29): https://www.nytimes.com/2019/01/29/magazine/sports-betting-washington.html

Schrotenboer, Brent. 2019. Bigger NFL problem may be owners. *USA Today* (March 28): 1C, 6C.

Schwab, Brendan. 2018. For athletes there are two systems of work. World Players Association (July 13): https://medium.com/@worldplayers/for-athletes-there-are-two-systems-of-work-4405bc397ed4

Silk, Michael L. 2004. A Tale of Two Cities: The social production of sterile sporting space. *Journal of Sport and Social Issues* 28, 4: 349–378.

Smith, Jason M. & Alan G. Ingham. 2003. On the waterfront: Retrospectives on the relationship between sport and communities. *Sociology of Sport Journal* 20, 3: 252–274.

Smith, R. Tyson. 2008. Passion work: The joint production of emotional labor in professional wrestling. *Social Psychology Quarterly* 71(2): 157–176.

Staff. 2018. When sports teams fleece taxpayers. *TheWeek.com* (October 29): https://theweek.com/articles/803881/when-sports-teams-fleece-taxpayers

Weiner, Evan. 2018. The NBA is expanding, not with additional teams, but by global footprint. (October 19): https://www.sportstalkflorida.com/nba/nba-news/the-nba-is-expanding-not-with-additional-teams-but-by-global-footprint/

Whyno, Stephen. 2017. Unions for athletes unveil change in "culture of sport." *The Associated Press* (December 15): online, https://www.apnews.com/ae22924bc360412eb81a8361b3aae868

Zillgitt, Jeff. 2019. NBA, FIBA plan to launch league in Africa in 2020. *USA Today* (February 18): 8C.

Zimbalist, Andrew & Allen Sack, 2013. Thoughts on amateurism, the O'Bannon case and the viability of college sport. The Drake Group. http://thedrakegroup.org/2013/04/10/drake-group-report-obannon-amateurism-and-the-viability-of-college-sport/

chapter

12

(*Source:* Alex Livesey/Getty Images)

SPORTS AND THE MEDIA

Could They Survive Without Each Other?

Sports is holding up the entire [media company] ecosystem. I call it the Jenga game: Pull out the sports block and the entire system collapses.

–Rich Greenfield, media analyst at BTIG Research (in Winkler, 2019)

NBA players . . . have grown up with access to phones and [their] brains have been warped by the machines in their pockets. . . . But [many] of them can't help but waste hours every day refreshing their feeds even if it means getting screamed at by strangers.

–Ben Cohen, sports journalist (2019)

. . . a historic lack of [mainstream media] exposure has forced female sports teams to be inventive, circumventing traditional media and in many cases leapfrogging the men's game in terms of innovation.

–Charlotte Rogers, senior writer Marketing Week (2018)

[Technology consulting firm,] Activate projects that in the United States esports will have more viewers than every professional sports league but the NFL by 2021.

–Syracuse staff, 2019

Chapter Outline

Learning Objectives

- Identify the major forms of media, what they provide to people, and the influence of commercial forces on media content.
- Discuss whether and how new media, including the Internet, change sport spectator experiences.
- Know the characteristics of fantasy sports, sports video games, and esports and explain how they change the sport-media landscape
- Identify factors that influence the images and narratives presented in the media.
- Discuss how sports and the media depend on each other for commercial success.
- Identify major trends in televised sports and media rights fees.
- Identify economic and ideological factors that influence relationships between sports and the media.
- Identify ideological themes around which the media coverage of sports is constructed.
- Describe the how gender, racial and ethnic, and national stereotypes have influenced media images and narratives in the coverage of sports.
- Discuss research findings on audience experiences and the media impact on sport-related behaviors, such as active participation, game attendance, and sports betting.
- Explain how sports journalism has changed during the last few decades and identify the factors that influence relationships between sports journalists and athletes.

Media pervade our cultures and our lives from billboards and newspapers to radio and television to multiple forms of digital media. Although each of us incorporates media into our lives in different ways, the things we read, hear, and see in the media are crucial parts of our experience. They frame and influence our thoughts, conversations, decisions, and actions.

We use media images and narratives as we evaluate ourselves, give meaning to other people and events, form ideas, and envision the future. This does *not* mean that we are slaves to the media or passive dupes of those who produce and present media content to us. The media don't tell us *what* to think, but they greatly influence what we *think about* and, therefore what we discuss in face-to-face and virtual conversations. Additionally, our experiences are clearly informed by media content, and if the media didn't exist, our lives would be very different.

Digital media, including the Internet, have added a new layer to our media experiences. They enable us to go beyond consumption and to create images and narratives that we present to others.

Sports and the media are interconnected parts of our lives. Sports provide content and context for all forms of media, and many sports depend on the media for publicity and revenues. To better understand these interconnections, five questions are considered in this chapter:

1. What are the characteristics of the media?
2. How are sports and media interconnected?
3. What images and messages are emphasized in media coverage of sports in the United States?
4. How are media involved in our sports participation and consumption?
5. What are the implications of new forms of digital media for sports journalism and sportscasting?

CHARACTERISTICS OF THE MEDIA

The media landscape is changing rapidly and dramatically. Personal computers, the Internet, wireless technology, and mobile communication devices have propelled us into a transition from an era of sponsored and programmed mass media into an era of multifaceted, on-demand, interactive, and personalized media content and experiences. In fact, the time spent each day listening to the radio and watching traditional television is far surpassed by digital media consumption. The pace and implications of this transition are influencing our personal and social lives in ways that we don't yet fully understand.

Although it's important to discuss new trends and explain what may occur in the future, it also is important to understand traditional media and their connections with sports.

Media research in the past often distinguished between print and electronic media. **Print media** included *newspapers, magazines, fanzines, books, catalogues, event programs,* and even *trading cards*—words and images on paper. **Electronic media** included *radio, television, and film.* But digital media and the devices used to consume, create, and distribute content have nearly eliminated the dividing line between these media forms.

Today, media provide *information, interpretation, entertainment,* and *opportunities for interactivity and content production.* When media content is provided for commercial purposes, entertainment is emphasized more than information, interpretation, or opportunities for interactivity and content production. In the process, media consumers become commodities sold to advertisers with the primary goal of promoting lifestyles based on consumption.

Media also put us in touch with information, experiences, people, images, and ideas outside the realm of our everyday, real-time lives. But much media content is edited and "re-presented" to us by others—producers, editors, program directors, programmers, photographers and videographers, writers, journalists, commentators, sponsors, bloggers, and website controllers. These people present us with information, interpretation, entertainment, and even opportunities for interactivity to achieve one or more of the following five goals: (1) make financial profits, (2) influence cultural values and social organization, (3) provide a public service, (4) enhance personal status and reputation, and (5) express themselves creatively or politically.

Commercial forms of sports and traditional media have always had a close relationship. Long before television, newspapers provided sports information, interpretation, and entertainment. Radio did the same. When television began to show people video images of the action, newspapers and radio, including sportswriters and announcers, were forced to change their approach to maintain sales and ratings. There are similar challenges for traditional media today as they compete with a nearly infinite supply of on-demand, interactive digital programming as well as privately produced content.

Power and Control in Sports Media

In nations where mass media (newspapers, magazines, radio, and television) are privately owned, the dominant goals are to make profits and distribute content that promotes the perspectives and interests of people in positions of power and influence (Smith, Evens & Iosifidis, 2015). These aren't the only goals, but they are the most influential. Years ago, media expert Michael Real explained that there was no greater force in the construction of media sport reality than "commercial television and its institutionalized value system [emphasizing] profit making, sponsorship, expanded markets, commodification, and competition" (1998, p. 17).

Of course, as the Internet and wireless technologies extend content and access, media sports reality is now constructed in diverse ways. This can be a contentious process as content providers compete for access to audiences.

In nations where mass media are controlled primarily by the state, the primary goals are to influence cultural values and social organization and provide a public service (Lund, 2007; Solvoll, 2016). However, state control has steadily declined as media companies have been privatized and deregulated, and as more individuals obtain online access to information, interpretation, entertainment, and opportunities for interactivity and content production.

Power relations in a society influence the priority given to the five goals that drive media content. Those who make content decisions for mass media programming act as filters as they select and create the images and messages to present. In the filtering and presentation process, these people usually emphasize images and narratives consistent with ideologies that support their interests in addition to attracting large audiences. As deregulation and private ownership have increased, the media have become hypercommercialized and media content focuses more on individual consumption and less on civic values and community. In fact, when groups with anticommercial messages have wanted to buy commercial time on television, media corporations and networks have refused to sell it to them.

There are exceptions to this pattern, but when people have tried to use mass media to challenge dominant ideologies, they encounter difficulties. This discourages transformational programming and leads people who create media content to self-censor it in ways that defer to the interests of the powerful.

This does not mean that those who control mass media ignore the truth and "force" media audiences to read, hear, and see things unrelated to reality or

(*Source:* Frederic A. Eyer.)

"Quick! Bring the camera—the viewers will love this crash!

Commercial media representations of sports are carefully selected and edited. Commentary and images highlight dramatic action, even when it's a minor part of an event.

their interests. But it does mean that, apart from content that individuals create online, average people influence mass media only through consumption and program ratings. Therefore, the public receives edited, or *mediated,* information, interpretation, entertainment, and interactive experiences that are constructed primarily to boost profits and maintain a business and political climate in which commercial media can thrive. In the process, people who control mass media are concerned with what attracts readers, listeners, and viewers within the legal limits set by government agencies and the preference parameters of individuals and corporations that buy advertising time. As they make programming decisions, they see audiences as collections of consumers that can be sold to advertisers.

In the case of sports, those who control mass media decide not only which sports and events to cover but also the images and commentary presented in the coverage. When they do this, they play an important role in constructing the overall frameworks that audiences use to define and incorporate sports in their lives (Allain, 2016; Boyle, 2014; Bruce, 2013; Burdsey, 2016; Groves & Griggs, 2016; Moraga, 2018; Pullen et al., 2019; Scott et al., 2018; Vincent et al., 2018).

Media Representations of Sports

Most people don't think critically about mass media content (Bruce, 2013). When we watch sports on television, we don't often notice that the images and commentary we see and hear have been carefully presented to create engaging narratives, heighten the dramatic content of the event, and emphasize dominant ideologies in our society, especially those that reaffirm the interests of sponsors as well as the media companies.

In the case of sports programming, the pregame analysis, camera coverage, camera angles, close-ups, slow-motion replays, the attention given to particular athletes, announcers' play-by-play descriptions, the postgame summary and analysis, and all associated website content are presented to entertain media audiences and keep sponsors happy. In some cases, sport leagues and their governing bodies hire their own writers and commentators to produce media content, or they deny press credentials to journalists who present content that sports officials don't like.

Sports media commentaries and images in the United States highlight action, competition, aggression, hard work, individual heroism and achievement, playing despite pain, teamwork, and competitive outcomes. Television coverage has become so seamless in its representations of sports that we often define televised games as "real" games–more real than what is seen in person at the stadium. Longtime magazine editor Kerry Temple explains:

> It's not just games you're watching. It's soap operas, complete with story lines and plots and plot twists. And good guys and villains, heroes and underdogs. And all this gets scripted into cliffhanger morality plays. . . . And you get all caught up in this until you begin to believe it really matters (1992, p. 29).

Temple's point is especially relevant today. The focus on profits has increased soap opera storytelling as a means of developing and maintaining audience interest in commercial media sports coverage. Sports programming is now "a never-ending series of episodes–the results of one game create implications for the next one (or next week's) to be broadcast" (Wittebols, 2004, p. 4). Sports rivalries are hyped and used to serialize stories through and across seasons; conflict and chaos are highlighted with a predictable cast of "good guys," "bad guys," and "redemption" or "comeback" stories; and the story lines are designed to reproduce ideologies favored by upper-middle-class media consumers–the ones that corporate sponsors want to reach with their ads.

Even though media coverage of sports is carefully edited and represented in total entertainment packages, most of us believe that when we see a sport event on television, we are seeing it "the way it is." We don't usually think that what we see, hear, and read is a series of narratives and images selected for particular reasons and grounded in the social worlds and interests of those producing the event and controlling the broadcast. Television coverage provides only one of many possible sets of images and narratives related to an event, and there are many images and messages that audiences do *not* receive (Galily, 2014). If we went to an event in person, we would see something quite different from the images selected and presented on television, and we would develop our own descriptions and interpretations, which would be different from those carefully presented by media commentators and commercial sponsors.

New York Times writer Robert Lipsyte (1996) described televised sports as "-sportainment"—the equivalent of a TV movie that purports to be based on a true story but actually provides fictionalized history. In other words, television constructs sports and viewer experiences. But the process occurs so smoothly that most television viewers believe they experience sports in a "true and natural" form. This, of course, is the goal of the directors, editors, and on-camera announcers who select images and narratives, frame them with the stories they wish to tell, and make sure they please sponsors in the process.

To illustrate this point, think about this question: What if all televised sports were sponsored by environmental groups, women's organizations, and labor unions? Would program content be different from what it is now? Would the political biases built into the images and commentary be the same as they are now? It is unlikely that they would be the same, and we would be quick to identify all the ways that the interests and political agendas of the environmentalists, feminists, or labor leaders influenced images, narratives, and overall program content.

Now think about this: Capitalist corporations sponsor nearly 100 percent of all sports programming in commercial media, and their goals are to create compulsive consumers loyal to capitalism and generate profits for themselves and their shareholders. Says media scholar Lawrence Wenner (2013): "The economic influences of media have changed sport, changed our associations with it, and have affected the stories that are told through sport, both in everyday communication and in the service of commerce." For those who are "tuned in" to the commercial media, their experiences as spectators are heavily influenced—that is, *mediated*—by the decisions of those who control programming and media representations (Oates & Furness, 2015; Rowe, 2018; Sherwood, Nicholson & Marjoribanks, 2017).

NEW DIGITAL MEDIA AND SPORTS

New digital media have altered relationships in the production and consumption of accessible content related to sports worldwide. They make possible individually created and selected information, interpretation, and entertainment. Additionally, personal

(*Source:* Associated Newspapers Ltd/Shutterstock)

New digital media give athletes (and their parents) an opportunity to promote themselves to millions of people. Sky Brown, a 10-year-old skateboarding phenom hopes to qualify for the 2020 Olympic Games in Tokyo. Helping her chances is the publicity of over a half million views on Instagram and 6 million views on her YouTube channel. High school athletes now do the same in hopes of attracting attention from college coaches (McGrath, 2019).

digital connections enable people to bypass the gatekeepers of content in the "old" media–that is, journalists, editors, and commentators–as they construct their own interpretations of events, athletes, and the overall organization of sports (Forde & Wilson, 2018; McHugh et al., 2015; McGrath, 2019; Yardley, Kennedy & Brolan, 2019).

In the case of sports, the recent proliferation of mobile devices and growing connectivity change the way many of us access and respond to sport media content. Additionally, many people now have the ability to produce and distribute sport content and commentary. We can interact with fellow fans, ask questions of players and coaches, follow them on twitter, identify scores and statistics, stream events on demand, and play online games that either simulate sports or are associated with real-time sport events around the world. This transforms media experiences and mediated realities in dramatic ways.

New Digital Media Consumption

Although people often access online sport content to complement content they consume in traditional media, there is a growing number of others who use new digital media to replace traditional content (Evans & Moran, 2017; Gong, 2019; McHugh et al., 2015; Pells, 2019; Winkler, 2019). This shift in consumption patterns concerns people in media companies that broadcast live sports worldwide, because their revenues in the past have depended on controlling this content and maintaining large audiences to sell to advertisers.

At the same time, sport organizations such as MLB, the NFL, the English Premier Football (Soccer) Division, and others have become more active in managing media representations of their sports so they can directly control information, analysis, and entertainment to promote themselves on their terms. For example, MLB.com offers a $116 per year subscription to access real-time coverage of all regular season games on multiple devices. The site also provides game previews, highlights, statistics, and general commentary, among dozens of other video, audio, and text materials on baseball. This enables MLB and other professional sports to provide media content *and* control the ways that their brands are represented.

Overall, new media allow people to control *when* and *how* they consume sports content, but this changes little from the days of traditional media when content was created by a limited number of powerful sources. The real transformational potential of new media rests in how people use them to produce content that offers alternatives to traditional media sources.

Digital Media Production

At the same time that corporations try to maximize control over online representations of sports, YouTube and other sites provide people opportunities to upload their own information and interpretation of sports as well as representations of sports events and performances (Christovich, 2019; Dumont, 2017; McGrath, 2019). For example, for more than three decades now, young people in alternative and action sports have found creative ways to photograph, film, and distribute images of their activities. Photos and VCR tapes were mailed and passed person to person, but distribution today occurs online with images accessible worldwide. Although these images represent what may be described as "performance sports," they're central to the media experiences of many young people who find highly structured, overtly competitive sports such as baseball or football to be boring, irrelevant, and uncreative.

In some cases, young people use new digital media to represent sports involving transgressive actions such as skating in empty private swimming pools at night or doing **parkour** ("PK"), *an activity in which young people use their bodies to move rapidly and efficiently through existing landscapes,* especially in urban areas where walls, buildings, and other obstacles normally impede movement (https://en.wikipedia.org/wiki/Parkour; www.americanparkour.com/). Research on new media representations of these activities is sorely needed. Videos of parkour have made it a global phenomenon as young men (for the most part) have become aware of the possibility of using the physical environments around them as "sport spaces" in which they can develop skills, express themselves, and even gain widespread recognition by doing things and posting videos that catch the attention of other PK athletes.

Researchers in many disciplines are now exploring these possibilities as the media landscape is changing in character and scope at a rate unprecedented in human history. Most of this research deals with how people use new digital media to complement or create informational and interpretive content related to sports already covered in mainstream media.[1] However, there also are a few studies of people using digital media to report on sports ignored by mainstream media (Antunovic and Hardin, 2015; Christovich, 2019; MacKay and Dallaire, 2014; McGrath, 2019).

This research highlights and describes exciting possibilities, but it also identifies factors that may undermine those possibilities. Powerful corporations have a high stakes financial interest in controlling new media and using it to add to their bottom line. This includes massive, monopoly-like companies that provide connectivity; mainstream media companies built around newspapers, magazines, radio, television, and film; and sport organizations that survive or prosper because of their financial relationships with mainstream media companies. Leaders in this industry are using their resources to enter the new digital media market, and retain and extend their control over how these media are used, who benefits from their use, and how content is regulated. Therefore, they continue to lobby federal legislators on copyright law, definitions of intellectual property, public domain parameters, liability laws, and a host of other issues that they can use to prevent anyone from threatening their financial interests. At the same time, they extend their control by using digital media in strategic ways. Fantasy sports and video games are examples of how they enlist people as allies to sustain their power.

The major sociological question related to new digital media is this: Will they democratize social life by enabling people to freely share information and ideas, or will they become tools controlled by corporations to expand their capital, increase consumption, reproduce ideologies that drive market economies, and maintain the illusion that we need them to provide pleasure and excitement in our lives? The answer to this question will emerge as the struggle for control over the media unfolds. At this point the struggle does not involve a fair fight, because people who will benefit from the potential democratizing effects of new digital media are not even aware of the fight–and the leaders of corporate media are doing all they can to keep it that way.

FANTASY SPORTS, SPORTS VIDEO GAMES, AND ESPORTS: MEDIA TRANSFORMED

Traditional media now have a 21st century set of digital triplets that they have cautiously adopted. This digital threesome–fantasy sports, sports video games, and esports–have grown so fast that many people in the sport-media realm, especially those over 40 years old, don't know what to make of them. Like real-life children, they are exerting significant influence on their traditional media parents and forcing them to make adjustments in what they do. At this time, it is difficult to know if these new triplets will grow up to challenge or complement their sport-media elders. What we do know is that they are changing audience demographics in the media-sport realm, altering how audiences define and consume mediated sports, and disrupting the meaning and organization of sports.

Each one of these triplets has unique characteristics that are changing as they grow and

[1]The major sources I've used to explore this issue are these: Boyle, 2014; Browning and Sanderson, 2012; Connolly and Dolan, 2012; Dart, 2014; Ferriter, 2009; Frederick et al., 2012; Galily, 2014; Gantz and Lewis, 2014; Hutchins, 2014; Oates and Furness, 2015; Ross, 2011; Wenner, 2014; Whannel, 2014.

gain experience. Their stories are compelling and important to consider from a sociological perspective.

Fantasy Sports: Changing How We Watch and Cheer

Fantasy sports is the first-born triplet, conceived in 1979 when a baseball fan created a game in which he and a few friends pretended to be the owners of imaginary Major League Baseball teams that competed against each other. In the process, they connected the passive activity of consuming traditional media with the active challenge of using their baseball knowledge to select their own "fantasy" teams from the active players in Major League Baseball and then use the performance statistics for their fantasy players to determine a score that could be compared to the scores of their friends' teams during and at the end of the season. This converted them from relatively passive fans into team managers and active competitors in a league of their own (Billings & Ruihley, 2014).

This fantasy game added a new dimension to their roles as fans. Now they read baseball coverage in newspapers and magazines more carefully to learn about individual players on all teams, not just *their* team. They tracked performance data on players and watched as many baseball games as they could to learn about the players they might select for their fantasy teams in the future and which players they may trade to other teams. The one thing that prevented this game from spreading around the United States faster than it did was the tedious job of collecting performance data for the players on all the fantasy teams and calculating team scores to determine who was the fantasy winner at the end of the season.

The internet boom in the late-1990s eliminated this tedious chore and opened the door for a massive influx of new fantasy sports gamers. Sports leagues along with media and tech companies developed online platforms that could serve millions of fantasy participants. As participants increased exponentially into the early years of the 21st century, newspapers and magazines hired fantasy sportswriters to create media content sought by fantasy sports participants, especially those who played fantasy football, the sport that attracted the most participation.

As the management and team owners in the NFL and other major sports leagues read studies showing that fantasy sports participants were their most engaged fans and consumed more media articles and programming than other fans, they supported and invested in the growth of fantasy sports. Other sports followed their lead. In addition to fantasy football, baseball, basketball, and hockey, there were fantasy leagues for auto racing, golf, tennis, global soccer, cricket, and even professional wrestling. Today you can manage fantasy teams selected from the National Women's Soccer League and the WNBA.

Fantasy sports changed as it grew, and around 2010, it came into contact with two startup companies: FanDuel and DraftKings. These companies were run by entrepreneurs who created short term competitions in addition to the season-long ones. They also pushed legal and moral boundaries as they introduced cash prizes for the short term winners. This attracted more participants and billions of dollars along with the attention of lawmakers who saw this as a form of illegal gambling. However, when the companies presented research evidence showing that success in fantasy sports depended on a participants' skills rather than random chance (as with poker and dice games), it was decided, after extended legal wrangling and the discovery of a loophole in anti-gambling laws, that their fantasy sports with cash prizes didn't fit the technical definition of gambling.

The companies that run fantasy sports operations today make money by charging entry fees, running advertising on their sites, and, in some cases, collecting a share of the money that people now legally bet on sports in an increasing number of states (Delventhal, 2019). In North America alone there were about 60 million people who played fantasy sports at some level in 2019, many of whom used the ESPN sports app. Revenues for the companies that run the fantasy league was nearly $8 billion (Deshbandhu, 2019; Rodriguez, 2017). In the UK there were 6 million participants in fantasy soccer, and worldwide, there were fantasy soccer leagues in 252 countries and territories (AlliAyewOKane, 2018). Companies in India now host fantasy cricket which is growing rapidly.

Most interesting for us in the sociology of sport is that fantasy sports have "gamified" media-sport consumption by turning consumers into virtual team managers who compete with each other. They also provide a research window through which we can study how participants engage with mediated sports content and how they use multiple media sources simultaneously (Deshbandhu, 2019; Nee and Dozier 2017). For example, fantasy participants continue to cheer for their favorite team, but they also cheer for players on multiple other teams because those players are on their fantasy teams. Therefore, they watch multiple games on multiple screens and are constantly online checking performance statistics as they are posted. Overall, they are deeply engaged with real-time sports in ways that people in the media-sport industry could only dream of in the past. For industry people, the challenge now is to use fantasy sports as a starting point for introducing interactive television–with the first-born triplet changing its adoptive parents in the process.

Finally, and maybe most significant, there is a close connection between fantasy sports and sports betting, each of which appeals to the same demographics and groups of fans (Fisher, 2019). The significance of this connection will increase as more states embrace sports betting and as commercial sports use the lure of gambling to increase their revenues. For example, one idea is to put betting chips in team and league merchandise to encourage people to make more prop bets. Therefore, when a football fan buys a New England Patriots hat, a chip in the hat-band would enable him to bet on whether quarterback Tom Brady will throw two touchdown passes in the first half of the season-opening game (Delventhal, 2019). Such a marketing strategy would contribute to the "gamblification of sports," a concept developed by sports media scholar, David Rowe (2018). This gamblification would further change the ways that sports and media are integrated into the lives of individuals, families, and communities. For example, it might increase rates of gambling addiction, family financial problems, and the need for community rehab programs. At the very least, it would change how many fans would consume traditional media coverage of sports.

Sports Video Games: Changing Sport Experiences

Video games that simulate sports is the second of the triplets. It is the sibling closest to esports, but like fantasy sports, its other sibling, it provides fans with the illusion of ownership and control in commercial sports. This aspect of video games was recognized over 30 years ago by Electronic Arts. Although Atari, Sega, Taito, Nintendo, and other companies created video game simulations of sports between the early 1970s and the late-1980s, it was Electronic Arts that did it the best. They began with the *Earl Weaver Baseball* video game in 1987 and *John Madden Football* in 1988, both of which used AI to provide realistic game playing experiences that set them apart from other game developers at that time.

The production of sport simulation games is tricky because it requires complex licensing agreements between a sports league, the league's players association, game developers, and a distributor. The realism of the games depends on the capabilities of software and hardware (computers and consoles) and the sophistication of other technologies such as motion-capture cameras. The importance of these things was recently demonstrated when *Madden NFL*, the best-selling sports video game for over 20 years, was surpassed by *NBA 2K*. As of mid-2019, *NBA 2K* had sold over 90 million copies, an accomplishment that led the NBA to extend its licensing agreement with 2K Sports (the game's developer) through 2026 for $1.1 billion (Kim, 2019).

The realism of the current *NBA 2K* games is produced by dressing every NBA player in a tight suit that has 60 reflective markers on it. Then they use

140 motion-capture cameras to film the player's moves on the court as infrared lights from each camera track the 60 markers. Each camera records images at 120 frames per second which gives the game creator 16,800 images for each second that the athlete is filmed (Pierno, 2019). This enables them to realistically represent the movements and expressions of the player, which are integrated with commentary that describes the athlete's moves in situations anticipated during game play. The realism of the resulting game action is increased as AI is used to learn the team strategies that lead to high percentage shots. In fact, it has even been shown that basketball players who play the game can increase their basketball IQ in the process (FoxSports, 2017).

At this point, we don't know if the realism of these video games leads those people to prefer them over watching real-time sports, or if it increases their consumption of traditional sports media programming. We do know that many NFL and NBA players are hooked on the video game versions of their sport. The realism of the latest NASCAR, Formula One, and Indy Racecar video games is so impressive that some professional drivers use games to familiarize themselves with the tracks on which their races are held. The details depicted in video games have even led tattoo artists to claim that they should receive a royalty for their original creations on the bodies of basketball players. In response to one such claim, LeBron James argued that his tattoos were part of *his* "persona and identity" and said, "If I am not shown with my tattoos, it wouldn't really be a depiction of me" (in Bailey, 2018). Who owns the copyright on an original tattoo? What constitutes "fair use" of the inked image? These are legal questions now being discussed in court cases.

Overall, the financial stakes associated with creating realistic and entertaining video games are significant. This constantly pushes designers to refine graphics, action, and game possibilities. It also leads them to talk with potential sponsors about product placements and advertisements built into the storylines and actions in the games. As more young people play video games, corporations, including sports leagues and their sponsors see them as vehicles for developing outposts in the heads of game players, outposts that can be used to deliver messages that encourage consumption and generate revenues for the corporations involved.

For us in the sociology of sport, these sports video games raise interesting questions. For example, if young people are introduced to a sport through a video game, are they more or less likely to play the real sport on which the game is based? If so, will their experiences in the video game influence their actions and feelings in real sport situations? Will young people be more or less likely to listen to coaches after being in control of players, game strategies, and video game conditions? Will they bring new forms of game knowledge to situations in which they play real sports? How many young people will choose to play sports video games rather than real sports? Will a high school or college student's status as a skilled and successful video game player rival or surpass a student's status as a skilled and successful athlete on a traditional sports team at their school?

Research is needed on these and additional questions related to the sociology of video games. In fact, over the next generation, there may be a time when the playoffs in the NBA 2K league attract as much attention as the NBA playoffs. This possibility leads to our consideration of the third triplet: Esports.

Esports: Transforming the Sport-Media Landscape

Fantasy sports and sports video games have altered the sport-media landscape, but esports is the triplet mostly likely to transform and colonize it in the future. Bryan Graham, long-time sports journalist and current deputy sport editor of *Guardian USA*, covers esports and has concluded the following: *The question is not whether esports is the future of sports entertainment, but whether there's any possible scenario where it's not* (Graham, 2019).

(*Source:* Jay Coakley)

The rapid evolution of "digital sports" is supported by influential investors and corporations. The Luxor casino in Las Vegas has added an ESPORTS ARENA to attract young people; other casinos and venture capitalists are doing the same worldwide. When betting on esports is legal, it will provide a major impetus for their growth.

The definition of esports is emerging as this third triplet grows and is increasingly embraced worldwide. At this point, ***esports** are organized, competitive video games played according to agreed-upon rules by individuals and teams.* In mainstream media discussions, there is a distinction made between the corporate-sponsored esports leagues and tournaments that involve professional gamers competing for millions of dollars of prize money, and local esports clubs and the rapidly expanding esports teams sponsored by high schools and colleges. The former is attracting attention from investors who see esports as a potential commercial rival of professional sports. Additionally, investors are tracking the commercial potential of gaming media platforms (portals) such as Twitch, Reddit, Discord, and various YouTube channels that are go-to streaming sites for millions of esports fans. This worries executives at mainstream television companies that have multi-billion-dollar rights deals with the NCAA and professional sports leagues. Even the executives at Netflix recently disclosed that "We compete with (and lose to) 'Fortnite' more than HBO" (Poletti, 2019).

As the global growth of esports has created a multi-billion-dollar media market, the people connected with the mainstream sport-media industry are taking notice (Wohn & Freeman, 2020). This is why the NFL and EA Sports sponsor the *Madden NFL Championship Series* that is streamed on EAMaddenNFL's channel on Twitch. In the process, the NFL hopes to recruit hardcore esports fans who will also consume media programming of football games (Edmunds, 2019). Similarly, FIFA sponsors the *FIFA19 Global Series* that attracted 61 million total views in June 2019. Some of the views were driven by the 20 million global players that participated in a series of tournaments leading up to the finals in the series. Like the NFL, FIFA uses the series to recruit young people as viewers of real FIFA soccer; unlike the NFL, FIFA has a much broader global appeal and potential.

The NBA has taken a slightly different long-term marketing route. It formed the NFL 2K League that now has 21 teams named after and located in NBA cities. Although weekly games seldom attract more than 30,000 viewers, the league is only 2 years old. NBA teams sponsor and subsidize their esports teams, and organize them like the real teams. There is a draft during which players demonstrate their skills and are selected (or not) by an NBA 2K team manager/coach. For those who make a team, the minimum base salary in 2019 was $33,000, although there is $1.2 million that is split into thirds and awarded to each team that wins one of three tournaments during the season. Additionally, travel to away games is paid by the NBA and each of the teams lives rent-free during the season in a nicely furnished house (Holmes, 2019).

A classic example of commercial esports was the 2019 Fortnite World Cup sponsored by Epic Games. It involved 40 million players who competed online during ten weeks of qualifying rounds to determine the 200 finalists who competed for $30 million in cash prizes at the Arthur Ashe Stadium in Flushing, New York. The finalists, all males, came from 34 countries and the $3 million first prize in the solo category was won by a 16-year old from the United States. There also were multimillion-dollar winners in other competition categories (Duos, Celebrity Pro/AM, and Creative); and the rest of the 200 finalists each took home $50,000. The 19,000 stadium seats were sold out for each of the three days of competitions. The media production truck had twice as many feeds as used by CBS during the 2019 Super Bowl. A full-color commentary broadcast was streamed on multiple platforms where many viewers had the option of choosing close-up camera shots of their favorite players (Graham, 2019).

Overall, the media audience for esports in 2019 was about 454 million people with expected growth to 645 million by 2022 (Pannekeet, 2019). With 1.5 billion people, mostly young people, who are aware of esports worldwide, the 2022 Asian Games designated esports as a medal event, and the International Olympic Committee is considering the inclusion of esports in its medal events in the future–a move that they hope will make the Olympic Games more attractive to young consumers globally.

A significant development in the United States is the number of colleges, over 200 as of 2020, that now sponsor esports teams and award scholarships to select team members. However, esports team members can also win money in the tournaments in which they play. Only 60 colleges designate esports as an official sport but Chris Haskell, coach of the Boise State University esports teams, recently predicted the following:

> *Collegiate esports is a coming wave. Somebody is going to become the Alabama football of esports. That seat is currently open. Why can't it be us? We just have to move quickly* (BallistixGaming, 2019).

NCAA president, Mark Emmert, is not as excited about esports as Coach Haskell at Boise State, even though the recent League of Legends World Championship had over twice the number of media viewers as the 2019 Men's Final Four games (Heilwell, 2019). When asked if the NCAA would include an esports division, he proclaimed the following:

> *We don't particularly embrace games where the objective is to blow your opponent's head off* (Kirshner, 2019).

This was an odd response coming from someone who heads an organization with nearly 800 colleges and universities that sponsor football teams on which players endure about 1500 head hits each year with some of them experiencing brain damage due to those hits. Of course, Emmert objected to the fictional violence in some video games (but not to the sexism or racism). However, Emmert has connections with universities that offer graduate degrees for people going into game design, and it would not be out of the question for them and their faculty to design challenging esports games in which heads aren't blown off and in which there is no sexism or racism (Stuart, 2019). If such a project were funded, and entertaining games with copyrights were created and used in college esports, they might even generate revenues to rival those generated by most NCAA sports.

High schools are likely to become leaders in creating esports teams. The National Federation of State High School Associations (NFHS) and the NFHS Network have already partnered with PlayVS, an online gaming provider, to initiate esports competition in high schools nationwide (https://www.nfhs.org/sports-resource-content/esports/). Seventeen states approved esports as official varsity or club sports. The teams have two seasons during the academic year, and PlayVS has the rights to multiple games approved by the state association, and schools can choose which ones they want to play. Teams have no travel expenses because they can compete with other schools through the PlayVS platform. This means that any school nationwide is a potential opponent. Additionally, each school can form as many teams as they want, and they can play as many games as they want during the seasons. To make things easier for the schools, the national federation will assist them in getting started with their esports programs.

As more schools embrace esports, young people will be introduced to new technologies, streaming platforms, gaming consoles, and the most entertaining video games in the world. Research is needed to see if this moves them away from traditional media and traditional sports. Will the introduction of esports teams change the culture of schools and alter the status of students on esports teams? Will teams be gender inclusive, and will the digital divide work to the disadvantage of students from lower-income families? More discussion of this topic is found in Chapter 14, Sports in High School and College. In terms of this chapter, it is clear that fantasy sports, sports video games, and esports have the potential to transform the current relationship between sports and the media.

SPORTS AND MEDIA: A TWO-WAY RELATIONSHIP

The media and commercialization are related topics in the sociology of sport. The media intensify and extend the process and consequences of commercialization. For this reason, much attention has been given to the interdependence between the media and commercialized forms of sports (Galily and Tamir, 2014). Each of these spheres influences the other, and each depends on the other for part of its popularity and commercial success.

Sports Depend on Media

People played sports long before media coverage of their events. When sports exist for participants only, there's no need to advertise games, report the action, publish results, and interpret what happened. The players already know these things, and they're the only ones who matter. It is only when sports become commercial entertainment that they depend on the media.

Commercial sports require media to provide a combination of coverage, publicity, and news. Sports promoters and team owners know the value of coverage, and they provide free access to reporters, commentators, and photographers. For example, the London Organizing Committee of the Olympic Games and Paralympic Games (LOCOG) accredited 21,000 journalists, media technicians, producers, and camera operators to cover nearly 15,000 athletes during the Olympics and Paralympics; another 6000 to 8000 were credentialed to cover nonsport aspects of the events. NBC sent 2700 people. The BBC deployed 756 staff, and the Associated Press (AP) had 200 journalists and photographers working full time during the games. This made the 2012 Olympic and Paralympic Games the most comprehensively covered event in history. Credentialed media personnel often are given comfortable seats in press boxes, access to the playing field and locker rooms, and summaries of statistics and player information. In return, promoters and owners expect and usually receive supportive media coverage.

Table 12.1 Annual media rights fees for major commercial sports in the United States, 1986–2019 (in millions of dollars)*

Sport	1986	1991	1996	2001	2008	2015	2019
NFL	400	900	1100	2200	3750	4950	8100
MLB†	183	365	420	417	670	1550	1500
NBA	30	219	275	660	765	925	2670
NHL‡	22	38	77	120	70	200	1200
NASCAR	3	NA	NA	412	560	683	660
NCAA Men's Basketball Tournament	31	143	216	216	560	720	804
WNBA	0	0	0	¶	¶	25	25
MLS	NA	NA	0	0	0	90	90

*Amounts are not adjusted for inflation. Data come from multiple sources, and amounts change when new contracts are negotiated data for 2019 are rounded to the nearest million or thousand.
†Amounts for baseball do not include local television and radio rights fees negotiated by individual teams, national radio rights fees negotiated by the league, or Internet revenues received by the league from subscriptions paid to receive games on MLB.com.
‡Includes US rights only for 2001 and 2006; Canadian and European rights included for 2015 and 2019.
¶Information has never been disclosed; the new contract that began in 2016 will pay $12 million annually.

Although commercial spectator sports depend on media, most have a special dependence on television because television companies pay for the rights to broadcast games and other events. Table 12.1 and Figure 12.1 indicate that "rights fees" provide sports with predictable, significant, and increasing sources of income. Once "rights contracts" are signed, revenues are guaranteed regardless of bad weather, injuries to key players, and the other factors that interfere with ticket sales and on-site revenue streams. Without these media rights contracts, spectator sports seldom generate much profit.

Television revenues also have greater growth potential than revenues from gate receipts. The number of seats in a stadium limits ticket sales, and ticket costs are limited by demand. But television audiences can include literally billions of viewers now that satellite technology transmits signals to most locations worldwide. For example, the IOC and sponsors of other sports mega-events seek to package the entire world's population into an audience that can be sold to sponsors.

Additional reasons for increased rights fees include the following:

- The deregulation of the television industry.
- A growing demand to watch certain spectator sports.
- Increased connectivity with satellite and cable worldwide.
- Sponsors willing to pay top prices for access to live sports audiences because commercials are seen by people rather than being skipped over in recorded programs.
- The growth of ESPN and other cable channels that collect money from cable and satellite companies as well as commercial sponsors, which gives them two sources of income.

These reasons have driven the increases in rights fees as shown Figure 12.1 and Table 12.1. In 1986 the NFL received $400 million in television rights fees, and in 2019 it received $8.1 billion. Similarly, the rights fees paid to televise the 1984 Olympic Games in Los Angeles amounted to $287 million—ten times *more* than was paid to televise the 1976

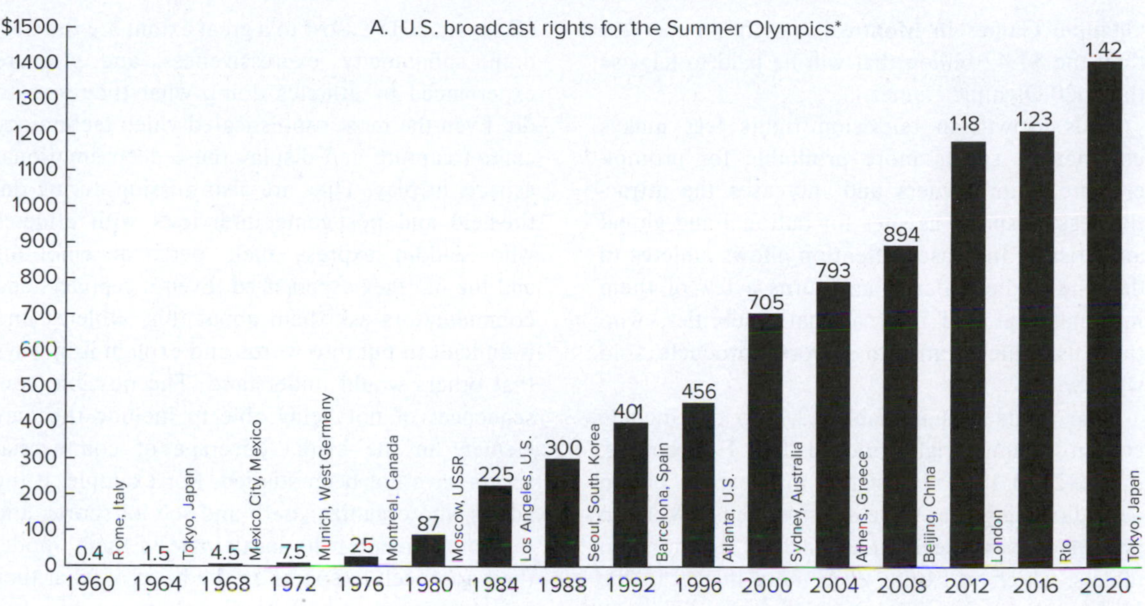

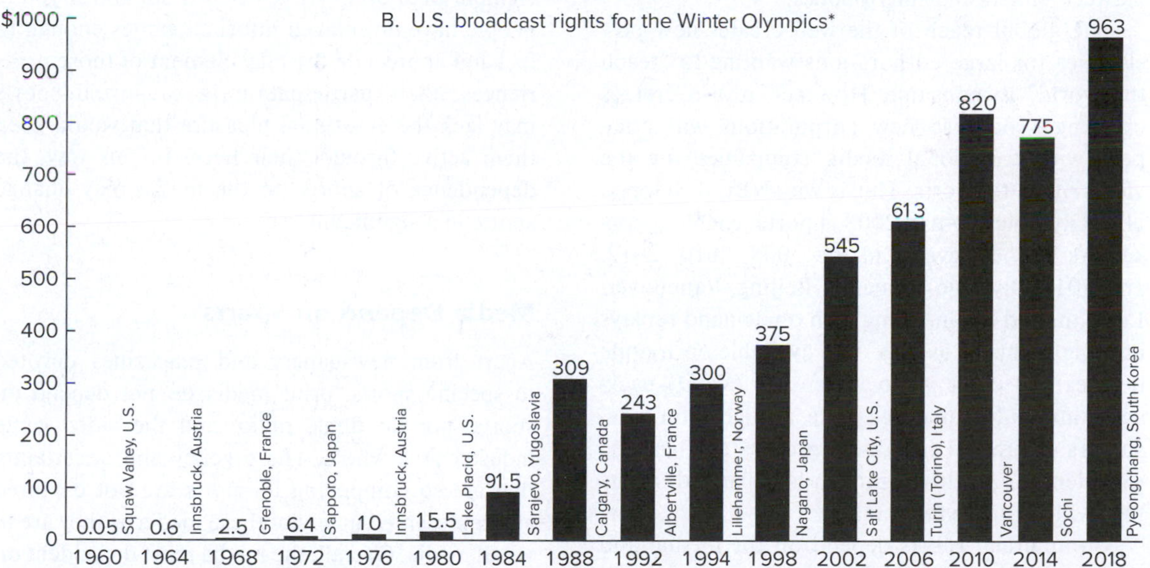

FIGURE 12.1 Escalating media rights fees paid by US media companies to televise the Olympics (in millions of dollars).

*The local organizing committee for the Olympic Games also receives rights fees from other television companies around the world. Europe, Japan, and continental Asia are paying increasingly higher fees. For US rights for Vancouver 2010 through the Summer Games in 2020, NBC Universal has paid the IOC $6.39 billion.

Olympic Games in Montreal, and five times *less* than the $1.42 billion that will be paid to televise the 2020 Olympic Games.

This growth in television rights fees makes commercial sports more profitable for promoters and team owners and increases the attractiveness of sports as sites for national and global advertising. Increased attention allows athletes to demand higher salaries and turns a few of them into national and international celebrities, who then use their status to endorse products sold worldwide.

The rights fees in Table 12.1 do not include certain streaming rights prior to 2019. For example, in late-2013 the NFL signed a 4-year $1 billion deal allowing games to be live-streamed on Verizon phones. But this deal did not include streaming on tablets, which will bring even more money to the NFL, and will force them to define the difference between tablets and smartphones!

The global reach of the web creates new possibilities for large corporations wanting to "teach the world" to consume. However, it also creates challenges because new corporations will compete with traditional media companies for the video rights to sports. This is why NBC developed NBCOlympics.com in 2008, a portal enabling consumers to view events in the 2008, 2010, 2012, and 2014 Olympic Games in Beijing, Vancouver, London, and Sochi, along with on-demand replays and highlights. Coverage was available on mobile devices and cable video-on-demand (VOD) packages, and other features were available for consumers interested in athlete profiles and gaming experiences. As this approach is expanded, rights fees will continue to increase.

Commercial sports depend on the media, and the media have clearly increased our access to sports events. But there is a downside to this development. As sports are covered and broadcast, what once were forms of play and games are converted into businesses and brands. In this process, the play element of sports is eclipsed by a combination of spectacle, seriousness, and rationality (Duncan, 2018). Lost to a great extent are the freedom, spontaneity, expressiveness, and pleasure experienced by athletes doing what they love to do. Even the most sophisticated video technology cannot capture and display these deep emotional aspects of play. They are also missing during on-the-field and post-game interviews with athletes who seldom express their personal emotions and the fun they experienced. Even if reporters and commentators ask them about this, athletes find it difficult to put into words and explain it in ways that others would understand. The possible consequences of not being able to include the play element in the media coverage of commercial sports have not been studied. For example, if the adults who organize youth and school sports, and the young people who participate in them, model their approach to sports on the basis of what they consume in the media, they may disregard a key element of sports experiences. If so, and if young people have not played informal games enough to feel and appreciate the play element of those experiences, their participation in organized sports may lack the emotional pleasure that would keep them active through their lives. In this way, the dependence of sports on the media may change sports in a significant way.

Media Depend on Sports

Apart from newspapers and magazines devoted to specific sports, print media do not depend on sports; nor do films, radio, and the video game industry as a whole. The urgency and uncertainty that are so compelling in sports are not captured and represented in any of these media as they are in visual media. Overall, the media most dependent on sports for commercial success are newspapers and television.

Newspapers Major North American newspapers give 25 percent of their daily news coverage to sports, more than any other single topic of interest, including business or politics. The sports section is the most widely read section of the paper. It accounts for at least one-third of the total circulation and a significant amount of the advertising revenues for big-city newspapers. It attracts local and online advertisers and online businesses that want to reach middle-aged males with ads for tires, automobile supplies, new cars, car leases, airline tickets for business travelers, alcoholic beverages, power tools, building supplies, sporting goods, hair-growth products, sexual performance products, testosterone, and hormone therapies. Ads for these products and services are unique to the (men's) sports section, and they generate needed revenues for newspapers.

As the Internet has become a primary source of information about big-time sports nationally and worldwide, many local, small-market newspapers have established online sites for breaking news, regular columns, and blogs. Their print editions may contain this content, but they focus more on local sports, including high school varsity teams, small college teams, and even youth sports. Despite this, the future of these newspapers is in serious jeopardy.

Television Major television networks in the United States now depend on the coverage of live sports as their primary revenue generators and they are willing to pay large amounts of money for the rights to broadcast them. Such high payouts for sports are a recent development. For example, the NFL's first television contract with CBS in 1962 amounted to $4.65 million, or $330,000 per team. In 2019 the NFL received $8.1 billion–a windfall of $255 million per team. Other sports don't have such lucrative deals, but most have also seen significant increases in their rights fees. For sports that don't share in this media bounty, it is difficult to survive at a professional or elite level.

At a time when television audiences are fragmented and new media capture the interests of many younger viewers, there is a collective urgency associated with certain men's sports and the Olympic Games that attracts large audiences that watch for long stretches without prerecording and editing out commercials. Sports now account for a growing proportion of media company income. Half of the operating income of the massive Disney Company is generated by ESPN, as it collects over $10 billion from fees paid by nearly 90 million cable, satellite, and streaming subscribers and it sells commercial time to its programming sponsors. Other channels feature sports programming, but ESPN produces thousands of hours of programming and accounts for nearly half of the live sport events televised in the United States.

In an effort to break ESPN's monopoly-like control of premium sports programming, Fox Sports launched Fox Sports 1 in 2013 as a new 24-hour sports programming channel. However, generating the revenues and viewer loyalty possessed by ESPN will be a formidable challenge. NBC Universal (owned by Comcast) has been successful in retaining its hold on the Olympic Games through 2020. Using its cable channels, CNBC, MSNBC, Bravo, and USA Network, it presented 6755 hours of the 2016 Olympic Games, not including the Paralympics.

An attractive feature of sport programming for the major US networks (ABC, CBS, Fox, and NBC) is that events often are scheduled on Saturdays and Sundays–the slowest days of the week for television viewing. Sports events are the most popular weekend programs, especially among male viewers who don't watch much television at other times. For example, NFL games have consistently accounted for 80 of the top 100 most-viewed television programs during recent years, and they provide sponsors access to young and middle-age males (Porter, 2018). Nearly all sport programming is ideal for promoting sales of beer, life insurance, trucks and cars, computers, investment services, credit cards, air travel and erectile dysfunction products. Sponsors realize that sports attract men who make purchasing decisions for hundreds, if not thousands, of employees, as well as for family members when it comes to buying beer, cars, computers, investments, and life insurance.

Golf and tennis are special cases for television programming. They attract few viewers and the ratings are exceptionally low, but the audience for these sports is very attractive to certain advertisers. It comprises people from upper-income groups, including many professionals and business executives. This is why television coverage of golf and tennis is sponsored by companies selling luxury cars and high-priced sports cars, business and personal computers, imported beers, investment opportunities with brokers and consultants, and trips to exclusive vacation areas. This is also why the networks continue to carry these programs despite low ratings. Advertisers will pay high fees to reach high-income consumers and corporate executives who make decisions to buy thousands of "company cars" and computers at the same time that they invest millions of dollars for employee pension plans or 401k plans. With such valued viewers, golf and tennis don't need high ratings to sell their television rights for high fees.

Women's sports also attract television coverage although they receive only 4–6 percent of the total coverage. Even though females make up 40 percent of sports participants in the United States women's events don't receive more coverage partly because female viewers of women's games have not been identified as a target demographic by advertisers who reach women through other means. Furthermore, men make up over half the viewing audience

(*Source:* PCN Photography/Alamy Stock Photo)

The media enable some athletes to become global celebrities and benefit from windfall income related to their popularity. However, photographers and reporters often enter spaces that athletes would like to keep private. Jessica Ennis, a popular British heptathlete, had her every move covered by British tabloids as she trained for and won the 2012 heptathlon (a seven-discipline event) with a record number of points. When she was physically and emotionally exhausted after her victory, the media documented the moment.

for most women's sports, but they also watch men's sports where sponsors already reach them.

Some cable and satellite television companies attract advertising money by covering sports that appeal to clearly identified segments of consumers. The X Games, for example, attract young males between 12 and 30 years old, which in turn attracts corporate sponsors selling soft drinks, beer, telecommunications products, and sports equipment such as helmets, shoes, skateboards, and dozens of other sport-specific products.

Over the past two decades, television companies have paid rapidly increasing amounts of money for the rights to televise certain sports, as indicated in Table 12.1. This is primarily because sports accounted for 86 of the top 100 television programs among 18-49 year-olds in 2018 with 63 of those programs being NFL or Olympics events. Additionally, rights fees are driven up due to competition from Amazon and communications tech companies that can offer platforms for streaming events, and from the rights owners themselves (NFL Network, MLB .com) who want to make money without using a media company (Siino, 2018).

As choices for sports television viewing have increased, audiences have fragmented and ratings for many sports have declined, especially during prime-time hours, even as the total number of people watching television sports has remained relatively steady. This means that rights fees for the very large events will remain high, but fees for other events, including "special-interest" events such as bowling, in-line skating championships, and international skiing races will be limited. When interest in special events is especially strong among particular viewers, pay-per-view (PPV) sports programming can push rights fees to high levels; this continues to occur for championship boxing, professional wrestling, and mixed martial arts. PPV can generate massive revenues, but events must be chosen selectively because most people are not willing to pay upfront for a single event on television. In the meantime, pay TV has become part of people's lives in the form of subscription fees for cable and satellite connections and special sports channels and packages.

Sports and the Media: A Relationship Based on Economics and Ideology

Global economic factors have intensified the interdependence between commercial sports and the media. Major transnational corporations need ways to develop global name recognition, cultural legitimacy, and product familiarity. They also want to promote ideologies that support a way of life based on consumption, competition, and individual achievement.

Media sports offer global corporations a means of meeting these needs. Certain sport events attract worldwide attention; satellite technology transmits television signals around the world; sport images are associated with recognizable symbols and pleasurable experiences by billions of people; sports and athletes usually can be presented in politically safe ways by linking them with local identities and then using them to market products, values, and lifestyles related to local cultures or popular forms of global culture. Therefore, powerful transnational corporations spend billions of dollars annually to sponsor the media coverage of sports. This in turn gives global media companies significant power over sports worldwide.

The long-time marriage of sports and media is clearly held together and strengthened by vast amounts of money from corporations whose executives use sports to increase profits and promote ideologies consistent with personal and corporate interests. Ideology is a key factor in the sport–media marriage. This is not a marriage based solely on money, but the goal of the sport–media partnership is to create a global family of eager consumers.

IMAGES AND NARRATIVES IN MEDIA SPORTS

To say that sports are "mediated" is to say that they consist of selected images and narratives. Much research in the sociology of sport has deconstructed these images and narratives and analyzed the ideas or themes on which they are based. The scholars who have done these studies assume that media sports are symbolic constructions, much like Hollywood action films, television soap operas, and Disney cartoons.

To say that a telecast of an American football game is a symbolic construction means that it presents the ideas that certain people have about football, values, social life, and the characteristics of the viewing audience. Although each of us interprets media images and narratives differently, many of us use mediated sports as reference points as we form, revise, and extend our ideas about sports, social life, and social relations.

Because media sports are part of everyday experience today, it's important to consider the following:

1. Media production and representation of sports.
2. Ideological themes underlying media coverage.
3. Media consumers and the ways they integrate media content into their lives.

Media Production and Representation of Sports

When media are privately owned and organized to make financial profits, sports are selected for coverage on the basis of their entertainment and revenue-generating potential. Media images and narratives are selected to represent the event so it meets the perceived interests of the audience and sponsors. Sports that are difficult to cover profitably usually are ignored by the media or covered only with selected highlights.

Sports coverage generally consists of images and narratives that exaggerate the spectacular, such as heroic injuries or achievements. Images and narratives also invent and highlight rivalries and explain why events are important. Furthermore, they create and maintain the celebrity status of athletes and teams. Cultural studies scholar Garry Crawford explains:

> The mass-media construction of celebrity often lacks depth of character, as figures are frequently painted in one-dimensional terms. . . . Much of the language used to describe sport stars . . . draws on the narrative of melodrama. Heroes rise and fall, villains are defeated, and women play out their roles as supporting cast members to men's central dramatic roles (2004, p. 133).

Narratives even redeem villains who demonstrate that they can be heroic warriors, with commentators describing them as "loyal blue-collar players"–"willing to take figurative bullets for their teammates"–and "always being there when the chips are down," even if they sometimes have broken rules in the past.

Mainstream media also emphasize elite, commercial sport events. For example, US newspapers and television networks increased their coverage of professional sports through the twentieth century and decreased coverage of amateur sports with the

A few powerful global media companies control most of the media representations of sports worldwide. This monopoly has serious implications for what sports we see or don't see.

exception of college football and men's basketball. This shift was accompanied by a growing emphasis on the importance of winning, heroic actions, and the desire to attract corporate sponsors and a mass audience. It's important to understand this process and the ways that particular images and narratives in media coverage inform popular ideas about sports and about social relations and social life in general.

Ideological Themes in Media Images and Narratives

Sports are represented in the media through images and narratives that are selected from a vast array of possibilities. The traditional media resemble windows through which we view what others choose to put in our range of vision and hear what others choose to say. Therefore, the only way to avoid being duped is to become a critical media consumer.

Becoming a critical media consumer involves learning to identify the ideologies that guide others as they construct media representations. In the case of sports, the most central ideologies that influence what we see and hear are those related to success, consumption, gender, race, ethnicity, and nationality.

Success Themes in Media Narratives Media coverage of sports in the United States emphasizes success through individual effort, competition, teamwork, aggression, and effective game plans. Also important are big individual plays such as home runs, long touchdown passes, and single-handed goals. The idea that success can be based on empathy, support for others, sharing resources, autonomy, intrinsic satisfaction, personal growth, compromise, incremental changes, or inclusiveness is seldom incorporated in media narratives, even though these elements often exist in sports.

Media representations exaggerate the importance of competitive rivalries as well as winning and losing in athletes' lives. For example, ESPN has organized its coverage of the X Games around the competitive quest for medals when, in fact, many of the athletes and the spectators aren't very concerned about competition or medals (Honea, 2009). Athletes in the X Games and similar events enjoy the external rewards that come with winning, and they certainly want to demonstrate their competence, but they often emphasize self-expression and creativity more than the final scores determined by official judges. Furthermore, friendships with others in the event are more important than media-hyped rivalries and competitive outcomes. However, media narratives highlight rivalries and the desire to win because this reaffirms widely accepted cultural values and can be used to attract sponsors and consumers who may not understand the culture and skills possessed by athletes in action sports.

The success ideology regularly emphasized in US media coverage is less apparent in the coverage that occurs in most other nations. Narratives in the United States focus on winners, records, and final scores. Even silver and bronze Olympic medals are often viewed as consolation prizes, and games for third place are seldom played or covered by the media. Sportswriters and announcers focus on "shootouts," sudden-death playoffs, dominating others, and big plays or big hits. Rare are references to learning, enjoyment, and competing *with* others, even though many players see their participation in these terms. Thus, the media don't "tell it like it is" as much as they tell it to reaffirm a discourse of competitive success that closely matches the interests of sponsors and advertisers. This ideological bias does not undermine the enjoyment of sports for most people, but it ignores that there are many ways to enjoy sports, even when they are organized to promote corporate interests.

Consumption Themes in Media Representations of Sports The emphasis on consumption is clear in most media coverage of sports. About 20 percent of televised sports coverage in the US consists of commercial time. Ads fill newspapers and magazines, and Internet sites use multiple strategies to present ads mixed with content. "TV time-outs" are now standard in football, basketball, and hockey games. And announcers remind media spectators that "This game is being brought to you by this or that corporation."

Commercials are so central in the telecast of the Super Bowl that the media audience is polled to rate them. Audiences for media sports are encouraged to express their connections to teams and athletes by purchasing objects that display team logos.

Gender Themes in Media Representations of Sports Masculinity rules in media sports. Men's sports continue to receive about 95 percent of sports coverage in the media. However, recent media coverage of concussions, serious injuries, permanent sport-related physical and cognitive impairments, athletes in major men's sports coming out as gay, and athletes supporting gay marriage has led to a more representative media narrative about masculinity in sport. References to men as warriors doing battle and sacrificing their bodies for victories are now occasionally accompanied by discussions of safer sports, athlete health, and acceptance of difference. One reason for this is to create a positive media image of sports and preserve lucrative revenue flows for media companies. Research is needed to track media narratives to see if this shift is more than superficial, if it exists across sports, and if it persists over time in various countries.

Media coverage of women's sports has never been a media priority, and research suggests that this has not changed over the past three decades. In fact, longitudinal research done by Cheryl Cooky, Mike Messner, and their colleagues at the Center for Feminist Research at the University of Southern California shows that sports news and highlights about women's sports have declined since data were first collected in 1989 (Cooky et al., 2013; Cooky, Messner & Musto, 2015; Musto, Cooky & Messner, 2017). When Messner and his colleagues issued their first *Gender and Televised Sports* report in 1990, they found that 5 percent of sports news and highlights were devoted to women's sports, but they incorrectly predicted that this percentage would increase as more girls and women played sports (Duncan et al., 2005). Despite significant sports participation increases among girls and women over the next 20 years, the media coverage given to women's sports actually declined.

The most significant positive change that has occurred recently is that when women's sports are covered, the quality of coverage has improved: it is more likely to be serious, and less likely to involve sexist jokes or comments that trivialize and sexualize women athletes. However, some coverage today remains characterized by a "gender bland sexism" as women's sports and female athletes are described with less excitement, urgency, and historical significance than is the case in coverage of men's sports and male athletes (Musto, Cooky & Messner, 2017; Yip, 2016). This difference may fade as more women with broadcast media experience cover women's sports and as their male peers learn to appreciate women as athletes and women's sports as exciting, even if it isn't gymnastics or figure skating during the Olympic games.

Another encouraging development is that during the 2019 Women's World Cup, some members of the US national team did not hide that they were lesbians, and some people in the media actually acknowledged this fact in supportive ways. A similar media acknowledgement occurred during NBC's coverage of the 2018 Winter Olympic Games as openly gay figure skater and bronze medal winner, Adam Rippon publicly owned his sexuality–a first in the Winter Olympics–and talked about his widely quoted objection to Vice President Mike Pence's stance on LGBTQ issues (Buzinski, 2018; Outsports, 2018; Robinson, 2019). In the process, he sparked a media conversation about him as a gay athlete.

Traditional patterns of dealing with gender in media coverage have been slow to change partly because sports media organizations worldwide have cultures and structures that have been shaped by heterosexual men. They've been organized and scheduled around men's sports, just like the work routines and assignments of sports reporters. Therefore, the coverage of women's events often requires changes in institutionalized patterns of sports media work. Furthermore, the vast majority of sports media personnel are men, and the highest-status assignments in sports media are those that deal with men's sports.

(*Source:* Alan Schwartz/Csm/Shutterstock)

There is no reason, other than the sexist preferences of fans and men working in broadcast media, that women are not hired as commentators for men's sports. After over 25 years of persistent work, ESPN assigned Doris Burke to do the color commentary for the 2019 NBA finals. Due in part to the respect that players have for her, she also hosted the trophy award ceremony when the Toronto Raptors won the NBA championship. In response, some viewers signed a petition on www.Change.org to "get this woman off of our TV's once and for all." Hopefully, ESPN will ignore them.

Female reporters and announcers today understand that their upward mobility in the sports media industry demands that they cover men's events in much the same ways that men cover them. If they insist on covering only women's events or if they are assigned only to women's events, they won't move up the corporate ladder in media organizations (Bruce, 2013). Advancement also may be limited if they insist on covering men's sports in new ways that don't reaffirm the "correctness" of the coverage patterns and styles developed by men.

Although women in the print media regularly cover men's sports, very few women have done regular commentary for men's sports in the broadcast media apart from occasional "sideline reporters" who interview players and coaches a few times during and after games. An exception to this pattern occurred in 2008 when Doris Burke was a color commentator for NBA playoff games. Online comments, nearly all from men, were generally supportive of Burke and praised her competence. But enough men complained that the network reassigned her to a sideline reporter role. Burke persisted and continued to earn the respect of players and coaches, and in 2017 became a regular NBA game analyst for ESPN–the first woman to have this position.

Race, Ethnicity, and Nationality Themes in Media Representations of Sports Just as gender ideology influences media coverage, so do racial and ethnic ideologies and the stereotypes associated with them (Coogan, 2015; Love and Hughey, 2015).

Research in the 1970s and 1980s discredited the assumed factual basis of racial and ethnic stereotypes at the same time that media studies identified the ways that ideology influenced sports coverage and commentaries, particularly in reference to black athletes. This made white journalists and commentators increasingly aware that the quality of their work depended on avoiding words and inferences based on discredited racial stereotypes. As a result, most of them chose their words more carefully.

But making these changes was difficult for white sports reporters and broadcast commentators who accepted dominant racial ideology and had never viewed it critically or from the perspectives of blacks, Latinxs, Asians, and Native Americans. Consequently, some media personnel made careless or naïve mistakes, and a few were suspended or fired for them.

Avoiding stereotypes and covering racial and ethnic relations in an informed way are two different things. Most sports coverage today pretends that race and ethnicity don't exist; it assumes that sports are racially and ethnically blind and that everyone in sports faces the same challenges and odds for success. But race and ethnicity are influential to such an extent that people cannot talk about them without discovering real, meaningful, and socially important racial and ethnic differences in what they think and feel. Ignoring facts about real differences allows whites in the media and media audiences to be comfortably color blind and deny the legacy and continuing relevance of skin color and cultural heritage in society and sports.

At the same time, blacks, latinxs, Asian Americans, and Native Americans are reminded that mainstream sport cultures have been shaped by the values and experiences of white men, and sport organizations and media companies are controlled by white men. This is simply a fact, and it is not meant to be an indictment of white men. But it does create tension for ethnic minority athletes and unique social dynamics in sports where players are racially and ethnically mixed. This in itself is a newsworthy story, but it would make many people, especially powerful white men, uncomfortable, and it would be difficult for most journalists to tell without being censored. But as long as it remains untold, white privilege in sports will persist without being recognized. Finally, if ethnic minority players or coaches try to tell the story, they're quickly accused of "playing the race card," being arrogant and ungrateful, promoting political correctness, or being bitter because of "imagined abuse."

Media coverage also reaffirms dominant racial ideology when whiteness is overlooked. For example, when journalists ignore the dynamics of living in a white-dominated, white-identified, and white-centered society, they unwittingly reproduce racial and ethnic stereotypes at the same time that they claim to be color blind.

Pretending to be color blind in a culture where a skin color–based racial ideology has existed for over three centuries ensures that white privilege is seamlessly incorporated into the media coverage of sports. It allows people in sports media to avoid asking why nearly all sports at the high school, college, and professional level are exclusively white or becoming so. It allows newspaper and magazine editors to never even think of publishing an article about the underrepresentation of ethnic minority athletes in most sports, even when they live in communities where hundreds of high school and college teams in swimming, volleyball, softball, tennis, golf, soccer, lacrosse, rowing, gymnastics, wrestling, and other sports are *all* white.

It also allows journalists to avoid asking critical questions about new patterns of residential and school segregation and growing income and wealth disparity that deeply influences who plays what sports in the United States today. They can put aside questions about why there are fewer African/Asian/Native American and Latinx professional golfers today than there were in 1981—15 years before Tiger Woods won his first PGA tournament as a professional in 1996. Most important, pretending to be color blind allows media people to ignore whiteness and all racial issues, thereby maintaining a high racial comfort level among white media consumers and advertisers. In this way, ignoring reality becomes an effective strategy for boosting profits.

Scholars in ethnic studies explain that this self-declared colorblindness denies the real history and relevance of skin color and ethnicity in societies where previously unquestioned racism has shaped the distribution of income and wealth and the everyday living conditions of nearly all people. When a color-blind approach governs the coverage of sports, media stories miss significant sport realities and reproduce the racial and ethnic status quo. This allows people in dominant racial and ethnic populations to see and use sports as forms of social escapism—as whitewashed worlds devoid of the complex, messy issues that characterize everyday life.

At the same time, a color-blind approach constantly reminds people in racial and ethnic minority populations that their histories, heritages, and experiences are unrecognized in sports. As a result, some ethnic minority people avoid some or all sports, or they use sports as sites for seeking recognition and respect in the dominant culture. When we view media critically, it becomes increasingly clear that they don't "tell it like it is" as much as they tell it as their target demographics and advertisers want it told.

Ethnicity and Nationality in a Global Context Themes related to ethnicity and nationality also exist in sports media coverage worldwide. Although some sports reporters and broadcasters are careful to avoid using ethnic and national stereotypes in their representations of athletes and teams, evidence suggests that subtle stereotypes and other motives regularly influence sports coverage (Allain, 2016; Coogan, 2015; Deeb & Love, 2018; Moraga, 2018; Vincent et al., 2018; Zenquis & Mwaniki, 2019). For example, some media coverage has portrayed Asian athletes as methodical, mechanical, machine-like, mysterious, industrious, self-disciplined, and intelligent. Their achievements are more often attributed to cognitive than to physical abilities, and stereotypes about height and other physiological characteristics are sometimes used to explain success or failure in sports. Latinxs, on the other hand, have been described as flamboyant, exotic, emotional, passionate, moody, and hot-blooded.

The sports journalists most likely to avoid such stereotypes are those who have worked to learn about national and ethnic histories and those parts of the world in which teams and athletes live. This is what all good journalists do when they cover events and people. For example, when 28 percent of MLB players are Latino and more players are coming from certain Asian countries, it is reasonable to expect the journalists covering baseball to do their homework and learn about the cultures and baseball histories in those countries, and about the experiences of the athletes who have grown up there.

It also would be professionally responsible for media companies to hire sports reporters and broadcasters who are bilingual and culturally informed so that they could talk meaningfully with players whose lives on and off the field are not understood by most baseball fans. These are important stories as all sports become increasingly globalized. For the media to ignore them is to ignore the reality of sports today.

The most effective way to reduce subtle forms of racial, ethnic, and national bias in the media is to also hire editors, photographers, writers, producers, directors, camerapersons, and statisticians from diverse racial, ethnic, and national backgrounds. Lip service is paid to this goal, and progress has been made in certain media, but members of racial and ethnic minorities are clearly underrepresented in nearly all sports newsrooms and media executive offices where over 80 percent of the full time reporters and editors are white (Lapchick, 2018).

This skewed pattern is unfortunate because ethnic diversity among media people would enrich stories and provide multiple perspectives for understanding sports and the people who play and coach them. Of course, neither skin color nor gender precludes knowledge about sports or the people involved in them, but knowledge is based on a combination of experience and the richness of the perspectives one uses to make sense of the ethnically and racially diverse social worlds that constitute sports today.

EXPERIENCES AND CONSEQUENCES OF CONSUMING MEDIA SPORTS

Media sports provide topics of conversation, occasions for social interaction, a sense of belonging and identity, opportunities to express emotions, and an exciting distraction for those who are passing time alone. However, few studies have investigated audience experiences to see how people give meaning to media sports coverage and integrate it into their lives. Similarly, we know that media images and narratives influence what people feel, think, and do, but few studies have investigated the consequences of sport media consumption at the individual or collective level.

Audience Experiences

Studies of audience experiences suggest that people interpret media content and integrate media sport consumption into their lives in diverse ways

(Bruce, 2013; Gantz, 2013; Wenner, 2013). More men than women are strongly committed to consuming media sports, and strongly committed consumers constitute less than a majority segment of the overall population in most societies, including the United States and Canada (Wenner, 2013). However, these studies don't tell us much about the ways that people give meaning to and include the consumption of media sports in their lives.

One exception is a creative study of twenty white men and a few women who had grown up in various towns in western Pennsylvania but had moved to Fort Worth, Texas (Kraszewski, 2008). By various means each person joined with others who had started a tradition of meeting in a sports bar where they watched Pittsburgh Steelers games from August through December. As they met each week their interaction focused on rekindling and nurturing their sense of western Pennsylvania as "home" and their identities associated with their geographical origins. In the process they created a place-image of western Pennsylvania that matched the blue-collar, white European-American, steelworker image of the Steelers. They wore Steelers jerseys, drank Iron City (Pittsburgh) beer in aluminum bottles, and were identified as Steelers fans by the Dallas Cowboys fans in the bar. They avoided talking about social class, race, and jobs and focused on "where they were from"–talking about roads, towns, and other features of the landscape of western Pennsylvania. For them, watching the Steelers on television was a social occasion for interacting with others who reaffirmed their sense of home and their regional identities, despite living over 1200 miles away from where they grew up.

When media scholar Walter Gantz (2013) studied male-female married couples in the United States, he found that they often watched televised sports together and that this usually was a positive activity in their relationships. Men watched sports more than women did and were more likely to be committed sports fans, but when women were committed fans, their patterns of watching and responding to sports on television were similar to men's patterns. Gantz did find that some couples experienced conflicts related to viewing sports, but most resolved them successfully. Partners usually learned to adjust to each other's viewing habits over time, and when they didn't, it usually meant that they had general relationship problems unrelated to watching sports.

In another study of viewing habits, Whiteside and Hardin (2011) found that even though women participate in sports more often today than in the past, they don't regularly watch women's sports as media spectators. Data indicated that women's leisure time is often spent doing things that fit the interests of other family members rather than using their leisure time for their own interests. They watched men's sports because they watched with the men in their lives. Under these conditions, watching women's sports seldom became a high priority for them.

Future studies will tell us more about the ways that people integrate media sports experiences into their lives and when media sports become important sites at which social relationships occur. For example, we know that social media magnify the voices of sport spectators and provide opportunities to raise their own issues in connection with sports (Millington and Darnell, 2014; Norman, 2012, 2014), but we don't know what that means in terms of their relationships and everyday lives at home, work, school, and in their own sport participation. It will be important to include the use of the Internet and video games in future studies.

Consequences of Consuming Media Sports

Research on the consequences of consuming media sports has focused on a wide variety of issues. Here we'll focus on three: active participation in sports, attendance at sport events, and betting on sports events.

Active Participation in Sports Does consuming media sports lead people to be more active sports participants or turn them into couch potatoes? This is an important issue, given the health problems associated with physical inactivity in many societies today.

When children watch sports on television, some copy what they see *if* they have or can make opportunities to do so. Children are great imitators with active imaginations, so when they see and identify with athletes, they may create informal activities or seek to join youth sports programs to pursue television-inspired dreams. However, participation grounded in these dreams usually fades quickly, especially after children discover that it takes years of tedious practice to compete successfully and reach the victory podium.

Research examining the legacies of the Olympics for people in the country hosting the games has shown consistently that watching sports on television is more likely to lead to more television watching than actively playing sports (Bretherton, Piggin & Bodet, 2016; Conn, 2012; Green, 2012; Kortekaas, 2012; Thornton, 2013). In light of this evidence it appears that a positive link between watching and doing sports may exist only when parents, teachers, or physical educators strategically connect media representations with everyday sports participation. Research is needed to explore this possibility.

Many adults don't play the sports they consume in the media, but some do. Research suggests that those who are not regular participants use media sports as entertainment, whereas those who are avid participants are the ones who use media sports as a source of inspiration for their own participation. In the absence of more research on this topic, we can say only that consuming sports through the media may be connected with activity or inactivity depending on the circumstances and the individuals involved.

Attendance at Sport Events Game attendance is related to many factors, including the consumption of media sports. On the one hand, many people say that they would rather watch certain events on television than attend them in person. On the other hand, the media publicize sports, promote interest, and provide information that helps people identify with athletes and teams and become potential ticket purchasers for events.

Although consuming media sports has generally been positively related to attending live events, this may be changing with widespread use of new media and the existence of large HD televisions. Whereas media companies in the past tried to duplicate the live-event experience on television, now stadium managers try to duplicate the home-viewing experience for those who attend live events. Spectators now demand broadband Wi-Fi and high-speed mobile phone connections in stadiums, large HD replay screens, and video screens by concessions and in restrooms so they don't miss the action they paid to see. These stadium upgrades are costly, but without them, more people may choose to stay at home, where they have access to everything they want during a game (Galily, 2014).

Additionally, there may be circumstances when people who normally pay for their ticket at the gate will stay home to watch a televised game rather than go to the stadium. This might occur when they expect that there will be a large crowd at the game, violent or uncivil behavior on the part of other fans, or bad weather. In light of these factors, those who manage venues and teams that depend on gate receipts must constantly create new forms of spectacle that cannot be experienced in a television broadcast. Unless fans are entertained in unique ways they may not buy as many season tickets or attend as many live events.

Sports Betting Consuming media sports is clearly connected with gambling, but there is no evidence that it causes people to bet on sports. However, as states continue to legalize sports betting, as bookmakers buy advertising time during sport broadcasts, and as mainstream media include programming focused on sports betting, this could change.

Current marketing studies predict that sports betting will increase as it is legalized, but they make no predictions about the impact that advertising and programming will have on betting behaviors (Broughton, 2018; Grove, 2016; Lopez-Gonzalez & Griffiths, 2018; Lopez-Gonzalez, Estévez & Griffiths, 2017; Minton, 2018; O'Malley, 2019; PwC, 2018; Ramsey, 2018). This is a topic for future research.

SPORTS JOURNALISM

Some people trivialize sport journalism by saying that it provides entertainment but is unrelated to important issues in everyday life. However, sports do matter–not because they produce a tangible product or make essential contributions to our survival, but because they represent ideas about how the world works and what is important in life.

Sports are not merely reflections of social worlds; they also are constitutive of those worlds–that is, they're sites at which social worlds are produced, reproduced, and changed. Sports journalists are key players in these constitutive processes, because their representations of sports can influence the ideas and beliefs that people use to define and give meaning to themselves, their experiences, and the organization of social worlds.

Sports Journalists Are Not All the Same

Entertainment is a focus for nearly everyone working in commercial media. Sportswriters generally provide specific information and in-depth analysis, whereas the announcers and commentators for visual broadcast media usually focus on providing images and narratives that create anticipation and a sense of urgency for their audience. Exceptions sometimes occur in sport talk radio when analysis and "call-in" interactivity are structured into program format. Additionally, television also includes some sports programming that provides analysis of social and economic issues, but this is relatively rare in its overall programming format.

As athletes, agents, team publicity directors, bloggers, and others contribute online content, traditional sports journalism is changing (Daum & Scherer, 2017). Independent investigative journalism has declined in favor of entertainment journalism that focuses on personalities and "celebrity chasing" rather than social and political issues in sports. Flashy infotainment now takes the place of hard news, media personalities present more opinions than fact-based stories, and stories holding the powerful accountable for their actions are usually censored or never produced.

There are capable investigative journalists working at *Sports Illustrated*, ESPN, and other content producers, but the entertainment emphasis of media companies limits independent reporting or fosters self-censorship by reporters. Independent journalists produce stories for blog sites such as *The Undefeated*, *Deadspin* and *SB Nation,* but they are paid as contract workers and rarely have resources for sustained investigative work. *Edge of Sports,* a weekly online column and podcast created by Dave Zirin, an independent sports journalist, asks critical questions and covers important social issues in sports. Zirin is a "go to" source for those of us in the sociology of sport, and he also is the sports editor at *The Nation*, a progressive news magazine and website.

Investigative journalism does not provide a good return on investment for media companies. For example, ESPN is owned by the Walt Disney Company, the largest media conglomerate in the world, and they can make more money providing escapist entertainment than presenting detailed stories on concussions and brain injuries, the sexual abuse of young athletes and sports administrators hiding the abuse, discriminatory employment practices in sports organization, tax-avoidance scams by sports teams and leagues, institutionalized corruption in powerful international sports organizations, and other important issues that require expensive, long-term investigations. This is why ESPN laid off many investigative journalists as millions of cable-cutting consumers caused their revenues to drop. With that said, ESPN also owns *The Undefeated*, a website that investigates "the intersections of race, sports, and culture," and produces *Outside the Lines*, a program that regularly covers social issues and asks critical questions about sports. However, due to accusations that ESPN had a liberal bias, and was too political, the new CEO of the company introduced a strict "stick to sports" approach (Curtis, 2017; Tracy, 2017). In the process, he questioned the merits of *The Undefeated* and hired new people to produce *Outside the Lines* (Strauss, 2019).

Like other media companies, ESPN is generally cautious when covering controversial social and political issues that might turn away some of its conservative consumers and create negative publicity. This was the case in 2013 when the company withdrew from a partnership with PBS (the Public Broadcasting System) on a *Frontline* program investigating the NFL's handling of head injuries (Miller & Belson, 2013; Sandomir, 2013a). The program, *League of Denial: The NFL's Concussion Crisis*, had just been completed when the NFL commissioner met the president of ESPN for lunch. Soon after, ESPN announced that it was no longer associated with the *Frontline* program, even though two of its top reporters (Mark Fainaru-Wada & Steve Fainaru) continued to work on the project. ESPN denied that its decision was influenced by its then $15.2 billion media rights contract with the NFL. However, ESPN reporters received a clear message: censor yourself, or others will do it for you when your news reporting could jeopardize company profits.

Another highly publicized case occurred in 2017-18 as Bob Costas, an announcer who worked for NBC for forty years and had become the face of NBC sports, was about to be part of the broadcast team for the 2018 Super Bowl. Costas, a recipient of 28 Emmys and eight National Sportscaster of the Year awards, was known for discussing controversial issues in sports. Beginning in 2011 he regularly included information about head trauma issues in the NFL as he announced *Monday Night Football* games. However, as research evidence on brain damage among many former NFL players became increasingly alarming, his criticisms of football became more poignant and attracted more attention. During a November 2017 appearance at University of Maryland journalism symposium, he declared the following: *The reality is that this game destroys people's brains–not everyone's, but a substantial number. It's not a small number, it's a considerable number. It destroys their brains* (in Fainaru-Wada, 2019). Although NBC executives did not say that the NFL influenced their decision, they told Costas he would not work the Super Bowl, and by the end of the year, Costas and the network parted ways.

(*Source:* Tom Pennington/Getty Images)

When Bob Costas, the face of NBC Sports for forty years, repeatedly updated NFL media audiences about research evidence on concussions, head injuries, and chronic traumatic encephalopathy (CTE) among NFL players, NBC negotiated his exit package. The network, with its 9-year, $8.55 billion deal to broadcast Sunday night games, may have been concerned about its relationship with the NFL if Costas kept speaking about the dangers of head trauma in football. If Costas wasn't safe, his peers in sports journalism may be inclined to censor their stories on issues that powerful sports organizations don't approve.

Overall, recent cases in which sports journalists were reprimanded or fired for comments and stories that were socially or politically controversial suggests that "a stick to sports" approach has become a prevailing norm in mainstream media organizations.

Exceptions to this exist among some print media journalists who are committed to investigative work and among independent journalists who can maintain their careers as they use a critical approach in their coverage of sports. At this point in time, the content and quality of sports journalism is a topic that needs attention in the sociology of sport (Forde & Wilson, 2018; Weedon et al., 2017).

Sport Journalists on the Job: Relationships with Athletes

As the amount of video coverage of sports has increased, sportswriters have had to create stories that go beyond describing action and reporting scores. This leads them to seek increasingly intimate information about the personal lives of athletes, and this creates tension in athlete–journalist relationships. Athletes today realize that they cannot always trust journalists to hold information in confidence, even if disclosures are made "off the record." Furthermore, the stakes associated with "bad press" are so great for athletes and teams that everyone in sports organizations limits what they say when talking with journalists. As a result, sports stories tend to contain similar and meaningless quotes from athletes season after season.

Salary and background differences between journalists and male athletes also increase tensions in their relationships (Kovacs & Doczi, 2018). Highly paid black and Latino athletes without college degrees have little in common with middle-class, college-educated, white, Euro-American journalists. As a result, some journalists don't refrain from disclosing personal information about athletes to enhance stories, and athletes define journalists as "outsiders" who can impact their lives without fully understanding who they are and what their athlete identity means to them.

Team owners and university athletic departments are so conscious of tensions between athletes and media personnel that they now provide players with training on how to handle interviews without saying things that might sound bad or be misinterpreted.

These tensions also call attention to ethical issues in sport journalism. Many, but not all journalists are aware that they should not jeopardize athletes' reputations simply for the sake of entertainment, and they should not hurt them unintentionally or without good reason. Latino journalist Dan Le Batard, who works for ESPN and formerly for the Miami Herald, explains that he tries to be "nonjudgmental" when he covers athletes because all people have flaws and exposing the flaws of athletes who disappoint you with their actions smacks of self-righteousness and raises the ethical issue of invasion of privacy (2005, p. 14). However, journalists constantly face gray areas in which ethical guidelines are not clear, and the need to present attractive stories often encourages them to push ethical limits.

In response to these tensions, many athletes now use social media to communicate directly with fans. Additionally, sites like *The Players' Tribune* offer opportunities for professional athletes to publish in-depth written and video content that accurately represents their feelings and thoughts and goes beyond the limits of other platforms such as Twitter and Instagram. This will not ease tensions with journalists, but it provides athletes with an opportunity to express themselves without depending on others.

summary

COULD SPORTS AND THE MEDIA SURVIVE WITHOUT EACH OTHER?

Media and media experiences have become ever-present in the lives of people living in many parts of the world today. This is why we study the relationship between sports and the media.

Media sports, like other aspects of culture, are social constructions. They're created, organized, and controlled by human beings whose motives and ideas are grounded in their social worlds, experiences, and ideologies. The media represent sports to us through selected images and narratives that usually reaffirm dominant ideologies and promote the interests of wealthy and powerful people who own media companies and the corporations that sponsor programming.

New media have altered the ways that people receive news, consume media content, interact with others who share their interests in sports, connect with athletes and teams, and even express their feelings about everything from on-the-field action to off-the-field management decisions. Therefore, new media extend the boundaries of what we study in the sociology of sport.

People now have access to sports content 24/7 on television, smartphones, tablets, and any Internet-connected device. This means that a person's identity as a fan can be reaffirmed at anytime, anywhere. Fans can also follow athletes on digital sites like Twitter, Instagram, Facebook, Tumblr, and blogs. This eliminates the mainstream media filter and provides them with information that comes directly from athletes.

Fantasy sports, sports video games, and esports now provide unique sport-related experiences unlike those occasioned by traditional media. Their rapidly growing popularity, especially among younger people, is changing the sport-media landscape and their impact on traditional sports media is likely to be significant in the near future.

Sports and the media have become increasingly interdependent as both have become more important parts of social worlds. They could survive without each other, but they would be different from what they are now. Commercial sports have grown and prospered because of media coverage and the rights fees paid by media companies. Without the publicity and money provided by media, commercial sports would be reduced to local business operations with much less scope than they have today, and less emphasis would be placed on elite, competitive sports in people's lives.

Media could survive without sports, but newspapers and television would be different from their current format if they did not have sports content and programming to attract young males and the sponsors who wish to buy access to that demographic. Without sports, newspaper circulation would decline, and television programming would be different and less profitable. The symbiotic relationship between commercial sports and for-profit media today exists because certain sports can be used to attract audiences that sponsors want to convert into consumers of their products and services.

Research indicates that media coverage of sports in the United States emphasizes images and narratives reproducing dominant ideologies related to success, consumption, gender, race, ethnicity, and nationality. As a result, current patterns of power and privilege are portrayed as normal and natural and remain taken-for-granted. This pattern exists worldwide.

Future research utilizing cultural, interactionist, and structural theories combined with a critical approach will tell us more about the various ways that people make sense of the media representations they consume. This is especially important in connection with the Internet and video games. Patterns of media sport consumption are changing rapidly, and it is important to study them in ways that promote critical media literacy rather than the uncritical celebration of media technology and the promotional culture of most sports coverage.

Few studies have investigated the experiences and consequences of consuming media sports. We know that people make sense of sports media images and narratives on their own terms and that this interpretive process of sense-making is influenced by the social, cultural, and historical conditions under which it occurs. People also integrate media sports experiences into their lives in diverse ways, but we know little about the patterns and consequences of this integration process. For example, research is needed to help us identify the conditions under which the consumption of media sports influences active participation in sports, attendance at live sports events, and gambling on sports.

To understand sports and the media, it helps to become familiar with basic features of sports journalism today. Journalists are key players in the overall process of representing sports to large audiences. In the process they influence ideas and beliefs about sports and social worlds.

However, journalists working for media companies that have large media contacts with sport leagues are cautious when they cover issues that may impact the profits of those leagues and teams. The interactivity made possible by new media makes journalists more accessible to their audiences while bringing members of the audience into the process of creating media content. Additionally, the need to create stories that capture the attention of media consumers has led journalists to seek stories that disclose private and personal information about athletes. This creates tensions between journalists and athletes, which then influence media representations of sports and the people who play them.

Sports and the media need each other, especially when making profits is a primary goal for each. Studying the dynamics of this relationship helps expand our understanding of sports in society.

SUPPLEMENTAL READINGS

Reading 1. New media: Consuming sports 24/7
Reading 2. Putting media to use: The NFL as a marketing machine
Reading 3. Live by the tweet, die by the tweet: Learning to use new media
Reading 4. Virtual sports: Play safe, stay home
Reading 5. Media rights deals: What sport has the best deal?
Reading 6. The stronger women get, the more men watch football: A prediction from 1990
Reading 7. People who don't watch sports on TV subsidize those who do.

SPORT MANAGEMENT ISSUES

- Athletes at your university have gotten into trouble using social media. You have been hired to create a social media policy for the athletic department. Identify the three main components of the policy, and describe how you would explain to the athletes why you created each of them.
- You're a new editor at *Sports Illustrated.* At your first editorial meeting the major item on the agenda is the February swimsuit issue. It is decided that it is economically unwise to drop the swimsuit issue, but it is also decided that if the swimsuit issue is continued, there must be other changes in the magazine to present a fair image of women in sports. As a new editor, you are called on to make some suggestions for changes. How would you respond?
- You are called in as an advisor to the President's Council on Fitness and Sports. The two topics being discussed are (1) whether television sports are turning people in the United States into couch potatoes and (2) whether the television coverage of professional sports is destroying people's interests in local high school, college, and amateur sports. The Council wants advice from you. What do you tell them?
- As a new employee in the student services office at a private college you are approached by a group of students who want the college to sponsor an esports team. It is up to you to write a proposal that will go to the college administrators. What are the 5 major points you would include in the proposal to support the addition of an esports team?

references

Allain, Kristi A. 2016. "The Mad Russian": Representations of Alexander Ovechkin and the creation of Canadian national identity. *Sociology of Sport Journal* 33(2): 156–168.

AlliAyewOKane. 2018. Fantasy Premier League demographics - 2017/2018. *Reddit.com*: Online, https://www.reddit.com/r/FantasyPL/comments/8w3ubd/fantasy_premier_league_demographics_20172018/

Antunovic, Dunja & Marie Hardin. 2015. Women and the blogosphere: Exploring feminist approaches to sport. *International Review for the Sociology of Sport* 50(6): 661–677.

Bailey, Jason M. 2018. Athletes don't own their tattoos. that's a problem for video game developers. *New York Times* (December 27): https://www.nytimes.com/2018/12/27/style/tattoos-video-games.html

BallistixGaming. 2019. Why universities are embracing esports. *BallistixGaming.com*: https://ballistixgaming.com/articles/why-universities-are-embracing-esports.html

Billings, Andrew C. & Brody J. Ruihley. 2014. *The fantasy sport industry: Games within games*. London/New York: Routledge.

Boyle, Raymond. 2014. Television sport in the age of screens and content. *Television & New Media* 15(8): 746–751.

Bretherton, Paul, Joe Piggin & Guillaume Bodet. 2016. Olympic sport and physical activity promotion: the rise and fall of the London 2012 pre-event mass participation 'legacy', *International Journal of Sport Policy and Politics* 8(4): 609–624.

Broughton, David. 2018. Media, gambling, new stadiums to push North American sports market to $80 billion. *SportsBusinessDaily.com* (November 5): https://www.sportsbusinessdaily.com/Journal/Issues/2018/11/05/Media/PwC.aspx

Browning, Blair, and Jimmy Sanderson. 2012. The positives and negatives of twitter: Exploring how student-athletes use Twitter and respond to critical tweets. *International Journal of Sport Communication* 5(4): 503–522.

Bruce, Toni. 2013. Reflections on communication and sport: On women and femininities. *Communication & Sport* 1(1/2): 125–137.

Burdsey, Daniel. 2016. One guy named Mo: Race, nation and the London 2012 Olympic Games. *Sociology of Sport Journal* 33(1): 14–25.

Buzinski, Jim. 2018. Openly gay Olympic skater Adam Rippon gets why it's important to be out. *Outsports.com* (January 12): https://www.outsports.com/2018/1/12/16882288/adam-rippon-figure-skating-winter-olympics-gay

Christovich, Amanda. 2019. Meet the superstars of youth basketball Instagram. *Wall Street Journal* (July 26): https://www.wsj.com/articles/meet-the-superstars-of-youth-basketball-instagram-11564142894

Cohen, Ben. 2019. Even the NBA has issues with social media now. *Wall Street Journal* (March 10): https://www.wsj.com/articles/even-the-nba-has-issues-with-social-media-now-11552223037

Conn, Jordan Ritter. 2015. The lingerie football trap. *Grantland.com* (July 23): http://grantland.com /features/legends-football-league-womens-lingerie-football-league-mitchell-mortaza/

Connolly, John, and Paddy Dolan. 2012. Sport, media and the Gaelic Athletic Association: The quest for the 'youth' of Ireland. *Media Culture Society* 34(4): 407–423.

Coogan, Daniel. 2015. *Understanding racial portrayals in the sports media.* Champaign IL: Common Ground Publishing.

Cooky, Cheryl, Michael A. Messner & Michel Musto. 2015. "It's dude time!" A quarter century of excluding women's sports in televised news and highlight shows. *Communication & Sport* 3(3): 261–287.

Cooky, Cheryl; Michael A. Messner & Robin H. Hextrum. 2013. Women play sport, but not on TV: A longitudinal study of televised news media. *Communication & Sport* 1(3): 203–230.

Crawford, Garry. 2004. *Consuming sport: fans, sport, and culture*. London/ New York: Routledge.

Curtis, Bryan. 2017. Sportswriting has become a liberal profession—here's how it happened. *The Ringer* (February 16): https://theringer.com/how-sportswriting-became-a-liberal-profession-dc7123a5caba#.4slzrb8s9

Dart, Jon. 2014. New media, professional sport and political economy. *Journal of Sport and Social Issues* 38(6): 528–547.

Daum, Evan & Jay Scherer. 2018. Changing work routines and labour practices of sports journalists in the digital era: A case study of Postmedia. *Media, Culture & Society* 40 (4): 551–556.

Deeb, Alexander & Adam Love. 2018. Media representations of multiracial athletes. *Journal of Sport and Social Issues* 42(2): 95–114.

Delventhal, Shoshanna. 2019. How FanDuel and DraftKings work. *Investopedia.com* (June 25): https://www.investopedia.com/articles/investing/122415/how-fanduel-and-draftkings-work.asp

Deshbandhu, Aditya 2019. Decoding fantasy football: A ludic perspective. Gamvironments 10: 85-116.

Dumont, Guillaume. 2017. The beautiful and the damned: The work of new media production in professional rock climbing. *Journal of Sport and Social Issues* 41(2): 99-117.

Duncan, Margaret Carlisle & Michael A. Messner. 2005. *Gender in televised sports: News and highlights shows, 1989-2004*. Los Angeles, CA: Amateur Athletic Foundation www.aafla.org/9arr/ResearchReports/tv2004.pdf

Duncan, Samuel Keith. 2018. Managed play: The media's impact on play in the Australian Football league. *Physical Culture and Sport: Studies and Research* 77: 5-16.

Edmonds, Nathan. 2019. Matt Marcou - Electronic Arts -The future of Madden NFL in esports. *Esportinsider.com* (February 28): https://esportsinsider.com/2019/02/matt-marcou-electronic-arts-the-future-of-madden-nfl-in-esports/

Evans, Alex & Gil Moran. 2017. L.E.K. Sports Survey – Digital Engagement Part One: Sports and the "Millennial Problem." *Executive Insights* 19(12): 1-4.

Fainaru-Wada, Mark. 2019. Bob Costas, unplugged: From NBC and broadcast icon to dropped from the Super Bowl. ESPN.com (February 10): https://www.espn.com/espn/otl/story/_/id/25914913/inside-story-how-legendary-nfl-broadcaster-bob-costas-ended-excised-football-nbc-espn

Ferriter, M.M. 2009. "Arguably the greatest": Sport fans and communities at work on Wikipedia. *Sociology of Sport Journal* 26(1):127-154.

Fisher, Eric. 2019. Research details heavy crossover between fantasy sports, wagering. *SportBusiness.com* (June 28): https://www.sportbusiness.com/news/research-details-heavy-crossover-between-fantasy-sports-wagering/

Forde, Shawn & Brian Wilson. 2018. Radical sports journalism?: Reflections on 'alternative' approaches to covering sport-related social issues. *Sociology of Sport Journal* 35(1): 66-76.

FoxSports, 2017. NBA 2K and the effects it has on basketball IQ In the NBA. *FoxSports.com* (June 30): https://www.foxsports.com/nba/story/nba-2k-and-the-effects-it-has-on-basketball-iq-in-the-nba-091716

Frederick, Evan L., Choong Hoon Lim, Clavio, Galen, Walsh, Patrick. 2012. Why we follow: An examination of parasocial interaction and fan motivations for following athlete archetypes on Twitter. *International Journal of Sport Communication* 5(4): 481-503.

Galily, Yair and Ilan Tamir. 2014. A match made in heaven?! Sport, television, and new media in the beginning of the third millennia. *Television & New Media* 15(8): 699-702.

Galily, Yair. 2014. When the medium becomes "well done": Sport, television, and technology in the twenty-first century. *Television & New Media* 15(8): 717-724.

Gantz, Walter, and Nicky Lewis. 2014. Sports on traditional and newer digital media: Is there really a fight for fans? *Television & New Media* 15(8): 760-768.

Gantz, Walter. 2013. Reflections on communication and sport: On fanship and social relationships. *Communication & Sport* 1(1/2): 176-187.

Gong, Yuan. 2019. Virtual collectivity through second screen: Chinese fans' WeChat use in televised spectatorship of European football. *Television and New Media* First Published June 19, https://doi.org/10.1177/1527476419857199

Graham, Bryan Armen. 2019. Fortnite World Cup: The $30m tournament shows esports' future is already here. *The Guardian* (August 1): https://www.theguardian.com/sport/2019/jul/30/fortnite-world-cup-esports

Green, Ken. 2012. London 2012 and sports participation: The myths of legacy. *Significance* 9(3): 2-48.

Grove, Chris. 2016. Esports and gambling: Where's the action? *Eilers & Krejcik Gaming* (August 15): Online, https://www.thelines.com/wp-content/uploads/2018/03/Esports-and-Gambling.pdf

Groves, Mark & Gerald Griggs. 2016. Riding in the shadows: The reaction of the British print media to Chris Froome's victory in the 2013 Tour de France. *International Review for the Sociology of Sport* 51(4): 428–445.

Heilweil, Rebecca. 2019. Infoporn: College esports players are cashing in big. *Wired.com* (January 21): https://www.wired.com/story/infoporn-college-esports-players-cashing-in-big/

Holmes, Jack. 2019. At the NBA 2K League draft, I witnessed the surreal future of what it means to go pro. *Esquire.com* (Martch 7): https://www.esquire.com/sports/a26684917/nba-2k-league-draft-esports/

Honea, Joy Crissy. 2009. *Sell-outs or outsiders?: Co-optation and resistance in action sport subcultures*. Riga, Latvia: Omniscriptum Publishing Group.https://www.pwc.com/us/en/industry/entertainment-media/assets/2018-sports-outlook.pdf

Hutchins, Brett. 2014. Sport on the move: The unfolding impact of mobile communications on the media sport content economy. *Journal of Sport and Social Issues* 38(6): 509–527.

Kim, Matt. 2019. 2K's new deal with the NBA for NBA 2K is reportedly worth a staggering $1.1 billion. *USGamer.net* (January 15): https://www.usgamer.net/articles/2k-games-nba-deal-renewal-1-billion

Kirshner, Alex. 2019. The extremely odd thing about the NCAA president's argument against esports. *SBNation.com* (January 25): https://www.sbnation.com/college-football/2019/1/25/18197240/mark-emmert-esports-ncaa

Kortekaas, Vanessa. 2012. Sports participation: Uphill task turning inspiration into perspiration. *The Financial Times* (August 19): http://www.ft.com/intl/cms/s/0/5486b32c-d7df-11e1-9980-00144feabdc0.html

Kovacs, Agnes & Tamas Doczi. 2018. The relation between Olympians and employees of the media in Hungary: Motivations, attitudes, rejection. *Physical Culture and Sport: Studies and Research* 78: 5–12.

Kraszewski, Jon. 2008. Pittsburgh in Fort Worth: Football bars, sports television, sports fandom, and the management of home. *Journal of Sport and Social Issues* 32(2): 139–157.

Lapchick, Richard. 2018. *The 2018 Associated Press Sports Editors Racial and Gender Report Card*. The Institute for Diversity and Ethics in Sport, University of Central Florida. Online, http://nebula.wsimg.com/2b640482e881dddc4dfb39e6aca52c2e1

Le Batard, Dan. 2005. Open look: Is it cheating if you don't understand the rules? *Es posible. ESPN The Magazine* 8.10 (May 23): 14.

Lopez-Gonzalez, Hibai & Mark D. Griffiths. 2018. Understanding the convergence of markets in online sports betting. *International Review for the Sociology of Sport* 53(7): 807–823.

Lopez-Gonzalez, Hibai; Ana Estévez & Mark D. Griffiths. 2017. Marketing and advertising online sports betting: A problem gambling perspective. *Journal of Sport and Social Issues* 41(3): 256-272.

Love, Adam & Matthew W. Hughey. 2015. Out of bounds? Racial discourse on college basketball message boards. *Ethnic and Racial Studies* 38(6): 877–893.

Lund, Anker Brink. 2007. The political economy of mass mediated sports. Keynote address at the ISHPES and ISSA Joint World Congress, Copenhagen (August 3).

MacKay, Steph & Christine Dallaire. 2014. Skateboarding women building collective identity in cyberspace. *Journal of Sport and Social Issues* 38(6): 548–566.

McGrath, Ben. 2019. The Brooklyn startup helping high-school athletes go viral. *The New Yorker* (June 19): https://www.newyorker.com/sports/sporting-scene/the-brooklyn-startup-helping-high-school-athletes-go-viral

McHugh, Josh; Po Bronson and Ethan Watters, eds. 2016. *The Future of Sports*. Delaware North. Online, http://futureof.org/sports/

Miller, James Andrew and Ken Belson. 2013. N.F.L. pressure said to lead ESPN to quit film project. *New York Times* (August 23): https://www

.nytimes.com/2013/08/24/sports/football/nfl-pressure-said-to-prompt-espn-to-quit-film-project.html

Millington, Rob, and Simon C Darnell. 2014. Constructing and contesting the Olympics online: The internet, Rio 2016 and the politics of Brazilian development. *International Review for the Sociology of Sport* 49(2): 190–210.

Minton, Michelle. 2018. Legalizing sports betting in the United States. *Competitive Enterprise Institute*, No. 243 (March 15): Online, https://cei.org/sites/default/files/Michelle%20Minton%20-%20Legalizing%20Sports%20Betting%20in%20the%20United%20States.pdf

Moraga, Jorge E. 2018. On ESPN Deportes: Latinos, sport media, and the cultural politics of visibilities. *Journal of Sport and Social Issues* 42(6): 470–497.

Musto, Michela; Cheryl Cooky & Michael A. Messner. 2017. "From fizzle to sizzle!" Televised sports news and the production of gender-bland sexism. *Gender & Society* 31(5): 573–596.

Nee, Rebecca Coates and David M. Dozier. 2017. Second screen effects: Linking multiscreen media use to television engagement and incidental learning. *Convergence* 23(2): 214–226.

Norman, Leanne. 2012. Gendered homophobia in sport and coaching: Understanding the everyday experiences of lesbian coaches. *International Review for the Sociology of Sport* 47(6): 705–723.

Norman, Leanne. 2014. A crisis of confidence: Women coaches' responses to their engagement in resistance. *Sport, Education and Society* 19(5): 532–551.

O'Malley, Andrew. 2019. NHL signs deal with William Hill as sports betting partner. *VegasSlotsOnline.com* (March 29): https://www.vegasslotsonline.com/news/2019/03/29/nhl-signs-deal-william-hill-sports-betting-partner/

Oates, Thomas & Zach Furness, eds. 2015. *The NFL: Critical and cultural perspectives*. Philadelphia PA: Temple University Press.

Outsports. 2018. Outsports person of the year: Adam Rippon. *Outsports.com* (December 20): https://www.outsports.com/2018/12/20/18148929/adam-rippon-person-of-the-year-2018

Pannekeet, Jurre. 2019. *Global esports market report. Newzoo.com*: Online, https://newzoo.com/insights/trend-reports/newzoo-global-esports-market-report-2019-light-version/

Pells, Eddie. 2019. Super Bowl: Last stand of live TV. *Denver Post* (February 4): p. 3B.

Pierno, Ian. 2019. Dunked on for science: How NBA 2K keeps the game realistic. *SlamOnline.com* (May 10): https://www.slamonline.com/archives/dunked-on-for-science-how-nba-2k-keeps-the-game-realistic/

Poletti, Therese. 2019. Netflix thinks 'Fortnite' is a bigger competitor than other streaming services. *MarketWatch.com* (January19): https://www.marketwatch.com/story/netflix-thinks-fortnite-is-a-bigger-competitor-than-hbo-2019-01-17

Porter, Rick. 2018. The top 100 primetime telecasts of 2018. *HolleywoodReporter.com* (December 31): https://www.hollywoodreporter.com/live-feed/top-100-primetime-telecasts-2018-1170761

Pullen, Emma, Daniel Jackson, Michael Silk & Richard Scullion. 2019. Re-presenting the Paralympics: (contested) philosophies, production practices and the hypervisibility of disability. *Media, Culture & Society* 41(4): 465–481.

PwC. 2018. At the gate and beyond: Outlook for the sports market in North America through 2022. *PwC Sports Outlook* (October): https://www.pwc.com/us/en/industries/tmt/library/sports-outlook-north-america.html

Ramsey, Eric. 2018. FanDuel becomes official DFS, sports betting partner for NHL. *LegalSportsReport.com* (November 5): https://www.legalsportsreport.com/25544/fanduel-nhl-sports-betting/

Real Michael. R. 1998. MediaSport: Technology and the commodification of postmodern sport. In L. A. Wenner, ed. *MediaSport* (pp. 14–26). London/NY: Routledge.

Robinson, Joanna. 2018. How Adam Rippon became the star of the 2018 Winter Olympics. *Vanity Fair* (February 12): https://www.vanityfair.com/style/2018/02/adam-rippon-olympics-video-2018-team-event-skate-who-is-adam

Rodriguez, Ashley., 2017. How the $7 billion US fantasy football industry makes its money in 2017. *Quartz* (September 3): Online, https://qz.com/1068534/how-the-7-billion-us-fantasy-football-industry-makes-its-money-in-2017/

Rogers, Charlotte. 2018. Why brands must rethink their approach to women's sports sponsorship. *Marketing Week* (February 8): https://www.marketingweek.com/brands-neglecting-womens-sports-sponsorship/

Ross, Philippe. 2011. Is there an expertise of production? The case of new media producers. *New Media Society* 13(6): 912–928.

Rowe, David. 2018. Cultural citizenship, media and sport in contemporary Australia. *International Review for the Sociology of Sport* 53(1): 11–29.

Sandomir, Richard. 2013. ESPN quits film project on concussions in N.F.L. *New York Times* (August 22): http://www.nytimes.com/2013/08/23 /sports/football/espn-exits-film-project-on-concussions.html

Scott, Olan Kees Martin, Andrew C. Billings, John Harris & John Vincent. 2018. Using self-categorization theory to uncover the framing of the 2015 Rugby World Cup: A cross-cultural comparison of three nations' newspapers. *International Review for the Sociology of Sport* 53(8): 997–1015.

Sherwood, Merryn; Matthew Nicholson & Timothy Marjoribanks. 2017. Access, agenda building and information subsidies: Media relations in professional sport. *International Review for the Sociology of Sport* 52(8): 992–1007.

Siino, Sal. 2018. The future of traditional television survival relies on live sports. *Thebusinessofsports.com* (October 2): http://www.thebusinessofsports.com/2018/10/02/the-future-of-traditional-television-survival-relies-on-live-sports/

Smith, Paul; Tom Evens & Petros Iosifidis. 2015. The regulation of television sports broadcasting: A comparative analysis. *Media, Culture, & Society* 37(5): 720–736.

Solvoll, Mona Kristin. 2016. Football on television: How has coverage of the Cup Finals in Norway changed from 1961 to 1995? *Media Culture Society* 38(2): 141–158.

Strauss, Ben. 2019. As ESPN tries to stick to sports, President Jimmy Pitaro must define what that means. *Washington Post* (July 26): https://www.washingtonpost.com/sports/2019/07/26/jimmy-pitaro-espn-president-politics/

Stuart, Keith. 2019. Not one of the Fortnite World Cup's 100 finalists was a woman. Why? *The Guardian* (July 29): https://www.theguardian.com/commentisfree/2019/jul/29/fornite-world-cup-100-finalists-female-gamer-esports-pro-sexism

Syracuse staff. 2019. With viewership and revenue booming, esports set to compete with traditional sports. *onlinebusiness.syr.edu* (January 18): https://onlinebusiness.syr.edu/blog/esports-to-compete-with-traditional-sports/

Temple, Kerry 1992. Brought to you by . . . *Notre Dame Magazine* 21, 2: 29.

Thornton, Grant. 2013. *Meta-Evaluation of the Impacts and Legacy of the London 2012 Olympic Games and Paralympic Games* (July; Report 5: Post-Games Evaluation). London: Department for Culture, Media and Sport.

Tracy, Marc. 2017. Claims of liberal bias in media now include sportscasters, too. *New York Times* (May 1): https://www.nytimes.com/2017/05/01/sports/espn-layoffs-sports-politics-bias.html

Vincent, John, John S. Hill, Andrew Billings, John Harris & C. Dwayne Massey. 2018. "We are GREAT Britain": British newspaper narratives during the London 2012 Olympic Games. *International Review for the Sociology of Sport* 53(8): 895–923.

Weedon, Gavin; Brian Wilson, Liv Yoon & Shawna Lawson. 2017. Where's all the 'good' sports journalism? Sports media research, the sociology of sport, and the question of quality sports reporting. *International Review for the Sociology of Sport* 53(6): 639–667.

Wenner, Lawrence A. 2014. On the limits of the new and the lasting power of the mediasport interpellation. *Television & New Media* 15(8): 732–740.

Wenner, Lawrence. 2013. The mediasport interpellation: Gender, fanship, and consumer culture. *Sociology of Sport Journal* 30(1): 83–103.

Whannel, Garry. 2014. The paradoxical character of live television sport in the twenty-first century. *Television & New Media* 15(8): 769–776.

Whiteside, Erin & Marie Hardin. 2011. Women (not) watching women: Leisure time, television, and implications for televised coverage of women's sports. *Communication, Culture and Critique* 4(2): 122–143.

Winkler, Elizabeth. 2019. Why the clock is running out on big media companies. *Wall Street Journal* (April 26): https://www.wsj.com/articles/why-the-clock-is-running-out-on-big-media-companies-11556290801

Wittebols, James A. 2004. *The soap opera paradigm: Television programming and corporate priorities*. Lanham, MD: Rowman and Littlefield Publishers, Inc.

Wohn, Donghee Yvette & Guo Freeman. 2020. Live streaming, playing, and money spending behaviors in esports. *Games and Culture* 15(1): 73–88.

Yardley, Elizabeth, Morag Kennedy & Liam Brolan. 2019. Footballer, rich man, celebrity, consumer: Media blindness and the denial of domestic abuse in the Stephanie Ward and Danny Simpson case. *Crime, Media, Culture* 15(3): 479–501.

Yip, Adrian. 2018. Deuce or advantage? Examining gender bias in online coverage of professional tennis. *International Review for the Sociology of Sport* 53(5): 517–532.

Zenquis, Manuel R. & Munene F. Mwaniki. 2019. The intersection of race, gender, and nationality in sport: Media representation of the Ogwumike sisters. *Journal of Sport and Social Issues* 43(1): 23–43.

chapter

13

(*Source:* Jay Coakley)

SPORTS AND POLITICS

How Do Governments and Global Political Processes Influence Sports?

Politics and sport have been bedfellows since at least the birth of the ancient Olympic Games some 28 centuries ago.

—Bryan Armen Graham, deputy sports editor, Guardian US (2017)

Soccer frequently serves as a barometer of political trends in the Middle East and North Africa. US intelligence officials have said that they routinely attended soccer matches in the region to glean clues as to where a country is headed.

—James M. Dorsey, Co-director, Institute of Fan Culture, University of Würzburg (2015)

NFL players have a huge platform, and using it to call attention to social justice is their right. Silencing their peaceful protest is the opposite of patriotism.

—Carrie Oillaux, Communications director, sportanddev.org (2018)

Playing the national anthem before our . . . games has become a lazy excuse for patriotism.

—Nancy Armour, Sports journalist, USA Today (2019)

Chapter Outline

Learning Objectives

- Know the differences between politics and government and between power and authority.
- Identify the major reasons for governments to be involved in sports.
- Provide examples of how government intervention in sports protects the rights and safety of athletes and nonathletes alike.
- Identify examples of how government intervention in sports may benefit some people more than others.
- Identify the traditional ideals associated with international sports and discuss those ideals in terms of the realities of international sports.
- Discuss why the Olympic Games are a socially valuable event, and what can be done to make them more socially sustainable.
- Explain the connections between cultural ideology and the sponsorship of sports by nation-states and transnational corporations.
- Discuss the political issues associated with the globalization of sports.
- Give examples of politics in sports, and explain why politics will always be a part of sports.

Organized competitive sports have long been connected with politics, governments, and global political processes. When people say that politics has no place in sports, they usually mean that there is no place in sports for politics that differ from their own.

Politics refers to the *processes of organizing social power and making decisions that affect people's lives in a social world.* Politics occur at all levels of social life, from the politics of friendship and family relationships to national, international, and global affairs (Volpi, 2006). In the sociology of sport we study political processes in communities, local and national sports organizations, societies, and large nongovernment organizations (NGOs) such as the International Olympic Committee (IOC) and the Fédération Internationale de Football Association (FIFA), the international federation that governs world soccer.

Governments are *formal organizations with the power to make and enforce rules in a particular territory or collection of people.* Because governments make decisions affecting people's lives, they are political organizations by definition. Governments operate on various levels from local parks and recreation departments to nation-states, and they influence sports whether they occur in a public park or a privately owned stadium that hosts international competitions. In the sociology of sport we often refer to "**the state**" because this concept *includes the formal institution of a national government plus those parts of civil society–such as education, family, media, and churches–that teach values and ideologies that extend the influence and control of the political agencies that make and enforce laws and govern a society.*

Politics often involve the actions and interactions of governments, but rule-making in sports today goes beyond the political boundaries of the state and occurs in connection with global processes. For example, soccer is a global sport because British workers, students, and teachers brought the game to South America and British soldiers and missionaries brought it to Africa, Asia, the West Indies, and other colonized areas of the nineteenth-century British Empire. Soccer grew around the world through the global processes of migration, capitalist expansion, British imperialism, and colonization–all of which involve politics.

Governments usually are involved in political processes, but today's world includes such rapid global movements of people, products, knowledge, ideas, technologies, and money that these processes transcend particular states and involve transnational corporations and nongovernmental organizations such as Greenpeace, the Red Cross, and sport organizations such as the IOC and FIFA.

This chapter focuses on the relationships between sports and politics. The goal is to explain the ways in which sports are connected with governments, the state, and global political processes. Chapter content focuses on four major questions:

1. Why do governments often sponsor and control sports?
2. How are sports connected with global politics that involve nation-states, transnational corporations, and nongovernmental organizations?
3. What is the role of the Olympic Games and other sports mega-events in global politics and processes?
4. How are political processes involved in sports and sports organizations?

When reading this chapter, remember that power and authority are the key concepts used when studying politics and political processes. **Power** refers to *an ability to influence people and achieve goals, even in the face of opposition from others* (Weber, 1922a). And **authority** is *a form of power that comes with a recognized and legitimate status or office in a government, an organization, or an established set of relationships.* For example, a large corporation, such as Nike or McDonald's, has power if it can influence how people think about and play sports and if it can use sports to achieve its goals. Sports organizations such as the IOC, FIFA, the NCAA, and a local parks and recreation department have the *authority* to administer particular sports as long as the people associated with those sports accept the organizations as legitimate governing bodies. This highlights the fact that *politics* refers to the power to make decisions that affect sports and sports participation.

THE SPORTS-GOVERNMENT CONNECTION

As sports grow in popularity, government involvement usually increases. Many sports require sponsorship, organization, and facilities–all of which depend on resources that few individuals possess on their own. Sport facilities may be so expensive that regional and national governments are the only entities with the power and resources to build and maintain them. Government involvement also occurs when there is a need for a third party to regulate and control sports and sports organizations in ways that promote the public good in a community or society.

The nature and extent of government involvement in sports varies by society, but it generally serves one or more of the following purposes (Houlihan, 2000):

1. Safeguard the public order.
2. Ensure fairness and protect human rights.
3. Maintain health and fitness among citizens.
4. Promote the prestige and power of a group, community, or nation.
5. Promote a sense of identity, belonging, and unity among citizens.
6. Reproduce dominant values and ideologies in a community or society.
7. Increase support for political leaders and government.
8. Facilitate economic and social development in a community or society.

Safeguard the Public Order

Governments are responsible for maintaining order in public areas, including parks, sidewalks, and streets, among other places. Here are two sections from the Los Angeles Municipal Code, enforced by the city in an effort to safeguard citizens and the public order:

> SEC. 56.15. BICYCLE RIDING–SIDEWALKS. No person shall ride, operate or use a bicycle, unicycle, skateboard, cart, wagon, wheelchair, roller skates, or any other device moved exclusively by human power, on a sidewalk, bikeway or boardwalk in a willful or wanton disregard for the safety of persons or property. (Los Angeles Municipal Code, 2013a)

> SEC. 56.16. STREETS–SIDEWALKS–PLAYING BALL OR GAMES OF SPORT. No person shall play ball or any game of sport with a ball or football or throw, cast, shoot or discharge any stone, pellet, bullet, arrow or any other missile, in, over, across, along or upon any street or sidewalk or in any public park, except on those portions of said park set apart for such purposes. (Los Angeles Municipal Code, 2013b)

Laws similar to these, full of bureaucratic language, exist in nearly all cities and towns. They set boundaries for where, when, and under what circumstances sports may be played.

Ideally, these laws promote safety and reduce conflict between multiple users of public spaces. For example, state and local governments in many countries ban bare-fisted boxing, bungee jumping off public bridges, and playing basketball on public streets. In the case of commercial sports, governments may also regulate the rights and responsibilities of team owners, sponsors, promoters, and athletes.

Local governments may regulate sports participation by requiring people to obtain permits to use public facilities and playing fields. Likewise, local officials may close streets or parks to the general public so that sport events can be held under controlled and safe conditions. Annual marathons in New York City, London, and other cities worldwide require the involvement of the government and government agencies such as city and state police.

Safeguarding the public order also involves policing sports events where safety may be threatened by crowds or unruly individuals. During the Olympics, for example, the host city and nation provide thousands of military and law enforcement officials to safeguard the public order. In the face of possible protests and terrorist actions, it is estimated that the Chinese government spent up to $6.5 billion to police and monitor the Beijing area in connection with the 2008 Olympic Games. The Chinese

(*Source:* Jay Coakley)

Local governments often regulate where and when certain sports can occur. This is true in Philadelphia's "Love Park," although "street skaters" have been known to break the rules on weekends, holidays, and late at night.

government also employed over 43,000 soldiers, 47 helicopters, 74 airplanes, 33 naval ships, 6000 security guards on 18,000 buses, 30,000 guards at bus stops and terminals, and the personnel to monitor tens of thousands of surveillance cameras in and around Beijing.

Governments also sponsor sports that are used in military and police training. Military academies in the United States sponsor sports for cadets, and the World Police and Fire Games are held every 2 years because people believe that sports participation enhances the physical abilities of soldiers, law enforcement officials, and firefighters to safeguard the public order.

When public officials believe that sports will keep young people—especially those labeled "at risk"—off the streets and thereby reduce crime rates, vandalism, loneliness, and alienation, they may provide funding and facilities for sport programs. However, these programs are seldom effective unless they are tied to other efforts to reduce the deprivation, racism, poverty, dislocation, unemployment, community disintegration, and political powerlessness that often create "at-risk youth" and social problems in communities and societies (Coakley, 2002, 2011; Coalter, 2015; Hartman & Depro, 2006; Huysmans et al., 2019; Nols, Haudenhuyse & Theeboom, 2017).

Overall, when safeguarding the public order is the reason for government involvement in sports, the focus of that involvement can influence sports in many ways—sometimes restricting certain forms of participation at the same time that other forms are supported.

Ensure Fairness and Protect Human Rights

Governments may intervene in sports by passing laws, establishing policies, or ruling in court cases that protect the rights of citizens to participate in public sports programs. A classic example of this is

Title IX in the United States and similar laws worldwide that other countries have passed to promote gender equity in sports.

Additionally, many national governments are considering or have already enacted laws mandating the provision of sports participation opportunities for people with a disability. For instance, in 2013, the US Department of Education's Office for Civil Rights clarified the existing legal obligations of schools "to provide students with disabilities an equal opportunity to participate alongside their peers in after-school athletics and clubs." It also noted that "schools may not exclude students who have an intellectual, developmental, physical, or any other disability from trying out and playing on a team, if they are otherwise qualified" (Duncan, 2013).

In other examples of government actions to guarantee fairness and human rights, the US Congress passed the Amateur Sports Act in 1978 and created the USOC, now the official NGO responsible for coordinating amateur sports in the United States. A major reason for doing this was to protect athletes from being exploited by multiple, unconnected, and self-interested sport-governing bodies that controlled amateur sports through much of the twentieth century. In 1998, the act was revised to require the USOC to support and fund Paralympic athletes because people with a disability were systematically denied opportunities to play elite amateur sports. However, people have differing opinions on how the act should be interpreted and this has led athletes with disabilities to file lawsuits to receive the support and funding that they and many others consider to be fair.

Most recently, the US Senate conducted an 18-month investigation of the sexual abuse of amateur athletes under the control of the United States Olympic and Paralympic Committee (USOPC) and affiliated National Governing Bodies (NGBs) for Olympic sports (Moran & Blumenthal, 2019). It's 235-page report summarized the criminal and negligent actions of sports officials, coaches, and medical personnel and provided an outline for the protection of athletes in the future.

Maintain Health and Fitness

Governments often become involved in sports to promote health and fitness among citizens. In nations with state-funded, universal health care programs, governments often sponsor sports and physical activities to improve health and reduce expenditures for medical care. Nations without universal health care may also sponsor or promote sports for health reasons, but they have a lower stake in preventive approaches and less incentive to fund them. For example, public schools in the United States have cut physical education programs and communities have defunded recreational sport programs because they are seen as too expensive to maintain.

Although people generally believe that sport participation improves health and reduces medical costs, there's a growing awareness that the relationship between sports participation and health must be qualified because certain sports have high injury rates. For example, local and state governments have or are in the process of passing laws mandating concussion protocols, banning collision sports for children under certain ages, and having athletic trainers at the practices and games of high school teams. Additionally, a US federal law–the Protecting Young Victims from Sexual Abuse and Safe Sport Authorization Act–was passed in 2018. It mandates that people working in sports organizations report allegations of abuse to local police or child protection agencies, and it established the United States Center for Safe Sport to investigate allegations.

As evidence about the relationship between sports participation and health indicates that some forms of sports and physical activities are better than others in producing positive health outcomes, governments are becoming more cautious about the kinds of sports they support for health purposes.

Promote the Recognition and Prestige of a Community or Nation

Government involvement in sports frequently is motivated by a quest for national recognition and prestige. This is especially the case for countries (and cities/regions) that host major sports events such as FIFA World Cups in soccer and the Olympic and Paralympic Games.

This quest for recognition and prestige also underlies government subsidies for national teams across a wide range of sports, usually those designated as Olympic sports. Government officials use international sports to establish their nation's legitimacy and visibility in the international sphere, and they often believe that winning medals enhances their image around the world. This is why many governments provide cash rewards to their athletes who win medals. For example, at the 2018 Winter Olympics in PyeongChang, the promise of payments hit record levels. Singapore offered $1 million USD for a gold medal, $500,000 for a silver, and $250,000 for a bronze medal. Other offers for gold medals varied by country: Indonesia offered $746,000; Kazakhstan, $250,000; Italy, $166,000; Russia, $61,000; Germany, $22,000; and Canada, $15,000 (Weliver, 2019). US athletes received no money from the government, but the USOPC paid medal winners $37,500 for gold, $22,500 for silver, and $15,000 for bronze.

Attempts to gain recognition and prestige also underlie local governments' involvement in sports. Cities fund sport clubs and teams and then use them to promote themselves as good places to live, work, locate a business, or vacation. Many people in North America feel that if their city does not have one or more major professional sport team franchises, it cannot claim world-class status.

Even small towns use road signs to announce the success of local high school teams to everyone driving into the town: "You are now entering the home of the state champions" in this or that sport. Public universities in the United States subsidize sport programs at colleges and universities for similar reasons: Competitive success is believed to bring prestige to the entire state as well as the school represented by athletes and teams; prestige, it is believed, attracts out of state and international students that pay high tuition rates at public, state-supported universities.

The downside of this approach is that when governments fund sports and sports facilities to boost the profile of a city or nation, they often become caught in a cycle where increased funding is regularly required to compete with other cities and nations doing the same thing with bigger budgets or newer facilities. This continuously increases the money and other resources that must be allocated to sports, and it decreases resources for programs having more direct and concrete positive impact on citizens. Government officials often find that using this strategy to boost prestige for a city or nation is costly relative to the public benefits created, especially when most of the direct and tangible benefits go to a relatively small and predominantly wealthy segment of their constituency.

Promote Nation Building

Political leaders have often used sports as a nation-building tool. Their belief is that the emotional unity created by successful national teams and athletes and by hosting major sports events will build national identity and pride among citizens. However, research indicates that the meaning, intensity, and expressions of national identity and pride are not static components of a population. They vary among people in a society and shift over time with many factors, including economic and political changes, involvement in international conflicts and wars, and patterns of immigration that alter a nation's demographic profile (Bowes & Bairner, 2019; Davis, 2016; Penfold, 2019; Sullivan, Chadwick & Gow, 2019; Tobar & Gusso, 2017; Whigham, Lopez-Gonzalez & Ramon, 2019).

Additionally, the emotional unity created by winning medals or hosting events is relatively shortlived and does nothing to change the social, economic, and political realities of everyday life for the vast majority of people in a society. Social distinctions and patterns of privilege and disadvantage that existed prior to the success of national teams or hosting events remain after events are over and the feel-good moments related to success have faded. Of course, there are some people in any society for whom winning medals and hosting events have special meanings that remain important over time, but they constitute a minority in any country. But even these meanings vary depending on the sport, the event, and the athletes involved. For example, the impact of hosting a table tennis event in the United States, or winning a table tennis event, would have little connection to feelings of national identity and pride compared to hosting and winning a basketball event. The fact that the entire US table tennis team consists of Asian-Americans, most of whom were not US-born would also be a factor.

Research on the impact of sporting success and hosting sports events on national identity and pride has produced mixed results. The largest and most recent study was done by scholars at the Danish Institute for Sports Studies (Storm & Jakobsen, 2019). They found that the level of national pride expressed by citizens in over 100 countries was not related to the sporting success of athletes from their country or to hosting major international events. This finding contradicts widespread beliefs about the impact of winning medals and hosting events on the general process of nation-building. In discussing this contradiction, the authors of the study note that winning medals and hosting events by themselves do not automatically produce national pride among citizens in a country. However, they also note that it may be possible for politicians and sports managers to deliberately design strategic initiatives that foster national unity, identity, and pride in connection with the success of their athletes and hosting events. It is up to future research to identify those strategic initiatives and the conditions under which they are most effective. Until then we cannot assume that sports automatically contribute to the nation-building process.

(*Source:* Richard Atrero de Guzman/NurPhoto/Getty Images)

Not everyone sees sports in the same way. For example, when extreme cost overruns and other contentious issues related to the 2020 Olympic and Paralympic Games became widely known in 2017, anti-Olympic protesters marched in Tokyo to protest against hosting the Games in and around their city. They wanted money being spent on the games to be used to reduce poverty in Japan and deal with other pressing issues. For the protesters and many others in Japan, hosting the Games did not contribute to national unity, pride, and identity.

Another nation-building issue is whether a nation's success in sports or hosting an international event makes people in other countries more aware of the nation's existence, attractions, accomplishments, and potential. This has not been studied in detail, but unless a nation receives extensive media coverage in connection with multiple sport events, it isn't likely that winning medals or hosting an event will lead to more than superficial knowledge about its history and heritage. Research is needed on this issue.

Reaffirm Dominant Political Ideology

Governments also become involved in sports to promote specific political values and ideas among their citizens. This is especially true when there is a need to reaffirm the idea that success is based on personal discipline, loyalty, obedience, and hard work, even in the face of hardship and bad times. Sports are useful platforms to promote these values and foster a particular ideology that contains taken-for-granted assumptions about the way social life is organized and how it does and should operate.

It's difficult to determine the extent to which people are influenced by sports that are represented in specific ideological terms, but we do know that in capitalist societies, such as the United States, sports provide people with a vocabulary and real-life examples that are consistent with dominant political and cultural ideologies.

The images, narratives, and the often-repeated stories that accompany sports in market economies emphasize that competition is clearly the best way to motivate people and allocate rewards in society, whereas alternative approaches emphasizing cooperation and collective benefits are ineffective, unnatural, and even immoral in the case of socialism and communism.

The Cold War era following World War II was a time when nations, especially the United States, the former Soviet Union (USSR–the Union of Soviet Socialist Republics), and East Germany (GDR–the German Democratic Republic), used the Olympics and other international sport competitions to make claims about the superiority of their political and economic systems and ideologies.

Now that the Cold War is over, powerful global corporations use sports to promote free-market ideology, but governments have not stopped using sports to promote values consistent with ideologies that support their interests. In fact, prior to 2009, NFL players did not stand for the national anthem because they remained in the locker room as it was performed. But in 2009 the Department of Defense (DOD) paid the NFL millions of dollars to move the players on the field during the anthem as a marketing ploy to make the players look like models of patriotism. Between 2011 and 2015 the DOD and the National Guard paid the NFL and other sports organizations nearly $13 million so they could unfurl gigantic flags on the field and hold colorful public ceremonies as part of their efforts to recruit young people into the military (Niles, 2017; Willingham, 2017). This paid patriotism and its impact on the minds of Americans set the stage for drama and debate when Colin Kaepernick "took a knee" to call attention to police brutality and racial injustice in the United States (see section titled, Athletes as Political Actors, pp. 485–488).

Increase Support for Political Leaders and Government

Government authority rests ultimately in legitimacy. If people do not perceive political leaders and the government as legitimate, it is difficult to maintain social order. In the quest to maintain their legitimacy, political officials have regularly used athletes, teams, and particular sports to boost their acceptance in the minds of citizens. They assume, as Italian political theorist Antonio Gramsci predicted, that if they support what people value and enjoy, they can maintain their legitimacy as leaders. This is why they attend highly publicized sports events and associate themselves with high-profile athletes and teams that win major competitions. US presidents traditionally have associated themselves with successful athletes and teams by inviting them to the White House for photo opportunities.

The sports involvement of political leaders in the United States is mostly symbolic. The agency responsible for overseeing sports is the Senate Committee on Commerce, Science, and Transportation (see https://www.rules.senate.gov/rules-of-the-senate). This committee deals primarily with the USOPC and NGBs, although they discuss sports only when there is a serious crisis.

In most countries, there is a Ministry of Sports with a cabinet minister that reports directly to the president or prime minister. This makes government involvement much more direct and consequential. The ministry provides funding for the National Olympic Committee, the NGBs, and a range of other sports programs. This enables the president, prime minister, or monarch to exert direct control over sports and use them to enhance their popularity and power. For example, in the family-based monarchies in Middle Eastern countries, one of the men in the ruling family will control all sports, including national teams, the top soccer clubs, and community sports. His control, as well as the goals he established for sports, are designed to affirm his power and the power of the ruling family. In countries where this approach is used, politics is structured into the DNA of all sports; there is no line separating them (Dorsey, 2016).

(*Source:* Chip Somodevilla/Getty Images)

The 2019 NCAA women's championship basketball team from Baylor, and their coach, Kim Mulkey, present US President Donald Trump with a jersey as they visited the White House. The University of Virginia men's championship team decided to skip their visit in a move that a number of players and entire teams have taken in response to racially insensitive comments made by the president.

Facilitate Economic and Social Development

Since the early 1980s, governments have supported or intervened in sports to facilitate a particular form of urban economic development (Boykoff, 2014). National and city governments now spend millions of tax dollars on bids to host the Olympic Games, World Cup tournaments, world or national championships, Super Bowls, College Bowl games, All-Star Games, high-profile auto races, golf tournaments, track-and-field meets, and well-marketed youth sports tournaments. In many cases, these expenditures of public money are connected with private entrepreneurial projects designed to increase personal and corporate capital and "renew" blighted or declining areas. By using a sports team, a new stadium, or a major sports event to justify spending public money, business-oriented public officials can partner with developers to gentrify declining or deteriorated urban neighborhoods by bringing in upscale businesses, shoppers, and residents, and moving out low-income and homeless people.

I am always amazed when I hear people saying that sport creates goodwill between the nations . . . Even if one didn't know from concrete examples . . . that international sporting contests lead to orgies of hatred, one could deduce it from general principles.

–George Orwell, The Sporting Spirit (1945)

Using sports is an effective way to create public support for this type of development project, but many of the projects are risky and controversial as public investments. Most fail to meet the optimistic economic impact projections provided by developers, and benefits are enjoyed by relatively few people (Kennelly, 2017; Kohe & Bowen-Jones, 2016; Müller & Gaffney, 2018; Orr & Jarvis, 2018; Pettigrew & Reiche, 2016; Yu, Xue & Newman, 2018).

Government involvement in sports may also be based on the presumed social effects of sports in a community or society. Many public officials believe the great sport myth and think that sports, in almost any form, bring people together and create social bonds that carry into other spheres of life and increase the social vitality of a city or society. Research generally contradicts this belief, often finding that relationships formed in connection with sports seldom carry over to other spheres, and that some relationships between individuals and groups are characterized by conflicts that can interfere with social development.

Overall, research indicates that sports may be associated with social development under certain conditions and that the social effects of this association may not be immediately observable in people's lives. This doesn't confirm the beliefs of public officials who use sports to promote social development as much as it provides information about how and when government can effectively facilitate social development and what can be expected in terms of social effects.

Critical Issues and Government Involvement in Sports

Advocates of government support for and involvement in sports say that it is justified because it serves the "public good." Of course, it would be ideal if government support and involvement provided equal benefits for all citizens, but differences between individuals and groups make this impossible. Therefore, public investments in sports tend to benefit some people more than others. Those who benefit most usually are the persons or groups who have the connections and resources to influence policy makers. This doesn't mean that government policies related to sports reflect only the interests of wealthy and powerful people, but it does mean that policy making is often contentious and creates power struggles among various segments of the population in a city or society.

Governments worldwide make decisions about allocating funds between elite sports and sports for all. Elite sports are highly organized, have strong backing from other organized groups, and base their requests for support on visible accomplishments achieved in the name of the entire country or city. Recreational sports serving large numbers of people are less organized, less likely to have powerful supporters, and less able to give precise statements of their goals and the political significance of their programs. This does not mean that government decision makers ignore mass participation, but it does mean that "sports for all" usually has lower priority for funding and support than elite sports have (Barboza Eiras de Castro et al., 2016; de Nooij & van den Berg, 2018; Schausteck de Almeida et al., 2012, 2018).

Those who believe the myth that there is no connection between sports and government are most likely to be ignored by public officials, whereas those who are aware of government involvement are most likely to benefit when it does occur. Sports are connected with power relations in society as a whole; therefore, sports and politics cannot be separated.

SPORTS AND GLOBAL POLITICAL PROCESSES

Most people have lofty expectations about the impact of sports on global relations. It has long been hoped that sports would serve diplomatic functions by contributing to cultural understanding and world peace. Unfortunately, the realities of sports seldom match ideals. Nation-states and transnational corporations (TNCs) regularly use sports to promote their interests and ideologies at the same time that athletes, teams, events, equipment, and capital investments cross national borders on a daily basis. Issues related to these global strategies and processes are closely linked with politics, so it is useful to understand them when studying sports in society.

International Sports: Ideals Versus Realities

Achieving peace and friendship among nations was emphasized by Baron Pierre de Coubertin when he founded the modern Olympic Games in 1896. For over a century, his goals have been embraced by many people who assumed or hoped that sports would do the following things:

- Create open communication lines between people and leaders from different nations.
- Highlight shared interests among people from different cultures and nations.
- Demonstrate that friendly international relationships are possible.
- Foster cultural understanding and eliminate the use of national stereotypes.
- Create a global model for cooperative cultural, economic, and political relationships.
- Establish processes that develop effective leaders in emerging nations and close the resource gap between wealthy and poor nations.

Recent history shows that sports can be useful in the realm of **public diplomacy,** which consists of *public expressions of togetherness in the form of cultural exchanges and general communication among officials from various nations.* However, sports have no direct impact on the outcomes of **serious diplomacy,** which consists of *discussions and decisions about political issues of vital national interest.* In other words, international sports provide opportunities for political leaders to meet and talk, but sports don't influence the content of their discussions or their policy decisions.

Likewise, sports bring together athletes who may learn from and about one another, but athletes have seldom tried to make or influence political decisions, and their relationships with one another have no serious political significance.

Recent history shows that most nations use sports and sports events, especially the Olympic Games and other major international events, to pursue their own interests rather than international understanding, friendship, and peace (Angelini et al., 2017; Dorsey, 2018a, 2018b, 2018c; Jamieson, 2015; Jennings, 2006; Schofield, Rhind & Blair, 2018; Usher, 2019; Whigham, Lopez-Gonzalez & Ramon, 2019). Nationalist themes going beyond respectful expressions of patriotism have been clearly evident in many events, and most nations regularly use sports events to promote their own military, economic, political, and cultural agendas. This was particularly apparent during the Cold War era following World War II and extending into the early 1990s. During these years, the Olympics were extensions of "superpower politics" between the United States and its allies and the former Soviet Union and its allies.

The inherent links between international sports and politics were so clear in the early 1980s that Peter Ueberroth, president of the committee that organized the 1984 Olympic Games in Los Angeles, said that "we now have to face the reality that the Olympics constitute not only an athletic event but a political event" (US News & World Report, 1983). Ueberroth was not being prophetic; he was simply summarizing his observations of events leading up to the 1984 games. He saw that nations were more interested in benefiting themselves than pursuing global friendship and peace. The demonstration of national superiority through sports has long been a major focus of world powers, and many nations that seek to extend their political and economic power have used sports to gain international recognition and legitimacy.

For smaller nations, the Olympics, World Cups, and international championships have been stages for showing that their athletes and teams can stand up to and sometimes defeat athletes and teams from wealthy and powerful nations. For example, when the cricket teams from the West Indies or India play teams from England, the athletes and fans from India and the West Indies view the matches as opportunities to show the world that they are now equal to the nation that once colonized their land and controlled their people. When their teams win, it is cause for political affirmation and great celebration.

National and city leaders know that hosting the Olympics is a special opportunity to generate international recognition, display national power and resources to a global audience, and invite investments into their economies. This is why the bid committees from prospective host cities and nations have regularly used gifts, bribes, and financial incentives to encourage IOC members to vote for them in the host city selection process. Illegal and illicit strategies were common during the bidding for the 2002 Winter Olympics, when officials from Salt Lake City offered to IOC members and their families money, jobs, scholarships, lavish gifts, vacations, and the sexual services of "escorts" as they successfully secured the votes needed to host the games (Jennings, 1996a, 1996b; Jennings and Sambrook, 2000). Efforts to influence votes and personally profit from decisions involving billions of dollars still occur, but they are usually done much more carefully and discretely (Booth, 2011; Jennings, 2013a, 2013b).

The link between sports and politics has been clearly exposed by protests and boycotts directed at the Olympics and other international sports events. For example, when Mexican college students used the 1968 Olympic Games hosted by Mexico City as an occasion for protesting police violence and the actions of an oppressive political regime, the police and military massacred hundreds of students and others in a public plaza in the Tlatelolco neighborhood of Mexico City (Poniatowska, 1975). Representatives of governments and National Olympic Committees said little or nothing about the murders because they wanted a "secure" Olympic Games.

In 1980, the United States and 62 of its political allies boycotted the Olympic Games in Moscow, the capital of the Soviet Union (USSR), to protest the decision of the Soviets to invade Afghanistan and eliminate Islamic rebels, because the rebels opposed Soviet control of the region. The United States supported the autonomy of Afghanistan, armed the rebels, including Osama bin Laden, and helped to create the terrorist infrastructure that later became Al-Qaeda.[1] In retaliation, the Soviet Union and at least 14 of its allies boycotted the 1984 Olympic Games in Los Angeles to protest the commercialization of the games and avoid terrorist actions they expected from Americans who had made threats against their teams and athletes.

Each of these Olympic Games was held despite the boycotts, and each host nation unashamedly displayed its power and resources to the world and touted the fact that they topped the medal count for the respective games. Neither boycotting nor hosting the games had any major effects on US or Soviet political policies, although they did intensify Cold War feelings and fears.

Global media coverage of sport mega-events has added new dimensions to the link between sports and politics. Television companies, especially the American networks, have used political controversies to hype the games and increase audience ratings, and they edit programming to highlight the American flag and melodramatic stories about athletes who overcame disadvantage to achieve success and participate in the American Dream (Angelini et al., 2017; Greider, 2006).

US media networks claim that Americans won't watch an Olympics unless the global power and cultural values of the United States are woven into the coverage. Of course, the US media aren't the only ones to do this, but their impact far surpasses the impact of nationalist and ethnocentric coverage in other nations, because the military and economic power and policies of the United States affect the world much more than do the power and policies of other nation-states.

Nationalistic themes in media coverage of international sports are now accompanied and sometimes obscured by images and narratives promoting capitalist expansion and the products and services of transnational corporations. These issues are discussed in the Reflect on Sports box "Olympism and the Olympic Games."

Nation-States, Sports, and Ideological Hegemony

Global politics often revolve around issues of ideological hegemony–that is, whose ideas and beliefs are most widely accepted worldwide and used to

[1]Al-Qaeda was then responsible for killing over 3000 people when it destroyed the World Trade Center Twin Towers in New York City and seriously damaged the Pentagon building in Virginia. This led to the global war on terror launched by President George W. Bush, a war in which over 500,000 soldiers, civilians, and terrorists have been killed over 18 years; as of early 2019, this war has cost the United States alone about $5,900,000,000,000 (DePetris, 2019).

The Olympic and Paralympic Games
Are They Special?

According to the Olympic Charter, the Olympic Games are based on a philosophy described in these words:

> Olympism is a philosophy of life, exalting and combining in a balanced whole the qualities of body, will, and mind. Blending sport with culture and education, Olympism seeks to create a way of life based on the joy found in effort, the educational value of good example, and respect for universal fundamental ethical principles.

This means that the Olympics should provide opportunities for people worldwide to learn about and connect with one another in ways that lead to respect and peace—a commendable goal given that our future and the future of the earth itself depends on global cooperation.

If the Olympic and Paralympic Games facilitate such an outcome, they are indeed special. But nationalism and commercialism exert so much influence on the organization and coverage of the Games that the goals of global understanding and peace receive only token attention.

One factor undermining the philosophy of Olympism is the current method of selling media broadcasting rights for the Olympic and Paralympic Games. Television companies buy media rights so they can re-present selected video images from the Olympics and Paralympics and combine them with their own narratives to attract audiences in their countries. Therefore, instead of bringing the world together around a single unifying experience, the coverage consists of many heavily nationalized and commercialized versions of the Games. Of course, media consumers give their own meanings to this coverage, but they consume images and narratives from only their nation as starting points for making sense of and talking about the Olympics.

Media consumers who want to use the Olympics to visualize a global community constructed around cultural differences and mutual understanding can do so, but current media coverage provides little assistance in this quest. Most coverage highlights the association between human achievement, selected cultural values, and corporate sponsors. In the process, many people come to believe that corporations really do make international sports possible. As they watch television coverage in the United States, about 25 percent of the programming consists of commercial messages from corporations, many of which claim to "bring you the Olympics."

People don't accept media images and narratives in literal terms, but corporate sponsors now bet billions of dollars on the possibility that associating their products and logos with the Olympics and Paralympics will discourage criticism of their products and policies, encourage people to consume those products, and normalize a lifestyle organized around consumption.

The overt commercialism that now pervades the Olympics has led some people to question the meaning of the games themselves. Bruce Kidd, a former Olympian and a physical and health educator at the University of Toronto, argues that if the Olympic Games are to be special, they must use sports to make people aware of global injustice and to promote social responsibility worldwide.

Kidd (1996) says that in the spirit of Olympism, athletes should be selected for participation in the games on the basis of their actions as global citizens as well as their athletic accomplishments. There also should be a curriculum enabling athletes to learn about fellow competitors and their cultures. The games should involve formal, televised opportunities for intercultural exchanges, and athletes should be ready to discuss their ideas about world peace and social responsibility during media interviews.

The IOC should sponsor projects enabling citizen-athletes to build on their Olympic and Paralympic experiences through service to others around the world. A proportion of the windfall profits coming from rapidly escalating TV rights fees should fund such projects, thereby giving IOC members opportunities to talk about real examples of social responsibility that they support. The "up close and personal" stories presented in the media could then highlight the socially responsible actions of athletes. Media consumers are increasingly aware that they don't live in isolation from the rest of the world and may find such coverage as entertaining as

Continued

reflect on SPORTS The Olympic and Paralympic Games (*continued*)

the current soap opera-like stories of personal tragedies and triumphs.

Additionally, the IOC could control nationalism and commercialism more carefully as it organizes the games and sells broadcasting rights. There is no single best way to do this, but here are six recommendations that would emphasize the spirit of Olympism:

1. *Add to each games "demonstration sports" native to the cultural regions where the games are held.* The IOC should specify that all media companies purchasing broadcasting rights and receiving press credentials must devote 5 percent of their coverage to these native games. Because the media influence how people imagine, create, and play sports, this would provide expanded images of physical activities and facilitate creative approaches to sport participation worldwide. At present, many Olympic sports are simply a legacy of former colonial powers that exported their games as they conquered peoples around the world. But there are thousands of folk games and indigenous sports that could inspire new forms of physical activities and sports today, if people knew about them and saw them being played.
2. *Use multiple sites for each Olympic Games.* The cost of hosting the summer Olympic Games was $14.6 billion for Athens in 2004; well over $40 billion for Beijing in 2008; about $15 billion for London in 2012, $13.1 billion for Rio de Janeiro; and about $21 billion for Tokyo. Such costs privilege wealthy nations and prevent other nations from hosting the games and highlighting their cultures. If Olympic events were split into three separate media rights packages many more nations could host one of the packages and enjoy the benefits of staging the events without accumulating the massive debts that burden local citizens for decades after the event and leave them with a legacy of underused facilities.
3. *Emphasize global responsibility in media coverage.* Television contracts should mandate an emphasis on global social responsibility in the media coverage of the games. Athlete committees, working with scholars from the Olympic Academy, could identify noteworthy efforts that have had a positive social impact in resource-deprived communities and assist media companies in producing coverage of these cases. Additionally, a mandated amount of media time should be dedicated to public service announcements from nonprofit human rights groups that work with athletes and sport organizations to promote social justice and sustainable forms of development. This would guarantee that media consumers receive information that is not created or censored by corporations and market forces.
4. *Integrate the Olympics and Paralympics.* Just as the Olympic Movement supports gender equality and opposes racial apartheid in sports, it should include Paralympic athletes in the Olympic Games. This

(*Source:* Barbara Schausteck de Almeida)

McDonald's and Coke have been longtime sponsors of the Olympic Games. Using marketing logic based on widespread acceptance of the great sport myth, the McDonald's Corporation and the Coca-Cola Company have spent billions of dollars in recent decades to link their logos with the Olympic rings. The hope is that beliefs in the purity and goodness of sports will be associated with their products that are difficult to market as pure and good.

would involve shared opening and closing ceremonies, awarding the same Olympic medals to all athletes, and referring to the entire event as the "Olympics." This would show the world saying that the full inclusion of people with a disability is an achievable goal in all spheres of life.

5. *Promote a fair method of calculating medal counts.* National medal counts are contrary to the spirit and official principles of Olympism. They foster chauvinism and hostility, present the achievements of athletes in divisive rather than unifying ways, and privilege large, wealthy nations with resources to train medal-winning athletes. To make medal counts fair, members of the Olympic Academy (scholars who study Olympism) should publish daily during each Olympic Games an "official medal count" in which the size and wealth of participating nations is statistically controlled.

Table 13.1 provides an example of how rankings would change if national population size were controlled. The list on the left side of the table ranks nations by the total number of medals won in all the Olympic Games from 1896 through 2018. The list on the right side of the table ranks nations in terms of the number of people in the overall population for each medal won by its athletes: the lower the population number per medal, the more efficient the country is in producing medal-winning athletes.

In this ranking system, the most efficient countries are Liechtenstein, Norway, Finland, and Sweden. Great Britain, ranked 24th, has had one medal-winning athlete for every 71,075 people in its population. The United States is 39th with one medal-winning athlete for every 110,853 people in its current population. Apart from Liechtenstein which is an exceptional case (see footnote at the bottom of the next column), this could be taken to mean that the systems of sports participation and elite athlete training in Norway, Finland, and Sweden have been much more efficient than the US system in producing athletes that win Olympic medals, and this does not take into account that the United States has a much higher gross domestic product (GDP) per capita than Finland and Sweden.*

6. *Replace the Olympic motto Citius-Altius-Fortius (Faster-Higher-Stronger) with Health-Unity-Peace.* The current motto creates problems for the Olympic Movement because athletes are reaching the limits of human performance in many sports. Therefore, the only way to go Faster-Higher-Stronger is to use performance-enhancing technologies that are often expensive and not accessible to many athletes worldwide. To ban some of these technologies and spend millions of dollars testing for them seems hypocritical when the current Olympic motto inspires athletes to use them. Therefore, it would be more in keeping with the philosophy of Olympism to adopt a new motto of Health-Unity-Peace.

Of course, people will dismiss these suggestions as idealistic, but the Olympic Movement was founded on idealism and intended to inspire visions of what our world could and should be. Additionally, Olympism emphasizes that progress comes only through effort and participation. If the Olympic and Paralympic Games of today are little more than marketing opportunities for transnational corporations and stages for power displays by large, wealthy nations with medal-winning athletes, now is a good time for those who value Olympic ideals to take action and turn them into reality.

*See http://www.indexmundi.com/g/r.aspx?v=67 for information on GDP per capita for all countries. *GDP per capita* is a measure based on purchasing power parity (PPP). *PPP GDP* is gross domestic product converted to international dollars that have the same purchasing power in a particular country as the US dollar has in the United States. This makes it a good statistic to use when comparing the standard of living from one country to another. For our example here, the PPP in the United States is 59,500. In Liechtenstein it is $139,100 (the wealthiest nation in the world); $70,600 in Norway, $52,300 in Sweden, and $44,000 in Finland (presented in terms of the value of the US dollar in 2017).

Continued

The Olympic and Paralympic Games (*continued*)

Table 13.1 Olympic medal count by total medals (left side) and population per medal (right side), 1896-2018

Rank	Country	Medals	Rank	Country	Medals	Population	Population per Medal
1	United States	2,827	1	Liechtenstein	10	36.476	3,647
2	Soviet Union	1.204	2	Norway	521	5,005,700	9.607
3	Germany	992	3	Finland	470	5,407,040	11.504
4	Great Britain	876	4	Sweden	652	9,490,683	14,556
5	France	836	5	Hungary	498	9,962.000	20,004
6	Italy	702	6	Switzerland	344	7,870,100	22.878
7	Sweden	652	7	Austria	319	8,452,835	26,497
8	China	605	8	Bahamas	13	353,658	27,204
9	Russian Federation	586	9	Denmark	195	5,580,516	28,618
10	Norway	521	10	East Germany	519	16,111,000	31,042
11	East Germany	519	11	Estonia	41	1,318,005	32,146
12	Australia	511	12	Bulgaria	223	7,364,570	33,024
13	Canada	499	13	Jamaica	78	2,705,827	34,690
14	Hungary	498	14	New Zealand	120	4,432,620	36,938
15	Japan	497	15	Netherlands	415	16,731,770	40,317
16	Finland	470	16	Australia	511	22,880,619	44,776
17	Netherlands	415	17	Cuba	219	11,241,161	51,329
18	Switzerland	344	18	Slovenia	40	2,057,540	51,438
19	South Korea	334	19	Grenada	2	110,821	55,410
20	Austria	319	20	Romania	307	19.042,936	62.029
21	Romania	307	21	Bermuda	1	64,237	64,237
22	Poland	304	22	Trinidad and Tobago	19	1,317,714	69.353
23	West Germany	243	23	Canada	499	34,771,400	69,682
24	Bulgaria	223	24	Great Britain	876	62,262.000	71,075
25	Cuba	219	25	Belgium	154	10.951,266	71,112
			39	**United States**	**2,827**	**313,382,000**	**110,853**

(*Source:* Adapted from http://www.medalspercapita.com/#medals:all-time; and http://www.medalspercapita.com/medals-per-capita:all-time).

guide everything from world trade to who starts wars with whom. In this process, sports usually serve the interests of wealthy and powerful nations. For example, when nations with few resources want to participate in major international sports, they must look to wealthy nations for assistance in the form of coaching, equipment, and training support. As this occurs, people in poorer nations often de-emphasize their traditional folk games and focus on the global sports developed around the values and experiences of nations powerful enough to export their games around the globe and make them the centerpieces of international competitions. If they want to play, those are the sports in which they must excel. To the extent that this makes poorer nations dependent, sports become vehicles for economically powerful nations to extend their control over important forms of popular culture worldwide–and to claim that it is part of the "foreign aid" that they give to poor people and struggling nations (Coakley and Souza, 2013; Cole, 2012; Darnell, 2012; Forde, 2013).

If people in traditional cultures want to preserve their indigenous sports and games, they must resist dependency status, but this is difficult in international sports when the rules and other structural characteristics of the sports reflect and privilege powerful nations. For example, when an American sport such as football is introduced to another country, it comes with an emphasis on ideas about individual achievement, competition, winning, hierarchical authority structures, physical power and domination, the body, violence, and the use of technology to shape bodies into efficient performance machines. These ideas may not be accepted by everyone who plays or watches football, but they reaffirm orientations that privilege US interests and obscure the cooperative values that are necessary for the collective survival of most traditional cultures. As an editor at *Newsweek* noted some years ago, "Sports may be America's most successful export to the world. . . . Our most visible symbol has evolved from the Stars and Stripes to Coke and the Nike Swoosh" (Starr, 1999, p. 44).

Ideally, sports facilitate cultural exchanges through which people from different nations share information and develop mutual cultural understanding. But true 50–50 sharing and mutual understanding are rare when nations have unequal power and resources. Therefore, sports often become cultural exports from wealthy nations that are incorporated into the everyday lives of people worldwide. Local people are free to reject, revise, or redefine these sports, but when "cultural trade routes" are opened through sports, nations that import sports often become increasingly open to importing and consuming additional goods, services, and ideas from the nations that brought them sports (Abbot, 2018; Jackson and Andrews, 2004; Peachey et al., 2018; Sanders, 2016; Sanders & Coakley, 2020). To avoid this outcome, the less powerful nations must increase their political power and economic resources; when an imbalance exists, it becomes more difficult to resist the political and economic dominance of wealthy and powerful nations.

Political Realities in an Era of Transnational Corporations

Global politics have changed dramatically since the 1970s. Massive corporations are now among the largest economies in the world today, and they share the global political stage with nation-states. This change occurred as nation-states embraced a policy of deregulation, lifted trade restrictions, lowered tariffs, and made it easier for capital, labor, and goods to flow freely around the globe. Although nation-states remain central in global relations, the differences between national and corporate interests have nearly disappeared in connection with sports. This was implied over 20 years ago by Phil Knight, CEO of US-based Nike, when he discussed shifts in fan loyalties in men's World Cup in soccer:

> We see a natural evolution . . . dividing the world into their athletes and ours. And we glory ours. When the US played Brazil in the World Cup, I rooted for Brazil because it was a Nike team. America was Adidas (Lipsyte, 1996, p. 9).

For Knight, teams and athletes represented corporations as much or more than nations; and corporate logos were more important than national flags at international events. When Nike paid to sponsor Brazil's national team and used its players to market Nike products, Knight was pushing consumption and brand loyalty over patriotism and public service as global values. For him, sports were outposts in the heads of sport fans and could be used as receptors and transmitters for the messages coming from Nike and other corporate sponsors seeking global capitalist expansion. Like executives from other transnational corporations (TNCs), he believes that sports contribute to the growth of global well-being when they are used to promote a lifestyle of consumption and the values that support it.

Corporate sponsors now exert significant influence over sports events, at least to the point of directing images and narratives toward spectator-consumers rather than spectator-citizens. Sports that can't be covered this way–such as those that aren't organized to attract spectators with high purchasing power, or those that don't emphasize competitive outcomes and setting performance/production records–are not sponsored. When spectators and potential media audiences are not valued consumers, and when sports don't represent an ideology of competition and winning, corporations seldom become sponsors and commercial media have little reason to cover them.

The global power of transnational corporations is neither unlimited nor uncontested. Individuals and local populations have used their own cultural perspectives to make sense of the images and narratives that come with global sports and give them meanings that fit with their lives (Chen, 2012; Maguire, 2019). However, research that combines cultural theory and a critical approach shows that global media sports and the commercial messages that accompany them often cleverly fuse the global and the local through thoughtfully and carefully edited images that combine local traditions, sport action, and consumer products in seamless and technically brilliant media representations (John and Jackson, 2011; Scherer and Jackson, 2010). The researchers doing this work argue that such fused images "detraditionalize" local cultures by representing local symbols and lifestyles in connection with consumer products that, by themselves, have nothing to do with those cultures.

On a similarly subversive level, Coca-Cola claims that it sponsors the Olympics because it wants the whole world "to move to the beat," to "live Olympic," and experience "unity on the Coke side of life." McDonald's used a similar approach as the Official Restaurant of the Olympic Games from 1996 through 2016. When asked about the message being sent by having Coca-Cola and McDonald's as sponsors, a spokesperson for the London Organizing Committee explained, "Without our partners such as McDonald's, the games simply wouldn't happen" (Cheng, 2012). A Coca-Cola representative added, "Without the support of sponsors such as Coca-Cola as many as 170 of the 200 National Olympic Committees would be unable to send athletes to compete" (Campbell and Boffey, 2012). A McDonald's spokesperson avoided questions about nutrition and health and stated, "Ultimately it's up to individuals to make the right food, drink, and activity choices for themselves" a classic neoliberal response (O'Reilly, 2012).

The goal of these corporations is to convince people that without them the pleasure and excitement of the Olympic Games would no longer exist. Of course, this is not true, although there would be less money for IOC expense accounts and the Games might be less glitzy and spectacular, but they could exist without fast-food and soft-drink sponsors. Commercial images and messages do not dictate what people think, but they certainly influence what people think about, and they become a part of the overall discourse that occurs in cultures around the globe.

This description of new global political realities does not mean that sports have fallen victim to a worldwide conspiracy hatched by transnational corporations. It means only that transnational corporations have joined nation-states in the global political context in which sports are defined, organized, sponsored, promoted, played, presented, and given meaning around the world.

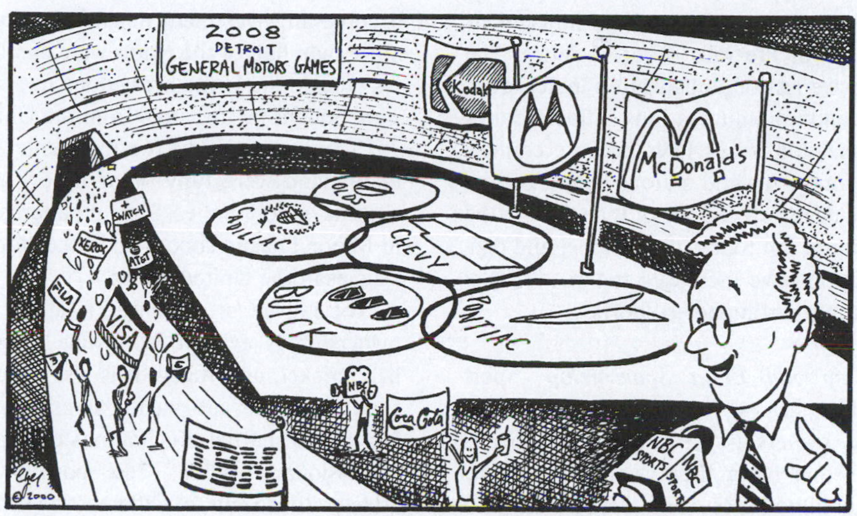

(Source: Frederic A. Eyer. All rights reserved. Used with permission)

"NBC Sports has eliminated nationalism in our Olympic coverage and replaced it with global consumer capitalism. Now our commentary will emphasize individualism, competition, and conquest. Enjoy the games—and the commercials that bring the games to you!"

Global politics today involve the interaction of nation-states and transnational corporations. As a result the media coverage of global mega-events is organized around images and messages that link transnational corporations with flags, anthems, and athletes representing nation-states. In the process, patriotic feelings and consumer desires are seamlessly woven together.

Political Realities in an Era of Globalization

Money, athletic skills, and sports media have all gone global. Even though we pretend that national political boundaries matter for the sake of patriots who track medal counts by country during the Olympics or cheer for their national teams in other events, those boundaries have become very porous for many sports. Today, sports are global businesses that transcend and blur political boundaries.

This is not to say that nation-states are unimportant (Rowe, 2013). Most national governments fund teams and training centers and present their athletes as representatives of the nation. Additionally, major sport leagues are generally nation-based, and national teams and athletes compete in the Olympic Games, World Cup tournaments, and World Championships. These structures sustain the importance of nations, but as sports become increasingly commercialized, super-rich investors buy teams in multiple countries; athletes, coaches, and technical personnel are recruited and seek opportunities and contracts worldwide; spectators follow sports, teams, and athletes outside their own countries; and sports are even transported around the globe as tourists and laborers visit or take up residence in new countries and maintain their connections with the sports of their birth nations. These patterns are not new, but they are more pervasive and growing faster than ever before. As a result, they raise political issues in and out of sports.

Globalization is *a process through which financial capital, products, knowledge, worldviews, and cultural practices flow through political borders and influence people's lives.* Globalization often involves *exchanges* of resources and elements of culture–but those exchanges are seldom equal, because some nations have more power to export and infuse their money and ways of life into other societies. The pace and pervasiveness of globalization increases as transportation and communications infrastructures expand. Globalization is not new, because connections between continents and nations began to grow and encompass nearly all regions of the world in the nineteenth century. But today, the Internet and digital communication have increased the pace of globalization, and this has impacted sports.

Team Ownership and Event Sponsorship Sport team ownership has gone global. Billionaires worldwide see ownership of professional teams as investments that bring them worldwide recognition. Oil-rich billionaires from Middle Eastern countries now own English soccer teams. Russians with billions of windfall dollars made by taking over companies previously owned by the state now own professional teams in top leagues around the world. Asian and North American entrepreneurs and global capitalists now see sport teams anywhere in the world as potential investments that come with publicity perks. In fact, the multi-billionaire co-founder of the Chinese company, Alibaba ("the Amazon" of the Eastern hemisphere) now owns the Brooklyn Nets in the NBA, the stadium in which they play, and the WNBA's New York Liberty.

Prior to this century it was unthinkable that a major professional sport team in any country would be owned by someone who was not a citizen of that country. Teams represented cities or well-defined regions, and local owners even hesitated to hire players who were "outsiders." But global media coverage of certain sports has given teams–especially those in the English Premier League, with soccer matches televised in more than 150 nations each week–the visibility needed to become global brands. At the same time the concentration of global wealth has created an international class of multibillionaire investors who see sport teams as investments that will provide good returns if they are marketed worldwide.

As a result, the English Premier League, the highest-profile sports league in the world, has become an investment magnet. During 2003–2013 more than half of the teams were purchased by owners outside the United Kingdom; five of those teams were bought by investors from the United States. In 2019, only eight of the twenty Premier League teams in England were fully or partly owned by English citizens or companies. Similar patterns are emerging in Major League soccer and other top professional leagues in the United States.

The impact of globalization at the level of team ownership is evident worldwide in soccer, basketball, cricket, and rugby. It is also occurs with event sponsorship for auto racing, tennis, golf, rodeo, boxing, mixed martial arts, various extreme sports, and professional wrestling. These sports have tours taking athletes to dozens of different countries each year, which makes them ideally suited for global corporations who want to sponsor sports with global appeal among identifiable demographic segments of populations across all countries.

Major golf and tennis organizations, including the PGA, LPGA, ATP, and WTA, now spread their officially sanctioned events across a number of different countries each year to attract spectators, sponsors, and future players worldwide. In fact, the LPGA has so many golfers from Asian countries that it has established a traveling language school to teach English and help native-English speakers learn the basics in other languages so they can communicate with other golfers.

Athletes Athletes have also gone global. Managers and scouts at soccer and baseball academies see athletes as global commodities that can be trained and then sold around the world to the highest-bidding teams. Professional and US college teams scout for athletic talent worldwide in the hope of finding regions or even towns where genetically gifted and "coachable" (that is, "controllable") athletes can be recruited to come away with them.

Skilled athletes in many sports now see their job market in global terms and are willing to travel any place in the world where they might be offered a desirable contract (Elliott, 2013). Their choices are informed by a hierarchy of "best places to work"– it is Sweden, Canada, or Russia for men's hockey; the United States or Japan for baseball; the United States or Germany for men's basketball; Germany, the United States, or Australia for women's basketball; England, Germany, or Spain for men's soccer; France, Spain, or the United States for women's soccer; France or Croatia for men's team handball; Denmark for women's team handball; England, India, or the West Indies for cricket; England, Australia, or New Zealand for netball; and Argentina, Brazil, or the United Kingdom for Formula 1 racing.

In basketball alone, as of 2019, more than 4,100 men and women from the United States were playing professionally in other countries and 3,428 players from outside the US played on US professional and college basketball teams during the previous 5 years (see http://www.usbasket.com/Americans-Overseas.asp). These numbers are growing as professional leagues prosper and new leagues are established in China, Russia, Japan, and countries in Eastern Europe and Latin America. For example, former NBA All-Star player Stephon Marbury played eight of his 22-year pro basketball career on three different teams in the Chinese Basketball Association (CBA). His teams won 3 CBA titles as he became one of the most popular players in China. After retiring in 2018, he became head coach of the CBA's Beijing Royal Fighters.

Athlete migration to US-based professional leagues and the athletic departments of major universities is significant. Athletes born outside the United States make up 71 percent of the players in the NHL, 56 percent of the players in the MLS, 28 percent of players on MLB teams, and 25 percent of NBA players. This has made "translator" a new job category in certain sports. It also creates new challenges for leagues and coaches that have taken on athletes who speak very little English.

(*Source:* JUAN MABROMATA/AFP/Getty Images)

The six-person US table tennis team at the 2016 Olympic Games in Rio de Janeiro consisted of three players born in China, including Zheng Jiaqi (top) and Wu Yue, both of whom migrated to the US because there are thousands of players competing to make the Chinese team. Thirty-eight Chinese-born players at Rio 2016 represented 21 countries other than China out of 56 countries that sent table tennis teams to the Games. Worldwide, 32-percent of the national table tennis players from all nations with teams were born in China (Keh & Quealy, 2016).

Data from the 2016 Olympic Games in Rio de Janeiro indicated that at least 120 athletes from outside the US were members of US college and university teams as they participated in the Games. When Olympic-level athletes want to attend school and remain amateurs while they train with top coaches and state-of-the-art technology, they seek scholarships in the United States. They know that every Division I university with a full athletic program has training facilities, coaches, and support staff that surpass what is available at the national training centers in most other countries.

Global migration also leads to mixed nationalities and more people with dual or multiple passports. For athletes, this makes country swapping possible. The athlete wants to know: What country shall I represent, or in what country do I have the best chance of making the national team and going to the Olympics? When long-time professional basketball player Becky Hammon was given notice that the US national team had no room for her in 2008, she became a Russian citizen and played for the Russian national basketball team during the 2008 and 2012 Olympic Games. She was widely criticized for doing this, even though she lived part-time in Russia while playing for a professional team there. However, this strategy is used by hundreds of athletes whose mixed ancestry allows them to make choices about which nation to represent. For example, 46 members of 2016 US Olympic team were born in other countries but represented the United States because they had dual citizenship.

Just as some athletes choose to represent one country over another, some countries poach athletes from other countries by promising them rewards and putting them on a very fast track for citizenship. Citizenship can be acquired in less than a day if the country wants the athlete and the athlete agrees to its terms. This form of government involvement in sports is relatively common, and nearly all countries have a "back door" through which athletes can gain citizenship to participate on a national team, or obtain work visas if a professional team wants them to sign to a contract.

The United States now has anti-immigrant policies, but it waives rules for professional athletes who are granted a special O-1 or P-1 visa, which makes them guest workers with no questions asked and allows them to change teams as many times as they wish. No other workers are given such treatment. This special exemption from US immigration rules allows the NHL, NBA, and other leagues to operate outside normal citizenship and employment restrictions, even if US athletes could be hired instead of athletes from other countries. Members of Congress, even those who are anti-immigration, have allowed this to occur because they see sports as special. However, research is needed to investigate the impact of changing immigration policies on the recruitment of top professional athletes into the United States and into Great Britain now that it is no longer a member of the European Union. If either country decided to "send them back to where they came from," it would have a major impact on professional sports.

When athletes move from one country to another, regardless of their reasons, it raises issues related to (1) personal adjustments by migrating athletes; (2) the rights of athletes as workers; (3) the impact of talent migration on the nations from and to which athletes migrate; and (4) the national identities of athletes and fans (Beissel, 2020; Elliott, 2016; Engh & Agergaard, 2015; Evans & Piggott, 2016; Evans and Stead, 2014; Faulkner, Molnar & Kohe, 2019; Fry & Bloyce, 2017; Velema, 2018).

The personal experiences of migrating athletes vary from major culture shock and chronic loneliness to minor homesickness and lifestyle adjustments. Some athletes are exploited by teams or clubs, whereas others make much money and receive a hero's welcome when they return home during the off-season. Some encounter prejudice against foreigners or racial and ethnic bigotry, whereas others are socially accepted and form close friendships. Some cling to their national identities and socialize with fellow athletes from their homelands, whereas others develop global identities unrelated to any one national or cultural background. Some teams and clubs expect foreign athletes to adjust on their own; others provide support for those who must learn a new language or become familiar with new cultural norms.

Worker rights vary by nation, and athletes may find that they have more or less protection than they anticipated when it comes to working conditions and how they are treated by management. Much of this depends on their contracts, but state regulations may also apply beyond the contract.

The nations from which athletes are recruited usually have less power and resources than the recruiting countries. Over time, there may be such a depletion of talent in a country that the infrastructure for a particular sport is destroyed and local people are forced to follow the sport as it is played in the country that has taken all their best talent. This form of "sport talent drain" has a significant impact on countries in Africa and Latin America, where athletes seek contracts in Europe and North America.

At this point little is known about the impact of athlete migration on the identities of the athletes themselves and the feelings of national identity among people in the countries from which they emigrate. Do athletes become citizens of the country to which they are recruited? Does the move to a new country intensify or decrease their sense of national identity? Do people in the country from which athletes are recruited feel resentment about losing their best athletes, or do they see this recruitment as an affirmation of their ability to produce talent in sports? Research is needed to answer these questions.

Fans Fans have also gone global. Top European soccer clubs along with top professional sport teams in the United states have fans worldwide. Now that many people can receive streamed or televised coverage of games, matches, and events, they often choose to give their allegiance to teams and athletes outside their own countries. For example, young soccer fans in Slovenia may pay little attention to club teams in their country because all the top Slovenian soccer players play on professional teams in other countries across Europe. Many Latin American and African fans do the same thing. But in the process they may develop an attachment to one or more teams outside their countries and follow them for much of their lives, even when players from their country are no longer on the rosters.

For this reason, the NBA created a subsidiary, NBA China, in 2008 with offices in Beijing, Hong Kong, and Shanghai (and Taipei, Taiwan). In 2015 the NBA signed a $500 million partnership deal with Tencent, a major Chinese tech firm with 900 million online users. The 2018 NBA finals attracted more than 2 billion views on Weibo, a social media platform, and today, the NBA is the favorite sport league among the Chinese people (Team Goldthread, 2019). With 1.4 billion potential sport fans and consumers in China, most sport leagues now cultivate interest there, although the NBA has been the most successful with more fans than the top three European soccer leagues combined.

Following its success in China, the NBA has launched a new basketball league in Africa. It has established youth training facilities in multiple African nations and it plans to use the league as the starting point for a pipeline of players who can play in the NBA and as a way to build basketball to be as strong as soccer across the continent (Nir, 2019).

Making Sense of Political Realities

It's not easy to explain the relationships between sports and global political processes. Are sports today merely tools of capitalist expansion and new forms of cultural imperialism? Are they being used by wealthy nations to make poor, developing nations dependent on them, or do they enable emerging nations to achieve cultural and economic independence? As globalization occurs, are indigenous sports and folk games being replaced by the organized, competitive sports favored by wealthy and powerful nations?

Finding answers to these questions requires research at local *and* global levels. Existing studies suggest that sports favored by wealthy nations are not simply imposed on people worldwide. Even when people play sports that come from powerful nations, they give them meanings grounded in local cultures. Global trends are important, but so are the local expressions of and responses to those trends (Chen, 2012; Cho et al., 2012; Doczi, 2012; Gilmour and Rowe, 2012; Jijon, 2013; J. Joseph, 2012, 2014; Kobayashi, 2012; Maguire, 2019; Shor and Galily, 2012; Silk and Manley, 2012; Tan and Houlihan, 2012). Power is a process, and it is always exercised through relationships and current forms of social organization. Therefore, research on sports worldwide must examine the processes through which powerful nations exert control over sports in other nations as well as the processes through which people in those nations integrate sports and sport experiences into their lives on their own terms.

POLITICS IN SPORTS

The term *politics* usually is associated with formal government entities in the public sphere. However, politics include all processes of governing people and administering policies at all levels of organization, both public and private. Therefore, politics are an integral part of sports, and local, national, and international sports organizations are generally referred to as "governing bodies."

Most sports organizations provide and regulate sports participation opportunities, establish and enforce policies, control and standardize competitions, and acknowledge the accomplishments of athletes. This sounds like a straightforward set of tasks, but they seldom are accomplished without opposition, debate, and compromise (Green and Hartmann, 2012). Members of sports organizations agree on many things, but conflicts often arise as decisions are made in connection with the following seven questions:

1. *What qualifies as a sport?* There is no universal definition of sport, so each nation, community, and international event, such as the Olympic Games, must develop a definition that makes sense within its circumstances. As a result, official as well as unofficial definitions of "sport" vary widely.
2. *What are the rules of a sport?* The rules in all sports are arbitrary and changeable. The governing bodies of sports often change them to fit their interests or the circumstances in which the sports are played.
3. *Who makes and enforces the rules in sports?* The official rules of every sport are determined by the sport's governing body, but confusion occurs when various organizations representing the interests of different people all claim to be the primary governing body of a sport.
4. *Who organizes and controls sports events?* Until recently, members of the governing body of a sport organized and controlled competitions, but events today may be organized and partially controlled by third parties such as sponsors, media companies, or management groups that specialize in event organization.
5. *Where do sports events take place?* When athletes decide where to play a sport, they choose a place that is convenient for them. When events are staged for commercial purposes, they take place wherever they can generate the most revenue. In the case of international events such as the Olympic and Paralympic Games, various cities make bids to be the host and the members of the organization that owns the event (e.g., the IOC) select the bidding city that provides the most attractive proposal.
6. *Who is eligible to participate in a sport?* Eligibility decisions take into account factors that are defined as relevant by members of a governing body or people managing an event. Age, skill level, academic performance, gender, race/ethnicity, nationality, citizenship, place of residence, and other factors have been used to limit eligibility depending on the concerns and beliefs of the people making eligibility decisions.
7. *How are rewards distributed to athletes and others associated with sports?* When rewards are associated with participating in or staging an event, the question of "Who gets what?" is crucial to everyone involved. Rewards may include affirmations of status, such as a Most Valuable Player

(*Source:* HOTLI SIMANJUNTAK/EPA-EFE/Shutterstock)

Outside Southeast Asia, Sepak Takraw might be called kick volleyball with no hands or arms allowed; only feet, head, knees, and chest may contact the ball. Based on cuju, an ancient Chinese game, Sepak Takraw has been played in Vietnam, Malaysia, Indonesia, Laos, Thailand, and Myanmar for five centuries. If these nations had conquered and colonized parts of the world and used this game to socialize colonial subjects into their cultures, as did Europeans with their sports, it would exist in enough countries to qualify as an Olympic sport. This is how politics has influenced global sport forms.

award, or monetary compensation as in the case of revenue-producing sports. The distribution of money often creates friction between the players and the people who organize and manage the team or event.

These questions are inherently political because answers are determined in contexts where there are differences of interest that must be resolved through negotiation (Green and Hartmann, 2012). Most people understand this, but they complain about politics in sports when the outcomes of negotiations are not the ones they favor.

Athletes as Political Activists

When it comes to politics in sports, athletes are not known as or expected to be political activists. In fact, most people see sports as apolitical activities, and they object when anyone mixes them with politics. They want sports to be an escape from the complex, confusing, and contentious issues that exist in the rest of the world. If athletes publicly raise contentious political issues, engage in political protests, or speak critically of the status quo in society, they incur the wrath of many people, especially those privileged by the status quo. According to those people, athletes should stick to sports and limit their civic participation to charity work with sick or poor children.

Athletes know this, and over the past century, most of them have carefully avoided statements or displays of political activism that are critical of the status quo. Yet there is a long history of athletes who have used their visibility to take a stand against oppression, discrimination, and social injustice in sports and society (Bryant, 2019; CNN. 2018; Edwards, 2018/1968; Lazzeretti, 2018; Wulf, 2019; Zirin, 2008). The lists of these athletes indicate that most of them are black men and a few women who have called attention to racial discrimination in sports and racial oppression and injustice in society. Additionally, there are women from multiple racial and ethnic backgrounds who have called attention to gender barriers and inequities in sports and gender discrimination in society. A few out LGBTQ athletes have engaged in public activism about the forms of exclusion and discriminatory treatment they experience in sports and society. Some white male athletes have also engaged in political activism, but it has focused mostly on labor issues in sports.

Prior to the 1960s, political activism in the United States generally involved individual athletes. They often had private support from family and friends, but public support was lacking. They alone suffered the consequences of their activism and were dependent on a mostly biased mass media to represent their positions to the public. There were no computers, smartphones, or social media sites enabling them to represent themselves and clarify the nature and intent of their activism. Consequently, they were labeled as traitors and radicals who threatened the assumed purity of sports and values of the nation.

Although most of these athletes broke racial, ethnic, or gender barriers in sports, and advocated changes consistent with stated American values, their personal lives and careers were seriously disrupted and damaged. For example, in 1947, when Jackie Robinson, the black grandson of a slave and the son of a black sharecropper, became the first African American to play in modern Major League Baseball, he faced brutal racism and hatred from white people on and off the field. For Robinson, "sticking to sports" was, in itself, a form of political activism. It was not until 25 years later, after a Hall of Fame career, when he was writing his book, *I never had it made (1972),* that he publicly stated, "*I cannot stand and sing the anthem. I cannot salute the flag; I know that I am a black man in a white world.*" This led many white people to condemn him for his "lack of patriotism." Shortly thereafter, at age 53, he died of a heart attack.

The 1960s and Emerging Political Activism The emergence during the 1960s of social movements promoting racial civil rights, women's rights, antiwar (in Vietnam) sentiments, and students' rights changed the social and political landscape. The college and professional athletes who aligned themselves with these movements supported each other. Some formed political action groups that made collective statements critical of the status quo. The most noteworthy of these was the Olympic Project for Human Rights organized in 1967 by Harry Edwards. As a visiting professor as San Jose State University, Edwards had previously organized a protest calling attention to discrimination against black athletes at the university. The protest led to the cancellation of the university's season-opening football game in 1967 and then grew into the Olympic Project for Human Rights (OPHR).

The initial goal of OPHR was to have black athletes boycott the 1968 Olympic Games in Mexico City as a protest against global and national racial oppression. Many, but not all, black athletes boycotted the Games. Among those who did not boycott were John Carlos and Tommie Smith who, after winning bronze and gold medals in the 400-meter run, took off their shoes, stepped onto the victory podium and raised gloved fists to protest global poverty and racism as the anthem played. This action caused them to be expelled from the US team and sent back to the United States, where they were widely criticized and demeaned for more than 20 years. Nearly four decades later–in 2005, and after their lives had been turned upside down by race-based hate–they received honorary doctorates from San Jose State University, where a 23-foot-high statue now commemorates their commitment to the transformative goals of racial justice and the elimination of poverty.

Harry Edwards continued his activism and helped to found the sociology of sport and popularize it among younger scholars during the late-1960s and 1970s. His 1969 book, *The revolt of the black athlete*, served as a wake-up call that recruited black athletes and a few white allies into political activism. The book was also used in some sociology of sport courses, including mine, during the 1970s. Edwards' activism connected him with key figures in the civil rights movement in addition to evoking death threats from angry white Americans. As a faculty member at the University of California at Berkeley, Edwards taught standing room only classes and established the Institute for the Study of Social Change that inspired, among other things, sociology of sport research focused on social issues. As a scholar-activist, Edwards has remained on the cutting edge of sport-based activism, working most recently with professional athletes, including those on the San Francisco 49ers NFL team.

The 1980s and Beyond Activism among athletes, and in the US generally, faded during the 1980s through the early 21st century. When the Black Lives Matter movement emerged in 2013, primarily in response to cell phone videos of police brutality against black men, a number of black athletes and a few white athletes expressed concern about persisting racial oppression in the United States (Gill, 2016). For example, LeBron James and Kyrie Irving wore "I Can't Breathe" shirts before a Clevland Cavaliers games in December 2014 (Coombs & Cassilo, 2017). The shirts referred to the last words of Eric Garner, an unarmed African American man, who had been killed by an illegal chokehold applied by a New York City police officer (who was eventually fired from the police force in 2019). About the same time, Tamir Rice, a 12-year-old African American boy was shot and killed by police on a Cleveland playground.

During the following two years–2015 and 2016–a record number of young black men were killed by police. They were killed at a rate that was nine times higher than was the case for young white men; in fact, one of every 65 deaths of young black men during that time was a killing by police (Swaine et al., 2015; Swain & McCarthy, 2016). Colin Kaepernick, the African American Super Bowl quarterback of the San Francisco 49ers studied this situation with the assistance of Harry Edwards and decided that he had to make people aware of this situation and call for investigations and action before more black men his age were killed. To do that, he sat and then knelt on one knee as the national anthem played before the preseason games in August and September 2016 and through most of the season. He was joined by teammates Eric Reid and Eli Harold (see photo in next column).

When first asked about his actions, Kaepernick said the following:

> *I am not going to stand up to show pride in a flag for a country that oppresses black people and people of color. To me, this is bigger than football and it would be selfish on my part to look the other way. There are bodies in the street and people getting . . . away with murder* (Wyche, 2016)

Then presidential candidate, Donald Trump, responded to Kaepernick by saying, *". . . maybe he should find a country that works better for him"* (The Irish News, 2017). Kaepernick clarified his motives by explaining, *Once again, I'm not anti-American. I love America. . . . That's why I'm doing this. I want to help make America better* (Mather, 2019); and he gave $2 million to community organizations working for change. In response, President Barack Obama stated the following:

> *I think he cares about some real, legitimate issues that have to be talked about. . . . I support our players when they want to see change in society, and we don't live in a perfect society* (Mather, 2019).

At the same time, white NFL fans booed Kaepernick and Reid during the 2016 season,

(*Source:* Thearon W. Henderson/Getty Images)

Eli Harold #58, Colin Kaepernick #7, and Eric Reid #35 of the San Francisco 49ers kneel during the national anthem prior to an NFL game in 2016. They and other black players initiated what has become a 3-year debate. Their supporters emphasize Kaepernick's stand on "the oppression of black people and people of color," whereas his detractors emphasize respect for the flag and national anthem. As with most debates that involve race in the United States, most white people resist acknowledging ongoing or even past racial discrimination and oppression. When people of color raise such issues, they are accused of being unpatriotic.

after which both players were released from the 49ers without explanation, and Kaepernick has not played since then.

The actions of Kaepernick, Reid and other NFL players who joined in their call for awareness of racial injustice spread through the United States. Players on high school and college teams knelt during the national anthem, as did Megan Rapinoe on the US women's national soccer team. This created a national discussion and debate with many white people saying that athletes should "stick to sports" and avoid politics, and many black people sticking up for and supporting Kaepernick and others. This led then President Donald Trump to say at the beginning of the 2017 NFL season that if a player did not stand at attention with hand on heart for the national anthem, the team owners should "*get that son of a bitch off the field right now. Out! He's fired. He's fired!*" (Graham, 2017)

With black players making up over 70 percent of NFL rosters, and with the vast majority of fans, especially those buying season tickets and luxury boxes being white men, the NFL faced a challenge (Smith & Tryce, 2019). The league provided $89 million to a coalition of black players who were against kneeling before games but wanted to engage in community action. That split the black players into two groups with media focused on their disagreements rather than the original issues raised by Kaepernick, Reid, and others (Fletcher, 2018). But those issues did not go away as the number of young black men killed by police hit near-record numbers in 2017 and 2018. Afraid that fans supportive of the issues raised by Kaepernick and his supporters were being alienated as teams refused to offer him a contract, the NFL joined with billionaire music mogul Jay-Z (Shawn Carter) and his Roc Nation in 2019 to plan halftime entertainment shows at games and to explore what could be done in a new NFL program called "Inspire Change."

Where this business alliance will lead is not clear. In the meantime, many black NFL players are skeptical of the alliance, and athletes across multiple sports continue to kneel during the national anthem as they call attention to racial injustice (Bieler, 2019a, 2019b; Brewer, 2019; Henao, 2019; Jones, 2019; Pascal, 2019). This spirit of activism spread to Major League Soccer (MLS) where some fans attending matches in 2019 displayed signs emphasizing that they support an "anti-fascist, anti-racist, and radically inclusive" position in their cities (Ruthven, 2019). MLS and stadium officials have banned the signs because political displays are not allowed by the MLS, but fans say that the signs refer to human rights rather than politics. At the same time, the US women's national soccer team has accused US Soccer of gender discrimination in connection with their pay and working conditions–an issue that they say transcends soccer in the US and affects women worldwide (Wrack, 2019).

The fact that athletes now have access to social media and can explain their political positions and inject them into public discourse over long periods of time has altered the connection between sports and politics in the United States. Athletes in Europe and Latin America have not been as politically involved and expressive as athletes have recently been in the US, but soccer fans in those parts of the world regularly express their political positions and occasionally confront the military and police who try to control them at the request of political leaders who reject those positions. Overall, it is difficult to predict the future of politics in sports except to say that they are intertwined in ways that cannot be eliminated.

Eliminating politics in sports is not possible. However, it is possible to shape political processes so that the voices of all parties impacted by decisions are heard and taken into account. Many sports organizations are notorious for their lack of transparency and accountability, and this often makes their decisions contentious because people don't know how or why they were made. There will always be differences of interest, but people are more apt to accept political decisions when they have participated in the process of making them and when they can hold accountable those who make them.

summary

HOW DO GOVERNMENTS AND GLOBAL POLITICAL PROCESSES INFLUENCE SPORTS?

Sports and politics are inseparable. Government involvement in sports is generally related to the need for sponsorship, organization, and facilities. The fact that sports are important in people's lives and can be sites for social conflict often leads to government involvement. The forms of involvement vary by society, but their purposes are generally to (1) safeguard the public order; (2) ensure fairness and protect human rights; (3) maintain health and fitness among citizens; (4) promote the prestige and power of a community or nation; (5) promote nation building; (6) reproduce values consistent with dominant ideology; (7) increase support for political leaders and government; and (8) facilitate economic development.

The rules, policies, and funding priorities set by government officials and agencies reflect political differences and struggles among groups within a society. This doesn't mean that the same people always benefit when government involvement occurs, but involvement seldom results in equal benefits for everyone. For example, funding priorities could favor mass participation instead of elite sports, but this is subject to debate and negotiation. This political process is an inevitable part of organized sports.

History shows that government intervention in sports usually favors groups with the most resources and organization, and with goals that support the interests of public officials. The groups least likely to be favored are those that fail to understand the connection between sports and politics or lack resources to effectively influence political decisions. When people believe that sports and politics are unrelated, they're likely to be ignored when officials develop policies and allocate funds.

The connection between sports and global political processes is complex. Ideally, sports bring nations together in contexts supportive of peace and friendship. Although this can and does occur, most nations use sports to satisfy their own interests. Displays of nationalism continue to be common at international events. For example, people who work with, promote, or follow the Olympics often focus on national medal counts and use them to support their claims for national status.

If mega events such as the Olympics are indeed special events with positive potential, efforts should be made to maximize that potential. Limiting nationalism and commercialism and emphasizing the interdependence of nations would be helpful and could be done many ways.

Powerful transnational corporations have joined nation-states as major participants in global political processes. As a result, sports are used increasingly for economic as well as political purposes. Nationalism and the promotion of national interests remain part of global sports, but consumerism and the promotion of capitalist expansion have become more important since 1991 and the end of the Cold War.

Within the context of global relations, athletes and teams now are associated with corporate logos as well as nation-states. Global sports events have political and economic implications. They are sites for presenting numerous images and narratives associated with the interests of nation-states *and* corporate sponsors. The dominant discourses associated with sports in the United States are clearly consistent with the interests of corporate sponsors, and they promote an ideology infused with the capitalist values of individualism, competition, achievement, and consumption.

Global political processes also are associated with other aspects of sports, such as the migration patterns of elite athletes and the recruitment patterns of sport organizations. Political issues are raised when athletes cross national borders to play their sports and when leagues and teams bring players from multiple national backgrounds into their countries. The globalization of sports affects the ownership of teams, the movement of athletes around the globe, and the allegiance patterns of sport fans worldwide.

These and other issues associated with global political processes are best understood when studied on both global and local levels. Data in these studies help determine when sports involve reciprocal cultural exchanges leading to mutual understanding among people and when they involve processes through which powerful nations and corporations exercise subtle influence over social life and political events in less powerful nations.

Politics also are part of the structure and organization of sports. Political processes exist because people in sports organizations must answer questions about what qualifies as a sport, the rules of a sport, procedures for enforcing rules, the organization and control of sports events, the locations of events, eligibility criteria for participants, and distribution of rewards. These political issues are central to sports, and they illustrate why the organizations that make decisions about sports are often described as governing bodies.

Finally, athletes over the past century have raised political issues in the context of sports. Although this occurred occasionally in the past, the political awareness and vested interests of athletes today has led some of them to engage in more frequent political demonstrations in connection with their sports participation. The fact that they can use social media to stay connected and support each other and present issues in their own words to the public, means that political expressions are likely to remain a part of sports in the future. Overall, sports are inseparable from politics and political processes.

SUPPLEMENTAL READINGS

Reading 1. Politics in organized sports
Reading 2. Protests and boycotts: Politics and the Olympic Games
Reading 3. There's nothing so over as the World Cup
Reading 4. Global politics and the production of sports equipment and apparel
Reading 5. Qatar and Slovenia: Two approaches to using sports as a developmental strategy
Reading 6. The soccer stadium as a political protest site: Looking back at the Arab spring

SPORT MANAGEMENT ISSUES

- You are working for a new office of Sport and Community Development in a midwestern city of 1 million people. As the new director begins to outline a 5-year plan, she asks you to list all of the ways that the federal, state, county, and local governments are involved in sports in the city, especially in terms of funding. Identify all the possibilities that you will check out as you begin the project.
- You've been appointed by the International Olympic Committee to a special commission charged with prioritizing possible reforms of the Summer Olympic Games. At the first meeting, each member of the committee must present and justify three suggestions for reform. What are your suggestions, and how do you justify them?
- You work in the personnel office of the Major Soccer League (MSL) in the United States. You must make recommendations about the league's policies related to players who are not US citizens. You must deal with two major questions: (1) Should there be a limit, for each team or the league as a whole on the number of players who are not US citizens? (2) How should the league and its teams provide support for the athletes who come from other countries? Explain your responses and discuss them in the general context of the globalization of sports.
- As a sport management consultant, you are asked by the NFL to advise the league on what to do in response to political displays by players during the playing of the national anthem. The league fears that game attendance and television ratings will fall no matter what they decide to do. How would you advise the NFL in an effort to preserve spectator interest over time? List three possible strategies and explain why each would be useful and which one you think would be most useful.

references

Abbot, Sebastian. 2018. *The away game: The epic search for soccer's next superstars*. New York /London: W.W. Norton & Company, Inc.

Angelini, James R.; Paul J. MacArthur, Lauren Reichart Smith & Andrew C. Billings. 2017. Nationalism in the United States and Canadian primetime broadcast coverage of the 2014 Winter Olympics. *International Review for the Sociology of Sport* 52(7): 779–800.

Armour, Nancy. 2019 Sports' anthem play an excuse for patriotism. *USA Today* (March 15): 2C.

Barboza Eiras de Castro, Suélen; Fernando Augusto Starepravo, Jay Coakley & Doralice Lange de Souza. 2016. Mega sporting events and public funding of sport in Brazil (2004–2011). *Leisure Studies* 35(3): 369–386.

Beissel, Adam S. 2020. Transnational corporations of football kin: Migration, labor flow, and the American Samoa MIRAB economy. *Journal of Sport and Social Issues* 44(1): 47–69.

Bieler, Des. 2019a. Jay-Z has 'moved past kneeling.' Some NFL players have a problem with that. *Washington Post* (August 20): https://www.washingtonpost.com/sports/2019/08/20/jay-z-has-moved-past-kneeling-some-nfl-players-have-problem-with-that/

Bieler, Des. 2019b. US fencer Race Imboden given 12-month probation for Pan Am Games protest. *Washington Post* (August 20): https://www.washingtonpost.com/sports/2019/08/21/us-fencer-race-imboden-given-month-probation-pan-am-games-protest/

Booth, Douglas. 2011. Olympic city bidding: An exegesis of power. *International Review for the Sociology of Sport* 46(4): 367–386.

Bowes, Ali & Alan Bairner. 2019. Three Lions on her shirt: Hot and banal nationalism for England's sportswomen. *Journal of Sport and Social Issues* 43(6): 531–550.

Boykoff, Jules. 2014. *Celebration capitalism and the Olympic Games*. London/New York: Routledge.

Brewer, Jerry. 2019. Athlete activism is growing and diversifying, just i*n* time for the 2020 Olympics. *Washington Post* (August 13): https://www.washingtonpost.com/sports/2019/08/13/athlete-activism-is-growing-diversifying-just-time-olympics/

Bryant, Howard. 2019. *The heritage: Black athletes, a divided America, and the politics of patriotism*. Boston MA: Beacon Press.

Campbell, Denis & Daniel Boffey. 2012. Doctors turn on No 10 over failure to curb obesity surge. *The Observer* (April 14): http://www.theguardian.com/society/2012/apr/14/obesity-crisis-doctors-fastfood-deals-ban

Chen, Tzu-Hsuan. 2012. From the "Taiwan Yankees" to the New York Yankees: The glocal narratives of baseball. *Sociology of Sport Journal* 29(4): 546–558.

Cheng, Maria. 2012. UK doctors criticize McDonalds' Olympic sponsorship, say ads could worsen obesity epidemic. *Huffington Post* (May 1): http://www.huffingtonpost.com/2012/05/01/london-olympics-sponsor-mcdonalds-doctors-blast_n_1467109.html

Cho, Younghan, Charles Leary & Stephen J. Jackson. 2012. Glocalization and sports in Asia. *Sociology of Sport Journal* 29(4): 421–432.

CNN. 2018. A timeline of social activism in sports. *CNN.com* (January 9): https://www.cnn.com/2016/12/12/sport/gallery/social-activism-in-sports/index.html

Coakley, Jay & Doralice Lange Souza. 2013. Sport mega-events: Can legacies and development be equitable and sustainable? *Motriz, Rio Claro* 19(3): 58–589.

Coakley, Jay. 2002. Using sports to control deviance and violence among youths: Let's be critical and cautious." Pp. 13–30 in Margaret Gatz, Michael A. Messner, and Sandra J. Ball-Rokeach, eds., *Paradoxes of Youth and Sport*. Albany, NY: State University of New York Press.

Coakley, Jay. 2011. Ideology doesn't just happen: Sports and neoliberalism. *Revista da Associación Latinoamericana de Estudios Socioculturales del Deporto,* 1(1): 67–84.

Coalter, Fred. 2015.Sport-for-change: Some thoughts from a skeptic. *Social Inclusion* 3(3): 19–23.

Cole, Teju. 2012. The white savior industrial complex. *The Atlantic* (March 21): http://www.theatlantic.com/international/archive/2012/03/the-white-savior-industrial-complex/254843/ (retrieved 9–15–13).

Coombs, Danielle Sarver & David Cassilo. 2017. Athletes and/or activists: LeBron James and Black Lives Matter. *Journal of Sport and Social Issues* 41(5): 425–444.

Darnell, Simon C. 2012. *Sport for development and peace: A critical sociology*. New York: Bloomsbury Academic.

Davis, Christopher P. 2016. The Indian Premier League, the spectacle, and the illusion of a nation. *Journal of Sport and Social Issues* 40(2): 107–123.

de Nooij, Michiel and Marcel van den Berg. 2018. The bidding paradox: Why politicians favor hosting mega sports events despite the bleak economic prospects. *Journal of Sport and Social Issues* 42(1): 68–92.

DePetris, Daniel R. 2019. The war on terror's total cost: $5,900,000,000,000. *The National Interest* (January 12) https://nationalinterest.org/blog/skeptics/war-terrors-total-cost-5900000000000-41307

Dóczi, Tamás. 2012. Gold fever(?): Sport and national identity–The Hungarian case. *International Review for the Sociology of Sport* 47(2): 165–182.

Dorsey, James M. 2015. Egyptian soccer player criticizes Sisi in reflection of mounting discontent. *The Turbulent World of Middle East Soccer* (July 4): http://mideastsoccer.blogspot.co.uk/2015/07/egyptian-soccer-player-criticizes-sisi.html

Dorsey, James M. 2016. *The turbulent world of Middle East soccer*. Oxford UK: Oxford University Press.

Dorsey, James M. 2018a. Gulf crisis upends fiction of a separation of sports and politics. *The Turbulent World of Middle East Soccer* (February 26): https://mideastsoccer.blogspot.com/2018/02/gulf-crisis-upends-fiction-of.html

Dorsey, James M. 2018b. 2018 World Cup potentially set to become latest Middle Eastern battlefield. *The Turbulent World of Middle East Soccer* (June 3): https://mideastsoccer.blogspot.com/2018/06/2018-world-cup-potentially-set-to.html

Dorsey, James M. 2018c. Trouble in sport paradise: Can Qatar overcome the diplomatic crisis? *Revista Crítica de Ciências Sociais* 116, online, http://journals.openedition.org/rccs/7479

Duncan, Arne. 2013. We must provide equal opportunity in sports to students with disabilities. *US Department of Education* (January 25): http://www.ed.gov/blog/2013/01/we-must-provide-equal-opportunity-in-sports-to-students-with-disabilities/

Edwards, Harry. 2018/1968. *The revolt of the black athlete: 50th anniversary edition*. Champaign IL: University of Illinois Press.

Elliott, Richard. 2013. New Europe, new chances? The migration of professional footballers to Poland's Ekstraklasa. *International Review for the Sociology of Sport* 48(6): 736–750.

Elliott, Richard. 2016. Football's Irish exodus: Examining the factors influencing Irish player migration to English professional leagues. *International Review for the Sociology of Sport* 51(2): 147–161.

Engh, Mari Haugaa & Sine Agergaard. 2015. Producing mobility through locality and visibility: Developing a transnational perspective on sports labour migration. *International Review for the Sociology of Sport* 50(8): 974–992.

Evans, Adam B. & David E Stead. 2014. 'It's a long way to the Super League': The experiences of Australasian professional rugby league migrants in the United Kingdom. *International Review for the Sociology of Sport* 49(6): 707–727.

Evans, Adam B. & David Piggott. 2016. Shooting for Lithuania: Migration, national identity and men's basketball in the east of England. *Sociology of Sport Journal* 33(1): 26–38.

Faulkner, Christopher, Gyozo Molnar, Geoff Kohe. 2019. "I just go on wi-fi": Imagining worlds through professional basketball migrants' deployment of information and communication technology. *Journal of Sport and Social Issues* 43(3): 195–218.

Fletcher, Michael A. 2018. Kaepernick rarely speaks but still dominates every NFL conversation. *TheUndefeated.com* (January 30): https://theundefeated.com/features/kaepernick-rarely-speaks-but-national-anthem-protest-dominates-nfl-super-bowl-conversation/

Forde, Shawn D. 2015. Fear and loathing in Lesotho: An autoethnographic analysis of sport for development and peace. *International Review for the Sociology of Sport* 50(8): 958–973.

Fry, John & Daniel Bloyce. 2017. 'Life in the travelling circus': A Study of loneliness, work stress, and money issues in touring professional golf. *Sociology of Sport Journal* 34(2): 148–159.

Gill, Emmett, Jr. 2016. "Hands up, don't shoot" or shut up and play ball? Fan-generated media views of the Ferguson Five. *Journal of Human Behavior in the Social Environment* 26(3–4): 400–412.

Gilmour, Callum & David Rowe. 2012. Sport in Malaysia: National imperatives and Western seductions. *Sociology of Sport Journal* 29(4): 485–505.

Graham, Bryan Armen. 2017. Memo to Trump after his NFL rant: sport is, and always has been, political. *The Guardian* (September 24): https://www.theguardian.com/commentisfree/2017/sep/24/donald-trump-nfl-nba-steph-curry-lebron-james-roger-goodell

Green, Kyle & Doug Hartmann. 2012. Politics and sports: strange, secret bedfellows. *The Society Pages* (February 3): http://thesocietypages.org/papers/politics-and-sport/

Greider, William. 2006. Olympic swagger. *The Nation* (February 28): http://www.thenation.com/doc/20060313/greider2

Hartmann, Douglas, and Brooks Depro. 2006. Rethinking sports-based community crime prevention: A preliminary analysis of the relationship between midnight basketball and urban crime rates. *Journal of Sport and Social Issues* 30(2): 180–196.

Henao, Luis Andres. 2019. Race Imboden kneels and Gwen Berry raises her fist: Americans protest on the medals stand at the Pan Am Games. *Chicago Tribune* (August 11): https://www.chicagotribune.com/sports/breaking/ct-race-imboden-gwen-berry-athlete-protest-20190811-gceardedn5fyjclxim5b7qexta-story.html

Houlihan, Barrie. 2000. Politics and sport. In Jay Coakley and Eric Dunning, eds., *Handbook of sport studies* (pp. 213–227). London: Sage.

Huysmans, Zenzi, Damian Clement, Meredith Whitley, Matthew Gonzalez & Tammy Sheehy. 2019. "Putting kids first": An exploration of the Teaching Personal and Social Responsibility model to youth development in Eswatini. *Journal of Sport for Development* 7(13): 15–32.

Jackson, Steven J., and David L. Andrews, eds. 2004. *Sport, culture and advertising: Identities, commodities and the politics of representation.* London/New York: Routledge.

Jamieson, Katherine M. 2015. Making the global turn: The USLPGA, commissioner rhetoric of difference, and "new imperialism." *Journal of Sport and Social Issues* 39(6): 501–520.

Jennings, Andrew, and Clare Sambrook. 2000. *The great Olympic swindle: When the world wanted its games back.* New York: Simon and Schuster.

Jennings, Andrew. 1996a. *The new lords of the rings.* London: Pocket Books.

Jennings, Andrew. 1996b. Power, corruption, and lies. *Esquire* (May): 99–104.

Jennings, Andrew. 2006. *Foul! The secret world of FIFA—bribes, vote rigging, and ticket scandals.* New York, NY: HarperSport.

Jennings, Andrew. 2013a. DavosMan takes control at FIFA. *Transparency in Sport News* (April 8): http://transparencyinsportblog.wordpress.com/2013/04/08/davosman-takes-control-at-fifa/

Jennings, Andrew. 2013b. Have the FBI got FIFA's bribe emails and offshore bank accounts? *Transparency in Sport News* (July 25):

http://transparencyinsportblog.wordpress.com/page/2/

Jijon, Isabel. 2013. The glocalization of time and space: Soccer and meaning in Chota Valley, Ecuador. *International Sociology* 28(4): 373–390.

John, Alastair, and Steve Jackson. 2011. Call me loyal: Globalization, corporate nationalism and the America's Cup. *International Review for the Sociology of Sport* 46(4): 399–417.

Jones, Jonathan. 2019. The sliver of hope for Jay-Z's NFL ambitions. *SI.com* (August 21): https://www.si.com/nfl/2019/08/21/jay-z-nfl-partnership-ownership-eric-reid-colin-kaepernick-blackball-kenny-stills

Joseph, Janelle. 2012. The practice of capoeira: Diasporic black culture in Canada. *Ethnic and Racial Studies* 35(6): 1078–1095.

Joseph, Janelle. 2014. Culture, community, consciousness: The Caribbean sporting diaspora. *International Review for the Sociology of Sport* 49(6): 669–687.

Keh, Andrew & Kevin Quealy. 2016. At least 44 table tennis players in Rio are Chinese-born. Six play for China. *New York Times* (August 17): https://www.nytimes.com/2016/08/18/sports/olympics/at-least-44-table-tennis-players-in-rio-are-chinese-born-six-play-for-china.html

Kennelly, Jacqueline. 2017. Symbolic violence and the Olympic Games: Low-income youth, social legacy commitments, and urban exclusion in Olympic host cities. *Journal of Youth Studies* 20(2): 145–161.

Kidd, Bruce. 1996. Taking the rhetoric seriously: Proposals for Olympic education. *Quest* 48(1): 82–92.

Kobayashi, Koji. 2012. Globalization, corporate nationalism and Japanese cultural intermediaries: Representation of bukatsu through Nike advertising at the global–local nexus. *International Review for the Sociology of Sport* 47(6): 724–742.

Kohe, Geoffery Z. & Will Bowen-Jones, 2016. Rhetoric and realities of London 2012 Olympic education and participation 'legacies': Voices from the core and periphery. *Sport, Education & Society* 21(8): 1213–1229.

Lazzeretti, Craig. 2018. Athlete activists who changed the world. *StadiumTalk.com* (October 12): https://www.stadiumtalk.com/s/most-influential-athlete-activists-changed-society-cfd0aedd8cf9428f

Lipsyte, Robert. 1996. One fell swoosh: Can a logo conquer all? *New York Times,* section B (February 7): 9.

Los Angeles Municipal Code. 2013a. Chapter IV, General welfare; Article 6, Public hazards; SEC. 56.15. Bicycle riding-sidewalks. Online: http://www.amlegal.com/nxt/gateway.dll/California/lamc/municipalcode?f=templates$fn=default.htm$3.0$vid=amlegal:losangeles_ca_mc

Los Angeles Municipal Code. 2013b. Chapter IV, General welfare; Article 6, Public hazards; SEC. 56.16. Streets–Sidewalks–Playing ball or games of sport. Online: http://www.amlegal.com/nxt/gateway.dll/California/lamc/municipalcode?f=templates$fn=default.htm$3.0$vid=amlegal:losangeles_ca_mc

Maguire, Joseph. 2019. The making of modern sports: Diffusion, emulation, and resistance. In Joseph Maguire, Mark Falcous & Katie Liston, eds. *The business and culture of sports: Sociocultural perspectives* (Vol. 2, pp. 223–238). Farmington Hills, MI: Macmillan Reference USA.

Mather, Victor. 2019. A timeline of Colin Kaepernick vs. the N.F.L. *New York Times* (February 5): https://www.nytimes.com/2019/02/15/sports/nfl-colin-kaepernick-protests-timeline.html

Moran, Jerry & Richard Blumenthal. 2019. *The courage of survivors: A call to action.* Washington DC: Offices of Senator Jerry Moran & Senator Richard Blumenthal. Online, https://www.moran.senate.gov/public/_cache/files/c/2/c232725e-b717-4ec8-913e-845ffe0837e6/FCC5DFDE2005A2EACF5A9A25FF76D538.2019.07.30-the-courage-of-survivors–a-call-to-action-olympics-investigation-report-final.pdf

Müller, Martin & Christopher Gaffney, 2018. Comparing the urban impacts of the FIFA World Cup and Olympic Games from 2010 to 2016. *Journal of Sport and Social Issues* 42(4): 247–269.

Niles, Emma. 2017. How the Pentagon paid for NFL displays of patriotism. *Truthdig.com* (September 26): https://www.truthdig.com/articles/pentagon-paid-nfl-displays-patriotism/

Nir, Sarah Maslin. 2019. The N.B.A. is pushing into Africa. Can It Compete With Soccer? *New York Times* (July 23): https://www.nytimes.com/2019/07/23/sports/basketball/nba-africa-league-senegal.htm.l

Nols, Zeno, Rein Haudenhuyse & Marc Theeboom. 2017. Urban sport-for-development initiatives and young people in socially vulnerable situations: Investigating the 'Deficit Model.' *Social Inclusion* 5(2): 210–222.

O'Reilly, Lara. 2012. McDonald's, Coke defend Olympic choice. *Marketing Week* (July 10): http:// www.marketingweek.com/2012/07/10/mcdonalds-coke-defend-olympic-choice/

Oillaux, Carrie. 2018. Sport versus patriotism. *SportandDev.org* (June 13): https://www.sportanddev.org/en/article/news/sport-versus-patriotism

Pascal, David R. 2019. Carl Lewis – Harsh words for Trump at Pan American Games. *thevoiceslu.com* (August): https://thevoiceslu.com/2019/08/carl-lewis-harsh-words-for-trump-at-pan-american-games/

Peachey, Jon Welty, Allison Musser, Na Ri Shin & Adam Cohen. 2018. Interrogating the motivations of sport for development and peace practitioners. *International Review for the Sociology of Sport* 53(7): 767–787.

Penfold, Tom. 2019. National identity and sporting mega-events in Brazil. *Sport in Society* 22(3): 384–398.

Pettigrew, Stephen & Danyel Reiche. 2016. Hosting the Olympic Games: An overstated advantage in sports history. *The International Journal of the History of Sport* 33(6/7): 635–647.

Poniatowska, Elena. 1975. *Massacre in Mexico* (original title *La noche de Tlatelolco;* translated by Helen R. Lane). New York: Viking Books.

Rowe, David. 2013. Reflections on communication and sport: On nation and globalization. *Communication & Sport* 1(1/2): 18–29.

Ruthven, Graham. 2019. MLS and Antifa: America's top flight grapples with political signage ban. *The Guardian US* (August 21): https://www.theguardian.com/football/2019/aug/21/mls-and-antifa-americas-top-flight-grapples-with-political-signage-ban

Sanders, Ben & Jay Coakley. 2020. Leveling the playing field: Investing in grassroots sports as the best bet for sustainable development. In Maguire, Joseph, Katie Liston & Mark Falcous, eds. *Palgrave Handbook of Globalisation and Sport*. London: Palgrave.

Sanders, Ben. 2016. An own goal in sport for development: Time to change the playing field. *Journal of Sport Development* 4(6): online, http://repository.uwc.ac.za/bitstream/handle/10566/2166/Sanders_own%20goal_2016.pdf

Schausteck de Almeida, Barbara, Suélen Barboza Eiras de Castro, Fernando Marinho Mezzadri, & Doralce Lange de Souza. 2018. Do sports mega-events boost public funding in sports programs? The case of Brazil (2004–2015). *International Review for the Sociology of Sport* 53(6): 685–705.

Schausteck de Almeida, Barbara; Jay Coakley, Wanderley Marchi Júnior & Fernando Augusto Starepravo. 2012: Federal government funding and sport: the case of Brazil, 2004–2009. *International Journal of Sport Policy and Politics* 4(3): 411–426.

Scherer, Jay & Steve Jackson. 2010. *Globalization, sport and corporate nationalism*. Pieterlen, Switzrland: Peter Lang AG.

Schofield, Edward, Daniel J. A. Rhind & Richard Blair. 2018. Human rights and sports mega-events: The role of moral disengagement in spectators. *Journal of Sport and Social Issues* 42(1): 3–22.

Shor, Eran, and Yair Galily. 2012. Between adoption and resistance: Grobalization and glocalization in the development of Israeli basketball. *Sociology of Sport Journal* 29(4): 526–545.

Silk, Michael L., and Andrew Manley. 2012. Globalization, urbanization & sporting spectacle in Pacific Asia: Places, peoples & pastness. *Sociology of Sport Journal* 29(4): 455–484.

Smith, Brent & Stephanie A. Tryce. 2019. Understanding emerging adults' national attachments and their reactions to athlete activism. *Journal of Sport and Social Issues* 43(3): 167–194.

Starr, M. 1999. Voices of the century: Blood, sweat, and cheers. *Newsweek* 134, 17 (October 25): 44–73.

Storm, Rasmus K. & Tor Georg Jakobsen. 2019. National pride, sporting success and event hosting: an analysis of intangible effects related to major athletic tournaments. *International Journal of Sport Policy and Politics*; published online: 06 Aug 2019.

Sullivan, Jonathan, Simon Chadwick & Michael Gow. 2019. China's football dream: Sport, citizenship, symbolic power, and civic spaces. *Journal of Sport and Social Issues* 43(6): 493–514.

Swaine, Jon & Ciara McCarthy. 2016. Killings by US police logged at twice the previous rate under new federal program. *The Guardian US* (December 15): https://www.theguardian.com/us-news/2016/dec/15/us-police-killings-department-of-justice-program

Swaine, Jon, Oliver McLaughland, Jamiles Lartey & Ciara McCarthy. 2015. Young black men killed by US police at highest rate in year of 1,134 deaths. *The Guardian US* (December 31): https://www.theguardian.com/us-news/2015/dec/31/the-counted-police-killings-2015-young-black-men

Tan, Tien-Chin, and Barrie Houlihan. 2012. Chinese Olympic sport policy: Managing the impact of globalization. *International Review for the Sociology of Sport* 48(2): 131–152.

Team Goldthread. 2019. How the NBA became China's favorite sports league. *Team Goldthread* (April 25): https://www.goldthread2.com/videos/nba-basketball-chinas-favorite-sport/article/3007773

The Irish News. 2017. A timeline of the NFL protests from Colin Kaepernick's to now. *The Irish News* (September 25): https://www.irishnews.com/magazine/daily/2017/09/25/news/a-timeline-of-the-nfl-protests-from-colin-kaepernick-s-to-now-1145483/

Tobar, Felipe & Luana Gusso. 2017. "Becoming Brazilian: The making of national identity through football." *The International Journal of Sport and Society* 8(2): 37–49.

US News & World Report. 1983. A sport fan's guide to the 1984 Olympics. *US News & World Report* (May 9): 124.

Usher, Lindsay E. 2017. "Foreign locals": Transnationalism, expatriates, and surfer identity in Costa. *Journal of Sport and Social Issues* 41(3): 212–238.

Velema, Thijs A. 2018. A game of snakes and ladders: Player migratory trajectories in the global football labor market. *International Review for the Sociology of Sport* 53(6): 706–725.

Volpi, Frederic. 2006. Politics. In Bryan S. Turner, ed., *The Cambridge dictionary of sociology* (pp. 445–447). Cambridge, UK: Cambridge University Press.

Weber, Max. 1968/1922a. *Economy and society: An outline of interpretive sociology*. Translated by G. Roth and G. Wittich. New York: Bedminster Press.

Weliver, David. 2019. How much do Olympic (both summer and winter) athletes earn? *MoneyUnder30.com* (March 19): https://www.moneyunder30.com/how-much-do-olympic-athletes-earn

Whigham, Stuart, Hibai Lopez-Gonzalez & Xavier Ramon. 2019. "Més que un joc?": Sport and contemporary political nationalism in Scotland and Catalonia. *Journal of Sport and Social Issues* 43(3): 219–244.

Willingham, AJ. 2017. The national anthem in sports (spoiler: it wasn't always this way).

CNN.com (September 25): https://www.cnn.com/2017/09/25/us/nfl-national-anthem-trump-kaepernick-history-trnd/index.html

Wrack, Suzanne. 2019. The US team's dispute over pay is a fight for women all over the world. *The Guardian US* (August 18): https://www.theguardian.com/football/2019/aug/18/us-women-soccer-pay-dispute-megan-rapinoe

Wulf, Steve. 2019. Athletes and activism: The long, defiant history of sports protests. *TheUndefeated.com* (January 30): https://theundefeated.com/features/athletes-and-activism-the-long-defiant-history-of-sports-protests/

Wyche, Steve. 2016. Colin Kaepernick explains why he sat during national anthem. *NFL.com* (August 28): http://www.nfl.com/news/story/0ap3000000691077/article/colin-kaepernick-explains-protest-of-national-anthem

Yu, Lin, Hanhan Xue & Joshua J. Newman. 2018. Sporting Shanghai: Haipai cosmopolitanism, glocal cityness, and urban policy as mega-event. *Sociology of Sport Journal* 35(4): 301–313.

Zirin, Dave. 2008. *A people's history of sports in the United States*. New York NY: The New Press.

chapter

14

(*Source:* Matthew Pearce/Icon Sports Wire/Getty Images)

SPORTS IN HIGH SCHOOL AND COLLEGE

Do Competitive Sports Contribute to Education?

The problem with sports is once you combine it with academics, it starts to take over. So you have to be constantly vigilant to control it and make sure you're sending kids a message about what's going to serve their interests for decades to come.

–Amanda Ripley, journalist and author (in Martin, 2013)

. . . under the right circumstances, school-based sports place the participant at the center of a social network that reinforces commitment to the school and mandates conformity to conventional expectations.

–Steven Overman, physical educator (2019)

What counts as misbehavior in this swamp [of big time college sports] is a murky subject. . . improvement of the multibillion-dollar entertainment industry that is parasitic off educational institutions must begin by forcing it to confront its foundational hypocrisy about amateurism.

–George Will, columnist, *Washington Post* (2019)

Look, football and school don't go together. They just don't. Trying to do both is like trying to do two full-time jobs. . . . "Any time any player puts into school will take away from the time they could put into football. They don't realize that they're getting screwed until it's too late.

–Josh Rosen, UCLA quarterback (in Hayes, 2017)

Chapter Outline

Learning Objectives

- Identify the arguments for and against interscholastic sports.
- Discuss the research findings about the experiences of athletes in high schools.
- Know the ways that varsity sports influence student culture and the overall social organization of high schools in the United States.
- Explain the conditions under which interscholastic sports may be valuable in high schools and in the lives of students who play sports.
- Identify differences between intercollegiate sports in big-time athletic programs and smaller, lower profile programs.
- Explain the research findings on the experiences of college athletes and how participation in sports is related to grades and graduation rates.
- Assess popular beliefs about the benefits of varsity sports for high schools and colleges.
- Identify the major issues faced by both high school and college sport programs, and explain how they might influence school-sponsored sports in the future.
- Identify the major scandals that have occurred recently in college sports and explain how the legal challenges now facing the NCAA may impact college sports in the future.
- Explain why some athletes of color have become socially isolated on predominantly white college campuses.

The emergence of today's organized sports is closely linked with schools in England and North America. However, the United States is the only nation in the world where it is taken for granted that high schools and colleges sponsor and fund interschool varsity sports programs. In most countries, organized sports for school-aged young people are sponsored by community-based athletic clubs funded by members or through a combination of public and private sources.

High schools and universities outside the United States may have teams, but they are not solely dependent on individual schools or school systems (Brown, 2015; Pot et al., 2014; Ridpath, 2018). Additionally, their meaning and purpose are unlike the meanings given to school teams in the United States, they often are organized and managed by students, and they are not integral to the culture and social organization of the schools.

Interscholastic sports are an accepted and important part of US high schools and colleges, but when they dominate the cultures and public profiles of schools, many people become concerned about their role in education.

This chapter is organized around four questions about interscholastic sports programs:

1. What claims do people make when they argue for and against the programs?
2. How are sports programs related to education and the experiences of students?
3. What effects do sports programs have on the organization of schools and the achievement of educational goals?
4. What are the major problems associated with high school and college sports programs and how might they be solved?

ARGUMENTS FOR AND AGAINST INTERSCHOLASTIC SPORTS

Most people in the United States don't question the existence of school-sponsored sports. However, budget cutbacks and highly publicized problems in some programs raise questions about the relationship between these sports, the development of young people, and the achievement of educational goals. Responses to these questions vary and almost always are based on strong emotions rather than good research evidence.

Program supporters claim that interscholastic sports promote the educational mission of schools and the development of young people. Critics claim that they interfere with that mission and distract students from learning and taking seriously their emerging responsibilities as citizens. The main points made on both sides of this debate are summarized in Table 14.1.

When people enter this debate, they often exaggerate the benefits or problems associated with interscholastic sports. Supporters emphasize glowing success stories, and critics emphasize shocking cases of excess and abuse. Research suggests that the most accurate descriptions lie somewhere in between these extreme positions. Nonetheless, supporters and critics call our attention to the relationship between sports and education. This chapter focuses on what we know about that relationship.

INTERSCHOLASTIC SPORTS AND THE EXPERIENCES OF HIGH SCHOOL STUDENTS

Do interscholastic sports affect the educational and developmental experiences of high school students? This question is difficult to answer. Education and development occur in connection with many activities and relationships. Even though interscholastic sports are important in most schools and the lives of many students, they constitute only one of many potentially influential experiences in the lives of young people.

Quantitative research on this issue has seldom been guided by social theories, and it generally consists of comparing the characteristics of athletes with the characteristics of other students. Qualitative research, often based on a critical approach and

Table 14.1 Claims made in arguments for and against interscholastic sports

Claims For	Claims Against
1. They involve students in school activities and increase interest in academic activities.	1. They distract students from academic activities and distort values in school culture.
2. They build self-esteem, responsibility, achievement orientation, and teamwork skills required for occupational success today.	2. They perpetuate dependence, conformity, and a power and performance orientation that is no longer useful in society.
3. They foster fitness and stimulate interest in physical activities among students.	3. They turn most students into passive spectators and cause too many serious injuries to athletes.
4. They generate unity and identification with the school that maintains it as a viable organization.	4. They create a superficial, transitory spirit unrelated to educational goals.
5. They promote parental, alumni, community, and government support for school programs.	5. They deprive educational programs of resources, facilities, staff, and community support.
6. They give students opportunities to develop and display skills in activities valued in society and to be recognized for their competence.	6. They create pressure on athletes and support a hierarchical status system in which athletes are unfairly privileged over other students.

guided by combinations of cultural, interactionist, and structural theories, has focused on the connections between interscholastic sports, the culture and organization of high schools, and the everyday lives of students.

High School Athletes[1]

Studies in the United States consistently show that high school athletes *as a group* generally have higher grade point averages, more positive attitudes toward school, lower rates of absenteeism, more interest in attending college, more years of college completed, greater career success, and better health than students who don't play school-sponsored sports.[2] These differences usually are modest, and it's difficult for researchers to separate the effects of sports participation from the effects of social class, family background, support from friends, identity issues, and other factors related to educational attitudes and achievement.

Membership on a school team is a valued status in most US schools, and for some students it seems to go hand in hand with positive educational experiences, reduced dropout rates, and increased identification with the school. However, research doesn't explain much about why sports participation affects students, and why it affects some differently from others.

[1]The term "student-athlete" is not used in this book because *all* members of school teams are students, just like band members and debaters. The NCAA promotes the use of this term as a political strategy to deflect the criticism that big-time college athletic programs are unrelated to the academic mission of universities and to prevent people from defining athletes as employees. I use the term "big-time" when referring to Division I universities and other colleges and universities that are Division I wannabes and operate that way.

[2]There are hundreds of these studies; the most methodologically respectable of these include the following: Brown (2015); Child Trends (2013); Eitle (2005); Fox et al. (2010); Guest and Schneider (2003); Hartmann (2008); Hoffman (2006); Hwang et al. (2016); Kniffin et al. (2015) Lipscomb (2006); Miller et al. (2005); Morris (2015); Pearson et al. (2009); Pot et al. (2014); Schultz (2017); Shakib et al. (2011); Shifrer et al. (2013, 2015); Troutman and Dufur (2007).

Why Are Athletes Different? The most logical explanation for differences between athletes on school teams and other students is that school-sponsored sports attract young people who have good grades and self-confidence, and are socially popular in school.

Most researchers don't have information about the pre-participation characteristics of athletes because they collect data at one point in time and simply compare students who play on sport teams with students who don't. These studies are limited because they don't show that playing school sports changes young people in ways that would not have occurred otherwise.

Fourteen- to 18-year-olds grow and develop in many ways whether they play school sports or do other things. This is an important point, because young people who play on varsity teams are more likely than other students to come from economically privileged backgrounds and have above-average cognitive abilities, self-esteem, and past academic performance records, including grades and test scores (Child Trends, 2013; Hartmann et al., 2012; Morris, 2015; Shakib et al., 2011; Shifrer et al., 2013). Therefore, students who try out for, make, and stay on school teams are different from other students *before* they play high school sports.

This *selection-in process* is common; students who participate in official, school-sponsored activities tend to be different from other students. This difference is greatest in activities in which student self-selection is combined with eligibility requirements and formal tryouts in which teachers or coaches select students for participation. Additionally, this combination of self-selection, eligibility, and coach selection, is an extension of a long-term process that begins in youth sports. Over time, students with lower grades and poor disciplinary records decide they don't want to be involved in sports, or they aren't academically eligible to participate, or coaches see them as troublemakers and cut them during tryouts.

Research also shows that students who play varsity sports for three years during high school are different from those who are cut from or quit teams. Those who are cut or quit are more likely to come from less advantaged economic backgrounds, have lower cognitive abilities, lower self-esteem, and lower grade point averages than those who remain on teams (Child Trends, 2013; Pearson et al., 2009; Pot et al., 2014; Shifrer et al., 2013). Furthermore, athletes who receive failing grades are declared ineligible and become "nonathletes" and have their low grades included in the "nonathlete category" when researchers collect data and compare the grades of eligible athletes with the grades of nonathletes. This creates unreliable research results.

A factor that has not been studied is the control that parents, teachers, and coaches have over the lives of athletes on school teams, especially when the athletes are "in season" and their daily activities, especially academic activities, are closely monitored by coaches and parents (Schultz, 2017). Homework checks, study halls, grade checks, class attendance, and even assessment of dress code conformity are standard procedures in the lives of athletes when their season is ongoing. Although this probably adds structure to daily schedules, its impact on learning, academic achievement, and general development is not known.

Overall, school sports have selection-in, filtering-out, and in-season control processes, each of which contributes to differences between athletes and other students even though these differences have nothing to do with the impact of sports participation itself on various aspects of development. To control for these processes and determine if and when playing sports produces unique, positive educational or developmental outcomes, researchers must collect data at regular intervals over multiple years from an entire sample of students so they can measure and track changes that are due to sports participation rather than other things.

Studying Athletes in Context Research published over the past half century presents mixed and confusing findings about the effects of playing school sports. This is because most researchers assume that playing on a school team has the same meaning in all contexts for all athletes in all sports and therefore must have the same consequences. But this is not true. Meanings vary widely depending on three factors:

1. The status given to athletes and sports in various school and community contexts
2. The identities that young people develop or fail to develop because they play sports
3. The ways that young people integrate sports and an athlete identity into their lives

For example, playing on a junior varsity team or being a mediocre player on a varsity fencing team often has different implications for the status and identity of a young man in comparison with being an all-state football or basketball player on a state-championship team–even if the fencer is on a team at a private school that has produced many college and Olympic champions in that sport. Similarly, being a young woman ranked the number-one high school tennis player in the state would involve different status and identity implications from being a young woman who is a substitute on the junior varsity softball team.

(*Source:* Jay Coakley)

Self-selection, combined with academic eligibility and coach selection, ensures that athletes often have different characteristics from other students before they ever play on school teams. Athletes may learn positive and/or negative things in sports, but it's difficult to separate those things from other forms of learning and development that occur during adolescence.

When researchers at the University of Chicago used data collected over 4 years from two large samples of high school students, they found that athletes at schools located in low-income areas were more likely to be identified as good students than were athletes playing at schools located in upper-middle-income and wealthy areas (Guest and Schneider, 2003). Additionally, having an athlete identity was positively associated with grades in schools located in lower-income areas but negatively associated with grades in wealthier areas where taking sports too seriously was possibly seen as interfering with preparing for college and careers. Therefore, the academic implications of being an interscholastic athlete depends on the different meanings given to playing sports and having an athlete identity in different social class contexts in American society (Hwang et al., 2016; Morris, 2015; Shakib et al., 2011; Shifrer et al., 2013, 2015; Wann et al., 2015).

Research also indicates that the meanings given to playing interscholastic sports vary by gender and have changed since the late 1960s (Fox et al., 2010; Miller et al., 2005; Miller and Hoffman, 2009; Pearson et al., 2009; Shifrer et al., 2013, 2015; Troutman and Dufur, 2007). For example, young women on school teams have had lower rates of sexual activity (that is, fewer sex partners, lower frequency of intercourse, and later initiation of sexual activity) than their female peers who didn't play sports. However, young men on school teams had higher rates of sexual activity than other young men in the schools (Miller et al., 1998, 1999). This difference persists because playing on school teams enhances the social status of young people and gives them more power to regulate sexual activity on their own terms (Kreager and Staff, 2009).

During the 1990s, it appears that many young women used this power to resist sexual relationships that they defined as inappropriate or exploitive, whereas young men used their power to gain sexual favors from young women. But these patterns identified in studies done twenty years ago could be different today or change in the future as the meanings given to being on school teams change and as there are shifts in students' ideas about sexual relationships.

Research also suggests that identifying oneself exclusively as an athlete in some US high schools connects a student with peers who are socially gregarious and more likely than other students to engage in risky actions such as heavy and binge drinking (Miller and Hoffman, 2009; Miller et al., 2005; Veliz et al., 2017). This issue needs more study, but it seems that playing on certain school teams provides students with more choices for aligning themselves with various cliques or social groups that have different priorities for what they like to do. The choices made by athletes probably influence how others identify them and where they fit into the overall social organization of the school. In some cases, this "positions" them with others who value academic work, whereas in other cases, it positions them so they focus on social activities with other who like to party even if it detracts from academic achievement.

Identifying the influence of playing high school sports in a person's adult life is much more difficult than identifying the changes that occur during late adolescence. The meanings people give to their own sports participation change over time and vary with a wide range of social and cultural factors related to gender, race and ethnicity, and social class. For example, when we hear that many CEOs of large corporations played sports in high school, it tells us nothing about the role of sports participation in the long, complex process of becoming a CEO. The occupational experiences of top CEOs, most of whom are white men, are strongly related to their family backgrounds and social networks, and cannot be separated from the gender, ethnic, and class relations that exist in the United States. This does not mean that these men didn't work hard or that playing sports was unrelated to their development, but the importance of sports participation cannot be understood apart from many other factors that are clearly related to becoming a CEO.

Overall, research in the sociology of sport indicates that the effects of playing school sports depend on the contexts in which sports are played, the organization of sports programs and teams, and the social characteristics of athletes (Crissey and Honea, 2006; Fox et al., 2010; Hartmann, 2008; Hartmann and Massoglia, 2007; Hartmann et al., 2012; Overman, 2018; Pearson et al., 2009). Therefore, when young, white women from upper-middle-class families play lacrosse in a small, private, elite prep school where grades are all-important, the effects of participation are likely to be different from the effects that occur when young ethnic minority men from working-class families play football in a large public school where they have opportunities to be noticed in positive ways and to connect with adult mentors that are missing in the lives of their peers (Zarrett, Veliz & Sabo, 2018).

Student Culture in High Schools

Sports are usually among the most important activities sponsored by high schools, and being on a school team can bring students prestige among peers, formal rewards in the school, and recognition from teachers, administrators, and people in the local community. Athletes, especially boys in high-profile sports, often are accorded recognition that enhances their popularity in student culture. Pep rallies, homecomings, and other sports events are major social occasions on school calendars. Students often enjoy these events because they provide opportunities for social interaction outside the classroom. Parents favor them because they're associated with the school and the students are controlled by school authorities; therefore, they will allow their children to attend games and matches even when they forbid them from going other places.

The popularity of school sports has led sociologists to ask questions about their impact on students' values, attitudes, actions, and experiences.

High School Sports and Popularity For many years, student culture was studied simply in terms of the factors that high school students used to determine popularity. Research usually found that male students wished they could be remembered as "athletic stars" in high school, whereas female students wished to be remembered as "brilliant students" or "the most popular." Although these priorities have changed over the last two generations, the link between popularity and being an athlete has remained relatively strong for male students (Shakib et al., 2011). At the same time, the link between popularity and being an athlete has become stronger for female students, although other characteristics, such as physical appearance and social skills, are also important–more important than they are for young men.

Most high school students today are concerned with academic achievement and attending college; furthermore, their parents regularly emphasize these priorities. But students also are concerned with four other things: (1) social acceptance, (2) personal autonomy, (3) sexual identity, and (4) becoming an adult. They want to have friends they can depend on, control their lives, feel comfortable with their sexual identity, and be taken seriously as young adults.

Because males and females in North America are still treated and evaluated differently, adolescents use different strategies for seeking acceptance, autonomy, sexual identity, and recognition. For young men, sports provide opportunities to demonstrate the physical and emotional toughness that is traditionally associated with masculinity, and successfully claiming a masculine identity is assumed to bring acceptance, autonomy, and recognition as an adult.

For young women, sports are not used so much to claim a feminine identity that brings acceptance, autonomy, and recognition as an adult, but playing sports is used to achieve and express the personal power that enables young women to achieve these things. My hypothesis is that young women in high school are less likely than their male peers to view sports as a self-identification focal point in their lives and more likely to view sports as part of

(*Source:* Danielle Hicks)

Sports participation often gives young women opportunities to establish personal and social identities based on skills respected by peers and people in the general community. However, even though playing sports often is enjoyable, as it is for members of this soccer team, it usually does not bring as much status and popularity to girls as it does to boys in US high schools.

a larger project of achievement that involves academic, social, and other personal accomplishments. If this is the case, the visibility and status gained by high school athletes have different implications for young men than for young women in high school student culture and beyond.

High School Sports and Ideology Sports programs do more than simply affect the status structures of high schools. When Pulitzer Prize–winning author H. G. Bissinger wrote the book *Friday Night Lights* about a high school football team in Odessa, Texas, he observed that football "stood at the very core of what the town was about. . . . It had nothing to do with entertainment and everything to do with how people felt about themselves" (1990: 237).

Bissinger noted that football in Odessa and across the United States was important because it celebrated a male cult of toughness and sacrifice and a female cult of nurturance and servitude. Team losses were blamed on coaches who weren't tough enough and players who weren't disciplined and aggressive. Women stayed on the sidelines and faithfully tried to support and please the men who battled on behalf of the school and town.

Attending football games enabled students and townspeople to reaffirm their ideas about "natural differences" between men and women. Young men who did not hit hard, physically intimidate opponents, or play with pain were described with nonmasculine terms. Additionally, a player's willingness to sacrifice his body for the team was taken as a sign of commitment, character, and manhood. At the same time, women who didn't stand by and support their men were seen as gender nonconformists.

Bissinger also noted that high school sports were closely linked with a long history of racism in Odessa, and that football was organized and played in ways that reaffirmed traditional racial ideology among whites and produced racial resentment among African Americans. Ideas about race and certain aspects of racial dynamics have changed since 1988 when many whites in the Odessa area referred to blacks with the n-word and blamed people of color for most of the town's social and economic problems. White people are not as likely today to say that black athletes succeed on the football field because of their "natural physical abilities" or that white athletes succeed due to character, discipline, and intelligence but some of these racial stereotypes appear in new forms today.

Bissinger's book fails to deal with many aspects of high school life, but a study by anthropologist Doug Foley (1990) provides a more complete description and analysis of the place of sports in a high school and the town in which it exists. Foley studied an entire small Texas town but paid special attention to the ways that people incorporated the local high school football team and its games into the overall social life of the school and the community. He also studied the social and academic activities of a wide range of students, including those who ignored or avoided sports.

Foley's findings revealed that student culture in the high school "was varied, changing, and inherently full of contradictions" (1990a, p. 100). Football and other sports provided important social occasions and defused the anxiety associated with tests and overcontrolling teachers, but sports were only one part of the lives of the students. Athletes used their sport-based status as a basis for "identity performances" with other students and certain adults, but for most students, identity was grounded more deeply in gender, social class, and ethnicity than sports participation.

Foley noted that sports were socially important because they presented students with a vocabulary they could use to identify values and interpret their everyday experiences. For example, most sports came with a vocabulary that extolled individualism, competition, and "natural" differences related to sex, skin color, ethnicity, and social class. As students learned and used this vocabulary, they perpetuated the culture and social organization of their school and town. In the process, traditional ideologies related to gender, race, and class continued to influence social relations in the town's culture, even though some people questioned and revised those ideologies and redefined their importance in their lives.

The point of Foley's study and other research on socialization as a community process is that the most important social consequences of high school sports are not their impact on grades and popularity but their impact on the overall culture of the school and community as well as young people's ideas about social life and social relations. Examples of this are highlighted in the PBS *Frontline* documentary "Football High" (Dretzin, 2011).

Foley's research in Texas is thirty years old. The reason I include it here is that it is one of the very few studies that even mention the impact of high school sports on the students who don't play on teams. This raises issues that have not been studied. For example, how do school sports impact those who try our for teams but do not make them or those who make a team one year and are cut the next? When sports are at the center of high school culture, how does this impact students who don't play sports and feel out of place when sports are seen as important by teachers and administrators? Additionally, we don't know how sports participation impacts students who play on community-based club teams or in sports that are not school sponsored. Do these forms of participation impact grades, identification with the school, social integration into student culture, popularity among students, educational aspirations, and college attendance? These questions become increasingly important as more adolescent athletes play sports on elite travel teams or do sports such as motocross, mountain biking, skateboarding, BMX, climbing, snowboarding, shooting, martial arts, and other sports that are not connected with school. Is the impact of participation for these young people the same as it is for students who play on school teams? At this point, we don't know.

High School Sports as Learning Experiences

Early in the twentieth century, educators included physical education and sports in US schools because they believed that learning should encompass body and mind. Physical activities and sports, they thought, could be organized to teach important lessons. But the widespread acceptance of the great sport myth and the related belief that "sports build character" led to the assumption that playing sports automatically transformed young people in positive ways, no matter how the sports were organized. There was no need for research to identify what participants learned or how to teach things beyond tactics and techniques. Individual testimonials about "sport making me what I am today" fueled the mythology that sports were like an automatic car wash: those who enter them will be cleansed, dried, and sent off with a shiny new look.

As a result, there are no "learning evaluations" at the end of seasons, coaches aren't held accountable as teachers, and there is an amazing lack of systematically collected evidence documenting the dynamics of teaching and learning in various sports played by over seven million high school students every year. The downside of this lack of knowledge is that we can't prove what young people learn in sports or when and why they learn certain things, either positive or negative. Nor can we rate the effectiveness of various coaching strategies for teaching what we want young people to learn in sports. And what is it that we want young people to learn? If we knew these things, we could present evidence to school boards when they make funding decisions. Too many people simply assume and say the same things: sport teaches discipline, teamwork, and the value of hard work. But they provide only anecdotal evidence about themselves or someone they know. What we need is systematic research identifying the conditions under which school teams provide worthwhile educational experiences for students (Overman, 2018).

INTERCOLLEGIATE SPORTS AND THE EXPERIENCES OF COLLEGE STUDENTS

Does varsity sports participation affect the educational and developmental experiences of college athletes?[3] This question cannot be answered unless

[3]This chapter focuses primarily on four-year institutions in the United States. Although junior colleges and two-year community colleges comprise 25 percent of all higher education institutions with intercollegiate programs and have about 10 percent of all intercollegiate athletes, there is little research on them.

we understand that college sports are very diverse. If we assume that all programs are like the ones we see or read about in the media, we are bound to have distorted views of athletes, coaches, and intercollegiate sports.

Intercollegiate Sports Are *Not* All the Same

The amount of money spent every year on intercollegiate sports varies from less than $100,000 at some small colleges to over $200 million at the University of Texas. There are 146 Division I universities with budgets over $100 million, not counting private universities that do not share budget data (Wolken, Berkowitz & DeMeyer, 2019). Large universities usually sponsor ten to eighteen varsity sports for men and a similar number for women, whereas small colleges may have only a few varsity sports and many club teams. The sociological implications of these differences are significant because they represent very different contexts for sports participation and the role of the athletic program in the culture and organization of campus life.

Schools with intercollegiate sports are generally affiliated with one of two national associations: the National Collegiate Athletic Association (NCAA) or the National Association of Intercollegiate Athletics (NAIA). The NCAA is the largest and most powerful association, with close to 1200 member institutions, nearly 500,000 athletes, and revenues of well over $1 billion per year for the national headquarters. Member institutions are divided into five major categories, reflecting program size, level of competition, and the rules that govern sports programs. Division I includes (in 2018–2019) 354 schools with "big-time" programs. This division contains three subdivisions:[4]

1. The Football Bowl Subdivision (FBS) consists of 130 universities that have big-time football teams; each institution is allotted eighty-five full scholarships for football players.
2. The Football Championship Subdivision (FCS) consists of 126 universities that have football programs and are allotted only sixty-three scholarships that can be awarded to or split between no more than eighty-five students.
3. The Non-Football (NF) subdivision consists of 98 universities that do not have football teams but have big-time basketball and/or other big-time sports.

NCAA Divisions II and III contain 319 and 449 schools, respectively. These schools have smaller programs and compete at less than a big-time level, although competition often is intense. Division II schools may award limited scholarships but rarely give a full scholarship to an athlete. Division III schools do not award athletic scholarships unless they sponsor one or more teams that compete at a Division I level. For example, Colorado College, a liberal arts school with about 2000 students has 16 varsity teams. Fourteen teams compete at the Division III level, and men's ice hockey and women's soccer compete at the Division I level.

Some colleges and universities choose to affiliate with the NAIA rather than the NCAA. The NAIA has about 250 member schools, an estimated 65,000 athletes, and annual revenues of about $8.5 million. NAIA schools can compete in 26 sports, 13 for men and 13 for women. Athletic scholarships are not common and seldom cover more than 25 percent of college costs Most member institutions are small private schools, many with religious affiliation, and their athletic programs have minimal budgets. The NAIA struggles to maintain members in the face of NCAA power and influence.

Christian colleges and Bible schools also have sports programs. About 90 of these are affiliated with the National Christian College Athletic Association (NCCAA), although some

[4]These numbers change regularly as conferences and universities position themselves to maximize revenue generation and minimize financial losses for their sports programs.

have dual membership in the NCCAA and either the NAIA or NCAA Division III. The National Junior College Athletic Association consists of about 525 junior and community colleges. Some of its 60,000 athletes receive scholarships, nearly all of which cover only partial expenses. Finally, there are hundreds of additional colleges that have intercollegiate sports programs without being affiliated with any of these organizations. We know little about them because there are no governing bodies that collect and publish data from them.

Even though the vast majority of intercollegiate sports are not big-time, people use what they see and read in the media to make conclusions about all college sports. But this is a mistake because most sports at most schools do not resemble the sports covered by the mainstream media. For example, the 130 FBS universities dominate media coverage, but make up only 11 percent of the 4-year schools that have sports programs. However, FBS universities have the largest athletic departments, the biggest budgets, the highest profile teams in football and basketball, and they award more athletic scholarships than other colleges and universities.

Although it's important to study the educational relevance of all college sports programs, most research focuses on Division I universities, mostly those in the FBS subdivision. Therefore, this chapter, based on the literature in the sociology of sport and other disciplines, provides a limited view of intercollegiate sports. This is important to remember when we discuss issues and problems because they vary widely from one division to the next.

Athletes in Big-Time Programs

College athlete is a term unique to higher education in the United States. Athletes in other countries may attend college, and college students may train and compete in a sport, but they are not identified as *college athletes*. They don't play on school-sponsored teams nor do the schools claim them as *their* athletes. For this reason, the young people who train and compete in a sport and attend college say that they have "dual careers," one as an athlete and the other as a student. Managing these dual careers is such a challenge that the European Union sponsors research on how young people handle it and what support they need to succeed as students *and* athletes (http://www.dualcareer.eu/). When dual careers are studied by European scholars, it is not assumed that being an athlete is a valued educational experience or that a college education is enhanced by playing a sport. If there are complementary connections between these careers, it is because young people have created ways to make their sports participation educationally relevant or make their university courses relevant to their sports participation (Stambulovaa & Wylleman, 2019). The challenge in Europe is to create support systems that will work across more than 30 countries most of which have different approaches to higher education and sports training.

This approach to higher education and sports sounds strange to most people in the United States. This is because Americans have created a narrative in which sports participation is assumed to be inherently educational, and education is assumed to be enriched by sports participation. This narrative is uncritically accepted to the point that universities collectively spend billions of millions of dollars to maintain athletic departments that involve a small proportion of students in sports without doing independent research that identifies if or what and when athletes learn as they participate in their sports. Coaches may identify team goals in locker room talks and booster club speeches, but there are no attempts to determine if athletes really learn discipline, teamwork, leadership, integrity, confidence, time management skills, fair play and other lessons that coaches say they instill in athletes. There is no curriculum committee to assess the pedagogy that coaches use to achieve the stated learning outcomes of playing a sport or how those outcomes fit with the educational mission of higher education. Despite billions of dollars spent annually and the emphasis that Americans put on intercollegiate sports, there is no independent research that regularly evaluates what athletes learn as they participate, how their participation complements their academic lives, or how the lessons learned might be applied apart from their sports.

Managing Dual Careers One of the things that we do know about college athletes in big-time sports programs today is that many of them have a difficult time managing their dual careers in ways that meet both academic and athletic expectations. Academic expectations and workloads for students have remained much the same over the past half-century, and it is the responsibility of students to allocate their time and energy to meet them. But expectations related to college sports participation have increased dramatically, even in sports that do not generate much revenue. The commitments of time and energy demanded of college athletes today are much greater than they were for past generations. Required commitments are no longer limited to a season. They exist throughout the year, often including summers. There is pre-season, in-season, and post-season training, and each is done with coaches aware of who meets the unstated requirements of team membership and scholarship renewal. Athletes' time, energy expenditures, and physical condition are monitored with new technologies by an increasing number of assistant coaches (Jones & Denison, 2018; Denison, Mills & Konoval, 2017; Hatteberg, 2018). The control that coaches have over athletes' lives is much more comprehensive than it has ever been, and they exercise that control as much as possible because they are expected to create and maintain teams that achieve excellence and enhance the school's public reputation.

Coaches have much more control over their athletes' lives than college teachers have control over students' lives. When students don't meet academic expectations, it's their problem; their teachers' careers are not jeopardized. But when athletes don't meet expectations, it's the coach's problem, and the coach's career depends on solving it. For young people managing their dual careers, this usually sets the stage for dual-career conflict, because there is not enough time in the day to meet both academic and athletic expectations. If they slack off and fail to meet athletic expectations, their coach has the power to change or end their careers in sports and, in many cases, to end their scholarships. If they slack off and fail to meet academic expectations, they can accept lower grades, register for classes with fewer expectations, change majors, seek assistance from academic support programs, cheat on assignments and tests, and simply meet the minimum requirements for athletic eligibility. This is not an easy choice, but there is more room for negotiation related to academic expectations than for athletic expectations. Under these conditions, priority is often given to meeting the latter.

Managing dual-career conflict is also influenced by the fact that grades are seen only by students, but athletic performances are public—possibly seen by millions of others. They are often presented and recounted in media coverage, recorded on film, assessed by multiple coaches and teammates, used to determine whether scholarships can be renewed, and possibly assessed by scouts for professional teams. They also evoke cheers and jeers from spectators and determine whether people perceive an athlete in positive or negative terms. In revenue-producing sports, especially Division I football and basketball, the performances of athletes have significant financial consequences for coaches, universities, and local businesses that depend on spectators coming to town for sports events, and media companies that have bought the rights to broadcast games. Additionally, the stakes associated with academic and athletic performances are different. Millions of dollars can be on the line when an athlete makes a jump shot during the NCAA men's basketball tournament or throws a touchdown pass to win a conference championship and guarantee a bowl appearance. From the perspective of an 18–23-year-old who has excelled in sports and has been known in terms of their sports identity through most of their formative years, giving priority to athletic expectations over academic expectations is common, even though graduation is important to nearly all of them.

This outcome is so incompatible with the goals of higher education and the stated goals of intercollegiate sports that Senator Chris Murphy from Connecticut initiated an investigation of college athletics in which he examined, among other things, "how programs fail to provide a full education to their student-athletes . . ." (Murphy, 2019a, p. 13). During Senator Murphy's investigation, he referred to the experiences of a young man who played football as a student at Kansas State University. The young man had planned to be a veterinarian, but meeting the expectations of his coach reduced the time and energy he had for his academic career. To manage this dual-career conflict, he redefined his academic plans, changed his major, and took less demanding courses to stay eligible and do what his coach and teammates expected. After he graduated, he had this to say:

> *The whole time...I felt stuck - stuck in football, stuck in my major. Now I look back and say, 'well what did I really go to college for?' Crap classes you won't use the rest of your life? I was majoring in football* (Murphy, 2019b, p. 2).

Senator Murphy also referred to a young man who played football at Oklahoma State University who used a different strategy to reduce his dual career conflict. He went to his academic advisors in the athletic department and they completed assignments for his courses. He explained that when he was assigned papers to write, "I would write them, and they would take them and just completely change everything about it . . . I never really learned how to write a paper, but I [stayed eligible for football]" (Murphy, 2019b, p. 2).

Of course, these are not the only ways to manage dual-career conflict, but they have been common enough to prompt Senator Murphy's investigation of the long-assumed educational relevance of intercollegiate sports. In fact, as he reviewed reliable evidence collected by journalists and scholars, he concluded the following:

> *Unfortunately, the NCAA and many of its member schools too often care more about the appearance of educating athletes than they do about actually educating them. That façade of educational opportunity manifests in too many former athletes left "worn, torn, and asking questions".* . . (Murphy, 2019b. p. 3).

Senator Murphy's conclusion was not a surprise to those of us familiar with studies of big-time intercollegiate sports over the past half-century. Research by sociologists Patricia and Peter Adler came to the same conclusion in the 1980s when expectations associated with sports training were less demanding than they are today. The Adlers didn't talk about dual-career conflict; rather, they focused on "role conflicts" between the athletic, academic, and social expectations in the lives of young men on a Division I basketball team. They used the concept of "role engulfment" to explain how the demands and rewards associated with being an athlete were so overwhelming and attractive that the young men were quickly "engulfed by it" to the exclusion of other roles (Adler & Adler, 1991). As this occurred, their athlete identity became so central to their

(*Source:* Paul W. Harvey)

Compared to men, women in Division I sports manage dual-career conflict more successfully. They are more likely to have academic support from teammates and they are less likely to give top priority to their athletic career or focus on a playing professionally in their sport.

sense of self that they had little time and energy to nurture their academic and other identities.

Research clearly shows that young people manage dual-career conflict in different ways depending on a combination of their personal resources and the support they receive from family, friends, teammates, teachers, coaches, mentors, and the school they attend. The availability of these resources and support systems vary depending on the socioeconomic status of the young person's family, the quality of their educational background, their past experiences in school and sports; their gender, race, ethnicity; their academic and athletic abilities; and the cultures of their team and campus (Bernhard, 2014; Bimper, 2016, 2017; Cooper, 2019; Dorsch et al., 2016; Feezell, 2015; Fuller & Bailey, 2018; Fuller, Harrison & Bukstein, 2017; Harper, 2018; Kaye, Lowe & Dorsch, 2019; Oseguera et al., 2018; Parietti, Sutherland & Pastore, 2017; Ridpath & Tudor, 2018; Rubin & Moses, 2017; Smith & Willingham, 2015). The influence of these factors is discussed in the following sections of this chapter.

Dual Careers and the NCAA The challenge of managing dual careers has not escaped the attention of the NCAA. Even though athletes nearly always manage to stay academically eligible when they are needed on the playing field, there have been highly publicized cases of individuals, teams, and entire athletic departments in which the academic careers of athletes had not been taken seriously or managed by athletic department staff so that athletes remained eligible despite doing little academic work (Benedict & Keteyian, 2013; Dohrmann & Evans, 2013c; Gurney, Lopiano & Zimbalist, 2017; Murphy, 2019b; O'Donnell, 2016; Smith & Willingham, 2015; Tracy, 2014). Over the years, these cases have damaged the reputations of the NCAA and major universities that otherwise were seen as being academically strong.

To avoid bad publicity and maintain athletic teams that generate significant revenues for athletic departments, the NCAA has periodically raised academic eligibility requirements. The assumption underlying this strategy was that it would encourage high school athletes to take education more seriously and encourage coaches to recruit athletes with stronger academic potential. The overall goal was to raise the grades and graduation rates of athletes to match those for the student body as a whole.

This sounds like a reasonable approach, and there were improvements in grades and graduation rates–a point that has been emphasized repeatedly by the NCAA (Hosick, 2018). However, a meaningful academic comparison of athletes and the rest of the student body is difficult to do because there are wide variations in the demands of academic courses, in the grading criteria used by faculty in different departments, and in graduation requirements in different colleges (engineering, business, arts and sciences) and departments. For example, research shows that athletes in certain sports are overrepresented in certain majors and courses–a phenomenon known as *clustering*. It occurs when athletes lack academic confidence and seek support from teammates in the same courses or major, when black athletes find a department where faculty members are aware of racial issues and treat them with respect, and when athletes register–often with guidance from athletic department staff–in classes involving little work or taught by faculty members known to give athletes high grades for little work.

Today, the NCAA publishes three academic assessment indicators. One is the *Federal Graduation Rate* (FGR) that is calculated by the US Department of Education. It is based on the percentage of first-time, full-time, first-year students who graduate within 6 years of entering a 4-year institution. A second indicator, created by the NCAA, is the *Graduation Success Rate* (GSR). It reports the percentage of scholarship athletes who earn a college degree on each team in the athletic department. The third indicator is the *Academic Progress Rate* (APR) that is calculated by giving each scholarship athlete on a team one point for remaining in school and another point for remaining academically eligible. The total points for each team are divided by the number of points possible on that team and then multiplied times 1,000 to arrive at the team APR.

Each of these measures is useful in certain ways, but each also has problems. First, the FGR counts all transfer students as "nongraduates" and includes part-time students in the general student body. This makes the graduation rate for athletes look better in comparison because they are full-time students with scholarships. Second, the GSR excludes athletes who leave the university in good academic standing and then includes them in the GSR of the program into which they transfer. But for every three athletes who leave a program when they are still academically eligible, only one transfers into another program. This means that about two-thirds of all transferring athletes (and about 16 percent of all athletes) are missing from the data. These athletes did not graduate, but the GSR formula counts them as if they did, thereby inflating the athlete graduation rate (Gurney et al., 2017; Murphy, 2019b). Third, neither the GSR nor APR involve comparisons with the rest of the student body, so there is no external baseline for comparing how athletes perform academically. These latter two measures treat athletes as a special academic category that is compared only to what athlete peers have done in the past.

Overall, these three measures of academic performance exaggerate academic success for athletes, teams, and athletic departments. For this reason, Richard Southall and his colleagues in the College Sport Research Institute (CSRI) at the University of South Carolina, developed the *Adjusted Graduation Gap* (AGG). It compares an adjusted FGR for the *full-time* students at a university with the FGR of athletes on Division I football, men's and women's basketball, softball, and baseball teams. As published in reports by the CSRI, the AGG data indicate that athletes generally have significantly lower graduation rates than the other students in their universities. Some of the most recent data available are presented in Table 2. As you can see, the AGG data make it possible to do comparisons by sport, conference, national team ranking, race, and gender.

Each number in Table 14.2 represents the percentage point difference between the graduation rate for athletes compared to the graduation rate for

Table 14.2 NCAA Division I conference average Adjusted Graduation Gaps for basketball and football players, 2018*

	AGG: All Athletes	AGG: Black Athletes	AGG: White Athletes
Men's Basketball			
Major conferences	−33	−35	−27
Mid-Major conferences	−18	−20	−15
Women's Basketball			
Major conferences	−19	−20	−21
Mid-Major conferences	−9	−10	−7
Football (2018)			
Power 5 conferences	−16	−22	−2
Group of 5 conferences	−10	−13	−2
Top 10 ranked teams	−26	−31	−9

Source: College Sport Research Institute, https://www.csri.org/

*Each number in the table represents the percentage point difference between the graduation rate for athletes compared to the graduation rate for their peers in the student body

Table guide:

Major conferences: American, Atlantic 10, Atlantic Coast, Big12, Big East, Big Ten, Conference-USA, Mountain West, PAC-12, Southeastern

Mid-Major conferences: 21 conferences that fill out Division I in basketball

Power 5 conferences: Atlantic Coast, Big Ten, Big XII, PAC-12, Southeastern

Group of 5 conferences: American, Conference-USA, Mid-American, Mountain West, Sun Belt

Top 10 ranked teams: final rankings for the college football playoff selections their peers in the student bodies of their universities. For example, all the male basketball players on teams in the 10 major conferences in Division I during the 2017-018 season had a graduation rate that was 33 percentage points below the graduation rate for the student body in their universities. The rate for black male players was 35 percentage points below the student body rate, and the rate for white players was 27 percentage points below the student body rate. The athlete graduation rates that were closest to the rate for their student bodies were for white football players in the Power 5 and Group of 5 conferences; their rates were only 2 percentage points lower than rates for their respective student bodies. Overall, the CSRI data over the past decade indicate the following:

- Athletes graduate at significantly lower rates than other full-time students.
- Female athletes graduate at lower rates than other full-time students, but at higher rates than male athletes.
- Athletes on top-ranked teams generally graduate at lower rates than other athletes in their sports.

CSRI data suggest that athletes experience more dual-career conflict than other students or handle it in a less balanced manner. The same pattern exists for male athletes relative to female athletes, black athletes compared with white athletes, and athletes playing on teams that are top-ranked nationally and in more elite conferences compared with athletes playing on lower-ranked teams in less elite conferences. None of these patterns is surprising, but it would be helpful if we had other studies that helped us understand why they exist and what causes them to vary the way they do.

Dual Careers and Division I Athletic Departments
In addition to the NCAA, people working in Division I athletic departments are aware of dual-career conflict among their athletes. They also know that as the financial stakes associated with winning have become intense' coaches are under pressure to recruit the best athletes even if their academic record and preparation are well below what they are for the rest of the student body (Rubin & Moses, 2017). Plus, most coaches know that top high school athletes have often focused more on their athletic than their academic careers.

As the NCAA has increased eligibility standards, coaches have faced a difficult choice. Either they can recruit only the athletes that meet the academic entrance requirements of their university or they can recruit the best athletes, even if they are poorly prepared for college. If they choose the second alternative–the choice that nearly all coaches make–academic support programs become a key part of big-time athletic departments. The financial stakes associated with winning are so high that they must provide academic support that maintains the eligibility of athletes, regardless of academic preparation or the athletes' interest in academic success.

The stated role of people working in an athletic department's academic support program is to facilitate the academic development and success of athletes. But the fact that the program is administered by and located in the athletic department raises questions about their goals. These questions are asked every time it is reported that academic support staff wrote papers and did other assignments for athletes, or even found people to take tests for the athletes (Benedict & Keteyian, 2013; Dohrmann and Evans, 2013c; Smith and Willingham, 2015). The regularity of academic fraud occurring in academic support programs has led David Ridpath, an expert on intercollegiate sports, to say that, "It makes no sense to have an academic support unit controlled by athletics" (in Kelderman, 2018). He adds that these programs should be organized and controlled by an academic unit and by faculty and staff that report directly to the top academic officer on campus. When the programs exist in athletic departments, there are too many vested interests and pressures to make sure that athletes are eligible no matter how it is done.

To understand this issue, imagine that you are an academic tutor making $35,000 a year in the athletic department at a university where the football team generates about $40 million per year. The coaches, including the nationally respected, highly paid and powerful football coach, are basically your bosses. With 3 days left in the summer semester, the football coach comes to you and says that the eligibility of an All-American running back is in jeopardy because he has not handed in a 20-page paper in a sociology class. The coach grips your shoulder firmly and says that if the running back is ineligible he will give you a bad evaluation that will jeopardize your job and your career in higher education. Additionally, if the running back does not play, it could prevent them from qualifying for a bowl appearance that would bring $35 million to the athletic department and increase the prospect of the athlete being drafted into the NFL. The athlete has never written a full paper and is busy with practice during the day and game film reviews during evenings. Under these circumstances, would you write the paper for the athlete to turn in to his sociology professor and receive the grade that will maintain his eligibility? If you answer "yes," you are not alone. Such decisions have resulted in cases of academic fraud at major universities with excellent academic reputations (Branch, 2011; Gurney, Lopiano & Zimbalist, 2017; Kelderman, 2018; Murphy, 2019b; New, 2016; Ridpath, Gurney & Snyder, 2015).

Academic support programs are seldom studied by independent researchers (Rubin & Moses, 2017; Steinberg et al., 2018). In part, this is because coaches and athletic directors do not want outsiders "snooping" around their programs and talking with staff and athletes about things that might make the athletic department and certain teams look bad. This is unfortunate because some support programs have 30-year histories and there is much to learn from experienced tutors and from athletes whose academic careers benefitted from the guidance and support they received. University presidents and academic administrators don't interfere with the programs because the coaches and athletic directors often have much higher salaries and are more widely known than anyone on campus, including the university president. Additionally, presidents use high-profile sports as public relations and fund-raising tools regardless of the grades or graduation rates of athletes. Similarly, the media companies that pay billions of dollars to televise college football games, and the corporations that sponsor teams and buy commercial time on telecasts care little about the academic careers of athletes as long as their teams generate the hype that sustains their profits. Nor are the owners of local businesses concerned about athlete graduation rates as long as spectators fill the town for every home game weekend and spend a lot of money.

Locating academic support programs in the athletic department, physically and administratively, is consistent with the growing social and academic isolation of athletes at universities with big-time athletic programs. Mixing with the rest of the student body, according to coaches and many athletes on high profile teams, is a distraction (Rubin & Moses, 2017). This is why opulent and expensive "athlete centers" are built to house academic support programs and other attractions that keep the athletes focused on their sport while they are under the watchful eyes of athletic department staff–much like a well-equipped detention center (Hatteberg, 2018) or a 21st-century plantation (Hawkins, 2010). Athletes generally see these centers as a refuge, a place where they can hang out together without dealing with people and issues that take time away from their athletic careers. But taking advantage of this refuge intensifies the process of role engulfment and undermines the development of relationships and identities that are not grounded in sports.

In some cases, this feels familiar to young men who were recruited as 14-year-olds into private, athletic-centric prep schools where they were used to build nationally ranked high school teams. Sport management and educational leadership expert, Joseph Cooper (2019) refers to this form of "flesh peddling" as central to the miseducation of black athletes in particular. As this occurs, these young men are immersed in a seductive system of sports-related encouragement and rewards that benefits others as it sidetracks holistic development among young people who play sports on high profile teams.

Building a Successful Dual Career System For nearly four decades the NCAA has tried to improve the academic experiences and graduation rates of college athletes. At the same time, research indicates that there has been a growing separation between the culture of intercollegiate sports and the general university culture (Cooper, 2019; Gurney, 2018; Gurney, Lopiano & Zimblist, 2017; Hawkins, 2010; Lawrence et al., 2007; Murphy, 2019b; Nixon, 2014; Ridpath, 2018; Smith and Willingham, 2015). This separation is fueled by historical, commercial, and political factors that currently shape the culture of college sports (Nixon, 2014). These factors are so powerful that a group of college professors formed The Drake Group (TDG, https://www.thedrakegroup.org/), the goal of which is to reform intercollegiate sports and defend academic integrity in higher education. TDG recently lobbied the US Congress, and asked it to investigate the nonprofit status of college sports teams that are organized to make money. When Congress formed an investigative committee, the NCAA lobbied Congress and highlighted academic success stories in college sports and the committee pulled back its investigation. TDG continues to be active and makes the case that the educational mission of universities will not be fully realized until college sports are monitored by an independent agency committed to higher education.

There is no shortage of recommendations to reform intercollegiate sports, but the power of commercial interests in the current system leads many of us who have studied college sports to be skeptical about the possibility of meaningful change. Others remain hopeful that the NCAA can make changes that enable all athletes to successfully manage dual-career conflict. My sense is that the vested interests in the current organization and financial payoffs generated by big-time intercollegiate sports are so great that meaningful changes will not occur until a crisis disrupts the system and forces people to save it by completely reorganizing it.

The Diversity of College Athlete Experiences

As noted in the previous sections, big-time revenue-generating intercollegiate sports programs are characterized by chronic problems, low graduation rates, and hypocrisy when it comes to education. However, there are programs that do not have big-time programs, and there are teams in nonrevenue-producing sports that are organized so athletes can successfully manage their academic and athletic careers. Additionally, the athletes in these programs and on these teams are usually similar to the rest of the student body in terms of academic preparation and they are seldom distracted by the dream of having professional sports careers.

Athletes on teams in which there is strong support for academic success may train hard and define athletic success as important, but most of them take education seriously and try to maintain a realistic balance between academic and athletic commitments. The athletes who do this most effectively are those with the following: (1) past experiences that consistently reaffirm the importance of education; (2) social networks that support academic identities and facilitate academic success; (3) perceived access to career opportunities following graduation; and (4) social relationships and experiences that expand confidence and skills apart from sports.

Coaches in programs that actively support academic success may schedule practices and games that do not interfere with coursework. Athletes may miss games and meets to study for or take tests, write papers, or give presentations. Team members may discuss academic issues and support one another's academic careers. In other words, there are programs and teams that neither subvert the academic mission of higher education nor undermine the academic careers of athletes. Usually they're found in NCAA Division III, some NAIA and many small Christian college programs, but they also exist in some low-profile, non-revenue-producing Division I and II sports and in many women's sports at all levels of competition.

However, teams at many of these schools are increasingly organized to emphasize "excellence," which means recording many more wins than losses at most schools. This pressures coaches to produce winning teams and championships to keep their jobs, and coaches put pressure on athletes to give priority to their sport. When this occurs, it is difficult for young people to balance their academic and athletic careers, even if they had a good academic record in high school. This may explain why the NCAA reported that of the 200 Division III schools providing graduation rates in their 2017 reports the overall rate for athletes was 68 percent, whereas football players and African American athletes had graduation rates of 51 and 46 percent, respectively (Burnsed, 2018). We can't meaningfully interpret these rates without having comparable rates for the rest of the student bodies at these schools, but it appears that even Division III athletes may struggle with dual-career conflict.

DO HIGH SCHOOLS AND COLLEGES BENEFIT FROM VARSITY SPORTS?

High school and college sports affect more than just athletes. In this section, we look at the influence of these programs on high schools and colleges as organizations. In particular, we examine school spirit and budgets.

School Spirit

Anyone who has attended a well-staged student pep rally or watched the student cheering section at a well-attended high school or college game realizes that sports can generate impressive displays of energy and spirit. This doesn't happen with all sport teams, nor does it happen in all schools. Teams in low-profile sports usually play games with few, if any, student spectators. Teams with long histories of losing records seldom create a spirited response among more than a few students. Many students don't care about school teams and resent the attention given to teams and athletes. But there are regular occasions when sports are sites at which students and others associated with a school come together and express spirited feelings about their teams and schools. These provide the scenes covered in the media and talked about by some people as they reminisce about their time in high school and college.

Proponents of varsity sports say that displays of school spirit at sport events strengthen student identification with schools and create solidarity among students. In making this case, a high school principal in Texas says, "Look, we don't get 10,000 people showing up to watch a math teacher solve X" (McCallum, 2003, p. 42). Critics say that the spirit created by sports is temporary, superficial, and unlikely to inspire positive actions apart from being a sports booster.

Being a part of any group or organization is more enjoyable when people have opportunities to collectively express their feelings. However, considerable resources in the form of time, energy, and money are devoted to producing this outcome in connection with sports. High school students prepare for games by making signs, planning social events in connection with games, and showing support for players. Cheerleaders practice and attend games. Athletes practice, play, and travel 10 to 20 hours a week, think about games, and view their "athlete" status as central to who they are in the school. Teachers attend games, mix with and "police" student spectators, serve as score and time keepers, and perform other game-related duties. Administrators devote time and energy to making sure the games, athletes, and students represent their schools in positive ways.

Parents pay participation fees, assist coaches with never-ending fund-raising events for teams, operate concession stands, and work behind the scenes to support their children who play or watch games. Coaches and school athletic program staff are paid, and they are part of a district and state structure consisting of people who are full-time sport management staff with offices and expense accounts. There also are people hired to do pre- and post-game cleanup of gyms, bleacher areas, and outdoor fields. Others are hired to groom and line the fields, repair damage to equipment and facilities,

(*Source:* Adam Glanzman/Getty Images)

Is this a display of school spirit? If it is, what does it mean? If these students didn't have football games to attend, would they study or identify with their school less? These questions should be answered before we assume that expressing spirit at a sports event has a positive impact on a school.

and set up bleachers and scoring tables. Referees are trained and hired, and the physical facilities of the entire school are managed to host up to three or four events per week smoothly and safely. Finally, local journalists and other newspeople come to and report on games as the only school activities worth covering in local news.

Now imagine if all this time, energy, and material resources were used to create curricula, engage in well-planned course projects, maintain classrooms and laboratories, train and pay teachers, reward students for academic accomplishments, present the school as a valuable learning site to the entire community, supervise student-generated intramurals and clubs sports, and guide teams of students in community service projects (Ripley, 2013a, 2013b). Would learning be defined as more central to students and in the overall organization of schools if these things replaced varsity sports? This is what occurs in many other post-industrial countries that are ranked far higher than the United States when it comes to student knowledge and test scores in math, reading, and world affairs.

In contrast, people, including educators, in the United States, uncritically assume that sports are so crucial in the organization of schools that no one even thinks of discussing this issue or what US education might be like if sports were community-based rather than school-sponsored activities (Ridpath, 2018). It seems that, the great sport myth is so widely accepted that it undermines critical thinking about the ways that school spirit might be more effectively generated and organized around something other than sport events in which most people are spectators (Ripley, 2013a, 2013b).

The spirit associated with high-profile intercollegiate sports is exciting for some students, but only a small proportion of the student body attends even highly publicized games. Either the students aren't interested or the athletic department limits student tickets so they can sell seats at a higher price to other fans, even when student fees subsidize athletic departments and teams.

The games of big-time sports teams often are major social occasions that inspire displays of spirit on many university campuses, but research suggests that this spirit has little to do with the educational mission of the university or creating general social integration on a campus (Clopton, 2008, 2009, 2011; Clopton and Finch, 2010; Pappano, 2012). It does create regular occasions for a segment of students, more often white males than women or ethnic minority students, to party, binge drink, avoid the library, and study less, especially when their team is successful and winning games regularly (Clotfelder, 2011; Higgins et al., 2007; Lindo et al., 2012).

Finally, we know that sports can generate impressive displays of school-related spirit in local communities. In fact, games played by teenagers, who often are perceived as "problems" in shopping areas and neighborhoods, become the main source of local entertainment in many towns and smaller cities in the United States. Does this lead to support for the schools and their educational programs, or does it focus attention more on sports rather than the academic performance of students?

Research is needed on this issue. People assume that support for teams translates into support for schools, but we don't know how or under what conditions this occurs. For example, people regularly watch, talk about, and cheer for high school and university sports teams at the same time that they vote down bond issues to fund local schools, or they vote for state legislators who cut billions of dollars from state university budgets. How and under what conditions do those cheering fans support funding for the high schools and universities that sponsor the teams they follow? We know little about this, although many people uncritically assume that spirit generated by sports is always good for education.

School Budgets

Public high schools and colleges have different budget issues because of how they are funded, although private high schools and colleges face similar issues. The financial stakes associated with big-time intercollegiate sports puts about 250 universities in a budget category of their own.

High Schools Most high school sports programs are funded through school district appropriations that come from property taxes. Declared expenditures for these programs usually account for less than two percent of school operating budgets. When certain sports have large budgets, money also comes from gate receipts and booster club donations.

In the face of recent budget shortfalls, many high schools have used various fund-raising strategies such as charging sport participation fees, fund-raising through booster clubs, and seeking corporate sponsorships. But each of these alternatives has a downside.

Participation fees privilege students from well-to-do families, discourage students from low-income families, and create socioeconomic divisions in the student body. But they are widely used and range from a low of $25 to a high of over $1000 for some sports that require big budgets to pay for equipment, travel, and facilities. Some families pay hundreds of dollars for their children to be on the rosters of school teams, which creates problems for coaches when parents who paid the fees make it known that they don't want their child sitting on the bench.

Relying on booster club support also creates problems because most community boosters want to fund boys' football or basketball teams rather than the athletic program as a whole, and many parent booster clubs focus only on the sports that their children play. This practice intensifies existing gender inequities and has led to Title IX lawsuits, none of which have been decided in favor of boosters who ignore girls' teams. Additionally, some boosters feel that they have the right to give advice to coaches and players, intervene in team decision making, and influence the process of hiring coaches and athletic directors. Community boosters often focus on win–loss records so they can tout their influence when they interact with friends and business associates; for them, educational issues may take a back seat to building a team that will win a state championship and boost their personal status.

Corporate sponsorships connect the future of high school sports to the advertising budgets and revenue streams of businesses. This means that schools can be left empty-handed when advertising budgets are cut or sponsorships are not paying off enough to satisfy company owners, stockholders, or top executives. Other problems occur when the interests of corporate sponsors don't match the educational goals of high schools. For example, promoting candy, soft drinks, and fast-food consumption with ads and logos on gym walls, scoreboards, and team buses contradicts health and nutrition principles taught in high school courses. This subverts education and makes students cynical about the meaningfulness of their curriculum. Additionally, certain corporations want to "brand" students as young as possible so they sponsor sports in the hope of turning students into loyal consumers.

High school budget issues have become increasingly contentious with the rising expectations of parents and athletes seeking athletic programs that match the individualized attention they've received in private club programs. As more students come out of club programs, they are focused on obtaining a college scholarship, and they expect to have high school coaches, trainers, equipment, and facilities that will help them achieve this goal, even if it is unrealistic.

This issue is not going away, even though budget crises are forcing some schools to drop all sports. The result is emerging inequality with public schools in upper-middle-class areas and private schools with students from wealthy families funding elaborate sports programs and facilities while schools in low-income areas struggle to maintain a few teams using outdated and rundown facilities and equipment.

Colleges and Universities The relationship between sports and school budgets at the college level is complex. Intercollegiate sports at small colleges are relatively low-budget activities funded through student fees and money from the general fund and the college president's office. The 2018–19 budgets at 130 NCAA FBS universities range from about 4.2 million (Coppin State) million to over $2.2 billion at the University of Texas, Austin. However, accounting systems vary from one university to the next, making it difficult to compare revenues and expenses from one sports program to the next. For example, some departments may "hide" profits to maintain their nonprofit status for tax purposes or to rise more money, and others may "hide" losses to avoid criticisms that sports teams are too costly to maintain.

There are at least 1700 intercollegiate sport programs in the United States, excluding nearly 450 junior and community college teams. As of 2019, the NCAA accounted for 1122 of those programs. Financial information for Division I is presented in Table 14.3. According to the NCAA's interpretation of that information, fewer than 25 of the athletic programs in Division I generate more money than they spend, although I count 28 in the *USA Today* presentation of NCAA data.[5] This is close to being true, but it is a deceptive conclusion because it is based only on the information in columns B, C, and the top dollar amount in each of the cells in column F. Therefore, if you take only *generated revenues* and subtract *total expenses* for each subdivision, the result is a *net deficit* in each case. For example, the net deficit for the FBS is -$1.13 billion, and the total net deficit for all three subdivisions is -$2.53 billion.

But these three columns tell only part of the story. Athletic departments also receive subsidies from *student fees* and money that comes from the *state or general university funds*. These are listed in columns D and E. When these subsidies are added to the generated revenues (column B), each subdivision shows an *operating profit*–the bottom number (*in italics*) in column F. For example, the operating profit for the FBS is $1.43 billion, and for all three subdivisions, it is $2.85 billion. The important thing about the operating profits is that the

[5]See https://sports.usatoday.com/ncaa/finances for these data. USA Today takes data directly from the financial information made public by the NCAA. Because 120 private colleges and universities in Division I do not provide the NCAA with their data, this list is incomplete, but it the only one available.

Table 14.3 University revenues, expenditures, subsidies, and net deficits for Division I by subdivisions, 2016–2017

Division I Subdivision	A Total Revenues (B+D+E)	B Generated Revenues*	C Total Expenses*	D Student Fees Subsidies	E State and University Subsidies	F Net Deficit (B-C) *Operating Profit*
Football Bowl Subdivision (N=130)	$8.35 billion	$6.92 billion	$8.05 billion	$597 million	$834 million	−$1.13 billion *+$1.43 billion*
Football Championship Subdivision (N=126)	$1.33 billion	$433 million	$1.32 billion	$339 million	$558 million	−$887 million *+$897 million*
Division I No Football (N=98)	$709 million	$188 million	696 million	$246 million	$275 Million	−$508 million *+$521 million*
TOTAL (N=354)	$10.39 billion	$7.54 billion	10.07 billion	$1.2 billion	$1.67 billion	−$2.53 billion** *+$2.85 billion***

***Generated revenues** come from gate receipts, media rights, and licensing fees, contributions, merchandise and concession sales, parking, game guarantees, bowl games, sports camps, endowments and investments earmarked for the athletic department. **Total expenses** include coaching and staff salaries, coaching bonuses, coaching severances, scholarships, facilities/overhead, game guarantees paid to other schools, bowl game expenses, medical and insurance, operational and utility costs, security, grounds maintenance, and other expenses.

**The difference between these two amounts is $5.85 billion.

Source: College Athletics Financial Information (CAFI) Database, Knight Commission on Intercollegiate Athletics, 2018; http://cafidatabase.knightcommission.org/about (Data source: USA Today's NCAA Athletics Finance Database, https://sports.usatoday.com/ncaa/finances).

Note: Financial data in this table come from each public institution in Division I, and each has its own accounting system. These are the most recent data available; some universities in the Power

athletic departments keep nearly all of this money. They don't return student fees to students or state money to taxpayers, although they may return a small amount of what they receive from university funds. This is important because instead of having a net deficit, universities in Division I actually have an operating profit. In fact, the difference between the two amounts is $5.38 billion.

Additionally, when the NCAA speaks about Division I finances, they exclude all private colleges and universities which constitute 34 percent of Division I members. Of those universities, including Baylor, Boston College, Brigham Young, Duke, Miami, Northwestern, Notre Dame, Rice, Southern California, Southern Methodist, Stanford, Syracuse, Texas Christian, Tulane, Tulsa, Vanderbilt, Wake Forest, the eight Ivy League universities, and others, there are probably a few that have revenues exceeding expenses.

Why would the NCAA, in their statements about the financial status of Division I schools, "hide" $5.85 billion from public view and lead people to think that 205 out of 230 (66 percent of Division I members) athletic departments lose money every year? When I analyze the data for 2017–18 (as presented by *USA Today*), I conclude that 111 Division I athletic programs in public colleges and universities report more total revenues than total expenses,

27 programs claim that they broke even for the year, and 92 say that they had more total expenses than total revenues. That means that 60 percent of all Division I athletic departments showed an *operational profit* for the year.

Of course, the NCAA would say that they are being honest when they report that only a few programs show a net profit, even if they do withhold data and do not say that they all private schools are excluded in their data. Others would say that the NCAA is not disclosing all relevant financial information about athletic programs (Ridpath, 2019). Critics suggest that NCAA claims of financial distress are used to justify one or more of the following factors that support their financial interests:

1. Their insistence that college sports are amateur activities, not commercial or professional activities–a point that they have made to defend themselves in dozens of lawsuits filed against them
2. Their nonprofit status that is approved by federal and state governments–which means that they don't pay taxes on income and wealthy donors can deduct their contributions to athletic departments on their tax returns
3. The use of student fees at a time when student debt is altering the lives of millions of students and their families to the point that it has become a national crisis (Hsu, 2019)
4. The use of state money allocated to the university at a time when academic departments face serious budget cuts that compromise educational quality
5. Their claims that athletic programs don't have enough money to pay compensation to athletes or allow athletes to make endorsement deals that would reduce the endorsements received by athletic departments

NCAA claims of financial distress ring hollow when Division I athletic departments have increased spending by 48 percent from 2011–2017. The argument made by coaches and athletic directors is that they must spend more money to win games if they want to increase their revenues, but economists say that they probably have it backwards: the athletic programs that win games increase their revenues and then increase their spending (Schroetenboer, Berkowitz & Schnaars, 2018). Apart from economic logic, FBS athletic programs have increased their spending at a time when many academic programs have been forced to reduce or hold constant their spending. Athletic department spending over the past decade was partly related to increased revenue from increasingly lucrative media rights contracts. But nearly all that media money went to the 65 schools in the Power Five conferences because media companies were hungry to televise their football and basketball games. In turn, the Power Five schools spent all that money in the hope that it would keep their teams competitive and nationally ranked. At the same time, other schools in the FBS and FCS subdivisions tried to keep up with the Power Five programs by spending themselves into debt and then asking for more subsidies from students and taxpayers.

This expensive arms race between athletics programs does not appear to be winding down to a sustainable level. In fact, new media rights contracts have pushed up revenues for Power Five schools to record levels. Table 14.4 shows that the 14 universities in the Big Ten each receives $51 million per year from media rights deals negotiated by the conference. With a less lucrative contract as of 2019, is the

Table 14.4 Media rights revenues for universities in Power Five conferences

Power Five Conference	**Annual Media Rights Revenue Per University***
Big Ten	$51 million
SEC	$43 million
Big 12	$37 million
Pac-12	$32 million
ACC	$28 million

* Rounded to nearest million; based on projections. Universities may also have individual deals with media companies.
Source: Ching (2018)

Atlantic Coast Conference; each of its 15 schools only receives $28 million annually, which is more than the total expenses at 117 of 230 Division I public colleges and universities.

Because football drives this revenue, these universities have dramatically increased what they spend to recruit football players (Estes, 2019; Gaines & Nudelman, 2017). Most Power Five schools have ignored their recruiting budgets and now spend two to four times more than they have in the recent past. For example, the University of Georgia spent $581, 531 for recruiting in 2013, but increased that amount to more than $7 million for the three-years, 2016-2018. In 2018 alone, they spent $2.63 million, with Alabama and Tennessee close behind. Vince Dooley, the former head football coach and athletic director at Georgia, was not surprised. He noted that to be competitive with the best you must recruit the best, and that means that there should be "No limit" to what they spend (Estes, 2019).

This way of thinking about college sports impacts many of the other Division I schools, because they also feel pressure to stay competitive, even though the realistic coaches and athletic directors know that they cannot match the Power Five schools when it comes to funding sports or winning on the playing field. For example, there are 11 universities in the Mountain West Conference, considered to be at the top of the second tier of conferences in Division I. Not one of those universities reports that they had more revenues than expenses in 2017–18. In fact, their net deficit is so high that they collectively received $238 million in subsidies from student fees plus state and university funds. That's an average subsidy of $21.6 million per university as they try to keep up with the Power Five schools that they compete with each year. In the meantime, many students, taxpayers, and a few state legislators with the courage to speak up are saying that this approach is unsustainable. Of course, the universities in the Mountain West Conference put pressure on universities in other second-tier conferences in trickle-down fashion.

Athletic programs in Divisions II and III schools are not impacted directly by Power Five spending patterns, but they often feel pressure to succeed because their achievements are used in their schools' institutional marketing and student recruitment strategies at a time when financial survival depends on student enrollment. Many administrators and others believe that spending money on sports teams is the best way to market their schools. However, they base their belief on anecdotal information rather than systematic research. This is ironic at institutions created, in part, to do systematic research. But they march in lockstep to the tune played by their Division I role models.

HIGH SCHOOL AND COLLEGE SPORTS FACE UNCERTAINTY

Despite their popularity, interscholastic sports face many uncertainties today. Some issues causing that uncertainty are similar for high schools and colleges, whereas others are unique to each level. In this section, we focus first on the similar issues and then deal with issues unique to each level of participation including esports; see pp. 524–525.

Issues Facing High School and College Sport Programs

High school and college sport programs both face issues related to cost containment and growing budget inequality between programs in schools at the same level of competition. The second issue is the changing orientations and rising expectations of parents and athletes, who now make their own sport-related goals a high priority when searching for a school and a sports program.

A third issue facing both high school and college programs is how to minimize concussions, repetitive head trauma, and other serious injuries that could significantly reduce participation in certain sports and bring about major changes in athletic departments and the sports they sponsor.

A fourth issue is how to create and maintain sports programs that support the educational mission of the school and the academic focus of teachers

Esports

A Fad or the Future of Interschool Sports

(*Source:* Josh Lefkowitz/Getty Images)

The emergence and rapidly growing popularity of esport teams in high schools and colleges has raised questions about the definition of sport and who counts as an athlete in schools. The challenge faced by many teams is to make them accessible and attractive to female students. The NCAA is unlikely to embrace esports because of it would raise gender equity issues and challenge its definition of amateurism.

What do scholars say about esports? Here are a few paraphrases based on my review of dozens of articles: *Esports are not sports, and they never will be* (Parry, 2018). *Esports are not sports, but they could become sports* (Hallmann & Giel, 2018). *It doesn't matter if esports are sports, but they are part of a sportification process in society* (Heere, 2018). *Esports may or may not be sports, but if we don't study them, we will miss out on an important social phenomenon* (Cunningham et al., 2018). And here is what a 20-year-old semi-professional gamer says: *Who cares if esport players are athletes or if esports are sports–they're fun, and competitors succeed based on their mental and physical abilities* (Brian, personal conversation, 2019).

Whether or not esports fit our preferred definition of sports, they are embraced by an increasing number of school administrators, teachers, and students as valuable student recruiting tools, unique learning experiences, and engaging and challenging activities. Overall, high school and college esports is a hot topic today. They are covered in mainstream media stories and have recently become a topic for articles in professional and scholarly journals.

There are many sociological questions to be asked about esports, but sociologists have been slow to ask them, and this is also true for the sociology of sport. In this chapter, one of our concerns is whether sports will merge with existing sports programs or enter secondary and higher education in other ways. So far, it appears that they are fully embraced by the National Federation of State High School Associations (NFHS). This organization has formed a partnership with Play VS, an online gaming platform provider, to coordinate esports competitions in high schools across the United States. This involves a process of introducing students to competitive gaming and making it clear that team members must meet the same eligibility rules used in traditional high school sports. Administrators, teachers, and coaches learn that esports participants are to be treated the same as traditional athletes in school announcements, convocations, and awards ceremonies. During the first esports season in 2019, five states held championships, and other states were ready to join them in 2020 (NFHS. 2019). To increase visibility and recognition, competitions are streamed for no charge on the NFHS Network (www.NFHSNetwork.com) with in-game coverage of students competing as their characters in *League of Legends*.

At this point, there are few systematic studies of high school esports and esports participants. We know little about how teams and team members they are integrated into student culture or how participation impacts educational experiences. From what I can tell, the teachers involved in sponsoring esports programs have tried to make them educationally relevant so that students experience them as more than a form of solitary entertainment.

College esports are neither as unified nor as universally supported as high school programs. Teams have been formed and scholarships are available for a limited number of gamers, but most teams are organized by students with assistance from faculty, student services, or a kindred spirit from the athletic department. Many varsity teams, as opposed to club and recreational teams, are sponsored by smaller colleges that belong to the NAIA or Division III of the NCAA. They see esports as a tool for recruiting students and engaging those who aren't interested in traditional sports.

Colleges and universities can join the National Association of Collegiate Esports (NACE), a nonprofit organization focused on "developing the structure and tools needed to advance collegiate esports in the varsity space" (https://nacesports.org/). Using an approach similar to the NFHS approach, NACE provides assistance in developing varsity programs and teams with guidelines for eligibility and a focus on graduation. It also sponsors competitions and awards scholarships. It's like the NCAA of esports without bureaucratic and control-oriented baggage. Collegiate esports leagues and tournaments are provided primarily by two other organizations: *Tespa* is a network of students, competitors, and club leaders that emphasizes students first, inclusion, and creating opportunities on and off campuses (https://tespa.org/about). It has partnerships with ESPN, Twitch, and other platforms that also provide media support. The Collegiate Starleague (CSL) is another gaming league for teams from accredited colleges and universities in North America (https://www.cstarleague.com).

The NCAA has toyed with the idea of esports, but it is unlikely to formally embrace them (Baker & Holden, 2018; Pizzo, Jones & Funk, 2019). The rights to games played in leagues and tournaments are owned by third parties which means that the NCAA would have to share control which is not part of its DNA. Some students who play on esports teams also win prize money and earn money through YouTube and Twitch streaming which the NCAA could not tolerate given its current definition of amateurism. The majority of gamers are males and that would create for the NCAA a bigger Title IX gender equity dilemma than it already has with 85-member football teams. Finally, it is unlikely that the emerging trajectory of esports could be bent to fit the highly regulated and archaic structure of the NCAA. Would gamers accept a 460-page NCAA rule book?

Despite being a poor fit with the NCAA, collegiate esports are generally described with a sport-oriented narrative to elicit popular and institutional support (Pizzo, Jones & Funk, 2019). This strategy–to put it in terms used in this book–is used to take advantage of the great sport myth so that people will come to see esports as essentially pure and good and believe that those who participate in them share in that purity and goodness. But building support on the basis of a myth is risky. Therefore, it may be wise to forget the NCAA and its governance model and practices, and create a student-oriented structure and culture that links esports explicitly and directly with academic priorities and post-graduate opportunities along with an emphasis on fun, identification with the school, interaction within and between teams, and horizontal relationships with coaches and faculty advisors.

Of course, there will be challenges along the way (Baker & Holden, 2018). Female students and their male allies may need support to develop new games that bring more females of all ages into competitive gaming. To patent a game that becomes popular would generate more revenues than a football team! Drug testing may be necessary to curb the use of cognitive enhancers by competitors. Time limits on training may be necessary to facilitate successful management of dual careers by esports team members who may also need guidance from physiologists and kinesiologists to avoid carpel tunnel syndrome and related problems. Nutrition and physical training will also be important for serious gamers. There may also be a need to discourage match-fixing if and when the stakes associated with betting on competitions become significant.

At this point, there are enough students in high schools and colleges interested in creating a future in which esports are integrated into secondary and higher education. If they succeed, they will alter the meaning and organization of sports in education. *What do you think?*

and students. Finally, both high schools and colleges continue to face the issues of gender inequities and the meaningful provision of sport participation opportunities for students with disabilities.

Viewed collectively, these five issues are bringing high school and college sports programs to a crossroads. The people running these programs face serious decisions on matters that can no longer be pushed aside and ignored. Dealing with these issues requires systemic strategies matched to individual schools and athletic departments, regardless of the competitive level at which their teams play. However, these issues are not just matters for sports. They have implications for the quality of education in the United States. Sports have become such a central component of US schools that strategies for dealing with them have implications far beyond the playing field and the lives of individual students.

Cost Containment and Budget Inequality The cost of programs at both high school and college levels has been increasing at a rate that far exceeds inflation and funding increases for academic programs. With growing pressure to contain costs, most sports programs today face serious budget questions. Money is tight across all of education, and those who administer sports programs cannot assume that such increased spending is sustainable.

As academic and athletic programs deal with funding issues, both have sought funding from outside sources including individual donors and corporate sponsors. High schools in areas that draw students from relatively wealthy families have been able to sustain and even increase spending as other schools face grim or desperate circumstances. In some schools, programs have been trimmed to teams in just a few sports, and in others the entire sports program has been dropped. But across all programs there is growing inequality in funding for sports, even among schools that compete at the same level.

Budget and program inequality among high schools is related primarily to the residential distribution of wealth across neighborhoods, towns, and even regions of the country. At the college level it is related to the distribution of media rights revenues, gate receipts, and fund raising connections. As a result, a relatively small percentage of programs enjoy the resources needed to build state-of-the-art facilities, attract skilled athletes, and pay qualified coaches and staff. At the same time other programs struggle to meet expenses and they cut corners that sometimes raise safety issues for athletes.

Exacerbating this inequality at the high school level is the emergence of private schools that have the resources to field excellent teams across a number of different sports (Johnson, Tracy & Pierce, 2015). These schools can recruit students without being limited by the geographical restrictions that exist for public schools, so they can pick the best athletes and offer tuition assistance or even full scholarships. If they also have an attractive academic program, students from wealthy families will bypass the public school in their area and attend a private school with a well-funded athletic department and highly skilled athletes.

As this occurs around the United States, schools with top teams in football and boys' and girls' basketball seek national ranking and play games out of state as they face off with the other high-budget teams across the country. Some people have suggested that there should be regional or even a national conference for these teams so they could play each other every year and sell broadcast rights to games. Inequality in high school programs has led officials in some states to reassign teams to different conferences and realign levels of competition to reduce the number of lopsided and embarrassing scores as well as injuries in contact sports. Private prep schools with well-funded and highly professionalized sports programs have become so dominant across all sports in some regions that other schools refuse to play them. At the same time, schools in low-income areas don't have the resources to maintain their sports programs with proper facilities, equipment, and coaching.

Sports program inequality is gradually becoming a castelike system that reproduces itself year after year. Adding to this trend is the fact that the best high school athletes are increasingly coming out of youth sports club programs in which participation costs are so high that they exclude well over half the young people in most regions of the country. This means that young people from relatively wealthy families have best opportunities to develop their skills, attend high schools with high profile sports programs, and then receive the majority of athletic scholarships in college–scholarships that, for some of them, have more status value than financial value, because they have enough money to pay college expenses.

These trends appear to be turning high school sports into pre-professional programs with excessive costs, well connected and demanding coaches, and opportunities that only economically privileged families can afford–and they do so willingly because they don't want to compete for scholarships with students from poor and working-class families (Farrey, 2017; Thompson, 2019). This may be one of the reasons why participation in high school sports decreased for the first time in three decades during the 2018-19 academic year, even though the number of students in high schools increased (Thompson, 2019). The high cost, high pressure programs eliminate potential participants whose families cannot afford them and those who are not willing to dedicate their high schools years to playing on professionalized teams.

The inequality in college sports programs is most visible and has the greatest impact in Division I of the NCAA. The absolute dollar differences in Division I budgets are staggering. For example, the the total expenses for the top five spending universities in Division I are greater than the total expenses for the 77 lowest spending universities in the same division. For all practical purposes the athletic programs in the universities that belong to the Power Five conferences exist in a totally different world than the programs in the other Division I universities. They basically operate quasi-professional programs and have organizational autonomy enabling them to make rules that fit their unique circumstances. The NCAA refers to this new approach as "reform," but it has further increased inequality in Division I without reducing dual-career conflict for the young people in their programs or meaningfully reducing the power that their coaches have over their lives.

Efforts to reduce inequality in the United States always run into massive resistance regardless of the context. The resistance to cost-containment policies and strategies to create more parity and possibilities for exciting competition between universities in any of the three NCAA divisions is deeply ingrained in US culture. As a result, program inequality will continue to shape the sports landscape in higher education.

Changing Orientations and Rising Expectations

As the stakes associated with sports participation have increased, there have been corresponding increases in the expectations and goals of parents and athletes. Young people today have been raised in a culture emphasizing self-improvement, growth, and achievement, and in no sphere of society is this emphasis stronger than it is in sports. At the high school level, a growing number of athletes seek opportunities to develop the skills and visibility that maximize their chances to receive a college athletic scholarship. They also believe that year-round involvement in a single sport is essential to achieving this goal, and they seek schools and coaches that fit their expectations.

When a local public school does not meet their expectations, parents and athletes seek other schools if they have a choice. If not allowed to switch public schools, they might seek a private school or even move into another area where there is a public school program that offers what they want. In either case, they expect to receive personal attention and coaching. Another alternative that is becoming increasingly popular in soccer, volleyball, lacrosse, and a few other sports is to remain on a high-profile club team that plays year-round and regularly goes to state, regional, and national tournaments scouted by college coaches. But these clubs are expensive, often costing $10,000 or more per year depending on travel and tournament expenses.

It is difficult to say how these changing orientations and rising expectations play out at the college level. Certainly there are more prima donna athletes focused on their personal goals. This results in more athletes switching schools to find the attention and opportunities they expect. Recently, it has also led to multiple lawsuits filed against the NCAA by parents seeking damages for the wrongful death of a child due to the negligence of a coach; athletes seeking damages for head injuries (over 200 separate lawsuits as of late-2019); injuries suffered during "extreme workouts;" the freedom to profit from the use of their own time (giving a "paid" speech, for example), names, images, and likenesses for commercial purposes; increased benefits from the revenues they generate through their athletic labor; more freedom to seek medical attention and insurance that covers treatments after graduation for injuries suffered while playing for a school team; more time to focus on meeting academic expectations; and more freedom to transfer and play immediately for another university, among other things.

Concussions, Repetitive Head Trauma, and Other Serious Injuries Concussions and the possibility of incurring short-term or permanent brain damage while playing school sports, especially football, is a hot-button issue for high school and college sports. It is also an anxiety-provoking liability issue for coaches, athletic directors, and school administrators. With football being the most popular and heavily promoted sport in high schools and colleges and a cash cow for a crucial segment of Division I universities, the fact that half of all reported concussions in organized school sports occur in football raises this anxiety level even further.

High school administrators know that the vast majority of athletes on school teams are under the age of informed legal consent, and that the school has a special responsibility to protect them while they are under their supervision. If studies continue to show that sport-related concussions or repetitive sub-concussive head trauma can cause death, permanent brain injuries, or an inability to meet academic expectations, they must find ways to drastically reduce head trauma during practices and games or eliminate football and other sports to protect the well-being of young people. Some teams now limit practice hours spent doing full contact drills and scrimmages, but they have increased the number of games that football teams play in a season, including playoffs (Brady and Barnett, 2015). Many coaches now teach tackling moves that limit head involvement, but these moves are difficult to make given the speed of real game action. New concussion diagnosis and treatment protocols are mandated in high school sports, but these only reduce the likelihood of playing with a head injury rather than preventing head injuries. High tech helmets are touted by football leagues at all levels as a way to protect athletes, but no helmet stops a brain from moving inside the skull when the head is hit or rotated with force; the helmet can reduce skull fractures but not brain cell damage (Connolly, 2019).

As research continues to show that repetitive subconcussive head trauma can cause temporary or permanent brain damage that could affect learning, test scores, grades, college admissions, future job prospects, and general health and well-being, lawsuits will be filed. Defendants in those lawsuits are high schools, coaches, athletic directors and principals, district and state athletic directors, and boards of education. Regardless of the possible legal outcomes, the mere threat of personal and school liability has caused insurance companies to rewrite policies in which damages due to head injuries in collision sports are not covered. As one insurance executive stated, "if you're [sponsoring] football, hockey or soccer, the insurance business doesn't want you" (in Fainaru & Fainaru-Wada, 2019). At the same time, executives from sports organizations claim that organized sports, especially those in educational institutions, cannot exist unless they have insurance protecting schools and coaches from liability for head injuries. This means that dealing with head trauma among athletes is no longer a choice. To avoid assertive actions puts schools, school districts, and state high school activities associations on the line as well as the careers and family assets of personnel associated with sports.

The issue of concussions and other serious injuries plays out in a slightly different way at the college level. Nearly all athletes in college have reached the age of (informed) legal consent. But this means that the NCAA, universities, athletic departments, and teams have the responsibility to fully inform athletes of the risks they agree to take in their sport. For many years, these parties have been slow to respond and grossly negligent. Universities have not provided in-depth education sessions to inform athletes of the risks they face in certain sport situations, despite having concussion and brain trauma experts on their faculties and in their medical schools, and despite claiming that college sports are important educational experiences (Tjong et al., 2017).

It appears that the NCAA and universities do not want to fully inform athletes in sports that involve regular head trauma about current research findings; coaches may fear that it will confuse them and reduce their motivation to put their bodies and brains at risk for the sake of their team. In the meantime, the NCAA denies any responsibility for brain injuries due to head impact despite knowing about those injuries for decades (Grossman, 2018; Hruby, 2019). This is why it has no meaningful head injury policy other than telling athletic departments in Power Five conferences that they must submit and have approved a concussion safety protocol, even though there is nothing *safe* about concussions. The other 290 Division I athletic departments have also been told to file a protocol but there is no evidence that the protocol policy has been meaningfully enforced. Knowing that the new policy might not free them of legal liability, the NCAA also created in 2017 and distributed to NCAA member institutions in 2019 a *Concussion Safety Protocol Checklist* to show that it is "an advocate for promoting and developing concussion safety management plans for each member school" (NCAA, 2019). Interestingly, the protocol contains information about when athletes can return to their sports after a concussion, but it lacks information about when they can return to classes and coursework after a concussion. Additionally, there is nothing in the protocol that deals with assessing its effectiveness or with the issue of athletes hiding symptoms of brain injuries so they can continue to play–a phenomenon that appears to be common (Davies & Bird, 2015).

As of late-2019, only one concussion lawsuit against the NCAA had been settled. It was filed in 2011 by a number of former NCAA athletes and settled in 2014 with the NCAA admitting no liability and paying no damages to an individual, but agreeing to establish a $70 million fund to pay for exams so the plaintiffs could be examined to see if they had neurological ailments that needed treatment for which the NCAA assumed no responsibility. They also agreed to provide $5 million for research on concussions (not on repetitive head hits). But then it took the NCAA three years to create a simple protocol and another two years to distribute it to NCAA member institutions. Overall, the settlement for the 2011 brain injury lawsuit was so ambiguous and unhelpful that former athletes have filed more than 100 additional lawsuits as of 2019, and most of them seek personal damages (Hruby, 2019). These lawsuits may be unified in a class action suit or they may be strung out one at a time for many years, which is the hope of lawyers for the NCAA. But sooner or later, the law of probabilities will catch up with the NCAA and lead to a settlement that forces institutions of higher education from sponsoring sports in which some students damage their brains.

In the meantime, research shows that before 2016 there was not one news article that could be found in which any college president talked about the issue of brain injuries in any university-sponsored sport or expressed concern about the damage that repetitive head hits may cause for athletes in any college sport (Igsvoog, 2015). This is certainly not due to chance. It appears that reporters from major media companies avoid the question because the financial success of their companies and the existence of their jobs depend on boosting the popularity of college football through uncritical and supportive coverage. At the same time, university presidents know that any statement of concern that comes out of their mouths will be used against the NCAA and university defendants in a court case. This is strange given that researchers in the medical schools and brain science departments at the presidents'universities are doing research on brain injuries among athletes and publishing findings that raise serious questions about the safety of playing any sport in which the head is forcefully hit hundreds of times each year (Frederick, 2019). It appears that the presidents are stuck between supporting the use of science to protect the health and well-being of athletes on their schools' teams versus supporting the football teams that provide universities with revenues and media publicity. So far, every president has opted for football over the health and well-being of athletes.

Educational Relevance As a form of physical activity and exercise, sports can be important in educational terms. However, this depends on how they are organized, the context in which they are played, and the meanings given to them. Unfortunately, when it comes to most high school and college sports we have ignored these conditional factors and used the great sport myth to assume that all sports are essentially educational and that playing sports always involves positive and valuable learning experiences.

The belief in the great sport myth has prevented educators, including coaches, from having critical discussions about what they want to happen in school-sponsored sports, how they can use teaching and learning theory (pedagogy) to make those things happen, and how they can determine if they've been successful. As a result, they have created a specialized form of elite, competitive sports in US schools without having systematically collected evidence or developed sound educational theory to justify their decision or guide its implementation.

These assumptions about sports participation are especially problematic when we consider the power of sports in US culture. Once sports are integrated into the culture and structure of schools, there is a tendency for them to dominate the public profile of the school; capture the attention of students, teachers, staff, and administrators; and take on a purpose and importance of their own–a purpose that is connected with winning records, championship trophies in the entrance of the school, public relations, entertainment, and media coverage (Ripley, 2013a). Overall, sports become both the symbolic and the real representation of the school itself.

When this occurs, sports are likely to collide with and overshadow the academic mission of the school (Nixon, 2014). Then people say that we have to have sports because they are the reason many of our students come to school every day. Or we need to have them because they are the only activities that "bring us together as a school community." Or we need them because they are the "front porch" of the university. And these statements are accepted without asking why our schools are so bad that students attend classes only because they must do so to play sports, or without asking what other ways we might come together as a community, or create ways to make Nobel Prize winners and cutting-edge knowledge the front porch of the university.

Without asking these critical questions, schools end up spending much more to support athletes than regular students (Marklein, 2013). To question these spending patterns in the United States is to invite widespread criticism grounded in highly charged emotions, defensiveness, and personal attacks. The criticism consists mostly of statements about "what sports meant to me" and "what sports mean to my kids." But these responses actually support the relevance of the question, because they clearly show how important sports have become in schools, and how people take this for granted without asking serious questions about their educational relevance.

Spending so much on sports would be viewed as strange by students from countries with highly rated educational systems, where they learn about teamwork, how to handle failure and success, how to work hard and complete projects, how to be resilient when learning is difficult in their classes, and through projects that they do with classmates (Ripley, 2013a, 2013b). This is not to say that young people from these countries do not play sports. They do, and sports are important to many of them. But for them, sports are community-based and do not dominate the social, cultural, and physical landscapes of their schools (Ridpath, 2018).

It is unrealistic to suggest that schools drop sports programs, although budget cuts are forcing some to do so. But it is not unrealistic to suggest that educators ask critical questions and take seriously the research that explains how and when sports alter the cultures and organization of their schools. Then they can make a decision to keep, change, or abandon sports programs. A good place to start is to ask what they would think about a higher education system where the highest-paid person in major universities is either a football or men's basketball coach, the most revered people on campus are football and male basketball players, and the university spends 6–12 times more money per capita to support athletes than to support students who are not athletes (Desrochers, 2012; HEP, 2018).

Gender Inequity A program in which students in the United States play the same sports across multiple generations ignores educational theory and fails to recognize the changing and diverse sport interests that exist in a culture that prizes individuality and innovation. For example, when high schools emphasize the same few power and performance sports for over a century, they discourage participation by some boys and many girls who prefer sports emphasizing pleasure and participation–sports that may not have existed 40 to 100 years ago. Progress that has been made toward achieving gender equity is due to adding new sports, and further progress toward equity requires additional changes that take into account racial and ethnic diversity as well as the new interests of girls and women. Sports played by their grandparents may not be what interests them.

Students who do not measure up to their bigger, faster, taller, and stronger classmates require alternatives to or modifications of traditional power and performance sports. Although sports like football and basketball receive much attention and many resources, there could be teams in Ultimate (Frisbee), disc golf, racquetball, flag football, in-line skating, orienteering, slacklining, wall climbing, mountain biking, BMX, water tube polo, roller hockey, skateboarding, and other sports for which there is enough local interest to field teams. With guidance, the students themselves could at least partially administer and coach these teams and coordinate exhibitions or meets and games with teams from other schools. Does there really have to be an official state champion for a sport to be educational?

Table 14.5 Girls and boys participating in high school sports, 1971–2019 (in millions)

Academic Year	Girls	Boys	Difference
1971–1972	0.29	3.66	3.37
1980–1981	1.85	3.50	1.65
1990–1991	1.89	3.41	1.52
2000–2001	2.78	3.92	1.14
2010–2011	3.17	4.49	1.32
2018–2019	3.40	4.53	1.13

Source: National Federation of High Schools; http://www.nfhs.org/ParticipationStatistics/ParticipationStatistics

Girls' sports in high schools continue to lack the support that boys' sports enjoy. This problem has a history that goes far beyond high school, but the result, as illustrated in Table 14.5, is that over a million more boys than girls play high school sports–nearly 1.13 million more in 2019.

Gender inequities at the college level are grounded in similar social and cultural dynamics, but the inequities go deeper and are manifested in many realms, such as operating budgets, recruiting money, and coaches' salaries. These differences in NCAA Division I programs for 2018 are shown in Figure 14.1. Even though women were 54 percent of the student body, they constituted only 44 percent of the athletes. Additionally, they received 47 percent of the scholarship dollars, 32 percent of recruiting dollars, 30 percent of the compensation for head coaches, and half of the operating budgets that men's teams receive.

Many people justify these gender inequities by noting that men's teams generate more revenues than women's teams. Others say that a portion of the revenues claimed by men, including football, comes from student fees more than half of which are paid by female students. This means that most NCAA Division I universities have not achieved gender equity, and this also is true for Divisions II and III, NAIA schools, and schools in the National

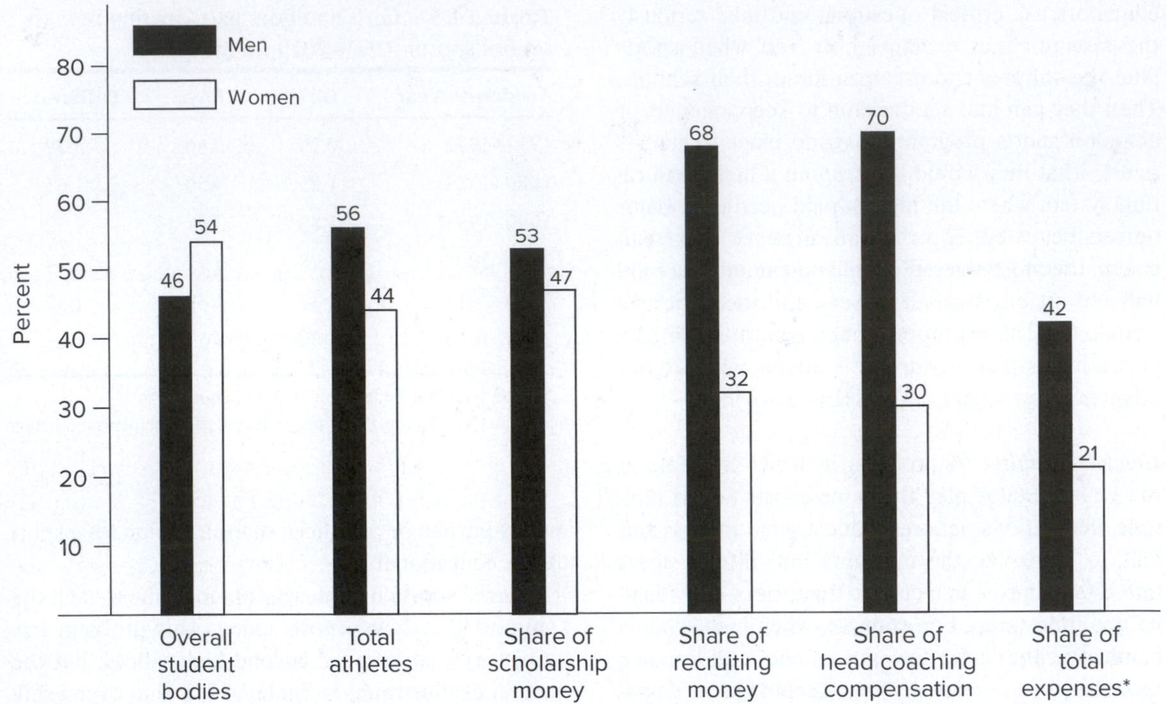

FIGURE 14.1 Gender inequity in NCAA Division I institutions, 2016. (*Source:* Wilson, 2018)
*37 percent of the operating budget is allocated to general administration, not specifically to men's or women's athletics

Christian College Athletic association, which has the largest gender disparity in the money allocated to men's and women's programs.

Gender-related participation inequities in high school and college are due primarily to the size of football teams and the increasing costs associated with fielding football teams. About 25 universities in the Power Five conferences (Atlantic Coast, Big Ten, Big 12, Pac-12, and Southeastern) have football and men's basketball teams that generate enough revenues to subsidize the budgets for all men's and women's sports, but as the expenses for football and men's basketball increase, student fees along with state and university money are used to cover athletic department expenses.

In terms of gender equity, the supporters of intercollegiate football face a glaring contradiction. On the one hand, they say that football is an educational activity and that they should not have to pay taxes on their increasing revenues or treat players as employees. On the other hand, when gender equity is discussed, they claim that college football is a business affected by objective market forces out of their control and that it should not be treated as an educational activity. This is why Title IX remains controversial–it exposes the contradictions of big-time sports programs and turns most college football supporters into flip-floppers and hypocrites. Achieving gender equity will continue to be difficult because football programs are expensive and they usually spend much more money than they generate, even in about 40 of the 65 universities in the Power Five conferences.

The other major reason for persistent gender inequities is that athletic programs remain grounded in a culture based on the values and experiences of men. This will not change until more women are hired as coaches of both women's and men's teams and as athletic directors. But the chance of this happening in the near future is remote for at least three reasons. *First*, most people working in school sports programs today are not familiar with the full meaning of gender equity as it is described in Title IX law, and certainly don't know how to implement the law (Staurowsky and Weight, 2011). *Second*, when football is the centerpiece of sports at the school and conference levels, women are not likely to be hired in top leadership positions because it is widely believed that they cannot effectively work with a football coach and team (Schull et al., 2013). *Third*, when women coaches or lower-level administrators raise questions about gender inequities, they are usually defined as troublemakers and marginalized in the athletic department or in the coaching job market (Fagan and Cyphers, 2012).

Changing the organization and culture of sport programs is a formidable task, and it is nearly impossible when those in charge see no reason to change or see change as a threat to their status and power. However, in the case of programs described and funded as "educational," there's no justification for paying women any less than men or defining women as unqualified for leadership jobs because some people believe that they cannot understand football or work effectively with powerful and highly paid football coaches. Even gender equity training programs are largely ineffective in changing athletic department cultures that have been created by and for men, and controlled by men.

Opportunities for Students with a Disability Where are disability sports in high schools and colleges? For all practical purposes, they are invisible. The National Federation of State High School Associations (NFHS) has sanctioned fourteen "adapted sports", but fewer than one percent of high schools–less than 200 out of over 19,500 US high schools–have teams in any of these sports. More than 7.9 million students play on "standard" high school sport teams and about 15,500 students play on adapted sport teams (NFHS, 2019).[6]

Some athletes with a disability play on standard teams, but apart from them, there is only one varsity athlete in adapted sports for every 510 athletes on high school teams. Students with a disability are "off the radar" for most high school sports programs. Consequently, students miss opportunities to play with and watch their peers with various (dis)abilities compete and share sports experiences with them. This is a missed educational opportunity for all students.

Colleges and universities have done little to nothing to provide sports for people with a disability. Only a dozen universities have recognized programs, and they are funded through student services rather than athletic departments. The programs are at the universities of Alabama, Arizona, Illinois, Missouri, Oklahoma State, Central Oklahoma, Oregon, Edinboro (Pennsylvania), Penn State, Rutgers, Texas at Arlington, and Wisconsin at Whitewater. The sports offered include men's and women's wheelchair basketball, track and road racing, tennis, golf, rowing, and wheelchair rugby (Gerber, 2015).

Although some Paralympians train in these programs, it is difficult to schedule games and meets with other university teams due to the distance between schools and the expenses associated with travel.

At a few of these universities participation occurs totally in-house in the form of training and intramural competitions. Despite recommendations and guidelines provided by the US Department of Education, few people in higher education have done anything beyond mentioning disability sports in passing conversations. The existence of the Paralympics has not had an impact on program development, even though it would make sense for universities to sponsor Paralympic sports just as they sponsor Olympic

---

[6]The "official" numbers of high school students playing sports do not take into account those who play more than one sport. If a school has 12 students with a disability, and each of them plays three sports, the official number of participants would be 36 instead of 12. The same is true for numbers provided by the NFHS.

sports in their athletic departments. As it is now, college students with a disability must seek opportunities to play sports outside the university, even though they pay student fees and should have access to the same opportunities that other students have.

It is difficult to predict how quickly educators will respond to the Department of Education guidelines and take seriously the sport participation of students with disabilities. It could take decades for measureable progress to be made and at least a generation before participation opportunities for students with a disability are a taken-for-granted part of secondary and higher education.

Issues in High School Sport Programs: A Focus on Sports Development

Some high school administrators, athletic directors, and coaches think that educational quality is somehow linked to the development of a sports program that focuses on winning records and being ranked highly among schools in the state or nation. Their goal is to achieve excellence, but their definition of excellence is often modeled after big-time intercollegiate programs. This leads to the emergence of a sports culture in which participants are expected to represent their schools and communities by giving priority to their training, being dedicated to achieving excellence, and being willing to make sacrifices for the team. Winning becomes proof of excellence and losing indicates a need for more training, dedication, and sacrifice. It has also led to building $70 million football stadiums, hiring 11 coaches for football alone, and creating high school academies that accept athletes only and give priority to developing athletic skills (Gay, 2018; O'Brien, 2016; Reagan & Schwartzel, 2017; Riddle, 2019).

People who focus on sports development often give lip service to keeping sports in proper perspective but fail to acknowledge that emphasizing sports in the school marginalizes many students with no interest in power and performance sports. In their zeal to create and maintain excellence on the field of play, administrators may overlook the educational needs of all students in the school.

Sports development today goes hand in hand with informal requirements that athletes specialize in a single sport year-round, even though this may limit their overall social and educational development. This approach turns off students who want to play sports but don't want to make them the center of their lives. At the same time, other students become so dedicated to sports that they see education as secondary in their lives at school.

Adherence to a sports development model often is driven by boosters and booster organizations that raise funds and provide other support to one or more teams in a school. However, individual boosters and booster organizations are seldom regulated by schools or school districts, and they exist primarily in wealthier areas, often giving unfair advantage to a single team in a school or an entire athletic program relative to programs in poor areas where resources are scarce and teams struggle to exist. Many boosters who provide resources, sometimes out of their own pockets, feel they have a right to intervene in the process of evaluating and hiring coaches, and they generally focus on coaches' win-loss records rather than their teaching abilities and knowledge of adolescent development.

Issues in College Sport Programs

This is a challenging time for college sports, especially at the big-time level. They are facing more issues today than at any time in the past century. Scandals and rule violations, lawsuits related to player compensation, and distorted racial and ethnic priorities are discussed in this section.

Scandals and Rule Violations Over the past decade there are too many scandals and major rule violations in NCAA athletic programs to list here (Dohrmann & Evans, 2013a, 2013b, 2013c, 2013d, 2013e, 2013f; Fitzsimmons & Tracy, 2018; Harper & Donnor, 2017). However, recent cases fall into four categories: sexual abuse and assault, academic fraud, college admissions cheating, and bribery involving coaches, sponsors, and athletes. They involve criminal actions as well as violations of NCAA and university rules. Overall, they suggest that some universities have lost institutional control of athletic departments, and the NCAA has been largely ineffective in deterring and punishing corrupt and criminal actions in college sports.

The *sexual abuse, sexual assault, and rape scandals* are among the most serious of recent cases. All of them involve long-term criminal activity by athletes, coaches, team doctors, athletic directors, and university administrators and staff. For example, a retired assistant football coach at Penn State used his affiliation with the football program to lure boys into relationships and sexually abuse them. When an assistant coach saw him sodomizing a boy in a football shower, he reported it to head football coach, Joe Paterno, rather than to local police or state child protection authorities. Paterno, who had suspected that his former coach sexually abused children, was in no rush to report it to Penn State officials. When he did, they took no action. After a former victim came forward, an official state investigation led to a conviction of the former coach on 45 counts of child abuse and child sexual abuse. The Penn State president, athletic director, director of campus security, head football coach, and the assistant coach were all fired for covering-up the actions of the former coach. For them, protecting the football program was a higher priority than following state law and protecting children from a sexual predator.

A Baylor University scandal fits a similar pattern. It involved over 100 reports of rape, sexual assault, and sexual harassment between 2011 and 2016. Fifty-two rapes and gang rapes were allegedly committed by at least 19 members of the football team. Athletic department personnel took no action when reports were made to them. Although court cases are ongoing, players have been convicted and given prison sentences. The university president, athletic director, and head football coach were forced to resign for their failure to respond to the alleged crimes (although the coach received an $18 million severance package, despite violating NCAA and university rules, if not criminal laws. Baylor received a minor punishment from the NCAA.

Michigan State University officials also failed to respond to reports that athletic department doctor, Larry Nassar was sexually abusing and assaulting young women (as he also had done to hundreds of girls training with USA Gymnastics. To avoid individual lawsuits, MSU is paying $500 million to 332 alleged victims of Nassar's assaults, a record amount paid by any university in a sexual abuse/assault case. It was also fined $4.5 million by the US Department of Education, in part for its collective failure to respond to reports of abuse that began in the late-1990s and continued through 2015. The MSU president, athletic director, a provost, and a medical school dean all resigned in the face of allegations that they violated a law mandating that suspected abuse must be reported immediately to local police or child protective services. Nassar was sentenced to 175 years in prison.

(*Source:* Jeff Moffett/Icon Sportswire/Getty Images)

Kenneth Starr, former president of Baylor University was just one of the top university officials to resign or be fired for failing to report sexual abuse and assault perpetrated by a person associated with an athletic team or the athletic department. Their desire to protect the reputation of the university and the athletic program took priority over doing the right thing.

The MSU president faces criminal charges because she lied to police about her knowledge of complaints about Nassar.

Academic frauds have occurred regularly in college sports (AP, 2016; Murphy, 2019b; New, 2016; O'Donnell, 2016; Ridpath & Gurney, 2015; Tracy, 2014). But "the mother of all academic frauds" occurred at the University of North Carolina between 1993 and 2011 (Smith, undated; Smith & Willingham, 2015). During those 18 years, over 3,100 students, over half of whom were athletes, took at least 200 bogus courses for which they received high grades (usually As) for doing no work, handing in no assignments, and attending no class sessions. The courses were offered in an African American Studies program, and they were listed as being taught by the head and only faculty member in the program. Over many of those 18 years, the courses were created and listed by the secretary for the program. She was an ardent fan of UNC sports and often took a day off to recover when the football or basketball team lost a game. She listed the classes, received class rosters, and turned in grades for students. Athletes were advised to take the classes by a number of academic counselors who saw that high grades were common in them and would keep athletes eligible. After some people suspected fraud, it took the university about five years to begin its own investigation.

Over the course of the fraud, athletes remained eligible and the UNC basketball team won three national championships. Some coaches knew about the fake courses, generally referred to as "paper classes," but said nothing. A 3-year NCAA investigation concluded that there was no fraud because its rule left such determinations up to universities, and UNC at that time claimed that the courses were legitimate. The NCAA also concluded that there were no rule violations because the bogus courses were open to all students and not offered exclusively for athletes (Bauer-Wolf, 2017). These conclusions protected everyone connected with UNC sports, and the NCAA did not penalize UNC or the athletic department, even though athletes and teams benefitted from major academic fraud. Full public disclosure of the fraud did not occur until Mary Willingham, a learning specialist, who often found that athletes in revenue-producing sports had decent grades but needed help in learning how to read. With assistance, she did her own investigation and reported what she found (Ganim & Sayers, 2014; Murphy, 2019; Smith, undated; Smith and Willingham, 2015; Wiseman & Kane, 2019).

A highly publicized *college admissions scandal* with connection to college sports involved payments by wealthy parents to have their children admitted to elite universities. In one part of this scheme, the former coach who orchestrated this cheating process knew that many coaches needed money or were under pressure from their athletic departments to raise money for their teams. He also knew that the applications of designated recruited athletes were regularly admitted to universities even when their academic qualifications did not meet minimum requirements. When a parent paid him he would fabricate an application in which their child was fraudulently presented as a highly recruited athlete in a particular sport, usually a low-profile sport in which coaches could give up one of their scholarships without it hurting team quality (Stripling, 2019). Then he would pay a coach in that sport at the desired university to request that the applicant receive a special admission reserved for talented athletes.

Because coaches have been approved to bypass the normal admissions process for these "special athlete admits," they became his accomplices. In this way, underqualified children of wealthy parents were admitted to the University of Texas, Yale, the University of Southern California, UCLA, Stanford, Wake Forest, Georgetown and the University of San Diego, among others. FBI investigations of this scheme exposed the lack of oversight related to special admissions for recruited athletes (Anderson & Syrluga, 2019; Hiltzik, 2019). Although formal criminal charges were filed in a number of cases, investigators estimated that hundreds of bogus "athletes" were admitted through this bribery scheme. An ongoing NCAA investigation will determine if penalties will be imposed on athletic departments, coaches, or athletic department personnel. However, the NCAA is notorious for allowing athletic programs to escape serious consequences even when there have been major rule violations.

Another *bribery scandal involving coaches, sponsors, and athletes* was uncovered by the FBI in 2017. The investigation identified representatives of Adidas who paid money to heavily recruited high school basketball players and their families if they promised to attend an Adidas-sponsored university such as Louisville, Kansas, or North Carolina State. Once the athletes accepted scholarships and attended an Adidas university, assistant coaches were paid money to steer the players to a particular sports agent if and when they entered the NBA draft. Everyone involved defined this as a win-win-win situation. Athletes received money for their labor in a revenue-generating basketball program, Adidas sold more shoes due to the publicity of having top players and college teams outfitted in their products, the basketball teams won games and usually qualified for the NCAA postseason tournament, assistant coaches received bonus money, and a pair of sports agents were in line to represent players likely to sign NBA contracts.

According to public information about the investigation, the universities involved were Arizona, Auburn, Creighton, Louisville, Miami, Oklahoma State, South Carolina, Southern California, and Texas Christian. Additional evidence of payments implicated Alabama, Clemson, Kansas, Kentucky, Lousiana State, Maryland, Michigan State, North Carolina, North Carolina State, San Diego State, Seton Hall, South Carolina, Texas, Utah, Washington, Wichita State, and Xavier. Money changed hands in many directions and in different amounts in one-time and multiple payments. When the investigation identified who was involved, players were declared ineligible, some assistant coaches were fired and a few were charged with crimes. Two Adidas employees were also charged along with two sports agents. On being questioned by the FBI, one of the agents admitted the following:

> *We were definitely paying players . . . Everyone was paying players. . . . They are the only people in college basketball who can't get paid. The idea that it's an amateur world is not real* (in Powell, 2019)

The fact that much of the evidence collected by the FBI was never disclosed has led investigative journalists to suggest that many Division I basketball programs are involved in similar schemes. The FBI analysis of the undisclosed evidence continues but there is no guarantee that it will be made public or used to file charges. In the meantime, no head coaches or top executives at Adidas were fired with the exception of Rick Pitino, the head coach at Louisville, but his termination was also tied to other incidents, including an affair with the wife of his team's equipment manager, paying her to have an abortion, and overseeing a basketball program in which assistant coaches supplied strippers and prostitutes to impress high school recruits and retain current players (Sokolov, 2018).

Player Rights and Compensation The NCAA has insisted for years that college sports are amateur activities and that college athletes are first and foremost students. This position has been the basis for its legal defense in dozens of major court cases in which the organization has been sued by athletes for not allowing them to have the same rights as other students, for not protecting their health, and for not allowing them to have a meaningful voice in determining the conditions of their sport participation. But this defense is becoming more difficult because Division I sports programs are highly commercialized and "professional-like" when it comes to revenues, the price of tickets to big-time college football and men's basketball games, sponsorship deals with major shoe and apparel companies, billion-dollar media rights contracts, and multimillion-dollar salaries for coaches, conference commissioners, and athletic directors (Branch, 2019). Additionally, college athletes in big-time programs now have regular access to information that has increased their awareness of issues that impact them negatively.

In the face of potential and real legal challenges to the NCAA concept of *amateurism*, officials in the organization regularly change its definition to fit their interests and the changing conditions of college sports. For example, when the NCAA appointed a committee in 2019 to examine the issue of athletes having the freedom–as all other students have–to benefit from the use of their names, images, and likenesses, they had this to say:

> *The group will not consider any concepts that could be construed as payment for participation in college sports. . . .[It]will study modifications of current rules, policies and practices [and]focus on solutions that tie any changes to education . . . and maintain the clear demarcation between professional and college sports; and further align student-athletes with the general student body* (Wolkin, 2019).

In other words, no matter what the committee recommends or what the NCAA decides, it will be consistent with its definition of amateurism as NCAA officials determine it to be.

The history of this strategy is clear (Wolkin, 2019). When football players resisted giving up their holiday and semester break to play in what were meaningless postseason bowl games, the NCAA approved giving the players gifts worth hundreds of dollars to quiet their objections; and they also explained that these gifts were not payments for participation. When a legal decision in a court case determined that athletes could be compensated for education-related expenses not covered by their scholarships, NCAA officials allowed universities to pay the "full cost of attendance." But they insisted that this was not a payment for participation in sports. The same thing occurred when a basketball player in the Final Four of the Division I basketball tournament explained that there were times when he and his teammates went hungry at night because NCAA rules prevented universities from feeding them beyond three times a day, despite their intense calorie-burning workouts. The NCAA changed this rule but insisted that this had nothing to do with payment for participation. This also was the case when NCAA officials decided that the families of athletes playing in bowl games and the Final Four tournament could be "reimbursed" for the travel expenses for attending the games. Most recently, after athletes were allowed to enter the NBA draft and return to their universities if they were not drafted or not satisfied with potential contract offers, the NCAA changed its longstanding rule that athletes were not allowed to seek the advice of agents without giving up their eligibility and scholarships. This meant that athletes could have agents to help them negotiate million-dollar deals, but remain amateurs (Waldron, 2019).

With this history, whatever is decided about athletes using their names, images, and likenesses for their benefit, the NCAA will insist that it is consistent with its definition of amateurism because it does not involve "payment for participation" (Wolkin, 2019). The NCAA has made such payments for athletes a line in the sand for the organization. Officials at the NCAA and at Division I universities say that going beyond this line will destroy college sports. However, other so-called amateur sports organizations, including the International Olympic Committee, have gone beyond that line and discovered that they can survive and even thrive. But crossing the line is a bit different for the NCAA because payment for participation would turn at least some athletes into university employees, an outcome that would create more work for coaches and athletic departments and deprive them of their total control over athletes' lives. This is because they would have to follow state and federal laws that protect the rights of workers, and athletes would be able to form unions through which they could negotiate the conditions of their employment.

It is difficult to predict all the consequences of such a change, but they would be significant. After paying athletes, there might not be enough money left to pay coaches the obscene salaries that some of them make as employees in tax-exempt nonprofit organizations (Johnson, 2018). Additionally, they would be subject to criminal charges if they had workouts in which athletes are pushed to the point of death or needing hospital treatment, as occurred recently at the Universities of Maryland, Oregon, Nebraska, and Iowa as coaches disregarded the health and safety of athletes to assert their power over them. The football coach at Maryland demanded the continuation of physically punishing drills even as one player crawled on the ground and was assisted by a teammate in an effort to complete the drill. As a result, the athlete died while obeying his coach (Hruby, 2018b; Jenkins, 2018; Maese & Stubbs, 2018).

Cases like this, as well as athletes being deprived of rights enjoyed by other students, have led elected officials at the state and federal levels to introduce laws giving college athletes the right to form unions and the right to profit from making endorsement deals, giving speeches, or running their own sport camps in the summer. For example, Nancy Skinner (who attended lectures by sociologist and human rights activist, Harry Edwards, when she was a student at Cal-Berkeley), as a new member of the California State Senate, introduced a bill allowing college athletes in California to receive payments for using their names, images, and likenesses to make marketing and endorsement deals if they had the chance, or to use their personal abilities and reputations to be paid if, for example, a water polo player or a swimmer offered lessons in their sport during the summer. Skinner's *Fair Pay to Play Act* (Senate Bill 206) was passed by a vote of 72-0 in September 2019 with support from liberal, moderate, and conservative senators. Gavin Newsom, the California governor, signed the bill into law which will take effect on January 1, 2023 (Murphy, 2019).

Of course, there was loud opposition to the bill from NCAA officials, the commissioner of the PAC-12 Conference, and coaches and athletic directors at California's major universities. They painted pictures of disruption, chaos, and post-apocalyptic despair if the bill becomes law. But they have their work cut out for them because there are similar legislative efforts being made in a number of other states and in the US Congress. My guess is that the US Supreme Court may have the last word on this. In the meantime, these changes are supported by many professional athletes, the National Labor Relations Board, the Steelworkers Union, The Drake Group, the National College Players Association, and the College Athletes Players Association (Bivens, 2017).

Lessons from Scandals and Legal Challenges Like most organizations that have power and resources, the NCAA is notoriously bad at self-policing and self-reform. Vested interests supporting the status quo are so strong that they limit the extent to which it investigates and punishes member institutions. After all, those institutions **are** the NCAA, and they are unwilling to make changes that might compromise their power and resources. This is why few members, especially influential members, are severely punished for actions that violate rules and why reforms come only when widespread public pressure or more powerful organizations force it to make changes.

From the examples in this section, it is clear that independent investigations are needed in cases that involve serious rule violations or criminal actions. However, pervasive public support for college sports and the universities that sponsor them, along with widespread sports-think grounded in the great sport myth, make it difficult to find independent investigators willing to critically assess the current organization and the everyday operations of sports programs. When people have strong attachments to universities and are fervent fans of college teams and college sports generally, they are hesitant to make decisions or recommendations that change what they love, even if the NCAA and big-time athletic programs engage in actions that are contrary to the mission of higher education and the values it professes.

When people take it upon themselves to ask critical questions about school-sponsored sports, conduct investigations, and identify problems that can be solved only by changing sports, they are generally ignored or they become targets of widespread scorn and personal attacks on their character and careers. This provides college (and high school) sports programs with a shield that is difficult to penetrate, even when the facts indicate that the shield should be laid to rest.

Distorted Racial and Ethnic Priorities In 2018, black students made up about 10 percent of the total student body at Division I universities, and the vast majority of them were students at predominantly white institutions (PWIs). Figure 14.2 shows that at the same time, black men and women were 21 percent of the athletes, 48 percent of football players, 56 percent of the men's and 47 percent of the women's basketball players. For example, at the University of Florida in 2016, black men comprised 2.2 percent of all undergraduate students, but comprised 78 percent of the men's basketball and football teams (Harper, 2018).

Seventy-seven percent of all black male athletes played football or basketball–the only sports that produced revenues and the sports with the lowest graduation rates. This also means that, in some Division I PWIs, black male athletes consistently generate revenues that fund other sport teams consisting of mostly or all white players from families that have much higher incomes than the families from which the black payers come–which is an interesting form of "welfare for white athletes" that is seldom discussed. The same revenues also pay multi-million dollar salaries to a growing number of white coaches and salaries of a million dollars or more to white

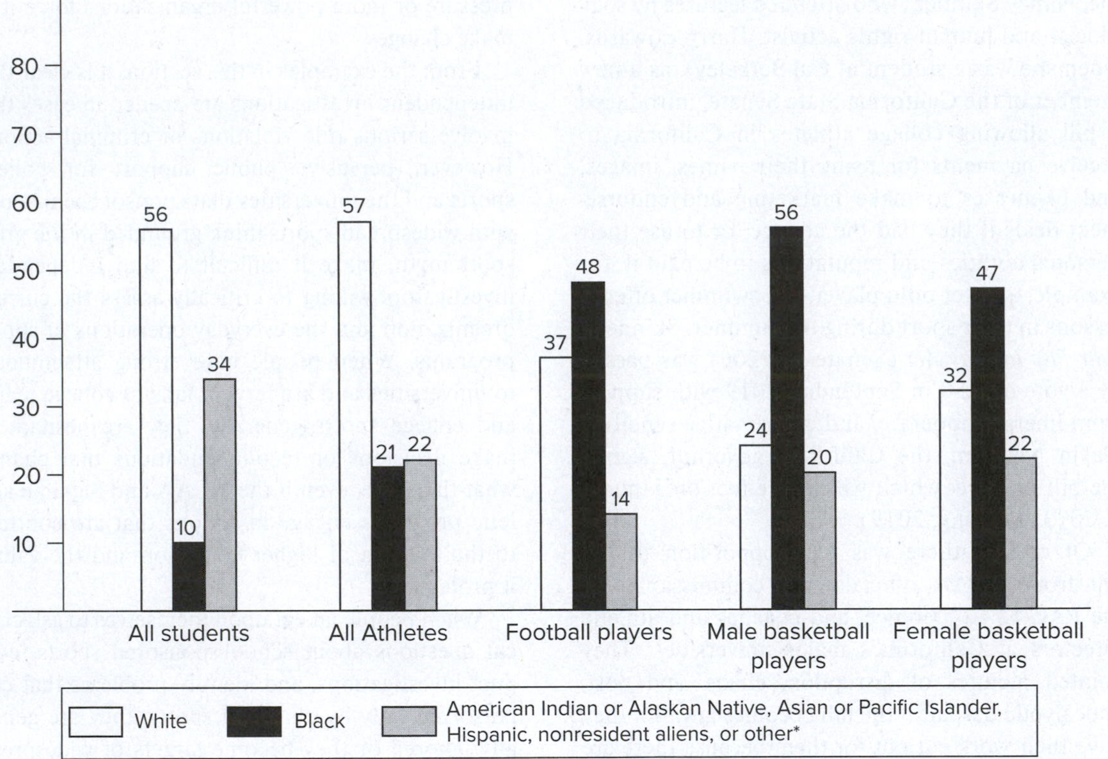

FIGURE 14.2 Percentages of students and athletes in football and men's and women's basketball in NCAA Division I universities by race and ethnicity, 2018. (*Source:* NCAA Research, http://www.ncaa.org/about/resources/research/ncaa-demographics-database)

athletic directors, an increasing number of white assistant and strength coaches, and conference commissioners as well as NCAA executives. As sociology of sport scholar, Billie Hawkins (2010), has said for many years, this situation resembles a contemporary plantation system in which the labor of black workers makes their white bosses wealthy.

Overall, these data suggest that if African Americans excel in revenue-producing sports, PWIs with big-time sports programs will actively identify and recruit them, but the same universities do a poor job of recruiting African American students who don't excel at scoring touchdowns or making jump shots. There is no denying that a few African Americans benefit from athletic scholarships. But the problem is that universities have capitalized on the racist myth that blacks can use sports to improve their lives, while ignoring their responsibility to recruit black students and change the social climate on campus so that black students feel welcome, supported, and respected, even if they don't score touchdowns or 20 points a game. In the meantime, the number of African Americans attending college is dropping, and 99.9 percent of all college age African Americans do not have athletic scholarships,

(*Source:* ELLEN OZIER/REUTERS/Newscom)

When African Americans attend historically white institutions of higher education, they often experience feelings of social isolation. This can be a problem for athletes when nearly all the coaches are white, along with the athletic director, faculty, advisors, administrators, and fans attending their games and meets. Most white students at these universities are unaware of this.

and most are unable to pay the costs of higher education.

A related problem is that many black athletes feel isolated on campuses where there are few black students, faculty, and administrators (Bimper, 2015; Bruening et al., 2005; Carter-Francique, Dortch & Carter-Phiri, 2017; Comeaux and Fuentes, 2015; Griffith, Hurd & Hussain, 2019; Harper, 2006, 2018; Hattery, Kiss & Smith, 2018; Hawkins, 2010; Hawkins et al., 2015; Hawkins, Carter-Francique & Cooper, 2016; Maples et al, 2019; Martin et al., 2010; Singer and Carter-Francique, 2013; Smith, 2009; Torres, 2009). This isolation is intensified by many factors, including these:

1. Racial and athletic stereotypes make it difficult for black athletes to feel welcome on campus and develop relationships that support their academic success.
2. Athletes must devote so much time to their sports that it is difficult for them to become involved in other spheres of campus life.
3. The lack of a proportional number of black coaches, faculty, and support staff available in the university and the athletic department for black athletes in need of knowledgeable guidance and mentoring.
4. Campus activities often fail to represent the interests and experiences of black students, who consequently often feel like outsiders.
5. When campus life is unrelated to their experiences, black athletes may withdraw from activities that could connect them with other students.
6. White students who lack experience in racially diverse groups may feel uncomfortable interacting with black students from backgrounds unlike their own.
7. When white students think that black athletes are privileged due to the scholarships that they may have, it creates tension that undermines meaningful interaction.

Feelings of social isolation are especially intense when most students have grown up in racially segregated neighborhoods with different levels of economic privilege, attended largely segregated K-12 schools with different levels of educational resources, and have little in-depth knowledge of race relations in the United States or in PWIs. This creates racial tensions that call for sensitive and effective interventions coordinated by campus administrators, professional staff, faculty, and student leaders, but such interventions rarely occur. Instead, athletic departments intervene and put athletes in their own dorm wings, create special academic support programs for them, and provide athlete centers where they eat and hang out with other athletes that share sport-related goals regardless of race. However, this strategy does nothing to improve race relations on campus and little to eliminate the isolation felt by black athletes.

After in-depth analyses of the racial dynamics in Power Five conferences in the NCAA, Shaun Harper, a professor in the schools of education and business at the University of Southern California and founder of the USC Race and Equity Center, has concluded the following:

> *Perhaps nowhere in higher education is the disenfranchisement of black male students more insidious than in college athletics* (Harper, 2006, 2018).

Most sociology of sport research on black players has focused on black men, so we know little about the experiences of black women who play sports in predominantly white institutions. Black women athletes face the dual challenges of complex racial and gender dynamics on campus *and* in the athletic department (Bernhard, 2014; Bruening, 2005; Bruening et al., 2005; Carter-Francique, 2014; Carter and Hawkins, 2011; Carter-Francique et al., 2011; Carter-Francique, Dortch & Carter-Phiri, 2017; Gabay, 2013; Hawkins, Carter-Francique & Cooper, 2016; Hughes, 2015; Milner & Braddock, 2016; Theune, 2016, 2019). They see few women of color in positions of power and authority in their schools and athletic departments, and this intensifies feelings of marginalization and powerlessness in both spheres.

A key issue for many black women is that Title IX has primarily benefited white women (Milner & Braddock, 2016; Theune, 2016, 2019). For example, 72 percent of all black women with athletic scholarships in Division I, including Historically Black Colleges and Universities (HBCUs), are members of basketball or track and field teams.[7] At the same time, black women receive less than 5 percent of the scholarships in all other women's sports. This is because most athletic departments in PWIs have attempted to meet Title IX equity requirements by adding sports such as rowing, golf, rifle, field hockey, lacrosse, ice hockey, fencing, skiing, beach volleyball, and water polo—all of which are played almost exclusively by white women from upper-middle-class families. In 2018, only 395 black women played on any of these teams, and many of those were the only black woman on their team in PWIs (teams in HBCUs are included in this total). As a result, it has intensified the feelings of isolation and powerlessness experienced by black female athletes, and by black female students.

Dealing with this situation is a goal for some of the few black female faculty and athletic department members working at PWIs. For example, when Akilah Carter-Francique, the 2018-2019 President of the North American Society for the Sociology of Sport, was a facuty member at Texas A&M University, she created the Sista to Sista™ leadership development program to provide black female athletes a "safe cultural space" on campus. The program fosters social connections built around an awareness of the dynamics of power on campus and in the athletic department, and around an affirmation of self-definition and self-valuation grounded in the history of black women's culture. From that vantage point, the women formulate strategies for representing their interests in a context where their voices have long been silenced (Carter-Francique, Dortch & Carter-Phiri, 2017). However, the structure and cultures of PWIs and Division I athletic departments where most of the coaches and athletic directors are white men, make it risky to express

[7] When computing these totals, I did not count members of both indoor and outdoor track and field teams because over 90 percent of them are the same people.

their voices. Speaking truth to power from a marginalized position nearly always evokes pushback and negative consequences that can affect academic and athletic careers. Additionally, to do this and successfully manage dual careers at the same time is nearly impossible. For this reason, it is best for them to work through organizations that have enough power and leverage to effectively represent their interests. But those organizations are scarce and usually have other priorities. In fact, this is one of the reasons that some of these women attend or transfer to HBCUs. These institutions have far fewer resources than Division I PWIs, but they have an abundance of safe cultural spaces in which to prepare for the future.

Racial inequities have long characterized historically white institutions of higher education. Expecting black athletes or all athletes of color to take on the challenge of resisting and changing their organizations and cultures is to be blind to the history and meaning of race in the United States. In fact, for young black men and women to attend those universities is in many ways an act of resistance in itself (Reddick, 2018). For those who are athletes, the challenge is to successfully manage their dual careers. Their academic careers are a high priority because only about two percent of them will have opportunities to play professional sports at a level that provides decent financial rewards for a few years.

From the perspective of PWIs, it is both naïve and unfair to recruit black or other ethnic minority athletes to campuses where they have little social support and feel that students and faculty don't know much about their history, heritage, experiences, and challenges faced on campus and the surrounding community. If universities effectively included racial and cultural diversity within all spheres of campus life, recruiting black athletes would not indicate a distorted set of campus priorities. When universities present to the world images of physically talented black athletes and intellectually talented white scientists, racism is perpetuated, whether intentionally or not, and the quality of education is compromised.

summary

DO COMPETITIVE SPORTS CONTRIBUTE TO EDUCATION?

The United States is the only nation in the world where it is taken for granted that high schools and colleges will sponsor and fund interschool sport programs. There are arguments for and against this practice, but most claims made on both sides are not based on good research.

Generalizing about high school and college sport programs is difficult because programs and the conditions under which participation occurs are so diverse. However, it's important to study school sports to determine if and when they contribute to positive educational outcomes for athletes, the overall effectiveness of the school, and students in general. At a minimum, if the programs provide no educational benefits for athletes, they cannot be justified as school-sponsored activities.

Research shows that young people who play on high school teams have better overall academic records than those who don't. But much of this difference is explained by the processes through which students are selected-in and filtered-out of school teams. Young people with characteristics consistent with academic achievement are favored in these processes, so it is not surprising that athletes, on average, have higher grades and other attributes that differ from students who don't make or stay on school teams.

The most effective way to determine what occurs in connection with school sports participation is to study athletes and teams in context over time. This enables a researcher to identify the factors that influence sports experiences, the meanings that young people give to those experiences, and how young people integrate them into their identities and everyday lives.

Sports experiences vary widely and are given different meanings that are influenced by gender, race and ethnicity, social class, (dis)ability, and the social and cultural context of the family, school, and local community. Although there is reasonably consistent evidence indicating that the social dynamics on certain high school sport teams increase the likelihood of binge drinking among athletes and higher rates of sexual activity and bullying by certain male athletes, most studies suggest that athletes have higher than average rates of educational achievement and fewer problems than other students.

Research also indicates that some schools, coaches, parents, and athletes lose sight of educational goals in their pursuit of competitive success in sports. Sports can be seductive, and people connected with high school teams usually require guidance to keep their programs in balance with academic goals. Unless teams are explicitly organized to achieve positive educational outcomes, the chances of achieving them decrease. When people assume that sports participation automatically builds character and enhances learning, it undermines the planning and evaluation that must be a part of any school activity, especially those that are as costly and popular as school sports.

The possibility that sports participation interferes with the education of athletes is greatest in big-time intercollegiate programs. The status and identity that often comes with membership on highly visible and publicized teams makes it difficult for many young people to focus on and give priority to their academic careers. This is especially the case among young men who see their destinies being shaped by athletic rather than academic achievements. Graduation rates among athletes vary widely by gender, race, and sport. However, research suggests that athletes in revenue-generating sports fail to graduate at the same rate as students in the rest of the university.

High school and college sports usually create spirited feelings among some students, faculty, and staff in schools. But little is known about the characteristics of this spirit or if and when it contributes to the achievement of educational goals—or disrupts the achievement of those goals. Although many different activities can be used to unite students and link them with community and society, sports often are used to do this in the United States. Sports are popular activities, but there is much to be learned about the conditions under which they are most and least likely to produce particular social, educational, and developmental outcomes.

Most high school sports programs don't seriously cut into funds for academic programs. The money they require is well spent if they provide students with opportunities to learn about their physicality, develop physical and interpersonal skills, and display their skills in ways that lead them to be recognized and rewarded by others. However, when budgets are strained, many programs depend on participation fees, donations boosters, and/or corporate sponsors to survive. When this occurs, schools in lower-income areas are at a serious competitive disadvantage. Over time, these strategies to fund school sports lead to and intensify social class and racial/ethnic divisions in and between schools and school districts.

Funding issues are complex and often confusing in intercollegiate sports. However, it's clear that very few programs are self-supporting and nearly all of them depend on subsidies from student fees and money from the state or general university funds. As intercollegiate programs increase their focus on achieving commercial goals, the likelihood of achieving educational goals usually declines. The allocation of state and general university funds and student fees to intercollegiate sports becomes an increasingly contentious issue when athletic departments and sport teams have become so separate from the rest of campus culture that some faculty and students see little reason to support them.

High school and college sports programs now face a number of crucial issues. These include cost containment and budget inequality between schools; rising expectations among athletes and their parents; dealing with concussions, repetitive head trauma, and other serious injuries; creating and sustaining programs with explicit educational relevance; eliminating gender inequity; and creating opportunities for students with a disability. Each of these issues creates a serious challenge for athletic directors and coaches.

Issues unique to high school sports programs consist of clarifying the meaning of sport development so that it is compatible with the education mission of schools and making sure that boosters and other community supporters understand what that means. The unique issues faced in college sports are reducing scandals and rule violations, coming to terms with issues related to athletes' rights and just compensation, and corrcting distorted priorities related to race and ethnicity in the university and in athletic departments.

The decisions made on these issues will have a significant impact on the future direction of high school and college sports.

SUPPLEMENTAL READINGS

Reading 1. Research faculty are not eager to study intercollegiate sports
Reading 2. A brief history of NCAA academic reforms
Reading 3. School–community relations
Reading 4. Ethnicity and sport participation among high school girls
Reading 5. Conformity or leadership in high school sports
Reading 6. Academic detachment in college sports

SPORT MANAGEMENT ISSUES

- You're a reporter for a newspaper in a small midwestern US city. A chronic budget crisis leads the local school board to consider dropping varsity sports. The board has scheduled a meeting to discuss this issue with people in the community. To prepare for the meeting, you review the arguments you expect to hear on both sides of the issue. What are those arguments, and who do you expect to be the most vocal proponents of each?
- You're a member of a school board in an urban school district. The board has just been presented with data showing that varsity athletes in the fifteen high schools in your district receive higher grades than nonathletes. A group of parents is using the data to request more funds for interscholastic sports in the district. What are the questions you would ask about the data, and why would you ask them?
- The academic experiences of athletes in colleges with big-time sport programs are different from the experiences of athletes in colleges with lower-profile programs. If you were talking to a group of high school seniors interested in playing college sports, how would you explain these differences?
- The intercollegiate sport programs at your school are in bad financial shape. Because of large losses, the students have been asked to increase their student fees by $100 per semester to maintain the programs. If the fee increase does not pass, all the intercollegiate sport programs will be dropped and replaced by low-cost, student-run club sports. How would you vote? Use material from this chapter to support your decision.

references

Adler, Patricia A., and Peter Adler. 1991. *Backboards and blackboards: College athletes and role engulfment*. New York: Columbia University Press.

Anderson, Nick & Susan Svrluga. 2019. Bribery scandal points to the athletic factor: A major force in college admissions. *Washington Post* (June 13): https://www.washingtonpost.com/local/education/bribery-scandal-points-to-the-athletic-factor-a-major-force-in-college-admissions/2019/06/12/b2fc39dc-7e3a-11e9-8bb7-0fc796cf2ec0_story.html

AP. 2016. Tutor says she took exams for Missouri athletes; probe started. *USA Today* (November 23): http://www.usatoday.com/story/sports/ncaaf/sec/2016/11/23/missouri-mizzou-tigers-athletics-tutor-exams/94369124/

Baker, Thomas A. & John T. Holden. 2018. College esports: A model for NCAA reform. *South Carolina Law Review* 70: 55–83.

Bauer-Wolf, Jeremy. 2017. NCAA: No academic violations at UNC. *InsideHigherEd.com*

(October 16): https://www.insidehighered.com/news/2017/10/16/breaking-ncaa-finds-no-academic-fraud-unc

Benedict, Jeff & Armen Keteyian. 2013. *The system: The glory and scandal of big-time college football*. New York: Doubleday.

Bernhard, Laura M. 2014. "Nowhere for me to go:" Black female student-athlete experiences on a predominantly white campus. *Journal for the Study of Sports and Athletes in Education* 8(2): 67–76.

Bimper, Albert Y. Jr. 2016. Capital matters: Social sustaining capital and the development of black student-athletes. *Journal of Intercollegiate Sport* 9(1): 106–128.

Bimper, Albert Y. Jr. 2017. Mentorship of Black student-athletes at a predominately White American university: critical race theory perspective on student-athlete development. *Sport, Education and Society* 22(2):175–193.

Bimper, Albert Y., Jr. 2015. Lifting the veil: Exploring colorblind racism in black student athlete experiences. *Journal of Sport and Social Issues* 39(3): 225–243.

Bissinger, H. G. 1990. *Friday night lights.* Reading, MA: Addison-Wesley.

Bivens, George J. 2017. NCAA student athlete unionization: NLRB punts on Northwestern University football team. *Penn State Law Review* 121 (3, May 14): 949-978.

Brady, Erik, and Josh Barnett. 2015. Stretching the season: Up to 16-game seasons spark debate on player safety. *USA Today* (December 18): 1C.

Branch, Taylor, 2011. The shame of college sports. *The Atlantic* (October): https://www.theatlantic.com/magazine/archive/2011/10/the-shame-of-college-sports/308643/

Branch, Taylor. 2019. What players deserve. *TIME Magazine* 193 (13, April 8): 19–21.

Brown, Letisha Engracia Cardoso. 2015. Sporting space invaders: Elite bodies in track and field, a South African context. *South African Review of Sociology* 46(1): 7–24.

Bruening, Jennifer E. 2005. Gender and racial analysis in sport: Are all the women white and all the blacks men? *Quest* 57(3): 330–349.

Bruening, Jennifer E., Ketra. L. Armstrong & Donna L. Pastore. 2005. Listening to the voices: The experiences of African American female student-athletes. *Research Quarterly for Exercise and Sport* 76(1): 82–100.

Burnsed, Brian. 2018. Diploma data. *Champion* (Spring): 62.

Carlson, Deven, Leslie Scott, Michael Planty & Jennifer Thompson. 2005. S*tatistics in brief: What Is the Status of High School Athletes 8 Years After Their Senior Year?* Washington, D.C: US Department of Education, Institute of Education Sciences, National Center for Educational Statistics (NCES 2005-303; http://nces.ed.gov/pubs2005/2005303.pdf)

Carter, Akilah R., and Billy J. Hawkins. 2011. Coping strategies among African American female collegiate athletes' in the predominantly white institution. In K. Hylton, A. Pilkington, P. Warmington, and S. Housee, eds., *Atlantic Crossings: International Dialogues in Critical Race Theory* (pp. 61–92). Birmingham, United Kingdom: Sociology, Anthropology, Politics (C-SAP), The Higher Education Academy Network.

Carter-Francique, Akilah R. 2014. The ethic of care: Black female college athlete development. In James L. Conyers, ed., *Race in American sports: Essays* (pp. 35–58). Jefferson, NC: McFarland and Company, Incorporated.

Carter-Francique, Akilah R., Deniece Dortch, Khrystal Carter-Phiri. 2017. Black female college athletes' perception of power in sport and society. *Journal for the Study of Sports and Athletes in Education* 11(1): 18–45.

Carter-Francique, Akilah R., Malia Lawrence, and J. Eyanson. 2011. Racial episodes in sport: voices of African American female athletes. *Intellectbase International Consortium* 4(4): 1–18.

Child Trends. 2013. *Participation in school athletics: Indicators on children and youth*.

Child Trends Data Bank (February): www.childtrendsdatabank.org

Ching, David. 2018. Big Ten's rights deal threatens to widen financial gap between even the biggest conferences. *Forbes.com* (April 17): https://www.forbes.com/sites/davidching/2018/04/17/big-tens-rights-deal-threatens-to-widen-financial-gap-between-even-the-biggest-conferences/#7cb38b035bf2

Clopton, Aaron W. & Bryan L. Finch. 2010. College sport and social capital: Are students 'bowling alone'? *Journal of Sport Behavior* 33(4): 333–366.

Clopton, Aaron W. 2008. College sports on campus: Uncovering the link between team identification and sense of community. *International Journal of Sport Management* 9(4): 1–20.

Clopton, Aaron W. 2009. One for the team: The impact of community upon students as fans and academic and social integration. *Journal of Issues in Intercollegiate Athletics* (Special Issue): 24–61.

Clopton, Aaron. 2011. Social capital and college sport: In search of the bridging potential of intercollegiate athletics. *Journal of Intercollegiate Sport* 4(2): 174–189.

Clotfelder, Charles T. 2011. *Big-time sports in American universities*. New York: Cambridge University Press.

Comeaux, Eddie, and Marcia V. Fuentes. 2015. Cross-racial interaction of Division I athletes: The campus climate for diversity. In Eddie Comeaux, ed., *Introduction to intercollegiate athletics* (pp. 179–192). Baltimore MD: Johns Hopkins University Press.

Connolly, Oliver. 2019. Helmets don't eliminate concussions. It's time for the NFL to ditch them. *Guardian US* (September 6): https://www.theguardian.com/sport/2019/sep/06/helmets-dont-eliminate-concussions-its-time-for-the-nfl-to-ditch-them

Cooper, Joseph N. 2019. *From exploitation back to empowerment: Black male holistic (under) development through sport and (mis)education*. New York: Peter Lang Publishing, Inc.

Crissey, Sarah R., and Joy Crissey Honea. 2006. The relationship between athletic participation and perceptions of body size and weight control in adolescent girls: The role of sports. *Sociology of Sport Journal* 23(3): 248–272.

Cunningham, George B., Sheranne Fairley, Lesley Ferkins, Shannon Kerwin, Daniel Lock, Sally Shaw & Pamela Wicker. 2018. eSport: Construct specifications and implications for sport management. *Sport Management Review* 21(1): 1–6.

Davies, Susan C. & Brenna M. Bird. 2015. Motivations for underreporting suspected concussion in college athletics. *Counselor Education and Human Services Faculty Publications.* Paper 44; online, http://ecommons.udayton.edu/edc_fac_pub/44

Denison, Jim; Joseph P. Mills & Timothy Konoval. 2017. Sports' disciplinary legacy and the challenge of 'coaching differently.' *Sport, Education and Society* 22(6): 772–783.

Desrochers, Donna M. 2012. *Academic spending versus athletic spending: Who wins?* Washington DC: American Institutes for Research. Online, https://www.air.org/sites/default/files/downloads/report/Academic-Spending-vs-Athletic-Spending.pdf

Dohrmann, George & Thayer Evans. 2013a. How you go from very bad to very good very fast. *Sports Illustrated* 119 (11; September 16): 30–41, online, https://www.si.com/vault/2013/09/16/106369342/how-you-go-from-very-bad-to-very-good-very-fast

Dohrmann, George & Thayer Evans. 2013b. Special report on Oklahoma State football: Part 1–The money. *Sports Illustrated* 119 (11, September 16): 34–41; online, https://www.si.com/vault/issue/1010920/35

Dohrmann, George & Thayer Evans. 2013c. Special report on Oklahoma State football: Part 2–The academics. *Sports Illustrated* (September 11): https://www.si.com

/college-football/2013/09/11/oklahoma-state-part-2-academics

Dohrmann, George & Thayer Evans. 2013d. Special report on Oklahoma State football: Part 3—The drugs. *Sports Illustrated* (September 12): https://www.si.com/college-football/2013/09/12/oklahoma-state-part-3-drugs

Dohrmann, George & Thayer Evans. 2013e. Special report on Oklahoma State football: Part 4—The sex. *Sports Illustrated* (September 13): https://www.si.com/college-football/2013/09/13/oklahoma-state-part-4-sex

Dohrmann, George & Thayer Evans. 2013f. Special report on Oklahoma State football: Part 5—The fallout. *Sports Illustrated* (September 16): https://www.si.com/college-football/2013/09/16/oklahoma-state-part-5-fallout

Dorsch, Travis E.; Katie Lowe, Aryn M. Dotterer & Logan Lyons. 2016. Parent involvement in young adults' intercollegiate athletic careers: Developmental considerations and applied recommendations. *Journal of Intercollegiate Sport* 9(1): 1–26.

Dretzin, Rachel. 2011. *Football high: Bigger and faster, but safer?* Frontline (PBS documentary). http://www.pbs.org/wgbh/pages/frontline/football-high/

Eitle, Tamela McNulty. 2005. Do gender and race matter? Explaining the relationship between sports participation and achievement. *Sociological Spectrum* 25, 2 (March–April): 177–195.

Estes, Gentry. 2019. Investigation: NCAA schools' spending on college football recruiting is skyrocketing. *Louisville Courier Journal/USA Today* (August 20): https://www.usatoday.com/story/sports/ncaaf/2019/08/20/college-football-recruiting-georgia-leads-pack-in-soaring-costs/2059273001/

Fagan, Kate & Luke Cyphers. 2012. Thanks but no thanks. *ESPN The Magazine* (June 11): 90–91.

Fainaru, Steven & Mark Fainaru-Wada. 2019. For the NFL and all of football, a new threat: An evaporating insurance market. *Outside the Lines, ESPN.com* (January 17): http://www.espn.com/espn/story/_/id/25776964/insurance-market-football-evaporating-causing-major-threat-nfl-pop-warner-colleges-espn

Farrey, Tom. 2017. The gentrification of college hoops. Theundefeated.com (March): https://theundefeated.com/features/gentrification-of-ncaa-division-1-college-basketball/

Feezell, Travis. 2015. Educated ignorance: What faculty don't know and why faculty can't lead intercollegiate athletics reform. *Journal of Amateur Sport* 1(1): 81–100.

Fitzsimmons, Emma G. & Marc Tracy. 2018. After Urban Meyer suspension, some at Ohio State see a culture of sports above all. *New York Times* (August 29): https://www.nytimes.com/2018/08/29/sports/ohio-state-urban-meyer.html

Foley, Douglas E. 1990. *Learning capitalist culture.* Philadelphia: University of Pennsylvania Press.

Fox, Claudia, Daheia Barr-Anderson, Dianne Neumark-Sztainer & Melanie Wall. 2010. Physical activity and sports team participation: associations with academic outcomes in middle school and high school students. *Journal of School Health* 80(1): 31–37.

Frederick, Eva. 2019. Just one season of playing football—even without a concussion—can cause brain damage. *Science Magazine* (August 7): https://www.sciencemag.org/news/2019/08/just-one-season-playing-football-even-without-concussion-can-cause-brain-damage

Fuller, Rhema D., C. Keith Harrison & Scott J. Bukstein. 2017. A study of significance of racial and athletic identification on educational perceptions among African American male college athletes. *Race Ethnicity and Education* 20(5): 711–722.

Fuller, Rhema & Eric Bailey. 2018. Artifacts and the academic motivation of African American male athletes. *The Journal of Higher Education Athletics & Innovation* published 5: 1–14.

Gaines, Cork & Mike Nudelman. 2017. The average college football team makes more money than the next 35 college sports combined. *Business Insider* (October 5): https://www.businessinsider.com/college-sports-football-revenue-2017-10

Ganim, Sara & Devon Sayers. 2014. UNC report finds 18 years of academic fraud to keep athletes playing. CNN Investigations (October 23): https://www.cnn.com/2014/10/22/us/unc-report-academic-fraud/index.html

Gay, Jason. 2018. A trip to Friday night lights. *Wall Street Journal* (November 9): A16.

Gerber, Charlotte, 2015. Colleges that offer adaptive sports programs for their students. *About Health* (December 11): http://disability.about.com/od /CareerDecisionsAndCollege/tp/College-Adaptive -Sports-Programs.htm

Griffith, Aisha N., Noelle M. Hurd & Saida B. Hussain. 2019. "I didn't come to school for this": A qualitative examination of experiences with race-related stressors and coping responses among black students attending a predominantly white institution. *Journal of Adolescent Research* 34(2): 115–139.

Grossman, Evan. 2018. The NCAA's concussion problem: Former players say league hid dangers of playing football. *New York Daily News* (March 25): https://www.nydailynews.com/sports/college/ncaa-players-league-hid-dangers-playing-football-article-1.3894488

Guest, Andrew, and Barbara Schneider. 2003. Adolescents' extracurricular participation in context: The mediating effects of schools, communities, and identity. *Sociology of Education* 76(2): 89–109.

Gurney, Gerald S. 2018. How to (maybe) reduce academic fraud in athletics. *The Chronicle of Higher Education* (January 28): https://www-chronicle-com.libproxy.uccs.edu/article/How-to-Maybe-Reduce-Academic/242350

Gurney, Gerald, Donna Lopiano & Andrew Zimbalist. 2017. *Unwinding madness: What went wrong with college sports and how to fix it*. Washington DC: Brookings Institution Press. https://www.brookings.edu/book/unwinding-madness/

Gurney, Gerald, Donna Lopiano, Eric Snyder, Mary Willingham, Jayma Meyer, Brian L. Porto, B. David Ridpath, Allen Sack & Andrew Zimbalist. 2017. *The Drake Group Position Statement: Why the NCAA Academic Progress Rate (APR) and Graduation Success Rate (GSR) should be abandoned and replaced with more effective academic metrics*. Online, https://thedrakegroup.org/2015/06/07/drake-group-questions-ncaa-academic-metrics/

Hallmann, Kirstin & Thomas Giel. 2018. eSports – Competitive sports or recreational activity? *Sport Management Review* 21(1): 14–20.

Harper, Shaun R. & Jamel K. Donnor, eds. 2017. *Scandals in college sports*. London/New York: Routledge.

Harper, Shaun R. 2006. *Black male students at public universities in the US: Status, trends and implications for policy and practice*. Washington, DC: Joint Center for Political and Economic Studies.

Harper, Shaun. 2018. *Black male student-athletes and racial inequities in NCAA Division I college sports*. University of Southern California Race and Equity Center. https://race.usc.edu/wp-content/uploads/2018/08/2018-Sports-Report.pdf

Hartmann, Douglas & Michael Massoglia. 2007. Re-assessing high school sports participation and deviance in early adulthood: Evidence of enduring, bifurcated effects. *The Sociological Quarterly*, 48: 485–505.

Hartmann, Douglas. 2008. High school sports participation and educational attainment: Recognizing, assessing, and utilizing the relationship. Report to the LA84 Foundation. Los Angeles: Amateur Athletic Foundation. Online, http://www.la84foundation.org/3ce/HighSchoolSportsParticipation.pdf

Hartmann, Douglas; John Sullivan & Toben Nelson. 2012. The attitudes and opinions of high school sports participants: an exploratory empirical examination. *Sport, Education and Society* 17(1): 113–132.

Hatteberg, Sarah J. 2018. Under surveillance: Collegiate athletics as a total institution. *Sociology of Sport Journal* 35(2): 149–158.

Hattery, Angela, Marissa Kiss & Earl Smith. 2018. Always the bridesmaid and never the bride: Coaching in college sports. *The Journal of Higher Education Athletics & Innovation* published 5: 37–47.

Hawkins, Billy J., Akilah R. Carter-Francique & Joseph N. Cooper, eds. 2016. *Critical race theory: Black athletic sporting experiences in the United States*. New York: Springer.

Hawkins, Billy, Joseph Cooper, Akilah Carter-Francique & J. Kenyatta Cavil, eds. 2015. *The athletic experience at historically black colleges and universities: Past, present, and persistence*. Lanham MD: Rowman & Littlefield.

Hawkins, Billy. 2010. *The New plantation: Black athletes, college sports and predominantly White NCAA institutions*. Palgrave Macmillan.

Hayes, Matt. 2017. Josh Rosen Q&A: UCLA QB on injuries, NCAA and post-NFL goal to 'own the world.' *BleacherReport.com* (August 8): https://bleacherreport.com/articles/2722587-josh-rosen-qa-ucla-qb-on-injuries-ncaa-and-post-nfl-goal-to-own-the-world

Heere. Bob. 2018. Embracing the sportification of society: Defining e-sports through a polymorphic view on sport. *Sport Management Review* 21(1): 21–24.

HEP. 2018. Massive spending gap between athletes and academics. *HigherEdDirect.com* (January 10): https://hepinc.com/newsroom/state-universities-spending-over-100000-per-athlete-8-to-12-times-more-than-academics/

Higgins, George E., Richard Tewksbury, and Elizabeth Ehrhardt Mustaine. 2007. Sports fan binge drinking: An examination using low self-control and peer association. *Sociological Spectrum* 27(4): 389–404.

Hiltzik, Michael. 2019. The admissions scandal is an example of the academic corruption caused by NCAA athletics. *Los Angeles Times* (March 13): https://www.latimes.com/business/hiltzik/la-fi-hiltzik-admissions-scandal-sports-20190313-story.html

Hosick, Michelle Brutlag. 2018. College athletes graduate at record high rates. National Collegiate Athletic Association (November 14): online, http://www.ncaa.org/about/resources/media-center/news/college-athletes-graduate-record-high-rates

Hruby, Patrick, 2019. The NCAA is running out of excuses on brain injuries. Deadspin.com (May 24): https://deadspin.com/the-ncaa-is-running-out-of-excuses-on-brain-injuries-1819854361.

Hruby, Patrick. 2018a. The NCAA is running out of excuses on brain injuries. *Deadspin.com* (May 24): https://deadspin.com/the-ncaa-is-running-out-of-excuses-on-brain-injuries-1819854361

Hruby, Patrick. 2018b. 'Junction Boys syndrome': How college football fatalities became normalized. *The Guardian* (August 19): https://www.theguardian.com/sport/2018/aug/19/college-football-deaths-offseason-workouts

Hsu, Hua. 2019. Student debt is transforming the American family. *The New Yorker* (September 2): https://www.newyorker.com/magazine/2019/09/09/student-debt-is-transforming-the-american-family

Hughes, Robin L. 2015. For colored girls who have considered Black feminist thought when feminist discourse and Title IX weren't enough. In Eddie Comeaux, ed., *Introduction to intercollegiate athletics* (pp. 2017–218). Baltimore MD: Johns Hopkins University Press.

Hwang, Seunghyun; Deborah L. Feltz, Laura A. Kietzmann & Matthew A. Diemer. 2016. Sport involvement and educational outcomes of high school students: A longitudinal study. *Youth & Society* 48(6): 763–785.

Idsvoog, Karl. 2015. *University presidents tackle football's future.* Culver City CA: Brave New Films, online, https://vimeo.com/141172993

Jenkins, Sally. 2018. Prehistoric college football coaches are killing players. It's past time to stop them. *Washington Post* (August 21): https://www.washingtonpost.com/sports/colleges/prehistoric-college-football-coaches-are-killing-players-its-past-time-to-stop-them/2018/08/21/5b0f67c2-a53b-11e8-8fac-12e98c13528d_story.html

Johnson, James E., Daniel R. Tracy & David A. Pierce. 2015. National review of interscholastic competitive balance solutions related to the public-private debate. *Journal of Amateur Sport* 1(1): 29–51.

Johnson, Richard. 2018. A history of skyrocketing college football coach salaries, from Walter Camp to Nick Saban. *SBNation* (October 4): https://www.sbnation.com/college-football/2018/6/4/17390394/college-football-coach-salaries-history-highest

Jones, Luke & Jim Denison. 2018. A sociocultural perspective surrounding the application of global positioning system technology: Suggestions for the strength and conditioning coach. *Strength & Conditioning Journal* 40(6): 3–8.

Kaye, Miranda P., Katie Lowe & Travis E. Dorsch. 2019. Dyadic examination of parental support, basic needs satisfaction, and student–athlete development during emerging adulthood. *Journal of Family Issues* 40(2): 240–263.

Kelderman, Eric. 2018. Who should oversee athletes' academic progress? *The Chronicle of Higher Education* (January 28): https://www-chronicle-com.libproxy.uccs.edu/article/Who-Should-Oversee-Athletes-/242351

Kniffin, Kevin M.; Brian Wansink & Mitsuru Shimizu. 2015. Sports at work: Anticipated and persistent correlates of participation in high school athletics. *Journal of Leadership & Organizational Studies* 22(2): 217–230.

Kreager, Derek A., and Jeremy Staff. 2009. The sexual double standard and adolescent peer acceptance. *Social Psychology Quarterly* 72(2): 143–164.

Lindo, Jason M., Isaac D. Swensen, and Glen R. Waddell. 2012. Are big-time sports a threat to student achievement? *American Economic Journal: Applied Economics, American Economic Association* 4(4): 254–274.

Lipscomb, Stephen. 2006. Secondary school extracurricular involvement and academic achievement: A fixed effects approach. *Economics of Education Review* 26(4): 463–472.

Maese, Rick & Roman Stubbs. 2018. Motivation or abuse? Maryland confronts football's fine line as new allegations emerge. *Washington Post* (September 30): https://www.washingtonpost.com/sports/colleges/motivation-or-abuse-maryland-confronts-footballs-fine-line-as-new-allegations-emerge/2018/09/30/e7ab028e-c3dd-11e8-b338-a3289f6cb742_story.html

Maples, Gordon, Nina Berger, Candace Collins & Michelle Healy. 2019. Student-athletes: academics and identity for black male college students in revenue-generating sports – a literature review. Online, https://sahe.colostate.edu/student-athletes-academics-and-identity-for-black-male-college-students-in-revenue-generating-sports-a-literature-review/

Marklein, Mary Beth. 2013. Division I schools spend more on athletes than education. *USA Today* (January 16): 3A.

Martin, Brandon E.; C. Keith Harrison, Jeffrey Stone & S. Malia Lawrence. 2010. Athletic voices and academic victories: African American male student–athlete experiences in the Pac-Ten. *Journal of Sport & Social Issues* 34(2): 131–153.

Martin, Michel. 2013. Should parents nix after-school sports? *National Public Radio, Tell Me More* (September 24): http://www.npr.org/2013/09/24/225747074/should-parents-nix-after-school-sports

McCallum, Jack. 2003. Thank God it's Friday. *Sports Illustrated* 99, 12 (September 29): 40–42.

Miller, Kathleen & Joseph H. Hoffman. 2009. Mental well-being and sport-related identities in college students. *Sociology of Sport Journal* 26(2): 335–356.

Miller, Kathleen E., Don F. Sabo, Michael P. Farrell, Grace M. Barnes, & Merrill J. Melnick. 1998. Athletic participation and sexual behavior in adolescents: The different world of boys and girls. *Journal of Health and Social Behavior* 39, 108–123.

Miller, Kathleen E., Don F. Sabo, Michael P. Farrell, Grace M. Barnes & Merrill J. Melnick. 1999. Sports, sexual behavior, contraceptive use, and pregnancy among female and male high school students: Testing cultural resource theory. *Sociology of Sport Journal* 16, 4: 366–387.

Miller, Kathleen E., Merrill J. Melnick, Grace M. Barnes, Michael P. Farrell & Don Sabo. 2005. Untangling the links among athletic involvement, gender, race, and adolescent academic outcomes. *Sociology of Sport Journal* 22, 2: 178–193.

Milner, Adrienne N. & Jomills H. Braddock. 2016. *Sex segregation in sports: Why separate is not equal*. Santa Barbara CA: Praeger.

Morris, David S. 2015. Actively closing the gap? Social class, organized activities, and academic achievement in high school. *Youth & Society* 47(2): 267–290.

Murphy, Brian. 2019. 'Shame on us': Colleges fail unprepared athletes, UNC whistleblower tells Capitol Hill panel. The News & Observer-Raleigh NC (July 25): https://www.newsobserver.com/sports/article233111249.html

Murphy, Chris. 2019a. *Madness, Inc.: How everyone is getting rich of college sports–except players* (report #1). Washington DC: United States Senate.

Murphy, Chris. 2019b. *Madness, Inc.: How colleges keep athletes on the field and out of the classroom* (report #2. Washington DC: United States Senate.

Murphy, Dan. 2019. California defies NCAA as Gov. Gavin Newsom signs into law Fair Pay to Play Act. *ESPN.com* (September 30): https://www.espn.com/college-sports/story/_/id/27735933/california-defies-ncaa-gov-gavin-newsom-signs-law-fair-pay-play-act

NCAA. 2019. *Concussion safety protocol management.* http://www.ncaa.org/sport-science-institute/concussion-safety-protocol-management

New, Jake. 2016. An 'epidemic' of academic fraud. *InsideHigherEd.com* (July 8): https://www.insidehighered.com/news/2016/07/08/more-dozen-athletic-programs-have-committed-academic-fraud-last-decade-more-likely

NFHS. 2019. Five state champions crowned in first esports season. National Federation of State High School Associations (March 12); online, https://www.nfhs.org/articles/five-state-champions-crowned-in-first-esports-season/

Nixon, Howard. 2014. *The athletic trap: How college sports corrupted the academy*. Johns Hopkins University Press.

O'Brien, Rebecca Davis. 2016. Friday night exclusive rights. *Wall Street Journal* (August 26): D8.

O'Donnell, Ricky. 2016. Everything you need to know about Syracuse's NCAA scandal. SBNation.com (November 6): https://www.sbnation.com/college-basketball/2015/3/9/8166543/syracuse-ncaa-scandal-explained-jim-boeheim

Oseguera, Leticia, Dan Merson, C. Keith Harrison & Sue Rankin. 2018. Beyond the black/white binary: A multi-institutional study of campus climate and the academic success of college athletes of different racial backgrounds. *Sociology of Sport Journal* 35(2): 119–131.

Overman, Steven J. 2019. *Sports crazy: How sports are sabotaging American schools*. Jackson MS: University of Mississippi Press.

Pappano, Laura. 2012. How big-time sports ate college life. *The New York Times* (January 20): http://www.nytimes.com/2012/01/22/education/edlife/how-big-time-sports-ate-college-life.html

Parietti, Megan L., Sue Sutherland & Donna L. Pastore. 2017. Parental involvement in the lives of intercollegiate athletes: Views from student-athletes and academic advisors for athletics. *Journal of Amateur Sport* 3(3): 106–134.

Parry, Jim. 2019. E-sports are not sports. *Sport, Ethics and Philosophy* 13(1): 3–18.

Pearson, Jennifer; Sarah R. Crissey & Catherine Riegle-Crumb. 2009. Gendered fields: Sports and advanced course taking in high school. *Sex Roles* 61(7–8): 519–535.

Pizzo, Anthony D., Gareth J. Jones & Daniel C. Funk. 2019. Navigating the iron cage: An institutional creation perspective of collegiate esports. *International Journal of Sport Management* 20(x): 171–197.

Powell, Michael. 2019. The most honest man in college basketball is going to prison. *New York Times* (May 3): https://www.nytimes.com/2019/05/03/sports/college-basketball-trial.html

Pot, Niek; J. van der Kamp, J. & Ivo van Hilvoorde, I. 2014. Sport socialisation in a digital age: sport games and sport identity. Paper presented at the 19th Annual ECSS-Congress (Amsterdam) with the abstract published in the European Database of Sport Science.

Reagan, Brad & Erich Schwartzel. 2017. Hollywood's schoolboy football factory. *Wall Street Journal* (October 28): A1

Reddick, Brianna. 2018. For black college students, balancing activism and mental health takes work. *The Nation* (September 18): https://www.thenation.com/article/for-black-college-students-balancing-activism-and-mental-health-takes-work/

Riddle, Greg, 2019. Big stadiums, bigger bucks: How Texas high schools are exchanging stadium naming rights for much-needed cash. *Dallas Morning News* (August 25): https://www.dallasnews.com/high-school-sports/football/2019/08/25/big-stadiums-bigger-bucks-how-texas-high-schools-are-exchanging-stadium-naming-rights-for-much-needed-cash/

Ridpath, B. David. 2018. *Alternative models of sports development in America: Solutions to a crisis in education and public health*. Athens OH: Ohio University Press.

Ridpath, Bradley David, Gerald Gurney & Eric Snyder. 2015. NCAA academic fraud cases and historical consistency: A comparative content analysis. *Journal of Legal Aspects of Sport* 25(2): 75–103.

Ridpath, David & Margaret Tudor. 2018. Does gender significantly predict academic, athletic career motivation among NCAA Division I college athletes? *The Journal of Higher Education Athletics & Innovation* published 5:B. 122–147.

Ripley, Amanda. 2013a. The case against high-school sports. *The Atlantic* (September 18): http://www.theatlantic.com/magazine/print/2013/10/the-case-against-high-school-sports/309447/

Ripley, Amanda. 2013b. *The smartest kids in the world, and how they got that way*. New York: Simon & Schuster (see, http://www.amandaripley.com/books/the-smartest-kids-in-the-world)

Rubin, Lisa M. & Ron A. Moses. 2017. Athletic subculture within student-athlete academic centers. *Sociology of Sport Journal* 34(4): 317–328.

Schroetenboer, Brent, Steve Berkowitz & Christopher Schnaars. 2018. Sports' deficits a rising concern. *USA Today* (June 29): 1C, 4C.

Schull, Vicki; Sally Shaw & Lisa A. Kihl. 2013. "If a woman came in ... she would have been eaten up alive": Analyzing gendered political processes in the search for an athletic director. *Gender & Society* 27(1): 56–81.

Schultz, Katie. 2017. Do high school athletes get better grades during the off-season? *Journal of Sports Economics* 18(2): 182–208.

Shakib, Sohaila; Phillip Veliz, Michele D. Dunbar & Donald Sabo. 2011. Athletics as a source for social status among youth: Examining variation by gender, race/ethnicity, and socioeconomic status. *Sociology of Sport Journal* 28(3): 303–328.

Shifrer, Dara, Jennifer Pearson, Chandra Muller, and Lindsey Wilkinson. 2015. College-going benefits of high school sports participation: Race and gender differences over three decades. *Youth & Society* 47(3): 295–318.

Singer, John N., and Akilah R. Carter-Francique. 2013. Representation, participation, and the experiences of racial minorities in college sport. In Gary Sailes, ed. *Sports in Higher Education: Issues and Controversies in College Athletics* (pp. 113-138). San Diego CA: Cognella Academic Publishing.

Smith, Jay M. & Mary Willingham. 2015. *Cheated: The UNC scandal, the education of athletes, and the future of big-time college sports*. Lincoln NE: Potomac Books.

Smith, Earl. 2009. *Race, sport and the American Dream.* 2nd ed. Durham, NC: Carolina Academic Press.

Smith, Jay M. undated. Academic fraud and commercialised collegiate athletics: lessons from the North Carolina case. In Transparency International, Global Corruption Report: Sport. Online, https://www.transparency.org/files/content/feature/5.2_AcademicFraudCollegiateAthletics_Smith_GCRSport.pdf

Sokolov, Michael. 2018. A university comes undone: How scandal and corruption brought down a college sports powerhouse. *The Chronicle of Higher Education* (September 28): https://www.chronicle.com/article/How-ScandalCorruption/244666

Stambulovaa, Natalia B. & Paul Wylleman. 2019. Psychology of athletes' dual careers: A state-of-the-art critical review of the European discourse. *Psychology of Sport and Exercise* 42(1): 74–88.

Staurowsky, Ellen J. & Erianne A. Weight. 2011. Title IX literacy: What coaches don't know and need to find out. *Journal of Intercollegiate Sport*.4(2): 190–209.

Steinberg, Mary Anne, Cheryl Walther, Maria Herbst, Jennifer West, Dixie Wingler & John Smith. 2018. Learning specialists in college athletics: Who are they and what do they do? *The Journal of Higher Education Athletics & Innovation* 4: 77–118.

Stripling, Jack. 2019. 'It's an aristocracy': What the admissions-bribery scandal has exposed about class on campus. *The Chronicle of Higher Education* (April 17): https://www.chronicle.com/article/It-s-an-Aristocracy-/246131

Theune, Felecia. 2016. The shrinking presence of Black female student-athletes at Historically Black Colleges and Universities. *Sociology of Sport Journal* 33(1): 66–74.

Theune, Felecia. 2019. Brown, Title IX and the impact of race and sex segregation on sports participation opportunities for Black females. *Sociology Compass*, 13(3), e12661.

Thompson, Derek. 2019. Meritocracy is killing high-school sports. *The Atlantic* (August 30): https://www.theatlantic.com/ideas/archive/2019/08/meritocracy-killing-high-school-sports/597121/

Tjong, Vehniah K. D, Hayden P. Baker, Charles J. Cogan, Melissa Montoya, Tory R. Lindley & Michael A. Terry. MD. 2017. Concussions in NCAA varsity football athletes A qualitative investigation of player perception and return to sport. *JAAOS Global Research & Reviews* 1(8): 1–6; online, doi: 10.5435/JAAOSGlobal-D-17-00070.

Torres, Kimberly. 2009. 'Culture shock': Black students account for their distinctiveness at an elite college. *Ethnic and Racial Studies* 32, 5: 883–905.

Tracy, Marc. 2014. The gold and blue loses a bit of its luster. *New York Times* (August 14): https://www.nytimes.com/2014/08/20/sports/ncaafootball/notre-dame-is-rocked-by-charges-of-academic-cheating.html

Troutman, Kelly, P. and Mikaela J. Dufur. 2007. From high school jocks to college grads assessing the long-term effects of high school sport participation on females' educational attainment. *Youth & Society* 38(4): 443–462.

Veliz, Philip; John Schulenberg, Megan Patrick, Deborah Kloska, Sean Esteban McCabe & Nicole Zarrett. 2017. Competitive sports participation in high school and subsequent substance use in young adulthood: Assessing differences based on level of contact. *International Review for the Sociology of Sport* 52(2): 240–259.

Waldron, Travis. 2019. The NCAA is losing its fight to keep exploiting college athletes. *The Huffington Post* (April 6): https://www.huffpost.com/entry/ncaa-pay-college-athletes-final-four_n_5ca61cb9e4b082d775e1d201

Wann, Daniel L., Paula J. Waddill, Matthew Brasher & Sagan Ladd. 2015. Examining sport team identification, social connections, and social well-being among high school students. *Journal of Amateur Sport* 1(2): 27–50.

Will, George. 2019. College basketball's murky swamp of misbehavior. *Washington Post* (April 3): https://www.washingtonpost.com/opinions/college-basketballs-murky-swamp-of-misbehavior/2019/04/03/fda7e4f0-556c-11e9-814f-e2f46684196e_story.html

Wilson, Amy S. 2018. *45 years of Title IX: The status of women in intercollegiate athletics*. Indianapolis IN: NCAA Research Department.

Wiseman, Steve & Dan Kane. 2019. NCAA committee endorses new rules to govern academic integrity. *Charlotte Observer* (May 17): https://www.charlotteobserver.com/sports/article230543689.html

Wolken, Dan, Steve Berkowitz & Tess DeMeyer. 2019. NCAA's Power 5 schools see steep raise in pay for non-revenue coaches. *USA Today* (August 12): https://www.usatoday.com/story/sports/2019/08/12/ncaa-power-5-schools-steeply-raising-pay-non-revenue-sport-coaches/1946843001/

Wolkin, Dan. 2019. More college athlete reform? That's tough when 'amateurism' means whatever the NCAA proclaims it does. *USA Today* (May 15): https://www.usatoday.com/story/sports/college/columnist/dan-wolken/2019/05/15/ncaa-reform-amateurism-means-whatever-ncaa-proclaims-does/3676682002/

Zarrett, Nicole, Philip Veliz & Don Sabo. 2018. *Teen sport in America: Why participation matters*. East Meadow, NY: Women's Sports Foundation.

chapter

15

(*Source:* Michael Zagaris/San Francisco 49ers/Getty Images)

SPORTS AND RELIGIONS

Is It a Promising Combination?

If athletes can endorse shaving cream, razor blades, and cigarettes, surely they can endorse the Lord, too.

–Don McClanen (1954), founder, Fellowship of Christian Athletes

Can you love your neighbour as yourself, and at the same time knee him in the face as hard as you can?

–Scott "Bam Bam" Sullivan, Christian pastor and MMA champion (in Blakely, 2014)

Not seeing people who look like us playing basketball meant it was not ingrained in our conscious that we, too, can compete. It is important now more than ever for Muslim women to be visible and diverse and integrate as much as possible.

–Asma Elbadawi, Sudanese-British basketball player (in Jones, 2017)

I've a wife and two kids to provide for and if it means killing you in the ring, that's what I will have to do. . . . I read the Bible quite a lot. . . . It gives me strength to know that if God is in my corner then no one can beat me.

–Tyson Fury, British and Commonwealth Heavyweight boxing champion (in Gore, 2010)

So for me, . . . [and] the other team pastors of the 30 teams in the NBA – our mission and our goal is to equip these young men to represent a life of accountability, integrity and responsibility.

–Earl Smith, chaplain, Golden State Warriors (in Ackerman, 2018)

Chapter Outline

How Do Sociologists Define Religion and Explain Its Connection with Society and Culture?

Similarities and Differences Between Sports and Religions

Modern Sports, Religious Beliefs, and Religious Organizations

The Challenges of Combining Sports and Religious Beliefs

Summary: Is It a Promising Combination?

Learning Objectives

- Understand why sociologists study religion in society.
- Discuss the similarities and differences between sports and religions, and why it may be difficult to make clear distinctions between them.
- Discuss why Christianity in general and Protestant beliefs in particular have become regularly connected with sports.
- Identify forms of world religions other than Christianity, and discuss why they have not become closely connected with sports and sport participation.
- Discuss challenges faced by Muslim women who want to play sports.
- Explain how Christian sports organizations have used sports.
- Identify the ways that Christian athletes and coaches have used religion in sports.
- Identify and discuss the conflicts faced by Christian athletes in violent spectator sports and explain strategies for dealing with them.
- Discuss what has occurred when sports and Christian beliefs have been combined in recent history.

As a 30-year-old Canadian student at the International YMCA Training School in Springfield, Massachusetts, James Naismith invented basketball in 1891. He did it to fulfill a requirement in a psychology of play graduate course he was taking at the same time that he needed an engaging activity that would keep football players physically active during their off-season. Naismith also wrote the first official rule book for basketball, founded the basketball program at the University of Kansas, became the first coach the university ever hired, and was an unordained Presbyterian minister who left his religious studies to work in the newly developing field of athletics.

Naismith's story is interesting because he did all these things at a time when many Christians in North America saw competitive sports as a tool of the devil–an activity that glorified the flesh rather than the spirit and focused the attention of young men on competition and winning when they should be using their body to honor God through work, reverence, and humility. Naismith knew these things but he was influenced by Muscular Christianity, a social movement started by Christian men who believed that religion had become so feminized that it ignored the connection between masculinity and living a Christian life.

At the risk of creating some discomfort, this chapter focuses on the many ways that sports and religion intersect in society. The major questions we'll discuss in this chapter are these:

1. How is *religion* defined, and how is it connected with society and culture?
2. What are the similarities and differences between sports and religions?
3. Why have people combined sports and religious beliefs, and why are Christians more vocal about this combination than are Jews, Muslims, Hindus, Buddhists, Sikhs, and others?
4. What are the issues and controversies associated with combining religious beliefs and sports participation?

When discussing the last question, special attention is given to the prospect of using religion as a platform for eliminating racism, sexism, deviance, violence, and other problems in sports and sports organizations.

HOW DO SOCIOLOGISTS DEFINE RELIGION AND EXPLAIN ITS CONNECTION WITH SOCIETY AND CULTURE?

A sociological discussion of religion often creates controversy because people tend to use their own religious beliefs and practices as their point of reference. Additionally, tensions are inevitable whenever people are asked to think critically and analytically about the beliefs they use to make sense of their experiences and the world around them.

In sociological terms, **religions** are *socially shared belief systems comprised of the words, symbols, metaphors, myths, and rituals that people use to think about their relationship with the supernatural realm and communicate their thoughts to others.* Religious beliefs and rituals usually link the supernatural realm with a divinity, including God or gods.[1]

Religions change over time and differ from one culture to the next due to the influence of prophets and theologians and decisions made by religious leaders. They are held together over time by believers who share beliefs about values and truths that transcend here and now reality. Related to these values and truths are the *norms* that believers use to assess the morality of individual actions, and identify good and evil in the world. In this sense, religions support the "moral and ethical backbone" of societies (Dorsey, 2019). As such, they can bring people together around shared values or they can drive people apart when values clash and create irreconcilable differences.

Religions are powerful because people use them as sense-making perspectives and guides for action. For this reason, they share certain characteristics

[1]The word *God* refers to the Supreme Being or the Creator in monotheistic religions. The words *god(s)* and *godliness* refer to deities across all religions, including polytheistic religions, in which people believe in multiple deities, or gods.

with ideologies. Both are parts of culture organized around beliefs accepted on faith or taken for granted; both are used to to guide choices and actions and explain the meanings of objects, events, and experiences. However, ideologies focus mostly on secular, here-and-now, material world issues, and they're neither automatically nor inevitably linked with a supernatural realm or a divinity. Religions, on the other hand, always bring a divinity or the supernatural into the sense-making process and connect meaning and understanding to a sacred realm that transcends the here-and-now material world.

Although ideologies are linked with the secular world and religions are linked with a supernatural realm, they often overlap, making it difficult to clearly differentiate them. For example, if people have a religious belief that God created male and female as two distinct human forms, they could use it to develop and support a gender ideology organized around male-female sex differences and the assumption that it is neither moral nor natural to blur or make light of those differences. When this occurs, secular ideologies take on moral significance and ideologically based actions become moral actions. This is why Islamic jihadist ideology is a powerful force in the world today–it establishes a connection between selected Islamist beliefs and a here-and-now quest for political control. As a result, the actions of jihadists are given moral urgency and legitimacy in their view of the world.

Because religion informs widespread views of the world and influences social relationships and the organization of social life, it also informs ideas and beliefs about the body, movement, physical activities, and sports. However, as we examine the relationship between religions and sports, it's useful to know that religions are linked with the supernatural and sacred–that is, with things that inspire awe, mystery, and reverence. For example, Christians define churches as sacred places by connecting them with their God. Therefore, the meaning of a church to Christians can be understood only in terms of its perceived link with the supernatural. On the other hand, sport stadiums are seen by most Christians secular places having no connection with the sacred or supernatural.They may be important to people, but they are understandable in terms of everyday, secular meanings and experiences.

The importance of distinguishing between the sacred and secular is illustrated by answers to the following questions. First, do you think that people in your town would object to a sport stadium having Pepsi, Budweiser, and McDonald's logos on scoreboards and signs placed around the venue? Second, do you think those people would accept the same logos placed on the pulpit and incorporated into its stained-glass windows in their church, temple, synagogue, or mosque? My guess is that having logos in the stadium is a non-issue, but putting them in a place of religious worship is certain to cause controversy, with people saying that they degrade the sacred meaning given to their (God's) house of worship and the sacred objects in it.

The diversity of religions and religious beliefs around the world is extensive. Human beings have dealt with inescapable problems of human existence and ultimate questions about life and death in many ways. In the process of creating answers and explanations, they've developed rich and widely varied religions. When sociologists study religions, they examine the ways that people use religious beliefs as they give meaning to themselves, their experiences, and the world around them. They also focus on the ways that religious beliefs inform people's feelings, thoughts, and actions. When religious beliefs set some people apart from others and connect power, authority, and wisdom in the secular world with a divinity or supernatural forces, religion has even deeper and more socially significant consequences.

The social influence of religion and religious beliefs varies widely, and it can produce the following consequences:

- Powerful forms of group unity and social integration, *or* devastating forms of group conflict and violent warfare
- A spirit of love and acceptance *or* forms of moral rejection and condemnation
- Humble conformity with prevailing social norms *or* righteous rejection of prevailing norms

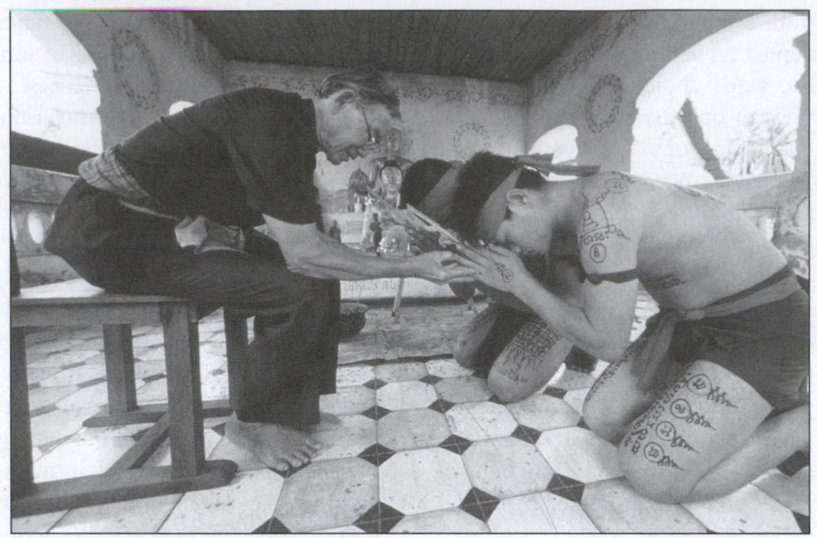

(*Source:* Patrick AVENTURIER/Gamma-Rapho/Getty Images)

In societies where Christianity is dominant, there usually are reasonably clear distinctions between the secular and sacred. In societies where Buddhism is dominant, it is very difficult to make this distinction because the secular and sacred are almost seamlessly merged in daily life. These boxers in Thailand make Buddhist prayers to their Master (teacher) before their competitions.

- A commitment to social equity *or* commitment to policies and practices that produce inequalities (between men and women, racial and ethnic groups, social classes, homosexuals and heterosexuals, and people with and without certain physical or intellectual impairments)

Of course, none of these consequences is inevitable. Each occurs only in connection with the ways that people interpret religious beliefs and incorporate them into their lives. But it is important to study the conditions under which specific consequences occur.

SIMILARITIES AND DIFFERENCES BETWEEN SPORTS AND RELIGIONS

Discussions about sports and religions often are confusing. Some people view sport as a form of religion, or at least "religion-like," whereas others assume that the "true and essential nature" of religion is essentially different from the "true and essential nature" of sport. Still others view sports and religions as two distinct sets of cultural practices, which may be similar or different depending on how people create, define, and use them. The purpose of this section is to explain and clarify each of these three positions.

Sport as Religion

Attending an NFL game or a World Cup soccer match and being a part of 75,000 or more people yelling, chanting, and moving in unison reminds some people of a religious experience. A few even say that sport *is* religion because it involves passion, dedication, identities, and ritualistic actions and it is played with bodies made in the image of God (Bain-Selbo, 2008, 2009; Bauer, 2011; Thoennes, 2008). Others stop short of this position and say that sports are sometimes religion-like because they share characteristics and produce similar consequences

SIMILARITIES: Both have	SPORTS have	RELIGIONS have
Special sites for events and communal gatherings	Stadiums, arenas, gyms, and parks	Churches, mosques, synagogues, and temples
Disciplined quests for perfection in mind, body, and spirit	Commitment to perfection through disciplined training and competitive performances	Commitment to perfection through disciplined study of holy books and quest for moral purity.
Structured organizations and a clear hierarchy of authority	Commissioners, owners/athletic directors, managers, and coaches	Prophets, popes/patriarchs/presidents, pastors, and priests
Events to celebrate and reaffirm shared values	Scheduled contests that celebrate competition, hard work, and achievement	Annual holy days that celebrate moral commitment, community, and redemption.
Rituals before, during, and after major events	Initiations, national anthems, pep talks, fist bumping, and marching bands	Baptisms, opening hymns, regular sermons, the joining of hands, and ceremonial processions
Heroes and stories about their accomplishments	Heroes are elected to halls of fame, and their stories are told by sports journalists, coaches, and fans	Heroes are granted sainthood, and their stories are told by religious writers, leaders, and believers
Occasions that inspire emotions and existential thoughts	Players and fans are inspired to contemplate the physical potential of human beings	Theologians and believers are inspired to contemplate the meaning of existence.
A focus that distracts attention from here-and-now social, political, and economic issues	Focus on athlete-celebrities, scores, win-loss records, records of achievement, and championships	Focus on salvation and a relationship with a deity and the supernatural realm

FIGURE 15.1 Similarities between sports and religions

(Baker, 2007; Forney, 2007; Serazio, 2013; Sing, 2013). In both cases, the proponents of the *sport as religion* and *sport as religion-like* positions refer to examples listed in Figure 15.1.

These similarities are striking, but most scholars also note that there are important differences between sports and religions. Some say that these differences are grounded in the unique essential natures of sport and of religion, and others say that they are inevitable differences grounded in the social and political histories of each. These positions are explained in the following two sections.

Sport and Religion Are Essentially Different

Some people argue that religion and sport each have a unique, separate truth, or essence. The essence of religion, they believe, is grounded in divine inspiration, whereas the essence of sport is grounded in human nature.[2] They argue that religion and sport reveal basic truths that transcend time and space, and people "live out" these truths every day, *but* the truths offered by religion are clearly different from the truths offered by sport.

People who think this way are **essentialists** because *they assume that the universe is governed by unchanging laws and that meaning and truth are*

[2]These people use the singular rather than the plural form when they refer to *sport* and *religion.* This is because they assume that all forms of sport contain and express the same essence, as do all forms of religion.

(*Source:* Jay Coakley)

This statue is created and sold by a Christian business. It illustrates that religions, like sports, are socially constructed cultural practices, which change in connection with larger social forces and contexts. To represent Jesus playing a heavy-contact sport that involves brutal body contact and borderline violence is to re-imagine biblical portrayals of him in light of the cultural importance of football in the United States.

inherent in nature. When they study religion and sport, they argue that the fundamental character of each is essentially different in the following ways:

- Religious beliefs, meanings, rituals, and events are fundamentally mystical and sacred, whereas sport beliefs, meanings, rituals, and events are fundamentally clear-cut and secular.
- The purpose of religion is to transcend the circumstances and conditions of the material world in the pursuit of eternal life, whereas the purpose of sport is to embrace material reality and seek victories through physical performance.
- Religion involves faith in the primacy of its beliefs and rituals, whereas sport involves competition to establish objective superiority.
- Religion emphasizes humility and love, whereas sport emphasizes personal achievement and conquest.
- Religious services highlight a collective process of acknowledging the sacred and supernatural, whereas sport events highlight a collective commitment to a here-and-now outcome with secular significance.

Essentialists argue that there are fundamental differences between Super Bowl Sunday and Easter Sunday, even though both are important days for many people. Similarly, they see fundamental differences between a hockey team's initiation ceremony and a baptism, a seventh-inning stretch and an evening prayer, a cathedral and a stadium.

Some essentialists are religious people who believe that religion and sport are fundamentally different because religion is divinely inspired and sport is not. They often claim that the essentially sacred character of religion is corrupted when combined with the essentially secular character of sport (Hoffman, 2010; White, 2008). Nonreligious essentialists don't believe in divine inspiration, but they also conclude that the cultural meanings and social consequences of religion and sport are fundamentally different.

Religions and Sports as Cultural Practices

Most sociologists who study religions and sports see them as cultural practices that are created by people as they live with each other and give meaning to their experiences and the world around them. This is a *social constructionist approach,* and it is based on evidence showing that religions and sports have diverse forms and meanings that are understandable only in connection with the social and cultural conditions under which people create and maintain them. Furthermore, these forms and meanings change over time as social and cultural conditions change.

Social constructionists generally use cultural and interactionist theories to guide their work. That is, they study social relations, power relations, and the meanings given to the body by people who have h religious beliefs. They also examine the ways that religious beliefs influence movement, physical activity, sports participation, and the organization of sports. They ask why sports and religions are male-dominated spheres of life and then study gender ideology in relation to religion, the body, and sports. They also investigate the ways that people combine religious beliefs with sports participation and the social consequences of those combinations in specific social worlds.

Social constructionists realize that the meanings and practices that constitute sports and religions vary by time and place. Religious beliefs and rituals change with new revelations and visions, new prophets and prophecies, new interpretations of sacred writings, and new teachers and teachings. These changes often reproduce the cultural contexts in which they occur, but there are times when they inspire transformations in social relations and social life. Sports are viewed in similar terms–as socially constructed and varying cultural practices that usually reproduce existing meanings and social organization but have the potential to challenge and transform them.

Studying Sports and Religions: An Assessment

The question of whether sports and religions are essentially the same or different does not inspire critical sociological analysis. More important to sociologists are the ways that people participate in the formation and transformation of social and cultural life and how sports and religions are involved in those processes.

Unfortunately, research on sports and religions is scarce. Scholars who study religions are seldom interested in studying sports, and scholars who study sports are seldom interested in studying religions. The studies that do exist focus primarily on Christian belief systems, particularly in North America. Therefore, we know little about sports and major world religions, even though it would be useful to understand how various religious beliefs are related to conceptions of the body, expressions of human movement, the integration of physical activity into everyday life, and participation in sports. Such knowledge could be used to create more culturally inclusive sports programs.

There have been recent studies of the influence of Islamic beliefs on the sport participation of Muslim women (Toffoletti, 2012 & Palmer, 2017; Walseth, 2016). For those who study sports and gender, it is helpful to understand that religious beliefs often define, in moral terms, expectations related to gender. This makes religion important to include in their analyses because these expectations regulate bodies and influence sports participation patterns in different cultures. Islam has received more attention than other religions in this regard, because it has very specific beliefs about the clothing that must be worn by women, especially when they might be seen by men.

Despite the relative shortage of information about sports and religions other than Christianity, issues related to this topic are discussed in the section, "Sports and World Religions" later in this chapter. But first, we focus on why certain forms of Christianity have become closely associated with organized competitive sports.

MODERN SPORTS, RELIGIOUS BELIEFS, AND RELIGIOUS ORGANIZATIONS

Despite important differences between the organization and stated goals of sports and religions, people have combined these two spheres of life in mutually supportive ways. In some cases, people with certain religious beliefs have used sports for religious purposes, and in other cases, people in sports have used religion to define and give meaning to their sport participation.

The frequency with which people combine Christian beliefs and sports raises interesting questions. Why have Christian organizations and beliefs, in particular, been linked to and combined directly and explicitly with sports? Why haven't other religions been linked with sports and sports participation to the same extent? How have Christian organizations used sports, and how have athletes and sports organizations used Christianity and Christian beliefs?

What are the dynamics and social significance of these connections? These issues are discussed in the following sections.

The Protestant Ethic and the Spirit of Sports

Historical evidence helps explain links between modern sports and contemporary Christian beliefs. In the late nineteenth century, German sociologist-economist Max Weber did a classic study titled *The Protestant Ethic and the Spirit of Capitalism* (1904/1958). His research focused on the connection between the ideas embodied in the Protestant Reformation and the values underlying the growth of capitalist economic systems. He concluded that Protestant religious beliefs, especially those promoted by the reformer John Calvin, helped create a social and cultural environment in which capitalism could develop and grow. Weber explained that Protestantism promoted a "code of ethics" and a general value system that created in people deep moral suspicions about erotic pleasure, physical desire, and all forms of idleness. "Idle hands are the devil's workshop" was a popular Protestant slogan.

Weber also used historical data to show that this "Protestant ethic," as he referred to it, emphasized a rationally controlled lifestyle in which emotions and feelings were suppressed in a dual quest for worldly success and eternal salvation. This orientation, developed further in Calvin's notion of predestination, led people to define their occupation as a "calling" from God and to view work as an activity through which one's spiritual worth could be proven and displayed for others to see. This was socially significant because it linked the economy and material success with moral worth: Being rich was a sign of "being saved"—as long as you didn't spend the money on yourself.

The Protestant work ethic has been integrated into different cultures in different ways over the past 500 years. However, it emphasized values consistent with the spirit that underlies organized competitive sports as they've been developed in Europe and North America over the past 200 years. Sociologist Steven Overman explains this in his book, *The Protestant Work Ethic and the Spirit of Sport: How Calvinism and Capitalism Shaped American Games (2011).* Overman shows that the Protestant ethic has emphasized a combination of the following seven key *virtues:*

1. *Worldly asceticism*—suffering and the endurance of pain has a spiritual purpose, godliness is linked with self-denial and a disdain for self-indulgence, and spiritual redemption is achieved only through self-control and self-discipline.
2. *Rationalization*—truth is discovered through human reason, and virtue is expressed through efficiency and measurable achievements.
3. *Goal directedness*—spiritual salvation and the moral worth of human action depend on achievement and success.
4. *Individualism*—salvation is a matter of individual responsibility, initiative, and choice, and people control their spiritual destiny by accepting a personal relationship with God/Christ.
5. *Achieved status*—worldly success is associated with goodness and salvation, whereas failure is associated with sin and damnation.
6. *The work ethic*—work is a calling from God and people honor God by working hard and developing their "God-given potential" in whatever they do.
7. *The time ethic*—time has a moral quality and wasting time is sinful and a sign of weak moral character.

Overman theorizes that these seven virtues are closely matched with the orientation and spirit that informs the meaning, purpose, and organization of modern sports, especially power and performance sports in societies that have been predominantly Christian for the past two cebturies. This theory is only partially supported by evidence because these virtues have been integrated into people's lives in many different ways, depending on historical and cultural factors. Furthermore, some of these virtues are not exclusive to Protestantism—they also exist in forms of Catholicism, Islam, and other religions, although no religion other than mainstream Protestantism is organized around a set of virtues the same as these seven.

Overman's theory helps to explain some of the ways that people in predominantly Protestant regions around the world view the body and sports. For example, most Protestants have emphasized that the body is a divine tool to be used in establishing mastery over the physical world (Genesis 1:28; I Corinthians 9:24–27; Philippians 4:13). The perfect body, therefore, was a mark of a righteous soul (Hutchinson, 2008; Overman, 2011). However, traditional Catholic beliefs emphasize that the body is a divine vessel–a "temple of the Holy Spirit" (I Corinthians 6:19). As a result, Catholics living in the nineteenth and early twentieth century were taught to keep the body pure through sexual abstinence and restraint, not through playing sports. Protestant beliefs have also supported the idea that individual competitive success

(*Source:* ChristianCycling.com)

Organized competitive sports emphasize work and achievement. These values are compatible with values underlying Protestant religious beliefs. Therefore, participation on a Christian cycling team is believed to be consistent with secular and Protestant-Christian values.

demonstrates a person's moral worth. Organized competitive sports, because they emphasize work and achievement, are logical sites for the application of Protestant beliefs. Unlike free and expressive play, sports often are worklike and demand sacrifice and the endurance of pain. Therefore, Protestant/Christian athletes can define sports participation as their calling (from God) and make the claim that God wants them to be the best they can be in sports, even if sports sometimes require the physical domination of others. Furthermore, Christian athletes can define sports participation as a valuable form of religious witness and link their efforts in sports to moral worth and personal salvation.

Evidence supports this aspect of Overman's theory in that athletes from Protestant nations disproportionately outnumber athletes from nations where people are primarily Muslim, Hindu, or Buddhist (Lüschen, 1967; Overman, 2011). Even the international success of athletes from non-Protestant nations is often traceable to the influence of cultures where Protestant beliefs are dominant. However, the recent and rapid global diffusion of work-related achievement values has decreased the influence of religious beliefs on athletic success. As a result, many athletes from non-Protestant nations excel in sports and win international competitions today. China and Japan are classic examples.

Sports and World Religions

Most of what we in North America know about sports and religions focuses on various forms of Christianity, especially evangelical fundamentalism. Little is written about sports and Buddhism, Confucianism, Hinduism, Islam, Judaism, Sikhism, Shinto, Taoism, or the many variations of these and other religions.

The beliefs and meanings associated with each of these religions influence how people perceive their bodies, define and give meaning to physical activities, and relate to each other through human movement. However, few people other than evangelical fundamentalist Christians use sports to publicly proclaim their religious beliefs, or use their religious beliefs to give spiritual meaning to sport participation.

It appears that no religion has an equivalent of the self-proclaimed "Christian athlete," which is a visible character in competitive sports in North America, Australia, New Zealand, and parts of Western Europe. This may be due in part to the Christian notion of individual salvation and how certain believers have applied it to everyday life. Additionally, some world religions focus on the transcendence of self, which means that believers seek to merge the self with spiritual forces rather than distinguishing the self by using sports participation to achieve personal growth and spiritual salvation. In fact, the idea of physically competing against others to publicly distinguish the self violates the core beliefs of many religions.

Unfortunately, our knowledge of these issues is limited. We know more about the ways that some North American athletes and coaches convert Zen Buddhist beliefs into strategies for improving golf scores, marathon times, and basketball teamwork than we do about the ways that Buddhism is related to sports and sports participation among the world's 500 million Buddhists. This is because much of our knowledge is grounded in Eurocentric science and limited personal experiences.

Buddhism and Hinduism: Transcending Self Buddhism and philosophical Hinduism emphasize physical and spiritual discipline, but they do not inspire believers to strive for Olympic medals or physically outperform or dominate other human beings in organized competitive sports. Instead, most of the current expressions of Buddhism and Hinduism focus on transcending the self and the material world. Beliefs emphasize that physical reality is transient and the human condition is inherently fragile–neither of which is consistent with training to be an elite athlete, signing endorsement contracts, or being inducted into a sport hall of fame. For example, 80 percent of the 1.3 billion people in India identify themselves as Hindu, and athletes from India have won fewer than 30 medals in Olympic history, compared with nearly 3000 won by US athletes. This is due to many factors, and religion is one of them. China, where Buddhism is

(*Source:* Frederic A. Eyer)

"Well, fans, this is the race we've waited for. The winner of this one will lead us to Ultimate Truth!"

Scholars who study religions and sports are not concerned with the truth or falsity of religious beliefs as much as they are concerned with the ways that religions influence the meaning, purpose, and organization of sports in society.

practiced by about 300 million people, sent teams to the Olympics only four times prior to 1984 and until recently was not very successful in the competitions. But during the past three decades, political interests have trumped religious interests and athletes from China are winning more medals in international competitions.

People revise religious beliefs as changes occur in their cultures and as belief systems travel from one culture to another. This is true for Buddhism and Hinduism as well as other world religions. Of course, there are many variations of Buddhist beliefs and practices, and most of them reflect the orientations of particular teachers or Masters. The island of Taiwan, off the southeast coast of China, is home to a form of "humanistic Buddhism" in which sports have been used to promote health and teach Buddhist principles (Yu, 2011). Competitive success is important, but more important is focusing on good everyday thoughts, words, and deeds.

Traditional Hindu practices in India are heavily gendered and call for women to be secluded and veiled–that is, confined to private, family-based spaces and covered with robes and scarves. For example, when Hindu girls were interviewed in a study about sports participation their responses indicated that "mothers and grandmothers still struggle with allowing girls to be physically active. One of the reasons could be the clothing they wear" (Araki et al., 2013). These traditions and practices were originally linked with a caste system in which religion was used to justify and maintain social inequalities. The caste system consisted of complex norms and beliefs that regulated activities and relationships throughout Indian society. Individuals were born into a particular caste, and their caste position marked their social status in society as a whole.

Officially, the caste system is illegal today, but its cultural legacy continues. This explains why women with a heritage traced back to middle and upper castes have considerable freedom, but women and many men from lower-caste heritage live with persistent poverty, unemployment, and illiteracy. Current patterns of sports participation are influenced by these factors, even though people may embrace "modernized" Hindu beliefs that accommodate increasing secularization in Indian society. Although the caste system was never grounded exclusively in Hindu religious beliefs, Hinduism was organized by upper caste people so that it reproduced the social importance of castes and caste membership.

This topic has yet to be studied in terms of its connection with sports and other physical activities. Additionally, there is a need for research on how Hindus in India and other countries combine religious beliefs with an intense passion for cricket.

Islam: Submission to Allah's Will Studying Islam and sports is a challenge because Muslims, like many Buddhists and Hindus, make few distinctions between the secular and the sacred. Religion is the foundation for personal identity for most Muslims and their every action is done to please Allah (God). This means that every part of their lives is an expression of worship. Religious beliefs and cultural norms are merged into a single theology/ideology, with an emphasis on peace through submission to Allah's will.

Muslims have long participated in physical activities and sports, but participation is regulated by their beliefs about what pleases Allah, and this varies among believers. The connection between sports and the mandate to submit to Allah's will has not been studied until recently (Dagkasa et al., 2011; Farooq and Parker, 2009; Jobey, 2012; Samie, 2013; Samie and Sehlikoglu, 2015; Toffoletti, 2012; Walseth, 2016).

There are noteworthy past and present examples of African American Muslims who excel in sports. However, the traditions of sports participation and the quest for excellence in sports are not as strong in Muslim countries as they are in secularized, Christian-Protestant countries, partly because low per capita income makes full-time training nearly impossible for many Muslims in rural and less materially developed regions of the world.

Although Muslim nations in many parts of Central and Southeast Asia have no religious restrictions on girls and women playing sports, Islamic beliefs in other parts of the world legitimize patriarchal structures and maintain definitions of male and female bodies that discourage girls and women from playing sports and restrict their everyday access to sports participation opportunities.[3]

Physical activities in many Muslim nations are sex segregated. Men are not allowed to look at women in public settings, and women must cover their bodies with robes and head scarves, even when they exercise. These norms are especially strong among fundamentalist Muslims, which is why national Olympic teams from some Muslim nations have few female athletes. The nations with the tightest restrictions include Iran, Afghanistan, Oman, Kuwait, Pakistan, Qatar, Saudi Arabia, the United Arab Emirates, and Sudan. However, an increasing number of women from Islamic countries have participated in recent Asian Games, and some countries now allow women to be spectators at men's soccer matches and other men's sport events (Alaei, 2019; Dorsey, 2018). The connection between gender, sport, and Islam is discussed further in the Reflect on Sports box "Allah's Will."

The popularity of sports among men in Islamic countries is often tied to expressions of political and cultural nationalism rather than religious beliefs. Similarly, when Muslims migrate from Islamic countries to Europe or North America, they sometimes play sports, but their participation is tied more to learning about life and gaining acceptance in their new cultures than expressing Muslim beliefs through sports (Amara, 2013). Muslim girls and women in non-Islamic countries have very low participation rates (Walseth, 2016), and Muslim organizations don't often sponsor sports for their members.

Judaism: Sports and Struggle The link between Judaism and sports is weak, but the link between Jews and sports participation is strong. This apparent contradiction is understandable when we remember that Jews constitute an ethnic population as well as a religion, and that Jews have faced discrimination in nearly every society in which they've lived, except Israel. The following two contradictory statements help us understand the confusion about sports participation among Jews:

> Jews are not sportsmen. Whether this is due to their physical lethargy, their dislike of unnecessary physical action or their serious cast of mind–it is nevertheless a fact . . . .
>
> –Henry Ford, 1921 (based on his anti-semitic stereotype of Jews)

> Sport valorized Gentile masculine values like aggression, strength, speed, and combativeness. . . . I loved it. Nothing my [Jewish] father could do or say stopped me from embracing baseball, basketball, or football over religion.
>
> –Alan Klein, 2008 (German-born Jew, anthropologist who studies sports and culture)

The first statement was made in 1921 by Henry Ford, founder of the Ford Motor Company and one of the most influential men in the United States at that time. The second statement was made by Klein (2008), who came to the United States just after the

[3]Patriarchy is a form of gender relations in which men are legally privileged relative to women, especially in regard their access to political power and economic resources.

Allah's Will
Challenges for Muslim Women in Sports

Imagine facing death threats whenever you play sports. Imagine winning an Olympic gold medal, receiving death threats from people in your country who brand you as an immoral and corrupt woman, and then being forced to live in exile. At the same time, imagine that you are a heroine to many young women, who see you as inspirational in their quest for equal rights and opportunities to play sports.

This was the situation faced by Hassiba Boulmerka, the gold medalist in the 1500 meters at the 1992 Olympic Games in Barcelona, Spain. As an Algerian Muslim woman, she believed that being an international athlete did not require her to abandon her faith or her commitment to Islam. But those who condemned Boulmerka said that although it is permissible for women to participate in sports, it was not permissible to do so in shorts or T-shirts, or while men are watching, or when men and women train together, or when facilities do not permit total privacy, or, if you are married, unless your husband gives his permission.

To complicate matters, some Islamic feminists accused Boulmerka of allowing herself to be used by a

(*Source:* Forough Alaei)

Women in some Muslim countries are not allowed to even enter a sports stadium as spectators. In this photo we see a young woman who has altered her appearance to join the men at a soccer game in Iran. The photographer, Forough Alaei, included this image in her "*Cry for Freedom*" series of photos that won 1st prize in the 2019 World Press Photo contest. Through her photos she gives voice to Iranian female soccer fans who are banned from stadiums.

Continued

reflect on SPORTS Allah's Will (*continued*)

sport system based on men's values and sponsored by corporations that promote a soulless, consumer culture. To participate in such a system, they said, was to endorse global forces that oppress humankind.

More recently, eighteen-year-old tennis phenomenon Sania Mirza from India was given heavy police security at a tournament in Calcutta, India, after receiving alleged threats from Muslim men saying that she violated Sharia Law stating that any woman in public must cover her entire body except for her hands and face. Mirza's shorts and sleeveless shirts were called "indecent" and "corrupting," and in 2008, the disputes over her tennis clothes led her to consider quitting her tennis career. Instead, she decided to boycott tournaments in her home country. At the same time, Indian corporations sought Mirza to endorse their products, knowing that many young Indian women looked up to her.

The issues facing Mirza were avoided by Bahrain-born sprinter Ruqaya Al Ghasara. Since 2004 she has been winning medals and setting records while wearing her trademark white headscarf and red bodysuit. When Al Ghasara won the 100-meters at the West Asian Games in 2007, she told reporters, "I have no problems with the hijab. I have a great desire to show that there are no problems with wearing these clothes. Wearing a veil proves that Muslim women face no obstacles and encourages them to compete in sport" (Algazeera, 2006). When pressed further, she said, "It's not just a matter of wearing a piece of cloth. There is something very special about wearing the hijab. It gives me strength. I feel lots of support from society because I am wearing the Islamic hijab. There is a relationship between the hijab and the heart" (IAAF, 2007).

Sadaf Khadem, a boxer from Iran pushed normative boundaries related to clothing in 2019 when she was the first Iranian woman to box in an official match in France against a French opponent (Pretot, 2019; Smith, 2019). She wore traditional boxing shorts and a tank top as other female boxers do, and this led Iranian authorities to issue a warrant for her arrest in her home country. To avoid jail, she canceled her trip home and stayed in Europe.

These four scenarios illustrate that the bodies of Muslim women are "contested terrain." Today, they remain at the center of deep political, cultural, and religious struggles about what is important, what is right and wrong, and how social life should be organized. Muslim women in sports embody and personify these struggles. On the one hand, these athletes are active subjects asserting new ideas about what it means to be a Muslim woman. On the other hand, they're passive objects used in debates about morality and social change in the world.

Of course, there are significant variations in the rights and autonomy of women in different countries where Islam is the dominant religion. But in general, struggles over issues of religion and gender will continue for Muslim women participating publicly in sports. At the same time, Muslim women living in predominantly Christian countries sometimes use sports played in private as a refuge and an opportunity to spend time with peers who share their beliefs. But coming to terms with "Allah's will" continues to be a challenge for many Muslim women. Their sports participation often depends on the support of people working in sports organizations. For those in sports management it raises an important question: *What strategies are most effective in promoting inclusion and accommodating religious diversity in programs and facilities?*

gas chambers had been shut down following World War II. Klein played sports, earned a Ph.D., and became an anthropologist noted for his excellent research on sports and human rights.

Like many Jews, Klein was attracted to sports as a reaction to anti-Semitism (Brenner and Reuveni, 2006). He played typical American sports to assimilate, to fit in at a time when being like everyone else kept him from feeling different in his school and community. Excelling in sports disrupted the anti-semitic stereotype that Jews were "thinkers instead of doers"–smart people with frail bodies. Similar dynamics led Jews to dominate professional basketball in the United States from 1920 through the late 1940s, and boxing from 1910 to 1940 (Klein, 2008).

Today Jews sponsor the quadrennial Maccabiah Games in the year following the Olympics. These games are cultural rather than religious in origin and purpose. They were founded to foster Jewish identity and traditions and to showcase highly skilled Jewish athletes. The 2017 Maccabiah Games, often described as "the Jewish Olympics," involved more than 10,000 athletes from 85 countries in 45 sports. In addition to sports competitions, there are cultural and educational programs, all designed to create strong ties with Judaism, Israel, and the global Jewish community (Chabin, 2013). In recent year the Maccabiah Games have added three new divisions for Juniors, Masters, and Paralympic athletes.

Shinto: Sumo in Japan Sumo, or traditional Japanese wrestling, is a combination of a sacred religious ritual and a fight to the death between two larger than life combatants. The wrestlers dress the part by wearing a mawashi or loincloth. They respect the priest-like referee and the history and cultural meaning of the sport. These coordinated presentations of self give spectators the feel of drama along with sport.

Sumo has strong historical ties to Shinto, a traditional Japanese religion (Light and Kinnaird, 2002). Shinto means "the way of the gods," and it consists of a system of rituals and ceremonies designed to worship nature rather than reaffirm an established theology.

Modern sumo is a nonreligious activity, although it remains steeped in Shinto ritual and ceremony.

(*Source:* Franck Robichon/EPA/Shutterstock)

Sumo wrestling in Japan is steeped in centuries-old Shinto rituals of purification. However, as sumo has become a more global sport, there is less awareness of and respect for its connection with religious beliefs and practices. As the Shinto foundations of sumo fade, its meaning in Japanese culture is changing.

The dohyō (sumo ring) in which the bouts take place are defined as sacred sites. Religious symbols are integrated into their design and construction, and the rings are consecrated through purification ceremonies, during which referees, dressed in priestly garb, ask the gods to bless the scheduled bouts. Only the wrestlers and recognized sumo officials are allowed in the dohyō. Shoes must not be worn, and women are never allowed to stand on or near an officially designated ring.

The wrestlers take great care to preserve the purity of the dohyō. Prior to their bouts, they ritualistically throw salt into the ring to symbolize their respect for its sacredness and purity; they even wipe sweat off their bodies and rinse their mouths with water presented to them by fellow wrestlers. If a wrestler sheds blood during a bout, the stains are cleaned and purified before the bouts continue. Shinto motifs are included in the architecture and decorations on and around the dohyo. However, wrestlers do not personally express their commitment to Shinto, nor do Shinto organizations sponsor or promote sumo or other sports.

In recent years, the popularity of sumo has declined at the same time that the sport has attracted participants from other parts of the world. Not being raised to know or respect Shinto and the traditional sacred rituals associated with the sport, these new wrestlers bring a secular orientation to the ring. This, combined with championships being won by non-Japanese wrestlers and recent match-fixing scandals, has eroded the religious foundations of the sport (McCurry, 2011; Sanchanta, 2011).

The exclusion of women from the doyhō was hotly contested in 2018 when a wrestler had a stroke in the ring and the only medical person close to the ring was a female nurse who was restrained from entering the ring to help the man (Yoshida, 2018). Feminists and progressive scholars protested and said that the exclusion of women was discriminatory and must be eliminated. Sumo and other male officials in Japan disagreed and the policy continues to exist although it is on shaky cultural grounds.

Religion and Life Philosophies in China Anthropologist Susan Brownell (1995, 2008) has studied physical culture and forms of Taoist, Confucian, and Buddhist ideas and practices in her comprehensive studies of the body and sport in China. She notes that each of these life philosophies is actually a general theory of the nature and principles of the universe. As with Islam, this makes it difficult to separate "religious beliefs" from cultural ideology as a whole. Each of these life philosophies emphasizes the notion that all human beings should strive to live in accord with the energy and forces of nature. The body and physical exercise are seen as important parts of nature, but the goal of movement is to seek harmony with nature rather than to overcome or dominate nature or other human beings.

Tai chi is a form of exercise based on this cultural approach to life and living. Some versions of the martial arts are practiced in this spirit, but others, including practices outside China, are grounded in secular traditions of self-defense and military training. China's success in recent international competitions, raises other questions about the possible connections between religious beliefs and sports participation. Therefore, research is needed to investigate the implications of Taoism, Confucianism, and Buddhism as they have been integrated into the lives of various segments of the vast and diverse Chinese population.

Native Americans: Merging the Spiritual and Physical Historically, Native Americans have often included physical games and running races in religious rituals (Nabokov, 1981). However, the purpose of doing this is to reaffirm social connections within specific native cultural groups and gain skills needed for group survival. Outside these rituals, sport participation has had no specific religious meaning.

Making general statements about religious beliefs and sports participation among Native Americans is difficult because beliefs vary from one native culture to another. However, many native cultures maintain animistic religious beliefs emphasizing the spiritual integration of material elements, such as the earth, wind, sun, moon, plants, and animals. Many native games contain features that imply this integration, and, when Native Americans play sports constructed by people from European or other backgrounds, they often use their religious beliefs to give their participation a meaning that reaffirms their ways of viewing the world and their connection with the sacred.

Anthropologist Peter Nabokov has studied running among Native Americans and notes that prior to their contact with Europeans they ran for practical purposes such as hunting, communicating, and fighting; but they also ran to reenact myths and legends and to reaffirm their connection with the forces of nature and the universe. More recently, Native American athletes whose identities are grounded in native cultures often define sports participation in terms of their specific tribal cultural traditions and beliefs. However, little is known about how they incorporate specific religious beliefs and traditions, which vary across cultures, into participation that occurs outside of their cultures or how young Native Americans who play sports connect their participation to religious beliefs. Again, research is needed.

Sports and World Religions: Waiting for Research We need more information about the connections between various world religions, ideas about the body, and participation in physical activities and sports. This information would help us understand the lives of billions of people who participate in various forms of physical activities and sports but do not connect them directly with religious organizations or use them as sites for religious witness. This is different from the tendency of some Christians to attach their religion to institutionalized, competitive sports that already exist for nonreligious purposes.

How Have Christians and Christian Organizations Used Sports?

Unlike other religions, Christianity has inspired believers to use sports for many purposes. These include (a) promoting spiritual growth; (b) recruiting new members and promoting religious beliefs and organizations; and (c) promoting fundamentalist beliefs and evangelical orientations.

To Promote Spiritual Growth During the mid-1800s, influential Christian men, described as "muscular Christians" in England and New England, argued that Christianity at that time had become feminized and promoted the idea that the physical condition of a man's body had religious significance. They believed that the male body was an instrument of good works and that meeting the physical demands of godly behavior required good health and physical conditioning. Although most Christians didn't agree with this approach, the idea that there might be a connection between the physical and spiritual dimensions of human beings grew increasingly popular (Baker, 2007; Guttmann, 1978, 1988; Watson et al., 2013).

The idea that the body had moral significance and that moral character could be strengthened with physical conditioning encouraged many religious organizations to use sports in their efforts to recruit boys and men. For example, the YMCA grew rapidly between 1880 and 1920 as the organization built athletic facilities in many communities and sponsored sport teams. Canadian James Naismith invented basketball in 1891 while he was a student at the Springfield, Massachusetts, YMCA. William Morgan, the physical activities director at a YMCA in Holyoke, Massachusetts, invented volleyball in 1895.

Religious beliefs about developing and strengthening the body were not applied to girls or women during the nineteenth and early twentieth centuries. For most people, "a female muscular Christian was a contradiction in terms [and] . . . Muscular Christianity represented a reaction against the 'femininization' of American middle-class culture" (Baker, 2007, pp. 44–45). In fact, when activist women opened the first YWCA in Boston in 1866 their focus was on "prayer, Bible study, and Christian witness" devoted to helping women find decent housing and obtain job training so they could work and support themselves; playing sports was not part of the program (Baker, 2007, p. 62).

Although mainline Protestants endorsed sports for boys and men through the end of the nineteenth century, some of them came to wonder about the religious relevance of the highly competitive sports that emerged during the first half of the twentieth century. Scandals, violence, and other problems in sports caused evangelicals, in particular, to question their value. Protestant leaders were also wary of women playing sports because it contradicted their belief that God created men and women to be different and that female athletes would subvert God's plan (Jonas, 2005).

It wasn't until the late 1940s that evangelical Christians again made a direct connection between sports and their religious beliefs (Ladd and Mathisen, 1999)–and they were not alone in embracing sports in the years following World War II. Protestant churches and congregations, Catholic dioceses and parishes, Mormon wards, the B'nai B'rith, and some Jewish synagogues also embraced sports as worthwhile activities for young men. These organizations sponsored sports and sports programs because their members and leaders believed that sports participation developed moral character and prepared young men for the military.

During the 1960s and 1970s, athletic-minded evangelical Christians began to focus on sport as a realm in which they could bring their religious beliefs to (male) athletes and then use the visibility and popularity of athletes to spread those beliefs to sports fans and the general public (Krattenmaker, 2010). The widespread acceptance of the great sport myth (see Chapter 1, p. 11) contributed to their success. People already believed that the essential purity and goodness of sports would be internalized by athletes willing to learn what sports would teach them. When athletes accepted and gave witness to Bible-based values, people saw the connection between sports participation and Christianity as logical and credible.

The connection between Christian values and the perceived purity and goodness of sports was clearly highlighted in 1971 by Billy Graham, the best-known and most highly respected evangelist of the later twentieth century. A long-time outspoken promoter of sports as a builder of moral character, Graham summarized the spirit in which many religious organizations have viewed sports over the last century:

> The Bible says leisure and lying around are morally dangerous for us. Sports keep us busy; athletes, you notice, don't take drugs. There are probably more committed Christians in sports, both collegiate and professional, than in any other occupation in America (in *Newsweek,* 1971, p. 51).

Graham's statement about drugs sounds naive today, but he accurately noted that many Christians see sports as activities that symbolize and promote moral development. This perception, despite evidence to the contrary, remains strong in North America.

To Recruit New Members and Promote Religious Beliefs and Organizations Using sports to promote particular religious beliefs was a key strategy of Christian missionaries who accompanied European and North Americans who colonized traditional cultures. Since the mid-1800s, this strategy was used to attract and recruit boys and men to churches and religious organizations, especially in England and the United States (Putney, 2003). This practice became so common in the United States after World War II that sociologist Charles Page referred to it as "the basketballization of American religion" (in Demerath and Hammond, 1969, p. 182).

In the early 1990s, for example, Bill McCartney, the former football coach at the University of Colorado, used sport images and metaphors as he founded a religious organization, The Promise Keepers, and recruited men to join. McCartney and others in the evangelical men's organization preached that a "manly man is a Godly man." Similarly, other Christian fundamentalist organizations have used images of tough athletes to represent ideal "Christian men." This strategy of presenting a "masculinized Christianity" was designed to attract men into churches so they could reclaim their status as moral leaders, honor their commitment to their wives and families, and present a masculinized version of biblical values (Beal, 1997; Randels and Beal, 2002). This approach continued in 2013 with a six-city Promise Keepers men's conference titled "Awakening the Warrior."

Church-affiliated colleges and universities in the United States have also used sports as recruiting and public relations tools. Administrators from these schools know that seventeen-year-olds today are likely to listen to recruiting advertisements that use terminology, images, and spokespeople from sports. Plus, a winning sports program can provide exposure and publicity for particular religious beliefs (Michaelis, 2011; Zillgitt, 2011).

Even a half century ago, when the famous preacher Oral Roberts founded his university in Tulsa, Oklahoma, he highlighted the importance of its sports program in this way:

> Athletics is part of our Christian witness. . . . Nearly every man in America reads the sports pages, and a Christian school cannot ignore these people. . . . Sports are becoming the No. 1 interest of people in America. For us to be relevant, we had to gain the attention of millions of people in a way that they could understand (in Boyle, 1970, p. 64).

Jerry Falwell, noted television evangelist, introduced intercollegiate athletics at his Liberty University in the 1970s with a similar explanation:

> To me, athletics are a way of making a statement. And I believe you have a better Christian witness to the youth of the world when you competitively, head-to-head, prove yourself their equal on the playing field (in Capouya, 1986, p. 75).

Then, in his opening prayer, Falwell declared, "Father, we don't want to be mediocre, we don't want to fail. We want to honor You by winning" (in Capouya, 1986, p. 72). More recently, university chancellor Jerry Falwell Jr. proudly stated that he was carrying out his father's vision (Pennington, 2012).

Other church-affiliated colleges and universities have used sports in similar but less overt ways to attract students. Catholic schools–including the University of Notre Dame, Gonzaga, Georgetown, and Boston College–have used football and/or basketball programs to build their prestige as church-affiliated institutions. Brigham Young University, affiliated with the Church of Latter Day Saints (Mormons), has also done this. Smaller Christian colleges around the United States formed the National Christian Collegiate Athletic Association (NCCAA) in the mid-1960s and today they continue to sponsor championships and recruit Christian student-athletes to their schools.

Some religious organizations are developed around sports to attract people to Christian beliefs and provide support for athletes who hold Christian beliefs. Examples include Sports Ambassadors, the Fellowship of Christian Athletes (FCA), Athletes in Action (AIA), Pro Athletes Outreach (PAO), Global Sports Outreach, Baseball Chapel, and dozens of smaller groups associated with particular sports. These organizations have a strong evangelical emphasis, and members are usually eager to share their beliefs in the hope that others will embrace Christianity as they do.

Christian organizations and groups also use sports as sites for evangelizing. For example, in 1996 the Association of Baptists for World Evangelism (ABWE) organized and supported hundreds of evangelical Christians as they were bused 260 miles from Chattanooga, Tennessee to Atlanta and back each day during the Atlanta Olympic Games (Hartman, 2016). They distributed over 500,000 booklets prepared for the spectators at the games and recorded over 600 professions of faith by the people they talked with during the two weeks. News of this success spread and inspired other evangelical organizations to send "missionaries" to every Olympic city to spread their beliefs. Most recently, highly organized teams of Baptists, Methodists, Presbyterians, Jehovah's Witnesses, and Mormons joined the United Christian Churches of Korea to engage in an Olympic outreach to spectators and athletes (Mulkey, 2018). The Jehovah's Witnesses alone sent 1000 missionaries to Gangneung and Pyeongchang, the host cities for the 2018 Winter Games. A key strategy used by missionaries was a to trade lapel pins, one of which was a "More Than Gold" pin that enabled them to redirect conversations to religious beliefs. They were so successful and there were so many of them that Olympic park officials banned them and began to confiscate religious materials that had been handed out and left in the park.

Evangelical Christian organizations also faced pushback in China after they had been banned by the Chinese government, but they took their evangelizing underground and spoke with uncounted Chinese people and spectators at the 2008 Olympic and Paralympic Games (4 Winds Christian Athletics, 2008; Associated Press, 2008). This led organizations to plan ahead for the strategies they would use at London 2012 and Rio de Janeiro

(*Source:* Jay Coakley)

The public profiles of some universities are linked to both sports and religion. This is the football stadium at the University of Notre Dame, with the library in the background. The outside wall of the library presents a mural image of Christ, now known as "Touchdown Jesus" among Notre Dame fans.

2016 where they experienced record success for passing out materials and encouraging professions of faith (Blazer, 2015; Cobb, 2016). This approach to sports evangelizing has also been used at the men's FIFA World Cup, the Pan American Games, and Super Bowls, among other sport mega-events.

Such efforts to evangelize are not new, but today they are highly organized and coordinated in connection with major events, such as the Super Bowl, FIFA World Cups, the Pan American Games, and other sports mega-events.

Apart from major events, the Fellowship of Christian Athletes publishes *Sharing the Victory (STV),* a widely circulated magazine that uses a biblically informed perspective to report on sports and athletes. Articles highlight Christian athletes and their religious testimony. Most athlete profiles emphasize that life "without a commitment to Christ" is superficial and meaningless, even if one wins in sports.

This method of using athletes to evangelize is now a key strategy. As the founder of the FCA asked over a half century ago, "If athletes can sell razor blades and soft drinks, why can't they sell the Gospel?" This approach corresponds with the fact that some high-profile media evangelists pair up with celebrity athletes whose statements about their fundamentalist Christian beliefs serve to promote the ministry of the evangelist.

A similar strategy has been adopted by top Catholic officials. In 2004, Pope John Paul II established a new Vatican office dedicated to "Church and Sport." Although its primary stated goal is to reform the culture of sport, it is also concerned with making Catholicism relevant in the lives of people, especially men, who are no longer involved in their parishes or using Catholic beliefs to guide their lives. Today, the office sponsors a talk radio sport program to attract Italian men who no longer see the Catholic Church as relevant to them; soccer is a central focus of the program on Vatican radio. It has also published books summarizing presentations on sports from a Catholic perspective and serves a guide for Catholics associated with sports (Pontifical Council for the Laity, 2006, 2008, 2011). Pope Francis has supported the connection between Catholicism and sport through many of his addresses on the topic. However, the emphasis among Catholic officials is less on evangelizing and more on preventing men from leaving Catholicism and urging athletes to use Catholic dogma to inform their involvement in sports.

To Promote Fundamentalist Beliefs and Evangelical Orientations Most of the religious groups and organizations previously mentioned, excluding Catholics, promote a specific form of Christianity–one based on a loosely articulated conservative ideology and a fundamentalist orientation toward life.

Religious fundamentalism is based on the belief that the secular foundation of modern societies is inherently corrupt and can be redeemed only if people reorganize their personal lives and the entire social order to manifest the absolute and unchanging Truth contained in a sacred text. Fundamentalists in all religions emphasize that this reorganization requires people to be personally committed to the supernatural or transcendent source of truth (God, Allah, Christ, Mohammed, "the universe," the spirit world), which provides answers to all questions. These answers are revealed through sacred writings, the verbal teachings of divinely inspired leaders and prophets, and personal revelations.

Fundamentalist movements in all religions arise when people perceive moral threats to a past way of life that was, according to their beliefs, firmly based on moral principles. Therefore, fundamentalists emphasize the "moral decline of society" and the need to return to a time when religious truth was the foundation for culture and social organization. This belief is so deeply held by some believers that it creates a social and political split between fundamentalists and the rest of society.

Ladd and Mathisen (1999) explain that most fundamentalist Christians in the United States have used sports, in part, to reduce their separation and gain acceptance from people in the rest of society. The ways that sports have been used by Christian fundamentalist movements in other predominantly Protestant societies suggest that this is seen to be an effective strategy although there are important variations between countries (Butterworth and Senkbeil, 2017).

How Have Athletes, Coaches, and Teams Used Religion?

Athletes, coaches, and teams use religion, religious beliefs, prayers, and rituals in many ways. Research on this topic is scarce, but there is much anecdotal information suggesting that religion is used for one or more of the following purposes:

1. To cope with uncertainty
2. To stay out of trouble
3. To give meaning to sports participation
4. To put sports participation into a balanced perspective
5. To establish team solidarity and unity
6. To reaffirm motivation and social control on teams
7. To achieve personal and competitive success

To Cope with Uncertainty Through history, people have used prayers and rituals based on religion, magic, and/or superstition to cope with uncertainties in their lives (Cherrington, 2012, 2014; Weber, 1922b/1993). Because sport competition involves uncertainty, it is not surprising that many athletes use rituals, some based in religion, to help them feel as if they have some control over what happens to them on the playing field.

A study of Olympic-level wrestlers in Europe found that some of them found reassurance through their prayers before matches. Saying silent meditative prayers, they explained, helped them relax their minds and gain control before stepping onto the mat (Kristiansen and Roberts, 2007). This strategy has been described by a German sport scientist as "Glaubensdoping," or "faith doping" (Güldenpfennig, 2001). This term would not be used in the United States, where prayers and religious rituals are commonly used prior to competition.

Not all religious athletes use prayer and religious rituals in this manner, but many call on their religion to help them face challenges and uncertainty. Therefore, many athletes who pray before or during games seldom pray before or during practices when uncertainty isn't an issue. For example, Catholic athletes who make the sign of the cross when they enter or are taken out of a soccer match, come up to bat in a baseball game, or shoot a free throw during a basketball game don't do the same thing when they walk on the field, bat, or shoot free throws during practices. It is the actual competition that produces the uncertainty and then evokes the prayer or religious ritual.

A national survey done in the United States by the Public Religion Research Institute (PRRI) found that when sports are important to people with a religious affiliation, they assume that sports also are important to their God. Consistent with this, nearly 40 percent of the Protestants and Catholics believed that God has a hand in the outcomes of competitive events (Jones & Cox, 2017). Dan Cox, the research director at PRRI explains that, "If you are an enthusiastic fan, why would God be absent from the [field of play]?" In the case of religious athletes, he noted:

> "If people believe in a personal relationship with God, it is not such a big step for them to say God rewards people who are faithful. For athletes, the rewards would be good health and success."

Cox also explained that 1 in 5 religious fans believe that if God is involved in sports, there will be times when their teams and athletes will be cursed and suffer negative consequences.

Sometimes it's difficult to separate the use of religion from the use of magic and superstition among athletes. **Magic** consists of *recipe-like rituals designed to produce immediate and practical results in the material world.* **Superstitions** consist of *regularized, ritualistic actions performed to give a person or group a sense of control and predictability in the face of challenges.* Thus, when athletes pray, it may be a form of religion or a form of magic and superstition, but for the person doing it, the purpose is usually to deal with the uncertainty in competitive sports.

To Stay Out of Trouble Christian athletes often say that religion helps keep them "on track" and avoid the risky lifestyles that often exist in the social worlds that develop around certain sports. For example, an NFL player said, "Before I found the Lord, I drank! I whoremongered! I cussed! I cheated! I manipulated! I deceived!" (in Corsello, 1999, p. 435).

The fact that religious beliefs may separate athletes from risky off-the-field lifestyles and keep them focused on training in their sports has not been lost on some coaches who are attracted to the possibility that religion may help athletes control their actions and avoid trouble that could disrupt team focus. This is why many professional teams–in the United States more than other countries–include Christian chaplains on their teams.

Some team owners also see "born-again athletes" as good long-term investments because they "are less likely to get arrested" (Nightengale, 2006). Religious beliefs also may keep athletes out of trouble by encouraging them to become involved in church-related and community-based service programs. This involvement also separates them from risky off-the-field lifestyles.

To Give Meaning to Sport Participation by Defining It as an Act of Worship Sports participation emphasizes personal achievement and self-promotion, and it involves playing games that produce no essential goods or services, even though people create important social occasions around sport events.

This makes sports participation a self-centered, self-indulgent activity. Although training often involves personal sacrifices and pain, it focuses on the development and use of personal physical skills, often to the exclusion of other activities and relationships. Realizing this can create a crisis of meaning for athletes who have dedicated their lives to personal achievements in sports.

One way to deal with this crisis of meaning is to define sport participation as an act of worship, a platform for giving witness, or a manifestation of God's plan for one's life (Hoffman, 2010; Krattenmaker, 2010). For example, US track-and-field athlete Jesse Williams put it this way at the 2012 London Olympics: "Jesus Christ is the reason why I am able to perform at this level, and I know He has a plan for me. That puts things into perspective before, during and after competition. I know God has put me in this place to represent Him." Many Christian athletes and coaches like to quote Colossians 3:23 in the Bible: "Whatever you do, work at it with all your heart, working for the Lord, not for men." This enables them to define their sports participation as a sacred rather than a secular activity. As a result, their doubts about the worthiness of what they do are eliminated because playing sports is sanctified as a calling from God. Additionally, it is comforting to know that your sport career is part of God's plan.

To Put Sports Participation into a Balanced Perspective It's easy to lose perspective in sports, to let it define you and foreclose other parts of your life. In the face of this threat, some athletes feel that religious beliefs enable them to transcend sports and bring balance to their lives. Domonique Foxworth, a former NFL player, explains that "there is no better way to calm an eager rookie before a big game than to put the game in perspective by reminding him of his spiritual beliefs" (Foxworth, 2005, 2D). This makes playing sports part of God's plan, and it becomes easier for athletes to face challenges and deal with the inevitable disappointments experienced in sports. In the process, they keep sports in perspective.

To Establish Team Solidarity and Unity Religious beliefs and rituals can be powerful tools in creating bonds between people. When they're combined with sports participation, they can link athletes together as spiritual teammates, building team solidarity and unity in the process. Many coaches know this, and some have used Christian beliefs as rallying points for their teams.

This use of religion can backfire when athletes object to being expected to pray using Christian prayers. This occurred at New Mexico State University when four Muslim football players filed a lawsuit accusing their coach of religious discrimination because he labeled them "troublemakers" after they objected to reciting the Lord's Prayer in a team huddle after each practice and before each game. The university settled the case out of court, suggesting that they agreed that a football coach doesn't have the right to turn his team into a Christian brotherhood (Fleming, 2007).

Objections to pregame prayers in public schools have led some US students and their parents to file lawsuits to ban religious expression in connection with sport events. However, coaches and athletes continue to insist that prayers bring team members together in positive ways and serve a spiritual purpose in players' lives. This controversial issue is discussed in the Reflect on Sports box "Public Prayers at Sport Events."

To Reaffirm Motivation and Social Control on Teams Religions also can sanctify norms and rules by connecting them with divinities. In this way, some Christians connect the moral worth of athletes with the quality of their play and their conformity to team rules and the commands of coaches. This combination of Christianity and sport is very powerful, and coaches have been known to use it as a means of motivating and controlling athletes. Coaches see obedience to their rules as necessary for team success, and religious beliefs can sometimes be used to promote obedience by converting it into a divine mandate.

To Achieve or Explain Competitive Success People often debate whether it is appropriate to pray for victories or other forms of athletic success. Some

(*Source:* Frederic A. Eyer)

"She says this prayer is 'voluntary.' Who's she trying to fool?!?"

When coaches use religious beliefs and rituals on sport teams, they may create solidarity or dissent. Coaches say that team prayers are voluntary, but players may feel pressure to pray or not play, regardless of their religious beliefs.

argue that using prayer this way trivializes religion by turning it into a training strategy. Others say that if prayers bring a sense of harmony and feelings of self-worth to an athlete, praying could enhance performance (Briggs, 2011; Krattenmaker, 2012).

Some Christian athletes believe that God intervenes in sports. For example, Colorado Rockies chairman and CEO Charlie Monfort assembled a Major League Baseball team that in 2007 had many Christians in management, coaching, and on the roster. When the team experienced success, Monfort said, "I think character-wise we're stronger than anyone in baseball. Christians . . . are some of the strongest people in baseball. I believe God sends signs, and we're seeing those." Dan O'Dowd, the team's general manager concurred with his boss, saying, "You look at some of the games we're winning. Those aren't just a coincidence. God has definitely had a hand in this."

Of course, athletes and others connected with sports list many different reasons for praying when they play sports (Hopsicker, 2009). But it is unlikely that nearly every major professional sport team in the United States would have a chaplain unless owners and managers thought it would improve performance. This also may be why 193 national teams at the 2012 Olympics brought chaplains with them to London. Reid Priddy, who led the US volleyball team to a gold medal at the 2008 Beijing Olympics, explained his success on the court in this way: "Right before the . . . Olympic Games I really felt the freedom from God to be a fierce competitor–not just a really nice and supportive teammate" (FCA, 2012).

THE CHALLENGES OF COMBINING SPORTS AND RELIGIOUS BELIEFS

Organized competitive sports and religions are cultural practices with different histories, traditions, and goals. Each has been socially constructed in different ways, around different issues, and through different types of relationships. This means that combining religious beliefs with sports participation requires adjustments–either in a person's religious beliefs or in the way a person plays sports.

Moral Dilemmas for Christian Athletes

Physical educator Shirl Hoffman (2010) has made the case that there are built-in conflicts between some Christian religious beliefs and the actions required in many power and performance sports. Christianity, he explains, is based on an ethos emphasizing the importance of means over ends, process over product, quality over quantity, and caring for others over caring for self. But power and performance sports emphasize winning, final scores, season records, personal performance statistics, and self-display.

Do these differences present a moral dilemma fore Christian athletes? For example, do Christian boxers and Mixed Martial Arts fighters wonder if pummeling another human being into senseless submission and risking the infliction of a fatal injury is an appropriate spiritual offering? Do Christian football players see problems associated with

Public Prayers at Sport Events
What's Legal and What's Not?

Prayers before sport events are common in the United States. They're said silently by individuals, aloud by small groups of players or entire teams in pregame huddles, and occasionally over public address systems by students or local residents.

Public prayers are allowed at private events, and all people in the United States have the right to say silent, private prayers for any purpose at any time–and this allows one or more students to kneel and say a private prayer before or after a game. As long as an event is not connected with a public, tax supported organization and as long as people pray privately, prayers are legal in connection with sports (Byrd, 2017; Green, 2016).

A 1962 US Supreme Court decision banned organized prayers in public schools when they are said publicly and collectively at sports events sponsored by state organizations, such as public schools. This ruling caused controversy in Texas in 1992, when two families near Houston filed a lawsuit requesting a ban on prayers in public schools. They appealed to the First Amendment of the US Constitution, which says, "Congress shall make no law respecting an establishment of religion." The federal district judge in the case ruled that public prayers are permitted as long as they are nonsectarian and general in content, initiated by students, and not said in connection with attempts to convert anyone to a particular religion. But this decision was qualified during an appeal when the appellate judges ruled that sports events are not serious enough occasions to require the solemnity of public prayer; therefore, the prayers are unconstitutional.

Despite this decision and a long list of similar court rulings between the early 1990s and today in the United States, people in many US towns have continued to say public prayers before public school sport events. These prayers often are "local traditions," and people object when federal government judges tell them that they are unconstitutional. They argue that it violates their constitutional right to "freedom of speech."

The issue of prayer related to public school teams continues to be contentious. In 2014, a high school coach in North Carolina was ordered to stop baptizing his players and leading his team in prayers (Stuart, 2014). A similar order was given in 2015 to a high school coach in Georgia when some of his players were baptized before practice. In front of a local news camera, the coach declared, "We did this right before practice! Take a look and see how God is STILL in our schools!" (Estep, 2015).

Although most of these incidents do not lead to lawsuits, local authorities have confirmed again and again that they violate the US Constitution–a conclusion reaffirmed whenever cases have gone to court.

Those who have filed lawsuits argue that the prayers affirm Christian beliefs and create informal pressures to give priority to those beliefs over others. They also say that those who don't join in and pray are subject to ridicule, social rejection, or efforts to convert them to Christianity. The people who support public prayers say they don't pressure anyone and that Christianity is the dominant religion in their towns and in the United States. However, they also assume that the public prayers will not be Jewish, Islamic, Hindu, Buddhist, Baha'i, or Sikh prayers and that they will not contradict their Christian beliefs.

When judges rule on these cases they consider what would occur if prayers at public school sports events represented beliefs that contradicted Christian beliefs. Would Christians object if public prayers praised Allah, the Goddess, or multiple deities? What would happen if Muslim students said their daily prayers over the public address system in conjunction with a basketball game, if teams were asked to pray to Allah or the Prophet Muhammad, or if all football games were rescheduled to accommodate Muslim customs during their three- to four-week observance of Ramadan in October? These are important questions because over four billion people in the world do not hold Christian beliefs and about 1 in 4 Americans have beliefs that are not Christian.

These are the reasons that judges have consistently ruled that public prayers are not allowed at sport events sponsored by state organizations such as public schools. This continues to create management challenges for officials in schools and sport programs, especially as local populations become increasingly diverse in terms of religious beliefs. *What would you do if you were a coach and half of your team members wanted to read out loud from the Koran/Qur'an in the lockerroom before games?*

using intimidation and "taking out" opponents with potentially injurious hits and then saying that such behaviors are "acts of worship"? Do athletes believe that they can use physically injurious actions as expressions of religious commitment simply by saying that they are motivated by Christian love?

For most of the twentieth century these questions were not asked, because it was assumed that sports, especially violent sports, were pagan rather than Christian activities. Athletes were not seen as representatives of Christian ideals. But acceptance of the great sport myth and the belief that sports participation imparts purity and goodness made it possible to claim that being a tough, aggressive athlete was consistent with Christian values.

Research suggests that Christian athletes combine their religious beliefs with sports participation in diverse ways (Baker, 2007; Butterworth & Senkbeil, 2017). However, in elite power and performance sports most self-described Christian athletes don't think about possible conflicts between their religious beliefs and their actions in sports (Oppenheimer, 2013; Sinden, 2013). At the same time, a few athletes do struggle with the conflict between the moral ethos of sports and the moral ethos of their Christian faith. To be selfless, a primary goal in most religious belief systems, including Christianity, is contrary to what is required to excel in sports. This has recently become an issue among some Christians who wonder if brain damage caused by head hits in football and MMA fights interferes with using those sports as a form of witness (Blakely, 2014; Watson and Brock, 2014; Krattenmaker, 2012).

Can you love your neighbour as yourself, and at the same time knee him in the face as hard as you can? –Scott "Bam Bam" Sullivan, a Christian pastor and MMA champion (in Blakely, 2014)

Although there is little research on this topic, Christian athletes in power and performance sports could use one or more of three strategies to solve moral dilemmas about the value of what they do in sports.

1. They could focus on the ascetic aspects of sports and see themselves as enduring pain for God's sake (Blazer, 2019).
2. They could strive to be the best they can be as athletes so they can more effectively use sports as a platform for evangelizing or doing good works off the field.
3. They could drop out of power and performance sports, and seek other sports and activities that fit more closely with their religious beliefs.

Figure 15.2 illustrates the two factors most likely to create conflict and doubts experienced by athletes and the strategies used to reduce them. On the basis of statements made by athletes on the FCA and AIA websites, it appears that Strategy B, options 1 and 2, would be most commonly used.

Moral Dilemmas for Female Christian Athletes

The Christian athlete movement worldwide has been male-dominated from its inception, especially in the United States. But female Christian athletes in the United States have embraced the movement to such an extent that they now constitute the majority of participants in the American sports ministry. As these athletes became immersed in sports, some of them learned things about gender, their bodies, and sexuality that caused them to rethink the meaning of specific evangelical beliefs that they had internalized during their childhood and adolescence.

This process of dealing with moral dilemmas created among young women who used sports as a form of Christian witness was studied by religious studies scholar and anthropologist Blazer (2015, 2019). Data collected through the use of ethnographic research methods enabled Blazer to investigate the ways that the sport experiences of young conservative Christian women pushed them to expand their ideas about gender and marriage, sexuality and same-sex attraction, and the impact of femininity and heteronormativity in their lives. Their embodied experiences as athletes prompted them to seriously reflect on the meaning of evangelical expectations in light of the realities they

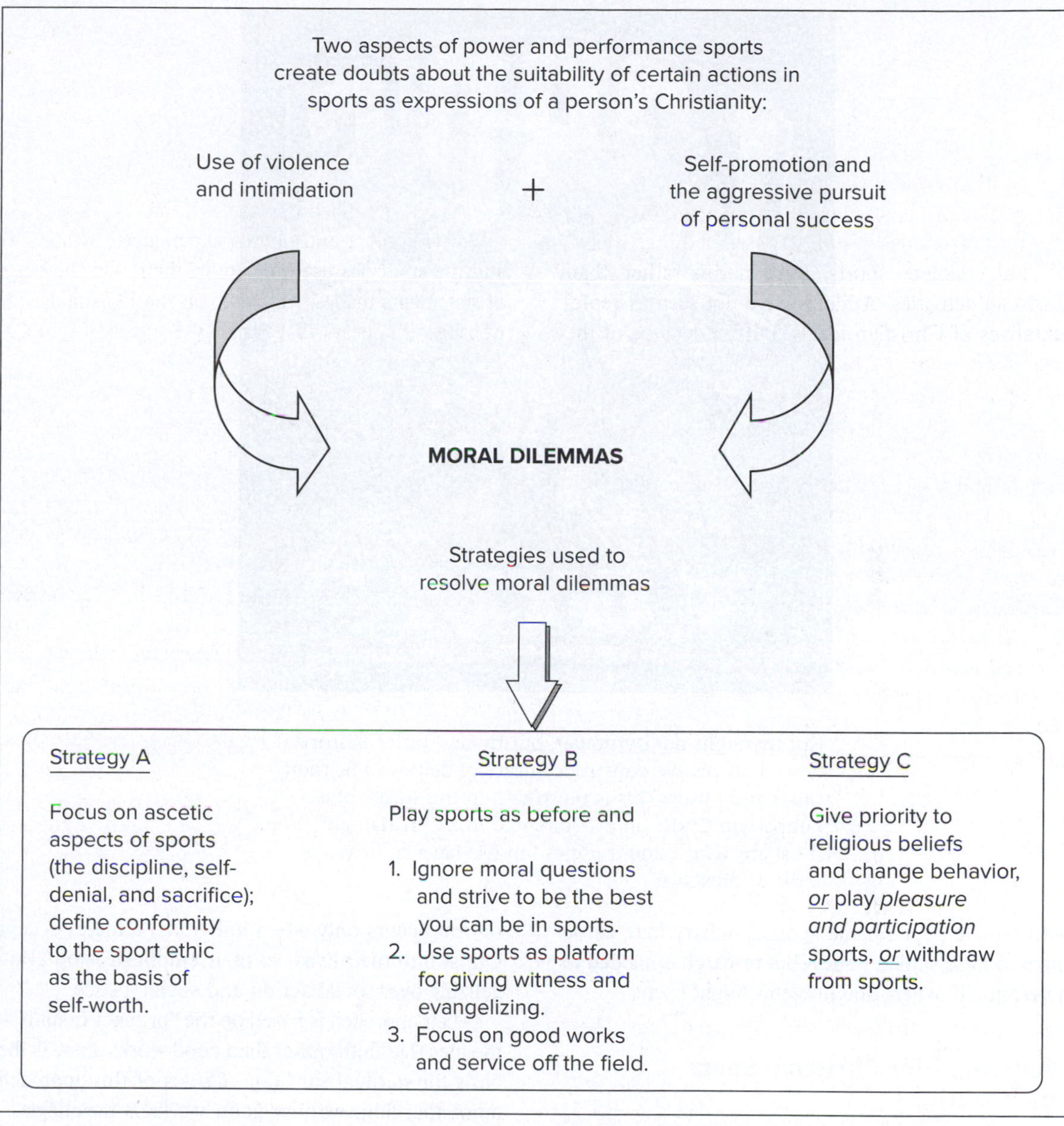

FIGURE 15.2 Christian religious beliefs and power and performance sports: a model of conflict, moral dilemmas, and resolution.

experienced in sports. In the process, they pushed the boundaries of their religious beliefs.

Blazer's research identified the struggles that some female Christian athletes experience as they make sense of their sports participation combined with traditional evangelical beliefs about what it means to be a Christian woman today. Although this gender-focused form of self-reflection seldom occurs among male athletes who combine witnessing and male-identified sports participation, their interaction

(*Source:* Jay Coakley)

"Not by might nor by power, but by my spirit." History shows that people construct images of deities to fit their values and ideals. This is illustrated in this image of a pumped-up Christ on a T-shirt sold in a Christian gift shop. Christians who value muscles tend to have an image of Christ as muscular.

with female peers in the sports ministry may cause them to raise similar issues—but research is needed to determine if, when, and how this might occur.

Challenges for Christian Sport Organizations

The record of Christian organizations indicates that they give primary emphasis to building faith one person at a time. Consequently, they do not devote many resources to eliminating problems in sports other than occasional condemnations of overcommercialization and drug use.

Noted sports historian William Baker points out that evangelical Christians generally assume that reform occurs only when individual athletes accept Christ into their lives, so their emphasis is on evangelizing over social action and social justice.

Their approach is based on the "primacy of faith"—the idea that faith rather than good works alone is the basis for spiritual salvation. Critics of this approach argue that faith without good works is meaningless, and that people who do good works can be saved even if they haven't given their lives to Christ. But this is a matter of faith rather than the sociology of sport.

Adapting Religious Beliefs to Fit Sports

Religions and sports change as people's values and interests change and as power shifts in society, but it appears that sports change little, if at all, when combined with religion. Instead, it seems that religious beliefs and rituals are called into the service of sports, or modified to fit the ways that dominant sports are defined, organized, and played in society (Oppenheimer, 2013).

Robert Higgs makes this point in his book *God in the Stadium: Sports and Religion in America* (1995). He explains that the combination of sports and Christian beliefs has led religion to become "muscularized" so that it emphasizes a gospel of discipline, duty, and self-righteousness rather than a gospel of stewardship, social responsibility, and humility. Muscularized religion gives priority to the image of the knight with a sword over the image of the shepherd with a staff. This approach, emphasizing a Christian's role as "the Lord's warrior," fits with the power and performance sports that are popular today.

Although a few Christian athletes have expressed concerns about social justice in sports, most have used Christian religious beliefs to transform winning, obedience to coaches, and a commitment to excellence in sports into moral virtues. Therefore, Christian beliefs generally reproduce sports as they currently exist. At this point, the only exception to this appears to be recreational sports where athletes have agreed upfront to use Christian beliefs to guide their actions during play.

Daniel Grano (2017), a communication studies scholar, has questioned the conclusion that sports never change in connection with religious beliefs. After identifying how media images expose myths and contradictions that exist in elite, commercial sports, he suggests that a critical theological approach may provide "a framework for imagining a 'wholly other' alternative to the political, economic, and social conditions of the present" in sports (p. 195). Grano's analysis leads him to conclude that this is a critical point in time because it is no longer possible to hold on to idealized versions of sport's past and present or to maintain narratives about the purity and goodness of sports. However, it remains to be seen whether theology or any major religious belief system will inspire demands to recreate sports so they match what many people believe them to be.

summary

IS IT A PROMISING COMBINATION?

Religion focuses on a connection with the sacred and supernatural, and religious beliefs influence the feelings, thoughts, and actions of believers. This makes religion significant in sociological terms.

Discussions about sports and religions often focus on how these two spheres of cultural life are similar or different. Certainly, they are socially similar because both create strong collective emotions and celebrate collective values through rituals and public events. Furthermore, both have heroes, legends, special buildings for communal gatherings, and institutionalized organizational structures.

On the other hand, those who assume that sport and religion each have essential characteristics that are fixed in nature argue that the inherent differences between these spheres of life are more important than any similarities. Some argue that sports corrupt religious beliefs.

Most scholars in the sociology of sport conceptualize religions and sports as socially constructed cultural practices with meanings that may overlap or differ, depending on social circumstances. This constructionist approach is based on evidence that sports and religions are subject to change as people struggle over what is important and how to organize their collective lives.

Little is known about the relationships between sports and major world religions other than particular forms of Christianity. It seems that certain dimensions of Christian beliefs and meanings have been constructed in ways that fit well with the beliefs and meanings underlying participation and success in organized competitive sports. Organized competitive sports offer a combination of experiences and meanings that are uniquely compatible with the major characteristics of the Protestant ethic.

Sports and certain expressions of Christianity have been combined for a number of reasons. Some Christians promote sports because they believe that sports participation fosters spiritual growth and the development of strong character. Christian groups and organizations have used sports to promote their belief systems and attract new members, especially young males who wish to see themselves as having "manly virtues." They also have used popular athletes as spokespersons for their messages about fundamentalist beliefs.

Athletes and coaches have used religious beliefs and rituals for many reasons: to cope with the uncertainty of competition; to stay out of trouble; to give meaning to sports participation; to put participation into a balanced perspective; to establish team solidarity and unity; to reaffirm motivation and social control on teams; and to achieve and explain competitive success.

Although the differences between the dominant ethos of Christianity and the dominant ethos of competitive sports would seem to create problems for Christian athletes and organizations, it appears that this rarely occurs. With the exception of sports played at the recreational level and sponsored by Christian organizations, Christian athletes define their religious beliefs in ways that generally reaffirm the ethos of competitive sports.

Neither Christian athletes nor Christian organizations have paid much attention to what might be identified as moral and ethical problems in sports. Instead, they've focused their resources on spreading religious beliefs in connection with sports events and sports involvement. Their emphasis has been on playing sports for the glory of God, using athletic performances as a platform for giving Christian witness, and working in church and community programs.

In conclusion, the combination of sports and religious beliefs offers little promise for changing dominant forms of sport, especially in the United States. Of course, individual athletes may alter their sport-related behaviors when they combine sports and religion in their own lives, but at this time such changes have had no observable effect on what occurs in elite, competitive sports.

SUPPLEMENTAL READINGS

Reading 1. Christian sports organizations
Reading 2. Ramadan as an issue for Muslim athletes
Reading 3. Self-indulgence for the "glory of God": Christian witness in high-performance sports
Reading 4. Skateistan: Skateboarding and gender barriers

SPORT MANAGEMENT ISSUES

- Your university has a growing number of Muslim students. The Muslim women have requested private access to a small gym in an older, secondary recreation center, because some of them are prohibited by their religion or their families from being seen by men while they exercise. Non-Muslim women in campus sororities object, saying that this is a case of granting Muslims special privileges. You have been asked to mediate what has become a potentially volatile campus issue. Describe two possible resolutions to this situation, and explain the rationale for each.
- You are working for USA Track & Field. Both the Fellowship of Christian Athletes (FCA) and Athletes in Action (AIA) have requested office space at your headquarters in Indianapolis. Along with other top staff you've been asked to explain your position on this matter. What issues would you raise in your statement at the upcoming staff meeting?
- You run the youth sport programs in the parks and recreation department of a midsize city, which has a diverse population that includes Muslims, Orthodox Jews, Hindus, and fundamentalist Christians. Each group has requested exclusive programs because they don't want their children to become confused about their religious beliefs as they play sports. The city government emphasizes policies of inclusion and has refused their requests. What management strategies might you use to defuse tensions as these different religious groups of people come together in each of your leagues?
- You have just taken a job with one of the top youth soccer clubs in the United States. It is

located in Denver, Colorado. Parents of a few players come to your office and say that they will switch to another club if you do not tell the coach of their 14-year-old sons that he can no longer have the entire team say the Lord's Prayer before every game. When you tell the coach this, he says that there is no rule against it because the soccer club receives no government funds and plays on privately owned soccer fields. How do you resolve this issue without losing the coach or the families making the complaint? Outline the steps you will take as you seek a resolution.

references

4 Winds Christian Athletics. 2008. 4 Winds Statement on Olympic Evangelism in Response to Franklin Graham. http://www.christiannewswire.com/news/430506606.html

Ackerman, Jon. 2018. Inside the NBA Chapel: How NBA players do "church" when they can't go to church. *SportsSpectrum.com* (May 31): https://sportsspectrum.com/sport/basketball/2018/05/31/inside-the-nba-chapel-how-nba-players-do-church-when-they-cant-go-to-church/

Alaei, Forough. 2019. Undercover: Female football fans in Iran. (April 15): https://www.theguardian.com/artanddesign/2019/apr/15/undercover-female-football-fans-in-iran

Algazeera. 2006. Glory for Al Ghasara. *Algazeera.net* (December 11): http://english.aljazeera.net/ NR /exeres/A3E2CB0F-A9CA-4327-A07B- 4675C98E13C7.htm

Amara, M. 2013. Sport, Islam, and Muslims in Europe: in between or on the margin? *Religions*, 4 (4): 644–656.

Araki, Kaori, Iku Kodani, Nidhi Gupta & Diane L. Gill. 2013. Experiences in Sport, Physical Activity, and Physical Education Among Christian, Buddhist, and Hindu Asian Adolescent Girls. *Journal of Preventive Medicine and Public Health* 46: S43–S49

Associated Press. 2008. Foreign missionaries defy ban during Olympics. *NBCnews.com* (August 21): http://www.nbcnews.com/id/26334578/ns/world_news-world_faith/t/foreign-missionaries-defy-ban-during-olympics/#.XMHlhehKiUk

Bain-Selbo, Eric. 2008. Ecstasy, joy, and sorrow: The religious experience of southern college football. *Journal of Religion and Popular Culture* 20 (Fall): online, http://www.usask.ca/relst/jrpc/articles20.html

Bain-Selbo, Eric. 2009. *Game day and God: football, faith, and politics in the American South*. Macon, FA: Mercer University Press.

Baker, William J. 2007. *Playing with God: Religion and modern sport.* Cambridge, MA: Harvard University Press.

Bauer, Olivier. 2011. *Hockey as a religion: The Montreal Canadiens.* Champaign, IL: Common Ground Publishing-Sport and Society.

Beal, Becky. 1997. The Promise Keeper's use of sport in defining "Christ-like" masculinity. *Journal of Sport and Social Issues* 21(3): 274–284.

Blakely, Rhys. 2014. Choke thy neighbour: cage fighting preachers who grapple for God The Times (April 4): https://www.thetimes.co.uk/article/choke-thy-neighbour-cage-fighting-preachers-who-grapple-for-god-lnfg7rtzx5h

Blazer, Annie. 2015. *Playing for God: Evangelical Women and the Unintended Consequences of Sports Ministry*. NYU Press

Blazer, Annie. 2019. An invitation to suffer: Evangelicals and sports ministry in the US *Religions* 10(11): 638, https://doi.org/10.3390/rel10110638 (open access).

Boyle, Robert H. 1970. Oral Roberts: Small but OH MY. *Sports Illustrated* 33(22; November 30): 64–66.

Brenner, Michael & Gideon Reuveni, eds. 2006. *Emancipation through muscles: Jews and sports in Europe*. Lincoln: University of Nebraska Press.

Briggs, David. 2011. In God NFL players trust: Teams, pubic pave path to deviance. *TheArda.com* http://blogs.thearda.com/trend/featured

/in-god-nfl-players-can-trust-teams-public-pave-path-to-deviance/

Brownell, Susan. 1995. *Training the body for China: Sports in the moral order of the People's Republic.* Chicago, IL: University of Chicago Press.

Brownell, Susan. 2008. *Beijing's games: What the Olympics mean to China.* Lanham, MD: Rowman & Littlefield.

Butterworth, Michael & Karsten Senkbeil. 2017. Cross-cultural comparisons of religion as "character": Football and soccer in the United States and Germany. *International Review for the Sociology of Sport* 52(2): 129–145.

Byrd, Don. 2017. Why is prayer over a loudspeaker at high school football games unconstitutional? *bjconline.org* (October 25): https://bjconline.org/why-is-prayer-over-a-loudspeaker-at-public-high-school-football-games-unconstitutional-102517/

Capouya, John. 1986. Jerry Falwell's team. *Sport* 77, 9: 72–81.

Chabin, Michelle. 2013. Maccabiah Games 2013: Athletes gather in Israel for 'Jewish Olympics'. *Huffington Post* (July 17): http://www.huffingtonpost.com/2013/07/17/maccabiah-games-2013_n_3606427.html

Cherrington, James. 2012. 'It's just superstition I suppose ... I've always done something on game day': The construction of everyday life on a university basketball team. *International Review for the Sociology of Sport* published 16 October 2012, 10.1177/1012690212461632.

Cherrington, James. 2014 'It's just superstition I suppose ... I've always done something on game day': The construction of everyday life on a university basketball team. *International Review for the Sociology of Sport* 49(5):509–525.

Cobb, John. 2016. #TruthAtTheGames: 2016 Summer Olympics outreach. (July 25): https://www.ligonier.org/blog/truth-at-the-games/

Corsello, Andrew. 1999. Hallowed be thy game. *Gentlemen's Quarterly* (September): 432–440.

Dagkasa, Symeon; Tansin Benn & Haifaa Jawad. 2011. Multiple voices: Improving participation of Muslim girls in physical education and school sport. *Sport, Education and Society* 16(2): 223–239.

Demerath, Nicholas J. & Philip Hammond. 1969. *Religion in social context: Tradition and transition*. New York: Random House.

Dorsey, James M. 2018. Saudi sports: The dark side of Crown Prince Mohammed's reforms. *The Turbulent World of Middle East Soccer* (January 11): https://mideastsoccer.blogspot.com/2018/01/saudi-sports-dark-side-of-crown-prince.html

Dorsey, James M. 2019. Want to curb violent attacks? Curb civilisationalism. *MidEastSoccerBlog.com* (May 1): https://mideastsoccer.blogspot.com/2019/05/want-to-curb-violent-attacks-curb.html

Estep, Tyler. 2015. Carroll schools investigating 'mass baptism' at football practice. *Atlanta Journal- Constitution* (September 2): http://www.ajc.com /news/news/local/carroll-schools-investigating-mass -baptism-at-foot/nnW2B/

Farooq, Sumaya & Andrew Parker. 2009. Sport, physical education, and Islam: Muslim independent schooling and the social construction of masculinities. *Sociology of Sport Journal* 26(2): 277–295.

FCA. 2012. US athletes in the 2012 London Olympics. *Fellowship of Christian Athletes*. Online, http://www.fca.org/2012/08/01/u-s-athletes-in-the-2012-london-olympics/#.UhWaH3-DmBY

Fleming, Scott. 2007. Sport and South Asian youth: The perils of 'false universalism" and stereotyping. In Alan Tomlinson, ed. *The sport studies reader* (pp. 289–297). London/New York: Routledge.

Forney, Craig A. 2007. *The holy trinity of American sports: Civil religion in football, baseball, and basketball*. Macon, FA: Mercer University Press.

Foxworth, Domonique. 2005. Ties that bind team begin with prayer. *Denver Post* (October 19): 2D.

Gore, Will. 2011. "I pray for my opponents before fights." *The Catholic Herald* (September 16): 7.

Grano, Daniel A. 2017. *The eternal present of sport: Rethinking sport and religion.* Philadelphia: Temple University Press.

Green, Lee. 2016. Prayer, religion-related activities at school athletics events. *National Federation of High Schools* (April 13): https://www.nfhs.org/articles/prayer-religion-related-activities-at-school-athletics-events/

Güldenpfenning, Sven. 2001. *Sport: Kritik und eigensinn: Der sport der gesellescahft.* Sankt Augustin: Academia.

Guttmann, Allen. 1978. *From ritual to record: The nature of modern sports.* New York: Columbia University Press.

Guttmann, Allen. 1988. *A whole new ball game: An interpretation of American sports.* Chapel Hill: University of North Carolina Press.

Hartman, Ingela. 2016. Game changer. *ABWE.org* (August 14): https://www.abwe.org/blog/game-changer

Higgs, Robert J. 1995. *God in the stadium: Sports and religion in America.* Lexington: University of Kentucky Press.

Hoffman, Shirl James. 2010. *Good game: Christianity and the culture of sports.* Waco, TX: Baylor University Press.

Hopsicker, Peter M. 2009. Miracles in sport: Finding the 'ears to hear' and the 'eyes to see'. *Sport, Ethics and Philosophy* 3(1): 75–93.

Hutchinson, Nichola. 2008. Disabling beliefs? Impaired embodiment in the religious tradition of the West. *Body and Society* 12(4): 1–23.

IAAF. 2007. A first for Bahrain. *IAAF Magazine* (Issue 1, June 1): http://www.iaaf.org/news/news /a-first-for-bahrain

Jobey, Liz. 2012. Everything to play for. *Financial Times* (July 13): Life and Arts, 1–2. Online: http:// www.ft.com/cms/s/2/2cf282dc-cbb4-11e1-911e-00144feabdc0.html#axzz215J4cFTL

Jonas, Scott. 2005. Should women play sports? Online: http://www.jesus-is-savior.com/Womens%20Page /christian_women_and_sports.htm (retrieved 7-8-2005)

Jones, Chris. 2017. Basketball star fights to lift FIBA's hijab ban. *Allblackmedia.com* (April 7): http://allblackmedia.com/2017/04/basketball-star-fights-lift-fibas-hijab-ban/

Jones, Robert P. & Daniel Cox. 2017. One-quarter say God will determine the super bowl's winner – but nearly half say god rewards devout athletes. PRRI, online, http://www.prri.org/research/poll-super-bowl-women-sports-god-athletes-marijuana/

Klein, Alan. 2008a. Anti-semitism and anti-somatism: Seeking the elusive sporting Jew. In Alan Klein, ed., *American sports: An anthropological approach* (pp. 1120–1137). New York/London: Routledge (also published in *Sociology of Sport Journal* 17(3): 213–228).

Klein, Alan. 2008b. Progressive ethnocentrism: Ideology and understanding in Dominican baseball. *Journal of Sport and Social Issues* 32(2): 121–138.

Krattenmaker, Tom. 2010. *Onward Christian athletes: Turning ballparks into pulpits and players into preachers*. Rowman and Littlefield.

Krattenmaker, Tom. 2012. Can faith help an Olympian? USA Today (August 6): 7A; online, http://www.usatoday.com/news/opinion/forum/story/2012-08-05/ryan-hall-religion-olympics-god/56809394/1

Kristiansen, Elsa, and Glyn C. Roberts. 2007. Religion as a coping strategy for stress among elite wrestlers. In Hannu ltkonen, Anna-Katriina Salmikangas & Eileen McEvoy, eds., *The changing role of public, civic and private sectors in sport culture* (pp. 224–227). Proceedings of the 3rd Conference of the European Association for Sociology of Sport, Jyvaskyla, Finland.

Ladd, Tony, and James A. Mathisen. 1999. *Muscular Christianity: Evangelical Protestants and the development of American sport.* Grand Rapids, MI: Baker Books.

Light, Richard, and Louise Kinnaird. 2002. Appeasing the Gods: Shinto, sumo and "true" Japanese spirit. In T. Magdalinski & T.J.L. Chandler, eds., *With God on their side: Sport in the service of religion* (pp. 139–159). London/New York: Routledge.

Lüschen, Günther. 1967. The interdependence of sport and culture. *International Review of Sport Sociology* 2: 127–141.

McClanen, Don. 1954. Don McClanen invitation letter (to join newly founded Fellowship of Christian Athletes). Sent in March: https://timeline.fca.org /don-mcclanen-invitation-letter-quote/

McCurry, Justin. 2011. Sumo wrestling hit by match-fixing scandal. *The Guardian* (February 2): http:// www.theguardian.com/world/2011 /feb/02/japan -sumo-wrestling-match-fixing

Michaelis, Vicki. 2011. Cougars come uncaged. *USA Today* (August 17): 1–2C.

Mulkey, Madeline C. 2018. At the Olympics, thousands of missionaries compete for souls. *ReligionNews.com* (February 22): https:// religionnews.com/2018/02/22/at-the-olympics -thousands-of-missionaries-compete-for-souls/

Nabokov, Peter. 1981. *Indian running: Native American history and tradition.* Santa Fe, NM: Ancient City Press.

Newsweek, 1971. Are sports good for the soul? *Newsweek* 77, 2 (January 11): 51–52.

Nightengale, Bob. 2006. Team's rebuilding effort focuses on Christianity, character. *USA Today* (May 31): 1A–2A.

Oppenheimer, Mark. 2013. In the fields of the lord. *Sports Illustrated* 118(4, February 4): 38–43.

Overman, Steven J. 2011. *The Protestant work ethic and the spirit of sport: How Calvinism and capitalism shaped American games*. Macon, GA: Mercer University Press.

Pennington, Bill. 2012. In Virginia's hills, a football crusade. *NYT* (November 10): http://www .nytimes.com/2012/11/11/sports/ncaafootball /in-virginias-hills-a-football-crusade.html

Pontifical Council for the Laity. 2006. *The world of sport today: A field of Christian mission.* Proceedings, November 2005 Vatican Seminar. Vaticam: Libreria Editrice Vaticana.

Pontifical Council for the Laity. 2008. *Sport: An educational and pastoral challenge.* Proceedings, November 2007 Vatican Seminar. Vaticam: Libreria Editrice Vaticana.

Pontifical Council for the Laity. 2011. *Sport, education, faith: Towards a new season for Catholic sports associations.* Proceedings, November 2009 Vatican Seminar. Vaticam: Libreria Editrice Vaticana.

Pretot, Julien. 2019. Boxing: Iranian female fighter cancels return home after arrest warrant issued. (April 17): https://www.reuters.com/article /us-boxing-women-iran-khadem-exclusive -idUSKCN1RT0YB

Putney, Clifford. 2003. *Muscular Christianity: Manhood and sports in Protestant America: 1880– 1920.* Cambridge, MA: Harvard University Press.

Randels Jr., George D. & Beal, Becky. 2002. What makes a man?: Religion, sport, and negotiating masculine identity in the Promise Keepers. In T. Magdalinski, T. and T. J. L. Chandler, eds. *With God on their Side: Sport in the Service of Religion* (pp. 160–176). London/New York: Routledge.

Samie, Samaya Farooq. 2013. Hetero-sexy self/ body work and basketball: The invisible sporting women of British Pakistani Muslim heritage. *South Asian Popular Culture* 11(3): 257–270.

Samie, Sumaya Farooq & Sertaç Sehlikoglu. 2015. Strange, incompetent and out-of-place: Media, Muslim sportswomen and London 2012. *Feminist Media Studies* 15(3): 363–381.

Sanchanta, Mariko. 2011. Match-fixing claims hit sumo wrestlers. *Wall Street Journal* (February 3): http://online.wsj.com/news /articles /SB10001424052748703960804576119481319525882#printMode

Serazio, Michael. 2013. Just how much is sports fandom like religion? *The Atlantic* (January 29): http://www.theatlantic.com/entertainment /archive/2013/01/just-how-much-is-sports -fandom-like-religion/272631/

Sinden, Jane Lee. 2013. The elite sport and Christianity debate: Shifting focus from normative values to the conscious disregard for health. *Journal of Religion and Health* 52(1): 335–349.

Sing, Susan Saint. 2013. *Play matters, so play as if it matters*. Phoenix, AZ: Tau Publishing.

Smith, Hannah Lucinda. 2019. They'll arrest me if I go back to Iran, says female boxer Sadaf Khadem. *The Times* (April 19): https://www.thetimes.co.uk/article/they-ll-arrest-me-if-i-go-back-to-iran-says-female-boxer-sadaf-khadem-q0nk082sx

Stuart, Hunter. 2014. School football coach ordered to stop praying with students. *Huffington Post* (February 5): http://www.huffingtonpost .com/2014/02/05/school-football-coach-baptism -prayer-ordered-to-stop-students_n_4725890.html

Thoennes, K. Erik. 2008. Created to play: Thoughts on play, sport, and the Christian life. In Donald Lee Deardorff & John White, eds., *The image of god in the human body: Essays on God Christianity and sports.* Lewiston, NY: Edwin Mellen Press.

Toffoletti, Kim and Catherine Palmer, 2017. New approaches for studies of Muslim women and sport. *International Review for the Sociology of Sport* 52(2): 146–163.

Toffoletti, Kim. 2014. Iranian women's sports fandom: Gender, resistance, and identity in the football movie *Offside. Journal of Sport and Social Issues* 38(1): 75–92.

Walseth, Kristin. 2016. Sport, youth and religion. In Ken Green & Andy Smith, eds., *Routledge handbook of youth sport.* London/New York: Routledge.

Watson, N.J. and Brock, B. 2014. Religion in the ring: Death, concussion and brain bleeds. *Theos, Public Theology Think-Tank*, London, Invited Essay (December 15): http://www.theosthinktank.co.uk/comment/2014/12/15/religion-in-the-ring-death-concussion-and-brain-bleeds

Watson, Nick J., Stuart Weir & Stephen Friend. 2013. The development of Muscular Christianity in Victorian Britain and beyond. Mississippi State University Archives, online, https://history.msu.edu/hst324/files/2013/05/muscular.pdf

Weber, Max. 1904/1958. *The Protestant Ethic and the spirit of capitalism* (trans. By T. Parsons). New York: Scribner's.

Weber, Max. 1922b/1993. *The sociology of religion.* Boston, MA: Beacon Press.

White, John. 2008. Idols in the stadium: Sport as an 'idol factory.' In Donald Lee Deardorff & John White, eds., *The image of God in the human body: Essays on Christianity and sports.* Lewiston, NY: Edwin Mellen Press.

Yoshida, Reiji. 2018. Banning women from the sumo ring: Centuries-old tradition, straight-up sexism or something more complex? *Japan Times* (April 30): https://www.japantimes.co.jp/news/2018/04/30/national/social-issues/banning-women-sumo-ring-sexism-centuries-old-cultural-tradition/#.XMHXnuhKiUk

Yu, Junwei. 2011. Promoting Buddhism through modern sports: The case study of Fo Guang Shan in Taiwan. *Physical Culture and port. Studies and Research* 53: 28–38.

Zillgitt, Jeff. 2011. Aspiring power has doubters. *USA Today* (August 18): 1–2C.

chapter

16

(*Source:* Mario Laporta/KONTROLAB/LightRocket/Getty Images)

SPORTS IN THE FUTURE

What Do We Want Them to Be?

If we truly care about sports . . . we need to be sports reformers and sports activists in our own way—even if that means just pushing for policy change at the local Little League board meeting.

—Ken Reed, Sport Policy Director, League of Fans, 2015

. . . there was no coach standing directly over you . . . There was no opponent directly across from you. And I loved that sense, so I started skating.

—Rodney Mullin, skateboarding innovator (in Atencio et al., 2018)

The latest shot-tracking technology in basketball is the latest sign of a profound shift in the making of professional athletes . . . There is now such a premium on shooting that it's spawned a technological arms race.

—Ben Cohen, Sports journalist, *Wall Street Journal* (2019)

. . . our games focused less on the physical aspect of the sport and more on addressing different social issues, questioning harmful practices in the community, teaching Self-Directed Learning methodology, and encouraging critical thinking with the participants.

—Coaches Across Continents (2019)

Chapter Outline

Envisioning Possibilities for the Future
Current Trends Related to Sports in Society
Factors Influencing Trends Today
Becoming Agents of Change
The Challenge of Transforming Sports
Summary: What Do We Want Sports to Be?

Learning Objectives

- Discuss how the power and performance model and the pleasure and participation model can be used to envision possibilities for what sports might be in the future.
- Explain why both power and performance sports and pleasure and participation sports will grow in the future.
- Identify and give examples of the five general societal trends that will influence sports in the near future.
- Distinguish between conservative, reformist, and radical goals for changing sports.
- Identify the pros and cons of the four different vantage points for making changes in sports.
- Discuss how cultural, interactionist, and structural theories can be used in the process of making changes in sports.

People often describe the future in science-fiction terms that arouse extreme hopes or fears. This sparks interest, but such images are rarely helpful because the future seldom unfolds as rapidly or dramatically as some forecasters would have us believe.

The future emerges in connection with social change, and social change is driven by the actions of people who create a reality that fits their visions of what life should be. Some people have more power and resources than others to turn their visions into reality, but they seldom want revolutionary changes because their privileged positions depend on stability and controlled, incremental change. This often impedes progressive changes in favor of increasing the efficiency and profitability of existing ways of life.

Although power relations cannot be ignored, people do have different ideas about what sports should and could be in the future. Accordingly, the goal of this chapter is to respond to the following questions:

1. What models of sports might we use to envision possibilities for the future?
2. What current trends must be acknowledged as we consider the future of sports?
3. What factors shape current trends, and how will they influence the future of sports?
4. How can we become effective agents in creating the future of sports?

ENVISIONING POSSIBILITIES FOR THE FUTURE

Sports are social constructions. This means that the sports that are funded and publicized the most at any particular place and time are likely to be consistent with the values, ideas, interests, and experiences of those who have power in a social world. However, sport forms are not accepted by everyone, and people often modify them or develop alternatives in the process of resisting or challenging them.

Dominant sports in most societies have been and continue to be organized around a **power and performance model.** However, people may reject all or part of power and performance sports as they seek experiences grounded in alternative values and interests. Many of these people create sports organized around one of more elements of a **pleasure and participation model.**

These two models do not encompass all possibilities for envisioning sports in the future, and there are many sports that combine features of both. But we can use them here as starting points for thinking about what we'd like sports to be in the future.

Power and Performance Sports

Power and performance sports will continue to be highly visible and publicized in the near future. They're based on key aspects of dominant ideologies in most post-industrial societies, as demonstrated by their emphasis on strength, power, speed, competition, and competitive outcomes.

Although power and performance sports take many forms, they're built around the idea that excellence is achieved through dedication, hard work, and competitive success. They stress setting records, pushing human limits, using the body as a machine, and employing science and technology in the process. According to many athletes in power and performance sports, the body is to be disciplined and monitored so as to meet the demands of sports.

Power and performance sports are exclusive in that participants are selected for their abilities to achieve competitive success. Those who lack such abilities are cut or relegated to lower-status programs. Organizations and teams have hierarchical authority structures in which athletes are subordinate to coaches and coaches are subordinate to owners and administrators. It is widely accepted that coaches can exceed standard normative limits when motivating and training athletes to outperform others. At the same time, athletes are expected to obey coaches and show that they are willing to make sacrifices in their quest for success.

The sponsors of power and performance sports stress the value of winning. Being endorsed by winning athletes and teams is important when selling products and promoting the sponsor's brand. Sponsors assume that their association with winners

(*Source:* XAVIER LEOTY/AFP/Getty Images)

Club sports and intramurals often include elements of both power and performance and pleasure and participation sports. Ultimate is a good example of such a hybrid sport.

enhances their status and makes them special in the eyes of people they wish to influence. As long as current sponsors desire this connection, power and performance sports will remain dominant for the foreseeable future in most societies.

Pleasure and Participation Sports

Although power and performance sports are highly visible, many people realize that there are other ways to organize and play sports that more closely match their values and interests. This realization has led to the creation of numerous sport forms organized around *pleasure and participation* and emphasizing freedom, authenticity, self-expression, enjoyment, holistic health, support for others, and respect for the environment. They focus on personal engagement and the notion that the body is to be nurtured and enjoyed in a quest for challenging experiences rather than trained and subordinated in a quest for competitive success.

Pleasure and participation sports tend to be inclusive, and skill differences among participants often are accommodated by using "handicaps" that allow everyone to experience challenges in organized physical activities. Sports organizations and teams based on this model have democratic decision-making structures characterized by cooperation, power sharing, and give-and-take relationships between coaches and athletes, if there are coaches. Humiliation, shame, and derogation are inconsistent with the spirit underlying these sports.

Pleasure and participation sports are characteristically sponsored by individuals, public and nonprofit organizations, and by corporations seeking exposure to a specific collection of consumers. Additionally, some corporations may sponsor these sports as part of an overall emphasis on social responsibility and a commitment to health promotion, among other commendable goals.

CURRENT TRENDS RELATED TO SPORTS IN SOCIETY

Becoming aware of current trends and the factors that influence them is the starting point for being effective agents in creating the futures we want to see. The complexity of social worlds complicates the identification of trends, so it's useful to think of the factors that support the growth of power and performance sports on the one hand, and pleasure and participation sports on the other. Making this distinction helps us clarify our goals and use social theories more effectively as we participate in the process of influencing the culture and organization of sports.

Factors Supporting the Growth of Power and Performance Sports

There are strong vested interests in power and performance sports among those who control resources in wealthy post-industrial societies. For example, when the goal is to use strength, power, and speed to outperform others, sports reaffirm gender differences and a form of gender ideology that privileges men. As long as men control corporate resources there will be an emphasis on sponsoring power and performance sports. Currently, this helps to explain why American football, the classic embodiment of these sports, has become the most popular spectator sport in the United States and continues to attract billions of dollars in television rights fees and other revenues. Athletes in the NFL and other power and performance sports are portrayed in the media as heroic figures, as warriors who embody a corporate emphasis on productivity, efficiency, and dedication to achieving goals in the face of all barriers. Spectators are encouraged to identify with these athletes and express their identification through the consumption of licensed merchandise and other products.

Because power and performance sports often involve pushing human and normative limits, they are relatively easy to market and sell when combined with storylines that resonate with consumers. This is why the media focus on individual athletes and their personal stories, often turning athletes into celebrities apart from the sports they play. Dedicated longtime fans are usually satisfied with coverage focused on the action and competitive strategies in matches and games, but less-knowledgeable fans are more likely to be entertained by narratives about players' lives.

Sportainment coverage is common in commercial power and performance sports, because it feeds and extends storylines that maintain audience interest even when action in the event is boring for many viewers. It also sustains interest in a sport between events and in the off-season and builds to a climax as the next event or new season begins. This boosts ratings and provides an opportunity to initiate and extend engaging narratives that foster consistent media sport consumption.

Factors Supporting the Growth of Pleasure and Participation Sports

Sports have always provided social occasions in people's lives, and people incorporate into them the things that give them pleasure or reaffirm their values and identities. Pleasure and participation sports today are popular to the extent that people define them as attractive alternatives to the more culturally dominant power and performance sports. Factors that motivate this search for alternatives today are (1) concerns about health and fitness; (2) participation preferences among older people; (3) values and experiences brought to sports by women; and (4) groups seeking alternatives to highly structured, competitive sports.

(*Source:* Jay Coakley)

Concerns about health and fitness frequently lead people to engage in pleasure and participation sports such as in-line skating. In Piran, Slovenia, people young and old negotiate town streets and sidewalks on their skates.

Concerns About Health and Fitness When health-care policies and programs emphasize prevention over treatment, people generally become more sensitive to health and fitness issues. In North America, health care and insurance companies now encourage strategies for staying well as they seek to cut costs and maximize profits. This encourages people to pursue activities with health benefits, and many pleasure and participation sports meet this need, whereas power and performance sports often undermine it due to high injury rates.

When people realize that healthy exercise can be incorporated into enjoyable pleasure and participation sports that connect them with others and their environment in enjoyable ways, they are likely to give higher priority to them–but this depends on how people choose to create the future for themselves, their families, and their schools and communities.

Participation Preferences Among Older People As the median age of the population increases in many societies and older people represent an increasingly larger proportion of the world's population, there will be more interest in sports that do not involve intimidation, physical force, the domination of opponents, and the risk of serious injuries (DeSchutter & Brown, 2016; Willing et al., 2018).

As people age, they're less likely to risk physical well-being to establish their status among peers. Older people are more likely to see sports as social activities and make them inclusive rather than exclusive (Horton et al., 2018; Pike, 2015). They also realize that they have but one body, and it can be enjoyed only if they cultivate it as though it were a garden rather than driving it as if it were a race car.

People in the baby-boom generation in the United States and Europe are now in their sixties and seventies. They grew up playing and watching competitive sports and are not likely to abandon them as they age, but most of them will avoid participation in power and performance sports that have high injury risk. Instead, they'll redefine what it means to be an athlete and they will play modified versions of competitive activities in which rules emphasize the pleasure of movement, connections between people, and controlled challenges (Dionigi et al., 2013; Klostermann and Nagel, 2012; Shell et al., 2016). Additionally, pleasure and participation sports will also be sites where older people challenge the notion that aging always involves increasing dependency and incapacity. "Seniors" and Masters sport programs will increase as people demand them. As a result, images of older people who are fit, healthy, and accomplished athletes will become more visible and serve as models for others seeking pleasure and participation.

Values and Experiences Brought to Sports by Women As women gain more power and resources, many will revise or reject traditional power and performance sports. For instance, when women play sports such as rugby, soccer, and hockey, they often emphasize inclusiveness and support for teammates and opponents in explicit ways that are less common in men's versions of these sports. The "in-your-face" power and performance orientation exhibited by some men is replaced by a more cooperative orientation that highlights connections between participants (Bush, 2016; MacKay & Dallaire, 2013; McGuire-Adams & Giles, 2018; Nieri & Hughes, 2016; Smith & Hardin, 2018).

Women often face difficulties when recruiting corporate sponsors for pleasure and participation sports, although this is beginning to change as people in corporations see that these sports can make employees healthier and create new realms of consumption for which products and services can be sold.

Groups Seeking Alternative Sports People who reject certain aspects of power and performance sports have a history of creating alternative sports and unique sport cultures organized around them. Studies of skateboarders, snowboarders, surfers, BMX and mountain bikers, in-line skaters, rock climbers, and others show that some people in these sports resist turning them into commercialized, competitive forms (Cohen & Peachey, 2015; Honea, 2013; Thorpe and Wheaton, 2013; Wheaton, 2013; Wheaton, Roy & Olive, 2017). This has occurred with skateboarding, snowboarding, surfing, BMX biking, Ultimate, and hundreds of other sports around the world. Most of these sports are created and maintained in connection with local cultures and remain confined to a particular geographical region. But regardless of where they exist, they remain popular because they retain an emphasis on elements of the pleasure and participation model and because people have integrated them into their everyday lives.

The alternative sports that are familiar to most of us in post-industrial societies are the ones that become popular among a particular demographic, such as young people, in multiple locations. Over time, some participants may add elements from the power and performance model to the sport and organize informal competitions among those who are highly skilled. As skilled participants attract attention, they may seek sponsors and try to have their sport included in competitive events. Skateboarding provides a classic example of this process. As participants who wanted skateboarding to be an officially recognized competitive sport were joined by entrepreneurs wanting to commercialize and grow the sport, it was included in the inaugural X Games held in 1995.

As some skaters focused on training and competitive success, the original culture of skateboarding changed to include an emphasis on power and performance. In response to this change, legendary skater Tony Hawk declared that the original spirit of skateboarding–a spirit emphasizing personal expression, creativity, and the sheer pleasure of participation–was being destroyed as the format of the sport was changed to meet the requirements of commercialized competitive events (Higgins, 2005). Hawk organized in 2002 what he branded as the Boom Boom HuckJam tour to preserve elements of pleasure and participation at the same time that it generated revenues to support elite athletes and attracted media coverage to grow the sport. Hawk succeeded in growing the sport, but his tour did not prevent skateboarding from becoming formally organized with national federations and an international governing body that was recognized by the International Olympic Committee in 2018.

Contrary to Hawk's efforts, skateboarding was added as a demonstration sport in the 2020 Olympic Games. Although many skaters saw this as an important affirmation of the value of their sport, others saw it as a loss of control over the meaning and organization of skateboarding. How this conflict plays out over the long-term is an interesting topic for research in the sociology of sport. Sociologist Joy Honea has suggested that skating, as well as other action sports facing similar conflicts, could exist in two parallel worlds, one emphasizing elements of pleasure and participation and the other emphasizing elements of power and performance (Honea, 2013). Recent research by Belinda Wheaton and Holly Thorpe (2018; Thorpe & Wheaton, 2019) at the University of Waikato in New Zealand led them to conclude that the power of the global sports market and influential sports organizations, such as the IOC and the federations that govern action sports, is formidable. But they also point out that it is possible for local groups of skaters to resist market forces and sustain a form of skateboarding that rejects the commercial and competitive ethos of power and performance sports.

This form of resistance is difficult to maintain over time, and the skaters who feel that they can sustain unique elements of their skate culture in the context of international competition may discover that this is difficult when their sport is part of an organizational structure shaped by the interests of global corporations and media companies. For those who prefer sports that emphasize pleasure and participation, there will always be alternatives, even if they must create them for themselves and shield them from the influence of powerful producers of contemporary popular culture.

Examples of alternative sports that are created and sustained over time are common among people who don't feel welcome or skilled enough to participate in mainstream power and performance sports. When people with physical or intellectual disabilities create alternative sports organized around elements of pleasure and participation, they are identified as "adapted sports." But this label is misleading because people who identify themselves as able-bodied also modify mainstream sports to fit their abilities and their desire to emphasize pleasure and participation. Of course, Paralympic sports often emphasize elements of power and performance, but most sports played by people with disabilities focus on pleasure and participation with concern and support for teammates and opponents as well as inclusiveness in terms of ability.

The Gay Games as organized on local, national, and international levels is another example of an alternative sport format in which people who feel marginalized in mainstream sports come together and experience participation, support, inclusiveness, and the enjoyment of physical movement. The tenth quadrennial Gay Games, hosted by Paris in 2018, attracted more than 10,000 athletes from 91 countries. They participated in 36 event categories, most of which have been adapted to meet the interests and preferences of people in LGBTQ communities worldwide. The sports are competitive, but they exist primarily to reaffirm supportive LGBTQ networks and a collective spirit of mutual recognition and acceptance.

The best examples of sports created by and for the people who participate in them exist in countries where cultural production is controlled by indigenous people who are not directly influenced by corporations and media companies that produce and promote forms of popular culture to serve their interests (Evers & Doering, 2019). Most of these sport forms are related to work or other community activities and integrated into everyday life. The meaning and organization of these sports generally changes over time to complement changing social and cultural conditions. A good example of this is Brazilian capoeira shown in the photo on this page. It has a 400-year history and is widely practiced in much of the country by males and females of all ages.

(*Source:* EDUARDO SOTERAS/AFP/Getty Images)

Capoeira was developed by enslaved Africans living in northeast Brazil during the 16th century. Escaped slaves used it as a survival tool when they needed to hide or defend themselves. Today it is considered a martial art and is included in both community festivals and sports events in Brazil. It is practiced by individuals, two "opponents," or in groups, often to the beat of drums played by other participants.

The range of sports that incorporate elements of the pleasure and participation model increases as people realize that sports are social constructions that can be created to fit even temporary interests and passing situations. This has been illustrated by people who have formed local adult kickball, footgolf, and gender-mixed flag football leagues; joined parkour and freerunning groups; and participated in sand surfing, bike polo, climbing, street surfing, fun runs, and pickup games of softball and futsal. Again, there are unlimited possibilities for creating pleasure and participation sports, as long as people don't fall for the myth that the only real sports are those that emphasize power and performance.

Although it often is a challenge to find corporate sponsors, various pleasure and participation sports usually survive because people are creative enough to find resources to maintain them. Furthermore, corporate or media sponsors are needed only when a sport hires administrators, coaches, and referees; stages large tournaments; and involves costly equipment and travel. When a sport exists simply for pleasure and participation, the primary resources needed are people wishing to play it and spaces in which it can be played.

FACTORS INFLUENCING TRENDS TODAY

When we're creating futures it's useful to know about factors that influence current trends. This enables us to anticipate possibilities, prevent or overcome resistance, and make more informed decisions as we participate in social worlds.

Many factors influence trends in sports, but the discussion here is limited to five: (1) a widespread commitment to organization and rationalization; (2) a cultural emphasis on commercialism and consumption; (3) the widespread use of digital media; (4) the growth of technology; and (5) the changing demographic composition of communities and societies.

Organization and Rationalization

Sports today focus on planning and productivity. "Fun" has been redefined so it is asociated with achieving goals rather than physical expression spontaneity, and joy. Process is now secondary to product, and the journey is secondary to the destination.

People in post-industrial societies live with the legacy of industrialization. They emphasize organization based on rational principles. Being organized and making plans to accomplish goals is so important that spontaneity, expression, creativity, and joy–the elements of play–are given low priority or may even be considered frivolous by parents, sports officials, coaches, and spectators. The implications of this emphasis on organization and rationalization were noted by legendary snowboarder Terje Haakonsen when he announced that he would not participate in the Olympics even though many people saw him as the best in the world. His explanation of the snowboarding experience provides interesting insights about sports:

> When I'm having fun snowboarding, it's like meditation. I'm not thinking about anything but what I'm doing right now. No past, no future. . . . [But today, too many] people get stuck and all they do the whole year is pipe, and that's too bad for them. They do the same routine over and over, get the moves down. It becomes like this really precise, synchronized movement, like they're little ballerinas or something. It's no longer this spontaneous sport, like when you're a kid screwing around (in Greenfeld, 1999).

Haakonsen felt that fun and effort merge together in sports when they are done on terms set by participants. This merger breaks down when sports are done for judges using criteria that ignore the subjective experience of participation.

These are important things to keep in mind when we think about what we'd like sports to be in the future. Many people today assume that sports should be organized primarily for the purpose of rationally assessing skills and performances. When this occurs, improvement takes priority over expression and creativity, and winning a medal or a championship is the ultimate goal. Haakonsen suggests that mastering a skill to expand possibilities for new experiences is one thing, but spending years perfecting a specialized skill to conform to single definition of technical perfection is another. Once this distinction becomes clear in our own sport participation, we become more creative when thinking about the future.

Commercialism and Consumption

Many people today are so deeply embedded in commercial culture that they think of themselves as customers rather than citizens. This changes the basis for evaluating self, others, and experiences. When commercial ideology pervades sports, play becomes secondary to playoffs and payoffs; games, athletes, and sport participation become commodities–things bought and sold for bottom-line purposes. Participation then revolves around the consumption of equipment, lessons, clothing, nutritional supplements, gym and club memberships, and meeting goals publicized by companies selling all these things. Identity becomes based on where you do sports, the equipment you use, the clothing you wear and your record of achievement–not the emotional joy and satisfaction gained through participation.

Many people are turned off by this approach, but unless they've experienced alternatives, it may be difficult for them to envision sports devoid of commercialism and consumption. This is why it's important to have public spaces where people can play sports that don't require fees, permits, or memberships. Creativity thrives in such spaces. In this sense, public policies at all levels of government can create or subvert possibilities for noncommercial sport futures.

(*Source:* Frederic A. Eyer. All rights reserved. Used with permission)

"Oh, Mom! I'm not going outside to play when I can play on my virtual World Cup Team right here."

The future of sports is difficult to predict. Will children prefer video games and virtual sports over the dominant sport forms of today? Will playing virtual sports serve as a "gateway" into real-time sports by teaching children the rules and challenges that characterize real-time sports?

In the United States and other societies where corporate capitalism is pervasive, it is common for popular culture to be produced through a top-down process. Even when cultural practices such as lifestyle and pleasure and participation sports are created at the grass roots level, the ones that become popular are often appropriated by corporations, turned into commodities, and sold back to the people who created them (Goodman & Dretzin, 2001). This continues to occur with sports that are created by and for people at the grass roots level.

Digital Media

Television, computers, game consoles, the Internet, smart-phones and other handheld devices provide images and narratives that many people use to imagine future possibilities for sports. This has led to the creation of video games, esports, and a vast array of screen-based activities. In this sense, people who create media-based experiences have had a major impact on how people define fun and spend their time. Additionally, the events, athletes, and stories represented in blogs, websites, and television coverage influence popular discourse about sports, and it is out of that discourse that people form their ideas about what sports could and should be in the future.

To understand this process, imagine that American football is the only sport you've ever seen on television and online. You would have a seriously limited sense of what sports are and what they could be. A version of this occurs as media companies select for coverage only those sports that generate profits. As a result, those are the sports that dominate popular discourse and influence our visions for the future. If we realize this, we can seek images and narratives about sports that are not represented exclusively through commercial media. When we do this, the digital media expand our experience and enable us to think more creatively about the present and future. The more versions of sports we see and talk about, the more we can create futures to match our interests and circumstances.

Although esports is the most popular new activity driven by digital media as I write this, future forms of sports will occur in augmented and virtual realities. We have already seen demonstrations of this with bike and car racing, golf, and skiing, but soon there will be virtual sports that provide varied and customized challenges for individuals and small sided teams.

Technology

Technology is the *application of scientific or other organized knowledge to solve problems, expand experiences, or alter the conditions of reality.* It is used to make sports safer, detect and treat injuries more effectively, assess physical limits and potential, and expand the experiences available in sports. It is also used to train more efficiently, control athletes' bodies, increase the speeds at which bodies move, analyze and quantify the risks involved in sports, enhance the size and strength of bodies, decrease recovery time after injuries, and alter bodies to match the demands of particular sports. Increasingly, we depend on technology to identify rule infractions more accurately, measure and compare performances with precision, analyze data and develop strategies for games and matches, improve the durability and functionality of equipment, and train in a virtual environment that mimics various conditions of competition (Booton, 2018a, 2018b; Fouche, 2017; Hurley, 2018; Kioussis, 2018; Millington, 2017; Pursell, 2016).

The major challenges we face with new technologies are how to assess and regulate them, and how to obtain the accurate information needed to make informed decisions about if and when we will use them. The governing bodies of sports try to regulate technologies used by coaches, officials, trainers, and athletes, but this is difficult because they are being introduced at such a rapid rate that officials cannot keep up with them. Assessing the implications of particular technologies is not easy. Consistent and sensible decisions about them are made only when we know what we want sports to be in the future.

As a case in point, consider genetic-enhancement technologies. They can be used to improve human performance, heal injured bodies, and eliminate some physical impairments. If we want to create a future in which sports are organized around the power and performance model, we would assess, regulate, and make decisions about using a particular technology differently than we would if we want sports organized around a pleasure and participation model. This is why it is important to have a clear sense of what we want the meaning, purpose, and organization of sports to be in the future.

Changing Demographics in Communities and Societies

Sports are social constructions, and some of the richest sport environments are those in which people have diverse cultural backgrounds and sport experiences. Even when people play the same sport, strategies and styles often vary with their cultural backgrounds. For example, Canadians created a secular and rationalized version of lacrosse that was different from the traditional, sacred game invented and played by Native Peoples in North America (King, 2007). People in the United States took the sport of rugby as played in England and adapted it to fit their preferences; the eventual result was American football, a game that is unique in the world. In 2004 the New York Mets hired a Latino general manager, signed notable Latino players, and developed a style of play that was fast, assertive, and spirited. This style is now accepted in Major League Baseball and it influences everything from on-the-field strategy to marketing the game to a diverse population of spectators.

Although demographic diversity presents challenges, it also presents possibilities for creating new forms and versions of sports. As geographical mobility, climate change, labor migration, wars, and political turmoil push and pull people across national borders, there will be opportunities to borrow and blend different sports, styles of play, and game strategies. If people take advantage of those opportunities without systematically privileging games from one culture and marginalizing games from other cultures, it will be possible to envision and create sports that fit a wide range of interests and abilities. This has occurred in music and there is no reason that it cannot occur in sports.

BECOMING AGENTS OF CHANGE

Understanding connections between sports and social worlds is a prerequisite for becoming effective agents of change. This is because social change involves identifying goals, choosing a vantage point for making changes, and using social theories to create strategies for achieving goals.

Identifying Goals

Change means different things to different people because their goals for the future are different. For most people in sports and sports management, the primary goal is *growth*—strengthening and expanding what exists today. For others, the primary goal is *improvement*—eliminating problems and promoting fairness in sports. And for a few people, the primary goal is *social transformation*–creating sports that are healthy, inclusive, humane, and widely accessible.

Growth is a **conservative goal** based on the belief that sports are inherently positive activities that should be strengthened and expanded in their current forms. Accomplishing this goal requires management and marketing techniques that expand and make sports organizations more efficient while maintaining the current culture and structure of sports. The belief is that increased efficiency will create resources that inevitably fuel growth. Most people in organized sports are dedicated to this goal for both ideological and personal reasons: they believe that the growth of sports as they now exist will improve society and increase opportunities for people to develop skills and achieve success.

Improvement is a **reformist goal** based on beliefs that sports participation produces positive consequences, that the ethical foundations and the inherent integrity of sports must be restored or maintained, and that participation opportunities must be increased. Accomplishing this goal requires changes that promote fair competition, responsible citizenship, and appropriate opportunities for everyone to participate. Cheating, deviance, and performance enhancing substance use must be controlled; discrimination must be eliminated from policies and programs; and participation must be made more accessible in schools and communities. Improvement is a widely accepted goal, although people may differ on the priorities for specific reforms. Reformist goals guided the people building "miracle fields," as described in Reflect on Sports, p. 524.

Transformation is a **radical goal** based on the belief that dominant forms of sports are systemically flawed and must be reorganized or replaced to create new meaning and purpose. Accomplishing this goal requires a critical assessment of dominant sports and the ability to create re-imagined or new sports in which previously disenfranchised people share power with others in determining policies, controlling sport resources and facilities, and developing opportunities that meet their needs and concerns. Few people associated with sports today are proponents of transformation, and those in positions of control usually are quick to use their resources to oppose transformation.

My experience indicates that most people who read this book give priority to *growth,* with *reform* being an important secondary goal. In the context of many sports organizations, reformers often are labeled as "anti-sport" and marginalized. People seeking the radical goal of transformation are especially unwelcome in those organizations.

Some people with radical goals have used sports as sites for challenging dominant definitions of masculinity and femininity, raising questions about the meaning of race, exposing the poverty and inequalities that prevent meaningful participation in society, destroying stereotypes about (dis)abilities, and critiquing the antidemocratic, exclusive, and hierarchical structures that characterize most organized sports today. In the process, they may inspire creative visions of what sports could be in the future and, in doing so, encourage others to critically assess sports and become involved in progressive programs in which political awareness and community activism are combined with playing sports.

Assessing Vantage Points

There are at least four vantage points or strategic positions for initiating changes in and through sports. We can work inside sports organizations, join opposition groups to resist or undermine certain sport forms, create new and alternative sports, or create new sport forms that are humane, accessible, and inclusive. Being aware of our personal vantage point is important because each comes with its own constraints and opportunities for making sports what we want them to be.

Working Inside Sport Organizations An "insider" vantage point is constraining because status, promotions, and job security generally depend on affirming the values and culture of the organization where you work. This means that even though you may favor certain reformist or transformational goals, your commitment to change will probably decrease as you move up the organization into positions of power.

reflect on SPORTS

Miracle Field
Creating Sport Spaces for People with a Disability

In 1997 a youth baseball coach in Conyers, Georgia, noticed that one of his five-year-old players came to every practice and game with his seven-year-old brother. The seven-year-old loved baseball, but there were no teams for children in wheelchairs. So the coach invited him to play.

This coach's action initiated a series of events. The following season, local adults organized the Conyers "Miracle League" for children with disabilities. It was the first baseball league of its kind, and the rules were adapted to fit the players. For example, every player on a team would bat each inning, all base runners were safe, and every player scored a run. Able-bodied young people and volunteers served as buddies, assisting players when the need arose.

During the first year there were thirty-five players on four teams. Watching them play inspired Dean Alford, a former Georgia state representative and president of the local Rotary Club. He saw that a conventional ball field with grass, dirt, and elevated bases created barriers for players who were blind or using wheelchairs, walkers, and crutches. Alford worked with local Rotary Clubs to raise money to design and construct a rubberized turf playing field plus accessible restrooms, concession stand, and picnic area. Three other grass fields were designed so they could be converted to synthetic surfaces as the Miracle League grew.

The field, 25 miles east of Atlanta, opened in 2000. It attracted national media attention and interest among the families of more than 75,000 children with disabilities in the Atlanta area. In 2019 there were 240 Miracle League organizations in the United States, Puerto Rico, and Canada, and they serve over 200,000 children and adults.

When people hear of the Miracle League, visit websites, and watch games, their idealism often pushes them to think further outside the box of traditional parks and playing fields. Some communities have built universally accessible playgrounds adjacent to the smooth-surface baseball fields. Playground designers today are more likely to create environments that attract children with varying physical (dis)abilities. This type of design enables families and friends to play safely as they encounter physical challenges and have fun regardless of abilities.

When people see a Miracle League game played on a barrier-free field adjoining a barrier-free play area, they usually say: "This makes so much sense," and then they ask, "Why doesn't my community have one of these?" This response along with the development of more sport programs like the Miracle League is heartening for over 6 million US children with physical impairments making it difficult or impossible to play sports in traditional programs that assume high ability among participants.

The more recent development of Miracle Leagues for adults is heartening to the thousands of veterans who returned from Iraq and Afghanistan with amputated limbs, sight and hearing impairments, and injuries that impede walking. Making sports accessible to them and others with a disability is both a political and a management challenge. It will require a revision of local priorities or the provision of incentives from state or federal government. *What do you think would be the most effective strategy for creating accessible facilities and leagues that meet the needs of people with a disability in your town?*

Once people reach those top positions, they tend to become more conservative and focus on growth and efficiency more than reform or transformation. This isn't inevitable, but it's common place.

On the other hand, an insider vantage point provides information about the structure and culture of sport organizations and enables a person to directly intervene in the processes that affect the meaning, purpose, and organization of sports. If a person reaches a position of power in a sport organization, the opportunities to make and influence changes increase but many reformist and nearly all transformational changes will be resisted by others in the organization.

Finally, it is especially difficult for athletes to change sports from their insider vantage points. They can come together and form players associations that are officially recognized by those who manage and control sports, but as individuals they seldom have the leverage or power to instigate meaningful changes in the culture and organization of a sport. The exceptions to this generalization are notable. Jackie Robinson played a key role in desegregating Major League Baseball and other professional sports. Arthur Ashe did the same in tennis. A lawsuit filed by baseball player Kurt Flood against the restrictive employment practices used in MLB led to changes in the legal status of MLB players and other athletes in professional team sports. Billie Jean King took the first steps to change the status of women in tennis and was a key advocate for the passage of Title IX that made sex discrimination illegal in public schools and their athletic programs.

These and other athletes who have advocated for racial and gender equity in sports and used lawsuits to change the legal status of professional athletes and the conditions under which NCAA athletes play their sports have usually paid a heavy price for their actions. Their careers have been disrupted or terminated, they've often received death threats and experienced significant personal losses. But they have inspired other athletes by showing that it is possible to change sports from an insider's vantage point.

Joining "Opposition" Groups History shows that the future often is influenced by groups that oppose the status quo and promote policies and programs that alter the organization of social life. For example, opposition groups in recent years have effectively lobbied against using public funds to build costly stadiums that primarily benefit wealthy people (Associated Press, 2019; Friends of McKalla, 2019; Kroman, 2018; Paulas, 2018; Scott, 2017). Opposition groups have recently experienced some success in opposing plans to host mega-events, such as the Olympics, and they may be even more effective in the future as research continues to document the debts and other problems that come with hosting such events.

Local groups opposing specific policies and programs have often been effective, whether it be to promote gender equity, build a new skatepark or disc golf course, or reserve public spaces for pleasure and participation sports. As these groups alter the sports landscape they create more diverse sports that meet people's needs more effectively.

Creating New Sports Altering the future of sports also occurs when people reject dominant power and performance sports and develop new sports grounded in alternative ideas about what sports should be. This is not easy to do because resources are seldom available to people seeking to transform sports programs and organizations. However, working from an outsider vantage point can be effective when it influences others to consider and participate in new sport forms.

Ultimate, created in 1968, and Quidditch, created in 2005, are among the most well known sports created by groups of people seeking new sports experiences. Both of these sports proved so popular that they have been formally organized in North America and internationally. The governing organizations sponsor annual tournaments and have been successful in raising funds to support full time staff. However, most new sports remain small-time with local participants who organize themselves as time and resources permit.

Canadian Bruce Kidd, a former Olympian with a deep knowledge of sports history, says that creating "alternatives to the commercial sport culture [is] . . . an uphill fight," but he also notes that efforts to create these alternatives "have a long, rich, and proud history" (1997, p. 270).

Working Outside Sports Creating the future of sports from outside vantage points requires foresight and a good grasp of how social change occurs.

(*Source:* Coaches Across Continents)

Coaches Across Continents (CAC) is an organization that uses sports as social impact tools in a process of facilitating community change in developing countries. The goal of CAC is to "ensure human rights by empowering communities with the knowledge and skills to create their own future" (https://coachesacrosscontinents.org/curriculum/#vision)

For example, when feminists created the women's movement during the 1960s it provided an opportunity for activists, educators, and progressive politicians to draft Title IX as part of the Education Amendments to the Civil Rights Restoration Act. When this act became law in 1972 it changed the legal context in which sports were organized, sponsored, and played in schools that received funds from the federal government. In turn, this dramatically altered sport participation patterns among females of all ages.

Similarly, people working in military veterans' organizations today may effectively change how "disabilities" are defined in US culture and, in the process, encourage others to draft laws and create programs that provide sports participation opportunities for people with a disability. In this sense, anyone who works to eliminate social injustice and create opportunities for new voices to be expressed and taken seriously in social worlds can also lay the groundwork for creating more humane, accessible, and inclusive sports in the future.

Using Theories

Throughout this book it is noted that sociologists study and explain social worlds in terms of culture, interaction, and social structure. Theories related to each of these dimensions of social worlds are useful when thinking about the future and developing strategies to change or transform sports and achieve particular goals. Theories provide systematic interpretive frameworks that make it possible to improve the odds of accurately anticipating the consequences of change-oriented strategies, regardless of the goals a person wants to achieve. In this sense, good theories are like road maps for navigating your way into desired futures.

Cultural Theories People who wish to be agents of change can use cultural theories to understand the processes through which social worlds are produced, reproduced, and transformed. These theories indicate that to change sports, we must change the symbols, values, norms, vocabularies, beliefs, and ideologies that people use to make sense of and give meaning to sports and sports experiences. For example, the process of creating gender equity in sports has involved, among many things, changing the vocabulary used by media announcers covering women's sports. In the past, female athletes were identified by their first names, which gave the impression that their sports were not as serious as those played by men. As this habit was identified, often by researchers in the sociology of sport, announcers changed how they talked about women athletes. This was a relatively minor change, but it altered narratives so that women's sports were eventually presented more seriously.

Overall, cultural theories focus attention on issues of ideology, representation, and power dynamics in society. They explain how people use power to maintain cultural practices and social structures that represent their interests, and they identify how people resist or oppose those practices and structures. This is important to know when developing effective strategies for changing sports.

Research using cultural theories helps us envision sports that are inclusive and empowering. Goals based on cultural theories usually are reformist, seldom conservative, and occasionally radical. For this reason, cultural theories may be seen as threatening by many people who want only to expand sports as they are currently defined and organized.

Interactionist Theories When people use interactionist theories, they focus on processes of social learning and the relationships through which people come to know and give meaning to the world. Interactionist theories explain that changing sports involves changing socialization processes, self-concepts and identities, and the priorities given to particular role models and significant others. For example, people often resist reformist and radical changes because their identities are grounded in and supported by the current culture and organization of sports. This is useful to know because it helps us anticipate that people will often be personally defensive in the face of efforts to change sports. Changes threaten their identities and provoke resistance. Therefore, strategies must be presented tactfully, based on clear research evidence, and implemented to include as allies those currently working in sports. Changing sports in this way requires patience, persistence, and a keen awareness of how others perceive and identify themselves with and through sports.

Interactionist theories can be used to support conservative, reformist, or radical goals, but they generally emphasize the need to include multiple voices and perspectives in the change process. The assumption underlying these theories is that when voices are effectively represented in social worlds, the organization of those worlds is more likely to support their interests and concerns. However, those using a critical approach usually combine interactionist theory with cultural theory and focus on power as well as representation. This often takes them in the direction of reform and transformation (Denzin, 2007).

Structural Theories When people use structural theories, they focus on social organization and who has access to power, authority, material resources, and economic opportunities. Structural theories explain that changing sports involves changing the context in which social relationships exist. Functionalism is a form of structural theory based on the assumption that all social worlds are organized around shared values and ultimately become more efficient and socially integrated. This approach appeals to people with vested interests in the status quo because it supports an emphasis on growth and minor reforms. As a result it is consistent with conservative and only slightly reformist goals.

Conflict theory, grounded in the ideas of Karl Marx, is another form of structural theory. It identifies the economic factors that create social-class divisions in society and determine life chances and lifestyles among people in all social classes. Conflict theory is most consistent with reformist or radical goals such as redistributing power and economic resources so that relationships are more egalitarian and social policies are more responsive to people with the greatest needs in a community or society. When strategies for changing sports are based on conflict theory, they identify the racism, sexism, nationalism, and militarism that distort the meaning, purpose, and organization of sports and they seek to eliminate the profit motive in sports organizations so that sports can be reorganized around the needs of those who play them rather than those who own them.

Social theories can be used to achieve conservative, reformist, or radical goals. But people interested in the sociology of sport are more likely than others, especially those working in sports organizations, to use a critical approach that focuses on reform and transformation (Donnelly et al, 2011, 2015). They focus on what can be done to make sports more democratic, accessible, and humane so that physical activities serve the needs of all people rather than simply expanding what already exists and more efficiently achieving the goals of those who currently control sports.

THE CHALLENGE OF TRANSFORMING SPORTS

Working to bring about changes that achieve conservative goals can be difficult, but people with power and resources often provide support for such goals, such as fostering growth and increasing efficiency. Creating changes to achieve reformist goals is more difficult and often contentious. Reform is generally resisted by people with a vested interest in the status quo and by those who fear the uncertainty involved when the status quo changes.

When existing forms of social organization–rules, relationships, and traditions–support a system of privilege for people involved in a sport, they see change as a threat to the benefits and privileges they define as normal. We continue to see this in public schools, where achieving gender equity requires that people revise or abandon the ideological perspectives that they have used in the past to predict, interpret, and influence the feelings, thoughts, and actions of males and females. Similar resistance occurs when change requires revisions of racial ideology or ideas and beliefs about ethnicity, nationality, social class, age, and (dis)ability. Even reforms designed to *simply* "level the playing field" become complex and contentious when people privileged by the status quo see the playing field as already level.

Challenges become even greater when changes require transforming the structure of sport, and changing rules, roles, relationships, reward systems, and the distribution of power in the process. Even talk about transformation creates defensiveness and resistance that is grounded in identities and taken-for-granted lifestyles. This is especially the case when people believe the great sport myth. They feel that sport is essentially pure and good and organized as it was meant to be. Additionally, the people who control mainstream sports, especially those organized around a power and performance model, have established legitimacy narratives that are very difficult to disrupt. As a result, even minor transformations are tenaciously resisted.

This can be seen by going to a meeting of Little League coaches and telling them that research shows that, to protect the developing arms of ten- to twelve-year-olds who throw "official" base balls thousands of times each year, the size and weight of the ball should be reduced to young players. Or try telling hockey coaches that players under thirteen years old should no longer be allowed to body check and that children under ten should play on smaller cross-rink surfaces instead of the full-length surface. For the most definitive evidence of resistance to transforming sports, tell youth and high school football coaches that tackle football is being replaced by flag football for all children under fourteen years old until we know more about the consequences of repetitive head trauma and concussions on young, developing brains. In both cases, resistance will be strong, but that does not mean that we should abandon efforts to bring about changes in sports.

Experience indicates that regardless of one's vantage point or theories used to develop strategies to change sports, being an effective agent of change always requires the following qualities:

1. Visions of what sports and social life *could* and *should* be like
2. Willingness to work hard on the strategies needed to turn visions into realities
3. Political abilities to rally the resources that make strategies effective in producing changes

Bringing these qualities together requires individual and collective efforts. If we don't make these efforts, the meaning, purpose, and organization of sports will be based on the interests of those who currently control and organize them.

summary

WHAT DO WE WANT SPORTS TO BE?

Sports are social constructions. This means that we play a role in making them what they are today and what they will be in the future. We can play this role actively by envisioning what we'd like sports to be and then working to make them so, or we can play it passively by doing nothing and allowing others to shape sports as they want them to be.

This chapter emphasized that the meaning, purpose, and organization of sports will become increasingly diverse in the future, and that power and performance sports will remain dominant because they continue to attract wealthy and powerful sponsors. Pleasure and participation sports will grow, but they will not attract as much sponsorship as is enjoyed by power and performance sports.

Sports at all levels of participation are sites for struggles over who should play and how sports should be organized. Current trends suggest that pleasure and participation sports are supported by concerns about health and fitness, the participation preferences of older people whose influence will increase in the future, the values and experiences brought to sports by women, and groups seeking alternative sports.

Current trends are influenced by many factors, including values supportive of increased organization and rationalization, a cultural emphasis on commercialism and consumption, new digital media and technologies, and the changing demographic composition of communities and societies.

Being an effective change agent in sports involves identifying goals, assessing what can be done from the vantage point that one occupies relative to sports in society, and using theories to plan effective strategies. Most people, especially those who are advantaged by the status quo, focus on the conservative goal of growth because they want to expand and strengthen sports as they are currently organized and played. Some people focus on the liberal goal of reform because they want more people to enjoy the benefits that sports have to offer. And a few people focus on the radical goal of transformation because they want to remake sports with new meaning, purpose, and organization.

The effectiveness of people who want to be agents of change requires a clear understanding of the vantage point they occupy in the relationship between sports and society. The four major vantage points are in (a) sport organizations; (b) opposition groups; (c) groups that create new and alternative sport forms; and (d) groups working to transform the larger society in ways that will change sports.

Efforts to bring about change can utilize strategies based on cultural, interactionist, or structural theories, regardless of goals. Cultural theories emphasize that the future of sports is linked with the symbols, values, norms, and ideologies that people use as they organize and give meaning to sports and sport experiences. Interactionist theories emphasize that changes occur in connection with socialization processes, identities, and the influence of peers and significant others. Structural theories emphasize that changing sports requires changes in the larger context in which sports exist.

Social theories can support conservative, reformist, or radical goals. Scholars in the sociology of sport tend to be reformist and occasionally radical rather than conservative, and they often focus on making sports more democratic, accessible, inclusive, and humane.

Regardless of one's goals, vantage point, or theories used to develop strategies, being an effective agent of change requires a clear vision of what sports could and should be in the future, a willingness to work hard to turn visions into realities, and possessing the political abilities to initiate and maintain strategies that produce results. Unless we work to make sports into what we want them to be, they will reflect primarily the interests of those who want us to play on their terms and for their purposes.

This leaves us with an interesting choice: we can be consumers who accept sports as they are, or we can be citizens who actively work to make sports humane and sustainable for diverse populations. The goal of this book is to prepare people to be critically informed and active citizens.

SUPPLEMENTAL READINGS

Reading 1. Sport fans as agents of change
Reading 2. Technology and change in sports
Reading 3. Working for change: Charity versus social justice
Reading 4. Using sports to make change: Does it work?

SPORT MANAGEMENT ISSUES

- You are the new director of community sports and recreation in a city of 300,000 people. The motto of your department is *Sport for All–Play for Life.* The programs with the most participants are organized around a pleasure and participation model. In the face of budget cuts, you hope to convince a large company in the city to sponsor those programs. List and explain the main points you will make in your presentation to the company officials.
- Your sport management and development consulting firm has been hired by a major city to develop a proposal for building a Miracle Field and forming a Miracle League. The proposal will be used to convince voters that they should support a bond issue that will be the source of funding for these things. Outline and explain the points you will include in your proposal.
- You are the director of student recreation at a major university with 30,000 students most of whom live on campus. The university president wants you to develop a gender-mixed and racially and ethnically inclusive intramural program. What are the sports that you would include in the program, how would you organize teams, and what rules would you establish to satisfy the president?
- You are an agent for five professional athletes—they all play different sports, but they live in the same city. They come to you as a group and say that they want to be meaningfully involved in creating a culture of sports participation in their city. They look to you for guidance in setting goals, and for creating effective strategies to

increase the community's physical activity and sports participation. Using material from this chapter, identify the issues they should consider as they create specific goals and plan their strategies to achieve them. Additionally, what advice would you give them in their roles as change agents?

references

Associated Press. 2019. Temple football stadium plans stall as opposition continues to grow. *NBCSports.com* (September 2): https://www.nbcsports.com/philadelphia/ncaa/temple-football-owls-stadium-plans-stall-opposition-continues-grow

Booton, Jen. 2018a. A rundown of sports technology innovation throughout 2018. *SportTechie.com* (December 27): https://www.sporttechie.com/rundown-of-sports-technology-innovation-throughout-2018/

Booton, Jen. 2018b. US Ski Team trained in virtual reality For Pyeongchang Olympics. *SportTechie.com* (January 23): https://www.sporttechie.com/u-s-ski-team-trained-virtual-reality-pyeongchang-olympics/

Bush, Lee. 2016. Creating our own lineup: Identities and shared cultural norms of surfing women in a US East coast community. *Journal of Contemporary Ethnography* 45(3): 290–318.

Coaches Across Continents. 2019. A week of reflection and growth for green Kenya. *CAC Blog* (July 31): https://coachesacrosscontinents.org/category/coaches-across-continents-blog/

Cohen, Adam & Jon Welty Peachey. 2015. Quidditch: Impacting and benefiting participants in a non-fictional manner. *Journal of Sport and Social Issues* 39(6): 521–544.

Cohen, Ben. 2019. Computers are the new basketball coaches. *Wall Street Journal* (July 19): https://www.wsj.com/articles/nba-technology-coaches-are-computers-11563478009

De Schutter, Bob & Julie A. Brown. 2016. Digital games as a source of enjoyment in later life. *Games and Culture* 11(1/2): 28–52.

Denzin, Norman K. 2007. *Symbolic interactionism and cultural studies: The politics of interpretation.* Oxford, UK: Wiley-Blackwell.

Dionigi, Rylee A.; Sean Horton & Joseph Baker. 2013. Negotiations of the ageing process: Older adults' stories of sports participation. *Sport, Education and Society* 18(3): 370–387.

Donnelly, Michele K., Mark Norman, and Peter Donnelly. 2015. *The Sochi 2014 Olympics: A Gender Equality Audit.* Centre for Sport Policy Studies Research Report. Toronto: Centre for Sport Policy Studies, Faculty of Kinesiology and Physical Education, University of Toronto.

Donnelly, Peter; Michael Atkinson, Sarah Boyle & Courtney Szto. 2011. Sport for Development and Peace: A public sociology perspective. *Third World Quarterly* 32(3): 589–60.

Evers, Clifton, Adam Doering. 2019. Lifestyle sports in East Asia. *Journal of Sport and Social Issues* 43(5): 343–352.

Fouché, Rayvon. 2017. *Game changer: The technoscientific revolution in sports.* Baltimore MD: Johns Hopkins University Press.

Friends of McKalla. 2019. Neighborhood group protests Austin FC–MLS sponsor. *GlobeNewsWire.com* (June 12): https://www.globenewswire.com/news-release/2019/06/12/1867396/0/en/Neighborhood-Group-Protests-Austin-FC-MLS-Sponsor.html

Goodman, Barak & Rachel Dretzin. 2001. *The merchants of cool.* PBS Video, Frontline; online, https://www.pbs.org/wgbh/pages/frontline/shows/cool/

Greenfeld, Karl Taro. 1999. Adjustment in mid-flight. *Outside* (February): http://outside.away.com/magazine/0299/9902terje_2.html

Higgins, Matt. 2005. A sport so popular, they added a second boom. *New York Times* (July 25): http://www.nytimes.com/2005/07/25/sports/othersports/a-sport-so-popular-they-added-a-second-boom.html

Honea, Joy C. 2013. Beyond the alternative vs. mainstream dichotomy: Olympic BMX and the future of action sports. *Journal of Popular Culture* 46(6): 1253–1275.

Horton, Sean, Rylee A. Dionigi, Michael Gard, Joseph Baker & Patricia Weir. 2018. "Don't sit back with the geraniums, get out": The complexity of older women's stories of sport participation. *Journal of Amateur Sport* 4(1): 24–51.

Hurley, Olivia A. 2018. *Sport Cyberpsychology*. London/New York: Routledge.

Kidd, Bruce. 1997. *The struggle for Canadian sport*. Toronto: University of Toronto Press.

King, C. Richard. 2007b. Postcolonialism and sports. In George Ritzer, ed., *Encyclopedia of sociology* (pp. 3547–3548). London/New York: Blackwell.

Kioussis, George N. 2018. Can a manager dope? Match analysis in the digital age. *International Review for the Sociology of Sport* 53(7): 824–836.

Klostermann, Claudia & Siegfried Nagel. 2014. Changes in German sport participation: Historical trends in individual sports. *International Review for the Sociology of Sport* 49(5): 609–634.

Kroman, David. 2018. Group pushes ballot measure to repeal Safeco funding. *Crosscut.com* (September 27): https://crosscut.com/2018/09/group-pushes-ballot-measure-repeal-safeco-funding

MacKay, Steph & Christine Dallaire. 2013. Skirtboarders.com: Skateboarding women and self-formation as ethical subjects. *Sociology of Sport Journal* 30(2): 173–196.

McGuire-Adams, Tricia D. & Audrey R. Giles. 2018. Anishinaabekweg dibaajimowinan (stories) of decolonization through running. *Sociology of Sport Journal* 35(3): 207–215.

Millington, Brad. 2018. *Fitness, technology and society: Amusing ourselves to life.* London/New York: Routledge.

Nieri, Tanya & Elizabeth Hughes. 2016. All about having fun: Women's experience of Zumba fitness. *Sociology of Sport Journal* 33(2): 135–145.

Paulas, Rick. 2018. Sports stadiums are a bad deal for cities. *The Atlantic* (November 21): https://www.theatlantic.com/technology/archive/2018/11/sports-stadiums-can-be-bad-cities/576334/

Pike, Elizabeth CJ. 2015. Assessing the sociology of sport: On age and ability. *International Review for the Sociology of Sport* 50(4–5): 570–574.

Pursell, Carroll. 2016. *From playgrounds to Playstation: The interaction of technology and play*. Baltimore: John Hopkins University Press.

Reed, Ken. 2015. *How can we save sports: A game plan*. Lanham MD: Roman & Littlefield.

Schell, Robyn; Simone Hausknecht, Fan Zhang & David Kaufman. 2016. Social benefits of playing Wii bowling for older adults. *Games and Culture* 11(1/2): 81–103.

Scott, Jason. 2017. Anti-tax group hopes to bar public money for stadiums. *AthleticBusiness.com* (May): https://www.athleticbusiness.com/stadium-arena/anti-tax-group-hopes-to-bar-public-money-for-stadiums.html

Smith, Allison B. & Robin Hardin. 2018. Female student-athletes' transition out of collegiate competition. *Journal of Amateur Sport* 4(3): 61–86.

Thorpe, Holly A., & Belinda Wheaton. 2013. Dissecting action sports studies: Past, present, and beyond. In David L. Andrews & Ben Carrington, eds. *A companion to sport* (pp. 341–358). Chichester, England: Blackwell Publishing Ltd.

Thorpe, Holly & Belinda Wheaton. 2019. The Olympic Games, Agenda 2020 and action sports: The promise, politics and performance of organisational change. *International Journal of Sport Policy and Politics* 11(3): 465–483.

Wheaton, Belinda. 2013. *The cultural politics of lifestyle sports*. London: Routledge.

Wheaton, Belinda & Holly Thorpe. 2018. Action sports, the Olympic Games, and the opportunities and challenges for gender equity: The cases of surfing and skateboarding. *Journal of Sport and Social Issues* 42(5): 315–342.

Wheaton, Belinda, Georgina Roy & Rebecca Olive. 2017. Exploring critical alternatives for youth development through lifestyle sport: Surfing and community development in Aotearoa/New Zealand. *Sustainability* 9 (2298): doi:10.3390/su9122298.

Willing, Indigo, Andy Bennett, Mikko Piispa & Ben Green. 2018. Skateboarding and the 'tired generation': Ageing in youth cultures and lifestyle sports. *Sociology* 53(3): 503–518.

NAME INDEX

C

D

I

J

SUBJECT INDEX

H